THE LAYMAN'S BIBLE COMMENTARY

NEW TESTAMENT

Dr. Mark Strauss
Consulting Editor

BARBOUR
PUBLISHING™

YOU are the reason we do what we do here at Barbour Publishing. We promise that we will always use our God-given talents to produce content with you in mind—and that we will remain biblically faithful, no matter what.

Thank you for being the heart of our business.

ISBN 979-8-89151-260-3

Produced with the assistance of Christopher D. Hudson & Associates. Contributing writers include Libby Britt, Stan Campbell, Beth Clayton, and Carol Smith.

Maps that appear in this volume are taken from *The Barbour Bible Atlas* (978-1-63609-771-8), published by Barbour Publishing, Inc.

Published by Barbour Publishing, Inc., 1810 Barbour Drive, Uhrichsville, Ohio 44683, www.barbourbooks.com

Our mission is to inspire the world with the life-changing message of the Bible.

Member of the Evangelical Christian Publishers Association

Printed in China.

CONTENTS

Introduction to the Gospels. 5
The Gospel of Matthew 11
The Gospel of Mark. 129
The Gospel of Luke 221
The Gospel of John 335
Acts 435
Romans. 539
1 Corinthians 591
2 Corinthians 641
Galatians. 671
Ephesians 705
Philippians 739
Colossians. 761
1 Thessalonians 785
2 Thessalonians 807
1 Timothy 821
2 Timothy 849
Titus. 867
Philemon. 881
Hebrews 891
James. 945
1 Peter. 967
2 Peter. 989
1 John 1003
2 John 1025
3 John 1031
Jude. 1037
Revelation. 1045

INTRODUCTION TO THE GOSPELS

THE GOSPELS

The first three Gospels in our New Testament—Matthew, Mark, Luke—are considered the synoptic Gospels. The word *synoptic* denotes that the separate Gospels were written "from a common view." These three narratives follow a similar chronological or structural outline, whereas the Gospel of John follows a different chronological or structural outline.

Although all four Gospels tell the story of Jesus carefully and accurately, they differ somewhat in content and considerably in what they want to say about Jesus. Each of the gospel writers adopted a different form or literary style, and even vocabulary. They each had a different theological purpose or intention. Furthermore, they each had a different audience in mind. Still, each individual writer was empowered by the Holy Spirit to use his specific giftedness to record faithfully the purpose of God.

The Gospels of Mark and Matthew are very similar in their narrative accounts. Luke is only slightly different, but still has much in common with Matthew and Mark. (It has been estimated that over 90 percent of the verses of Mark are found in Matthew.)

Both Matthew and Luke follow Mark's basic narrative form. Mark was probably the first of the Gospels written, then Matthew, followed by Luke. Matthew and Luke supplemented Mark's narrative with additional material to meet the unique theological purpose and audience each had in mind.

THE GOSPELS IN THE LIFE OF THE CHURCH

The most likely dates for writing the synoptic Gospels range from the early 60s AD to the mid-70s AD. Even if Matthew was written earlier, as some believe to be true, several of Paul's epistles (Galatians, 1 and 2 Thessalonians, Romans, 1 and 2 Corinthians) were likely written before the Gospels. In the early days of the mission and expansion of the church, the need for the Gospels was not as great since the apostles and other apostolic men were still alive and active. Then, as the church spread and as the apostles were dying, the gospel message needed to be formalized.

Furthermore, as the gospel spread to distant lands and among different Gentile cultures it became necessary to explain the story of Jesus in terms the new communities of believers or would-be believers could understand. It became necessary to interpret the significance of Jesus for a second generation of believers, namely, Gentile Roman and Greek seekers. Hence there arose a need for Gospels that would explain Jesus to a Roman audience (Mark), a Jewish audience (Matthew), and a Greek audience (Luke). Some years later, in the region of Asia (Turkey), it became necessary for John to retell the story of Jesus to a church that was being challenged by new false doctrines about Jesus' divinity and human form (John).

The Gospels are often described as accounts of Jesus' death, burial, and resurrection with extended introductions to provide backstory. They explain why the death of this seemingly marginal Jew, Jesus, was so significant. The Gospels give reasons why people should respond to a radical call to discipleship, surrender their lives to this Jesus, and follow Him wherever that might lead, possibly even to a martyr's death. (Remember that martyrdom for Jesus was a real threat to Christians during the first three centuries.)

Although we cannot date the four Gospels precisely, all four were certainly written before the end of the first century AD. They are the only early and reliable historical accounts of the life and ministry of Jesus. The later so-called "apocryphal Gospels"—such as the Gospel of Thomas, the Gospel of the Truth, and the Gospel of Phillip—either borrowed from the four canonical Gospels or were created from legendary stories.

THE NATURE OF THE GOSPELS

It is important to understanding that we ask this question: "What kind of literature do we have in these Gospels?"

The four New Testament Gospels are fundamentally a different kind of literature from the New Testament Epistles. The Gospels incorporate a number of literary styles (parables, teaching materials, narrative materials) as they tell their stories. Keeping these literary styles in mind gives us a framework to interpret the Gospels accurately.

BIOGRAPHIES?

The Gospels don't fit the category of modern biographies in that they describe only a short period of Jesus' life. They do fit in the category of ancient biographies in that ancient hero biographies did not attempt to tell everything about a hero, but only those matters that were important to the story. Nevertheless, to simply define the Gospels as biographies comes up short.

HISTORY

Some have attempted to define the Gospels as historical narratives. Although there was an interest in setting the story of Jesus into a historical context, there is obviously more than mere historical facts in the Gospels. Jesus was a historical person who actually lived, died, and rose again, although outside of scripture it would be difficult to prove the historical nature of His resurrection. However, there is enough other material in the Gospels that touch history to affirm that the Gospels are accurate. The Gospel writers were concerned with reliable testimony as they told the significant facts of Jesus' life and ministry. So, do the Gospels relate the story of Jesus in historical terms, constructs, or contexts? The answer is yes, but this is not their primary concern.

THEOLOGY

The Gospels are in fact theological writings, telling the story of Jesus (biographical facts significant to their purpose) and placing Him into a historical context (historical testimony significant to their story), but more importantly, explaining why He had the right to be considered the Son of God, the Messiah, and the Christ ("the anointed").

Some have suggested that the Gospels are really the story of Jesus' suffering, death, burial, and resurrection—with extended introductions. These lengthy introductions explained who this Jesus was, why His life was significant, and what discipleship of Jesus entails.

THE THEOLOGICAL FOCUS OF THE INDIVIDUAL GOSPELS

Each of the synoptic Gospels was written for a particular audience or community, with the purpose of explaining how the message of Jesus related to that group's needs and interests.

Mark wrote to a group of persecuted believers to demonstrate that Jesus was the mighty Messiah and Son of God, but that He suffered and died to pay for sins. His is a call for believers to take up their own crosses and follow Jesus through suffering to victory.

For the Jewish mind-set, and especially those Jewish Christians that were displaced after the destruction of Jerusalem, Matthew wrote to establish Jesus' rightful claim to be the Messiah, the King of God's kingdom.

For a mainly Gentile audience, Luke wrote demonstrating that Jesus was the Son of God who was truly interested in people and who had died to save people from sin. Jesus, in Luke, is the Savior of the world—He is the healer of mankind.

THE NEED AND PURPOSE OF THE GOSPELS

Several factors lay behind the need for the gospel story to be written down in reliable form. We can group them under the following categories:

- **Apostolic Preaching**. The need to preserve the preaching message of the apostles was becoming urgent as the apostles were being persecuted and dying as martyrs for the cause and message of Christ. In time, our four Gospels became a form of apostolic presence.
- **Gentile Missions and Expansion of the Church.** The dramatic expansion of the New Testament church created a situation that demanded a firm and reliable record of the apostolic preaching in the form of the written message. It was simply impossible for the apostles and apostolic evangelists to cover all of the new bases and churches in the Gentile world.
- **False Teaching.** There was a need to correct false ideas about Jesus and His mission that began to arise in the church.

We continue to need the perspective of all four Gospels to this day. They teach us that Jesus was a real person of history and that God, from even before His birth, was involved in the events that took life in the person of Jesus. They teach us that Jesus performed miracles to prove His divinity and mission, that He died according to the plan and will of God, that He was resurrected in history on the third day, that He now reigns in God's kingdom, and that He will return as predicted in scripture to judge the world in righteousness.

THE GOSPEL OF MATTHEW

INTRODUCTION TO MATTHEW

Although this is a commentary on the Gospel of Matthew, and this Gospel can stand alone as an independent witness to Jesus, it is helpful to our understanding of it to see it in relation to the other Gospels, especially Mark and Luke. As noted in the introduction to this volume, Matthew, Mark, and Luke are referred to as the synoptic Gospels because they are similar accounts and see the story of Jesus "through the same eyes." The Gospel of John had a unique view or approach to the gospel story.

Although Mark's Gospel appeared first and was early accepted by the church, Matthew soon became the church's favored Gospel. For a number of reasons, throughout the centuries Matthew has continued to be the most prominent of the three synoptic Gospels (Matthew, Mark, and Luke). Here are some possible reasons:

- It is commonly believed to have been written by one of the original apostles.
- It is more comprehensive than Mark, containing messianic genealogy, birth narratives, and a considerable amount of Jesus' teaching material.
- It contains more than 90 percent of Mark's Gospel since Matthew used Mark as a basis for his Gospel.
- Its incorporation of large blocks of Jesus' teaching material, especially the Sermon on the Mount, has met the educational and liturgical needs of the church through the centuries.

AUTHOR

Our earliest records claim that the apostle Matthew wrote this Gospel. Early church tradition was almost unanimous in this regard. While there remains some continuing discussion about Matthew's authorship, the Gospel itself was accepted without question by the early church and incorporated into the New Testament canon.

PURPOSE

It is obvious that Matthew's Gospel was addressed to a Jewish-Christian audience or community. Matthew presented Jesus to this audience as God's messianic King.

HISTORICAL CONTEXT

Some scholars date Matthew after AD 70, sometime after the destruction of Jerusalem, while others date it earlier, in the 60s.

In this commentary we will follow the view that Matthew's community was a group of Jewish Christians or Jewish church communities who had escaped Jerusalem between AD 66 and the destruction of Jerusalem in AD 70. Needing to know that their faith should not be focused on Jerusalem and the temple, which was now destroyed, but on Jesus the Messiah, Matthew wrote for these dislodged Jewish Christian communities who needed to refocus their faith and discipleship.

THEMES

Several characteristics of Matthew's Gospel are immediately apparent:

A strong Jewish interest. Matthew used a number of literary devices that indicate a Jewish audience.

A strong sense of messianic expectation and fulfillment in Matthew. Matthew made much of fulfilled prophecy in his narrative. Quoting heavily from the Old Testament, Matthew claimed that fifteen Old Testament prophecies were fulfilled in Jesus' ministry. He showed great interest in Jesus' teaching on the Law of Moses. Jesus' statement that He came to fulfill the law rather than abolish it is found exclusively in Matthew (5:17–20).

Universalism and Missions. Although Matthew wrote for a Jewish community, he was not a Jewish zealot. He saw Christianity reaching beyond the Jewish nation to the Gentiles. (Note his condemnation of the Jewish leadership in Matthew 23 and the Great Commission in 28:18–20.)

Pastoral and Ecclesiastical Interest. Matthew is in every sense of the word a church Gospel:

- It is the only Gospel to include the term *ekklesia*, meaning "church" (16:18; 18:17).
- Matthew was interested in the church's corporate life and the issues of living in a close-knit body (18:15–20).
- Matthew emphasized Jesus' role as an authoritative teacher (7:29).
- Matthew emphasized Jesus' instruction regarding the kingdom (Chapter 13).

Messianic Kingdom Interests. From the first paragraph of the Gospel, Matthew was concerned with Jesus as the Messiah, the King of God's kingdom. His purpose was to show that Jesus was the long-expected Messiah.

Eschatological Interests. Matthew manifested significant interest in the final age of history, the end times. He included several parables that had themes relating to the final judgment, including:

- The parable of the tares (13:24–30)
- The parable of the ten virgins (25:1–13)
- The parable of the talents (25:14–30)

Matthew described the destruction of Jerusalem in much greater detail than Mark and Luke. In Matthew, three chapters are devoted to the destruction of Jerusalem and the confusion of the disciples over the final end of the age (23–25). Mark and Luke used only one chapter for this discussion (Mark 13; Luke 21).

STRUCTURE

Careful examination of the Gospel of Matthew reveals a deliberate and careful literary structure with a specific theological purpose. The literary structure of Matthew alternates between six blocks of narrative material, five of which are each followed by a block of sayings or discourse material. Many draw a parallel between the five books of Moses (the Law) and the five discourses of Jesus. In Matthew's case, these discourses were not discussions of Christian law, as the books of Moses are, but teachings discussing the meaning of discipleship in the kingdom.

NARRATIVE 1	Matthew 1:1–4:25	Preparation for Ministry
Discourse 1	Matthew 5:1–7:29	The Sermon on the Mount
NARRATIVE 2	Matthew 8:1–9:38	The Authority of the Messiah
Discourse 2	Matthew 10:1–42	The Limited Commission
NARRATIVE 3	Matthew 11:1–12:50	Opposition and Rejection
Discourse 3	Matthew 13:1–58	The True Nature of the Kingdom
NARRATIVE 4	Matthew 14:1–17:27	Final Days of Preparation
Discourse 4	Matthew 18:1–35	Community—Humility and Forgiveness
NARRATIVE 5	Matthew 19:1–22:46	Toward Jerusalem—The Final Week
Discourse 5	Matthew 23:1–25:46	The Apocalyptic Discourse
NARRATIVE 6	Matthew 26:1–28:20	The Messiah's Final Week

OUTLINE

NARRATIVE 1

PREPARATION FOR MINISTRY 1:1–4:25

- The Genealogy of Jesus 1:1–17
- The Virgin Birth 1:18–25
- The Wise Men 2:1–12
- The Flight to Egypt 2:13–23
- The Ministry of John the Baptist 3:1–12
- The Baptism of Jesus 3:13–17
- Jesus' Temptation 4:1–11
- The Beginning of Jesus' Galilean Ministry 4:12–17
- The Call of the Disciples: Peter and Andrew, James and John 4:18–25

DISCOURSE 1

THE SERMON ON THE MOUNT 5:1–7:29

- The Disciples' Character: The Beatitudes 5:1–12
  - On the Mountain 5:1–2
  - The Poor in Spirit 5:3
  - Those Who Mourn 5:4
  - The Meek 5:5
  - Those Who Hunger and Thirst for Righteousness 5:6
  - The Merciful 5:7
  - The Pure in Heart 5:8
  - The Peacemakers 5:9
  - Those Who Are Persecuted for Righteousness' Sake 5:10
  - When Men Revile You and Persecute You 5:11–12
- The Disciples' Influence: Salt and Light 5:13–16
- The Disciples' Righteousness: To Exceed That of the Scribes and Pharisees 5:17–20
- The Six Antitheses 5:21–48
  - Antithesis one—Murder 5:21–26
  - Antithesis two—Adultery 5:27–30
  - Antithesis three—Divorce 5:31–32
  - Antithesis four—Oaths 5:33–37
  - Antithesis five—Retaliation 5:38–42
  - Antithesis six—Love 5:43–48
- The Disciples' Piety: Deeds of Righteousness 6:1–18
  - Almsgiving 6:1–4
  - Prayer 6:5–15
  - Fasting 6:16–18
- The Disciples' Ambition 6:19–34
  - True Riches 6:19–21
  - Two Parables 6:22–24

Trust and Anxiety 6:25–34
The Disciples' Pitfalls 7:1–20
Judging One Another 7:1–6
Prayer, Faith, and the Golden Rule 7:7–12
False Teachers 7:13–20
Commitment to Jesus and to the Will of God 7:21–27
Jesus' Authority 7:28–29

NARRATIVE 2

THE AUTHORITY OF THE MESSIAH 8:1–9:38

Cleansing a Leper 8:1–4
The Centurion's Servant Healed 8:5–13
Peter's Mother-in-law Healed 8:14–17
Impulsive and Reluctant Would-Be Disciples 8:18–22
The Storm Stilled 8:23–27
Demons Cast Out 8:28–34
A Paralytic Forgiven and Healed 9:1–8
Matthew's Call 9:9–13
The Questing about Fasting 9:14–17
The Issue of Blood Stopped and the Dead Raised 9:18–26
The Blind See, and a Demon Is Exorcised 9:27–34
The Need for Workers 9:35–38

DISCOURSE 2

THE LIMITED COMMISSION 10:1–42

Commissioning the Disciples 10:1–4
The Mission of the Apostles 10:5–15
Warnings of Opposition to the Preaching 10:16–42
Persecution 10:16–23
The Disciple and His Followers 10:24–33
The Disciple and the Cross 10:34–39
The Disciples' Message and Reward 10:40–42

NARRATIVE 3

OPPOSITION AND REJECTION 11:1–12:50

John the Baptist's Question 11:1–6
Jesus' Estimate of John the Baptist 11:7–19
Judgment on the Unrepentant 11:20–24
The Revelation of the Father 11:25–30
Lord of the Sabbath 12:1–8
Jesus Heals on the Sabbath 12:9–14
Jesus Heals Many 12:15–21

The Charge of Blasphemy 12:22–37
The Scribes and Pharisees Seek a Sign from Jesus 12:38–45
Jesus' True Family 12:46–50

DISCOURSE 3
THE TRUE NATURE OF THE KINGDOM 13:1–58
The Parable of the Sower 13:1–9, 18–23
Why Did Jesus Teach in Parables? 13:10–17
The Parable of Wheat and Tares 13:24–30
The Grain of Mustard Seed 13:31–32
The Parable of the Leaven 13:33–35
The Wheat and the Tares Explained 13:36–43
The Hidden Treasure and Pearl of Great Price 13:44–46
The Dragnet 13:47–51
The Conclusion to the Kingdom Parables 13:52–58

NARRATIVE 4
FINAL DAYS OF PREPARATION 14:1–17:27
The Death of John the Baptist 14:1–12
Feeding the Five Thousand 14:13–21
Jesus Walks on the Sea 14:22–36
Ceremonial and Real Defilement—Washing Hands 15:1–20
The Canaanite Woman and Tyre and Sidon 15:21–28
The Feeding of the Four Thousand 15:29–39
The Pharisees and Sadducees Demand a Sign from Heaven 16:1–4
The Leaven of the Pharisees and Sadducees 16:5–12
Caesarea Philippi and Peter's Confession 16:13–20
Jesus Foretells His Death, Burial, and Resurrection 16:21–23
Radical Discipleship 16:24–27
The Son of Man Coming in His Kingdom 16:28
The Transfiguration 17:1–13
Healing of the Epileptic Boy 17:14–21
Jesus Again Foretells His Death and Resurrection 17:22–23
The Shekel in the Fish's Mouth and the Temple Tax 17:24–27

DISCOURSE 4
COMMUNITY—HUMILITY AND FORGIVENESS 18:1–35
Humility 18:1–9
Finding the Lost Sheep 18:10–14
Solving Personal and Community Problems 18:15–20
Christian Forgiveness 18:21–35

NARRATIVE 5

TOWARD JERUSALEM—THE FINAL WEEK 19:1–22:46

Jesus Answers the Pharisees on Marriage and Divorce 19:1–12
Jesus Blesses Little Children 19:13–15
The Rich Young Ruler 19:16–30
The Parable of the Householder 20:1–16
Jesus Again Foretells His Death and Resurrection 20:17–19
The Son of Man Came to Serve, Not Be Served 20:20–28
Healing Two Blind Men near Jericho 20:29–34
The Triumphant Entry into Jerusalem 21:1–11
Cleansing the Temple 21:12–17
The Barren Fig Tree 21:18–22
Chief Priests Challenge Jesus' Authority 21:23–27
The Parable of Two Sons 21:28–32
The Parable of the Wicked Tenants 21:33–46
The Parable of the Marriage Feast 22:1–14
The Messiah, Taxes, and Caesar 22:15–22
The Sadducees and the Resurrection 22:23–33
Which Is the Greatest Commandment? 22:34–40
Jesus' Unanswerable Question to the Pharisees 22:41–46

DISCOURSE 5

THE APOCALYPTIC DISCOURSE 23:1–25:46

Jesus' Condemnation of the Scribes and Pharisees 23:1–36
The Lament over Jerusalem 23:37–39
Jesus' Judgment of the Temple and Jerusalem 24:1–35
The Disciples' Question 24:1–14
The Destruction of Jerusalem 24:15–28
The Coming of the Son of Man 24:29–31
The Sign of the Fig Tree 24:32–35
The End of the Age 24:36–25:46
The Need for Watchfulness 24:36–44
Faithful and Unfaithful Servants 24:45–51
The Parable of the Ten Virgins 25:1–13
The Parable of the Talents 25:14–30
The Parable of the Sheep and Goats 25:31–46

NARRATIVE 6

THE MESSIAH'S FINAL WEEK 26:1–28:20

The Sanhedrin Plots to Kill Jesus 26:1–5
Jesus Anointed by Mary at Bethany 26:6–13
The Bargain of Judas 26:14–16
The Last Passover Supper 26:17–25

The Lord's Supper Instituted 26:26–29
Peter's Denial Foretold 26:30–35
Jesus in Gethsemane 26:36–46
Judas Betrays Jesus 26:47–56
Jesus Is Taken Before Caiaphas, the High Priest 26:57–68
Peter's Denial of Jesus 26:69–75
Jesus Is Delivered to Pilate by the Sanhedrin 27:1–2
Judas's Suicide 27:3–10
Jesus Before Pilate 27:11–26
The Crucifixion of Jesus 27:27–56
The Burial of Jesus 27:57–61
The Tomb Sealed and Guarded 27:62–66
The Empty Tomb and Resurrection of Jesus 28:1–10
Bribing the Soldiers 28:11–15
The Great Commission 28:16–20

MATTHEW 1:1–4:25

NARRATIVE 1: PREPARATION FOR MINISTRY

The Genealogy of Jesus	1:1–17
The Virgin Birth	1:18–25
The Wise Men	2:1–12
The Flight to Egypt	2:13–23
The Ministry of John the Baptist	3:1–12
The Baptism of Jesus	3:13–17
Jesus' Temptation	4:1–11
The Beginning of Jesus' Galilean Ministry	4:12–17
The Call of the Disciples: Peter and Andrew, James and John	4:18–25

Setting Up the Section

This first block of narrative in Matthew is sometimes overlooked in the misconception that it's not quite as important to the Gospel as, say, the Sermon on the Mount of Matthew 5–7 or the great Kingdom Parables of Matthew 13. It may be seen as simply the backdrop or story setup. However, it actually presents one of the most striking and significant theological emphases of the Gospel. This narrative lays the foundation for Matthew's arguments regarding the messiahship of Jesus.

1:1–17

THE GENEALOGY OF JESUS

Matthew begins his theological argument for the messiahship of Jesus in proper Jewish style, with an appropriate genealogy—although it is a theologically shaped one. It is obvious from a comparison of other Old Testament genealogies (1 Chronicles 1–9) that Matthew leaves out some levels of Jesus' family tree and repeats some names.

Because Matthew's genealogy underlines matters of fundamental theological importance, he grounds his narrative upon several Old Testament quotations and intends to provide a strong sense of fulfillment. To further emphasize the theological impact of this genealogy, he begins with its most significant elements—"Jesus Christ the son of David, the son of Abraham."

Matthew numbers the generations from Abraham to Jesus as three groups of fourteen. This has generated much speculation. Though we cannot be certain of Matthew's meaning, he seems to take it for granted that his first century Jewish readers will understand.

Most importantly, in Matthew's carefully constructed genealogy, it is obvious that Jesus is the descendant of Abraham and David, two significant persons in the genealogy of Israel. By the time Matthew wrote his Gospel, *Son of David* had become a messianic title. Matthew is clearly demonstrating through this historical/theological genealogy that Jesus is the rightful Son of Abraham and Son of David, namely, the Messiah.

Furthermore, it is Mathew's purpose to demonstrate that the promises to Abraham were fulfilled through Jesus. This would be important for a Jewish believer to know. (In his letter to the Galatians, Paul makes a similar argument—that Jesus is the seed of Abraham, thus fulfilling the promise of God to Abraham.) For Matthew's Jewish audience, Jesus' being the seed of Abraham has both messianic and promise implications. You can read God's promises to Abraham in Genesis 17:5–7.

The genealogy of Matthew differs from that of Luke. Matthew traces a heritage from Abraham through David to Jesus through the royal or legal lineage. His goal is to show that Jesus is the legitimate king of Israel. Luke also follows the line of David and Abraham, but traces his genealogy from Jesus through Mary all the way back to Adam. Luke's genealogy, like Matthew's, is meant to fulfill a theological purpose, demonstrating that Jesus is the Savior for all people everywhere.

1:18–25

THE VIRGIN BIRTH

Joseph is pledged (NIV) to Mary. This indicates something similar to modern engagement, only with a stronger legal implication. It was, in fact, the beginning of the marriage "ceremony." The pledge was as legally binding as the marriage contract. It could only be broken according to the Jewish laws of marriage and divorce. In this case, since it appears that Mary is no longer considered clean since she is pregnant with Jesus, it is within the law for Joseph to divorce her. Imagine the sensitivity of Joseph in this matter. When it is revealed by an angel that Mary's pregnancy is the work of the Holy Spirit and part of God's purpose, Joseph takes her as his wife.

The virgin birth of Jesus is fundamental to the Christian faith and to Matthew's theology. Throughout this section, Matthew emphasizes the role of the Holy Spirit. He wants his readers to know that this conception is unusual, that it transcends the purely historical or earthly, that Jesus' conception and birth involve the direct involvement and action of the divine. The central point in this birth narrative is not simply that Jesus is born of a virgin, true as that may be, but that His conception and birth is the result of direct divine intervention (the Holy Spirit), and that it forms an integral part in God's saving activity in history.

To reinforce this point, Matthew argues that Jesus' birth is a fulfillment of prophecy, namely, Isaiah 7:14. For Jewish ears, this is a powerful argument demonstrating that Jesus is a fulfillment of God's prophetic activity, that He has a legitimate place in God's promises to Abraham, and that He, in fact, stands in the direct line of God's redemption.

Critical Observation

As early as Matthew 1:22, we are introduced to a fascinating aspect of Matthew's theological style. We encounter the first of ten significant fulfillment passages in Matthew. Although Matthew quotes from or cites many Old Testament and prophetic texts, these ten are unique because they are introduced as fulfillments. Singling them out in this manner, Matthew draws out their theological implications for Jesus' ministry as Messiah. The other nine similarly unique citations are: 2:15, 17, 23; 4:14; 8:17; 13:35; 21:4; 26:56; and 27:9. Matthew's use of these quotes fits with his determination to demonstrate that Jesus legitimately fulfills the role of Messiah.

In his opening chapter Matthew makes two significant theological claims regarding Jesus.

1) He is the son of Abraham and David, thus supporting Matthew's claims that Jesus is legitimately the Messiah.
2) His birth is not ordinary; it is the result of the direct intervention of God.

2:1–12

THE WISE MEN

With this narrative, Matthew sets the scene for a major theme he will develop throughout the Gospel. It concerns those who acknowledge Jesus and worship Him. The ones you would anticipate as welcoming and worshiping Jesus as the Messiah, do not. It is those from whom one would least expect worship that Jesus receives homage.

Matthew sets this account of the Wise Men in a historical context—during the reign of Herod the king (Herod the Great, AD 47–4 BC). Because we know the date of Herod's death, a key event in this story, we have a firm time marker—one that is somewhat surprising. If Jesus was born while Herod was still ruling, then Jesus was born before 4 BC.

Herod the Great was not popular with the Jews for several reasons.

1) He was not a pure Jew, but an Idumean. (Idumea lay to the south and southeast of Judea and the Dead Sea. Some associate Idumea with Edom and the Edomites, but this is only part of the Idumean heritage).
2) He had been appointed by the Roman government to rule over Israel.
3) He was a harsh ruler. Even the Roman Emperor, Augustus, acknowledged the ruthlessness of Herod.

It is difficult to identify the Wise Men with any degree of certainty. The word used to describe them here is *magoi* (*Magoi* could refer to magicians or a priestly caste from Persia). In all probability, they are a group of Persian priests familiar with reading the formations of the stars. When the Wise Men (not necessarily three wise men, since Matthew does not actually number them) see the star in the East and follow it, they come to Jerusalem and Bethlehem, anticipating something important. They recognize that a new king has been born.

Did they really understand the significance of this baby to Israel? We do not know all that this realization involved—only that it was significant enough to bring them to Jerusalem to inquire about the new king. Word of this disturbs Herod so much that he assembles the chief priests and asks where the Christ was to be born. Fascinating. Herod immediately identifies this new king with the messianic expectation of Israel. So do the chief priests, since they immediately cite the prophecy in Micah 5:2. Matthew's use of this text is in keeping with the Jewish rabbinic practice of making an indirect theological emphasis by the giving of a narrative account. The fact that Herod and the chief priests immediately consider a messianic text in this situation is an indirect support for Matthew's argument that Jesus is indeed the same Messiah that had been prophesied to be born in Bethlehem, a small town about five miles south of Jerusalem.

The Wise Men (Persian Gentiles) acknowledge Jesus as the king and worship Him and give Him gifts of costly aromatic herbs or ointment. Many have seen a symbolic significance in these three gifts: gold for royalty, incense for deity, myrrh for burial. It is unlikely that the Magi saw this significance, but Matthew's readers may have seen it.

Being warned in a dream not to return to Herod, the Wise Men leave for their own home country. Herod and the chief priests do not receive Jesus and pay Him homage, but Gentiles from afar worship Him. Matthew continues to work this theme into his Gospel.

2:13–23

THE FLIGHT TO EGYPT

Again we have divine intervention—an angel of the Lord warns Joseph to flee into Egypt.

Matthew cites Hosea 11:1 as his second fulfillment prophecy. While this Hosea text pertains to the nation of Israel, Matthew uses it in regard to the Messiah. In doing this, he emphasizes that what is happening to Joseph, Mary, and Jesus is not an accident; it is part of God's ongoing work of salvation throughout history.

Herod's response to the possible presence of the Messiah is to have all male children in Bethlehem who are two years old and under killed. Matthew cites Jeremiah 31:15 as a prophetic reference for this. Again, Matthew takes an Old Testament text and paraphrases it. This text is the third of the fulfillment texts in Matthew. Jeremiah 31:15 is in the specific historical context of the deportation of the Hebrews to Babylon. Matthew applies the prophecy regarding that historical situation to the grief and the weeping over the cruel work of Herod. He again uses this parallel to connect the events surrounding Jesus' birth with an Old Testament fulfillment and God's divine plan.

After Herod's death, God intervenes once again. An angel of the Lord tells Joseph to return to Israel. After Herod's death no one is appointed king, but Herod's son, Archelaus, becomes governor over Judea. Archelaus, like Herod, is not a pure Jew; he is half Idumean and half Samaritan. Because of Archelaus's reputation, Joseph is warned not to return to Judea (which included Bethlehem and Jerusalem), but instead to go to Galilee, the district in the north over which Archelaus is *not* governor. Joseph and his family settle in Nazareth.

Matthew resorts to his fourth fulfillment text to support this (v. 23). The problem is that it is almost impossible to find this prophecy's precise source. This would not be a problem for Jews familiar with first-century application of Old Testament passages. Matthew's purpose is, again, to connect Jesus with, or place Him firmly within, God's saving activity in history. Some say the background behind this text is the Nazarite vows of Judges 13:5, 7 and 16:17, but we can't be sure that the Judges verses are the source.

3:1–12

THE MINISTRY OF JOHN THE BAPTIST

The expression "In those days. . ." (NIV) is a Hebrew statement that draws attention to a period of time that should hold significant interest.

Matthew spends no time explaining who John the Baptist is. He feels no need; every Jew at this time would have known something about John the Baptist, and Matthew is writing for a Jewish-Christian audience. On the other hand, Luke, writing for a Gentile Greek audience, spends considerable time on John's birth (Luke 1:5–25, 39–80). While for Matthew no introduction of John is necessary, John's ministry and his introduction of Jesus are important to Matthew's message.

John the Baptist begins preaching in the wilderness. His message—"Repent, for the kingdom of heaven is near" (NIV)—is a short statement with significant theological content. It is exactly this message that Jesus came preaching (4:17). Each word is loaded with meaning:

- *Repent* (turn to God). Recognizing the time is fulfilled and that Jesus is about to usher in the last days, there is a sense of urgency in the air. God is about to restore His kingdom through His Messiah, Jesus. When the Pharisees and Sadducees come out for baptism not manifesting repentance, John calls them a brood or generation of vipers—in other words, poisonous snakes (3:7).
- *Kingdom of heaven.* It was normal for the Jews to substitute something similar in the place of the word *God*, hence Matthew uses the expression *kingdom of heaven* rather than *kingdom of God*. When the Bible speaks of the "kingdom of God," it is referencing the reign of God. The reign of God from heaven through His messianic king is about to break into human experience in a unique and powerful manner.
- *At hand* (near). This term can mean close or near, but in certain contexts a term can take on heightened importance. In this case, it takes on the sense of something that is already here or something that is so certain that it can be spoken of as if it already exists. In the context of John's preaching, this means that the kingdom of heaven/God is so certain (and in the person of Jesus is already among them) that the Jews need to repent immediately. Later, in Matthew 12:28, Jesus will say, "but if I drive out demons by the Spirit of God, then the kingdom of God has come upon you" (NIV), indicating that the kingdom in His person was already there.

In keeping with his already established policy, Matthew introduces John with a fulfillment passage, but this is not one of the ten specifically formulaic passages. In this case, Matthew (as did Mark and Luke when they cited the Old Testament) quotes from the Septuagint, a Greek version of the Old Testament scriptures.

Matthew's quote stresses that John's ministry takes place in the wilderness, away from the religious establishment. It is in the wilderness that John is preparing for the ministry of the Messiah, whose ministry also begins outside of Jerusalem's influence. Notice that when the Pharisees and Sadducees come out for baptism, John severely warns them to repent because judgment (an axe) is ready to take place over them. They will be judged by God for their rejection of the Messiah.

Even John's clothes set him apart from the religious leaders of the day. His dress is that of a desert monk (and his diet that of a desert survivalist), reminiscent of the great prophet Elijah (2 Kings 1:8). The religious leaders would have worn fine garments reflecting their high position.

John likewise distances himself and his ministry from that of the Messiah. He baptizes in (or with) water based on repentance, but Jesus' ministry and baptism come in the fullness and power of the Holy Spirit. In Matthew 3:6 John preaches a baptism related to the forgiveness of sins. Mark described it simply: "John the Baptist preached in the desert. He preached that people should be baptized because they were sorry for their sins and had turned from them. And they would be forgiven" (Mark 1:4 NLV). What is the difference between this baptism of John and the Christian baptism shortly to be proclaimed by Jesus? Both are based on repentance and are for the forgiveness of sins, yet some of those that are baptized according to John's baptism need to be rebaptized later as Christians (Acts 19:1–5).

Although John's baptism is for the forgiveness of sins, it is a transitory baptism, shortly to be replaced by a baptism that Jesus commands (Matthew 28:19–20; Mark 16:15–16). The difference is the sacrificial system upon which they were built. John's baptism existed under the yearly sacrificial system of animal sacrifices; Christian baptism was, and remains, under the permanent, once-for-all-time, sacrifice of Jesus. John's baptism was under a temporary sacrificial system to last only until the permanent sacrifice of Jesus. Also, Jesus commanded His disciples (apostles) to go and make disciples of all nations (Matthew 28:19–20; Mark 16:15–16). John's baptism was only for the Jews.

John's description of Jesus in verse 12 relates to judgment. A reference to the harvesting and processing of wheat, it describes a procedure in which harvested wheat is gathered onto a threshing floor. The rough wheat is then thrown into the air so that the breeze can catch the lighter chaff and blow it away. In this way, the good, nutritious wheat is separated from the useless chaff.

3:13–17

THE BAPTISM OF JESUS

The baptism of Jesus was so important to His ministry that all three of the synoptic Gospels (Matthew, Mark, Luke) record the event. In convincing John to go through with the baptism, Jesus claims His baptism will fulfill all righteousness, or do everything that God requires of them. Jesus' baptism represents both divine empowerment and divine affirmation for His ministry. It is the inaugural event of His public ministry.

The Gospel of Luke adds an interesting undertone to the significance of the baptism, exemplifying the Pharisees' perspective: "But the proud religious law-keepers and the men who knew the Law would not listen. They would not be baptized by John and they did not receive what God had for them" (Luke 7:30 NLV). In this light, their refusal to be baptized is not simply the rejection of a custom; it is tantamount to rejecting the purpose of God.

God had evidently instructed John to baptize for repentance and forgiveness of sins (Matthew 3:6; Mark 1:4). Baptism as a cleansing rite, based on faith and repentance and for the forgiveness of sins, was important to the ministry of both John the Baptist and Jesus. Christians in the early centuries continued to practice baptism based on faith, accompanied by repentance, for the forgiveness of sins. (See Acts 2:38; 8:34–39; 16:33; 22:16.) From Romans 6:4 and Colossians 2:12 we learn that baptism is a symbolic burial with Jesus. Jesus commands baptism, based on faith and repentance, in His plan of salvation for the Christian faith (Matthew 28:18–19; Mark 16:15–16).

Immediately, when Jesus is baptized, God gives His approval. Again, we notice the activity of the Holy Spirit in the life and ministry of Jesus, reinforcing the aspect of divine intervention. On this occasion the Holy Spirit descends on Jesus like a dove, giving visual manifestation of His presence. Following that, a loud voice proclaims that Jesus is the Son of God, and that God is pleased with Him. Divine approval. We see two Old Testament passages brought together at this point, Isaiah 42:1 (Jesus as God's servant) and Psalm 2:7 (Jesus as God's Son), tying Jesus into the line of God's saving activity from the Old Testament to the present. In Judaism, the term *Son of God* had already become a phrase associated with the Messiah. (This same voice would again affirm Jesus in Matthew 17:5 at His transfiguration.)

Jesus' baptism plays a significant role in affirming Jesus' Sonship.

4:1–11

JESUS' TEMPTATION

Though the record in Mark is only two verses, the temptation of Jesus is found in all three synoptic Gospels (Matthew 4:1–11; Mark 1:12–13; Luke 4:1–13), indicating the significant role of the event. Matthew and Luke make more of this event than Mark does, and their records differ in order:

TEMPTATIONS	MATTHEW	LUKE
First	Stones into loaves	Stones into bread
Second	Pinnacle of temple	Kingdoms of the world
Third	Kingdoms of world	Pinnacle of temple

Luke's order for the temptations ends at the temple, a place that plays a central role in Luke's narrative. Matthew's order ends on the mountain, and mountain revelations play a major role in Matthew's narrative (for instance, the Sermon on the Mount).

Matthew's purpose for recording the temptations is more theological than chronological or historical. This should not be taken to mean that the temptations did not occur; it simply means that Matthew is making theological applications, not just reciting an event.

At a Glance: The Temptation of Christ			
TEMPTATION	**NATURE OF THE TEMPTATIONS**	**SATAN ARGUES**	**JESUS ANSWERS FROM SCRIPTURES**
Stones into loaves	Physical temptation: hunger	If you are the Son of God, tell these stones to become bread.	Man doesn't live on bread alone, but on every word God speaks. (Deuteronomy 8:3)
Pinnacle of temple	Physical temptation: personal safety	If you are the Son of God, throw yourself down and angels will catch you. (Psalm 91:11, 12)	Do not put God to the test. (Deuteronomy 6:16)
Kingdoms of world	Spiritual temptation: power	If you'll worship me, I'll give you all these kingdoms.	Worship the Lord God and serve Him only. (Deuteronomy 6:13)

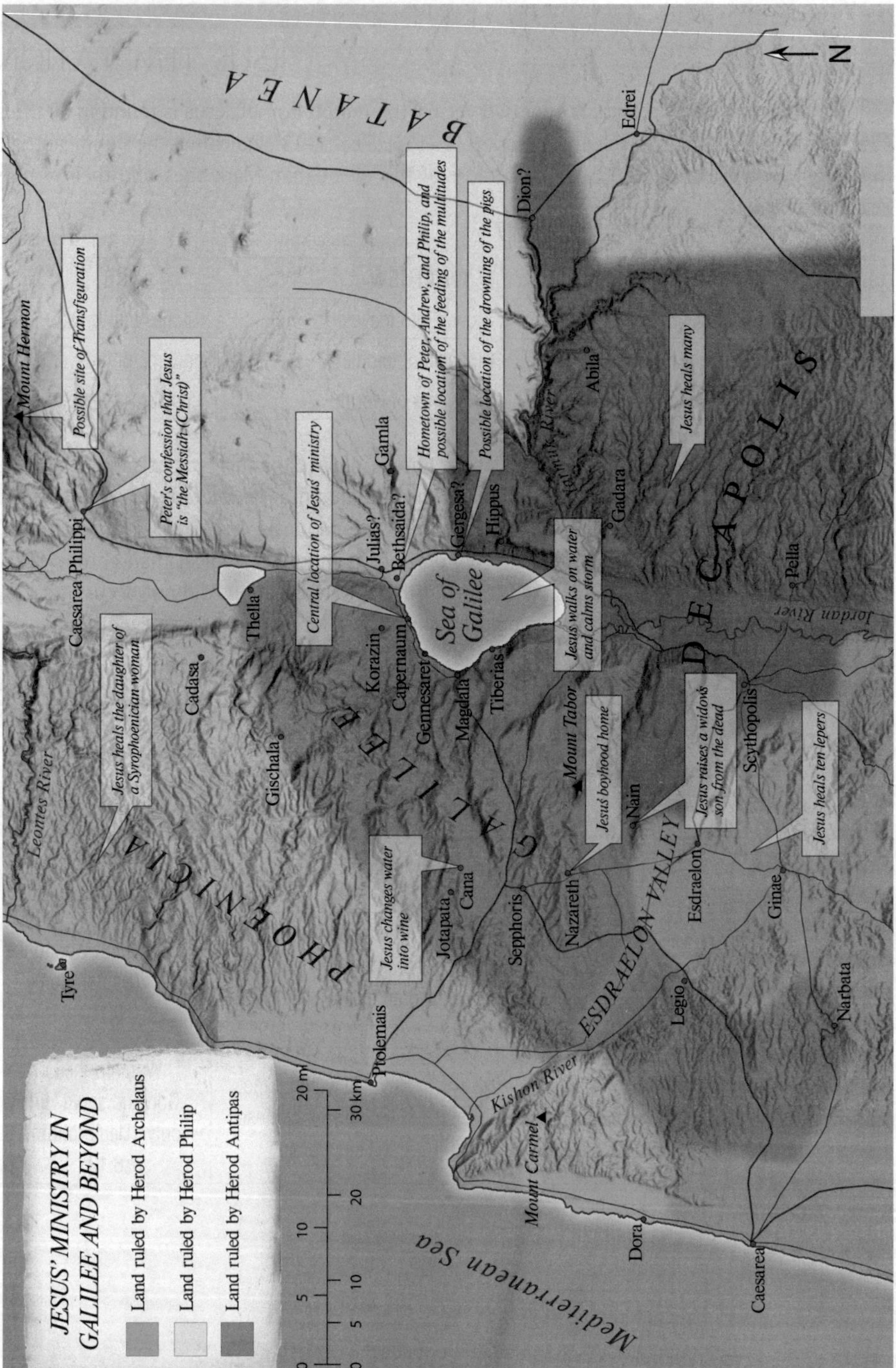
JESUS' MINISTRY IN GALILEE AND BEYOND
Land ruled by Herod Archelaus
Land ruled by Herod Philip
Land ruled by Herod Antipas
0 5 10 20 m
0 5 10 20 30 km
N
Mediterranean Sea
PHOENICIA
GALILEE
BATANEA
DECAPOLIS
ESDRAELON VALLEY
Sea of Galilee
Tyre
Leontes River
Mount Hermon
Caesarea Philippi
Cadasa
Thella
Gischala
Korazin
Capernaum
Gennesaret
Magdala
Tiberias
Julias?
Bethsaida?
Gamla
Gergesa?
Hippus
Gadara
Abila
Yarmuk River
Dion?
Edrei
Pella
Jordan River
Scythopolis
Mount Tabor
Nain
Nazareth
Sepphoris
Cana
Jotapata
Ptolemais
Esdraelon
Ginae
Legio
Narbata
Kishon River
Mount Carmel
Dora
Caesarea
Jesus heals the daughter of a Syrophoenician woman
Peter's confession that Jesus is "the Messiah (Christ)"
Possible site of Transfiguration
Central location of Jesus' ministry
Hometown of Peter, Andrew, and Philip, and possible location of the feeding of the multitudes
Possible location of the drowning of the pigs
Jesus walks on water and calms storm
Jesus heals many
Jesus changes water into wine
Jesus' boyhood home
Jesus raises a widow's son from the dead
Jesus heals ten lepers

Take It Home

There is a strong connection here between Israel's ancient story and Jesus' story. Jesus' forty days in the wilderness are analogous to Israel's forty years wandering in the wilderness. The three Old Testament passages Jesus cites are all from Israel's wilderness wanderings. When put to the test, Jesus succeeds where Israel had failed. This seems to be the central analogy in the temptation account.

There are several applications for us in the story of Jesus' temptation or testing in the wilderness.

1) Jesus is prepared for the temptation. He has been taken there by the Spirit, and He has fasted.
2) Jesus is identified as the Son of God. Satan himself recognizes that fact.
3) Jesus does not use His divine power to defeat Satan. He becomes a man, is tempted as a man, and dies as a man.
4) As a man, Jesus turns to God and His Word for strength and deliverance from temptation.

We can follow Jesus' pattern by practicing spiritual disciplines that will prepare us for temptation and by turning to God's Word for the strength and guidance we need to stay strong. Jesus came here to face the life we live so that He could show us how to better live (1 Corinthians 10:13).

4:12–17

THE BEGINNING OF JESUS' GALILEAN MINISTRY

The return to Galilee at the news of John's imprisonment is the first of several retreats Jesus makes. While Matthew mentions John's imprisonment here, it is not until Matthew 14:3 that he explains the reason: John had preached against Herod's marrying Herodias, his brother Philip's wife. John's arrest must have been a politically tense topic in Judea because he was popular with the community, having preached successfully in the wilderness and baptized many (Matthew 3:5 states all the region went out to hear him).

After visiting Nazareth, Jesus goes to Capernaum. From this point on, Capernaum becomes Jesus' home base. (All four Gospels inform us that Jesus moves to Capernaum at this point.) John adds that during the journey, Jesus spends a few days in Samaria, where He speaks to the woman at the well about living water (John 4:1–42).

Matthew introduces this narrative by referring to his fifth fulfillment passage, an application of Isaiah 9:1–2. In Isaiah, this prophecy pertained to the promised restoration of Israel. While the cities mentioned seem to be the tie-in for this prophecy, there is more. For so many years, particularly in captivity, Israel remained in a national and spiritual darkness, always with the hope of the light-bearing Messiah who would usher in God's salvation. Matthew is applying this hope to the beginning of Jesus' ministry. With this comment, Matthew adds that Jesus begins to preach. His message is that of John's—"Repent, for the kingdom of heaven is at hand" (NIV).

Critical Observation

Matthew 4:17 and 16:21 are key verses identifying a topical outline for Jesus' ministry. These two texts form pivotal points in the ministry of Jesus, separating or defining the periods of public and private ministry:

Matthew 1:1–4:16	Preparation for Ministry
Matthew 4:17–16:20	Public Ministry: Jesus' ministry to the Jews primarily in Galilee and Judea. He teaches as He performs miracles and clashes with the Jewish leadership.
Matthew 16:21–28:20	Private Ministry: Jesus' ministry to His disciples in the last week of His life prepares them for His trial, death, burial, and resurrection.

4:18–25

THE CALL OF THE DISCIPLES: PETER AND ANDREW, JAMES AND JOHN

All four of the New Testament Gospels describe the calling of the first disciples. The accounts of Matthew and Mark (Mark 1:16–20) are shorter than those of Luke (Luke 5:1–11) and John (John 1:35–42).

Peter and Andrew were brothers, as were James and John. They worked as partners in the fishing business. When Jesus calls the two groups of brothers, they immediately leave their fishing boats and their families and follow Jesus. The emphasis on *immediately* stresses the radical nature of discipleship to which they are called by Jesus.

The radical nature of discipleship will become a major theme in Matthew's Gospel. Luke recounts that henceforth the disciples will be catching people, not fish (Luke 5:10).

After the call of the first disciples, Jesus travels throughout Galilee and the Roman province of Syria, which included the Decapolis (a ten-city federation) and Judea. He teaches in the synagogues, local Jewish teaching centers, preaching the gospel of the kingdom and healing every disease and infirmity of the people, as well as casting out demons. Jesus' ministry, in all its aspects, is a fulfillment of His mission as Messiah (Matthew 11:2–6; 12:28; Luke 4:16–21).

MATTHEW 5:1–7:29

DISCOURSE 1: THE SERMON ON THE MOUNT

The Disciples' Character: The Beatitudes	5:1–12
On the Mountain	5:1–2
The Poor in Spirit	5:3
Those Who Mourn	5:4
The Meek	5:5

Those Who Hunger and Thirst for Righteousness	5:6
The Merciful	5:7
The Pure in Heart	5:8
The Peacemakers	5:9
Those Who Are Persecuted for Righteousness' Sake	5:10
When Men Revile You and Persecute You	5:11–12
The Disciples' Influence: Salt and Light	5:13–16
The Disciples' Righteousness: To Exceed That of the Scribes and Pharisees	5:17–20
The Six Antitheses	5:21–48
Antithesis one—Murder	5:21–26
Antithesis two—Adultery	5:27–30
Antithesis three—Divorce	5:31–32
Antithesis four—Oaths	5:33–37
Antithesis five—Retaliation	5:38–42
Antithesis six—Love	5:43–48
The Disciples' Piety: Deeds of Righteousness	6:1–18
Almsgiving	6:1–4
Prayer	6:5–15
Fasting	6:16–18
The Disciple's Ambition	6:19–34
True Riches	6:19–21
Two Parables	6:22–24
Trust and Anxiety	6:25–34
The Disciples' Pitfalls	7:1–20
Judging One Another	7:1–6
Prayer, Faith, and the Golden Rule	7:7–12
False Teachers	7:13–20
Commitment to Jesus and to the Will of God	7:21–27
Jesus' Authority	7:28–29

Setting Up the Section

To fully understand The Sermon on the Mount, it's best to know the context of the theology of Matthew and the discourse that grows out of his first narrative (Matthew 2–4). Matthew's theology is that Jesus is the Messiah, the King of God's kingdom, that He does the works of the Messiah, and that He calls disciples to follow Him and make disciples of all nations.

At the conclusion of the first narrative, Jesus has called disciples to follow Him. In Matthew 4:17 Jesus passes from His preparation for ministry into His public ministry.

The Sermon on the Mount picks up from the calling of the disciples and offers the called disciples information about what kind of person a disciple must be—character development. A key thought is that disciples are different in righteousness, piety, and ambition from the scribes and Pharisees (Jewish religious leaders), and from the Gentiles (non-Jews).

The Sermon can be broken down into seven sections:

- **Matthew 5:1–12 The Disciples' Character: The Beatitudes**
- **Matthew 5:13–16 The Disciples' Influence: Salt and Light**
- **Matthew 5:17–48 The Disciples' Righteousness: To Exceed That of the Scribes and Pharisees**
- **Matthew 6:1–18 The Disciples' Piety: Deeds of Righteousness**
- **Matthew 6:19–34 The Disciples' Ambition**
- **Matthew 7:1–27 The Disciples' Pitfalls**

5:1–12

THE DISCIPLES' CHARACTER: THE BEATITUDES (INTRODUCTION)

The word *Beatitudes* derives from the Latin *beatitudo* (supreme blessed, happy). The popular use of the term *beatitude* and its meaning of happiness derived from its Latin background lead to the unfortunate concept that these verses have to do with some form of happiness.

Actually, the Beatitudes teach what kind of person Jesus expects His disciples to be. They address the desired character of the disciples, but are given in the form of a blessing to those who manifest this character.

The term *blessed* carries with it the sense of deep spiritual richness. The Greek term that Matthew uses in chapter 5 is drawn from the Old Testament concept of blessedness that is found in the Wisdom Literature, especially the Psalms (Psalms 1:1; 2:12; 32:1) and in other Old Testament passages such as Isaiah 56:2; Jeremiah 17:7; and Daniel 12:12. When interpreting the word in Matthew 5, be careful to keep the meaning within this context.

Critical Observation

An interesting factor in the study of the Sermon on the Mount is a comparison of Matthew's account of the sermon to Luke's (for instance, Luke records fewer Beatitudes and in a different order than Matthew). Scholars are somewhat divided as to whether the sermons are the same sermon or whether both Matthew and Luke created their sermon from sayings delivered by Jesus on different occasions.

It's important to remember that each Gospel writer reported Jesus' sermon in a manner that suited his purpose and his particular audience. The sermons, however, have the same historical roots—they are true and reliable accounts of Jesus and His ministry.

To understand this passage, we need to understand it from two different perspectives. First, we should hear it from the perspective of Jesus' original listeners. He was addressing Jews who were longing for God to restore His kingdom to Israel.

Then we must understand it in terms of Matthew's original audience in the late first century. Matthew

CONTINUED

was writing for Jewish Christians who were struggling to understand the Messiah's role in light of the recent destruction of Jerusalem. They may have hoped for the Messiah to bring a political triumph for Jerusalem, but if so, it was obvious when the temple was destroyed that this triumph had not come about. So they had to sort through what Jesus' ministry and message meant, rather than what they had expected it to mean.

5:1–2

THE BEATITUDES: ON THE MOUNTAIN

The region north of the Sea of Galilee is mountainous. Several important events take place on mountains—Jesus' temptation (4:8); Jesus praying (14:23); healing (15:29); and the Transfiguration (17:1).

Jesus assumed the authority of a rabbi with His teaching style and pose:

- He sat down, the customary position for teaching rabbis in Palestine.
- He opened His mouth, a Semitic idiom for public address.
- He began to teach.

5:3

THE BEATITUDES: THE POOR IN SPIRIT

Poor in spirit means spiritually destitute without God. There are two Greek words for poor. The one used here means not simply "poor," but "abject poverty." It is only when the disciple understands that he is destitute without God that he can truly be blessed and filled by God.

Kingdom of heaven, the inheritance of the poor in spirit, is the same as kingdom of God. (See the discussion of this in Matthew 3:2.) *Kingdom* means the reign of God from heaven, or the reign of Christ. The kingdom or reign of God demands complete surrender to God. Only the poor in spirit, those who recognize that without God they are spiritually destitute, can surrender completely to the reign of God.

5:4

THE BEATITUDES: THOSE WHO MOURN

Only those who mourn truly understand the need for comfort.

The background to this Beatitude is Isaiah 61:2–3. This passage is in the context of God's promise of restoration for those who repent. This is also the text that Jesus uses to introduce His ministry at Nazareth (Luke 4:18). Although this Beatitude carries the concept of mourning in general, within the context of Jesus' ministry the mourning is specifically for personal sin and estrangement from God.

5:5

THE BEATITUDES: THE MEEK

The Greek word translated "meek" means gentle, humble, considerate, and unassuming. Jesus did not simply have in mind those who were gentle and kind, but rather those who were humble and downtrodden and oppressed. These will be the true heirs of God's promise and covenant with Abraham.

5:6

THE BEATITUDES: THOSE WHO HUNGER AND THIRST FOR RIGHTEOUSNESS

Those who hunger and thirst after righteousness are the poor, downtrodden, and oppressed, who are longing for the relief promised by God to His people. The term *righteousness* is a popular religious concept in both the Old and New Testaments. In the context of the Beatitudes (poor, downtrodden, grieving) it is best understood as justice. In this instance, it is best to understand righteousness as not just personal moral righteousness, but societal righteousness, or justice.

5:7

THE BEATITUDES: THE MERCIFUL

Justice and mercy were significant themes of the Old Testament prophets. On several occasions Jesus challenges the Pharisees and religious leaders of His day with the idea that God wants their mercy, more than their sacrifice. Jesus has in mind passages such as Hosea 6:6 and Micah 6:6–8. Mercy is obviously a fundamental characteristic of a disciple of Jesus.

5:8

THE BEATITUDES: THE PURE IN HEART

To see God is a Hebrew saying for standing before God (Psalm 11:7), or having fellowship with God in His kingdom. It is only those with a pure heart who are able to stand before God. This Beatitude recalls the thrust of several psalms such as Psalm 24:3–4.

5:9

THE BEATITUDES: THE PEACEMAKERS

The term translated as "peacemakers" is only found twice in the New Testament, here and in Colossians 1:20. The reason for this Beatitude lies most likely in the turbulent days of Israel under Roman rule. The violence came to a head for Judea and Jerusalem in the late 60s AD and the destruction of Jerusalem in AD 70.

Late in Jesus' ministry (according to John 13:35), He encourages the apostles to understand that the world will know that they are His disciples because they love one another. Here in Matthew He adds that it is those who are peacemakers who will be called children of God. The stress on peace, and following after things that make for peace, becomes a significant motif for disciples in the New Testament (Romans 12:16–18; 14:19; Hebrews 12:14; James 3:18; 1 Peter 3:11).

5:10

THE BEATITUDES: THOSE WHO ARE PERSECUTED FOR RIGHTEOUSNESS' SAKE

Righteousness in the Jewish sense had to do with a person's relationship with God. The righteous were in a right relationship with God. Because of that relationship, disciples would be persecuted. Persecution was synonymous with discipleship in the first three centuries of the Christian faith.

Jesus later warns the disciples that their discipleship will lead them into opposition with their families, the authorities, and the world. Many will die for their faith. He ties the blessedness of persecution to *suffering for righteousness sake*, not merely suffering for any reason. The reward of suffering persecution faithfully is a share in the kingdom (reign) of God. This is the very message of Revelation—if you die as a martyr for your faith in Jesus, you reign with Jesus in His kingdom.

5:11–12

THE BEATITUDES: WHEN MEN REVILE YOU AND PERSECUTE YOU

This Beatitude is obviously an expansion on the previous one regarding persecution. Jesus warns that being a disciple will cause some people to react harshly. In Jesus' day Christianity certainly was a threat to the Pharisees, Sadducees, and others who did not see in Jesus the kind of political Messiah they hoped for.

SUMMARY OF THE BEATITUDES:

- The Beatitudes addressed the disciples' character.
- They are set in the context of Old Testament theology and Jewish expectation.
- The blessedness they promised is a deep, inner spiritual richness, not a superficial happiness.
- They stress the radical nature of Christian discipleship.

5:13–16

THE DISCIPLES' INFLUENCE: SALT AND LIGHT

In regard to the influence that disciples have, notice that Jesus does not say the disciples should be *like* salt and light. He says they are salt and light. Disciples are expected to be an influence on those with whom they come into contact.

With reference to salt, Jesus picks a common metaphor. Everyone listening would know about salt and its unique characteristics. Whether Jesus is focusing more on the preservative nature, the seasoning nature, or the purifying nature of salt is impossible to determine. All three have relevant applications.

The salt that loses its saltiness is likely a reference to the impure salt drawn from the Dead Sea, which contained other minerals. Normally today, salt does not lose its saltiness, but the common salt of Jesus' day may well have been known for this characteristic. Whatever the case, salt that does not produce saltiness is worthy of being discarded.

The reference to light is intriguing. Typically light is a common metaphor referring to God rather than His followers (Isaiah 60:19–20; John 8:12; 1 John 1:5). Light was often opposed to darkness as an illustration of the radical difference between God and evil.

Jesus is the light of the world; His disciples are to reflect that light. The result of lives used properly to reflect the light of the kingdom will result in praise and glory being given to God.

5:17–20

THE DISCIPLES' RIGHTEOUSNESS: TO EXCEED THAT OF THE SCRIBES AND PHARISEES

The major thrust of this section is that the disciples' righteousness must exceed that of the scribes and Pharisees—the Jewish religious leaders of the day. Also, the disciples' righteousness must be the right kind of righteousness. Here Jesus is pointing out that it's not *how* one becomes righteous, but rather the *nature* of that righteousness. At this time, the scribes and Pharisees held that righteousness could only be possible if one obeyed every minutia of the law as taught by the Jewish system and the traditions associated with it.

Jesus begins by stressing that His purpose is not to destroy the Law, but to establish its real purpose. In doing this, He addresses the scribes' and Pharisees' attitudes through six opposing conceptions or antitheses. Jesus wants the attitude of a disciple to address the deeper matters, the root issues for which the Law was intended, those which the scribes and Pharisees had missed.

The fact that Jesus intends to fulfill Jewish Law is vitally important to His ministry. In fact, He repeats the saying twice in a parallel form. But what exactly does Jesus mean by *fulfill*? The word translated "fulfill" can mean to accomplish, to complete, to finish, to bring to an end, to validate, to confirm, to establish, to uphold, or to bring out the intended meaning.

To emphasize His conviction that He has no intention of destroying the Law, Jesus adds that heaven and earth will pass away before He removes one *jot* (smallest letter, comma) or *dot* (period, tittle, little stroke) from the Law. The jot is a translation of *iota*, the letter "i" in English and the smallest letter in the Greek alphabet or the *yod*, one of the smallest letters in the Hebrew alphabet. The dot is one of the minute markings of a written text.

Matthew 5:20 is the clinching statement, or what this section is all about. It is possibly the key and pivotal statement to what follows in the Six Antitheses, and in Jesus' understanding of righteousness. His point: Kingdom righteousness is different from that of the established scribes and Pharisees. Jesus does not deny that the scribes and Pharisees have some form of righteousness. However, He stresses that their righteousness is not adequate for kingdom righteousness.

Critical Observation: Matthew's Understanding of Righteousness

Although the word *righteousness* is not often found in Matthew, the concept of righteousness is fundamental to Jesus' and Matthew's teaching. We can summarize Matthew's use of righteousness as:

1) the right relationship to God and His will, and

2) the right conduct that flows from that relationship to God.

In the Sermon on the Mount (here at 5:20, but also at 6:1 and 6:33), the point Jesus makes is that the behavior that flows from the disciples' relationship with God must be deeper and more extensive than that of the scribes and Pharisees, whose concept of righteousness was limited to superficial deeds in accordance with their interpretations of the Law.

5:21–6:48

THE SIX ANTITHESES (INTRODUCTION)

The expression "you have heard that it was said. . ." (NIV) is repeated in five of the antitheses and is included in similar form in the third antithesis. The use of this phrase was a typical device by which the teaching rabbis demurred from pitting their views against scripture, or even readily commenting on scripture. It was their custom to refer back to the teachings and conclusions of previous rabbis with the expression, "you have heard that it was said," contrasting their views with the rabbinic tradition rather than scripture.

Jesus sets His teaching against the rabbinic tradition with this same traditional saying but then draws His conclusions from scripture, correcting the rabbinic tradition. Jesus' teaching, therefore, carries a much stronger scriptural authority. It is no wonder that at the end of the Sermon on the Mount, the crowds are astonished because He teaches with authority (7:29).

5:21–26

ANTITHESIS ONE—MURDER

In Jesus' mind, the rabbinic teaching "You shall not kill; and whosoever kills shall be liable to judgment" misses the meaning and purpose of the sixth commandment (Exodus 20:13). The quotation of the commandment is precisely as stated in Exodus 20:13 and Deuteronomy 5:17; the concluding comment regarding judgment is an interpretation of the commandment.

It is difficult to determine with any certainty what was meant in the rabbinic tradition by *judgment*. In all probability, it referenced the judgment and death penalty of the Jewish Sanhedrin. If we move from that Jewish understanding, and remember that Jesus and Matthew are speaking to Jews, then we should interpret Jesus' teaching from within that Jewish context. The Jewish court system was similar to our present day court system, ranging from local county courts to state courts up to state supreme courts and the national supreme court. The Jewish system had a local Sanhedrin comprised of twenty-three male members, and then the Jerusalem Sanhedrin was comprised of seventy-one male members. Cases would move from the local court to the Jerusalem Sanhedrin.

The mention of "the fire of hell" certainly has eschatological (end times) judgment overtones. The phrase is from a Hebrew word meaning Valley of Hinnom, a valley which lay just outside the city of Jerusalem to the south. This was a smelly, smoky place where the city refuse was burned. In earlier pagan days it had been the place of human sacrifice. This valley became a suitable Jewish metaphor for the final judgment.

Jesus goes right to the heart of murder, addressing anger that grows to insult and finally into open denigration, which often lies at the heart of murder. The strict adherence to the sixth and other commandments was admirable, but fell short of the divine intent of the commandments.

In Matthew 22:36–40 Jesus observes that to love God and one's neighbor is the sum of the commandments, and in Matthew 19:16–22 Jesus tells the rich young man that there is more to eternal life than merely keeping the letter of the commandments. Jesus is teaching that there is more to the sixth commandment than mere murder.

The next verses (5:23–26), regarding making things right with your brother before taking an offering to the altar of sacrifice, drive home the point that God wants more than mere sacrifice. He wants love, mercy, and righteousness. This reinforces Jesus' message that love comes before the strict literal performance of the commandments. This does not diminish the need to respect and keep the commandments. It does, however, demand the correct understanding of the meaning of the commandments.

5:27–30

ANTITHESIS TWO—ADULTERY

This quotation of the seventh commandment is verbatim from Exodus 20:14 and Deuteronomy 5:18. The word translated "adultery" is the normal word for the breaking of the marriage covenant in extramarital sexual intercourse.

Like the previous teaching of Jesus on murder, this teaching goes straight to the heart of the commandment—not the mere commission of the act, but the inner thought and being of the person. Jesus describes the heart of the sin—the lust of the eye and mind, the desiring or imagining a sexual relationship. From Jesus' perspective, this lustful desire of the eye and heart is the same as committing adultery, only this adultery is perhaps more serious than the act itself, for it speaks of the heart of man rather than merely his actions.

The plucking out of the offending right eye and right hand is a Hebrew idiom or hyperbole stressing the seriousness of the action or offense. This antithesis on adultery leads straight into the third antithesis on divorce.

5:31–32

ANTITHESIS THREE—DIVORCE

Unlike the previous two antitheses, this one is not based on one of the commandments, but arises out of the command against adultery. Jesus will again comment on divorce in Matthew 19:3–12, where He is tested by the Pharisees on Deuteronomy 24. The debate on Deuteronomy 24 was obviously one that engaged the scribes and Pharisees considerably.

Although Jesus comments briefly on divorce and remarriage in this section, He does so because of the previous discussion on adultery. Jesus does not get involved in a lengthy discussion on divorce, but uses the occasion to address the problem of divorce. The proximity of this teaching to adultery leads one to believe that adultery and divorce both arise in the lustful heart of men. Whatever Jesus says about divorce and remarriage must be seen in the context of what He has most recently been discussing—adultery.

The current teaching was that all a man had to do was to give his wife a certificate of divorce in accordance with Moses' instruction (Deuteronomy 24). Jesus' response challenges the superficiality of that practice. In the discussion among the rabbis on divorce and remarriage in Jesus' day, two opinions held sway, that of Rabbi Hillel and that of Rabbi Shammai. Rabbi Hillel interpreted Deuteronomy 24 loosely so that divorce was granted for almost any reason. Rabbi Shammai interpreted Deuteronomy 24 narrowly so that divorce was granted only in cases of unchastity or sexual immorality. (See Demystifying Mark," page 180.)

Again, as in the case of the previous two antitheses, Jesus takes the more difficult road that challenges the inner heart of a person rather than the superficial nature. In this third antithesis Jesus takes the narrower view of divorce indicating that kingdom ethics on the matter of marriage and divorce are different from the laissez-faire ethic of much of the current attitude of His day. In Jesus' radical view of discipleship, more is expected of in the kingdom than is manifest in the practice of the day. (In Matthew 19:10, Jesus' attitude is so narrow that even the disciples have problems with it.)

5:33–37

ANTITHESIS FOUR—OATHS

In this case Jesus is not taking issue with how the scribes and Pharisees treated a commandment, but rather against the lax rabbinic rationalization in the treatment of oaths. Jesus is addressing a crystallization of several teachings (Leviticus19:12; Numbers 30:2; Deuteronomy 23:21–23; and possibly Exodus 20:7).

In this day and time oaths were used to assure the truth of the one making a promise, similar to a witness swearing to tell the whole truth with his or her hand on the Bible. Oaths could be sworn on many things. Swearing by heaven, the temple, earth (the footstool of God), Jerusalem, or one's head were typical examples of how rabbinic thinking shifted the oath to a lesser one which was not as binding as an oath before God.

Jesus teaches that kingdom ethics demand absolute integrity rather than the easy way out offered by lesser oaths. Kingdom ethics demand that the disciples' word be binding regardless of an oath. Jesus is not teaching against oaths taken, but against the attitude that lesser oaths are not binding. Nor is Jesus teaching against taking oaths, since Jesus takes an oath in Matthew 26:63–64 and God swears by His promise and His person (Luke 1:73; Acts 2:30; Hebrews 6:16–18).

5:38–42

ANTITHESIS FIVE—RETALIATION

Rabbinic practice in response to the law that permitted recompense for loss (Exodus 21:24; Leviticus 24:20; Deuteronomy 19:21) permitted equal recompense for loss by one's neighbor. A legalistic response to personal loss was not what this original law was intended to accomplish. Jesus' understanding of these laws is that they were intended to restrict *excessive* retaliation rather than empower retaliation. Jesus' teaching runs in opposition to the current practice and normal human reactions. In broad sweeping terms, He teaches that kingdom ethics elicit no retaliation at all. Illustrating the extent of kingdom ethics, Jesus encourages the disciples when taken to court over a coat (inner garment) to surrender a cloak (outer garment) as well.

5:43–48

ANTITHESIS SIX—LOVE

The command to love your neighbor is drawn directly from Leviticus19:18, and later Jesus will teach that this is the second most important commandment. The second part of rabbinic teaching, to hate your enemy, is not commanded or taught directly, but may be a summary drawn from such passages as Psalm 139:21–22; 26:5; or Deuteronomy 7:2 and 30:7. Following centuries of aggression against Israel's enemies in the occupation of Canaan and Palestine, it is natural that Jews would see hating one's enemy as a legitimate attitude.

Jesus' response is a radical departure from current Jewish attitudes toward enemies, and the Jews had many enemies among the Roman occupation armies. In contrast to hating, Jesus teaches love for one's enemies, and prayers for those persecuting the disciple. Since persecution is to be a major part of discipleship for several centuries, this teaching will be a critical aspect of future kingdom ethics and behavior.

6:1–18

THE DISCIPLES' PIETY: DEEDS OF RIGHTEOUSNESS (INTRODUCTION)

Setting Up the Section

In this section on the disciple's piety we find three important emphases:

1) Almsgiving
2) Prayer
3) Fasting

These three elements were important religious practices of Jewish religious lives.

6:1–4

THE DISCIPLES' PIETY: ALMSGIVING

The main thrust of this section is that the disciple's piety, almsgiving, and prayer are not to be like that of the hypocrites who did their righteous deeds to be seen and admired by others. The disciple's prayer is also to be different from that of the Gentiles.

Although disciples are to let their lives shine as light (5:14), they are not to do so in order to be seen and admired by others. The reward of a public display of deeds is the public acclamation of others. The reward of righteous piety is the reward from the Father in heaven. Jesus is reacting to the public performance of piety practiced by many of the Jewish leaders of His time.

Matthew appropriately connects piety with the practice of almsgiving (6:2). The practice of giving money to the poor was common among the Jews. We have already noticed Jesus' concern for the poor in Matthew (5:3).

This was a Jewish problem of considerable concern to Jesus, as can be seen in His strong language. The English word *hypocrite* comes from a word that originally referred to one who performs in front of others, an actor. This is Jesus' opinion of the righteousness of the scribes and Pharisees. He sees in the Jewish leaders of the day an insincerity that is not befitting of the kingdom.

The expression, "do not let your left hand know what your right hand is doing. . ." (NIV) is a Hebrew idiom indicating the discretion needed in the process of doing benevolent works.

6:5–15

THE DISCIPLES' PIETY: PRAYER

Public prayer can be a challenge, especially to the one leading the prayer. There is the danger of it being said to impress others rather than being addressed to God. Here Jesus takes exception to the prayers of both the Jews and the Gentiles.

Apparently some people prayed in public to be seen by others. Jesus again observes that those who pray to be seen by others have their human reward in the acclamation of others, but those who pray unobtrusively will be seen by God.

In regard to the Gentiles, the empty phrases (babbling, rambling, repeating) are apparently attempts to manipulate God into fulfilling some desire of the petitioner by repeating a supposed magic formula, not merely the repetition of words. From Jesus' instruction and His own religious lifestyle, prayer should be an important aspect of the disciple's righteousness.

What follows is commonly referred to as the Lord's Prayer. Some take exception to this name and prefer to call this the Model Prayer. Certainly this is intended to be a model prayer—Jesus' words opening Matthew 6:9 indicate this clearly—but in contrast to model prayers taught by others (John the Baptist to his disciples) this is Jesus' model prayer, so it can legitimately be referred to as the Lord's Prayer.

Luke records that in this prayer, or at least on a similar occasion, Jesus' disciples ask Him to teach them to pray "as John taught his disciples. . ." (Luke 11:1 NIV).

From what we know of Judaism in Jesus' day, His model prayer is shaped by the prayer tradition and pattern of the synagogue. The primary concern is a redemptive theme, not concern for mundane, earthly matters.

Note the remarkable structure of the opening of this prayer. All three of these parallel clauses are modified by the last clause of the petition: on earth as it is in heaven. What this means is that disciples are to pray that:

God's name would be holy. . .as it is in heaven, so on earth;
God's kingdom would come. . .as it is in heaven, so on earth;
God's will would be done. . .as it is in heaven, so on earth.

This is not a prayer that God's kingdom would come sometime in the near future, but a prayer that God's kingdom would be presently on earth just as it is in heaven. How? By His name being holy and His will being done.

The second petition of the Lord's Prayer (6:11) looks simple on the surface, but just what does Jesus mean by His request for daily bread? The Greek reads, "The bread of ours for tomorrow give us today." If this is a simple prayer for physical food, then it is the only emphasis on the physical in The Lord's Prayer. All the other petitions are for spiritual concerns. While there may be several interpretations, Jesus is not simply concerned for the mundane physical food (although this would fit well into the prayer for daily sustenance), but also for the spiritual food that sustains us for the future.

The next petition for forgiveness (6:12) is a prayer for the forgiveness of sins or, perhaps better put, shortcomings. The point in this petition is that disciples should pray to God on a regular basis for the forgiveness of their sins, but also that disciples must be forgiving like their Father in heaven.

The final petition (6:13) relates to temptation. First, the word often translated as "temptation" can mean both temptation and testing. While James 1:13 informs us that God does not tempt His children, God does allow His children to be tested. This is one of the secondary lessons we learn from the Old Testament book of Job.

However, this petition cannot be fully understood until put in context with the request for deliverance from evil. Perhaps it is better to translate *evil* as "the evil one." This petition is a plea to God that He deliver, rescue, guard, and protect those facing trials.

The final verses of this section (6:14–15) repeat the warning and encouragement to forgive one another as the Father forgives the disciple. However, here the statement is in a conditional form—if you forgive. . .your Father will forgive your trespasses.

6:16–18

THE DISCIPLES' PIETY: FASTING

Again, Jesus contrasts the disciple's righteous behavior with that of the Jewish leaders whose fasting had become a performance of righteousness.

Fasting is an interesting subject. This is a Jewish practice that is more traditional than biblical in the sense that fasting was not commanded but practiced. We read of people in scripture fasting, but nowhere does it seem that it is commanded. Rabbinic tradition informs us that the stricter Jews fasted regularly on special days such as Monday and Thursdays.

From what we learn in the Gospels, Jesus is neither proposing that disciples fast nor condemning the practice of fasting. He simply speaks out against hypocritical fasting, which had as its goal to be noticed. Some fasting Jews disfigured their faces, didn't keep their hair tidy, or smeared ashes on their faces. It was this ostentation that Jesus speaks out against. Anointing the head (with oil) and washing the face, which Jesus suggests, has the opposite effect of the facial disfiguration or the smeared ashes.

Though fasting is less in the forefront today, the principles Jesus gives are still relevant. If a disciple chooses to fast as an occasion of deep spiritual mourning or commitment, this is admirable and to be commended. However, it should be a private matter and not become a spectacle. Demanding others fast or indirectly communicating that fasting is a sign of one's spiritual superiority over another is an abuse of this fine practice.

6:19–34

THE DISCIPLES' AMBITION (INTRODUCTION)

Setting Up the Section

The general thrust of this section is this: The disciple's ambition should be toward being rich in God, not in worldly things. The key to this passage relates to the problem we all have with anxiety over the things of this life. Disciples must know that their hope and comfort lie not in Jerusalem or this world but in the future prepared by God for His people.

6:19–21

THE DISCIPLES' AMBITION: TRUE RICHES

This passage serves as a key to the upcoming discussion on anxiety. It was common in the Jewish tradition to see good works as being the treasures that one lays up in heaven—not good works as merit, but good works as serving. The result of true discipleship (loving service, good works) is a treasure waiting in heaven. Jesus promises a treasure in heaven to those who give to the poor (19:21).

6:22–24

THE DISCIPLES' AMBITION: TWO PARABLES

Jesus reinforces His point with two parables, one regarding the problem of covetousness and lust, the other the problem of serving two masters.

The good (single, clear, unclouded) eye is contrasted with the bad (evil, diseased) eye. In both instances, Jesus is speaking figuratively of covetousness and lust. The thought carries over from the previous discussion on treasure—what a person covets or lusts after shapes his or her life.

The second parable of two masters is clearly understood in a culture familiar with slavery. The term *mammon* (money, wealth, property) illustrates the anxiety of physical earthly matters as opposed to spiritual heavenly matters. In Luke 16:9–11, Luke adds the term *unrighteous* mammon (tainted, dishonest, worldly), contrasting this focus in life with true righteousness that derives from a right relationship with God.

The expression of hating the one and loving the other (6:24) was a common Jewish idiom that stressed the contrast between absolute and partial commitment. The love-hate terminology found in both Judaism and Jesus' teaching should not be taken literally, but should be understood as an idiom stressing the absolute priority of certain matters over others.

6:25–34

THE DISCIPLES' AMBITION: TRUST AND ANXIETY

This section is also found in almost the same content in Luke 12:22–31, although some of the terms used by Luke differ from those used by Matthew. Both Matthew and Luke find this teaching of Jesus to be fundamental to their teaching, stressing the proper focus and commitment of discipleship.

Jesus reminds the disciples that life is full of matters more necessary than food and clothing. As important as physical concerns may be, they must never dominate the disciples' dedication. Jesus' illustration of the birds and flowers is most meaningful and beautiful. The God who is able to take care of and provide for His natural creation can surely take care of and provide for His ultimate and spiritual creation—mankind.

In contrast to this, Jesus encourages disciples to seek other goals and priorities in life that hold better and more lasting hope. This is the climactic teaching of the whole section, and perhaps of the entire Sermon on the Mount—seek first His kingdom, and everything else will follow (6:33). Perhaps these words are some of the best known of all Jesus' teachings. But what do they mean?

The first priority of the disciple is to seek the reign of God in one's own life. This whole section is an encouragement to refocus one's life, and a warning against anxieties that interfere with ultimate matters such as God's reign and a right relationship with God.

The admonition to not be anxious about tomorrow (6:34) is similar to the prayer of Matthew 6:11 for daily bread. The disciple should be more concerned for the present today than for what might happen tomorrow, over which we have no control. Do not be anxious of tomorrow or the future. Leave that to God; He will provide.

7:1–20

THE DISCIPLES' PITFALLS (INTRODUCTION)

Setting Up the Section

In this section the disciples are warned of the pitfall of constantly judging one another (as was the practice of the Pharisees), and are encouraged to treat one another as they would like to be treated (the Golden Rule). Finally, Matthew includes admonitions by Jesus to be alert to false teachers, and a call to commitment to the teachings of Jesus and the will of God.

7:1–6

THE DISCIPLES' PITFALLS: JUDGING ONE ANOTHER

Apparently the tendency to judge one another was widespread in the first century and has been common in religious groups throughout history.

Although Christianity should be an exception to this weakness (the basic ethical foundation to the Christian faith is that disciples, being children of God, should love one another since love is the fulfillment of the law, and God is love [see John 13:34, 35; 1 John 3:11; 4:7]), but human nature still leaves Christians open to this sin.

When Jesus says, "Judge not...," He is not saying that believers should not be discerning or should never point out sin. Jesus is not implying that disciples should never make personality or relational decisions, sometimes even judgments, but that they should beware that this does not become habitual. There are certainly times when disciples must make fellowship decisions (1 Corinthians 5:9–13; 2 Thessalonians 3:6–13), and other times when disciples must simply decide that they cannot share in the lifestyle of others. But the warning is against becoming judgmental and continually pointing to the faults of others, instead of loving them and looking out for their best interests.

Jesus' amusing story of a man with a log in his eye, trying to take a speck out of another's eye, is one of the most powerful and telling illustrations of human foolishness manifest in many of our judgmental situations. If we took our own imperfections seriously, we would have little time for judging others. Jesus' warning is punctuated by the harsh term *hypocrite*, which, as before, implies a play actor. Those who make a habit of judging others are playacting in the Christian faith.

The next short section has raised several problems for interpretation. The parable in itself is not difficult. One should not give to the unclean (dogs and swine) that which is clean or holy.

However, does *the unclean* refer to Gentiles, or simply to the undeserving? Does it perhaps refer to the hypocrite of 7:5? It is difficult to determine what holy thing Jesus is referring to at this point as it relates to the previous admonition against judging. It may be in the larger picture that in the kingdom, disciples who love one another should not destroy the harmony of the kingdom by their sinful tendency to constantly be judging one another. The nature of a disciple's life in the kingdom, or the nature of the harmony of the kingdom, is that which is holy.

7:7–12

THE DISCIPLES' PITFALLS: PRAYER, FAITH, AND THE GOLDEN RULE

The next pitfall disciples face is the loss of faith (7:7–12). Jesus encourages His disciples to keep on asking, seeking, and knocking, for true faith never loses heart and quits.

Again, Matthew follows this encouragement of Jesus with a saying that seems to be detached, the Golden Rule, but it does have some connection to the previous admonitions of Jesus. Disciples are to be like their heavenly Father. They are to love one another and be constant in their faith.

The Golden Rule, as this saying is commonly known, is not unique to Jesus or Christianity, for it is found in most religions in some form. In Judaism it is found in the negative form. Rabbi Hillel summarized it as follows: "What is hateful to yourself, do to no other." The Christian form as given by Jesus is, however, more positive and powerful than the negative form, which does not deny the good intention of the negative form. Again, this proverbial saying is simply another way of expressing the fundamental kingdom ethic of loving one another. The Golden Rule, expressing the law of love, is what the law and prophets were all about (7:12).

7:13–20

THE DISCIPLES' PITFALLS: FALSE TEACHERS

The following three admonitions, all demonstrating pitfalls the disciple faces, are related. They address the problem of false teachers and commitment to the teachings of Jesus.

We are again introduced to the Jewish idiom of two opposing ways—here, one is the narrow way, the other way broad. The narrow way is the more difficult. Jesus knows that the road ahead for disciples will call for opposition and even serious persecution. Faced by such choices, disciples will be tempted to choose the easier way, perhaps that of retaining their Jewish religion based on law rather than following God in freedom.

The New Testament is replete with warnings against false teachers, indicating the seriousness of the problem faced by the early church. However, false teachings in the New Testament do not refer to differences of biblical interpretation or church doctrines. In the New Testament the truth or sound doctrine refers to teachings regarding the nature of Jesus as the Son of God, the Messiah. Apostasy is a denial of the divinity of Jesus and His death, burial, and resurrection. False teaching is that which denies the all-sufficiency of Jesus and the gospel of grace through faith that was preached by the apostles.

7:21–27

COMMITMENT TO JESUS AND TO THE WILL OF GOD

Jesus is fully aware that many will follow Him, but on their own terms or when it is convenient. Obedience to the will of God will be the hallmark of true discipleship. In the context of the Sermon, with its heavy emphasis on righteousness as the right relationship with God and His will, it is not surprising the Jesus closes with this teaching. Failure to submit to and do the will of God will result in Jesus' denial of the disciple.

Jesus refers to entering the kingdom in the future (7:21). The verb in the future tense indicates that Jesus has in mind the future eschatological kingdom that one will enter after the judgment day—not the present reality of the inaugurated kingdom we currently enjoy. This is also supported by the words *on that day* (7:22). This is a common Jewish reference to the judgment day and is found in many instances in both the Old and New Testaments (Isaiah 2:20; Amos 8:9; 9:11; Zephaniah 1:10, 14; Zechariah 14:4; 2 Thessalonians 1:10; 2 Timothy 4:8).

The parable of the two builders (7:24–27) provides a powerful conclusion to this section on commitment to the will of God, as well as to Jesus' emphasis on the necessity of doing the will of God.

7:28–29

JESUS' AUTHORITY

When Jesus finishes teaching, the crowds are astonished at the authority with which He spoke to them. A statement like this can be found at the conclusion of each of the great discourses in Matthew. In each of these formula endings to the teachings of Jesus, Matthew draws attention to the authoritative role of Jesus:

- Matthew 5–7 He teaches the crowds (The Sermon on the Mount)
- Matthew 10 He teaches His disciples (The Limited Commission)
- Matthew 13 He teaches the disciples (The Kingdom Parables)
- Matthew 18 He teaches the disciples (The Christian Community)
- Matthew 23–25 He teaches the disciples (The Apocalyptic Discourse)

This is one of Matthew's tools that emphasizes the unique character of Jesus.

MATTHEW 8:1–9:38

NARRATIVE 2: THE AUTHORITY OF THE MESSIAH

Cleansing a Leper	8:1–4
The Centurion's Servant Healed	8:5–13
Peter's Mother-in-law Healed	8:14–17
Impulsive and Reluctant Would-Be Disciples	8:18–22
The Storm Stilled	8:23–27
Demons Cast Out	8:28–34
A Paralytic Forgiven and Healed	9:1–8

Matthew's Call	9:9–13
The Questing about Fasting	9:14–17
The Issue of Blood Stopped and the Dead Raised	9:18–26
The Blind See, and a Demon Is Exorcised	9:27–34
The Need for Workers	9:35–38

Setting Up the Section

In this section we move from one miracle to the next as we see Jesus performing the works expected of the Messiah. The focus here is on the messianic deeds Jesus performs. Matthew follows Mark in recording a string of Jesus' miracles, with a few observations included by Matthew. As in Mark, Matthew demonstrates Jesus' power over physical illnesses of all types, the demon world, as well as His power over the physical world of nature. The miracles of restoration and healing recorded here also indicate the presence of the kingdom of God (Isaiah 29:22–24; 35:3–10).

While Jesus continues to do the powerful works expected of the Messiah, He is not accepted by the scribes and Pharisees.

8:1–4

CLEANSING A LEPER

Leprosy was a common ailment in the ancient world, and one Israel had encountered throughout its history. It was a most dreaded illness. Biblical leprosy is not the same as modern leprosy (Hansen's disease). In the Bible, the word *leprosy* refers to a variety of skin ailments, some serious and some not—but all rendered its sufferer unclean. Thus, the issue of leprosy has as much to do with ritual uncleanness as great danger to health or imminent death.

Having been declared a leper, a person was considered dead. Leprosy was so serious a problem that the Mosaic Law addressed the condition of the leper and the process of being cured from this dreaded illness (Leviticus 13–14). Jesus heals this man and instructs him not to tell anyone about his healing, but to do as the Law of Moses commanded regarding cleansing from leprosy.

Jesus' instruction not to tell anyone about the cleansing is in line with His desire not to be followed because of sensationalism. Jesus simply does not wish to be followed because of mistaken understandings of His messianic role.

Jesus' instruction for the leper to show himself to the priest as proof (a witness) is interesting. The proof was in keeping with the Jewish legal requirements for a cleansed leper's return to society. Jesus' requiring this demonstrates His support of the Jewish law.

8:5–13

THE CENTURION'S SERVANT HEALED

The centurion was either a Syrian or Roman, probably a Roman. He was a soldier in command of 100 soldiers. Groups of Roman soldiers were posted throughout the Empire. The encounter between Jesus and this man introduces a major theme that Matthew develops throughout his

Gospel: The Jewish religious leaders who should have believed in Jesus do not, and the Gentiles, who had no real reason to believe, do (remember Herod and the Wise men of Matthew 2:1–12).

There are some questions as to whether the specific word that Matthew uses in verse 6 should be translated as "son" or "servant." Luke's parallel of this account uses a word that undoubtedly translates as "servant." Either way, Jesus' response and the significance of the account remain the same.

The relationship of Greek words in Jesus' response—I will come and heal him—is interesting. The Greek reads "I, having come, will heal him." The sentence indicates that Jesus has no hesitancy in entering the Gentile's house and healing his son or servant. The centurion realizes the problem and, sensitive to Jewish concerns, indicates his unworthiness to have Jesus in his home. Jesus is amazed at the depth of this man's faith and confidence. Thus His remark that nowhere in all Israel has He found such depth of faith.

Demystifying Matthew

The comment regarding those from the east and west (Gentiles) sitting with Abraham, Isaac, and Joseph is striking, and would be shocking to the Jewish mind. That Gentiles would sit with Jews at the eschatological banquet (Jewish eschatological expectation of the end-of-the-world banquet with God) was in keeping with Matthew's purpose in challenging his Jewish-Christian community to engage in a worldwide mission to include the Gentiles (Matthew 28:18–20). Jesus declares that those to whom the kingdom should have belonged will be thrown into outer darkness, obviously because of their refusal to accept God's Messiah.

8:14–17

PETER'S MOTHER-IN-LAW HEALED

Upon entering Peter's house in Capernaum and learning that Peter's mother-in-law is ill with a fever, Jesus heals her. Many others hear of this and gather at Peter's house. Jesus heals all who are sick and demon possessed. Matthew sets this series of miracles in the context of one of the ten unique fulfillment prophecies he builds into his text. The citation is obviously of Isaiah 53:4, but is apparently a free translation by Matthew. The brevity of this section, describing the powerful miracles of Jesus, highlights the incomparable authority of Jesus as the Messiah.

8:18–22

IMPULSIVE AND RELUCTANT WOULD-BE DISCIPLES

First a scribe, then another would-be disciple are challenged by Jesus to understand the radical nature of discipleship.

The scribe promises to follow Jesus wherever He goes, not realizing the true nature of the radical call to discipleship. That call means leaving all, including home and its comforts.

The second would-be disciple is a reluctant follower who likewise does not understand the commitment demanded by discipleship. Removed from the Jewish setting, this saying of Jesus is difficult to understand, but left in the Jewish context it has considerable meaning. The context is the Nazarite vow of Numbers 6:6–8 and the priestly service of Leviticus 21:11. In both cases, touching a dead body resulted in ceremonial uncleanness. Both called for a radical dedication and sanctification. Discipleship of Jesus calls for the same sanctification from the world and dedication to service. Kingdom service is total commitment to Jesus.

Take It Home

This section dramatizes the dedication demanded by messianic discipleship. The full force of the radical call to discipleship must be set in the context of Jesus' own disciples and the reaction of the Jewish leaders to Jesus, and then in the context of Matthew's community and their settlement in a new and hostile Gentile community. However, even today, the call to discipleship must be accompanied by a willingness to make a radical change in lifestyle. Following Jesus still demands a willingness to leave everything, including our "boats" and follow Jesus.

8:23–27

THE STORM STILLED

The miracle of stilling the great storm is a lesson on faith, or the need for faith in seemingly impossible situations. The disciples are still struggling to understand the full nature and power of Jesus. This section also speaks clearly on the nature of discipleship. Disciples are people of deep faith, even in the face of the impossible and unbelievable.

The Sea of Galilee was surrounded by hills and was susceptible to sudden and violent storms. Matthew indicates that the sea was extremely rough and dangerous. The disciples' frantic reaction is a natural one. Jesus' response and His reference to little faith pick up on one of Matthew's themes: people of little faith who should have great faith. Jesus' response to the disciples' fear is found five times in Matthew (6:30; 8:26; 14:31; 16:8; 17:20), and is well translated "O men of little faith" as in the Revised Standard Version, or "you of little faith" in the New International Version.

The disciples marvel that Jesus can still the sea, and ask the rhetorical question, "What sort of man is this, that even the winds and sea obey Him?" (NRSV). The answer is obvious—this man is not an ordinary man, because only God can command the waves and sea and they obey the command.

Note the following psalms with which Jesus and His disciples would have been familiar, and surely Matthew's community would have known:

- Psalm 89:8–9: "O Lord God Almighty, who is like you? You are mighty, O LORD, and your faithfulness surrounds you. You rule over the surging sea; when its waves mount up, you still them" (NIV).
- Psalm 65:5–7: "You answer us with awesome deeds of righteousness, O God our Savior, the hope of all the ends of the earth and of the farthest seas, who formed the mountains by your power, having armed yourself with strength, who stilled the roaring of the seas, the roaring of their waves, and the turmoil of the nations" (NIV).

8:28–34

DEMONS CAST OUT

Crossing the Sea of Galilee to the eastern shore of the Gadarenes (Luke calls them the Gerasenes), Jesus encounters two persons possessed by demons (a common phenomenon of that day).

The exact location indicated by Matthew and Luke can't be known with complete certainty. This possibly refers to a town called Gergasa (modern Khersa or Kursi), which is among cliffs overlooking the Sea of Galilee.

Critical Observation

Another problem encountered in this section, and which we encounter on other occasions when we compare Matthew with Mark and Luke, is that Matthew's account includes two demoniacs—Mark's (Mark 5:1–20) includes one man, and Luke's includes one man (Luke 8:26–39). This should not pose a serious problem, with Matthew's predilection for truth being established by two witnesses. He includes both men rather than only describing one of them. In another event, Mark (Mark 10:46–52) describes one blind man, but Matthew (Matthew 20:29–34) describes two.

In contrast to the Jewish leaders in Matthew (scribes and Pharisees), here at least two demons recognize Jesus as the Son of God. The little expression "before the appointed time" (NIV) in verse 29 indicates the Jewish understanding of an end-time judgment. The demons recognize that in Jesus the end was already near.

In keeping with their request, Jesus casts the demons out and they enter a herd of pigs, causing them to rush over the cliff into the sea. The Gadarenes obviously do not understand and are fearful of Jesus, possibly believing Him to be a powerful magician. They ask Him to leave the area. After all, they have just lost a herd of pigs. The fact that they had a herd of pigs indicates that they were Gentiles, not Jews.

9:1–8

A PARALYTIC FORGIVEN AND HEALED

Returning to His own city (Capernaum), Jesus enters a house and a paralytic is brought to Him. Jesus does a startling thing for the man—He forgives his sins. The scribes are beside themselves because they know only God can forgive sins, and Jesus is doing just that. In their eyes this is a grievous sin—blasphemy (taking or using God's name falsely or inappropriately). Their problem is that they have not taken note of His messianic signs and will not believe that He is the Messiah.

In verse 5 Jesus asks which is easier, to say someone's sins are forgiven or to tell a paralyzed person to walk. While claiming to forgive sins is easier (Anyone can claim this, and who could disprove them?), the healing proved He had the power to forgive sins.

Demystifying Matthew

The connection of sickness and sin lay deep in the Jewish psyche and could be taken all the way back to the Fall (Genesis 3). All sickness, suffering, and death can be traced back to the Fall and God's condemnation of sin. However, the Jewish religious leaders took this to the extreme: They blamed sickness on individual sin or the sin of the parents. Jesus did not follow that line of thought, but nevertheless the connection between the Fall and sickness and death cannot be overlooked.

The cross of Jesus overshadows this section; Jesus could forgive sins for He was the Son of God. It would be much easier to heal a man than to forgive sins. The forgiveness of sins was the greater gift of the Messiah, connecting His ministry to His primary reason for coming, that is, to die on the cross for sins.

We encounter one of Jesus' early "Son of Man" sayings in this section. Jesus uses the term in the tradition of Daniel 7:13–14 to demonstrate that He has the authority to forgive.

9:9–13

MATTHEW'S CALL

This is the only Gospel in which the first disciple is called Matthew. Both Mark and Luke call him Levi. Many suggestions have been given for the difference in names. The simplest and most likely is that Matthew had two names, Matthew and Levi. This was not uncommon in ancient times, especially among the Jews.

All three synoptic authors identify Matthew/Levi as a tax collector. Tax collectors were despised for their avarice, being self-serving and dishonest. Furthermore, they were the agents of the despised Roman power. They were considered by the Jews to be among the worst of sinners. In fact, Jews viewed tax collectors to be as lowly as the Gentiles. When accused by the Pharisees of fraternizing with tax collectors and sinners, Jesus responds by saying that it is the sick who need a physician, not the healthy. This did not mean that Jesus saw the Pharisees as healthy, but that He saw the tax collectors as those in need of help. He then follows this with a searing reference to Hosea 6:6, the scathing implication of which would have been clearly understood by His audience. Jesus adds furthermore that His purpose in coming is not to call those who saw themselves as righteous, but to call those who would see their need, the sinners. This passage draws attention to the growing antagonism between the Pharisees and Jewish leaders and Jesus.

9:14–17

THE QUESTING ABOUT FASTING

Fasting was a cultural-religious practice with a spiritual depth almost synonymous with righteousness among the Jewish religious leaders. The Day of Atonement was the only annual national fast day set out in Jewish Law. The requirement for this fast was repentance for sin (Leviticus 16:29, 31; 23:27, 32; Numbers 29:7).

Demystifying Matthew

There are several references to personal fasts that involve smaller groups and individuals. These are likewise associated with occasions of mourning and penitence, or are associated with prayers of supplication (1 Kings 21:27; Numbers 30:13). After the Jews' return from exile, a number of annual public fasts were instituted (Ezra 8:21–23; Nehemiah 9:1). Of particular interest would be the fast at the time of Purim (Esther 4:16).

- During the period between the Old and New Testaments, fasting as a sign of spiritual devotion was associated with prayer and almsgiving.
- By New Testament times, fasting as a sign of mourning and for personal sin, as well as its association with prayer, had become synonymous with the righteous life.
- During the time of Jesus, the practice of the Pharisees was to fast twice a week, once on Monday, then again on Thursday.
- Jesus gave instruction regarding fasting in the Sermon on the Mount, warning against the hypocrisy of the scribes and Pharisees (Matthew 6:16–18).

In this section, the setting for the discussion of fasting arises from the question of why the disciples of John fasted, but Jesus' disciples do not. Fundamental to the situation was that John and his disciples were expectantly waiting for the Messiah. Jesus knows that the messianic age is breaking in through Himself. The presence of the Messiah is not an occasion of mourning, but one of rejoicing. In other words, while the Messiah is present, fasting is not called for. In the coming days, when the Messiah will no longer be with them, there will be time for fasting.

Jesus follows His answer with two proverbial sayings: the first regarding new cloth and old garments, the second regarding new wine and old wineskins. The core of these two proverbial statements is that you do not mix the old and the new. Perhaps there is an indication in Jesus' response that the old message of Torah thinking should not be mixed with the new messianic ways and that the coming of the kingdom inaugurated a new age of salvation for all people, not just a reforming of Judaism.

9:18–26

THE ISSUE OF BLOOD STOPPED AND THE DEAD RAISED

Matthew's narrative that includes these miracles is much shorter than Mark's. This indicates that Matthew's purpose in recording them is different from that of Mark. Mark's emphasis is on the remarkable power of Jesus. Matthew's purpose is to demonstrate the remarkable faith in the woman and the ruler of the synagogue.

The first story regarding the ruler (Mark and Luke revealed his name as Jairus, a ruler in the synagogue) is abruptly broken off for a while by the intrusion of the woman with the twelve-year hemorrhage. Matthew does not explain to his Jewish audience that the man is a ruler of the synagogue.

First, the healing of the woman. We do not know for certain the nature of her hemorrhage, but assume that it is a hemorrhaging of the womb. If this is the case, then her problem is two-fold:

1) The difficulty of a physical problem she has endured for twelve years.
2) The ceremonial uncleanness that would have been pronounced on her by Jewish custom because she is bleeding (Leviticus 15:19–23).

She is unclean, yet she reaches out and touches the fringes of Jesus' garment. Jesus evidently follows the Jewish instructions regarding the four fringes to be at the four corners of the garment (Numbers 15:38–41; Deuteronomy 22:12).

It is obvious that this story is about the simple faith of the woman. She is convinced that if she can only touch the fringes of His garment, she will be healed. Jesus acknowledges her faith and encourages her to take heart, for her faith has made her well. Instantly she is healed.

Now to Jairus, the ruler of the synagogue, and his daughter. Jairus's faith is also the point of this section, indicating that some of the Jewish leadership believed. His confidence in Jesus is such that all Jesus has to do is reach out His hand and touch his daughter and she will be healed. (Luke's Gospel tells the story from the beginning when Jairus's daughter is dying. Matthew tells the story from the point where Jesus gets into the action, when Jairus first contacts Him.) By the time Jesus gets to Jairus's house, the girl is dead. When Jesus says the girl is not dead, the crowd laughs because they know she is dead. Jesus knows, however, that her death is not permanent, for He is about to raise her up from death.

9:27–34

THE BLIND SEE, AND A DEMON IS EXORCISED

In striking contrast to the Jewish leaders, two blind men recognize Jesus and confess their faith by calling Him the Son of David. (Notice Matthew's reference to *two* blind men. This is significant in a Jewish context because two witnesses were required for any testimony.) Jesus asks whether these men really believe He can heal them, and they confess they do. They not only demonstrate great faith, but acknowledge Him as Lord, something the Jewish leaders refused to do. Jesus immediately restores their sight. Again, Matthew demonstrates the necessity of great faith in Jesus, and the acknowledgement of His lordship.

Jesus, fearing that the crowds would acclaim Him Messiah for the wrong reason, strictly charges the two men not to tell others of their healing. This proves to be an impossible task, for soon the news of this spreads throughout the region.

Without much fanfare, Mathew recounts that Jesus also has power to cast out demons, for a demoniac is healed. The crowds marvel and observe that nothing like what Jesus is doing has been seen in Israel. In contrast to the two blind men, the demoniac, and the crowds, the Pharisees refuse to believe in Jesus, and charge that Jesus has cast out demons by Satan, the prince of demons. There's no response from Jesus listed here, but in chapter 12 a similar charge is made with a response from Jesus included.

Critical Observation

Matthew 9:35 marks the beginning of a transitional passage connecting Jesus' messianic deeds and Matthew's second discourse. Here's a review of the flow of Matthew's Gospel thus far:

- Narrative One established Jesus' right to be the Messiah, and was devoted to the preparation for His ministry. His genealogy and birth narrative emphasized the divine intervention aspect of His birth. Narrative One closed with the radical call of the disciples (Peter, Andrew, James, and John.)
- Discourse One, the Sermon on the Mount, described the character, influence, righteousness, and ambition of a disciple, and introduced the radical nature of discipleship. We learned what kind of person a disciple of Jesus should be.
- In Narrative Two Jesus performed astonishing miracles and demonstrated the ministry of the Messiah. There was a developing contrast between the Jewish leaders, who should have believed in Jesus but were blind to His ministry and messiahship, and the great faith of those who had no great reason to believe other than their need. There was also developing opposition from the Jewish leaders. The emphasis in this narrative section was on Jesus performing the powerful deeds of the Messiah.

9:35–38

THE NEED FOR WORKERS

Jesus continues to preach and teach the gospel of the kingdom in the synagogues, performing great messianic deeds. Matthew emphasizes that Jesus has compassion on the crowds because they are harassed and are without a shepherd. The Jewish leaders (scribes and Pharisees) should have been providing this leadership, but were not.

With the observation that the harvest is plentiful, Jesus means that there are many people who will believe in the gospel of the kingdom. The scribes and Pharisees should have been laboring in the kingdom, but were more interested in their religious position. Jesus' instruction is for the disciples to pray for the Lord of the harvest to send laborers into the ministry of the kingdom.

MATTHEW 10:1–42

DISCOURSE 2: THE LIMITED COMMISSION

Commissioning the Disciples	10:1–4
The Mission of the Apostles	10:5–15
Warnings of Opposition to the Preaching	10:16–42
Persecution	10:16–23
The Disciple and His Followers	10:24–33

The Disciple and the Cross 10:34–39
The Disciples' Message and Reward 10:40–42

Setting Up the Section

In the second narrative (Matthew 8–9), Matthew paralleled Mark's basic narrative of Jesus' powerful messianic ministry as He went from place to place, performing the powerful works expected of the Messiah. At the conclusion of this narrative, Jesus encouraged the disciples to pray that the Lord of the harvest would send laborers.

At this point, Mathew's narrative takes a dramatic turn, for the laborers sent out into the harvest turn out to be the disciples themselves. Here, Matthew discusses the commissioning of the twelve apostles in greater detail than do Mark and Luke (Mark 6:7–13; Luke 9:1–6).

We call this section the limited commission because Jesus limits the scope of the effort to the Jews. The disciples are told not to preach to the Gentiles or the Samaritans at this stage, but only to Israel. Later, in Matthew 28:19–20, Jesus charges His followers to make disciples of all nations—that passage is often referred to as the Great Commission.

Mark and Luke also record this commission (Mark 6:7–13; Luke 9:1–6), but neither of them limit the commission to only Israel. Since Mark and Luke are writing to Gentile audiences, the point is not as relevant, particularly in light of the later, greater commission. However, Matthew is writing to a Jewish audience who should have been able to understand that the gospel is intended first for their nation, who were to be God's special people and a light of revelation for the Gentiles (Isaiah 49:6).

10:1–4

COMMISSIONING THE DISCIPLES

In verse 1, Matthew refers to Jesus' closest followers as the twelve disciples, but then in the second verse he calls them twelve *apostles*. The term *apostle* means "one sent out," or a person commissioned to go.

The names of the twelve apostles differ in some traditions or accounts. In John 1:45, Nathaniel is listed rather than Bartholomew. In some manuscripts, Thaddaeus is known as Labbaeus, and in Luke 6:15, Simon the Cananaean (Aramaic for "zealous one") is called Simon the Zealot. Notice that Matthew groups the names into six groups of two. In similar fashion, in Luke 10:1, Luke records Jesus sending seventy disciples out in groups of two. This is significant in the Jewish culture in that two witnesses were required to affirm truthful testimony.

10:5–15

THE MISSION OF THE APOSTLES

After His resurrection, Jesus will again commission the apostles (Acts 1:6–8), when He charges them to begin witnessing first to Jerusalem, then to Judea, Samaria, and finally to the end of the earth. The kingdom is to begin with Israel, but is not to be limited to Israel. On the day of Pentecost (Acts 2) Peter preaches the first gospel sermon to the Jews; in Acts 8 Philip preaches to the Samaritans; then in Acts 10 Peter preaches the first gospel sermon to the Gentiles (Cornelius and his household).

The content of the gospel to be preached by the twelve apostles in the limited commission is the same as that preached by Jesus, "The kingdom of heaven is near" (4:17 NIV). Along with this preaching, the apostles are to perform the messianic deeds of healing, identifying their message with that of the Messiah.

Jesus' instruction to take no provisions on the journey and to stay with those who welcome them is within the tradition of traveling rabbis or teachers in both the Jewish and Gentile cultures. Traveling or itinerant teachers and philosophers were common in the Jewish world, and it was expected by good Jewish communities to welcome and care for such itinerant rabbis (Romans 15:19–24; 1 Thessalonians 2; 2 John; and 3 John). In Matthew 10:15, Jesus adds a sense of finality on those who do not accept the apostles and the message they preach, comparing them to Sodom and Gomorrah.

10:16–42

WARNINGS OF OPPOSITION TO THE PREACHING (INTRODUCTION)

Setting Up the Section

In four alarming paragraphs, Matthew records Jesus warning the disciples of serious opposition and persecution that will result from preaching the kingdom message.

10:16–23

WARNINGS: PERSECUTION

Because of their testimony, the disciples will be hated and faced with death. The apostles are not to be overly concerned as to how to react in such circumstances, for the Holy Spirit will give them the words they need.

You can hear throughout this text not only Jesus' concern for His disciples, but also Matthew's concern for his community as they testify to their faith in a hostile Jewish and Gentile context. Persecution is sure to arise and threaten.

Jesus uses the puzzling expression that they will not go through all the cities before (or until) the Son of Man has come. This expression could refer to:

1) the transfiguration of Jesus (Matthew 16:28 and 17:1–2);
2) the destruction of Jerusalem itself (Matthew 24:30);
3) some other unusual event such as the day of Pentecost (Acts 2);
4) the coming of Jesus at any time as a demonstration of His final judgment (Revelation 1:7; 2:16; 22:7, 12);
5) Jesus' second coming at the end of the world (Matthew 24:28).

Keep in mind that Jesus' words were originally spoken *before* the destruction of the temple in Jerusalem, while Matthew's Gospel was probably written afterwards. Jesus' original listeners and Matthew's later readers encountered these ideas from differing perspectives. If the coming of the Son of Man referred to the destruction of Jerusalem, and Matthew was writing *after* the destruction of Jerusalem, it is possible that Matthew's purpose in recording this was to challenge his Jewish church community to move on to Jesus' greater commission to disciple the Gentiles, not just the Jews. Jesus obviously had a vision of a later Gentile mission beyond the cities of Israel and the destruction of Jerusalem, but at the time that He spoke these recorded words, His focus was still on the apostles and their early Jewish mission.

10:24–33

WARNINGS: THE DISCIPLE AND HIS FOLLOWERS

Jesus warns His disciples that they should expect nothing less than what He, their teacher, will receive from the Jewish leaders. Since the Jewish leaders had called Jesus "Beelzebul"—a Hebrew name for Satan (9:27–34), they would also malign Jesus' disciples. Jesus warns the apostles not to fear those who could, and would, kill them, but rather to fear the One who had the power to destroy both body and soul in hell—God Himself.

The term for "hell" is the Hebrew *Gehenna*, meaning the valley of Hinnom, or the place of destruction. It was a euphemism for the Christian concept of hell. (This is a different concept than *hades*, the place of the dead.) The apostles are encouraged not to fear persecution because God knows them and will ultimately protect them. This does not mean that they will not have to die, but it means that they do not have to fear the destruction of hell. Jesus will acknowledge before God those who faithfully testify to Him as Messiah.

10:34–39

WARNINGS: THE DISCIPLE AND THE CROSS

Jesus explains that His coming will bring suffering for those who believe in Him. Parents and family will turn against the disciple because of Jesus. The radical nature of messianic discipleship is that disciples must choose Jesus before all family allegiance. Those who will not choose Jesus over all others are not worthy disciples. Jesus adds a brief statement about disciples taking up their crosses and following Him. He will again take up this thought in Matthew 16:24–28. Taking up one's cross is a picture of being willing to die for Jesus—it means far more than accepting one's responsibilities. Those who faithfully preach the gospel will have to make this decision in the first three centuries of Christianity.

10:40–42

WARNINGS: THE DISCIPLES' MESSAGE AND REWARD

Jesus assures the apostles that whoever receives them and their message receives both the Son and the Father. Jesus follows this with a proverbial saying about the righteous receiving their just reward. Jesus' closing statement in this section sets the scene for a discussion Matthew will take up in Chapter 18, namely, that of taking care of the little ones. At first glance this might be construed as a reference to children, but Jesus will later describe these little ones as those who believe in Him (18:6). In Matthew 11:25 Jesus will comment on the Father revealing things to babes. The context here indicates that the babes are the ones who have received the Father's revelation, that is, the disciples. But why call the disciples babes and little ones? Because disciples, like little children, are vulnerable to abuse. We should remember that these comments in Matthew 10 are in the context of disciples being abused and persecuted simply because they believe in and proclaim Jesus as the Messiah.

MATTHEW 11:1–12:50

NARRATIVE 3: OPPOSITION REJECTED

John the Baptists' Question	11:1–6
Jesus' Estimate of John the Baptist	11:7–19
Judgment on the Unrepentant	11:20–24
The Revelation of the Father	11:25–30
Lord of the Sabbath	12:1–8
Jesus Heals on the Sabbath	12:9–14
Jesus Heals Many	12:15–21
The Charge of Blasphemy	12:22–37
The Scribes and Pharisees Seek a Sign from Jesus	12:38–45
Jesus' True Family	12:46–50

Setting Up the Section

Jesus continues the powerful works expected of the Messiah but receives increasing opposition from the Jewish leaders. The events of these chapters are somewhat paralleled by those described in John's Gospel at the time when many disciples were leaving Jesus because He did not meet their expectation of a militant messiah who would lead them to freedom from Rome (John 6:60–69).

Also, there is an increasing emphasis on the kingdom of God and its glory.

11:1–6

JOHN THE BAPTIST'S QUESTION

It is difficult to know exactly what is going on in John the Baptist's mind while in prison. Matthew has already informed his readers that John had been arrested by Herod (4:12). In chapter 14, Matthew records John's death. Here in chapter 11, we encounter what seems to be the troubling doubt of John regarding Jesus' messiahship. However, there may be another way of looking at John's question.

At this time John is incarcerated in the fortress of Machaerus, in the wilderness east of the Dead Sea. His future is certainly discouraging. Emotionally, he must be at a low point in his life. The kingdom he had predicted as imminent has not materialized. It would have been natural that some questions and doubts could be plaguing John.

An alternative view is that John is turning his disciples away from himself to Jesus. He may be asking questions for the benefit of his disciples.

Jesus' response to John's question draws attention to His messianic ministry. He has been doing what had been prophesied the Messiah would do (Isaiah 61:1–3; 35:5–6; Luke 4:16–19): healing the sick, blind, lame and deaf, and taking care of the poor. Jesus' messianic ministry should have been all the witness John and his disciples needed.

11:7–19

JESUS' ESTIMATE OF JOHN THE BAPTIST

Jesus continues the discussion on John the Baptist by asking what kind of person the Jews had set out to see when they went to the Jordan River to witness John's baptisms. His somewhat colloquial language reflects that they had not gone out to see a weak person, but a bold prophet. Jesus cites Malachi 3:1 in support of John's ministry of preparing the way for the Messiah. Following this He pays John a great compliment—there is no one greater than John.

The last statement could be interpreted as contradictory, or at least vague. Jesus (and Matthew by his record of Jesus' words) is laying the foundation for kingdom business. John is great, yet in the kingdom, it is the humble servant that is the greatest. The kingdom of Jesus is different from all earthly kingdoms, and Jesus' and John's disciples need to know this.

Jesus continues that God did not intend to inaugurate His kingdom. Instead, it will be realized fully only through the death of the Messiah. This is a lesson that the zealous Jews (Zealots) cannot accept, and that the disciples will have trouble understanding (16:21–23).

Finally, Jesus again returns to John the Baptist and his testimony. John the Baptist is the expected Elijah who was to come and testify to God's messianic plans. However, the Jewish religious leaders of Jesus' day are like children—fickle and easily swayed. They will accept John the Baptist, but reject the Messiah he proclaims. When things get tough they will say that John has a demon, and that Jesus is only a friend of tax collectors and sinners.

11:20–24

JUDGMENT ON THE UNREPENTANT

Chorazin and Bethsaida were small towns just to the north of the Sea of Galilee and the town of Capernaum. Jesus had performed powerful signs in those towns, but they refused to believe in His ministry and messiahship. If the miracles performed in these two cities had been performed in the Gentile towns of Tyre and Sidon, the Gentiles would have believed.

Because a great revelation had been made to these places, a great accountability would be leveled against them. Jesus pronounces judgment on Chorazin and Bethsaida. Then, He pronounces a worse judgment on Capernaum than on Sodom, the Old Testament city with a reputation for great sinfulness. (Genesis 18–19 records God's judgment of fire that destroyed the city of Sodom, a place where not even ten righteous men could be found.)

11:25–30

THE REVELATION OF THE FATHER

In this passage, Matthew exhibits his rabbinic skill. The literary form of this text is in the genre of a Jewish revelation text, which was comprised of three sections:

1) Thanksgiving for the revelation from the Father (11:26)
   a. Thanksgiving to God for revealing the kingdom message
   b. The wise and understanding—a reference to the Jewish leaders who in their so-called wisdom did not receive the revelation regarding Jesus.
   c. The babes or little children are the disciples.
2) The revelation itself (11:27)
   a. All things or everything that had been given to Jesus related to the kingdom message regarding Jesus, the Messiah.
   b. The Son revealed the will and plan of God regarding the kingdom.
3) An invitation arising out of the revelation (11:28–30)
   a. An invitation to become a disciple of Jesus
   b. Promised rest to the poor and heavy-laden
   c. The gentle nature of the kingdom of God
   d. The promise to make the disciples' burden of sin and suffering light through the glorious kingdom message of redemption

This passage must be seen in the context of Jewish rejection of Jesus and His message. The learned ones rejected Jesus' message; the poor, needy, and humble ones believed and followed Him.

Critical Observation: The Religious Leaders

Here is a brief discussion of the makeup of the Jewish religious and political groups—the Pharisees, scribes, Sadducees, Herodians, Essenes, and Zealots.

- **Pharisees.** A variety of resources exist from which to learn about the Pharisees, and with that wealth of information there can be some confusion as to their exact identity. Some refer to them as a sect, some as a school, some as a political movement, some as a group of scholars, others as a middle class group of Jews, and on it goes. In all probability, all these concepts can be found in the term *Pharisee.* At different points in the history of the Jewish nation, the Pharisees played different roles—political, religious reformers, separatists, and social. The long history of this group's members makes it difficult to define them or their role with precision. The existence of the Pharisees can be traced back to about 134 BC. In Josephus's writings, they are often pictured in conflict with the Sadducees. Although not definitive, it is held by some that the Pharisees resisted Hellenization (adoption of Greek culture) as opposed to the Sadducees, who were more comfortable with Hellenization. When we encounter the Pharisees in the Gospels, they had formed a popular religious reformer group that included scholars of the Law. The Pharisees manifested a political messianic inclination but possessed little political power. They held to a strict observance of the Mosaic Law and interpreted the Torah in a broader sense than the Sadducees, including

CONTINUED

the remainder of the Jewish cannon as well as the vast rabbinic tradition in their legal code. They believed in a judgment for the Gentiles and the resurrection of the dead.

- **Scribes.** The term *scribe* meant those who were primarily secretaries. They were responsible for recording both the religious and legal aspects of Jewish life. Most were sympathetic to the Pharisees and some were even members of the Pharisees (Mark 2:16). As such they were the scholars on the Law upon whom the Pharisees depended for their interpretation of the Law. They were not so much a sect as a social or scholarly group.
- **Sadducees.** Like the Pharisees, it is difficult to define the Sadducees as a group. Sometimes they acted as a sect, at other times as a political movement. Their history is difficult to determine with precision, but like the Pharisees they can be traced in Josephus's historical writings, the New Testament, and rabbinic writings. Sociologically, they were mostly upper class and wealthy members of society. They therefore possessed greater political influence than the Pharisees. They were also more comfortable with Hellenization and social conformity than were the Pharisees. The Sadducees were often in religious conflict with the Pharisees. They only believed the Torah, the five books of Moses, to be inspired Scripture. They adopted a free will mind-set in regard to life, and rejected personal immortality and the resurrection.
- **Herodians.** The Herodians are mentioned only three times in the Gospels: Matthew 22:16; Mark 3:6; and Mark 12:13. Little is known of them other than they formed a political royalist group in support of the Herodian family. In the Gospels they aligned themselves with the Pharisees in opposition to Jesus, obviously in opposition to any kingdom He might inaugurate. Under normal conditions, the Pharisees would not have been associated with the Herodians, but they subordinated their differences to form an alliance against Jesus.
- **Essenes.** The origin of the group is uncertain. Some were monastic and some were not. There are some indications that they were opposed to the temple sacrificial system, believing that mainstream Judaism was corrupt. Remains of animal bones carefully buried indicate some possibility that they offered animal sacrifices apart from the temple. They held to the Mosaic Law and interpreted it literally, and treasured ancient literature. A strict code and ceremony of admission into the group was followed, with a strong code of communal living. It is believed that they adopted orphans from the mainstream of Jewish life. They held to a form of the afterlife. Most scholars consider the group that produced the Dead Sea Scrolls to be Essenes who lived at Qumran near the Dead Sea.
- **Zealots.** The term *zealot* derives from the concept of "zeal for God and the Law." The Zealots took pride in past heroes who had stood adamantly for God and the Law against all odds. They stood against any form of idolatry and offenses against the Law. Later they became revolutionaries against the opposing overlords, especially against Roman Imperialism. (This was not the only revolutionary group during the late Roman period. The historian Josephus lists five such groups.) The Zealots were a coalition of a lower group of priests, Jerusalem insurgents, and refugee bandit groups. During the time of Jesus, their zeal was for the overthrow of Rome. Jesus did not fit their ideal of a revolutionary king. We read little of the Zealots in the Gospels other than Simon, one of the apostles, who was a member or former member of the group (Luke 6:15).

12:1–8

LORD OF THE SABBATH

In a series of encounters with the Jewish leaders, Matthew 12 narrates the building controversy between Jesus and the scribes and Pharisees.

Matthew records that it is on the Sabbath that Jesus and His disciples are traveling through the grain fields. The disciples, being hungry, pluck grain to eat. To the Pharisees this was a serious violation of the Sabbath Law—resting from all work on the seventh day—as recorded in Exodus 20:10; 34:21 and Deuteronomy 5:14.

Rabbinic tradition listed at least thirty-nine classes of work the rabbis saw covered by this law. The overzealous literal application of the legal principle obviously overlooked a deeper principle to which Jesus holds the Pharisees. He corrects their understanding by referring to two examples in the Jewish writings (Torah), which were obvious exceptions to the legal application of the Law. Furthermore, He finally explains the place of the Law in God's purpose.

Jesus' opening statement, "Have you not read. . . ," is somewhat of a rebuke or reminder of what they should have known regarding David and his men eating bread of the Presence in the Tabernacle, which was bread reserved only for the priests (1 Samuel 21:1–6; Leviticus 24:5–9). When this occurred, the priest brought no condemnation against David and his men, and obviously in the mind of Jesus this occasioned no sin.

Jesus' next argument is that the priests broke the literal interpretation of the Sabbath Law every Sabbath as they served in the temple, yet the Pharisees took no offence at this. Obviously, this was another occasion when the Sabbath law should not be taken legalistically.

Jesus' next statement raises several questions. What does He mean by one who was greater? In all probability Jesus has in mind the new system of grace that had come to take over from the legal system of Law. This seems to fit, since Jesus then refers to a principle often brought up in the Torah, especially in Hosea 6:6 and Micah 6:8, God's desire for mercy rather than sacrifice.

Finally, Jesus makes the remarkable statement that the Son of Man is Lord over the Sabbath. The Gospel of Mark (Mark 2:27) records this saying of Jesus more fully to include the concept that the Sabbath was in fact made for mankind, not mankind for the Sabbath. Jesus is setting the Torah in a more mature expression or context than the Pharisees of His day did.

The Pharisees are not content with Jesus' rebuff and return to similar themes again in other settings, as in the next section.

12:9–14

JESUS HEALS ON THE SABBATH

Matthew's use of the expression *their synagogue* sets the synagogue of the Jews in contrast to the community of believers, namely, the church. When a man with a withered hand appears, the Pharisees take advantage of this to raise another question and accuse Jesus regarding lawful activity on the Sabbath. In this instance, Jesus knows that rabbinic practice permits the rescuing of an animal on the Sabbath (Luke 14:5). Arguing that it is far more important to heal a person than an animal, Jesus heals the man's withered hand. The Pharisees, obviously dissatisfied with Jesus, take council on how to destroy Him.

12:15–21

JESUS HEALS MANY

Jesus withdraws. Rather than incite the Pharisees further, Jesus seeks out quieter climes away from areas where the Pharisees frequented, but continues His healings. Matthew draws attention to one of the Servant Songs in Isaiah (Isaiah 42:1–4) to demonstrate that Jesus, as the Messiah, is involved in messianic works.

12:22–37

THE CHARGE OF BLASPHEMY

When a blind demoniac acknowledges Jesus as the Son of David (a term that had come to refer to the Messiah and was Matthew's favorite title for Jesus), the Pharisees take exception, charging that it is by the power of Beelzebul, the Prince of demons, that Jesus cast out demons.

Critical Observation

Be-elzebul, sometimes spelled Be-elzebub, or Ba-alzebub.

In Matthew, Mark, and Luke this term is another name for Satan. The etymology of this name has been difficult to determine with any degree of finality; the term has been thought to mean "Lord of the Flies," "Lord of Dung," "Lord of heaven" (a star god), "Master of the House," and "Fly Lord" (flies being demons).

Whatever the case, the term as used by the Pharisees was a pejorative one, intended to be an insult to Jesus.

When the Pharisees once more charge that Jesus cast out demons by the power of Satan, Jesus responds with three basic arguments and a startling announcement:

Argument 1. A house divided against itself will fall. If Jesus was casting out demons by the power of Satan, then Satan's house was divided.

Argument 2. To what power did the Pharisees attribute the power of their own disciples to cast out demons?

Argument 3. Before one can enter a house and plunder the goods of the house, one must first overpower the owner. If Jesus had entered Satan's house and plundered his goods (those people held captive by demons), this must mean Jesus had overpowered Satan.

Jesus' startling announcement is this: Since He is indeed casting out demons by the power of the Spirit of God, then the kingdom of God has come. Not that it *will* come, but the kingdom has already come and is upon them.

Jesus continues His rebuttal of the Pharisees' charge of blasphemy with another remarkable statement that has given problems to scholars and ministers—the unforgivable sin (v. 32). This section begins with the word *therefore* (12:31 NASB), which connects this discussion to the previous one in which the Pharisees had attributed the work of God through His Holy Spirit as a work of Beelzebul, or Satan. To attribute the work of God through His Holy Spirit as a work of Satan is the worst kind of blasphemy possible.

While there are many differing opinions regarding the unforgivable sin, it is possible to understand the meaning in this section as it relates to the previous discussion of the Pharisees' blasphemy against the Holy Spirit. To set this section in context:

1) The Pharisees had blasphemed the Holy Spirit, charging that Jesus cast out demons by the power of Satan, whereas He claimed to cast them out by the power of the Holy Spirit.
2) To deny, or blaspheme, the work of the Holy Spirit is to blaspheme the Holy Spirit Himself and to deny the very process of new birth, regeneration, and sanctification.
3) To deny the work of the Holy Spirit is to remove oneself from the process of forgiveness and to place oneself outside the process of God's atonement, and to undercut the very possibility of experiencing the reality of God's salvation.
4) To oppose the Holy Spirit is the same as opposing the very mission of Jesus Himself.
5) Although rejecting Jesus' divine ministry has catastrophic consequences, Jesus Himself stressed that the denial or blasphemy of the Holy Spirit has ultimate, unforgivable results.

To summarize: The blasphemy against the Holy Spirit that is unforgivable is a denial of the working of the Holy Spirit in God's system of atonement. Jesus considered this blasphemy even worse than blasphemy against Himself. To reject the saving power and work of the Holy Spirit is ultimately to reject God's working His salvation in the individual.

Jesus closes this encounter with the Pharisees with a pronouncement of judgment on them for the careless words they had just uttered. In their haste to deny Jesus, they had in fact blasphemed the very working of God through His Holy Spirit. Their words, uttered in the heat of their hatred, were not thought about, and through their cavalier treatment of Jesus and the Holy Spirit, they had brought judgment on themselves.

12:38–45

THE SCRIBES AND PHARISEES SEEK A SIGN FROM JESUS

Joining the Pharisees, the scribes ask Jesus for a sign. There is nothing wrong in seeking a sign, as long as the seeker is sincere. It is apparent that the scribes and Pharisees are not sincere, for they have already witnessed many miracles of Jesus and still refuse to believe. In fact, as in the previous section, they attribute the power of His miracles to Satan.

In a striking analogy, Jesus makes reference to the sign of Jonah, the prophet. Unlike the people of Nineveh, the scribes and Pharisees would not believe and repent. The sign of Jonah here is the analogy between Jonah in the belly of the large fish and Jesus' burial and resurrection. Jesus knows that the scribes and Pharisees will not even believe in His resurrection as a sign. So Jesus reprimands and condemns them for their unbelief. (In Matthew 16:4 the sign of Jonah is used to refer to the unbelief of the Jews in general.) Twice in the Gospels, both times in Matthew in the context of the sign of Jonah, Jesus refers to these religious leaders as evil and spiritually adulterous.

Jesus concludes this encounter with a parable of an unclean spirit leaving a man and returning to find his house clean. The spirit returns with seven more spirits and moves into the house. Jesus compares the generation of the scribes and Pharisees with this spirit. Those who do not respond will find in the end their situation is worse off than it was in the beginning. Obviously, Jesus has in mind that by refusing His message, the scribes and Pharisees face certain judgment. Did Jesus have in mind the eschatological judgment at the end of the world, or the impending judgment of the destruction of Jerusalem? Possibly Jesus and Matthew had both in mind.

12:46–50

JESUS' TRUE FAMILY

This is the first reference to Jesus' family in Matthew. The last reference to Mary was in Matthew 2. The next reference to family will be in Matthew 13:55–56, where the Jews attempt to find Jesus' significance in His family of origin by asking if He's the carpenter's son, if His mother is Mary, and if His brothers are James, Joseph, Simon, and Judas.

In this encounter with His family, Jesus is not rejecting them, but demonstrating that kingdom relationships take precedence over physical relationships. The section serves as a transitional passage, as Matthew moves on to the third discourse and the teachings on the kingdom.

MATTHEW 13:1–58

DISCOURSE 3: THE TRUE NATURE OF THE KINGDOM

The Parable of the Sower	13:1–9, 18–23
Why Did Jesus Teach in Parables?	13:10–17
The Parable of Wheat and Tares	13:24–30
The Grain of Mustard Seed	13:31–32
The Parable of the Leaven	12:33–35
The Wheat and the Tares Explained	13:36–43
The Hidden Treasure and Pearl of Great Price	13:44–46
The Dragnet	13:47–51
The Conclusion to the Kingdom Parables	13:52–58

Setting Up the Section

The previous narrative was about the opposition and controversy to Jesus' identity and message. The events described came approximately at the same time as the events described in John 6, when many of the disciples were leaving Jesus, disappointed with His claims of messiahship. They did not understand the nature of the kingdom of God and had anticipated more of a political physical kingdom, whereas Jesus' kingdom was a spiritual relationship with God. Jesus asks His closest disciples whether they, too, are about to leave Him. Peter has answered that there is nowhere else to go because Jesus alone has the words of eternal life (John 6:68).

13:1–9, 18–23

THE PARABLE OF THE SOWER

This is not a parable about sowing—it is a parable about hearing. Mark begins his version with a call to listen (Mark 4:3). Luke ends his version with the call to his readers to be careful how they listen to the message (Luke 8:18). To his version, Matthew adds the Jewish proverbial saying that whoever has ears, should listen well (Matthew 13:9). The parable—the simple analogy of a farmer sowing seed in Palestine—is about how a person hears and understands the message of the kingdom.

PARABLE AT A GLANCE

The soil	The seed	The application
The path	The birds ate them.	Those who hear don't understand, and so Satan snatches them away.
Rocky or stony places	They developed no roots so were scorched by the sun and withered.	Those who hear receive with joy, but fall away when faced with persecution.
Among the thorns	They were choked out by the growing thorns.	There are those who hear, but worries and wealth prevent the seeds from bearing fruit.
Rich, fertile soil	They produced a great crop.	Those who hear and understand produce the crop God intended.

The point is that in order for the message of the kingdom to germinate and flourish, the mind has to be prepared for hearing and understanding the kingdom. A stubborn and rebellious heart cannot receive the Word.

This parable had borne itself out with those who heard the message of the kingdom (John the Baptist's and Jesus' preaching): some were snatched away, others fell away when discipleship became difficult, some heard the truth but could not sacrifice their own lives to follow, others heard and followed and brought others. Those disciples who had been willing to hear, who had prepared their minds and hearts and believed and repented, were able to understand the message that had brought forth fruit in their faith and lives.

Take It Home

The significant lesson for us today from the parable of the sower and the soils is that we must prepare our minds and hearts for the Word of God before it can take root and grow. Paul commends some first-century Christians in Thessalonica in the same way, thanking God that they received God's Word, not as the teaching of humans, but for what it really is—the Word of God (1 Thessalonians 2:13).

The message for Jesus' disciples (and for us) is simply this: Some will never receive the Word, some will begin and fall away, some will keep on growing. The difference will be in how they hear and understand. Do not expect the same from everyone because not everyone is willing to hear and understand.

13:10–17

WHY DID JESUS TEACH IN PARABLES?

Parable teaching was a favored rabbinic teaching style. The Jews were familiar with parable teaching. Also, Jesus explains that the crowds surrounding Him are expecting some teaching, though they are not ready for the deeper matters of the kingdom, or willing to understand the true spiritual nature of the kingdom. Jesus is well aware that the crowds are willing to hear Him but are not willing to hear His message. His understanding of the mysteries of the kingdom is not in step with theirs.

The next proverbial statement–that those who have will receive more and those who have not will lose even what they have–was well known in rabbinic Judaism. It implies that if one does not take the opportunities presented, the opportunities will be denied. Since the Jewish leadership refuse to believe in Jesus, even the opportunities to believe will be denied.

Jesus' reference to Isaiah 6:9–10 must be seen in relation to the calling and commissioning of Isaiah. Isaiah was to preach to the rebellious Israel even though many would not repent and believe His message. One must be sensitive to the poetic form of Isaiah 6 to understand the message it conveys. Israel cannot in its unfaithful heart see and hear. In this condition, for Israel to turn to God for healing is ludicrous.

In contrast to the stubborn Jewish leaders, the disciples believe. To them the secret things of the kingdom will make sense. For this reason, Jesus teaches in parables. The Jewish leaders who are looking for the wrong kind of kingdom will still find some message in Jesus' teachings in parables, but the disciples who believe will be in a position to receive and accept the deeper spiritual nature of the kingdom.

Critical Observation

There are two fundamental principles in interpreting a parable:

1) Determine the context of the parable in the light of its origin and setting in the overall text. How does the parable fit into the full story or narrative that it is intended to enlighten? What was going on historically when the parable was told?

CONTINUED

2) Determine the central truth or lesson the parable is intended to illustrate or teach. While you may apply a parable in a variety of ways, it had only one central lesson or principle when it was originally used. Maintain the interpretation within that principle or lesson. Remember that a parable is an earthly story with a central spiritual truth or lesson.

It is not difficult to determine the nature of the parables in Matthew 13, for in each instance Jesus either relates the parable to the kingdom, or says "the kingdom of heaven is like. . ." (13:24 NIV). These are parables about the kingdom.

What is the historical setting for the parables in Matthew 13? Jesus is running into increasing opposition from the scribes and Pharisees. Many of the disciples are leaving Jesus because they do not understand the nature of His messianic reign or kingdom (spiritual rather than a physical). Thus, He teaches them about the kingdom.

13:24–30

THE PARABLE OF WHEAT AND TARES

This parable, like the sower, receives additional attention and explanation by Jesus (13:36–43). The parable is also similar to the kingdom parable of the dragnet (13:47–52).

The parable of wheat and tares explains that in the kingdom of God one can expect a mixed crop. This is first because of human fallibility and weakness. But also, Satan is busy working on human minds. He plants seeds, sometimes of false teaching, sometimes of doubt. Whatever the case, a mixed crop is the result.

The temptation for the disciples is to intervene and attempt to pluck out what they consider to be the bad seed. Disciples must refrain from this since they are not in a position to determine all of the circumstances involved. The parable emphasizes that the judgment of crops (a person's faith) is beyond the disciples and must be left to the reaper himself (Jesus). Jesus explains in Matthew 13:36–43 that it will be the Son of Man and His angels who will do the reaping and judging. Even the well-meaning can judge a person too soon.

13:31–32

THE GRAIN OF MUSTARD SEED

In this time, the mustard seed was considered the smallest of seeds. The size of the mustard seed would have been well known among those hearing Jesus tell this parable. The size and slow growth of the mustard seed is an excellent metaphor for the humble beginnings of the kingdom. The Jews expect a triumphant arrival of the kingdom and expulsion of the Gentile enemy, but that is not how the kingdom of God is going to work. The Messiah came not to a princely house, but to the house of a lowly carpenter. The beginnings of the kingdom are in fact small—12 apostles and about 120 other believers (Acts 1:13–15).

Despite its humble beginnings, the kingdom slowly matures and grows significantly. The mysterious growth of the kingdom is the working of God's grace and power in human lives, not the result of human intervention and work.

The meaning of the parable for Jesus' disciples is simple. The kingdom begins small, but given time will grow into something significant. Do not expect too much too soon. The lesson for the church today is likewise one of encouragement and warning—give the seed of the kingdom time, give people time to grow, give God time to work in people's lives.

There is also a significant lesson and warning for the church today regarding triumphalism (expecting the church to burst in and be great by human standards). The church will always be made up of humans who are not yet "there." We experience the work of God in our lives and grow, but it is only when we reach the end, the eschatological goal of the Christian age, when we will be fully triumphant. We experience many wonderful victories over Satan and the world, but there remain yet many battles to be fought and much weakness to be revealed. However, the final victory has been secured by Jesus' death and resurrection. It will be fully revealed at the end.

Matthew's church needed to hear this message as keenly as did Jesus' disciples in those early days of the kingdom. But so do we today, 2,000 years later.

13:33–35

THE PARABLE OF THE LEAVEN

This brief parable, whose images are well-known to the disciples and Jesus' audience that day, repeats much of the same message as the mustard seed. Baking bread was an everyday experience in ancient days, especially among the Jews. It is widely known that leaven spreads throughout the loaf, but the maturing of the leaven and its leavening power take time. Hurry the process and you end up with a lump of hard bread that is useless and inedible. Give the leaven time and it produces a wonderful loaf of bread.

So it is with the message of the kingdom. Do not expect too much too soon. Interfere with the process of slow leavening and growth and you end up with a catastrophe. Give the power of God time to work in people, and do not expect too much too soon.

13:36–43

THE WHEAT AND THE TARES EXPLAINED

This section continues to develop as the parable of the wheat and tares. The message is simple—judging is not the role of the disciple. The mission of discipleship is planting, not reaping. Jesus will take care of the reaping and do a far better job than humanly possible.

The message is especially meaningful to the disciples who must have been disappointed that many did not believe and receive Jesus, and that many were leaving. Likewise, the message must be meaningful to Matthew's disciples who now find themselves in a Gentile and hostile world that deserves judgment. Perhaps the meaning is just as powerful today in church life, when members are prone to judge others and in many cases even write them off.

13:44–46

THE HIDDEN TREASURE AND PEARL OF GREAT PRICE

These two parables are similar in meaning and application. The kingdom is of inestimable value, and those who find it are greatly enriched. However, the richness of the kingdom is not out on the surface to be seen by all. It takes a discerning (believing) eye to understand and find the richness of the kingdom. Furthermore, these parables teach that one must search to find the mystery and richness of the kingdom.

Perhaps the most significant message of these parables is that when one finds the richness of the kingdom, one must be prepared to give up everything to attain it. Matthew will develop this point later when he narrates Jesus' encounter with the rich young ruler (19:16–30). These parables also fit in with the theme of radical discipleship—the willingness to give up everything for the sake of gaining the kingdom. Many of the disciples in Jesus' day were not willing to pay this price, so when they learned the radical nature of the kingdom, they left.

13:47–51

THE DRAGNET

This parable is reminiscent of the parable of the wheat and tares, for it emphasizes judgment. The kingdom of God involves judgment. It is for this reason that John the Baptist and Jesus demanded repentance in view of the arrival or breaking in of the kingdom.

Jesus sets this parable in the context of the end of the age by emphasizing that the angels will come to separate the evil from the righteous and throw the evil into the fire of judgment (typical Jewish and rabbinic images of the final judgment). It is a sobering thought that one's attitude toward Jesus and His kingdom involves final judgment.

13:52–58

THE CONCLUSION TO THE KINGDOM PARABLES

This little section is thought of by some to be an eighth parable. However, it is best seen as a concluding statement to all the preceding Kingdom Parables.

The thought is in the form of a proverbial saying. The scribes, the learned scholars of the Law, should have been trained for the purpose of revealing all the mysteries of the kingdom. However, the scribes of Jesus' day are blinded by their reaction to Jesus and the nature of His message and kingdom.

Jesus has revealed the richness and mysteries of the kingdom—both the old thoughts of the kingdom and the new ideas and thoughts of the kingdom. His disciples, by learning from Him about the kingdom, can bring together the promise of the old covenant with the fulfillment of the new.

As in each of the other four blocks of discourse or teaching material, Matthew concludes the discourse with a transition into the next section. In this discourse, the focus has been on the true nature of the kingdom and matters that disciples should know regarding the kingdom.

When Jesus finishes teaching these parables, He goes away from that place and comes to Nazareth, where the people are amazed at His teaching but are reluctant to follow Him because they feel they know Him too well. After all, was this not the carpenter's son? Because of their lack of faith, Jesus does few of His miracles in Nazareth. It was not because they simply did not believe; it was because they would not believe. Sometimes prejudice obscures faith.

SUMMARY

1) These Kingdom Parables came to their original audience at a crucial point in Jesus' ministry. Many disciples were turning back because the kingdom offered by Jesus did not meet their expectations and desires. The radical call to discipleship and the radical nature of the spiritual kingdom were too much for them.
2) These parables were also of extreme importance for Matthew's church, since his readers had just given up all for the kingdom and needed encouragement that their decision was worthwhile. They needed reminding also that it was not their prerogative to begin judging their Gentile neighbors, for God could also work His power in the life of the Gentiles and bring them into His kingdom. Making disciples by teaching the message of the kingdom is the ministry of disciples; judging belongs to the Son of Man and His angels.
3) Growth in the kingdom is by the power of God, and not human endeavor. Disciples need to give the seed of the kingdom time and space to mature. The kingdom begins small in human hearts, but nurtured and sustained by God's power and grace, matures slowly into something beautiful and useful.
4) The kingdom involves radical commitment with the promise of accountability to God. One cannot escape the kingdom and its message by walking away. There will be a judgment, and Jesus' followers will be judged by their reaction to the message, the kingdom, and the King.

Take It Home

In Matthew's description of Jesus commissioning His disciples, there was a challenging message for Matthew's original audience, as well as for us today. When we pray earnestly that the Lord will send laborers into the harvest, it might be that we turn out to be the laborers that the Lord of the harvest has in mind.

MATTHEW 14:1–17:27

NARRATIVE 4: FINAL DAYS OF PREPARATION OF DISCIPLES

The Death of John the Baptist	14:1–12
Feeding the Five Thousand	14:13–21
Jesus Walks on the Sea	14:22–36
Ceremonial and Real Defilement—Washing Hands	15:1–20
The Canaanite Woman and Tyre and Sidon	15:21–28
The Feeding of the Four Thousand	15:29–39
The Pharisees and Sadducees Demand a Sign from Heaven	16:1–4
The Leaven of the Pharisees and Sadducees	16:5–12

Caesarea Philippi and Peter's Confession	16:13–20
Jesus Foretells His Death, Burial, and Resurrection	16:21–23
Radical Discipleship	16:24–27
The Son of Man Coming in His Kingdom	16:28
The Transfiguration	17:1–13
Healing of the Epileptic Boy	17:14–21
Jesus Again Foretells His Death and Resurrection	17:22–23
The Shekel in the Fish's Mouth and the Temple Tax	17:24–27

Setting Up the Section

A report of John's death is found in all three synoptic Gospels (Matthew, Mark, and Luke), but briefer in Luke. Luke gives none of the details described in Matthew and Mark. Mark includes the sending out of the twelve disciples, which Matthew has included earlier in his Gospel (Mark 6:7–13).

While John's death is described here, chronologically his death actually occurred earlier on the time line. His imprisonment is mentioned in Matthew 4:12. The details given here are in light of the connection made by Herod about the possible return of John the Baptist. It was a common perception that some of the prophets would return to introduce the end of the age.

14:1–12

THE DEATH OF JOHN THE BAPTIST

"At that time. . ." (niv) is a favorite transition for Matthew. In this instance it merely highlights Herod's reaction to Jesus and introduces the section on John the Baptist's death. The description of John's death is a flashback, prompted by Herod's speculation that Jesus might be John the Baptist raised from the dead.

This Herod is Herod Antipas, one of the sons of Herod the Great. He is identified by Matthew as the tetrarch, and by Mark as the king. Herod had divorced his first wife and married his brother Philip's wife, Herodias. John the Baptist had repeatedly warned him of this sin. Herod, frustrated with John and in an attempt to silence him, had imprisoned him in the fortress of Machaerus, eventually executing him as a result of the schemes of Herodias and her daughter (Salome).

Herod evidently feels guilty for beheading John, and so when he hears of another prophet (Jesus), he superstitiously wonders whether John has come back from the dead.

Matthew mentions this for two reasons:

1) To narrate the events of John the Baptist's death
2) To focus attention on the importance of Jesus' ministry and the concerns this raised for Herod Antipas, the ruler of Jesus' home region

Critical Observation: The Herodian Dynasty

Herod the Great (37 BC–4 BC) was the great builder of the temple, palaces, and fortresses. He had many children by several marriages. Three of his sons ruled after him: Antipas, Philip, and Archelaus. The Herodian dynasty can be confusing, because of rulers who shared common names and because of much intermarriage. The Philip mentioned here in Matthew 14:3 (Mark 6:17) is a fourth son of Herod the Great.

- Herod Antipas (4 BC–AD 39) was the tetrarch (ruler over a fourth of the kingdom). He ruled over Galilee (Jesus' home province) and Perea. He married Herodias, his brother Philip's wife. He also murdered John the Baptist.
- Herod Philip (4 BC–AD 34) was tetrarch of Iturea and Traconitis (Luke 3:1). He was the son of Herod the Great and Cleopatra of Jerusalem.
- Herod Archelaus (4 BC–AD 39) ruled over the province of Judea. He was titled an ethnarch (ruler of the people).
- This Philip is not well attested in history. He was apparently the first husband of Herodias and the father of Salome—facts we discover through information regarding Antipas.

14:13–21

FEEDING THE FIVE THOUSAND

This is the only miracle of Jesus recorded in all four Gospels. The section begins a series of situations focused on the need for faith and the failure of the disciples and others to have adequate faith.

The narrative of the miracle of the feeding of more than five thousand people has more than historical significance. It drives home the point that Jesus, as the Messiah, could take care of His people. The feeding of the five thousand has an obvious connection to God feeding the children of Israel with manna in the wilderness after they left Egypt. It also has insights into the messianic banquet at the end of time when God's redeemed will sit at God's banquet table and be sustained.

The miracle itself is simple. Taking five loaves and two fish and multiplying them into food enough for more than five thousand is no test to God's sovereign power. The power of this miracle lies in two points:

1) The disciples' failure to have faith in Jesus' ability to feed them
2) The illustration of Jesus' ability to take care of every need His disciples might have, with an emphasis on the spiritual food symbolized by the Old Testament manna and the New Testament loaves and fish

The spiritual significance of this miracle is extremely important to Matthew's late first-century community, which needs to understand that the Messiah can take care of its spiritual needs apart from Jerusalem and the temple (which had been destroyed).

14:22–36

JESUS WALKS ON THE SEA

This is one of two miracles common to all four Gospels, the other being the feeding of the five thousand. Several items stand out in this striking section.

1) The sea. To the Hebrew mind the sea was sinister and a symbol of evil.
2) Jesus' power over nature. Jesus had previously calmed a tempestuous sea (8:23–26).
3) The distress and lack of faith in the disciples
4) The recognition of those in the boat that Jesus was the Son of God

This miracle is not as much about the natural elements, other than Jesus' power over them, but is more about Peter and the disciples' faith. The situation surrounding Jesus' ministry required Him to have time to Himself for prayer and spiritual strength. He compels His disciples to get in a boat and set out to sea. A storm arises in the middle of the night (the fourth watch, between 3:00 a.m. and 6:00 a.m.), and the disciples are struggling with the waves. They are about a mile out at sea (a *stadia* [NASB], being about 200 yards). They see Jesus walking on the water and think He is a ghost.

Jesus calls out to them not to fear. An expression similar to this is found eight times in Matthew, indicating that having faith in Jesus drives away fear. He also tells them to take heart, for "it is I" (NIV) or "it's me." The Greek phrase that is translated here may be an allusion to the divine name of God, who is the great "I am" (Exodus 3:14). In the context of a Jewish gospel and a Jewish community, this certainly would carry the significance of a symbol of the presence of God in Jesus. The recognition of the disciples that Jesus is the Son of God supports this thought.

The narrative indicates that Peter initially steps out in faith, but that his faith wavers, resulting in his sinking into the sea. But Jesus saves him. It is easy to find fault in Peter for his wavering faith, but where were the other disciples? Still in the boat. Jesus gently rebukes the disciples for being men with little faith.

The striking thing about this event following immediately after the feeding of the five thousand is that the disciples still have a lot to learn about faith and trusting Jesus. Faith is something that needs time and experience to develop.

15:1–20

CEREMONIAL AND REAL DEFILEMENT—WASHING HANDS

Once again, the Pharisees and scribes accuse Jesus of desecrating the Jewish tradition of the elders, this time because His disciples do not wash their hands before eating. The Pharisees were experts in interpreting the tradition of the elders, but that was not the same as the actual Torah (Genesis, Exodus, Leviticus, Numbers, and Deuteronomy). Translating this into contemporary contexts, human interpretations are opinions, and not the law or doctrine itself. These traditions in themselves are good, but when they are put on the same level as God's Law, then mankind's opinion has been set on the same level as God's Word. This is the mistake the religious leaders have made.

In this instance, the Pharisees have not only put their interpretation on the level of God's Torah, but in fact have put one of their traditions above God's Law. Jesus focuses His answer on this. The problem is their interpretation of Corban (also Qorban or Korban), a vow permitted by a righteous Jew to maintain a sacred offering to fund the temple. Korban was not a command of God, but was a practice of the day. In this case, the Pharisees allow a person to offer this monetary gift to the temple rather than use it to support their parents—a fulfillment of God's command to honor one's parents (Exodus 20:12). The Pharisees are setting their tradition above the direct command of God.

There is another sense in which the Pharisees are speaking out of turn. They charge that the disciples are transgressing the tradition of the elders by not washing their hands before eating. In this case, though, they are applying instructions given for the sake of ceremonial purity (the priests carrying out sacrifices) to the normal household matters of eating. These two things were not the same (Exodus 30:17–21; Leviticus 15:11).

Jesus' condemnation of the Pharisees is scathing. He likens them to the Jews in Isaiah's day who honored God with their lips but whose hearts were far away from God (Isaiah 29:13). The Jews in Isaiah's day had taught their own opinion and thoughts on an equal level with the sacred scriptures. The Pharisees were blind guides leading blind men, resulting in everyone falling into a pit. It is not what goes into the mouth that defiles people, but instead what proceeds out of their hearts and mouths.

Take It Home

Understanding the mistake of the religious leaders of Jesus' day offers the modern church an opportunity to examine its own heart. Do we honor our beloved traditions above the greatest commandments—loving God and loving our neighbors? Are we sometimes blinded to what God is doing in the world around us because we are so focused on our religious customs that, while based on our understanding of the Bible, are not scripture themselves?

Just as Jesus called the scribes and Pharisees to open their eyes and look beyond their own religious structure to see what unexpected thing God was doing—so He calls to the church today.

15:21–28

THE CANAANITE WOMAN AND TYRE AND SIDON

This section continues the story of the need for faith, and the lack of faith, on the part of the Jewish leaders.

Jesus leaves Capernaum and travels west into the Gentile region of Tyre and Sidon, where He is met by a Canaanite woman whose daughter is possessed by a demon. In her plea to Jesus she acknowledges that Jesus is the Lord and messianic king, crying out "Have mercy on me, Lord, Son of David" (nrsv). Because she was a Gentile, the disciples would have sent her away, but Jesus simply remarks that His ministry is to the Jews, not the Gentiles. She remains persistent, so Jesus offers a proverbial statement that His ministry is not for the unclean (dogs), but for the children of God. Her response indicates that she understands His remark, but observes that even dogs (a derogatory term commonly used by the Jews to refer to Gentiles) eat food from the Master's table. Jesus commends her for her great faith and heals her daughter.

The point of this narrative is this: The Jews, who should have accepted Jesus and believed in Him, did not, but this Gentile woman, who had no reason to believe in Jesus, did. Jesus finds great faith where no one would have expected it, but no faith where it should have been. The lesson for the members of Matthew's community is that they, too, should not ignore the Gentiles among whom they now lived, for one can find faith also among the Gentiles.

15:29–39

THE FEEDING OF THE FOUR THOUSAND

Jesus returns from the region of Tyre and Sidon to the Sea of Galilee. Sitting with a large crowd on the mountainside, He performs many miracles. Again, Jesus wants to feed the crowd. The disciples, seemingly with a short memory, ask where they can get enough food to feed the crowd. After Jesus takes the seven loaves and few small fish and feeds more than four thousand people, there are more than seven baskets of food left over.

The point of this narrative is, again, that Jesus can take care of the needs of His people, no matter how little they have and how great the need. A secondary lesson is that the disciples' faith still needs much maturing.

The location of Magadan (and in Mark's account, Dalmanutha) is unknown in both cases. This is the only mention of Magadan and Dalmanutha in ancient literature.

16:1–4

THE PHARISEES AND SADDUCEES DEMAND A SIGN FROM HEAVEN

The Pharisees are now joined by the Sadducees to continue the attack on Jesus. These two theological and political enemies join together in their opposition to Jesus, illustrating their frustration and desperation. We have not heard of the Sadducees since Matthew 3:7 and will hear of them in Matthew only seven times (four times in Matthew 16, and twice in Matthew 22).

The request for a sign (from heaven, which also meant from God) is intended to trap Jesus and provide evidence that they might use against Him. Jesus' response draws attention to the fact that they already have all the signs they need. His comment about their ability to read natural signs indicates the duplicity of their request.

Jesus' strident rebuke likens them to an adulterous generation, which has all the evidence it needs yet still rebels against God. Therefore, they are guilty of committing spiritual adultery. This is the second time Jesus refers to the sign of Jonah. The first was in Matthew 12:40. In both cases Jesus is referencing His resurrection from the dead. Jonah was in the belly of the fish for three days and nights, and Jesus will be in the grave for the same period.

16:5–12

THE LEAVEN OF THE PHARISEES AND SADDUCEES

Jesus warns the disciples to beware of the leaven (yeast) of the Pharisees and Sadducees. The disciples associate this with physical bread, which they have forgotten to bring with them. Reminding them of His miracles with the five thousand and four thousand, Jesus warns them again. Finally, the disciples understand Jesus' warning regarding the Pharisees' and Sadducees' teaching and refusal to believe, and the need they have for faith. Since the disciples continued to display little faith (17:20), this warning is entirely appropriate.

16:13–20

CAESAREA PHILIPPI AND PETER'S CONFESSION

The confession of Peter is a crucial turning point in the Gospels of Matthew, Mark, and John. It is only here in Matthew, though, that the high status in the church is assigned to Peter at the end of the passage. In fact, this section is one of the central texts in the Gospel of Matthew, and it is certainly central for the existence of the church as the messianic community.

The discussion begins with the seemingly neutral questioning of the disciples by Jesus, regarding who people think He, the Son of Man, is. The response is mixed–John the Baptist, Elijah, or one of the prophets (a sign of the end times and God's imminent judgment).

When Jesus asks more specifically who the disciples think He is, Peter responds with the famous confession, "You are the Christ, the Son of the living God" (NIV).

Jesus' response recognizes that Peter's understanding is the result of the revelation of God. This does not necessarily mean that at that instance God had revealed this to Peter. It most likely means that human ingenuity could not have full credit for Peter's conclusion. The hand of the Father can be seen in the process that has led to Peter's understanding. God has been working His plan, attested to by both prophetic utterance and the powerful miracles of Jesus.

Critical Observation

Jesus' response to Peter—calling Peter a rock on whom Jesus will build His church—opens the door to much speculation and debate.

The Greek word for Peter is *petros.* The Greek word for rock is *petra.* Both petros (masculine) and petra (feminine) mean rock. But in the original conversation, Jesus may have been speaking Aramaic. In that language there is only one word, *kepha,* which means rock. Whether you consider the language Jesus is probably speaking in or the language that Matthew is writing in, Jesus is making a play on words.

While looking back through Protestant-Catholic history, there have been many discussions about the connection between this passage and the role of Peter as Pope. But keep in mind that this was not an issue for Matthew. It's important to look at this text as it was meaningful to those for whom it was written.

It is possible that the rock-like confession of Peter is the play on words Jesus is making, and that it is on the confession of the divinity of Jesus that He will build His messianic community. It is in this manner that thinkers such as Calvin, Zwingli, and John Locke understood the expression. The focus of the discussion can be seen in the parallelism between Peter's confession and Jesus' confession.

CONTINUED

This section clearly states that Peter's confession and apostolic office are the bedrock of the messianic community Jesus claimed He would build—the church.

The word *church* appears here, then again in Matthew 18:17. Elsewhere the reference to the messianic community is to the kingdom of heaven or kingdom of God. The Aramaic word underlying the Greek is normally translated as "synagogue." In most instances in the New Testament, *church* is the favored word, although *synagogue* is occasionally used in references to the church.

It is interesting that Jesus distances His messianic community from the Jewish synagogue, and that Matthew makes this distinction for the sake of his community that had just been uprooted from the temple. It could no longer identify with the Jewish synagogue, for the Jewish synagogue was not the messianic community of Jesus.

The word used here that some versions of the Bible translate as "hell" actually references another place—Hades—the realm of the dead or the underworld. Jesus is stating that not even death or the realm of the dead will prevail against this establishment of the church. This probably refers to His own imminent death (the next section in Matthew develops this), but some would include in His meaning the fact that death and martyrdom will not hinder the establishment and growth of the church.

The keys of the kingdom that Jesus offers Peter represent authority. Historically, it is Peter who preaches the first gospel sermon that leads to the salvation of the first Jewish converts to Christianity after the resurrection of Jesus (Acts 2:17–40), which then leads to the first Gentile converts to Christianity (Acts 10–11).

Binding and *loosing* were rabbinic expressions found in many places in the Jewish tradition that had a variety of usages. Fundamentally it involved including and excluding people from the community, and setting the rules for behavior in the community. It is to the apostles, beginning with Peter, that the responsibility is given to establish the church and the community life within. In Matthew 16 this has reference to Peter, but later this authority is expressed in regard to all of the apostles (18:18). It is to the apostles that, through their preaching, authority is given to shape the New Testament church.

16:21–23

JESUS FORETELLS HIS DEATH, BURIAL, AND RESURRECTION

Matthew 16:21 marks a dramatic turning point in Jesus' ministry. From this point on He turns away from the crowds and to His disciples in a personal ministry intended to prepare them for His imminent suffering and death. Although there have been some allusions to Jesus' coming suffering and death (9:15; 12:40), this is the first real announcement by Jesus.

Mathew's Gospel continues to narrate accounts of Jesus' powerful healings, but these are no longer the main focus of the narrative. From this point on, Matthew will develop the necessity and inevitability of Jesus' suffering and death. This is the first of four predictions by Jesus of His death, burial, and resurrection, the others being Matthew 17:22–23; 20:17–19; and 26:2.

The focus will also shift to the development of the radical nature of the call to discipleship, and the central meaning of the Gospels—Jesus' sacrifice and resurrection.

Matthew records that Jesus begins to show His disciples that He has to go to Jerusalem. In doing so, He demonstrates that His suffering and death are not accidents, but part of God's will, purpose, and plan. It is necessary by God's will and purpose for Jesus to do four things:

1) Go to Jerusalem
2) Suffer at the hands of the ruling power of the Jews
3) Be put to death
4) Then be brought back to life on the third day

This passion statement (*passion* is used here as a technical term for Jesus' death, burial, and resurrection) becomes the central theme of the gospel message (1 Corinthians 15:1–4). It is certainly the central theme of Peter's preaching on Pentecost (Acts 2) and to Cornelius (Acts 10:34–43).

Peter's comment "God, forbid it, Lord" (16:22 NRSV) may be better translated as "far be it from. . ." or "may God be gracious to you and forbid this. . . ." Peter still does not understand the full implication of Jesus' messianic ministry as the suffering servant described by Isaiah (Isaiah 53), and of God's purpose for and in Jesus. But who would have understood this fully at that time?

Jesus' response is a strident and harsh rebuke. A paraphrase of Jesus' response might read "Peter, you are a hindrance to God's purpose for me. You are functioning under the influence of Satan."

A major lesson we learn from this exchange is again the radical nature of Jesus' ministry and our discipleship. Jesus' purpose, contrary to human tendencies, was not to take the easy solution to the problem. Our discipleship is radical because our Master is radical.

16:24–27

RADICAL DISCIPLESHIP

The unsettling and radical thrust of Jesus' passion pronouncement is followed by an equally unsettling and radical revelation from Jesus on the cost of discipleship—true discipleship must entail a willingness to die for one's faith. Discipleship must be modeled on Jesus' pattern of being the suffering servant of God—denying one's self and taking up one's cross just as Jesus did. In other words, do as I do, follow My example.

Taking up our crosses for Jesus can have a lot of contemporary applications, as we sacrifice in order to follow Him closely. However, in the context of Jesus' discussion and Matthew's community's needs, coupled together with what Jesus has taught His disciples in Matthew 10:16–39, and especially verses 34–39, we should understand this as a radical call to discipleship and if necessary, martyrdom.

This understanding comes from the discussion that follows, in which Jesus elaborates and it seems to best fit the context of martyrdom. Martyrdom was a very present reality to Christians in the first century. In fact, by the second century of Christianity, discipleship held the threat of martyrdom for many.

Jesus speaks of losing one's life for His sake. The word translated "life" here can also be translated as "soul" (16:26 NIV). Reading the entire passage, "life" fits the context better in this instance.

In the Greek school of thought (Plato), a person was merely a physical body in which a spirit dwells. Not so in the Jewish view of humanity. In the Jewish view, a person was seen as an integrated spiritual being, not merely the housing of a spirit. The Jewish view did not separate the physical and spiritual life, but conceived them to be a unit. Thus, as written in the book of Romans, death is the consequence of sin (Romans 6:23), implying both physical and spiritual death. Considering this, it is appropriate to understand *life* in this passage to include the soul, which represents the whole being of mankind, both physical and spiritual.

Life is valuable and we treasure it, but by seeking to save one's life (not being willing to die for Jesus) one does in fact lose it. Notice the irony of Jesus' statement. What we treasure so much, we lose by trying to keep it.

Earlier in Matthew, Satan had sought to tempt Jesus by offering Him the kingdoms of the world (4:1–10). If Jesus had accepted Satan's offer, He would not have had to die on the cross. He could have saved His life, but in saving His life He would have lost everything.

Jesus' next statement adds a dramatic note to the discussion. Those who seek to save their lives by denying Jesus will be judged by this at the end of the age.

16:28

THE SON OF MAN COMING IN HIS KINGDOM

As in Matthew 10:23, Jesus uses the puzzling expression that something will not be completed before (or until, or till) the Son of Man comes. This expression could refer to:

1) the transfiguration of Jesus (Matthew 16:28 and 17:1–2);
2) the destruction of Jerusalem itself (Matthew 24:30);
3) some unusual event such as the destruction of Jerusalem (Matthew 24) or the day of Pentecost (Acts 2);
4) the coming of Jesus in judgment at any time as a demonstration of His final judgment (Revelation 1:7; 2:16; 22:7, 12);
5) Jesus' second coming at the end of the world (Matthew 24:27–28).

Within the Judeo-Christian understanding of eschatology (end times), any event in the eschatological age (from the coming of the Messiah to the final end of the age) is referred to as an eschatological event, and is an act of the Messiah coming in some form of dramatic action. Thus the destruction of Jerusalem is an expression of the coming of the Son of Man in power or in an eschatological act of judgment. And Jesus coming in judgment on one of the seven churches in Asia (Revelation 2, 3) can be spoken of as a coming of the Son of Man in judgment.

17:1–13

THE TRANSFIGURATION

Matthew's mention of six days having passed is interesting in that Luke mentions eight days having passed. This indicates that the precise timing is not the central point of this section. The central point is the glory of Jesus and God's acknowledgement of His divine role.

The fact that this section appears in all three Gospels immediately after Jesus' prediction of His death is striking. The passion prediction must have left a dark cloud over the disciples. They needed encouragement and hope. The Transfiguration and God's approving statement regarding

Jesus provide a ray of light and encouragement for the immediate circle of disciples (Peter, James, and John), and for Matthew's readers, too.

Jesus, taking only Peter, James, and John with Him onto the mountain, indicates His need to maintain a sense of secrecy and quietness in the matter of His messianic glory. Throughout the Gospel accounts of Jesus' ministry, He has tried to keep the crowds away to avoid sensationalism. Jesus later takes these same three men with Him into the Garden of Gethsemane to pray (26:37). We have no real indication why it is these three that seemingly formed the inner circle among the disciples.

The miracle of the Transfiguration is one of the truly great experiences of the story of Jesus. He is transformed. The shining of His face like the sun and the brightness of His garments are reminiscent of the Shekinah Glory of God that shone from Moses after his encounters with God on Mt. Sinai (Exodus 34:29–35).

The proposal by Peter that they build three tents has prompted much speculation as to what Peter had in mind. It is doubtful the tents were intended to be three shrines for worship because in Israel the booths were not for that purpose. Booths of branches were built for shelter on pilgrimages to Jerusalem, not worship. The simplest conclusion here is that Peter is proposing they spend more time in this transformed state with Jesus, Moses, and Elijah.

While Peter is still speaking, a bright cloud surrounds them (again an indication of the presence of God and God's involvement in this experience) and the great voice of God speaks in recognition of Jesus. This is the same message heard at the baptism of Jesus (3:17) with its inherent allusions to Psalm 2:7 and Isaiah 42:1. However, on this occasion God adds an allusion to Deuteronomy 18:15, the admonishment for those present to listen to Jesus. Most likely Moses represents the Torah Law given at Sinai, and Elijah represents the prophets, but now the authority to speak for God is transferred by God Himself to Jesus. Moses and Elijah had been the voice of God and the interpreters of the Torah, but from now on it will be Jesus who will interpret.

Following what was a magnificent experience—and frightening for Peter, James, and John—Jesus warns them not to tell others of this experience until after His resurrection.

The disciples are still confused about the expectation of the return of Elijah during the end times and question Jesus in this regard. Jesus explains that Elijah had returned in John the Baptist, but people were not ready to receive John and his message. In a similar vein, neither are they willing to receive the Son of Man and His message, and because of this, the Son of Man has to suffer at the hands of the Jewish leaders.

17:14–21

HEALING OF THE EPILEPTIC BOY

The disciples are not able to heal this epileptic boy of his demon possession. The boy's father pleads with Jesus to heal the boy, which Jesus does. The healing is not the striking point of this section, since we already know that Jesus could, and did, heal many. Neither is the faith of the father the central point. It is the lack of faith, or weak faith, of the disciples that is at issue. Jesus is again working to build the faith of His disciples. His comment that faith can move mountains is a Hebrew proverb that meant faith can move immovable obstacles. The emphasis is not on the literal moving of mountains, but on the insurmountable problems that the disciples and all Christians face in life. John will write later that it is faith that is the victory that overcomes the world (1 John 5:4).

Matthew 17:21, the statement that prayer and fasting are required for this kind of feat, is missing in the more reliable ancient manuscripts. The verse appears in Mark's parallel (9:29) and was likely added by a later copyist to harmonize the two accounts.

17:22–23

JESUS AGAIN FORETELLS HIS DEATH AND RESURRECTION

For some reason, possibly because the disciples are still struggling over Jesus' statement at Caesarea Philippi regarding His passion, Jesus again tells His disciples that He must be delivered into the hands of men and be killed, and then be raised by the power of God. Matthew reveals that the disciples are greatly distressed. Mark records that they don't understand but are afraid to ask (Mark 9:32). Luke records that it is hidden from them and they don't understand (Luke 9:45). These parallels reinforce the fact that the disciples are still struggling with the fate of the Messiah.

This section reinforces that Jesus' ministry falls within the will and purpose of God. The people of Matthew's community may have still been struggling with this and similar questions regarding Jesus' death, and their own subsequent suffering. They need to be assured that God is in control, that He is working His purpose, and that they are part of the plan of God.

17:24–27

THE SHEKEL IN THE FISH'S MOUTH AND THE TEMPLE TAX

It is not surprising that Matthew is the only recorder of this experience, since it involves Jesus' attitude toward the temple. This would not be that important to either Mark's or Luke's audience. It is important to Matthew's community, which is struggling with the destruction of the temple. It is only the servants of the temple who need to pay the temple tax, and Jesus as the Son of God does not need to pay this tax, for sons are free of taxation. But to show His regard for the temple and for all it really stood, Jesus pays the tax anyway. However, the disciples and Matthew's community need to know that Jesus is greater than the temple, and whereas before His death the temple had been a focal point of Jewish faith, now it is Jesus who is the center of faith.

MATTHEW 18:1–35

DISCOURSE 4: COMMUNITY—HUMILTY AND FORGIVENESS

Humility	18:1–9
Finding the Lost Sheep	18:10–14
Solving Personal and Community Problems	18:15–20
Christian Forgiveness	18:21–35

Setting Up the Section

This discourse covers several topics vital to successful church community life. It is introduced by the topic of the previous narrative in which Jesus focuses His attention on the disciples, preparing them for His death and resurrection. In this discourse Matthew takes the preparation of the disciples one step beyond the Resurrection, namely, on how they will live in a Christian community after Jesus is gone.

This discourse would have been essential for Matthew's readers in the late first century. They, as a community, had established themselves in new territory. In the same way, this discourse is also essential for churches today.

18:1–9

HUMILITY

Still struggling with the true nature of the kingdom, the disciples are concerned with who will be greatest in the kingdom. Jesus' answers in the following verses demonstrate that the disciples are struggling with matters of position, power, and authority. His response that the disciples should be like little children indicates that greatness in the kingdom has nothing to do with power and position, but everything to do with one's attitude toward self and others. Jesus has already noted that true greatness has to do with serving (11:11). He will return to this theme again when the mother of James and John seeks a high position for her sons (20:20–21). Luke 22:25–27 also drives this point home.

Jesus' response to the disciples that they must *turn* (convert, change) indicates a radical turn. The word translated as "turn" is a word commonly used to imply a moral turning or repenting. Jesus admonishes the disciples to make a radical turn in their mind-set regarding greatness in the kingdom. They need to become like little children. The point is that disciples need to be humble servants. However, we learn from the discussion that follows there is also the sense that, as humble servants, the disciples will be vulnerable to abuse. Humble disciples open themselves to abuse from others outside of the community of believers. Yet, Jesus explains, unless a disciple is willing to turn and be humble, he or she will not become a member of the kingdom, let alone be great in it (18:3).

Jesus continues by observing that to receive (welcome, accept) a disciple in the name of Jesus is the same as receiving Jesus Himself. However, to reject a vulnerable disciple (little one) is tantamount to leading the disciple to stumble or sin. The Greek word translated "stumble" or "sin" has the connotation of a snare or trap. In the religious or biblical sense, to stumble is equated with falling into sin or losing one's faith.

The discussion on humility is developed by Jesus to reflect on how disciples treat one another and influence other disciples. To cause a vulnerable disciple to stumble or lose his or her faith in Jesus is a serious matter, one in which judgment is compared by Jesus to having a millstone tied around one's neck and being cast into the depths of the sea and drowned. It seems from other references (Revelation 18:21) that this figure of speech may have been an idiom in Judaism for severe condemnation. Jesus closes this point with the interesting analogy of cutting off one's bodily members if they cause one to stumble (to lose faith and thus the kingdom).

Take It Home

What does it mean for the disciple to be humble? Unless one is willing to deny self and give up all for Christ, placing other disciples before self, one is not able to understand the kingdom. Faith and humility go hand in hand. Without both, the kingdom is impossible, for the kingdom is permitting God through Christ to reign in one's heart and life.

Consider Jesus' answer to the disciples' question regarding who is greatest in the kingdom. The one who humbles him- or herself like a little child is greatest in the kingdom, for as Jesus had previously taught, it is the servant who is greatest.

18:10–14

FINDING THE LOST SHEEP

To demonstrate further the importance of vulnerable disciples (all disciples are vulnerable), Jesus uses the illustration of the man who had 100 sheep, of which one got lost. Jesus concludes that this analogy reflects the love and concern of the Father in heaven for any one lost sheep.

Disciples are vulnerable to stumble and be lost. Disciples must be concerned for the vulnerable and lost and be sensitive to the needs of fellow disciples. Pride and seeking for greatness are not fitting for the kingdom. Having concern for fellow disciples, those who are vulnerable and easily lost, is key to kingdom understanding.

18:15–20

SOLVING PERSONAL AND COMMUNITY PROBLEMS

Hardly is there a passage that has more implications for Christians living in the kingdom than this one. In most English translations verse 15 opens with, "If your brother sins against you. . ." (NIV). Some very reliable manuscripts, from which these English versions of the Bible are translated, omit "against you." (The parallel passage in Luke 17:3 omits this.)

After reading verse 15 with the "against you" included, some have concluded that this passage refers *only* to a private sin. This is probably not the case, particularly considering the fact that the context of this section is community life and concern for disciples in general. The mention of the church later in this section (18:17–18) sets these verses firmly within the action of community life and discipline. Personal concerns do have a significant impact on congregational life, so the truth of this passage relates to both sin that is personal and private as well as sin that impacts the life of the church community.

The principles laid down by Jesus in this section are essential to resolving ruptured personal relationships, and mediating conflict. The instruction on how to handle such matters is firmly set in the threefold procedure established in Deuteronomy 19:15–21:

1) The process begins first on the personal level.
2) Then it proceeds to the second level of two witnesses.
3) The third level is bringing the matter before the community of believers.

In Deuteronomy 19:17, the final community level is considered the same as being in the presence of the Lord. Note Jesus' teaching in Matthew 18:20 that where this process is followed in His name, there He is present.

An interesting construction is evident in verses 15–17. Each initial clause in these statements of Jesus begins with "If." The careful construction of these verses indicates that Matthew has taken the time to set the verses up in a parallel structure styled in the form of a church discipline saying. The "if" clauses indicate the strong possibility, even probability, that in community life such occasions will occur and will require the appropriate corrective practice, which Jesus sets out.

1) Speak to the individual in person without publicizing the problem.
2) If an appropriate response is not forthcoming, take another person with you (at the mouth of two persons truth is established [Deuteronomy 19:15]).
3) As a last resort, bring the matter before the appropriate persons in the church community (possibly recognized leaders, elders, or even if necessary, the whole congregation). If no repentance is forthcoming, and no forgiveness requested, then the sinful person should be treated as a pagan (Gentile), meaning that the community should have no further fellowship in a brotherly sense with the sinful person.

There are other instances where instruction is given to the church on how to handle such matters. For instance, Galatians 6:1 relates closely with this section. On at least two other occasions, Paul instructs churches on matters of church discipline (1 Corinthians 5:1–13; 6:1–6; 2 Thessalonians 3:6–15).

In Matthew 18:15–20, Jesus concludes His instruction with the remarkable observation that action taken by the community in good Christian order is sanctioned in heaven and in fact becomes His own action.

The emphatic expression "truly" (v. 18 NASB) translates the Greek *amen* and adds a note of sincerity and genuineness to the saying that follows. Whatever is decided by the community in regard to settling community problems, when carried out in the appropriate manner, is accepted in heaven. The word translated as "bound" was used in marriage contracts, but in the context here implies a contract that will be honored in heaven. The full saying in Matthew 18:18 is in the form of a proverbial or idiomatic saying inferring that heaven acknowledges the decisions of the Christian community action.

The comment regarding two agreeing and two or three gathering in Jesus' name adheres to the Jewish belief that two witnesses settle a matter. The gathering together has no reference to a small gathering of the church on the Lord's Day for worship, which has become a partial excuse for a small assembly, but is a euphemism in reference to the group or community gathering in proper order to resolve problems. The community is reminded that Jesus is always present when His community gathers in His name, or under His will and lordship.

"In My name" (18:20 NIV) is a Hebrew euphemism for "in the person of Jesus" or "under His will."

18:21–35

CHRISTIAN FORGIVENESS

The principles of Christian forgiveness are as essential to successful church community life as are the ones for resolving conflicts involving sin, as depicted in the previous section. Whereas the previous section initially presupposed a lack of repentance and focused on the other party, this section focuses on the first person, or the self. It asks not what the other person should have done, but what should *I* be doing?

This section begins with Peter asking how often he should forgive another person. Peter recognizes that forgiveness is vital to the process of church discipline and resolving broken relationships. His suggestion of forgiving seven times is generous. Rabbinic teaching suggested three times as the standard. Peter has chosen a favored Jewish number for completeness, but Jesus responds with a greater number—seventy times seven—indicating that there is no limit to the number of times one should be willing to forgive.

The fascinating and powerful parable that Jesus teaches drives home the need for Christians to learn how to forgive. The parable is set in the context of the kingdom, emphasizing Matthew's interest and concern for kingdom matters. When Jesus is reigning in disciples' lives and the kingdom is something real in their experience, more is expected than passive membership or church-going.

In the parable, the first servant owes the king an unpayable debt, 10,000 talents, estimated by some to be in the high millions or even billions of dollars in present-day currency. In 4 BC the total taxes for all of Judea, Samaria, and Idumea was only 600 talents. The king is merciful and forgives the first servant completely. Then there is a sudden change of events. The first servant is owed 100 denarii by another, about 100 days' wages (there were 6,000 denarii in one talent) and a payable debt. The first servant shows no mercy and no forgiveness. When the king hears, he throws the first servant in jail until he pays the full 10,000 talent (unpayable) debt. The application of this parable is timeless, applying to the first disciples, Matthew's community, and all Christians today.

We are reminded that this discourse begins with the disciples inquiring about who is greatest in the kingdom, which indicates a faulty understanding of kingdom life. Jesus' answer challenges the disciples to understand humble service in the kingdom. The discourse moves on to the need for all disciples to be concerned for all disciples, since disciples are vulnerable to sin and loss of faith. The value of one lost disciple is driven home by Jesus' teaching on the lost sheep. Jesus then moves on to community behavior and the need for disciples to resolve problems in the appropriate manner. Finally, the need for mercy and forgiveness is driven home by the powerful kingdom parable of the king and the two servants.

MATTHEW 19:1–22:46

NARRATIVE 5: TOWARD JERUSALEM—THE FINAL WEEK

Jesus Answers the Pharisees on Marriage and Divorce	19:1–12
Jesus Blesses Little Children	19:13–15
The Rich Young Ruler	19:16–30
The Parable of the Householder	20:1–16
Jesus Again Foretells His Death and Resurrection	20:17–19
The Son of Man Came to Serve, Not Be Served	20:20–28
Healing Two Blind Men near Jericho	20:29–34
The Triumphant Entry into Jerusalem	21:1–11
Cleansing the Temple	21:12–17

The Barren Fig Tree	21:18–22
Chief Priests Challenge Jesus' Authority	21:23–27
The Parable of Two Sons	21:28–32
The Parable of the Wicked Tenants	21:33–46
The Parable of the Marriage Feast	22:1–14
The Messiah, Taxes, and Caesar	22:15–22
The Sadducees and the Resurrection	22:23–33
Which Is the Greatest Commandment?	22:34–40
Jesus' Unanswerable Question to the Pharisees	22:41–46

Setting Up the Section

In the final week of Jesus' ministry, He continues to prepare His disciples for His death. His conflict with the Jewish leaders sharpens, leading up to exasperation and judgment on the scribes and Pharisees and on Jerusalem and the temple.

19:1–12

JESUS ANSWERS THE PHARISEES ON MARRIAGE AND DIVORCE

As in Jesus' previous discussion of the divorce and remarriage issue, this discussion is set in the context of the Pharisees attempting to test and trap Jesus. This discourse on divorce and remarriage is not the final testament on the issue, but a serious answer to a trap by the Pharisees. Certainly, Jesus touches on several major issues in the debate on divorce and remarriage, but only within the context of the Pharisees' question.

The test question posed by the Pharisees is one that had troubled the rabbis for generations, in fact, since Moses had spoken to the issue in Deuteronomy 24:1. The question that arose from Moses' declaration was how to interpret the kind of indecency that would justify a man divorcing his wife. The issue placed before Jesus is not simply one on divorce, but relates to the justifiable grounds for divorce.

Two rabbinic schools of thought prevailed at the time the Pharisees posed this question:

- Rabbi Shammai interpreted the word *indecency* as unchastity or sexual immorality.
- Rabbi Hillel interpreted this loosely as any form of uncleanness on trivial grounds.

Jesus' response moves the argument back beyond Moses' permission for divorce to God's ideal for marriage. Marriage is to be for life, and what God has joined, man is not to break apart (Genesis 2:24).

Since Moses permitted divorce under the limited condition of unchastity (Deuteronomy 24:1, Shammai), we are introduced to a significant point that must impact our understanding of this perplexing dilemma: We have God's original instruction on His ideal for marriage. We have in Moses' permission the limited practical application of God's ideal.

The Pharisees' return argument is that Jesus has spoken in opposition to Moses. Jesus corrects them by showing that what Moses had done was not a command but permission. The Pharisees had attempted to place Jesus in opposition to Moses and the Law. Jesus again, as in the Sermon on the Mount, demonstrates that the Pharisaic interpretation of the Law does not take into consideration the real spirit of purpose of the Law. Moses' permission was purely because of human hardness of heart. By adding the except-for-unchastity clause, Jesus is reminding the Pharisees of the narrowness of God's permission. The narrowness of Jesus' response disturbs the disciples, indicating how lax Jewish attitudes had become in regard to marriage and divorce. Their observation is that it might be better for one not to marry if Jesus' interpretation is correct.

Jesus' response speaks of three groups of eunuchs—two literal, one metaphorical.

1) Those born impotent and therefore eunuchs
2) Those made eunuchs by others such as in the case of the Ethiopian eunuch of Acts 8, sometimes occurring in slavery
3) Those who chose to live celibate lives for the kingdom as in the case of the apostle Paul

Jesus' response to the disciples' concern again illustrates the radical nature of discipleship in the kingdom. Disciples are to live by God's ideals rather than permissiveness resulting from sinful weakness.

Although this is not the place for a full discussion of the marriage and divorce issue, note that Paul takes the argument beyond the narrow confines of Judaism and Israel as the covenant people of God into a discussion of marriages involving non-believers. Perhaps Paul's discussion is more relevant for contemporary issues and may be parallel to Moses' permission. Disciples in the kingdom should be shaped, however, more by kingdom issues and God's ideals than by permissiveness.

19:13–15

JESUS BLESSES LITTLE CHILDREN

This little section in which the disciples seek to drive children away provides Jesus with another occasion to remind the disciples that the kingdom belongs to those who have learned to be humble like children. It is not uncommon for disciples to bring worldly standards of greatness into the kingdom. Followers of Jesus throughout the centuries have struggled with the principle of humble servant leadership, with many seeking positions in the church for the wrong reasons—personal importance rather than humble service.

19:16–30

THE RICH YOUNG RULER

The narrative regarding the rich young ruler focuses again on radical discipleship and the true nature of the kingdom. Matthew does not identify the young man as a ruler, but Luke does so in his parallel narrative in Luke 18:18–27. Obviously the young man is not only rich, but also a person of position, possibly a ruler in the synagogue. On this occasion the rich young man addresses Jesus regarding eternal life, asking what good thing he must do to inherit eternal life (referring to the afterlife, not an eternal earthly life).

Jesus' question about the man's meaning of *good* is interesting. Rabbinic tradition defined the Torah as the good. Jesus explains that it is by keeping the commandments that one will experience eternal life. When the young man explains that he has done this, Jesus accepts his claim. One can be righteous through keeping the law, for Paul claims such (Philippians 3:6). Maintaining righteousness should not be equated here with being sinless, but instead seen as merely a claim to having maintained a right relationship with God through observing the Torah.

Jesus' instruction to the young man gets to the heart of his problem—riches. When he learns that discipleship in the kingdom involves placing kingdom matters and discipleship above personal possessions, the young man goes away sad, for the cost of discipleship is too high. His reaction reminds us of Jesus' teaching in the Sermon on the Mount, that your heart will be where your treasure is (6:21).

Jesus continues the discussion begun by the young man. He does not say it is impossible for a rich person to enter heaven, but only that it is difficult. (This Greek word for *difficult* is found in the New Testament only on this occasion in Matthew, Mark, and Luke.) Illustrating how difficult it would be for a rich person to enter the kingdom, Jesus uses the analogy of a camel going through the eye of a needle. Attempts to soften this by interpreting *camel* and *eye of a needle* in a more reasonable way fail to grasp the irony of Jesus' statement. He is using exaggeration to make a point. The reason some attempt to soften this saying is that it seems to make it impossible for a rich person to be saved. The disciples catch this and are amazed and ask who can be saved. This is when Jesus gets to the point—salvation is not the work of humanity, but of God. Even though it would be difficult for a rich person to be saved, it is not impossible for God, but it would necessitate the rich person turning away from this world and to God for His saving grace. No one can be saved by human effort. It is only through the grace and working of God that all people can be saved.

When Peter, troubled by Jesus' seemingly harsh statement, asks what will happen to them for they have given up all for the kingdom, Jesus responds that in the new world they will sit on thrones with Jesus and judge the world with Him. All who give up everything for Jesus and the kingdom's sake will inherit eternal life.

Jesus' reference to the new world (the regeneration, the renewal of all things, when the Son of Man sits on His throne) uses a Greek word that means rebirth or regeneration. The word is found in the New Testament only twice, here and in Titus 3:5, but has a rich heritage in historical writings and the Jewish rabbinic tradition. In most cases, it references a future age or occasion of renewal, rebirth, or restoration. Here Jesus links it to the time when the Son of Man will sit on His throne and reign over the kingdom. The apostles who have given up all will then sit with Him and judge Israel with Him. This is supported in Revelation, where John writes that those who have died as martyrs sit with Jesus on thrones (Revelation 2:26–28; 20:4–6).

Jesus concludes this discussion with the proverbial statement that the first will be last. Given the context of the rich young man, one must assume that the first must be in reference to the rich who believe that because of their position in life they should be privileged. In the kingdom this is not the case, for as we have already learned, it is the humble who benefit from the kingdom, not the proud (5:1–12), and it is the humble servants who are greatest in the kingdom (18:1–4).

20:1–16

THE PARABLE OF THE HOUSEHOLDER

This parable connects back to the closing statement of Matthew 19:30 and illustrates the principle of the first being last, and the last being first. It is a parable that speaks to behavior in the kingdom. But it is also an illustration of the great kingdom principle of grace.

The householder (who represents God) hires a series of workers at different times of the day. He promises the first a day's wages (a denarius). At the close of the day he pays all the workers the same wage, but those who were hired first are upset that they'd worked longer for the same pay as those that were hired on late. The householder's closing remarks demonstrate a great principle of grace: Can't I do what I want with what belongs to me? Do you resent my generosity toward others?

Jesus closes the parable by returning to the proverb, but in this case reverses the order—the last will be first.

20:17–19

JESUS AGAIN FORETELLS HIS DEATH AND RESURRECTION

As Jesus draws near to Jerusalem, He again instructs the twelve regarding His death, burial, and resurrection. This time, though, He elaborates briefly on several other things: His suffering, condemnation by the Jewish leadership, trial before the Gentiles, and the mocking and scourging He will receive.

20:20–28

THE SON OF MAN CAME TO SERVE, NOT BE SERVED

We see again in this section the difficulty the disciples have understanding the true nature of discipleship and the kingdom. On this occasion the mother of James and John asks Jesus for positions of honor for her sons in the kingdom. We should not think too poorly of this mother, or of the other disciples for being indignant over her request. The temptation to see leadership positions as power rather than opportunities to serve still exists today in the church.

Jesus asks the two disciples whether they are willing to drink the cup that He is about to drink, and they respond that they are. The metaphor of drinking the cup is in reference to His suffering and death, which He has just talked about (20:17–19). The background for the use of a cup in reference to suffering can also be found in the Old Testament in passages such as Psalm 75:8 and Isaiah 51:17, 22. The immediate response of the two disciples seems to indicate they do not fully understand the implications of Jesus' remark.

Jesus follows His comments with a clear, real-life analogy. In this world the greatest are served while the least do the serving. The kingdom of God works in the reverse. The greatest are those who serve. Jesus uses a reference to Himself as the Son of Man to illustrate this. As the Son of Man, He deserves being served by others, but this is not His purpose. He came to be a servant. Luke records similar words from Jesus (Luke 22:25–27). Paul also writes of Jesus' humble service (Philippians 2:5–11).

20:29–34

HEALING TWO BLIND MEN NEAR JERICHO

As Jesus and the disciples are passing through Jericho they see two blind men.

The synoptic Gospels—Matthew, Mark, and Luke—record different details. In Luke's Gospel Jesus and His disciples are coming into Jericho, as opposed to Matthew's record that they are leaving. Mark and Luke refer to one man, while Matthew, making the story more reliable to a Jewish audience, records two men. Mark includes the name of the man, Bartimaeus. But these details are not contradictory. Each writer brings out the details that serve his purpose best in the retelling.

The two blind men call out to Jesus, referring to Him as the Son of David and begging Him to heal them, which He does. The narrative draws attention to the fact that even the blind recognize Jesus as the Messiah, yet the seeing—Pharisees, scribes, and Sadducees—do not recognize the Messiah. This narrative fits in well with the preceding discussion of the greatest being last and the least being first.

21:1–11

THE TRIUMPHANT ENTRY INTO JERUSALEM

This event and narrative is shared by all four Gospels (Mark 11:1–11; Luke 19:29–44; John 12:12–19).

Bethphage was a small village, possibly on the Mount of Olives near Bethany, but we do not know its exact location. The name means "house of unripe figs." We read of Bethphage only in this account in Matthew, Mark, and Luke.

Jesus' entry into Jerusalem is a turning point in the Gospel narrative. It ends His Galilean ministry and journey to Jerusalem and begins the tragic passion narrative. It is an event marked by the capriciousness of the people and manifests a mixture of truth and irony. The truth is that Jesus really is the Messiah. The irony is that His very identity as the Messiah is the reason He is rejected by the Jews, particularly the Jewish leadership. When He enters Jerusalem He is welcomed as the Son of David, but is almost immediately rejected as the Messiah and mocked by the people. When Jesus shows that He is a different kind of Messiah than they expected, He is rejected.

Jesus deliberately stages His ride into Jerusalem to fulfill Zechariah 9:9, an Old Testament passage that was interpreted with reference to the Messiah by the rabbis. Matthew's use of Zechariah 9:9 is one of the ten fulfillment passages unique to his Gospel. He combines Zechariah 9:9 with Isaiah 62:11.

Mark, Luke, and John record one animal, an ass or donkey, while Matthew records an ass that had a colt with her. Some commentators think that Matthew has misunderstood the poetic parallelism in Zechariah 9:9 to refer to two animals instead of one. But this is not necessary. Matthew's account makes sense when we recognize that—as Mark tells us—Jesus is riding on a colt on which no one has previously sat. The mother animal is therefore brought along to calm the colt as Jesus rides on it.

The crowd welcomes Jesus jubilantly, spreading their garments on the road for Him to ride into Jerusalem in kingly style, and crying "Hosanna to the Son of David" (21:9 NASB) followed by a blessing from Psalm 118:26. The term *Hosanna* in Aramaic means "O save" or "God save," but had come to be a simple term of praise. The people praise Jesus as their king, their Messiah. Yet, they also recognize Him merely as the prophet from Nazareth.

21:12–17

CLEANSING THE TEMPLE

The cleansing of the temple narrative is found here at the close of Jesus' ministry in Matthew, Mark, and Luke, but in John's Gospel it appears at the beginning of His ministry. There is also a difference in the order of the event in Matthew and Mark. Matthew has the cleansing of the temple immediately, or on the same day that Jesus enters Jerusalem. Mark has it on the following day and inserts the narrative of the barren fig tree between the Jerusalem entry and the cleansing of the temple. The fact that John places this cleansing early in Jesus' ministry, and that Mark places it on the second day after Jesus enters the city, indicates that chronological exactness is not of prime importance to the Gospel writers, and takes a secondary role to theological interests.

Matthew has the cleansing on the same day that Jesus is acknowledged as king, indicating that the cleansing is a messianic duty. John places it at the beginning of Jesus' ministry indicating that Jesus truly is the Son of God. Theological interests are primary to Matthew and John rather than historical or chronological concerns. It is a stretch of imagination to suggest two cleansings of the temple, since such a dramatic action would have been too remarkable for any of the writers not to mention a second one.

The authority Jesus claims for cleansing the temple is to cite scripture. "It is written" (21:13 NIV) was a recognized rabbinic expression. He quotes Isaiah 56:7 as His authority for overturning the tables of the moneychangers and the seats of the pigeon sellers. Consideration of the verses surrounding Isaiah 56:1–7 adds to the significance of Jesus' actions. Particularly notable is the fact that Isaiah 56 refers to the Gentile inclusion in God's kingdom.

There in the temple, Jesus continues His ministry of healing the blind and the lame. However, when the chief priests see the wonderful miracles of Jesus, and hear the children acclaiming Jesus as the Son of David, they are indignant and rebuke Jesus. Jesus responds by referring to Psalm 8:2, with His declaration that perfect praise can come from the mouths of babes or children.

Leaving the temple, Jesus goes to stay in Mary and Martha's home in Bethany.

The cleansing of the temple sets Jesus in open conflict with the Jewish leaders and is the first of a series of confrontations which culminates in His condemnation of the scribes and Pharisees (Matthew 23) and judgment on the temple and Jerusalem (Matthew 24). It is not surprising that Matthew places the cleansing of the temple immediately after His entry into Jerusalem and follows it with the narrative of the barren fig tree, an event which amounts to condemnation of the Jewish leaders.

21:18–22

THE BARREN FIG TREE

Mark's account of this event is in two narratives separated by the cleansing of the temple and is in greater detail than Matthew's.

The barren fig tree is a lesson on faith. However, it is also a lesson on the absence of faith. The point is that Jesus expects fruit on the fig tree. Fig trees in Palestine, as many places elsewhere, bore two crops of fruit, an early crop known to Palestinians as *taqsh*, and a later crop of fully formed figs. The presence of leaves indicates that the early fruit of the fig should have been present, but Jesus finds none. The harshness of His condemnation is symbolic of His condemnation of the Jewish leaders for their lack of faith. Faith should have been the trademark of the Jewish religious leaders, but had not been a typical response from them.

Jesus' statement regarding faith moving mountains is a Hebrew type of expression indicating that with faith great things can be achieved.

21:23–27

CHIEF PRIESTS CHALLENGE JESUS' AUTHORITY

Upon entering the temple again, Jesus is confronted by the chief priests and elders who challenge His authority. Jesus responds with a challenge regarding the baptism of John the Baptist—was it from heaven or from men? This backs the Jewish leaders into a corner, for if they claim John's baptism was from heaven, they will blacken their own eyes that they hadn't believed John. If they answer that his baptism was from men, the crowds who followed John could turn on them. Stymied, they simply respond that they do not know. In similar fashion, Jesus answers that He will not tell them by what authority He acts. This exchange illustrates well the growing tension and opposition from the Jewish leadership and Jesus' firm response.

21:28–32

THE PARABLE OF TWO SONS

The next parable involved two sons—one initially refuses to work but then works, another initially agrees to work, but never goes. The first son references the tax collectors, prostitutes, and general sinners who turn away from God but then repent. The second represents the Jewish leaders who claim to be righteous but do not repent. Those who should inherit the kingdom will not, but those who do not deserve the kingdom receive its benefits. Jesus gets very personal in Matthew 21:32 by speaking directly to the Jewish religious leaders. He confronts them on their character assassination of Him and John the Baptist as well as their refusal to repent.

21:33–46

THE PARABLE OF THE WICKED TENANTS

The parable of the wicked tenants is again a reference to the religious leaders who should take care of the master's vineyard, but do not. When the master sends servants, the tenants kill the servants, and then go on to kill the heir of the master who comes in the master's name.

When asked by Jesus what should happen to the wicked tenants, the chief priests and Pharisees rightly respond that the wicked tenants deserve death. What they do not see is that Jesus is referencing them in the parable. These religious leaders had rejected the prophets and now they are rejecting the heir of the master, the Son of God. Jesus challenges the chief priests and Pharisees from Psalm 118:22–23. They are rejecting the chief cornerstone to the building of God—the true holy temple, which is the people of God—and do not recognize the error of their ways.

Jesus' next comment is a scathing rebuke—the Jews will lose the kingdom of God and the Gentiles will receive it. Finally, the chief priests and Pharisees see that Jesus is speaking about them. If not for their fear of the crowds who follow Jesus, they would arrest Him.

22:1–14

THE PARABLE OF THE MARRIAGE FEAST

Chapter 22 continues Jesus' condemnation of the Jewish leaders with the parable of the marriage feast. It also includes further discussion with the Pharisees and Sadducees which leads into Jesus' scathing condemnation of the scribes and Pharisees in Matthew 23.

Demonstrating Matthew's end-times perspective, this parable is addressed as a parable of the kingdom of heaven and draws heavily on the Jewish concept of a final banquet to which those who are righteous and worthy are invited. The book of Revelation likewise draws on this concept (Revelation 19).

There might have been a sense that those who refused to come were the Jewish leaders, but by this point in Jesus' ministry the rejection had spread beyond the leaders and into the general populace. Possibly those who are invited but refuse to come are those who think they are righteous—but are not. The second group invited from the thoroughfares is both bad and good. It is interesting that Jesus mentions the bad before the good, emphasizing that it is not the righteous that come, but the sinners. The righteous do not see the need to respond.

Some say that the king sending out his army to punish the offenders might be a reference to the judgment and destruction of the scribes, Pharisees, and Jerusalem that are described in greater detail in Matthew 23–25. This might not be the case since the figure of kings sending soldiers out to punish offenders was a common one in ancient parables and narratives.

Of the many that do respond to the invitation, one man is present who is not wearing a wedding garment. Questions exist among scholars as to whether the king had provided the wedding garments for his guests, and whether this was a common practice. These details are not mentioned in the parable. It is, after all, simply a parable rather than a historical account. Not all the details are necessary to the story, nor are they pertinent to the lesson of the parable. What is pertinent to the lesson is that the man is not properly attired for a wedding and is thrown out.

The significant question is the exact meaning of the wedding garment. In the context of the parables and events in Jesus' life at this point, it is apparent that wearing the appropriate wedding garment represents being clothed by faith and righteousness, both of which are absent in the chief priests and Pharisees who are attempting to be part of the messianic kingdom on their own terms, not the terms of the king.

The final verse of this parable gets to the heart of things—many are called (invited), but few are chosen. All are called, but only those characterized by faith and righteousness are the chosen.

22:15–22

THE MESSIAH, TAXES, AND CAESAR

The question of the Pharisees places Jesus between the horns of a dilemma. Whichever way He answers the question, He will be in trouble with some group of leadership. If He answers that it is permissible to pay taxes to Rome, He will meet with opposition from the crowds as well as the Pharisees—the Roman tax was despised by the Jewish nation. If He answers that tax should not be paid to the Romans, He will meet with opposition from the Herodians and the Romans themselves.

Critical Observation

Seeking for means to entrap Jesus, the Pharisees joined forces with the Herodians (the Jewish party in support of the ruling Herod family) and hypocritically questioned Jesus regarding the Roman tax system. What is significant about this event is the apparent collusion between the Pharisees and Herodians, who under normal situations would not have had anything to do with one another. Since the Herodians were political supporters of the Herodian rulers, they were not favored by the religiously inclined populace and Pharisees who rejected the Herodian monarchy. In this case though, the Pharisees compromise by sending their disciples with the Herodians to trap Jesus. By adopting this stance, the Pharisees kept a bit of distance yet allied themselves with a group that was more politically astute.

Jesus understands the entrapment. His answer serves to give neither group grounds for uprising or arrest. Stumped again by Jesus, they leave Him and go away—for a time.

22:23–33

THE SADDUCEES AND THE RESURRECTION

Next, it is the Sadducees' turn at trapping Jesus. The Sadducees were the more traditional or conservative among the Jewish sects, holding that it was only the first five books of scripture that were authoritative and comprised the Torah of God. Because of this, they rejected anything not addressed in Genesis through Deuteronomy. The resurrection of the dead was not explicitly taught there and was thus rejected by the Sadducees, along with belief in angels. The Sadducees also differed with the Pharisees on matters of ceremonial purity and civil law.

Like the Pharisees in the previous section, the Sadducees, seeking to discredit Jesus, address Him as teacher as they question Him in regard to His interpretation of the Torah. It's easy to suspect that the address "teacher" is less than sincere.

The setting of the Sadducees' question is the Mosaic Levirate law of Deuteronomy 25:5–10. According to this law, if a woman's husband dies before she bears a son to carry on the family inheritance, then a brother of the deceased husband takes the widow as his wife. The son that she bears by this man is considered the son of her dead husband, thus that man's inheritance is kept intact. Potentially, as this woman loses husbands in death, she could continue to marry the next brother in the hopes of producing an heir.

The problem the Sadducees are addressing is who then would the woman belong to in the resurrection. This poses no problem for the Sadducees if the resurrection does not exist. However, if the resurrection does exist, this poses a serious problem to them.

Jesus' answer is both direct and stern–the Sadducees' problem is that they know neither the scriptures (a serious challenge and insult) nor the power of God (which addresses the core of the Sadducees' problem with the resurrection). Jesus' challenge to the Sadducees regarding their lack of knowledge comes directly from a scripture the Sadducees have to accept–Exodus 3:6, 15. Since these verses are in the present tense, the implication is that at the time God was speaking these words to Moses, Abraham, Isaac, and Jacob, they were alive, even though centuries had passed since their deaths were recorded in Genesis. This could be possible only if the resurrection were real and true. Jesus' point, then, is that to deny the resurrection is to misunderstand scripture. This is quite a challenge to a group that defines itself by its attention to scripture.

Rather than undermine Jesus' standing as a teacher, the Sadducees reinforce it, for the crowds are astonished by Jesus' teaching.

Take It Home

We, like the Sadducees, might not have a full understanding of what life will be like in the resurrection (afterlife), but unlike the Sadducees, we believe in the power of God and leave the uncertainties to later fulfillment and understanding. Somewhat like Paul, we now see in a mirror dimly, but we'll one day see face-to-face. We know in part for now, but then we'll understand fully (1 Corinthians 13:12).

22:34–40

WHICH IS THE GREATEST COMMANDMENT?

The fact that Jesus has stood up against both the Pharisees and Sadducees does not cause the Pharisees to back off from challenging Him. Their next challenge is a concerted group effort. They come together and, through a scribe (a lawyer, or expert in the Torah), the Pharisees pose a serious legal test question—which is the greatest commandment? Jesus' answer to this question will place Him either among the fringes of Jewish teachers, or within the mainstream of Jewish legal interpretation.

One wonders what must have motivated this particular question. Perhaps it was Jesus' previous teaching which seemed to go contrary to the scribes interpretation of the Torah (5:17–48). Jesus' answer, though, gets to the heart of the law by way of an orthodox path. He quotes part of the Shema (Deuteronomy 6:4–9), a passage that was quoted twice every day by all serious Jews: "Love the Lord your God with all your heart and with all your soul and with all your strength" (6:5 NIV). Jesus then follows this with a quotation from Leviticus 19:18: "Love your neighbor as yourself" (NIV).

A close examination of the Ten Commandments reveals that loving God and one's neighbor is what the Ten Commandments and the Torah are all about. Jesus' final comment that the Law and the prophets depend on these two commandments leaves the scribe silent. Neither the Pharisees nor the scribe have a response.

22:41–46

JESUS' UNANSWERABLE QUESTION TO THE PHARISEES

While the Pharisees are still together, Jesus takes the initiative and asks them whose son the Messiah is. They answer, "The son of David" (22:42 NIV). This was a typical rabbinic answer of the day, for it was held and stated that the Messiah would be a descendant of King David. In fact, the term had become synonymous with the Messiah.

Jesus' question is not simply one designed as a clever trap for the Pharisees, but is one with serious implications for His own identity and calling as the Messiah. The question does, however, pose a serious interpretive problem for the Pharisees. How could David call the Messiah his Lord (Psalm 110:1) when the Messiah was to be a human descendant of his?

The core of Jesus' question addresses the issue of a human being (a son of David) being the divine messianic Lord (which is what Psalm 110:1 implied). This question and how it is answered lies at the very core of Matthew's Gospel and theology. Disciples must believe that Jesus (a human being) is at the same time a divine being (this is what the virgin birth narrative demonstrates), and the divine Messiah.

This question from Jesus, and the Pharisees' inability to answer it, closes this series of challenges in this major narrative section. However, the Pharisees' inherent denial of Jesus' messiahship, and their inability to answer His final question, set the scene for the final major discourse in Matthew, in which Jesus condemns the scribes and Pharisees and pronounces judgment on Jerusalem and the temple.

MATTHEW 23:1–25:46

DISCOURSE 5: THE APOCALYPTIC DISCOURSE

Jesus' Condemnation of the Scribes and Pharisees	23:1–36
The Lament over Jerusalem	23:37–39
Jesus' Judgment of the Temple and Jerusalem	24:1–35
The Disciples' Question	24:1–14
The Destruction of Jerusalem	24:15–28
The Coming of the Son of Man	24:29–31
The Sign of the Fig Tree	24:32–35
The End of the Age	24:36–25:46
The Need for Watchfulness	24:36–44
Faithful and Unfaithful Servants	24:45–51
The Parable of the Ten Virgins	25:1–13
The Parable of the Talents	25:14–30
The Parable of the Sheep and Goats	25:31–46

Setting Up the Section

There are four components to this discourse:

1. **Jesus' Condemnation of the Scribes and Pharisees**
2. **The Destruction of Jerusalem Predicted by Jesus**
3. **Comments Regarding the End of the Age, or the End of the World**
4. **Warnings to Be Prepared for the Final End**

23:1–36

JESUS' CONDEMNATION OF THE SCRIBES AND PHARISEES

Jesus begins this significant judgment by acknowledging the scribes and Pharisees as teachers of the Torah, but warns the disciples not to imitate their actions. The problem is that the scribes and Pharisees make their interpretation of keeping the Torah a matter so strict that no one can bear the burden of their interpretation. Furthermore, the Pharisees make a show of their position and righteousness in contrast to drawing people's attention to their God and His laws.

The point Jesus is stressing in this passage is that the disciples have only one true interpreter and teacher of the Torah—Jesus—not the scribes and Pharisees. Likewise, the disciples have only one spiritual Father and that is God Himself. The scribes and Pharisees are not to be seen as the spiritual fathers of the disciples.

Jesus' seven judgments on the religious leadership—absolute in their condemnation—begin with verse 13. He refers to these leaders as

- Blind guides
- Blind fools
- Hypocrites
- Murderers
- Serpents
- Vipers
- Whitewashed tombs

The fact that Matthew clusters the judgments of Jesus against the scribes and Pharisees into seven woes is both significant and vital to this final discourse. Matthew's intention is to demonstrate that Jesus' condemnation of the scribes and Pharisees has final judgment implications. The unique structure around the seven woes sets the tone for the following two chapters (24 and 25).

Demystifying Matthew

The King James Version of the Bible has eight woes in this section, but that may be a stretch. There are sometimes a variety of ancient manuscripts to consult when translating a version of the Bible. Careful consideration of the differing manuscripts for this text indicates that the most reliable manuscripts contain only seven woes. Most other English translations either omit verse 14 or set it apart in some way (italics, parentheses, as a note rather than text). The opinion of text critics is that verse 14 is a later insertion and not original to Matthew.

There is a sense of parallelism in the content and structure of these seven woes.

1) Each begins similarly with a woe. This is a classic prophetic expression pronouncing judgment.
2) Six of the woes are pronounced against the scribes and Pharisees, the rabbinic teachers of Jesus' day who rejected both His identity as the Messiah and His interpretation of the Torah. One of the woes, the third, refers to these leaders only as blind guides.
3) Six of the woes refer to the scribes and Pharisees as hypocrites. Since this word implies a play actor or pretender, it strikes at the insincerity of the scribes and Pharisees.

The final condemnation of the scribes and Pharisees as murderers summarizes the depth of their rejection of God, His prophets, and His messengers, and predicts the coming persecution of the Christian apostles, prophets, and evangelists.

In the sense of corporate responsibility, the scribes and Pharisees of Jesus' day are responsible for the deaths of all the righteous persons and prophets of God since the murder of righteous Abel (Genesis 4) down to the most recent murder of the prophet Zechariah. Scholars debate who this Zechariah might be. Some cite the prophet Zechariah of 2 Chronicles 24:20, since 2 Chronicles was the last book of the Jewish canon, but this Zechariah was identified as the son of a priest name Jehoida while the Zechariah mentioned by Jesus is the son of Barachiah. We might not be able to identify this Zechariah, but he must have been a recognizable person of historical significance for Jesus to mention him as He does here.

Jesus' closing condemnation adds even more gravity to the woes. His inclusion of the whole generation brings the Jewish populace into the condemnation, for they side with the scribes and Pharisees in the events leading up to Jesus' crucifixion.

23:37–39

THE LAMENT OVER JERUSALEM

This section is one of the saddest exclamations that can be made, and ranks with the one made by the disciple John when he states that Jesus comes to His own, but they do not accept Him (John 1:11).

The personification of Jerusalem adds to the tragedy of Jesus' denunciation of the great city, which in both the past and the present has rejected God's servants and stoned and killed them (and will do the same in the imminent future).

The desolation (abandonment, desertion) of Jerusalem's house draws on Old Testament language and situations in which Jerusalem had been judged by God and destroyed (Jeremiah 22:5; 12:7 for example).

However, no matter how drastic and complete Jesus' condemnation of the scribes, Pharisees, and Jerusalem, He does not give up hope. He instead pronounces redemption for those who believe in Him and surrender their lives to Him. He offers future hope in the midst of tragedy.

This brief section sets the scene for the next two chapters (24–25), including Jesus' prediction of the destruction of the temple and the city of Jerusalem, as well as the disciples' question regarding the end of the age.

24:1–35

JESUS' JUDGMENT OF THE TEMPLE AND JERUSALEM (INTRODUCTION)

Setting Up the Section

This discourse, as with all the other materials in this Gospel, must be understood within the context of Matthew's Gospel and the Jewish context of Jesus' ministry. Jesus is addressing the scribes and Pharisees and pronouncing judgment on Jerusalem.

Critical Observation

In order to be able to follow the flow of thought and the shifts in emphasis in this section, here are several factors vital to understanding this discourse:

1) We have already noticed that Jesus begins this discourse in an apocalyptic context (the end-times connotations contained in the seven woes). He continues by keeping His discussion in an apocalyptic kind of language.
2) Any judgment on Jerusalem and the temple, and any destruction of Jerusalem and the temple, would be interpreted by a Jew as the end of the age or world. To a Jew, nothing could be worse than a judgment on Jerusalem and the Jewish religious system.
3) The disciples are so shocked by Jesus' denunciation of the Jewish religious leaders, the temple, Jerusalem, and that generation that they ask Jesus two questions, although they see them as one question: When will this be, and what are the signs of Jesus' coming?
4) Jesus responds, treating their questions as two events, not one. He separates the destruction of Jerusalem as one event and His coming and the end of the age as a separate event.
5) Jesus first discusses erroneous views or predictions of His coming (theologically, we refer to this as His second coming). He then draws on the imagery of Daniel 9:27 to describe the desecration of the temple and a great final crisis and warns the disciples to flee the city. These signs can be clearly seen and understood.
6) He draws on clearly understood apocalyptic imagery (Matthew 24:29–31) to demonstrate that this is a political enemy, and that the destroying enemy is an agent of God. (This is the genius of the unique apocalyptic genre adopted by Jesus.)
7) He makes it clear that these events will come upon the generation He is addressing.
8) Then Jesus turns to discuss the second question asked (What will be the sign of His coming and the end of the age?) and responds that there will be no sign. He warns His disciples to be alert and watchful, for no one will be able to predict when the Son of Man will come again.
9) Matthew 25 and the three parables illustrate how the disciples must be alert, watchful, and prepared for the sudden and unannounced coming of the Son of Man.

24:1–14

JUDGMENT: THE DISCIPLES' QUESTION

The disciples are so shocked by Jesus' condemnation of Jerusalem, that as they are near the temple—the bastion of Judaism—they draw Jesus' attention to the temple. Jesus responds in a manner intended to help the disciples see that the temple, however important it was to Judaism, is not to play a part in the messianic kingdom and ministry. The temple is to be destroyed.

To a Jew, and the disciples are Jews, this is inconceivable and unbelievable—the temple to be destroyed? When will such a significant event take place? Surely such an event has to be the end of the age. What will be the sign of Jesus' coming, or the end of the age?

Jesus warns that many will falsely predict His coming, but before such an event the gospel has to be preached throughout the world. Jesus encourages His disciples to not be misled by wars, earthquakes, and other such events, which false prophets will use to lure followers away. He encourages His disciples to endure such catastrophes and persecutions; those who endure will be saved in the end (He is speaking of final, eternal salvation, not the present salvation we enjoy in the Christian life).

The point Jesus is making to the disciples in this section is that they should not be lead astray by false predictions or claims that Jesus has come or is about to come. They are not to confuse the destruction of Jerusalem and the temple with the end of the world or the coming of the Son of Man.

24:15–28

JUDGMENT: THE DESTRUCTION OF JERUSALEM

Jesus begins His discussion of the destruction of Jerusalem by making reference to language and events with which all Jews were familiar, the language of Daniel 9:27 and 12:11—the abomination that causes desolation. The event prophesied by Daniel had taken place in 168 BC when Antiochus Epiphanes captured Jerusalem and desecrated the temple by erecting an altar to the god Zeus there. Jesus uses this well-known imagery to describe the events surrounding the destruction of Jerusalem in His prophecy.

Most scholars identify this event with the destruction of Jerusalem by the Romans in AD 70. The historical accounts of the Roman siege and destruction of Jerusalem fit well with the language used by Jesus in this section.

Jesus warns the disciples to immediately and hastily flee Jerusalem when they see the approaching desolation. For those pregnant and with small children, the flight will be difficult. The disciples should pray that their flight will not be necessary on the Sabbath (because of the Jewish travel restrictions on the Sabbath) and that it not be in the winter.

Eusebius, the Father of Church History, recorded that in the year AD 66, when the Christians saw the approaching Roman armies, in keeping with Jesus' admonition, they fled Jerusalem for the region that is now the nation of Jordan (Ecclesiastical History, 3.5.3).

Again, Jesus warns the disciples not to believe those who might proclaim that these events usher in His second coming. In Matthew 24:22–25 Jesus repeats His previous warning—that He will come just as the lightning strikes, suddenly and without warning.

At this point, Jesus has twice warned His disciples not to interpret world events as signs of His eschatological coming.

The last saying of this section (24:28) falls firmly within the apocalyptic tradition. Some commentators interpret the eagle as the insignia on the standards or banners of the Roman legions, but this is unlikely. The word can mean either "eagle" or "vulture" and refers to a bird that eats dead flesh. The imagery expresses that there will be much bloodshed and death when the abomination that causes desolation comes (24:15).

24:29–31

JUDGMENT: THE COMING OF THE SON OF MAN

Demystifying Matthew

This short section has generated considerable discussion among scholars through the centuries. Without question, it is a difficult passage, especially if the reader does not consider the strong apocalyptic genre in which it is so obviously couched. The terms used in the passage have a long and rich history in the Old Testament and apocalyptic literature, and must be seen in line with this tradition. Failure to understand this tradition will lead to speculation, but not necessarily the truth.

The apocalyptic genre and tradition is the literature of persecution, tribulation, and suffering. It is generally pessimistic regarding the potential of human endeavor and history to solve the suffering, but is especially optimistic regarding God's ability to provide a solution. Apocalyptic writings often describe a great and final persecution of God's people and God's intervention to destroy the wicked, save the righteous, and establish His eternal kingdom.

There is a tendency in apocalyptic writing to bring several well-known scriptures together in a collage of thoughts as a symbol of what is taking place. The story is presented as bigger than life in order to make the point that this is not merely a human story, but God's divine intervention and judgment on history and mankind.

The use of the word *immediately* (v. 29) can, at first read, make it seem that the coming of the Son of Man at the end of the age is to happen just after the destruction of Jerusalem. But historically and theologically this does not happen, and Jesus has warned against such interpretation (24:5–14).

In this case, *immediately* is a transitional term that connects the section under discussion directly and dynamically back to the previous discussion, namely, the destruction of the temple and Jerusalem. This makes the case that the destruction of the temple and Jerusalem are the direct judgment of God and the Son of Man, not merely historical occurrences.

The Christian faith is familiar with concepts that have both a now and a then nature. We experience salvation now that is only to be fully experienced in eternity. We participate now in the resurrection of Jesus, but that resurrection will only be realized at the final resurrection. Any event in the Christian age partakes of end-of-the-world significance. If you believe in Jesus now, it has end-of-the-world significance. If you deny Jesus now, this, too, has end-of-the-world significance. The point is that in apocalyptic contexts one can describe present events with end-times terminology without implying the end of the world. Unfortunately, this is the pitfall the original disciples fall into when they confuse the destruction of Jerusalem with the end of the age. Knowing that Jesus has taught the imminence of the fall of the temple, the disciples naturally assume the imminence of Jesus' second coming. In their minds the two are inseparable. They can't conceive of the fall of Jerusalem apart from the end of the age, as the question of 24:3 indicates. Nevertheless, although Jesus teaches the imminent fall of Jerusalem, He does not teach the imminence of His second coming. He leaves the latter to the undetermined future.

24:32–35

JUDGMENT: THE SIGN OF THE FIG TREE

The attempt to tie Matthew 24:29–31 to the Second Coming creates difficulties with this section, especially regarding how to interpret or understand the reference to the current generation (24:34). To apply this section to the second coming of Christ, for which there will be no warning signs (24:42–44), is to stretch beyond the context of this section.

Typically, the pronouns *this* and *these* refer to what is closest at hand in time or in space. Note that in Matthew 24:36 Jesus speaks of *that* day or hour. The pronoun *that* indicates something further away in time or space. In Matthew 24:32–35 the signs are for what is closer or nearer. The context of the discussion and the interpretation of the warning signs point to the judgment and destruction of Jerusalem rather than the second coming of Christ.

Summary

Jesus predicts the destruction of Jerusalem and the temple. This disturbs the disciples who interpret this as the end of the age. We associate the end of the age with the second coming of Christ.

Jesus separates the destruction of Jerusalem from the Second Coming, warning the disciples to be able to interpret the signs of the coming tribulation and destruction of Jerusalem and to flee from the city before that event occurs. He warns that some will interpret the signs as indicators of His coming and clearly warns them not to be misled by such predictions. Before the final eschatological end, the gospel has to be preached to all the world.

Jesus sets the discussion of the destruction of Jerusalem in apocalyptic language to demonstrate that the destruction will not simply be the work of the Roman army, but will in fact be the work of God through the Son of Man. The Roman army will simply be God's destroying agent.

In the next section, Jesus responds to the second part of the disciples' question, and argues that there will be no sign for His second coming.

24:36–25:46

THE END OF THE AGE (INTRODUCTION)

Setting Up the Section

We saw in the last four sections (Matthew 24:4–35) that Jesus warns His disciples not to confuse the signs for the coming destruction of Jerusalem and the temple with signs of His second coming.

As this next section opens, Jesus shifts from the signs for events that can be experienced (destruction of Jerusalem) to events for which there can be no signs—the Second Coming. The first clause of Matthew 24:36 introduces a discussion of a different day from the destruction of Jerusalem, namely, the day of the Second Coming.

24:36–44

THE END OF THE AGE: THE NEED FOR WATCHFULNESS

Verse 36 introduces the idea that not even the angels of heaven or the Son of Man know when that day will be. That decision lies not in the will of the Son of Man, but solely in the will of the Father. Jesus makes a similar statement about the coming of the Holy Spirit. God sets those times by His own authority (Acts 1:7).

Since this is the case, it would be folly for the disciples and anyone else in Jesus' day to attempt to predict the second coming of the Son of Man. Likewise, today, it is the height of both folly and arrogance to predict the time or date of the second coming of Jesus or the end of the world.

In Matthew 24:38–41 Jesus introduces Noah, two men in the fields, and two women at the grinding mill. These are illustrations Jesus uses to make the point that the eschatological coming of the Son of Man will be sudden and without warning.

Matthew 24:42 gets to the heart of Jesus' teaching about the unexpected coming of the Son of Man. The disciples are to be ready, watchful, and alert, for they do not know on what day their Lord will come. As the thief does not announce in advance his coming, so the Son of Man will not announce His coming in advance. Therefore the disciples must always be ready.

24:45–51

THE END OF THE AGE: FAITHFUL AND UNFAITHFUL SERVANTS

The faithful and wise servant is the one who, when His master comes home, is busy doing what he is supposed to be doing. Jesus highlights the point by warning that the unfaithful and foolish servants are hypocrites who will be punished. This is a clear warning that eternal punishment awaits those disciples who are not ready and waiting expectantly.

Serving God involves waiting expectantly for the return of the Son of Man. How does one wait appropriately for the return of the Son of Man? In the following three parables, all part of Jesus' final apocalyptic discourse, Jesus explains how one alertly waits His eschatological return.

25:1–13

THE END OF THE AGE: THE PARABLE OF THE TEN VIRGINS

The Greek word often translated as "virgin" can also be translated as maiden, or young woman. In the context of Jesus' parable, the emphasis indicates that these are young, unmarried women—similar to today's bridesmaids.

Of the ten maidens, five are prepared and five are not. The unprepared are excluded from the marriage feast. The connection of the marriage feast with the end-times banquet anticipated by Judaism and Christianity is obvious. Disciples that are not prepared will be excluded from that banquet.

How exactly should one be prepared? Jesus answers that question in the next two parables.

Before moving on to the discussion of preparedness, think about the wise maidens who will not lend oil to the foolish maidens. That raises an important question: Why not help those in need? In response, in this case, the necessities—personal faith, repentance, baptism, personal holiness, personal service, and personal preparedness—can't be borrowed.

25:14–30

THE END OF THE AGE: THE PARABLE OF THE TALENTS

In this parable the talent is an amount of money.

Critical Observation

Originally a talent was a measure of weight, but when applied to silver coinage it became an amount of money. One talent was equal to 6,000 denarii or 6,000 days' wages. Thus one talent was a considerable amount of money.

In this parable, a master leaving on a journey entrusts an amount of money to each of his three servants. The first two servants trade and double the investment. The third one, for fear of his master, buries his talent of silver and returns it to his master. The master casts this third servant into outer darkness (again, indications of the final judgment are evident in this parable). The other two servants are rewarded for their diligence.

To make His point clear, Jesus then references the proverbial saying that to those who have will be given more (because they use what they have), and to those who have not (or have little) and who do not use it, will have it taken away.

The point of the parable is that disciples must use the giftedness that they have, whatever it may be. Disciples do not all have the same giftedness, but all disciples must use what they have in service of the Master. Being involved is part of being prepared.

Is it possible that the scribes and Pharisees, who were so busy with religion, had not prepared themselves properly for the works of the Messiah, and were relying on the faith of Abraham and Moses rather than developing true faith for themselves?

25:31–46

THE END OF THE AGE: THE PARABLE OF THE SHEEP AND GOATS

In this parable, the warnings of Jesus regarding watching, being alert, and being ready reach a disturbing highpoint. The reference to the final judgment is obvious and clear.

The sheep, those on the right hand, are blessed and inherit the kingdom prepared for them from the beginning of the world. The goats, on the other hand, are cursed and cast into eternal fire. But what are the criteria for this judgment? What has the one group done that the other group has not?

The goats are so busy with their religion and hypocritical worship of God that they do not take time for the poor and helpless. The sheep recognize that true worship of God involves taking care of the poor and helpless (Micah 6:6–8; Psalm 51:17; James 1:27).

It is obvious that these qualities are absent or lacking in the scribes and Pharisees who are so busy with religion that they are missing what their charge really is—to be shepherds to the lost and disenfranchised. This is the work of the Messiah that they do not understand, and for this they are judged and condemned by Jesus.

Summary

This fifth and final discourse in Matthew's Gospel comes at the time when Jesus enters Jerusalem and faces rejection, first from the Jewish leaders, then from the crowds. At the root of the rejection is the nature of Jesus' messiahship. He is not the kind of Messiah the crowds are looking for, namely, a political Messiah. Furthermore, His interpretation of the Torah challenges that of the scribes and Pharisees.

Frustrated with the hypocrisy of the scribes and Pharisees, Jesus soundly and severely condemns them (Matthew 23). His condemnation of Jerusalem and the temple (personified) leads to the disciples' concern and sense of insecurity (Matthew 24).

Jesus warns the disciples to be prepared for the destruction of Jerusalem, but not to confuse this with the second coming of the Messiah, or Son of Man (Matthew 24). Before the final end, the gospel has to be preached throughout the world (Matthew 24), but the eschatological coming of the Son of Man is certain to take place, though no warning signs will be provided.

Since the Son of Man will come suddenly without warning, the disciples must be watchful, alert, and ready. Being alert and ready necessitates being prepared for the coming of the Son of Man, being involved in messianic ministry, and being concerned for the lost.

The real issue for the disciples is that their messianic hope should not be fixed in the temple and Jerusalem, nor in the scribes and Pharisees' example of no faith in Jesus. Faith should be in the Messiah Himself and in what God is doing in and through the Messiah. This would be particularly significant to Matthew's community, which has just recently experienced the destruction of Jerusalem and the temple, and is now struggling to understand the true nature of discipleship apart from the temple.

Take It Home

One of the applications of this section is that rather than predicting the day of the coming of the Messiah, the followers of Jesus should be busy doing the work of the Messiah. We must be prepared for the coming of the Messiah by living alertly and watchfully, involved with the more important aspects of faith such as serving the lost, poor, and needy.

Another application is that Christian hope must not be in human effort, in the church, or in persons, but in Jesus Himself and what God is doing through Him. Christian hope is not fixed in the ability to get doctrine all sorted out and correct. Neither is it to be based on our own ability to achieve perfect obedience. Of course, we should make every effort to understand scripture correctly and to follow sound doctrine, but our Christian hope is fixed in our faith in Jesus and what God is doing through Jesus.

MATTHEW 26:1–28:20

NARRATIVE 6: THE MESSIAH'S FINAL WEEK

The Sanhedrin Plots to Kill Jesus	26:1–5
Jesus Anointed by Mary at Bethany	26:6–13
The Bargain of Judas	26:14–16
The Last Passover Supper	26:17–25
The Lord's Supper Instituted	26:26–29
Peter's Denial Foretold	26:30–35
Jesus in Gethsemane	26:36–46
Judas Betrays Jesus	26:47–56
Jesus Is Taken Before Caiaphas, the High Priest	26:57–68
Peter's Denial of Jesus	26:69–75
Jesus Is Delivered to Pilate by the Sanhedrin	27:1–2
Judas's Suicide	27:3–10
Jesus Before Pilate	27:11–26
The Crucifixion of Jesus	27:27–56
The Burial of Jesus	27:57–61
The Tomb Sealed and Guarded	27:62–66
The Empty Tomb and Resurrection of Jesus	28:1–10
Bribing the Soldiers	28:11–15
The Great Commission	28:16–20

Setting Up the Section

This final narrative offers the account of the final days of Jesus' life, but also the climax of the Gospel—the passion (death, burial, and resurrection) of Jesus. In fact, some have described the substance of the Gospels as this upcoming passion narrative and the preceding chapters as simply an extended introduction to this narrative.

Here you find the fulfillment of God's plan of salvation for mankind.

26:1–5

THE SANHEDRIN PLOT TO KILL JESUS

Matthew's mention of the Passover is not intended to simply provide a time reference. Instead, it sets the purpose of the passion narrative in a specific theological framework. Central to the original Passover event was the lamb whose blood, smeared on the doorposts, saved the Israelites from death (Exodus 12–14). Here, in the Gospel, Jesus is the lamb prepared for the deliverance and redemption of humanity.

Critical Observation: The Passover Feast

The roots of the Passover Feast go back to Exodus 12:1–28 and the exodus of Israel from Egyptian slavery (Exodus 12–14). The feast was to be a perpetual reminder (memorial) that God had delivered Israel from Egypt and had spared the firstborn of every house that had sprinkled the two doorposts of the lintel with the blood of the sacrificial lamb. The Passover was initially to be celebrated in homes as a family celebration. During the feast the participants were dressed for travel, sandals on their feet, and staff in hand, indicating they were ready to leave home in a hurry.

The Passover feast was celebrated beginning on the fifteenth day of Nisan, which in the year of Jesus' crucifixion fell on a Saturday, or the Sabbath day. Being defined by the Jewish calendar, the fifteenth day of Nisan would have begun that year at sunset on Friday evening. The Passover meal would have been eaten on Friday evening.

The Passover was combined with another feast, the Feast of Unleavened Bread. The Feast of Unleavened Bread was a seven-day feast that began at the same time as the Passover feast, in that it began on the evening of the fourteenth day of Nisan, and lasted for seven days. During this feast no leavened food was to be eaten. In time the two feasts were combined in practice into one feast, and both became holy days.

After the initial celebration of the Passover in Egypt, the feast became an annual one, not celebrated just anywhere, but in a place determined by the Lord as the place of His presence. (See Deuteronomy 16:1–8.) In time the feast became a pilgrimage to Jerusalem for the celebration—so it was in Jesus' day.

After the destruction of the temple and Jerusalem, the Passover was celebrated in homes in local towns.

Conflicting reports have come down through the centuries as to the exact details of the feast. It seems that in later centuries successive cups of wine (either three or four) were part of the celebration as was eating the lamb and unleavened bread with bitter herbs. To these were added prayers, blessings, and reading of the Psalms, especially Psalms 113–118.

The celebration was conducted by the head of the family with the children present. The youngest boy in the family would ask, "Why are we celebrating the Passover?" This would give occasion for the head of the family to recite the history of God delivering Israel out of Egypt and nurturing them in the wilderness. The theology of the Passover was a focus on the nurture of Israel by God. It was a reminder of God's deliverance.

Demystifying Matthew: The Jewish Calendar

The Jewish calendar was based on a lunisolar or lunar system, fixed by the first appearance of the new moon. Through the centuries differing methods were used to determine the length of the months. The days of a month ranged between 29 and 30 days, depending on the cycle of the moon.

CONTINUED

Depending on how the months were calculated, there might be anywhere between 354 and 364 days in the year.

Scholars believe that the names of the Jewish calendar were influenced by both Canaanite and Babylonian names. The months of the Jewish calendar (compared to the modern calendar and seasons) and Jewish feasts are as follows:

Nisan Iyyar Sivan Tammuz Ab Elul	Passover Unleavened Bread	March–April May June July August September	Spring Summer
Tishri Marcheshvan Chislev Tebeth Shebat Adar	Atonement, Booths	October November December January February March	Fall Winter

It is two days before the Passover (26:2) when Jesus again foretells His passion and crucifixion. Since in this year the Passover falls on the Sabbath (Saturday), the Passover meal will been eaten on Friday evening. Therefore, Jesus speaks these words to the disciples on Wednesday.

The chief priests and elders (most likely the ruling members of the Sanhedrin) gather in the palace of Caiaphas, the ruling high priest, to decide how to arrest Jesus and have Him killed. They are concerned that this be done with stealth for fear of rioting, which is of concern to the Roman authorities. Being such a time of heightened Jewish religious fervor, the Romans are on guard for disturbances.

26:6–13

JESUS ANOINTED BY MARY AT BETHANY

This event occurs in the home of Simon the Leper, only mentioned in the New Testament on this one occasion. The fact that Simon has been cured is implied by the fact that they are meeting in his home, something that would not have been permissible otherwise under Jewish law. Simon lived in Bethany, a small town two miles from Jerusalem on the eastern slope of the Mount of Olives.

Luke records a similar experience (Luke 7:36–39), but in his description the event happens in Simon the Pharisee's home, and the woman is identified only as a sinner. The events and discussion recorded by Luke differ from that in Matthew, Mark, and John.

A woman anoints Jesus with ointment that obviously is very expensive. John's gospel identifies the woman as Mary of Bethany, sister to Lazarus (John 11:2). Observing her actions, the indignant disciples miss the point of her action—her love for Jesus. Instead, they raise questions as to why the gift has not been spent on the poor.

Mark (14:4) merely mentions that some present were indignant, while John adds that it is

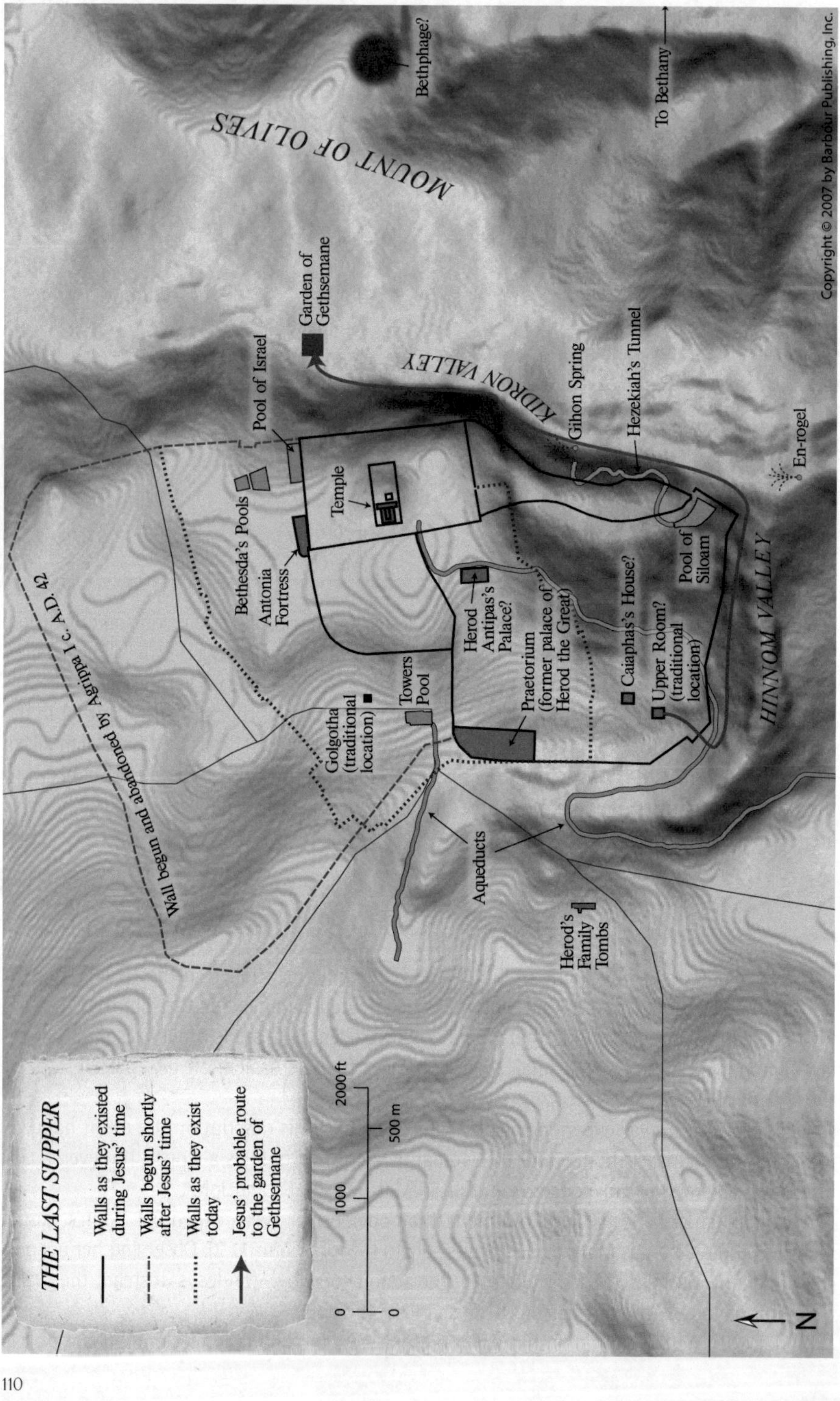
THE LAST SUPPER
Walls as they existed during Jesus' time
Walls begun shortly after Jesus' time
Walls as they exist today
Jesus' probable route to the garden of Gethsemane
0
1000
2000 ft
0
500 m
N
Mount of Olives
Bethphage?
To Bethany
Garden of Gethsemane
Kidron Valley
Gihon Spring
Hezekiah's Tunnel
En-rogel
Pool of Siloam
Hinnom Valley
Pool of Israel
Bethesda's Pools
Temple
Antonia Fortress
Wall begun and abandoned by Agrippa I c. A.D. 42
Herod Antipas's Palace?
Caiaphas's House?
Upper Room? (traditional location)
Praetorium (former palace of Herod the Great)
Towers Pool
Golgotha (traditional location)
Aqueducts
Herod's Family Tombs

Judas who objects (John 12:4). Perhaps the objectors are beckoning to Jesus' predilection for the poor, but the Master reminds the disciples that they will always have the poor, but they will not always have Him present with them as He now is.

The theological point of this narrative is that Jesus interprets the woman's action in light of His approaching death and burial, not simply as an act of devotion. That is not to say that the woman made that connection–she has acted only out of love. Nevertheless, in the context of His imminent passion, Jesus breathes new meaning into her love.

The remarkable prediction of Jesus that her act will become a memorial to her has happened through the history in Matthew's Gospel.

26:14–16

THE BARGAIN OF JUDAS

In what is perhaps one of the most tragic events in history, Judas makes plans to betray his Lord. Matthew identifies Judas by his full name–*Judas* (a form of the Hebrew *Judah*) and *Iscariot* (after the town in Judea called Kerioth). Except for Judas, the remaining disciples were from Galilee.

The sum of the betrayal agreement is thirty pieces of silver, a sum considered by scholars to be the equivalent of the price of a slave. The insubstantial sum has led some to suggest that Judas's motivation for the betrayal is not greed, but possibly disappointment in Jesus' messiahship. Some have suggested that Judas might have been motivated by the same frustrations seen in the zealots who would have been looking for a militant political messiah who would lead them in victory over their Roman overlords.

Luke identifies Satan as the motivation behind Judas's betrayal (Luke 22:3). John agrees with this conclusion (John 13:2).

26:17–25

THE LAST PASSOVER SUPPER

There are some apparent variations in the Gospel accounts of the preparation and eating of the Passover. Working across four Gospels, each with its own theological purpose and each with a different audience in mind, this is not surprising. However, there are reasonable explanations for the variations.

Although we are not informed of all the details, Jesus sends His disciples to find a man in whose home Jesus intends to eat the Passover. Apparently, Jesus has made some arrangement with the man, but we are not informed regarding this. Mark and Luke add to the narrative by recording Jesus telling the disciples to follow a man carrying a water jar to the house where He intends to eat the Passover (Mark 14:13–15; Luke 22:10–12). This man would have been easily recognized since women normally carried water.

Jesus does not eat the Passover in Bethany, but in Jerusalem where the Passover should have been eaten as prescribed by the Torah. It was only after AD 70 and the destruction of Jerusalem and the temple that Jews ate the Passover in a variety of towns and villages.

Critical Observation

The term *Last Supper* is not found in scripture, but is one adopted by the Christian faith to describe this last meal, or last Passover meal, Jesus celebrated with His disciples.

The term *Lord's Supper* is not found in the synoptic Gospels, but is found in 1 Corinthians 11:20. In early post–New Testament Christianity the term *Lord's Supper* soon gave way to the term *Eucharist*, which prevailed for many centuries until the modern Protestant era. *Lord's Supper* along with the term *Communion* have become favored descriptions in many Christian circles for this memorial feast.

Jesus' Death and Resurrection

Each gospel records the events leading up to Jesus' death and resurrection. Below are the key events and where they occur in each gospel.

	Matthew	**Mark**	**Luke**	**John**
Jesus in Gethsemane	26:36–46	14:32–42	22:39–46	18:1
The Betrayal and Arrest	26:47–56	14:43–52	22:47–53	18:2–12
Trial Before Annas				18:13–14, 19–23
Trial Before Caiphas	26:57	14:53	22:54	18:24
Peter Denies Jesus	26:69–75	14:66–72	22:54–62	18:15–18, 25–27
Trial Before Sanhedrin	27:1	15:1	22:66–71	
The Suicide of Judas	27:3–10			
Jesus' Appearance before Pilate	27:2, 11–14	15:1–5	23:1–5	18:28–38
Jesus' Appearance before Herod			23:6–12	
Jesus' Second Appearance before Pilate	27:15–26	15:6–15	23:13–25	18:39–19:16
Crowd Asks for Barrabas	27:19–21	15:6–11	23:18	18:39–40
Jesus Whipped	27:26	15:15		19:1–5
Pilate's Judgment	27:23–25	15:14	23:20–25	19:7–16
Soldiers Mock Jesus	27:27–30	15:16–20		
Jesus Led to the Cross	27:31–34	15:20–23	23:26–33	19:16–17
Jesus on the Cross	27:35–56	15:24–41	23:33–49	19:18–37
Jesus Is Buried	27:57–66	15:42–47	23:50–56	19:38–42
The Resurrection	28:1–20	16:1–8	24:1–53	20:1–21:25

The order of the wine and bread discussed in the Passover meal by Matthew, Mark, and Luke differs somewhat, although not significantly. Matthew follows the order of the meal in Mark, but Luke differs in speaking of a cup being drunk before the bread followed by another cup. However, this is a Passover meal and three or four cups are involved. John does not discuss the Passover meal in his Gospel, leading some to question whether the meal eaten by Jesus with His disciples in John 13–17 was in fact the Passover meal.

The stern warning of Jesus regarding the one who will betray Him must have sobered both Judas and the disciples who still did not know the extent of the betrayal. Luke indicates the continuing uncertainty of the disciples over the matter of the betrayal (Luke 22:23). Jesus, however, indicates that the betrayal and consequences are according to scripture (Matthew 26:24).

26:26–29

THE LORD'S SUPPER INSTITUTED

Jesus intends this institution, often referred to as the Lord's Supper, to be a way for the disciples (and later the church) to commemorate His death. As the Passover was intended to be a perpetual commemoration of God's deliverance of Israel from Egypt, so the Lord's Supper is intended to be a perpetual commemoration of Jesus' death. The eating of the Supper is intended to be a proclamation of His death as well as an interpretation of that death. The bread and wine are intended to symbolize His body and blood given for the deliverance of mankind from bondage to sin. Just as the annual Passover rite memorialized and personalized the Passover in Egypt and deliverance from Egypt, the Lord's Supper likewise not only memorializes the death of Jesus, but personalizes it as well.

The institution of the Lord's Supper is essential to the life of the church. For this reason, most Protestant churches have identified the Lord's Supper along with baptism as the two sacraments of church life. Sacraments are those religious practices that associate or identify Christians with the church, or the body of Christ. Sacraments involve a promise or commitment. Thomas of Aquinas and Augustine considered the sacraments to be signs of a holy alliance.

We are not certain at which stage of the Passover Jesus takes the bread and breaks it, but in the Passover seder (ceremony related to the Passover), breaking the bread was associated with the promise of a future redeeming Messiah.

Jesus gives the bread to the disciples and says that it is His body. Interpreting what Jesus meant by this has led to centuries of division in church doctrine relating to the Lord's Supper. The Roman Catholic tradition interprets this as "this becomes my body." This Catholic doctrine is called transubstantiation, in which the bread literally becomes the body of Christ. Protestants have objected to this, and a variety of views have surfaced.

In this context Jesus probably means that the bread symbolized His body. This is how many Protestant churches understand the expression. Jesus is implying that the bread symbolizes His whole person, His whole life, and all that His life means. By eating the bread we are reminded of all that Jesus stood for, lived for, and died for. Eating the bread is a sacrament in that it is a pledge to live the life of Jesus.

Jesus then takes the cup, the wine, and gives thanks (also used in Matthew 15:36) for it. It is because of this act of giving thanks that some Christian communities call the Lord's Supper the Eucharist.

Christian church traditions have been divided over whether the wine means grape juice or actual wine. Because of their puritan and temperance heritage, many churches insist that this can only mean grape juice. Churches from the Greek Orthodox and Eastern Orthodox traditions, and others not of the puritan temperance heritage, insist that it simply means wine.

Consider these things:

- The Greek phrase translated "fruit of the vine" in some translations (26:29) is a Hebrew euphemism for wine.
- The cups of the Passover were cups of wine, not grape juice.
- Wine drinking in the time of Christ was not socially or religiously looked down upon (though drunkenness was).
- We have several instances in the New Testament in which wine drinking is socially and religiously acceptable.
- Jesus turned water into wine at the wedding in Cana (John 2:1–11).
- Paul wrote to Timothy and encouraged him for medicinal purposes to drink a little wine for his stomach's sake (1 Timothy 5:23).

The attempt to translate or understand the drink Jesus offered as grape juice rather than wine is a modern socio-religious problem, not a biblical one. The key here is not what we use today in our traditions of celebrating the Lord's Supper, but that we do celebrate it, and when we do, we understand the purpose of that celebration.

Jesus says the wine is His blood. As in the case of the bread, this means the wine represents or symbolizes the blood of the covenant. The new covenant prophesied in Jeremiah 31 was fulfilled in the blood shed by Jesus on the cross. Those drinking the cup in the Lord's Supper, which symbolizes the blood of Jesus, are reminded of the promises of the new covenant and they participate in those promises. The fulfillment of the new covenant is described in Hebrews 8:10–12: the promise of God's people holding His Word in their hearts, of their becoming, in a unique manner, His people, and of God's mercy and grace and forgiveness of sins. It is the new covenant of deliverance empowered by Jesus' blood (through His atoning death).

The final statement of Jesus before He and the disciples sing the Hallel hymn of the Passover is an affirmation that He will drink the cup with them again, but not until He does so in His Father's kingdom (26:29). Jesus is somewhat mysterious in this comment. Does Jesus mean until He drinks it with them in the Eucharist, or does He mean until He drinks it with them in the final new-world banquet?

Possibly either or both. Not only are Christians reminded of what God did for them on the cross, but they are encouraged to look ahead to the final end and the great wedding banquet. It was for this reason that early Christians favored the term *Eucharist* (thanksgiving) to define the experience of the Lord's Supper. The Eucharist should be a celebration, not just an occasion of mourning remembering Christ's death.

26:30–35

PETER'S DENIAL FORETOLD

This sad narrative stresses the tragic frailty of human effort. We don't know exactly what prompts Jesus to warn the disciples of the frailty of their faith, but His warning indicates His knowledge of their coming weakness and denial.

Jesus' statement about scattering sheep suggests He may have intended the events that followed to be seen as a fulfillment of the prophecy in Zechariah 13. Nevertheless, Jesus' warning of the falling away of the disciples obviously disturbs them. First Peter, then all the disciples, deny that they will fall away and disown Jesus. Jesus, however, forewarns Peter of his disowning Him.

The one positive element of the section is the statement that Jesus will rise and go before the disciples to Galilee. In spite of their weakness, Jesus has not given up on them. He expects to see them again in Galilee. The steadfast love of the Lord endures forever.

26:36–46

JESUS IN GETHSEMANE

The Garden of Gethsemane, as it is known from John's Gospel (John 18:1, 26), was actually an olive orchard on the east side of the Kidron Valley on the lower slopes of the Mount of Olives. Matthew simply called it a plot of ground or a place rather than a garden. "Gethsemane" is the Greek equivalent of the Hebrew *gat semane* (oil press). It was a quiet place off the regular beaten pathway, a place where Jesus could be alone in prayer.

This poignant narrative stands as a monument to Jesus' agony and fear of suffering and dying as a human, but also as a monument of His willingness to submit to the will of His Father in heaven. Adding to the tragedy of this occasion is that this is the last account of Jesus spending time with His disciples before dying on the cross. At the moment that He needs them most, they fail Him miserably.

Jesus takes with Him the three disciples with whom He obviously has the closest relationship—Peter, James, and John. As a human being He needs the company of friends as He faces the most difficult time of His life and as He agonizes in prayer.

Twice He encourages (perhaps begged) the three disciples to keep watch (stay awake) with Him, and once to pray with Him. However, on both occasions they fail Him and fall asleep. Perhaps they are tired, but perhaps also they do not understand the depth of His concern and anguish. In His second encouragement to the three, He warns them not to fall into temptation (the spirit is willing, but the flesh is weak), indicating His own struggles as well as His awareness of the disciples' struggles.

Jesus' mention of the cup is a Hebrew metaphor that refers to the suffering He is about to experience. His reference to the hour at hand is not simply an indication that it is soon, but rather that it is certain and so certain that it is already upon Him. He comments that the Son of Man is betrayed in the present tense, indicating that the events are already underway.

26:47–56

JUDAS BETRAYS JESUS

Judas arrives with a great crowd armed with swords and clubs as though Jesus were a robber or insurrectionist. John informs us that there were possibly temple guards and Roman soldiers in the crowd (John 18:3) as well as chief priests and elders, or the Sanhedrin.

Judas, by agreement with the mob members, kisses Jesus to identify Him as the one they are seeking. The eastern kiss was a sign of greeting. Judas adds the words, "Greetings, Rabbi" (26:49 NIV), which was a traditional eastern greeting.

One of Jesus' disciples—John informs us that it is Peter (John 18:10–11, 26)—takes a sword and cuts off the ear of the chief priest's slave. Only Luke records that Jesus heals the slave's severed ear (Luke 22:51).

26:57–68

JESUS IS TAKEN BEFORE CAIAPHAS, THE HIGH PRIEST

Caiaphas was the high priest at that time. He was the son-in-law of Annas, who previously had been the high priest. Caiaphas had been appointed to the position by the Roman procurator, Valerius Gratus, the predecessor of Pontius Pilate. Caiaphas had been the main instigator for the arrest and trial of Jesus.

The chief priests, scribes, and elders, namely, the Sanhedrin, have gathered in anticipation of Jesus' arrest. Jesus is brought before the Sanhedrin gathered at Caiaphas's palace.

The hypocrisy for which Jesus has condemned the scribes and Pharisees comes to the forefront in the false testimony the Sanhedrin seeks against Jesus. In several attempts to gather enough testimony against Jesus to condemn Him to death, which is their purpose, they finally get two false witnesses to come forward with statements that Jesus had claimed to be able to destroy the temple and rebuild it in three days. Obviously they were taking several strands of Jesus' teachings and weaving them into ridiculous charges. When Jesus refuses to answer the charges of the high priest, the high priest places Him under oath and asks Him whether He is the Christ, the Son of God. Jesus' answer is actually a direct answer in the affirmative, a Hebrew idiom that indicates a qualified yes (Mark 14:62 records that Jesus says, "I am").

Jesus' additional comments are drawn from Daniel 7:13 and Psalm 110:1. They are so loaded with apocalyptic symbolism that the high priest immediately understands what Jesus is claiming—to be the One seated "at the right hand of Power," (26:64 NASB) and the One who will come in judgment on them. The word *power* implies God but adheres to the Jewish tradition of not saying God's name out loud.

After requesting the death penalty, those present in the Sanhedrin begin to mistreat Jesus. Their evil scheming has come to fruition. However, the Jews under Roman rule did not have the authority to carry out their condemnation of death. Only the Romans could carry out that sentence. That is why, after Matthew's description of Peter's denial of Jesus, Jesus is led bound to Pilate, the Roman governor.

26:69–75

PETER'S DENIAL OF JESUS

Peter, we learn in Matthew 26:58, has followed the crowd that arrested Jesus, but at a distance. In the courtyard of the high priest's palace, he is confronted by a maid who recognizes him as a follower of Jesus. After his denial, Peter is again confronted with similar charges because of his Galilean accent. Again, but this time with an oath, Peter denies the charge. After a while the bystanders accuse Peter again. He begins to invoke a curse on himself and to swear that he doesn't know Jesus.

Peter's response reveals his heart. Though he failed Jesus, his own actions grieve him.

27:1–2

JESUS IS DELIVERED TO PILATE BY THE SANHEDRIN

Early Friday morning (still 14 Nisan which began the previous evening with the Passover meal), the Sanhedrin meets in full session to confirm the decision in Caiaphas's palace that Jesus should be put to death. It is Luke's Gospel that confirms it is a full session (Luke 22:66–71).

It is necessary for the Jewish leaders to take Jesus before the Roman authorities in order to legally put Him to death. Pilate, who is governor over Judea, is conveniently in Jerusalem at this time. The rulers of the Sanhedrin bring Jesus before Pilate, hopeful that he will confirm their judgment.

Critical Observation

Technically, Pilate's title was *prefect*. Matthew refers to him as the governor of Judea. Luke identifies him as Pontius Pilate (Luke 3:1). Pilate was governor of Judea from AD 26/27–36. His official residence was in Caesarea Maritima (beside the sea). He was perhaps visiting in Jerusalem for the Passover to maintain stability and Roman control during the feast.

27:3–10

JUDAS'S SUICIDE

Judas's conscience begins to work against him. When he hears that Jesus has been condemned to death, he is deeply troubled and attempts to return the thirty pieces of silver to the chief priests. He confesses he has betrayed an innocent man, but the callous chief priests will not take back the money. Matthew records that Judas is overcome with remorse (27:3).

What is ironically tragic is that the chief priests recognize earnings from betraying someone as blood money (27:6). They know they cannot put the money into the treasury since these kinds of earnings were condemned in the Torah (Deuteronomy 23:18). Yet they have knowingly provided the money for this very reason, to betray Jesus. Their duplicity apparently does not trouble them. It is no wonder Jesus condemns them as whitewashed tombs full of dead men's bones (Matthew 23:27).

Matthew merely reports that Judas goes out and hangs himself (27:5). Luke relates that he buys a field and falls dead in it (Acts 1:18–19). Some scholars see in the different descriptions of Judas's death a probable contradiction, but what we have here are merely two different accounts of what happened. Judas commits suicide for his betrayal; the field where he dies is called the field of blood since he has betrayed Jesus for blood money, and the field had been purchased with the chief priests' blood money.

Matthew clearly sets Judas's betrayal in the context of God's eternal plan. His quote combines ideas from Zechariah 11:12–13 and Jeremiah 19:1–13. For Matthew, all the scriptures come to their climax in Jesus. This is the last of the ten fulfillment passages Matthew uses in his Gospel to demonstrate that Jesus' life and death are within the eternal purpose of God.

27:11–26

JESUS BEFORE PILATE

Pilate asks Jesus if He is the king of the Jews. Notice he does not ask Jesus if He is king over Israel, which could seem a more politically threatening title. Pilate's political sensitivity to Roman concerns, and his ability to see that this was a Jewish matter, framed the question. Jesus' answer to Pilate, "You say so" (27:11 NRSV), implies a simple yes.

When Pilate questions Jesus further, He remains silent, reminiscent of the prophet Isaiah's description of the Messiah as a silent lamb led to slaughter (Isaiah 53:7).

At the feast, Matthew informs us, it is the governor's practice to release a Jew from prison. Although we have no external evidence for such practice other than the Gospels, this seems in accord with what the governor would have done in order to show some sort of clemency to the Jews. The person to be released would be someone meeting the crowd's request. The description of the prisoner Barrabas could be understood to mean an insurrectionist, a bandit, or murderer. Some ancient manuscripts suggest that Barabbas's first name was Jesus, a common name among Jews of the day. There may have been a play on names in Pilate's mind as he suggests two persons by the name of Jesus, hoping that the Jews will see the vast difference between Jesus, the son of Joseph, and this Jesus, the insurrectionist. Pilate knows that it is out of envy that they have condemned Jesus and want Him dead.

Romans paid much attention to warnings from divination and dreams, like the one Pilate's wife had. As Pilate attempts to remove himself from the process by symbolically washing his hands, he is indicating publicly that he does not find Jesus worthy of death. The crowds' statement that the blood of Jesus will be on their hands and those of their children was a well accepted expression from the Old Testament that spoke to full responsibility in an act (Lamentations 5:7).

The scourging with the Roman lash, which contained sharp objects for tearing the flesh, was commonly administered to those about to be crucified, possibly to so weaken them that they would not linger on the cross indefinitely. After having Jesus scourged, Pilate hands Him over to his soldiers to be crucified. Had Jesus been a Roman citizen, His death by crucifixion would have been prohibited.

27:27–56

THE CRUCIFIXION OF JESUS

What is striking in all of the Gospel accounts is the brevity of Jesus on the cross. We fully recognize the agony of Jesus and the suffering both emotionally and physically that He endures on the cross, but this is not played up in the Gospel accounts. In light of the Gospel theology, this death of Jesus is pictured as dramatic, but it is to be seen as a victory—the victory of God and Jesus over Satan and sin. The Gospels do not trivialize the atoning death and victory of Jesus, but simply describe it as a fact of history and God's divine plan.

After mocking Jesus in the worst manner, the Roman soldiers take Jesus out to Golgotha, the place of the skull, to crucify Him between two robbers. These men were possibly insurrectionists or bandits. Luke refers to them as criminals (Luke 23:32 NASB).

Simon, the man from Cyrene (North Africa) who carries Jesus' cross, was in all probability a Jewish pilgrim to the Passover Feast. Tradition has it that Simon later becomes a Christian.

Layers of church tradition have obscured the precise location of Golgotha, but it must have been just outside the city walls and on a well-traveled thoroughfare, for it was the practice of the Romans to carry out crucifixions in full view of people, and a road into Jerusalem would have served the Roman publicity purpose well.

The drink offered to those dying on the cross was sometimes mixed with gall, which could be a bitter, poisonous or noxious substance, which might explain why Jesus refuses to drink it when He tastes it. Most likely though, it was spoiled or bitter wine. Later, when offered vinegar on a sponge (27:48), He drinks it. The vinegar was a form of sour or cheap wine, which was known to relieve thirst better than water.

All four Gospels record that Pilate has an inscription nailed to the cross, proclaiming "THIS IS JESUS, THE KING OF THE JEWS" (27:37). John adds that it is in all three languages of the area—Hebrew, Latin, and Greek—and that the Jews object to the inscription. Pilate rejects their objection.

Matthew records that the crowds and the chief priests, elders, and scribes mock (blaspheme) Jesus as He hangs on the cross. The robbers, too, join in the mocking of Jesus. Luke records the exchange between Jesus and the two criminals dying beside Him (Luke 23:39–43), one mocking Him and the other defending Him.

It is difficult for any interpreter to fathom all that went on in the death of Jesus on the cross. It certainly was attended by supernatural occurrences and some remarkable events. The death of Jesus is not only the climax of the Gospel narrative, but more so it is the climax of the purpose of God for the person of Jesus. To die for mankind is precisely what He came to do.

From the sixth to the ninth hour (from noon to 3:00 p.m.) there is darkness over all the land, possibly meaning the region of Judea. The darkness is similar in significance to a divine judgment over the land.

Twice in Matthew's account Jesus cries out with a loud voice, once here and in verse 50. The first time He adds the words in Aramaic, but Matthew translates them for us into Greek: "My God, my God, why hast thou forsaken me?" (29:46 KJV). Scholars have been divided over exactly what Jesus meant by this expression in which He quoted Psalm 22:1, a lament psalm. (Lament psalms were characterized by a similar structure: first a complaint, then trust, then deliverance, and finally praise.) Matthew offers no explanation for Jesus' cry, but several proposals have been made:

1) Some feel it is the cry over the fact that, because of the enormity of humanity's sins, God abandoned Jesus in the moment of His death (see Isaiah 53:4, 10).
2) Others believe that Jesus felt abandoned by God in His intense suffering. However, this overlooks the nature of Psalm 22 as a psalm of lament.
3) Some feel that Jesus understood the lament meaning of Psalm 22 and used it as a prayer for God's help in His moment of anguish. In such suffering and aloneness at crucifixion, He must have felt abandoned. He was in fact abandoned by His people (Israel), the Romans, the crowds, and His disciples. While Psalm 22 is a lament psalm, it is also a psalm of confidence in God's deliverance and help. Jesus would have understood it this way. When Jesus cried this psalm out, it would have been a cry of aloneness and for help from the God in whom He trusted, not a cry of abandonment.

Some of the bystanders mistake Jesus' cry as a cry to Elijah to come and rescue Him. This is understandable from the similarity of the words *Eli* and *Elijah*.

When Jesus finally dies, Luke records that He verbally commits His spirit into God's hands (Luke 23:46).

Matthew describes the event of Jesus' death in terms of supernatural events:

- The temple curtain is torn in two.
- The earth shakes.
- Rocks are split.
- Tombs open.
- Saints are raised from the tombs and go into the city where they are seen by many.

Matthew and Mark both include the comment regarding the temple curtain being torn from top to bottom, but the remaining supernatural events are found only in Matthew.

What is strange regarding these supernatural events is that neither Matthew nor Mark explain the theological nature of the torn curtain, the earthquake, and the dead being raised. The interpretation of the events is left to the reader. But to any Christian (especially in the first century and to Matthew's community), they are loaded with significance.

Nevertheless, the meaning of the events is fairly obvious. There can be little doubt that the supernatural events support God's involvement in the death of Jesus and His approval of Jesus' atoning sacrifice. These miraculous events can happen only by God's divine intervention. The theological implication of the torn temple curtain signifies a new system of entry into the Holiest of Holies through the death of Jesus (Hebrews 9:11–14; 10:19–23). The earthquake and split rocks indicate apocalyptic judgments of God on Jerusalem, and the dead raised after the resurrection of Jesus indicates Jesus' power over death, the source of life and resurrection, and the guarantee of a future resurrection.

What is not explained or commented on by many commentators on Matthew or Mark is the historicity of the events. What complicates the problem of the historicity is that, to our knowledge, there are no Roman or Jewish records of the three-hour darkness, the temple curtain being torn, or the dead saints being seen in the city. There are some late Christian and rabbinic allusions, but since these all come much later than the destruction of Jerusalem, it is not possible to fix these allusions to the Crucifixion. They seem rather to be allusions to what happened in the temple at the destruction of the temple and Jerusalem.

The miraculous is often without scientific, empirical, or historical verification, but to deny the miraculous on such grounds is to deny the very existence of God and His Holy Spirit. There are many instances of divine intervention for which there are no reasonable empirical explanations, but they are accepted by reliable testimony. The resurrection of Jesus is in fact one such miraculous event of divine intervention that cannot be proven by empirical means, yet based on reliable testimony is believed by most to be historical.

At the root of questions regarding the historicity of certain acts of divine intervention in human affairs is the question of the miraculous. Scholars who have difficulty with the historicity of divine intervention often have questions regarding the possibility of the miraculous.

Perhaps the most important event in this section of the Gospel narrative is the comment of the Roman centurion and his companions—"Truly this man was God's Son!" (27:54 NRSV). These people saw what the Jewish leaders did not see. Luke adds the following regarding the centurion—that he praises God and claims Jesus' innocence (Luke 23:47).

Matthew records that there are women who have followed Jesus, watching from afar. Named among them are Mary Magdalene, Mary the mother of James and Joseph, and the mother of James and John, the sons of Zebedee. Neither Mary is mentioned in the Gospel prior to this occasion, but later both are witness to the risen Christ. We are uncertain who James and Joseph were as both were common names. We are not sure what Matthew means by their ministering to Jesus, but according to Luke there is a group of women, including Mary Magdalene, that has supported Jesus' ministry (Luke 8:2–3). It is surprising that Matthew mentions none of the eleven disciples as being present. Neither Matthew, Mark, nor Luke mention any of the disciples, but John in his Gospel does mention that the disciple Jesus loved (John himself) is there with the women (John 19:25–27).

John adds two other details as well.

- The request to break the legs of the three being crucified, which leads to the soldier's discovery that Jesus is already dead (John 19:31–33)
- The piercing of Jesus' side with the spear (John 19:34–37)

27:57–61

THE BURIAL OF JESUS

According to Deuteronomy 21:22–23, it was a Jewish requirement that dead bodies of executed criminals not be left hanging on trees overnight. On Friday evening, just before the Sabbath begins (the other Gospels inform us that it is on the Day of Preparation, just before the Sabbath begins, for instance, Mark 15:42), Joseph, a rich man from Arimathea and a disciple of Jesus, asks Pilate for Jesus' body in order to bury Him. Pilate gives the order for Jesus' body to be given to him. We are uncertain where Arimathea is located, but it could have been a town by the name Ramathaim, a town in Judea. Joseph takes the body of Jesus, wraps it in a clean linen shroud, and lays it in his own new tomb. A great stone rock is rolled to the door of the tomb, sealing it. Mary Magdalene and the other Mary are there, sitting opposite the tomb.

27:62–66

THE TOMB SEALED AND GUARDED

This narrative becomes significant in view of charges made by many against the resurrection of Jesus. It is unique to Matthew simply because it had greater significance to a Jew and Jewish Christians than it would to Gentiles (Mark, Luke, and John were written for Gentile readers). On the Sabbath, the day after the Day of Preparation (Friday) the chief priests and Pharisees request that Pilate set a guard at the tomb lest the disciples steal the body of Jesus and claim that He has risen.

The guard is to make the tomb secure. This is the Sabbath, and by now Jesus has been in the tomb all of Friday night. It is certain that the guard would have inspected the tomb. The tomb being made secure must have implied some sort of official seal.

Remember that the chief priests and Pharisees know of Jesus' prediction that He will be raised on the third day (16:21), but they do not believe it. The resurrection of Jesus was not then something unknown, unexpected, or unpredicted. The Jewish authorities knew about it, they did not believe it, and expected the disciples to make some form of effort to steal the body. Any attempt to steal the body was, therefore, rendered highly improbable.

The duplicity of the chief priests and Pharisees can be seen by what follows after the resurrection of Jesus when it is discovered that Jesus' body is no longer in the tomb. They pay the soldiers to claim the disciples stole the body while they were sleeping, promising to keep the soldiers from punishment for the dereliction of duty that their lie implies (28:11–15).

28:1–10

THE EMPTY TOMB AND RESURRECTION OF JESUS

Setting Up the Section

Matthew 28 focuses chiefly on the final aspect of the Gospel narrative—the resurrection of Jesus. This is the climax of the Gospel story—Jesus' resurrection and His triumph over death and sin.

The narrative does not describe the actual resurrection of Jesus, only the results of the resurrection, namely:

1. **The empty tomb and appearances of Jesus to the two women named Mary**
2. **The narrative of the bribing of the Roman soldiers**
3. **The appearance of Jesus before the disciples in Galilee and the giving of the Great Commission**

There is some disagreement about the opening phrase of this section—"After the Sabbath" (28:1 NIV). The early Christians would have understood this to mean "After the Sabbath had closed and early on the first day of the week." It is because of the resurrection of Jesus on Sunday that Sunday became the holy and special day of worship for Christians. Christians, because of this, worshiped on the first day of the week (Acts 20:7; 1 Corinthians 16:2), and the day became known as the Lord's Day (Revelation 1:10).

The two women go to the tomb, most likely to mourn the death of Jesus. As in the previous chapter there is a great earthquake, signifying some divine intervention, and an angel appears and rolls back the stone, sealing the mouth of the tomb. It certainly would have been too heavy for two women to roll it back. The angel's appearance is so striking that the guards (notice, they are still there) fall down like dead men, in great fear.

Offering to show them the empty tomb, the angel encourages the two women not to be afraid, but to go quickly and tell the disciples that Jesus has risen from the tomb. They are to tell the disciples to meet Jesus at Galilee, for Jesus has gone on ahead. The words of the angel to the women are interesting, "He is not here, He is risen" (28:6 NIV).

The women leave quickly with mixed emotions—fear and great joy. Fear because remarkable and strange things have happened. Jesus has risen! An angel has appeared! There was a great earthquake! Any one of these events would cause fear in most people. But they are also filled with great joy—Jesus is not dead and He is going to meet the disciples in Galilee.

Shortly after this, Jesus greets the women. His greeting is the first words spoken by the risen Christ, and they are spoken to two women. But why first to the two women? Perhaps simply because they were there—they cared enough to be there at the tomb. The women humbly worship Jesus, and He encourages them not to be afraid and gives them the instructions for the disciples. An interesting point is that Jesus continues to call His disciples His brothers. He has done this on several occasions in Matthew (12:48–50; 25:40), and continues to do so even though they have denied and forsaken Him.

Critical Observation

The fact that no one witnessed the actual resurrection of Jesus has led some critical scholars, especially during the first half of the 20th century, to question whether the Resurrection could in fact be considered historical. Since belief in the resurrection of Jesus is considered by Christians to be fundamental and essential to Christian faith, the narratives of Matthew 28 and the parallel sections in the other Gospels, as well as the testimony of other New Testament writers, are of prime importance to the gospel message.

1) None of the alternative explanations of the resurrection of Jesus—a stolen body, a Jesus who only swooned, or a mistaken tomb—is adequate to explain the total range of phenomena that must be explained historically (Matthew 27–28; Mark 15–16; Luke 23–24; John 19–20).
2) Jesus appeared after His resurrection on at least twelve different occasions:
    - Mary Magdalene (Mark 16:9; John 20:14).
    - Two disciples on the road to Emmaus (Mark 16:12; Luke 24:13–15)
    - Peter (Luke 24:34; 1 Corinthians 15:5)
    - Ten disciples in the upper room—Thomas absent (John 20:19)
    - Eleven disciples in the upper room—Thomas present, Great Commission (John 20:26; Luke 24:36; Mark 16:14)
    - The disciples at the Sea of Tiberias (Galilee) (John 21:1)
    - The eleven disciples on the mountain in Galilee—Great Commission (Matthew 28:16–20)
    - Five hundred men (1 Corinthians 15:6)
    - James (1 Corinthians 15:7)
    - All of the apostles (1 Corinthians 15:7)
    - At the Ascension (Mark 16:19; Luke 24:50; Acts 1:3)
    - Paul on the road to Damascus (Acts 9:3–8; 1 Corinthians 15:8; 1 Corinthians 9:1)
3) Paul, in 1 Corinthians 15:1–4, discusses the Resurrection as a vital and essential ingredient of the gospel message of salvation.

28:11–15

BRIBING THE SOLDIERS

It isn't surprising that the duplicitous chief priests and the Sanhedrin would have to do something to keep the guards at the tomb quiet. As they have done before, they are willing to pay a bribe to achieve their purposes. They tell the guards to say that the disciples had come during the night and stolen the body. The chief priests will take care of any concerns the governor would have that the soldiers had not adequately guarded the tomb. As a result the story of the disciples stealing the body of Jesus spread quickly. However, it is surprising that no disciple ever confesses to stealing the body of Jesus or knowing of those who did steal the body, even under dire circumstances—persecution and martyrdom.

28:16–20

THE GREAT COMMISSION

This narrative of Jesus meeting His disciples in Galilee is unique to Matthew's Gospel.

Matthew 28:18–20 is a key to the whole Gospel narrative. It concerns making disciples of all nations. Matthew's Jewish community would need to know this, and that Jesus had commissioned His apostles for this purpose—including Matthew's readers.

The eleven disciples meet Jesus on a mountain in Galilee, just as Jesus had instructed them through the two women. Traditionally this mountain has been identified as Mt. Tabor, but we have no certain information on this other than tradition. Mt. Tabor is about thirteen miles west of the southern tip of the Sea of Galilee.

When the disciples see Jesus, they worship, but still some doubt (hesitate). It is not surprising they worship Him, but what does Matthew mean by the doubts? The Greek word translated by most versions of the Bible as "doubt," can also mean hesitate. It is found only two times in the New Testament, both in Matthew (28:17; 14:31). It occurs in Matthew 14:31 when Peter walks on the sea and begins to sink; Jesus asks him why he doubts.

Here in Matthew 28:17, perhaps it would be better to understand the meaning as doubt that lies in hesitancy rather than doubt that lies in disbelief. But one might ask, why uncertainty or hesitation rather than joy? Remember the trauma experienced by the disciples, as well as the guilt they felt over abandoning Jesus in His hour of trial. How will Jesus relate to them now? Matthew does not develop this point since it does not fit into the theological scheme of this last climactic paragraph of his Gospel. To learn of Jesus' reaction one should refer to John 21, where Jesus goes fishing with the disciples, encourages them, and speaks tenderly to Peter.

For Matthew's Jewish community, the point of the Great Commission focused on Jesus' messianic authority and His charge to His disciples to make other disciples of *all* nations. Its appearance is unique in several ways:

1) **Jesus' messianic authority.** The verb translated "give" is understood as a divine action in which God is the one who in His divine sovereignty gave Jesus the authority as the Messiah to function as the king over God's kingdom (one of the major themes of Matthew's Gospel—Jesus is the messianic king over God's kingdom). Divine authority over the kingdom is in fact divine authority over all existence, both in heaven and on earth.
2) **The charge to make disciples.** The controlling imperative of the Great Commission was the simple charge to *make* disciples. This is the only verb in the commission that is actually a command. It is not a surprising command since this is what we learned from the limited commission Jesus had given earlier in Matthew 10. The remainder of the words of the Great Commission explained how disciples are to be made, and of whom disciples are to be made. There are three key participles—going, baptizing, and teaching—that explain how the making of disciples was supposed to be carried out.

   How does one make disciples? A disciple is a learner, one who has been instructed by a teacher and who has followed the teacher. The process of making disciples hinges around who the disciple is to follow. In the Christian case, disciples are disciples of the Messiah, or Jesus. People need to be taught about Jesus and how to follow Him.

3) **The charge to go.** Remember, the word *apostle* implies one sent or commissioned to go on behalf of the sender. In the context of both the eleven disciples/apostles and Matthew's community of disciples, they were to go. The tendency for a Jew would be to remain in Jerusalem or wherever he or she was in his or her community. But to carry out their messianic ministry of making disciples, the apostles were to go. In fact, this participle should be translated "you must go." This would be important to both the apostles, and especially to Matthew's community who were now living in a Gentile world. They were to leave the comfort of their own circle and go.

   But where were they to go to? Jesus has already qualified this in His expression in delineating *all* nations. Neither the apostles nor Matthew's community were to limit their messianic ministry only to the Jews (10:6) as in the earlier limited commission. Because of this we know this commission as the Great Commission, for it was for all—the Jews and the Gentiles. For Matthew's community this would have had significant meaning, as it does today to the Christians who often are satisfied to wait for people like themselves to come to church to be converted to become even more like themselves.

4) **The charge to baptize them in the name of the Father, Son, and Holy Spirit.** Disciples become disciples of Jesus by being united with Him. In the Christian community one is united to Jesus by being baptized into Jesus (Romans 6:1–9; Galatians 3:25–29). It is obvious that before being baptized, the potential disciple must be told who to believe in—Jesus—and then how to believe. We see this in Acts 16:25–33 in the case of the Philippian jailor who first had to be informed and then was baptized.

   The disciples were to be baptized in the name of the Father and of the Son and of the Holy Spirit (28:19), which probably means baptizing them as though the Father, Son, and Holy Spirit were baptizing the disciples.

5) **The charge to teach them to observe all that Jesus had commanded.** Disciples, once baptized into the fellowship of Christ and the Christian community, need to be taught. Fundamentally, they need to be taught what the life of a disciple is all about: the character of the disciple, the ministry of the disciple, the meaning of kingdom membership, how to live as disciples in a Christian community, and where to fix their hope. There are certain fundamentals of the Christian faith that new disciples need to be taught, and this teaching is an ongoing, unending process. There are always new challenges to discipleship. Disciples need to be taught the primary lesson of discipleship in Matthew's Gospel—discipleship is a radical life.

   In the context of Matthew's Gospel, the expression translated "all that I have commanded you" refers to the lessons of discipleship learned from Jesus through the Gospel message.

"I am with you always, to the very end of the age" (28:20 NIV) implies an ongoing mission, especially one that reaches beyond the recent tragedy in the lives of Matthew's community, namely, the destruction of Jerusalem and/or the trauma that Jesus' disciples experienced in the Crucifixion. Through whatever lies ahead, the disciples are promised the ongoing presence of Jesus.

The expression "end of the age" is reminiscent of Matthew 24:3 and the final expression of that narrative in Matthew 24:14, "then the end will come" (NIV). The point Jesus is making is that before the close of the age or the end, there will be the need for the preaching of the gospel. Jesus' precise words are, "And this gospel of the kingdom will be preached throughout the whole world, as a testimony to all nations; and then the end will come."'

In commissioning His disciples and sending them out as apostles to make disciples of all nations, Jesus promises always to be with them. The apostles will not be alone as they preach; Jesus will be with them in power and spirit. His presence will be real.

Take It Home

We do not become disciples on our own terms. This we have learned from the Gospel of Matthew. Discipleship is a radical decision to leave self and follow Jesus. The Sermon on the Mount explained what kind of person a disciple should be. The Limited Commission explained what disciples do. The Kingdom Parables taught how to understand the life of a disciple in the kingdom. The Discourse on the Christian Community taught how Christians relate to one another in a Christian community. The Apocalyptic Discourse explains the central focus of the messianic kingdom—not Jerusalem, but the Messiah. The man who tried to enter the marriage banquet without wedding garments was cast out, indicating that one does not gate-crash the kingdom on one's own terms. As disciples, we must understand these principles about following Jesus and the kingdom of God.

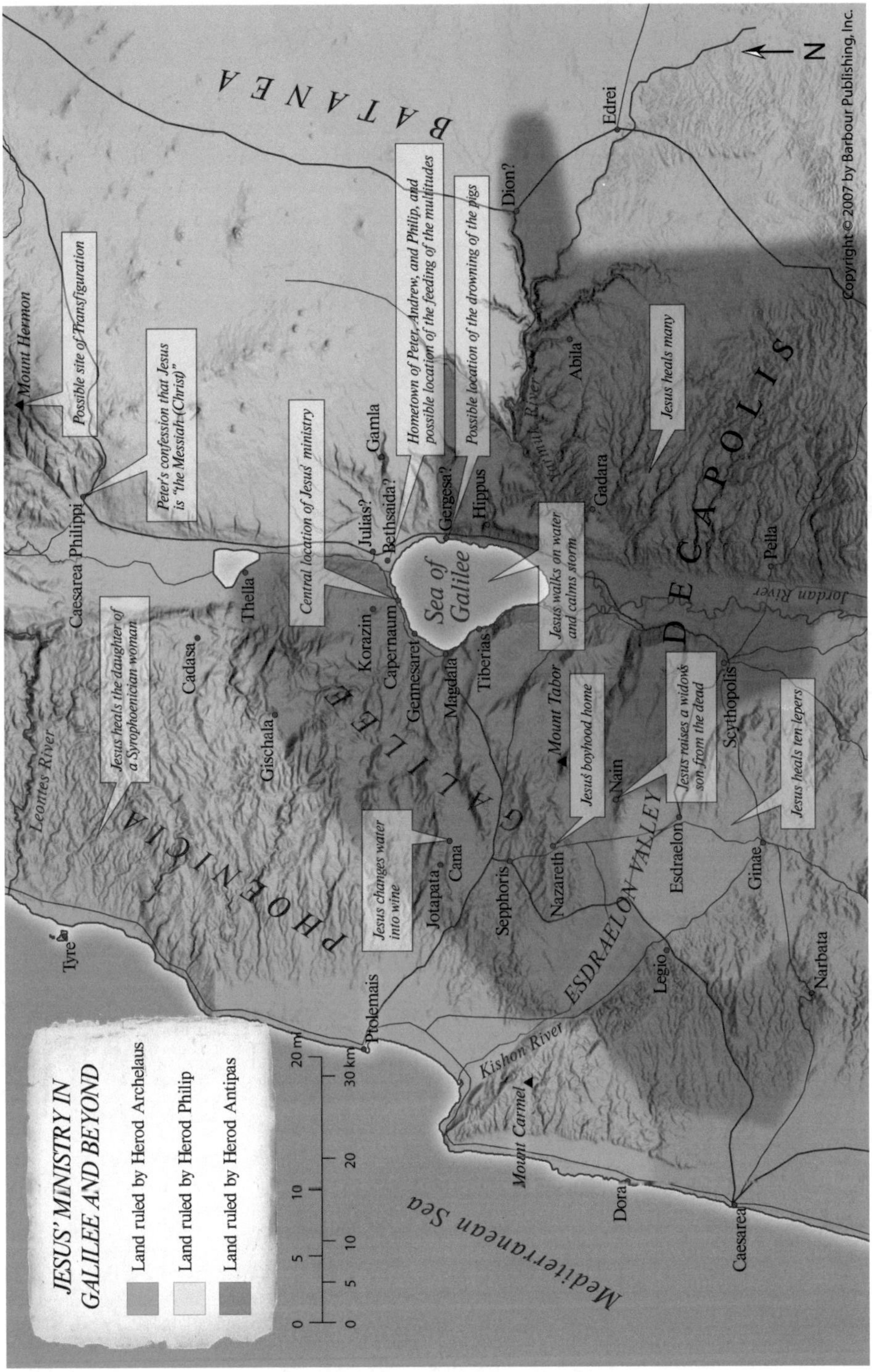
JESUS' MINISTRY IN GALILEE AND BEYOND
Land ruled by Herod Archelaus
Land ruled by Herod Philip
Land ruled by Herod Antipas
0 5 10 20 m
0 5 10 20 30 km
Mediterranean Sea
PHOENICIA
GALILEE
DECAPOLIS
BATANEA
ESDRAELON VALLEY
Mount Hermon
Possible site of Transfiguration
Peter's confession that Jesus is "the Messiah (Christ)"
Caesarea Philippi
Leontes River
Jesus heals the daughter of a Syrophoenician woman
Tyre
Cadasa
Gischala
Thella
Central location of Jesus' ministry
Julias?
Bethsaida?
Gamla
Hometown of Peter, Andrew, and Philip, and possible location of the feeding of the multitudes
Gergesa?
Possible location of the drowning of the pigs
Hippus
Dion?
Edrei
Sea of Galilee
Korazin
Capernaum
Gennesaret
Magdala
Tiberias
Jesus walks on water and calms storm
Gadara
Yarmuk River
Abila
Jesus heals many
Pella
Jordan River
Mount Tabor
Jesus' boyhood home
Nain
Jesus raises a widow's son from the dead
Scythopolis
Jesus heals ten lepers
Jesus changes water into wine
Jotapata
Cana
Sepphoris
Nazareth
Esdraelon
Ginae
Ptolemais
Legio
Narbata
Kishon River
Mount Carmel
Dora
Caesarea
N
Copyright © 2007 by Barbour Publishing, Inc.

THE GOSPEL OF MARK

INTRODUCTION TO MARK

The book of Mark is the shortest of the four Gospels and is considered by many to be the oldest. It may well have served as a source for the Gospels of Matthew and Luke. Numerous church leaders (Papias, Irenaeus, Clement of Alexandria, Origen, Jerome, and others) associated this Gospel with John Mark, the disciple of Peter. It was the opinion of the early church that Mark recorded the gospel that Peter preached.

AUTHOR

The writer of Mark never identifies himself, yet no serious suggestion of an author other than Mark has been put forward. John Mark was a young disciple who had traveled with Paul and Barnabas on their first missionary journey (Acts 13–14), but deserted them. His actions later caused such a rift between the two missionaries that they went their separate ways (Acts 15:36–41). Yet Mark's subsequent spiritual growth and faithfulness eventually earned Paul's trust once more (2 Timothy 4:11).

PURPOSE

Mark probably wrote from Rome to an audience primarily comprised of Gentile Christians to provide them with a defense of the gospel and encourage them in their faith. The content of the Gospel contains several indications of Mark's Roman and Gentile audience. He used ten Latin words, some of which are found nowhere else in scripture; he made a point to explain Jewish traditions; no genealogy is found for Jesus, as in Matthew and Luke; and he doesn't go into geographic or historic detail because his audience would not have been familiar with such Palestinian matters.

HISTORICAL CONTEXT

The date of Mark's writing is debated. Some people have estimated that his Gospel could have been written as early as AD 45. Most, however, agree that it was written no later than AD 60 to 70.

Not long after the death of Jesus, persecution began to intensify for His followers. For a while the Roman authorities had paid little attention, assuming Christianity was just an offshoot of Judaism, which they had under control. But as the early church began to grow and spread out, believers experienced more and more conflicts with the Roman Empire. By the time of Mark's writing, persecution had become an ongoing concern, so he presented the life of Jesus to illustrate His willingness to suffer and sacrifice.

In the early to mid-60s (AD) the letters of Paul were beginning to circulate to the churches. It was also the time of Nero's reign, which brought more targeted persecution to believers. A horrendous, destructive fire broke out in Rome in AD 64, suspected to have been ordered by Nero himself, and further rumored to have been blamed on the Christians as a cover-up. In the wave of persecution that followed, Peter was among those martyred for their faith (AD 64 or 67).

THEMES

Several themes and emphases can be seen in Mark's Gospel, but foremost among them are Mark's positioning of Jesus as both Son of God and Son of Man.

Son of God—Some scholars suggest that Mark 1:1 serves as a title to Mark's Gospel: "The beginning of the gospel of Jesus Christ, the Son of God" (ESV). As soon as Jesus is mentioned, He is identified as the Son of God. Throughout His life, others confirm this fact about Jesus (1:11; 3:11; 9:7; 15:39). The title alone, however, would not have meant much to a Roman audience unless Jesus also displayed the power of God. So Mark wastes no time getting to the ministry of Jesus and His performance of many amazing miracles.

Son of Man—Jesus never denied that He was the Son of God and the Messiah (Christ). However, His emphasis was not on power or politics, but on servanthood and suffering. So His preferred term of self-description was "Son of Man." Mark uses this title for Jesus fourteen times—mostly while quoting Jesus Himself.

"Son of Man" was a far less politically heated term, though certainly messianic, originating from Daniel's prophecy (Daniel 7:13–14). The Jewish people had been anticipating the arrival of a Messiah for centuries, but they were looking for a military figure to set them free from Roman domination. Throughout His ministry, Jesus slowly reinterpreted His Messianic ministry. He certainly had power, yet He refused to use His power against those in control. And His arrival did indeed bring freedom—not immediate victory over Roman rule, but spiritual triumph over fear and death available only through the suffering and sacrifice of the Son of Man. Half of Mark's Gospel (beginning with 8:31) is dedicated to Jesus' suffering, death, and resurrection.

CONTRIBUTION TO THE BIBLE

About 95 percent of Mark is found in either Matthew or Luke. Yet Mark's Gospel has a fresh and immediate tone not to be missed. His writing has a fast flow of action, moving rapidly from story to story. He records details not found in the other Gospel accounts that make the events more vivid. For example, he frequently notes the emotional reactions and gestures of Jesus. Only two discourses of Jesus are provided (4:1–32 and 13:1–37) and only four parables (Matthew recorded eighteen parables, and Luke, nineteen). Yet Mark contains eighteen of Jesus' miracles—about the same number as Matthew and Luke. So Mark's Gospel gives us a bold, concise, action-filled look at Jesus' life.

STRUCTURE

Ancient tradition considered Mark's Gospel "disorderly." Some have proposed that Mark's Gospel is best seen as a passion narrative with an extended introduction. Jesus' suffering and death is the dominant theme around which the Gospel narrative is structured. Most scholars break Mark into two main parts: 1:1–8:30 and 8:31–16:8 (with 8:27–9:1 as the transition). Some break Mark into three parts, the third beginning with Jesus' entry into Jerusalem (Mark 11:1).

While Matthew and Luke begin their Gospels with birth accounts of Jesus and genealogies to prove who He was, Mark skips the events surrounding Jesus' birth and quickly hastens into Jesus' public ministry. Mark 1:14–9:50 examines Jesus' ministry in Galilee, from His widespread popularity to His conflicts with the religious leaders to His withdrawal and preparation of His disciples. Mark 10 describes Jesus' ministry in Judea and Perea. And chapters 11–16 detail Jesus' final week, concluding with His resurrection.

OUTLINE

PREPARING FOR SOMETHING NEW 1:1–13

Two Titles 1:1
John the Baptist 1:2–8
Spiritual Ups and Downs 1:9–13

JESUS' MINISTRY BEGINS 1:14–45

The Time Has Come 1:14–20
Unprecedented Power 1:21–34
First Solitary, Then Surrounded 1:35–45

A MINISTRY TO THE "SICK" 2:1–17

The Faith to Move Rooftops 2:1–12
An Unusual Choice to Be a Disciple 2:13–17

CONFLICT INTENSIFIES 2:18–3:6

The Conflict Over Fasting 2:18–22
The Conflict Over Picking Grain on the Sabbath 2:23–28
The Conflict Over Healing on the Sabbath 3:1–6

FAME AND FOLLOWERS 3:7–19

Enduring the Crowds 3:7–12
Calling Disciples 3:13–19

FAMILY AND FOES 3:20–35

Even Jesus Had Family Problems 3:20–21
A Harsh (and Inaccurate) Accusation 3:22–30
An Expanded Definition of Family 3:31–35

THE PARABLE OF THE SOWER 4:1–25

Master of Parables 4:1–9
Why Parables? 4:10–12
The Real Meaning 4:13–20
Applying the Parable 4:21–25

MORE PARABLES ABOUT SEEDS 4:26–34

The Parable of the Growing Seed 4:26–29
The Parable of the Mustard Seed 4:30–34

JESUS' ACTIONS VERIFY HIS TEACHINGS 4:35–5:20

Even the Wind and Waves Obey Him! 4:35–41
Helping a Wild Man 5:1–20

A PLANNED AND AN IMPROMPTU MIRACLE 5:21–43

A Helpless Father 5:21–24
A Desperate Woman 5:25–34
Hope in the Face of Death 5:35–43

REJECTION INCREASES 6:1–30

Rejection at Home 6:1–6
The Apostles Are Sent Out in Pairs 6:6–13
The Death of John the Baptist 6:14–29
The Report of the Disciples 6:30

AN UNUSUAL STROLL AFTER AN UNUSUAL MEAL 6:31–56

The Miraculous Meal 6:31–44
The Miraculous Lake Crossing 6:45–56

CLARIFYING SOME TWISTED LAWS 7:1–23

To Wash or Not to Wash 7:1–13
The Source of "Uncleanness" 7:14–23

OVERWHELMED WITH AMAZEMENT 7:24–37

Crumbs Are Enough 7:24–30
Deaf and Speechless No More 7:31–37

REPEAT PERFORMANCES 8:1–26

Another Feeding of the Masses 8:1–13
The Problem with Yeast 8:14–21
A Miracle in Stages 8:22–26

THE BEGINNING OF THE END 8:27–9:1

The Great Confession 8:27–30
Suffering and Death 8:31–33
Humility and Sacrifice 8:34–9:1

THE UNIQUENESS OF THE CHRIST 9:2–29

Jesus' Transfiguration 9:2–13
A Difficult Exorcism 9:14–29

GREATNESS: AN EXAMPLE AND SOME OBSTACLES 9:30–50

A Model of Greatness 9:30–37
Teamwork or Competition? 9:38–41
A Strong Warning against Offenses 9:42–50

THE HEART OF THE MATTER 10:1–31

Divorce: A Touchy Subject 10:1–12
Little Children: A Model for Us All 10:13–16
The One Who Got Away 10:17–31

LEARNING TO SEE STRAIGHT 10:32–52

Unclear Spiritual Vision 10:32–45
Unclear Physical Vision 10:46–52

JESUS' FINAL TRIP TO JERUSALEM 11:1–10

Humble Service 11:1–6
Necessary Deliverance 11:7–10

A NONPRODUCTIVE FIG TREE AND A DISRESPECTFUL TEMPLE 11:11–26

The Cursing of the Fig Tree, Part I 11:11–14
The Expulsion of Merchants from the Temple 11:15–19
The Cursing of the Fig Tree, Part 2 11:20–26

CONTROVERSIES IN THE TEMPLE, PART I 11:27–12:17

Controversy: Jesus' Authority 11:27–33
Controversy: The Rejection of Israel 12:1–12
Controversy: The Payment of Taxes 12:13–17

CONTROVERSIES IN THE TEMPLE, PART II 12:18–44

Controversy: Marriage at the Resurrection 12:18–27
Controversy: The Greatest Commandment 12:28–34
Controversy: The Identity of David's Son 12:35–37
Controversy: The Scribes Contrasted with the Widow 12:38–44

WATCH AND WAIT 13:1–13
The Destruction of the Temple 13:1–11
Signs to Watch For 13:5–13

THE END OF THE AGE 13:14–37
True Signs of the End of the Age 13:14–23
The Return of the Son of Man and the Gathering of His Elect 13:23–27
Certain and Uncertain Truths about the Return of Jesus 13:28–37

A FINAL MEAL TOGETHER 14:1–26
A Remarkable Gift 14:1–11
The Institution of the Lord's Supper 14:12–26

ARRESTED AND CHARGED 14:27–72
Abandoned in Gethsemane 14:27–42
Arrested and Tried 14:43–65
Peter's Three Denials 14:66–72

JESUS' ROMAN TRIAL 15:1–20
The Trial Before Pilate 15:1–15
Jesus Before the Soldiers 15:16–20

JESUS' CRUCIFIXION, DEATH, AND BURIAL 15:21–47
Jesus' Crucifixion 15:21–32
The Death of Jesus 15:33–41
Jesus' Burial 15:42–47

BETWEEN DEATH AND RESURRECTION 16:1–8
Worry 16:1–3
Alarm 16:4–6
Fear 16:7–8

AN ADDENDUM TO THE GOSPEL OF MARK? 16:9–20

MARK 1:1–13

PREPARING FOR SOMETHING NEW

Two Titles	1:1
John the Baptist	1:2–8
Spiritual Ups and Downs	1:9–13

Setting Up the Section

Mark quickly moves from the appearance of Jesus on earth to His adult ministry. After eight verses about John the Baptist, Jesus is baptized and sets to work, calling disciples and healing.

1:1

TWO TITLES

Before Mark introduces John the Baptist as the forerunner to Jesus, he provides two significant titles for Jesus that succinctly describe who He is and what He came to do. The first, *Christ*, represents what Jesus came to do. Rather than a name, the word *Christ* is a title (the Greek translation of the Hebrew for *Messiah*) that means "Anointed One." Jesus was anointed to perform the redemptive work of being prophet, priest, and king of His people. He is the divinely appointed, commissioned, and accredited Savior of humankind. (See Hebrews 5:1–4; Isaiah 11:2–4; 49:6; John 5:37; and Acts 2:22).

The second term, *Son of God*, refers to Jesus' nature rather than His office. He isn't the Son of God because of anything He has done (miraculous birth, incarnation, resurrection, etc.), but rather because of who He is. Mark uses Son of God in its messianic sense and links it closely to "Messiah."

In the ancient way of thinking, a man's life was continued in his son. A son would inherit the property of his father—and the firstborn received a double portion. A son was perceived as the extension of the father's rule and position in the house. So Jesus' title "Son of God" shows that even when He was separate from the Father, He lived to do the will of God and shared His very nature.

1:2–8

JOHN THE BAPTIST

The prophets had foretold not only a Messiah to come, but also a messenger—an "Elijah"—to prepare the way. Verses 2 and 3 are quotes from Isaiah 40:3 and Malachi 3:1. Mark inserts these reminders to introduce John the Baptist. John preaches about the forgiveness of sins that would follow repentance (1:4), and he baptizes those who respond to his message.

Demystifying Mark

People of Jesus' day would expect a messenger to precede the arrival of any important person. It was the messenger's job to: (1) ensure the roads were in proper repair; (2) arrange for food, lodging, and a proper reception of the dignitary; and (3) announce the arrival of the important person. John the Baptist performed the role of messenger prior to the appearance of Jesus.

Mark's physical description of John the Baptist (1:6)—his unique diet and style of dress—creates an additional connection between the new prophet and the Old Testament Elijah (2 Kings 1:8). Even though John must have been a powerful presence, his message of repentance is based on the anticipation of "one more powerful than I" (1:7 NIV). John's comment about his own unworthiness to untie Jesus' sandals—the work of a slave—is a vivid image of the homage he pays to Jesus and the work He will do (1:7). And although John is baptizing people with water, Jesus will baptize with the Holy Spirit (1:8).

1:9–13

RESISTING TEMPTATION

Even though John had proclaimed Jesus to be much greater than himself, Jesus came to be baptized by John (1:9). At this time, God makes a statement about Jesus (1:11) that He has never made about anyone after the fall of Adam. Because of the prevalence of sin, no human being can please God. Yet Jesus came to do for us what we are unable to do for ourselves.

Critical Observation

Coming out of Nazareth (1:9) didn't do much for Jesus' reputation to begin with. Nazareth was such an obscure village that it is mentioned nowhere in the Old Testament, the writings of Josephus, or rabbinic literature. While the small community was not held in high regard, archeological evidence confirms its existence.

The opening of the heavens (1:10) suggests a divine intervention and a new revelation of God after centuries of silence (Isaiah 64:1). With the advent of Jesus, we might conclude that God is becoming accessible to an extent not previously known. The descent of the Holy Spirit upon Jesus is described in a simile to symbolize the same type of beauty and majesty as a dove in flight. And God himself confirms what Mark has already told us: Jesus is indeed the Son of God who pleases His heavenly Father and is beloved (1:11). The blessing conferred on Jesus contains important allusions to Psalm 2:7 and Isaiah 42:1. Also, His empowerment with the Spirit was predicted in Isaiah 11.

Yet, immediately after this high point in Jesus' life, He goes into the wilderness where He is tempted by Satan. Matthew and Luke provide more extensive accounts of Jesus' temptation, but Mark includes additional details. We discover in verse 12 that the Holy Spirit *sends* Jesus into the desert. It was God's will for Jesus to prove Himself by resisting the temptation to sin—something no human has ever been capable of doing. Just as the Israelites went into the wilderness for forty years and failed, Jesus is in the desert for forty days and succeeds. Having triumphed over the enemy, Jesus can now go forth and call a new people who will share His spiritual inheritance.

Mark also mentions wild animals present in the wilderness (1:13). God had placed Adam in a beautiful and peaceful garden over which he had dominion, yet Adam lost that privilege due to his sin. Jesus is sent into a dangerous setting, yet overcomes physical dangers and spiritual temptations to reestablish the kingdom of God on earth—a kingdom that would be marked by peace and righteousness (Isaiah 11:6–9; 35:9). It seems clear that Jesus' spiritual temptations are severe, because angels are there to minister to Him and encourage Him (1:13).

With just thirteen verses, Mark deals with the life of Jesus prior to His public ministry. From this point onward, Jesus will be a teacher and healer, each day closer to His inevitable sacrifice on the cross.

Take It Home

It is a common experience to feel a significant letdown after a spiritual mountaintop experience. During such times, some people start to doubt and think what they felt must not have been real. But in this passage we see that even Jesus plunged from the heights of spiritual confidence at His baptism to a dark and challenging time of testing immediately afterward. What confidence should we pull from knowing that Jesus resisted where I would have succumbed? What hope can I draw from knowing that my Savior has the power to resist the devil?

MARK 1:14–45

JESUS' MINISTRY BEGINS

The Time Has Come	1:14–20
Unprecedented Power	1:21–34
First Solitary, Then Surrounded	1:35–45

Setting Up the Section

As Mark begins his account of Jesus' ministry, he maintains a focus on Jesus' proclamation and demonstration of the nearness of the kingdom of God. Jesus proclaimed by teaching and preaching; He demonstrated by performing miracles. Mark wants his readers to see that Jesus is more than a prophet—He is the Messiah and the Son of God. As such, His ministry is powerful.

1:14–20

THE TIME HAS COME

Jesus' ministry begins in Galilee and the surrounding regions. Mark's Gospel shows how Jesus regularly moves from place to place, which stresses the urgency of His message about the kingdom of God. Some of the travel is in Gentile territory, foreshadowing an outreach that is central to the establishment of the kingdom of God.

Jesus begins His public ministry as John the Baptist is completing his. John had been put in prison (1:14) and would not emerge alive (6:17–29). Jesus continues John's message that the kingdom of God is near, and people should repent and believe the good news (1:15; Matthew 3:1–2). The good news is twofold: (1) Because of Jesus, the kingdom of God had come to earth; and (2) Through Jesus, salvation is given to all who believe. The only way to enter God's kingdom is by believing the good news that Jesus came to take the punishment of humankind. By believing in Him, the very righteousness of God will be bestowed as a person is reconciled to God.

Critical Observation

God expects believers to repent—to turn from their sins. Yet repentance alone is not enough to save us. Repentance without faith is just self-improvement; faith without repentance is just religion. What is necessary is both repentance *and* belief in Jesus.

To help spread His message, Jesus begins to call disciples. Mark first describes the call of two pairs of brothers, all fishermen–Andrew and Simon (Peter), and James and John. Jesus promises to make them "fishers of men" (1:17). The facts that these followers would set aside their livelihoods to be in the service of Jesus and be immediately willing to follow are indications of Jesus' authority.

1:21–34

UNPRECEDENTED POWER

Jesus' authority as a teacher is authenticated by the power He displays. The first miracle Mark records is the casting out of an evil spirit from a possessed man at a synagogue in Capernaum. The crowd is already amazed at Jesus' teaching (1:22), but becomes even more astounded when He rids the troubled man of the evil spirit. Note that the demon knows exactly who Jesus is–in regard to both His humanity ("Jesus of Nazareth") and His divinity ("the Holy One of God"). And even though Jesus sternly commands the spirit to keep quiet, news about Jesus quickly spreads (1:28).

Demystifying Mark

Synagogues may have originated during the Babylonian exile when the Jewish people had no access to the temple. A synagogue was not a place for sacrifice, but rather for reading the scriptures, praying, and worshiping God. The services were led by laymen, supervised by a board of elders, and presided over by a ruler. A synagogue could be organized anywhere there were ten or more Jewish men above the age of twelve.

When Jesus and His followers leave the synagogue, they presumably go to the home of Simon and Andrew for their Sabbath meal. There they find Simon Peter's mother-in-law in bed with a fever–a very serious condition in the first century. Jesus' healing allows her to rise immediately and begin to wait on her guests–an honor for a woman during this time.

The Sabbath ended at sundown, at which time "the whole town gathered" (NIV) at the house

(1:33). And they didn't simply bring hordes of sick and demon-possessed people; they kept on bringing people for Jesus to tend to.

1:35–45

FIRST SOLITARY, THEN SURROUNDED

Even after the long healing session at Simon Peter's house, Jesus arises very early the next morning and finds a solitary place to pray (1:35). His solitude doesn't last long, however, because the crowds are soon looking for Him again. But Jesus opts to move on to other places. He had come to spread the Word of God, not just to heal the sick. The people Jesus healed would still die eventually. Physical healing—which was another indication of His authority—was simply proof that Jesus' message of spiritual healing should be heeded.

While traveling on through Galilee, a man with leprosy approaches Jesus, asking for healing. This man would have been considered ceremonially unclean to Jesus and His followers. Jesus seems aware that no one had been permitted contact with this man for a long time. Yet Jesus not only touches the man, but heals him, making him clean once again. The leper is expected to follow the legally prescribed course to verify healing (Leviticus 14:1–32).

Jesus warns the man not to say anything about what had happened, but the man is so overjoyed that he tells everyone he sees (1:45).

This is Mark's first mention of a pattern of Jesus' ministry that some refer to as the "Messianic Secret." He never encouraged public excitement about His healing ministry lest it create a problem with the Jews and the Romans. The Jews would want to follow Jesus only because of His power to heal and the Romans would think He was a Jewish insurrectionist trying to overthrow the government. Thus, Jesus would tell people that He had healed to keep quiet (1:44; 3:12; 5:43; 7:36-37; 8:26, 30; 9:9). In this case, as in some others, the healed man was so overjoyed that rather than keep Jesus' secret, he told everyone he saw.

From a theological standpoint, Jesus was secretive because He did not want His miracles to be seen as the central piece of His ministry. They were only meant to confirm that He was indeed who He said that He was. His miracles proved that His words should be heeded and His death and resurrection provided the power behind the promises that He made.

The tests for leprosy provided in Leviticus 13:1–46 present a symbolic picture of the problem of sin. Like sin, leprosy is beneath the surface (Leviticus 13:3); it spreads (Leviticus 13:5–8); it defiles and isolates (Leviticus 13:45–46); and it renders things fit only for the fire (Leviticus 13:52).

As word spreads about Jesus' ability to heal even leprosy, Jesus tries to avoid towns and seek out remote places. But wherever He is, the people find Him and congregate.

Take It Home

According to Mark, people were first amazed at the teachings of Jesus (1:22). Then they were even more amazed when they witnessed firsthand the power of God Jesus displayed through His miracles. In fact, the desire to see the miracles seemed to have superceded their willingness to respond to what He was saying. In your own life, to what extent do you depend on signs to confirm what you believe to be true about Jesus? Are the teachings of the Bible enough to convince you, or do you desire additional proof?

MARK 2:1–17

A MINISTRY TO THE "SICK"

The Faith to Move Rooftops 2:1–12
An Unusual Choice to Be a Disciple 2:13–17

Setting Up the Section

Mark has wasted no time describing the immense popularity of Jesus as He begins His public ministry. But now Jesus does something that many cannot understand: Rather than associating with only the elite of the culture, He instead chooses to hang around with the outcasts of His society. He even selects members of this group to be included among His closest companions.

2:1–12

THE FAITH TO MOVE ROOFTOPS

Jesus returns to Capernaum, and again, huge crowds assemble to hear Him speak. This time He is in a house, and it is filled beyond capacity. Most Palestinian homes had one to four rooms, and the crowd at this one fills the house and sprawls outside.

The "word" Jesus preaches (2:2) is the good news that the kingdom of God is near (1:15). Indeed, the kingdom was arriving through His incarnation and ministry.

While Jesus is speaking, five men arrive: four carrying a fifth who is paralyzed. When they realize they can get nowhere close to Jesus, they improvise a plan to go through the roof. Many first-century homes had an outside staircase leading to a flat roof made of branches and sod. It would not be difficult to make an opening in the roof and lower their friend.

Considering the unusual entrance of the man, Jesus' first words to him are surprising (2:5). For one thing, Jesus surely knows the man has come for physical healing, not spiritual forgiveness. For another, His words trigger a negative response from the teachers of the law among the crowd.

Jesus perceives the faith of the five men (2:5), and Mark frequently associates the presence of faith with the performance of miracles by Jesus. Even though Jesus uses the passive voice in making His statement, His intent is not missed by skeptical listeners. The Jews believed that only God was capable of forgiving sin. Similar claims by anyone else were blasphemy (irreverent, profane, impious speech about God that held a sentence of death for those found guilty [Leviticus 24:16]).

Jesus knows the thoughts of the religious leaders and preempts their objections by asking a question (2:9). Clearly, the forgiveness of sin (spiritual healing) requires much more authority than performing merely a physical healing. Yet His observers know it is much easier to *say* that the man's sins are forgiven because forgiveness cannot be verified, while healing can. But to Jesus, the granting of healing and forgiveness are equally the work of God. So He heals the paralyzed man to validate His authority to forgive sins. Mark writes that as the man stands up and carries His mat out, "everyone" (NIV) is amazed, but he is probably referring to the general effect on the crowd. As we will soon see, the religious leaders are still resistant to the ministry of Jesus.

Jesus makes a very important connection here for the people watching this miracle (2:8-10). In book of Isaiah (chapters 29; 35; 61) God said when the Messiah arrived on earth that not only would God forgive sins and restore the broken hearted, but the Messiah would also bring healing to the lame. When Jesus pronounces forgiveness of sin and then backs up this declaration with a healing, He is fulfilling what the Scriptures said the Messiah would do (Isaiah 61:1).

Critical Observation

This is the first place in Mark where Jesus calls himself "the Son of Man" (2:10), although Jesus would use this term as His favorite self-designation. The vagueness of the phrase carried overtones of both humanity and deity (Daniel 7:13–14). By using it, Jesus forced people to make up their own minds about Him. If He had spoken publicly of being the Messiah (Christ), it would have quickly created problems in the politically and religiously charged culture of the time.

2:13–17

AN UNUSUAL CHOICE TO BE A DISCIPLE

Mark has already told us that Jesus had been calling disciples to follow Him (1:16–20). Simon, Andrew, James, and John seemed decent choices, even though they were simple fishermen and not among the prestigious crowd. But Jesus' choice of Levi in this passage is even more startling. (Levi is identified in Matthew's Gospel as "Matthew," but the name change is not explained in scripture.)

As usual, Jesus is surrounded by a large crowd. He is walking along and teaching them when He comes upon Levi, a tax collector sitting in his booth. Levi immediately responds to Jesus' invitation to "Follow Me" (2:14), and soon Jesus is having dinner at his house. But Jesus' willing association with tax collectors and "sinners" (2:15–16) creates instant indignation among the teachers of the law.

This is where Mark first introduces his readers to the Pharisees, a party of laymen who devoted themselves to keeping the law, especially its oral interpretation. The name probably meant "separatists," perhaps in reference to their separation from the common people—the "sinners" mentioned in this passage. The scribes, referred to by Luke as lawyers, were the official interpreters of Jewish law. The scribes and Pharisees were separate groups, though some Pharisees were also scribes.

Tax collectors were on the opposite end of the scale from the Pharisees. Roman tax collectors were despised because of their dishonesty, use of intimidation and force, and contact with Gentiles. The Jewish tax collectors appointed by King Herod weren't liked much better.

Demystifying Mark

Those who live in modern, Western society may have difficulty comprehending just how scandalous it was for Jesus to associate with tax collectors and other social outcasts. In Semitic society, table fellowship was one of the most intimate expressions of friendship. The Jewish leaders could not understand how Jesus could regard Himself as a religious person and still dine with such spiritual rebels. But Jesus defied many of the conventions of His society.

The religious leaders do not question Jesus directly (2:16). Even as they are looking down on His behavior, it seems they are still afraid to confront Him because of the power He displayed in both words and deeds. But Jesus overhears and responds directly. He clarifies that His purpose is not to affirm the good works of self-righteous people, but rather to bring healing and righteousness to those who realize their own insufficiencies. For Jesus to refuse to associate with sinners would have been as foolish as for a doctor not to associate with the sick.

Take It Home

Jesus showed love for all kinds of sinners. He took the initiative in seeking them out. He accepted them as friends, and chose to have close fellowship with them. His response to outcasts provided a new and revolutionary model for both religion and social behavior. And sadly, it might still be new and revolutionary in our own culture. Why is it hard to show love for sinners? What gets in the way of showing unconditional love? How does the love that Jesus had for sinners give us hope that we can one day love sinners?

MARK 2:18–3:6

CONFLICT INTENSIFIES

The Conflict Over Fasting	2:18–22
The Conflict Over Picking Grain on the Sabbath	2:23–28
The Conflict Over Healing on the Sabbath	3:1–6

Setting Up the Section

In this section of his Gospel, Mark has collected five accounts to chronicle the growing conflict Jesus experienced with the religious leaders of Israel. We have already seen two: their reluctance to Jesus' authority to forgive the sin of the paralyzed man (2:1-12) and their disgust at his association with tax collectors and "sinners" (2:15-17). Now we look at three more conflicts and see how quickly the conflict escalated.

2:18-22

THE CONFLICT OVER FASTING

The Old Testament only prescribed fasting one day a year: on the Day of Atonement (Leviticus 16:29-31), although other traditional fasts had begun later (Zechariah 7:5; 8:19). But by the first century, the Pharisees made a habit of fasting every Monday and Thursday (Luke 18:12). Other occasional fasting was common following personal loss, as an expression of repentance, in preparation for prayer, or even as a meritorious act.

Jesus and His disciples did not practice the rigorous fasting of the Pharisees, or even of John the Baptist's disciples, so a group of people asked about this discrepancy. Jesus responded to their question with a question of His own—a common tactic in rabbinic debates. In essence, Jesus clarified that there were appropriate and inappropriate times to fast. His appearance on earth was a special time; He was not unlike a bridegroom at a wedding, and His disciples were like guests. For them, it was not a time to fast, but to celebrate.

In this context, Jesus' two short parables (2:21-22) make sense. The fasting of the Pharisees was not necessary because it represented an old way of doing things. With the onset of the kingdom of God on earth, certain things were going to change. The traditions of scribal Judaism were like the old garment and the old wineskin. The "old" was not inherently wrong, but its time had passed. The old ways would not smoothly merge with Jesus' new teachings; they had to be replaced with something better.

2:23-27

THE CONFLICT OVER PICKING GRAIN ON THE SABBATH

The Old Testament clearly forbade work on the Sabbath (Exodus 20:8-11), but the scribes had so meticulously defined "work" that they had a list of 39 different prohibitions. Third on their list was "reaping," which was their accusation against Jesus and his disciples (2:23). Since Jesus' followers were only feeding themselves, Jesus had a ready response. He referred His accusers to the story of David (1 Samuel 21:1-6) who used "consecrated bread" out of the tabernacle to feed his men. He emphasized that the Sabbath was created for people to cherish, not to enslave them with legalistic restrictions (2:27-28).

Demystifying Mark

For anyone unfamiliar with the Old Testament, Jesus' example may confuse more than clarify. Twelve loaves of bread were placed in the tabernacle every Sabbath, probably to symbolize God's presence and provision (Exodus 25:30; Leviticus 24:5-9). The bread was designated to be eaten only by the priests (Leviticus 24:9). Yet when David and his men showed up at the tabernacle, famished and with no other food available, the priest used the bread to feed them. Jesus' point was that human need should take precedence over ceremonial laws.

3:1-6

THE CONFLICT OVER HEALING ON THE SABBATH

For the Pharisees, Sabbath observance was one of the more important elements in Judaism and a noticeable distinction between Jews and Gentiles. When Jesus began to challenge their long-held standards, they became enraged. And when the conflict wasn't quickly resolved, they even began to plot to kill Him.

On one particular Sabbath, Jesus and His disciples were in the synagogue. So were the Pharisees. And so was a man with a shriveled hand. The Pharisees allowed healing to take place on the Sabbath—but only if a person's life was in danger, which was certainly not the case in this account. By this time, Jesus' opponents were looking for any opportunity to accuse Him, so apparently they were more interested in watching Him than in worshiping. Again, Jesus appeared to know their thoughts, so He made a public display of having the deformed man stand in front of everyone. His question (3:4) lifted the issue of Sabbath observance to a level above a list of prohibitions. His question suggested that to heal is to do good; not to heal is the equivalent of doing evil. To Jesus, merely resting on the Sabbath was not enough when the day could be used to accomplish good. And after He received no argument in response to His question, He healed the man. He then raised the analogy even higher by suggesting that failing to save a life would be equivalent to murder. The irony here is that while Jesus is doing good on the Sabbath, His opponents are plotting murder!

Critical Observations

In all of ancient literature, the Herodians are only referred to in Mark (in 3:6 and 12:13) and once in Matthew (22:16). They were a Jewish political party devoted to the Roman emperor and his deputy (Herod). Ordinarily the Pharisees would have nothing to do with such a group that submitted willingly to the government of Rome, but their common hatred of Jesus would unite these two parties at opposite ends of the political scale.

Jesus became angry that these so-called religious leaders were so hard-hearted that they would resist the healing of a person in distress. The Sabbath was created for rest and relief, yet they used it to burden people. Jesus' anger was directed at the insensitivity toward suffering as well as the entire system of legalism where the letter of the law is given more weight than the needs of the people it is supposed to help.

Mark provides this series of conflicts so we can see the tension that was developing between Jesus and His adversaries. And this certainly won't be the last of the disagreements.

Take It Home

In this account we see that Jesus got angry, so anger itself is not a sin. It was a natural response at the culmination of a long series of conflicts. Yet Jesus didn't lose control. Does your anger tend to be more in regard to offenses against God, or do you get upset more often at personal offenses? And how well do you stay in control when anger rises within you?

MARK 3:7–19

FAME AND FOLLOWERS

Enduring the Crowds	3:7–12
Calling Disciples	3:13–19

Setting Up the Section

Much of what Mark has already introduced is continued in this section. Crowds continue to vie for Jesus' attention as He continues to assemble a team of disciples to assist Him in His ministry. Yet Mark provides new bits of information with each new story.

3:7–12

ENDURING THE CROWDS

Mark had just described the beginnings of a plan to have Jesus put to death. Here we read that Jesus "withdrew" to the Sea of Galilee (3:7). The word *withdrew* in this context apparently meant "flee from danger." At this point Jesus chooses to withdraw rather than debate the Pharisees because His ministry is still in the early stages, and He wants to extend it beyond the towns in Israel. In fact, several of the locations mentioned in verse 8 had large Gentile populations. It doesn't take long for Jesus' message to spread beyond the bounds of traditional Jewish locales.

The dastardly plot of the Pharisees stood in sharp contrast to how the crowds respond to Jesus. By this time, He can hardly travel anywhere without a swarm of people around Him. Many are even beginning to push and shove to get close to Him (3:10)—seemingly much more interested in being healed than in hearing what He has to say about salvation. From a similar account in 4:1 it seems likely that the boat was not intended for escape, but to provide Jesus with a podium—a buffer between Himself and the crowds.

Again, Jesus encounters evil spirits (1:23–24, 34). This time they are acknowledging Him as the "Son of God" (3:11), but He forces them to remain quiet about His identity.

This is another example of what some refer to as the Messianic Secret. Jesus often encouraged those that he helped to keep the miracle to themselves (1:44; 3:12; 5:43; 7:36-37; 8:26, 30; 9:9). While this secret kept Jesus from unwanted, untimely attention from both the Jewish leaders and the Romans, there was a more significant theological reason. Jesus did not want His miracles to be seen as the central piece of His ministry. His miracles were only meant to confirm that He was who He said that He was.

Demystifying Mark

James writes that, "Even the demons believe [that there is one God]—and shudder" (James 2:19 NRSV). Here in Mark's account, the demons are aware of who Jesus is and what He came to do. Nevertheless, they are already condemned and beyond salvation. They were not declaring Jesus' lordship as a confession of submission, but out of fear. And because it was premature for Jesus to proclaim His true identity, He had them silenced. His authority would ultimately be confirmed at the cross.

3:13–19

CALLING DISCIPLES

Mark had already written about Jesus' call of Andrew, Simon, James, and John (1:14–20), and later Levi (2:13–14). Here he provides the list of the twelve disciples chosen from the rest. They would be designated *apostles*, meaning "sent ones" (3:14), in contrast to crowds of other disciples who followed Jesus as well.

It's interesting to note the various lists of the apostles in the New Testament. There are four: Matthew 10:2–4; Luke 6:13–16; Acts 1:13; and this one in Mark. In each case, Simon Peter is always listed first, Philip fifth, James the son of Alphaeus ninth, and Judas Iscariot last.

Sometimes the names of the apostles can be a little confusing. We've seen that Matthew 3:18) is sometimes called Levi. Similarly, Bartholomew is probably the same as Nathanael, and Thaddaeus may be another name for Judas (the son of James).

These would be the twelve people Jesus would spend most of His time with, preparing them for a time when He would no longer be around to lead them. They would be the first to understand His plan of redemption and to spread the good news of that plan around the world.

Critical Observation

The number twelve recalls the tribes of Israel, God's people in the Old Testament. The twelve apostles will become the nucleus of the new, restored people of God, later to be known as the church.

Jesus retreats to a mountain to summon His twelve primary followers. The call of Jesus is always for a purpose, not just for status. The apostles are called to serve a missional purpose. Mark provides two aspects of their calling: (1) to be with Jesus (one of the most important aspects of being a disciple); and (2) to proclaim the advent of the kingdom of God by preaching and exorcising demons (3:14–15).

Mark maintains a focus on Jesus' supernatural power over both the physical world and the spiritual world. His apostles would have the privilege of sharing and using that power. Similarly, today's disciples are not expected to minister in their own strength, but to be empowered by their omnipotent Savior (2 Corinthians 12:9–10).

Take It Home

Many people find personal ministry to others fulfilling and rewarding—as long as it doesn't become too demanding. However, as we look at the ministry of Jesus we see a continual stream of people physically pressing in on Him and demanding His attention. In addition, He is getting up early to pray, making time to call and train disciples, and maintaining the important, essential aspects of ministry. How do you respond when the demands of ministry require more than the time you have allotted? What other options do you have in such situations?

MARK 3:20–35

FAMILY AND FOES

Even Jesus Had Family Problems 3:20–21
A Harsh (and Inaccurate) Accusation 3:22–30
An Expanded Definition of Family 3:31–35

Setting Up the Section

Jesus' teachings were unlike anything the people of Israel had ever heard, and the reactions of the crowds toward Him were frequently unpredictable. Even those closest to Him didn't know what to think. In this section we see that, at times, Jesus' human family didn't respond to Him much differently than those who strongly opposed Him. Mark is here setting up his theme that while many of Jesus' own reject Him, outsiders and outcasts accept Him (John 1:11).

This is the first time Mark uses the literary device common to his Gospel called bracketing or sandwiching. In this section, Mark sandwiches one account in the middle of another. He brings two stories together to support the same point. In this case, it is to show that no one—not the religious leaders and not His own family—truly understood who Jesus was and what He came to do. Other examples of Mark's sandwiching in the Gospel are 4:1–20; 5:21–43; 6:7–29; 11:12–26; 14:1–11; 14:53–72.

3:20–21

EVEN JESUS HAD FAMILY PROBLEMS

As we look back about 2,000 years to the ministry of Jesus, knowing what we do, it's natural to think that it would have been exciting to be there, witnessing all the newness of His power and teaching. But if we read scripture closely, we see quite a variety of responses—many of them not what we might expect.

Here we see that Jesus' own family is not only embarrassed by Him but literally thinks He is out of His mind (3:21). With all the crowds flocking to Him everywhere He goes—in this case He and His disciples are not even able to eat (3:20)—His own family does not perceive Him to be anything special.

Mark's reference to family is not a statement that Jesus' mother rejected Him, but it emphasizes that even those closest to Him did not fully understand His purpose and power. Mark will say more about Jesus' family a few verses down, but he first inserts another incident between Jesus and the scribes.

Critical Observation

Who were Jesus' "brothers"? Some people think these were children of Joseph from a previous marriage. Others believe Mary and Joseph had children after Jesus was born. Although skeptical at first, some of Jesus' brothers would eventually become church leaders and epistle writers.

3:22–30

A HARSH (AND INACCURATE) ACCUSATION

Many times in the New Testament we read of someone who "came down" from Jerusalem (3:22). The reference is geographical as well as spiritual. Jerusalem, God's holy city, was on a hill, so anyone who departed, by necessity, had to go "down."

Apparently the scribes had followed Jesus, and it didn't take them long to express their criticism. This time, however, they actually accuse Jesus of being possessed. Beelzebub (3:22) was the Greek form of a Hebrew name that meant "lord of flies," and was the name given to the prince of demons. In essence, the religious leaders are accusing Jesus of being possessed by Satan.

Jesus uses logic to refute their accusations. He says it is foolish to think that someone possessed by the prince of demons would go around casting demons out of other people. He uses three consecutive short parables to make His point (3:25–27). The first two are self-explanatory. The third one, however (3:27), can be confusing. The "strong man" is a reference to Satan, who possesses a number of people. The one capable of entering his house and carrying off his possessions is Jesus, who came to earth and began setting people free by exorcising demons. He would soon break the hold of sin and death for good with His sacrificial death.

Jesus' statement in verses 28–29 has been a source of discussion and debate for centuries. To begin with, we should not miss the emphatic opening that all the sins and blasphemies of people will be forgiven. Jesus' use of "Verily" (KJV) (or "Truly" [NASB, ESV, NRSV] or "I tell you the truth [NIV])" is a declaration that what follows is absolute truth. The term *blasphemy* refers to slandering another, in this case, being irreverent or defiant toward God. It is the notion of abusing the name of God by something one says or does. And what Jesus is stating so strongly is that such offenses will be forgiven.

It's the second part of His statement that creates the confusion, that whoever blasphemes against the Holy Spirit will never be forgiven (3:29). To understand this verse, we have to understand the context. Jesus has recently cast out a number of demons, using the miraculous power of God. But the scribes accuse Jesus of acting under the power of evil. Jesus explains that those who attribute the power of the Holy Spirit to Satan have no way of being forgiven. This sin is apparently quite rare because it requires being faced with the power of Jesus and then declaring it the work of the devil.

Demystifying Mark

Blasphemy was a serious sin, punishable by death in the Old Testament (Leviticus 24:10–16). The people took this matter so seriously that they would not speak the name of God at all. At the same time, it was rather easy for accusers to charge someone with blasphemy. It would be the official charge at Jesus' trial (Matthew 26:64–66) as well as the reason Stephen was stoned (Acts 6:11), even though in both these cases those accused were speaking only truth.

Verse 30 clarifies this a bit more. Mark tells us that Jesus' statement was made in response to the scribes saying that He had an evil spirit. Theirs was not a single act, but a habitual attitude that was influencing their actions. And it's noteworthy that the sin was committed by religious scholars and authorities, not laypersons.

3:31–35

AN EXPANDED DEFINITION OF FAMILY

As Jesus faces skeptics and doubters both within and outside His family, we see quite a difference in scale. Jesus' family members thought He was crazy, yet they weren't as off-base as the scribes.

Still, when His family members show up asking to see Him, He doesn't give them priority. It seems they didn't want to go inside and get Him personally, so they sent someone with a message that they were waiting for Him outside. Jesus' response (3:33–35) shows a shift in thinking. Jesus is now speaking of God's family, not His own human family unit.

This passage surely encouraged Mark's Gentile readers, as it does modern Christians. It is difficult to think of a more meaningful symbol than inclusion in the family of God. Jesus came to bring salvation to the world, not just to a single family unit or ethnic subgroup. As a result, every new day brings additional growth to the family of God.

Take It Home

Jesus redefined family, expanding it to include everyone who responds to His message and does God's will. Mark's account suggests that being part of God's family may require adjusting or even severing relationships with one's earthly family. Have you found this to be true at all? And how do you feel about being in God's family? Do you feel more like a full-fledged child with all the rights and privileges, or more like a distant cousin or ugly stepchild? What could you do to feel more at home in God's family?

MARK 4:1–25

THE PARABLE OF THE SOWER

Master of Parables 4:1–9
Why Parables? 4:10–12

The Real Meaning 4:13–20
Applying the Parable 4:21–25

Setting Up the Section

To this point, Mark has been providing a narrative account of Jesus' public ministry. Here, however, he inserts a series of Jesus' parables, the first being the Parable of the Sower. Mark's point is to announce the gospel of Jesus Christ and to help explain why Jesus' message will receive mixed reviews.

4:1–9

MASTER OF PARABLES

When we think of biblical parables, we tend to immediately think of Jesus. While parables can be found in the Old Testament and were used by other teachers, Jesus carefully employed this literary device. His parables weren't intended as entertainment; Jesus used them for a very specific reason, as Mark will explain.

The "lake" (NIV) where Jesus is teaching (4:1) is the Sea of Galilee. The miracle ministry of Jesus has become so popular that it has spawned a following of mass proportions. Because of the size of the crowd, Jesus teaches from a boat in the lake while the people stand ashore. But His teaching this day is about farming.

Jesus begins and ends the parable by telling His audience to listen thoughtfully (4:3, 9), indicating that the meaning of parables is not always self-evident. The Parable of the Sower is short, clear, and true to what is known about Palestinian agriculture. Unlike the modern method of planting, seeds were first sown and then plowed underground. The sower held a quantity of seed in an apron with one hand and used his other hand to broadcast it. Naturally, some seeds would fall on the hardened path through the field, some where the soil was too shallow, and some among thorns. (The stones and thistles that infest Palestinian fields to this day are legendary.)

Critical Observation

The one atypical element in the parable is the abundant harvest (4:8). Due to primitive agricultural techniques, an average harvest in ancient Palestine was probably no more than seven or eight times the amount of seed sown; a good harvest might yield ten times more. So the parable makes a significant point: To achieve so high a return, much of the seed needs to take root in good soil. Even as He was speaking this parable, Jesus' words were like the seed being scattered and taking root only in the hearts that were fertile soil—which turned out to be quite a small percentage in this case.

Even though most everyone can understand what Jesus is saying about farming, they can't comprehend what He really means by telling the parable.

4:10–12

WHY PARABLES?

Some may assume that Jesus used the simplicity of parables to clarify what He was saying, but that's not the case. After He tells the Parable of the Sower, His disciples immediately asked about its meaning. Before answering, Jesus tells them that the mystery of the kingdom of God will be revealed in the form of parables. The parables serve to reveal truth to those with spiritual insight, those who have been redeemed by placing their faith in Jesus. Indeed, many parables are set in the context of a confrontation between Jesus and the religious leaders of Israel. Jesus condemns the rebellious religious elite while initiating a new covenant with Israel, as promised in Jeremiah 31:31–34.

In addition to revealing truth to those capable of understanding, parables also *conceal* truth from the rebellious. Quoting Isaiah 6:9–10, Jesus reminds His listeners of a time when God, as a form of judgment, said He would not allow the people to hear the word of salvation. Their pride had drawn them away from Him, and He would allow them to experience the consequences. The same was true of those too arrogant or insensitive to comprehend God's truth contained in the parables. Martin Luther wrote that the use of Isaiah 6:9–10 by Jesus shows that "divine foreknowledge is referred to, that God conceals and reveals to whom He will and whom He had in mind from eternity" (*Complete Sermons of Martin Luther Vol. 1.2* [Grand Rapids: Baker Book House, 2000], p. 123).

Demystifying Mark

The parables are the means through which God provides two opposing works: revelation and concealment. In the revelation of the kingdom of God, His people are trained and instructed in the requirements of the kingdom. In the concealment of the kingdom, those who oppose God are prevented, as a form of punishment, from ever understanding the true nature and requirements of the kingdom. Unless one understands this dual purpose of the parables, there will be no proper interpretation, and therefore the clear and intended meaning of the parables will be lost.

4:13–20

THE REAL MEANING

Jesus' questions to His disciples are not meant to discourage them, but to force them to consider the real meaning of parables as well as the state of their hearts. If they don't provide "good soil" for the seed He is spreading, how can they ever understand what He is trying to teach?

Jesus' explanation of the parable provides surprising insight. The symbolism of the sower is not explained, but the context indicates he is Jesus. Seed is the Word of God. Soils are different kinds of hearers. Birds represent Satan. Thorns are the worries of life. No wonder Jesus tells everyone to pay close attention!

Jesus seems to say that there are those who can hear His message, respond for days, months, or even years, and still not have the gospel take root in their lives. But those who hear and respond will bear spiritual fruit, with varying yields.

4:21–25

APPLYING THE PARABLE

The Parable of the Sower sets the stage for the ministry of Jesus and the kingdom of God on earth. Jesus' follow-up statements make direct application of the parable to the lives of the disciples. It is very important to understand the application because it lays the groundwork for the work of the apostles and believers who would follow.

Jesus explains that He and His followers are providing light to the world (4:21), yet light serves little use if it is hidden. Their challenge would be to let the light of God shine brightly. As spiritual light is provided, the hidden mysteries of God would be revealed. Although Jesus is using parables to intentionally keep some of the mysteries of God hidden from those who resist His ministry, soon the truth will become clear and brought out into the open (4:22).

Jesus concludes with another warning to pay close attention to the Parable of the Sower, because the better His hearers understand the revelation of this mystery, the more opportunity they will have to proclaim it (4:24–25). As they respond to the teaching of Jesus, they will be given responsibility commiserate to their understanding. Verse 25 is frequently taken out of context and used to create unfounded financial formulas, but Jesus is speaking of comprehension and ministry. In what may be a veiled reference to Judas, Jesus concludes by warning that whoever does not understand these truths will lose his or her ministry.

Take It Home

The Parable of the Sower raises questions for every reader:

- Which of the soils best represents my responsiveness to the Word of God?
- Am I hard-hearted to the extent that it never sinks in to begin with?
- Was I eager to respond at one time, but now rootless and dry?
- Do I allow people and circumstances to capture all my attention, so that God's Word gets choked out?

MARK 4:26–34

MORE PARABLES ABOUT SEEDS

The Parable of the Growing Seed	4:26–29
The Parable of the Mustard Seed	4:30–34

Setting Up the Section

Mark follows Jesus' Parable of the Sower (4:1–25) with two more related parables about seeds. Both are short, yet each one provides a bit more information about the kingdom of God.

4:26–29

THE PARABLE OF THE GROWING SEED

The Parable of the Growing Seed is the only parable unique to Mark's Gospel. Like the Parable of the Sower, it presents a comprehensive picture of the coming of God's kingdom: sowing, growing, and harvesting. The emphasis, however, is on the growing stage. The opening statement (4:26) could be literally interpreted "The kingdom of God is as follows: It is like. . . "

The initial phase of the growing seed occurs when the sower scatters seed on the ground. In phase two the sower is present, but not active. He has planted the seed and left it to germinate, sprout, and grow. Meanwhile, he goes about his other daily duties. The soil ("the ground") produces grain, which develops to maturity in successive stages in a way the sower cannot understand. The growth occurs without visible cause, without the help of human intervention. It is God who works in the life-bearing seed that, when planted in good soil, grows stage by stage and produces grain.

The sower's ultimate interest is in phase three, the harvesting of the seed. When the grain is ripe, the sower immediately puts the sickle to it.

The point of this parable is that as the disciples work to "scatter the seed" (NIV) of the gospel, the ultimate results are the work of God. The sowers are not in charge of the hearts of the people, nor can they change others. All they can do is scatter the seed and trust God for the outcome. Followers of Jesus must understand that they do not cause the harvest; but they must spread the seed.

4:30–34

THE PARABLE OF THE MUSTARD SEED

Although an herb, the mustard plant begins as a tiny seed and can grow to heights of ten to twelve feet with a stalk three to four inches in diameter. It is clear that the mustard plant symbolizes the extreme contrast between the tiny beginning and ultimate result of the kingdom of God. Mark is writing his Gospel at a time near the beginning of the growth cycle when the kingdom might not have appeared very significant in contrast to other earthly kingdoms such as the Roman Empire. Yet this parable points to a much greater impact to come.

Critical Observation

The mustard seed was not literally the smallest seed in the world (though it may have been the smallest known in Palestine). However, it was used proverbially to indicate small size (much as we might refer to the head of a pin). Bible critics might point to Jesus' statement that the mustard seed is "the smallest of all seeds" (4:31 NLT) and declare that the Bible contains errors. But Jesus was merely using a popular idiom to better communicate with His listeners.

Some people misinterpret this parable, questioning whether the growth depicted is desirable and pointing out that birds are sometimes symbols of evil. They suggest that an abnormally large herb with its branches filled with birds represents an overgrown, apostate, institutional church. Yet such an interpretation is completely at odds with the two previous parables and as a description of "the kingdom of God" (4:30). The reference to the birds merely implies that just as birds inhabit a large tree, so, too, will people take rest and comfort in the great work of God that had such a humble beginning.

Mark concludes this section by pointing out that he is only recording a few of the parables that Jesus told (4:33). And he makes it clear that even though the crowds might have been confused by some of the things Jesus was saying in His parables, He later explained everything to the disciples when they were alone.

Take It Home

Jesus compares the growth of the kingdom of God to a seed that is planted and then grows on its own. Nothing people do can hasten its growth. In light of this teaching, how do you feel about the emphasis many churches put on growth and the tendency to measure success with numbers? Do you think Jesus was downplaying evangelism? If not, how do you think evangelism fits into what He is saying?

MARK 4:35–5:20

JESUS' ACTIONS VERIFY HIS TEACHINGS

Even the Wind and Waves Obey Him!	4:35–41
Helping a Wild Man	5:1–20

Setting Up the Section

Mark follows three parables about the kingdom of God (the Sower, the Growing Seed, and the Mustard Seed) with accounts of four miracles of Jesus. The miracles are signs that the kingdom of God is near, revealing the power of Jesus as the Son of God. It would take a long time for people to truly understand, but from the beginning, Jesus' works vindicated His words.

4:35–41

EVEN THE WIND AND WAVES OBEY HIM!

Most of the recorded miracles of Jesus were healings and exorcisms. This miracle, however, is important because it establishes Jesus' authority over nature just as His healings show His power over humanity. Jesus is the Lord of nature as much as He is Lord of individuals.

Jesus had been teaching in a boat (4:1). When He finished, He and the disciples decided to cross the Sea of Galilee and leave the crowd behind.

Critical Observation

The Sea of Galilee was—and still is—infamous for sudden squalls. Surrounded by mountains at most points, the waters swirl violently when a strong wind bears down. A storm can swell up with little advance warning.

After a long day of ministry, Jesus is tired and fell asleep. He continues sleeping even as a furious squall arises, nearly swamping the boat. Jesus' sound sleep demonstrates two things: (1) His humanity, as He felt fatigue just as humans would; (2) a confidence in God that allowed Him to rest as those around Him were panicking.

Finally the disciples wake Him, filled with fear (4:38). Remember that the group included a number of veteran fishermen, so this must have been quite a severe storm. The disciples rebuke Jesus for not caring about them. Jesus responds by rebuking the storm. (He had used very similar words to cast out an evil spirit on a previous occasion [1:25].)

The disciples should have been catching on by this point that Jesus was doing things only God could do. God's power to calm a storm is mentioned specifically in Psalm 107:29–30, so Jesus rightly questions the disciples on their faith. Their "terrified" response (4:41 NIV) reveals that they acknowledged an experiential glimpse into the real nature of Jesus. Their fear stemmed from a sudden understanding that they had met divine power in this teacher. They knew Jesus was a great man with great power, yet they never imagined *this* kind of power could exist.

They were astounded, but their faith remained weak. Mark will show his readers that the mystery of who Jesus is will continue to be an issue up to His death, resurrection, and beyond. It would take the resurrection of Jesus and the indwelling of the Holy Spirit to get His followers to see Him clearly.

5:1–20

HELPING A WILD MAN

After the brief but terrifying storm subsides, Jesus and the disciples continue sailing across the lake. No sooner do they get out of the boat than Jesus is encountered by a man with an evil spirit. Based on their locale, the possessed man is probably a Gentile.

Demystifying Mark

Ancient Greek manuscripts, translations, and quotations vary on the location of this passage. Most likely, Mark is referring to a known village on the eastern shore. The village has steep hills and cave-tombs about a mile to the south. But one thing is for sure: This event occurred in Gentile territory—the first of Mark's account set outside of Palestine.

The word translated "evil spirit" (5:2 NIV, NLT) literally means "unclean spirit" (KJV, NASB, NKJV, NRSV, ESV). The ancients believed that the caves where people were buried were dwelling places of demons. The description of the man (5:3–5) emphasizes the demonic destruction of his personality to the point of insanity and the ostracism and brutal treatment he had received from his townspeople.

The demon within the man recognizes Jesus (5:7) and is afraid. In contrast to the disciples' recent fear that was based on their ignorance, the demon's fear is a result of knowing with whom he is dealing.

The spirit gives his name as "Legion," which was a term used to describe a Roman force of 4,000 to 6,000 men. It is unclear whether the word in this sense refers to a proper name, an arrogant boast, or an attempt to avoid providing an actual name. The usual interpretation is that many demons actually possessed this man.

The demon(s) realize Jesus is in complete control of what is going to happen. Rather than being cast out of the area, they beg to move into a nearby herd of pigs. When Jesus grants them permission, the entire group of 2,000 pigs runs directly into the lake and drowns (5:13).

The man, now freed of his demonic tormentors, is most grateful. He begs to go with Jesus, an indication that he realizes Jesus is not only a miracle worker, but someone to be followed. Jesus denies his request but gives him a different mission—one that is assigned to every disciple (5:19).

The surrounding townspeople are not so happy, however. They have not only just lost a significant source of income, but they are afraid of Jesus. Because of their superstitions, they are terrified of anyone displaying so much power, so they beg Jesus to leave.

This account shows that, even as important as Jesus' miracles are in Mark's presentation of the ministry of Jesus, they do not always serve to prove who Jesus is or to compel faith. The primary response in this case was fear. Yet the wild man was widely known, and the personal testimony of his healing would have a dramatic effect in the area.

The Decapolis (5:20) was a loosely connected group of ten Gentile cities that had been set free from Jewish domination by the Roman general Pompey when he occupied Palestine in 63 BC. Mark probably saw the healed man as the first missionary to the Gentiles and a preview of the Gentile mission that flourished during the quarter century before the writing of his Gospel.

Take It Home

As Mark shows us, ignorance of who Jesus really is can create a response of fear. However, clear insight into who He is can as well. Which case do you think is true of more people you know today? Is the fear of God based on what they don't know about Him, or on what they do?

MARK 5:21–43

A PLANNED AND AN IMPROMPTU MIRACLE

A Helpless Father	5:21–24
A Desperate Woman	5:25–34
Hope in the Face of Death	5:35–43

Setting Up the Section

Mark has been presenting Jesus as the Son of God, and as such, the only way to salvation. He has just shown Jesus' power over nature (4:35–41) and over demons (5:1–20). He continues now by emphasizing Jesus' power over sickness and death.

Here is another example of Mark's sandwiching technique. In this case, he interposes the story of the woman with the bleeding disorder into the story of the healing of Jairus's daughter. Examples of Mark's sandwiching in the Gospel are 4:1–20; 5:21–43; 6:7–29; 11:12–25; 14:1–11; 14:53–72.

5:21–24

A HELPLESS FATHER

Jesus and the apostles have come back across the Sea of Galilee (5:21) after His healing of the demon-possessed man in Gentile territory. He is quite possibly back in Capernaum, and certainly among another Jewish crowd that knows His reputation and is eager to be around Him.

One who came with a specific request is a synagogue ruler named Jairus, but his request is not for himself. He knew of Jesus' reputation for laying hands on people to heal them, and his twelve-year-old daughter (5:42) is near death.

A synagogue ruler was an important and highly respected person. In some cases, Jesus faced strong opposition from leaders of synagogues (Luke 13:14), but this man shows surprising faith. What set Jairus apart from other leaders, and from the scribes and Pharisees in general, is that he believed Jesus could, and would, heal someone he loved.

Jairus implores Jesus to come heal his daughter, and Jesus starts off with him. As usual, a large crowd presses in on Jesus as He walks.

5:25–34

A DESPERATE WOMAN

One person in the crowd actually shouldn't be there: a woman with a twelve-year bleeding issue. Mark isn't specific as to her problem, but it was probably uterine bleeding, which would have made her ceremonially unclean. She would have been an outcast for twelve years, with people having no contact with her, and yet here she is among the crowd.

Her desperation is understandable. She had been to numerous doctors and had only gotten worse (5:26). She had in mind to quietly walk up to Jesus, touch His clothes, and be healed. And as soon as she touched Him, that's exactly what happened (5:28–29)! Keep in mind that Mark has just shown how Jesus' family rejected Him, His disciples did not fully understand who He was, and the Gentiles were afraid of Him. Yet this unidentified, unclean, and very sick woman trusts Him completely.

The miracle is extraordinary because it takes place without conscious effort on Jesus' part. As Jesus realizes that healing power has left His body, He asks who has touched Him (5:30). It must have seemed a crazy question to the disciples and most of the swarming crowd. Yet the woman knew what He meant and confesses, somewhat fearfully.

Jesus gently assures her. He offers her more than just physical healing. He gives her peace of mind and security that her faith was placed in the right person. She goes away healed, both physically and spiritually.

5:35–43

HOPE IN THE FACE OF DEATH

Just as the woman is leaving with fresh joy and peace, some messengers from Jairus's house are arriving to let him know it is too late, that his daughter has died. They assume Jesus' time would be better spent elsewhere (5:35). Jesus hears, but ignores them. He tells Jairus to "just believe" (5:36 NIV).

Upon arrival at Jairus's house, Jesus' comment about the girl not being dead but asleep (5:39) is met with scoffing laughter by the mourners. So He takes only the girl's parents along with Peter, James, and John into the girl's room with Him. This inner circle of disciples is singled out on other significant occasions as well (9:2; 14:33; etc.).

Consider that Jesus could have made a public display of bringing the girl back to life, silencing and shaming His critics. But it is a private moment, an incredible miracle to be witnessed only by those with considerable faith. At Jesus' command, the dead girl immediately stands up and walks (5:42).

Critical Observation

It was not unusual to have professional mourners at funerals to provide profuse commotion and wailing (5:39), although in this instance there might not have been time to procure them. The Jewish *Mishna* (completed about AD 220), quotes Rabbi Judah as saying that for a burial, even the poorest in Israel should hire two or more flutes and one weeping woman. A ruler of the synagogue, of course, was not likely a poor man and could probably afford professional mourners.

Jesus instructs the parents to feed the girl and not to tell anyone what He has done (5:43). He wants no publicity. Yet this healing—the resurrection of the dead—represents a crescendo of Jesus' ministry. Mark emphatically makes his point that Jesus is the Son of God, proven by His power over nature, evil spirits, disease, and even death.

Take It Home

Both of these miracles require an undistracted faith. Is your faith distracted by love of this world or fear that God's plan is not the best plan for your life? What might you do to remove the distractions that hinder your faith?

- How strong would you say your own faith in Jesus is at this point in your life?
- On a scale of 1 (least) to 10 (most), how would you rate it?
- What might you do to increase your faith?

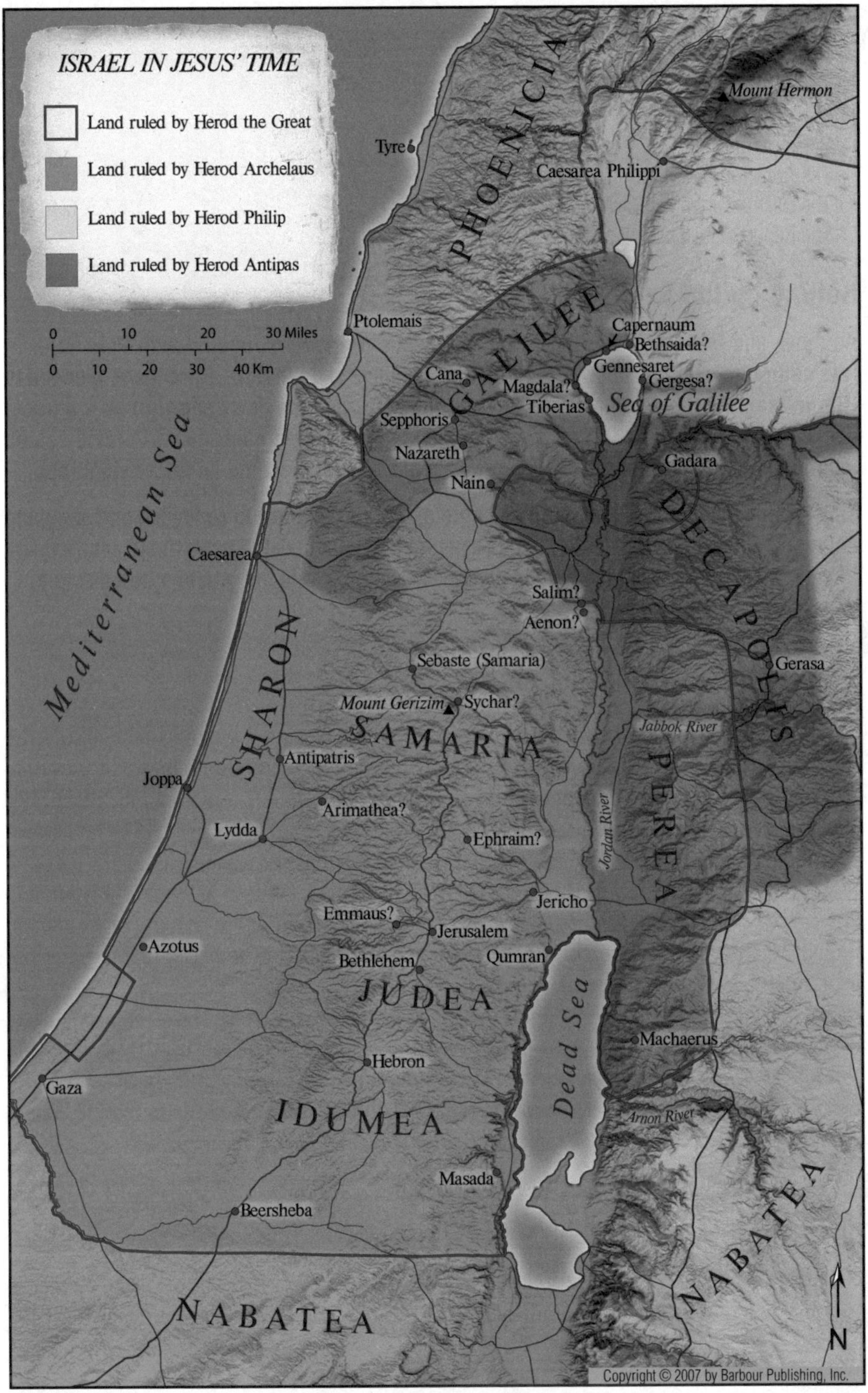
ISRAEL IN JESUS' TIME
Land ruled by Herod the Great
Land ruled by Herod Archelaus
Land ruled by Herod Philip
Land ruled by Herod Antipas
0 10 20 30 Miles
0 10 20 30 40 Km
PHOENICIA
Mount Hermon
Tyre
Caesarea Philippi
GALILEE
Ptolemais
Capernaum
Bethsaida?
Gennesaret
Gergesa?
Cana
Magdala?
Tiberias
Sea of Galilee
Sepphoris
Nazareth
Nain
Gadara
Mediterranean Sea
DECAPOLIS
Caesarea
Salim?
Aenon?
SHARON
Sebaste (Samaria)
Gerasa
Mount Gerizim
Sychar?
SAMARIA
Jabbok River
Antipatris
Joppa
PEREA
Jordan River
Arimathea?
Lydda
Ephraim?
Jericho
Emmaus?
Jerusalem
Azotus
Qumran
Bethlehem
JUDEA
Dead Sea
Machaerus
Hebron
Gaza
Arnon River
IDUMEA
Masada
Beersheba
NABATEA
NABATEA
N
Copyright © 2007 by Barbour Publishing, Inc.

MARK 6:1–30

REJECTION INCREASES

Rejection at Home	6:1–6
The Apostles Are Sent Out in Pairs	6:6–13
The Death of John the Baptist	6:14–29
The Report of the Disciples	6:30

Setting Up the Section

As more and more people who witnessed Jesus' ministry struggled with their faith, it was natural to expect a degree of rejection. We have seen that the Gentiles responded to Him in fear, the disciples are running hot and cold, and the Jews see Him as a miracle worker but are slow to respond in obedience and faith. This passage will provide some additional instances of rejection—a preview of what will become an increasing trend.

This section includes yet one more example of Mark's tendency to sandwich one story into another in order to make a point. In this case, both episodes—the news about John's death in the midst of the sending out of the disciples—demonstrate the role of a true disciple.

6:1–6

REJECTION AT HOME

In bringing a fearful father's daughter back to life and healing a woman who had suffered for twelve years (5:21–43), Jesus witnesses two examples of great faith followed by gratitude for what He has done. He then goes home to Nazareth (6:1), where things change drastically.

Because He is a well-known speaker and healer, Jesus is invited to speak at His hometown synagogue. A large crowd is there. The people are amazed at His teaching (6:2), but not in a positive way. Instead, they question His credentials. They knew Him as well as anyone and were aware that He had never studied with a rabbi. They consider Him nothing more than an ordinary craftsman—no different than His brothers and sisters, and no better than anyone else in Nazareth.

This is Mark's last reference to Jesus' teaching in a synagogue. Jesus knew the people were offended, so He quotes a popular proverb (6:4). In spite of all the acclaim He is receiving throughout Israel, He is utterly rejected in His hometown. As a result of the lack of faith, He heals only a few people and then moves on (6:5–6). In fact, there is so little faith that Jesus is *amazed* (6:6). They don't merely doubt Him; they aggressively reject Him.

6:6–13

THE APOSTLES ARE SENT OUT IN PAIRS

After such rejection in Nazareth, Jesus and the disciples start going from village to village. His emphasis during this time is on teaching. It is through His teaching that people hear the

Word of God, and through hearing the message of salvation that they can respond in faith (Romans 10:14–15).

At this time Jesus sends out the disciples to share the message He has been preaching. They travel in pairs, which was a common Jewish practice. Jesus gives them authority to speak for Him, and power over evil spirits.

Jesus' instructions (6:8–11) suggest the urgency of their mission and the necessity of trusting God for provisions. The bag they are prohibited from taking might refer to either a beggar's bag or a knapsack. The extra tunic probably is an outer garment often used as a blanket. This is a mission of faith in which the disciples will be dependent on God providing for them through the hospitality of their hosts.

The purpose of the injunction in verse 10 is to prevent the travelers from moving if they happen to find better accommodations in the same town. Yet they weren't expected to stay where they weren't welcome. In that case, the disciples were to move on.

Demystifying Mark

Jews returning to their homeland from other countries would remove the foreign dust from their shoes and clothing in order not to defile the land. Jesus adopted this symbolic action in the tradition of the ancient prophets to indicate first a warning and then judgment if rejection of the message and messengers persisted.

The six pairs of disciples go out with the same message of repentance (6:12) that had begun with John the Baptist (1:4) and Jesus (1:15). They heal the sick and drive out demons (6:13). Oil (usually olive oil) was often used medicinally, although here the anointing probably serves as a symbol of the presence, grace, and power of God.

6:14–29

THE DEATH OF JOHN THE BAPTIST

When Herod hears of the power of Jesus and His followers, he grows worried that John the Baptist has risen from the dead, so Mark provides us with the account of John's death at this point. It's also an early warning that the preaching of the gospel can be so offensive to some that it would cause those who proclaimed the truth to lose their lives.

Critical Observation

The Herod of this account was Herod Antipas, the tetrarch of Galilee and Perea from 4 BC to AD 39 (Luke 3:1). He should be distinguished from Herod the Great, his father, who was the Roman client-king of all Palestine from 40 BC to 4 BC and from Herod Agrippa I, who was client-king from AD 41–44. Herod is called "king" (Mark 6:14), but the title is a token of respect. Technically, Herod was only the regional governor.

It seems that Herod has fallen in love with his sister-in-law, Herodias, and has divorced his wife and convinced Herodias to divorce her husband in order to get married. John the Baptist has criticized the marriage, and Herodias wants to have him killed. Herod believes John to be a righteous and holy man (6:20), but he has him arrested and imprisoned to keep him out of the public eye. But even in prison, Herod likes to listen to John preach.

However, Herodias sees an opportunity at Herod's birthday banquet. She has her daughter (named Salome, according to the historian Josephus) perform a dance for the assembled group of "leading men of Galilee" (6:21 NIV, NASB, ESV). We can speculate that the dance was seductive and the dinner guests inebriated. At any rate, Herod promises the young dancer anything. At her mother's urging, she asks for the head of John the Baptist on a platter (6:25). With all eyes on him, Herod has little choice but to comply, even though he is distressed. John's disciples come to claim his body and bury him.

6:30

THE REPORT OF THE DISCIPLES

It's interesting that Mark inserts the story of John the Baptist between the sending out of the apostles and their report. No doubt they were encouraged and amazed to have experienced the power of Jesus in their individual ministries. But the death of John seems to foreshadow their report. Indeed, most of them would also eventually die martyrs' deaths.

Take It Home

Do you know anyone who has at some point attempted a purely faith-based ministry like the apostles did in this account? If so, what was the result? How do you think it would feel to go from town to town with no assets and no plans? What do you think Jesus was trying to teach His followers?

MARK 6:31–56

AN UNUSUAL STROLL AFTER AN UNUSUAL MEAL

The Miraculous Meal	6:31–44
The Miraculous Lake Crossing	6:45–56

Setting Up the Section

Mark has just reported on the death of John the Baptist and the sending out of the apostles. Now he returns to focus on Jesus. With two more amazing miracles, Jesus is still trying to teach His disciples who He really is, yet they are still slow to comprehend.

6:31–44

THE MIRACULOUS MEAL

After their return from ministering to the surrounding villages, the apostles are weary. They had hoped to retreat to a quiet place and rest (6:31), but the crowds won't allow it. Even when they leave on a boat, the people note the direction they are headed and run "from all the towns" (6:33 NIV, NASB, ESV) to get there ahead of them. But arriving to find large crowds doesn't upset Jesus. Instead, He sees their spiritual need, has compassion, and begins to teach them.

Demystifying Mark

"Sheep without a shepherd" (6:34 niv) is an Old Testament image of Israel without spiritual leadership (Numbers 27:17; 1 Kings 22:17; Ezekiel 34:5). Jesus is pictured as the Good Shepherd who feeds the new Israel since its current spiritual leadership was not doing the job. Jesus understood the excitement of the people as they listened to the Word of God and saw His power applied to the sick and hurting among them.

The word translated "compassion" is used in the New Testament only by or about Jesus. It is an emotion that compels action, not merely a feeling of pity. Jesus saw not only physical need but also spiritual lostness. So first He feeds the crowds with His teaching and then addresses their physical hunger.

The disciples see a problem arising, and try to head it off (6:35–36). But rather than sending the people home, Jesus tells the apostles to feed them. Having just returned from their mission, they should have had a sense of what God was capable of doing. But rather than using faith, they figure out how much it would cost to feed everyone and determine it can't be done!

Jesus sends them to collect whatever food they can find, which turns out to be meager indeed (6:38). The loaves are smaller and flatter than modern bread. The fish are dried and salted. And the headcount is 5,000 men (plus women and children).

The "green grass" (6:39) suggests springtime in Palestine, which would have placed this event sometime around Passover. And the terminology befits a Passover meal, as it does the Lord's Supper: "taking," "gave thanks," "broke," "gave" (6:41 NIV). Jesus miraculously provides not only enough food to fill everyone but also enough to collect baskets of leftovers (6:42–43). Parallels to this event include Elisha's feeding of a hundred men with twenty barley loaves and some grain (2 Kings 4:42–44) and the miraculous feeding of the people of Israel with manna in the desert (Exodus 16; Numbers 11).

6:45–56

THE MIRACULOUS LAKE CROSSING

The disciples were tired before this event, so afterward they must have been exhausted. Jesus has them get in a boat and head toward Bethsaida. He was going to spend a little more time with the people and then have a private time of prayer. From His prayer spot on the mountainside, Jesus can probably see His followers struggling to row against the wind.

Critical Observation

Mark used Roman standards of timekeeping in this passage. The Jews divided a night into three watches, the Romans four. The first watch was 6:00 p.m. to 9:00 p.m., the second 9:00 p.m. until midnight, the third midnight until 3:00 a.m., and the fourth between 3:00 a.m. and 6:00 a.m.

In the wee hours of the morning, Jesus walks across the lake, catching up with the disciples. The Old Testament spoke of God walking on water (Job 9:8; 38:16), and Jesus is proving it true. It is debated what is meant by, "He was about to pass by them" (6:48 NIV). Some suggest it means He was going to outpace them so they would acknowledge His greatness. More likely, He simply wanted to pass in view of the disciples so they would see Him.

They certainly see Him, and they become terrified (6:49–50), thinking He must be a ghost. Mark makes a somewhat harsh notation that the apostles' hearts were hardened and that they didn't really understand the miracle that Jesus had just performed with the loaves and fish (6:52). So when Jesus identifies Himself with "It is I" (6:50), perhaps it is a reflection of God's identification of Himself to Moses as "I am who I am" (Exodus 3:14).

The notation that the disciples were "greatly amazed" (6:51 NKJV) makes the point that they should have learned by now that nothing was beyond the power of Jesus, because the power of Jesus was the power of God.

In contrast to the developing faith of the disciples is the response of the crowds when the boat lands (6:53–56). What is not stated, but implied, is that their reaction to Jesus is faith-inspired. The "fringe of his cloak" (6:56 NASB) was probably the tassel that pious Jews wore in accordance with Numbers 15:38–41 and Deuteronomy 22:12. And the word translated "cured" can also be interpreted as "saved," indicating that Mark saw in physical healing a sign of spiritual healing as well.

Take It Home

One might think that the apostles would have the best insight into the true character of Jesus and what He was capable of doing. Yet in spite of everything they had seen to this point—healings, exorcisms, the calming of a storm, feeding the 5,000, and even a resurrection from the dead—they were still disturbed and amazed to see Him walking on water. Why do you think this was true? And do you think the same thing happens today? In spite of their personal experience, do believers still tend to place limits on what they feel God can or will do?

MARK 7:1–23

CLARIFYING SOME TWISTED LAWS

To Wash or Not to Wash 7:1–13
The Source of "Uncleanness" 7:14–23

Setting Up the Section

Mark has just described a phenomenal response to Jesus' healing ministry (6:54–56). The stir concerning Jesus has led to the hope—if not outright belief—that the Messiah had arrived. But the ruling religious authorities would never support anyone who did not believe exactly as they did. The things Jesus did were always within the law God had given Moses, yet they did not always conform to the numerous laws that had been tacked on over the centuries. Consequently, a perpetual state of conflict resulted.

7:1–13

TO WASH OR NOT TO WASH

This time the Pharisees' complaint is that Jesus' followers eat meals before washing their hands. The issue is not one of hygiene but of ritual purity and is an excellent case in point to describe how oral law had become much more stringent than what Moses had recorded. In the Old Testament, priests had been instructed to wash prior to certain ceremonies (Exodus 30:17–21; 40:12). But by the first century, the scribes and Pharisees had started washing before every meal and apparently expected everyone else to do so as well. In addition, they call for the washing of "cups, pitchers, and kettles" (7:4 NIV, NLT). Mark provides a parenthetical explanation of their habits (7:3–4).

The "tradition of the elders" (7:3) is a reference to the oral, scribal interpretation of the written, Mosaic law. These laws were later collected and recorded in the Mishna (ca. AD 220). The "elders" were scribes, Pharisees, leaders of synagogues, and revered persons in general.

In response to the Pharisees' query, Jesus quotes Isaiah 29:13 (Mark 7:6–7) to clarify that external observance of religious ceremony is no substitute for inward piety. Their insistence on external righteousness is not in accordance with the scriptures, and they are missing the whole point. It is they who were unclean and not Jesus' disciples.

Critical Observation

Not every Old Testament passage quoted in the New Testament is word for word. That's because the New Testament writers used the Septuagint—a Greek translation of the Hebrew Bible.

But Jesus doesn't stop with the Isaiah passage. He labels His critics as hypocrites (7:6) and accuses them of substituting human tradition for God-given law (7:8). He also gives a specific example to show how ludicrous their traditions have become.

Demystifying Mark

"Corban" (7:11) is the English transliteration of the Greek transliteration of a Hebrew word meaning "a gift dedicated to God." The Hebrew word occurs about 80 times in Leviticus, Numbers, and Ezekiel. Corban was an offering that involved an irrevocable vow of dedication to God. As a result, the thing offered to God could not be used for any other purpose. However, there was no prescribed way the offering had to be used, so what was supposedly a sacred vow to God had actually become a loophole to impede observance of other clear laws of God.

It seems that it had become common practice to make an offering of one's financial wealth and devote it to God by invoking a vow (Corban). It sounds quite spiritual and selfless. But what such an action actually meant was that the person would retain his wealth throughout his life, and it would go to the temple/priests when he died. If his parents needed assistance in their old age, the person could refuse to provide funds because they were set aside for God. This twisted tradition was just a way to sidestep the clear command to honor one's mother and father.

Notice the progression Jesus describes: First the Pharisees have "let go" of God's law (7:8 NIV), then have become experts at "setting aside" the commands of God (7:9 NASB), and eventually "making void" the word of God (7:13 NRSV, ESV) with their improper traditions. Furthermore, the rigidity of the Corban vow was not an isolated instance of scribal manipulation of the law, but only one of many instances. The Pharisees used their traditions for their own profit and glory—not God's.

7:14–23

THE SOURCE OF "UNCLEANNESS"

At this point Jesus broadens His conversation from just the Pharisees to include the surrounding crowd. The scriptures dealing with "clean" and "unclean" foods (Leviticus 11; Deuteronomy 14:1–21) had been creating questions and confusion that would continue to be addressed by the early church for a number of years. But here Jesus makes it clear that food is not the real issue. Impurity, He says, is not the result of failing to follow a ritual, but rather is the condition of an unredeemed and unregenerate heart.

(Depending on the manuscript used for translation, some Bibles omit 7:16. This statement is not found in the earliest and best manuscripts.)

Jesus' disciples seek further clarification of what He is saying (7:17). Jesus thinks they should comprehend Him by now, yet explains that the real problem with uncleanness is not the result of eating an unclean animal or eating approved food with unwashed hands. Such food goes through the body without affecting the state of the heart. The "heart" in the Bible is a symbol of the rational, intellectual, decision-making element in human beings rather than the emotional, affectionate element.

Jesus goes on to explain that the source of uncleanness is already inside a person. He provides specific examples: evil thoughts, sexual immorality, theft, murder, adultery, greed, malice, deceit, lewdness, envy, slander, arrogance and folly (7:21–22). His point is that uncleanness is moral rather than ritual.

At this point in his Gospel (7:19), Mark inserts a parenthetical comment that Jesus' statements are a declaration that all foods are from then on considered "clean." After Jesus' resurrection, Peter will soon receive a confirmation of this new concept (Acts 10:9–23).

Take It Home

The religious segment of society had gotten off track in Jesus' time. By trying so hard to adhere to rules and laws, the religious had gone astray. Spiritual laws had been stretched so far that they became a burden for people. Legalism impeded the freedom God intended for His people—and perhaps it still does. Do you see similar problems in the church today? In your own life, do you find following God to be something of a burden, or is it a freeing experience?

MARK 7:24–37

OVERWHELMED WITH AMAZEMENT

Crumbs Are Enough 7:24–30
Deaf and Speechless No More 7:31–37

Setting Up the Section

After Jesus' debate with the religious leaders over the issue of "clean" versus "unclean," Mark follows with two accounts of miracles in Gentile territory. Jesus is teaching that purity has more to do with the condition of one's heart than the adherence to legal rules and ceremonies. This concept will become clearer as a ministry to the Gentiles is initiated.

7:24–30

CRUMBS ARE ENOUGH

Tyre was a city on the Phoenician coast about thirty-five miles northwest of the Sea of Galilee. No explanation is provided for why Jesus goes there, other than perhaps to attempt to escape the crowds and be alone for a while. If that is His intent, it doesn't work (7:24).

A woman finds out Jesus is in the area and rushes to ask Him to heal her daughter who is possessed by an evil spirit. Prostration (7:25) was a sign of both grief and reverence. By falling at His feet, the woman is showing the utmost respect for Jesus.

This woman was from Syrian Phoenicia, not to be confused with Libyan or Carthagenian Phoenicia, which was located in North Africa. Phoenicia (modern Lebanon) was part of the Roman province of Syria. It was Gentile territory. That fact, coupled with the condition of her daughter, would indicate an emphatic state of ritual uncleanness. Still, the woman approaches Jesus with a request.

Critical Observation

Jews often used the word *dogs* to refer to Gentiles, and even though it seems out of character for Jesus to have done so, He almost certainly used it in this way (7:27). The harshness of the statement is softened somewhat by the use of the diminutive form that could indicate "puppies" or "house pets." In context, Jesus' comment was not an insult, but a comparative statement to say that the Jews, for a while, would take precedence over the Gentiles. Paul later echoed this same sentiment (Romans 1:16). And perhaps Jesus' apparent harshness in this case was to test the woman's faith.

When Jesus challenges her "right" to His attention, she responds with intelligence and determination. She does not deny the precedence of Israel, but also suggests that the Gentiles can be included as well. Even "dogs" get scraps under the dinner table, she says, indicating that Jesus' willingness to perform a miracle for her daughter will not in any way diminish the ministry He is doing among the Jews.

Although this account says nothing about the woman's faith, it is certainly implied in Jesus' statement. Jesus responds to her and grants her request. When she gets home, she finds her daughter well, with the demon gone (7:30).

7:31–37

DEAF AND SPEECHLESS NO MORE

Mark describes Jesus as traveling from Tyre to Sidon and then to the Sea of Galilee and the region of the Decapolis (7:31). This would be like going from Chicago to Dallas via Minneapolis. We can speculate that since Jesus has been hoping to escape the crowds (7:24), He may have chosen a circuitous route. He is still beyond Israelite territory in the lands of the Gentiles.

A group brings a deaf and mute man to Jesus (7:32), but He takes the man aside, away from the crowd. Jesus is going to heal the man, but doesn't want the crowds to misinterpret the miracle. The miracle will be a sign authenticating Him as being the Messiah, not an indication that the earthly kingdom of God had arrived in its fullness where everyone could expect to walk around in perfect bodies.

Demystifying Mark

Ancient healing practices included touching a person, using saliva, uttering deep groans—all of which Jesus did in this account. However, this in no way suggests that Mark invented the details to conform to the usual practice. Because Jesus could not communicate with the man through ordinary methods (speech and hearing), it would be natural for Him to express His concern through touch.

Jesus first opens the man's ears. Mark provides us the interpretation of the Aramaic word *Ephphatha* (7:34). Only after his ears are "opened" is he able to speak. This miracle illustrates a running theme in Mark: Only those who have ears to hear can speak with faith.

After enabling the man to speak clearly, Jesus commanded him and his friends not to tell anyone (7:36). But who could blame this no-longer-mute man for telling others what had happened to him? The witnesses were "overwhelmed with amazement" (7:37 NIV), and the miracle could not be concealed. Mark quotes the people who said, "He has done everything well," (ESV) and "He even makes the deaf hear and the mute speak" (NIV, ESV). These are poetic references to the messianic age (based on Genesis 1:31 and Isaiah 35:5-6). Jesus' admonition to the people to keep quiet is another example of what some refer to as the Messianic Secret. Jesus did not want people talking about His miracles—He did not want His miracles to be seen as the central piece of His ministry. Jesus' miracles were only meant to confirm that He was who He said that He was. Until the cross, the miracles could not be placed within their proper context.

Take It Home

The response of the crowds to the miracles and ministry of Jesus was that they were overwhelmed with amazement (7:37). When is the last time you can remember having a similar response to a work of God in the world or in your life? What might you need to do to be more aware of God's work in life and in the world? Try keeping a record of prayer requests and answers to prayers for one year. How would that help you become more aware of God's work in the world?

MARK 8:1–26

REPEAT PERFORMANCES

Another Feeding of the Masses	8:1–13
The Problem with Yeast	8:14–21
A Miracle in Stages	8:22–26

Setting Up the Section

Mark 8 includes events similar to those he's already recorded. Mark wanted the reader to see and understand that Jesus was more than a good teacher and was indeed the Lord of the universe. As the disciples witnessed repetition of His miracles, this truth was being reinforced in their lives.

8:1–13

ANOTHER FEEDING OF THE MASSES

Jesus and His disciples are still in the region of the Decapolis, a group of cities populated mainly by Gentiles. Crowd after crowd forms to see and hear Him. In this case, a group has been with Him for three days (8:2). Mark doesn't even mention whether Jesus is teaching or healing. Instead, he moves right to the compassion Jesus feels for the people, who are surely hungry after such a long time.

It is hard for those in the modern western world to perceive a time when food was not readily available, although the same conditions exist in many places outside the western world today. There was a very real danger of collapsing from hunger and exhaustion on the way home, and Jesus wasn't willing to send everyone away without a meal.

The disciples are woefully shortsighted. As soon as Jesus expresses the desire to feed the crowd, they immediately respond with the impossibility of finding enough bread "in this remote place" (8:4 NIV). Lest we forget, they had not so long ago witnessed Jesus feeding a larger crowd with less food (6:30–44). It seems that even though the disciples have witnessed a great number of Jesus' miracles, they are still perceiving them as one-time events rather than seeing Jesus as the divine Son of God.

Jesus instructs the people to sit down, and He gives thanks for the seven loaves and few small fish that are available (8:5–7). He is about to multiply the food, but He does so out of a thankful heart for the provision of His heavenly Father.

The word used to indicate a basket here (8:8) is not the same as the one used previously (6:43). This time the reference is to a large basket made of wicker or rope, used for carrying provisions. So the seven basketfuls of leftovers in this account may well have contained more than the twelve basketfuls in the previous miracle.

The exact location of Dalmanutha (8:10) is not known. A cave in the area called Talmanutha may indicate where Jesus goes with His disciples.

The "sign" the Pharisees request there (8:11) is not another healing, exorcism, or feeding. They want to see some kind of apocalyptic manifestation (the sun disappearing, angels appearing, or some similar sign) that will prove beyond all doubt that Jesus has God's approval. Jesus' response (8:12) is likely a sigh of anger because He knows they aren't sincere in their request—they only want to trip Him up and lessen His influence on the crowds. Jesus did not perform miracles to convince the hard-hearted; He used them to cure those in need and to show compassion on those hurt by sin.

Mark almost certainly sees an indication of Jesus' displeasure toward the Pharisees in His departure (8:13) and perhaps even a symbolic picture of the rejection of Judaism as the divinely approved religion.

8:14–21

THE PROBLEM WITH YEAST

As Jesus and the disciples go back across the sea, He warns them to beware of the "yeast" (or "leaven") of the Pharisees and Herod (8:15). Most references to yeast or leaven in the New Testament almost always are symbolic references to evil. (Matthew 13:33 is one exception.) Just as a little yeast changes the complete nature of dough, so, too, a slight influence of pharisaical teachings could corrupt the truth of the gospel.

In spite of everything the disciples have seen Jesus do, they are coming dangerously close to unbelief. Even in response to Jesus' comment, they misunderstand and think He is speaking about their shortage of bread. The disciples no doubt are aware of the evil influence of Herod, but Jesus is saying the evil of the Pharisees is just as bad. He chides those closest to Him for still being hard-hearted and failing to see and hear all He has been doing.

Critical Observation

Some people speculate that Jesus may have only performed one great miracle of feeding the masses, which is reported more than once. But in His reasoning with the disciples (8:17–21), He speaks clearly of two separate events.

Jesus' references to eyes that fail to see and ears that fail to hear are reminiscent of Old Testament judgment passages such as Isaiah 6, Jeremiah 5:21, and Ezekiel 12:2. The disciples, like the people of ancient Israel, are failing to comprehend God's presence. In fact, at this point the unbelief of the disciples is bordering on that of Jesus' enemies!

8:22–26

A MIRACLE IN STAGES

This is the one time when Jesus conducts a healing that requires additional attention. Because of where it is in the narrative, it can be considered an object lesson—a physical demonstration of the spiritual condition of Jesus' disciples.

Some people of Bethsaida ask Jesus to heal a blind man. Jesus applies saliva to the man's eyes, lays His hands on him, and asks what he saw (8:23). The man's vision has improved because he can see the shapes of people, but they look "like trees walking around" (8:24 niv, nlt). Jesus again places His hands on the man, and this time the man can see clearly. Similarly, although the disciples' spiritual "vision" is not yet 20/20, they will eventually come to see clearly who Jesus was.

Take It Home

It's easy to be critical of the disciples who, even after seeing Jesus feed a crowd of at least 5,000 people, were helpless when He gave them the opportunity to feed a smaller crowd. Yet perhaps we do no better. Do you know anyone who has had an encounter with Jesus where they came face-to-face with His greatness, and then went on to live as if it were a one-time event? Or can you recall a recent, seemingly impossible event where you were quick to panic rather than call on the God for whom nothing is impossible?

MARK 8:27–9:1

THE BEGINNING OF THE END

The Great Confession	8:27–30
Suffering and Death	8:31–33
Humility and Sacrifice	8:34–9:1

Setting Up the Section

This section of Mark records a significant transition. To this point, Jesus' disciples have witnessed (and even initiated) a number of miracles. They have not only heard Jesus teach, but have also been privy to His interpretation of parables and other private instruction. Yet Jesus has repeatedly pointed out their inability to comprehend exactly who He was and what He was doing. They haven't acted in faith when given the opportunity. But here they begin to understand. As they do, Jesus reveals more of what they can expect ahead of them.

8:27–30

THE GREAT CONFESSION

It was common practice in rabbinic circles for students to ask questions and have the teacher provide the answers. But Jesus would frequently pose a question, as in this case (8:27), and see what his students had to say. This was an essential question to help the disciples solidify who Jesus is, and this was one time when they come up with the correct answer.

Critical Observation

Caesarea Philippi (8:27) was a rebuilt, enlarged version of the ancient city of Paneas, the site of a grotto dedicated to the god Pan. When Herod the Great acquired the territory, he built a temple in Paneas and dedicated it to the emperor Augustus. His successor, Philip the tetrarch, renamed the city for Augustus (Caesar) and for himself. Another city named Caesarea was built on the Mediterranean Sea, but Caesarea Philippi was located in a beautiful setting at the foot of Mt. Hermon next to some gushing springs that were one of the sources of the Jordan River.

A number of popular opinions were being expressed about who Jesus was (8:28; 6:14–16), as had been the case with John the Baptist. While such beliefs expressed a degree of respect and acclaim for Jesus, they were still inadequate. So Jesus goes from the popular opinion to personal opinion by asking His disciples directly: "But what about you? . . .Who do you say I am?" (8:29 niv).

The answer would reveal a lot in regard to the disciples' spiritual condition. It is not necessary to understand everything about what one believes. For example, a person can believe that a plane can fly and take a cross-country flight without fully understanding the mechanics involved. Similarly, someone can believe Jesus is the Messiah without comprehending all the "hows" involved.

Peter acts as the spokesman for the group, so his confession is as much theirs as it is his. And he affirms their belief that Jesus is "the Christ" (8:29). The term *Christ* has not been used in Mark since the opening verse, so it is especially noteworthy here. Peter's confession of Jesus as the Christ (or Messiah or Anointed One) went beyond that of popular opinion.

Yet we also discover that the disciples still have much to learn. They had a typical Jewish understanding of "the Christ" as a military conqueror who would free them from foreign domination (Acts 1:6). They aren't ready to spread the word about Jesus, so He warns them not to tell anyone (8:30).

8:31–33

SUFFERING AND DEATH

Up to this point Jesus had been revealing the Messiah's power and authority. Here, He begins to reveal His suffering role, clarifying for His followers what was involved in God's plan for the Messiah. It would involve not only suffering at the hands of others, but ultimately His death as well.

Demystifying Mark

We find three predictions of Jesus' death in the middle of Mark's Gospel: 8:31–32; 9:31; and 10:33–34. Clearly, Jesus foresaw His death and resurrection. It was planned, and no mistake or oversight. But because His role as Messiah/Christ was not what people had been expecting, they were slow to catch on to what He was teaching about having to suffer and die.

Jesus' teachings about His death are specific. He makes it clear that it is God's will, and that it will be at the hands of the Jewish leadership. The very nation that brought forth the Messiah will endorse His execution. Yet death will not be the end; "after three days" He will rise again (8:31).

But even after Peter's bold confession, he doesn't want to hear what Jesus is saying about suffering. He is envisioning a victory without suffering, and rebukes Jesus. But Jesus returns the rebuke. His comment to "Get thee behind me" (8:33 kjv) is commonly interpreted as a command for Peter to get out of sight and stop tempting Him. What Peter might plan was not what God had planned, as Jesus goes on to explain.

8:34–9:1

HUMILITY AND SACRIFICE

Not only will Jesus suffer, but so will His followers. To announce this new concept, Jesus calls the crowd to hear, along with His disciples.

To deny oneself (8:34) is not a call to asceticism, self-rejection, or self-hatred. Rather, it is to replace the desires of self with the will of God, to set aside all personal rights and live for the glory of God and the mission of extending His kingdom.

Denial of self might indeed involve taking up a cross, which would have had a much more severe implication in the first century. Many of Jesus' early followers literally died by crucifixion. Today the phrase is more symbolic, though it should never be cheapened by use in reference to minor irritations or common burdens.

Jesus challenges His listeners to think of long-term effects of their daily choices (8:34–37). Everyone either lives for self or lives for God. While living for self will have certain benefits, none come close to eternal life with a loving God.

Living for Jesus includes speaking up for Him, even when persecuted by a wicked and adulterous generation (8:38). But on the positive side, Jesus makes a promise to "some who are standing here" (9:1 NIV). What does Jesus mean that some will "not taste death before they see the kingdom of God come with power" (NIV)? The answer comes in the next section of Mark (9:2–13).

Take It Home

Peter's confession at Caesarea Philippi was a special moment in his relationship with Jesus (although a bit short-lived). Jesus' closest followers should have a different perspective on Him than the rest of the general population. If Jesus were to ask the same questions today, how would you respond? Who do people say He is? And how about you? Who do you say He is?

MARK 9:2–29

THE UNIQUENESS OF THE CHRIST

Jesus' Transfiguration 9:2–13
A Difficult Exorcism 9:14–29

Setting Up the Section

Context is always important in Mark's Gospel. In the previous passage Jesus has been quite frank about His impending death. Yet from the beginning of his writing, Mark's goal has been to show that Jesus is the Son of God, and death would not be the end. Ultimately, Jesus would be glorified, and we see a preview of that in this section.

9:2–13

JESUS' TRANSFIGURATION

The reference to six days (9:2) is significant. Jesus has revealed to His disciples that He will soon suffer and die, and He challenges the crowds to deny themselves, take up a cross, and follow Him. Yet He also promises that some of those present will not die before they witnessed "the kingdom of God come with power" (9:1 NIV, KJV).

Only six days later, three of those people—Peter, James, and John—are invited to climb a high mountain with Jesus. There He is "transfigured" in their presence. His clothes become supernaturally white, and Moses and Elijah appear and talk with Him.

Demystifying Mark

The "high mountain" referred to in verse 2 is traditionally thought to be Mt. Tabor in lower Galilee. Though only 1,929 feet above sea level, it is compared in the Old Testament to both Mt. Hermon (Psalm 89:12) and Mt. Carmel (Jeremiah 46:18). Mt. Tabor was beautiful, appealing, and convenient for pilgrims. Biblical references to a "high mountain" often indicate places of revelation, which was certainly true in this case.

Transfiguration refers to a radical change in form or appearance. In this account it was a physical change, as Jesus' appearance is temporarily transformed from that of a human being to a divine being in all His glory. In other places where the word is used, it refers to a dramatic moral transformation from sinner to saint (Romans 12:2; 2 Corinthians 3:18).

The Greek text implies that the garment of Jesus becomes "intensely white" (9:3 ESV). The brightness recalls the shekinah glory of God in the Old Testament—a glory beyond physical equal on earth.

Moses and Elijah (9:4) represent the law and the prophets. Jesus was the fulfillment of the ancient scriptures. Christianity would not be a new religion, nor a correction of Judaism. Rather, it is the fulfillment of what had been proclaimed through the Old Testament writings.

Peter isn't always presented well in this account, largely due to fear (9:6). First, on such a significant occasion, he addresses Jesus as "Rabbi," a less flattering title than Lord or Master. Then he asks to erect three "shelters" (9:5 niv). What was likely intended as a tribute was actually something of a put-down because he was placing Jesus on the same level as Moses and Elijah—who were great men, to be sure, but only men. Peter wanted to capture and preserve the moment, but doing so would have short-circuited the cross. The transfiguration was just a *preview* of Jesus' glory. His true glory would come after, and as a result of, the completion of His mission by dying on the cross.

Critical Observation

The "shelters" Peter wanted to construct were probably similar to those used to commemorate the Feast of Tabernacles. During such times the Israelites would leave their homes to live in "booths" as a reminder of God's deliverance from Egypt (Leviticus 23:39–43; Hosea 12:9).

Even though Peter says and does the wrong thing in the presence of God's glory, we see the mercy of God in that there is no punishment or recrimination for his shortcoming. It *was* a lot to take in. Jesus is transfigured into a state of glory. A cloud envelops the group. A voice from the cloud declares that Jesus is the Son of God and instructs the disciples to listen to Him. No wonder Peter, James, and John are scared.

Then, abruptly, the event is over. The three disciples are alone again with Jesus. As they descend, Jesus is again discussing His death with them, instructing them not to tell anyone what they had just witnessed until He has risen from the dead (9:9). This is the last time Jesus will tell people not to relate what they had seen, and the only time He includes a time limit. But from this instance, we can infer that the reason He had prohibited people from talking (1:43–45; 7:36) was that the magnitude of His miracles could only be fully understood in the context of His death and resurrection. Still, the disciples have little idea what He means (9:10).

They are also confused about the prophecies that Elijah must come prior to the Messiah (9:11). They had just seen Elijah—was that what the prophecies meant? Or is all Jesus' talk of rising from the dead a reference to Elijah?

Jesus explains that Elijah had already come, meaning John the Baptist (Matthew17:10–13). The prophesied suffering and death would be the burden of the Messiah, not Elijah.

9:14–29

A DIFFICULT EXORCISM

While the three disciples with Jesus are struggling to understand what He is trying to teach them, the nine they left behind are having troubles of their own. A man has brought his demon-possessed son for healing, and they are unable to cast out the spirit. A large crowd has gathered as the teachers of the law argue with the disciples.

The disciples had previously been able to exorcise demons (6:13), and apparently assumed they could do so whenever they wished. But in this case they lack faith. Spiritual power is not a resource that, once possessed, will always be available. It must be maintained and renewed.

Meanwhile, the young man with the spirit is in terrible shape (9:18, 20–22). As Jesus approaches, the evil spirit responds by throwing the youngster into a convulsion. The father feels helpless, and his faith is weak. But Jesus affirms that all things are possible to whomever believes. The father has wisely placed what faith he has in Jesus, so Jesus casts out the demon (9:25–26). The result is that the boy appears dead for a short time, until Jesus takes his hand and helps him up.

The disciples are frustrated and confused about not being able to cast out the demon on their own. While Jesus has spoken about faith on numerous occasions, here He adds the importance of prayer as well (9:29). The two go hand in hand. Prayer is the avenue to faith. The power the disciples lacked could come only from God, and therefore was available only through faith and prayer.

Take It Home

We can take comfort in seeing how long it took the disciples—those who spent the most time in direct contact with Jesus—to understand what He was trying to teach them. Similarly we can rest assured that God is patient and compassionate. We do not have to have everything figured out to be in a relationship with Jesus. What are some of the areas of spiritual life that you tend to struggle with? As you struggle, how strong is your faith? As you struggle, how distracted is your faith? Do you bolster your faith with prayer, scripture, Bible teaching, and Christian fellowship? How do those disciplines help create an undistracted faith?

MARK 9:30–50

GREATNESS: AN EXAMPLE AND SOME OBSTACLES

A Model of Greatness 9:30–37
Teamwork or Competition? 9:38–41
A Strong Warning against Offenses 9:42–50

Setting Up the Section

At this point, Mark indicates that Jesus' public ministry in Galilee is over. This trip through Galilee will be the first leg of His journey to Jerusalem and the cross.

9:30–37

A MODEL OF GREATNESS

Jesus is again seeking privacy for Himself and His disciples, but this time it is not due to danger from Herod (6:14) or the teachers of the law (9:14). Rather, He wants to continue to instruct His disciples about His upcoming betrayal, death, and resurrection. The word *betrayed* (9:31) means "given over" or "handed over." The same word is used to refer to Judas' betrayal of Jesus as well as the fate of the Old Testament prophets, John the Baptist, and eventually Jesus' disciples. Some think the "handing over" in this case was God's delivering His Son over to sinful men to be a sacrifice for sins

Jesus' suffering and death would be the result of a friend's action. Yet Jesus was well aware of what was about to happen. His death was no mistake. It was part of the plan of God, the defining characteristic of His life. And His resurrection would prove that He is both the Son of God and the Messiah.

Mark again emphasizes the dullness of the disciples (9:32). By this time, they are even embarrassed to ask Jesus to explain what He means. Jesus knows their minds are on less noble things. When He asks what they are discussing, they won't respond. But Mark informs us that they are arguing about which of them is the greatest (9:34).

They have come to a house in Capernaum (possibly Peter's and Andrew's home previously mentioned in 1:29), so Jesus sits them down for a serious talk. Perhaps the disciples' debate on greatness was a result of three of them being chosen to accompany Jesus during His transfiguration (9:2–8). They believed Jesus was getting ready to establish an earthly kingdom (Acts 1:6) and were probably seeking key positions within that government. But Jesus quickly corrects their mistaken thinking. His use of a small child (9:36–37) is an object lesson to reinforce what He is saying. To welcome (9:37) such a person is a way of receiving both God and Jesus. Greatness in His kingdom consists not of position, but of ministry.

Critical Observation

In first-century society, the roles of both children and servants were considered lowly. Jesus elevated the role of the servant to the primary position in His kingdom. And He used a child as an example of someone whom His followers should care for, if indeed they cared for Him.

9:38–41

TEAMWORK OR COMPETITION?

The disciples were accustomed to thinking of spiritual leadership in terms of exclusivity. The scribes and Pharisees, for example, were exclusive groups. So when the disciples come upon someone else driving out evil spirits in the name of Jesus, they instruct him to stop. And they tell Jesus, thinking He would be pleased.

But Jesus makes it clear that anyone who does anything sincerely "in My name" is to be accepted as an ally. Jesus is beginning to promote a mind-set of acceptance rather than rejection.

Jesus' reference to "a cup of water" has come to be viewed as a symbolic act of hospitality. Yet in the semiarid climate of the Middle East, the act can just as rightly be interpreted literally. And Jesus quickly shifts the emphasis from the actions of one stranger to include "you" and "anyone" (9:41). While we have our own support groups, we should not be surprised to find people active for the kingdom of God whom we do not know. And perhaps we should be much slower to criticize than were Jesus' disciples.

9:42–50

A STRONG WARNING AGAINST OFFENSES

"One of these little ones" may refer to the child Jesus is holding (9:36) or perhaps to new believers who are spiritually immature and weak. The word translated "millstone" (9:42) refers to a large stone that required a donkey to turn it (as opposed to a smaller stone that women sometimes used).

Jesus makes a subtle shift here, moving from actions that may cause someone else to sin to those that might allow oneself to sin. He uses hyperbole and metaphor (9:43–48) that should not be taken literally. Yet because of the emphasis He places on these instructions, neither should they be ignored. Followers of Jesus must not only watch over others; they must watch over themselves as well.

Believers should do away with harmful habits that endanger spiritual life as completely as a surgeon amputates a limb that endangers the rest of the body. Jesus speaks of hell as a very real place of very real torment, and something to be avoided at any cost.

Demystifying Mark

The word translated "hell" (9:43, 45, 47) is *gehenna*, a Greek transliteration of two Hebrew words meaning "valley of Hinnom." The site was a deep valley on the south and west side of Jerusalem. It had once been a place for child sacrifice to the god Molech, and certain Israelites seem to have adopted the practice during periods of spiritual decline (2 Kings 23:10; Jeremiah 7:31; 32:35). Later it became the garbage and sewage dump of Jerusalem and a symbol of the place of punishment because worms and fires were so closely associated with the location.

"Salted with fire" (9:49) is an unusual phrase, particularly in this context. Jesus has just mentioned *fire* in a sense of judgment and punishment (9:43, 48). Here, however, both fire and salt are symbols of refinement and purification. Jesus has been talking about His own suffering and death (9:31). Here He expands the possibility of persecution to everyone who follows Him.

In conclusion, Jesus teaches that the "salt" of the earth (believers) must not lose what makes it distinctive—its saltiness. The salt gathered from the Dead Sea contained so many impurities that much of it was essentially worthless for providing flavor or preserving foods. Pure salt, however, cannot lose its saltiness.

Jesus is saying that believers must strive to remain salty by welcoming all people, protecting the weak, acknowledging fellow believers, and watching out for their own souls. Much of this would occur in the context of suffering, but truly "salty" believers would not lose their influence.

Take It Home

Jesus' teachings about greatness were not what His disciples were expecting to hear. Indeed, they still sound strange in modern culture. Can you think of any examples of someone attempting to be "first" by becoming the very "last," and a servant to all? And what do you think are the characteristics of a little child that Jesus wanted the surrounding group of adults to consider?

MARK 10:1–31

THE HEART OF THE MATTER

Divorce: A Touchy Subject	10:1–12
Little Children: A Model for Us All	10:13–16
The One Who Got Away	10:17–31

Setting Up the Section

Every story in Mark 10 deals with the heart of a person (or group) who comes into contact with Jesus. Some hearts are filled with arrogance and self-interest, while others contain childlike faith and eagerness to serve God and His kingdom. This passage (Mark 10:1–31) covers three stories; the following passage (10:32–52) will examine two more.

10:1–12

DIVORCE: A TOUCHY SUBJECT

By this time, it seems that everywhere Jesus went He was the target of the Pharisees and other religious leaders. On this occasion, they "test" Him (10:2) on the topic of divorce. The matter is of extreme interest to the people in the crowd. Herod Antipas and his wife (Herodias) had both gotten divorced to marry each other. (John the Baptist had died for publicly pointing this out [6:17–29]). In addition, two prominent rabbis of the time expressed very different opinions. Therefore, much debate takes place to determine what constituted justifiable grounds for divorce, according to the scriptures.

Demystifying Mark

To better understand the test the Pharisees were giving Jesus, it helps to know that His peers would have been exposed to the teachings of Rabbi Hillel and Rabbi Shammai, two noted scholars born a generation or so before Christ. Both had great wisdom, though they disagreed on a great many topics. For example, after both rabbis had studied Deuteronomy 24:1, the conservative school of Shammai ruled that "something about her that he doesn't like" meant adultery. The liberal school of Hillel, however, claimed that a man could divorce his wife for *anything* that displeased him, even burning a meal. If Jesus had sided with either of these men's teachings on divorce, He might well have lost the following of all those who supported the other.

Jesus is in the territory of Herod, so perhaps His questioners hope to get Him to say something that will incur Herod's displeasure, as John the Baptist had done. But Jesus counters their question with one of His own (10:3), which sends them back to their scriptures. He then explains that Moses wasn't by any means promoting divorce, yet had allowed for it in extreme cases. It was God's intention for marriage to last a lifetime, yet He knew that people's "hearts were hard" (10:5 niv) and had created a contingency plan.

The response of Jesus' critics is not noted. But Jesus goes into even greater detail when alone with His disciples. His comments (10:10–12) are quite contrary to the traditions of Judaism at that time. According to Jewish law, a wife could commit adultery by having relations with another man; a man (single or married) could commit adultery against another man by having relations with that man's wife. But a husband could not be charged with adultery against his own wife by being unfaithful to her. By insisting that a husband can commit adultery against his own wife, Jesus greatly elevates the status of wives and women in general.

Jesus' statement in 10:12 is found only in Mark. In ancient Jewish society, a wife did not have the right to divorce her husband. But in the first century, if a Jewish woman wanted a divorce, she could obtain one on the basis of Roman law even though her decision might cut her off from Jewish society.

We need to understand that the issue of divorce is complicated. Jesus was not saying all that could be said about divorce. He was speaking to people who would leave a spouse for no good reason and move from partner to partner. He condemned divorce as contrary to God's will and set forth the highest standards of marriage for His followers. But He did not address other potential reasons for divorce, such as spousal abuse and similar horrendous issues that have recently plagued society. We must be careful not to apply His teaching beyond its original context.

10:13–16

LITTLE CHILDREN: A MODEL FOR US ALL

Jesus had recently used a little child as an example of a helpless, humble person who should be welcomed by His followers (9:35–37). But apparently His disciples had missed the point. In this case, people are bringing little children for Jesus to touch (bless), and the disciples are trying to discourage them. The disciples are probably trying to protect Jesus' time, assuming He is too busy or too important to be bothered by such trivial matters.

The Gospels contain only a few instances where Jesus expresses anger, but this is one of them. He grows "indignant" (10:14) with His disciples for their treatment of the small children. Anyone who comes to Jesus, regardless of age, should do so with the simple faith and trust of a child. He or she is not to be hindered, but encouraged and supported.

In ancient society, children were considered irrelevant, totally without social status. Here, the traits of children that Jesus is probably referring to are their lowliness and dependence on others. In essence, he is telling His disciples they must be humble and absolutely dependent on God to enter the kingdom. For us as well, these values help us find and enter the kingdom of God.

Note that God's kingdom is to be both received and entered (10:15). The blessings of the kingdom are to be received as a gift, yet we enter the kingdom through responsive faith. Jesus takes the children in His arms to visually demonstrate that the blessings of the kingdom are available to those who choose to come to Him (10:16). Through faith, all believers are accepted in the arms of Jesus and blessed by Him.

10:17–31

THE ONE WHO GOT AWAY

When Mark points out that Jesus is "on his way" (10:17 niv), it is a reminder that Jesus is headed toward Jerusalem and the cross. On the way He encounters a man who asks what needs to be done to inherit eternal life. But the man's reference to Jesus as "Good Teacher" is what caught Jesus' attention.

In Jewish thought, God was preeminently "good"—so much so that it was unusual to apply the term to anyone else. So first, Jesus responds to the man with a query (10:18) that essentially asks, "Are you consciously calling me God, or was that just a mistake?"

Then Jesus continues with information from scripture that the man is already aware of. In fact, the man is convinced he has kept the laws perfectly since his childhood, which should certainly merit his entrance into God's kingdom.

He must have been sincere about his thinking, because Mark tells us that Jesus "looked at him and loved him" (10:21 niv). Jesus goes on to explain how a true keeper of the law would behave (10:21)—with unbridled compassion for the needy. Jesus is expressing love and compassion for this man and asks him to do the same for others.

Jesus' command to "sell all you possesss and give to the poor" (nasb) should not be applied literally to every professing Christian. It is used in this case to demonstrate that someone who obeyed the law to the point that this man *thought* he did would have such a heart of love for others that he would be ready to take the next step and give them all he had.

The man can't do as Jesus asks and "went away sad" (10:22 niv). Even though Jesus promises him "treasure in heaven," he is unwilling to let go of what he already possessed. This is the only example in Mark of someone being called to discipleship, but refusing.

Critical Observation

The story of Jesus and the rich man must be understood in light of the Jewish attitude toward riches. The dominant Jewish view was that wealth was an indication of divine favor and a reward for righteousness. Although provision was made for the protection and assistance of the poor, rarely was poverty associated with piety. So the teaching of Jesus was revolutionary in its time, and remains scandalous even today.

After the man leaves, Jesus and His disciples discuss the difficulty of rich people entering God's kingdom (10:23). Jesus' comment about a camel going through the eye of a needle has prompted much discussion. The suggestion that He was referring to a small gate in the wall of Jerusalem called "The Eye of a Needle" has no supporting evidence, and first arose in the ninth century, long after the destruction of Jerusalem. But clearly, the contrast between the largest Palestinian animal and one of the smallest openings is meant to teach the impossibility of entering God's kingdom on our own merits.

This idea is confirmed in 10:26–27, which contain the key to understanding the entire passage. Salvation, eternal life, and entry into God's kingdom are impossible for any human being, but not for God.

After Peter takes a stab at saying the disciples had tried to do as Jesus said (10:28), Jesus turns from warning to promise. Jesus is not encouraging people to walk away from their families (10:29–30), but is telling His followers to keep their priorities straight. Following Jesus can be costly, because along with blessing comes persecution. Yet ultimately the eternal rewards will far outweigh any sacrifices made in order to obtain them.

Finally, Jesus doesn't intend for us to be preoccupied with rewards (10:31). As we learn to serve the people He places in our path, He will see to rewards beyond anything we can ask or imagine (Ephesians 3:20).

Take It Home

Wealth can be a temptation, a hindrance, and a diversion from ongoing spiritual maturity. It provides false security that makes radical trust in God difficult. Yet Jesus never condemned riches as evil in themselves. Have you experienced any personal tension between your assets and your spiritual growth? How do you maintain a balance you feel good about? Do you perceive a need to make any changes in your financial attitudes or practices in order to become a more dedicated follower of Christ?

MARK 10:32–52

LEARNING TO SEE STRAIGHT

Unclear Spiritual Vision 10:32–45
Unclear Physical Vision 10:46–52

Setting Up the Section

As he did in the previous section (10:1–31), Mark continues to provide his readers with stories that reveal what is in the hearts of those who surrounded Jesus. While Jesus appears to know what people want from Him, He still encourages them to verbalize their desires before He responds.

10:32–45

UNCLEAR SPIRITUAL VISION

Jesus and His disciples are "on their way up to Jerusalem" (10:32 NIV)—a literal statement in this case. The road from Jericho to Jerusalem climbs about 3,300 feet in a twenty-mile stretch. The phrase is also used as a common expression for going to the Holy City on a pilgrimage or for some other important purpose.

Demystifying Mark

Several times in Mark's Gospel, Jerusalem is used as a symbol of opposition to Jesus. See, for instance, 3:22 and 7:1. And in this account, Jesus is heading to Jerusalem to die.

Mark describes Jesus leading the way, resolutely pressing toward His goal, deliberately striding toward His death (10:32). Twice already Jesus had begun to instruct the disciples about His upcoming death (8:31–32; 9:30–32). This time, however, He provides many more details (10:33–34), including being handed over to the Gentiles and suffering a number of humiliating indignities.

Yet again, Jesus' disciples demonstrate complete incomprehension. No doubt Mark's readers/hearers had difficulty understanding the full significance of Jesus' death and resurrection, and they benefited by realizing that Jesus' original disciples had a similar difficulty.

The disciples are still anticipating an earthly reign, and they want positions of authority when the time comes. In Jewish thought, the right hand (10:37) of the king was the place of greatest prominence; his left hand was the second most coveted seat. But James and John are missing the point. Jesus doesn't rebuke them directly, but indicates they do not realize the implications of their request.

The "cup" that Jesus refers to (10:38) symbolizes the wrath of God. His use of "baptism" is not the sacrament we know, but a metaphor for being immersed in calamity. It is ironic that even though James and John don't know what they are asking, Jesus foretells their participation in His "cup" and "baptism" (10:39).

By aspiring to positions of greatness, the disciples are thinking like Gentile rulers (10:42). And as a result, dissention runs through their ranks (10:41). Jesus emphatically states that His disciples must be like servants—even slaves (10:44). And He is about to demonstrate just what He is teaching them.

Jesus' subsequent statement about His own purpose—to serve and give His life as a ransom—is often considered an appropriate theme verse for Mark's whole Gospel (10:45). Humankind was in bondage to sin and pride, but Jesus' sacrifice was the necessary ransom. This usage of the word *ransom* indicates the price paid to free a slave or someone in prison. Jesus not only demonstrated humility but also freed us, enabling us to see what true humility is and then strive to emulate it.

10:46–52

UNCLEAR PHYSICAL VISION

When Jesus and His disciples reach Jericho, they encounter a blind man name Bartimaeus among a large crowd (10:46). Bartimaeus addresses Jesus as "Son of David" (10:47–48). The crowd tries to shush the blind man, but he is determined to get Jesus' attention. Jesus finally calls him forward. Mark provides the interesting detail of the man casting off his cloak (possibly used as a pallet), showing that Bartimaeus was casting aside everything to stand before Jesus. He had real and passionate faith. And when Jesus asks what he wants, he is quick with his response (10:51).

Critical Observation

Just as the healing of the blind man at Bethsaida (8:22–26) introduces the second major division of Mark, so the healing of Bartimaeus concludes it. Both stories contain exact geographical references—something unusual in Mark. Bracketing this section of Mark as they do, these accounts tie together the work of Jesus in providing physical sight for the blind and spiritual insight to His disciples. Bartimaeus becomes a picture of what was happening to the apostles—they were beginning to understand who Jesus was and what He came to do.

Again Mark emphasizes the importance of faith (10:52). The man calls out to Jesus, and Jesus saves him. His eyes are opened. He is healed physically and saved spiritually. And he immediately begins to follow Jesus.

Take It Home

The story of Bartimaeus is the last healing miracle in the Gospel of Mark. It provides an example of someone who understood who Jesus was, responded immediately to His call despite discouragement from others, believed in Him, and followed Him as a disciple. And it remains as an example for others to follow. Suppose you were to encounter Jesus today and He asked, "What do you want Me to do for you?" What would you say? What is it that Bartimeaus saw in Jesus that excited his faith to call out to Jesus?

MARK 11:1–10

JESUS' FINAL TRIP TO JERUSALEM

Humble Service 11:1–6
Necessary Deliverance 11:7–10

Setting Up the Section

For a while now, Mark has emphasized that Jesus was deliberately moving toward Jerusalem, where He would suffer and die. In this section, He arrives on what will become the original Palm Sunday. The focus of Mark's Gospel is on the humility of Jesus during His entry into the city. In Jesus' humility, we begin to see the foundation for victory in our own Christian lives.

11:1–6

HUMBLE SERVICE

Jesus is making His way to Jerusalem to prepare for the single most important moment in human history, the moment when He would take the place of sinful humankind and die. His entry into the city is of extreme importance because it sets the stage for how He is going to carry out the work He was called to do.

Jesus is fully in control of this moment. From His perspective, the event had been planned and prepared far before the foundations of the world. It had been prophesied more than 400 years previously by the prophet Zechariah (Zechariah 9:9). Jesus is not improvising as He goes along.

A common question is how Jesus knew about the colt, and why someone would just give it away when the disciples asked for it (11:2–3). Had Jesus made arrangements with the owner ahead of time, or was this some kind of divine miracle? There is no record of Jesus talking to the man beforehand. With the long anticipation of the moment, it is not too much to believe that God worked in the man's heart to let him know that his animal would be used to fulfill the Old Testament prophecy. Regardless, it is certain that Jesus is fulfilling the scriptures to the letter. So the disciples do as Jesus instructs and obtain the colt (11:4–6).

Critical Observation

The fact that the colt used by Jesus had never been used has symbolic overtones. In the Old Testament, whenever God designated an animal to be used for religious purposes, it was always without defect and never previously used for other purposes (Numbers 19:2; Deuteronomy 21:3). So the donkey's colt chosen by Jesus would be appropriate for His mission.

Jesus' choice of a donkey's colt is very important because it demonstrates an unusual level of humility. Those who rode donkeys were usually people of humble means. If a king rode a donkey into a city, it was to proclaim peace rather than to declare war. Therefore Jesus enters Jerusalem, making a statement of humility and peace. He is not coming to claim the military or political leadership of Israel.

Without such a display of humility by Jesus, we would never be able to understand the level of humility that God loves and expects from us. Jesus humbly served God so that we might receive the power to choose humility as well. If He had not humbly entered Jerusalem to willingly die on a cross, we would have been swallowed up in our own pride and left to our many selfish ambitions.

Although Jesus is exemplifying complete humility, He enters Jerusalem fully intending to look like the Messiah. Until this point, Jesus had been reluctant to tell the crowds following Him that He was the Messiah. Here, His bold approach to the city finally confirms their thoughts, but it also sets into motion His death. Jesus knows this dramatic entrance will trigger a response from the religious leaders.

11:7–10

NECESSARY DELIVERANCE

The crowds recognize the significance of Jesus' entrance into Jerusalem and respond with signs of respect (11:8–10). The spreading of garments pays homage to royalty (2 Kings 9:13), as do the waving of branches (Psalm 118:27 NIV). The verbal shouts (11:9–10) are additional signs of honor. Although Jesus demonstrates complete humility in what He is doing, He is also fulfilling the mission He has come to do, and is glorifying God in the process. So God ensures that, at least for this short ride into Jerusalem, Jesus receive worship and honor.

The cries of the people are meaningful. *Hosanna* is Hebrew for "Save us, now." Originally a cry for help, it had become a shout of praise for deliverance. "Blessed is he who comes in the name of the Lord" was a cry that applied to every pilgrim who approached the temple, but no doubt Mark intends his readers to understand that the phrase has particular significance when applied to Jesus. And "Blessed is the coming kingdom of our father David" expresses the expectation that Jesus will not only deliver, but also bring the kingdom of God to earth.

Demystifying Mark

It is important to keep in mind that Jesus was entering Jerusalem just prior to the Passover celebration. As the Jewish people recalled and celebrated God's deliverance of Israel from Egypt, their hopes for the eventual deliverance from Rome naturally ran high. In fact, the Roman Empire maintained troops in Jerusalem during this time in case riot control became necessary.

Although the people are celebrating Jesus' appearance, most of them miss the significance of the deliverance He is bringing. They are looking for political deliverance, but Jesus is bringing spiritual deliverance, which is much more essential. He is the only One capable of removing the oppressive burden of sin under which humankind suffers and struggles. Yet when He doesn't do anything about the oppression of Rome, many of the same clueless people who were cheering Him on this Sunday are crying for His execution less than a week later.

Take It Home

In spite of all the excitement of the people, they would eventually reject Jesus because He did not meet their expectations. When you think of the Savior, what image comes to mind? Are you willing to respond to someone who sets you free from pride and the burden of sin, or are you holding out for someone who allows you to hold on to your pride and is still willing to make your life better? What preexisting ideas, thoughts, dreams, plans, or agendas in your life keep you from seeing Jesus as a humble servant who obeyed God in order to follow His example in a greater humility and obedience?

MARK 11:11–26

A NONPRODUCTIVE FIG TREE AND A DISRESPECTFUL TEMPLE

The Cursing of the Fig Tree, Part I	11:11–14
The Expulsion of Merchants from the Temple	11:15–19
The Cursing of the Fig Tree, Part 2	11:20–26

Setting Up the Section

Upon reaching Jerusalem, it doesn't take Jesus long to begin to address things that need attention and correction. The improprieties He witnesses in the temple cause His immediate response, and His cursing of a fig tree serves to symbolize the unfruitful spiritual state of the religious leaders of His day.

This section includes yet one more example of Mark's tendency to sandwich or bracket one story into another in order to make a point. In this case, He first tells of Jesus cursing the fig tree, then moves on to His experience in the temple. Then Mark again returns to Jesus at the fig tree, stacking the image of the fruitless fig tree against the image of the fruitless religion found in the temple.

11:11–14

THE CURSING OF THE FIG TREE, PART I

If Jesus and His disciples have walked the twenty-one miles from Jericho to Jerusalem—most of it uphill—it makes sense that it would be late by the time He arrives (11:11). It also explains why the crowd disperses and Jesus takes no public action. Still, note that He doesn't just enter the city that evening, but the temple as well. Then He and the disciples go on to Bethany (about two miles away), where they will stay during this final week of Jesus' life.

It's not surprising that Jesus is hungry. The first meal of the day wasn't eaten until midmorning, and the prospect of figs is encouraging. Israel had been compared to a fig tree throughout the Old Testament (Jeremiah 29:17; Hosea 9:10, 16; Joel 1:6–7; Micah 7:1). So "not the season for figs" (11:13) is as much a reflection on the spiritual state of Israel as for the fruitless tree. Both the tree and the nation appear to be healthy and complete, but neither is in season or productive. Both create disappointment rather than satisfaction.

Jesus addresses the fig tree (11:14) within earshot of the disciples. This will be important the following day, as will be seen (11:20–26).

11:15–19

THE EXPULSION OF MERCHANTS FROM THE TEMPLE

The event in this passage is frequently called "the cleansing of the temple." In this case, the temple or temple area refers to an outer court—the only place Gentiles are allowed to worship. Yet it is here where the moneychangers provide shekels required for the temple tax in exchange for Roman currency. Other sellers provide doves, the prescribed offering for the poor who cannot afford a larger animal to sacrifice.

Critical Observation

The Tyrian shekel was the closest equivalent for the annual temple tax payment required from all Jewish males. According to the Jewish *Mishna*, the tax was due two weeks before the Passover, so exchange tables were set up in the temple five days prior to the due date.

Jesus takes immediate action to rid the temple of the moneychangers and animals (11:15–16). As He drives them out, He quotes Isaiah 56:7 and Jeremiah 7:11 to remind everyone that God's house is intended to be a place of worship, not business. Mark is the only Gospel writer with the reference to all nations (11:17) in Jesus' quotation. Perhaps he had in mind Isaiah's prediction that the Gentiles would one day have a place among the people of God and in the temple of God (Isaiah 56:6–7).

While the pilgrims in Jerusalem would have benefited from the services of the moneychangers and animal sellers, the temple was not a proper location to conduct business. Even if the merchants weren't price gouging, they were "robbers" (11:17) in the sense that they were robbing the Gentiles of unhindered worship opportunities.

The responses to Jesus' actions are quite mixed. The crowds are amazed at His "teaching" (11:18), a word that probably indicates both His words and His symbolic act of expelling the merchants. In contrast, the chief priests and teachers of the law are afraid of Him, and begin to look for a way to kill Him.

Perhaps Jesus waits until evening to leave (11:19) for His safety, as the time for His crucifixion has not quite arrived.

11:20–26

THE CURSING OF THE FIG TREE, PART 2

After witnessing the clearing of the temple, the disciples may have had second thoughts about the significance of Jesus' previous cursing of the fig tree. When He had said, "May no one ever eat fruit from you" (11:14), did His meaning extend beyond the single tree to include the nation of Israel? And if so, what did that mean to the apostles, who were from that nation?

When Peter sees that the tree has indeed withered by the following morning (11:20–21), he brings it to Jesus' attention. Jesus minimizes the alarm and fear the disciples may be feeling by focusing on the importance of faith. Despite the cursing of the fig tree (Israel), God was still accessible. The temple would no longer be the way to Him, however. Faith and prayer would be the way to God—an approach equally available to Jews and Gentiles.

Jesus' words (11:22–23) are sometimes taken out of context. They are not intended to apply to spectacular miracles, but as an encouragement in accomplishing the Christian mission. He is saying that if a person walks by faith, no difficulty can overwhelm him or her—not even a mountain-sized one.

Similarly, His statement on prayer (11:24) is not to be universalized and applied without exception. But neither is it to be limited to the original disciples and ignored as having no current practical value. Faith is an indispensable element in prayer. When faith is exercised, the pray-er can be confident of an answer.

In addition to faith, forgiveness is also an essential aspect of prayer (11:25). Believers must pray in a way that reflects the gospel they promote. A healthy relationship with God cannot be maintained apart from proper relationships with one's fellow human beings. Standing (11:25) was probably the most common posture for prayer at the time.

Verse 26 has been omitted from some Bibles. The sentence is found in a large number of medieval manuscripts, but not in the older and more reliable ones. It reads, "But if you do not forgive, neither will your Father in heaven forgive your trespasses" (NKJV).

It was most likely added under the influence of Matthew 6:15. But Jesus' point is not to be missed: Forgiveness is critical to every part of our relationship with God.

Take It Home

What are some of the obstacles in your life that get in the way of sharing the gospel with a family member or a friend? What encouragement comes from this text as you consider the hope of this passage? Who do you need to forgive so that you can carry on God's will in an undistracted manner?

MARK 11:27–17

CONTROVERSIES IN THE TEMPLE, PART I

Controversy: Jesus' Authority	11:27–33
Controversy: The Rejection of Israel	12:1–12
Controversy: The Payment of Taxes	12:13–17

Setting Up the Section

This section begins a series of seven conflicts between Jesus and the religious authorities. (Three will be examined in this segment; four in the next one.) These stories show how Jesus refutes the errors of the Jewish leaders and why they reject Him. The accounts were also helpful for first-century readers in seeing how Jesus faced opposition to His teachings, something the early church had to do as well.

11:27–33

CONTROVERSY: JESUS' AUTHORITY

Upon Jesus' return to the temple, He is confronted by a delegation of chief priests, teachers of the law, and elders (11:27) from the Sanhedrin—the Jewish religious ruling body. They want to know by whose authority He had driven out the temple moneychangers and animal sellers.

Authority was a big issue, as Mark has regularly noted (1:22, 27; 2:10; 3:15; 6:7; etc.). The religious leaders feel Jesus had gone too far—they were supposed to be in charge of the temple. But Mark is seeking to demonstrate that Jesus is the Christ, the Son of God. As such, He possesses all authority.

Rather than defend His actions, Jesus answers their question with a question of His own (11:29–30), posed to show that their motives are not about seeking the truth as much as staying in power and maintaining popularity. He isn't attempting to evade their question, but rather to establish the source of His authority in the spiritual realm.

At issue is the authority of John the Baptist. The clear implication of Jesus' question is that John's ministry was divinely authorized. And if so, since John had endorsed the ministry of Jesus, then the religious leaders should recognize Jesus' authority. Of course, the religious authorities would never concede that John was a prophet from God. But John had been popular with the crowds, so the religious leaders don't dare voice their opinion. Their only option, in response to Jesus' question, is to say, "We do not know" (11:33).

In rejecting John, they have rejected God's truth. So Jesus refuses to respond to them. They already know the answer to their question of authority (11:28). But if they hadn't listened to John, neither will they listen to Jesus.

12:1–12

CONTROVERSY: THE REJECTION OF ISRAEL

This parable of the wicked tenant farmers is very similar to a prophecy of Isaiah (Isaiah 5:1–7). In both cases, the vineyard clearly represents Israel, and the owner, God. In the Isaiah account, the problem was that the vineyard failed to produce the fruits of righteousness. In Jesus' variation, the problem is with the overseers (the religious authorities) who refuse to serve the owner due to their wickedness (greed, dishonesty, violence, and murder). The servants (12:2–5) are the prophets whom God had sent, yet who had been rejected, abused, and sometimes even killed. And the owner's beloved son is Jesus (1:11; 9:7).

Jesus is saying that the current tenants (the Jewish religious authorities) will lose their coveted position. God's vineyard will soon be the church, which He will use rather than the nation of Israel to advance His kingdom. Yet the church will include both Jewish and Gentile believers, grafted into the same olive tree (Romans 11:17–24).

Demystifying Mark

If no living person claimed ownership of a piece of land, its occupants could acquire it. By doing away with every representative of the owner, the tenants in the parable thought they could possess complete control over their land. To kill the owner's son was bad enough, but to leave a corpse unburied was the ultimate insult and showed complete contempt.

The "cornerstone" or "capstone" reference (12:10–11) is a quote from Psalm 118:22–23 used two other times in the New Testament (Acts 4:11; 1 Peter 2:7) in addition to the parallel Gospel accounts (Matthew 21:42; Luke 20:17). The Jews had understood the prophecy to refer to their nation, which was rejected by other nations but would be restored by the Lord. The early Christians, however, realized the rejected stone was a reference to Jesus (Ephesians 2:20).

The religious leaders who continue to oppose Jesus realize this parable is about them (12:12). If Jesus was right, it meant that God would soon reject them. But rather than change their opinion, they are all the more determined to have Jesus arrested. This is an irony in Mark's Gospel that while previous parables concealed the truth from the religious leaders, this one reveals it to them and so provokes Jesus' crucifixion.

12:13–17

CONTROVERSY: THE PAYMENT OF TAXES

A short time later a group of Pharisees and Herodians (see "Critical Observation" for Mark 3:1–6) go to Jesus in an attempt to "catch Him in His words" (12:13 NIV, KJV, NKJV). Although what they say about Jesus (12:14) is true, Mark reveals their shady motives by showing that it is insincere flattery.

Jesus sees right through their hypocrisy and calls them on it. Ironically, Jesus doesn't have a coin, but His opponents do. The insertion of this fact might be another indication that they implicitly recognized the authority of the emperor, therefore exposing them as hypocrites.

Critical Observation

A poll tax was imposed on all residents of Judea, Idumea, and Samaria in AD 6. Although the tax was only one denarius a year—a day's wage for an agricultural laborer—it was a symbol of foreign domination. In addition, the tax had to be paid with a coin bearing both the image of the emperor (in this case, Tiberius) and an offensive inscription claiming a status of deity for the ruling emperor.

The Pharisees think they had Jesus in a no-win situation. If He advises them to pay the tax, He will surely lose much of His popularity with the people. If He advises against it, He will become a target of Rome. But Jesus ingeniously sidesteps their trap (12:15–17).

A coin minted by the emperor with his picture was considered his property even while in circulation. So Jesus says to give it to him, acknowledging that God's people have an obligation to the state. But a far greater obligation is to God. If coins bearing the image of an emperor ought to be returned to him, how much more should human beings bearing the image of God devote themselves to their Lord? Believers should present their lives to God as an act of worship (Romans 12:1).

Jesus teaches that obedience to a secular power does not necessarily conflict with one's obedience to God. Later New Testament writings would reaffirm this fact (Romans 13:1–7; 1 Timothy 2:1–3; Titus 3:1–2; 1 Peter 2:13–17).

People who hear Jesus are "amazed" at Him (12:17). But that doesn't stop His opponents from trying to trap Him. More controversies follow in the next section of Mark.

Take It Home

Not many people live under the rule of an emperor these days, but we can still encounter situations where faith and secular authority create conflict. Can you think of any such circumstances in your own experience? How do you handle situations where your faith and your other commitments seem to be at odds with one another?

MARK 12:18–44

CONTROVERSIES IN THE TEMPLE, PART II

Controversy: Marriage at the Resurrection	12:18–27
Controversy: The Greatest Commandment	12:28–34
Controversy: The Identity of David's Son	12:35–37
Controversy: The Scribes Contrasted with the Widow	12:38–44

Setting Up the Section

The conflict between Jesus and those hoping to destroy His credibility continues in this section of Mark. The previous section (11:27–12:17) contained three separate controversies. But in the four that follow, we find a few positive examples amid the attempts to discredit Jesus.

12:18–27

CONTROVERSY: MARRIAGE AT THE RESURRECTION

The Sadducees (12:18) are mentioned only here in Mark's Gospel. Little is known about them, but they had some different viewpoints on certain matters of theology. One distinction was that they did not believe in the resurrection of the dead.

Demystifying Mark

The Sadducees seem to have emerged as an identifiable party during the second century BC. They were wealthy aristocrats who were politically liberal and theologically conservative. They were usually associated with the temple and the office of the high priest, although only one high priest was explicitly identified as a Sadducee. (Their name may have derived from Zadok, a high priest in David's time [2 Samuel 20:25].) None of their own literature has survived, so all references to them are in the writings of their adversaries, and therefore questionable. One thing for certain is that they rejected the oral tradition of the scribes and Pharisees, which created some interesting discussions and debates.

The preposterous supposition they have concocted (12:20–23) has probably been used many times in their debates with the Pharisees. It is based on a teaching found in Deuteronomy 25:5–10, intended to provide for any widow who had been left childless after her husband's death.

Jesus again uses a question (12:24) to reveal ignorance and take the discussion to a higher plane. He points out two errors of the Sadducees: (1) not knowing the content and/or proper interpretation of the scriptures; and (2) not having personally experienced the power of God in their lives. Therefore, they are missing the whole point of the argument.

Jesus teaches that resurrection life will be different from earthly life. "Like the angels" (12:25 NIV, NLT) may indicate either a sexless state or an emphasis on serving and worshiping God. Relationships in heaven will be of such a degree that they will satisfy better than the best relationships on earth. Sin, grief, and loss will be left behind as believers experience the surpassing joy of new and more powerful relationships.

And as far as the Sadducees' disbelief in resurrection, Jesus quotes from Exodus 3:6 (12:26). When God spoke in present tense of being the God of Abraham, Isaac, and Jacob, He indicated that those patriarchs were still alive—an implication of resurrection. And to make things perfectly clear, Jesus emphasizes that the Lord is not God of the dead, but of the living (12:27).

12:28–34

CONTROVERSY: THE GREATEST COMMANDMENT

No sooner has Jesus answered the Sadducees than a scribe approaches with another question. But this time, the questioner seems to be more sincere. He wants Jesus' opinion on which He considers to be the greatest commandment, and quite a challenge it is. The scribes had gone through the law and identified 613 separate commandments: 365 prohibitions and 248 exhortations to obey. They also categorized them as "heavy" or "light" based on what they felt was more or less important.

Jesus quotes from Deuteronomy 6:4–5 (the first part of the Jewish *Shema*) and Leviticus 19:18. In doing so, He teaches that in loving God and one's neighbor, a person fulfills the entire law of God. Jesus brings together and virtually merges the commands to love God and to love fellow human beings.

Critical Observation

The Shema is the declaration of Deuteronomy 6:4–9. Its foundation is Deuteronomy 6:4 which declares that God is the one true God. The name *Shema* is derived from the first Hebrew word of the verse, "hear." This passage is recited three times a day as part of the religious Jew's spiritual practice. It is also part of the synagogue Sabbath service.

The response of the scribe (12:32–34) is found only in Mark. It is the only place in the Gospels where a scribe is described as being favorably disposed toward Jesus. But it's enough to demonstrate that not all scribes and Pharisees were unwilling to listen and respond to what Jesus had to say.

And it's noteworthy to notice exactly what they agree on: the elevation of an ethical quality over sacrificial worship. This scribe understands that Jesus is exactly right—love for God and for one's neighbor is more important "than all burnt offerings and sacrifices" (12:33).

By deeming the man "not far from the kingdom of God" (12:34), Jesus is encouraging him to go the rest of the way with wholehearted devotion. Whether he did so cannot be known.

12:35–37

CONTROVERSY: THE IDENTITY OF DAVID'S SON

Jesus has proven Himself authoritative on taxes, resurrection, and the law, so at this point He raises a question of His own (12:35). Throughout the Old Testament, the prophets had written that the Messiah would be from the line of David, and "Son of David" would be a regular title in the New Testament. However, fathers in ancient Israelite society did not refer to their sons—much less their distant descendants—as "lords." So why did David refer to his future descendant as "Lord" (12:37)?

Critical Observation

When David wrote, "The Lord said to my Lord. . ." in Psalm 110:1, quoted by Jesus in Mark 12:36, two different words are used for "Lord." The first usage is a clear reference to God (Yahweh). The second word (*Adonai*) is sometimes used of God, but not always. So a paraphrase of the statement might be, "God said to my superior. . .'"

Jesus is not denying that He is David's descendant or the Messiah. However, those terms were too limiting. Jesus is more than the "Son of David." He is also the "Son of Man"—the representative of all humanity who has to suffer before He is exalted at God's right hand (Daniel 7:13–14). Still more importantly, Jesus is the Son of God!

In a veiled way, Jesus is telling everyone that the Messiah is not to be a warrior-king like David. And yet He will be greater than David. To hear such deep thoughts explained brings "delight" to Jesus' listeners (12:37).

12:38–44

CONTROVERSY: THE SCRIBES CONTRASTED WITH THE WIDOW

Jesus refutes the showiness that has come to symbolize "proper" worship (12:38–39). The reference to long or flowing robes probably refers to the *tallith*, a shawl worn during formal prayers and ceremonies. Some scribes might have worn one to attract attention. "Greetings in the market places" (NASB) were expressions of deference to a religious authority. The "most important seats" (NIV) in the synagogue were on the bench facing the congregation or near the chest that contained the scrolls. At a banquet, the choicest seats were near the host.

But such religious gestures were hollow. The same people putting on such a pretense would "devour widows' houses" (12:40). Scribes were forbidden to receive payment for their teaching. However, some may have ingratiated themselves to widows in hopes of being willed their homes. Others might have found technicalities in the law, allowing them to lay claim to the houses of defenseless persons, or perhaps expected generous sums from widows after praying for them.

In contrast to this unscrupulous habit of taking from helpless people stands the example of the widow (12:41–44). The "treasury" (12:41) where this takes place appears to be in the court of women where thirteen trumpet-shaped receptacles were placed to collect both the temple tax and money given voluntarily for various purposes.

The amount of each of the widow's two coins (12:42) would have been 1/64 of a denarius—a denarius being equal to a day's wage. Jesus observes her selfless gift and points out that the amount of a gift is weighed by how much remains for one's personal use afterward. The widow's giving of everything she has to live on demonstrates her absolute trust in God—a far more significant gift than anyone else had given.

Take It Home

There were no shortage of controversies between Jesus and the established religious leaders of His day. What controversies are you aware of in the church today? Based on what He said to His critics, how do you think Jesus would respond to each issue that confronts the church today?

MARK 13:1–13

WATCH AND WAIT

The Destruction of the Temple 13:1–11
Signs to Watch For 13:5–13

Setting Up the Section

Mark 13 has been given a variety of names, including the eschatological discourse, the prophetic discourse, the Olivet discourse (since it was given on the Mount of Olives),

and the "Little Apocalypse." Jesus foretells God's judgment, a great cataclysm in the world, and Jesus' eventual return. This passage is the longer of two of Jesus' extended discourses found in Mark's Gospel (the other being 4:1–34). At this point in Mark's account, Jesus begins to reveal to the disciples some of the specifics of what will happen as the ministry of the church begins to unfold in the world.

13:1–11

THE DESTRUCTION OF THE TEMPLE

The Olivet discourse is initiated by a random comment by one of the disciples about the temple (13:1). Jesus acknowledges the greatness of the buildings, but predicts a day when "not one stone here will be left upon another" (13:2). Naturally the disciples want more details (13:4), so Jesus sits them down on the Mount of Olives where they can look down on the temple and the city of Jerusalem. The Mount of Olives was also prominent in Old Testament prophecies about the return of the Lord (Zechariah 14:4).

Critical Observation

The "massive stones" of the temple (13:1 NIV) were indeed magnificent. According to the writings of Josephus, a first-century historian, some of the stones were thirty-seven feet long by eighteen feet deep by twelve feet high. The few stones that remain from portions of the southeast corner and the western wall are not quite that large, yet are still considerably larger than the stones used during the medieval rebuilding of the walls. In Jesus' day, before its destruction, the temple was truly a masterpiece of architecture.

Jesus gives His followers signs to look for, but not specifics. He *doesn't* say that the Jews will rebel against the Romans in AD 66 and that the Romans will obliterate the temple in AD 70 as a result. Yet the disciples realize that if the temple were to fall as Jesus said, it would surely be as a result of greater events that would throw the world they know into chaos. So Jesus lays out a number of events for them to watch for.

13:5–13

SIGNS TO WATCH FOR

In Jesus' expansive answer to the disciples' questions (13:4) He identifies four signs that will indicate the coming destruction of Jerusalem and/or the end of the world.

(1) False Messiahs (13:5–6)

It's interesting to note that Jesus' first warning sign is deceit—many people will come, claiming to be the Christ, and will recruit a lot of followers. One of the ongoing challenges of living in a fallen world is discerning false teaching that appears to be true. At the heart of this false teaching will be people who claim to be (or to represent) the Messiah. So Jesus repeats the warning to "watch out," "beware," and "be on your guard" throughout the discourse

(13:5, 9, 23, 33, 37). Despite the horrendous physical calamities He is about to describe, the spiritual dangers are far greater.

(2) Wars (13:7–8)

The Roman Empire had risen to greatness through conquest, and would continue to do so. The reference in 13:7 is to the war soon to be fought between Israel and Rome. After the Jewish rebellion of AD 66 and fall of the temple in AD 70, Jewish opposition to Rome will be ultimately quashed at the fortress of Masada in 73 or 74. Although it will be hard for Jewish people to believe at the time, Jesus indicates that these events will *not* be a sign of the end of the world or of His return. Wars will continue and worse things will happen.

(3) Natural disasters (13:8)

Earthquakes and famines will be only the beginning of the problem. The reference to birth pains (or pangs) should have been familiar to any Jewish people with a knowledge of their scriptures. It was a common metaphor to symbolize anticipation of a significant event (Isaiah 13:8; 26:17–18; Jeremiah 4:31; 50:43; Hosea 13:13; Micah 4:9–10; etc.).

(4) Persecution (13:9, 11–13)

The followers of Jesus will be opposed and handed over to the courts where they will be sentenced to punishment or death. The gospel will be rejected as the religious establishment seeks to silence the message of Jesus.

None of these signs can silence the gospel (13:10). Even in the midst of horrendous times and catastrophic events, God's Word will continue to be preached and His kingdom will advance. Consequently, persecution won't be just one of the signs of the end of the world, but a way of life for believers. So Jesus includes some guidelines for handling persecution: Continue to testify for Him (13:9), depend on the Holy Spirit to know what to say (13:11), and stand firm to the end (13:13).

Demystifying Mark

Verse 11 is one of the few references to the Holy Spirit found in Mark's Gospel. It is not a prohibition against preparation, but against anxiety.

When Jesus tells His followers to endure "to the end" (13:13), He likely means the end of each individual's life rather than the end of the age or any other specific date. The promise of being saved is in a spiritual, not a physical, sense.

The readers of Mark's Gospel were facing the birth pangs of persecution. These words were no doubt of great comfort to them as they were assured that God would certainly reward those who are faithful to Him.

Take It Home

Mark's purpose in writing was to provide assurance about the true identity of Jesus and confidence about His eventual return. Yet his repeated warnings against being deceived were intended to dampen

CONTINUED

uncontrolled enthusiasm and speculation about the future. In the 2,000 years since Jesus died, many groups and individuals have been deceived and/or mistaken about the end times. When you think about such things, what is your response? (Some may want to hide, others want to talk about nothing else, etc.) What do you think Jesus' intent was in sharing so much general information with His followers, but not giving them (us) a detailed schedule of when everything would take place?

MARK 13:14–37

THE END OF THE AGE

True Signs of the End of the Age	13:14–23
The Return of the Son of Man and the Gathering of His Elect	13:24–27
Certain and Uncertain Truths about the Return of Jesus	13:28–37

Setting Up the Section

Whenever the return of Jesus is discussed, it's not unusual to find a number of different opinions. Mark reports what Jesus has to say, but it is interpreted in different ways by different people. This passage almost certainly refers to the coming siege of Jerusalem in AD 70. Even so, it's a debated passage that looks far ahead into our future.

13:14–23

TRUE SIGNS OF THE END OF THE AGE

"The abomination that causes desolation" (13:14 niv) is a phrase found in Daniel's prophecies (Daniel 9:27; 11:31; 12:11). The word *abomination* indicates something repulsive to God and His people. *Desolation* suggests that as a result of its profanation, the true people of God abandon the temple. Daniel's prediction came true when Antiochus IV Epiphanes of Seleucid Syria erected a statue of Zeus Olympus in the Jerusalem temple in 167 BC.

Demystifying Mark

In addition to the "abomination that causes desolation" of Antiochus IV Epiphanes, later temple desecrations (prior to Jesus' statement in Mark) included one in 63 BC when the Roman general Pompey conquered Jerusalem and entered the Most Holy Place, and another when the governor, Pilate, introduced idolatrous standards into the city in about AD 26–27. Later ones would include the unsuccessful attempt by Caligula to erect his statue in the temple (AD 40) and the intrusion of the Zealots when they gained control of the temple during the Jewish rebellion in AD 66–70.

Jesus' use of the phrase most likely refers to the coming profanation of the temple by the Romans just prior to its destruction in AD 70. During this siege, Titus will enter the Most Holy Place and remove various items, taking them to Rome to adorn his victory procession. However, a second meaning can also be taken to refer to a future sacrilege by another profane and oppressive person, possibly the one of "lawlessness" Paul writes about in 2 Thessalonians 2:1–12.

The call to "let the reader understand" may be an insertion by Mark rather than part of the statement of Jesus, calling the reader to think about the significance of this statement in light of previous revelation in Daniel 9:23, 25. Some scholars think that Mark is pointing the original readers to events taking place at that time, and that the destruction of Jerusalem is imminent. This would date the Gospel to the late 60s of the first century.

The danger Jesus describes (13:14–16) is so great that there is no time for any delay. Palestinian houses had flat roofs for relaxation and cooling off during summer evenings, and were built with outside staircases. Jesus' warning is to flee without even going inside. Nor should field workers stop to retrieve their outer cloaks (removed while working). The time will be especially bad for "pregnant women and nursing mothers" (NIV) because of their weakened condition and inability to hurry. And winter will be an especially bad time because rivers will be high and hard to cross.

The "days of distress unequaled from the beginning, when God created the world, until now" (13:19 NIV) is another reference to Daniel (Daniel 12:1). This tribulation will be so severe that it could cause even the true children of God to despair (13:20), but God will not allow it to go that far.

One reason Jesus is being so frank with His disciples is that "false Christs and false prophets" will arise and deceive a lot of people. To prevent His followers from being misled, Jesus is carefully telling them "everything in advance" (13:23 NASB).

13:24–27

THE RETURN OF THE SON OF MAN AND THE GATHERING OF HIS ELECT

Verse 24 signifies a contrast, showing that the return of the Son of Man (13:26) is a distinct event that follows the fall of Jerusalem and other sufferings of the present age, though no time frame is provided. The scene described in 13:24–25 is an allusion to Old Testament passages such as Isaiah 13:10; Ezekiel 32:7–8; and Joel 2:10, 31. Some people interpret these as literal events; others see them as symbolic. The point in either case is there will be a clear sign that precedes the return of Jesus Christ. God will make the event known.

The return itself will also be public (13:26). This presumably means that all persons—not just disciples—will observe Jesus' return. It is significant that the title "Son of Man" is used here. It means that the same One who humbly ministered on earth (10:45) and who suffered and died (8:31) will return with "great power and glory." Glory is an Old Testament characteristic of God, so Jesus' glorious return is further indication of His deity.

In Mark's account, Jesus says nothing about future judgment (either punishment or rewards), resurrection, or reigning. The emphasis is on the gathering of God's scattered "elect" (13:27)—those who are chosen and blessed. The word itself gives no indication of why this group is chosen, but the concept of gathering the scattered people of God runs throughout the Old Testament (Deuteronomy 30:3–4; Psalm 147:2; Isaiah 11:12; 43:6; Jeremiah 32:37; Ezekiel 11:17; 34:13; 36:24). The emphasis in Mark is that Jesus will regather His people from wherever they have been scattered. This will be comforting for Mark's readers who are about to be scattered due to mounting persecution.

13:28–37

CERTAIN AND UNCERTAIN TRUTHS ABOUT THE RETURN OF JESUS

Jesus concludes His Olivet discourse with a collection of sayings and parables that deal with the uncertainty of the end times and the need to be ready. The mini-parable in 13:28–29 compares the coming of the Son of Man with the approach of summer. Jesus uses a fig tree in His example because so many other trees in Palestine are evergreens. But the fig tree loses its leaves in winter, and the reappearance of leaves is a sign of summer. Similarly, the signs Jesus has been describing are certain to lead to His return.

Critical Observation

This is an important teaching: As the condition of the world goes from bad to worse, it is not a sign that Jesus is losing the spiritual battle, but that His victorious return and final judgment are only getting closer.

"This generation" (13:30) refers to the contemporaries of Jesus. Some of them—particularly some of His disciples—will not die until the events of 13:5–23 have taken place, including the destruction of the temple. To a limited extent, 13:30 is the answer to the question asked in 13:4.

Verse 32 affirms that no one except God knows the exact time of the coming of Christ. But by referring to the event as "that day," Mark taps into the richness of the Old Testament writings about the Day of the Lord—a day of judgment for both Israel and the surrounding nations (Amos 5:18–20; Zephaniah 1:7, 14–16). The day marks the end of the present evil age and the beginning of the coming age of righteousness.

Another mini-parable in 13:34 once more reminds Mark's readers to be watchful. People in his day didn't usually travel by night (13:35), but might do so if returning from a late banquet or from abroad. They were not to sit around doing nothing while waiting for something to happen. The proper way to be prepared was to go about one's assigned tasks (13:34). Ignorance of the date or laziness (13:36) was no excuse to be caught unprepared.

Finally, Jesus gives one concluding reminder to "Watch!" (13:37). And He makes it clear that He is not only talking to His disciples; the discourse is for all Christians of all times.

Take It Home

Jesus spent a lot of time trying to inform His followers about the end times. What is the variety of emotional responses to this teaching? Why are there a variety of responses? How have you responded to this teaching in the past? What is your response today? How is this teaching meant to encourage us?

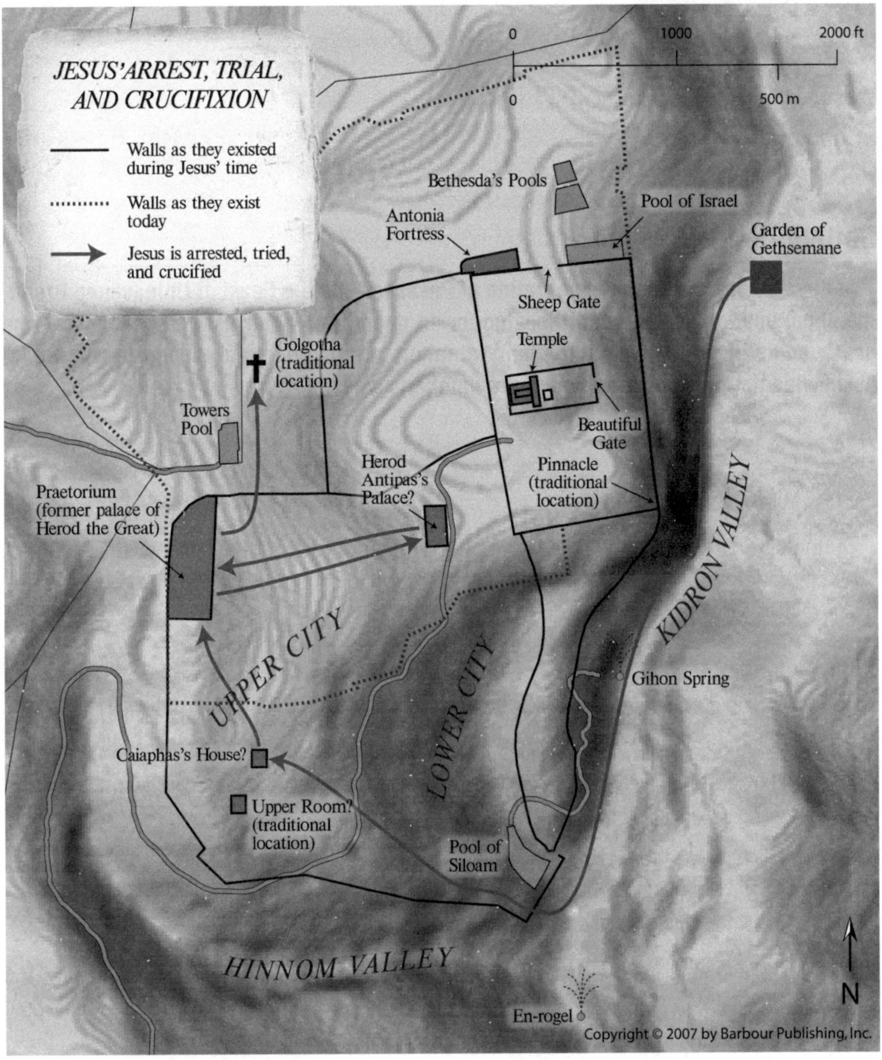
JESUS' ARREST, TRIAL, AND CRUCIFIXION
Walls as they existed during Jesus' time
Walls as they exist today
Jesus is arrested, tried, and crucified
0
1000
2000 ft
0
500 m
Bethesda's Pools
Pool of Israel
Antonia Fortress
Garden of Gethsemane
Sheep Gate
Temple
Golgotha (traditional location)
Towers Pool
Beautiful Gate
Herod Antipas's Palace?
Pinnacle (traditional location)
Praetorium (former palace of Herod the Great)
KIDRON VALLEY
UPPER CITY
LOWER CITY
Gihon Spring
Caiaphas's House?
Upper Room? (traditional location)
Pool of Siloam
HINNOM VALLEY
En-rogel
N

MARK 14:1–26

A FINAL MEAL TOGETHER

A Remarkable Gift	14:1–11
The Institution of the Lord's Supper	14:12–26

Setting Up the Section

Two days before the annual celebration of Passover and the Feast of Unleavened Bread, the opponents of Jesus are still looking for an opportunity to arrest and kill Jesus—and finally come up with a workable plan. Yet others are beginning to recognize who He is, acknowledging Him in verbal and more emphatic ways.

14:1–11

A REMARKABLE GIFT

During annual festivals, the population of Jerusalem swelled to three or four times normal. So even though a contingent of religious leaders is still looking for a way to put Jesus to death, it is afraid of a riot among the people.

Demystifying Mark

The Passover and the Feast of Unleavened Bread began on the same day, but the Feast of Unleavened Bread lasted seven days. It both celebrated the barley harvest and recalled the time when Israel ate unleavened bread during the exodus from Egypt. Passover commemorated the "passing over" of the angel of God who spared the firstborn sons in homes with blood on the door (Exodus 12:1–28). The Passover lamb could be killed only in the temple and eaten only within the city of Jerusalem. The emphasis on God's leading people from slavery to freedom, connected with the slaying of innocent lambs, made the timing and symbolism of Jesus' death highly significant.

Jesus is still popular, in large part due to His acceptance of people who were normally ignored or looked down on by other leaders. Here Mark shows that Jesus is at a party given by a man identified only as "Simon the leper" (14:3)—perhaps someone Jesus had healed.

While Jesus is reclining at the table (the traditional posture during more formal meals and dinner parties in that time and culture), a woman approaches Him. That is unusual in itself, because Jewish women didn't normally attend banquets for men except as servants. But in addition, she breaks a jar of very expensive nard (aromatic oil probably imported from India) and pours the entire contents on Jesus' head. Mark doesn't explain the woman's motives. (John indicates this woman is Jesus' friend, Mary [John 12:3]).

The woman's actions result in criticism from many of those present (14:4–5). But Jesus not only recognizes her motives, but also publicly defends her. It isn't that He doesn't share the others' concern for poor people, but the world would have only one Messiah and one death for their sins, so those facts were of greatest importance at this point. Only the woman had recognized the significance of the moment.

Verse 8 reveals Jesus' perception of the woman's actions, whether or not it had been her intent. And His prophecy in 14:9 was fulfilled as Mark recorded the event.

In stark contrast to the woman's devotion to Jesus, Mark inserts Judas's decision to betray Jesus at this point (14:10–11). Mark had only mentioned Judas once previously, and that was in a list of the disciples (3:19). Nothing is said of Judas's motive. Was he disappointed about Jesus' refusal to become a political Messiah? Was he attempting to force Jesus to take decisive action against His enemies? Had he been a spy all along? No one knows for sure. But Judas's cooperation sets in motion the plan of the religious leaders to have Jesus put to death.

14:12–26

THE INSTITUTION OF THE LORD'S SUPPER

Three important aspects to this section support Mark's theme that Jesus is the Christ, the Son of God: (1) Jesus is the fulfillment of the Passover; (2) Jesus is not taken by surprise by His captors; and (3) Everything Jesus does is in accordance with the scriptures.

The unique manner in which a house was arranged for the Passover meal echoes the arrangements Jesus makes to secure the colt to ride into the city (14:13–16; 11:1–6). The "man carrying a jar of water" (14:13 NIV) should have stood out because women ordinarily transported water.

Large upper rooms (14:15) were rare in Palestinian homes, which usually consisted of from one to four rooms on a single level. A furnished room would have provided carpets, couches, and vessels.

Jesus has already made it clear that He will be betrayed and put to death. The observation that Jesus' betrayer is a close friend (14:17, 20) is intended to show the extent of Judas's crime. In ancient Semitic society, eating together was one of the most meaningful indications of friendship. Few actions were more despicable than betraying a friend at, or immediately after, a shared meal.

Critical Observation

The Passover meal was special. In addition to the main course of a specially sacrificed lamb, it began not with the traditional breaking of bread, but by dipping bread and bitter herbs into a bowl containing dried fruits, spices, and wine or vinegar. Wine was mandatory at Passover, but much more rare at other meals (at least among common folk). Passover was celebrated in the evening rather than late afternoon. Reclining while eating was more common at formal meals than ordinary ones. And a traditional dinner did not conclude with a hymn.

The very celebration of Passover is a reminder that death is necessary to provide salvation. Yet the one who betrays Jesus will face a horrible consequence. The word *woe* (14:21) carries with it intense condemnation. At the time, all the disciples are afraid Jesus might be talking about them (14:19).

At some point during this Passover, Jesus institutes a new meal for His followers (14:22–24). It begins with giving thanks, followed by the proclamation that the bread is Jesus' body and the cup (wine) His blood. Up until this point, Passover recalled the lamb that was slain to preserve life just prior to Israel's exodus from Egypt. In the future, however, the celebration would become a remembrance of the body of Jesus offered up as our substitute and His blood shed to provide the forgiveness for our sins. "Poured out" (14:24) indicates the shedding of blood would be violent.

This will be Jesus' last meal together with His disciples (14:25). The "hymn" (14:26) is probably Psalm 118. The Hallel, a Jewish prayer/recitation of Psalms 113–118, was used during Passover and other holidays.

Events will now unfold that bring about the death of Jesus. He has instituted a formal remembrance, but will continue to prepare those He loves for what is about to happen.

Take It Home

When this woman saw Jesus for who He was, she responded with a wholehearted act of worship. What did she see in Jesus that caused her to respond with such a sacrifice of worship? What do we learn about how a person views Jesus by his or her response of praise and worship? How would you evaluate your view of Jesus by your response to His person?

MARK 14:27–72

ARRESTED AND CHARGED

Abandoned in Gethsemane	14:27–42
Arrested and Tried	14:43–65
Peter's Three Denials	14:66–72

Setting Up the Section

After all the predictions and preparations by Jesus, the time has finally come for His arrest and trial. The whole process, including His death and resurrection, will only take a weekend. Yet the emotional toll of dread, denial, betrayal, physical abuse, and everything else will be horrendous.

14:27–42

ABANDONED IN GETHSEMANE

At the Passover dinner Jesus had predicted His betrayal by "one of you" (14:18). On the way to the Mount of Olives He foretells that *all* His disciples will "fall away" (14:27). Yet Jesus is already looking beyond their failure to His reunion with them (14:8).

Peter makes a bold and arrogant claim (14:29), and Jesus just as boldly corrects him. This emphatic statement that Peter will deny Jesus not only once, but three times, is punctuated with Mark's final use of Jesus' phrase, "I tell you the truth" (14:30 NIV). It was certain to happen.

The vehemence of Peter's affirmation of loyalty (14:31) makes his failure all the greater. The fact that scripture portrays its main characters with such honest and unflattering examples is one indication of its trustworthiness. In addition, the Bible affirms that positive results can come from negative experiences, so the utter failure of Peter should encourage later followers of Jesus who fail in similar ways.

"Gethsemane" (14:32) is a transliteration of two Hebrew words meaning "oil press." It was probably an olive grove, and the exact location is unknown.

Another translation of 14:34 might be, "Horror and dismay came over Him." Jesus knows what it would mean to be forsaken by God, and He is seeking prayer support from His closest friends. The observation that Jesus "fell to the ground" (14:35 NIV) indicates a spirit of desperation.

In praying that "the hour might pass from Him" (14:35), Jesus is not regretting what He had come to earth to do. But in His humanity, He seeks another way to get the job done. When there is none, He leaves everything in His Father's hands: Yet "not what I will, but what You will" (14:36). Jesus' use of "Abba" in addressing God is unique in Judaism and shows His unique relationship to the Father.

The disciples, as usual, are lost as to what is really happening. When Jesus checks on them, they are sleeping off a good meal. The reason Peter (and all the others) will soon let Jesus down is that they are sleeping while Jesus is preparing His Spirit and His flesh to obey God. Even after Jesus specifically asks them to pray with Him, they fall asleep a second time. . .and a third (14:37–41).

By then, the hour has come—in a literal sense. The time is here for Jesus to be betrayed and put in the hands of sinful people.

14:43–65

ARRESTED AND TRIED

Even as Jesus is waking Peter, James, and John for the third time, Judas appears with an armed crowd. Judas knows Jesus' specific plans and has arranged for Jesus' enemies to pick Him up when there won't be much of a crowd. Using a kiss as a sign—the way someone would greet a close friend—shows the ugliness of the betrayal (14:44–45).

We know from John's account of this story that the disciple with the sword (14:47) is Peter (John 18:10). He makes an initial futile effort to defend his Master, but he is a fisherman, not a soldier.

Jesus repairs the damage Peter has done to the servant's ear (Luke 22:51), and then addresses the crowd (14:48–49). His comments point out the wickedness and deception of His adversaries. It is safe to speculate that the guards and weapons were not present as protection against Jesus, but because the religious leaders feared His followers. Yet being so outnumbered, Jesus' disciples "all forsook him, and fled" (14:50 KJV).

Demystifying Mark

The unusual notation about the young man who ran away naked (14:51–52) has led to much speculation that he was John Mark, the author of the Gospel. The upper room where Jesus had celebrated Passover might have been owned by Mark's mother, and Mark could have followed the group after dinner. The word translated "naked" could mean completely naked, or wearing only a loincloth.

Peter has run away, yet he trails the crowd and follows Jesus all the way into the courtyard of the high priest. He can't witness the trial, but it isn't going very well from the perspective of the prosecutors.

They have made an arrest, but have no evidence to formally charge Jesus. The trial should have been public, but they are trying to get it done under the cover of night. Before imposing a death penalty, Jewish law required the agreement of two (if not three) witnesses, but no two people will agree (14:56). The religious leaders' scheme is backfiring, so Jesus has no need to speak. His silence during this period fulfills prophecies such as Psalm 38:13–14 and Isaiah 53:7.

Finally the high priest asks Jesus directly, Are you "the Son of the Blessed One?"(14:61). The question is phrased this way because the Jews did not like to speak the name of God, lest they accidentally profane it. But Jesus knows what he means, and gives a direct and detailed response (14:62) which references the Old Testament prophecies of Psalm 110:1 and Daniel 7:13–14. After so much secrecy about His identity to this point, His openness seems quite surprising. But He is leaving no doubt—neither for His accusers nor His followers. Not only is He the Messiah, but He is also going back to His Father and will return to earth one day in all His power.

That's all the high priest needs to hear. Tearing one's clothes (14:63) was usually a dramatic symbol of grief or alarm; in this case it was an official act expressing indignation. By claiming to sit at God's right hand, predicting a return from heaven, and using the divine name "I am," Jesus is clearly claiming to be God. He is accused of blasphemy and "condemned. . .as deserving death" (14:64).

Critical Observation

Under Roman rule, the Jewish leaders could sentence someone to death, but could not execute him. That was left to the Romans, which is why Jesus was sent on to Pilate after His trial before the Sanhedrin.

The irony in 14:65 becomes apparent in retrospect. The hostile crowd beats Jesus and challenges Him to "prophesy" because they think He can't. Yet their very actions are fulfilling His own previous prophecy (10:33–34) as well as Old Testament prophecies such as Isaiah 50:6; 53:3–5 and Micah 5:1.

14:66–72

PETER'S THREE DENIALS

Meanwhile, Peter waits in the courtyard. He is trying to remain anonymous, but to his credit, he has at least tried to stay close to Jesus. A servant girl thinks she recognizes him as a member of Jesus' group, but Peter claims ignorance. Later she asks him again, this time including "those standing around" (14:69 NIV). Peter responds with a second denial. But by then he is attracting attention. A group (presumably including men) tries to get him to admit an association with Jesus. This time Peter begins "to call down curses on himself" (14:71 NIV), and he swears he doesn't know Jesus. As soon as the words leave his mouth, a rooster crows a second time and Peter recalls Jesus' prediction that he would deny Him three times (yet another of Jesus' prophecies coming true even as a hostile crowd is challenging Him to "prophesy").

In response, Peter "broke down and wept" (14:72). His great failure is recorded in all four Gospels. There is no attempted cover-up of the fact that the man who insightfully confessed Jesus' messiahship at Caesarea Philippi (8:29) later denies Him three times.

Take It Home

Peter thought that he could follow Jesus everywhere in the power of the flesh—he failed to understand that following Jesus must be done in the power and strength of the Spirit. In your life have you ever sought to follow and serve God in the power of the flesh? What was the outcome? Have you ever served God in a spirit of dependence upon the power and strength of God? What was that like? How do you depend upon the Spirit in your life—what does it look like?

MARK 15:1–20

JESUS' ROMAN TRIAL

The Trial Before Pilate	15:1–15
Jesus Before the Soldiers	15:16–20

Setting Up the Section

Jesus has just been arrested, tried, and sentenced to death. Judas has betrayed Him, Peter has already denied Him three times, and the rest of His friends have deserted Him. That was the treatment He received from His own people. Now He has the Romans to deal with.

15:1–15

THE TRIAL BEFORE PILATE

Mark makes regular notations about the time in this passage. Chapter 15 is divided into four periods of three hours each: "very early in the morning" (15:1), "the third hour" (15:25), "the sixth hour. . .until the ninth hour" (15:33), and "evening" (15:42).

As soon as it is morning, the chief priests meet with the scribes, elders, and the entire council to present the conclusion of their findings—that Jesus had declared He was God and therefore should be handed over to the Roman government for execution.

The Roman ruler at this time is Pontius Pilate, the fifth Roman governor of Judea after the deposition of Archelaus in AD 6 (Matthew 2:22). Although the governors usually resided at Caesarea, they often came to Jerusalem at festival times in order to be at the site should disorder arise among the thousands who attended the fest.

Critical Observation

Pilate was governor from AD 26–36. Both Josephus and Philo described him as being cruel and without any sensitivity for Jewish religious beliefs or practices. (One of his atrocities is briefly mentioned in Luke 13:1.) By the time of Mark's writing, Pilate was so well known in Christian circles that he needed no detailed description.

Pilate's first question to Jesus (15:2) gets right to the heart of the charge. The phrase *king of the Jews* doesn't appear in Mark until this point, yet it is used six times in chapter 15. By doing so, Mark calls attention to the fact that Jesus died as the king of the Jews.

Jesus' affirmative response is quick and direct (15:2). Pilate wasn't too concerned if Jesus were only a religious leader. But if Jesus saw Himself as someone seeking to overthrow the Roman government, He would surely be executed.

Mark doesn't specify what other charges the Jewish leaders bring against Jesus (15:3). Whatever they are, Jesus again remains silent (15:4–5; 14:60–61). Pilate is amazed, probably because he has never seen anyone refuse to defend himself in such a situation.

The custom of releasing a prisoner (15:6) is probably unique to Pilate. No records exist to suggest this was an official Roman practice. Most likely, it was a ploy for popularity.

Mark records another irony with his account of Barabbas (15:7–11). After showing how the religious leaders have gone to such lengths to position Jesus as a threat to Rome, Pilate then places Him up against an already convicted insurrectionist. It seems that Pilate is attempting to see that Jesus is set free.

Pilate's attempt to release Jesus is probably based less on motives of humanity and justice than his contempt for the men who are railroading Jesus. It surely wasn't hard for a politically astute ruler to see that the Jewish leadership was envious of Jesus and that the entire procedure was a sham. Just as clear to see would have been Jesus' pure and moral character. Indeed, if Jesus really had been vehemently opposed to Roman rule, it is highly unlikely that the Jewish leaders would have turned Him in.

The crowd's defense of Barabbas (15:11) is influenced by the chief priests. Pilate has unconditional power of amnesty and can release both prisoners if he wishes. But Mark suggests that Pilate sees the potential for a riot and makes the politically correct decision.

As the momentum shifts and the people turn against Jesus, they begin to demand His crucifixion (15:13). Yet when Pilate presses the point and asks what crimes Jesus has committed, they have no answer (15:14). As a result, Jesus is falsely accused by the Jews and condemned by Pilate for the very offense for which Barabbas is guilty.

15:16–20

JESUS BEFORE THE SOLDIERS

The Praetorium (15:16) probably refers to whatever building(s) constituted the residence and office of the governor. The Praetorium was not always a fixed place, but was designated wherever a high Roman official conducted business—many times outdoors.

The "whole company of soldiers" (NIV) was a cohort—a Roman force of between 200 and 600 men. It was typical of Roman soldiers to humiliate as well as torture condemned prisoners. Purple cloth was very expensive, so the color purple (15:17) is associated with royalty. The "crown" of thorns is a mocking parody of the emperor's laurel wreath. The soldiers' shout, "Hail, king of the Jews," is an imitation of their salute, "Hail, Caesar the Emperor."

During all this time of mocking, Jesus is also being beaten and spat upon. All had been prophesied in the Old Testament: the mocking (Psalm 22:7; Isaiah 53:3), the beating (Isaiah 50:6; 53:4–5; Micah 5:1), and the spitting (Isaiah 50:6). Jesus had also foretold these very offenses (Mark 10:33–34).

Demystifying Mark

Flogging was a severe punishment in itself, yet was also used as a preliminary to crucifixion (perhaps to hasten death). Roman flogging must be distinguished from the "forty lashes less one" that were sometimes administered as a synagogue punishment. The Romans embedded bits of metal, bone, or glass in leather thongs, which shredded the flesh of victims until bones or entrails were exposed. Occasionally flogging was fatal.

The usual Roman procedure was to strip the convicted person and flog him along the way to the place of execution. But Jesus has already been flogged (15:15) and can bear no more. He will even need help along the way to carry His cross.

Take It Home

How do you feel when you read about the different groups that mistreated Jesus: the so-called religious leaders who twisted truth and incited crowds; the Roman soldiers who were so merciless; and even the disciples who betrayed, denied, and deserted Jesus? Lest we be too hard on them, we need to realize that what they did would be no different than what *anyone* would have done. It is Jesus' sacrifice on the cross that allows us to find salvation and treasure the love of God within us. Barabbas was a symbol for us all. Our ongoing response should be one of wonder and gratitude.

MARK 15:21–47

JESUS' CRUCIFIXION, DEATH, AND BURIAL

Jesus' Crucifixion	15:21–32
The Death of Jesus	15:33–41
Jesus' Burial	15:42–47

Setting Up the Section

The plot to have Jesus put to death is finally implemented. After a number of debates, disagreements, and outright conflicts with Jesus, the Jewish religious leaders finally get

what they want. Yet even in His death, there is additional evidence that Jesus is who He claimed to be—the Messiah and the Son of God.

15:21–32

JESUS' CRUCIFIXION

We know that Jesus started toward Golgotha bearing His own cross (John 19:17). But the fact that Simon is recruited to help Him carry it (Mark 15:21) indicates that Jesus must be very weak at this point. Some people speculate that Simon was a Gentile, but a colony of Jews had lived in Cyrene, North Africa, since the fourth century BC, so Simon could just as easily have been a Jewish pilgrim in Jerusalem for Passover. The passing reference to "Alexander and Rufus" indicates they were probably church members who would have been familiar to Mark's readers.

Golgotha (15:22) is a Greek form of the Aramaic word for "skull." None of the Gospel writers provide a location or description of the place. Both Jews and Romans customarily executed people in public places, but outside the city. It is possible that the name reflects a place of unnatural death.

Crucifixion (15:24) was one of the most horrifying forms of execution ever devised. After being stripped and flogged, the victim was lashed and/or nailed to a wooden pole. Death usually came slowly as a result of exposure and exhaustion. Inasmuch as no vital organ was damaged, it often took two or three days for the subject to die, although death could be hastened by breaking the legs, making breathing much more difficult. The usual practice was for the condemned person to carry the crossbar to the place of execution where he was affixed to it before being hoisted upon the vertical pole that was permanently fixed.

Demystifying Mark

Crucifixion seems to have been invented by the Persians, adapted by the Carthaginians, and then learned by the Romans. It was the ultimate punishment for slaves and provincials, but never used for Roman citizens. There were different kinds of crosses, including a single upright pole with two crossed poles in the shape of an X. But the most common seems to have been a vertical pole with a horizontal crossbar on or near the top to form a T shape.

The Babylonian Talmud records a tradition of the women of Jerusalem providing those condemned to die with a narcotic drink–possibly based on Proverbs 31:6–7. The "wine mixed with myrrh" offered to Jesus (15:23) may have had this purpose, but He refuses it. He faces death in complete control of His senses and willingly endures the pain. Jesus endures the fullness of suffering and death so human beings would never need to. Because He has faced the worst, He can see us through any future sufferings.

Roman custom allotted the clothing of the victim to the executioner (15:24). Clothing held much more value in ancient times than today. Casting lots for Jesus' clothing calls to mind Psalm 22:18.

The "third hour" (15:25) was 9:00 a.m. The written inscription (15:26) was usually a placard containing the condemned man's charges that he wore around his neck to the execution site, where it was then affixed to the cross. However, we learn from other Gospel accounts that Pilate himself was responsible for the sign designating Jesus as "king of the Jews." Again, what he surely meant as something to aggravate the Jewish religious leaders, unwittingly proclaimed the truth about Jesus.

The word translated "robbers" (15:27) probably means "insurrectionists" or "rebels." Perhaps these men were among the group Barabbas was involved with (15:7). The statement, "one on his right" and "one on his left" recalls the recent request of James and John (10:37) and provides insight into what it means to occupy "places of honor" in the kingdom of God.

Verse 28, not found in all Bible translations, was probably a study note (a reference to Isaiah 53:12) inadvertently added to the text by a copyist at a date after Mark's writing.

While on the cross, Jesus is mocked yet again (15:29–32; 14:65; 15:16–20). The repeated taunts for Jesus to save Himself reveal much ignorance. If Jesus had miraculously come done from the cross, He would not have saved Himself *or* others. Only by dying on the cross could He "give His life as a ransom for many" (10:45).

15:33–41

THE DEATH OF JESUS

Mark records two apocalyptic signs that accompany the death of Jesus. The first is eerie darkness (15:33) for three hours (noon until 3:00 p.m.). Jesus' cry out to God (15:34) reveals His mental state. Even throughout His horrendous physical and emotional ordeal, He has been quiet. But here, while He bears the sins of the world, God cannot be with Him. Jesus has to experience the abandonment that sin creates in order for the wrath and justice of God to be fulfilled. His quotation of Psalm 22:1 expresses His feeling of aloneness. Not only have His friends all deserted Him while His enemies have tortured and crucified Him, but now even His heavenly Father is distant.

As Jesus hangs on the cross, many diverse attributes of God are displayed at once. His love and mercy for sinners is clearly evident, as is justice and wrath against sin, which His righteousness demands.

The observers' mistaken belief that Jesus is calling for Elijah (15:35–36) is understandable. The Jews believed not only that Elijah would return, but also that one of his tasks would be to help those in need. The offer of wine vinegar fulfilled Psalm 69:21.

Most people who were crucified grew gradually weaker over a long time and quietly expired. But Mark's account suggests that Jesus' death is sudden and violent, that He voluntarily and deliberately dies with the forceful shout of a victor (15:37).

The second of Mark's recorded apocalyptic signs occurs at the moment of Jesus' death. The tearing of the temple curtain (15:38) represents the climax of the replacement of the temple motif throughout Mark (11:12–25; 13:2; 14:58). The death of Jesus removes the barrier to the Most Holy Place, opening the door to God.

Jesus' death has an immediate effect on one of the people closest to Him—a Roman centurion. Although crowds have mocked and taunted Him while He is on the cross, the centurion sees the way Jesus dies and is convinced of His deity (15:39). The fact that a Gentile is the first to recognize that Jesus' status as Son of God is confirmed through His suffering is quite significant. In fact, it foreshadows the expansion of the gospel mission beyond the Jews into the Gentile nations.

Mark also introduces a group of female disciples, three who were named, who are observing Jesus' death "from a distance" (15:40). Members of their group will also be at His burial and later at the empty tomb. Although Jesus has been forsaken by His male disciples, these women display great strength and courage.

15:42–47

JESUS' BURIAL

The Romans did not always permit burial of executed criminals, often leaving the bodies on the cross to rot or be devoured by animals and birds. But the Jews believed a quick and decent burial of the dead—including enemies and criminals—was an act of piety.

"Preparation Day" (15:42) was the Friday prior to the Sabbath. Since sunset was the starting point, Jesus' body needed quick attention to prevent profaning the Sabbath and to comply with burial instructions in Deuteronomy 21:22–23.

It was unusual to release a body to someone not a relative. Yet Jesus' mother seems to have left the scene (John 19:26–27) and nothing is said of His other family members. None of the Twelve have the courage to ask for the body, but a high-ranking Jewish leader steps forward. Joseph of Arimathea is a secret disciple (John 19:38) who volunteers to see to Jesus' burial, at risk to his own reputation, if not his life.

Pilate's surprise that Jesus is already dead (15:44) is not unusual. But the fact that he releases the body of one charged with treason may further indicate that he recognizes Jesus' innocence.

Critical Observation

Burial in caves or in rock chambers of abandoned quarries was much more common among ancient Jews than burial in the ground. Such tombs were sealed with large rocks to keep out animals and grave robbers. But upscale tombs often had a disk-shaped rock similar to a millstone that rolled back and forth in a channel. The channel sloped toward the opening so that it was easy to seal the grave, but difficult to remove the stone and uncover it.

As Joseph wraps Jesus' body and places it in his own tomb (Matthew 27:60), he is seen by two of Jesus' previously mentioned female disciples (Mark 15:40, 47). They note the location of the tomb and plan to return to anoint Jesus' body, but their plans will be surprisingly changed.

Take It Home

During His crucifixion, the worst experience known to humans, Jesus refused substances that would have deadened the pain. Why do you think He did so? What hope do you gain from knowing that Jesus endured the full pain of the cross? What help does this give to us as we face the trials and suffering that come from following Jesus?

MARK 16:1–8

BETWEEN DEATH AND RESURRECTION

Worry	16:1–3
Alarm	16:4–6
Fear	16:7–8

Setting Up the Section

We are accustomed to moving quickly from any consideration of Jesus' death to the joy and certainty of His resurrection. But for His first-century disciples, the emotions following the death of their leader are dark and severe indeed. It is these emotions that help to put the significance of His resurrection into a clearer perspective.

16:1–3

WORRY

Due to the onset of the Sabbath, the women who have followed Jesus' ministry have not been able to attend to His body after His death as they wished. But they are already set to go at sunrise on Sunday morning. They are prepared to anoint His body with oils and spices that were probably bought immediately after sunset the previous night when stores opened briefly after the close of the Sabbath.

The devotion these ladies feel for Jesus is evident in their purchasing of the spices and even more so in their willingness to anoint a body already dead for a day and a half. Also evident is the fact that they are certainly not anticipating a resurrection. They are prepared to see Jesus dead, in the grave, and already beginning to decompose in the Middle East heat. Mark shows his readers that not even Jesus' closest friends and most loyal allies truly understand what He had come to do, even when the great miracle of God was taking place right before their eyes.

Critical Observation

The Jews did not embalm. The use of spices was not to prevent decomposition of the body, but to offset its stench. John's Gospel informs us that Joseph of Arimathea, accompanied by Nicodemus, had already wrapped Jesus' body in about 75 pounds of myrrh and aloes (John 19:38–40). The women didn't seem to know about this, even though they had noted the location of Joseph's tomb (Mark 15:47).

In addition, they are worried about how they might be able to remove the stone that covered the grave (16:3). Tombstones were large to prevent grave robbers from taking clothes and other memorabilia placed in the tomb with the dead. It wasn't unheard of for murderers to hide their victims in tombs. And in Jesus' case, as we learn from Matthew's Gospel, the tomb even had the seal of Rome and guards stationed outside to prevent anyone stealing the body and creating a story that Jesus had risen from the dead.

The male disciples are still in hiding, so the women are on their own. It is natural for them to worry, and they are expecting nothing supernatural. But soon their worry will turn to alarm.

16:4–6

ALARM

On arriving at the tomb, they discover they had worried for nothing. The stone is already rolled away—not to make their access easier, but to reveal that Jesus is no longer there. The young man wearing a white robe (16:5) is an angel who confirms that Jesus has indeed risen from the dead. This unexpected event fills them with alarm. They are not only startled, but afraid as well.

The angel tries to comfort them by assuring them they will see Jesus again and by giving them directions (16:7). The oldest and most reliable versions of Mark's Gospel do not include any post-resurrection accounts of Jesus, but Mark makes it very clear in this passage that Jesus has risen. His body has not been stolen or misplaced. He has been resurrected and is alive again.

Demystifying Mark

The angel's reference to "Jesus of Nazareth" (16:6) is an ongoing reminder that Jesus was a real person who can be traced to specific history and geography.

And as miraculous and hard-to-comprehend as this event was, it rings true largely because of the presence of the women. Since women in the first century weren't even allowed to testify in court, no one would have made up a story where the primary witnesses were all female. The truth of this account is unusually verifiable because the story is too countercultural to be concocted.

Still, the events of the early morning are a shock to the women. Their alarm quickly intensifies into fear.

16:7–8

FEAR

The angel has attempted to comfort the women, and his instructions to them are intended to comfort others (16:7). The news is almost too good to believe: They will see Jesus again, "just as He told you." And this message is to be delivered immediately to the disciples (because they had all fled in Gethsemane) and specifically to Peter (because he, in particular, had denied Jesus). The angel's message implies forgiveness and eventual restoration to fellowship with their Lord. Jesus had previously shared this very plan with them (14:27–28), and it was still intact.

This should have been terrific news, yet the women flee from the tomb just as the disciples had fled from Jesus' arrest. They run out "trembling and bewildered," and "said nothing to anyone, because they were afraid" (16:8 NIV). Other Gospel accounts report that the women also experienced great joy intermingled with their fear. Why did Mark record only the fear? Perhaps he wanted his readers to see the humanity of the women and to comprehend the reality of human interaction with Jesus.

In some manuscripts, this was how the Gospel of Mark originally ended. He concluded with this stark reminder that human faith may fail at times, and trust will waver. Even so, Jesus had not deserted those He loved, and was planning to reunite with them soon.

Take It Home

The women and the disciples did not fully understand the full extent of the cross and thus fear overcame their hearts. How does our lack of understanding the cross bring about fear in our own lives? In light of this text, what insight can we gain from 1 John 4:18? Can you think of an example from the book of Acts where the knowledge of the cross gave the first century believers courage?

MARK 16:9–20

AN ADDENDUM TO THE GOSPEL OF MARK?

Setting Up the Section

Most Bible scholars feel that the Gospel of Mark ended at 16:8 and that verses 9–20 were added considerably later to smooth out the abrupt ending. Although these closing verses are not considered to be part of the scriptures to the extent of the rest of Mark's Gospel, they are an honest attempt to complete the story of Jesus.

Because the other Gospels provide such full accounts of appearances of Jesus after His resurrection, it is curious and somewhat frustrating that Mark's writing stopped at 16:8. Perhaps he had written more, but his ending was lost. The scribes who added verses 9–20 pulled from other scriptures as well as historical witnesses to the post-resurrection lives of the apostles. Therefore, the events recorded here are true, but not a part of Mark's original record.

It seems that two attempts are made to complete Mark's work: one in verses 9–18, and a second in verses 19–20. These passages are largely comprised of details taken from the other Gospels or Acts, with a few additions from early church traditions.

Verses 9–11, seemingly taken from John's Gospel, explain how Mary Magdalene is the first to see the risen Christ. The two of them mentioned in verses 12–13 are a reference to the appearance of Jesus to the two disciples at Emmaus (Luke 24:13–32). And verse 14 has parallels in the other Gospels, though the exact occasion referenced here is not clear.

Even though these verses were most likely added to Mark's Gospel as a footnote, they are still in harmony with the rest of the book. Themes of believing and not believing permeate this section. Although the verses may not be from the pen of Mark, they are nevertheless consistent with his previous writing and with the rest of the Gospels.

The great commission of Matthew 28:18 is reflected in verses 15–16. Belief in Jesus leads to salvation; unbelief is itself a condemnation.

Most of the signs mentioned in verses 17–18 are found either in the Gospels or the book of

Acts. The exception is drinking poison without being harmed, which is mentioned in writings of the early church. Yet the writer does not suggest that these particular signs are provided all the time and for everyone. They were unique events used to authenticate the message of the apostles (Hebrews 2:1–4).

Critical Observation

Though God still performs miracles today, we must not assume that the signs recorded in Mark 16:17–18 still apply in every instance today. The text describes what occurred after the gospel was preached, and does not prescribe action for the church. In other words, a believer bitten by a poisonous snake is not assured continued health should he choose not to seek treatment. We should accept the miracles of God gratefully if and when they occur. But our minds should be set on God's kingdom, not merely on its signs.

The final two verses (19–20) may have been a second addition to Mark's writing. They describe a brief triumphal ascension of Jesus, the apostolic mission of evangelism, and the manner in which the preaching of God's word was vindicated by the results.

The section of Mark 16:9–20 is not part of scripture, so should not be used as a basis for establishing doctrine. However, we may accept these closing verses because they agree with scripture and are a valuable summary of the beliefs of the early church.

Take It Home

Suppose this section of Mark had not been added and you were left hanging with the women "trembling and bewildered" as they fled from Jesus' tomb. What would you have wanted to recall, either from previous portions of Mark or your knowledge of other portions of scripture, to bring closure to this Gospel?

THE GOSPEL OF
LUKE

INTRODUCTION TO LUKE

As author of this Gospel and its sequel, the book of Acts, Luke is responsible for over a fourth of the content of the Greek New Testament. He brings a distinctive perspective to the writing as well. While many of Jesus' followers had the reputation of "unschooled, ordinary men" (Acts 4:13 NIV), Luke's writing in his opening paragraph displays the sophisticated style of Greek historians, and then he moves into smooth, everyday vernacular. His eye for detail is evident in numerous places.

AUTHOR

Luke doesn't identify himself in either of the books he wrote, but there has been little dispute that he was the author of both. He was a physician (Colossians 4:14), and notes specifics in several of Jesus' healings that other writers do not. Aside from the Colossians reference, Luke is mentioned only two other times in the New Testament (2 Timothy 4:11; Philemon 24). People have theorized that he might have been Lucius of Cyrene (Acts 13:1), one of the seventy-two disciples sent out by Jesus (10:1–17), one of the Greeks mentioned in John 12:20, or even the other disciple with Cleopas on the road to Emmaus (24:13–35). But there is no biblical or historic evidence for any of these speculations.

More reliable is the assumption that Luke knew Jesus' mother, Mary. Therefore, his Gospel includes the wonderful account of the shepherds visiting the manger, the story of Elizabeth and Zechariah and the birth of John the Baptist, the mention of Simeon and Anna when Jesus was presented in the temple, and the story of Jesus questioning the religious leaders in the temple at age twelve (1–2).

Luke also traveled on some of Paul's journeys, which is evident from passages in the book of Acts that switch from third person to first person. And he must have been more than a mere acquaintance because Paul refers to him as a dear friend (Colossians 4:14).

PURPOSE

Evidence points to Luke being a Gentile believer who wrote for a Gentile audience. The primary recipient of both his books was "most excellent Theophilus" (Luke 1:3 NIV; Acts 1:1), a title that suggests someone of wealth and authority—perhaps a ranking official. Luke tended to give details about Jewish locations that wouldn't have been necessary for Jewish readers. These and other clues suggest that Luke's intent was explaining the story of Jesus to Gentiles.

OCCASION

Theophilus may have been a financial backer for Luke's travels and/or writing. However, while he may have been the first recipient of Luke's words about Jesus, it isn't likely he was intended to be the sole reader. Theophilus had already heard about Jesus; Luke was writing to confirm the authenticity and validity of the gospel. Luke began with eyewitness accounts and then personally investigated them to ensure accuracy (1:1–4). He showed that the faith of Theophilus—and all those who believed in Jesus Christ—had a strong foundation.

THEMES

In his concern for Gentiles, Luke's portrayal of the gospel is more encompassing than that of the other Gospel writers. He stresses an individual's privilege and ability to repent and be forgiven—and the joy that results from each such decision (15:7, 10, 32). Numerous Samaritans, women, children, Roman officials, and other traditional outsiders are shown in a positive light, providing a natural segue into his book of Acts and the worldwide mission of the church. Luke alone tells of the thief on the cross who repents and is promised a place in paradise with Jesus (23:39–43).

Luke had a high regard for women, as seen in stories such as the faith of Elizabeth (1:5–80), Anna in the temple (2:36–38), and the dilemma between Mary and Martha (10:38–42). He records Jesus' gentle words toward women of faith (7:13; 8:48; 13:12, 15–16; 23:28–31), and he credits the women who traveled with Jesus and supported Him (8:1–3). In doing so, Luke introduces his readers to thirteen women who appear nowhere else in scripture.

Luke has much to say about money. More accurately, he records much of what Jesus had to say about wealth that other writers didn't include. For example, Luke is the only source for Jesus' Parable of the Rich Man and Lazarus (16:19–31). He also tells of how first the twelve disciples, and then another seventy-two, were sent out with no provisions in order to see for themselves that God would provide (9:1–6; 10:1–17). And the theme of money is carried throughout the Gospel, as he notes attitudes toward the poor as well as toward the rich.

Though he doesn't usually elaborate, Luke also highlights the prayer habits of Jesus (3:21–22; 5:16; 6:12; 22:41–44; etc.). Because of His example, Jesus' disciples began to ask about improving their own prayer habits (11:1).

HISTORICAL CONTEXT

Luke establishes times within his Gospel by citing rulers of the period (1:5; 2:1–2; 3:1; etc.). However, the actual date of his writing is difficult to determine. Neither of his books makes reference to the fall of Jerusalem (AD 70) or even Nero's persecution of the early Christians (AD 64). It is commonly estimated that Luke was written after Mark, which was probably written in the mid to late 60s.

CONTRIBUTION TO THE BIBLE

Over half of Luke's Gospel contains content found nowhere else in scripture. In addition to what has already been mentioned (Elizabeth and Zechariah, the Nativity stories, Jesus at age twelve, the repentant thief on the cross, the Rich Man and Lazarus, etc.), Luke includes seven miracles of Jesus and nineteen of His parables that are unique to this Gospel.

Were it not for Luke's Gospel, we would miss out on many of the most-read and appreciated portions of scripture: the parables of the Good Samaritan (10:30–37) and the Prodigal Son (15:11–32), Jesus' visit to see Zacchaeus (19:1–10), one of the accounts of a resurrection from the dead (7:11–17), the healing of the ten lepers (17:12–19), the two disciples on the road to Emmaus after Jesus' resurrection (24:13–35), Jesus' "Father, forgive them" prayer from the cross (23:34 NIV), and more.

On a related note, Luke tended to notice and record the artistic, poetic expressions of the people he researched. He alone includes the songs or canticles of Elizabeth (1:41–45), Mary (1:46–55), Zechariah (1:67–79), Simeon (2:29–32), and even the angels announcing Jesus' birth (2:13–14).

STRUCTURE

The commentary for this book is laid out by chapters for ease of use, but here is a look at the broader structure of this book of the Bible:

Jesus' Birth and Preparation for Ministry	1:1–4:13
Jesus' Ministry in Galilee	4:14–9:50
Jesus' Journey to Jerusalem	9:51–19:27
Jesus' Ministry amidst Conflict in Jerusalem	19:28–21:38
Jesus' Arrest, Trial, and Crucifixion	22:1–23:56
The Resurrection and Ascension	24:1–53

OUTLINE

A MIRACLE BIRTH (BEFORE JESUS') 1:1–80

Luke's Salutation	1:1–4
Zechariah's Encounter with Gabriel	1:5–25
Jesus' Birth Predicted	1:26–56
John the Baptist Is Born	1:57–80

THE ARRIVAL OF THE MESSIAH 2:1–52

The Birth of Jesus	2:1–20
The Infant Jesus at the Temple	2:21–40
The Boy Jesus at the Temple	2:41–52

TWO MINISTRIES BEGIN 3:1–38

The Voice of One Calling in the Desert	3:1–6
Q & A with John the Baptist	3:7–20
Jesus' Family Tree	3:21–38

TEMPTATION, REJECTION, AND HEALING 4:1–44

Forty Days in the Wilderness	4:1–13
The Hometown Crowd Turns on Jesus	4:14–30
Jesus Demonstrates His Power	4:31–44

CHOOSING DISCIPLES AND DEFINING DISCIPLINES 5:1–6:11

A Shift of Emphasis	5:1–11
Healing a Leper and a Paralytic	5:12–26
Levi Becomes a Disciple and Throws a Party	5:27–39
Sabbath Issues	6:1–11

A DIFFERENT WAY OF SEEING THE WORLD 6:12–49

Designating the Top Twelve	6:12–16
Blessings and Woes	6:17–26
A Very Different Perspective	6:27–49

SAVING FAITH AND A FAITHFUL SAVIOR 7:1–50

The Faith of a Gentile	7:1–10
Jesus Brings a Widow's Son Back to Life	7:11–17
A Message for John the Baptist	7:18–35
Unusual Insight from a Woman "Sinner"	7:36–50

PARABLES, MIRACLES, AND FAMILY MATTERS 8:1–56

Spiritual Wisdom and the Parable of the Soils 8:1–21
Two Fear-Inspiring Miracles 8:22–39
Two More Amazing Miracles 8:40–56

HIGHS AND LOWS OF MINISTRY 9:1–62

Paired Up and Sent Out 9:1–9
Jesus Feeds Five Thousand 9:10–17
Peter's Confession and Jesus' Transfiguration 9:18–36
Some Shortcomings of the Disciples 9:37–56
Excuses Not to Follow Jesus 9:57–62

SEVENTY-TWO MISSIONARIES, A GOOD SAMARITAN, AND SIBLING RIVALRY 10:1–42

The Seventy-two 10:1–24
The Good Samaritan 10:25–37
Mary and Martha Disagree about What's Important 10:38–42

PRAYER, DEMONS, SIGNS, AND WOES 11:1–54

Lessons on Prayer 11:1–13
Jesus vs. Beelzebub 11:14–36
A Long Series of Woes 11:37–54

WARNINGS AND ASSURANCES 12:1–59

Beware Bad Yeast 12:1–11
Hoarding vs. Trust 12:12–34
Two Contrasting Scenarios 12:35–59

CLEARING UP SOME MISCONCEPTIONS 13:1–35

Why Do Bad Things Happen? 13:1–9
Resentment in Response to a Healing 13:10–17
Two Short Parables 13:18–21
Take Nothing for Granted 13:22–35

BANQUET ETIQUETTE 14:1–35

Dinner Conversation 14:1–14
A Banquet Parable 14:15–24
Seeing Things Through to the Finish 14:25–35

LOST AND FOUND (X 3)	15:1–32
The Lost Sheep	15:1–7
The Lost Coin	15:8–10
The Lost Son	15:11–32
TWO CHALLENGING PARABLES	16:1–31
The Shrewd (Dishonest) Steward	16:1–18
The Rich Man and Lazarus	16:19–31
FAITH, SERVICE, AND EXPECTATION	17:1–37
Sin and Forgiveness	17:1–10
A 10 Percent Return of Gratitude	17:11–19
Missing the Obvious	17:20–37
PERSISTENCE AND PENITENCE	18:1–43
A Persistent Widow vs. an Unjust Judge	18:1–8
A Pharisee and a Tax Collector	18:9–14
Little Children and a Rich Ruler	18:15–34
A Loud Blind Man	18:35–43
LAST JOURNEY TO JERUSALEM	19:1–48
A Tax Collector in a Tree	19:1–10
In the Absence of the Master	19:11–27
Jesus Arrives at Jerusalem	19:28–48
QUESTIONS OF AUTHORITY	20:1–47
By What Authority?	20:1–18
Taxes and Resurrection	20:19–40
Son of David or Lord of David?	20:41–47
THE FUTURE: INDICATIONS AND INSTRUCTIONS	21:1–38
A Widow's Special Gift	21:1–4
The Coming Fall of Jerusalem	21:5–24
Signs and Promises	21:25–38
BETRAYAL, DENIAL, ARREST, AND ANGUISH	22:1–65
A Traitor among the Group	22:1–6
The Last Supper	22:7–38
Jesus' Arrest	22:39–65

JESUS' TRIALS AND CRUCIFIXION 22:66–23:56

The Trials 22:66–23:25
Jesus' Crucifixion 23:26–43
Jesus' Death 23:44–56

RESURRECTION AND SECOND CHANCES 24:1–53

The Empty Tomb 24:1–12
Cleopas and His Friend 24:13–35
A Final Training Period 24:36–53

LUKE 1:1–80

A MIRACLE BIRTH (BEFORE JESUS')

Luke's Salutation	1:1–4
Zechariah's Encounter with Gabriel	1:5–25
Jesus' Birth Predicted	1:26–56
John the Baptist Is Born	1:57–80

Setting Up the Section

Luke begins his Gospel of Jesus not with the account of Jesus' birth, but with the announcement of the miraculous, approaching birth of John the Baptist. The Jewish people had been told to expect the coming of Elijah prior to the arrival of their Messiah (Malachi 4:5–6). John the Baptist would fulfill the Elijah role of preparing for and announcing the coming of Jesus (Matthew 11:11–14). And Zechariah and Elizabeth prove to be dedicated and influential parents just as Mary and Joseph were.

1:1–4

LUKE'S SALUTATION

Luke immediately acknowledges that numerous people have been writing about Jesus, but he wants to ensure his readers that they will have a trustworthy account based on eyewitnesses (1:1–2). He personally sets out to investigate carefully before writing. "Most excellent" (1:3 NIV) was a title of respect. While nothing is known of Luke's recipient, Theophilus, he may have been a Roman official who became a Christian. He very well might have been a Gentile, and perhaps even Luke's financial backer. Regardless, since Luke is writing to an individual concerned with the truth of the gospel of Jesus, his Gospel is appropriate for all interested readers.

1:5–25

ZECHARIAH'S ENCOUNTER WITH GABRIEL

The Herod referred to in verse 5 is Herod the Great, who would rule until 4 BC. A number of other Herodian leaders are mentioned in the Bible—all descendants of Herod the Great.

Luke's description of Zechariah and Elizabeth reveals their childlessness as well as the qualities for which they found favor with God, and which were the basis for God's selection of them as the parents of John.

Zechariah (or Zacharias) was not a prominent religious leader, but he was a faithful priest. Unlike later New Testament religious figures who exemplify self-righteousness and completely twist the intent of God's law, Zechariah stands out as someone "upright in the sight of God" (1:6 NIV). His wife Elizabeth is equally righteous. However, their inability to conceive a child may have been seen as a sign of God's displeasure for some offense (an opinion soon to be disproved).

Many priests were available to serve in the temple, so various duties were assigned "by lot" (1:9 NASB). The duties were allocated according to the divisions of priests (1 Chronicles 24). When it came time for the order of Abijah's division to perform the temple duties, Zechariah is chosen for the very high privilege of burning the incense, which he did either in the morning or the evening. This was such a high privilege it might be done by a priest only once in a lifetime. It was a very coveted task. Some of the priests would never have the honor of going into the Holy Place alone and providing fresh incense that burned continually on the special altar before the Most Holy Place. But while Zechariah is there, the angel Gabriel appears to him.

After getting past the initial shock and fear (1:12), Zechariah hears that his wife Elizabeth will soon have a child—a very special child (1:13–17), whose purpose will be to prepare the people for the coming of the Lord. He will be filled with the Holy Spirit from His mother's womb (1:41, 44).

While it's understandable from a human perspective that Zechariah has difficulty believing this amazing thing is happening to him, there were a number of examples of supernatural births in the Old Testament with which he is certainly familiar. Abraham and Sarah had a son in their old age, as did Hannah and the parents of Samson.

Critical Observation

The instructions for John's upbringing as specified by Gabriel are conditions of the Old Testament Nazirite vow (Numbers 6:1–21). Samson and other biblical figures were also Nazirites (Judges 13:2–5).

Zechariah is understandably confused and skeptical because of his and Elizabeth's advanced age. Because of his doubts, and to signify that something special has indeed occurred, Zechariah's ability to speak is temporarily suspended. It will be restored when the promised child is born (1:20).

The people outside the temple are growing restless (1:21). Zechariah is supposed to lead a blessing when he comes out, and it shouldn't have taken very long to light the incense. In addition, the people waiting would be well familiar with the story about the sons of Aaron, who were put to death because they had performed this very function with an improper attitude (Leviticus 10:1–2). Even after Zechariah emerges from the temple, it takes them all a while to determine what has happened. But it doesn't take long for Gabriel's prophecy to come true (1:24–25).

1:26-56

JESUS' BIRTH PREDICTED

Gabriel's announcement to Mary is significant for many reasons, including the declaration that Jesus will be the Messiah who will fulfill God's promise to King David (1:32–33). This promise is recorded in 2 Samuel 7, particularly verses 10–16. Nathan's prophecy from God was that King David's family (of which Jesus would be a descendant) would rule forever.

Mary is quite a contrast to Zechariah in age, gender, and marital status. Yet Gabriel gives her a similar impossible prediction. After her initial surprise at being addressed as "highly favored" (1:28 NIV), she is also confused at how she can be pregnant having never had sex (1:34). This is an additional contrast: Zechariah had been somewhat doubtful, but Mary is only seeking clarification in order to comply with God's message. Mary quickly absorbs what Gabriel is asking her to do, and her response is exemplary (1:38).

Both Mary and Elizabeth are learning that nothing is impossible with God (1:37). Gabriel identifies them as relatives, but their relationship is never explained. We aren't told how much each woman knew of the other's story prior to Mary's visit. Nor do we know exactly when Mary conceived God's child. But no sooner has Mary greeted Elizabeth than Elizabeth's child "leaped in her womb" (1:41 NIV). Filled with the Holy Spirit, Elizabeth immediately recognizes the importance of the child Mary will bear, as well as the significance of the son she is carrying (1:41–45).

We aren't told that Mary, too, is filled with the Holy Spirit, but can assume so. Her song (called the *Magnificat*) reflects a great depth of spiritual understanding. Her praise (1:46–55) is buoyed with numerous Old Testament references and allusions. It begins with her personal expression of humility and expands to reflect God's grace to His chosen people, Israel.

Elizabeth is six months' pregnant when Mary arrives (1:36), and Mary stays three months (1:56). We can speculate that she stays until the birth of John, and then returns home to complete her own pregnancy.

Critical Observation

Luke tends to notice and record creative expression more than other Gospel writers. He alone recorded Elizabeth's Spirit-inspired proclamation (1:42–45). He also included several songs or canticles.

Mary	1:46–55 "The Magnificat," Latin for "magnify," from Mary's opening words.
Zechariah	1:68–79 Called "The Benedictus," which is Latin meaning "blessed."
Angelic chorus	2:14 Called "Gloria in Excelsis," Latin for "Glory to God."
Simeon	2:29–32 Called the "Nunc Dimittis" because these are the first two words of the Latin translation of the prayer. It translates into English as "now depart."

1:57–80

JOHN THE BAPTIST IS BORN

When the time comes for Elizabeth to have her baby, neighbors and relatives gather (1:57–58). But a conflict arises at the baby's circumcision because the crowd of supporters assumes the child will be named after Zechariah. The name, however, has already been assigned by Gabriel (1:13), which Elizabeth knows. But the others resist her and go to Zechariah, who asks for a writing tablet. As soon as he gives written confirmation that the child's name will be John (1:63), he regains his speech and immediately begins praising God.

In first-century Middle East culture, being named after a father or other family member indicated intent to follow in his steps. But John will not become a priest like Zechariah. He will have his own distinct ministry.

Luke also notes that these very important events are not first announced to the religious elite of the day, or even in the temple in Jerusalem. The first to hear of the arrival of the kingdom of God (and to respond in awe) are the simple people in the hill country (1:65). The announcement foreshadows the later ministries of Jesus and John, who come not to the healthy and the righteous, but to the sick and to sinners (Matthew 9:12–13).

As Elizabeth and Mary had done previously, Zechariah uses his renewed power of speech to praise God. His Spirit-inspired proclamation (1:67–79) is more personal and prophetic than Mary's, laying out John's purpose in life as well as his relationship with Jesus. Yet John's individual ministry is seen in the context of the nation of Israel.

Luke's concluding statement for this account (1:80) is short, but summarizes about thirty years of John's life. Zechariah's and Elizabeth's child will grow not only physically, but will also become strong in his spirit. His strength will be developed in solitude for eventual use in public ministry.

Take It Home

In light of the significant events taking place in this passage, the participants all seemed to prepare for their roles in solitude. Mary and Elizabeth went into seclusion. Zechariah found solitude in silence. And John went into the wilderness. To what extent is solitude a part of your regular spiritual growth? Do you make time to be alone with God, or is most of your spiritual commitment tied to fellowship and interaction with others? Are you satisfied with your current balance of time devoted solely to God and time devoted to others?

LUKE 2:1–52

THE ARRIVAL OF THE MESSIAH

The Birth of Jesus 2:1–20
The Infant Jesus at the Temple 2:21–40
The Boy Jesus at the Temple 2:41–52

Setting Up the Section

Luke interweaves the birth stories of Jesus and John the Baptist. In the previous passage he provided the angelic foretelling of both miraculous births, and provided the story of John's birth. In this passage, he moves on to the details of Jesus' birth and early life.

Luke 2 has three major sections. Verses 1–20 depict the birth of Jesus and the worship and witness of the shepherds. Verses 21–40 feature an account of the presentation of Jesus at Jerusalem, and the inspired testimony of Simeon and Anna. Verses 41–52 describe Jesus' visit to the temple, His Father's house, busy with His Father's business.

2:1–20

THE BIRTH OF JESUS

The details of Jesus' birth are surprisingly scarce in the Bible. Mark and John ignore them altogether. Matthew provides a few stories surrounding the birth. Luke is the only Gospel writer to cover the birth itself.

Demystifying Luke

Remember that Luke's recipient, Theophilus, could have been a Roman official. The term "most excellent," which Luke uses in chapter 1 (1:3 NIV), is also used by Luke three times in Acts (23:26; 24:3; 26:25), each time in reference to a political official of high standing. While we may care little that Quirinius was governor of Syria (2:2), this fact would have been significant to Theophilus. Luke was providing facts that showed Theophilus that faith in Jesus had historical validity—something not true of the other "gods" of the time.

The census (2:1–3) not only inconveniently forced people to their hometowns; it was also a painful reminder that the Jewish people were under the rule of a pagan power. Yet it serves to send Mary and Joseph to Bethlehem (2:4–5), the place where the prophet Micah had long ago predicted the Jewish Messiah was to be born (Micah 5:2). The journey from Nazareth to Bethlehem is more than sixty miles and will take at least three days.

Luke properly points out that Joseph and Mary are "pledged to be married" (2:5 NIV) at this point. Matthew calls them husband and wife (Matthew 1:19, 24)—titles used as soon as an engagement was formally announced. But to ensure the purity of the bride, the engagement was followed by a one-year period of abstinence and waiting. At the end of the year, the marriage ceremony would be held, the relationship consummated, and the couple would begin living together. When Mary is found to be pregnant during the waiting period, Joseph's initial instinct is to get a quiet divorce. But after being informed by an angel what is happening, Joseph breaks tradition and takes Mary into his home. However, the official consummation and beginning of their marriage will not take place until after the birth of Jesus (Matthew 1:18–25).

Much of the imagery that has become a part of the Christmas and Nativity tradition has been supplied by our filling in the gaps of Luke's account. What we are told is that there is not room in the inn. In this case, the word *inn* probably refers to a guest room. It was the custom of the day for the Jews of Jerusalem to have enough guest rooms to accommodate their guests. Joseph and Mary must have expected this would be the case, but when they arrive in Bethlehem, such accommodations aren't available.

Joseph and Mary's not having a place to stay results in the baby Jesus being wrapped in rags or strips of cloth and placed in a cattle feeding trough for a crib (2:6–7). We do not know if Jesus is born in a stable or in a cave. The feeding trough could have been borrowed, so if the baby may have been born under the stars. Mary may have preferred the privacy. The trough would have provided a soft place for the baby to sleep and the strips of cloth, wrapped around the child, would have kept his arms and legs tucked in and kept the cold out, especially if the family was camped in the open, out in the elements. In addition, the baby being wrapped in cloths and lying in a manger would be a sign for the shepherds (2:12).

The Egyptians in the days of the Old Testament looked down on shepherds (Genesis 46:33–34), yet Israelite leaders such as David and Moses were shepherds. God Himself is described as a shepherd. The shepherds described by Luke seem to be godly men—men who are looking for the coming of Israel's Messiah. All the others of those who are directly informed of the birth of the Messiah in Matthew and Luke are described as godly people, and so it seems to be true of the shepherds as well. After all, news of His coming would not be good news (2:10) unless they were seeking Him. The haste of these shepherds to the place of Christ's birth (2:15–16) also testifies to their spiritual preparedness and eagerness for the coming of the Messiah.

To these humble shepherds the angel of God appears in a blaze of glory, which causes them to be greatly frightened (2:9). The angel assures them that he brings them good news, and tells them of the birth of the Messiah. This is to be the cause of joy for all the people—all the nations, and not just Israel, would benefit from His birth. Suddenly, the angel is joined by a host, as a divine confirmation of the angel's announcement.

The angel has promised a sign to the shepherds—they will find the child wrapped in strips of cloth and lying in a cattle feeding trough (2:12). The sign is not designed to convince the shepherds of the truth of the angelic announcement. Surely the splendor of the angel, compounded by that of the heavenly host, is convincing enough. This sign is for the purpose of identification. The way that they will recognize God's Messiah is by His swaddling clothes and by His unusual crib. No other child will be found in such a setting.

These signs do even more than simply identify Jesus. They allow Him to identify with the shepherds. One of the names of Messiah is Emmanuel, which means "God with us." The circumstances of our Lord's birth uniquely identify the Lord Jesus with the shepherds. The Lord seemingly has no roof over His head, no house to dwell in. Neither do the shepherds, who, we are told, sleep under the stars as they care for their flocks (2:8). Jesus is poor and of no reputation, as are they. And Jesus is to be both the sacrificial Lamb of God (see Isaiah 53:4–6; John 1:29) and the Good Shepherd (Psalm 23:1; Ezekiel 34:23; John 10:14).

The shepherds' arrival at the manger (2:16) must have been comforting for Mary and Joseph. Both have been told by their own angelic messengers about the significance of the child they will parent, but surely it is reassuring in this faraway place to get confirmation from other sources. And after seeing Jesus, the shepherds spread the word about what they have been told, amazing all who hear them (2:17–20).

2:21–40

THE INFANT JESUS AT THE TEMPLE

Several ceremonies were required after the birth of a child.

1) The circumcision was to take place the eighth day after the birth of a son (Leviticus 12:3) because the mother would be ceremonially unclean for seven days after giving birth. The child was usually assigned a name at this time.
2) A second ceremony was the presentation and consecration of a firstborn son (Exodus 13:1–2, 12).
3) Then there was the purification of the mother, celebrated forty days after the birth of a son or eighty days after having a daughter (Leviticus 12:1–5).

It is the second ceremony, the presentation of Jesus at the temple, which is most prominent in Luke's account (2:27). It is on this occasion that Simeon and Anna appear to attest and announce that the baby Jesus is God's Messiah, the Savior of the world.

Critical Observation

Jesus' circumcision is not prominent in this passage, but it is noteworthy. First, this record attests to the fact that the parents of our Lord did everything according to the Law (2:39). Second, the circumcision of Christ parallels that of John, described earlier (1:59–79). Finally, it was at the circumcision of Christ that His name was formally given.

Jesus' name was predetermined and had been announced by Gabriel (Matthew 1:21; Luke 1:31). The Hebrew form of the name was Jeshua, derived by combining two root words that meant "the Lord" and "to save." So the name *Jesus* means "the Lord is salvation."

During His presentation, the identity and significance of Jesus is twice more confirmed. The first to praise Jesus is an old man named Simeon, who has been told by the Holy Spirit that he will not die before he has seen the Christ (2:26). The only things we are told about Simeon are those which matter most to God—things pertaining to his faith, his character, and his relationship with God. We are told that Simeon is righteous and devout (2:25), which speaks of his personal walk with God and his integrity. He is a man of faith and hope, for he looked for the restoration of Israel through the coming of the Messiah. Finally, Simeon is a man who is filled by the Holy Spirit. It is the Holy Spirit who has revealed to Simeon that he will not die until he has seen the Messiah (2:26). It is also the Holy Spirit that directs Simeon to the temple on the particular day that Jesus' parents bring Him to be presented to the Lord. Finally, in some unspecified way, it is the Spirit of God who reveals to Simeon that this child is indeed the Messiah.

Recognizing Jesus to be the Messiah, this elderly man takes the child in his arms and blesses God. He reveals that He will become a light of revelation to the Gentiles and glory for Israel (2:32). He also is the first to acknowledge the suffering that will come to Jesus and those connected to Him (2:34–35).

Up to this point in Luke's Gospel, all of the inspired utterances pertaining to the Lord Jesus have been very positive, speaking with reference to His ruling on David's throne, setting right the things that are wrong, and bringing peace and salvation to people. But now Simeon unveils the other side of the story, which is also a part of the Old Testament prophecies, such as those of Psalm 22 or Isaiah 53—prophecies of the rejection, crucifixion, and death of the Messiah. More pointedly, Simeon's words prepare Mary for the grief she must suffer, as the rejection of Her Son by men will cause her to witness His death on the cross.

Simeon's revelations are confirmed by Anna, an eighty-four-year-old prophetess who never leaves the temple. While we are told less about what she actually says, we are given more information about her background than Simeon's. Anna is of the tribe of Asher, one of the ten lost tribes of Israel, which were scattered in the Assyrian captivity. She is also a prophetess. She was married for seven years before her husband died, and has lived the rest of her life as a widow. Day and night she is in the temple praying and fasting. She gives thanks to God and speaks of Jesus' role in the redemption of Jerusalem (2:38).

The inspired utterances of Simeon and Anna completely overshadow the ceremony of Christ's presentation. The occasion for the appearance of our Lord at the temple is His presentation, but nothing is actually said about this ceremony. We have no record of the ritual, nor are we given the names of any of the priests involved in the ceremony. We are only told of Simeon and Anna and of their proclamations. It is not the ceremony itself, the ritual of the presentation of Jesus, which is most important, but the proclamation of these two saints.

2:41–52

THE BOY JESUS AT THE TEMPLE

Luke's next story fast-forwards twelve years to the only inspired, biblically recorded incident in the life of Jesus between His birth and His adult ministry. After an annual trip to Jerusalem to celebrate Passover, Jesus is found missing on the return trip home to Nazareth. His parents backtrack to Jerusalem and finally find Him in the temple with the teachers, listening and asking questions (2:46).

After a rebuke by His frustrated mother, Luke provides the earliest known words of Jesus: "Why were you searching for me? . . . Didn't you know I had to be in my Father's house?" (2:49 NIV). Or as some translations render it, "Did you not know that I must be about My Father's business?" (NKJV).

Although Jesus' parents don't understand what He means, Jesus is already preparing Himself for His adult mission. At thirteen Jewish males joined the adult community, and Jesus has an opportunity at the temple to learn things His parents can't teach Him. (This is the last time Joseph is mentioned in Jesus' life.)

This story is bracketed by two separate notations about the growth of Jesus (2:40, 52). Just as all humans do, Jesus went through a growth process—not just physically, but spiritually, intellectually, and relationally as well. And even though Jesus had made His point at the temple, He returns with His parents to Nazareth and is obedient to them (2:51).

Take It Home

When people put God first in their lives, they can expect benefits—and occasional problems. Mary and Joseph had the unique privilege of rearing the Savior of the world, but they found themselves homeless in Bethlehem and confused twelve years later in Jerusalem. And even today, those who choose to follow God are sometimes left without explanations for bad events in their lives. Have you experienced problems or disappointments as a believer? If so, how do you deal with them?

LUKE 3:1–38

TWO MINISTRIES BEGIN

The Voice of One Calling in the Desert	3:1–6
Q & A with John the Baptist	3:7–20
Jesus' Family Tree	3:21–38

Setting Up the Section

The first four chapters of Luke's Gospel intertwine the accounts of the birth of both John and Jesus, along with significant childhood events. Thus, when we come to the ministry of John the Baptist in chapter 3, we are finding John in the spotlight, as he has been before, as the forerunner of the Messiah. In fact, all four Gospels begin Jesus' public ministry with the ministry of John the Baptist.

3:1–6

THE VOICE OF ONE CALLING IN THE DESERT

Luke tells us that Jesus is about thirty years old when He begins His public ministry (3:23), and John the Baptist precedes Him. So while John has an important calling and a bold, emphatic message, he is by no means old. He apparently shows much maturity for a young man.

There is not one instance in the Gospels where we are told that John performs a miracle. John does not heal people, like our Lord, so far as the text informs us. Those people who witnessed the ministry of Jesus, in the very place where John had formerly preached and baptized, testified that John never performed signs (John 10:41). This means that it is only John's preaching that attracts the crowds. He must have been some preacher. (No doubt it was the messianic nature of his message that caused such excitement.) John's ministry seems to give hope of the coming of the kingdom, as it is intended to do (3:15–17).

Several of the names Luke mentions at the opening of chapter 3—Pontius Pilate, Herod, Philip, Annas, and Caiaphas—serve to ground Jesus' ministry in actual historical events (3:1–2).

Some people consider John the Baptist the last of the Old Testament prophets. Luke associates the ministry of John with Isaiah's prophecy of the voice in the wilderness, preparing the way for the Lord (3:4–6). He extends the quotation to include Isaiah 40:5—beyond what Matthew and Mark include—which states that all humanity will see God's salvation. This passage is especially significant from Luke's Gentile perspective because it foretold not just the coming of Israel's deliverer, but someone who will enable all humankind to see God's salvation (3:6), which is a key theme for Luke.

Like the prophets of old, John preaches a message of repentance that includes a call to both personal response and responsibility.

3:7–20

Q & A WITH JOHN THE BAPTIST

John stays in remote areas all around the Jordan River (3:3). He doesn't seek out the leadership of the nation or the elite population segments; instead, all kinds of people go out to hear him.

Other Gospel writers provide more complete physical descriptions of John (Matthew 3:4; Mark 1:6) in addition to the essence of his message. But Luke alone shares some of the interaction between John and various groups in his audience.

Surrounded by soldiers, tax collectors, and others, John speaks frankly. Addressing them as poisonous snakes (3:7), he talks of coming wrath and the need for repentance. He also tells the Jewish people in the crowd that they can't count on their national heritage (having "Abraham as our father" [3:8 NIV]) to ensure God's favor. Rather, they are to repent and produce good fruit (3:7–9).

When pressed for specifics, John's responses are simple and straightforward. People with extra food and possessions are to share with those who have none. Tax collectors are to be honest and not collect more money than they are due. Soldiers are instructed to be content with their pay and stop extorting money or falsely accusing people (3:10–14).

Critical Observation

Luke's Gospel will continue to address the proper use of material goods. Many of the parables of Jesus that Luke chose to include in his writing will center on the subject of money and/or wealth.

The crowds seem to take John's message to heart. In fact, John's presentation is so impressive that they are hoping to hear that he is the Messiah (Christ) they have been told to expect. But John makes it quite clear that there will be no mistaking the two (3:15–16). John may have seemed impressive, but Jesus will be more powerful. John will baptize with water, Jesus with the Holy Spirit and fire. Jesus will separate the useful wheat—those with true faith—from the worthless chaff and burn up the chaff (3:17).

Demystifying Luke

A "winnowing fork" (3:17 NIV) was a shovel-like tool used to toss grain into the air so the outer chaff would either fall and be burned or blow away in the wind and only the good wheat would remain. This was a familiar process in an agrarian community of the first century.

John's message may sound harsh to modern ears, yet it was good news for his listeners. However, his boldness will later lead to his arrest and death (Matthew 14:3–12; Luke 3:19–20).

3:21–38

JESUS' FAMILY TREE

Although John has publicly declared his unworthiness to even untie the thongs of Jesus' sandals (3:16)—a task designated for the lowest of slaves—Jesus still acknowledges John's ministry and comes to him to be baptized. All four Gospels include Jesus' baptism by John, but only Luke notes that Jesus is praying when heaven opens and the Holy Spirit descends on Him in the form of a dove (3:21–22).

When God's voice from heaven calls Jesus His Son (3:22), the words suggest more than just a Father/Son relationship. As God established kings for Israel in the Old Testament, He invites them into a relationship of sonship (2 Samuel 7:14; Psalm 2:6–12). So here at Jesus' baptism, God designates Jesus as the King of Israel, confirming what Gabriel had told Mary prior to Jesus' birth (1:31–33). And the additional comment, God's approval of Jesus, calls to mind Isaiah 42:1–4, the prophetic foretelling of the coming servant of the Lord who brings God delight.

Verses 23–38 contain Luke's genealogy of Jesus. Matthew provides one as well (Matthew 1:1–16), but the two versions have considerable differences. One obvious distinction is that Matthew begins with Abraham and tracks the line of descent to Jesus—clearly something that would interest Jewish readers. Luke begins with Jesus and goes backward through history to Adam, suggesting a more Gentile-friendly perspective that Jesus' significance was for the entire human race and not just the Hebrew people. In addition, the difference in placement should be noted. Matthew began his Gospel with Jesus' genealogy—His "credentials." Luke waited until he introduced the public ministry of Jesus, placing the genealogy right between Jesus' baptism and His temptation. Another significant difference is that Matthew traces the royal line through David's son Solomon while Luke traces it through David's son Nathan.

Critical Observation

The variations in names used in Luke's version of Jesus' genealogy compared to Matthew's suggest that Matthew may have been tracing the kingly line of Christ through His father, Joseph, while Luke recorded the ancestors of Jesus through His mother, Mary.

The baptism of Christ identifies Christ as Israel's king, and demonstrates that He has the Father's approval and the Spirit's anointing. The genealogy shows that our Lord has the right lineage—that He is indeed of the "throne of David." The temptation proves that our Lord has the godly character to reign. In every way, Luke shows Him to be qualified for the task He has been given.

Take It Home

Luke recorded the specific response of John the Baptist when tax collectors and soldiers asked what they should do in order to "produce fruit in keeping with repentance" (3:8 NIV; 3:10–14).

- To the crowd, he said to share its resources.
- To the tax collectors, he said to be honest and just.
- To the soldiers, he said to not take advantage of their power and to be content with their pay.

Suppose someone from your own profession had been there and asked the same question. What do you think John would have told them?

LUKE 4:1–44

TEMPTATION, REJECTION, AND HEALING

Forty Days in the Wilderness	4:1–13
The Hometown Crowd Turns on Jesus	4:14–30
Jesus Demonstrates His Power	4:31–44

Setting Up the Section

After Jesus' baptism (3:21–22), He is tempted by the devil for a period of forty days. There are several reasons why the temptation accounts are of importance to us. From the standpoint of Jesus' ministry and calling, His mission is contingent upon His victory over every temptation of Satan. Also, by studying the temptation of our Lord by Satan, we learn a great deal about our adversary, Satan, and the means by which we can withstand his attacks.

Afterward Jesus begins a public ministry of teaching and healing, and quickly becomes a well-known and popular figure...except in Nazareth, where He had been raised.

4:1–13

FORTY DAYS IN THE WILDERNESS

Jesus' baptism may have been a high point in His life, with the descent of the Holy Spirit and the voice of His heavenly Father expressing His love and approval (3:21–22). Yet the Spirit immediately leads Jesus into the wilderness to be tempted. It seems safe to presume that these temptations are a barrage by the devil to strike when He is the weakest.

Satan's first temptation appeals to Jesus' physical hunger. After forty days with nothing to eat, Jesus would be more than just hungry. A physical body deprived of food that long, apart from divine intervention, would be weakened to the point of near death. Yet Satan's taunt to turn a stone into bread (4:3) is not effective. We know from Matthew that John the Baptist subsisted in the wilderness on locusts and wild honey (Matthew 3:4) and from Mark that wild animals were in the wilderness (Mark 1:13). So Jesus could find food, but He isn't there to eat, as indicated in His response (4:4).

Jesus had a need for food as well as the power to meet that need. While many people would consider that a formula to immediately satisfy the need, Jesus chooses to remain focused on God rather than fulfill His own desire at the moment.

Critical Observation

Why was Jesus led to be tempted in this passage when He later taught His disciples to pray, "lead us not into temptation" (Matthew 6:13 NIV)? The word *temptation* can be used in two very different senses. One is clearly a solicitation to sin—which is always the case with Satan. But from God's point of view, a better word is *test*, which is an opportunity for someone to be proven righteous. So Abraham was tested when told to offer Isaac (Genesis 22:1–2), and Job was similarly tested (Job 1–2). Although Satan attempted a full-out temptation of Jesus in the wilderness, from God's point of view it was a test (which He passed with flying colors).

The devil's second temptation is an offer of power and authority as he parades all the kingdoms of the world before Jesus in an instant (4:5–7). Jesus and Paul both recognized Satan as the ruler of this world in the sense that he dominates fallen human beings through the power of sin and death (John 12:31–32; 16:11; 2 Corinthians 4:3–4; Ephesians 6:12). The devil may influence kings and kingdoms, yet he is not in control. Jesus is the One who is in sovereign control of history. God could not foretell the future if He did not control it. So Jesus' second response (4:8) is a reminder to keep God foremost in one's thoughts.

Satan's third temptation (4:9–11) reveals his acknowledgement of Jesus as the Son of God. For anyone else, a leap off the pinnacle of the temple would be certain suicide. Jesus has already twice used scripture to refute temptation (Deuteronomy 6:13; 8:3), so this time the devil uses scripture, perhaps attempting to enhance his proposition (Psalm 91:11–12). But Psalm 91 was not a promise of protection for Israel's Messiah. Rather, it was a promise of protection from God's wrath for all who take refuge in God. The devil's motive may be to disqualify Jesus as Messiah, weaken His faith and trust in God, bring about a premature introduction of Jesus as Messiah, or maybe even kill Him. Regardless of his intent, Jesus curtly rejects his proposal with a third quotation from scripture (4:12; Deuteronomy 6:16).

It would be a mistake to assume that Satan's words should be accepted at face value. Scripture calls him the father of lies (John 8:44). It is not at all certain that just because Satan claims to possess all the kingdoms of the world (4:5–6) that he really does have the right to offer them to Christ. Satan is always offering others that which he does not possess. For example, he encouraged Adam and Eve to help themselves to the forbidden fruit of the tree of the knowledge of good and evil and thus to a new level of knowledge. Our Lord offers people what He possesses, what He has purchased (for instance, salvation by His blood), but Satan offers what is not his.

Having failed after trying his best, the devil leaves Jesus alone. But he isn't finished with his temptation. He is merely waiting for another opportunity (4:13).

Demystifying Luke

Luke tells us Jesus' temptation lasted forty days, often a significant number in scriptural accounts. Perhaps most significant, it was the same number of years that the Israelites wandered in the wilderness, a time of testing after their lack of faith to enter the promised land.

Jesus' temptation also drew a significant analogy to the temptation of Adam and Eve in the garden. In the New Testament Jesus is described as the second Adam. Just as Adam was tempted and fell, Jesus was tempted and stood strong. In many ways, Jesus came to undo what Adam did. This parallel is highlighted even more in the fact that Luke refers to Adam as the son of God (3:38) and Satan confronts Jesus as the Son of God (4:3).

4:14–30

THE HOMETOWN CROWD TURNS ON JESUS

It is clear that Jesus has become a much talked about personality (4:14–15). When He decides to return to Nazareth, the town where He grew up, He goes to the synagogue on the Sabbath. There He is called on to read from the book of Isaiah, and the passage is a prophecy of the Messiah who will have a preaching and healing ministry (4:16–19; Isaiah 61:1–2). When He finishes reading, He then declares that He is fulfilling the scripture (4:21). In other words, Jesus is claiming to be Israel's Messiah.

Isaiah 61 was a significant passage for the people to hear from Jesus. They viewed themselves as the poor and oppressed that God was promising to bless with healing and deliverance. First, the people respond very positively to Jesus' claim. Luke informs us that the people are amazed at what Jesus says (4:22). Unfortunately, the warm response to Jesus' words is the result of a distorted concept of the Messiah.

Jesus points out that if His ministry were correctly understood, He would be rejected like all the other prophets of Israel's history. Prophets were not received by Israel, but spurned, persecuted, and even killed, and this without exception (1 Kings 19:10; Jeremiah 35:15; 44:4–5; Acts 7:52). Jesus not only cites the principle that Israel's prophets were never honored by their own people, He shows that the Gentiles received blessings from the prophets (4:24–27). He cites the case of Elijah's stay with the Gentile widow at Zarephath (1 Kings 17:9) and of the healing of Naaman, the Syrian, a military leader of the army that was successfully attacking Israel (2 Kings 5:1–14).

In both cases, the prophet of Israel brought blessings to Gentiles, which the Jews, his own people, did not receive. It is this key point that makes the people of Nazareth furious. They, like the Jews later described by Luke in the book of Acts (13:46, 50; 22:21–22), violently react to Jesus' words. There is not even an attempt to "sanctify" their actions by trumping up false charges, which is what will happen at His trial and crucifixion. Anyone who speaks of the blessing of the Gentiles instead of the Jews is a traitor!

The crowd rushes Jesus from the synagogue and presses Him toward the precipice of a nearby cliff, attempting to force Him to fall to His death. Jesus does not escape by fleeing, or by "taking a back way out." Instead, He walks through the midst of His opponents (4:30). Just as the waters of the Red Sea parted to allow Moses and God's people to pass through, so the angry crowd parts to allow Jesus to pass through its midst, unharmed, untouched. This is the one and only miracle that this crowd will witness.

There is a similar incident recorded by Matthew and Mark that many scholars consider to be descriptions of the same event (Matthew 13:53–58 and Mark 6:1–6).

Demystifying Luke

Luke's prominently Gentile audience would certainly have been encouraged by this account of Jesus. Some must have wondered, How can a Jewish Messiah, dying in fulfillment of Jewish scriptures, obtain salvation for a Gentile? Yet centuries before, God had promised Abraham that "all peoples on earth will be blessed through you" (Genesis 12:3 NIV). The Jews would initially reject Jesus, and the Gentiles would be included in God's invitation of salvation to all people.

4:31–44

JESUS DEMONSTRATES HIS POWER

Jesus moves on to Capernaum where, as in Nazareth, He begins to teach. The people in the synagogue are amazed at His teaching. (There was a similar reaction in Matthew's Gospel, immediately after Jesus had delivered the "Sermon on the Mount" [Matthew 7:28–29].) What is it that distinguished Jesus' teaching from that of the scribes and Pharisees, and made His teaching authoritative, when their teaching was not? The difference does not seem to be a matter of style, so much as of substance. Jesus taught with personal authority. Hearing Him speak would have been more like hearing from someone who authored the book, rather than someone who had simply read the book.

Jesus is soon interrupted by a man with an evil spirit. The demon controls the man's voice, and screams out at Jesus in a loud and disruptive manner. Even so, the evil spirit recognizes Jesus' identity and purpose (4:33–34). With a stern rebuke, Jesus drives the demon from the man and he is not harmed. Between Jesus' teaching and power, news about Him spreads quickly (4:36–37).

Later that day Jesus gives a command to heal the fever of Peter's mother-in-law, allowing her to immediately get up and attend to her guests (4:39). And when the sun goes down, ending the Sabbath, crowds of sick and possessed people seek Him out and He heals them.

Early the next morning Jesus goes to a solitary place, yet the people keep coming. They desperately want Him to stay in Capernaum, but Jesus is committed to a broader teaching ministry to all the villages of Galilee. They want to see miracles, but He has come to proclaim the kingdom of God. The healings and exorcisms are not an end in themselves, but are meant to demonstrate the powerful arrival of the kingdom of God—a message that everyone needs to hear. His fellow townspeople in Nazareth are not interested in this message and even those in Capernaum seem more interested in physical healing than in Jesus' proclamation of the kingdom. So Jesus moves on.

Take It Home

In some of the most stressful conditions possible, Jesus withstood Satan's strongest temptations. And He did so in a manner available to all of us: He simply quoted scripture. Each of His responses to the devil came directly from our Old Testament.

Jesus offers us a model to follow in so many ways. As we observe those who responded to Him, and the wide breadth of their responses, it leaves us examining how we respond to God's presence in our own lives. Do we rejoice? Do we misunderstand? Do we obey?

LUKE 5:1–6:11

CHOOSING DISCIPLES AND DEFINING DISCIPLINES

A Shift of Emphasis	5:1–11
Healing a Leper and a Paralytic	5:12–26
Levi Becomes a Disciple and Throws a Party	5:27–39
Sabbath Issues	6:1–11

Setting Up the Section

If Luke chapter 4 focused on the ministry of Jesus to the masses, chapter 5 begins to focus on the ministry of Jesus with respect to the leadership of Israel. So far in Luke's account, Jesus has been portrayed as a solitary teacher moving from place to place, teaching in the synagogues. In this passage He begins to call disciples to travel with Him in His ministry of teaching and healing. But when He and His disciples don't conform to established norms, they soon encounter opposition.

5:1–11

A SHIFT OF EMPHASIS

Luke's reference to the "Lake of Gennesaret" (5:1 NIV) is what other Gospel writers usually call the Sea of Galilee. With a crowd of people pressing around Jesus at the water's edge, He borrows Peter's boat so He can sit down and teach. When He finishes, He tells Peter to sail out to deep water and drop the nets. Peter doesn't really want to, but does as Jesus instructed.

Critical Observation

Was this Jesus' first encounter with Peter, Andrew, James, and John? Not likely. His progressive calling of the disciples seems to roughly follow this sequence:

1) At the suggestion of John the Baptist, some of his disciples begin to follow Jesus (John 1:36–51).
2) Jesus calls Peter, Andrew, James, and John to follow Him, which they begin to do as they continue their fishing business (Matthew 4:18–22).
3) After the miraculous event in this account, the four fishermen/disciples leave their boats to follow Jesus full time (Luke 5:1–11).
4) Jesus calls Levi, also known as Matthew (Luke 5:27–28).
5) Jesus calls the rest of the Twelve, but the specifics are not recorded in the Gospels.
6) Others wish to follow Jesus, but the cost of discipleship is high (Matthew 8:18–22).
7) Jesus spends a night in prayer prior to appointing twelve disciples as His apostles (Luke 6:12–16).

Peter's words in verse 5 indicate that he and his partners are tired from working all night. Besides that, they have just finished washing their nets. They will have to do it all over again. Also, Peter indicates that their efforts had been futile. Night was the best time to fish. If they had not caught anything at night, why in the world should they catch anything in the daytime, the worst possible time to fish? In addition, there seems to be a hint of irritation here. Jesus' order could have certainly seemed naive.

Yet when Peter's obedience results in a miraculous catch of fish that almost sinks two boats, he humbly acknowledges his sinfulness (5:6–8). Peter thought he was the expert, but now sees that Jesus is Lord of the sea as well. Peter doubted that they would make a great catch, and feared that his efforts would be wasted. Now he sees his Lord's sovereignty and his own sin.

Jesus' response to Peter can seem perplexing. Peter confesses his sinfulness. Why does Jesus tell him not to be afraid (5:10)? Peter is probably fearful because he not only recognizes his own sin but also the Lord's righteousness. His words reveal his awareness of Jesus' greatness.

Ultimately the Lord's provision for Peter's sin is even more abundant than His provision of fish. That provision will be made at the cross of Calvary, where He will die in the sinner's place. Communion and intimacy with God is abundantly provided by the Lord's sacrificial death. It is too early for Peter to know about this, and so he is simply assured, without any specific details being given.

At this point Peter, Andrew, James, and John leave their boats behind to follow Jesus full time. Before calling them to catch people (5:10), Jesus lets them experience every fisherman's dream—a catch of a lifetime. Yet their most significant accomplishments lay ahead.

Take It Home

It's important to remember this text is not teaching that those who are most committed to Christ must leave their secular jobs to be His disciples. The disciples left their jobs, but that was necessary in order for them to be with Jesus while He was physically present on the earth.

After His resurrection and ascension, Jesus is present with all of us through His Holy Spirit. Our calling goes deeper than our physical location or occupation. While we may not need to relocate to be in His presence, we are called—like the disciples—to leave behind all of our other allegiances and follow Him completely in every situation.

5:12–26

HEALING A LEPER AND A PARALYTIC

The term *leprosy* could include a number of different skin diseases, but Luke (a doctor) notes that one particular man who approaches Jesus (5:12) is covered with the disease. Normally, a person in this condition would have no contact with those who were "clean" or not infected. Yet Jesus touches the man before healing him (5:13). Jesus is doing several significant things here.

1) He is touching a leper before he is cleansed, showing that He is not tainted by the uncleanness of others, but rather makes unclean people clean.
2) He is instantly producing physical healing of a very serious disorder.
3) He is not only healing the man, but pronouncing him to be cleansed, which was the role of the priest as described in Leviticus 13–14.

Jesus did not always explain His motives. But in this case, by telling the healed leper to show himself to the priests, it is to be a testimony to them (5:14). Jesus also orders the man not to tell anyone else, but how does a healed leper explain his instantaneous recovery without giving credit to the man who helped him? So news about Jesus spreads even more (5:15).

Jesus keeps trying to seek out solitary places where He can pray (5:16). Jesus' retreat for prayer is an expression of His dependence upon the Father. It puts His successes in perspective, for He does everything in obedience to the Father's will and in the power of His Spirit (4:14). These times keep Jesus' perspective and priorities in line with those of the Father.

Jesus is beginning to attract curious religious leaders who critique what He says. This is the case once when He is speaking in a home where four men bring a paralytic to be healed (5:18–19). The house is overflowing with people, including many Pharisees (5:17). Luke includes a detail about these Pharisees—they are sitting, even in a packed room with standing room only. This may be because the sitting position is the position of authority for the teacher. A teacher in those days did not stand to teach; he sat to teach (4:20–21). For these teachers to stand may seem like a concession to Jesus' authority.

The scene might have been a bit comical with the crowd of religious leaders— falling debris and the sudden appearance of a man on a suspended pallet (5:18–19). But it is no joke to Jesus, who sees the faith of the man's friends and tells him, "Friend, your sins are forgiven" (5:20 NIV).

Jesus' response is not what any one of them really want to hear. The man's friends are surely expecting a healing for their friend after all their work and ingenuity. Even more, the Pharisees are taken aback that Jesus would claim to forgive sins. It is blasphemy to them (5:21). Forgiveness of sins is something that only God can do. Thus, to tell a man his sins are forgiven is to claim to be God.

But Jesus knows what they are thinking. He asks which is easier, to heal or to forgive (5:23). There is no visible proof that sins have been forgiven. One can claim that ability without having to prove it. But to command a paralyzed man to walk—the proof is visible. Jesus has set up this circumstance to show that He has both the power to forgive sins and to make the paralyzed walk (5:25–26).

5:27–39

LEVI BECOMES A DISCIPLE AND THROWS A PARTY

Luke says little about Jesus' call of Levi (referred to later in 6:15 as Matthew). Jesus calls Levi from his tax booth to follow, and Levi gets up and goes (5:27–28).

Demystifying Luke

Tax collectors such as Levi were not only often dishonest, but they were a painful reminder of the fact that Israel was not a free nation, but subject to Roman rule and authority.

Luke has already revealed one of the evils of which many tax collectors were guilty when he recorded what John the Baptist told the tax-gatherers who came to be baptized—don't collect more than you've been ordered (3:12–13). Thus, at the least we know that many tax collectors were guilty of abusing their position by using the power of the state to charge excessive taxes and keep the profits from their evil deeds. Luke himself will later inform us of one instance in which a sinful tax collector (Zacchaeus) repents and makes restitution for his misconduct (19:1–10).

Since nothing is said of Levi's desire to make restitution for previous dishonesty (as will be the case with Zacchaeus [19:1–10]), perhaps he is an upright and honest person—and maybe that is why Jesus chooses him.

To celebrate, Levi hosts a banquet for Jesus, and the guest list includes both Pharisees and fellow tax collectors. Luke tells us that the guests included "tax-collectors and others" (5:29 NIV). This is different from Matthew and Mark, who identify the guests as "tax-collectors and 'sinners' " (Matthew 9:10 NIV; Mark 2:15 NIV). When the Pharisees see Jesus and His followers drinking and associating with those they consider beneath themselves, they ask the disciples (not Jesus) why Jesus allowed it. Jesus, however, answers their question.

Jesus' answer in verses 31–32 reflects the difference between the heart of God and the heart of Pharisaism. The Pharisees thought that holiness required them to remain separate from sinners, to refuse to have contact with them. Jesus was holiness incarnate, and yet His holiness was not diminished by His contact with sinners. In order for God to call sinners to repentance, God found it necessary to have contact with them, which is the reason for our Lord's incarnation—of His taking on human flesh, living among men, touching and being touched by them.

Apparently Jesus' response isn't what they want to hear, so they press the point (5:33) of Jesus' and John's differencing practices. John the Baptist ate a rather unusual diet of desert foods (locusts and wild honey [Matthew 3:4]) and did not drink wine (1:15). It is quite plain, then, that what John did not drink, namely wine, Jesus did.

Jesus tells two short parables (5:36–39) to explain that sometimes new things must replace old things; trying to incorporate the two just doesn't work. The Pharisees are entrenched in old ways—trying to follow the Law to the letter in order to obtain righteousness. It isn't working, and never will. Jesus and the "sinners" are happy, enjoying life, and developing relationships. The guests are in the presence of the bridegroom, and it is a time to celebrate.

6:1–11

SABBATH ISSUES

Luke is not concerned here with providing a precise chronology. This can be seen by the broad time references ("one Sabbath" [6:1 NIV]; "on another Sabbath" [6:6 NIV]). Luke's purpose is to prepare his readers for the rejection, arrest, conviction, and execution of Jesus by His opponents by laying the groundwork early in the book. The Pharisees reject Jesus because He claims God's own authority (5:17–26), because He associates with sinners (5:27–39), and now, because He does not keep the Sabbath as they interpret it (6:1–11). These issues will dominate the relationship between the Pharisees and Jesus, culminating in His crucifixion.

While in chapter 5 the Pharisees (first mentioned by Luke in conjunction with the pronouncement to the paralytic that his sins were forgiven) object to Jesus' authority to forgive sins, they do not seem to have yet resolved a way to oppose Him. When we come to verses 6–11 in chapter 6, they have their minds made up. They are no longer looking for evidence as a basis for making a decision about Jesus; they are looking for proof to validate their rejection of Him. What began with curiosity, and led to concern, has, by the time we have reached our text, become condemnation and criticism.

In verses 1–5, some of Jesus' disciples begin to strip heads of grain from the field, rub them in their hands to separate the grain from the sheaf, and pop the grain into their mouths. This, to the Pharisees, is technically harvesting and threshing grain, something which one could do on any other day, but not on the Sabbath. Jesus' disciples are breaking the Pharisees' interpretation of "work" on the Sabbath and so the Pharisees challenge them.

In response, Jesus cites an Old Testament story (1 Samuel 21:1–6), where David and his men had eaten food that, according to law, should only be consumed by the priests. But the conditions warranted such an action, and since the Pharisees revered David, they could understand making an exception in that case. However, they don't think much of Jesus, and He and His followers aren't afforded the same tolerance. Yet that doesn't keep Jesus from making it perfectly clear that He is "Lord of the Sabbath" (6:5 NIV). As such, He—not the Pharisees—will have the final say in what is appropriate to do or not do on the Sabbath. Jesus' argument, as outlined by Luke, is based upon a very simple premise: Who you are determines whether you have the authority to define what is and is not a true Sabbath violation.

In Jesus' response, He refers to Himself as the "Son of Man" (6:5 NIV). This term has only once been used previously by Luke, and that at the time of the Pharisees' rejection of Jesus' authority to forgive sins. Jesus' use of the title is drawn especially from its messianic significance in Daniel 7. Jesus begins to use the title for Himself at the first evidence of rejection.

The expression, "Lord of the Sabbath" (6:5 NIV) is also significant. Besides affirming His position as Messiah, Jesus may also be saying that the rest associated with the Sabbath has come in Christ: "Come to Me, all who are weary and heavy-laden, and I will give you rest" (Matthew 11:28 NASB).

The second story in verses 6–11 is even more telling of the Pharisees' legalistic attitudes. The Pharisaical view of the Sabbath would reluctantly allow for one to render aid to a dying man, to one in such dire straits that he would not live till the Sabbath had ended. But Jesus heals a man with the withered hand—this does not fit into the Pharisees' category. The man's malady is not life-threatening. The Pharisees therefore believe that Jesus should have waited to heal this man. Jesus, by His actions, is raising the question, "Why?"

His question highlights the bad logic of the Pharisees. If the Sabbath was for good, then doing good on the Sabbath could hardly be wrong. It is that simple. Why was the Sabbath given, for good or evil?

Jesus could have easily avoided the issue by waiting until they weren't watching to heal the man. But He turns the tables with a piercing question (6:9). It is perfectly permissible to save a life on the Sabbath and, in a sense, His healing of the man is an act of salvation. And since Jesus only speaks, the Pharisees can't even accuse Him of doing any work. Still, they begin to plot against Him. They will continue to confront Him throughout His ministry.

By this point, the Pharisees are the bitter enemies of Jesus. They are not interested in following Him. They are no longer open to the possibility of His being the Messiah. They only wish to be rid of Him, something they will only later be able, in the providence of God, to achieve. The Sabbath controversy is, for them, the last straw. They are deadlocked in an irreconcilable conflict so long as they stubbornly resist.

Take It Home

Numerous debates continue as to whether old ways or new ways are better when it comes to religious things. Are the old hymns better than newer praise music? Is casual clothing in church appropriate? Is worship lessened or heightened by the presence of a band rather than an organ or a cappella? We all have our preferences, and draw lines as to what is inappropriate. Where do you stand in the old-vs.-new debate? How do you prevent Pharisaic legalism from creeping in while holding strong to what you feel Jesus would have you do?

LUKE 6:12–49

A DIFFERENT WAY OF SEEING THE WORLD

Designating the Top Twelve 6:12–16
Blessings and Woes 6:17–26
A Very Different Perspective 6:27–49

Setting Up the Section

This passage contains Luke's parallel to Matthew's Sermon on the Mount. The two versions contain many similarities but more than a few distinct differences. Luke has recently provided a number of accounts of Jesus' encounters with the Pharisees and has shown how legalistic attitudes had twisted the intended meaning of the gospel. Here Jesus provides His own outlook on how people should live.

It's important to read Jesus' words in terms of the principles of the law, not just specific actions. For instance, Jesus' teaching on "turning the other cheek" is not simply a mechanical kind of response to a right cross punch, but a principle that should govern our relationships with our enemies. We honor the sermon best when we apply it in the broad strokes of our lives.

6:12–16

DESIGNATING THE TOP TWELVE

By this time Jesus has attracted a number of followers. (Seventy-two would soon be sent out to various towns [10:1].) Luke regularly notes Jesus' commitment to prayer, as he does here (6:12). After spending a night in prayer, Jesus designates twelve of His disciples to become apostles. Luke has already recorded the call of Peter, Andrew, James, John, and Matthew (referred to as Levi in 5:27–29). At this point he completes the list (6:13–16).

In every biblical list of the apostles, Peter is listed first and Judas last. Yet this does not suggest that Jesus recruited Peter to be "the rock" and Judas a traitor. It takes all the disciples a long while to figure out who Jesus really is and what their roles should be. It is likely during their extended learning process that Peter eventually rises to prominence and Judas falls away to become a thief and betrayer.

6:17–26

BLESSINGS AND WOES

After calling the Twelve, Jesus is surrounded by a great crowd. The extent of Jesus' popularity with the people is evident from two major facts mentioned by Luke. First, the large number of people who are there, even in such a remote place. Second, the great distance from which people are coming. Here, we are told by Luke that they have come from all over Judea, Jerusalem, and even from the coast of Tyre and Sidon (6:17). A large number have come to benefit from Jesus' great power to heal diseases and remove evil spirits. And while the great throng is assembled, Jesus begins to teach the people (although Luke records that He primarily addresses His disciples [6:20]).

Critical Observation

There are a number of differences between Luke's account of the Sermon on the Mount (6:17–49) and that of Matthew (chapters 5–7).

- Luke's version of Jesus' sermon is considerably shorter than Matthew's (Matthew 5–7; Luke 6:17–49).
- Matthew used third person to speak of those who are blessed; Luke uses second person ("you").
- Matthew addressed characteristics that are a bit more spiritual, while Luke's traits are physical (poor in spirit vs. poor, hunger and thirst for righteousness vs. hunger, etc.).
- Matthew's account deals only with blessings, while Luke's includes a list of curses that correspond to each one (rich vs. poor, well fed vs. hungry, etc.)

Care must be taken when reading these passages blessing the poor. Jesus does not attribute any intrinsic benefit to being poor, or any automatic evil in being rich. Jesus says, "Blessed are you who are poor," not, "Blessed are all who are poor." Luke's account identifies the poor as the disciples who have chosen poverty in order to follow Him. So also, those who are rejected and persecuted are treated this way because of their faith (6:22). It is not simply being poor that is blessed, but being poor for Christ's sake. There is no intrinsic merit in being rejected and persecuted, but only in being thus treated on Christ's account (1 Peter 2:20). The joy of serving Jesus will more than compensate for the things disciples give up in order to serve.

Take It Home

The point of the passage is clear. People must make a decision as to their values and their priorities. We must all choose to forsake some things in the pursuit of others. Not everyone must forsake wealth to follow Christ, although all must forsake the love of money. Life involves choices. We must choose what in life to pursue. Every choice has both benefits (blessings) and a price to pay. The gospel of Jesus Christ is the good news of a gift, the gift of eternal life, which is of infinite value (Philippians 3:7–11).

6:27–49

A VERY DIFFERENT PERSPECTIVE

Jesus' teaching is 180 degrees different from what people are accustomed to hearing. Not only does He teach love for one's enemies, He even refuses to justify retaliation/revenge for offenses (6:27–30). This is the context for the familiar Golden Rule (6:31). Jesus' challenge is to rise above the status quo of relationships and initiate a higher level of love and care than is being demonstrated by others (6:32–36).

Critical Observation

Measures of grain were sometimes carried in the folds of the loose clothing worn in the Middle East. So if we want to receive a good measure (a lap full) of forgiveness poured out on us, we should not be stingy offering it to others (6:38).

Jesus warns against judging and condemning others. Giving and forgiving are the appropriate antidotes (6:37–38). Status seeking and hypocrisy only cause difficulties in life: The blind have difficulty leading other blind people, students should seek to imitate their teachers rather than seeking higher status, and it's foolish to try to remove a speck of sawdust from someone's eye with a plank in one's own eye (6:37–42).

It is foolish to pretend to be someone you aren't. Just as trees are recognized by their fruit, people are identified by their actions. People with good hearts can't help but produce good deeds, just as evil in one's heart will produce evil in one's life. And whatever is in the heart—good or bad—will certainly be reflected in one's speech (6:43–45).

It's easy to give lip service to Jesus and consider oneself a believer (6:46); it's much harder to love enemies, freely give to someone who is trying to take from you, keep from judging others, and maintain a mind-set of humility. But genuine believers obey even the difficult commands of Jesus. In the closing parable, also recorded in Matthew's account (Matthew 7:24–27), one homebuilder digs a deep foundation on rock (6:48). The other doesn't even bother with a foundation. So when a torrent falls on the two homes, the first one stands firm while the second is completely destroyed (6:46–49).

Take It Home

Jesus called His followers to extraordinary responses. It's a natural and ordinary response for people to love those who love them, but we Christians are called to love our enemies. We are to do so because God has loved us while we were His enemies. We are to do so because God is the One who will bless us for obeying His commands.

LUKE 7:1–50

SAVING FAITH AND A FAITHFUL SAVIOR

The Faith of a Gentile	7:1–10
Jesus Brings a Widow's Son Back to Life	7:11–17
A Message for John the Baptist	7:18–35
Unusual Insight from a Woman "Sinner"	7:36–50

Setting Up the Section

At this point in Luke's narrative, Jesus has been in public ministry for a while. Yet He is still coming across people who stand out from others in the crowd. A Roman centurion displays faith greater than any witnessed in Israel. A woman recognizes the significance of Jesus and anoints Him. And Jesus gives tribute to the faithful ministry of John the Baptist.

7:1–10

THE FAITH OF A GENTILE

After Jesus' famous sermon (6:17–49), He goes to Capernaum where He encounters a delegation sent by a Roman centurion. The official is requesting Jesus' healing of a servant. Although the Jewish people didn't much care for the Romans as a whole, this particular man is an exception. Not only has the centurion shown respect for the Jewish nation and helped with the construction of a synagogue, he also values his servant who is sick—a servant who might very well be Jewish (7:2–5).

Demystifying Luke

There are some differences between Luke's account of the centurion and that of Matthew. It is not difficult to conclude that the accounts in Matthew 8:5–13 and Luke 7:1–10 are a record of the same incident. However, Luke's Gospel makes a point of telling us that the centurion never personally spoke with Jesus, while Matthew's account clearly gives us this impression. How, then, can we explain the apparent contradictions in these two accounts?

It would have been a reasonable explanation that Matthew understood that a delegation sent by this man was the same as the man himself coming to Jesus. But more importantly, we don't always need to feel an obligation to reconcile the differences between accounts, particularly when they are not central to the significance of the story. The Gospel writers were aware of the writings of others (Luke 1:1–2), and yet they felt free to have differences in their accounts—perhaps differences which remind us that we have only partial accounts of any incident in the life of Christ and that each is remembered differently by different people. That doesn't take away the value of understanding what Jesus did.

Jesus accommodates the request. Yet while still on the way to the man's house, additional messengers from the centurion intercept them, explaining that the centurion doesn't need Jesus to actually go to his home. He understands authority, and believes that Jesus can simply speak and heal his servant. The centurion's faith is revealed not just in the fact that he recognizes Jesus' authority, but that he recognizes that Jesus' authority is the result of a higher authority. The centurion's faith attests to Jesus' identity in a way that the religious leaders have yet to understand (7:7). Jesus is amazed that the man has such faith, because no one in Israel has yet shown that level of belief in Him. By the time the messengers get back to the centurion's house, the servant is well (7:9–10).

Critical Observation

The story of the centurion's faith is very similar to the Old Testament account of Naaman and Elisha (2 Kings 5). In both cases, a Gentile official sought help from a Jewish man of God to find relief from a serious illness. (Naaman had leprosy; the Roman centurion's servant was near death.) Yet Naaman had been initially reluctant to follow the course of action prescribed by Elisha, while the Roman centurion showed exemplary faith in Jesus.

7:11–17

JESUS BRINGS A WIDOW'S SON BACK TO LIFE

About twenty-five miles southwest of Capernaum was the town of Nain (7:11). It is there two large crowds converge. One crowd is traveling along with Jesus and His disciples. The other is a group of townspeople in a funeral procession. A widow's only son has died, which in that culture leaves her essentially helpless. As the two crowds merge, Jesus sees what is happening and His heart goes out to the woman (7:13).

Jesus approaches the coffin (which would not have had a top if made according to Jewish tradition), and the pallbearers stand still. Then He reaches out and touches the coffin, an unusual move since it would have rendered anyone else ceremonially unclean for doing so. With no ceremony, Jesus simply instructs the boy to arise, which is immediately evident by his sitting up and speaking (7:15). Not surprisingly, the crowds of people are all filled with awe. They acknowledge Jesus as a great prophet and begin to praise God (7:16–17).

This story, like that of the healing of the centurion's son, also brings to mind the healings of the prophets Elijah and Elisha. Jesus' raising of the dead son reminds us of a similar incident in Elijah's ministry (1 Kings 17:17–24) and in that of Elisha as well (2 Kings 4:18–37). In the case of Elijah, especially, there are parallels to the raising of the son of the woman who lived at Nain. Both boys were the only son of a widow. Both boys were raised from the dead by a prophet of God. Both Elijah and Jesus presented the boys to their mothers. Both raisings proved that a true prophet of God was present. But the more labored and time-consuming resurrections performed by the Old Testament prophets were overshadowed by this instantaneous raising of Jesus.

Critical Observation

These two miracles, the healing of the centurion's son and the raising of the widow's son, serve several purposes in the developing message of Luke's Gospel.

- They testify to the fact that Jesus is who He claimed to be—Israel's Messiah.
- They serve as a backdrop for the questions of John the Baptist, which are to be introduced in the next section.
- They are samples of the kind of faith that we should have today.

7:18–35

A MESSAGE FOR JOHN THE BAPTIST

The last Luke has said about John the Baptist is that Herod had imprisoned him (3:20). John is still following the ministry of Jesus through messengers, though. Yet apparently he isn't hearing what he expected. He sends two of his disciples to Jesus, asking directly if He is the promised Messiah or if everyone should be looking for someone else (7:18–20).

Critical Observation

Believers sometimes have a "pious bias" and assume that righteous people don't have the same doubts and difficulties of less religious people. John's lack of certainty that Jesus was the Messiah may seem like a shortcoming. Yet in spite of their spiritual connection, as far as we know John and Jesus had very little physical contact. In addition, Jesus was trying to avoid publicly identifying Himself as "the Messiah" because the term meant different things to different people. He was not planning, for example, to overthrow the Roman government and set up His own kingdom on earth (as many people were hoping).

Perhaps John is encouraging Jesus to declare His spiritual credentials–maybe he is even daring Him to speak up, in a sense. But Jesus doesn't declare Himself the Messiah as John may have hoped. Nor does He go work things out with John. Instead, He merely tells John's disciples to go back and report what they were seeing: blind and lame people healed, lepers cured, the dead raised, and the good news of the gospel preached to the poor (7:22). These were all signs from Isaiah (Isaiah 29:18; 35:5–6) of the coming of God's end-time salvation. In effect, Jesus is simply telling John to do what every first-century Jewish seeker needed to do–compare the prophecies of the Old Testament with the deeds and declarations of Jesus Christ. If Jesus fulfills these prophecies, then the Bible bears witness to the fact that He is the Messiah.

Jesus doesn't appear at all upset that John has questioned Him. Just the opposite: After John's disciples have gone, He gives John a glowing tribute (7:28). However, He adds that the least person in the kingdom of God would be even greater. In other words, John anticipated the kingdom of God. Jesus identified John as the one who had been prophesied to prepare the way for the Messiah. But those who will come after John will understand more clearly Jesus' death and resurrection and the redemption His suffering will bring.

Most in the crowd agree with what Jesus says about John. Only the Pharisees and the experts in the Law have refused to be baptized (7:30). Jesus points out that some people just can't be pleased. They criticize John's ascetic lifestyle, even suggesting he has a demon (7:33). But then they accuse Jesus of gluttony and drunkenness because He eats and drinks with regular people (7:34). Yet spiritually discerning people can see the validity of both Jesus' and John's ministries (7:35).

7:36–50

UNUSUAL INSIGHT FROM A WOMAN "SINNER"

All four Gospels include an account of the washing of Jesus' feet by a woman (Matthew 26:6–13; Mark 14:3–9; Luke 7:36–50; John 12:1–8). Despite a few similarities, the story in Luke seems to be a separate event from the one described in Matthew, Mark, and John.

We are not told precisely when this incident occurs, or the name of the city. The principle characters are Jesus, Simon the Pharisee, and the woman with a soiled reputation. It is interesting that Luke gives us the name of the host, but not of the woman. Omitting her name may have been an act of grace, purposely done.

Jesus may have had a reputation for associating with tax collectors and "sinners," but on this occasion He has accepted a dinner invitation from a Pharisee. The host's intent is not clear because this is during a phase where the Pharisees are increasing their opposition against Jesus (6:11).

While Jesus is eating, an uninvited guest appears with a fancy jar of perfume. Since Jesus and the others eat while reclining at the table, His feet are away from the table rather than under it, as in Western dining. So the woman washes His feet with her tears, dries them with her hair, and then anoints them with the perfume. To make things worse, the host (and perhaps many others) knows of the woman's reputation, and assumes Jesus isn't much of a prophet if He doesn't know as well.

Jesus not only knows all about the woman; He knows what His host is thinking. The story He tells makes the point that those who are forgiven most, love most (7:40–43).

Critical Observation

In verse 47 it would appear that Jesus is telling the woman that she is forgiven because she loved much. To love because you are forgiven is a natural response to grace. To be forgiven because you love could be interpreted as earning forgiveness through works. But that is not what the parable teaches. In the parable, the one who is forgiven much loves much in response. The forgiveness precedes the response of love. A better translation of verse 47 would be "I tell you, her many sins have been forgiven—as her great love has shown" (TNIV).

Jesus' body language in verses 44–47 is significant. All through the dinner, Jesus' back is to the woman, who is anointing and kissing His feet. He is, at the same time, facing His host, Simon. Now, once Simon's rejection of Jesus is revealed, in contrast to the woman's worship, Jesus turns His back on Simon and faces the woman, even though He is still addressing Simon (7:44). Jesus is, by His actions, rejecting Simon and accepting the sinful woman.

This woman's motives are pure and her actions are genuine. (Perhaps it was the host's inattention to Jesus that had motivated her to improvise the washing and drying of Jesus' feet when she had no pitcher of water or towel.) Yet it is her faith that impresses Jesus most of all. He forgives her sins and sends her on her way in peace, leaving the dinner guests wondering if He really has the authority to do so (7:44–50).

Take It Home

Jesus wanted His Pharisee host to realize that those who are forgiven most tend to love most. The Pharisee's accusation that Jesus associated with sinners was good news to the woman who understood the depth of His forgiveness. Even today, the better we comprehend Jesus' forgiveness—and the less we are concerned with proving our own righteousness—the better equipped we are to show love to others.

LUKE 8:1–56

PARABLES, MIRACLES, AND FAMILY MATTERS

Spiritual Wisdom and the Parable of the Soils	8:1–21
Two Fear-Inspiring Miracles	8:22–39
Two More Amazing Miracles	8:40–56

Setting Up the Section

Jesus' ministry has become very active. He is teaching the crowds, training His disciples, healing all kinds of diseases, casting out evil spirits, and even performing an occasional phenomenal miracle or resurrection of the dead. In this passage, Luke records a bit of each of these aspects of Jesus' ministry, along with brief mentions of His supporters and family.

As we look more closely at the description of the ministry of Jesus in the Gospels, we discover that very soon the party that accompanies our Lord becomes quite large. One of the few texts that informs us about this large group is Luke 8. In addition, Luke informs us of the vital role a large number of women play in supporting the ministry of Jesus and His disciples.

8:1–21

SPIRITUAL WISDOM AND THE PARABLE OF THE SOILS

Jesus has spent a year or so wandering around Galilee and preaching. In the early days He was often pictured as alone or with a few disciples. At this point, however, it seems He begins a new phase of ministry, traveling again through Galilee (8:1). But this time He is beset by crowds everywhere He goes, along with a rather significant following of disciples (in addition to the Twelve) and supporters (8:2–3).

Luke names three of Jesus' female sponsors, revealing a great diversity in background and social status: Mary Magdalene (from whom the seven demons had been cast out); Joanna the wife of Cuza, Herod's steward (this may explain one of Herod's primary sources of information about Jesus and His ministry [9:7]); and Susanna, who is not mentioned again in the scriptures (8:2–3). The women all seem to have this in common: Jesus has miraculously delivered (healed) them of conditions for which there is no human solution. Some, like Mary Magdalene, were delivered of demon possession. Others were healed of sicknesses and disease. They went with Jesus to be of help to Him because they had experienced His help in their lives. Luke is clear that these women are not mere "hangers-on." They are active contributors to the proclamation of the gospel of the kingdom.

Jesus uses and encourages women in ministry. Luke's account of these women who follow Jesus and support the Galilean campaign is a tribute to them and to their ministry. It commends the women for their faithfulness and commitment to the Lord and it values their ministry as a partnership in the gospel (8:3).

Critical Observation

Jesus' practice of allowing women to support Him and His followers gave approval to the general principle of supporting those who proclaim the gospel. Our Lord set the precedent that those who proclaim the gospel should be supported by those who benefit from that preaching. This is seen earlier in the Old Testament prophets (1 Kings 17:7ff; 2 Kings 4:8–10), and is taught in principle by the apostle Paul (1 Corinthians 9).

Jesus seems to be making several shifts in the way He ministers:

1) In the first Galilean campaign of our Lord, the emphasis was on His identity as Israel's king. Now, He seems to be concentrating more on the nature of the kingdom itself.
2) There is a change of method. Jesus is now teaching by means of parables—more indirectly than before.
3) Jesus is beginning to spend more time with His disciples. In His first Galilean campaign, it would seem that His disciples were not always present. From now on, Jesus pours more effort into the teaching of His disciples (not just the Twelve but the larger group of His followers).

Why the shift to parables? Parables can reveal God's truth to those with spiritual awareness, even while concealing it from those intent only on opposing Jesus (8:10). Some people aren't as interested in truth as in maintaining their religious status, so they will discover no truth in Jesus' parables.

The Parable of the Soils (8:4–15) makes this very point. It is found in all three of the synoptic Gospels (Matthew 13:1–23; Mark 4:1–20; Luke 8:4–15). It has become quite a familiar illustration to many modern-day believers, but imagine the disciples' confusion after first hearing only the parable without the explanation (8:5–8). The Parable of the Soils describes what becomes of seed that is sown in four different types of soil.

1) Soil that is the hardened soil of the pathway. This seed does not penetrate the soil at all, but is quickly snatched up by the birds of the air.
2) The rocky soil, a shallow layer of earth, barely covering the rock below. The seed that falls upon this type of soil quickly germinates, aided by the warmth retained by the rock, but is hindered by a lack of depth and by a lack of moisture. The seed that germinates quickly also terminates quickly.
3) Soil populated with thorns. The seed falling into this soil germinates and begins to grow, but is eventually crowded out by the hardier thorns.
4) The fruitful soil, which produces a bountiful crop.

Thankfully, Jesus gives His followers a clear interpretation (8:11–15). As He sows the Word of God, His hearers will respond in numerous ways: some not at all (hardened), some enthusiastically at first but soon falling away (rocky), others trying to add His teachings to an already full life rather than changing priorities (thorny). Some, however, will hear the Word, retain it, and become productive for God's kingdom (fruitful).

Yet immediately after using a parable to intentionally cloud the truth from the religious leaders who follow Him, Jesus teaches that light is meant to shine and that everything hidden will be disclosed (8:17). When the time is right—after His death and resurrection—His disciples will be prepared to bring everything He has told them out into the open.

Demystifying Luke

It would not be long after this that the cult of Gnosticism would form. This group proposed that secret spiritual knowledge was attainable by only a privileged few. That's not what Jesus was teaching here. Even while attempting to keep His role as Messiah low key, He was training His disciples and giving them full explanations. They could then provide the early church with all the truth Jesus taught them (Colossians 1:25–26).

Spiritual wisdom is not something to take for granted. It is acquired by careful listening, and can be lost through apathy and inattention (8:18). Indeed, Jesus even begins to define relationships in terms of those who hear God's Word and put it into practice (8:19–21). Those who practice such spiritual disciplines are considered family by Jesus, even more so than His flesh-and-blood family, which doesn't yet believe in Him (Mark 3:21; John 7:5).

8:22–39

TWO FEAR-INSPIRING MIRACLES

The account of the stilling of the storm is the first of three miracles recorded by Luke in chapter 8. It is followed by the healing of the demoniac, then the raising of Jairus's daughter, interrupted by the healing of the woman with the issue of blood. The two central threads that run through these miracles are fear and faith.

Every biblical account of Jesus' calming the storm is surprisingly short and succinct (Matthew 8:23–27; Mark 4:35–41; Luke 8:22–25). What comes through clearly, however, is Jesus' expectation that by now the Twelve should have faith in Him. Even a raging storm that could terrorize experienced fishermen is no problem for Jesus' power. After He speaks, not only does the storm dissipate, but the sea immediately becomes absolutely calm. In response, the disciples are amazed and fearful (8:25). It would seem that their reaction to what Jesus has just done is even more startling than the life-threatening storm itself. They are beginning to catch on that maybe they are scared of the wrong things.

Failing to trust in Christ dishonors and displeases Him and is detrimental to men. The disciples' lack of faith does not please our Lord here, nor does it do so elsewhere (Matthew 14:31; 16:8). It is dishonoring to Christ, for it shows that the disciples do not trust Him as the Son of God. In addition, the disciples' lack of faith causes them much unnecessary consternation and fear.

Faith involves a decision for which people are responsible. Our Lord's rebuke of His disciples, regardless of how gentle it was, indicates that the disciples were expected to have faith, and are held accountable for failing to have faith. While faith is, in one sense, a gift of God, it is also a gift that may be accepted or refused. Faith involves choices—though sometimes it means moving and sometimes it means waiting.

Yet no sooner have they landed than they have another frightening encounter. In a relatively remote stretch on the other side of the Sea of Galilee, they find a demon-possessed man living among tombs (8:26–39). He no longer wears clothes. People have tried to secure him for his own protection, but chains cannot hold him.

Critical Observation

The Bible never explains how people became demon-possessed. But it addresses possession by evil spirits as a very real and distinct problem, not merely a form of mental illness.

When Jesus asks his name, it is the demons who answer. The name Legion suggests a multitude of demons (8:30). Yet they recognize Jesus and His power to determine what happens to them (8:28, 31). Take note of the fact that although the demoniac falls at Jesus' feet, it is not an act of worship, as it will be when the demons are cast from the man. The demons do recognize Jesus' identity, and they also acknowledge His superiority and authority over them. They recognize, for example, that He can do with them as He pleases. Their petitions are addressed as those of inferior beings to One who is infinitely superior to them, but not in devotion or worship; only in fear.

It seems that the demons need to be embodied in something, if not someone, and beg Jesus to allow them to go into a nearby herd of pigs. Jesus grants the request, but the pigs immediately rush down a steep bank into the sea and drown (8:32–33).

The men who are watching the pigs, run into town to report what has happened. By the time they get back, the previously possessed man is dressed and rational. Seeing him there and fully cured, the townspeople are overwhelmed with fear (8:34–37). They desperately want Jesus to leave, and the cured man begs to go with Him. But Jesus tells him to go home and tell what God has done (8:38–39). Who better to not only describe but also to demonstrate the healing power of God?

This account is important for us for several reasons. First, it teaches us much about the demonic forces that oppose our Lord and His church. It reminds us of the supernatural forces at work contrary to the Christian. It reminds us, as well, that Jesus Christ has power over the demonic forces, indeed, even over an entire "legion" of demons. This description of Legion provides us with a kind of "untouched photo," unmasking Satan's deception and destruction. Second, the deliverance of the demoniac draws our attention to a fear of God, which is unholy and unhealthy, one which causes men to draw away from God, or, as in our text, to ask the Son of God to withdraw. Finally, the townspeople's response reveals the resistance and fear that can come against the good that Jesus can do.

8:40–56

TWO MORE AMAZING MIRACLES

Although Jesus has sailed across the Sea of Galilee, enduring a storm and facing off with a demon-possessed man, a crowd is still waiting for Him when He gets back to shore. A ruler of the synagogue named Jairus meets Him, pleading for Him to come and heal his dying daughter. Jesus agrees, and they head for Jairus's home, but the going is slow because of the crushing crowds surrounding Jesus (8:42). So imagine the disciples' surprise when Jesus stops and asks who touched Him (8:45).

They aren't aware that a woman who has suffered from a bleeding disease for twelve years has sneaked up and, in faith, touched the edge of Jesus' cloak. She shouldn't be there because the bleeding makes her unclean. It is very likely a menstrual problem, so even if she can get Jesus' attention in the crowd, it will be horribly embarrassing to request healing.

But Jesus will not allow the woman's faith to go unnoticed. She is a positive example for everyone. In addition, she might feel guilty about "stealing a healing" later on, or afraid that in telling the story to others they might interpret the results as magic rather than faith. So Jesus waits until the woman comes forward (trembling) and explains what she has done (8:47). He acknowledges her faith and sends her home in peace.

In the meantime, however, word arrives that Jairus's daughter has died. Jesus isn't fazed, and He encourages Jairus to believe that she will be healed (8:50). When they arrive, mourners are already wailing, and they laugh when Jesus suggests the girl is only sleeping (8:52–53). They don't laugh long, though, because the girl stands up at Jesus' command. He tells her parents to feed her and not to tell anyone what has happened. Perhaps Jesus' command for silence is primarily directed to the faithless scoffers who wait outside (Matthew 9:23–25). Not only do they miss seeing this outstanding miracle, they also will be denied hearing about it firsthand. Lack of faith has any number of drawbacks.

Take It Home

Much is said about fear in this passage: the disciples during the storm, the people who knew the demon-possessed man, the woman standing before Jesus, etc. In particular we should notice Jesus' admonition to Jairus not to fear, even after hearing the worst about his daughter. Can you think of a time when it seems God has been slow to act? If so, how did you respond while waiting for Him? What is your initial response to crisis situations: fear or faith? How might you increase your faith so that such times will feel less stressful in the future?

LUKE 9:1–62

HIGHS AND LOWS OF MINISTRY

Paired Up and Sent Out	9:1–9
Jesus Feeds Five Thousand	9:10–17
Peter's Confession and Jesus' Transfiguration	9:18–36
Some Shortcomings of the Disciples	9:37–56
Excuses Not to Follow Jesus	9:57–62

Setting Up the Section

Any business or ministry that undergoes rapid growth will almost always experience corresponding problems. Jesus' ministry is no exception. In this passage the apostles are given more responsibility, resulting in some successes as well as some failures. Some of them are beginning to see Jesus for who He really is, yet argue about which of them is the greatest. Jesus is still popular with crowds, but now has Herod's attention as well. Meanwhile, His miracles continue.

9:1–9

PAIRED UP AND SENT OUT

One day Jesus gathers the apostles, puts them in pairs, and sends them out to preach about the kingdom of God and to heal (9:2). He gives them "power and authority to drive out all demons and to cure diseases" (9:1 NIV), and He forbids them to take any provisions. They are to go village to village, in each place finding a willing host to allow them to stay and do their work. If none is found, they are to "shake the dust off [their] feet" (9:5 NIV)—a gesture that demonstrates complete separation and disdain.

Critical Observation

In this instance the apostles were expected to be completely dependent on God for food, lodging, the right words to say, and the power to act. But we are not to assume that God always expects such total absence of planning or provision. Later Jesus will instruct this same group to prepare and take all it needs (22:35–36).

While there are people in the remote villages who may not have heard much about Jesus or His message, Herod certainly has. He is curious about Jesus (9:9). He is a Jew and probably knows something about the Messiah. He might have heard talk of the kingdom of God and feels threatened. He could be haunted by guilt and fear that John the Baptist (whom he has killed) has risen. Or maybe he just wants to see a miracle (23:8).

9:10–17

JESUS FEEDS FIVE THOUSAND

When the disciples return from their ministry, Jesus tries to provide them a place and time for a little retreat (9:10). But the crowds find them and gather, so Jesus continues to teach and heal.

When the crowds don't go home, and it is time to eat, the disciples tell Jesus to send everyone away. But He tells the disciples to feed the crowd. They have just returned from living day to day by the provision of God, yet they balk at this challenge. They see five thousand men (plus women and children) and only see five loaves and two fish. They see no way to feed the crowd without going out to buy food for everyone (9:13–14).

So Jesus takes over. He gives thanks for the food and begins to divide it. Envision at least one hundred groups of fifty people each, with the twelve apostles distributing the seemingly never-ending source of food from Jesus' hands. It is not likely a coincidence that there are twelve baskets of leftovers—one for each of the still spiritually short-sighted apostles (9:17).

9:18–36

PETER'S CONFESSION AND JESUS' TRANSFIGURATION

Luke's next story shows that the apostles are beginning to glean some insight about Jesus that the masses are missing. There is no clear consensus about who Jesus is. Everyone seems to agree that He is a specially designated man sent from God, but no one is saying He is the Messiah (9:19).

Critical Observation

It can be safely said that Luke places a heavy emphasis on prayer. He is careful to link prayer with great manifestations of God's grace and power. This is true in both the Gospel of Luke and the book of Acts. Look at these instances, including verse 18, when the disciples make their confession, in which prayer shortly precedes a great event.

In Luke's Gospel:		
Text	**Prayer**	**Event**
1:5–20	Prayer of Zechariah	Announcement of John's birth
3:21–22	Jesus prays at His baptism	Father appears, speaks (3:21–22)
4:42	Jesus' private prayer	Galilean ministry (4:43 and following)
6:12	Jesus in prayer	Choosing the twelve disciples
9:18	Jesus in prayer	The great confession
9:28–29	Jesus in prayer	The transfiguration

In the Book of Acts:		
Text	**Prayer**	**Event**
1:14	Disciples in prayer	Pentecost
4:31	Prayer of church	Powerful witness in Jerusalem
7:59–60	Stephen's prayer	Saul's conversion
9:11	Saul in prayer	Saul's sight regained and filled with Holy Spirit
10, 11	Prayer of Peter, Cornelius	Gospel spreads to Gentiles
12:5	Church in prayer for Peter	Peter's release
13:1-3	Fasting and prayer	First missionary journey
16:25	Prison prayers	Earthquake, release, conversion of jailer

So Jesus asks the Twelve, "Who do you say I am?" (9:20 NIV). Peter usually gets credit for the answer, but he is probably speaking for the group. He identifies Jesus as "the Christ of God" (9:20 NIV), a bold proclamation that Jesus is the Messiah.

Peter has recognized that the teaching and actions of Jesus have shown Him to be the Messiah. And yet the apostles are far from a complete understanding of their Master. Jesus instructs them not to tell others about this. He wants to provide them with a fuller understanding of a Messiah who will (for now) be a suffering servant rather than a military victor or political figure. And He begins to prepare them for their own suffering: denial of self, taking up a cross, and possibly even loss of life (9:23–27). But He also promises that some of them will personally witness "the kingdom of God (9:27 NIV)."

Eight days later, three of them find out what He means (9:28). He takes Peter, James, and

John up a mountain to pray with Him, and they witness His transfiguration. Jesus' clothing, and even His physical appearance, changes. He becomes "as bright as a flash of lightning" (9:25 NIV), and Moses and Elijah appear and speak about His departure (9:29–31).

Both Moses and Elijah had departed the earth with some mystery. Moses was buried by God (Deuteronomy 34:6). Elijah was carried to heaven in a whirlwind (2 Kings 2:11). These men speak to Jesus about His departure, meaning His exit from earth and return to heaven. The word translated "departure" harkens back to Moses' exodus from Egypt when he led God's people to freedom, an apt parallel for the work of Christ.

The disciples have been very sleepy, but when awakened, see the full glory of Jesus. As the two heavenly visitors begin to leave, Peter proposes building shelters for them, possibly in an attempt to extend their stay. Or maybe he thinks if Jesus' kingdom is established now, they all could skip the suffering, rejection, and death that Jesus has been talking about. Whatever Peter's intent, Luke tells us he doesn't know what he is saying (9:33).

Even as Peter is speaking, he is interrupted by the voice of God (9:35). After the voice has spoken, Jesus is again alone, and the three disciples keep it to themselves (9:36).

9:37–56

SOME SHORTCOMINGS OF THE DISCIPLES

Meanwhile, the other nine apostles have been asked by a desperate father to cast an evil spirit out of his son (9:38–40). Although Jesus has given His disciples authority to drive out demons (9:1), they are unable to help this young man. Jesus merely speaks, the spirit comes out, and the boy is healed (9:42).

Luke doesn't specify to whom Jesus is speaking when He expresses frustration with lack of faith (9:41). Very likely, He is referring to the entire "generation" (9:41 NIV), which would include the father, the people in the crowds, and even His disciples. And when Jesus tries to tell the disciples about His impending betrayal and death, they are still clueless about what He means (9:44–45).

The apostles may not have completely understood Jesus' teaching about His kingdom, but that doesn't stop them from arguing about who will have the highest position in it (9:46). In response, Jesus calls forward a small child as an example of the least on earth who will become the greatest in the estimation of God (9:48).

This act must have reminded them of a stranger they had seen driving out demons in the name of Jesus. They had tried to stop him (9:49). (Quite an irony: They had been unable to cast out a demon, and equally unable to stop someone who could!) Jesus tells them not to interfere with people who are working toward the same goals they are (9:50).

Critical Observation

Verse 51 marks a turn in Luke's Gospel. This is a critical narrative turning point as Jesus resolves to go to Jerusalem. It is the beginning of what some scholars refer to as Luke's travel narrative, which will run through chapter 19. This next section of Luke also shows Jesus preparing His disciples for their second mission.

Luke notes that the time is approaching for Jesus to be taken to heaven (9:51). This is a reference beyond Jesus' death and resurrection to His ascension. Luke's Gospel describes the ministry of Jesus before His ascension; the sequel, Acts, reports what happens after Jesus' ascension through His disciples (Acts 1:2).

The disciples are far from ready, yet Jesus sets out for Jerusalem. When denied permission to stay in a Samaritan village, James and John express indignation and ask Jesus if they can call fire from heaven to destroy the offending village. Jesus rebukes them and simply goes elsewhere.

Demystifying Luke

The spiritual and ethnic differences between Jews and Samaritans created problems on a regular basis. This tension was even stronger when the Samaritans realized that Jews were on their way to Jerusalem. Jewish travelers would frequently go around Samaria, but Jesus hadn't chosen to do so.

9:57–62

EXCUSES NOT TO FOLLOW JESUS

Along the road Jesus meets a series of people who want to follow Him. . .sort of. The first person seems to give up the idea when faced with uncertainty (9:57–58). Two more want to put off following until they can attend to other matters—important matters to be sure, but things that prevent them from going with Jesus.

At first reading, Jesus may seem cold and heartless. But in reality, essentially everyone who chooses not to follow (or not to do so wholeheartedly) can come up with a really good reason to justify his or her actions. As Jesus has resolutely set out for Jerusalem, He expects people to decide if they're with Him or against Him.

Take It Home

What are some of the excuses you've heard about why people don't want to follow Jesus? To what extent do you think each excuse is valid? Can you detect any excuses that you sometimes use in order to justify not doing as much as you might feel you ought to do?

LUKE 10:1–42

SEVENTY-TWO MISSIONARIES, A GOOD SAMARITAN, AND SIBLING RIVALRY

The Seventy-two	10:1–24
The Good Samaritan	10:25–37
Mary and Martha Disagree about What's Important	10:38–42

Setting Up the Section

Luke chapter 9 is the immediate backdrop for our text in chapter 10. It began with the sending out of the twelve disciples. The report of Herod's concern with the identity of Jesus is followed by the feeding of the five thousand. After this, Peter's great confession is recorded, followed immediately by the transfiguration of Jesus.

The first words of verse 1 in chapter 10 ("After this. . ." NIV) show the close link between the sending out of the seventy-two and the preceding context. The sending out of the disciples is thus related both to the sending out of the Twelve (9:1–6) and the Lord's instruction on discipleship (9:37–62).

Just as Jesus has sent out the Twelve in pairs to experience firsthand ministry (9:1–6), He now sends out seventy-two more. They are thrilled with what they learned from this teaching method. Jesus also teaches an expert of the Law with a classic parable and teaches two sisters an important lesson on priorities.

10:1–24

THE SEVENTY-TWO

Jesus' sending out of the apostles in pairs (9:1–6) is described in three Gospels, but only Luke tells of the subsequent sending out of seventy-two in pairs. (Some manuscripts say that seventy went out rather than seventy-two.) And considerably more is said about the appointing of the seventy-two than the mission of the Twelve.

While there are similarities between the two groups that were sent out, there are significant differences in the instructions given.

The Twelve Luke 9	The Seventy-two Luke 10
The Twelve are known individuals.	The seventy-two are not.
Sent out in Galilee	Sent along the route Jesus will be taking to Jerusalem
Told specifically not to preach to the Gentiles or the Samaritans	There is a clear hint of this sending including the Gentiles. This seems to be a more Gentile territory, and there would be no need to speak of what is eaten if they were only in Jewish homes.
This sending seems to conclude Jesus' ministry in Galilee.	This sending seems introductory.
Sent out in place of Jesus	Sent out as forerunners, sent ahead of Jesus, who would be passing by this way (10:1)
Sent out from village to village, and the impression is that they went to those remote, previously missed places. This seems to have been a rural, remote mission (9:6).	Sent to the towns and cities (10:8, 10, 12)

Jesus tells the larger group not to speak to people along the road (10:4) and to eat whatever is set before them (10:8). Seemingly, Jesus is intentionally expanding His ministry—not only going to larger cities than previously, but also beginning to include Gentile territory. (Otherwise, there would have been no need to address the food issue [10:7–8].) But still He instructs His messengers to go only where they are welcomed (10:10–16).

It can seem strange that Jesus would command the disciples to refrain from the normal social amenity of a friendly greeting on the road. His instruction actually implies the urgency of the task: Don't stop for chitchat; get to the business of spreading the good news. Just as Jesus is resolved to go to Jerusalem, so the disciples must be resolved to proclaim the message.

Jesus perceives the world as a vast harvest, with only a few workers (10:2). He makes it clear that the seventy-two are "like lambs among wolves" (10:3 NIV), but He gives them power to heal and authority to preach (10:9, 16).

Demystifying Luke

Korazin and Bethsaida (10:13) were cities on the north side of the Sea of Galilee—the area where Jesus conducted a number of miracles early in His ministry. Capernaum (10:15) was Jesus' home base during His adult life. Jesus contrasted these cities with Tyre and Sidon (10:13–14), two predominantly Gentile cities where He had not taught or worked miracles.

The experience must have been very positive because they return with joy, reporting to Jesus that even demons submitted to them in Jesus' name (10:17). It would seem that their ability to cast out demons was the ultimate evidence of the power and authority they exercised in the name of the Lord Jesus. It is easy to see how they would have come to this conclusion. After all, the nine disciples had been unable to cast a demon out of a boy (9:37–41). If the nine were the "A squad," and they could not cast out a demon, and the seventy-two, the "B squad," were successful, this was cause for great joy. The casting out of demons is proof to the disciples that they have great authority in Jesus' name.

Jesus tells the overjoyed disciples that their ability to cast out demons is evidence of even greater issues than they have imagined. They see their success only in terms of their having authority over the demons; Jesus is also watching their success, seeing Satan in the beginnings of his demise (10:18). Satan is falling down lightning fast. The coming of Christ, and more specifically the cross of Christ, is Satan's defeat, and the mission of the seventy is but a preview of what is to come.

Jesus doesn't want to diminish their joy, but He does try to redirect it. If the destruction of Satan is good news and cause for rejoicing, their salvation is even better news and cause for deepest joy. In a very gentle way, Jesus tells them that they should rejoice in the fact of their salvation, rather than the fact of Satan's downfall and defeat (10:20). On another occasion He will speak of those who have the power to cast out demons, yet He calls them evildoers (Matthew 7:22–23).

Jesus is also full of joy. Although He has "resolutely set out for Jerusalem" (9:51 NIV) to die, He is filled with the Holy Spirit at this point and praises God for the opportunity, at last, for people to witness what the seventy-two have seen. He tells them privately that they have witnessed what prophets and kings have long wished to see (10:23–24), and that God is revealing spiritual insights to them that will remain hidden from the wise and educated (10:21). How can they not feel joy?

10:25–37

THE GOOD SAMARITAN

One day Jesus is approached by "an expert in the law" (10:25 NIV). He asks Jesus about the scriptural prerequisites for inheriting eternal life. Jesus turns the question back on the man, who cites commands from Deuteronomy 6:5 and Leviticus 19:18—to love God with all one's heart, soul, strength, and mind, and to love one's neighbor as oneself. Jesus agrees with the man's answer, adding, "Do this and you will live" (10:28 NIV).

But in order to justify himself, the man asks a second question: "And who is my neighbor?" (10:29 NIV). In response, Jesus tells the Parable of the Good Samaritan. The Jewish priest and Levite, both of whom hold respected religious positions, choose to ignore a severely injured man on the road. The fact that they are going down the road (10:30–32) suggests they are coming from Jerusalem and aren't rushing to some important obligation at the temple. They even go out of their way to cross the road to avoid close contact.

In contrast, a Samaritan—a man who would have been despised by the Jews— sees the same man. He stops, treats his wounds, transports him to an inn, cares for him, and pays the innkeeper to watch over the injured man until he can return. He does everything he can possibly do. So Jesus asks the lawyer which of the three men acted as a neighbor.

The expert in the Law can't even bring himself to say, "The Samaritan." Rather, he responds, "The one who had mercy on him." And Jesus says, "Go and do likewise" (10:37 NIV).

That's twice that the man asks Jesus a question, answers his own question, and is told by Jesus to do what he has said. He thought he was doing a good job of justifying himself by his works, but Jesus quickly shows him it isn't as easy as he thought. Love for God is demonstrated by love for others—all others.

It might appear from the story of the Good Samaritan that Jesus is advocating salvation by works. Jesus is, in reality, doing the opposite. He is attempting to show this expert in the Law that in order to be saved through law-keeping, he will have to do that which he has not been able to do (that is why he felt the need to justify himself), and that no one can do, for salvation through the Law requires perfect, progressive obedience to the Law, without one failure.

Critical Observation

Luke has briefly mentioned the tension between the Jews and Samaritans (9:51–56), but the problem had existed for centuries. When the Assyrians defeated the Israelites in the mid-700s BC, they took many people into exile and brought their own people in to resettle Samaria and other areas. The remaining Israelites eventually intermarried with the Gentiles. When the Jews came out of captivity and returned to their homeland, they faced opposition from the inhabitants, and the mutual dislike of Jews and Samaritans continued from that point forward. But the hostility reached its peak around the time of Jesus' ministry.

10:38–42

MARY AND MARTHA DISAGREE ABOUT WHAT'S IMPORTANT

In another story recorded only by Luke, Jesus is invited to have dinner at the home of Martha, who has a sister named Mary. (They also have a brother named Lazarus [John 11:1–2], whom Jesus raised from the dead.) Martha appears to be the older of the two sisters. In Luke 10 verses 38 and 40, Martha is depicted as the hostess, who invites Jesus into her home. Martha seems not only to be the older, but the more aggressive and outspoken of the two women. It is she who went out to meet Jesus after Lazarus died, and to inform Him that this would not have happened if He would have been there sooner (John 11:20–21).

Mary sits at the feet of Jesus while Martha is busy preparing a meal in the kitchen, which finally aggravates Martha to the point where she goes and asks Jesus to tell Mary to help her (10:40). It's easy to assume that Mary is clearly the more spiritual of the two, yet Martha has a point. This is no small meal. Jesus has His disciples with Him (10:38), which at the time might have been a number much larger than twelve. Who can blame Martha for wanting help? For Luke's first-century audience, Martha's role seems much more understandable than Mary's. They would have been shocked by Mary's behavior—in Judaism, women did not learn at the feet of a rabbi.

Still, Martha seems more angry than jealous. It must be hard to hear that Mary has made the better choice (10:42). Jesus shows no anger toward Martha. Nor does He impose a stereotypical "woman's role" on either of the women. He merely tries to clarify what should have been the highest priority at that moment. And He deals more with their attitudes than their actions.

The story of Martha and Mary underscores the importance and priority of learning at the feet of Jesus, that is, being His disciple. It was not the frantic activity of Martha that won

Jesus' commendation, but the quiet activity of Mary, who sat at the feet of her Savior, listening intently to His teaching.

Take It Home

Are you by nature more like Mary or Martha? At church meetings or similar gatherings, are you more attentive to the needs of the group or the content being discussed. . .or are they equally important to you? Regardless of your natural tendencies, how can you ensure that you stay focused on what is better—the one thing that is needed (10:42)?

LUKE 11:1–54

PRAYER, DEMONS, SIGNS, AND WOES

Lessons on Prayer	11:1–13
Jesus vs. Beelzebub	11:14–36
A Long Series of Woes	11:37–54

Setting Up the Section

People are beginning to respond to Jesus' ministry in various ways. He has preached and healed, but has also taught by personal example. Now His disciples begin to ask about how to pray. Onlookers speculate as to how He casts out demons. People start to expect fantastic signs from Him. And the Pharisees increase their opposition to Him.

Up to this point, the emphasis of Luke has fallen on the prayer life of Jesus. But here a certain unnamed disciple sees the Lord's practice as a pattern, one which each disciple should follow, and thus Jesus is asked to teach the disciples to pray as well. The prayer life that characterizes our Lord will, in the book of Acts, characterize the disciples as well. Luke is paving the way, laying the foundation for that constant communion with God in prayer.

11:1–13

LESSONS ON PRAYER

One day when Jesus had just finished praying, one of the disciples asks Him to teach their group to pray. Perhaps the curious disciple had previously been a follower of John the Baptist (11:1). In response, Jesus provides what has become known as the Lord's Prayer (11:2–4), although Luke's version is a bit shorter than the more familiar version found in Matthew 6:9–13.

The prayer Jesus gives to His disciples as a pattern is a short one. This prayer does not include all of the elements of prayer. The prayer is a skeletal one, one which can be filled in with much greater detail, but it is also one that does outline the essential elements of our prayers. It underscores three areas of need:

1) The coming of the kingdom of God. This is a desire for the authority of the Father to be fully established on the earth, and for His glory and splendor to be revealed.
2) Physical needs. The Father is the provider for His children, and thus the disciples are taught to ask Him for their daily needs. The bread represents not just food in a general sense, but all of the areas of physical need.
3) The spiritual needs of saints who still sin. Salvation delivers one from the penalty of sin, but only the return of Christ will rid the saint of the presence of sin. Thus, Jesus taught His disciples to pray for forgiveness for their sins. In order to enjoy fellowship with God, the barrier of our sins must be removed by His forgiveness. There is an ongoing need for this, and it is for this that Jesus taught us to pray.

In this case Jesus does not initiate the discussion of prayer. He has modeled it enough for others to notice and become curious. When asked, He follows His model of prayer with additional instructions. Having provided a model, Jesus moves to the motivation for prayer. To do this He tells two parables. The first parable deals with one's request of a friend (11:5–10); the second with the request made of one's father (11:11–13).

The parable in verses 5–8 demonstrates the need for persistence in prayer. If people can be swayed to change their minds in response to their friends, even at inconvenient times, then how much more is a loving God willing to respond to His followers? The result of persistence is receiving as much as one needs. Yet it is important to ask, seek, and knock (11:9–10) rather than assume God will drop all we need into our laps with no thought.

In the second parable, Jesus teaches that God is like a father who wants only the best for his children (11:11–13). Human fathers give their children good things when asked, rather than potentially harmful substitutes. So a loving, heavenly Father who knows our needs will certainly provide much more for His children. But rather than give us everything we ask for (much of which is not necessarily needed or helpful), God provides the Holy Spirit to those who ask. With the wisdom, strength, and comfort provided by God's Spirit, there is little else we actually need (11:13).

11:14–36

JESUS VS. BEELZEBUB

Jesus has cast out evil spirits from people on numerous occasions. So have the apostles (9:1) and the seventy-two disciples (10:17). Even people they didn't know were driving out demons in the name of Jesus (9:49). But on this occasion, Jesus' onlookers decide to challenge Him.

They can't deny that a miracle has taken place, because a previously mute man is speaking clearly after the removal of the spirit (11:14). So Jesus' critics (Pharisees and teachers of the Law, according to Matthew 12:24 and Mark 3:22) try to question the motive behind the miracle. They accuse Jesus of having the power of Beelzebub, "the prince of demons" (11:15 NIV).

Demystifying Luke

The Old Testament Philistines had worshiped their god Baal under the name Baal-Zebub. The Greek version became Beelzebub, meaning "lord of flies." Perhaps it was an intentional variant spelling of Beelzeboul, which meant "lord of the dwelling." Beelzebub came to be used as a name for Satan (11:18).

Jesus immediately points out the illogic of their speculation. Why would anyone working in league with Satan go around removing evil spirits (11:17–18)? In addition, asks Jesus, how about other Jewish people who drive out demons, or for that matter, the Jewish belief that the power of God could remove evil spirits (11:19)? Is their work of the devil? And even more important: What if they are wrong about Jesus? If indeed He is using the power of God, they are guilty of resisting the kingdom of God (11:20).

Jesus' response quickly shows how foolish such a conclusion is. It was as if Jesus had said, "Who willingly and knowingly shoots himself in the foot?" Satan would not do harm to himself, would he? The opponents of Jesus are foolish to make such a charge against Him. Not only is it false; it isn't even logical.

Jesus has probed their logic (which is faulty), and He has pressed it to a very uncomfortable conclusion (their disciples or followers are operating by Satan's power, too, for they also cast out demons). Now, He gives them one more logical thrust: If they are wrong and He is operating in the power of God, then they must admit that the kingdom of God has come and that Jesus is the Messiah. This is the very thing they most dread, and Jesus has just reminded them of what good logic must conclude: He is the King, whom they refuse to receive.

The second argument of Jesus is just as forceful as the first. Not only are Jesus' opponents wrong in attributing His power to Satan because Satan would not attack himself, but they are also wrong because the One who would attack Satan must be more powerful. No one can take away the possessions of a powerful man without first overpowering the person. The powerful man must first be overpowered, then disarmed, and finally bound, so that his goods can be plundered. Satan is indeed strong (11:21); he takes possession of certain people. But Jesus is stronger (11:22), capable of overpowering him and freeing those who have been bound.

So Jesus soundly refutes the supposition that He might be using the power of the devil, but He also responds to numerous other speculations in this passage. When a woman tries to praise Jesus' mother, He again shifts the focus from His flesh-and-blood relatives to a broader sense of family—all those who hear the Word of God and obey it (11:28; 8:21).

For those in the crowd who may have been trying to remain neutral on the issue, Jesus warns what can happen to those who try to cleanse themselves using their own power. The power of God is necessary to effectively and lastingly deal with the problem of sin and evil (11:24–26).

Then there are those who are asking for a sign (11:16)—probably one of the day-of-the-Lord signs foretold in the Old Testament (such as Joel 2:30–31). Even when John the Baptist had sought additional confirmation about Jesus, He had simply said to look at what He was doing (7:22). If the cure of a mute man is not enough, what else do they want?

Jesus has very strong words for those who request a sign from heaven. His words inform us that this is evidence of a wicked generation of Israelites, and so much so that the "belief" of two

Old Testament peoples puts them to shame. The people of Nineveh accepted the "sign of Jonah" (11:29 NIV) and repented, and the Queen of the South believed the reports about Solomon's wisdom (11:31). For this, they will testify in the day of judgment against this generation for their unbelief (11:32).

Critical Observation

Jesus' mention of the Ninevites (Jonah 3:5–10) and the Queen of the South (1 Kings 10:6–9) is telling. First, because both are Gentiles, and they, because of their belief, condemn the unbelief of this generation of Israelites. Second, both parties believed with much less evidence than what Jesus' audience had seen. The Ninevites repented at the preaching of Jonah, which, as we find it recorded in the book of Jonah, may have been only one short proclamation that they had forty days to straighten up or they would perish. The Queen of the South also was convinced of Solomon's wisdom when she merely heard his words.

The responses of all of these people within the crowd that witnessed Jesus' deliverance of the demoniac were varied, but the end result and the problem was the same in every case: They did not believe in Jesus as their Messiah. And this unbelief was rooted in their rejection of Jesus' words, which led them to a misinterpretation of His works. These who looked beyond the clear manifestations of God's power would receive no other signs (11:29–32).

In the final paragraph of this section, Jesus now exposes the real problem. In verse 33 Jesus says that the purpose of a lamp is to illuminate, and thus a light is put in a prominent place. Since He came to illuminate people (Luke 1:79; John 1:4–18), He does not speak or act in secret, but in the open. His light, as it were, is brightly exposed to people. His generation will not perish for lack of light.

The eye, Jesus says, is the gateway to the person's entire being, his whole body. If the eye is good, if it lets in the light, the whole body is illuminated. If the eye is defective, if it lets in little light, the whole body is dark. Jesus is saying that everyone who fails to interpret the evidence of this miracle as they should has done so because of a defect in their ability to see the truth, not because of any deficiency in the evidence (11:34).

11:37–54

A LONG SERIES OF WOES

It seems odd that after refuting the Pharisees so soundly, one of them invites Jesus to eat with him (11:37). The washing that Jesus decides to forego is not the kind of washing up that mothers insist on before a meal, the washing required by good hygiene. The concern here is not dirty hands but ceremonial defilement. This is a washing that is required by the traditions of the Pharisees, rather than by the Law itself (Mark 7:1–4). It seems He may have intentionally passed on the opportunity in order to challenge the Pharisees on their habits. They remain highly focused on looks and external matters, but have lost sight of the inward purity God desires for His people (11:39–41).

Critical Observation

The word *Pharisee* may very well be derived from a term that means "to separate." The origin of the Pharisees as a sect seems to have been in or around the second century BC. They were not known as a primarily political group as much as the zealots who wanted change through revolution. The Pharisees sought to produce spiritual holiness and spiritual reformation. They recognized that Israel's condition was the result of sin, specifically a disobedience to the Law. It was their intention to identify, communicate, and facilitate obedience to God's law, thus producing holiness and paving the way for the kingdom of God to be established on the earth.

The problem with the Pharisees is not in what they believed, and not even in what they hoped to do, but in what they actually became and did. Their goals were noble and their presuppositions were essentially correct, but they were sidetracked. Instead of being the first to recognize Jesus as the Messiah, they were the first to reject Him. Rather than turning the nation to Him, they sought to turn the nation against Him.

Jesus' response to the Pharisee (11:39–41) is an answer to his surprise at the Lord's avoidance of ceremonial washing. While our Lord is addressing His host, He is also confronting the evils of the whole Pharisaic system (11:39), of which this man is a part.

Jesus' words here can be difficult to follow because the imagery changes so quickly and so often. The overall thrust is the contrast between the outside, which is secondary, and the inside, which is primary. Jesus begins by talking about the washing of the outside of a cup or a dish, but then moves to the inside of a man. He then moves back to the dish imagery and tells His host that He can make the dish clean by emptying its contents and giving them to the poor.

The overall impact of Jesus' words is clear. Jesus differs from His host and the other Pharisees by seeing the inside as more important than the outside—the heart more important than appearances, one's attitudes and motives more important than one's actions. The Pharisees believed that a man is made holy by working from the outside, in. Jesus believed that holiness (and defilement) came from the inside, out.

When it becomes obvious that His host is uncomfortable with His refusal to wash, Jesus unleashes a series of three "woes" on the Pharisees as a group.

1) They emphasized minute points of law while missing the basic fundamentals (11:42).
2) They were preoccupied with position, prestige, and praise (11:43).
3) They had become a source of defilement rather than purification (11:44).

Similarly, the experts in the Law, who should have been the elite subset of the Pharisees, are offended. But Jesus proclaims three woes for them as well.

1) Their teaching resulted in burdens rather than blessings on the people (11:46).
2) They had the same attitude as their forefathers who had persecuted and even killed God's prophets (11:47–51).
3) These self-proclaimed experts had not only lost sight of God's knowledge, but they were hindering others from discovering it as well (11:52).

Not surprisingly, after Jesus addresses the Pharisees and experts of the Law, they get together in fierce opposition to Him (11:53).

Of what did the Pharisees accuse Jesus?	Of what were the Pharisees accused in the Gospels?
1) Eating/associating with sinners—Matthew 9:11; Mark 2:16; Luke 5:30; 7:39; 15:2	1) Hypocrisy—bring forth fruit worthy of repentance—Matthew 3:7–8
2) Not fasting as they did—Matthew 9:14; Mark 2:18; Luke 5:33	2) Honoring God with mouth, but heart far away—Matthew 15:7–20
3) Operating in power of Satan—Matthew 9:34	3) Justifying selves in men's sight, but God knows hearts—Luke 16:15
4) Disciples violating Sabbath by eating—Matthew 12:2; Mark 2:24; Luke 6:2	4) Self-righteousness—Luke 18:10–14
5) Jesus violating Sabbath by healing man with withered hand—Mark 3:1–5; Luke 6:6–10	5) Not having works sufficient to get them into kingdom—Matthew 5:20
6) Healing man with dropsy on Sabbath—Luke 14:1-6	6) Placing their traditions above the Law—Matthew 15:1–20
7) Violating Sabbath, He cannot be Messiah—John 9:16	7) Focusing on externals, not internals—Luke 11:39–41
8) His disciples didn't wash their hands ceremonially—Matthew 15:1–20; Mark 7:1–9	8) Demanding a sign—Matthew 16:1-4; Mark 8:11-12
9) Under what conditions can a man divorce his wife? —Matthew 19:3–12; Mark 10:2–12	9) The leaven of/in their teaching—Matthew 16:5-12
10) Claiming, by inference (sins forgiven) to be God—Luke 5:17–25	10) Being ignorant of the scriptures—Matthew 19; 21:42, and of power of God (Matthew 22:29).
11) Testing Jesus as to what to do with woman caught in adultery/application of the Law—John 8:3–11	11) Elevating themselves and seeking prominence—Matthew 23:2, 5-6
12) Jesus appearing as His own witness—John 8:13–19	12) Shutting off kingdom of heaven from men—Matthew 23:13
	13) Using technicalities as excuses for disobedience of law—Matthew 23:16-24
	14) Focusing on trivial but missing the main points—Matthew 23:23–28
	15) Being lovers of money—Luke 16:14
	16) Disdaining the crowds, who knew not the Law—John 7:49

Take It Home

One of the temptations we face as Christians, and which our text clearly exposes, is to focus on outward acts or appearances rather than on inward motivation. We are often guilty of taking new Christians aside and trying to rid them of their evil behaviors, as though cleaning up the outside purifies the inside. Jesus teaches us that when we clean up the inside, when our attitudes and our motives are pure, our outward lives will clean up. Often, cleaning up only the outside tends to corrupt the inside more. Now, having cleaned up the outside, we find pride and self-righteousness to be added to our list of inner evils. Let us learn from our Lord that holiness begins inside and works out, and not the reverse.

LUKE 12:1–59

WARNINGS AND ASSURANCES

Beware Bad Yeast	12:1–11
Hoarding vs. Trust	12:12–34
Two Contrasting Scenarios	12:35–59

Setting Up the Section

After having just publicly confronted the Pharisees and teachers of the Law, Luke moves to an instance where Jesus gives specific instructions to His apostles about the problems of hypocrisy. He also addresses proper stewardship of the gospel, possessions, and the use of our time.

12:1–11

BEWARE BAD YEAST

Jesus and His followers are surrounded by a trampling crowd of thousands (12:1). Yet Jesus seems to ignore the masses and speaks directly to the disciples.

Jesus states clearly that the "yeast" (12:1 NIV) of the Pharisees is hypocrisy—and the danger is that it permeates and spreads like yeast throughout the entire lump of dough. They tend to know little about true religion and act as if they do. On the outside, they look fine. They have long, pious-sounding prayers, and they have all of the trappings of men of dignity and holiness. But inside, Jesus says, they are full of greed and wickedness (11:39). But how can the disciples possibly be tempted to be hypocritical, like the Pharisees?

Critical Observation

Hypocrisy can take many forms:

- Hypocrisy can be a conformity to the values and expectations of someone else, bowing to the idol of other people's values, which are not really our own. Hypocrites adjust and accommodate their appearance to what other people think or feel.
- Hypocrisy can be an inconsistency. It's the discrepancy between what appears and what is, between the way things seem and the way they are. The Pharisees appeared to be righteous on the outside but, in reality, they were wicked.
- Hypocrisy can be a deception by our actions or our words, acting in such a way that people will come to the wrong conclusion. This, to a large degree, was true of the Pharisees.

Hypocrisy is a problem no matter what the motivation. Whether we are hypocritical either to achieve men's praise as the Pharisees or to avoid their persecution, perhaps as the disciples, Jesus calls us to something different.

Jesus seems to suggest that a more likely problem for His disciples is knowledge of the complete truth yet being reluctant to speak out. Perhaps that's why He speaks of hidden things being made known (12:2–3) and fear of those who can physically threaten (12:4). But He also makes clear each person's worth and God's awareness of each person and situation (12:6–7). He tempers His comments on the fear of God by addressing His listeners as "friends" (12:4 NIV).

Jesus challenges His followers to stand firm for Him when the time comes, promising that He will be their heavenly advocate (12:8–9). The unforgivable sin of blasphemy against the Holy Spirit is better defined in Matthew 12:31–32, and Mark 3:23–30 as attributing the work of the Holy Spirit to Satan. If someone does not acknowledge the role of the Holy Spirit in faith and salvation, no other course of forgiveness exists. Indeed, it is the Holy Spirit who will instruct believers on what to say during times of trial and persecution.

We see a number of examples of those who stand firm in the power of the Spirit in the book of Acts. Peter and John, when arrested, boldly preach the gospel as their defense (Acts 4). Stephen, when arrested and charged before the crowd, powerfully preaches the gospel as his defense (Acts 6–7). So, too, with Paul (Acts 22). The Holy Spirit gives people under duress a special sense of God's presence (Acts 7:55–56), thus comforting and assuring them. He also gives them the words to speak and the power to speak them boldly.

12:12–34

HOARDING VS. TRUST

Still surrounded by a great crowd, a voice breaks through while Jesus is talking to His disciples (12:13). Jesus is a rabbi, a teacher. He has not come to oversee probate court, and He lets the man know (12:14). It is unclear to whom the following parable is directed, whether the disciples, the crowd, or maybe even the questioner and his brother who are disputing their inheritance. Yet Jesus clearly identifies the root of the problem: greed (12:15).

The Parable of the Rich Fool (12:16–21) teaches that a person's view of the future determines his or her present conduct. The rich man does well to think in terms of the future; his failure is in not recognizing where his wealth has come from. Jesus clarifies that it is the ground that produces a good crop (12:16). God has provided the wealth, but the man is seeking to cash it in and store it.

Critical Observation

Modern readers of the Parable of the Rich Fool may be a bit discomfited to realize that his plans for the future are not very different from many people's goals for retirement. Jesus' teaching in the following passage (12:22–34) helps put the teaching of this parable in context. Whether wealthy or poor, we should keep our focus on real treasure (12:33).

The rich man is a fool because he perceives his possessions as his security. He has great wealth, but doesn't use it for anyone except himself. However, Jesus is not condemning wealth per se in this parable. His own interpretation is that this is how it will be for anyone who stores up wealth but is not rich toward God (12:21). Concern for the future, He says, should not escalate into worry (12:22). Just as rich people can become preoccupied with accumulating wealth, so can those of lesser means.

Jesus' statement that life is more than food (12:23) reflects His rebuke of the devil during His temptation (4:4). When we worry about clothing or food we fail to focus on what is most important in life. Additionally, such worry is foolish when we consider God's marvelous provision for His creatures in nature (12:24–28). Believers should put God's kingdom first, and everything else will fall into place (12:30–31).

It seems that Jesus isn't putting His disciples into the category of poor people, because He tells them to sell their possessions and give to the poor (12:33)—a general rule, not a broad-sweeping command. What is in one's heart is inextricably connected to his or her idea of treasure. In the long run, heavenly things endure as earthly ones deteriorate (12:33–34).

12:35–59

TWO CONTRASTING SCENARIOS

Jesus then tells two parallel stories, both of which emphasize the importance of readiness for His coming, yet with vastly different results. In the first (12:35–38), a master has attended a wedding banquet and his servants are anticipating his return. Keeping the lamps burning (12:35) was important in a culture without electricity or streetlights. And when the master gets home and finds his servants faithfully waiting, he serves them (12:37). Keep in mind how counter-cultural this image would be in the first century—a master serving his slave!

In contrast, Jesus speaks of a homeowner who has no interest in visitors (12:39–40). In this case, the return of the Son of Man is described in terms of an unexpected thief who breaks into the house.

In both stories the coming of someone is unscheduled. The difference, however, is the relationship between those in the house and the one who will be arriving. The faithful servants—those that are alert and ready—are rewarded for their watchfulness.

The disciples are confused, and as usual, it is Peter who speaks up to ask Jesus to clarify (12:41). Jesus doesn't respond directly, but gives additional clues to what He means (12:42–48). If directed to individuals, Jesus' words are uncomfortably severe. Another interpretation, however, is that the nation of Israel is the servant who knows what his master wants (12:47). Because they are not ready to receive Jesus, the Jews are cut to pieces (dispersed) and assigned a place with the unbelieving Gentiles (12:46). The Church (including both believing Jews and Gentiles) will eventually be put in charge of the Master's possessions (12:44). Whether eagerly anticipated or dreaded, one's attitude toward the Lord's second coming is the result of his or her response to His first coming.

Demystifying Luke

Throughout the Bible, fire is closely associated with the presence and power of God. It is figuratively and literally an instrument of divine wrath exercised against sinful people—both Jews and Gentiles. Biblical prophecy speaks of fire yet to come, including the fire of divine judgment linked with the Messiah. At the outset of his ministry, John the Baptist spoke of the coming Messiah as bringing fire (3:16–17).

Jesus continues with some additional alarming statements in verses 49–59. He speaks of coming fire (12:49), division of families (12:52–53), and the possibility of prison for those who don't reconcile with the magistrate (12:58). Jesus' ministry will not bring peace to everyone. He is going to judge sin, and unrepentant sinners will be punished before God's kingdom can ultimately be established. Yet the passing of judgment will not only be painful to sinful people; it is painful to God as well. In addition to God not wanting to see anyone perish (2 Peter 3:9), there will be the literal pain Jesus will experience. It is a baptism He dreads (12:50). His love for humankind will motivate Him to go through with it, yet not all the consequences will be positive.

Take It Home

Opposition in the disciples' day took the form of the raised fist; today it frequently takes the place of the raised eyebrow. People don't want to be looked down on, or even questioned as to their motives when it comes to spiritual things. To what extent are your own religious beliefs (or more specifically, your public statements of faith) influenced by the actions and attitudes of others? Do you detect any hypocrisy? Greed? An air of superiority?

LUKE 13:1–35

CLEARING UP SOME MISCONCEPTIONS

Why Do Bad Things Happen?	13:1–9
Resentment in Response to a Healing	13:10–17
Two Short Parables	13:18–21
Take Nothing for Granted	13:22–35

Setting Up the Section

In this passage Luke describes Jesus in a number of settings. He is still healing and teaching, but the tone of His message has changed. He speaks of punishment, weeping, gnashing of teeth, and the coming desolation of Jerusalem. Yet He also tells of God's patience and the ongoing opportunities for people to participate in God's rapidly growing kingdom.

13:1–9

WHY DO BAD THINGS HAPPEN?

Verses 1–9 seem to take place in the same setting as before, where Jesus and His disciples were surrounded by a crowd of thousands (12:1). Some of those present bring up news of a recent tragedy: Pilate had ordered people killed while they were offering sacrifices in the temple (13:1). This was more than a mere statement of fact; it was an assumption that the people killed were somehow more guilty of sin than others, and God had allowed them to die. Similarly, a common belief was that a person's prosperity was proportional to his or her piety.

In response, Jesus speaks of a different tragedy—the collapse of a tower inside the wall of Jerusalem that had killed eighteen people (13:4). The two tragedies are quite similar. In both cases, people had died suddenly and unexpectedly at places where they probably felt most secure. One group was offering sacrifices to God; the other was adjacent to a structure that had been erected for the group's defense.

In both cases, Jesus emphatically refutes the assumption that the victims had done anything to expedite their deaths. Rather, He teaches His listeners to view the two events as symbolic of the kind of death that everyone who doesn't repent will face (13:3, 5).

He follows His comments with a parable about a fig tree (13:6–9). The lack of fruit certainly applies to Israel, as confirmed by other statements and parables Jesus has been teaching. Yet in spite of the nation's stubborn rebellion and sin, the parable emphasizes God's patience and an extended period of grace (13:7–9).

Demystifying Luke

A fig tree was a common biblical symbol for the nation of Israel, which is likely the case in Jesus' parable (13:6–9). Many gardens in the area were planned with a fig tree planted in the center. If the tree failed to produce fruit, it only made sense to remove it to use the space for something more productive.

13:10–17

RESENTMENT IN RESPONSE TO A HEALING

The setting for this section changes from that of a crowded street to a synagogue where Jesus is teaching. (This will be Luke's final mention of Jesus teaching in such a location.) While there, He sees a woman who has been crippled for eighteen years, calls her forward, and heals her. It is the Sabbath, and the synagogue leader becomes upset.

Previously, Pharisees who had opposed Jesus' healings on the Sabbath had challenged Him personally. The synagogue leader uses a different tactic: He starts telling the people to come for healings only on the six days suited for work (13:14).

Jesus calls him on his hypocrisy. First, how likely will it be that anyone will be healed there on a workday if Jesus is not present? Second, as the healed woman and numerous onlookers are praising God (13:13, 17), the very person in charge is trying to shut down their enthusiasm. And finally, Jesus points out that the man isn't even giving the woman ("a daughter of Abraham" [13:16 NIV]) the same respect he would give his ox or donkey (13:15–16 NIV).

13:18–21

TWO SHORT PARABLES

The Parable of the Mustard Seed (13:18–19) is frequently interpreted as showing how quickly the kingdom of God would grow. However, another interpretation is possible. In the original language, the seed was not so much planted as thrown, or cast aside. Perhaps the mustard plant wasn't planned or provided for, yet grew surprisingly large and strong. If this is the case, perhaps Jesus is suggesting that His rejection by the Jewish people is like being cast aside, yet the end result will be a strong kingdom that provides for all believers, including Gentiles. In contrast to the well-tended but fruitless fig tree in danger of being destroyed (13:6–9), the mustard plant will thrive.

Similarly, the next parable (13:20–21) can have different interpretations. It may be that the woman mixed the yeast into the flour. Or perhaps her intent was to hide the yeast (another acceptable translation). If the latter, the woman's efforts certainly backfired because a little yeast would quickly permeate a large amount of dough. If, like the synagogue leader in verse 14, the leaders of the Israelites are attempting to hide the gospel—especially from the Gentiles—their efforts are futile.

Critical Observation

Yeast (leaven) is usually a symbol for spiritual corruption. Luke has already recorded Jesus' warning to "be on your guard against the yeast of the Pharisees, which is hypocrisy" (12:1 NIV). But this case is an exception where yeast is used as a positive symbol.

13:22–35

TAKE NOTHING FOR GRANTED

Jesus is continuing toward Jerusalem (13:22), where He knows He will be put to death. A voice in the crowd calls out, "Lord, are only a few people going to be saved?" (13:23 NIV).

Jesus doesn't respond to the question directly, but rather begins to speak in terms of a door and limited time to enter (13:24–25). The door is narrow, but at least it is currently open.

Salvation will involve more than mere association with Jesus, such as sharing a meal or listening to His words (13:26). Some people who assume entitlement to God's kingdom are considered "evildoers" by Jesus (13:27 NIV). In the kingdom of God, many who consider themselves first will be last, and those who are last will become first.

At this point in His ministry, Jesus is not to be deterred from His mission—not even by rumors of Herod's desire to kill Him (13:31). While Herod is hoping to meet Jesus (9:9) he also fears Him, thinking He might be the resurrected John the Baptist, whom Herod himself had executed (9:7–9). Jesus isn't swayed. He gives the Pharisees a return message, though it is doubtful they will have the courage to deliver it (13:32–33).

Jesus knows exactly what to say, and again He expresses sorrow for what He sees. He concludes this section of His teaching with a fondness for Jerusalem and her people (13:34–35). Yet He keeps moving in that direction to do what He has come to do.

Take It Home

Some people today may not be too different from the Israelites who assumed that they would enter the kingdom of God based on their credentials—not because of an individual relationship with Jesus. Have you witnessed this among friends or peers? What are some things that people think will get them into heaven?

LUKE 14:1–35

BANQUET ETIQUETTE

Dinner Conversation 14:1–14
A Banquet Parable 14:15–24
Seeing Things Through to the Finish 14:25–35

Setting Up the Section

In recent passages, Jesus has been teaching some difficult lessons, and He continues in this one—once at a dinner and again while beset by crowds as He travels. Much of what He says is easy to understand, even though His listeners might be reluctant to acknowledge it. Some of His teachings are, and have always been, a bit difficult to comprehend without considerable thought and reflection.

14:1–14

DINNER CONVERSATION

If it seems suspicious that Jesus is invited to eat with a prominent Pharisee, such suspicions are confirmed when we read He is carefully being watched (14:1). Also quite dubious is the diseased man coming to Him on the Sabbath (14:2). Jesus is clearly aware of what is going on because He asks His fellow diners whether they believe it is lawful to heal on the Sabbath. Since the Sabbath forbade work, the rabbis typically debated whether it was lawful to do good, such as healing, on the Sabbath. Different rabbis had different opinions. Generally it was considered that only life-threatening disease or injury could be treated on the Sabbath.

When no one is willing to speak up, Jesus heals the man with dropsy and sends him on his way (14:4). Jesus is aware that the Pharisees wouldn't hesitate to make an exception to their traditions about "work" if one of their sons, or even one of their animals, needed help on the Sabbath. Still, they try to impose their legalistic standards on others, so Jesus doesn't hesitate to call them on their hypocrisy. Even after Jesus' miracle they have nothing to say (14:6).

Demystifying Luke

Dropsy (14:2) was a medical condition noted only by Luke (a doctor) in the New Testament. Now called edema, it occurs when fluid accumulates in the body and causes soft tissue to swell. If prolonged, the problem can be terminal.

The Pharisees' air of superiority is reflected in their table manners as well.

Certain seats, usually those nearest the host, were considered places of honor. (This was true not only for the Pharisees, but throughout the Greco-Roman world.) It had become something of an art to secure one of the better seats at any occasion. It wasn't unlike musical chairs as grown men jockeyed for the best positions at social functions. Jesus points out that it would be much more preferable to be asked by the host to move up rather than be humiliated by being asked publicly to yield your seat to a more distinguished person (14:7–11). Ironically, Jesus is probably in the lowest position as He tells the group that "everyone who exalts himself will be humbled, and he who humbles himself will be exalted" (14:11 NIV). In other words, the way up is down. Those who wish to be honored must be humble. The ways of the kingdom of God are not man's ways.

Critical Observation

In Israel the meal table played a very important role, not only in the family, but in society as well. When an Israelite provided a meal for a guest, even a stranger, it assured him not only of the host's hospitality, but of his protection.

Jesus also challenges the dinner guests to provide meals for those who cannot afford to throw parties—the poor, crippled, lame, and blind (14:12–14). When planning a banquet, the temptation is to invite those who are most likely to benefit us in return. Thus, one thinks first of inviting family members or rich friends, who will reciprocate in kind. We are tempted to give in order to get. Jesus teaches that this practice should not only be revised, but reversed. In this world, people invite their friends and the rich, in order to gain from their reciprocal invitations and hospitality. In God's economy, people should be gracious to the helpless and to those who cannot pay them back, and when the kingdom of God is established on the earth, they will receive spiritual rewards. Rather than seeing one's hospitality repaid as it would be by family or friends, the more satisfying result would be blessings and eternal rewards.

14:15–24

A BANQUET PARABLE

The ambience of the dinner party is probably a bit tense at this point, so perhaps the man's comment in verse 15 is an attempt to lighten the mood. However, it also emphasizes the Pharisaical belief that they will be the ones around the table in God's kingdom.

Demystifying Luke

The mention of a feast that would happen in God's kingdom (14:15) is a reference to Isaiah 25:6–8. God's salvation is portrayed as a great final banquet with the Lord as the host. This is actually an important theme that runs through Luke—look at all the meal scenes!

The parable Jesus tells in response (14:16–24) confirms that, indeed, the leaders of Israel should be at the banquet. The invitations have been sent out well in advance of the event, and it appears that the recipients have responded that they will be coming. But when the big day arrives and a messenger is sent to escort them to the banquet hall, they all give reasons why they cannot attend. They are expecting the master of the banquet (which certainly must represent God) to excuse them.

The excuses cited by Jesus are telling. Staying home with a new wife (14:20) is a poor enough excuse, but the others are even more ludicrous. One person wants to go see a field he has apparently bought sight unseen (14:18). The second person has supposedly bought a pair of oxen without even trying them out (14:19). Not only are these people making last-minute excuses, the excuses aren't even good ones!

The master becomes angry when he receives his servant's report. He sends the servant right back out with instructions to bring in all the street people he can find. The servant rounds up all the poor, crippled, blind, and lame people he can find (14:21 [also see 14:13]), but there is still room. So the master sends him to the outer roads and country lanes to gather enough to fill the house. The original elite who declined the invitation are no longer welcome. But the others who would normally be considered outsiders (probably an allusion to the Gentiles) are compelled to come. For them, the master will not take no for an answer.

The Pharisee's dinner guest is correct. It will be a blessing to eat at the feast in the kingdom of God (14:15). But the guest list will be very different from what any of those present can imagine.

Take It Home

In verses 1–6, self-interest is at the heart of the sinful actions and attitudes of the Pharisees. Self-interest caused the Pharisees to angrily reject Jesus because He spent great amounts of time and energy with "sinners" and the unsuitable people rather than with them. In verses 7–11, it was also self-interest which motivated each person to seek a seat in the places of honor at the dinner table, which very likely left Jesus at the place of lowest honor. In verses 12–14, self-interest is once again the culprit. It prompts us to invite those who can reciprocate rather than to waste a meal on someone too poor or unable to return the favor. Finally, in verses 15–24, it was self-interest that caused the Israelites of Jesus' day to reject Him as Messiah.

These are examples of people who want to enter into the kingdom of God, but do not want to create any pain, displeasure, or sacrifice for themselves. They stand as reminders of how self-interest can paralyze our ministries, our worship, and our Christian journeys. We, too, can become so involved with our own traditions and social customs that we miss the point of what God wants to do in us and through us.

14:25–35

SEEING THINGS THROUGH TO THE FINISH

It is customary for people to follow Jesus wherever He goes (14:25), but in this instance Jesus begins to talk about what it means to really follow Him as a disciple. His expectations are high—and perhaps seem exceptionally high at first. Since Jesus has been teaching love of enemies and the importance of peacemaking, His instructions to "hate" one's own family must sound peculiar indeed. But a true disciple will not put anything before a relationship with his master. . .not even parents, a spouse, or children (14:26). In addition, discipleship includes a cross of one's own (14:27).

Critical Observation

Jesus' use of the word *hate* (14:26 NIV) is not what we first may think. In biblical phrasing, it frequently refers to a lesser relationship. For example, God loved Jacob but hated Esau (Malachi 1:2); to serve other gods was to hate the Lord (Exodus 20:5); etc. In such cases, no literal hatred (as we understand it) was involved, yet the word makes clear the difference in affection.

Jesus' two examples help make sense of what He is saying. Anyone who begins a building project but runs out of money (14:28–30) has only a monument to his incompetence. And any king who is outnumbered two to one (14:31–33) is well advised to make peace before fighting begins, or he is likely to have to surrender and be at the mercy of his enemy.

In His conclusion (14:34–35), Jesus makes it clear that He expects commitment and dedication from His disciples. He is very honest and up-front about His expectations. Better to have a few followers who finish what they start than a great number who lose their "saltiness" (14:34 NIV) before getting the job done.

Jesus' closing words, "He who has ears to hear, let him hear," (14:35 NIV) are found several times in the Gospels. The words are used in a context where our Lord is not understood by the majority, and where Jesus encourages His listeners to ponder His words carefully to learn their meaning. They serve as a reminder to contemporary readers as well, to dig deep and understand the broad applications of Jesus' teachings, and to apply them, however painfully, to our own lives.

LUKE 15:1–32

LOST AND FOUND (X 3)

The Lost Sheep	15:1–7
The Lost Coin	15:8–10
The Lost Son	15:11–32

Setting Up the Section

Jesus' debate with the Pharisees continues in this passage. They cite a complaint, and Jesus responds by telling three seemingly related parables, including what has become known as the Parable of the Prodigal Son. But on closer examination, the three parables—each of which describes the finding of a lost item, and each of which describes the joy and celebration that resulted—aren't as similar as they first appear.

15:1–7

THE LOST SHEEP

As Jesus continues to move toward Jerusalem, teaching as He goes, He begins to attract a crowd of tax collectors and sinners (15:1). Jesus treats them with respect, and His willingness to associate with them draws criticism from the Pharisees (15:2).

Jesus' rebuke of the Pharisees in Matthew 23 sheds some light on the constant conflicts Luke describes between them:	
The Pharisees loved to draw attention to themselves (Matthew 23:5).	Jesus spent time with people that held no prominence, thus would not enhance the image of the Pharisees (14:7–11).
The Pharisees took an elitist view as to who could enter God's kingdom (Matthew 23:13).	Jesus, by association with the masses, threatened to pollute this pure group of pious people.
The Pharisees focused on the technicalities (Matthew 23:16–24) based (to some degree) upon their expertise in very complex rules and regulations that left everyday people in a fog.	Jesus taught simply. He threatened to undermine the complicated, technical teaching of the Pharisees, and thus they opposed people pursuing Him to hear His teaching.
The Pharisees protected and promoted their own hypocrisy by concentrating on external sins (behaviors), rather than inner attitudes and motivations (Matthew 23:13–14, 25–36).	Jesus emphasized the internal aspects of sin (Matthew 5–7).

So Jesus tells a series of three stories. The first asks His listeners to put themselves in the place of a man who has one hundred sheep, but loses one. So he leaves the ninety-nine to go find the single lost sheep. When he finds it, he carries it home on his shoulders and then calls his friends and family, asking them to celebrate with him (15:5–6).

This is a story the Pharisees can relate to. Most people have experienced the joy of finding something valuable they had considered lost. Jesus is using this universal feeling to explain that there is rejoicing in heaven when even one sinner repents (15:7).

15:8–10

THE LOST COIN

Jesus' second story is very similar to the first. This time a woman owns ten coins and loses one. She sweeps and searches the house until she finds it. Then she, like the man in the first story, calls together her friends and neighbors to celebrate. And again Jesus observes that, "there is rejoicing in the presence of the angels of God over one sinner who repents" (15:10 NIV).

So far so good. Aside from the fact that the celebrating might seem a bit excessive in both cases, Jesus has said nothing to upset His listeners.

Critical Observation

The critical difference between Jesus and the Pharisees is that the letter cared about possessions, while Jesus cared about people. The Pharisees grumbled that Jesus could eat with and gladly receive repentant sinners and rejoice in their return, yet the Pharisees would diligently search for lost possessions and celebrate when they found them. Among other things, these first two parables indirectly expose the misplaced compassion of the Pharisees. The stories also contrast the kind of love for that which was lost in the Pharisees with that of the Lord Jesus.

The Pharisees were out of sync with heaven. Why were they unwilling to seek out sinners and unable to rejoice at their repentance? Why were they unwilling to associate with them? This is what the third parable will tell us. The third parable depicts the loving and forgiving heart of God (in the father), the repentance of the sinner (in the younger brother), and the sullen joylessness of the Pharisees (in the older brother).

15:11–32

THE LOST SON

Although this passage has come to be known as the Parable of the Prodigal Son, it would be more appropriately titled the Parable of the Two Sons. The younger son who asks for his share of the estate (15:12) might have received a third of the father's wealth. (The older son would have been entitled to a double portion.) The assets shouldn't have gone to either son until the death of the father, yet the father grants the son's request.

It doesn't take long before the younger boy has "squandered his wealth in wild living" (15:13 NIV). Not only does he become the hired hand of a pagan landowner, but his work involves feeding pigs—one of the most degrading jobs a Jewish person could think of. So he eventually comes to his senses and decides to return home with a different attitude. Meanwhile, the father appears to have been watching for him because he spots his son "while he was still a long way off" (15:20 NIV). The boy is repentant and ready to work as a servant, but is instead immediately restored to full status as a son.

It is not until this point in the story that Jesus begins to reveal the thoughts and attitudes of the older son: He is incensed that his brother is back home and having a party thrown in his honor. The older brother had worked hard and is upset that he never had such a celebration. The father tries to point out that their relationship is supposed to be reason enough to celebrate (15:31), but the story ends without the older brother being satisfied.

The closing terminology of this story (15:32) echoes the first two: The younger son had been just as "lost" as the sheep and the coin. And now that a personal relationship was at risk, the celebration at finding what was lost should have been even greater. Luke doesn't record the response of the Pharisees, but surely they see their own attitudes reflected in that of the older brother.

Demystifying Luke

Sometimes the Parable of the Prodigal Son is perceived primarily as a source of comfort for all parents with wayward children, and in one sense it is. But in the context of the two preceding stories, this last parable shocks the readers with the grace of the father compared to the lack of grace of the brother (representing the Pharisees). This last parable emphasizes the theme of joy at finding the lost, and by doing so it reveals the Pharisees' lack of concern for the lost.

It is interesting to note that Jesus' story never attempts to minimize the foolishness or serious offense of the younger son. Yet his repentance is equally serious and sincere. If heaven rejoices over one sinner who repents (15:7, 10), the son's return would indeed be a time for such rejoicing. Yet the Pharisees would throw parties for retrieved sheep and coins but not celebrate the "finding" of an actual human being who had been "dead" but was made alive again (15:32).

Whether or not His listeners detect it, Jesus points out a number of similarities between the two sons. Both want a celebration that doesn't include the father (15:13, 29). Neither has a genuine love or appreciation for the father, even though he loves them both. Both sons were slaves—the younger because he squandered his money in a faraway land and the older because of his attitude while working for his father. Both are materialists. And both are sinners.

Only one, however, is on record as being repentant and restoring a good relationship with the father. It is not a lack of love on the father's part, but a lack of repentance on the part of the older son (and the Pharisees) that will prevent receiving all the father has to offer.

Take It Home

The message these three parables brought home to the Pharisees and scribes is painfully clear: They cared too little for lost people. The Pharisees wrongly believed that it was good works that merited God's favor, rather than His grace manifested toward sinners. The older brother was angry with the father because he felt he did not get what he deserved (a banquet), while the younger brother got what he didn't deserve (a banquet). The older brother's works didn't work, but the younger brother's repentance did. That is the way God's grace is—it is bestowed on unworthy people, sinners, who do not trust in their good works but in God's grace.

Part of the Pharisees' logic in not caring for people like the lost son is that they seemed to believe their degree of holiness was measured by the distance they kept from "sinners." The Bible actually speaks of holiness in terms of the closeness we keep to Christ. In the Gospels we find Christ closely associating with, and having compassion on, people whose behavior the religious establishment took exception to. This can be a challenge to us to understand our own ideas of holiness in a different light. Do we shun the very people Christ engaged, invested in, and celebrated the return of?

LUKE 16:1–31

TWO CHALLENGING PARABLES

The Shrewd (Dishonest) Steward 16:1–18
The Rich Man and Lazarus 16:19–31

Setting Up the Section

The entire 16th chapter of Luke revolves around one's attitude toward and use of material possessions. This subject is one that Luke has been speaking to throughout this Gospel. What we find in chapter 16 is not the final word on the subject, but it is more specific in its application than previous references.

Jesus continues to teach His disciples, aware that the Pharisees are listening in on everything He is saying. The Pharisees are lovers of money, so Jesus tells two parables about rich men. One man has a crooked employee he is about to fire, and the other finds himself suffering in hell after a lifetime of selfish luxury.

LUKE 16:1–18

THE SHREWD (DISHONEST) STEWARD

Luke has had a lot to say about wealth and possessions so far in his Gospel: attitudes toward tax collectors, blessings on the poor, sending disciples out without provisions, invitation lists to banquets, and more. In this passage the topic begins to get more emphasis.

The rich man's steward has been "wasting his possessions" (16:1 NIV)—not unlike padding an expense account or perhaps even embezzling. In effect, he is asked to first give an account of his management and then turn in his resignation.

The steward is panicked at first. He is too proud to beg and not cut out to do manual work. So instead he comes up with a plan to make allies who will help him after he is out of work. He offers deep discounts to his master's clients, pulling each one of them into a knowing co-conspiracy against the business owner (16:5–7). Then, in a surprise ending to the parable (16:8), the master commends the steward because he has acted shrewdly.

How can a man who has just been "ripped off" by his employee, a man who has suffered a substantial and irretrievable loss, commend a crooked employee? The answer to this question is in verse 8.

Our Lord's words here indicate several important realities.

1) Both the unrighteous steward and his master valued the same thing—shrewdness. You don't commend a man for something you disdain.
2) Both the unrighteous steward and his master were members of the group that our Lord characterized as people of the world rather than people of the light. The contemporary expression, "it takes one to know one" fits here.
3) Neither the master nor his steward is a member of the group identified as sons of light.

We are accustomed to assuming any master in a parable is a symbol for God. Did Jesus tell this parable because He, too, commended such behavior? After all, He had told His disciples to be "as shrewd as snakes" (Matthew 10:16 NIV). Is He encouraging His followers to be like this crooked businessperson?

Not at all. Jesus makes His purpose clear: His disciples are to use worldly wealth wisely to achieve eternal ends (16:9). If believers are to follow the steward's example at all, it should be to make friends by the use of material possessions (16:9). The unjust steward saw that his days were numbered, and that he would not be able to take his master's money with him. He then began to use his master's money in such a way as to make friends, because they would outlast his master's money. While we should have an eternal motivation over mere survival, we can use money in such a way that will last forever by building relationships with people who will gratefully receive us in heaven.

Demystifying Luke

The proper interpretation of a Greek or Hebrew word always depends on its context. Just as "being tempted" and "being tested" sound much alike to us but are very different biblical concepts, the word *shrewd* also has quite diverse interpretations. Jesus' use of the word in Matthew 10:16 had a positive connotation of being "wise." The serpent in the Garden of Eden was also shrewd, but the meaning there is closer to "crafty." Most commentators would say that Jesus is saying here that the children of God should be just as shrewd in preparing for their eternal welfare as the sinful children of this age are in protecting their welfare in this life.

The rest of Jesus' commentary seems to be a direct contrast with the actions of the steward. Anyone who can't be trusted with little certainly can't be trusted with much (16:10). If we're not trustworthy with worldly wealth and other people's property, how can we expect to be responsible with really important things (16:11–12)? Even though the master in the parable commends the actions of his steward, Jesus makes it clear that following God is an either/or decision. If He doesn't have our complete hearts, we aren't really serving Him (16:13).

Although Jesus has been speaking to His disciples (16:1), He has critics among the surrounding crowd (16:14). Luke clearly states at this point that the Pharisees loved money, so it's not surprising that they are scoffing at Jesus' comments. Jesus has previously pointed out their hypocrisy at various times, and here points out their underlying problem—the Pharisees are seeking approval from the wrong source, and they are seeking to be judged according to the wrong standard. They are striving to be justified by men, so their standard has to be that which people can see and evaluate—outward appearances (16:15).

This simple observation explains the actions and reactions of the Pharisees. To get the approval of people, they acted in a way that would attract attention to themselves and make them look righteous, as people might judge it. Their actions included:

- long prayers
- obvious fasting and contributions
- places of prominence at banquets and ceremonies
- ostentatious clothing
- a proud distance from anyone considered sinful, thus beneath them
- meticulous ceremonial washings

In all of this, Jesus says they are hypocrites because their hearts are not really righteous at all. Understanding this about the Pharisees also explains why they value money so highly. It was an external proof of piety. After all, had God not promised to prosper His people Israel if they kept His laws (Deuteronomy 28:1–14) and to bring them great poverty and adversity if they disobeyed (Deuteronomy 28:15–68)? The Pharisees' love of money is an indication of their attachment to external standards and appearances, so that they can obtain the approval of other people. But in the process of seeking men's praise, they also obtain God's condemnation.

Critical Observation

Jesus' mention of "the Law and the Prophets" (16:16 NIV) was a reference to the entire Old Testament. In this context, His use of the phrase was significant. The Pharisees highly regarded the Law—the five books of Moses. But it was the section of the Prophets that spoke of the coming Messiah. The prophets also had much to say about the "heart issues" of life. God's revelation in the Old Testament was not seeking mere outward conformity, but inward conformity to the will of God. The Pharisees were overlooking a lot of the significance of that portion of scripture.

Jesus also affirms that He is not attempting to do away with the Law that the Pharisees hold in such high esteem (16:17). Including both the Law and the prophets was a way of referring to the complete Old Testament scriptures, not simply the first five books of the Law. The Pharisees had always seen themselves as the keepers of the Law. But after hearing the message of John the Baptist and then Jesus, people are responding to the news of the kingdom with force, in other words, they are so eager they are forcing their way in (16:16).

The reference to divorce at this point (16:18) seems abrupt, but is just one example of how the usually conservative and legalistic Pharisees have adopted a liberal interpretation to justify their own actions, expanding the parameters of the acceptable reasons for divorce until their customs don't reflect what the Law of God taught. Men of this culture and era have come to enjoy the freedom to change wives, and the Pharisees, the self-proclaimed custodians of the Law, function in this area as its corrupters.

16:19–31

THE RICH MAN AND LAZARUS

Jesus begins this parable exactly as He has the previous one: "There was a rich man. . ." (16:1, 19 NIV). Most parables don't provide names for the characters; this is the sole exception. The description of poor Lazarus couldn't be more different from that of the rich man. But only three verses describe their lives. The majority of the parable takes place after their deaths, when the contrast is exactly reversed. Lazarus is carried to "Abraham's bosom" (16:22 KJV), a term Jewish rabbis used for the home of the righteous. From hell (Hades), the rich man can see Lazarus in the distance, and can even communicate with Abraham, but a great chasm prevents any other interaction.

The rich man first appeals for brief relief from his agony, and then for a messenger to be sent to his family members so they can avoid the same dreadful experience in the afterlife. Both requests are denied. He is told that those who would ignore "Moses and the Prophets" (16:31 NIV) would not even be swayed by a personal message from beyond the grave.

We aren't told the Pharisees' response after Jesus' second parable, but after hearing His opening descriptions of the two characters (16:19–21), based upon appearance alone, one can see how the Pharisees would have judged these two men. Since the Pharisees equated prominence with the blessing of God, they would have justified the rich man and condemned Lazarus.

The fate of the two men after their deaths shows the Pharisees' judgment to be wrong. Not only that, it is an indirect blow to the Pharisees. Since they would have related more to the rich man's role in the parable, the fact that God rejects the rich man is an indictment of them (16:24–26).

Take It Home

The two parables in this passage both involve rich characters who don't have God's perspective on life. And Jesus made it clear: "You cannot serve both God and Money" (16:13 NIV). But that doesn't mean Jesus stood opposed to all wealthy people. What do you think is the appropriate balance for us to maintain regarding money and the kingdom of God?

LUKE 17:1–37

FAITH, SERVICE, AND EXPECTATION

Sin and Forgiveness	17:1–10
A 10 Percent Return of Gratitude	17:11–19
Missing the Obvious	17:20–37

Setting Up the Section

At first this passage may not seem to have much coherence between the topics:

- **Not causing your brother or sister to sin—17:1–2**
- **What to do when your brother or sister sins—17:3–4**
- **Faith and the disciple—17:5–10**
- **The healing of the ten lepers and the gratitude of one—17:11–19**
- **The coming of the kingdom of God— 17:20–37**

It takes some effort to determine what the relationship is between these "parts" of the whole. Yet, in the context of Jesus' recent debates and confrontations with the Pharisees, it is likely that His teaching and healing is being done here in full awareness of their prying eyes and listening ears. So what He says and does can be interpreted in light of increasing opposition from Israel's religious leaders.

17:1–10

SIN AND FORGIVENESS

Many times, sin is not a solitary problem. Temptations often arise when we get around other people. Jesus seems to acknowledge this problem in verse 1. And He holds accountable those who lead others into sinful actions. His words as recorded by Luke (17:2) are ominous, but a similar statement following His Parable of the Weeds (Matthew 13:40–42) is even worse.

When people acknowledge their sins against others, forgiveness is important. When offended by someone's sin, it is appropriate to rebuke the person (17:3). Yet if he or she repents (apparently, a verbal expression should be sufficient), forgiveness should be extended. And even if the same person commits seven offenses in the same day and repents seven times, forgiveness should be offered in each instance.

The term "brother" (or "sister," 17:3 NIV) refers to a fellow believer. By using this expression, Jesus may well be implying a couple of important truths.

1) He may be informing His disciples that they are not responsible to correct and rebuke mankind in general, but only those whom they know, with whom they closely identify. The Pharisees (not to mention many of us) seemed to love to condemn those outside of their own circles. Jesus tells us that we are responsible to correct those whose sins are personally known to us.
2) He may be reminding the disciples that their sinning brother is still their brother. We cannot, like the self-righteous older brother in the Parable of the Prodigal Son, disown those close to us who sin.
3) The fact that we are responsible to rebuke and to forgive our brother implies that we must also be alert to the kinds of sin that he is most likely to commit. If this brother is close to us, then he is also like us, which means that we must begin by being sensitive to those sins that so easily can beset us. How easy it is to focus on the visible sins of others, rather than on the perhaps more socially acceptable sins of which we are guilty.

From the wording of verse 3, one may wonder if Jesus taught that forgiveness should only be granted if the sinner repents. Does repentance precede forgiveness? Certainly not in the case of our Lord. On the cross, He cried out, "Father, forgive them. . . " (23:34 NIV). Forgiveness is first granted, and then it is experienced by those who repent. Jesus taught that forgiveness was to be granted if the sinner repented, not because we are to withhold forgiveness, but because not all sinners repent. Repentance may not occur, but when it does, we dare not withhold forgiveness. The point here is also that this forgiveness is to be verbalized at the time the sinner repents.

In response, the apostles ask Jesus to increase their faith (17:5). Note the subtle shift from "disciples" (17:1) to "apostles" (17:5).

Critical Observation

Remember that Jesus had already given His apostles power and authority for all kinds of healing and driving out demons (9:1). Yet when He started giving instructions about forgiving one another, they asked for an increase of faith (17:5). This suggests not only the importance but also the difficulty of forgiveness.

The apostles' request implies that what Jesus required necessitated great faith, and that their supply was deficient. Thus, they ask Jesus for more faith, assuming they do not have enough. Jesus' answer is that it takes only a very little quantity of faith to achieve much. With the quantity of faith equivalent to that of a mustard seed—a very small seed indeed—they could uproot a tree and transplant it into the sea (17:6). Did they then need more faith—really? Jesus' answer seems to question their premise that they had too little faith.

The story Jesus tells about the servant and the master (17:7–10) seems to suggest that in addition to faith is the necessity of doing one's duty. In the first instance, it is the master who is not obligated to have gratitude toward the obedience of his slave. Good servants simply do what they are expected to do without fuss or expectation of praise. Perhaps that attitude is lacking among Jesus' apostles.

Demystifying Matthew

If Jesus were making up the parable about the servant and master (17:7–10) in a contemporary setting, He might have told the story of the man who filled out his income tax form. The form was neatly filled out, with all the supporting facts and figures. Along with the form, mailed before April 15th, there was a check for the taxes that were due. Surely, Jesus might say, this man would not expect a call or a thank you note from the IRS or from the president of the United States, expressing the government's gratitude for obedience to the laws of the land. Paying taxes is our duty—one for which we expect no gratitude if we obey exactly as required, but one for which we expect punishment for failing to perform.

Jesus' words in verses 6–10 serve to correct the erroneous thinking of the apostles, who asked for greater faith. The important thing, Jesus says, is not the amount of faith, but the attributes of faith. Here faith is not a matter of quantity, but of quality. The disciples' thinking is that they lack sufficient faith. Jesus' answer is that they lack an accurate understanding of the nature of faith. It appears Jesus is condemning what we might call Pharisaical faith, which is based more upon the possessor of it than its object, a faith based more on one's performance than on God's character.

17:11–19

A 10 PERCENT RETURN OF GRATITUDE

If Jesus had the Pharisees in mind (even while addressing His disciples [17:1]), they would have rankled at being compared to servants who had to clean themselves after working in the fields before preparing and serving supper. And it is at this point that Luke inserts the story of the healing of the ten lepers. (The Gospel writers did not always write chronologically, but frequently recorded various accounts around a particular theme.)

Of the ten lepers, two things set the one who returns apart from the others: He praises God in a loud voice and thanks Jesus, and he is a Samaritan (17:15–16). The inference is that the others are Jewish. And it isn't that their actions are rude or malicious. After all, Jesus has told them to show themselves to the priests, who need to make an official ruling on the healing (17:14). Yet Jesus' questions suggest that taking the time to stop and express their gratitude would have been appropriate (17:17–18). Again, following the law to the letter—but not taking the spirit of the law into their hearts—was indicative of the Pharisees.

All ten lepers are healed. But only one—the Samaritan who returns to acknowledge Jesus for who He is and thanks Him—is told, "Your faith has made you well" (17:19 NIV). Jesus' comment suggests salvation in addition to physical healing.

Luke, of course, has a special message in this, for the one man is not a Jew at all but a Samaritan. Jesus makes a point of referring to this one grateful leper as a "foreigner" (17:18 NIV). Once again, we are being prepared for the gospel to be proclaimed and accepted by the Gentiles, while spurned by the Jewish religious leaders. This one grateful Gentile is a prototype of the many Gentiles who will believe and will praise God.

Take It Home

Jesus' story of the ten lepers is one to think about. It's easy to look down on the nine lepers who didn't stop to express their thanks to Jesus for what He had done for them. Yet today it is still possible—and perhaps too easy—to fall into a rigid obedience of all the things God tells us to do while losing the joy, gratitude, and spontaneity that ought to be involved in the abundant life promised to Christians. Can you think of any such examples in your own life, or in the lives of friends or family members? What can be done to ensure a response more like the Samaritan from now on?

17:20–37

MISSING THE OBVIOUS

Whether or not the previous events had a specific application for the Pharisees, what happens next is clearly directed to them. They approach Jesus and ask about the timing of the coming of the kingdom of God (17:20). He tells them that they won't be able to figure it out with their careful observation. In fact, they have already missed it because it is within (17:21). Perhaps Jesus meant it was a spiritual, inner matter. Others think the word *within* is better translated "among," and that Jesus meant that the kingdom of God was already in the midst of both the Pharisees and the disciples through His own presence and actions, though neither group was yet capable of realizing that fact.

Jesus' answer meant that they would not be able to simply point to the Messiah or the kingdom and say, "Here it is," or, "There it is." Why? Probably because the expectations of what the kingdom would be like were so distorted that the holders of those expectations would never recognize the real thing. The concept of the kingdom was so secular, so earthly, so materialistic, that the kingdom of our Lord was never seriously entertained as an option. Jesus simply did not fit the preconceived expectations of the Pharisees, and on the whole, they seemed to have no thought of changing those expectations. And this was in spite of the fact that Jesus did produce many signs, attesting His identity as Messiah (John 9:16; 11:45–47; 12:37).

While it was difficult to recognize Jesus for who He really was, it had been done. Luke has already told of how Mary, Elizabeth, Zechariah, Simeon, Anna, and John the Baptist had honored Jesus as the Messiah. The words and works of Jesus should have been evidence enough for others, too, but people's hearts are hard and don't always see the obvious.

Demystifying Luke

Luke's term "careful observation" (17:20 NIV) was a phrase used at the time to describe a doctor who closely monitored the symptoms of a patient over time. Since Luke was a physician, the term is quite appropriate.

Jesus speaks to the Pharisees about His first coming (17:20–21) and to the disciples about His second coming (17:22–37). He knows that eventually His followers will be looking for Him in earnest, and tells them not to waste their time chasing down every rumor and impostor (17:22–25). When He comes again, people will know! Yet His coming will be sudden, and humankind will not be prepared any more than it was for the judgments that took place in the days of Noah and Lot (17:26–32).

Some people interpret Jesus' words in verses 34–36 as a reference to the rapture, when believers are called into heaven to be with the Lord and spared the judgment of God:

- Some translations mention two men in the first scenario. Others render the phrase to be a man and wife. The Greek is not gender specific, but simply refers to "two" people. Keep in mind that this passage is not commenting on sexuality, but on the day-to-day events that will be affected by this "taking." In those days there were no bedrooms as we know them today. Often thus the whole family slept together on the floor, on what must have been mats, at best.
- The second case is that of two women, both of whom are going about their daily duties in the grinding of grain. One is taken, and the other is left. But where is the one taken to?

It is possible here to see these scenarios as references to the rapture, but the surrounding context makes it much more likely that the ones taken will be those who are being ushered off to face their final judgment. This interpretation would explain why, when the disciples seek additional information (17:37), Jesus' response is bleak.

The discussion is dropped abruptly. But Jesus will return to the topic of what to expect in future times in Luke 21.

LUKE 18:1–43

PERSISTENCE AND PENITENCE

A Persistent Widow vs. an Unjust Judge	18:1–8
A Pharisee and a Tax Collector	18:9–14
Little Children and a Rich Ruler	18:15–34
A Loud Blind Man	18:35–43

Setting Up the Section

In this section Jesus continues teaching His disciples about the kingdom of God. He uses a number of contrasts to teach some important lessons. He contrasts a persistent widow with a self-centered judge, a Pharisee and a tax collector, little children and annoyed adults, and the priorities of the kingdom of God with those of a wealthy young man. He also continues to heal the sick as He approaches Jerusalem to face His death.

18:1–8

A PERSISTENT WIDOW VS. AN UNJUST JUDGE

Sometimes Jesus would tell a parable that left even His closest followers confused about what He meant. Here Luke first explains why Jesus is telling the story—to show the disciples "that they should always pray and not give up" (18:1 NIV)—before actually recording the parable.

This story is sometimes called the Parable of the Unjust Judge, and sometimes the Parable of the Persistent Widow. After an initial reading, it is clear that the woman is the one who models the lesson of persistence that Jesus intends to teach. But a closer look also shows that He directs His listeners (the disciples) to the words of the judge (18:6).

Jesus' point is that even a self-centered, uncaring person could bring about justice if pestered enough to do it. How much more surely, then, would a loving God respond when asked persistently by His "chosen ones" (18:7 NIV)? God surely stands ready to act on behalf of the ones He loves. We never pester Him with our prayers; indeed, our repeated prayers remind us that He is there and in charge. It is only if we give up that we stand to miss out. When Jesus returns He will be looking for faithful people who are ready for Him (18:8).

There is another inference from this paragraph we need to note carefully. The words of our Lord indicate there will be no real, complete, and ultimate justice on the earth until He returns and establishes it on the earth. We must persistently pray for justice and not lose heart because there will be much injustice until He comes again. There are some who seem to be saying these days that Christ will only come to the earth after we (the church) have established justice. That is not true, either to this text or to the rest of the scriptures pertaining to the coming of His kingdom. The Sermon on the Mount speaks of present pain, mourning, persecution, and sorrow, and of ultimate blessing when He comes with His kingdom.

18:9–14

A PHARISEE AND A TAX COLLECTOR

Still on the subject of prayer, Jesus tells the Parable of the Pharisee and the Tax Collector. But His focus has changed. Rather than addressing the disciples (18:1), He addresses a group of self-righteous people (18:9). In the first parable, it is the character of the one who is petitioned that is in focus; here, it is the character of the one praying who is highlighted. In the first parable, it is justice that is sought; in this second parable, it is mercy and forgiveness. This story is for those who trust in themselves rather than God—who look down on others and prefer their own righteousness to God's mercy and grace.

The Pharisee's words in this parable (18:11–12) are a stark contrast to the tax collector who can't even hold his head up before God. But Jesus is also able to speak for God, and declares the second man justified rather than the first (18:14). This parable helps explain why those are blessed who weep and mourn (6:21).

The previous parable taught persistence in prayer; this one emphasizes humility. According to Jesus, no one is too sinful to be saved—only too righteous. The Pharisee not only does not want God's grace, He disdains it. The reason, in his mind, is that he does not need it, for his righteousness (in law-keeping as he defines it) is sufficient, indeed, more than enough. The penitent sinner goes away justified by grace, while the Pharisee goes away condemned by his own works and words.

Critical Observation

This is not to say that self-righteous Pharisees are beyond saving. They are not! By his own confession, one of the most self-righteous of all Pharisees—Saul of Tarsus—was saved to become an apostle to the Gentiles. But in order to be saved, Saul, who became Paul, had to render all of the things in which he had formerly taken great pride as worthless.

18:15–34

LITTLE CHILDREN AND A RICH RULER

Some commentators believe the theme of humility is continued into the account of the children brought to Jesus to be blessed (18:15–17). But humility doesn't seem to be the characteristic Jesus is referring to (18:16–17). Children can be quite demanding. Others suggest it is faith, yet children are more gullible than faithful. Luke provides an insight missing in the other Gospels. He reveals that the little children brought to Jesus are actually infants.

There are several questions that are essential to understanding this incident, its meaning, and its application:

1) Why did Jesus react so strongly to their efforts to hinder the children from being brought to Him? The gospel itself is at issue. The way in which children were freely accepted by Jesus was similar to the way in which all people must enter into the kingdom of God.

2) Why did the disciples seek to prevent the parents from bringing their children to Jesus? Probably for the same reason Jesus welcomed them—they had nothing to offer but themselves.
3) What is the specific characteristic of childlikeness to which our Lord is referring, which is necessary for anyone to enter into the kingdom? While many claim it is the humility or the faith of these children, since they were merely infants, it is more likely the fact that they are helpless to save themselves. They can't earn any bit of the grace bestowed on them. Throughout Luke's Gospel, it is the lowly and the outcast who receive salvation blessings. The fact that these children had almost no status in first-century society made them an apt image of those that Jesus came to reach.

The next account, that of the rich young ruler, drives home the point that we can do nothing to earn our place in the kingdom of God. The young man tries to justify himself to Jesus because of behavior and attitudes he has held since he was a boy (18:21). Jesus deals with the rich young ruler by focusing his attention on the matter of goodness. Jesus' point is not to affirm whether he himself is good or not, but to challenge the man's concept of what is good. True goodness is perfection, so only God is good. We are all therefore dependent on God for salvation.

Critical Observation

The accounts of the children being brought to Jesus and His discussion with the rich young ruler are found in Matthew, Mark, and Luke—paired together in each instance (Matthew 19:13–26; Mark 10:13–27; Luke 18:15–27). The contrast between childlikeness as a positive trait and wealth as an impediment to following Jesus seems to be a clear thread that ties these two stories together.

To his credit, the young man seems to realize that following the law (as he is convinced he has done) is not enough for salvation. Jesus doesn't really answer the young man's original question. Instead, He tells him what he needs to do to become a disciple. In that event, his earthly treasure will be gone—distributed to the poor—but he will have treasure in heaven (18:22).

That certainly isn't the answer the young man anticipated. It is the one thing he is unwilling to do. The man is unwilling to give up that which gives him security (his wealth) and trust wholly in God. His failing is self-trust over trust in God.

The disciples are still thinking like the Pharisees, assuming that wealth and privilege are signs of God's favor. So this man, who is rich and religious and also seems to be genuinely seeking involvement in God's kingdom, appears to be more than qualified. So naturally they ask, if he can't be saved, then who can (18:26)?

Some may interpret Jesus' answer—with God all things are possible (18:27)—to mean that salvation for the rich is impossible without God's help. But the truth is, God's power is necessary for anyone to be saved no matter their possessions or wealth.

Peter's response (18:28) receives Jesus' commendation (18:29). But Jesus' words to His disciples in verses 31–34 are intended to put their sacrifice into perspective. Do they think that they are giving up everything for the kingdom of God? In reality, they are not giving up, but gaining. There is really only one sacrifice on which the kingdom of God is based, and that is the sacrifice that the Lord Jesus will make.

In Luke's Gospel there is a progressively revealed indication of Jesus' suffering. Luke has informed us that Jesus will be

- rejected by the Jewish leaders (9:22–23)
- betrayed by one of His own (9:44–45)
- rejected by His generation (17:24–25)
- rejected and crucified by the Gentiles (18:31–34)

Luke, in writing this Gospel for a Gentile audience, points out the non-Jews' own role in the rejection and crucifixion of the Messiah. The prophecy of His suffering and death given in 18:31–34 is very specific and detailed.

Yet with such a specific prophecy, the disciples don't understand (18:34). The reason for their lack of understanding is given in our text: The meaning was hidden from them—God deliberately withheld it. They were not ready for it. They would only understand Jesus' rejection, crucifixion, and death after His resurrection.

Jesus had already made specific statements recorded in Luke, directly referencing His death. Yet, as with 18:31–34, the disciples were not ready to understand the full implications.	
Luke 9:20–31	When Jesus questioned His disciples about His own identity, and Peter made his great confession, Jesus made it clear that He would "suffer many things and be rejected by the elders, chief priests and teachers of the law, and he must be killed and on the third day be raised to life" (9:22 NIV).
Luke 9:43–45	After Jesus stepped in and drove a demon from a little boy who the disciples had failed to heal, He told them that He would be "betrayed into the hands of men" (9:44 NIV).
Luke 17:24–25	Jesus told His disciples that before He could return again, He "must suffer many things and be rejected by this generation" (9:25 NIV).

18:35–43

A LOUD BLIND MAN

As Jesus walks toward Jericho, a blind man (Bartimaeus, according to Mark 10:46) hears He is passing. Although he is told that Jesus of Nazareth is passing by, he calls out for "Jesus, Son of David" (18:38 NIV). "Son of David" is a title for the Messiah, suggesting that Bartimaeus isn't spiritually blind.

This is a scene that is both tragic and comic at the same time. Bartimaeus is sitting by the road as it leads into Jericho (18:35). Beggars always have certain spots picked out where the traffic is more frequent, and where, for some reason, there seems to be more generosity expressed (e.g. outside the temple). He cannot see, so his begging is triggered by what he hears—a footstep, the sounds of passers-by talking, etc.

He keeps yelling for Jesus until he annoys everyone around him. But it works. Jesus calls him forward, restores his sight, and declares that his faith has healed him (18:39–42). At this point, the Gospel of Mark exposes the hypocrisy of those who once tried to silence Bartimaeus, for now they tell him to take courage (Mark 10:49). Mark also tells us that the man jumps up, throws off his coat, and goes to Jesus (Mark 10:50).

And as soon as Bartimaeus can see where he is going, the blind man starts following Jesus—quite a contrast to the rich man who had sadly walked away (Mark 10:17–22; Luke 18:18–23).

Take It Home

This passage has much to say about the prayer life of a believer. We are to be persistent in our communication with God, all the while exercising humility. The power of Jesus to save and heal is an ongoing source of hope, even as His willing sacrifice gives renewed meaning to any relationship with Him. Which of these areas needs the most attention in your life? How can you improve your prayer habits and better connect with the One most concerned for you?

LUKE 19:1–48

LAST JOURNEY TO JERUSALEM

A Tax Collector in a Tree	19:1–10
In the Absence of the Master	19:11–27
Jesus Arrives at Jerusalem	19:28–48

Setting Up the Section

Not even halfway through his Gospel, Luke wrote: "As the time approached for him to be taken up to heaven, Jesus resolutely set out for Jerusalem" (9:51 NIV). All the events of Luke 10–18 have occurred along the way.

The subject of the coming kingdom of God has been in view since the Pharisees first asked about when it would come in chapter 17. In chapter 18, the focus changed from the timing and circumstances of the coming kingdom to who would enter into it. Jesus taught that those who would enter His kingdom would not be those who expected to enter. And so the self-righteous Pharisee is not justified, but the penitent tax collector is (18:9–14). Jesus taught His disciples that while the rich young ruler, and those like him, would have much difficulty getting into the kingdom (18:18–27), those who were childlike would possess it (18:15–17).

And in this section, Jesus finally arrives in Jerusalem. As the time of His death nears, His teachings and actions seem to become more intentional and direct.

19:1–10

A TAX COLLECTOR IN A TREE

Jericho (19:1) was about seventeen miles from Jerusalem. At this point in His ministry, Jesus is still beset by crowds as He travels. A tax collector named Zacchaeus desperately wants to see Him, but is very short and doesn't have much of a chance among the hordes of people. So even though he is a man of wealth and position (19:2), he decides to climb a tree so he can get a better view.

Unlike the blind man in the previous story (18:35–43) who had yelled until he got Jesus' attention, Zacchaeus seems to desire anonymity. Yet when Jesus surprisingly stops beneath him and invites Himself to dinner, Zacchaeus welcomes Him (19:6).

Jesus had associated with tax collectors throughout His ministry, yet He never stopped receiving criticism for it. We might even wonder if the people who complained (19:7) included the apostles. Jesus doesn't demand that Zacchaeus sell all his possessions to benefit the poor as He had the rich ruler (18:18–23), but Zacchaeus's response is voluntary and generous (19:8). And regardless of the attitudes of others, Jesus celebrates the salvation of Zacchaeus (19:9–10).

Jesus explains to Zacchaeus that He has come to seek and save what is lost (19:10). Jesus did not come to associate with the rich and powerful. He did not come to provide positions and power for the disciples. He came to save sinners, people like Zacchaeus, the hated and evil tax collector. To do so, He had to associate with sinners. Thus, while it may offend the sensitivities and the social mores of His day, Jesus would go where sinners were, so that the gospel could come to them and they could be saved. If one's goal is to save sinners, then associating with sinners is simply a means to that goal.

Jesus' climactic statement about seeking and saving the lost provides a beautiful summary of this whole Gospel—it is the lost (the outcast, the sinners, the Samaritans, etc.) He has come to save. Those who recognize their need of salvation are being saved, while the self-righteous are losing out.

Critical Observation

When you compare Zacchaeus's story with the story of the blind man named Bartimaeus (18:35–43) you see an interesting picture of the tension that is maintained here between the sovereignty of God and the responsibility of humanity. The blind man called out to the Savior for mercy and received it. Zacchaeus did not call upon the Lord, but the Lord called to him. The scriptures clearly teach that no one who truly comes to Jesus for mercy, on the basis of faith, will be turned away. The scriptures also teach that anyone who comes to Christ for salvation does not come on their own initiative, but is drawn by God. Both of these perspectives are true. God seeks us, and we give ourselves to Him, and it all happens only through the faith that He enables in us.

19:11–27

IN THE ABSENCE OF THE MASTER

Jesus' Parable of the Ten Minas (19:11–27) is usually considered another version of the Parable of the Talents found in Matthew 25:14–30, although there are considerable differences. In Luke's account, Jesus reveals the attitudes of the people toward the nobleman who left and came back as king (19:14–15). And in this version, the servants are given the same amount of money (19:13) and told to put it to use. (A "mina" was a wage one could earn in about 100 days.)

The first servant, who earned a tenfold return on his mina, is rewarded with responsibility over ten cities and verbal praise from his master. The second servant, with a profit of five times the original amount, receives charge of five cities (though no praise is noted). But the bulk of the parable dwells on the third servant. He expresses fear of the master to justify his inaction, and is judged by his own words. His fear should have at least motivated him to invest the money in a bank account to get interest. Consequently, he loses his portion of money to the one who had proven to be faithful with the ten minas. And as for the citizens who badmouthed their leader, they are put to death (19:27). (Perhaps the servants represented Jesus' followers while the citizens symbolized unrepentant Israel who rejected Jesus.)

Jesus tells this parable as He is just about to enter Jerusalem. He will soon be going away and leaving responsibility for His ministry to others. When He returns, it will be as King. Clearly, what His followers do in the meantime will be important. Those who are faithful will be rewarded.

Perhaps the third servant may have failed to do business with his master's money simply because he felt that time was too short to engage in business. At the beginning of this parable, Luke tells us that Jesus spoke the parable in addition to His other words, because the people were looking for the kingdom to come immediately (19:11). One of the things a short-term mind-set does is discourage long-term planning and investing. If you receive a check for $10,000 but know that you will have to write a check for that same amount in a day, you generally will not seek to buy a certificate of deposit with it, or to buy a savings bond, or to put the money in your savings account. You will deposit the money in your checking account simply because you know that it will only be a short time before it will be gone.

In the context of Luke's Gospel, this parable now begins to make sense. Jesus is nearing Jerusalem. Expectation is at an all-time high. Everyone expects the kingdom to commence upon our Lord's arrival. This parable is then given by our Lord. The departure of the king to a distant land, and his later return, signals a time delay in the arrival of the kingdom of God. The people expect the kingdom to be established almost immediately, but this parable teaches that there are some intervening events which must take place first.

Take it home

Here is a very real tension in Christian living. We must hold two truths in tension as we seek to apply them. On the one hand, we must live in the light of Jesus' imminent return. Christ may come at any moment, and we should be both ready and watching for His return. But we must also live wisely, making good investments for His kingdom, knowing that His return may not be as soon as we think or hope. Many foolish things have been done by those who feel that the kingdom was imminent. On the other hand, many foolish things have been done by those who feel Jesus' coming is distant. We can count on the return of our King, yet there is ample opportunity to be productive for Him as we are waiting.

19:28–48

JESUS ARRIVES AT JERUSALEM

Jesus' arrival in Jerusalem comes at a time of heightened emotions. People close to Him have heard numerous comments about kingdoms and the Messiah and such. Maybe they are hoping for something eventful to occur. After all, everyone knew from Old Testament writings that Jerusalem would be where the Messiah would be enthroned as king. In addition, it was Passover when pilgrims gathered in Jerusalem and fueled the fires of spiritual and messianic expectations. The crowds have no idea how right they are—and how wrong.

One can hardly grasp the mood of many at this moment in history. They are looking for the Messiah, and Jesus is a likely candidate. The moment is right. They look for Him, watching carefully for any indication of His identity. In contrast, the Pharisees and religious leaders are determined that He is not the Messiah, and that He will have no opportunity to be acclaimed such by the masses who wish He was their King. They are intent on putting Him to death, and are only looking for the right opportunity. These opponents of our Lord fear the crowds, and seek to do away with Jesus out of their sight.

Jesus sends two disciples ahead to secure a colt (19:28–31). The fact that it had never been ridden would have qualified it to be used as an offering to God (Numbers 19:2; Deuteronomy 21:3–4). The willingness with which it is given up suggests both a foreknowledge of Jesus and the owners' awareness of who the "Lord" is who needed it (19:32–35). And the fact that it is secured by the disciples acting on the authority of Jesus is a preview of how the church will operate after Jesus' physical departure.

The remaining distance to Jerusalem is negligible, and nothing is said of Jesus riding an animal at any other point. So why now? Jesus is not only declaring Himself to be the king that has been foretold, He is also fulfilling prophecy to the letter (Zechariah 9:9).

His ride into Jerusalem has come to be known as the "triumphal entry." A great crowd of people praise Him with its words and actions (19:36–38). Yet the crowd surrounding Jesus is likely comprised of His followers—not the city as a whole. And even among that crowd, no one fully understands what is going on. Just as Jesus will say that those who crucified Him didn't really understand what they were doing (23:34), so we see that the people in the crowd do not know what they are doing here, either.

The triumphal entry serves to publicly identify Jesus as the king of Israel. Many were wondering if He were the Messiah. His act of riding into Jerusalem on a donkey is His way of affirming His role as king of Israel and Son of God, thus His right to be worshiped by all people.

The Pharisees ask Jesus to silence the people, but Jesus says that praise will come from the very stones if nowhere else (19:39–40). Still, Jesus doesn't seem to consider His entry "triumphal." Rather, He weeps for the city of Jerusalem. What a contrast between the joy of the crowd and the sorrow of the Savior. Jesus knew what lay ahead for this wayward, wrong-thinking nation. Instead of the Messiah's coming bringing about the demise of Rome, the rejection of Jesus as Messiah meant the destruction of Jerusalem, at the hand of Roman soldiers. Jesus therefore speaks of the coming destruction of Jerusalem, which takes place in AD 70 (19:41–44).

It was neither by the Messiah's use of force and power, nor by the death of the Messiah's enemies that the kingdom was to be brought about, but by the Messiah's death at the hand of His enemies. It was not triumph that would bring in the kingdom, but the tragedy (from a merely human viewpoint) of the cross. God's ways are never man's ways. Man would have brought about the kingdom in many ways, but man would never have conceived of doing so by a cross, by apparent defeat and the suffering of the Messiah Himself, for the sins of His people.

Demystifying Luke

Jesus' deity is implied in a number of ways in this passage: His right to use the possessions of humankind (19:29–35), His right to receive praise and worship from humankind (19:36–40), His right to repossess the temple (19:45–48), and His right to institute His kingdom the way He sovereignly chose (suffering that leads to a cross) rather than using the means humankind might prefer (overthrowing enemies that leads to a crown).

Did the Israelites expect Jesus to immediately wage an attack on Rome and on its rule? Jesus does not do so. What Jesus does is attack the Jewish religious system itself and renounces its evils. He marches on the temple and casts out the money changers. This was the holiday season—Passover—and business there in the temple area must have been booming. But instead of using the temple for a place of prayer and worship, the religious leaders made it a place for personal gain.

Jesus' attack on the religious system of His day is strongly reacted to by those with a vested interest—the chief priests, the teachers of the Law, and the leaders of the people. They are not yet able to kill Jesus, due to the crowds, but they are intent on putting Him to death at the earliest possible moment. The battle lines are drawn, but it is not between the Messiah and Rome, but rather between the Messiah and religion. In spite of Jesus' popularity with the people, the religious leaders are more determined than ever to kill Him. They just can't come up with a workable plan—yet (19:47–48).

Take It Home

The "wee little man" song about Zacchaeus may relegate the account to a children's story in our minds. But even though the actions of the tax collector were quite childlike, that isn't a bad thing in Jesus' opinion (18:16–17). Jesus stopped and initiated a conversation with Zacchaeus, but first Zacchaeus had planned and taken action to get as close as possible to Jesus. (He didn't seem to mind that he had a reputation in the community.) How far would you go to be closer to Jesus?

LUKE 20:1–47

QUESTIONS OF AUTHORITY

By What Authority?	20:1–18
Taxes and Resurrection	20:19–40
Son of David or Lord of David?	20:41–47

Setting Up the Section

Jesus has arrived in Jerusalem to spend the final week of His human life. He has, by His actions, announced His identity as Israel's Messiah. He possessed the donkey (19:29–35), the praises of the people (19:36–40), and finally His temple (19:45–48).

Up to this point, the principle source of opposition to Jesus has been from the party of the Pharisees, who seem to have been dogging the heels of the Savior from very early on in His ministry (see 5:21 and following). Both the Pharisees and Sadducees (teachers of the law or scribes) were political/religious parties, and members from both groups served on the Sanhedrin (the official leadership of Israel). The Sadducees had their primary powerbase in Jerusalem and among the priestly hierarchy, and the Pharisees appear to have been more influential among the synagogue communities, but both were present in Jerusalem.

It is at the Lord's possession of His temple in Luke 19:45 that we see the torch of opposition to Jesus being passed from the Pharisee party to the priests, the scribes, and the elders (20:1). The Jerusalem leaders may not have been overly concerned with Jesus' ministry and influence in the outlying parts of Israel, but became threatened when Jesus invaded their turf. They wanted to stop Him, but the Lord's popularity with the masses was too great to ignore or to challenge (19:48). Thus, they waited for their chance. Their first attack came in the form of an official challenge to the authority by which Jesus did the things He had done (20:2).

The issue that underlies this entire section of scripture is that of authority.

20:1–18

BY WHAT AUTHORITY?

After arriving in Jerusalem, Jesus spends a lot of time in the temple both teaching the people and preaching the gospel (20:1). The religious leaders, who had tolerated His ministry through gritted teeth as long as He had been a wandering rabbi, are now more concerned because He is in their center of operation. This is their territory, their turf, the Jerusalem leaders believe, and thus they confront Jesus in the temple in the context of His teaching there. Their question in verse 2 is two-pronged, not simply one question put differently the second time. There are two questions in view:

1) Just who do You think You are to do these things, anyway?
2) Who gave You the authority to do these things?

The first question has to do with Jesus' personal authority. Jesus is acting as though He owns the place, and so He does. The simple answer is, "I am the Messiah." But while the people are entertaining this at least as a possibility, the leaders reject the thought out of hand. No way! The second question has to do with Jesus' official accreditation—Who sent Him? These leaders seem to think that they are the accrediting agency. Jesus has not received their permission to come to town as He has, or to accept men's praise, or to take over the temple. If the nation's highest spiritual leadership has not authorized Jesus, then who has? That is the issue. It is the issue of authority, both Jesus' innate authority and His delegated authority.

Jesus' reply (20:3–4) isn't an attempt to change the subject. The issue is broader than Jesus, for John the Baptist had introduced Jesus to Israel as the Messiah. If the Jerusalem leaders are going to pronounce on Jesus' authority, they also have to deal with John's, for if John was a divinely appointed prophet, a spokesman for God, then Jesus is the Messiah. Furthermore, if they refuse to accept John's witness, then they surely will not receive Jesus, either. Let them declare themselves, then, on the authority of John. What authority did he have? Who sent him? If they answer this question, then Jesus will answer theirs.

Luke provides the heart of the religious leaders' discussion (20:5–6), which is both comic and tragic. They don't bother discussing the right answer to Jesus' question. Instead, they spend their time trying to justify their answer. When they cannot safely say what they really think, they have to say they don't know (20:7), which must be very frustrating for such self-proclaimed authorities. And because they refuse to answer, so does Jesus (20:8).

Jesus continues by telling the Parable of the Tenants (20:9–16). It seems clear that the vineyard represents Israel, and the owner, God. In time, the tenants decide to take possession of what they are only renting. Each time the owner sends servants (the prophets) to check and collect some of the fruit, they beat the messenger and send him away empty-handed. The owner finally sends his son (Jesus), thinking they will surely respect him. But they see the son's visit as an opportunity to take complete control by killing him.

This parable builds a powerful picture. Men like John the Baptist were prophets, and thus had the authority to speak for God. John, as a divinely appointed spokesman for God, proclaimed Jesus to be the Messiah. But just as Israel's leaders had rejected other prophets, so they had done with John as well. Jesus, in this parable, is telling His audience that He is not just a prophet; He is the Son. That is the basis of His authority. He owns the vineyard. He has been sent by His Father to possess what is His. But they will reject Him and put Him to death. And they do so with the full knowledge that He is the Son. They kill Him because He is the Son. This, we recall, is what Jesus' opponents have already purposed to do (19:47). It is not so much that they do not know who Jesus is, but that they will not accept His authority.

The people hearing the parable are horrified. But in verses 17–18, Jesus cites another prophecy to verify His meaning (Psalm 118:22; Isaiah 8:14, 15). The stone that is overlooked and rejected by the builders of the nation will eventually become the capstone (or cornerstone). The stone will also be an object of judgment (20:18)—one that opponents to the gospel will continue to stumble over.

20:19–40

TAXES AND RESURRECTION

The religious leaders know Jesus is talking about them (Matthew 21:45), but He is so popular with the people that they can't do as they wish—arrest Him on the spot (20:19). Instead, they resort to stealth and subversion. They watch Him closely and send spies to act nice and try to catch Him saying something they can use against Him. Then they can turn Him over to the government (20:20).

Their plan shows how desperate they have become. To begin with, all that would be needed to "get some dirt" on most people is to watch their actions and catch them doing something wrong. They realize, however, that this will not work with Jesus. Instead, the goal of the leaders of the people is reported here by Luke:

- They purpose to catch Jesus in His words. It was by His words that Jesus put these leaders to shame. It is by Jesus' words, the leaders suppose, that Jesus will be eliminated. It is significant that the leaders of the people cannot and will not attempt to discredit Jesus in any of His actions.
- They seek to deal with Jesus politically. The solution to their problem, as the Jewish leaders reason, is a political one, not a spiritual one. They do not seek to deal with Jesus in any way prescribed by the Old Testament law. They turn instead to a secular government that has the power to execute, the very government that they despise, rather than have Jesus govern them.

The spies go right to a sensitive topic: the payment of taxes (20:21–22). By their thinking, if Jesus is posing as the Messiah and they get Him to say there is no further need to pay taxes to Caesar, then they can alert Rome, get Him charged with treason, and He will trouble them no more. But Jesus sees through them (20:23).

Jesus' response surely takes everyone by surprise. No one expects Him to advocate paying taxes to support the Romans. He acknowledges a distinction between government and God, but doesn't assume they have to be in opposition to one another. Indeed, Jesus will soon give Caesar His very life, so taxes are a small matter. While tax money may belong to governments, people belong to God (20:24–25).

Critical Observation

The denarius Jesus used in His response to the tax question was not just referencing money, though it was that. In Jesus' day there were different kinds of money. The denarius was the form of money used for paying taxes to Caesar. Matthew told of how Jesus paid the two-drachma temple tax (Matthew 17:24–27). The tax was not paid with a denarius, but with the drachma. This is the reason why the money changers were exchanging money in the courts of the temple—the temple tax could not be paid with a denarius. When Jesus asked to see a denarius, it was with a specific purpose in mind.

After the spies fail to trap Jesus and are silenced, the Sadducees come along with another question (20:27–33). This question revolves around a command found in Deuteronomy 25:5–6. If a man died without having sons, his brothers had a responsibility to marry the widow and give her sons. If a brother did so, the son born to the widow carried on the deceased brother's heritage.

The purpose of this legislation was to assure that each family and tribe in Israel was perpetuated by the bearing of children. When the oldest brother married, but died before having any children, the younger brother was to take the widow as his wife so that the first son would carry on the name and the leadership of the deceased. Other legislation assured that the inheritance of land would remain in the tribes and families. Here was a very practical law, given to assure future generations. One can especially see the importance of this legislation when you recall the fact that the Messiah would be born of a woman (Genesis 3:15), from the tribe of Judah (Genesis 49:9–10), of the line of David (2 Samuel 7:8–16). How crucial it was for the tribes of Israel to perpetuate, for from such the Messiah would be born.

Since the Sadducees didn't believe in the resurrection, their query is almost certainly contrived and theoretical, meant to be a stumper. The argument of the Sadducees is based on this premise: Life in the kingdom of God will be just like it is on earth. Consequently, the present institution of marriage is assumed by the Sadducees to continue on in the kingdom. Thus, a woman who was married to seven brothers would be in a terrible predicament in heaven, for she would have to choose one of them to live with.

Demystifying Luke

This is Luke's first mention of the Sadducees, a priestly aristocracy who focused more on political matters than religious ones. In addition to not believing in resurrection of the dead, they downplayed the existence of angels and spirits, and they only viewed as authoritative the books of Moses (the first five books of the Old Testament). The traditions and interpretations of the Pharisees meant little to them. Because of their refusal to believe in resurrection, we hear more about them in the book of Acts—after the death and resurrection of Jesus. We also hear about them more in Acts because their power base was in Jerusalem, where the church was established, rather than Galilee, where most of Jesus' early ministry was conducted.

Jesus' response is concise, yet points out two major errors in the Sadducees' thinking. First, He distinguishes between this age and that age (20:34–35). He specifically mentions the resurrection from the dead (20:35), when people neither experience death nor participate in marriage. Second, He even goes back into the books of Moses to show that, in fact, God had made reference to resurrection at the burning bush (20:37–38). The Sadducees' mistaken assumption was that Moses rejected the doctrine of the resurrection of the dead. Jesus demonstrates that Moses was a believer in the resurrection of the dead, contrary to the belief of the Sadducees.

Jesus' answer is so powerful, His adversaries have to commend Him. The Pharisees enjoy the way that Jesus has silenced their opponents, the Sadducees, when they sought to entrap Jesus in such a way as to give credence to their rejection of the resurrection of the dead. Thus they cannot restrain themselves from praising Jesus for His response (20:39), even though they have set out on a course of trying to catch Jesus in His words. The praise of the Pharisees will be short-lived, however, for in the next question, raised by our Lord Himself, Jesus will show the Pharisees they do not understand the scriptures.

20:41–47

SON OF DAVID OR LORD OF DAVID?

After answering the Sadducees' tricky question, Jesus asks one of His own: If David called the Messiah "Lord," then how could the Messiah be David's son? (20:41–44). "Son of David" was a messianic title all Jesus' listeners would have been aware of. So Jesus asks how it is that David had referred to his descendant as "Lord."

By citing this passage from Psalm 110, Jesus makes it clear that they not only have a grievance with Jesus, who claims to be both human and divine, but more so, they are inconsistent with the Old Testament scriptures, even those written by King David. The citing of Psalm 110 by our Lord brings the central issue into focus, and shows it to be a truth taught clearly by the scriptures. The question that Jesus raises in this conundrum is how can the Messiah be greater than his "father" David? There is no explicit claim to deity, but rather the intriguing point that the Messiah must be more than David's son, and so more than Jewish expectations about the Messiah.

Throughout his Gospel, Luke stresses both the humanity and messiahship of Jesus. It is only by the miracle of the incarnation that the Messiah can be both human (a descendant of David) and divine. Jesus never fully answers His own question, but the religious leaders know the source He provided and are aware of what He is saying to them.

Critical Observation

Jesus' choice to refer to Psalm 110 over all other available texts worked well for several reasons:

1) Since the Messiah was commonly understood to be a "son of David," who could speak with more authority on his son than David?
2) The 110th Psalm went far beyond the issue of the Messiah's humanity and His deity, referring to His coming in power to overthrow His enemies.
3) Psalm 110 reveals the attitude of David, as Israel's leader, to the superiority of his son.
4) Psalm 110 clearly teaches both the humanity of the Messiah (a son of David) and His deity (David's Lord).

One question Jesus doesn't ask, yet would be implied from the passage He quoted, is, "Who are the enemies of the Messiah?" If Jesus is the Messiah, as He claims and as John had testified, then they are His enemies. They are the ones whom God will overthrow. And this is precisely what Jesus had suggested in the parable of the vineyard and the vine-growers earlier in this chapter (20:9–18).

Jesus addresses His disciples, but knows that everyone else is listening. His indictment of the teachers of the Law (20:45–47) must be leaving them with their ears burning. They had hoped to catch Jesus in something He said (20:20), yet they can't deny the truth of His charges.

Take It Home

We, too, have to decide what we will do with God's authority. When we reject it, we do not become the masters of our souls and the captains of our fate. When we spurn God's authority, we place ourselves under the dreadful authority of sin, and ultimately of Satan himself. Imagine it. The people of Jesus' day rejected Him, saying they had no king but Caesar (John 19:15). They gladly traded a traitor (Barabbas) for the sinless Son of God. When we reject God's authority, God's rule, we consign ourselves to the dominion of sin and of Satan. The "freedom" that Satan offers people is the freedom from a righteous life, and the bonds of sin and death.

We must deal with God's authority both personally in our own lives and in our lives as a community, the church. We, like these first-century Jewish leaders, can forget that the church belongs to Christ. It is His church, not ours, and He is the one who is to benefit from it. But how often church leaders begin to look on the church as their own, and to protect their power and positions rather than use them as avenues of service. And how often we all go to church expecting (even demanding) to gain from it, but forgetting that it is God who has the right to expect and to get gain. The church, like Israel, belongs to God, and its ultimate reason for existence is not our gain, but His.

LUKE 21:1–38

THE FUTURE: INDICATIONS AND INSTRUCTIONS

A Widow's Special Gift	21:1–4
The Coming Fall of Jerusalem	21:5–24
Signs and Promises	21:25–38

Setting Up the Section

Jesus and His disciples have arrived in Jerusalem, and Jesus has begun to teach at the temple every day. His time is short, and He is trying to give special attention to His followers. Yet each day large numbers of people arise early and show up at the temple to hear what He has to say.

It seems these first four verses (21:1–4) are placed here by Luke in contrast to the Pharisees, to show how God's ways differ so greatly from those of men. The Pharisees loved riches, and they viewed wealth as an evidence of piety. God, in their minds, would be impressed by the wealthy, and would be especially pleased by the size of their contributions.

21:1–4

A WIDOW'S SPECIAL GIFT

Jesus has just been warning His disciples about the abuses of the teachers of the Law and their misplaced priorities. Among His specific charges are that, "they devour widows' houses" (20:47 NIV), indicating a certain level of deceit in their dealings with helpless people. Then, almost as He is speaking those words, He looks up and points out a widow making an offering. Her two small coins, each worth about one-eighth of a cent, surely seem pathetic in contrast to the showy gifts of the wealthy.

Demystifying Luke

The temple treasury was in the court of women, where thirteen collection bins received the gifts of worshipers. The two tiny coins of the widow must have seemed a puny gift, but Jesus was well aware of the sacrifice being made by the woman.

Yet Jesus is pleased with her offering, realizing she is trusting God with all she has to live on (21:4). It's interesting that although Jesus points out the woman's complete selflessness to His disciples, it doesn't seem that He says anything to the woman. Nor are we told the disciples' response to Jesus' comment. But we soon discover their minds aren't on simplicity and sacrifice.

There is an implied contrast between the widow's offering in verses 1–4 and the disciples' admiration for the temple in verse 5 and following. Jesus is impressed with what took place in the temple—with the widow's offering. The disciples are impressed with the temple itself—with its beauty and splendor. Man truly looks on the outward appearance and God on the heart, here, as always.

21:5–24

THE COMING FALL OF JERUSALEM

The disciples, who may not have come to Jerusalem often, are not unlike tourists taking in the sights. The tax collector, fishermen, and others are simple men who find themselves in one of the greatest architectural achievements of their day (21:5). Luke alone among the Gospel writers informs us that some of these adornments were the result of gifts that were donated.

The disciples are understandably impressed. Was it possible that the disciples' attachment to the temple was based upon some false assumptions concerning it? For example, if the disciples believed that Jesus was about to establish His throne in Jerusalem, would He not make the temple His headquarters? Did this not mean that their offices would be in the temple? If such was their thinking, then no wonder they are impressed with this building. What great facilities this building would provide them.

But this is not at all to be the case. Jesus is aware of the not-too-distant fall of the holy city. Even though the temple is still under construction, Jesus tells the disciples of a time "when not one stone will be left on another" (21:6 NIV). They immediately want to know when the destruction will take place and what to look for. But rather than merely satisfy their curiosity, Jesus instead addresses their conduct—how to respond when the time comes.

Critical Observation

The construction of Herod's temple was not only a magnificent work of architecture but was also built to accommodate Jewish sensitivities. Since only priests were allowed in certain parts of the interior, one thousand of them were trained to do the masonry and carpentry in those portions. Temple service was never interrupted from the beginning of construction in 20–19 BC through the completion of the surrounding buildings and courts in AD 64 .Yet all that beautiful white marble fell in ruins in AD 70.

His warning is widespread (21:8–24), including both the soon-to-come fall of Jerusalem and His considerably later second coming, and what to expect for both believers and nonbelievers. Yet rather than distinguish the events, Jesus is intent to intertwine them. Some of the predicted events will even occur more than once, such as the trampling of Jerusalem by the Gentiles (21:24). It falls in AD 70, and the book of Revelation predicts another similar event (according to many interpretations, at least) at a point in the future (Revelation 11:2).

Jesus provides three primary instructions for His followers:

1) Watch out for false messiahs (21:8). When times get bad, people always arise with answers. But the bad times He is describing will be the judgment of God, and no human solution will remedy the situation.
2) Don't be frightened by wide-scale world events or personal persecution (21:9–19). Jesus will provide words and wisdom to get His disciples through such times (21:15). Yet Jesus' promise that "not a hair of your head will perish" (21:18 NIV) must be viewed in light of His statement in verse 16, that some of the disciples will be put to death. (His predicted betrayal by parents, brothers, relatives and friends [21:16] helps explain Jesus' previous

insistence on putting Him even before family members [14:26].) Followers of Jesus will not perish eternally, though they may pay a high price for discipleship. Luke, in his second volume, the book of Acts, gives a historical account of some of the sufferings of the saints in the days after our Lord's ascension.

3) Do not flee to Jerusalem for safety when it is under siege (21:20–24). Normally people would flock to fortified cities during wartime, but Jerusalem will not stand. This will happen in the lifetime of the disciples who are with Jesus. In Acts, Luke writes, "a great persecution began against the church in Jerusalem, and they were all scattered throughout the regions of Judea and Samaria, except the apostles" (Acts 8:1 NASB).

Jesus' words surely redirect the disciples' thoughts.

- They should lay to rest the disciples' visions of an immediate kingdom, with Jerusalem and that temple as its headquarters.
- They spell out hard times ahead for those who will follow Him, rather than happy days, as nearly all, including the disciples, hope for. This is true for the disciples and for the early church (see Acts), but it is just as true for saints of all ages (2 Timothy 3).
- While it may not seem so, times of adversity are legitimate times for continuing to spread the gospel. The gospel is light to those in darkness, and it offers hope to those in despair.

But Jesus still has more to say.

21:25–38

SIGNS AND PROMISES

From the predictions for what will happen in and around Jerusalem, Jesus moves on to heavenly signs (21:25). Here He appears to be speaking specifically to His second coming (21:27), so the same signs produce quite different responses. Those who don't know Christ will "faint from terror" (21:26 NIV), while believers should stand with their heads lifted up in anticipation of their final redemption (21:28).

Jesus intentionally doesn't give His followers a list of specific times and dates. His Parable of the Fig Tree (21:29–31) explains why. Farmers and gardeners don't operate by calendar dates, but in response to the conditions they observe. Jesus expects His disciples to have sensitivity to the season of His return. He doesn't want them ignorant of what to expect, but neither does He want them to suspend their watchfulness until some specified date in the future.

Ongoing debate takes place over Jesus' promise that "this generation will certainly not pass away until all these things have happened" (21:32 NIV). His second coming is included in "all these things," so how can a single generation span such a time period? Some people redefine *generation* more broadly to mean "humankind" or "Israel," although that seems to stretch the context of Luke's writing (and the very definition of *generation*). Another possibility is that "all these things" will occur twice—once for the disciples in Jesus' generation and again for disciples at a future time. Thus, Jerusalem is sacked in AD 70, in fulfillment of our Lord's words. And so, too, Jerusalem will be trodden under the feet of the Gentiles again, during the tribulation (Revelation 11:2).

Jesus' second promise is that His "words will never pass away" (21:33 NIV). He speaks with an authority far greater than even the prophets had. He speaks as God. His words are divine revelation.

Jesus concludes three specific evils that will distract His followers from watching for the signs and understanding their significance (21:34). (These warnings are reminiscent of what He already taught in 12:22–34.)

- Dissipation is the hangover after drinking too much. It would be tempting, in light of the difficulties of life ahead, for Jesus' followers to overindulge in many ways, and then be rendered dull and insensitive to what is really going on around them.
- Drunkenness, directly related to dissipation, would also be a temptation for the suffering, afflicted, persecuted disciple, who is also aware of the chaos taking place in the created universe and who wishes to blot out the danger and the pain by anesthetizing his brain.
- Worry, or the preoccupation with the anxieties of life, would seem justifiable. According to Jesus, though, worrying about the details of life only misappropriates our energies to worthless efforts.

The antidote for all three will be to always watch and pray (21:36). An ongoing relationship with Jesus is the only way really to face all that will take place.

Biblical teachings about the last days can be confusing and a source of fierce debate. But at this time, Jesus' words are eagerly received by crowds of people at the temple (21:37–38). Yet His teaching days are almost at an end.

Take It Home

What is your understanding of the last days and second coming of Jesus? When you read passages like this one, are you more comforted, scared, or confused? The day of the Lord should be a truth that radically changes the Christian's lifestyle. Knowing that the material world will vanish, we should not place too much value on material things. Knowing that the Word of God will never pass away, we should find it of infinite, eternal value. Rather than tempting us to dull ourselves or worry ourselves to death, Jesus' return should motivate us to live a mindful life marked by self-control and a sense of mission.

LUKE 22:1–65

BETRAYAL, DENIAL, ARREST, AND ANGUISH

A Traitor among the Group 22:1–6
The Last Supper 22:7–38
Jesus' Arrest 22:39–65

Setting Up the Section

Luke's Gospel moves abruptly from Jesus' teaching in the temple after His triumphal entry to the events leading to His crucifixion. Remember the broader setting in which the Last Supper is found. The Jewish religious leaders in Jerusalem have already determined that Jesus must die. After He cleansed the temple, the sparks really began to fly, with the religious leaders making every effort to discredit Him or to get Him into trouble with the Roman authorities (20:19–20). When these efforts, as well as their attempts to penetrate the ranks of our Lord's disciples, miserably failed, the chief priests were delighted to have Judas approach them with his offer. It was only a matter now of waiting for the right chance.

22:1–6

A TRAITOR AMONG THE GROUP

Luke's version of Judas's betrayal of Jesus is considerably more concise than that of the other Gospel writers. Prior to this point, Luke has said nothing about Judas by name other than including him (last) in the list of disciples (6:16).

Critical Observation

Other Gospel writers provide a bit more insight into Judas's nature. He was not only the treasurer of the group, but also a thief (John 12:4–6). It was Judas's offer to betray Jesus that seemingly hastened Jesus' death. Were it not for Judas, the religious officials had planned to wait until after the Passover celebration to kill Jesus because they feared a riot (Mark 14:1–2). But in reality, Judas's betrayal was on God's timetable, because Jesus knew ahead of time about His betrayer (Luke 22:21).

Judas had been among the Twelve when they were paired up to teach and heal (9:1–6). His faults prior to Jesus' betrayal didn't seem much worse than those of the other disciples. So perhaps the best explanation for what makes him decide to betray his master is Luke's short comment that "Satan entered Judas" (22:3 NIV), prompting him to go to the chief priests and strike a deal to turn Jesus over to them (22:3–6).

Luke gives the account of Judas's agreement with the chief priests and officers (22:3–6) just before the Lord's instructions concerning the preparation for the last supper (22:7–13). This order of events is significant, for had Judas known in advance the place where the Passover was to be eaten, he could have arranged for Jesus' arrest there.

22:7–38

THE LAST SUPPER

Jesus' instructions for finding a place to celebrate the Passover (22:7–13) are just as cryptic as those for acquiring a donkey to ride into Jerusalem (19:28–35). But Peter and John faithfully obey, and the upper room is secured.

Demystifying Luke

The Passover itself began at the exodus of the Israelite nation from Egypt. The word that Moses brought to Pharaoh from God, "Let My people go. . ." (Exodus 5:1 NIV), was challenged by Pharaoh: "Who is this God, that I should obey Him?" (Exodus 5:2). The plagues were God's answer to this question. But while Pharaoh often agreed to release the people of Israel, he would renege once the pressure was off. The final plague was the smiting of the eldest son of the Egyptians, which resulted in the release of the Israelites. The firstborn sons of the Israelites were spared by means of the first Passover celebration. The Passover animals were slaughtered, and some of the blood was placed on the doorposts. When the death angel saw the blood on the doorposts, he "passed over" the house. This celebration was made an annual feast for the Israelite nation.

Luke writes of Jesus first taking the cup (22:17), then the bread (22:19), and then the cup again (22:20). Current Lord's Supper sacraments normally begin with the bread and follow with the wine. But if Jesus were following a traditional Passover celebration, there would have been four cups during the dinner.

None of the Gospels hint strongly that the Last Supper will eventually become as significant as it is to the church. The symbolism and weight of the event becomes evident in retrospect, but the disciples are not aware at the time. They don't notice that Jesus is instituting a new covenant and fulfilling the old covenant (22:15–16).

Luke's account of this event emphasizes the fact that the Last Supper has two distinct meanings. Verses 15–18 refer to the significance of the Passover for the Lord Jesus. The reference to eating (the bread, presumably) and drinking has its own meaning for Him as Israel's Messiah. The reason why He can say that He has eagerly desired to eat the Passover is revealed in verse 16: He will not eat it again until its fulfillment in the kingdom of God. So, too, for the cup. He will not drink the cup again until the kingdom of God is fulfilled (22:15, 17, 19–20).

Normally, we tend to look at the Passover as being a prototype of the death of Christ on the cross. Jesus looks beyond the cross, to the crown. The joy set before Him is the kingdom, and the suffering of the cross is the way this joy will be realized. Thus, Jesus focuses on the joy of the fulfillment of the Passover and is encouraged and enabled to endure the cross because of it.

In Matthew and Mark's parallel accounts of the Last Supper, Jesus is said to have indicated to His disciples that one of them would betray Him. The disciples are greatly saddened, and one by one each asked if he could be the traitor (Matthew 26:21–25; Mark 14:18–21). Luke's account adds an interesting comment (22:21–24). He passes over the sorrow of the disciples and informs us that the conversation quickly deteriorates into a finger-pointing session, where the disciples seem to look more at one another to find the culprit than to look within themselves. They actually end up in an argument over which of them is the greatest. From a search for the great sinner, the disciples move to a scrap over the greatest success among them.

Jesus responds with the criteria of greatness He expects from His followers (22:24–26). He exhorts His disciples to demonstrate servanthood and promises that their efforts will be rewarded—not only with their inclusion in His kingdom, but also with authority (22:27–30). When Jesus tells His disciples that the greatest must be the servant of all, He is simply reminding them that they must be like Him. He is not asking them to do anything that He is not doing Himself.

The disciples' preoccupation and debate over their own position, prestige, and power is inappropriate for several reasons:

1) This is the way the heathen behave.
2) It is the opposite of the way Jesus has manifested Himself, even though He is the greatest of all.
3) The preoccupation with greatness is untimely, for that which the disciples are seeking will not come in this life but in the next.

At some point during the evening, Jesus singles out Peter and warns him of a specific temptation the disciples will face (22:31). Just as Satan was at work in turning Judas against Jesus, the evil one is also about to attempt to test the other disciples (22:31). Although Peter will be singled out as one who will soon deny his Lord, the "you" in verse 31 (NIV) is plural. Jesus is warning them all. The word picture regarding wheat is this: In the process of getting from the fields into the storehouses, wheat is cut down, trampled, and tossed about. Jesus' followers could expect a similar experience before becoming productive members of the kingdom.

Jesus' reference to Peter (the nickname Jesus gave him, meaning "the rock") as Simon must have hurt, too. Simon was Peter's name before he met the Master. Looking back to this moment from what we know of history, it suggests that Peter would be acting like his old self, and not as a disciple of the Lord when he denied Jesus.

Peter thinks he is ready to withstand any kind of suffering—even death. But Jesus states, in no uncertain terms, that by morning light Peter will already have denied Him three times (22:33–34).

Verses 35–38 raise numerous questions. Jesus had previously told the disciples not to take provisions with them when they went out (9:1–6). Is Jesus changing His mind? Yes and no. The key to proper interpretation is verse 37, a reference to Isaiah 53. The passage in Isaiah, detailing various aspects of an unpopular, suffering Savior rather than a victorious Messiah, was not even considered messianic until after Jesus had died. The Greek word translated as "transgressor" (NIV) or criminal here refers to a rebel, someone defiant of God.

The fact that Jesus is crucified between two criminals does fulfill the prophecy of Isaiah 53:12, but it does so in a kind of symbolic way, so that it also leaves room for a broader, more sweeping fulfillment. Jesus is numbered (perhaps, as has been suggested, allows Himself to be numbered) among transgressors, and the two thieves are definitely that. But it could also be said that since Jesus is now dealt with as a criminal, His disciples are regarded in the same way. Jesus and His disciples are considered transgressors.

Yet Jesus is surely speaking figuratively about purchasing swords. When He says, "That is enough" (22:38 NIV), He probably doesn't mean two swords are enough. Indeed, one sword is too many in the garden during His arrest. And never in the rest of scripture are believers told to use force against their enemies. The only swords they wield are spiritual ones (Ephesians 6:17). So Jesus' comment very likely means they have partaken of quite enough foolish talk because His statement concludes their dialog on greatness, power, and priority.

22:39–65

JESUS' ARREST

After the Last Supper in the upper room, Jesus and the disciples go "as usual" to the Mount of Olives (22:39 NIV)—more specifically, to Gethsemane (Matthew 26:36). This was apparently a regular stop for Jesus, and private. Perhaps Judas knew he could lead Jesus' opponents to Gethsemane without the likelihood of encountering Jesus' adoring crowds.

First, though, Jesus asks the disciples to pray and then goes off by Himself to do the same. Like any other human being, He doesn't want to die. But He is fully committed to God's will and carrying out His part of the plan. Luke's account of the agony of our Lord in Gethsemane is considerably shorter than those of Matthew and Mark. Luke, for example, does not set the three disciples (Peter, James, and John) apart from the other eight, even though these three are taken by our Lord, to watch with Him at a closer distance. Neither does Luke focus on Peter, although in the other accounts, Jesus specifically urges Peter to watch and pray. While Matthew and Mark indicate three different times of prayer, with our Lord returning twice to awaken His disciples and urge them to pray, Luke refers to only two. Luke's record of Jesus sweating drops of blood is also unique to this Gospel (22:44). This reference may refer to the physical condition in which a person's stress response causes capillaries to break and blood to mix with his perspiration. Or, it may be a reference to the fact that Jesus is sweating so profusely that it is as if He is bleeding.

Though He is in such great sorrow and anguish that an angel comes to minister to Him, He doesn't ask for the disciples' prayer support. Rather, He asks them twice to pray that they won't fall into temptation (22:40, 46). He knows what is coming and wants them to prepare, but they fall asleep instead. Jesus' prayer, while it has three sessions and takes up a fair amount of time, can be summed up in His surrender to the will of God if the suffering could not be taken way (22:42). Jesus speaks of what is to come as a "cup." In other places in scripture, a cup is used as a visual image of the wrath of God (Habakkuk 2:16; Revelation 14:10). Jesus' agony is due to the cross that looms before Him. He is not in agony because He will be forsaken by men, but because He will be forsaken and smitten by God. Jesus is dreading, suffering in the anticipation of His bearing of the sins of the world and the wrath of God, which they deserved.

Demystifying Luke

Perhaps Luke's interest as a physician motivated him to record that Jesus' "sweat was like drops of blood" (22:44 NIV). Hematidrosis is a very rare condition in which severe stress results in people literally sweating blood. Scripture does not say this was the case for Jesus, but it is a possibility. In either case, Jesus was undergoing unprecedented, supernatural suffering. Luke also noted that the disciples weren't merely sleepy, but that their great fatigue was the result of their sorrow (22:45).

Jesus rouses the disciples and goes out to meet the crowd that has come for Him (Matthew 26:46; Mark 14:42). Luke's account of the arrest is again more concise than other Gospels. He dwells not on what is done to Jesus, but on what Jesus says and does.

1) Jesus rebukes Judas for betraying Him with a kiss (22:48).
2) Jesus orders a cease-fire and is obeyed, by both His own disciples and by the crowd of armed men who have come to arrest Him (22:49–51).
3) Jesus heals the servant's ear, so that all damages are corrected. (Luke again uses his eye for detail to note it was the right ear [22:50–51].)
4) Jesus rebukes the religious leaders for the way in which they deal with Him (22:52–53).

Luke reveals Jesus to be in control of the situation—a willing arrestee for whom they have no need for all their weapons (22:52). They expected a fight, but Jesus does not resist. They find Jesus unshaken. It is these arresting officers who are shaken up. John's account informs us that they actually draw back and trip over themselves when Jesus identifies Himself to them (John 18:6).

The disciples aren't prepared for crisis. They all flee (Matthew 26:56), but Peter follows at what he thinks is a safe distance. When recognized, he quickly denies knowing Jesus. Before long two others have associated Peter with Jesus, and then as he is making his third denial, a rooster crows (22:60). If that isn't bad enough, Luke tells us Jesus turns and looks straight at Peter (22:61). Jesus' prediction (22:34) certainly comes rushing back to Peter, and he can do nothing but leave and weep bitterly (22:62). Luke's account of Peter's denial gives us no explanation for Peter's presence there in the courtyard of the high priest's house. Neither does he give us the reason why Peter denied his Lord when confronted with the fact that he was one of His disciples. Luke simply gives us a straightforward account of Peter's three denials.

Meanwhile, Jesus is being blindfolded, mocked, beaten, and insulted by His guards (22:63–65). Notice that they are not abusing Jesus as though He were a hardened criminal or a violent man who has caused others to suffer and so deserves to suffer as well. They are mocking Jesus as a prophet. They want Him to give them some kind of magical display of His powers. In the process they are fulfilling Jesus' own words, that a prophet is persecuted, not praised, for his work. Thus, Jesus is here identified with the prophets who have gone before Him to Jerusalem, to be rejected and to die.

Take It Home

With faith so seldom challenged these days, how many believers really know how strong their faith is? Are they like Peter, verbally bold and even overconfident, only to stumble at the first real trouble? How do you evaluate your own level of faith? Can you look back at a turbulent time and see that your faith was either shaken and/or grew stronger as a result? Do you think your daily life would be much different if your faith were stronger?

LUKE 22:66–23:56

JESUS' TRIALS AND CRUCIFIXION

The Trials	22:66–23:25
Jesus' Crucifixion	23:26–43
Jesus' Death	23:44–56

Setting Up the Section

After Jesus' betrayal by Judas, arrest in Gethsemane, and denial by Peter, He undergoes a series of trials where He is rejected by both the Jews and the Gentiles. It seems that Pilate tries, but fails, to spare His life.

He is crucified between two thieves and buried in a borrowed tomb. The events surrounding the death of our Lord, as described by Luke, fall into several distinct sections. The first of these is the Via Dolorosa ("Way of Sorrow"), the way to the cross, described in 23:26–32. The second is the actual crucifixion scene, the events surrounding the execution of our Lord, taking place on Calvary, in 23:33–43. The final section, in 23:44–49, is the account of the death of our Lord, along with Luke's description of the impact of these events on some of those who witnessed it—namely, the centurion, the crowd, and the women who had accompanied Jesus from Galilee.

22:66–23:25

THE TRIALS

No time is wasted in passing sentence on Jesus. Only hours after His nighttime arrest, the elders convene. By law, they have to wait until the break of day (22:66). Jesus is brought before the group and drilled as to whether or not He is the Christ.

Other Gospels delve more into the scheming of the religious leaders. The Sanhedrin had to resort to another illegal ploy. Could they somehow trick Jesus into bearing witness against Himself? While the law of that day had its own fifth amendment, which prevented the accusers from forcing a man to testify against himself, could they somehow get Him to acknowledge that He is the Messiah, and even better, that He is the Son of God? If so, then they could find Him guilty of blasphemy, a crime punishable by death?

Critical Observation

The official Jewish council that oversaw Jesus' trial was the Sanhedrin, a final court of appeals. Certain members of the seventy-member body were sympathetic to Jesus (23:50–51), but apparently they were either absent or out voted.

Luke is again content to show that Jesus is in control. Jesus' retort (22:67–69) shows that He realizes this trial is little more than a sham. He isn't tricked or coerced into saying what His accusers want to hear; He speaks because His time has come.

Jesus affirms He is the Messiah. You can imagine the Sanhedrin's response when Jesus indirectly confirms He is the Son of Man. This expression, found in Daniel's prophecy (Daniel 7), implied not only humanity, but deity. Will He admit He is the Son of God? Jesus' response is a grudging admission that implies something like, "yes, but not the way you understand messiahship." Nevertheless, it gives the Sanhedrin the grounds it needs to accuse Jesus.

The Jewish officials, of course, consider His words to be blasphemy (although Jesus spoke the truth). No matter how they had mistreated Jesus, disrespecting His human rights, now all they need is the cooperation of the state to kill Him—they could pass a death sentence, but couldn't carry it out.

So the next stop was to present their case before the governor of Judea, Pontius Pilate. Luke's account of the secular trial of Jesus is quite distinct from the other accounts.

- Luke is the only account to include the trial before Herod.
- Luke's account describes Pilate more in terms of his intentions and desires, than in terms of his actions.
- He tells us that Pilate proposes that he will punish Jesus, and then release Him.
- He does not emphasize the external pressures brought to bear on Pilate, as the other Gospels do.
- He emphasizes Jesus' silence.
- He most strongly emphasizes Jesus' innocence.

Luke informs us in verse 2 that members of the Sanhedrin (who apparently all came along to bring charges, see verse 1) press three charges against Jesus, all of which are political (that is, against the state), and none of which are religious. The charges against Jesus are:

1) stirring up unrest and rebellion;
2) opposing taxation by Rome; and
3) claiming to be a king (23:2).

Pilate appears to have been a savvy politician. He passes right over the first two charges. If Jesus were a revolutionary, would not the Romans have known about Him much sooner? Indeed, did not the Romans know of Jesus? Surely they had long ago determined that He was no threat. Revolutionaries there were, but Jesus was not among them. And neither did the Roman IRS have any evidence that Jesus had ever so much as implied that the Jews should not pay their Roman taxes. And, as Jesus had emphasized to His arresters, had He not taught publicly, day after day, so that His teaching was a matter of public record (see 22:52–53)?

Pilate does address the third charge (23:3) asking Jesus only to respond as to whether or not He is the king of the Jews. When he can find no foundation (23:4) he tries to dismiss the charges. After all, even if Jesus claimed to be a king, He had no military backing or political power.

The chief priests and the crowd protest, insisting that Jesus stirs up the people all over Judea by His teaching, starting in Galilee. By doing so, they have disclosed that Jerusalem is simply the last place where Jesus has created some measure of unrest. He is not a Judean, a man of Jerusalem, but a Galilean. Thus Pilate delights in ruling that this case is really not in his jurisdiction. The case must go to Herod the Tetrarch, for he is the one who rules over Galilee (3:1). And so Jesus, along with the religious leaders and the rest of the crowd, are sent, still early in the morning, to bother Herod.

While Pilate seemingly had little interest in Jesus and virtually no previous contact with Him, Herod at least had a fair amount of indirect contact. One of the women who followed Jesus and helped to support Him was Joanna the wife of Chuza, Herod's steward (8:2; 24:10). Also, there was Herod's relationship with John the Baptist. So there were several reasons that Herod would have been informed about Jesus' ministry. Herod is pleased to meet Jesus in person (23:8) and is hoping to see a miracle, or at least interview Jesus. But Jesus does not respond. Herod has Jesus dressed in an elegant robe and returns Him to Pilate after he and his soldiers get tired of mocking Him (23:11). Surprisingly, this experience forges a friendship between Pilate and Herod, who were previously enemies (23:12).

Why does Luke include this incident with Herod while no other Gospel writer does? Perhaps to show that everyone rejected Jesus as the Messiah, including Herod. It was necessary for Rome and the Gentiles to share in the rejection and the crucifixion of Christ so that all people, not just the Jews, might be guilty of His innocent blood.

It seems, not only from verse 13 but also from the parallel accounts, that Pilate takes Jesus aside after He is brought back from His trial before Herod, and that he attempts to satisfy himself concerning Jesus' guilt or innocence. When he comes out, Pilate calls the chief priests and rulers of the people (for it is they who are pressing him for a guilty verdict) and reiterates that he is unconvinced of any criminal charges that merit the case presented against Jesus, reminding them that by his actions, Herod had also acknowledged the innocence of Jesus.

Demystifying Luke

In verse 18 the name of Barabbas appears. The editors of the NIV and the NASB have chosen to omit verse 17 because it is not included in the oldest and most reliable manuscripts. The content of the verse though—the custom of releasing a prisoner—is clearly mentioned in the parallel accounts (Matthew 27:15–26; Mark 15:6–15; Luke 23:18–25; John 18:39–40). The custom may have come about as a kind of goodwill gesture on Pilate's part.

With Jesus again in Pilate's jurisdiction, Pilate tries three more times to convince the crowd to release Jesus (23:18–22). Yet they even insist on releasing Barabbas, a convicted murderer, rather than Jesus, a man of peace. And even after Pilate attempts to satisfy them by having Jesus beaten, they still insist on His crucifixion (23:23–25).

23:26–43

JESUS' CRUCIFIXION

There are two major incidents described in Luke's Gospel, both of which occur on the way to Calvary. The first is the commandeering of Simon of Cyrene. The second is Jesus' response to the wailing women. These two incidents are both prophetic of the unpleasant things to come for the nation of Israel, and specifically for those who lived in Jerusalem.

Normally, convicted criminals carried their own crosses (the horizontal piece) to the execution site, but Simon of Cyrene is commandeered by the Roman soldiers to carry the cross for Jesus (23:26). Presumably, the beatings and other demands of the evening have been too physically strenuous for Jesus. Simon was an innocent bystander, so far as the rejection and crucifixion of Christ was concerned. He was a man from a faraway place—Cyrene, a city in Africa (see Acts 2:10; 6:9), and he was not in Jerusalem but was heading there from the country. He was as removed from the rejection of Jesus as was possible.

Jesus' words to the women of Jerusalem—to weep for themselves and their children rather than Him—places the sorrow on them as He tells them what to expect (23:27–31). The future destruction of Jerusalem, which caused Jesus to weep as He entered that city (19:41–44), is the same destruction over which the women of Jerusalem are now told to weep. These women should not mourn so much over Jesus' death (after all, it would be the cause of their salvation), but they should mourn over that destruction that will take such a terrible toll on them and on their children.

Jesus' presence among humankind had been a remarkable, though generally unrecognized, blessing. His words in verse 31 say, in essence, "If the very Son of God is in your city, and the Roman army deals with Me this way, what do you think your destiny will be in My absence?" While crucifixion was not a Jewish means of executing men, nor was it all that common at the time of our Lord's death, crucifixion would be the rule of the day when the Romans came to sack the city of Jerusalem. It is said that thousands were crucified, at least, and that there was a shortage of crosses and of wood to build them due to the demand.

Critical Observation

Luke's account is unique, making contributions omitted in the other Gospel accounts. He included three incidents which are not reported elsewhere in the Gospels:

1) the words of Jesus to the women of Jerusalem (23:27–31),

2) the conversion of the thief on the cross (23:38–43), and

3) the words of our Lord, asking God to forgive His tormentors (23:34).

The place called the Skull (23:33) is the meaning of *Calvary* (Latin), or *Golgotha* (a Greek transliteration of an Aramaic word). Crucifixions were gory and gruesome, yet Luke spares us many of those details. He says simply that Jesus is crucified along with criminals. Matthew and John show how Jesus' death fulfilled Old Testament scripture; Luke remains focused on the love and salvation of the Messiah.

- Even as Jesus is being nailed to a cross, and people are gambling for His clothes, He prays for their forgiveness (23:34).
- And while hanging on the cross, when one of the thieves has an abrupt change of heart, Jesus still responds (23:43).

Demystifying Luke

The belief and salvation of the thief is recorded only in Luke's Gospel, and was pivotal to the tone of Jesus' crucifixion. Prior to that point Jesus receives only scoffing and other verbal and physical abuse; afterward such things are no longer mentioned, and Jesus' death takes on a somber and supernatural dignity.

23:44–56

JESUS' DEATH

The sixth hour is noon, by Jewish timekeeping. So the darkness must be eerie as the sun stops shining for three hours in the middle of the day (23:44–45)—an appropriate setting for the Savior of the world to, at last, commit His spirit into the hands of His heavenly Father (23:46). Meanwhile, the curtain in the temple that veiled the Most Holy Place and Ark of the Covenant is torn in half. With the death of Jesus, people will henceforth be able to approach God boldly, without requirement of animal sacrifice or priestly intervention. Jesus forever fulfills both essential roles: sacrifice and priest (Hebrews 4:14–16).

The response of the onlookers to Jesus' death is quite a contrast to what was recorded during His trial and during the first stages of His crucifixion. His death prompts a confession of faith from the Roman official in charge, declaring Jesus' innocence (23:47). Luke's record of this declaration is a thread in the theme of innocence that he weaves through the trial and crucifixion account.

Even the crowd's response becomes more subdued. People leave in sorrow and/or contrition. And Jesus' female followers simply stand and watch (23:48–49).

It is a member of the Sanhedrin who makes the official request to tend to Jesus' body. Joseph of Arimathea (with the help of Nicodemus [John 19:39]) goes to Pilate, takes Jesus' body, prepares it with spices (75 pounds) and wrappings, and places it in Joseph's brand-new tomb (23:50–53; John 19:38–42). This was done in the final hours before sunset when the Sabbath began and such a task would not be allowed.

Joseph and Nicodemus were both, to a great degree, outsiders. What they did seemed to be because of their position and authority. What they did, as far as we know, they did apart from any involvement on the part of the disciples of our Lord or the women who had long been following along with Him. While the disciples of John the Baptist claimed the body of John and buried it (Mark 6:29), the disciples of Jesus did not do so.

The women who are concerned for Jesus want to anoint His body, but the best they can do is gather their spices and wait until the Sabbath is over (23:54–56).

Critical Observation

The sequence of events in Jesus' crucifixion is not always clear, and Luke leaves out a number of phenomena that the other Gospels include, so that we cannot tell for certain the exact order of the events. Here is a general idea, however, of how the events appeared, keeping in mind the accounts of all the Gospel writers:

- The victims were nailed to their crosses, which were raised and fixed in position.
- Either prior to this or shortly after, drugged wine was offered to deaden the pain.
- The clothing of Jesus was gambled for and divided among the four soldiers.
- Railing accusations and mocking occurred throughout the ordeal—the crowd somehow seems to file or pass by the cross.
- Jesus cried out, "Father, forgive them. . ." (Luke 23:34 NIV).
- The criminals joined in reviling Christ.
- The thief on the cross came to faith in Jesus as his Messiah (Luke 23:40–43).
- Darkness falls over the scene, from the sixth hour (noon) till the ninth hour (3:00 p.m.).
- Jesus cried out, "my God, my God, why have you forsaken me?" (Matthew 27:46 NIV; Mark 15:34 NIV).
- Jesus said, "I am thirsty" (John 19:28–29 NIV) and drank a sip of vinegar.
- Jesus said, "It is finished" (John 19:30 NIV).
- Jesus bowed His head and said, "Father, into your hands. . ." (Luke 23:46 NIV) and died.
- Immediately, the curtain of the temple tore in two, top to bottom.
- An earthquake and the raising of dead saints occur (Matthew 27:51–54).
- The legs of the other two were broken, but Jesus' legs were not broken, since He was already dead (John 19:31–37).
- A soldier pierced Jesus' side with a spear—blood and water gushed out (John 19:34).
- A centurion (and the other soldiers who witnessed it) recognized He was the Son of God (Matthew 27:54; Mark 15:39) or the righteous/innocent one (Luke 23:47).
- The crowds left, beating their breasts, while the Galilean followers stayed on, watching from a distance.

Demystifying Luke

When Luke wrote that it was the day of preparation (23:54), he was referring to the Sabbath laws. Since there was no work to be done on the Sabbath (from Friday evening until Saturday evening), which included no cooking, preparations had to be made on Friday for the family's meals on Friday evening and Saturday (the Sabbath). The same "no work" laws would have kept the women from tending to Jesus' body on Saturday, so Sunday morning was their next opportunity.

Luke gives no clue as to the women's state of mind during their wait, but it must have been a sorrowful time indeed. Just a week before, Jesus had ridden into Jerusalem to the acclaim of the crowds. He had been teaching daily in the temple. The suddenness of His Thursday night arrest and Friday afternoon death and burial, coupled with their inability to do anything on the Sabbath, was surely cause for intense grief and perhaps even hopelessness. But what none of them yet realized was that the story of Jesus was far from over.

Take It Home

It can be disheartening to see that, after Jesus invested so much of His time in His apostles, His final hours were spent alone. His old friends seemed to have betrayed, denied, and deserted Him. Yet at the same time, new disciples (Joseph of Arimathea and Nicodemus) had a burst of faith and courage that enabled them to go public and tend to His body and burial. If you are a long-time follower of Jesus, what can you learn from this account? What can you learn if you are a new believer?

LUKE 24:1–53

RESURRECTION AND SECOND CHANCES

The Empty Tomb	24:1–12
Cleopas and His Friend	24:13–35
A Final Training Period	24:36–53

Setting Up the Section

After the bleakness and despair of Jesus' horrid crucifixion, His followers have an assortment of amazing epiphanies. The women discover an empty tomb and angelic messengers announcing His resurrection. Two disciples on the road have a heart-burning conversation before they realize their fellow traveler is Jesus Himself. And finally the apostles get to see Jesus and hear His explanation for everything that had happened. Consequently, even the absence of Jesus' physical presence would not deter their worship and praise of God.

24:1–12

THE EMPTY TOMB

The women who had wanted to anoint Jesus' body on Friday have not been able to, but they have marked the location of the tomb where He was laid (23:55). Perhaps they even noticed that someone had already anointed His body (since seventy-five pounds of spices had been used [John 19:39]), but they want to see to it themselves.

Even at this point, the apostles aren't involved. Surely the women could have used help carrying their load of spices or protection for travel in the dim morning light (24:1), but they travel alone for their discomfiting task.

When they arrive, they see the stone has been rolled away (24:2). They enter the tomb and hardly have time to wonder what has happened before two angels address them. The angels' clothing is fiercely radiant, probably allowing the women to see clearly that Jesus' body is not there. So that it cannot be said that the women merely forgot the burial place of Jesus and went to the wrong tomb, Luke (along with the other Gospel writers) reports that the angels inform the women that they have come to the right place, seeking Jesus, but that He is not there (24:5–7; Matthew 28:5–6; Mark 16:6). Matthew tells us that one angel invited the women to see the place where He once lay (Matthew 28:6).

The women are looking for the living among the dead (24:5). The angels confirm that Jesus' body isn't just gone; He has risen (24:6). To further explain, the angels remind the women of Jesus' own words (24:6–7; 9:22), and the women begin to remember and comprehend what Jesus had taught them.

Critical Observation

Luke doesn't mention it, but Judas had killed himself by this time (Matthew 27:1–10; Luke will briefly describe Judas' suicide in Acts 1:18–19). He begins referring to the apostles as the Eleven (24:9, 33), although other biblical writers continue to refer to them as the Twelve.

The women return to tell the apostles, but the Eleven don't believe them. Still, Peter decides to check out their story (along with John [John 20:1–9]), and runs to the tomb. He sees the open tomb and wrappings for the body, but registers no understanding or belief that something miraculous has happened (24:9–12).

24:13–35

CLEOPAS AND HIS FRIEND

Two more disciples are discouraged (24:17) as they walk the seven miles from Jerusalem to Emmaus, discussing the events of Jesus' death. We do not know the exact location of the small village of Emmaus, only its distance from Jerusalem. If they did not live in Emmaus, they may have been staying there, in the suburbs as it were, for the Passover celebration. The huge influx of people may have necessitated finding accommodations outside the city.

One of these disciples is named Cleopas (24:18); the other is not named. By virtue of the length of this account, it seems that Luke places a great deal of importance on this incident. It takes up much of his account of our Lord's post-resurrection appearances.

Along the way Jesus joins them, although they don't recognize Him (24:15–17). This might only mean that Jesus appears to the men in His resurrected body, but it seems to mean that He appears to them in a body that is not immediately recognizable. This could mean, for example, that the nail scars were not apparent, so all the telltale indications of His identity would have been concealed.

Jesus asks what they are talking about, and they tell Him what little they know (24:17–24). It was, they said, the third day since He had died. This could be a reference to Jesus' words that He would rise again on the third day. What was more, some of the women, they told Jesus, had gone out to the tomb and found it empty. The women further claimed to have seen angels, but alas they did not see Jesus. The very things that seemed to point to the resurrection of Jesus had no impact on these two men at all.

Jesus gently scolds them for not comprehending what the prophets had written in light of all that had happened (24:25–26). They had a partial understanding, like many of the Israelites of their day, but perhaps they chose to overlook the prophecies about the suffering of the Messiah while dwelling on the portions declaring His victory and glory. So Jesus teaches them what was said in all the prophecies (24:27).

When they get to Emmaus, Jesus gives them the opportunity to let Him walk away. But they insist that He stay with them (24:28–29). For one thing, it is late. But perhaps they are also interested in all He has been telling them. They sit down to eat, and as Jesus gives thanks and breaks bread, they recognize Him (24:31). At that instant, He disappears.

In a sense this breaking of bread with these two men was a prototype of heaven and of the joys that await the Christian. At the Last Supper, Jesus spoke of the kingdom in terms of a banquet meal (22:24-30), at which time He would serve His followers (12:37). Jesus said that He would not eat the Passover again until it was fulfilled in the kingdom of God (22:16). Jesus disappears because that great day is yet ahead when they will fellowship at His table in the kingdom. But this meal made the joy and anticipation of that occasion even greater.

They get up at once, driven by a burning in their hearts (24:32), and return to Jerusalem to tell the Eleven. By that time, Jesus has also appeared to Peter (24:34; 1 Corinthians 15:5), so they begin swapping their joyful stories.

24:36–53

A FINAL TRAINING PERIOD

In his account of the post-resurrection appearances of Christ, Luke's emphasis is on what takes place in Jerusalem, not so much on what happens in Galilee (as, for example, Matthew recorded in 28:16–20). There are many appearances, some of which are described in one or more Gospels, and others of which may be described by another. There were probably a number of appearances that were not even mentioned.

While the disciples are discussing their experiences, Jesus appears again. Jesus' first words to this group are of peace (24:36). This is not the disciples' response, however. They are startled, Luke tells us (24:37). Why are they not overjoyed? Why are they frightened and upset? The use of "startled" (NIV) suggests that the disciples are caught off guard, as though they never expected to see Jesus. They think He is a ghost (24:36–37).

It is easier for the disciples to believe in a ghostly Jesus than in a Jesus who is literally and physically present. The issue really comes down to belief or unbelief. The disciples thought they really believed. They say that they believe (24:34). But their response seems to communicate something else.

The thrust of verses 36–43 is Jesus' provision of physical evidence for His resurrection. The first evidence is the Lord, standing before them. He is not, as they supposed, a ghost. He encourages them to touch Him, and to see that He has flesh and bones (24:39). He also encourages them to look at His hands and His feet (24:39). The inference is clear that both His hands and His feet bare the nail prints that He had from the cross. In this sense, at least, His body is like the body He had before His death. Finally, Jesus eats some of the fish that they are eating, the final proof that His body is, indeed, a real one (24:41–43).

As Jesus reasons with the startled group, He opens their minds to allow them to understand what the biblical prophecies had meant (24:44–45). Paul will later reaffirm that it is only through God's revelation that anyone can properly interpret and understand the truths of scripture (1 Corinthians 2:6–16; 2 Corinthians 3:14–18).

Demystifying Luke

This final section of Luke (24:24–53) is compressed. Luke later tells us that forty days passed between Jesus' resurrection and His ascension (Acts 1:3). The teachings in verses 45–49 were likely taught and reinforced throughout that period.

Jesus reminds them of the prophecies about Himself:

1) the rejection, suffering, death, and resurrection (24:46);
2) the proclamation of the gospel to all nations (24:47); and
3) the promise of the Holy Spirit (24:48–49).

While Jesus makes it clear that His death and resurrection are for all nations (24:47), it will later take a lot of discussion and debate (as well as divine revelation) before the early church fully understands that Gentile believers are as entitled to salvation as Jewish ones. The universality of the gospel—the fact that the Messiah would die for the sins of all who would believe, Jew or Gentile—was one of the greatest irritations for the Jewish religious leadership, especially for those who did not see themselves as sinners. Yet even the Abrahamic covenant, the great promise upon which Judaism was based, revealed this very truth: "And I will bless those who bless you, and the one who curses you I will curse. And in you all the families of the earth will be blessed" (Genesis 12:3 NASB).

In the light of the fact that the salvation that the Messiah came to bring was for all nations, the Great Commission comes as no new revelation, but as an outflow of the work of Christ on the cross of Calvary and of the Old Testament prophecies that foretold of the salvation of men of every nation. Notice that Luke (both here and in Acts 1:8) records the Great Commission, not so much as a command but as a promise, a certainty (24:47–48).

As one final miraculous assurance that Jesus has been sent from God, He is taken up into heaven as they all watch (24:50–53). He leaves them with a blessing and they worship Him. In addition, they "stayed continually at the temple" (24:53 NIV).

Luke seems to end his Gospel rather abruptly. But his "ending" isn't intended to be the final word. He continues the story right at this point in the book of Acts.

Take It Home

Christians today can fall into the very same trap into which the first-century disciples fell. We read and study the scriptures through the grid of our own sin, desires, ambitions, and preferences. We arrive at our own idea of what God should be like and what His kingdom should be, and then we are tempted to rearrange the scriptures to suit our ideas. How often we do this in those areas of tension, where two seemingly contradictory things are somehow linked. We would be wise to be like the Old Testament prophets, who heard the Word of God but couldn't always fathom its meaning based on their life experiences. Sometimes when we don't understand, we have to hold two truths in tension, seeking and praying to understand their interrelationship. We have to trust that even if we, in this life, can't see exactly what God has for us in the future, we can still trust Him to reveal Himself in His own time.

THE GOSPEL OF JOHN

INTRODUCTION TO JOHN

While the Gospels of Matthew, Mark, and Luke are identified together as the synoptic Gospels because of their similarities, the Gospel of John stands apart in style and in content. John's style is simple in vocabulary, yet profound and even sometimes poetic. As for content, he records events that the synoptic Gospels don't. Jesus' teaching also has a different focus. In the synoptic Gospels, Jesus' teaching focuses on the kingdom of God, but in John His teaching centers more on His own identity and how His presence manifests God the Father.

DISTINCTIVES

John's Gospel does not record Jesus' parables or some of the well-known events recorded in the other Gospels—such as His baptism, temptation, and transfiguration. It does, however, include the accounts of eight miracles performed by Jesus, only three of which appear in the other Gospels. While the other Gospels describe works of Jesus without much explanation, John's Gospel, providing fewer events, includes more exchange about the people involved and the significance of each event to those people.

AUTHOR

The author of this Gospel does not identify himself by name, though he is referred to as "the disciple that Jesus loved." Through the years, a variety of possible authors have been proposed, yet the apostle John, of the original twelve disciples, still seems the most likely candidate.

John was identified in the New Testament as the son of Zebedee and Salome, and as the younger brother of James. Jesus called James and John the "Sons of Thunder" (Mark 3:17). John was working as a fisherman when Jesus called him as a disciple.

PURPOSE

John states his purpose for writing in the Gospel's closing:

Jesus did many other miraculous signs in the presence of his disciples, which are not recorded in this book. But these are written that you may believe that Jesus is the Christ, the Son of God, and that by believing you may have life in his name (John 20:30–31 NIV).

The central theme of this Gospel is Jesus' revelation of God the Father and the connection that revelation enables between humanity and God. This Gospel is a call to faith as well as an encouragement to those continuing in their faith. Some compare it to a first-century tract written to explain Jesus' identity and to inspire others to have faith in Him.

HISTORICAL CONTEXT

There is some disagreement as to when John's Gospel was written, but most scholars date it in the late first century.

John probably wrote the Gospel while he was ministering in Ephesus, an important coastal city on the western shore of modern Turkey. Before John, first-century leaders such as Paul, Timothy, and the ministry couple Priscilla and Aquila influenced Ephesus.

While the early Christian movement had a presence in the area, it was not without conflict. The famous Temple of Diana and the trade from the manufacture of idols associated with the temple were part of the fuel for the conflict. By the time John was ministering in Ephesus, there was also opposition from the Jews. The first-century Christian church began as a predominantly Jewish movement, but by the late first century, those ties had been broken. In fact, John may have been dealing with opposition from the Jews reminiscent of the opposition that his Gospel describes Jesus facing.

THEMES

John's dominant theme is Jesus' identity as the Messiah, Son of God, the revelation of the Father. He also thematically points out the foolishness of the Jewish leaders who rejected Jesus as the Messiah. Several other themes run throughout the Gospel:

- **Eternal life.** In John's Gospel, eternal life is equated with knowing God, which happens through knowing Jesus.
- **The Holy Spirit.** Jesus' work will continue in and through His followers by the work of the Spirit who will guide, direct, and mediate the presence of the Father.

CONTRIBUTION TO THE BIBLE

Along with this Gospel, John wrote three short letters included in the Christian New Testament, identified as 1, 2, and 3 John. Many also believe he wrote the book of Revelation. The Gospel of John is often the first book a faith seeker reads in the Bible. John 3:16 stands as a hallmark of the love of God, often the one verse people of all backgrounds are familiar with.

STRUCTURE

The commentary for this book is laid out by chapters for ease of use, but here is a look at the broader structure of this book of the Bible:

Prologue	1:1–18
Jesus' Ministry—The Seven Signs	1:19–12:50
Jesus' Farewell Address, Trial, Death, and Resurrection	13:1–20:31
Epilogue	21:1–25

OUTLINE

THE PROLOGUE OR INTRODUCTION 1:1–18

The Deity of Christ 1:1–5
John: The Forerunner of Christ 1:6–8
The Light of Christ 1:9–13
The Incarnate Christ 1:14–18

THE WITNESSES 1:19–51

The Witness of John the Baptist 1:19–28
The Second Witness of John the Baptist 1:29–34
The First Disciples 1:35–51

THE PUBLIC MINISTRY OF JESUS 2:1–25

The First Sign
2:1–11
Scriptural Faith vs. Superficial Faith 2:12–25

A MEETING AT NIGHT 3:1–21

Nicodemus 3:1–21
The Final Witness of John the Baptist
3:22–36

A MEETING BY THE WELL 4:1–54

The Woman at the Well 4:1–26
The Harvest 4:27–42
Knowing Christ 4:43–54

THE POSITION OF JESUS 5:1–47

The Authority of Jesus 5:1–18
Jesus Claims to Be God 5:16–24
The Power and Authority of Jesus 5:25–29
The Witnesses of Jesus' Deity 5:30–47

REVEALING HIMSELF 6:1–71

The Awesome Power of Jesus 6:1–15
The People of Glory 6:16–29
The Bread of Life 6:30–40
Rejection and Revelation 6:41–71

CHALLENGES TO RESPOND 7:1–8:11

The Response of Jesus' Family 7:1–13
Spiritual Insight 7:14–24
Ignorance in Wisdom's Clothing 7:25–36
Come and Drink 7:37–52
A Woman Caught in Adultery 7:53–8:11

FROM PRESENTATION TO CONDEMNATION 8:12–59

The Light of the World 8:12–20
The First Condemnation of Israel 8:21–30
Genuine Faith 8:31–32
The Corruption of Man 8:33–36
Man's Only Security 8:37–47
Spiritual Ignorance 8:48–59

THE BLIND MAN 9:1–41

What the Blind Man Saw 9:1–41

JESUS CONFRONTS THE LEADERSHIP 10:1–42

Woe to the Shepherds 10:1–21
The Deity of Jesus 10:22–42

THE PRIVATE MINISTRY OF JESUS 11:1–57

A Faith That Is Larger than Life 11:1–44
The Plan of Men—the Plan of God 11:45–57

THE FAITHLESS AND THE FAITHFUL — 12:1–50

The Priority of Worship — 12:1–8
The Beginning of the End — 12:9–26
The Power of the Cross — 12:27–36
The Unbelief of Israel — 12:37–50

FINAL WORDS — 13:1–38

Love in Action — 13:1–17
A Traitor in the Camp — 13:18–30
The Distinguishing Mark of the Church — 13:31–38

HOPE FOR THE DISCOURAGED — 14:1–31

Hope for the Hopeless — 14:1–3
Clarity for the Confused — 14:4–31

FINAL INSTRUCTIONS — 15:1–27

Abide in Jesus — 15:1–11
Abide in Love — 15:12–17
The Cost of Abiding — 15:18–27

A HELPER FOR DIFFICULT DAYS — 16:1–33

A Final Word on Persecution — 16:1–4
Better Days Are Yet to Come — 16:5–15
The Transforming Work of the Spirit — 16:16–33

JESUS' PRAYER — 17:1–26

Jesus Prays for Himself — 17:1–5
Jesus Prays for His Disciples — 17:6–19
Jesus Prays for All Believers — 17:20–26

JESUS' TRIALS — 18:1–39

The Sovereign Control of Jesus — 18:1–11
Humanity's Corruption and Jesus' Innocence — 18:12–27
What Is Truth? — 18:28–39

JESUS' DEATH 19:1–42

Behold, the Man 19:1–16
The Culmination of History 19:17–42

JESUS CONQUERS DEATH 20:1–31

The Empty Tomb 20:1–18
Jesus and the Disciples 20:19–31

EPILOGUE 21:1–25

Fishing Instructions 21:1–14
Breakfast by the Sea 21:15–25

JOHN 1:1-18

THE PROLOGUE OR INTRODUCTION TO THE GOSPEL OF JOHN

The Deity of Christ	1:1–5
John: The Forerunner of Christ	1:6–8
The Light of Christ	1:9–13
The Incarnate Christ	1:14–18

Setting Up the Section

This first chapter of John is a summary of the message of the entire Gospel—Jesus has come as the light of the world, and some reject and others accept. The first eighteen verses of chapter one offer an outline of his letter. Each topic that John will show us about Christ is introduced in these first verses.

1. The Deity of Christ (1:1–5)
2. The Forerunner of Christ (1:6–8)
3. The Rejection of Christ (1:9–11)
4. The Acceptance of Christ (1:12–13)
5. The Incarnation of Christ (1:14–18)
These topics represent the foundation of Christianity.

1:1–5

THE DEITY OF CHRIST

As we study the Gospel of John we find its purpose is to present Jesus as God's Son so that we might believe in Him and have eternal life. In fact, John gives us the two-fold purpose of his Gospel in 20:30–31:

1) That you might believe that Jesus is the Christ (Messiah), the Son of God
2) That believing in Him you might have life in His name

Throughout this Gospel, John shows us Jesus as the self-revelation of God and the various responses of the people around Him to that revelation. Some reject this truth and others accept it.

These first five verses reveal five truths about the deity of Christ:

1) *The Eternality of Christ (1:1).* John's first words draw the attention of the reader to the opening lines of Genesis, where Moses writes, "In the beginning God" (Genesis 1:1 NIV). Another way to say this is that before time began the Word was there.

Critical Observation

Why does John call Jesus the "Word" (Greek: *Logos*)? One reason could be because this would make a point to both Jews and Greeks.

- **For the Jewish mind** this described the LORD God because the LORD (*Yahweh*) was a God who spoke. Each day of creation begins with, "Then God said . . ." God's power was manifested through His spoken word.
- **For the Greeks**, all of the little gods that they worshiped were just a part of the one big god of reason and philosophy. The name of this power source in Greek religion is also the Logos ("the Word")—the power source that created everything and the power source that sustains everything.

2) *Jesus Is Distinct from God (1:1).* When John says that "the Word was with God" (NIV), it means more than one person in the room with another person. The Greek word used here carries the idea of being intimately related or facing each other. John is saying that Christ was distinct from the Father, and yet, in union with Him. This was a stumbling block to the Jews of Jesus' day. They believed in one God. Then Christ comes and declares that He is God, yet distinct from God the Father. This is the foundation of the teaching known as the Trinity, that there is one God, but He exists as three distinct "persons"—Father, Son, and Spirit. John presents Jesus the Son as fully God, but distinct from the person of the Father.
3) *Jesus Is God (1:1).* John is not saying that Jesus is simply divine, as if He is an extension of God. He is saying that Jesus is God in bodily form, and He is God completely. This is why Jesus tells the disciples in John 14:9, "Anyone who has seen me has seen the Father" (NIV).
4) *Jesus Is Creator of All Things (1:2–3).* This is both a negative and a positive statement. All things came into being by Jesus, which means nothing came into existence without Him.
5) *Jesus Is the Source of Spiritual Life (1:4–5).* Life and light are reoccurring themes in John. The concept of *life* here applies to the spiritual life of a person. John refers to Christ as the source of life more than fifty times in this Gospel. In addition, Jesus is the source of light. Some Bible translations say the darkness couldn't *understand* the light. Others say the darkness couldn't overpower the light. The Greek word can mean either of these things. It is possible that the author is making a play on words and that both meanings are intended.

1:6–8

JOHN: THE FORERUNNER OF CHRIST

This passage introduces not only John the Baptist, but also a complex aspect of early Christianity—the transition from the Old Testament to the New Testament. Why did the Gospel writer introduce John the Baptist at this early point? Because his message is critical in understanding Jesus as the Messiah.

John the Baptist was the connection to the Old Testament to point people to Christ. He was the last Old Testament prophet and the first New Testament evangelist. In verse 7, we get a clear and simple description of his message—he came as a *witness*. As it does still today, this word has a connotation of a person who gives testimony in court so that people might be convinced of the truth.

The Gospel writer adds one last comment about John the Baptist—that he was not the light, but came to bear witness to the light. This is important because the Jews were looking for a Messiah. They had not heard from God through a prophet in over four hundred years. Many wondered if John was the Messiah himself. If the messenger was misunderstood in this way, then the message that he preached could be lost (Acts 19:1–7).

1:9–13

THE LIGHT OF CHRIST

The author draws a contrast between John the Baptist and Jesus in verse 9. Jesus is the true light that gives light to all mankind. Does this mean that Jesus placed an understanding of Himself in every person? No. It is the idea that Christ came and shined His light upon all people. This forced humanity to make a decision about who He was.

This is a key theme in John's Gospel—that Jesus' light forces people to come to grips with their sin. John uses the imagery of light more than twenty times to refer to Jesus. He continues to draw a distinction between the world in darkness and the light of Jesus.

Verse 10 describes Jesus as the creator of the world. He shined His light upon the world, and they did not know Him. Jesus came to His own, the Jews, yet they—particularly the religious leaders—did not receive Him (1:11). With key exceptions, Jesus was not recognized by those who had creation as a witness or by those who had scripture as a witness. But verses 12–13 reveal the hope of those who do recognize and make themselves a part with Christ—they are given the right to be called children of God. (See Romans 8 for Paul's teaching on this adoption into God's family.)

Take It Home

As a Christian, you are part of God's family. You are brought into fellowship with God in which:

- You are a son and not a slave.
- You are valued and not discriminated against.
- You are accepted and not rejected.

These things come to those who believe in His name. It does not matter that people did not see Jesus, for Jesus came to this dark place to take on mankind's sin so that God would save mankind.

1:14–18

THE INCARNATE CHRIST

"The Word became flesh" (1:14 NIV). This is what we call the incarnation—God becoming human. Jesus was not a man who became divine—He was divinity that took on humanity. This belief of Jesus taking on humanity is central to Christianity.

The word translated as *dwelling* or *living* (1:14) means "to pitch a tent" or "take up residence." This is an image referring back to the Old Testament when God was believed to reside in the tabernacle, and then in the temple. Jesus lived on earth for thirty-three years as the presence of God on earth.

The *glory* of God (1:14) does not refer to a shining light or phenomenon. It is simply the sum of all of His attributes. Jesus revealed the grace and truth of God on earth in His nature and His work. That is what the disciples saw.

John the Baptist (1:15), as the witness of Jesus, is the link between the Old Testament and the New Testament. By mentioning John the Baptist, someone who was still well known when this Gospel was written in the mid-to-late first century, the Gospel writer includes a credible witness in identifying Jesus as the Messiah. John's words describing Jesus, communicate a paradox—Jesus came after him, yet existed before him.

There are a variety of interpretations of the phrase "fullness of his grace" in verse 16 (NIV). It could refer to Jesus' abundance of grace, or the replenishing nature of His grace, or a number of other possibilities. Whatever the exact meaning of that phrase, the grace we have received in Jesus is enough and does give good things to us over and over again. And while that grace does contrast with the Law of Moses (1:17) both reveal God's nature to us.

Critical Observation

The Old Testament law anticipated the grace of a future sacrifice. Ancient people came to God by faith just as we do. What did they have their faith in? It was not the Law, but in what the Law pointed them to. The Law showed them that God would provide a sacrifice that would take the guilt of their sin. So, the Old Testament worshiper trusted in the future grace that would come—the Messiah. When Jesus came, He was the fulfillment of the hope that was only understood in part in the Old Testament.

"No one has ever seen God" (1:18 NIV). While the Old Testament does describe times when God was revealed to people by appearing as a man or through some representative, God did not ever fully show Himself to people, for His holiness would consume them. Yet, Jesus Christ has revealed God to us. He is God put on display.

The description of Jesus in verse 18 focuses on the intimate relationship between Jesus and the Father. To be at the side of the Father means that Jesus is uniquely related to the Father. God the Father and God the Son share an intimate relationship with each other, as a result of being one (Hebrews 1:1–2).

Demystifying John

This next section begins a different writing style for John. The first eighteen verses of this chapter were primarily doctrinal statements concerning the deity and humanity of Jesus Christ. We now move to the actual narrative of the book. John 1:19–12:50 is often referred to as a collection of signs because it includes seven miracles that reveal Jesus' revelation of God the Father. Rather than looking at statements to evaluate their meaning, we look at conversations and events to determine their significance.

Remember that this Gospel is not as much a chronological history of Jesus as it is a photo album. Each story is like a snapshot. These stories are a collection of events in the life of Christ that prove that He is the manifestation of God the Father.

JOHN 1:19-51

THE WITNESSES

The Witness of John the Baptist	1:19–28
The Second Witness of John the Baptist	1:29–34
The First Disciples	1:35–51

Setting Up the Section

This first account begins with John the Baptist and the inquisition of the religious establishment. It introduces the first of many question-and-answer times with the Jewish leadership.

1:19–28

THE WITNESS OF JOHN THE BAPTIST

There were rumors that John was the Messiah himself. That's why it was essential to these religious leaders to explore his identity. John was baptizing and ministering to the people, so these men were justified in their need to confirm or deny his work as being from God.

Demystifying John

John records quite a few dialogues between Jesus and the Jewish religious leaders. While he often refers to these leaders simply as the Jews, they are made up of several groups. Understanding who they are can help us understand the significance of the questions they ask or the way that they respond.

- **Jews:** This term appears more than seventy times in the Gospel of John. In many cases it does not refer to the Jewish people as a whole (Jesus and His disciples were also Jews!), but to the religious leaders who opposed Jesus. That is why some translations render the word as "Jewish leaders" in certain contexts.
- **Priests:** The priests oversaw the temple worship. They were commissioned to determine whether or not a person's sacrifice was proper. They were in charge of all worship.
- **Levites:** The Levites, in general, were the ones in charge of caring for the temple, as well as keeping order in the worship. A certain family of the Levites—the descendants of Aaron, Moses' brother—served as priests.
- **Pharisees:** A group or sect of religious leaders within Judaism who devoted themselves to keeping the Law, especially its oral interpretations and applications.

In this Gospel, these names appear often, and the interplay between the groups is significant to the story. Though there are exceptions, typically the various religious groups were somewhat antagonistic toward each other. Yet, we see them work together in their opposition to Jesus.

When the priests and Levites ask John the Baptist who he is, he knows what they are really asking. So he responds immediately that he is not the Christ (1:20).

The inquiry as to whether he is the Old Testament prophet Elijah (1:21) relates to a prophecy in Malachi 3:1 and 4:1–6, of the coming day in which the enemy of Israel would be destroyed by God. Before this great day of the Lord, God said that Elijah would come and restore the hearts of the people. John assures them he is not the Old Testament prophet.

The next question, whether John is "the Prophet" (1:21 NIV), may refer to the "prophet like [Moses]" of Deuteronomy 18:15 (NIV). Again John answers, "No." When asked for his identity, John gives them a significant description from Isaiah 40:3: "the voice of one calling in the desert, 'Make straight the way for the Lord'" (1:23 NIV). He is saying that he is the fulfillment of this prophecy. God had called him to prepare the hearts of Israel for the coming of the Messiah:

1) By calling people to repentance
2) By baptizing those who repented

Critical Observation

Throughout history, before a great move of God, the people were to consecrate themselves (cleansing and setting themselves apart from sin) so they would be prepared. For John the Baptist, the cleansing was accomplished through repentance. The setting apart was accomplished through baptism.

Those questioning John either did not understand his answer or did not believe him, for this next question shows little regard for the powerful answer he has just given. The delegation begins a second line of questioning concerning the authority under which John practices his baptisms (1:24–25). Baptizing was not the role of just anyone.

John's answer to this question is important (1:26). John's water baptism is less significant than the baptism of the Spirit. John's baptism is not the act of salvation, but rather the preparation for it. Notice John states that the Messiah is already present.

John said he was not fit to untie Jesus' sandals (1:27). The household servant who untied someone's sandals was the lowest of the lowest slave. So John is saying that he was not even good enough to be the lowest servant to this man.

The Bethany most commonly mentioned in the Gospels lies a short distance southeast of Jerusalem, on the road to Jericho. The Bethany mentioned here (1:28) is a region located on the other side of the Jordan.

1:29–34

THE SECOND WITNESS OF JOHN THE BAPTIST

This section includes John's second testimony—the witness that Jesus is the Son of God.

Jesus comes on the scene the day after John is questioned by the religious leaders (1:29). If we were to harmonize this chronology with the synoptic Gospels (Matthew, Mark, Luke), Jesus would probably be coming back from the wilderness after being tempted. John has already baptized Jesus, and so he has already had one encounter with Him.

John makes the mighty declaration that Jesus is "the Lamb of God, who takes away the sin of the world!" (1:29 NIV). John's original hearers would have taken this phrase as a reference to the prophecy of Isaiah. Isaiah 53:4–9 describes the Messiah who would sacrifice Himself willingly, like a lamb at slaughter.

Critical Observation

John uses the singular form of the word *sin* rather than the plural. He's talking about the root of sin as a whole, not just the individual sins committed one at a time. By taking care of the root of sin universally, he then takes care of the fruit of sin, or individual sins.

John the Baptist continues his description of Jesus by tying together a previous sermon that he preached about the coming Messiah (1:30). John had already preached that the Messiah would be greater because the Messiah existed before John. In that first-century culture, the older person had more status. To acquire age was to acquire wisdom, which was the prize of life. John identifies Jesus as the Messiah, but John is the older man of the two. Yet Jesus existed before John—He existed as God.

Demystifying John

John's Gospel is noted for its irony. People miss the obvious point of conversations with Jesus. Words are used with ironic double meanings. In John the Baptist's case, he presents Jesus as the one who existed before John, even though Jesus is younger than John. These kinds of twists run throughout the Gospel.

John describes his role in preparing the way for Jesus. He admits that he did not at first recognize Him (1:31). It is not that he did not know Jesus at all, but rather, he could not come to the full realization of Jesus' messiahship or His role on earth. Nevertheless, John's role was to baptize so that Israel might be ready for the coming of the Messiah—to call the Israelites back to God so that they would be ready for the Messiah.

How did John know that Jesus was really the Messiah? He was given a sign by God, and that sign was revealed at Jesus' baptism—the Spirit came down like a dove and rested on Jesus (1:32–34).

1:35–51

THE FIRST DISCIPLES

This passage reveals five witnesses that testify to the nature and work of Jesus Christ.

- John the Baptist. John sees Jesus coming again and tells his disciples that He is the Lamb of God (1:36). The disciples do not need anything more than that designation for them to understand who Jesus is. They understand this to mean that this is the one who takes away the sins of the world. John's words were enough to convince them to follow Jesus (1:37).
- Andrew. Verse 40 reveals that Andrew is one of the two disciples described in verses 35–39. At the time that this Gospel was written, Peter was the more prominent disciple, so Andrew is identified as the brother of Peter. For the sake of the non-Jewish reader, the Gospel writer defines the word *rabbi* (1:38)—master or teacher. The word originally came from a root word meaning "a great man," but came to be used of a respected teacher. By calling Jesus "Rabbi" they are showing their respect to Him. In asking where He is staying, they imply a desire to, in essence, set up an appointment to learn from Him.

Demystifying John

Verse 39 mentions it being the tenth hour when Jesus spent time with Andrew and the other disciple. Both Romans and Jews tended to count hours from sunrise, so this would make it about four o'clock in the afternoon. Some scholars, however, think it was 10:00 a.m., counting ten hours from midnight.

Andrew's witness is immediate (1:41)—he has found the Messiah. Notice that John translates *Messiah* as "Christ" for his Greek readers. Both *Messiah* (Hebrew) and *Christ* (Greek) mean "anointed one" or God's chosen instrument. By the first century the term *Messiah* had come to refer specifically to the Savior from King David's line who would deliver God's people.

Andrew brings his brother Simon to meet Jesus, but Jesus knows him already, identifying him by name, then giving him the nickname *Cephas*, an Aramaic word that John translates into Greek for his readers as Peter (*petros*). Both *Cephas* and *Peter* mean a "rock" or "stone." Jesus is laying claim to Simon. He speaks about his role in Jesus' kingdom. Simon will be a key player for Jesus in the next three years of ministry.

- Philip. In verse 43, Jesus calls Philip. The focus of this Gospel is not the calling of the apostles, but the divine nature of Jesus, so these interactions are summaries. Philip was from the same region as Andrew and Peter. In turn, Philip told Nathanael.

Take It Home

Philip's response to Nathanael is the response that we should all have when we share Jesus with someone—come and see for yourself. We need to show the nature of who Jesus is and trust God for the results.

- Nathanael. Nathanael does not think that Jesus is the Messiah (1:46), so he meets Jesus with questions. When Jesus reveals what no ordinary human could have known (1:47–48), this supernatural insight moves Nathanael to confess two things:
  1) Jesus is the Son of God; the one to whom God gave His Spirit.
  2) Jesus is the King of Israel, therefore the ruler of Israel.

  Nathanael probably does not understand the full implications of his declaration (1:49). He believes that this was the anointed one who will sit on the throne of David. Nathanael sees Jesus as more than a great teacher; he sees Him as Israel's king to be worshiped.
- Jesus. In verses 50–51, Jesus makes a declaration about Himself. Jesus' description of angels ascending and descending on the Son of Man is a reference to Jacob's famous dream in Genesis 28. Jacob dreamed that a ladder appeared from heaven to earth with angels climbing up and down the ladder. In essence, Jesus was saying that He is that ladder, the connection between mankind and God. More than eighty times in this Gospel, Jesus refers to Himself as the Son of Man as He does here (1:51).

Critical Observation

Verse 51 begins with the words, "I tell you the truth" (NIV), or as some translations say, "Verily, verily." In the Greek, it is the word *amen* repeated twice. This is a word that carries the idea of an absolute and binding truth that is not to be contradicted. This is why we often finish our prayers with the same word. Jesus begins statements this same way at least twenty-five times in the book of John.

JOHN 2:1–25

THE PUBLIC MINISTRY OF JESUS

The First Sign 2:1–11
Scriptural Faith vs. Superficial Faith 2:12–25

Setting Up the Section

Chapter 1 focused on the words of testimony about Jesus. Now Jesus' actual works witness to the truth that He is the Messiah.

- **Seven miracles—all of which show the glory of God dwelling in Jesus' body**
- **Seven "I Am" statements—which are Jesus' declaration of Himself**
- **Four interviews—in which Jesus discusses with people about Himself**
- **Various discourses—in which Jesus explains the gospel to individuals**

All of this is given to provide a testimony that Jesus Christ is the self-revelation of God.

2:1–11

THE FIRST SIGN

The miracle of Jesus changing the water to wine in this section is the first of seven signs that John offers as proof of Jesus' identity as the Son of God.

Verse 1 begins on the third day of Jesus' journey. This verse draws our attention back to John 1:43, in which Jesus is making His way to Galilee. The idea is that it probably took two days to get to Galilee, and on the day after He arrives, He goes to a wedding.

Mary, Jesus' mother, was invited to this wedding. Jesus probably arrives with His disciples, and they are allowed to attend as well.

Critical Observation

Weddings in first-century Judea were big affairs. Generally they lasted about a week, even longer if the family was wealthy. Every night there was a party, and every night they would parade the couple around town in their wedding clothes. Usually, in the middle of the week, the couple would actually have the ceremony and then spend the rest of the week with the family before they could be alone.

A wedding was an important part of life, for it was the time when the family members of the groom would establish themselves by the type of party that they would throw. If people had a bad time at the wedding—if they did not get enough food to eat or wine to drink—it would reflect poorly on the family. Poorly enough for even the bride's family to think, *What kind of family did we just release our daughter into?*

Running out of wine was a critical situation (2:3) at a first-century wedding. Notice that Mary alerts Jesus to the problem. This might mean that the family was related to Mary, so she was "in the know" on a problem like this.

Demystifying John

Some have claimed that the wine in Jesus' day was not fermented, but there is no evidence to support that claim. All wine in that day became fermented by nature of the fact that there was no refrigeration in an intense climate. You could not stop the fermenting process. Yet wine was often diluted with water and used as a purifying agent, since water was often contaminated and unhealthy to drink. The scriptures caution against drinking to the point of being drunk.

Jesus' nature is revealed in His interaction with His mother (2:3–4). His response that His time has not come appears harsh, but it is not. Jesus also calls His mother "woman" (2:4 NIV). In that day this was the equivalent of saying "lady", or "dear lady." It was a respectful term, yet a distant term. It is a word that one would use to refer to someone who is not a relative, but yet is close and deserves respect.

Many believe that Joseph was dead by this point in Jesus' life. This seems to be supported by the fact that he is not mentioned after Jesus' childhood and the fact that Jesus commends Mary into John's care at his death. If Joseph had already passed away, Jesus, as the firstborn, would be responsible for His mother. This lends some insight into why she would come to Jesus with this problem. Mary, knowing who Jesus is, understands that He will take care of the problem in His time, so she instructs the servants to obey Him (2:5).

Stone water pots were used for the custom of purification (2:6). The law required several types of cleansing, including the cleansing of the hands and the feet before a meal. That is probably what these pots were used for.

Jesus wants the water pots full of water, which is no small task. They will hold, when He is done, 180 to 240 gallons of wine. Filling the water pots required significant effort going to the well and back.

In the first century, the headwaiter was something of a party coordinator. This was necessary because the entire town showed up for a wedding. The servants testified to this particular headwaiter that they have indeed put water into the pots. Then he verifies the quality of wine in the same pots (2:10).

What is the significance of this miracle? John tells us it reveals Jesus' glory. Remember that the purpose of the Gospel of John is to show that Jesus is the self-revelation of God. What Jesus does in the miracle is to display the glory of God in Himself. Note that it is the disciples whose faith is strengthened by seeing this miracle (2:11).

Take It Home

The disciples believed by faith in chapter 1, and then they saw the truth for themselves in chapter 2.

That is the process that we all go through. We all start by faith, without much knowledge. All we know is that at one point we were blind and now we see. We then spend the rest of our spiritual journey seeing Jesus for who He really is and having our faith strengthened as we grow in knowledge and understanding of Him.

2:12–25

SCRIPTURAL FAITH VS. SUPERFICIAL FAITH

In this section, John contrasts the faith of the disciples with the lack of faith of the Jewish leaders and the shallow faith of the crowds. This contrast provides a theological foundation to help us understand the rest of the Gospel.

Critical Observation

There are seven miracles, or signs, that Jesus performs between John 2 and John 11 that show His power and identity.

1. Changing water into wine (2:1–11)
2. Official's son healed (4:43–54)
3. Disabled man healed by the pool (5:1–15)
4. Feeding five thousand men plus women and children (6:1–15)
5. Walking on the water (6:16–21)
6. Healing a man born blind (9:1–12)
7. Lazarus raised after death (11:1–44)

Verse 12 offers the detail that Jesus is going to Capernaum. He will quite often return to this base of operation throughout His ministry in Galilee.

Verse 13 begins the account of Jesus in the temple during the Passover. This was a time set aside for the Jewish nation to remember the deliverance from Egypt that God provided its ancestors (Exodus 12). In this situation it seems that the temple has been turned into a place for merchandising. However, this kind of merchandising was tied into the sacrificial system. Typically the Levites offered an opportunity for worshipers who had traveled to Jerusalem to buy their animals for sacrificing right there at the temple. The money changers were there to convert foreign currency into the currency of the temple so that traveling worshipers could give the proper offering (2:14). This service was intended to be convenient for the worshipers so that they could be free to celebrate and worship. Unfortunately, this temple business took over the courtyard. They all lost the focus of the Passover in their attempt to consolidate and streamline. It is this loss of focus that Jesus rails against. Why does He make a whip (2:15)? Because He has to move sheep out of the temple, and the whip is the best tool to move them quickly.

Note the responses of the people to Jesus' actions. The disciples' minds go to Psalm 69:9 (2:17), a psalm in which David was hounded unjustly because of his love for the temple. The disciples are progressively connecting Jesus with the scriptures. The Jews (and keep in mind that John typically uses this term to refer to Jesus' Jewish opposition), on the other hand, challenged Jesus (2:18) to show them His credentials of authority to create such an uproar. Unfortunately, they missed the obvious—Jesus Himself is the sign of God, not simply the miracles He performs.

Jesus' response refers to tearing down the temple (2:19). There are a couple of Greek words for "temple." One word usually refers to the temple grounds or larger courtyard area (*hieron*) while the other refers to the temple building itself (*naos*). Jesus uses the latter here. This makes an important connection because Jesus is the place God is now dwelling on earth. The religious leaders miss the point of Jesus' comment (2:20–21).

The essence of verses 23–25 is that there are others who believed in the name of Jesus on the basis of His signs, "but Jesus would not *entrust* himself to them" (1:24 NIV, emphasis added). When the text says that He does not entrust Himself, the idea is that He does not connect Himself to these people like He does the disciples because He knows their hearts.

JOHN 3:1–36

A MEETING AT NIGHT

Nicodemus	3:1–21
The Final Witness of John the Baptist	3:22–36

Setting Up the Section

This passage of scripture includes some of the most popular verses in the Christian world. John 3 is the most quoted chapter from the New Testament, and holds within it one of the first verses ever memorized by many American Sunday school children, John 3:16.

This text is popular not only because it sets forth for us the great love of God for humanity, but also because it lays out, in very direct terms, the gospel message. Therefore, it is a treasured chapter in the scriptures for its concise teaching of the nature of humanity, the need for regeneration, and the nature of the Messiah and His great love and work for humanity. We find here a very clear presentation of the gospel and the essentials of salvation and faith.

3:1–21

NICODEMUS

We are told two things about Nicodemus (3:1):

1) He is a Pharisee, a Jewish sect devoted to keeping the Law of Moses.
2) He is a ruler of the Jews, a member of the seventy-member Jewish ruling council called the Sanhedrin.

Nicodemus' first statement (3:2) reveals who he and others think that Jesus is:

- He is from God.
- He is a teacher.
- God is with Jesus on the basis of the signs that He has performed.

His statement also implies a question: Is there more that I should know about who you are?

Jesus begins His reply in verse 3 with the famous, "Verily, verily" (KJV), or the more modern, "I tell you the truth" (NIV). He does this as well in verses 5 and 11. In Greek, the word used here is *amen*, which means "this is the binding truth."

Basically, Jesus says Nicodemus will be unable to understand who He is and the true nature of His life unless he is radically transformed—born again (3:3).

When Nicodemus fails to understand, he responds to the idea of rebirth literally (3:4). Nicodemus has a physical understanding of the kingdom of God rather than a spiritual one. Notice in verse 3, Jesus says that one cannot see (perceive) the kingdom of God unless he is born again, and in verse 5, Jesus says that one cannot enter (experience) the kingdom of God unless he is born of water and Spirit.

What does this mean to be born of water and Spirit? In order to understand we must look from Nicodemus's point of view. While John the Baptist had baptized in water to prepare for redemption, Christian baptism (as a symbol of redemption through Christ) is not a custom yet. Jesus chastises Nicodemus for not understanding (3:10), so Jesus' reference is to something Nicodemus would have heard. In this case it is an Old Testament passage that Nicodemus would be very familiar with—Ezekiel 36, specifically verses 25-27.

In this passage, Ezekiel describes what needs to happen in order for Israel to partake of the kingdom of God—to be washed clean in the water of God and to have God's Spirit placed within. Jesus is telling Nicodemus that he needs to have the birth of water and Spirit—the same birth mentioned in Ezekiel 36. Nicodemus needs to understand that Jesus is not talking about a physical rebirth, but a spiritual one (3:6).

Demystifying John

Jesus' illustration of the wind in verse 8 means, in essence, you must have faith, then understanding will come. Even if you do not know what causes the wind, it does not stop you from believing in it. (Remember this is before our contemporary understanding of meteorology, so there was not the understanding of wind and weather that we have today.)

Jesus' point to Nicodemus in verse 10 is that the truth has been in the scriptures all along. Yet Nicodemus may have spent his life teaching that adherence to the Law of God was the condition to enter the kingdom of God. That was certainly the impression given by the Pharisees of his day.

Nicodemus's failure is a lack of wisdom, not of explanation. It is a failure to believe (3:11–12). Jesus is the one who came from heaven as the revelation of God (3:13). Jesus is God explained. What Nicodemus needs to do if he is going to understand these things is come to grips with Jesus Christ.

The event Jesus refers to in the life of Moses is recorded in Numbers 21:4–9 (3:14–15). A bronze snake on a pole was the means God used to give life to the children of Israel when they were bitten in a plague of snakes. If they looked to the serpent Moses held high, they survived the plague. In the same way, Jesus must be lifted up—on the cross. There He will die and take on humanity's punishment for its sins. Nicodemus is being challenged to turn to Jesus for new birth, just as the ancient Israelites were commanded to turn to the bronze snake for new life.

The word *believe* as used here by Jesus (3:15) means to place trust and faith in something. In this context, it means that your entire relationship with God is resting on this one thing, Jesus Christ.

Verses 16–21 are Jesus' instructions to Nicodemus, explaining in detail the nature of the Messiah so that Nicodemus could understand who the object of his faith should be. In the famous John 3:16, Jesus is explaining to Nicodemus the true nature of God toward the world, the fact that God is love, and that His love extends past Israel to all the people in the world.

Critical Observation

To someone who believed that the world was pagan and deserving of God's judgment, Jesus' proposal that God loves the whole world would have been a surprising thought. Jesus is saying that God did not choose the Jews so that by nature of Judaism they would be saved. God chose the Jews so that through that race the Messiah would come and save people all over the world, Jews included. This was a revolutionary thought for a first-century Jewish Pharisee to take in.

The traditional translation "begotten" used in some versions of John 3:16, is probably better translated as "one of a kind" or "unique." Jesus is the one who is from God, and therefore shares the nature of God. His glory is not just a part of God; He shares in the full nature of God.

There are two types of believing. One type is to mentally understand something. The other type is a belief in something so much that you place all of your hope and trust in that which you believe. Here Jesus means the latter, that all who place their faith in the work of Jesus on the cross will have eternal life.

Jesus next deals with judgment. As a Pharisee, Nicodemus believes that God will pour out His wrath on the world and restore Israel to her position of glory. Jesus' mission is one of salvation, not judgment (3:17). At first this seems a contradiction to verses like John 9:39, in which Jesus pronounces His judgment. But these are different kinds of judgment. The type of judgment that Jesus talks about in 9:39 is the final judgment in which the wicked will be cast away forever, and the righteous will be established in the kingdom of God. Jesus did not come the first time for that judgment. That will be part of His second coming. And that is the kind of judgment He mentions in verse 18.

When He says those who do not believe are judged already (3:18), He is saying that they stood condemned before God prior to Christ, and now they just add to their judgment by rejecting Christ.

Also John doesn't only write that judgment comes from not believing in Jesus, but from not believing in His *name* (3:18). The name of someone in first-century Judaism represented his or her character or nature. To not believe in the name of Jesus is to deny His character or nature.

Verses 19–21 provide the basis for the judgment of which Jesus spoke. This judgment is described in metaphorical terms—light and darkness. The light that enters the world is the coming of God in the person of Jesus Christ. That humanity loved darkness means that humanity preferred to live without the knowledge of God. Why? Because of a fundamentally evil nature.

Notice the contrast in verse 21. The ones who practice the truth actually walk toward the light with no fear at all. *Practicing the truth* comes from a Jewish phrase that means to act faithfully. It is the idea of living out the very standard of God.

Jesus is explaining that those who have been born again do not run away from the accountability of the light. They run toward it. There are two contrasts that Jesus is pointing out about the nature of man in these verses.

1) The person who loves the darkness practices evil and the one who loves the light practices righteousness.
2) The one who loves the darkness shuns the light out of fear of exposure, shame, and conviction; and the one who loves the light comes to the light, not on the merit of his works, but on the works that God has done through him.

Take It Home

The truths given to Nicodemus are important for each of us:

1) A person needs to be born again if he is to have eternal life. A well-lived life is not good enough.
2) Salvation happens when a person looks to the cross of Jesus Christ.
3) A person will never understand God, the things of God, or even the scriptures unless he comes to grips with Jesus Christ first.

Therefore it's no use to only use human logic and human wisdom to convince someone that God exists. We must offer the testimony of Jesus.

3:22–36

THE FINAL WITNESS OF JOHN THE BAPTIST

This section includes more testimony from John the Baptist, confirming for us that Jesus is God and that He is the only way to salvation.

Jesus and His disciples come into Judea (3:22), yet if we look back to the preceding chapter, it's clear that they were already in Jerusalem, which is in Judea. Probably then, they went into the outlying areas of Judea where John the Baptist is also ministering (3:23).

Jesus is doing two things:

1) Spending time with His disciples
2) Baptizing or at least overseeing the baptisms (4:1–2)

The mention of John the Baptist gives us a time frame—he is not yet in prison (3:24; Matthew 14:3–5). This means that this account happens early in the ministry of Jesus. All the other Gospels go from the temptation of Jesus to the imprisonment of John, skipping this account. But this Gospel writer wants us to see the overlap of the ministries.

A discussion is brewing on the part of John's disciples and a Jew or a group of Jews (3:25). (Some early manuscripts have the word *Jew* in the plural, and others refer to one Jewish person.) The issue of this discussion is Jewish purification, the custom of ritual cleansing. In short, any time a person became ceremonially unclean for any reason—such as sickness or making contact with something unclean—that person was to cleanse with water. This act symbolized purity in devotion to God, and the cleansing of all defilement from the world. In some cases, the person just cleaned a part of the body, and in other cases he or she washed entirely.

This topic takes on added meaning when you put it in the context of a key component of John the Baptist's ministry—baptism with water. Somewhere in the discussion, the disciples of John are alerted to the fact that Jesus is also baptizing people—many people. So they alert John (3:26).

John's response makes the point that it is the sovereign hand of God that makes ministry happen. If people come, it is because God brought them, and if people go to Jesus it is because God sent them to Him. John's disciples are taking too much credit for what God does.

Critical Observation

In all the Gospels, John the Baptist is presented as a man who is very clear about his role in God's kingdom (3:27). His own testimony about Jesus can be found in John 1:29–31 (also see Matthew 3:11–15). In verse 29, John explains his role as a best man in a wedding. Being best man gives him no rights to the bride. The wedding doesn't center around him. His role as best man is to make sure the wedding happens smoothly and the bride is safely placed into the hand of the groom.

John the Baptist feels joy and excitement as he sees the bride (the believers in Christ) being delivered into the hands of the bridegroom (Jesus). Thus, his perspective is that of the two of them, only Jesus should become greater (3:30).

John the Baptist offers five reasons that Jesus must gain emphasis and he must step back:

1) Jesus came from heaven, and therefore is above everyone on the earth (3:31).
2) Jesus speaks from a firsthand knowledge of the kingdom of God (3:32).
3) Jesus says and does all that God would say and do on earth because He is God (3:33).
4) Jesus speaks the words of God (3:34).
5) Jesus is the sovereign ruler of the world and all that is in it (3:35).

John's point to his disciples is that Jesus is God the Father revealed; therefore, the central religious question is, who is the object of your faith (3:36)? If Jesus is rejected as the focus of a person's faith, then that person has to face the consequences of sin—the eternal wrath of God. This wrath does not imply a sudden burst of anger but simply the reaction of God's righteousness to humanity's unrighteousness.

JOHN 4: 1–54

A MEETING BY THE WELL

The Woman at the Well	4:1–26
The Harvest	4:27–42
Knowing Christ	4:43–54

Setting Up the Section

The Gospel writer John is continuing to show us that Jesus is the revelation of God the Father, and in this text, he uses Christ's conversation with a Samaritan woman.

4:1–26

THE WOMAN AT THE WELL

Verse 1 connects us to the previous chapter, in which we are told that more people are coming to Jesus and His disciples to be baptized than to John the Baptist for baptism. This piques the interest of the Pharisees who consistently opposes Jesus (4:1–2). As Jesus becomes aware of the Pharisees' interest, He moves out of Judea to avoid an untimely confrontation.

John writes that Jesus has to pass through Samaria (4:4). On a map of Israel, you find Judea on the bottom and Galilee on the top. Sandwiched in between is Samaria. The Jews and the Samaritans had an extreme prejudice toward each other, dating back as far as 450 BC. They only had dealings as a last resort, and, if time and resources allowed, would probably go out of their way to minimize contact with each other. Jesus' purpose in going through the region has to do with His mission—it is essential to meeting the woman who would be at the well.

Demystifying John

There were several key historical events that contributed to the animosity between the Jews and the Samaritans.

- In 720 BC, Assyria took over the northern kingdom and replaced most of the Jews with people from other lands. The nationalities mingled and the Samaritan people were born. The Jews were very particular about intermarrying and, therefore, looked down on the Samaritans who even in their first generation were only half-Jewish.
- In 450 BC, when Jerusalem was being rebuilt, the Samaritans wanted to help, but the Jews refused to let them. This contributed to the animosity.
- Manasseh, a Jewish man (not the king by the same name), built a temple on Mt. Gerizim because that is the place that Moses proclaimed the blessings of the covenant to the people. The Samaritans worshiped at this temple, which greatly offended the Jews who worshiped in Jerusalem.
- In addition, the Samaritans only followed the first five books of the Old Testament and rejected the rest of the Old Testament scriptures.

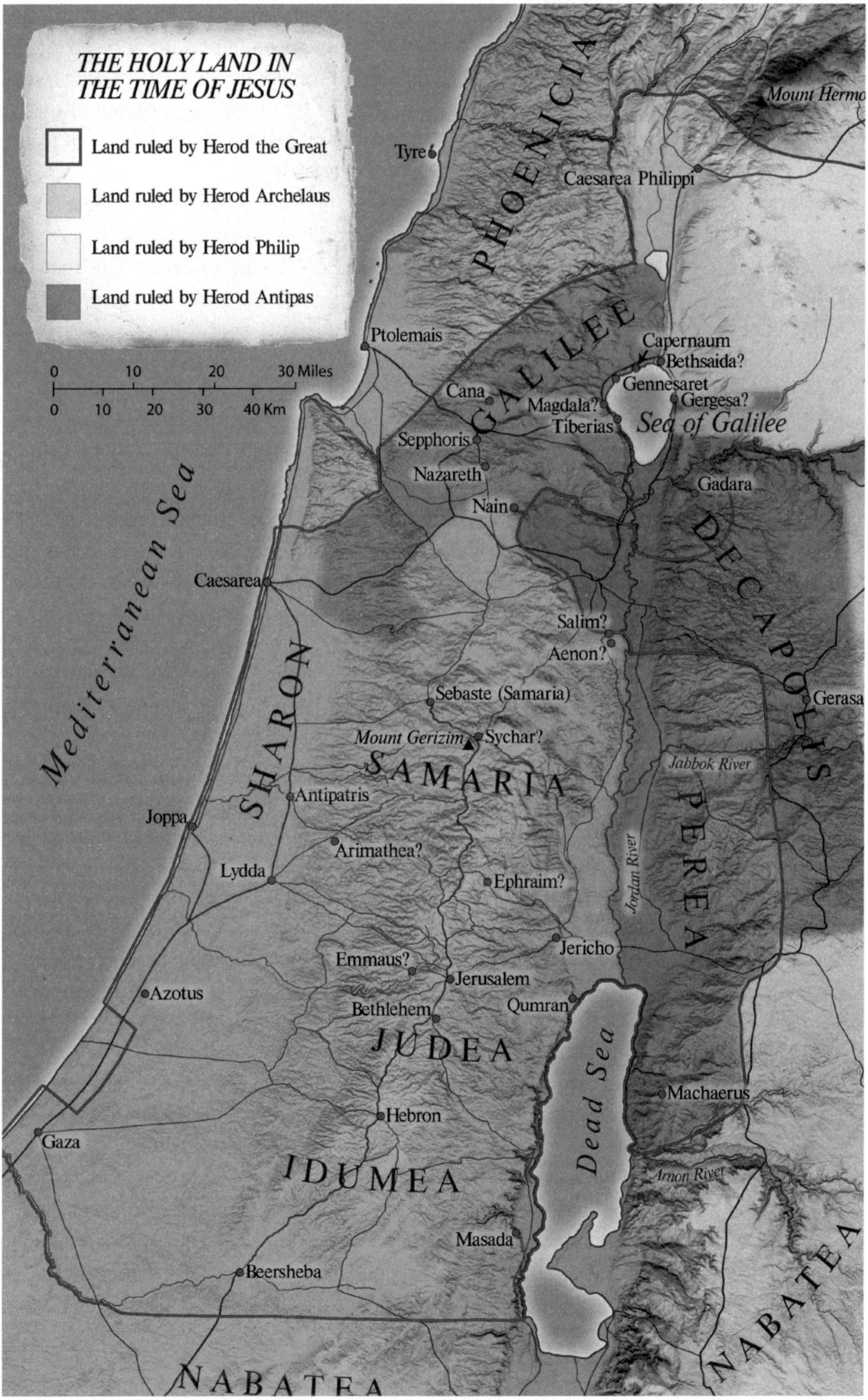
THE HOLY LAND IN
THE TIME OF JESUS
Land ruled by Herod the Great
Land ruled by Herod Archelaus
Land ruled by Herod Philip
Land ruled by Herod Antipas
0 10 20 30 Miles
0 10 20 30 40 Km
Mediterranean Sea
PHOENICIA
Tyre
Mount Hermo
Caesarea Philippi
GALILEE
Ptolemais
Capernaum
Bethsaida?
Gennesaret
Gergesa?
Cana
Magdala?
Tiberias
Sea of Galilee
Sepphoris
Nazareth
Gadara
Nain
DECAPOLIS
Caesarea
Salim?
Aenon?
SHARON
Sebaste (Samaria)
Gerasa
Mount Gerizim
Sychar?
SAMARIA
Jabbok River
Antipatris
Joppa
PEREA
Arimathea?
Jordan River
Lydda
Ephraim?
Jericho
Emmaus?
Jerusalem
Azotus
Qumran
Bethlehem
JUDEA
Dead Sea
Machaerus
Hebron
Gaza
IDUMEA
Arnon River
Masada
Beersheba
NABATEA
NABATEA

The property on which Jesus stops is not only significant because it had a well; it also had historical significance. It is a piece of property that Jacob, an important ancestor of the Jewish nation (1 Kings 18:31), bought and then gave to his son, Joseph (4:5–6). The Samaritans felt that they had the same heritage as the Jews (who reject them), so they would feel as connected to this property and its history as the Jews would. Jesus stops at the well at the sixth hour, which probably means about 12 noon (4:6; see 1:39).

The fact that the Bible mentions only this woman at the well is a noteworthy detail (4:7). Going to the well was typically a task women did as a group.

Jesus' request for a drink from her is a break in tradition for several reasons. In that day and time,

- Men did not talk with women in public.
- Rabbis did not talk to women.
- Jews did not talk with Samaritans (the woman even gave voice to this custom [4:9]).

In John's added explanation, the phrase "have no dealings with" (4:9 NASB) meant that Jews would never even touch a utensil of a Samaritan, for in doing so they would become unclean.

With his next statement, Jesus turns the tables (4:10). At the beginning of this conversation Jesus is thirsty, and the woman has the source to quench His thirst. Now Jesus turns it to the fact that she is thirsty, and He has the source to quench her thirst. The Greek words translated "living water" refer to a well that is fed by an underground spring; therefore it always produces fresh water.

The woman first responds with what is obvious to her—Jesus doesn't have anything with which to draw the water. To her this is foolishness (4:11–12). She, like Nicodemus in chapter 3, is missing a spiritual truth and responding to a physical impossibility (3:4).

Jesus draws a contrast between earthly water and spiritual water. The word "well" (4:14 NASB) again refers to a spring-fed well with a continual source.

It would seem from the woman's response that she is motivated by convenience (4:15). Would living water keep her from having to walk out to the well each day?

Jesus then starts to deal with her heart, asking questions that will delve into her lifestyle and reveal His power (4:16–19).

The woman's question about where people should worship seems to be on a different track from the conversation (4:20). The Samaritans worshiped on Mt. Gerizim, and the Jews worshiped in Jerusalem. Jesus responds to her question with three truths (4:21–24):

1) He states that worship as she understands it will be rendered obsolete.
2) He states that salvation springs forth out of Judaism. Since the Jews include the writings of the prophets, they have all the promises there—including those of the Messiah.
3) He explains in detail the nature of true worship. The point of this statement (4:23–24) is that true worship is not based on location but on the condition of the worshiper's heart.

When the woman refers to the Messiah—the first reference in John's Gospel—Jesus actually declares Himself to be that Messiah (4:26). It is a significant twist that the first person Jesus declares His messiahship to is a Samaritan, a woman, and a social outcast.

4:27–42

THE HARVEST

The way the Greek manuscript is worded at the beginning of 4:27 makes the point that the disciples walked into the conversation as Jesus is declaring Himself to be the Messiah (4:26). Knowing that makes it surprising that they choose to comment on Jesus' talking with a woman.

In some translations, verse 28 says that when the woman runs to town to spread the news, she goes first to the men. If so, this would be because women in this culture could not hold any position of authority. The men, who had more power within that society, could evaluate and determine if Jesus was the Messiah.

The misunderstanding that occurs between Jesus and the disciples regarding food is that same misunderstanding that occurs throughout the Gospel of John—the things of the earth versus the things of heaven (4:31–33). In verse 34, Jesus moves the disciples from the physical world to the spiritual world by describing His devotion to the will of God and how that devotion is what drives Him in all that He does.

Demystifying John

The exact four months that Jesus refers to in verse 35 is not clear, but it is clear that the time for the harvest of souls is at hand. In verse 36, Jesus is continuing the metaphor of the harvest time. In that day, when it was harvest time, the man who sowed the seed would hire reapers. It was the reaper's job to harvest the fruit. When a reaper completed his section, he was paid. Jesus is saying that we do not need to wait for the spiritual harvest time—it is here!

In verse 37, Jesus gives a key principle in understanding the work of God: In the work of the kingdom, there will be some who sow and others who reap, and the work of God is dependent upon each of these factors. Then, in verse 38, Jesus gives the disciples their commission. This will be the first of many times that Jesus explains to the disciples their purpose. Jesus tells them that they will be reaping a crop they have not worked for. In a specific sense, they have done nothing in Samaria, but more generally, they are building on the works of others—Moses, John the Baptist, and obviously, Jesus.

It is significant that the townspeople believe the word of a woman—a woman who is probably a social outcast (4:39–42). Yet it is equally significant that as the people spend time with Jesus, they recognize the truth of who He is in a way that His own townspeople hadn't (4:41–42).

4:43–54

KNOWING CHRIST

Jesus is finishing the trip He started at the beginning of this chapter (4:43; see 4:3). He was leaving Judea because it is not time for the confrontation to begin there between the Pharisees and Himself. While verse 44 can seem out of context, it foreshadows the fact that Jesus is headed home, specifically to the site of His first miracle, and rejection is waiting there.

At first it seems that the Galileans believe in Jesus (4:45), but their belief was based on the miracles that Jesus does rather than who Jesus is. Then the royal official approaches Jesus and begs Him to come and heal his son (4:46–47). If you compare the request of the centurion in Matthew 8:5–13 to this man's request, you can see the difference between a request based on a knowledge of who Jesus is and one that is not. The centurion based his request on Jesus' authority and the authority of God. This official seems to only know Jesus' reputation as a miracle-worker.

When Jesus responds with somewhat of a rebuke in verse 48, He is responding to the fact that these people are looking for Jesus to do His tricks, His signs and wonders. They will not believe in Him based upon His Word. Look at the contrast in verse 42—the Samaritans believed based upon His Word.

In verse 49, the royal official reveals the limitations he believes Jesus faces. He asks Jesus to come before his child dies because he believes that after death there is nothing Jesus can do. Yet when Jesus declares the child healed (without being present with the child), the man believes.

The synchronized details that John includes—the child being healed at the moment Jesus spoke—reveals that it was the word of Jesus that healed the boy. Jesus did not have to conjure up spirits, make a potion, or speak a magic spell. Jesus' very words were the power to save this boy. This man suddenly does not look at the miracle, but at Jesus, and believes. The miracle serves as a vehicle to show that Jesus is the revelation of God.

This healing is the second of the seven signs that John offers in this section as proof of Jesus' identity as the Son of God.

Take It Home

The account of the woman at the well teaches us that God uses many different people, despite our prejudices, and many different means to prepare the hearts of others. It is our job to be faithful to the call and the task that He has for us. The good news is for everyone.

The account of the royal official leaves us asking, who do we see Jesus as? Is our faith placed in what He can do for us (some kind of divine room service), or in whom we believe Him to be? This Gospel writer wants us to see the Man behind the miracle, the Savior of the world. Have we come to grips with Him, as these people did?

JOHN 5:1–47

THE POSITION OF JESUS

The Authority of Jesus 5:1–15
Jesus Claims to Be God 5:16–24
The Power and Authority of Jesus 5:25–29
The Witnesses of Jesus' Deity 5:30–47

Setting Up the Section

The struggle that we experience individually as we seek to surrender ourselves to God's will is similar to what plagued Jesus' relationship with the religious leaders of His day. As He exercised His authority as God, the religious leaders became increasingly angry—not wanting to believe Him to be God or to have authority over them—and desired to kill Him. They did not want a new leader to work outside of their system. They didn't want a new way of doing things. Therefore, when Jesus required them to submit to Him, they rejected Him. This conflict became the source of the anger that built in the Pharisees and caused them to seek to kill Jesus.

5:1–15

THE AUTHORITY OF JESUS

In the previous chapter, Jesus traveled from the southern region, Judea, northward to Galilee. Here He travels south again, back down to Jerusalem.

John does not mention the particular feast that brings Jesus back to Jerusalem (5:1), but it is important to note that Jesus went to these festivals, such as Passover. The festivals were given by God to the Jews to celebrate the various aspects of God's work on behalf of Israel. They were required under the Jewish law.

Jerusalem was a city with a wall around it. There were multiple gates through which a person could enter the city, such as the Sheep Gate (5:2). As the name implies, it was the gate through which the shepherds brought their sheep in and out to graze. The pool near the gate had five entrances and was probably spring fed, which means that it would bubble up every time the fresh water came in. This bubbling is what the people would wait for, hoping to be healed.

Verse 4, in some translations, is marked with parentheses or an asterisk, or footnoted, or may not even appear. The verse, an explanation, does not appear in some of the oldest manuscripts of the New Testament that we have access to. It is probably a footnote added later to explain how the people of that day interpreted the bubbling up of the water.

When Jesus asks questions to open a dialogue with a man waiting to be healed (5:5–6), we learn about the man through his answers (5:7):

1) He has no friends there to assist him.
2) He is disabled in such a way that he can't move well.

With three simple commands Jesus heals the man (5:8–9): Get up, take up your bedding (probably a mat made of straw that could be rolled up), and walk. Notice that the man said nothing of record. He does not argue with Jesus; he just jumps up, rolls up his bed, and walks. Why? Because Jesus spoke with the ultimate authority of God.

At the end of verse 9, John offers what becomes a sticking point for the rest of Jesus' ministry—Jesus heals this man on the Sabbath.

Critical Observation

The Old Testament had forbidden work on the Sabbath. The rabbis divided work into thirty-nine classes, including picking something up and taking it from one place to another (unless it was an act of mercy, like moving a paralytic). Therefore, on the Sabbath, a Jew had to be very careful not to transgress any of these thirty-nine classes of work.

It's obvious from the response of the religious leaders that they have a greater concern for their rules than they do a miracle from God (5:10–13). This is because they could not fathom that anything good could come outside their laws. Their system was the system that the Messiah would come through, and anything outside of that system was surely evil.

Jesus' later words to the healed man make it appear as if this man's condition was a result of some sin (5:14). Jesus addresses the man's behavior. We get no further background explanation, but it is interesting to the note the man's response once Jesus confronts him (5:15).

This healing is the third of the seven signs that John offers in this section as proof of Jesus' identity as the Son of God.

5:16–24

JESUS CLAIMS TO BE GOD

When the healed man identifies Jesus as the man who has made him well, the conflict is set between Jesus and the religious establishment (5:15–16). The core of this conflict was who had the authority—Jesus the Messiah, or the Pharisees, the interpreters of the Jewish religious system.

Note two things in Jesus' initial response to the religious leaders (5:17):

1) God does not stop working on the Sabbath, so Jesus won't. The emphasis of the Sabbath when God established it (Genesis 2:1–3) was not that God stopped working all together. He rested from the work of creation.
2) Jesus is claiming an exclusive relationship with God ("My Father" [NIV]).

Both elements of Jesus' response declare that He is God. Jesus did not bow to the Pharisees authority; He establishes His authority and calls for them to submit to Him. And they understand His meaning, thus begin to plot murder (5:18).

Jesus begins His reply in verse 19 with the famous "Verily, verily" (KJV), or the more modern, "I tell you the truth" (NIV). He does this as well in verses 24–25. In Greek, the word used is *amen*, which means "this is the binding truth." Then Jesus goes on to explain emphatically that He is God because He:

- Implements God's will (5:19–20)
- Exhibits God's power (5:21)
- Judges with the same authority (5:22)
- Receives equal honor (5:23)

All these things together leave no doubt that Jesus claimed to be one with God. In verse 24, He lays down the gauntlet before the religious establishment—only those who believe in Him will escape judgment.

5:25–29

THE POWER AND AUTHORITY OF JESUS

Verses 25–29 expound upon Jesus' declaration in verses 21–22. He is the source of life, and if you reject that life, you will be judged by Him. This passage shows Jesus' power to raise the dead.

Jesus opens verse 25, affirming the truth of what He is about to say, and that what He is about to say will happen very soon. He is telling the Jewish leaders that they are at the precipice of the time when the dead will live—salvation.

Demystifying John

If we understand what *dead* means, then we can understand just what condition man is in before He is saved. A dead person is insensitive to life. Stick a pin in that person, and he or she will not feel it. In a spiritual sense, to be dead is to be insensitive to the things of God. It means that person has no desire to be a part of God, has no ability to ever get to God, and has no senses to react or respond to God. As far as any true spirituality, a person is unable to respond because he or she is a spiritual corpse.

Verse 26 tells us why the Son of God is able to give this life: Because the Son is life. Jesus also has been given the authority to execute judgment (5:27).

Notice that when Jesus is referred to as the giver of life in verse 25, He is called the Son of God. When Jesus is referred to as the judge of all of mankind, He is referred to as the Son of Man (5:27). This concept of the Son of Man is not a new one to the Pharisees. They knew from their study of the Old Testament that the Son of Man would be the judge of the earth, and would come to have authority over the earth.

Verses 28 and 29 describe a different kind of resurrection. At this judgment, there will be two groups of people there: those who are going to heaven and those that are going to hell. And the determination of where a person will be going is his or her works. This does not imply that salvation comes through works, but it is evidence that real faith is seen through works, because faith leads to good works.

5:30–47

THE WITNESSES OF JESUS' DEITY

Jesus just finished, in verse 29, His declaration that as God, He will be the judge of all mankind. Coming out of this statement, Jesus reiterates one of the key principles of this entire discourse, the key point His argument with the Jews is based upon: Jesus and the Father are one (5:30).

The idea behind verses 31–32 is that the tremendous burden of proving the claims of Jesus is not placed solely in His testimony but upon the testimonies of others. In this first-century culture, a testimony alone is no testimony. According to Deuteronomy 17:6 and 19:15, every testimony needed at least two or three witnesses to confirm that it was the truth.

In verses 33–39, Jesus offers four testimonies to confirm His deity:

1) John the Baptist pointed Jesus out to the Jewish religious leaders as the Messiah. He declared Jesus the Lamb of God (5:33; see 1:19–34). Jesus talks about John the Baptist in the past tense, so he is probably already in prison or perhaps already killed (Mark 6:17–29). The word that the Gospel writer uses for "light" in talking about the great preacher and prophet (5:35) does not mean that he was the source of light, but that he was a lamp that shed light.
2) Jesus' own work testifies of His deity (5:36). No one could do the miracles that Jesus did. Only God can do these miracles. Jesus says this in the context of healing a man who was lame for thirty-eight years (5:1-9).
3) God the Father testifies to the deity of Jesus Christ (5:37). God gave His witness at Jesus' baptism (Matthew 3:16–17). The way to hear the witness of God is to believe in the Son, and if you fail to believe in the Son, you do not receive the witness of the Father.
4) The scriptures certainly bear witness of the Messiah. Some translations of the Bible open verse 39 as a command for the Jewish leadership to search the scriptures. Others open verse 39 as an observation that these men do search the scriptures. With either interpretation the end result is the same—these men knew the scriptures but came to the wrong conclusion about who Jesus is.

In verses 40–44, Jesus explains Himself. The fact that He points out their error in not believing who He is has nothing to do with winning their approval. Since Jesus has God's approval, the fact that the religious leaders disapprove of Him is what condemns them.

There were others rising up in Jesus' day, claiming to be the Messiah (5:43–44). Some of them won a lot of recognition, even religious acclaim. Some fit more of the popular idea that the Messiah would come to fight a political battle rather than a spiritual one. The fact that the leaders don't recognize the real thing, from the scriptures they had based their lives on, is their condemnation (5:45–47). Some examples of the writings of Moses that point toward the Messiah are Genesis 3:15 (the descendant of Adam that will defeat the serpent), Numbers 24:17 (the star that will rise out of Israel, Jacob's descendants), and Deuteronomy 18:15–18 (the prophet that God will raise up).

JOHN 6:1–71

REVEALING HIMSELF

The Awesome Power of Jesus	6:1–15
The People of Glory	6:16–29
The Bread of Life	6:30–40
Rejection and Revelation	6:41–71

Setting Up the Section

Chapter 6 continues within the ministry of Jesus in Galilee, and it provides the same basic structure as chapter 5. In chapter 5 we see Jesus performing a miracle and using that miracle to proclaim His deity as Lord of the Sabbath. In chapter 6 we see Jesus performing a miracle and then using that miracle as a platform to proclaim His deity as the Bread of life.

6:1–15

THE AWESOME POWER OF JESUS

Chapter 6 begins with John referencing previous events before Jesus goes on His way (6:1). What does John mean when he says "after this" (NIV)? If you look at John 5:1, you will observe that Jesus went to Jerusalem, and it is there that He healed a man and had His first confrontation with the religious leaders. Then, if you look at 6:1, you will notice that He is crossing to the other side of the Sea of Galilee. Somewhere between verses 5:47 and 6:1 Jesus went to Galilee. Remember, the purpose of John is not to give a chronological history of Jesus' life, but rather to give us snapshots of the deity of Jesus Christ.

Of the many months spent in Galilee, John focuses on this particular account, which is in the later portion of Jesus' ministry in Galilee. Therefore, between verses 5:47 and 6:1 there is approximately six months to one year that has passed. For more of the Galilean ministry, read Matthew 4:12–15:20.

John 7:1 tells us why Jesus moved into Galilee—because the Jewish leaders in Judea wanted to kill Him. Because it is not time for Him to die, He avoids Judea and spends some time concentrating on Galilee.

Verse 2 introduces us to the multitudes that are pursuing Jesus—approximately fifteen thousand people. They are following Jesus because of His miraculous healings.

Jesus goes to the mountain (6:3) to be alone with the disciples and instruct them. If we compare this scripture to Mark 6, we discover that the disciples just returned from their first ministry assignment, and Jesus wants to debrief them from that experience.

Critical Observation

Verse 10 states that there were five thousand men. That count does not include women, children, and servants. If you add in a conservative guess of those groups left out, there could be at least fifteen thousand people, and some even estimate there were as many as twenty thousand.

Jesus poses the dilemma of feeding the crowds to Philip (6:5–6), who was from that area and would know most about the resources that were available. Of course verse 6 reveals that Jesus already knows what He intended to do. The denarius (6:7 NASB) used in Philip's calculations was equivalent to one day's wage.

The barley loaf that is part of the solution that Andrew offers is not equivalent to a contemporary loaf of bread. It would have been more like a muffin. That's why the boy had five. The fish were probably pickled fish that were spread on top of the cakes. This was a common meal in that day. The main part of the meal was the bread, and the fish served as a topping. This meal reveals to us that this boy is probably poor, since barley loaves were the meal of the poor at this time.

In the Greek there are two different words that some versions of the English Bible translate as "men." One word typically means mankind in general, and the other typically means men as a gender. Verse 10 first refers to people in general, but the count included in the verse is for actual men who were present.

In Mark's account of this story, Jesus asks that the people sit in groups of fifty and one hundred (Mark 6:39–40). Notice the dedication of the disciples in that they have no idea how Jesus will feed the people, yet they followed His directions in organizing them.

In the Jewish catechism, the children are taught that if you do not thank God for your food, it is equal to stealing from God, for food is a gift from God. Thus we see Jesus' prayer of thanks in verse 11. A typical Jewish thanks for a meal would have been something like this: Blessed are you, O Lord our God, King of the universe, who brings forth bread from the earth.

Jesus then bypasses the natural order of things, and transforms five muffins and two fish into thousands of portions. Verses 12–13 paint the picture of each disciple with a basket full of miraculous leftovers. Jesus uses the need of these people to teach the disciples a lesson—that He is greater than any need.

The people's response to the miracle (6:14) is a reference to Deuteronomy 18:15–18, the promise to bless the children of Israel with a prophet like Moses who will speak the words of God. These people believe that Jesus is that prophet.

The point that they failed to see was that Jesus wasn't going to be their king until they repented. If they had fully understood the passage in Deuteronomy, they would have realized that they should have fallen before Him in sorrow and repentance. But instead they are telling Jesus what He must do. The people fail to really listen to Jesus' words; they want Jesus on their own terms.

This miracle of feeding the crowd is the fourth of the seven signs that John offers in this section as proof of Jesus' identity as the Son of God.

Take it Home

Philip's reaction to Jesus' question likely mirrors what our reaction would have been in the same situation. When God tests us, our first instinct is to calculate the feasibility of a solution and try to determine ourselves if it will work or not. But God's solution is most often only seen by faith.

6:16–29

THE PEOPLE OF GLORY

In this passage, Jesus deals with the multitudes: those who want the theology of glory and not the theology of the cross. He has just miraculously fed close to fifteen thousand people then escapes before they forcefully claim Him as their king.

"Evening" in verse 16 (NIV) probably refers to late afternoon, just before sunset. The disciples had a five to seven-mile journey ahead of them to Capernaum.

The Sea of Galilee is six hundred feet below sea level, in a cup-like depression among the hills. When the sun sets, the air cools; and as the cooler air from the west rushes down over the hillside, the resulting wind churns the lake. Since the disciples are rowing toward Capernaum, they are heading into the wind; consequently, they would make little progress in the storm (6:18).

The disciples are about halfway across the lake by the time they see Jesus approaching (6:19). Other accounts of this story reveal that they think Jesus is a ghost.

Once they realized it is Jesus and He gets in the boat, they instantly reached Capernaum. The Gospel writer moves on without drawing any conclusions, but it is clear that the disciples have just witnessed two miracles (including the feeding of the large crowd) that reveal Jesus as the Master of the earth.

This miracle of Jesus walking on the water is the fifth of the seven signs that John offers in this section as proof of Jesus' identity as the Son of God.

Verses 22–25 reveal that the crowds are watching Jesus closely. They realize only one boat started across the sea, and Jesus wasn't on it. So how did He get to the other side?

Jesus begins His charge in verse 26 with the famous, "Verily, verily" (KJV), or the more modern, "I tell you the truth" (NIV). He does the same as well in verses 32, 47, and 53. In Greek, the word used here is *amen*, which means "this is the binding truth."

Jesus' charge is that their pursuit is not because they saw signs, but because their bellies were filled (6:26). The people looked at the miracle, and stopped there. They failed to recognize what that miracle meant. There was something much more significant than just the feeding of the crowd: Here was the Messiah putting Himself on display for all to fall before Him in repentance and worship. These people are coming to Jesus to have their needs met, not to be redeemed.

In that day, many people could not read, so when the king wanted people to understand that a decree was his, he would place his seal on it. The seal was the recognizable stamp that allowed people to know that something was approved of by the king. Jesus says that the Father has placed His seal, His mark of approval, upon Him as the sole dispenser of eternal life. Jesus is saying, "Do not trivialize My coming as simply a source of food. God sent Me to dispense life" (6:27).

The people respond by focusing their attention on work (6:28). They have no idea that salvation is a gift of God, given by grace and mercy, acquired by faith. The multitudes ask for a work to do to be saved, and Jesus responds with faith in Himself (6:29).

6:30–40

THE BREAD OF LIFE

Jesus is in the middle of a conversation with the multitudes. He has just told them that they must look to the food that gives eternal life, not just to the food that feeds the body. They ask what they must do to get this food, and Jesus has told them that they must place all of their trust in Him. It is at this point that this passage begins.

Verses 30–33 can be broken down into two thoughts: first, the demand of the people to have Jesus prove His claim, and then the response of Jesus to that demand.

The people are asking for a sign before they will place their trust in Jesus. Their fathers ate manna in the wilderness (Exodus 16:1–5), how could Jesus top that? Note that asking for a sign is evidence of their lack of faith. Asking for a sign is an act of pride that makes God subject to the people, not the other way around.

Jesus responds that the people have made four errors in their understanding of the Old Testament, and it has affected their understanding of Him, as well as their understanding of salvation (6:32–33).

1) Moses didn't give the bread, God did. In the same way, it is God who gives them the true bread from heaven. Both are gifts from God, not the miracles of mere humans.
2) Jesus is not just interested in satisfying bellies, but in satisfying the souls.
3) Manna is physical, not spiritual. All manna really did was paint a picture of what the true eternal manna (sustenance) is going to be like.
4) Manna was only for Israel, the true bread is for the world. Spiritual bread is not exclusive to a particular group; it is for everyone.

Again, a demand—give us this bread (6:34)—and Jesus' response. In calling Himself the Bread of life, Jesus is saying people must partake of His nature and His life in order to have the hunger of the soul satisfied. It is important that people understand the key role that Jesus plays in connecting humankind to God.

Critical Observation

Jesus made seven "I am" statements, starting with John 6:35.

- "I am the bread of life" (6:35 NIV).
- "I am the light of the world" (8:12 NIV; 9:5 NIV).
- "I am the [door or] gate" (10:7 NIV).
- "I am the good shepherd" (10:11, 14 NIV).
- "I am the resurrection and the life" (11:25 NIV).
- "I am the way and the truth and the life" (14:6 NIV).
- "I am the true vine" (15:1 NIV).

In verse 36, Jesus shifts gears a little and begins confronting the people on their fundamental problem—they do not truly believe in Him (6:36). There is more to it than simply seeing Jesus as a prophet or as an earthly king or as a great man. He wants us to see Him as God in the flesh and realize that our life amounts to nothing apart from Him.

In verses 37–39, Jesus explains the nature of salvation. The role of the Father is to turn on the light of understanding in humanity. The role of the Son is not to cast out or drive away those that come. Jesus is going to protect and preserve those who have come to Him.

Demystifying John

This issue of Jesus rejecting the Jews was a common question in the time that John wrote this Gospel, so it is historically significant that he included this teaching of Jesus. The foundation for why Jesus rejects his Jewish opposition is here in John 6:37. He would never cast away a true child of God, only those who were not given to Him by the Father.

Many people were confused in the latter first century as to how Christianity and Judaism fit together. The problem was not Judaism itself, but a dependence on the Law to be saved instead of faith in Christ's work on the cross.

In verse 38, Jesus wants the people to hear that it is His role to do what the Father wants—He is not an independent leader. Jesus has come down from heaven to do the Father's will, and what is the Father's will? To keep hold of those given to Him and to raise them up on the last day (6:39). The last day is simply the final judgment when the righteous will enter the kingdom, and the unrighteous will go to eternity in hell. This would hold great meaning to a first-century Jewish listener. The Jews longed for the day of resurrection. It is such a key part of Jewish theology that even today a devoted Jew would not have his body cremated for in doing so he might hinder the process of this resurrection.

In verse 40, Jesus reiterates the message of verses 38–39.

The words used here to describe looking to Jesus, depict the same kind of looking a person does at a table full of food at Thanksgiving; as you look, you want to have some of the food. To believe, in this context, means to no longer rely on yourself and your own way of thinking, but to trust in and rely on the mind, will, and way of Jesus Christ. It is acting on what you see in Jesus.

Notice the promise for those who do this: Jesus will raise them up on the last day and guarantees eternal life to those who trust in Him for salvation and life.

As for His Jewish listeners, Jesus just reworked their theology. They thought that they were going to be raised up on the last day by being obedient Jews. But Jesus just said that they must abandon all that they hold sacred and simply trust in Him for salvation.

6:41–71

REJECTION AND REVELATION

In verse 41 the Gospel writer moves from Jesus' conversation with the multitudes to a conversation with the religious leaders. This shift gives us the theological content of what happened.

Critical Observation

Remember that John moves from one situation to another by simply focusing on what Jesus said and the various responses to Him. As a result, this Gospel often combines the dialogue of various accounts that all teach the same thing. John gives us a theological account rather than a strict chronological account of the ministry of Jesus Christ.

Jesus' Jewish opposition has a problem with one aspect of His teaching. It is the claim of deity. The Jews grumble because Jesus' claim puts Him on par with God—the ultimate arrogant and criminal blasphemy. These men think that they know Jesus—the Son of a Galilean carpenter (6:42). They know His mom and His dad, and they know where He came from. They refuse to accept that He is from God, and therefore, they refuse to go through Him to get to God.

Jesus simply tells these men that grumbling will get them nowhere—what they need is the hand of God. Notice that Jesus states that He is the source of the resurrection from the dead (6:43–44).

Jesus offers the Jewish opposition a description as to how God draws people to Himself, and by doing so, offers an indictment. He refers to an Old Testament teaching found in both Isaiah and Jeremiah, and implied in many other passages. The quoted material in verse 45 is just a rephrasing of a passage in Isaiah, claiming God's restoration of His people (Isaiah 54:13–14). The simple reality is that God teaches His people, allowing them to understand the message of Christ, and He instructs them as to what is truth and what is not.

The point of God's teaching is in verse 46. No man has ever seen God except Jesus. He came from God as the explanation of God. He is the revelation that we need to understand.

Verses 47–48 provide the foundational point that Jesus wants the religious leaders to hear—if they will believe in Him, they will have eternal life. Next, He exposes the error of their thinking by referring back to the manna. In essence He says, if you reduce God to just an earthly God and His provision to just physical provision, you have nothing. Then in verse 50, Jesus contrasts the benefits: Manna prolongs the death process, but the bread out of heaven gives life. Verse 51 summarizes the heart of the issue at stake. They are to look to Jesus Himself as the spiritual Bread.

Verse 52 says that the Jews are arguing with each other. This could mean they are angry at the statements Jesus made, and so they are standing around shouting about it. Perhaps more likely though, they are divided in their opinions as John has noted on other occasions. Note the progression—in verse 41 the people are complaining, but by verse 52 they are angry.

Jesus responds to these men by first explaining the sacrifice of His body. Notice that in verse 53, He adds that they must not only eat His flesh but also drink His blood, or there is no life. This would have been even more troublesome for Jesus' listeners. To the Jews, drinking blood was a major offense; they were forbidden to ever drink blood.

Jesus offers three benefits that come when a person looks to Him for salvation.

1) Eternal life (6:54–55)
2) Unity with Jesus (6:56–57)
3) Abundant life (6:58)

The use of the word *disciple* in verse 60 is a reference to all the people that are following Jesus at this point. In saying that Jesus' teaching was hard, they are implying it is difficult to accept (6:60).

When Jesus asks them if His words offended them (6:61) or made them stumble, He is using a word that describes an old-fashioned trap for an animal—a box held up by a stick with bait attached. Over time, this word developed the connotation of anything that trips someone up.

Jesus' question about ascending to heaven (6:62) means, in essence, if you saw Me going back to heaven, then would you believe that I came from heaven?

In verse 63, He deals with the problem that the multitudes had concerning their need and His provision of that need. In the middle of verse 63 the central issue of true discipleship surfaces again: The words of Christ are the dividing line between life and death.

After asking His questions, Jesus identifies the problem (6:64)—unbelief. Salvation is not a question of intelligence; it is a question of faith. In this text we are indirectly introduced to Judas. John adds this insight of Jesus because he wants us to see that not even Judas is beyond the knowledge of Jesus. Jesus is fully aware of the unbelief of the people and fully aware of the nature of Judas.

Verse 65 is the theology behind Jesus' statement—it takes a work of God for a person to believe.

There are two aspects to Peter's answer to Jesus (6:66–69)—faith and faithfulness. Speaking for the group, Peter declares that they do not stumble over Jesus' claims. Rather, they believe Jesus' claims. That is the faith, but notice also the faithfulness. It is at the beginning of Peter's statement. Peter says they will stay with Jesus. They are committed to His teaching, to going where He goes. His words do not make them run away from Jesus, instead, they make them run to Jesus.

Notice Jesus' response to Peter's statement (6:70–71). He chose the disciples. The multitudes came on their own accord but the disciples were called. And He chose one who would betray Him. Judas's presence is a part of the plan of God. Jesus purposely picked one who would betray Him.

Take It Home

John's Gospel makes it clear that faith and faithfulness are the core foundations of true discipleship. Believing and sticking are the marks of the Christian life. We have also seen that the mark of a false disciple is one who accepts the person of Jesus, and is willing to accept the miracles of Jesus, but rejects the words of Jesus. They refuse to live by what Jesus taught. What kind of disciple are you?

JOHN 7:1–8:11

CHALLENGES TO RESPOND

The Response of Jesus' Family 7:1–13
Spiritual Insight 7:14–24
Ignorance in Wisdom's Clothing 7:25–36
Come and Drink 7:37–52
A Woman Caught in Adultery 7:53–8:11

Setting Up the Section

From chapter 7 of the Gospel of John, the focus is more on the reaction of the people to Jesus. A theme from this point on will be people's inability to understand who Jesus is.

Another theme that runs throughout this Gospel is Jesus' divine timetable. John will show that Jesus' will only happens at God's appointed time.

7:1–13

THE RESPONSE OF JESUS' FAMILY

Verse 1 gives us the reason that Jesus trained His disciples in Galilee rather than Jerusalem. If Jesus were to perform a public ministry in Judea, it would create such a stir that His death would likely be carried out before the appointed time. Therefore, Jesus stayed in Galilee.

The feast mentioned in verse 2, the Feast of Tabernacles ("dwellings") or Booths, had a twofold purpose: It celebrated the harvest that God provided for that year, and it looked back to the provision that God gave Israel while her people were living in tents in the desert. It looked to the present as well as to the past. During the celebration, all the Jewish males were to come to Jerusalem, set up tents, and celebrate. The tents symbolized the tents that the Israelites lived in during their wandering (described in the book of Numbers).

Verse 3 mentions Jesus' brothers, of which He has four. It is in the setting of the feast that Jesus' brothers make a request of Him: They want Jesus to get out of the villages and go to the city where the leaders and the people can see what He does and listen to His claims. This request, though, does not come from their faith (7:5). They are saying, *if* what you are doing really proves you are from God, then go and have it verified.

Jesus gives the reasons He will not go in verses 6–9:

1) It's not the right timing. Revealing Himself in Jerusalem precipitates His trial and death. It's not yet time for that.
2) Those He would teach would resent Him for revealing the sin in their lives. While His brothers would be free to go, His visit would have greater ramifications.

In the end, Jesus does go to Jerusalem, but in secret (7:10–13). As He had described, people were looking for Him, so His appearance in the open would go unnoticed. While there is discussion about His identity, it is a somewhat taboo subject amid the resentment that is building in the religious leaders.

Critical Observation

Jesus' interaction in Jerusalem reveals a typical scenario played out every time He seeks to teach in the temple.

1) Jesus teaches.
2) The religious leaders react.
3) Jesus confronts them.
4) The people react.
5) Jesus confronts again.
6) The leaders remain even more committed to killing Him.

7:14–24

SPIRITUAL INSIGHT

After Jesus points out the importance of timing to His brothers (7:6–8), John is very specific that He arrives at the temple in the midst of the feast, perhaps Wednesday or Thursday of the week. There would have probably been a full audience, since people were already in the midst of celebrating.

John doesn't focus on the content of Jesus' sermon, but rather the response that people have to His teaching. The point of this passage is that Jesus does come in and teach, not before the religious leaders, but before all the people.

Notice that the religious leaders are astonished at the way Jesus handles the text of scripture, yet point out that His teaching is not grounded in the systems of the day (7:15). In that day, all true learned men had a teacher, and that teacher authenticated them. This way they could wash out self-proclaimed prophets and false teachers.

Jesus responds both to their comments on His teaching and their comments on Him as a teacher (7:16–17). He tells them that His teaching is indeed based on someone else (implying God Himself) but that a person must have full and complete faith in God before he can ever assess whether Jesus' teaching is from God or not.

These people raise the question of Jesus' teaching, and Jesus in return raises the question about their ability to hear and understand. In essence, Jesus says, "You are not in any position to evaluate what I say because you don't want to do the will of God." Jesus then moves from their attack on His teaching to their attack on the teacher (7:18). One of the primary differences between Jesus and all the false messiahs is who received the glory from the teaching. Jesus says that if He seeks the glory of God, then He must be pure and righteous.

Next, Jesus exposes the impure motives of His accusers—they want to kill Him. How can they proclaim themselves followers of the Law if they are intent on murder (7:19; see Exodus 20:13)?

The crowds do not believe such a thing could be true about their leaders. A demon must be the source of Jesus' seemingly insane behavior (7:20). But Jesus reveals the problem with the religious leaders. He refers back to something that was recorded in John 5 (7:21–23). Jesus healed a man, and then told the man to arise and take up his mat. It was illegal, according to Jewish laws, to carry anything on the Sabbath, and therefore, by Jesus telling this man to carry his mat, Jesus was going against the man-made laws of the Sabbath.

In His response, Jesus also refers to circumcision, a practice that God had instituted through Abraham (Genesis 17:10–12). The Law stated that a male is to be circumcised on the eighth day; Jesus points out to the leaders that they will circumcise a child even if the eighth day falls on the Sabbath. The leaders did not consider it wrong to do work on the Sabbath if it was in obedience to God's Law. Therefore, to them it was not against the Sabbath to circumcise, but completely consistent with the Sabbath.

In verse 23, Jesus highlights the fact that the leaders would regularly break their Sabbath laws in order to keep the Law of Moses. Yet Jesus performs one work, and they hated Him for it. What Christ is doing is completely consistent with what Moses taught. The problem, then, is not that Jesus is out of line with Moses, but that the leaders do not really understand the Law of Moses.

Jesus goes one step further in exposing their problem (7:24). They have been judging according to appearances. Jesus' work for the man in John 5 was a symbol of the work of God in the lives of every believer. But because these leaders were caught up in their own legalistic standards, they were not able to evaluate or understand Jesus at all. Their judgment was based on appearances, not the heart behind the laws of God.

7:25–36

IGNORANCE IN WISDOM'S CLOTHING

Verse 25 introduces the reaction of the residents of Jerusalem. This reaction not only confirms the fact that the leaders want to kill Jesus, but it also illustrates the ignorance of the people regarding Jesus. The fact that the Jewish leaders are allowing Jesus to speak publicly causes the people to wonder if the leaders know that Jesus really is the Messiah (7:26). But they rule out that idea based on their misunderstanding of Old Testament prophecy (7:27).

There was a prevalent misinterpretation of Malachi 3:1, and portions of Isaiah 53, that the Messiah would appear out of nowhere. This created a belief that no man will know where the Messiah will come from. Their logic is this: Since they know Jesus is from Nazareth He cannot possibly be the Messiah.

Jesus' shouted response (7:28–29) opens with a possibly sarcastic phrase, almost equivalent to, "So you know Me, do you?" The point of His response is that He comes not from Nazareth, but from God. He is not a self-proclaimed prophet, but a sent one. The implication then is that these people do not know the God whom Jesus really comes from.

As throughout this section of John's Gospel, Jesus' words bring about anger for some and belief for others (7:30–31). The religious leaders are ready to take definite action against Him (7:32). Jesus' response (7:33–34), in its most basic meaning, is that He will return to heaven, and they will not be able to follow. Yet even that simple message is misunderstood. Jesus' listeners thought He was literally going away somewhere (7:35–36). They want to know if Jesus is saying He is going to the outcast Jews that lived among the Greeks. The idea of this passage is not that these Jews were simply scattered in Greece, but to indicate that they were scattered among Greek-speaking people—the Gentiles.

7:37–52

COME AND DRINK

On this last day of the feast, Jesus gives Israel the call of faith that the entire Old Testament was longing for. This moment in Israel's history is a defining one. For on a very strategic day, Jesus will offer Israel the salvation that was promised since creation and anticipated through all of Israel's history.

The last day of the Feast of Tabernacles was the high point of this celebration of God's provision for the Israelites during their forty years of desert wandering. On the last day of the feast, a golden chalice was filled with water from the pool of Siloam and was carried in a procession by the High Priest back to the temple. As the procession approached the Water Gate, the door in the temple wall that gave access to the water hole, three blasts from the shofar—a special trumpet—was sounded.

The water was offered to God at the time of the morning sacrifice, along with the daily drink offering, wine. The wine and the water were poured into their own special bowls, and then poured out on the altar. The Feast of Tabernacles was related in Jewish thought both to the Lord's provision of water in the desert and to the Lord's pouring out of the Spirit in the last days. Pouring at the feast refers symbolically to the Messianic age in which a stream from the sacred rock would flow over the whole earth.

It is on this day that Jesus proclaims Himself the source of water for thirsty people (7:37–38). The scriptures have already declared that the result of believing in Him is, from the depth of your being, flowing rivers of living water. This is reminiscent of the living water Jesus spoke about with the Samaritan woman at the well in John 4.

The outpouring of the Holy Spirit will not be in its full form until Jesus returns to heaven. That is why John adds an interpretation for the reader (7:39). The coming of the Spirit is a theme that will emerge again in John, as Jesus tells the disciples that when He goes, the Holy Spirit will come (14:16).

At this point, the people divided into several veins of thought:

1) Some thought that Jesus was the fulfillment of Deuteronomy 18:15 (7:40). Many Jews in that day interpreted this verse to mean a great prophet that would arise to come alongside of the Messiah—a prophet in the magnitude of Moses, or any of the great men of God. These Jews were placing Jesus in that category of great leaders of Israel.
2) Others referred to Jesus as the Christ (7:41) or Messiah. There were some who believed in His claims and declared that they believed in Him.
3) Still others ruled Him out as Messiah on the basis that He came from Galilee rather than from Bethlehem as was prophesied (7:41–42). They have no idea that Jesus was born in Bethlehem, therefore, they are mistaken. Had they asked, or researched, they would have discovered that Jesus was from the city of David, and the line of David, and therefore, qualified as the Messiah.

There is division among the people (7:43–44) and a conflict among the leadership. The guards failed to seize Jesus because they are so awed by His words. In response to this, the Pharisees pointed out that while some of the people may have fallen for Jesus out of ignorance of the law, the religious leaders know better (7:47–49).

Then Nicodemus speaks up (7:50–51). This is the Pharisee who had come to Jesus secretly, saying, "Rabbi, we know you are a teacher who has come from God. For no one could perform the miraculous signs you are doing if God were not with him" (3:2 NIV). Nicodemus was one who was willing to consider that Jesus was from God, unlike many of his peers. He offers a point of reason—they are wrong in the way that they are dealing with Jesus. By law they should at least hear Jesus and attempt to validate His claim.

The Pharisees rebuff Nicodemus, but not without mockingly asking if he is motivated to validate Jesus because he is from the same place, Galilee (7:52).

7:53–8:11

A WOMAN CAUGHT IN ADULTERY

Some Bible translations do not include John 7:53–8:11. It was not originally part of this section of John's Gospel. While it was not a part of the earlier manuscripts of John, it is unlikely that it is totally fiction. It is probably an added snapshot of Jesus' ministry, inserted later from oral tradition. While the language of the story does set it apart from the rest of this Gospel, the event is completely in line with Jesus' character and ministry.

What has led up to this moment? The Pharisees have become increasingly angered at Jesus. He has repeatedly confronted them. Since they can't arrest Him, or get the people to stop believing, they decided to trap Him with a situation in which there is no right answer. This is an effort to get Him to contradict the Law of Moses.

The Mount of Olives, where the people came to hear Jesus teach (8:1), was one of His places to pray, and He is there often from this point on in John's Gospel. It is not unusual that Jesus sits down to teach (8:2). This was typical for a Jewish rabbi—he sat and the people stood.

It is both the scribes and the Pharisees who come to Jesus with the adulteress woman. While it was common to bring religious questions to a rabbi to answer, in this case, the ulterior motive was to trap Jesus (8:3–6).

Critical Observation

The scribes studied and copied the Old Testament Law. Because of their familiarity with it, they are sometimes called lawyers or teachers of the Law. This familiarity also made them experts on the application of the Law—religious and ethical practices. Since this was a culture that centered around the law, the scribes held an essential role. If anyone had a question concerning some practical outworking or technical subtlety, he would consult a scribe.

The Old Testament law taught that those who commit adultery should be killed because their action attacks the very heart of the family and society (Leviticus 20:10). However, adultery was so common in Jesus' day that often this law was ignored. The people of the day did not agree with the practice of killing for adultery, and the Roman authorities banned the practice by the Jews.

Thus, when the religious leaders bring a woman caught red-handed in adultery, Jesus is being asked to choose between the Law of Moses and the legal and accepted practice of the day. If He suggests they stone the woman, He is breaking Roman law. If He chooses mercy, He breaks Moses' Law. Because these men do not understand the plan of God, they can't understand how justice and mercy can become reconciled.

The Bible does not reveal what Jesus writes in the ground (8:6). When He does respond, His answer is based on Deuteronomy 13:9 and 17:7, which instructed those who had witnessed a crime to be the first to inflict the punishment for that crime. Since the religious leaders are the ones who caught this woman, they are the ones who should actually make the first move. Therefore, Jesus is upholding the law entirely.

Jesus' response also places the execution of this woman on the shoulders of those who brought her. There is the implication that you cannot accuse someone of something that you yourself have done, or are guilty of. The question is not whether or not the Law of Moses should stand in this case, but whether or not these men are qualified to be this woman's judge. Their hearts are not bent on the glory of God, but rather on causing Jesus' downfall. Their own hypocrisy disqualifies them.

While Jesus does write in the dirt again, verse 9 makes it clear that the religious leaders leave because they heard Jesus' statement, not because they read what He wrote. Notice the order in which they leave: The older ones left first. The retreat continues until only Jesus and the woman are left. Finally, she moves from being the object of an evil plot to the object of God's mercy. In showing mercy (8:10–11), Jesus addresses both her position and her practice.

- The positional statement: I do not condemn you.
- The practical statement: From now on sin no more.

Her position might be forgiven, but she must now practice righteousness.

Take It Home

We are to live with the same instruction Jesus gave the adulteress woman—this is the life of the Christian. We are forgiven. And as a result we walk in righteousness. Christ's death on the cross did two things: It forgave human sin—literally all of the wrongs that were committed against God—and second, it conquered the power of sin in a person's heart. That is the power of the cross, the place where God's mercy and God's justice meet.

JOHN 8:12–59

The Light of the World	8:12–20
The First Condemnation of Israel	8:21–30
Genuine Faith	8:31–32
The Corruption of Man	8:33–36
Man's Only Security	8:37–47
Spiritual Ignorance	8:48–59

Setting Up the Section

For eight chapters John has been detailing the claims of Jesus Christ. Jesus has given sufficient evidence that He is the Messiah. He has declared Himself the object of the Passover, the object of the Feast of Tabernacles, the source of light, the source of life, the source of eternal life, and the only way to heaven. Jesus has backed up His claims with the miracles that the scriptures said would accompany the Messiah.

How have the Jews responded? The crowds have seemed motivated to follow Jesus as long as He fed them and healed them. Unfortunately, in the following chapters, what has started as a hope that Jesus is the Messiah, will, by the end of chapter 8, turn to an attempt to murder Jesus.

At this point, Jesus changes from a public presentation of Himself to a public condemnation of Israel. This is a turning point in the Gospel of John. Israel is being chastised for her rejection of the Messiah.

8:12–20

THE LIGHT OF THE WORLD

Jesus is in the court of the treasury when He makes His next claim (8:12, 20). That treasury is located in one of the outer courts of the temple. It is actually located in the court of women, the innermost place women could go into the temple. It's also where people brought their money to give as offerings.

John's mention of this detail—Jesus in the treasury—is a good example of the kinds of details that give this Gospel an eyewitness kind of authenticity.

To fully understand the power of Jesus' claim to be the light of the world (8:12), look back at a prophecy of the Old Testament prophet Malachi (Malachi 4:2) that concerns the spiritual healing that God will provide through the sun (rather than Son) of righteousness. Throughout the Old Testament, light is a metaphor for God's presence and work and of the future Messiah:

- The glory of God's presence was represented by light (Exodus 13:20–22).
- The protection of God was represented by light (Exodus 14:19–20).
- The psalms described God as light and salvation (Psalm 27:1).
- God's Word, His truth, is described as a light (Psalm 119:105; Proverbs 6:23)

- God's light is His revelation (Ezekiel 1:4–8) and salvation (Habakkuk 3:3–4).
- The light of God's face was His people's strength and victory (Psalm 44:3).

There are many other examples, but in short, the coming of the Messiah was light to a dark world.

To the darkness of	Jesus is the light of
falsehood	truth
ignorance	wisdom
impurity	holiness
sorrow	joy
death	life

Jesus is laying claim that He is the promised sun of righteousness. And He adds a consequence for those that respond to His claim: Those who follow Him will not walk in darkness (8:12). This is a parallel to God's presence with the Israelites on their journey out of Egypt described in the Old Testament—a pillar of fire to guide them by night (Exodus 13:20–22).

Jesus' claim is one that this crowd would have understood because of its familiarity with Isaiah's great prophecy of the coming of the Messiah: Those in darkness will see a great light (Isaiah 9:2–7). Jesus is telling the people that Isaiah's prophecy is fulfilled in Him. In order to receive the blessings promised in this prophecy, they must follow Him.

In light of the Pharisees' challenge (8:13), Jesus reveals the basis for His claim.

1) His origin. His witness is true because He came from heaven and speaks with divine approval. Unfortunately, these people still see Him as someone from Galilee. They don't understand His true origin (8:14).
2) His ability to judge. The point here is not that Jesus will never judge, but rather, that Jesus does not use the same superficial standard for judging that these people are using (8:15). Jesus says that His judgment will not be based on human wisdom because He is God (8:16).
3) Divine testimony. Since Jewish law requires two witnesses to confirm any testimony, Jesus is saying He has two witnesses: Jesus and God, His Father, because they are one. This should satisfy the demand of the Law (8:17–18). Again, the people look at Jesus' response from a small, human perspective—where is His father (8:19)? They are proving that they have no idea who Jesus is. Therefore, Jesus places His finger on the problem by saying, "You do not know me" (NIV). Their inability to recognize Jesus testifies that they really do not know God Himself.

Jesus' statements would have been outrageous to those who did not believe in Him. The conflict for these religious leaders is building, yet God's timing is still in effect (8:20).

8:21–30

THE FIRST CONDEMNATION OF ISRAEL

The tenor of Jesus' ministry changes as He begins to pronounce the judgment that the people of Israel will face for rejecting their Messiah. They cannot go where He is going because of their lack of faith in Him (8:21).

The Jews, which in John's Gospel refers to the Jewish leadership, miss this solemn warning. They suggest that He might be talking about suicide (8:22). In rabbinical teaching, anyone who committed suicide would be placed in the darkest part of Hades forever. Their response, then, is filled with an arrogant undertone. The only place that Jesus could go that they would not find Him would be the recesses of Hades, so He must be talking about killing Himself. They miss the point of Jesus' statement entirely.

Jesus' response to these leaders turns the tables. In essence He says, "I am not the one who is going to go to the pit; actually, you are from that pit" (8:23). These leaders thought that their religious practices had enabled them to transcend the world, but in all reality, they were engulfed in the world's system.

Next Jesus addresses their unbelief (8:24): They will die in their sins unless they believe in Him. If they fail to believe, they will not only be sinners by nature, but they will also be sinners by choice, which will seal their fate.

Jesus defines belief very specifically–faith in Himself (8:24). In response, these leaders give Jesus an opportunity to clarify Himself (8:25).

Critical Observation

Verse 26 is the turning point at which Jesus switches from His public ministry to Israel to a public condemnation of Israel's leaders. Jesus says His judgment comes from God and, therefore, is true. He reveals the stark reality of their situation.

In verse 27, John tells us that these leaders miss the point that Jesus was sent from God. Therefore, Jesus introduces a function of the cross: to reveal who Jesus is (8:28). In verse 29, He drives the same point home, which has been a contention all along with the religious leadership—Jesus will always do that which pleases God. Many of the people believe in Jesus because of His words (8:30), but the conflict with the religious leaders continues on.

8:31–32

GENUINE FAITH

Jesus defines genuine faith as that which holds to His teaching (8:31–32). To "hold to" (8:31 NIV), in this context, means to "remain" or "continue" for the long term. It conveys the idea that a person will not fall away. True discipleship means living Jesus' teaching so continuously that it becomes part of the believer's life, a permanent influence and stimulus in every area of life. Jesus is not saying you must prove by staying the course that you have good enough faith. He is saying that as you continue in His teaching, then it becomes obvious that you are one of His true disciples.

Take It Home

In verse 32, Jesus says that by making Christ's word the rule of our lives, and accepting Him as guide and teacher, we will come to the knowledge of the truth that only a life of devotion can bring. Holding to the teaching of Jesus is the very source of wisdom and understanding in the believer's life. But not just wisdom and understanding are found in the truth—there's freedom as well.

8:33–36

THE CORRUPTION OF MAN

Jesus has just defined true faith as that which abides or continues in His teaching. His listeners respond by touting their heritage—we are descendants of Abraham, why would we need to be set free by Your truth (8:33)? They believed that because they were Jewish, they were inwardly free, even though they were outwardly in bondage as a nation. They misunderstood that when God called the Jews as His people, He was not calling them to a salvation meant exclusively for them, but rather to be the people that His salvation would come through.

Jesus begins His reply in verse 34 with the famous, "Verily, verily" (KJV), or the more modern, "I tell you the truth" (NIV). He does the same as well in verses 51 and 58. In Greek, the word used here is *amen*, which means "this is the binding truth."

Jesus outlines the seriousness of humanity's problem with sin in verses 34–36. Simply, it is that sin affects every aspect of our being. In other words, the whole person is corrupted by sin. We may not have allowed sin to run its full course in our lives, but sin is slavery whether it runs its full course or not. Jesus describes to His listeners that not only does a person sin by action, but actually, they are sinners in the very depth of who they are. They are enslaved to that sin.

Building on that slavery image, Jesus sets up a contrast between a slave and a son (8:35). The son has a permanent place; the slave is only kept as long as he or she is useful. There is a prophetic undertone to this statement. Jesus has been warning them that they will be rejected if they don't believe in Him.

The only one who can set a slave free would be the rightful heir of the family. Only the father or the firstborn son can do this (8:36). That means Jesus can set humanity free from the enslavement of sin. What an offer. Only the heir of the house is allowed to set a slave free, and only Jesus can set any of us free from our sin.

8:37–47

MAN'S ONLY SECURITY

In verse 33, the Jewish leaders make the claim that they are not slaves to sin if for no other reason than because they are Abraham's descendants. In verses 34–36, Jesus clarifies that all humanity is corrupted by sin. In verses 37–41, He then questions the notion that these leaders are true spiritual descendants of Abraham. Physical lineage does not denote spiritual lineage.

In a physical sense, the Jews who oppose Jesus are the descendants of Abraham. Yet that is not enough to make them a part of the family of God. If they are truly children of Abraham, they would not be seeking to kill the Messiah. They are outwardly conformed to the law, but inwardly their hearts are bent on murder (8:37). They have not given Jesus' teaching permanent residence in their lives, as Jesus talked about in verse 31.

Jesus' next statement is a cutting one—those who oppose Him speak a different language than He does and have a different father. While the Jewish leaders maintain their family ties with Abraham (8:39), Jesus points to Abraham's works of faith (Hebrews 11:8–12, 17–19). These Jews who oppose Jesus are self-righteous workers who find their security not in God's promises and His power to fulfill those promises, but in their own works.

Notice the progression of the statement made by Jesus in verse 40. They want to murder a man who has told them the truth about their situation, God's truth. They are rejecting God's revelation. Abraham loved the truth and did not run from it. Abraham sought to serve God, and sought to follow the truth, not do away with it. Thus, they are not the spiritual children of Abraham (8:41).

In response, they claim not to be illegitimate children—God is their Father if for no other reason than because of their Jewish heritage. Jesus' point remains: If God were truly their Father, then they would love Jesus because He came from the Father. How could you be of God if you hate the Messiah (8:42)?

In telling them that they are unable to hear Him, Jesus is addressing a fatal flaw (8:43). The problem is His communication is not the obstacle; it is their ability to understand Jesus that is the issue. Because they cannot hear Jesus, they fail to grasp the true meaning of His words. This logic leads them to a startling conclusion in verse 44: Their system, their beliefs, and their hearts are grounded in evil. Satan's desires are murdering and lying, and these have become the desires of these Jewish leaders. Jesus speaks the truth (8:45) and they don't recognize it. They are content with a lie. They want to kill Him, and find no problem with that. Jesus is clear both about who they are and who He is (8:46–47).

8:48–59

SPIRITUAL IGNORANCE

Jesus continues in His dialogue with the religious leaders. He has been clear with these men about who He is, and what He came to do. In addition, He has been clear about their spiritual condition and their need to trust in Him as the Messiah.

In verses 42–47, Jesus had confronted the leader, saying that their inability to recognize Him as God's Son revealed the fact that, spiritually, they were not God's children. Though they were Jews by heritage, their faith did not prove them to be the spiritual sons of Abraham.

In response to Jesus' bold claims, the Jewish leaders pose a question that reflects how they feel about Jesus. They ask Jesus how they can come to any conclusion other than that He is both a Samaritan and possessed by a demon (8:48). While there are other places in the Gospels where Jesus is accused of working under the power of Satan, this is the only place where He is accused of being a Samaritan.

Critical Observation

To fully understand the accusation posed by the Jewish leadership in verse 48, examine the feelings of the Jews toward the Samaritans. The Jews believed that the Samaritans were, first of all, traitors to Israel. It was the Samaritans' forefathers—Jews of the northern kingdom of Israel—who, during the early stages of the captivity under Nebuchadnezzar, married outside of the Jewish nation, and therefore their offspring were not fully Jewish. These descendants took on the customs and religious practices of the nations that they married into and so practiced a corrupt version of Judaism. The Jews of the southern kingdom rejected these mixed marriages and the mixed culture that they produced.

Keep in mind that Jesus has just criticized these men at a tender spot–their heritage as the descendants of Abraham. For them to attack Jesus' heritage is to respond in kind. In calling Jesus a Samaritan, these leaders are accusing Him of betraying Judaism in the same way they believed the Samaritans had.

Jesus does not respond to the accusation that He is a Samaritan (8:49). Jesus loved the Samaritans (John 4). He does, however, flatly deny that He is possessed. Jesus is concerned with honoring God (8:50). He doesn't respond to attacks that have nothing to do with that role.

Then Jesus returns the conversation to the purpose of His time on earth–all who keep His word will not "see death" (8:51 NIV). The word *see* in this verse means "to look with understanding" or "to experience." Jesus is saying that when you place your faith in Him, you will not experience eternal separation from God. Therefore, physical death is nothing but the journey from this life into eternity with God forever, skipping the horrors of separation from God's mercy and grace.

The response Jesus receives to this statement is based on a physical understanding of death. These Jewish leaders miss the spiritual truth of what Jesus is saying (8:52–53). In taking offense, they merely wonder, *Who does He think He is?*

Jesus' answer to their query angers them even more. He tells these men first that He is not out to honor Himself by offering eternal life. His goal is not to demean Abraham but to honor God the Father (8:54–55). Abraham was overjoyed at the promise of the Messiah, yet these men stand in the Messiah's presence and reject Him. But when Jesus points this out (8:55), the Jews' response once again diminishes His statement to a simple physical fact: Jesus isn't old enough to have known Abraham (8:57).

For these argumentative religious leaders, though, Jesus' claim in verse 58 is unmistakable. Jesus calls Himself *I am*. That is the personal name of God used in the Old Testament when God spoke to Moses (Exodus 3:14). Jesus is saying, "I am God."

Leviticus 24:16 states that anyone who claims to be God, and thus blasphemes God, should be stoned. This is why, in verse 59, the men pick up stones with intent to execute Jesus.

JOHN 9:1–41

THE BLIND MAN

What the Blind Man Saw 9:1–41

Setting Up the Section

Chapter 9 is a key chapter in the Gospel of John because it serves two purposes. First, it serves as a theological summary of the entire Gospel of John. Second, it is a transition between Jesus' public ministry to Israel and His public condemnation of Israel. Because the leaders reject Jesus as God and the Messiah, Jesus will condemn them. Because they failed to honor Jesus as Lord and Messiah, they will suffer the consequences.

In this section of John's Gospel, made up of seven signs or miracles, the healing of the man born blind is the sixth sign.

9:1–41

WHAT THE BLIND MAN SAW

Some believed that any physical infirmity was a result of a sin committed by that person or someone related to that person. This may have been based on a misunderstanding of verses like Exodus 34:7. Thus, the disciples ask who is at fault for the man's blindness (9:1–2).

Jesus gives the simple answer that no one sinned (9:3). The reason for this man's blindness is that God's power will be put on display in this man's life. Verse 4 is a call to make the most of the time that God has given. Jesus uses a workday illustration to make His point. There is an appointed amount of work that God has planned for Jesus, and Jesus must complete that work while He is here on earth (John 17:4).

In verse 5, Jesus tells the disciples His purpose—He is the light of the world, the revelation of God on earth. He is showing the glory of God to everyone.

The way that Jesus heals this man—the mud on his eyes and the command to wash in the pool (9:6–9)—contains several possible allusions to the Old Testament. It is clearly reminiscent of the Old Testament prophet Elijah healing a man named Naaman of leprosy by having him wash in the Jordan River (2 Kings 5:1–14). Some also connect the word *Siloam* to the river called Shiloah in the Old Testament. Isaiah 8:6 speaks metaphorically of Israel rejecting "the gently flowing waters of Shiloah" ([NIV] meaning God's sustenance) and allying itself with the king of Syria. Another possible allusion is to Genesis 49:10, "the scepter will not depart from Judah. . .until Shiloh comes" (NASB), a passage interpreted by the rabbis with reference to the Messiah. Whether these allusions are present or not, by interpreting the word Siloam as "sent" John links the pool of Siloam to the Messiah—the one "sent" by God (3:16; 4:34: 5:23, 37; 7:28; 8:26, etc.)

Naturally, the people want to see who it was who caused such a miracle, but because the man never saw Jesus he cannot point Him out to them, though He calls Him by name. This is the second time in John that Jesus is accused of transgressing the Sabbath. In chapter 5,

He healed a man on the Sabbath, and the leaders were more upset about Jesus' breaking the Sabbath than they were awed at the miracle. In this case, Jesus could be accused of breaking three Sabbath rules:

- He had healed a man.
- He had made a mud pack.
- He had anointed a man.

There are three interrogations performed by the Pharisees to get to the bottom of the incident.

1) 9:13–17. The Pharisees question the man. Their questions center around the process Jesus used to perform the healing, concerned more about the rules than God's glory.
2) 9:18–23. The Jewish leaders then interview the parents. They could discredit the miracle if the man had not been born blind. Unfortunately for them, the parents, out of fear, only confirm their son was born blind, and then defer any other questions to him. They were afraid of disagreeing with the Pharisees and being excommunicated, or cut off from the synagogue. If they were cut off, they would not be able to work, they would be kicked out of their home, forced to live as outsiders, and not be welcomed into heaven when they died.
3) 9:24–34. The leaders again call this man to be questioned. They cannot deny the fact that he was blind from birth; therefore, the only thing left is to attack the character of Jesus. If Jesus is a sinner, then it does not matter what miracle He performs—it is all evil. The one thing this man will not relinquish, though, is that he was blind and now he sees (9:25).

The man's answer—asking if they want to be disciples of Jesus—could be a sarcastic response (9:27). It was probably obvious that their interest was not motivated by a desire to be Jesus' disciples.

Next, the Jewish leader elevate themselves by claiming they are disciples of Moses (9:28–29). When they refer to God speaking to Moses, they are referring to Moses' special connection with God. The idea of Moses and God conversing together conveys God's approval and blessing. This reveals how much the leaders reject everything that Jesus has said. Jesus has said over and over that He is from heaven and that He and God are one.

The healed man's response reveals a spiritual common sense that is lacking in the religious leaders. What the man finds remarkable is not that Jesus healed him, but the unbelief of the officials (9:30). Jesus just performed an amazing miracle, and yet they refuse to admit that Jesus is God.

The man's logic works this way (9:31–33):

1) We know that God does not hear sinners.
2) God hears those that do His will.
3) To heal someone blind from birth must be a miracle of God.
4) Since it is a miracle of God, the person who performed this miracle must have been obeying God. God heard Him.
5) Therefore, if Jesus were not from God, God wouldn't have empowered Him to work this miracle.

Responding in anger, the leaders curse the man and throw him out of the synagogue (9:34–35). Because of that, Jesus seeks the man out and asks him if he believes in the Son of Man. The word *believe* means trust, and the title *Son of Man* refers to Jesus being the Messiah, the revelation of God on earth (Daniel 7:13–14). Keep in mind that when the man asks who the Son of Man is, he has never actually seen Jesus. His eyes had been covered with mud, and then he was taken to the water where he received his eyesight.

Critical Observation

Notice the progression of the man's increasing faith in Jesus:

"The *man they call Jesus* made some mud and put it on my eyes" (9:11 NIV, emphasis added).

"He is a *prophet*" (9:17 NIV, emphasis added).

"If this man were not *from God,* he could do nothing" (9:33 NIV, emphasis added).

"Then the man said, 'Lord, I believe,' and he worshiped him" (9:38 NIV, emphasis added).

When Jesus speaks about judgment, He is not referring to the final judgment of the world, but rather the judgment that causes a decision to be made—to accept or to reject.

Jesus uses the illustration of sight. If you don't know you are blind, you have a problem. It's the same with spiritual sight. The Jewish leaders are spiritually blind, but are unaware of it (9:40–41).

Take It Home

Jesus' words are a warning for all who believe they see the truth. The Jewish leaders were convinced that they were right, that they could see the truth, but they missed what God was doing through Jesus. The only way to be free is to fall before Jesus and exchange all that you are for all that He is. When you admit you are blind, then you will receive sight.

JOHN 10:1–42

JESUS CONFRONTS THE LEADERSHIP

Woe to the Shepherds	10:1–21
The Deity of Jesus	10:22–42

Setting Up the Section

Jesus is continuing to answer the question that was asked by the Pharisees in 9:40. They wanted to know if they are blind, and they are. And because they are blind, chapter 10 goes on to explain, they are not the true shepherds of Israel. Instead, they are false shepherds that harm the sheep.

Verse 22 marks the end of a very important part of the life of Jesus. In the last part of this

chapter, Jesus will end His public ministry to the leaders of Israel, and begin His private ministry to the disciples.

Though this is the last in a series of confrontations between Jesus and the leaders of Israel, the same theme emerges: The leaders question Jesus, and Jesus declares that He is God. The dialogue will cover the same ground covered in the past several chapters, yet the religious leaders remain unconvinced.

10:1–21

WOE TO THE SHEPHERDS

Jesus begins His allegory with the famous, "Verily, verily" (KJV), or the more modern, "I tell you the truth" (NIV). He does the same as well in verse 7. In Greek, the word used here is *amen*, which means "this is the binding truth."

Critical Observation

Jesus' illustration (10:1–5) centers on first-century sheepfolds. The sheepfolds of Jesus' culture were large enclosures, open to the sky, but walled around with reeds, stone, or brick to protect against robbers, wolves, and other beasts.

The shepherd entered the sheepfold through a large door, though sometimes animals and robbers clambered over the walls elsewhere in order to prey upon the sheep.

At the doors of the large sheepfolds, some large enough to hold thousands of sheep, a porter, or doorkeeper, remained on guard. This doorkeeper would only admit those who have the right to enter. All those who climb into the sheepfold some way other than by the door are robbers or attackers.

The King James Version refers to Jesus' teaching here as a "parable" (10:6), but a better translation of the Greek word would be "illustration" or "analogy." Jesus expands on this illustration (10:7–9) by calling Himself the door to the sheepfold. Anyone who wants to be a part of the kingdom of God must go through Him. When He refers to all who came before Him as criminals, He is not teaching that Moses and the prophets were among that group. He is referring instead to the more recent history—the teachers and leaders who are in power at the time.

In verse 10, Jesus continues to explain the true heart of the leaders of Israel and compares them with Himself. Jesus uses the picture of thieves at the sheepfold to communicate that if a teacher is pulling his followers away from faith in Christ, that teacher is destroying them. This is aggressive language for Jesus to use in a direct confrontation with the leaders questioning Him.

In contrast to death and destruction, Jesus brings life, abundant life. When a person comes to the door of Christ for salvation, he or she is given a life that is full, complete, and not lacking anything.

Jesus continues to compare Himself with the religious leaders of the day (10:11–13). He is the shepherd; they are the hired help. In calling Himself the shepherd, Jesus claims Himself not only the path to salvation (the door or gate) but also the provision of salvation.

There is a bond between the sheep and the shepherd (10:14–15). Included in this bond between Jesus and His sheep is the bond between Jesus and His Father. Both relationships are secure. The true shepherd cares for the sheep in such a way that He gives His all. That is the depth of the relationship between Jesus and the sheep.

In verse 16, Jesus speaks of the Gentiles as the other sheep outside of Israel that He will redeem. He will bring those to the fold, and they will become one with the Jewish believers. They will have one single flock, with one single shepherd. That is what His sacrifice will bring.

The death of Jesus is not something that Jesus is forced to do (10:17–19). It is not something that Satan does to Jesus—it is something that Jesus does on His own initiative. It is the power and authority of Jesus that causes Him to give His life, and it is the very authority of God that Jesus possesses that causes Him to rise from the dead.

The reactions Jesus receives are not unusual (10:19–21):

- Rejection—He has a demon and is insane.
- Consideration—How can He be a demon or insane if He heals the blind?

Throughout Jesus' ministry, He meets with these reactions. Some reject Him outright. Others look at what He does and wonder if He is for real.

10:22–42

THE DEITY OF JESUS

Some time has passed between verses 21 and 22, probably a couple of months. It is winter, and the Feast of Dedication is happening. Jesus is walking around the portico of Solomon. This was one of the only fully enclosed places in the temple, and therefore, in the winter months this is where you would find many of the rabbis and religious leaders, as well as most of the people.

Demystifying John

The Feast of Dedication is also called Hanukkah. This feast is not a feast required in the Law of Moses. It was one added later in Israel's history during the four hundred-year period between the events recorded in the Old Testament and the events recorded in the New Testament.

In 167 BC, the Syrian king Antiochus Epiphanes overran Jerusalem and polluted the temple, setting up a pagan altar to displace the altar of Israel's God. Eventually a leader emerged, Judas Maccabeus, who developed an army, and led the Jews in what we today would call guerilla warfare. They recaptured the temple and spent eight days rededicating it to God. It was decreed that a similar eight-day feast of dedication should be held every year. Hanukkah begins on the twenty-fifth day of the Jewish month of Kislev, a date that varies throughout December on our calendar.

It is during this Feast of Dedication that the Jews press in on Jesus in the temple and ask Him to reveal once and for all if He is the Christ (10:24). *Christ* is a title rather than a name. It's the

Greek equivalent of the Hebrew *Messiah*. Both words mean "anointed one."

Keep in mind that the Jews want a champion leader like Judas Maccabeus to conquer Rome for them. If Jesus is that man, He should speak now. If not, He should be killed—that is the pressure behind this question.

When Jesus says that He has already answered them (10:25), He is not referring to a specific statement, but rather to the works that were done in the Father's name. Those works were witnesses to Jesus' role as Messiah. But the religious leaders failed to believe. In verse 26, Jesus begins to explain why they did not believe—because they were not sheep of His flock. Jesus has continued to tell them through His miracles and His claims that He is the Messiah, but they cannot hear because they are not of the sheep of God.

Take It Home

While verses 28–29 continue Jesus' explanation of the distinction of those who are God's sheep, they also teach us about Jesus' role as our shepherd. Not only does He know the sheep, but He protects the sheep. He gives them eternal life. The reason that we have eternal life is that we have the life of Christ within us, and therefore, we become partakers of that perfect eternal life that preserves us. We are protected in the hand of God.

Notice that in verses 28–29, Jesus refers to His hand and to God's hand interchangeably. This is one more subtle illustration of a truth given directly in verse 30—Jesus is fully God.

The Jewish leaders have challenged Jesus to define Himself again for them. Jesus does and declares Himself as God. For the Jewish opposition, Jesus' claim is blasphemy. They respond by preparing to stone Him (10:31) for the second time (the religious law required that anyone who claims to be God be stoned to death). To these first-century Jews, God did not dwell in human bodies or in idol forms. You could not get close to Him or you would die. From that perspective then, how could Jesus, who is human and bound to this earth, actually be God?

When the leaders threatened to stone Jesus previously (8:13–59), Jesus disappeared. This time He remains and asks them a question. Jesus had manifested the works of God on earth (as prophesied in Isaiah 61:1). Of these works of God, Jesus wants to know, which ones render Him deserving of death (10:32)?

In response to the accusations of blasphemy (10:33), Jesus refers these men to Psalm 82:6. In Psalm 82, God called out to the unjust rulers. He had appointed them as "gods," His sons, His representatives on earth. The title *gods*, in this context, implies authority or ruler (10:34). Jesus makes an argument from the lesser to the greater (10:35–38). If these men could be called sons of God, and without performing any great works of God, could He not rightly be called the Son of God, having manifested God's works? All that Jesus has done has been the work of the Father. No one could have done what Jesus did.

Since they remain unconvinced, He leaves, waiting for the right timing (10:39). This time He travels beyond the Jordan (10:40).

Critical Observation

From here on out in the Gospel of John, Jesus will focus on teaching His disciples and preparing the way for His death, resurrection, and the future church. The people to whom Jesus ministered, who in turn came to believe in Him, are in sharp contrast to the leaders who failed to believe. This serves as the point of transition. The leadership of Israel rejected, but the people in the villages believed the preached word of John the Baptist and the works of God manifested in the life of Jesus. All the people needed to do was hear the message, and they believed (10:41–42).

JOHN 11:1–57

THE PRIVATE MINISTRY OF JESUS

A Faith That Is Larger Than Life 11:1–44
The Plan of Men—the Plan of God 11:45–57

Setting Up the Section

The issue here is faith. As a group of people struggle with death, the ultimate conqueror, will they believe that Jesus is even more powerful than death? The disciples believe that Jesus is going to die when He goes back to Judea. The sisters of Lazarus believe that death has conquered their brother. It seems it has not yet occurred to anyone that Jesus' power is greater than death.

11:1–44

A FAITH THAT IS LARGER THAN LIFE

Not much has been said about Lazarus until this miracle. In fact, more people know Mary and Martha, so John's Gospel gives them as a point of reference to know who their brother is (11:1). Mary's anointing of Jesus' feet (12:1–8) must have been a well-known story by the time this Gospel was written because John references it here (11:2) even though the story hasn't appeared in this narrative yet.

Lazarus is noted as someone Jesus loves (11:3). This term of endearment, of course, signifies a close relationship. Jesus had healed others He had never met; surely He would come and heal this man who means so much to Him.

Critical Observation

Verse 4 is key to this account. Jesus declared that Lazarus' sickness would not result in death. Lazarus will die, but his death will not be final. This sickness will provide the occasion for God to be revealed through the power of Jesus raising Lazarus from the dead.

This issue of the mutual glory of Jesus and the Father is one of the sore spots for the Jewish religious leaders. They believe they honor the Father, and yet, at the same time, they are dishonoring Jesus. Jesus has been telling them that there is mutual glory shared between the two, and therefore, if you dishonor Jesus you dishonor God.

Notice the tension in verses 5–6. Jesus has a deep affection for Lazarus and his sisters, yet He waits two days to respond to them. Why does He wait? It is clear to us now that Jesus waits so that Lazarus will be dead when He arrives, and Jesus can then raise him from the dead.

The last time that Jesus had been in Judea, the religious leaders tried to kill Him (11:8). This is why the disciples are hesitant to return. Jesus responds to their fear with the image of the safety of daylight (11:9–10). In that culture there were no street lamps or lightbulbs, so for the most part, work stopped at sundown. A person working at night would not be able to see well and would stumble around accomplishing nothing. If that same person works in the daylight, he does not stumble because he can see. In other words, as long as the disciples are in the presence of the light, nothing will get in the way of their mission.

When Jesus describes Lazarus as asleep, the disciples miss His point (11:11–16). Lazarus is actually dead, not asleep, and they are charged with a divine mission, not just a mandate to escape danger. Thomas's almost fatalistic comment in verse 16 reveals that their eyes still were not open to the bigger issues going on around them.

The four days (11:17) Lazarus's body was in the tomb was sufficient to confirm that he was dead. As was the custom of the day, relatives and neighbors would have come to care for the family in this time of grief. In addition, at most funerals, the family would hire a funeral band to play sad music, and professional mourners. This would have been a large gathering of people, all centered on the grieving family members to mourn with them (11:18–19).

While perhaps not obvious at first, Martha's comments reflect a lack of faith. While she is sure that Jesus *could have* done something about Lazarus, now that he is dead, she is just as sure that Jesus can do nothing about the situation. Her interpretation of Lazarus's potential resurrection is the final judgment resurrection (11:20–24).

Critical Observation

In verse 25, we see the lesson of the story. Jesus is changing the focus of the conversation from the eventual resurrection of the dead to the fact that He is the one with the power and authority over death. Jesus is the source of resurrection and life (11:25–26).

In response to Jesus' claim, Martha's statement of faith models the ideal response. In the midst of all the rejection Jesus received from the religious leaders, Martha sees Jesus for who He is, and believes (11:27).

It seems that Martha makes the attempt to be discreet when she alerts Mary that Jesus has come, yet those watching follow on her heels. Mary's words to Jesus echo those of her sister's in verse 21 (11:28–32).

Amid Martha and Mary's grief, and the looming question of whether Jesus had waited too long to do anything about the situation, Jesus is deeply moved (11:33) or deeply agitated. At first it appears that Jesus is weeping with them, as the Jews interpret His actions (11:35–36). However, there are several elements of this situation that would have been disturbing, for instance the limited faith of His close friends. The word "troubled" (11:33 NIV) could communicate that kind of idea. Why would Jesus be upset at their grief? Perhaps because they were acting as if there is no hope. They reduced the power of Jesus to His earthly presence instead of trusting Him as the Son of God.

The crowd refers back to the miracle Jesus performed in chapter 9. If He had healed a blind man, couldn't He have saved Lazarus?

Lazarus's tomb was typical for that time—a cave carved into rock with a stone to block the entrance (11:38). These tombs were often large enough for people to move around inside, since it was common for more than one body to be buried there. This grave was similar to the one Jesus would soon be raised from.

As Jesus stands before the grave, calling for the stone to be moved, Martha struggles to look beyond her circumstance to see the glory of God as Jesus promised (11:39–40). In this context, the glory of God does not refer to a grand light show. It simply refers to an authentic display of who God is. As throughout the Gospel of John, Jesus is that display of God's glory.

Jesus' prayer of thanks reaffirms the claim that He has made throughout this section of John's Gospel—that He has been sent from heaven and is the physical manifestation of the Father (11:41–43).

The grave clothes on Lazarus were typical for that culture. Embalming was not a part of Jewish burial customs. The body was typically washed, dressed, and wrapped in linen, but was not put into a coffin. Instead it was carried into the tomb and left in a prepared place, perhaps a carved shelf or shallow grave. Spices and perfumes were placed in the grave clothes and in the tomb to mitigate the odor of decay. A separate piece of cloth covered the head.

When Lazarus is raised, the fact that his body is restored after four days of decay is a part of the miracle.

11:45–57

THE PLAN OF MEN—THE PLAN OF GOD

When Jesus calls Lazarus from the grave, the responses are divided (11:45–47). The leaders do not see Lazarus's resurrection as a sign that Jesus is the Messiah. Instead, they see it as competition. The council they convene is made up of both the Pharisees and the chief priests. Most of the chief priests were from the party of the Sadducees. Typically, the Pharisees and the Sadducees did not get along, yet, in this case, they were united in one purpose—opposing Jesus.

Demystifying John

The Sanhedrin was the highest Jewish authority, sometimes referred to as the high council. It was composed of seventy-one members, one high priest (Caiaphas, in this case) presiding over seventy men. Most of the members were Sadducees, but there was a minority of Pharisees.

Typically, the Sanhedrin sat in semicircular rows so that its members could see each other. Clerks sat at either end. Students, often disciples of the scribes, also attended. While the trial of Jesus involved some irregularities in the procedure of this ruling body, it was typically a group known for a high interest in fairness and justice.

It is obvious from this text that miracles alone will not convert the human heart. The leaders do not deny the miracles of Jesus. In this case, they are not as upset by Jesus' miracle as they are about the numbers of people believing in Him. If Jesus is allowed to go unchecked, then more will believe that He is the Messiah, and the status quo will be threatened. If the Jews begin to see Him as a king, then Rome could become involved (11:48).

Notice these things about their response:

1) They still call Jesus a man (11:47), even in light of His miracles.
2) Their fears are exaggerated (11:48). Jesus' followers were often divided. Particularly when He taught about the cost of discipleship, many fell away.
3) They come to illogical conclusions (11:48). Jesus' mission is not to be king in the earthly sense. They seem to have forgotten, even as religious men, that God is more powerful than Rome. They should fear His displeasure more than Rome's.

Caiaphas is the high priest. In fact he served for eighteen years (AD 18–36) as an appointment of Rome. Notice his words in verses 49–50. He is saying, in essence, that it would be in the best interest of the religious establishment if Jesus is used as a scapegoat. There is no real ground under Roman law that Jesus should be executed, yet Caiaphas seems to feel His death would keep some perceived peace with Rome.

Under Roman law, the Jews were allowed to govern themselves, but they were not given the authority to execute anyone. So, if the goal is to execute Jesus, these men are faced with a dilemma because Jesus never broke the Roman law.

John says that Caiaphas does not make his statement about Jesus' death on his own initiative (11:51). Caiaphas thinks he is speaking of the destruction the leaders are plotting, but his statement is more meaningful in light of the sacrifice Jesus will make to provide eternal life for so many (11:52). Jesus' death is going to bring the lost and scattered souls from every tribe and every nation together into one body. Caiaphas has no idea that what he thinks he has devised is really the plan of God. He seeks destruction, but God has planned life.

With the commitment the leadership has made to end Jesus' life (11:53), the stakes have changed, and Jesus withdraws (11:54). It was the previous Passover mentioned in John's Gospel at which Jesus, on the Sabbath, healed the man who had been lame for thirty-eight years. He then declared Himself God, with full rights to break the man-made Sabbath laws (John 5). The conflict that surrounded that Passover has only grown over time.

Take It Home

God is sovereign over the plans and motives of people. In this case, God has a plan for the evil heart of the leaders. God uses both good and evil, and God even uses the things that do not make sense to us.

Therefore, if someone has wounded or inconvenienced us, or even falsely accused us, we can still have faith in God, and believe that even in the worst of times He is in control. Jesus' sense of timing throughout His ministry speaks of the kind of faith that rests in God's timetable rather than fear of the power of people and their opinions.

JOHN 12:1–50

THE FAITHLESS AND THE FAITHFUL

The Priority of Worship	12:1–8
The Beginning of the End	12:9–26
The Power of the Cross	12:27–36
The Unbelief of Israel	12:37–50

Setting Up the Section

In the previous chapter Jesus raised Lazarus from the dead, revealing Himself to be the resurrection and the life. This miracle created a lot of attention for Jesus, which increased the anxiety of the religious leaders over Jesus' ministry.

This passage begins with a contrast of a faithful heart, Mary, and a deceitful heart, Judas.

12:1–8

THE PRIORITY OF WORSHIP

Jesus is in Bethany at a dinner with Lazarus and his family (12:1). If you read the same accounts of this story in the other Gospels, you will find that Jesus is in the house of Simon the Leper, and He is there with the disciples (Matthew 26:6–13; Mark 14:3–9). It is six days before the Passover (12:1), the beginning of Jesus' final week before His death and resurrection.

A distinction of John's account is his focus on the feet of Jesus. The other Gospels describe Jesus' body being anointed. John may have focused his account this way because in chapter 13, foot washing will become a major teaching point of Jesus.

Mary pours about twelve ounces of a valuable perfume (nard) on Jesus' feet (12:3). It was not uncommon for a special guest in that day to be anointed with a perfume when he arrived. The region was hot and dusty, and the people did not have showers in which to clean up. People were typically dirty and a little smelly. When a special guest would arrive, sometimes they were greeted with a douse of perfume to help the smell.

In anointing Jesus, Mary broke several customs of the day:

- She approached Jesus at the table. In that day men and women dined at different tables.
- She let her hair down in public. Women did not let their hair down in front of men. That was a sign of intimacy, only to be shared between husband and wife.
- She wiped His feet with her hair. Not only did a woman not let her hair down in public, but she certainly would not have touched a man with her hair.

Mary was placing all that she had at the feet of Jesus. She was humbling herself in front of Him, and presenting everything to Him out of a heart of love and devotion. She was literally foreshadowing Romans 12:1, presenting herself as a living sacrifice. Her act was one of devotion. It also foreshadowed Jesus' death. In a sense, Mary was anointing Jesus for His death and burial (Matthew 26:12; Mark 14:8).

In this passage, Mary's actions stand in contrast to the actions of Judas. When John adds the detail that Judas will later betray Jesus, he isn't saying that Judas was already intending to betray Jesus. His Gospel was written years after the fact, and Judas's betrayal was common knowledge. John's addition of detail here adds weight to Judas's comments. Judas is upset that this perfume is wasted on Jesus (12:4). His question (12:5) reflects two key areas of defect in him: what little regard he has for Jesus, and his sinister heart. Judas was the one in control of the finances, and because he was greedy, he would steal from the money box. If the perfume had been sold, he could have gotten access to the cash (12:6).

In defending Mary's actions to Judas (12:7–8), Jesus is making the point that Judas needs to get his priorities straight. Nothing is to be more important than the glory of God. Nothing is to take center stage more than the worship of God.

12:9–26

THE BEGINNING OF THE END

When people hear that Jesus is in Bethany, they come to see Him (12:9). However, the crowd is interested in the miracles Jesus performs, not necessarily worshiping the Messiah. It is because of these crowds that the chief priests decide to not only plot Jesus' death, but Lazarus's death as well. Lazarus's presence gives testimony to Jesus (12:10–11). A movement is continuing to form around Jesus that threatens the current religious leaders.

The next day, when the crowd gathers to meet Jesus as He enters Jerusalem (12:12), the people do two things:

1) They bring palm branches. Greeting a hero with palm branches was a custom of that day. It symbolized honor for a leader, national pride, and a conquering warrior. By laying down palm branches they reveal that they see Jesus as a political Messiah sent to reestablish Israel as a nation. They are worshiping Jesus with the right words but with the wrong motives.

2) They call out, "Hosanna!" This comes from Psalm 118, and it was a common scripture that was quoted during this time of the year. Psalm 118 originally was used to describe a Jew making his way to Jerusalem for worship. Because many Jews were making their way to Jerusalem for the Passover, this psalm would be sung along the way. Also, in many Jewish writings of the time, there was a messianic connection to this psalm, signifying that this verse is talking about the coming of the Messiah. Because of this teaching, these people are

standing in the street, proclaiming their allegiance to Jesus, whom they are hoping is their Messiah and will conquer Rome.

This misunderstanding of Jesus' role prompts some fear in the religious leaders. They see the people of their nation beginning to center around Jesus as their national hero, and they think for sure that Rome will intervene and further take away their independence.

Jesus' entrance into Jerusalem (12:14–15) fulfills the Old Testament prophecy of Zechariah 9:9. In John's account, the details are left out, yet he still confirms that Jesus fulfills it. The quotation here is not an exact quotation.

Demystifying John

In Zechariah 9:9–11, God promised that a king would come to Israel and three things would happen:

1) The wars in Israel would end.

2) Peace would be proclaimed.

3) Because of the blood of the covenant, prisoners would be released.

The context of this passage is victory in Israel. This victory is being proclaimed by Jesus, but it is being accomplished not by a war, but by Jesus' death. That is the significance of the donkey, in that day a sign of someone coming in peace. Jesus accepted their praise, but He also showed the people that He was not out to conqueror Rome but to conquer sin. While they have their eyes on politics, Jesus has His eyes on their souls.

It is not until Jesus ascends into heaven that the disciples are able to look back and understand that the scriptures declared He would ride in on a donkey as the Messiah, and that the kingdom that He would destroy would be the kingdom of sin. At the point of Jesus' acclaimed entry into Jerusalem, they miss the paradox of life in death, of greatness in humility, of hope in suffering.

Verses 17 and 18 tell us that the people who are with Jesus are enthralled by His display of power, but not focused on identity. In John 11:57, the leaders directed anyone who saw Jesus to report His location so He could be arrested. In chapter 12, the people obviously ignore that order (12:19).

Verses 20–22 preview what is to come. The "Greeks" John mentions are probably "god-fearers"—Gentiles who worshiped the God of Israel but had not fully converted to Judaism. They have come to worship during the Passover. These Gentiles serve to signify that Jesus is the Savior of the whole world. And so with the blindness of Israel being confirmed by the plot of the leaders and the ignorance of the people, John offers a picture of salvation offered to the Gentiles.

Jesus' response to the inquiry of these Gentiles is that the time has come for Him to be glorified (12:23–28). For the Jewish listeners around Him, Jesus' words might be mistaken for a statement that it is time for Him to take Rome, which, of course, is not what Jesus has in mind.

The illustration of the kernel of wheat that is useless until it dies and produces a harvest (12:24) reveals that Jesus' glorification will happen through His death. Verse 25 describes the result of His death upon the lives of His true followers. This truth is critical to Christian discipleship: Those who have contempt for themselves will be the ones who live eternally, but those who have a high regard for themselves will lose their lives.

Jesus begins His illustration in verse 24 with the famous, "Verily, verily" (KJV), or the more modern, "I tell you the truth" (NIV). In Greek, the word used here is *amen*, which means "this is the binding truth."

Take It home

In Jesus' day, those who were simply hoping for a conquered Rome missed the important truths of God's kingdom. There was a cost to following in Jesus' footsteps: a death to self. This is a message for us today. What are we expecting from our faith? Miracles? Life made easier? Answers to prayers? Or humble obedience as Jesus' disciples? Throughout history, humanity has tried with all sorts of religious acts to please God in the hopes of a variety of returns, but only in death to self, and a complete devotion to Jesus, is God truly pleased.

12:27–36

THE POWER OF THE CROSS

After speaking about the importance of giving up one's life, Jesus now faces that very sacrifice. He is deeply anxious, and asks if He should pray for deliverance. Instead, Jesus basically says to God the Father, "If My death and agony bring You glory, then I'll do it" (12:27).

After Jesus declares His desire to the Father, the Father speaks to Him in an audible voice (12:28). There are only two other times in the Gospel accounts in which God speaks audibly—at Jesus' baptism (Matthew 3:17; Mark 1:11; Luke 3:22; compare John 1:29–34) and His transfiguration (Matthew 17:1–8; Mark 9:2–8; and Luke 9:28–36). When God spoke at Jesus' baptism, He expressed His approval, authenticating His Son. Why? Because people around Jesus were thinking about a great Jewish nation, and Jesus was talking about His own death.

When Jesus says that God is speaking for the people's sake (12:30), He means that the Father did not speak from heaven because Jesus needed confirmation, but because the crowd needed confirmation that Jesus' death will bring glory to God. That is the centerpiece of God's plan. In verses 31–33, Jesus explains.

Critical Observation

The background of Jesus' description of the "prince of this world" (12:31 NIV) being driven out is found in Genesis 3, the story of the fall of Adam and Eve. God promised a struggle between Eve's seed (that which would be born of her, her descendants) and the seed of the serpent who had tricked her (Genesis 3:15). Jesus is the fulfillment of this promise. The cross is the place where we see God, but it is also the place where Satan's power will be broken.

Notice that Jesus says that He will draw all people to Himself (12:32). The words we translate as "all people" don't mean that Jesus will draw to Him everyone ever created. It means that He will draw all those who put their faith in Him throughout history.

Look at the response. The people understand that Jesus is saying He must die, but they can't reconcile that with the idea that the Messiah will live forever (12:34). They miss the simple reality that the Old Testament says both about the Messiah, that He will die but that He will also live forever.

Jesus' reply points them to the urgent necessity to act on the light that they have (12:35-36). They must give up their preconceived notions and act on the revelation that Jesus is giving them, and then their questions will be answered. In essence, you must first become a child of the light if you are going to walk in the light.

The next public revelation will come at His crucifixion. Jesus spends the remainder of His days preparing the disciples for what is to come.

12:37–50

THE UNBELIEF OF ISRAEL

John inserts verses 37–50 to show his readers that the rejection of Israel is all a part of what God had said would happen, and therefore, it is not a reason to deny that Jesus is the Messiah. Instead, it is a sign confirming that Jesus is the Messiah (12:38–41). He quotes from two passages of Isaiah: 53:1 and 6:10. Both of these passages talk about the blindness of Israel in relation to the Messiah. That blindness was produced by God as a form of judgment. There is a segment of people who believe, but they are afraid of the stigma of admitting it (12:42–43).

Verses 44–50 summarize Jesus' teaching and public ministry. This is not a literal response to the leaders mentioned in verse 42. It is probably from a series of messages that Jesus had preached to the leaders and is now condensed for the readers of this Gospel. The idea that Jesus cries out these words (12:44) means that whenever they are spoken, they are shouted out. This signifies their importance.

The point in verse 47 is not that Jesus will never judge sin or faithlessness, but that His mission for the time being is not about judgment. Judgment will happen in the future (12:48-49).

JOHN 13:1–38

FINAL WORDS

Love in Action	13:1 17
A Traitor in the Camp	13:18–30
The Distinguishing Mark of the Church	13:31–38

Setting Up the Section

Chapter 13 begins a very concentrated description of the love of God as seen through the sacrifice of Jesus.

The Passover was a celebration that pointed in two directions. It pointed backward to the great exodus from Egypt, God's deliverance. But it also pointed forward to God's final salvation. Isaiah and other Old Testament prophets described a new and greater exodus that God will accomplish when He delivers His people and establishes His kingdom (Isaiah 11:10–16; 40:1–5).

Jesus is that once-for-all Passover Lamb who will accomplish this new exodus. Jesus knows that He is about to die and become the fulfillment of what the Passover meal pointed to. John tells us that Jesus is fully aware of what is taking place (13:1).

13:1–17

LOVE IN ACTION

In verse 1, the word "hour" (NIV) refers to the whole period of the crucifixion, not just the hanging on the cross. John is making the point that Jesus knows He is ending His full-time public ministry and, therefore, will die, then ascend into heaven, completing the task of redemption.

For Jesus to love His own "to the end" (NASB) is another way of saying that Jesus loves them with a complete love, a love that will carry them through to the end. To love someone to the end means to love someone to perfection. It's unconditional love. The cross is the place where Jesus' perfect and complete love is manifested.

John refers to Judas's betrayal but leaves out any details concerning it (13:2). Jesus is in the room with a man who is in a conspiracy with Satan to seek His execution.

When Jesus lays aside His outer garment and takes the towel to wash the disciples' feet, He is putting on the clothes and taking on the role of the lowest of servants (13:3–5). This is why Peter is so unsettled (13:6). His view of leadership would have rejected a leader doing such a thing. His interpretation of leadership was that of being served, not of serving. Once Peter understands the cross, the foot washing will make more sense (13:7).

Critical Observation

In that day people usually wore sandals. Walking on dusty, sometimes filthy, roads would make their feet dirty. It was the role of the lowest slave to actually clean the feet of the guests as they arrived. At the home the disciples used for this meal, there were no servants, and therefore, their feet did not get washed.

In verse 10, Jesus responds to Peter's request for a bath (13:8–9) with a principle of forgiveness. If a person has taken a bath before he goes to a gathering at someone's house, when he arrives he does not need to get an entire bath again. All he needs is to have the dust of his feet washed off. The rest of his body is already clean. The point—you do not need to go beyond what Jesus offers for salvation. His work is enough for a lifetime. That is why it is a perfect love.

The point of Jesus' explanation of the foot washing is for these men to understand their roles in a new way (13:12–17). The example that Jesus has set is that of humility. True love is an enduring love that seeks to serve others at expense to self. The only way for the world to see what Jesus did to save mankind is for His followers to model before the world that kind of humility.

13:18–30

A TRAITOR IN THE CAMP

In verses 12–17, Jesus explains to His disciples that they are to show true love by their humble service to each other. In the midst of this lesson, Jesus changes gears and begins to talk about Judas. John has already mentioned the betrayal of Judas in his Gospel as early as John 6:70–71.

Jesus' point in verse 18 is simple: The commands and the blessing of obedience do not apply to Judas. As He said in verse 10, one man in the room is not really a true disciple and therefore does not or will not ever receive any blessing from God. Yet Judas fits into the divine design that God established for the redemption of mankind.

Jesus tells the disciples that His betrayal was predicted in the Old Testament; it fulfills scripture (13:18). He's referring to Psalm 41:9, a psalm of King David. David says in essence, that "his betrayer has lifted up his heel against him." This phrase can carry the idea of an attacker who, after wounding a person until he or she is defenseless, picks up his foot and drives it into the person's neck to inflict more damage. It also can refer to the heel of a horse, raised for a swift kick.

Demystifying John

King David had a son named Absalom with whom he was in conflict. Absalom tried to overthrow David's kingdom with the help of Ahithophel. Ahithophel was a counselor to both David and Absalom, and so Ahithophel betrayed David in favor of the rebellious Absalom (2 Samuel 15–17). David wrote Psalm 41, from which Jesus quotes here, in light of this betrayal.

In verse 19, Jesus once again refers to Himself as the *I Am*, the name God called Himself when commissioning Moses. His revelation of a betrayer will one day serve as a confirmation that He is who He claims to be. Verse 20, then, follows the chain of command. If Jesus and God are one, then those that Jesus sends out are included in that connection.

Note the response of the disciples to Jesus' announcement about a traitor. These men have labored together, yet they don't immediately suspect Judas (13:22). They are at a loss. This reminds us that their lives and relationships were as complicated and mysterious as our own can sometimes be.

While people of this day often ate sitting on the floor, it was also the custom at special meals to eat reclining at the side of a table. Each person reclined on his left arm, and ate with his right arm. In this way, since John was in a place of honor beside Jesus, John's head would be close to Jesus. This is why he would have been in a position to observe Jesus and to ask about the identity of the betrayer (13:23–25).

Jesus offers the bread dipped in sauce to Judas, signifying to John that Judas is the betrayer (13:26–27). Ironically, offering bread to a guest was a sign of friendship.

John mentions Judas's being possessed by Satan (13:27). This highlights the fact that the conflict is not between Jesus and the Pharisees, or the Romans, or even Judas. It is between Jesus and Satan. So when Jesus speaks to Judas, He gives Satan the approval to start the chain of events to bring about His crucifixion, though the disciples still don't understand the significance of those instructions and come to their own conclusions (13:28–29).

Light and darkness are a constant theme in John. It is symbolic that when Judas leaves, the Gospel makes it clear that it is night (13:30).

13:31–38

THE DISTINGUISHING MARK OF THE CHURCH

In this passage, Judas has already left the room, and Jesus is talking with the remaining disciples.

Son of Man (13:31) is a historical phrase that Jesus uses in the Gospels to refer to Himself. It is a title introduced in the Old Testament book of Daniel (7:13–14). In Daniel 7:13 (NIV), Daniel speaks of "one like a son of man" (meaning a human figure) who comes before the Ancient of Days (God Himself) and is given authority, glory, sovereign power, and an eternal kingdom. It is this portrait of the exalted Messiah that Jesus is drawing on when He refers to Himself as the Son of Man.

The word "glorified" (13:31 NIV) means to reveal with honor. Contemporary English describes a son who looks just like his father as a glorified version of his dad. Notice that, in this case, Jesus ties His glory in with His death. It is in the death of Jesus that His glory, the presence of God, is revealed. God will put Jesus on display (13:32).

Critical Observation

Keep in mind that on the cross Jesus performed a great act of love. By doing this, He manifested the Father and therefore was glorified. Consider this:

- On the cross Jesus redeemed mankind from hell.
- On the cross Jesus disarmed Satan and destroyed the power of sin.
- On the cross Jesus paid the price that God's justice demanded for humanity's sin: death.
- On the cross Jesus offered His body as the perfect sacrifice to God.
- On the cross the justice of God and the law of God were fully satisfied.

Jesus tells the disciples that they are not allowed to come with Him (13:33). He had told the Jewish leadership this same thing in an earlier confrontation (8:21). There is a difference in the meanings, though. Jesus told the Jews that they would die in their sins and could not come with Him into eternal life. He is telling the disciples that they cannot come with Him to the cross.

Then, in verse 34, Jesus gives the requirement of the mission with which He will leave the disciples. He calls this a new commandment, though God had already commanded the Jews to love each other (Leviticus 19:18). This is a new commandment because of the standard of this love. Jesus says that they are to love each other even as Jesus loves. The result will be that the disciples are recognized as followers of Jesus by the way they love (13:35).

All four Gospels record the claim Peter makes to lay down his life for Jesus (13:37; Matthew 26:35; Mark 14:31; Luke 22:33). His words echo those of Jesus when He describes the work of the shepherd laying down his life for the sheep (10:11, 15, 17). As bold as Peter's claim is on behalf of Jesus, Jesus predicts here Peter's denial (13:38)—which happens that very night (18:17, 25–27).

JOHN 14:1–31

HOPE FOR THE DISCOURAGED

Hope for the Hopeless	14:1–3
Clarity for the Confused	14:4–31

Setting Up the Section

Jesus is giving His final address before His death. Some have compared His words to Moses' last address to his people before his death (Deuteronomy 31–33).

In this passage, Jesus offers some very specific encouragement regarding the Spirit of God, and the role He will play in the lives of the disciples. Then, in the following chapters (15–16), He offers instructions on how He wants them to act, and speaks of the persecution they are to expect from this point on.

14:1–3

HOPE FOR THE HOPELESS

Jesus first tells His disciples what not to do: Don't be troubled (14:1). He does not want the current situation to create fear and sadness. This is actually a night of rejoicing.

Next He tells them to believe in Him. Jesus is redirecting their faith and focus from their circumstances to the God who controls those circumstances. First, Jesus tells the disciples that He is preparing a place for them; second, that His return is as sure as His departure; third, Jesus tells them that they will be unified with Him as a result of His return (14:2–3). Being united with Jesus in heaven will be the full consummation of the disciples' faith. His leaving is not a sign that He is out of their lives, but rather a sign of His desire to be with them forever.

Critical Observation

Jesus' comment about God's house having many rooms (14:2) has sparked many images of a heaven with specific dwellings in it. Another understanding of Jesus' words has less to do with a place in heaven and more to do with the access that we have to God through Jesus' work. Jesus is providing a way for His followers to be *with* God. The way we do that as people is to go to someone's house.

14:4–31

CLARITY FOR THE CONFUSED

Jesus tells the disciples they already know both the place and the way to where He is going, and that both the location and the way to that location are bound up in Him. When Thomas asks about this, Jesus makes another *I am* statement, identifying himself as the way, the truth, and the life (14:4–6). In Jewish wisdom literature following "the way" meant living life by God's standards. The "truth" and the "life" further that explain the way. Jesus is the only true path that leads to eternal life with God.

The disciples do not recognize Jesus for who He truly is (14:7). When He tells them they will eventually know who He is, He is referring to all that is to come—His resurrection, ascension, the coming of the Spirit—then they will fully know Him, and in knowing Him they will know the Father.

Philip's request reveals that he wants his confidence to be grounded in his physical and earthly experience (14:8). Jesus' rebuke reiterates His same point—Jesus is the revelation of the Father on earth. Jesus is not enough for Philip because Philip does not truly understand or believe this (14:9).

Jesus makes three key points in verses 10–12:

1) His unity with the Father. Jesus asks a question that forces the point (14:10): Do they believe He is one with God?
2) A call to faith. Only God could do the works that Jesus has done (14:11).
3) Those who believe in Jesus will do His same works and even greater (14:12). The word *greater* indicates the idea of "greater in depth." What could be greater than raising the dead? Preaching the gospel of eternal life.

Jesus shares with them in verses 13–14 that the gap between the Father and the disciples is closed by Jesus. They now have access to the Father. They have the resources of heaven at their disposal.

Verse 15 carries the idea that a person cannot say that they love Jesus and disobey Him. Intrinsic to faith is obedience.

Jesus says that He will intercede before the Father and ask that the Helper, or Counselor, be given (14:16). The word translated *helper* or *counselor* means one who "comes alongside to intercede or to support." This is not the idea of a therapist's role, but more like a lawyer who pleads a case for you. The helper is the Spirit of truth (14:17). He reveals the truth to those who believe.

In verses 18–19, Jesus moves on to the eternal relationship His followers will have with Him. Because of His resurrection and departure, He is giving them the Spirit, access to God, the ability to work the miracles of heaven, and a promise of abundant life on earth and eternal life in heaven. They are not orphans; they have a new home in heaven. When the Spirit comes, they will understand these things (14:20).

In verse 21, Jesus goes back to the importance of obedience. True love is marked by obedience. Those who truly obey are one with Jesus, one with the Father, and truly understand who Jesus is (4:21). Jesus reveals Himself to those who obey Him.

There were two Judases in the original twelve disciples. John is clear here which is asking the question (14:22). Judas's question probably comes from a misunderstanding of prophecies such as Isaiah 11, which describe the coming of the Messiah in terms of worldwide recognition and a change in the entire world system. He is wondering why Jesus wouldn't be revealed to the whole world.

To answer Judas's question, Jesus explains the nature of salvation (14:23–24). Those who do not obey out of faith will not come to the realization of who Jesus is. The disclosure is not an automatic reality for everyone; it is only a reality for those who are truly devoted.

Then Jesus reminds them that when He goes, things will get a little more difficult but He will send the Holy Spirit to empower them (14:26). They are required to obey, preserve, guard, and protect all that Jesus has taught. That is something that is impossible in the flesh. Yet, with the Spirit's help, it can be done.

The discouragement of the disciples initiated this conversation, so Jesus reminds them of the peace that only He can give (14:27).

Critical Observation

One idea of *peace* is the absence of war—knowing that your nation and your home are secure. Peace was to be the supreme result of the Messiah's coming. The *Pax Romana*, peace of Rome, was achieved through military power, and the Jews of that day easily thought that the messianic peace would have to come through a mightier military power than that of the Roman army. Yet the peace of Jesus was achieved through the death of a righteous man.

Jesus refers to His departure for the sixth time in this chapter (14:28). Each time, He has shown the disciples some theological error in their belief. In this case, Jesus directly challenges their love for Him. Why? To produce faith (14:29).

Take It Home

In this text, Jesus gives us two great descriptions of what it means to be a Christian:

First, to obey Jesus' words. Obeying Jesus is more than just a series of dos and don'ts. It's a way of life in which all that you do and believe is conformed to the image and character of Jesus.

Second, to be devoted to Christ's glory. A true believer seeks to glorify Jesus even at expense to himself.

JOHN 15:1–27

FINAL INSTRUCTIONS

Abide in Jesus	15:1–11
Abide in Love	15:12–17
The Cost of Abiding	15:18–27

Setting Up the Section

Central to the heart of Jesus' message, and especially clear in the Gospel of John, is the fact that Jesus declares that He is what the Old Testament longed for. Jesus is the resolution. He is the one promised as early as Genesis 3:15, the great redeemer of humanity.

Chapter 15 moves from Jesus' first discourse of encouragement to His second discourse of instruction.

15:1–11

ABIDE IN JESUS

Jesus says, "I am the true vine" (15:1 NIV). (This is the seventh time Jesus makes an *I am* statement in John's Gospel.) The disciples are already connected to the vine, not on the basis of their works or adherence to the law, but based upon the Word Jesus spoke to them (15:3). The idea around the word "clean" (15:3 NIV) is that of being purified from sins in order to be used by God. Unlike Old Testament Israel, who failed to produce the fruit of obedience, the disciples' hearts are cleansed from their sin so they can produce fruit.

Demystifying John

Jesus explains the Father is the vinedresser. The role of a vinedresser is to care for and protect the vine and the branches. The act of pruning the dead branches is the act of protecting the good branches to ensure that they get the maximum amount of sap for growth (15:2). The Father is actively a part of the fruit-bearing process.

Jesus reiterates His point that the disciples must maintain their faith in Him (15:4; see John 8:31–32). The idea of maintaining means not breaking fellowship. The disciples must keep an undivided heart and an undivided faith. They cannot bear fruit without being connected to the vine. Therefore, it is essential that they completely trust Jesus, or they will not be connected to the source of life (15:6).

Verse 7 declares that if we are in this union with Jesus, our prayers will be heard and answered. Because of our union with Jesus, He is able to hear and answer us. God intended for His character to be manifested through the fruit that is produced by a person who is in union with Him (15:8).

Jesus has shown His disciples the same love that the Father has shown to Him. He wants the same relationship between His disciples and Himself as He has with the Father. That relationship is marked by Jesus' complete devotion to the commandments and love of the Father. In the same way, if a person keeps His commandments, that person abides in Jesus (15:9–10).

Jesus tells the disciples all this so that they might experience the joy that He possesses (15:11). If they abide in Jesus, then they will have that perfect joy.

15:12–17

ABIDE IN LOVE

Jesus gives the commandment that His disciples should love one another as Jesus loved them (15:12). This is the application of verse 10—abide in Jesus' love by loving others the way that Jesus loved.

Verse 13 reveals God's definition of love. At one level, this verse lays out the standard of love Jesus' disciples are to show to one another; at another level, it refers to Jesus' death on behalf of His friends. It is this level of sacrifice that Jesus wants the disciples to associate with love. Jesus shows these men that they have been the recipient of this type of selfless love, and it is upon that basis that they are to love each other. The implication in verse 14 is obvious—Jesus is going to lay down His life for them.

In verse 14, it might appear that Jesus is saying that you are a friend of Jesus if you are obedient. Notice the last part of this verse: Jesus tells them that they are His friends "if you do what I command" (NIV). It's not their obedience that makes them friends, but rather their friendship is characterized by obedience. The point is that Jesus lays down His life for them, and they, as a result of this love, become completely devoted to Him.

How have they been a recipient of Jesus' love?

1) They've gone from being called a slave to being called a friend (15:15).
2) They will produce lasting fruit (15:16).

Jesus, out of His love, chose these men. Their relationship with God is a result of *His* choice, not theirs. Not only were the disciples chosen, but they were chosen for a purpose: that they should be sent to bear fruit. The idea around the word "appointed" (15:16 NIV) is the word *ordained*. They have been set apart for a particular purpose. Inherent to their salvation is their mission. This is true for every believer.

Take It Home

When you see the way that Jesus loves you, it becomes easier to love others with that same humility. What does God do when you fail? He lovingly and patiently restores you—go and do the same for others. When we grasp this point we begin to comprehend what it means to be a disciple, and what it means to disciple others. Love must be at the heart of who we are and what we do.

15:18–27

THE COST OF ABIDING

In order to help the disciples deal with the fear of the future persecution that awaits them, Jesus instructs them about suffering. In verses 18–21, Jesus identifies two reactions that the world (in this context, anyone who is not devoted to Jesus) will have to the disciples: hatred and persecution.

The second half of verse 20 shows a division. Everywhere that Jesus went there was a mixed reaction—those who hated what Jesus said and those who believed. The disciples will receive the same mixed reactions.

Jesus sums up His point by telling the disciples why they will face persecution (15:21)—because they are associated with Jesus and because their opposition does not know the Father. It is clear in verse 22 that Jesus is talking about the Jewish leadership. It is not as if the coming of Jesus introduced sin and guilt to these people. Rather, by coming and speaking to them, Jesus revealed the most central and most controlling sin, that of the human heart to choose the darkness over the light. Jesus not only revealed God, He revealed humanity's heart.

The sin that Jesus is referring to in verse 22 is the sin of rejection. If Jesus had not come, the rejection in the Jewish leaders' hearts would have never been made evident. Jesus' coming caused people to either accept or reject Him—which is the same as rejecting the Father (15:23). Jesus did works among them that displayed the glory of the Father to the Jewish leaders, and in rejecting Jesus they rejected the Father (15:24).

Demystifying John

Verse 25 is a quote from two psalms: Psalm 35:19 and 69:4. These are psalms of David, in which David is being hunted down because he was the chosen king of Israel. Jesus connects Himself to these psalms. If David, the lesser king, was hated without a cause, how much more would Jesus, the greater king of Israel, be hated without a cause?

When Jesus goes to heaven, His testimony on earth will not go to heaven with Him, but will stay and be proclaimed by the Holy Spirit. Not only will the Spirit bear witness, but the disciples will bear witness as well. In the face of these witnesses, Jesus' opposition will continue to reject the message just as it did when He walked the earth (15:26–27).

JOHN 16:1–33

A HELPER FOR DIFFICULT DAYS

A Final Word on Persecution	16:1–4
Better Days Are Yet to Come	16:5–15
The Transforming Work of the Spirit	16:16–33

Setting Up the Section

In the last several chapters, Jesus has warned the disciples about the difficulties they will face. John 16 continues on this same topic. This way, when these men face the persecution Jesus has described, they will not be surprised. In fact, it could confirm their faith.

16:1–4

A FINAL WORD ON PERSECUTION

The Jewish leaders had already expelled from the synagogue those who believed in Jesus (9:22; 12:42). This will certainly continue and will happen to the disciples (16:1–2). By the time John was writing this Gospel, the Christian movement had broken ties completely with the synagogues, which once had been the conduits for Jesus to speak to His countrymen.

Critical Observation

Stephen became the first Christian martyr (Acts 7:54–60), with Saul, the yet unconverted Paul the apostle, looking on. Saul's perspective was very much what Jesus describes in verse 2. He saw his persecution of Christians as his service to God (Galatians 1:13–14; Philippians 3:6). These deaths happened for the very reason that Jesus described—the persecutors didn't know the Father and didn't understand the connection between God the Father and His Son, Jesus.

16:5–15

BETTER DAYS ARE YET TO COME

In verses 5–6, Jesus identifies a major problem in the heart of the disciples: their self-focused minds. Sorrow has filled their hearts because it seems they are going to lose everything when Jesus goes away. This is the second time that Jesus has shown the disciples their self-centeredness (14:28). They can't see past the persecution that is to come to see the bigger picture of what Jesus is accomplishing through His departure.

Jesus focuses now on one aspect of His departure, that of the Holy Spirit (16:7). The role of the Holy Spirit on earth cannot be understated. The Spirit is the Helper, or advocate, of those who believe and the accuser of those who don't. He duplicates the work of Jesus on earth.

The ministry of the Spirit to the world centers on conviction of sin (16:8–10). The word *convict* means "to expose, refute, or convince." The Spirit will also proclaim the end of Satan's reign (16:11). The Spirit will testify that Satan and his system have already been condemned by God.

Jesus is beginning to draw His instruction to a close (16:12). It is time for them to endure the next few days. After that, the Spirit will work on their behalf (16:13–15).

16:16–33

THE TRANSFORMING WORK OF THE SPIRIT

Jesus' point, that He will go and then return (16:16), confuses the disciples (16:17–18). They are trying to reconcile all that Jesus said to them. This is the first that we have heard from the disciples since Judas's question in chapter 14, but in this case they are only wondering among themselves out of earshot of Jesus. Aware of their confusion, Jesus articulates the question that they do not ask Him (16:19).

Demystifying John

The King James Version (also NKJV) includes the phrase, "Because I go to the Father," at the end of verse 17. This phrase, which does not occur in the earliest Greek manuscripts, was probably added by a later copyist to help the reader understand verse 17. Jesus has said throughout His instructions that He was going to the Father.

Jesus tells the disciples their sorrow will be turned into joy (16:20); notice not *replaced with joy* but *turned into joy*. This means the very event that plunges them into grief will be what lifts them into joy. What is the thing that will plunge them into sorrow? The cross.

Jesus illustrates this principle with childbirth (16:21). Before the baby is born, there is sorrow. The pain is astounding. But once the baby is born, the focus suddenly shifts from the pain to the joy of having a baby. The event becomes a day of celebration, where once a year the birth of this child is remembered, not as a day of pain but a day of joy. The event did not change, only the focus of the event. And the birth becomes a greater day than the sorrow. And the sorrow is only temporary, but the joy is eternal (16:22).

Critical Observation

Jesus continues to explain. There will come a time of understanding. They will be able to approach God directly in the name of Jesus and He will answer them (16:23). This is a tremendous change from the Old Testament Judaism that required a mediator between humanity and God (16:24). This is not a rebuke; rather, Jesus is explaining to the disciples that they will have this new relationship with the Father, and He encourages them to go the Father and receive His response. And the result: full joy.

It is one thing to have joy; it is another thing to have *full* joy. Full joy comes from a person who has an active prayer life with the Father. Those who are in such a relationship, where the Father is granting their prayers, have their joy strengthened because they are experiencing a relationship with the Father.

Some translations have the world *parable* in verse 25, others say *figurative language*. The meaning is "a veiled or hidden truth." Because Jesus speaks in this kind of language, the disciples will be dependent upon Him for the understanding.

The point of verse 26 is that Jesus does not need to do all of the requesting for them anymore. Now they can pray on their own because they will pray in accordance with God's will—because they know God's will. They now have the understanding to be able to come before God and pray.

The reason that Christ will not intercede for His disciples is that the Father Himself loves them. The Father does not need to be persuaded to be gracious to them (16:27–28). Because they place their faith in Jesus and are completely devoted to Him, they are able to enjoy a relationship with the Father in which they can now approach Him on their own.

In verse 28, Jesus restates the truth that must be believed: Christ came from heaven, therefore, He manifests God. He'll return to heaven, completing the perfect work of salvation. Christ's heavenly origin is important, else He would not be our Savior. But His heavenly destination is also important, for it is witness to the Father's seal on the Son's saving work.

Verse 29 is the first public response of the disciples since chapter 14. In verse 30, they ascribe their understanding to the fact that Jesus is from God because He knows everything. They think that because they understand His answer that they now understand what is going on. But this is not the case. If they truly understand, then they will not have such a fearful reaction when Jesus' trials start.

Observe Jesus' response to their aggressive answer (16:31–32). In less than twenty-four hours they will experience their first set of trials, and those trials will continue for the rest of their existence. But Jesus wants them to fully understand that His peace will allow them remain stable in the turbulent world around them. And the reason that His peace will do this is because His peace has overcome the world (16:33).

Take It Home

Just as Jesus promised the Spirit's help to the disciples, that help is here for us. We are not alone, left to fend for ourselves. God's Spirit still points us to Jesus. And it is upon His power that we become His witnesses.

We must continue to look to Jesus to live the Christian life and to accomplish the work that He set out for us to do. We must believe in the presence of the Holy Spirit, here to give us the strength to continue on in that work, no matter what we face.

JOHN 17:1–26

JESUS' PRAYER

Jesus Prays for Himself	17:1–5
Jesus Prays for His Disciples	17:6–19
Jesus Prays for All Believers	17:20–26

Setting Up the Section

This chapter offers a pre-cross preview of the post-cross work of Jesus: the work of intercession—praying on behalf of believers. Jesus prays for Himself, for His disciples, and for believers of every age and every generation. His prayers reveal even more about the beautiful relationship between Jesus and the Father.

17:1–5

JESUS PRAYS FOR HIMSELF

Today we often bow our heads in reverence when we pray. In the first-century Jewish culture, a common prayer posture was standing with eyes lifted to heaven (17:1). It signifies two things:

1) that the person praying acknowledges God's place in heaven on the throne, and

2) that the person praying is coming to God with a clean and pure heart.

Jesus prays that the will of God will be done in His life. He acknowledges that God's plan, appointed in eternity past, is ready to be carried out. He prays:

1) That the cross would bring God glory

2) That the cross would save people

Jesus also prays for the consequence of the cross (17:2). The essence of this prayer is that Jesus desires that eternal life be given to all of those who have been given to Him.

In verse 3, Jesus speaks to an essential element of salvation: the understanding of God. Eternal life is not a measure of time; it is the life of God in man or woman. This is why Jesus has told the disciples that they are to have His peace, His joy, His love, and all that Jesus has. Jesus' role is to dispense all that He is to those whom the Father has given Him.

Verse 4 reveals the perfect obedience of Jesus. He finished the work that God called Him to do. Because of that, He prays that He will return to the union that He shared with the Father before He came to earth (17:5).

17:6–19

JESUS PRAYS FOR HIS DISCIPLES

In verse 6, Jesus prays for the specific followers who were commissioned to bring the message of the Messiah to the world. These followers are described as those who kept the Word of God. Jesus made known to them the Word of God, and they responded to it and upheld it as a way of life.

Critical Observation

Some translations of this verse mention Jesus revealing God's name to His disciples. To reveal the name of God simply means to show the full character of God. This is one of the key roles of Jesus particularly highlighted in John's Gospel: to reveal the Father. Jesus revealed God to these people, and ultimately, they came to believe that Jesus was indeed from heaven as He claimed (17:7–8).

Jesus is saying that these disciples are a part of His family (17:9), true believers. He then prays for their unity.

There is a reason that this is a specific prayer for a specific group of people, and that reason is found at the end of verse 10 and at the beginning of verse 11. Jesus is preparing to leave the world, and His disciples are going to put Jesus on display to the world as He has displayed the Father.

In verses 11–12, Jesus prays for protection for these men. The idea is that the Father will protect them in the same way that Jesus did while He was on earth. But even more than protect them, He will uphold them so that they will remain an ever visible representation of Jesus Christ on earth.

Jesus calls God "Holy Father" (17:11 NIV). The word *holy* means "to be separate, or set apart." In this context, it means someone who is set apart from sin and this world. The idea is "holy and separate Father, protect them from the world that You are not bound to."

In verse 12, the one that was lost is a reference to Judas Iscariot. Judas's betrayal was predicted in the Old Testament (Psalm 41:9; 109:4–13). He was given to Jesus to fulfill the role of betrayer. In 17:12 the word "perdition" (KJV), or some translations use "doomed to destruction" (NIV), refers to someone who is utterly lost with no hope of ever being saved. A subtle point here is that the will of the Father was accomplished in both Judas and the other eleven disciples.

In the midst of all of the persecution and hatred, Jesus prays that His joy would fill these men (17:13). Not only does Jesus want them to have joy on the basis of the Father's care for them, He also wants them to be sanctified as a result of the Father's protection.

Because they, like Jesus, are not a part of the world's system, they will be hated (17:14). Jesus is not asking that they be taken away from the hatred (17:1–5). Instead of escape, they need protection from Satan so that they will be set apart from the world (17:16).

Verse 17 is the other side of the coin of protection. Not only are they to be protected from Satan, they are also to be holy, or sanctified. To be *sanctified* is to be set apart for a specific purpose. It is the idea of being a holy vessel in the hands of the Master. How does a person become sanctified? By the Word of God.

In verse 18, Jesus, in prayer, sends the disciples out. Then in verse 19, Jesus sets Himself apart. Upon His work the disciples were sanctified and are sent out to continue His mission.

17:20–26

JESUS PRAYS FOR ALL BELIEVERS

Jesus prays a three-fold prayer for future generations of believers (17:20)—unity, glory, and love.

1) Unity. That the disciples would know the oneness that exists between the Father and the Son (17:21). This oneness is revealed when the life of God is living in a person (17:22–23). Because of Jesus' work with the disciples (revealing the Father), they have His life within them and are to be unified just as the Father and the Son are one.
2) Glory. Jesus prays to the Father that we will experience the full glory of Himself in heaven (17:24).
3) Love. Jesus prays that we will have His love within us. One of the functions of the revelation of the Father was to place the unending love of God within those who believe (17:25–26).

Take It Home

Jesus' prayer makes it clear that Christians need to be one in the perfect unity of God so that they will have a testimony in this world. Without this unity, there is no testimony. Our ability to be unified in thought, mind, word, and deed shows the world that Jesus is from God.

How are the Father and the Son one? They are both separate from sin, and they both are devoted to the revelation of the other. And in that sense, we are to be one in this body. We are to be holy, and we are to be devoted to each other's best interests.

JOHN 18:1–40

JESUS' TRIALS

The Sovereign Control of Jesus 18:1–11
Humanity's Corruption and Jesus' Innocence 18:12–27
What Is Truth? 18:28–40

Setting Up the Section

Chapters 18–21 make up the final section of the Gospel of John—the death and resurrection of Jesus. John's focus in this account remains true to the rest of the Gospel—even in the account of the crucifixion, Jesus reveals the Father. This is not the picture of a weak and feeble man who is being taken by surprise by the events. Instead, the point here is that Jesus is actually in control of all of the events that are going on.

This is Jesus' moment. It is God's plan and not the plan of the Jews. The death of Jesus was ultimately the will of God—John's Gospel makes this clear.

18:1–11

THE SOVEREIGN CONTROL OF JESUS

Verse 1 transfers us from Jesus' prayer to His walk to the garden where He is going to be betrayed and arrested. The Garden of Gethsemane is the place where Jesus went often to pray.

Judas knew that this is where He would be (18:2), and Jesus would have been aware of that. Jesus is not being taken by surprise; He is giving up His life. Jesus knew that Judas was plotting to turn Him over to the Jews. He went to the garden because it was His time to die.

Verse 3 reveals what Judas was doing when he left the Passover meal (13:30). The Jews now have Judas working for them, and the leaders put an entire army together to arrest Jesus. There are two groups of people mentioned:

1) The Roman cohort. This represents about six hundred soldiers. During Passover, the Romans would usually double their guards to create a show of force to eliminate the beginnings of any insurrection.
2) Officers from the chief priests and the Pharisees. The chief priests hired a group of temple police to enforce the Jewish laws. These officers were the ones who arrested Jesus.

At this point in the year there would have typically been a clear sky and a full moon, which means there would be need for just a few lanterns. These people came with torches, lanterns, and weapons—this implies that they were prepared for a search and, if necessary, a fight.

Instead of putting up a fight, Jesus goes to these men before they can come to Him (18:4). Notice that the Gospel writer makes it clear that Judas is standing with the guards, not the disciples (18:5).

Jesus responds with another *I am* statement, confirming His identity as God, who introduced Himself in the Old Testament as "I AM." Jesus is not simply saying that He is Jesus; He declares Himself the revelation of God. When He does this, close to seven hundred people fall to the ground because of the power of His name (18:6). This detail is a continuation of John's theme of Jesus as the revelation of the Father. It also further emphasizes that Jesus is offering Himself. It is God's will that He be arrested, not human will.

Jesus asks a second time who these men are looking for. The essence of this question is, "Whose name is on the arrest warrant?" (18:7–8). These officers may have wanted Jesus' disciples arrested as well. But there was, in essence, only one name on the warrant; and so Jesus, the one to be arrested, instructs the officers to let the others go.

In His prayer Jesus had just claimed that He would lose none of the disciples. Here, Jesus is preserving the disciples (18:9).

In verse 10, Peter, at the height of passion, attempts to defend Jesus with his sword. The particular Greek word for *sword* used here implies a small dagger. This kind of dagger would have been used to gut fish and could have been used to defend oneself in close combat. Given that Peter was a fisherman, it was not strange for him to carry this kind of weapon.

There is a good possibility that Peter was not aiming for the ear, but rather swinging for the head. In Luke's Gospel, we are told that Jesus put the ear back on Malchus (Luke 22:50–51), but John focuses on Peter's mistake—Peter failed to see Jesus as being in control. Jesus rebukes Peter and tells him to put his sword away (18:11).

Critical Observation

Peter gets a lot of attention in this chapter because He goes from the height of passion in defending Jesus, to the depth of despair in denying Jesus. But both are equal in their disobedience. Neither is an act of faith.

Passion, zeal, and excitement for God are not pleasing to Him if not in accordance with the divine will of God. Peter is still trying to prevent the cross from happening. He is trying to protect his Friend and Teacher, but he is actually standing in God's way.

Notice the word *cup* in verse 11. In Jewish thought this word is sometimes associated with judgment—the cup of God's wrath, or the cup of judgment (Revelation 14:10). Peter missed the point. His flesh produced a zeal that tried to defend Jesus, but in all reality Jesus did not want or need to be defended by him.

18:12–27

HUMANITY'S CORRUPTION AND JESUS' INNOCENCE

The Romans and the Jewish officers of the high priest worked together to arrest Jesus (18:12). Typically, these groups did not work together; in fact they were often in opposition.

Jesus is led to Annas, the father-in-law of Caiaphas (18:13). Annas was a powerful man. Annas, for several years, operated as the high priest, and then continued his influence through his son-in-law's role as high priest. Annas's control of Caiaphas was generally recognized by the people.

Critical Observation

Annas was the man who ran the concessions at the temple. The concessions were where the animals were sold for sacrifice, and foreign currency would be exchanged. Annas functioned as a businessman, making money and wielding power. He bought his way into power, and could often pay off the Romans to get his way.

In verse 14, John reminds his readers that Caiaphas was the one who said that it is better to kill Jesus than to lose the entire nation (11:49–50).

John's Gospel moves us from an introduction of the leaders to the failure of Peter, a failure that reveals that even with the best of intentions (13:37–38), it is impossible to be faithful to God in one's own power. Peter is following behind (18:15). In addition to Peter following, there is another disciple who is not named. This disciple might not be one of the eleven. Other followers of Jesus are also referred to as disciples, for instance Nicodemus (7:50) or Joseph of Arimathea (19:38).

This other disciple was known in the court of the high priest and is able to get Peter in to see what will happen (18:16). As Peter goes through the door, he is questioned, and he denies his association with Jesus (18:17). Then he goes to the fire to warm himself with the officers who have just been part of the arrest (18:18).

Critical Observation

One of the corruptions of this trial is that Jesus is the one being asked about His teaching. According to Jewish law, if you bring an accusation before a person, there must be witnesses. A defendant was supposed to be presumed innocent, and therefore would not have to answer any questions until the evidence is secured. In addition, a person accused of a crime was not allowed to be convicted based on his own testimony.

When the high priest questions Jesus about His teaching and His disciples (18:19), Jesus responds by asking why He is being questioned. He has already spoken openly before hundreds (18:20–21). Jesus' comments expose two things—His innocence and the illegalities of the trial. They should not be questioning Him without confirmed witnesses.

It was also illegal to strike a prisoner. The wording used for the officer striking Jesus (18:22) carries the idea that the officer hit Jesus hard, as one would strike an insubordinate criminal who was mouthing off to the authorities. There is a possibility that the officer did not use his hands, but actually used a stick. The wording used to describe the blow that Jesus received could be translated as a punch or a hit with a stick. There was no evidence offered to warrent Jesus' being hit in this situation (18:23–24).

Jesus is sent to the high priest for the next phase of the trial (18:24). While all of this is going on, Peter is still mingling in the courtyard. When asked if he is a disciple, again he says no

(18:25). Then, one of the servants of the high priest, a relative of Malchus, recognizes Peter and asks him if he is a disciple (18:26), and Peter says no a third time (18:27). When this happens, the rooster crows, just as Jesus had predicted (13:38).

18:28–40

WHAT IS TRUTH?

It is at this point that Pilate is brought into the story. The Jews did not have the authority to enforce the death penalty. Therefore, they needed to have the Romans find Jesus guilty, and then the Romans could put Him on a cross.

The Praetorium, or palace (18:28), is the Roman court, the hall of judgment. It is early when they lead Jesus to Pilate. This was a hurry-up process. Jesus has been up all night in an illegal trial, and now they bring Him before Pilate early in the morning before anyone can stop them.

Observe the hypocrisy in verse 28. The Jews are illegally running Jesus through a false trial, they are seeking to murder an innocent man, yet they do not want to go to into the house of a Gentile and be considered ceremonially unclean. (This is an example of John's Gospel highlighting the corruption of the process and the innocence of Jesus.)

Pilate's inquiry about the charges against Jesus exposes the motives of the Jews (18:29). They respond, in essence, with "Take our word for it" (18:30). They want Pilate to work for them and to execute Jesus on the basis of their judgment. They are not interested in a trial, only an execution. The Jews want death by crucifixion because it will portray Jesus as a lowly criminal, not someone to be followed. Another consequence might turn Jesus into a martyr and increase His following (18:31–32).

John gives us some important information in verse 32—the desire to crucify Jesus is not a cause for discouragement. The leaders are falling into God's plan. Jesus had told Nicodemus that He would be lifted up (3:14). The idea is that He would be lifted onto the cross. Psalm 22, considered a psalm about the Messiah, speaks to the crucifixion (Psalm 22:1, 18).

Pilate launches his own investigation (18:33). He's been led to believe that Jesus is an insurrectionist, declaring Himself king and, therefore, is leading a mass rebellion against Rome. This would have fed into the thoughts Rome had of the Jews all along. Rome feared any insurrection and, therefore, had guards and soldiers around Israel to minimize any attempts of rebellion.

The exchange between Pilate and Jesus reveals that Pilate doesn't have any idea why Jesus is being accused. The interview does provide Jesus an opportunity to explain that He is a king, but the kingdom of which He is a part doesn't exist within earthly boundaries (18:34–37). Jesus is not subject to the affairs of this world. Even His wording—that He came into this world—implies that He existed outside of it.

When Pilate asks about the truth, it is as if he is saying the truth cannot be found, that there is no absolute answer. Yet Jesus spoke the truth. Pilate finds no fault in Jesus, but the custom that makes releasing Barabbas a possibility, negates Pilate's view of Jesus' innocence (18:38). The Jewish leaders choose a robber over God's Son (18:39–40).

Take It Home

Pilate's role in the trial of Jesus reminds us that we all have to answer the same question: What are we going to do with Jesus? Will we trade Him for someone more like us? Will we wash our hands of Him rather than deal with the havoc His reign might wreak in our lives? Will we acknowledge who He is and surrender our lives? Will we make our choices based on that truth?

JOHN 19:1–42

JESUS' DEATH

Behold the Man 19:1–16
The Culmination of History 19:17–42

Setting Up the Section

Pilate will try over and over again to get rid of Jesus. He has already tried in chapter 18. He put Jesus up against a real insurrectionist named Barabbas, but the accusers chose Barabbas. Therefore, Pilate will attempt to avoid having to face Jesus and having to come to a point of action concerning Him.

19:1–16

BEHOLD THE MAN

Pilate's first attempt to rid himself of Jesus is centered on punishment (19:1). Maybe if he gives Jesus the most severe punishment, short of execution, that would satisfy accusers.

The Roman scourge was a stick wrapped in leather with long leather strips hanging off the end. Attached to the leather strips were bits of brass, lead, and bones filed to sharp points. The victim was strapped to the ground with his back up, tied to a post, or actually hung in the air. Scourging involved forty lashes on the back. This process could expose the arteries and even the internal organs. It shredded the skin. This was such a horrendous torture that no Roman citizen could ever legally be scourged, only the enemies of Rome. Many did not survive.

Critical Observation

Luke's Gospel records that before Pilate ordered Jesus to be scourged, he sent Jesus to Herod in the hopes of moving the case. Herod was the governor of the entire region of Palestine. Herod sent Jesus back, finding no fault in Him (Luke 23:6–12). It was at this point that Pilate ordered Jesus to be scourged, hoping that this would be enough punishment to satisfy His accusers.

Jesus is mocked as well as whipped (19:2–3). The idea in the description is that the soldiers keep mocking Jesus while they continue to beat Him.

Pilate again declares Jesus' innocence (19:4). At this point, Jesus has been beaten almost to death. His face would have been swollen, His body shredded, and He would have been covered in blood. There is also a crown of thorns on His head (19:5), piercing His skull and causing even more blood to pour down His face. He is also wearing a purple robe to signify that no one who is in the position to decide believes that Jesus is a king.

In displaying Jesus (19:5), Pilate tries to make the point that this man is no threat and certainly no king. Perhaps Pilate hoped this would satisfy the Jewish leaders. But nothing will keep Jesus from the cross.

The leaders call again for Jesus' crucifixion, hearkening back to the accusation of blasphemy. While Pilate reiterates that he has no official grounds on which to execute Jesus, the people explain their view on blasphemy (19:6–7). Pilate, scared and confused, makes His second attempt to free Jesus (19:8).

Critical Observation

Matthew's Gospel adds the detail of Pilate's wife. According to her dream, Pilate's dealings with Jesus would only bring suffering (Matthew 27:19). She sent a message to this effect to Pilate, increasing his discomfort with the situation.

Pilate wants to know if Jesus is a god (19:9). Jesus sits quietly, reminiscent of the lamb silent at his slaughter as described by the Old Testament prophet, Isaiah (Isaiah 53:7).

After Pilate reminds Jesus of his own power, Jesus responds, but only to put Pilate in his place (19:10–11). Any authority Pilate has is a delegated authority. Therefore, Jesus is not concerned about the outcome. The future of Jesus does not rest in the hands of Pilate; it ultimately rests in God.

From that point, Pilate moves from trying to persuade Jesus, to trying to persuade the Jews in the face of their threats to paint him as an enemy of Caesar (19:12).

Demystifying John

History records that the Jews had already complained to Caesar once about Pilate. Pilate had brought Roman votive shields, which the Jews viewed as idols, into Herod's palace in Jerusalem. When the Jews complained to Caesar, Caesar ordered Pilate to remove the shields, humiliating him.

If the Jews went to Caesar again and said that Pilate refused to execute a man who was trying to take over the Roman kingdom, Pilate might lose his position.

Pilate resorts to political pressure. He goes to the place where official judgments were made. Once a judgment was made from this place, it was permanent and binding. Pilate puts Jesus on display one more time in the robe, thorns, and with wounds and blood (19:14). John's Gospel points out that it's almost the sixth hour. The Passover celebration is at hand. A judgment needs to be made.

Pilate wants to put the pressure of the decision on the Jewish leaders. If Jesus is going to be crucified, it will be because they made the decision. And thus in a hypocritical expression of loyalty to Caesar, the Jewish leaders call for Jesus' death (19:15–16).

19:17–42

THE CULMINATION OF HISTORY

In verses 17–18, John shows the crucifixion simply and clearly. John's focus is the glory of Jesus, not the horror of the cross.

Demystifying John

The crucifixion of Jesus is a central event in human history. Jesus came so that God would be made known, and He died so that man would have eternal life.

The Gospel of John's main purpose is to present Jesus as the manifestation of God. Therefore, in writing the Gospel, John highlights accounts that speak to the issue of Jesus' deity. As we come to the account of Jesus' crucifixion, John will show us the majesty of Jesus in the midst of what His enemies hoped was His humiliation.

The "place of the skull" (19:17 NIV) is *Golgotha* in Hebrew and *Calvaria* in Latin. It is, of course, from the Latin that we use the English word *Calvary*. This was a hill, so the crucifixions would be seen by many. The public nature of Calvary was a visual reinforcement of Rome's power to control.

Jesus carries His own crossbeam. The vertical posts were already in the ground. Victims were led through the streets with the crossbeams on their backs.

Critical Observation

We are told in other accounts that before Jesus got to the foot of the hill, He became so weak that a man named Simon was asked to carry Jesus' crossbeam. When Jesus got to the place of execution, the crossbeam was nailed to His hands, He was hoisted up on to the vertical post, and the crossbeam was set into a notch on the horizontal beam already in the ground. (For other accounts of Jesus' crucifixion, see Matthew 27:27–54; Mark 15:25–39; Luke 23:26–47).

On this hill Jesus is hung between two thieves. This is significant because Isaiah 53:12 prophesied that the Messiah would be "counted among the rebels" (NLT).

Pilate's sign, made for the top of the cross, becomes a center of controversy (19:19). Pilate believes Jesus to be innocent, yet, for political reasons, he gives in to the crucifixion. It was a

Roman custom to place the offense of the person being crucified on the top of the cross to announce what the person did to warrant execution. Pilate's sign simply identifies Jesus as the King of the Jews, and is written in Aramaic, Latin, and Greek (19:20) so that all onlookers will be able to read it. Verse 20 tells us that the place where Jesus is crucified is near the city, and therefore, everyone can see the sign.

It is unusual that the sign has no disgrace to it, at least none for Jesus. But it does have some disgrace for the Jews. The leaders look guilty because they just crucified their king. In light of this, these Jews want the sign changed to put the offense back on Jesus—that He only *claimed* to be king (19:21). Pilate refuses (19:22), which may be a way of retaliating for the difficult position they put him in.

The next aspect of Jesus' glory relates to scriptures that He fulfilled.

Jesus' outer garments would have been His shoes, the belt, the headdress, and the outer cloak. The inner garment is one piece, therefore, the soldiers gamble to see who will get it (19:23–24). These soldiers fulfill Psalm 22:18.

There are four ladies at the foot of the cross (19:25), but almost all of the disciples are nowhere to be found. The first lady mentioned is Mary, Jesus' mother. When Mary brought Jesus to the temple as a baby, she was told by Simeon that there would come a day when her own heart would be pierced. The other ladies there are Mary's sister, Mary's sister-in-law, and Mary, the one in which Jesus cast out seven demons. All of these ladies loved Jesus and are there to be with Him until His death.

Even on the cross, Jesus fulfills His duty as Mary's son in seeing to it that she is cared for (19:26–27). Jesus places her into the care of John. From that point on, John treats Mary as his own mother and cares for her.

After Jesus completes His duty to His mother, He knows that everything that was to be accomplished has been (19:28). He then fulfills the final prophecy concerning what He would say on the cross and says, "I thirst" (19:28; Psalm 69:21). In response He is given sour wine—vinegar (19:29).

Jesus is given the vinegar with a branch of hyssop, a reedlike branch significant in Jewish culture. The hyssop was used in the first Passover in Egypt to spread lamb's blood on the doorpost of the house so that the angel of death would spare the firstborn son. Each time hyssop is used, it would remind a Jewish person of this event. And so in this moment the Passover is coming to life in the death of Jesus.

Finally, Jesus exclaims, "It is finished" (19:30 NIV). This does not simply mean that His earthly life is over. Rather it means His task is accomplished—the plan is fully realized. Therefore, with that, Jesus physically dies.

Exodus 12:46 declares that the Passover lamb is not to have any broken bones. Therefore, since the Passover is a picture of the cross, Jesus was not to have any broken bones, and He does not (19:31–37). Jesus dies before they need to break His legs.

Demystifying John

The custom of breaking a crucified person's legs functioned to hasten death. To die by crucifixion was actually to die by asphyxiation. As the person hung, he could breathe in, but it became increasingly difficult to breathe out. In order to do so, he would have to gather his strength to push himself upward on feet that had been pierced. That effort would have also scraped his back, already raw from flogging. If a person was surviving too long on the cross, breaking his legs took away any ability to support himself in order to breathe.

The piercing of Jesus' side (19:34) is the completion of what was prophesied in Zechariah 12:10.

Often in this day, victims of crucifixion were buried in a common grave. In Jesus' case, though, Joseph of Arimathea and Nicodemus, two Jewish leaders that had become disciples of Jesus, ask Pilate for the body and take care of the funeral arrangements (19:38–42). Even in this, the scriptures are fulfilled. Isaiah 53:9 says that the Messiah would be a rich man in death. Though Jesus died the death of a wretched man, in a twist of circumstances, He was allowed to be buried in a rich man's tomb.

Take It Home

Jesus' deity is evident in the sign that Pilate made, the scriptures fulfilled, the selfless love, the supernatural knowledge, and the final scriptures concerning His death. What this shows us is that Jesus is God, and as God He perfectly redeemed us. Jesus is the perfect sacrifice for humanity.

JOHN 20:1–31

JESUS CONQUERS DEATH

The Empty Tomb	20:1–18
Jesus and the Disciples	20:19–31

Setting Up the Section

Jesus controlled death; death did not control Jesus. He died in humanity's place and then rose from the dead, conquering the bondage of death. John's Gospel offers evidence that Jesus rose from the dead and, therefore, if we believe in the person and work of Jesus, we will have life.

20:1–18

THE EMPTY TOMB

John records Mary's trip to the tomb (20:1). This is not an exhaustive picture of the event—just a snapshot. When Mary discovers that Jesus' body is gone, she runs to get Peter and John to tell them that someone has taken the body of Jesus away (20:2). When John, Peter, and Mary arrive at the tomb, they find the burial clothes of Jesus lying there (20:3–6).

If Jesus' body had been moved by someone, then the burial clothes would not be lying there. They would still be around the body. If someone stole the body, he or she would not likely unwrap it. Something else happened to the body—this is the first evidence of the resurrection.

The second piece of evidence John offers is Jesus' face cloth (20:7). While the body of the deceased is wrapped in strips of cloth, somewhat mummy-like, the face cloth is laid over the head. This piece of cloth is folded up and placed away from the wrappings. Again, this is unlikely to be the work of grave robbers, who would not likely take the time to fold up the cloth even if they chose to unwrap the dead body.

This is evidence of not only the spiritual resurrection of Jesus, but the bodily resurrection. Jesus doesn't just rise as a spirit. He rises from the dead in a body that is able to pick up the head covering and fold it and place it in another part of the room.

John enters the tomb with Peter, and when he sees the burial clothes, he believes (20:8). When John sees the cloths lying there and the head piece folded up, he is convinced that Jesus has risen from the dead.

At this point, the disciples still have not understood all that Jesus had spoken about His resurrection. John believes the prophecies, but does not fully understand that they are being fulfilled before his eyes (20:9–10).

John's next piece of evidence regarding the resurrection is the claim of Jesus. Mary sees two angels, one by the head and the other by the feet of where the body had been lying (20:11–12). John's Gospel does not focus on Mary's reaction to the angels, but rather focuses on their question (20:13). The presence of angels confirms this as a divine moment. They ask Mary a question, not because the angels need the answer—Mary needs to know it. Mary thinks Jesus' body has been stolen. She thinks that Jesus is gone, and has no idea what has taken place. The implication of the angels' question is that there is nothing to weep about. This is a day of rejoicing, not of tears.

Jesus had said that the disciples would be in a state of deep sorrow while the world is in a state of rejoicing (see John 16:20). But Jesus said that He would not leave them in a state of sorrow. Mary finds herself face-to-face with Jesus, but she has no idea that it is Him (20:14). Mary does not recognize Him because He looks different after the resurrection (1 Corinthians 15:35–49).

Critical Observation

Mark 16:12 says that Jesus appeared to the disciples in a different form after the resurrection. He had a glorified body. While we know He had a physical body, it was in a different form than what He had before He died.

Jesus asks Mary a question: "Why are you crying?" (20:15 NIV). Jesus asks the same question as the angels. Mary has all love and no faith.

In John 10, Jesus said that His sheep know His voice, and He, as the good shepherd, calls them by name. That is what happens to Mary (20:16). Jesus speaks her name, and suddenly she sees that it is Jesus. She responds to Jesus and calls Him *Rabboni*, a title of great respect. It is like calling someone master, or even supreme master. It could even be used to describe God.

She sees that it is Jesus, and she automatically humbles herself before Him. She also clutches Jesus, and will not let Him go.

In verse 17, some translations describe Jesus as saying, "Do not touch me," but a better translation would be, "Don't cling to me." Jesus must ascend to the Father. The relationship is going to change, and Mary cannot cling to Him physically. She must now learn to cling to Jesus spiritually.

Mary is to announce Jesus' ascension to the disciples (20:17–18). Remember, Jesus had told the disciples in chapters 14–16 that He would ascend to the Father. Notice that Jesus calls the disciples "brothers." Now that He has risen from the dead, their relationship has changed. They have a new life in Him and are in the family of God.

Take It Home

Jesus calls the disciples brothers because they are now a part of the family of God. Hebrews 2:11 tells us that we, by the virtue of Jesus' death, also become siblings of Jesus. His life is placed within us, and we, therefore, can call His Father our Father. We do not fear death anymore because of our new life in Him.

20:19–31

JESUS AND THE DISCIPLES

When Jesus appears to the disciples, they are locked in a house because they are still afraid of being arrested and tried as Jesus was (20:19). Jesus says to them, "Peace be with you!" (20:19 NIV). To wish someone peace was to wish them all of the fullness and happiness that God intended. When Jesus uses this greeting, it carries a deeper significance because Jesus wishes the disciples the fullness of life and peace that is found in Him. It is within this context that Jesus gives them the precursor to their great commission (20:20–21). Just as God sent Jesus on a mission, so Jesus is sending the disciples on a mission. They are to be the manifestation of Jesus on earth, continuing the work He started.

The Holy Spirit is essential to the disciples' mission (20:22). The Spirit is the power and ability to accomplish what needs to be done. Jesus had promised the Holy Spirit would come after He ascends to heaven, but this event is not exactly the same as the coming of the Holy Spirit described in Acts 2. Here, it is Jesus connecting the Holy Spirit with the mission of the disciples in anticipation of what will happen after His ascension.

Verse 23 describes the disciples' right to speak on behalf of God. The disciples are not able to forgive sins, but they are charged with telling those who believe, that their sins have been forgiven through Jesus' sacrifice.

Thomas was not with the other disciples in the room when Jesus gave the commission, though the other disciples obviously explained it to him. He responds in his famous skepticism (20:24–25), wanting physical confirmation. Jesus does appear again, announces peace, and then offers the physical evidence that Thomas has been looking for (20:26–27).

Jesus knows Thomas's doubts even though He wasn't in the room when Thomas voiced them. This is another way in which John's Gospel emphasizes Jesus' sovereignty over everything. He knows Thomas's doubts, and He meets Thomas at his point of need (20:28).

Take It Home

In verse 29, Jesus lays out a principle: It is one thing to believe when you have seen Jesus; it is a greater thing to believe if you have never actually seen the physical resurrected body of Jesus. Since that day, there have been millions of people who have believed without seeing, only trusting in the Word of God. That is real, undeniable faith.

John states his purpose for writing this Gospel here. He wants the reader to believe that Jesus is God manifested, that on the cross He bore all people's sin, and that when He rose from the dead He gave humanity life (20:30–31).

JOHN 21:1–25

EPILOGUE

Fishing Instructions	21:1–14
Breakfast by the Sea	21:15–25

Setting Up the Section

Chapter 21 is the epilogue of this great Gospel. Jesus gives His disciples a living illustration that He is their provider, and that He is the sovereign Lord of the universe.

In Peter's restoration, we learn what it means to love Jesus and what it means to follow Jesus. This becomes a fitting conclusion of the Gospel of John.

John offers this final account of one of Jesus' post-resurrection appearances to not only confirm the resurrection of Jesus, but to also illustrate one last time the fact that Jesus is truly the manifestation of God.

21:1–14

FISHING INSTRUCTIONS

After Jesus' resurrection, He is in His glorified body, and only appears to those who know Him.

Seven disciples are fishing (21:1–3). They are not returning to their old trade, but they are continuing to fish in this transition time. They are no longer with Jesus daily, and yet the Holy Spirit has not come and empowered them to preach. They are waiting for their mission to start.

They have fished all night and have caught nothing. After Jesus offers instructions, they are unable to haul in the load because there are too many fish. John realizes that the man on the shore is Jesus. Who else controls the fish in the ocean? (21:3–7).

Note Peter's zeal in verses 7 and 8. The rest of the disciples are left to carry the load of fish in by themselves as Peter is swimming to the shore.

Jesus serves the disciples with a hot breakfast. There are 153 fish in the catch—Jesus has provided abundantly (21:9–11).

By the time Jesus invites the disciples to eat breakfast, they all recognize Him (21:12). When this Gospel was written, years later, these kinds of statements offered proof for those who questioned whether the resurrection was a reality. John tells us that this is the third manifestation of Jesus to the disciples, and it is an experience filled with service and compassion (21:13–14).

21:15–25

BREAKFAST BY THE SEA

When breakfast is over, Jesus is ready to deal with Peter. In John 13:37, Peter had declared he would lay down his life for Jesus. Since this was said in the context of Jesus' recognizing Judas's potential betrayal, Peter's words had the implication that he would be faithful even if the rest of the disciples were not. Yet later that same night, his failure—in denying Jesus—was monumental.

Jesus' question addresses the heart of the problem (21:15). Peter does not understand the nature of love. He loves Jesus with passion, enthusiasm, and emotion, but his love is lacking simple obedience. Peter's answer declares Jesus as the center of His affection. Jesus wants that love and affection channeled through tending His lambs.

The idea around the word *tend* is that of feeding. Peter is to be sure Jesus' flock is kept healthy. If Peter truly is devoted to Jesus, then it will show when he cares for the lambs of God in the same way Jesus cares for His disciples. The point is, if Peter loves Jesus then he will love and value the things that Jesus loves and values.

Jesus asks the question again (21:16), and this time His directive to Peter has to do with nourishing, caring for, and treating the sheep as if they are an extension of his own body. It is more than just pet-sitting; it is engaged nurture.

Jesus asks the question a third time, which grieves Peter (21:17). He takes it personally that Jesus has not trusted his responses, but Jesus is restoring Peter. For each time Peter looked out for himself at the expense of obedience by denying Jesus, he will be restored. This last time, Jesus charges Peter to make sure he take Jesus' lambs as his primary responsibility.

Jesus begins verse 18 with the final, "Verily, verily" (KJV), or, "I tell you the truth" (NIV) statement of the Gospel of John. Remember, this is Jesus doubly affirming His point. The idea is that this is binding and absolute truth.

In Peter's denial he showed compassion only for himself, and in his subsequent denials he showed that he was afraid of death. Jesus now addresses Peter's death (21:19). We know that Peter was indeed crucified. Church tradition claims that he went to the cross and asked to be crucified upside down because he did not want to die in the same way as Jesus.

In light of this information, Jesus calls Peter to follow Him. The implication of the Greek word for "follow" (21:19 NIV) is that Peter is to follow Jesus constantly and consistently as opposed to the sporadic nature in which he had followed in the past.

Peter turns and sees John and asks Jesus a question that we would all be prone to ask, "What about John?" (21:20–21). Is John going to have a violent death as well? Jesus simply states that His plans for John are of no concern to Peter.

At one time, it was believed that Jesus' response to Peter's inquiry (21:20–21) about John meant that John was going to live forever. Here, as Gospel writer, John clears up the rumor and says that Jesus is not giving a prophecy (21:22–23).

Take It Home

This Gospel account ends here (21:24–25) to illustrate to us that we must follow Jesus as Lord, and follow Him wherever He has called us. In following Jesus we will all be called into one body, but into different places in that body. Some will have a difficult struggle in their walk, and will constantly be under attack for faith. Some will experience prosperity on earth, and will be used to advance the kingdom. Some will die early, and some will live long.

The key is to follow God where He has planted you. Do not seek what He has not given you, and do not be ungrateful for what He has given you. Rather, follow God whatever the cost, wherever the location. That is what Jesus wanted Peter to know.

ACTS

INTRODUCTION TO ACTS

One of the earliest titles for this book of the Bible was simply "Acts," with other early titles being, "Acts of Apostles," "Acts of the Holy Apostles," and the popular, "The Acts of the Apostles," which wasn't really accurate. The acts of Peter and Paul are highlighted in this book, yet many of the other apostles are hardly mentioned. A more accurate title might be, "The Acts of the Holy Spirit," but many modern Bibles have reverted to simply using "Acts" as the title.

AUTHOR

As was the case with his Gospel, Luke doesn't identify himself as the writer of Acts, though his authorship is seldom questioned. The information he provided in the book of Luke was a result of his research to verify the testimony of eyewitnesses (Luke 1:1–4). His involvement in Acts is even more personal. Much of this book, like Luke's Gospel, is written in the third person. But certain sections (16:10–17; 20:5–15; 21:1–18; 27:1–28:16) switch to first person. It is evident that Luke accompanied Paul on various legs of his missionary journeys.

Luke was a doctor (Colossians 4:14) who had an eye for detail. He seems particularly interested in seafaring, and he provides vivid descriptions as he narrates. Many of his first-person accounts are when Paul is traveling by ship.

PURPOSE

Like his Gospel, Luke's book of Acts is addressed to Theophilus (1:1). The purpose of the Gospel account was "so that you may know the exact truth about the things you have been taught" (Luke 1:4 NASB). With his follow-up book of Acts, Luke is sending his primary recipient (and perhaps his financial sponsor) a well-researched account of the spread of Christianity throughout both Jewish and Gentile communities. Since Luke was personally involved in the growth of the church, he was able to provide both an insightful historical overview and a corresponding apologetic emphasis.

OCCASION

Each of the four Gospel accounts provides a distinctive look at the life, death, and resurrection of Jesus. But none deal with what happened to Jesus' followers after He ascended into heaven and returned to His Father. In Luke's Gospel, we are told only that the disciples stayed at the temple, praising God (Luke 24:53).

The book of Acts picks up at that point to describe the coming of the Holy Spirit on the Day of Pentecost and records the growth, challenges, and miraculous happenings in the early church. Jesus had commanded His followers to make disciples of all nations (Matthew 28:19). Acts details the work of the Holy Spirit and the spread of the gospel "to the ends of the earth" (Acts 1:8). The offer of God's forgiveness and salvation is extended to the Gentiles, and new opportunities open up for mission.

God's Word went out in ever-widening circles from Jerusalem. Even as the book of Acts concludes, Paul had just arrived in Rome to speak before the emperor there. Though beset by relentless opposition and persecution, the followers of Jesus persevered and continued to carry the gospel wherever they went.

THEMES

From start to finish, the book of Acts emphasizes the work of the Holy Spirit. The Spirit was first evident in the lives of Jewish believers in Jerusalem on the Day of Pentecost, but later was evidence that Gentiles, too, were experiencing the forgiveness and salvation of God.

The establishment and expansion of the church is Luke's ongoing concern in Acts. The followers of Jesus first congregate in a single group and create a unique and exemplary model of community. As they increase in number and persecution pushes them out of Jerusalem, they gather in various other locations, led by pastors and elders. And rather than each body seeing itself as independent, the churches look after one another's needs, financially and spiritually.

The persecution of believers is repeated throughout Acts as well. It was persecution that drove the church out of Jerusalem into surrounding areas. Paul was regularly persecuted during his travels. And at times when Paul could not be located, his associates were persecuted instead. More intense and organized persecution would come later, but Luke describes many of the initial attacks against the early church.

Luke also records a number of impassioned speeches throughout the book of Acts. Many are presentations of the gospel by church leaders such as Peter, Stephen, and Paul. Every episode contributes in some way to the central theme of the book: the expansion of the church from Jerusalem to the ends of the earth, and from a Jewish beginning to a Gentile expansion.

HISTORICAL CONTEXT

Since Luke's coverage of world events makes no mention of Nero's persecution of Christians (AD 64 and following), the destruction of Jerusalem in AD 70, or Paul's death in AD 68, many scholars believe he wrote the book of Acts around AD 60–62. He had traveled with Paul to Rome at this time, and may have been writing Acts while Paul was writing his Prison Epistles.

CONTRIBUTION TO THE BIBLE

The book of Acts holds a distinctive place in scripture. It is the only follow-up provided for the Gospels and provides a revealing look at the interaction, blessings, and problems of the believers in the early church. The Gospels highlight the ministry of Jesus; Acts highlights the ministry of the Holy Spirit. Only when viewed together do readers get the complete picture of God's plan, and how He chose to include humankind in the work of His kingdom.

More importantly, Acts shows how the expansion of the church from Jerusalem to Rome and from Jews to Gentiles was the work of God and part of His plan of salvation. The accounts of this time period provided by secular historians are helpful, to be sure, but they were written by people outside the church, looking in. Luke's account as a participant and believer gives us a trustworthy report that emphasizes things important to those who share his faith. His book of Acts provides much information that amplifies our understanding of other portions of scripture.

In addition, Luke's mostly chronological account of Paul's travels is invaluable in establishing dates for and better comprehension of his Epistles. By combining Paul's references in his letters with Luke's in Acts, the details of Paul's ministry become much clearer.

OUTLINE

MAKING A BIG TRANSITION 1:1–26

- Forty Days of Assurance 1:1–3
- Jesus' Ascension 1:4–11
- Replacing Judas 1:12–26

THE ARRIVAL OF THE HOLY SPIRIT 2:1–47

- A Sight, a Sound, and Strange Speech 2:1–13
- Peter's Explanation 2:14–41
- The Church Gets Underway 2:42–47

PERSECUTION BEGINS 3:1–4:31

- Power in the Name of Jesus 3:1–10
- Peter's Second Sermon 3:11–26
- Trouble with the Authorities 4:1–22
- The Response to Persecution 4:23–31

NEW PROBLEMS FOR THE NEW CHURCH 4:32–5:42

- One in Heart and Mind 4:32–37
- Two Exceptions. . .and the Consequences 5:1–11
- Phenomenal Healing and Continued Growth 5:12–16
- Another Brush with the Authorities 5:17–42

THE CHURCH'S FIRST CASUALTY 6:1–8:3

- The Problem with Success 6:1–7
- The Brief Ministry of Stephen 6:8–15
- Stephen's Defense 7:1–53
- The Death of Stephen 7:54–60
- Persecution as a Way of Life 8:1–3

FROM JERUSALEM TO SAMARIA TO ETHIOPIA 8:4–40

- The Ministry of Philip, Part I 8:4–8
- The Gift That Can't Be Bought 8:9–25
- The Ministry of Philip, Part II 8:26–40

THE SURPRISE CONVERSION OF SAUL 9:1–31

- On the Road to Damascus 9:1–9
- Saul in Damascus 9:10–25
- Saul in Jerusalem 9:26–31

INCLUSION OF THE "UNCLEAN" 9:32–11:30
Peter Heals Aeneas and Raises Tabitha 9:32–43
The Vision of Cornelius 10:1–8
The Vision of Peter 10:9–23a
Gentiles Are Baptized into the Church 10:24b–48
Peter in Jerusalem 11:1–18
Barnabas and Saul in Antioch 11:19–30

PETER'S PRISON BREAK 12:1–24
Persecution to Please the Crowds 12:1–3
Peter's Arrest and Prison Escape 12:4–19a
The Death of Herod 12:19b–24

THE GOSPEL MOVES OUTWARD 12:25–13:52
The Call of Barnabas and Saul 12:25–13:3
Ministry in Cyprus 13:4–12
Ministry in Pisidian Antioch 13:13–52

COMPLETION OF THE FIRST MISSIONARY JOURNEY 14:1–28
Ministry in Iconium 14:1–7
Ministry in Lystra 14:8–20
Ministry in Derbe and the Return Home 14:21–28

THE COUNCIL IN JERUSALEM 15:1–35
The Issue at Hand 15:1–4
Discussing the Issue 15:5–21
Addressing the Issue 15:22–35

A SECOND JOURNEY, A DIFFERENT PARTNER 15:36–16:40
An Irresolvable Dispute 15:36–41
A New Partner, a New Recruit 16:1–5
A New Direction 16:6–15
A Jailer Finds Freedom 16:16–40

MOVING THROUGH GREECE 17:1–34
Ministry in Thessalonica 17:1–9
Ministry in Berea 17:10–15
Ministry in Athens 17:16–34

WRAPPING UP THE SECOND MISSIONARY JOURNEY 18:1–22

Ministry in Corinth 18:1–8
First a Promise, Then a Test 18:9–17
Home Again 18:18–22

THE THIRD MISSIONARY JOURNEY BEGINS 18:23–19:41

Introducing Apollos 18:23–28
Clarifying the Truth in Ephesus 19:1–20
Christianity vs. Commerce 19:21–41

A FORLORN FAREWELL 20:1–38

Ministry in Macedonia and Greece 20:1–6
An All-Night Sermon. . .and Its Consequences 20:7–12
Good-bye to Ephesus 20:13–38

EXPECTING TROUBLE, BUT MOVING AHEAD 21:1–26

Sailing Back to Jerusalem 21:1–9
Advance Warning 21:10–16
Rebutting a Rumor 21:17–26

TROUBLE IN JERUSALEM (AS PREDICTED) 21:27–22:29

Same Problem, New City 21:27–32
Paul's Arrest and Defense 21:33–22:21
The Rights of the Accused 22:22–29

PAUL'S TRIAL BEGINS 22:30–23:35

Disorder in the Court 22:30–23:11
The Plot to Murder Paul 23:12–35

PAUL'S TRIAL BEFORE FELIX 24:1–21

The Case for the Prosecution 24:1–9
Paul's Rebuttal 24:10–21

A SECOND TRIAL IN CAESAREA 25:1–26:32

Festus Tries Paul 25:1–12
Festus and Agrippa 25:13–22
Paul and Agrippa 26:1–32

PROBLEMS ON THE WAY TO ROME 27:1–44

Sailing West 27:1–12
Into a Hurricane 27:13–26
Shipwrecked, but Ashore 27:27–44

ROME AT LAST 28:1–31

Winter in Malta 28:1–10
From Malta to Rome 28:11–16
Ministry in Rome 28:17–31

ACTS 1:1–26

MAKING A BIG TRANSITION

Forty Days of Assurance	1:1–3
Jesus' Ascension	1:4–11
Replacing Judas	1:12–26

Setting Up the Section

The book of Acts picks up where the Gospel of Luke ends. Jesus has been making occasional post-resurrection appearances, but He is about to depart for good. He leaves His followers final instructions, and while they await the promised Holy Spirit, they try to attend to some business.

1:1–3

FORTY DAYS OF ASSURANCE

Luke again addresses his writing to Theophilus as he did in his Gospel (1:1). The use of the title "most excellent" (Luke 1:3) suggests that Theophilus had a position of high social status. Perhaps he was a Roman court official with whom Paul was scheduled to meet, and Luke hoped to provide him with a less prejudicial and more reliable opinion of Christianity. If so, Luke was not only a skilled historian, but he was also an astute diplomat and knowledgeable apologist who argued convincingly for the cause of Christianity.

Luke also emphasizes in his opening statement that the entire earthly ministry of Jesus was only a beginning. What Jesus had begun would continue to expand in geographic and spiritual significance (1:1).

Jesus' public ministry had lasted about three years. Then, after His resurrection, He appeared numerous times in various settings over a forty-day period to prove that He was alive (1:3).

Critical Observation

The Bible records a number of appearances of Jesus between His resurrection and ascension. He appeared to Mary Magdalene (John 20:14–18), a group of women (Matthew 28:8–10), two men on the road to Emmaus (Luke 24:13–35), and numerous times to His disciples (Matthew 28:16–20; Luke 24:36–49; John 20:24–29; 21:1–24). He also appeared to Peter (Luke 24:34; 1 Corinthians 15:5), his brother James (1 Corinthians 15:7), as well as a group of more than five hundred people (1 Corinthians 15:6).

1:4–11

JESUS' ASCENSION

Luke describes four stages of development Christ instituted for disciples in the early church:

1) He chose them (1:2). None of the apostles were self-appointed.
2) He commissioned them (Matthew 28:16–20; Acts 1:2). He gave them specific instructions.
3) He showed Himself to them (1:3). It was no ghost or apparition that appeared to them during that forty-day period. In this passage He ate with them (1:4). These disciples were irrefutable eyewitnesses to the reality of Jesus' resurrection.
4) He promised them the Holy Spirit (1:5), who would provide the power and authority they needed to carry out His instructions.

The instructions of the resurrected Jesus to His followers were very specific (1:4–6). He gave them a command (not to leave Jerusalem) and a promise (they will be baptized with the Holy Spirit).

On what appears to be a later occasion when they were again together, the disciples had a question of their own (1:6). In his Gospel, Luke noted numerous times when the apostles either misunderstood Jesus or seemingly ignored what He was saying as they held their own discussions about position and power. It's not surprising that Jesus once again had to steer their attention to the need for simple obedience and witness rather than establishing rank in God's kingdom (1:7–8).

The clarification from Jesus in verse 8 provides an outline for the book of Acts. Reading through Luke's account, we first see the witness of the disciples in Jerusalem, then the surrounding areas of Judea and Samaria, and if not literally to "the ends of the earth," at least to Rome, Turkey, Greece, Africa, and perhaps even Spain. And perhaps Jesus had His followers begin in Jerusalem because that had been their source of greatest failure. Just a few weeks before, they had all abandoned Him in His moment of greatest need. But after they received the Holy Spirit, they would never again be the same. They would be witnesses first among the people who knew them best—those who were especially aware of their weaknesses.

The disciples' own lives would be the first to change, and then they would touch many others. Jesus' inclusion of Samaria in their mission (1:8) is significant because of the spiritual, cultural, and racial barriers between the Jews and Samaritans. Right off the bat, Jesus is drawing His followers out of their comfort zones.

Some people argue that the statement about Jesus being taken up (1:9) reflects a naïve and prescientific view of cosmology, with heaven being somewhere above us and hell somewhere below. Yet such an argument seems to press the point too far. Christ's ascension is not about the order of the universe or the physical location of heaven. Rather, it shows a distinct break as Jesus leaves His human companions and returns to His Father. He had been appearing and disappearing for forty days. What better way to show He would not be coming back than to let everyone observe His final departure into the clouds? Angels confirmed with certainty that He wouldn't be returning for quite some time (1:10–11).

No one had witnessed Jesus' resurrection, yet they saw its effects in the continued presence of the risen and living Lord. And they did witness His ascension, but not the effects—at least not for a while. Their understanding would begin ten days later when the Holy Spirit arrived.

1:12–26

REPLACING JUDAS

The number of believers that gathered after Jesus' ascension was a meager 120 (1:15). With the exception of Judas Iscariot, all the apostles were present (1:12–13). And by this time, Jesus' brothers, who previously hadn't believed in Him (John 7:5), were also among the believers (1:14). Though somewhat small, the group was constantly in prayer (1:14).

Peter's awareness of scripture led him to propose finding a replacement for Judas. The Bible never provides the reason that Judas betrayed Jesus. Luke refers to his wickedness (1:18); other translations of the original language describing Judas refer to his "infamy," "villainy," and "crime." Opinions are divided as to whether Judas was trying to save his own skin, acted out of greed, had come to feel out of place among the close-knit group of apostles, or was simply trying to coerce Jesus into declaring His role as Messiah and taking a stand against Rome. Whatever his motive, Judas's real tragedy is that, after realizing his mistake and experiencing remorse, he didn't attempt to seek forgiveness and restoration. His gruesome death (1:18–19) stands in stark contrast to the new life and fresh start the other apostles would receive.

Demystifying Acts

Matthew wrote that Judas went out and hanged himself (Matthew 27:5). The additional details in Acts 1:18–19 may suggest that considerable time passed before he was cut down. Another possibility is that an alternate biblical definition of *hanging* involved a large sharpened pole instead of rope. The person would be impaled on the pole and left there to hang.

Peter quoted portions of two psalms (69:25; 109:8) that had typologically predicted the betrayal of Jesus and what should be done in response (1:20). These two passages seemed to provide adequate guidance for what action they should take. With Jesus no longer available to consult, and prior to the arrival of the Holy Spirit, the apostles were using scripture to guide their decision-making and the discerning of God's will for their lives.

In determining who should replace Judas, they looked for someone who had belonged to their group from the beginning of Jesus' public ministry and had witnessed His resurrection (1:21–22). Two possible candidates were named (1:23). To ensure that the decision was God's and not theirs, they prayed and cast lots to determine which person should be selected (1:24–26).

Casting lots may seem like tossing a coin to us, but it had long been a highly respected method of determining God's will (Leviticus 16:7–10; 1 Samuel 14:40–42; Nehemiah 10:34; Proverbs 16:33; etc.). Yet it is interesting to note that scripture says nothing more of Matthias, the one chosen. In addition, this is the final mention of casting lots in the Bible. After the arrival of the Holy Spirit, it was no longer necessary.

Some people believe the apostles acted hastily and that Paul was intended to be the twelfth apostle. However, Paul would not have met either of the criteria they were using, and he was aware that his calling was quite unlike that of the others in Jesus' inner circle (1 Corinthians 15:7–8).

It's not fair to evaluate the importance of characters based on the amount of attention they receive in scripture. Many of the original Twelve remain essentially invisible throughout Acts. The very fact that Joseph and Matthias were chosen for consideration at all is testimony to their dedication and high moral character.

Take It Home

When we think of the apostolic nature of the church and realize that God chooses to work through His people, it is easy to rush forward and start trying to do things our own way. We design a plan to accomplish the mission of God and go full steam ahead only to discover many times that we've made a mess of things. Along with Jesus' promise that His followers would receive power and authority was His command to wait (1:4). Can you think of a time when you should have waited for God and suffered because you didn't? How about a time when you did wait and it paid off? What can you do to ensure that in the future you will wait on God to provide a clear calling and vision for your task?

ACTS 2:1–47

THE ARRIVAL OF THE HOLY SPIRIT

A Sight, a Sound, and Strange Speech	2:1–13
Peter's Explanation	2:14–41
The Church Gets Underway	2:42–47

Setting Up the Section

Prior to His crucifixion, Jesus had tried to tell His followers that the Holy Spirit would come to replace Him after His departure (John 14:15–27; 16:5–16). After His resurrection, just prior to His ascension into the heavens, He instructed them to go to Jerusalem and await the Holy Spirit. He hadn't set a time frame, but their wait was only about ten days. The coming of the Holy Spirit was an unmistakable event that transformed the believers and initiated the establishment of the church.

2:1–13

A SIGHT, A SOUND, AND STRANGE SPEECH

The annual celebration of Pentecost (2:1) was significant in both an agricultural and historical sense. It was originally known as either the Feast of the Harvest or the Feast of Weeks, and was the middle of three annual Jewish harvest festivals. *Pentecost* means "fiftieth," and relates to the fact that the event was held fifty days after the Sabbath of Passover week (Leviticus 23:15–16). During the years prior to the birth of Christ, Pentecost also came to be celebrated as the anniversary of the giving of the Law at Mount Sinai, because the event was thought to have taken place fifty days after the Exodus from Egypt.

It is no coincidence, then, that Yahweh's two covenant promises were fulfilled on the day of Pentecost. He had promised through His prophets to send His Spirit (Ezekiel 36:27) to the people of Israel, and to put His law in their minds and write it on their hearts (Jeremiah 31:33). While the people were ready to celebrate the harvest, the specific occasion would also become a memorable event regarding the "harvest" that Jesus had been concerned with (Luke 10:2). And the sound, fire, and speech that had been present atop Mount Sinai occurred once again on the Day of Pentecost (2:2–4).

The sound was that of a violent wind. The fire took the shape of tongues that came to rest on everyone present. And the speech was perhaps the most impressive sign of all. The group of uncultured and unschooled Galileans was suddenly able to present the gospel in the various native languages of all the visitors gathered in Jerusalem for the Feast. It was not a gift of hearing; it was a gift of speech.

Luke's list of peoples represented in Jerusalem included fifteen groups named (approximately) geographically from east to west (2:5–11). The fact that they all heard the gospel clearly explained in their own language represented the voice of God and the universality of the message.

Reactions to this amazing occurrence were mixed. Many people were amazed and perplexed (2:12). After all, these were the same people who had been too timid to even admit knowing Jesus during His trial and crucifixion. Yet here they were boldly proclaiming the wonderful things God had done (2:11). After experiencing such fresh new power, the followers of Jesus would never be the same. Yet other people weren't so impressed with the believers and looked for other explanations (2:13).

2:14–41

PETER'S EXPLANATION

Peter made it clear that the phenomenon the crowds had witnessed was not the result of too much wine—especially not at 9:00 a.m.! He then used three passages from the scriptures to explain what was happening.

The first (2:16–21) was from Joel 2:28–32. Joel was a rather gloomy book, written during a period when an invasion of locusts had destroyed every green plant and created a national disaster in their rural, agricultural economy. And rather than attempting to soothe the people with promises of comfort and hope, Joel told them that their situation would get worse. The locusts were only a symbol of the more intense divine judgment to come. Yet in this context was the passage cited by Peter of God's promise to pour out His Spirit and provide salvation for everyone who calls on His name.

Peter's boldness on this occasion is striking. He had already stood and raised his voice to address the large crowd (2:14). And while it was one thing to quote scripture, Peter's additional remarks summarized the essence of the gospel and held his listeners accountable for their actions (2:22–36). He told them that Jesus, sent from God, was handed over to them. And, yet, they were the ones responsible for His death (2:23).

Critical Observation

The tendency for overzealous Christians to blame Jews for the death of Christ stands as one of the black eyes in the church's past. It is a fact of history that Jewish leaders did conspire to have Jesus executed, and the Gospels record that the crowd on Good Friday called for His blood (Matthew 27:25; Luke 23:23). Yet the Romans were the ones to crucify Him, and all the water in the world cannot wash Pilate of the blood that is on his hands for the death of Jesus. But at a more basic level, it is the sin of each and every individual that is responsible for putting Jesus on the cross.

Peter was addressing fellow Jews and all of those who lived in Jerusalem (2:14). He held his own people accountable for their actions (2:23). But the word *wicked* can also mean "lawless," and those without the law were the Gentiles. However, the act of putting Jesus to death is soon overshadowed by God's action of raising Him from the dead (2:24).

Peter's second passage is from Psalm 16:8–11, a psalm of David. Although this poem was written a thousand years before Christ and contains statements that apply literally to the Old Testament king of Israel, one portion could not possibly have referred to David. In Peter's speech, he pointed out that David's tomb was there in their midst (2:29), so David's body had certainly seen decay. Jesus was therefore the Holy One referred to in Psalm 16:10, who had overcome death and the grave as prophesied by David long ago (2:30–33).

Peter's third passage was from another psalm of David (Psalm 110:1). This verse is quoted or referred to in the New Testament at least twenty-five times. In the original Hebrew, the first reference to "Lord" is *Yahweh* or *Jehovah*, referring to the great God of Israel. The second word interpreted "Lord" is *adonai*, meaning an individual greater than the speaker. So David is saying that God invites another person, someone greater than David, to sit at His right hand. Peter again clarifies that this significant individual is none other than the Messiah.

Demystifying Acts

One might wonder how Peter is suddenly such a profound source of spiritual insight and theological acuity, enabled to realize that Jesus was the fulfillment of so many Old Testament prophecies. Perhaps a clue is found in the story of the two disciples on the road to Emmaus (Luke 24:13–35). As Jesus walked with them, "beginning with Moses and all the Prophets, he explained to them what was said in all the Scriptures concerning himself" (Luke 24:27 NIV). Similarly, Jesus spent numerous sessions with His disciples during His post-resurrection appearances discussing the kingdom of God (Acts 1:3). In light of the resurrection, surely the apostles began to grasp a better understanding of what had happened. And with the presence of the Holy Spirit, Peter was able to concisely summarize the facts and persuade his listeners.

It was painful for many in the crowd to hear that the person whose crucifixion they had endorsed had been made both Lord and Christ by God (2:36). Yet, rather than assigning blame or amplifying feelings of guilt, Peter promises forgiveness and salvation for those who would repent and be baptized. He warned them and pleaded with them, and in response, about three thousand people became believers that day (2:40–41).

2:42–47

THE CHURCH GETS UNDERWAY

In one day church membership increased twenty-five times its original number, and new people were added every day (2:47). In a modern setting, such growth might create numerous problems. Yet in its earliest stages, it seemed that the new and growing church was doing everything right. It was, and continues to be, a model for worship (both collectively in the temple and in smaller groups in homes), in discipleship, in showing care for others, in evangelizing, and in serving. The godly awe that filled the people (2:43) was reflected in their attitudes, relationships, giving, and every other aspect of their lives.

Take It Home

In our post-modern world, the twenty-first century church has many of the same challenges that the first-century church faced. Christianity is again becoming a minority voice among the other beliefs in our nation and our world. In some countries, Christians are persecuted with the same cruel intolerance as the members of the early church were soon to face. What can we learn from their positive examples to make our body of believers stronger today? What can be done collectively? What might you do personally to make a difference?

ACTS 3:1–4:31

PERSECUTION BEGINS

Power in the Name of Jesus	3:1–10
Peter's Second Sermon	3:11–26
Trouble with the Authorities	4:1–22
The Response to Persecution	4:23–31

Setting Up the Section

As the early church is formed, Peter quickly emerges as the prominent leader. After making an impassioned and persuasive speech to a large crowd (2:14–36), he soon begins to demonstrate spiritual power and authority similar to what Jesus had modeled. In this section he heals a beggar who had been crippled from birth. And as had been the case with Jesus, the healing didn't go unnoticed by the Jewish religious leaders, who respond with a show of their own power.

3:1–10

POWER IN THE NAME OF JESUS

Peter and John were on their way to the afternoon prayer when they encountered a crippled man who, we find out later, was over forty years old (4:22). Lame from birth and unable to get around on his own, he was completely at the mercy of others (3:2). No doubt his location outside the temple was a planned strategy to appeal to people on their way to prayer. He was hoping to benefit from their desire to gain merit as a result of almsgiving.

The temple gate that was called Beautiful (3:2) is usually considered to be the Nicanor Gate—the main eastern gate to the temple precincts from the court of the Gentiles. The story was told that the gate had been transported from Alexandria to Jerusalem by ship when a terrible storm began. The gate was about to be jettisoned, and a man named Nicanor requested to be thrown overboard along with it. When both survived the storm, it was considered a miracle, and the name and gate were forever associated. Josephus the historian described the gate as being seventy-five feet tall with double doors made of Corinthian brass. The beggar must have appeared a pathetic creature indeed at the foot of this gleaming, magnificent gate.

He asked Peter and John for a contribution, as he did everyone else who came along. But their response was different (3:4–5). The beggar had hoped for money, but what he received was much more valuable (3:6–8). Perhaps Peter had been observant when Jesus raised Jairus's daughter from the dead (Luke 8:54) because he didn't merely tell the man to get up; he gave the command, and then extended his hand to help (3:7).

The healed beggar's reaction is noteworthy (3:8). He praised God verbally while simultaneously walking and jumping. His physical enthusiasm was certainly praise as well. And as onlookers saw the commotion and recognized the man who was leaping around, they were amazed (3:10).

3:11–26

PETER'S SECOND SERMON

Even in his unbridled enthusiasm, the healed beggar held on to Peter and John (3:11). Consequently, it didn't take long for a crowd to form.

Solomon's Colonnade (3:11), next to the outer court of the temple, was a roofed porch supported by rows of tall stone columns. It was here that Peter, for a second time, found himself surrounded by curious onlookers wanting an explanation for the awe-inspiring events they had witnessed (2:14–36). He began by telling them, essentially, "Don't look at me. John and I didn't perform this miracle!" (3:12). The power, he said, should be attributed to God who has glorified Jesus (3:13).

Peter used imagery of the suffering Savior (Isaiah 52:13–53:12), an unfamiliar concept for many in the crowd who still anticipated a heroic military Messiah. He went on to provide three specific ways that Jesus had suffered at the hands of the people:

1) They—including those in the crowd—had demanded that Jesus be killed even after Pilate tried to exonerate Him (3:13).

2) They had demanded release of a murderer rather than God's own Son (3:14).
3) They had killed the very One who made life possible for them, but God had raised Him from the dead (3:15).

It was only through Jesus' power that they were able to heal the crippled man (3:16). And it must have been difficult to hear that, even though God had foretold that His Christ would suffer (3:18), the suffering had been at *their* hands.

Still, Peter wasn't attempting to instill guilt. He acknowledged that the people had acted ignorantly (3:17). Yet as a result of their actions, they needed to repent. They had missed the significance of Jesus and allowed Him to die; they must not overlook His eternal significance as their only source of restoration and salvation (3:19–21).

Peter made another point that would have been important to the people in the crowd. They hadn't just missed out on the message of the prophets concerning Jesus; even Moses (whom they revered) had told them to look for a prophet like him (Deuteronomy 18:15–19; Acts 3:22–23). The other prophets from Samuel onward had then reaffirmed Moses' message of a coming servant of God (3:24–26). Moses and the prophets had done as God had instructed, and now it was up to the people to do the same by turning from their wicked ways (3:26).

4:1–22

TROUBLE WITH THE AUTHORITIES

As with Peter's first sermon, the second one had mixed reactions. Many people believed what Peter was saying and responded in faith (4:4). In fact, the church swelled from around three thousand people (1:15; 2:41) to five thousand men (4:4). (Many times, biblical head counts included only the males, referring to family units.)

Yet Peter's teachings about Jesus' resurrection had also gotten the attention of the Sadducees, who didn't believe that people were resurrected after they died (Luke 20:27). They came, along with security officers from the temple, and seized Peter and John. This was no small scrap with the law; the captain of the temple guard (4:1) held a priestly rank second only to the high priest, and he was responsible for the maintenance of law and order. Since it was already late in the day, the apostles were jailed for the night (4:3).

Demystifying Acts

The Sadducees were a ruling class of wealthy aristocrats. Politically they ingratiated themselves to the Romans and followed a policy of collaboration. Theologically they believed that the messianic age had begun during the Maccabean period (around 160 BC), so they were not looking for a Messiah. They also denied the doctrine of the resurrection of the dead, so naturally they viewed Peter and John as both heretics and agitators.

The purpose of their overnight incarceration was to convene the Sanhedrin (frequently referred to simply as "the council" in scripture). This was a seventy-member body plus its president, the high priest, comprised of members of the high priest's family, experts in the law (including scribes and Pharisees), and other respected members of the community (elders). They sat in a semicircle as they served as both the Supreme Court and Senate of the nation of Israel.

During their night in jail it surely occurred to Peter and John that they were about to stand before the very group that had condemned Jesus to death less than two months before. Was history about to repeat itself? They surely couldn't count on justice from this court that had listened to false testimony and unjustly condemned Jesus. Fear would have been justifiable, since many of the same authorities that had sentenced Jesus to death were presiding (4:5–6).

But the next day, rather than being afraid, Peter was filled with the Holy Spirit (4:8). His response is an emphatic demonstration of the truth of what Jesus had previously promised His followers (Luke 21:12–15). Peter certainly received the words and wisdom that Jesus spoke of. As soon as Peter and John were challenged to explain themselves (4:7), Peter took the offensive. There were three parts to Peter's defense:

1) He focused on the healing of the crippled man as being an act of kindness, brought about by the name of Jesus Christ of Nazareth (4:8–10). Peter was neither ashamed nor afraid to testify about Jesus.
2) He drew attention to the fact that the same Sanhedrin trying his case had been responsible for the death of Jesus, but God had vindicated the Lord by raising Him from the dead (4:10–11). He considered their actions a fulfillment of prophecy (Psalm 118:22). Jesus was the overlooked and rejected stone that had become the capstone, the crowning piece of God's creative work in the world.
3) He changed the topic from healing to salvation (4:12). He started by replying to a query about physical and temporal restoration, and moved from there to the subject of spiritual and eternal restoration. The healing of the crippled man was a picture of the salvation available to all people through Jesus.

Peter's use of "no other name" (4:12) proclaimed the positive uniqueness of Jesus. His death, His resurrection, His exaltation, and His authority constitute Jesus as the one and only Savior for humankind.

The Sanhedrin was astonished at the courage of Peter and John. Jesus had been an insightful and formidable opponent to the religious authorities who had repeatedly debated and criticized Him. These two were clearly ordinary men (4:13). But that had been an early assumption about Jesus as well (John 7:15).

The council members had to make a judgment, and the healed man stood before them, physically regenerated (4:14). So they could not deny the miracle, but neither would they acknowledge it. Even the miraculous power of God could not penetrate the Sadducees' preoccupation with protecting their vested interests. They shut themselves off from seeing and responding to the miracle that occurred. But they also realized that the crowds of people were certainly taking notice of what had happened (4:17).

The best they could do was to solemnly forbid Peter and John to speak at all in the name of Jesus. The ban on the apostles was intended both to serve as a warning and to provide a legal basis in the event further action should be needed. But the powerful Sanhedrin was certainly not expecting the apostles' response to its admonition (4:19–20). As with the prophets of old, God's Word was in the apostles' hearts like a burning fire, and they could not remain silent.

With all the people praising God for the miraculous healing of the crippled man, the council could see no way to punish Peter and John. So it threatened them more and then let them go (4:21).

Critical Observation

Consider Peter's newfound boldness in this passage. He had always been the impulsive one in the group of apostles. He got out of the boat and walked on water, only to falter and begin to sink (Matthew 14:27–31). He was quick to speak up but frequently said the wrong things (Matthew 16:22–23; Luke 9:32–36). Within hours of promising to go to prison and to death with Jesus, he had denied Him three times (Luke 22:33–34, 54–62). Yet immediately after the coming of the Holy Spirit, we see him stand boldly and proclaim the gospel to a large crowd, use the power of God to heal someone of a forty-year ailment, and defend his faith before an authoritative and rather resistant group of religious leaders.

4:23–31

THE RESPONSE TO PERSECUTION

At this stage in the early church, the believers were all together "and had all things in common" (2:44 NKJV). So when Peter and John had been arrested, imprisoned for the night, and tried before the Sanhedrin, all the other church members had a stake in what would happen to them. The fact that Peter and John were released with nothing more than a slap on the wrist was a cause for great rejoicing.

And their joy was not misplaced. While some may have felt a great sense of relief, the believers immediately lifted their voices in prayer and praise (4:24). They acknowledged God as sovereign Lord and Creator. And the words of Psalm 2:1–2 came to mind and took on new significance. The psalmist had written of nations, peoples, kings, and rulers gathering together to oppose God (4:25–26). Those same groups were still standing in opposition: Jews, Gentiles, Herod, and Pontius Pilate (4:27).

But at this point, after the resurrection of Jesus had put things into better perspective, they could see Jesus' (and their own) persecution as events that God had ordained (4:28). The believers did not pray for God to eliminate, or even reduce, their sufferings. Rather, they asked for boldness in the face of threats and opposition (4:29). And they asked for God's power, not to use against their persecutors, but so they could continue to heal and minister in the name of Jesus (4:30).

God acknowledged the believers' prayers, responding by shaking their meeting place and filling them all with the Holy Spirit. As a result, their boldness was intensified.

The believers withstood this initial problem of persecution from those outside their ranks and grew stronger as a result. The next threat, however, would come from within.

Take It Home

Notice in this passage that what the beggar was asking for was not what he really needed. He was looking for handouts from others, which had gotten him by for over forty years. But after Peter and John saw his real need and used the power of God to heal him, the man was absolutely jubilant. What can believers learn about their prayer habits from this story? Do you ever pray for something that is more of an immediate want than a real need? Could it be that the reason God sometimes doesn't answer prayers is because He is more concerned with meeting our needs than in fulfilling our current desires?

ACTS 4:32–5:42

NEW PROBLEMS FOR THE NEW CHURCH

One in Heart and Mind	4:32–37
Two Exceptions. . .and the Consequences	5:1–11
Phenomenal Healing and Continued Growth	5:12–16
Another Brush with the Authorities	5:17–42

Setting Up the Section

Led by the Holy Spirit, and inspired by recent positive results after an encounter with the Jewish authorities, the newly forming church is a model of unity and mutual sacrifice. So when the first threat to that unity is exposed, the consequences are severe indeed. Yet the believers get past that problem and continue to teach, heal, and share with one another. Meanwhile, opponents continue to intensify their persecution of the believers, which only strengthens the faith of Jesus' followers.

4:32–37

ONE IN HEART AND MIND

From the arrival of the Holy Spirit on the Day of Pentecost, every mention of the gathering of believers has emphasized their unity. Here they are of "one heart and soul" (4:32 NASB). Beyond being just a mental attitude, the proof of their love for one another was seen in their selfless giving. Even though believers were by this time numbering in the thousands (4:4), none among them were in need of anything because they didn't even claim possessions as their own. The willingness of those with wealth to share with others more than covered the needs of the group. This was but one of the results of the grace that was on them all (4:33).

Generosity even reached the point where some people would sell their houses and property to donate to the needs of the church (4:34–35). One such person was named Joseph, yet he would become known throughout the rest of the New Testament as

Barnabas, a nickname meaning "Son of encouragement" (4:36).

The response of the church to such large (and public) gifts is not noted. With everything else said about the church to date, however, one would think that much praise would be given to God, with heartfelt appreciation expressed to the donor(s). Yet with the steadily growing numbers, it was only a short time until problems arose to jeopardize the unity the believers felt and the sharing they practiced.

5:1–11

TWO EXCEPTIONS. . .AND THE CONSEQUENCES

The account of Ananias and Sapphira is one of the more difficult biblical passages to deal with. The offense of the couple seems insignificant in contrast to other sins that were quickly forgiven. From all appearances, Barnabas and Ananias did the same thing. Both sold a piece of property. Both brought the proceeds of the sale to the apostles. The only difference might appear to be that Barnabas brought all he received, while Ananias held out a little for himself.

Yet Ananias was guilty of the double sins of dishonesty and deceit. He and his wife agreed to misrepresent the selling price when reporting to the church. It is understandable that they might have wanted a positive reputation and the respect of their peers. But instead of acclaim, they both were put to death by God immediately after Peter's explanation that they had lied (5:3). They weren't killed because they held out some of the money for themselves; that was their right. Instead, what they thought was a subtle attempt to make themselves appear better was actually a lie to God (5:4, 9).

The church members became fearful after hearing what happened (5:5, 11). The situation was a classic example of what Paul would later teach: "Do not be deceived: God cannot be mocked" (Galatians 6:7 NIV). And the story is a graphic reminder that there are no "little" sins.

Critical Observation

Perhaps the severity of the punishment of Ananias and Sapphira was the result of their being the first to break the unity within the early church. Throughout scripture, as God leads His people to new opportunities and a closer relationship with Him, those who are first to disobey are treated more harshly. A few examples include:

- Nadab and Abihu, two sons of Aaron who tried to make an offering of incense in a different manner than God had prescribed (Leviticus 10:1–2)
- Achan, who stole and hid plunder after the fall of Jericho (Joshua 7)
- Uzzah, who touched the Ark of the Covenant against God's instructions, even though he had the best of intentions (2 Samuel 6:6–7)

5:12–16

PHENOMENAL HEALING AND CONTINUED GROWTH

As the story of Ananias and Sapphira spread throughout the community, the result was beneficial. Although verse 13 says that no one else dared join the apostles and believers, the reference appears to be to those who might be joining merely out of curiosity or with less-than-total commitment. The very next statement clarifies that additional men and women continued to be added to their number (5:14).

Those who chose to be involved with the new movement were witness to incredible things. Few of the numerous signs and wonders (5:12) are detailed other than healing of the sick and those tormented by evil spirits (5:16). Yet the method of healing listed is but a single clue as to the great spectacle of how God was at work among His young church (5:14). People began to flock in crowds to Jerusalem as news spread of the many wonderful things taking place (5:16).

5:17–42

ANOTHER BRUSH WITH THE AUTHORITIES

The Sadducees weren't happy that the apostles had ignored their warnings to quit talking about Jesus (4:18, 21), so this time they had a larger group arrested and jailed (5:17–18). Their real motive is recorded as well: jealousy (5:17). Clearly, God was at work among the believers in Jesus, and all the Sadducees could do was observe (and complain) as outsiders.

The apostles were supposed to be in prison overnight, but their sentence was commuted by an angel who released them (5:19). Rather than take the opportunity to hide or escape, the apostles followed the angel's orders to go tell people about the gospel.

The truly miraculous aspect of the apostles' prison break was that no one knew they were gone. The cells were still locked and the guards still at their posts. It wasn't until the Sanhedrin had assembled and sent for the apostles that they were discovered missing. Someone finally had to tell the council that the apostles were teaching in the temple courts—one of the most public places in Jerusalem (5:25).

To avoid a potential stoning by the people, the temple officials decided to use tact instead of force to summon the apostles (5:26). The high priest interrogated them, wanting to know why they ignored the previous warnings they had received. Their answer was short and clear, and they followed it with a mini-sermon about the significance of Jesus and the Holy Spirit, and how the Jewish leaders had contributed to Jesus' death (5:29–32).

The response angered the council to the point where its members wanted to kill the apostles. The translation of the New English Bible is on target: "They were touched to the raw" (5:33). But a cooler head prevailed. Gamaliel, a highly respected rabbi, used logic, reason, and historical precedent to justify a policy of laissez-faire. The apostles claimed to be obeying God (5:29), but he advised his peers to wait and see if God was really behind this movement. After all, two previous movements had collapsed as quickly as they had arisen (5:35–39).

Demystifying Acts

Gamaliel appears in Acts with no introduction, but he was a significant person on the council. He was the grandson of the famous rabbi Hillel. Saul of Tarsus (the apostle Paul) was one of his students. He was a Pharisee with a reputation for scholarship, wisdom, and moderation. And he wasn't just scholarly; the people had a high regard for his opinion. He was a welcome model of reason and sanity in this emotionally charged situation.

Gamaliel's words swayed the Sanhedrin, and though spoken by a non-believer, the council proved to be prophetic for the whole book of Acts. He points out that if God is behind this movement, no one will be able to stop it. Sure enough, throughout Acts no one and nothing can stop the progress of the gospel, proving that this is indeed God's work. Yet, though it was swayed, the council didn't simply release the apostles this time.

Before letting them go—with additional orders not to talk about Jesus any more—the council had them flogged (5:40). But rather than being despondent from pain and shame, the apostles rejoiced that they had been deemed worthy of suffering in the same way that Jesus did. They had the honor of being dishonored, and the grace to be disgraced.

As for the orders of the Sanhedrin, silence was not an option. If anything, the apostles' experience only intensified their fervor to spread the good news about Jesus (5:41–42).

Take It Home

Sometimes committee work, or even fellowship within the church, can take on the tone of a business meeting, with varying opinions stated strongly and persuasively and little room for compromise. What can you learn from Gamaliel's advice (5:38–39), or from his example in general, to ensure that human argument doesn't short-circuit God's will during a hotly debated issue in the future?

ACTS 6:1–8:3

THE CHURCH'S FIRST CASUALTY

The Problem with Success	6:1–7
The Brief Ministry of Stephen	6:8–15
Stephen's Defense	7:1–53
The Death of Stephen	7:54–60
Persecution as a Way of Life	8:1–3

Setting Up the Section

To this point the commentary on the new and growing church has been overwhelmingly positive, even though problems are beginning to arise. The apostles have been imprisoned and flogged. Two members have died dramatic deaths as a result of lying to God. And this section describes another problem from within: discrimination. Yet the church does such a good job of resolving the problem that one of the people chosen to help attracts too much outside attention and becomes the church's first martyr.

6:1–7

THE PROBLEM WITH SUCCESS

With the number of disciples steadily increasing in the church (6:1), problems were to be expected. But discrimination should not have been among them.

Demystifying Acts

"Grecian Jews" (NIV) or better, "Hellenistic Jews" (TNIV; *Hellenistai*), were Jews who had at one time lived outside of Palestine. They spoke Greek as their primary language and were culturally and socially distinct from the Hebraic Jews (*Hebraioi*). These latter had never left Palestine and spoke Aramaic as their native tongue. The tension between these two groups is understandable, but it prevented the complete unity of the church (6:1).

To say the apostles waited on tables (6:2) may sound condescending today when we think of the wait staff in a contemporary restaurant, but that was not the apostles' intent here. Their leadership role involved teaching and preaching, and they wanted to maintain their focus on what God was calling them to do. So they enlisted a group of other people who were called to minister in a more physical, material way. Yet the fact that the apostles sought out people known to be full of the Spirit and wisdom (6:3) indicated that the waiting-on-tables ministry was just as much a spiritual calling as teaching and preaching.

In addition to acknowledging the spiritual significance of this new ministry, the plan of the disciples was wise for a number of other reasons. They did not appoint a committee; they appointed a ministry team and delegated the responsibility and authority to get the job done. In addition, they chose seven people to oversee the new program rather than a single person. There is great wisdom in the plurality of leadership in the church, with ministry exercised in community. Finally, the names of the people chosen were Greek (6:5). The church selected people who would be most understanding of the problem of discrimination, striving to be inclusive rather than exclusive.

The apostles' proposal pleased everyone, so the seven candidates were commissioned with prayer and laying on of hands (6:5–6). After the new ministers went to work, the church not only kept growing, but also began to see Jewish priests coming to believe in Jesus in large numbers (6:7).

The book of Acts will have more to say about Stephen and Philip, the first two of the seven listed (6:5). Philip reappears in Acts 8. Stephen's story follows immediately.

6:8–15

THE BRIEF MINISTRY OF STEPHEN

Only one verse (6:8) is devoted to the wonderfully positive ministry of Stephen before we read of the conflicts he encountered. Yet his upright character becomes evident in contrast to the actions and statements of his accusers.

The Synagogue of the "Freedmen" (6:9), or Libertines, may have been composed of descendants of Jewish prisoners of war enslaved by the Roman general Pompey when he conquered Palestine in 63 BC. Later released, they formed a synagogue community of "freedmen." It is unclear whether Luke has in mind one synagogue, made up of Jews from various places (Cyrene, Alexandria, Cilicia, and Asia), or whether he is referring to two or more synagogues. In any case, these Jews opposed Stephen's preaching about Jesus.

The topic of their argument with Stephen is not mentioned, but they were no match for his wisdom. Yet rather than concede that he knew more than they did, they used the same tactic the Pharisees had used with Jesus: Get him to say something and then enlist false witnesses to twist his words (6:11).

Stephen's supposed offense was a double charge of blasphemy: speaking against the temple and the Law of Moses (6:13). The Law was God's Word, and the temple was God's house. So for Jews to speak out against either one was to speak against God Himself. Once more in Acts, the Sanhedrin was convened for a hearing about the new teachings of Christianity (6:12). Yet even before the trial began, everyone there noticed that Stephen's face was like that of an angel (6:15). Many believe that his face glowed with divine glory as Moses' had after he had spent time in the presence of God (Exodus 34:29–35).

7:1–53

STEPHEN'S DEFENSE

The high priest (president and moderator of the Sanhedrin) began by asking if the charges against Stephen were true (7:1). In response, Stephen launched into a lengthy sermon that was, in fact, his answer to the question. In the panorama of God's dealings with His people, Stephen focused on four main epochs of Israel's history, each one with a major character.

Abraham (7:2–8)

It was thanks to Abraham's obedience to God that the Israelites got to Israel in the first place. He had left a comfortable home in Mesopotamia only because God told him to. He was later rewarded with land, a child of his own, and descendants too numerous to be counted. It was through Abraham that God's covenant of circumcision was established. God also shared with Abraham what would happen during the next phase of history—slavery in Egypt.

Joseph (7:9–19)

It was thanks to Joseph's obedience to God that the Israelites didn't starve during a seven-year famine. Joseph's brothers' hostility toward him had actually been God's method of placing Joseph in Egypt, where he was put in charge of Pharaoh's kingdom. It was at Pharaoh's invitation that Joseph's entire family moved to Egypt to survive the famine. But four hundred years later the family had grown into an immense force that threatened the Egyptian leaders who no longer remembered Joseph. Therefore, the members of the family of Israel (the Israelites) were enslaved.

Moses (7:20–43)

God had told Abraham that his descendants would become slaves in Egypt, but that He would punish the nation that enslaved them (7:6–7). It was thanks to Moses' (reluctant) obedience to God that the Israelites at last departed from Egypt and (after numerous trials and lapses of faith) finally made it to the promised land. Had Moses' parents obeyed Pharaoh's instructions, Moses would have been put to death as an infant. But through a series of God-directed events, he grew up as Pharaoh's grandson instead. He spent forty years in the palace, forty years in a lonely existence in the wilderness, and forty years leading his people. His final forty years were especially challenging because the people continually complained to him, wishing they were back in Egypt and constructed a golden calf as soon as Moses was gone for a while.

David and Solomon (7:44–50)

While in the wilderness, the Israelites had a portable tabernacle, created just as God instructed, that allowed the priests to operate and the people to worship and offer sacrifices. Joshua continued with it into the promised land. David wanted to build a permanent structure ("dwelling place" [7:46]) for God, but his request was denied. Instead, God allowed Solomon to construct the temple. But Solomon realized at the time, and Stephen reiterated in his speech, that God cannot be limited to any physical space—not even a temple dedicated in His name (1 Kings 8:27).

Why did Stephen single out these four periods of Israel's history? They were not random thoughts. The connecting feature of these four epochs is that in none of them was God's presence limited to any particular place. On the contrary, the God of the Old Testament was a living God, a God on the move who was always calling His people to fresh adventures and always accompanying them wherever they went. God does not live in buildings made by the hands of people.

Critical Observation

Peter and Paul would later build on Stephen's theme and explain that the Spirit of God now dwells in the hearts of believers, and together we are the living stones of God's house (Ephesians 2:19–22; 1 Peter 2:4–5).

Stephen appears to be one of the first Christians to understand, and certainly the first to declare it publicly, that God could never be contained in the buildings or boxes we try to put Him in. Heaven is God's throne and earth is His footstool. Stephen also understood that the patterns of the Old Covenant were passing away.

The false witnesses had accused Stephen of two blasphemies—that he spoke against the holy place (the temple) and that he spoke against the holy law (6:13). In response to both accusations, his defense was that nothing he said had been out of line with scripture. He showed that the Old Testament placed less emphasis on the temple and more emphasis on the Law than did his accusers.

At this point, Stephen the accused became the accuser. He used unflattering names to call out the members of the Sanhedrin and put them in the same category with their ancestors who had resisted the Holy Spirit and persecuted God's prophets (7:51). Although they placed such an emphasis on circumcision, their eyes and ears remained "uncircumcised"—just like those of the unbelieving Gentiles. And not only had they not obeyed the Law they claimed to hold so highly, they also had betrayed and murdered Jesus (7:52–53).

7:54–60

THE DEATH OF STEPHEN

Stephen's words were not at all well received (7:54). The furious council members could hardly control themselves. It was then that Stephen saw a vision of Jesus and told them what he had observed (7:55–56). His use of the title "Son of Man" is significant. It had been how Jesus most often referred to Himself and subtly combined both the human and divine nature of His messianic role. (This is the final use of the term in the New Testament.) In addition, biblical references to Jesus at God's right hand refer to Him as seated (Psalm 110:1; Colossians 3:1; Hebrews 8:1; etc.). The fact that He is standing here, some speculate, is to receive Stephen into His presence.

The Sanhedrin was supposed to be a Supreme-Court-like body with strict rules and procedures. But here its members acted no better than a lynch mob (7:57–58). They didn't have the authority to carry out a death sentence, yet they dragged Stephen outside the city and began to stone him. It is here where we find the first biblical mention of a young man named Saul who would soon, due only to the grace of God, become the dynamic apostle Paul (7:58). Stonings could be messy, so Saul was tending to the coats of the participants—a role that indicates his endorsement of what was going on.

But in his final moments of what was intended to be agony, Stephen was still filled with the Holy Spirit (7:55) and responded very much the same way Jesus had during His crucifixion. Like Jesus, Stephen had been charged with blasphemy, and false witnesses were produced to testify against him. And Stephen's two final statements reflected two of his Lord's last words from the cross. First, he asked Jesus to receive his spirit, and then he prayed for forgiveness for those who were in the process of killing him (7:59–60). Finally, he fell asleep, a common biblical euphemism for death (7:60).

8:1–3

PERSECUTION AS A WAY OF LIFE

The church was shocked by the martyrdom of Stephen and the violent opposition that followed, but with the benefit of hindsight we can see how in God's providence it was used to help fulfill the Great Commission. Stephen's death was the occasion of a great persecution that led to the scattering of the disciples out of Jerusalem and into Judea and Samaria (8:1). Yet wherever they went, they took the gospel with them.

Meanwhile, Saul quickly moved from tending coats into full-scale persecution of believers. He was both cruel and heartless, going from house to house and dragging off both men and women to be imprisoned—all in his desire to destroy the church.

Paul's story is dropped abruptly at this point, but will be picked up again in Acts 9.

Take It Home

Stephen was the first Christian martyr, but certainly not the last. Dying for one's beliefs is not a problem that has been left in the past. According to statisticians, more Christians died for their faith during the twentieth century than in all the previous centuries combined. These days we may hear more about suicide bombers dying for radical Islamic causes than about Christians dying around the world, but both are realities. The freedoms of the Western world may make martyrdom seem distant and unreal to us. So perhaps the harder question for the Western church is not, "Do you think you would be willing to die for your faith if it came down to it?" but instead, "Are you willing to live out your faith boldly and publicly?" On an individual level, are you making the most of the spiritual freedom you enjoy?

ACTS 8:4–40

FROM JERUSALEM TO SAMARIA TO ETHIOPIA

The Ministry of Philip, Part I	8:4–8
The Gift That Can't Be Bought	8:9–25
The Ministry of Philip, Part II	8:26–40

Setting Up the Section

Jesus had told His followers that they would be His witnesses in Jerusalem, Judea, and Samaria, and to the ends of the world (1:8). Until the stoning of Stephen, they had remained in Jerusalem with an idyllic unity and spirit of fellowship. In this section, however, persecution will drive them out of Jerusalem into the surrounding territories of Judea and Samaria.

8:4–8

THE MINISTRY OF PHILIP, PART I

Change is seldom easy. It must have been difficult, if not a bit traumatic, for the church members in Jerusalem to disperse. Most descriptions so far in Acts have portrayed the church as an exciting and contagious place to be. Members ate in one another's homes. No one had any financial needs. Property was shared. Much time was devoted to prayer and learning from the disciples. There was power in the early church. Miracles took place, and new believers were added daily.

The few problems faced so far had been dealt with quickly, allowing the group to keep ministering and growing. The ministries of the newly designated Seven had started very well, especially the work of Stephen.

Then, with no warning, Stephen had been seized, carried before the Sanhedrin, and stoned to death. The crowd's hostile feelings toward Stephen extended into a great persecution against the church in Jerusalem. The apostles remained in Jerusalem and the church eventually survived there, but many members were scattered to new locations (8:1). They left the wonderful unity they had shared to settle elsewhere and begin new communities. Meanwhile, Saul was passionately seeking out and imprisoning all the believers he could find.

They might have been resistant to change, yet they preached about Jesus wherever they went and began to see positive things happening. Philip, another of the Seven, went to preach in Samaria. When he was no longer needed to disperse food to widows, Philip became an effective evangelist. Like Stephen, he was empowered to perform great miracles (6:8; 8:6). He drove out evil spirits and healed many paralyzed and crippled people, resulting in great joy.

8:9–25

THE GIFT THAT CAN'T BE BOUGHT

As it turned out, Philip's display of God's power was overshadowing the work of a sorcerer named Simon who had made a living in Samaria for a while (8:9). Simon's boast to be the Great Power (8:10) may have been a claim of divinity, or perhaps it was enough for him to claim an association with some unseen power. In either case, his ability to amaze the Samaritans with his magic came to an end when they saw Philip performing genuine miracles in the name of Jesus. Even Simon counted himself among the believers and was baptized with numerous other Samaritans. Yet Simon appeared to be more a follower of Philip, with an intense curiosity about the power he was using, than a follower of Christ (8:13).

But one great miracle had not yet been observed in Samaria. For some reason, the belief and baptism of the Samaritans were not accompanied by the receiving of the Holy Spirit, as all previous conversions had been. Peter and John had been sent from Jerusalem to observe for themselves the response of the Samaritans to Philip's preaching. When they arrived, they prayed for the Samaritans to receive the Holy Spirit, and the new believers did (8:14–17). Luke does not specify exactly what confirmed the presence of the Holy Spirit, yet it was very apparent because Simon the sorcerer witnessed something that impressed him. It is frequently assumed that the sign was speaking in tongues as it had been on the Day of Pentecost.

Peter had promised the gift of the Spirit to all who repented and were baptized (2:38–39), so why the delay in the arrival of the Holy Spirit in this one instance? The long history of tension (and even hatred) between the Jews and the Samaritans may help explain. Hostility had existed between the Jews and the Samaritans for centuries, and a schism had formed because of racial and theological differences. The mutual animosity was intense. For the Samaritans to believe in the same Savior and be baptized in the same Name as the Jews was an unprecedented event. The delay in the coming of the Holy Spirit allowed Peter and John to witness the event so they could return to the church in Jerusalem and confirm God's work among their former enemies. In addition, Philip's ministry as an evangelist was validated among the Samaritan people.

Critical Observation

It is rather ironic that John was one of the representatives sent to witness the coming of the Holy Spirit to the Samaritans. One of the last times he had been in Samaria, he had asked Jesus about calling down fire on the people (Luke 9:52–56). The very disciple who previously wanted God to pour out His judgment on the Samaritans was there to see God pour out His Spirit and His blessing instead.

Peter and John had laid their hands on the Samaritan believers prior to their receiving the Holy Spirit. Simon the sorcerer witnessed what happened and tried to bribe the two apostles to give him the same ability (8:18–19). Peter's response not only revealed the shallowness of Simon's previous "conversion," but also created great fear within the sorcerer (8:20–24). Judging from Simon's heart not right before God, wickedness, bitterness, and captivity to sin, it is doubtful that he had ever made a sincere decision to repent and follow Jesus. Even after Peter's harsh rebuke, Simon wouldn't pray to God directly but looked for someone else to pray for him (8:24). The word *simony* arose from this story, meaning the buying or selling of ecclesiastical pardons, offices, and such. Early church tradition also says that Simon originated the cult of Gnosticism and led believers astray with his false teachings.

In contrast to the reluctance of Simon was the enthusiasm of Peter and John. On their way back to Jerusalem, they preached the gospel in many other Samaritan villages (8:25). The love of Jesus was beginning to heal a rift that had existed for centuries.

8:26–40

THE MINISTRY OF PHILIP, PART II

After such rousing success in Samaria, the angel's instructions to Philip don't seem to make much sense (8:26). Gaza is the most southerly of five Philistine cities near the Mediterranean coast. The road between Jerusalem and Gaza stretched through the desert for fifty or sixty miles. Why leave the crowds of eager-to-hear Samaritans to go into isolation in the wilderness? Yet Philip seemed to respond with no reservations.

Along the way he saw a chariot and was told by the Spirit to stay close to it (8:29). Inside was a man reading from the book of Isaiah. It was common practice in antiquity to speak aloud when reading. So Philip had the ideal opportunity to ask if the man in the chariot understood what he was reading. He had no idea.

It turned out that the man was an important official from Ethiopia, in charge of the queen's treasury. The reference to Ethiopia in this passage is not the contemporary country east of Sudan, but rather an area that would currently extend from southern Egypt into central Sudan. Candace (8:27) was actually a traditional title for the queen mother, who was responsible for performing the more mundane duties of the reigning king.

The queen's treasurer had traveled a great distance to worship in Jerusalem, but the fact that he was a eunuch may have prevented his inclusion in the ceremonies because Hebrew law forbade it (Deuteronomy 23:1). Perhaps he had gone all that way, only to be turned away from the temple and all the other worshipers.

If so, it is all the more significant that he was reading about someone else who was humiliated and without descendents (8:33). It was also all the more frustrating that he didn't really understand the scriptures. So Philip climbed up in the chariot with him and started with that very passage to tell him the good news about Jesus (8:31, 35). Jesus had no children, yet as our Messiah and Savior He created a whole new family of faith with His Father in heaven where there is room for us all.

When they traveled past some water, the Ethiopian asked to be baptized, and Philip complied (8:36–38). But as soon as the two came up out of the water, Philip disappeared under the power of the Spirit of the Lord. The Ethiopian never saw him again, but left rejoicing.

Demystifying Acts

Verse 37 is missing from many current Bible translations because it is not found in the original manuscripts and is thought to have been added later. It makes the Ethiopian's request to be baptized conditional on his belief, and provides his testimony: "I believe that Jesus Christ is the Son of God."

It appears that when the Ethiopian got back home, he started a family—not a physical one, but a spiritual one. The Christian church in Ethiopia sprang up and continued to grow, perhaps as a result of the Ethiopian's newfound understanding of the gospel, although there is no direct proof.

As for Philip, he turned up in Azotus (the Old Testament city of Ashdod), miles away from where he had been. He made his way north to Caesarea, preaching throughout various towns as he traveled (7:40). He appears to have settled in Caesarea (21:8).

Take It Home

The account of the belief and salvation of the Samaritans and their early inclusion into the church provides a good lesson for today's believers. Can you detect any people or groups who tend to be excluded from church involvement—either locally or worldwide? Do you think it's better for the church to remain somewhat segregated, or should God's people strive harder for total unity? What do you think it would take to resolve the conflicts and become more united, regardless of race, economy, political affiliation, etc.?

ACTS 9:1–31

THE SURPRISE CONVERSION OF SAUL

On the Road to Damascus	9:1–9
Saul in Damascus	9:10–25
Saul in Jerusalem	9:26–31

Setting Up the Section

After the arrival of the Holy Spirit, shortly after Jesus' ascension, the followers of Jesus were in for a lot of surprises. The apostles stopped cowering in seclusion and began to speak boldly in the streets and temple courts—even at risk of arrest and imprisonment. Priests and Samaritans were among those adding to the number of believers. But the biggest surprise yet is found in this section, where one of the foremost among Christian persecutors has a dramatic encounter with Jesus and becomes one of the foremost among New Testament evangelists.

9:1–9

ON THE ROAD TO DAMASCUS

Saul's experience on the road to Damascus is the most famous conversion in all of church history. Paul will later share his story with other people, which Luke also records, so the account is found three times in the book of Acts. But so far, each of the three mentions of Saul (7:58; 8:1, 3) has portrayed him as a relentless opponent of Christ and His church.

That hostile image continues in Acts 9:1–2. Saul had been involved, to an extent, with the stoning of Stephen (7:58). We don't know whether or not he actually participated in killings of other believers, but based on verse 1, that might be the case.

In any event, he had gone out of his way to secure official permission and paperwork needed to imprison any believers he found in Damascus. Believers weren't yet being called Christians. Jesus had referred to Himself as the way, the truth, and the life (John 14:6), so at this point the movement of His followers was sometimes called "the Way" (9:2). This term is found several times throughout Acts.

Critical Observation

The trip to Damascus was a commitment in itself. The city was about 150 miles from Jerusalem—a journey that would require almost a week. But a lot of Jewish people lived in Damascus, and the synagogues would be a good place to seek out adherents of the new Christian religion.

Saul wasn't alone. He had traveling companions, perhaps members of the temple police to help transport any believers he might find back to Jerusalem. Saul and his group were almost to Damascus when he saw a light from heaven and heard clearly the voice of Jesus (9:3–4). Saul fell to the ground and responded, and the voice confirmed that, indeed, He was Jesus. It's worthwhile to note that Jesus didn't accuse Saul of persecuting the church; it was Jesus Himself who was being persecuted. Saul would later come to understand the close interrelationship between Jesus and His followers, and would incorporate the concept into his Epistles.

Jesus told Saul to go on into Damascus and wait to be told what to do (9:6). The men with Saul heard a noise, but did not discern that it was a voice speaking to him. When he arose to comply, he discovered he was blind and had to be led by the others into the city. He was there three days, and unwilling to eat or drink anything. It was quite a humbling turn of events. Saul had come to Damascus to arrest anyone who believed in Jesus; instead he was arrested by Jesus, whose light shone not only in his eyes, but also in his heart. He had expected to enter the city with pride in his prowess as a self-confident opponent of Christ, but found himself humbled and blinded, a captive to the very One he had opposed.

9:10–25

SAUL IN DAMASCUS

Jesus was calling Saul to an exciting new ministry, but first He called a believer named Ananias for a short-term assignment (9:10–12). Saul had traveled to Damascus for the express purpose of imprisoning believers—which would perhaps result in their subsequent deaths. Ananias had full knowledge of Saul's mission (9:14), so it was no small matter for him to approach Saul to extend a favor and treat him as a believing brother. He expressed his concerns to the Lord, and was assured that Saul was a different person.

In Jesus' comments to Ananias, we learn a lot about Saul. His hometown is mentioned for the first time (9:11). Tarsus is still a city in Turkey, and having been in existence for more than six thousand years, may be the oldest city on earth. (Another contender for the title is Damascus.) It had a good reputation as an intellectual city. Tarsus is mentioned only five times in the Bible, each time in connection with Paul.

Demystifying Acts

Though it's not commonly heard today, *Ananias* was a common name in the Mideast during the first century. This passage tells of a disciple in Damascus by that name. Acts 5:1–11 told of the death of another Ananias and his wife, Sapphira. And later in Acts (23:1–5), Paul will defend himself before a high priest named Ananias.

Jesus' instructions to Ananias also explain that Saul would become His representative to the Gentiles and their kings, as well as his fellow Israelites (9:15). Later chapters in Acts will show Saul (Paul) before Roman rulers and various other groups of Gentiles. Ananias was also told of the suffering Saul would endure (9:16). Over the course of his life, Saul was beaten eight times for his faith. Once he was pelted with rocks and left for dead. On various occasions he spent a lot of time in prison. And tradition says that eventually Saul was beheaded in Rome by order of Caesar.

But none of these outward signs of belief had taken place in Saul's life as Ananias responded in great faith and went to the house where Saul was staying. Straight Street (9:11) shouldn't have been hard to find. Damascus is filled with short, crooked roads, but two parallel streets ran east to west to connect the city walls. Ananias even addressed Saul as "Brother Saul" (9:17), as he explained why he was there. After laying his hands on Saul, something like scales fell from Saul's eyes and he could see again. The first thing he did was go to be baptized. Then he ate for the first time in three days (9:18–19).

A subtle distinction is made between the appearance of Jesus to Ananias and His appearance to Saul. Ananias saw Jesus in a vision (9:10). But Saul had an encounter with the resurrected Jesus (9:17), which he confirms later in his writing (1 Corinthians 15:3–8).

Saul spent several days with the Damascus disciples. The reference to many days (9:23) was probably a three-year period. In retelling his story, Paul later adds the fact that he went to Arabia during this time—perhaps to study, meditate, pray, and discern God's will for his life (Galatians 1:13–18). During his time in Damascus, he immediately began to preach in the synagogues that Jesus is the Son of God (9:20). The antagonist of the believers had become a protagonist. The persecutor became a proclaimer. Right from the start, Saul was a powerful witness and defender of the faith. His sudden commitment to his newfound faith was confusing to people at first, of course. But when the Jews tried to challenge what he was saying, he bewildered them with his persuasive observations. No one could refute his arguments (9:21–22).

As days passed and Saul attracted more and more attention, the Jews in Damascus began to conspire to have him killed. The Roman governor was in on the plot as well (2 Corinthians 11:32–33). They set up a twenty-four-hour surveillance of the city gates and planned to catch him leaving the city, but he learned of their plot. The Damascus believers lowered him in a basket down the outside of the city wall during the night, after which he made it safely to Jerusalem (9:23–25).

9:26–31

SAUL IN JERUSALEM

Back in Jerusalem, Saul was a man with no place to go. He, of course, wanted to unite with the believers there, but they didn't know what had happened to him in Damascus. He needed someone to reach out to him, as Ananias had done in Damascus. That person turned out to be Barnabas, the "Son of Encouragement," who had already been such an example of generosity in the early church (4:36–37). We aren't told that Barnabas received a vision or special divine instruction to provide the courage to meet with Saul. Perhaps he did it because he thought giving someone a chance for repentance and forgiveness was simply the right thing to do.

With Barnabas as his ally, Saul met with the church leaders (9:27). He recounted the events of his trip to Damascus and stayed with them. He also spoke boldly about Jesus throughout Jerusalem. And in very little time, he became embroiled in debates with the Jews there until they, too, conspired to kill him. When the Jerusalem believers discovered their plot, they sent Saul to Tarsus (9:30).

Saul had been perceived as such a monumental threat to the established Jewish way of life, that once he was removed from the geographic area the Jews didn't even bother to persecute the other believers. The church throughout the whole area—Judea, Galilee, and Samaria—had a period of peace. It continued to grow both in spiritual depth and in numbers (9:31).

Saul will be absent from Luke's narrative for the next few chapters, with Peter's ministry taking prominence. But then the account picks up with Saul again and continues throughout the rest of the book of Acts.

Take It Home

It's almost impossible to consider how the history of the church would have been different if Saul (Paul) had not played the part he did. Yet twice in the early stages of his faith, it was other people who played important roles in helping him find his place in the church. Ananias is only mentioned in this account and once more as Paul recounts his conversion (22:12). Barnabas is a bit better known, but not nearly as recognized as Paul. Yet the fearless service of Ananias and Barnabas should not go unnoticed. The church is always in need of those who will go out of their comfort zones to connect with people who both need to know more about Jesus and who have much to contribute. Do you know anyone who seems like a modern-day Ananias or Barnabas? Can you think of any opportunities you might have to reach out to someone, even if the prospect seems a bit frightening?

ACTS 9:32–11:30

INCLUSION OF THE "UNCLEAN"

Peter Heals Aeneas and Raises Tabitha	9:32–43
The Vision of Cornelius	10:1–8
The Vision of Peter	10:9–23a
Gentiles Are Baptized into the Church	10:24b–48
Peter in Jerusalem	11:1–18
Barnabas and Saul in Antioch	11:19–30

Setting Up the Section

The early chapters of Acts show Peter as the primary leader of the church. He will soon fade from prominence as Saul (Paul) begins his ministry. And the previous section made clear that Saul was chosen to go to the Gentiles. However, in this section we discover that God also called Peter to a ministry that included Gentiles as well as Jews. Male or female, slave or free, Jew or Gentile—anyone who believes in Jesus can be included in His church.

9:32–43

PETER HEALS AENEAS AND RAISES TABITHA

After Stephen's death, persecution had broken out against all the believers. Many left the city, but the apostles had determined to stay in Jerusalem (8:1). However, Saul's conversion had attracted much attention and prompted his departure for Tarsus, so the pressure was off of the other church leaders, and they enjoyed a respite from persecution.

Peter took the opportunity to get out of the city and engage in an itinerant ministry. He was probably offering encouragement to the various churches that had formed from the believers who had fled Jerusalem. Among his travels throughout the country he visited believers in Lydda (9:32), a town about twenty-five miles northwest of Jerusalem at the intersection of one highway from Egypt to Syria and another from Jerusalem to Joppa (on the coast). It was a decent-sized village according to the historian Josephus.

In Lydda, Peter came across a man named Aeneas who had been paralyzed for eight years and was currently bedridden. We aren't told of any preliminary conversation between the two. It appears that Peter simply declared Aeneas healed in the name of Jesus and told him to get up and walk, which Aeneas immediately did (9:34).

In many of Jesus' miracles, healing had been in response to a person's declaration of faith. Yet faith is not the power that brings about miracles. Faith is rather the preparation for the miracle—anticipation of what God will do not only in the person's body, but also in his or her spirit. There are instances in scripture, as in this one, where the person made no expression of faith prior to being healed. It appears that in certain cases healing initiates faith. On this occasion, all those in Lydda and Sharon (a fifty-mile stretch of fertile land along the coast of Palestine) who heard about the healing of Aeneas turned to the Lord (9:35).

Meanwhile, Peter was approached by two disciples from Joppa, urging him to go with them. Joppa was Judea's main seaport, only about twelve miles away. A faithful believer there had just died. Her name was Tabitha (Aramaic) or Dorcas (Greek). Both versions of the name mean "gazelle." Tabitha was a skilled seamstress who had a wonderful reputation for helping the poor and doing good, and many people were mourning her death (9:36, 39).

The Bible records three instances when Jesus raised someone from the dead, but none of His followers had ever attempted a miracle of this magnitude. It is possible that the believers in Joppa had sent for Peter only for his consolation and prayer support during this difficult time, although it seems that they were expressing the faith that he would perform a great miracle.

Peter had been present when Jesus had raised Jairus's daughter (Luke 8:51–56), and he followed much the same procedure here. He sent out all the mourners, then kneeled down and told the woman to get up. When she opened her eyes, he took her hand and helped her stand up. This miracle, like the healing of Aeneas, caused many people to believe in Jesus (9:42).

Peter then spent several days in Joppa, perhaps at the urging of the people there. The fact that he stayed in the home of a tanner (9:43) indicates a new level of inclusion. By most Jewish standards, someone who worked with dead animals would be ceremonially unclean and therefore looked down on. Peter's willingness to stay with Simon is a prelude to the story that follows.

10:1–8

THE VISION OF CORNELIUS

Previous sections of Acts have hinted at a ministry to the Gentiles. The great response of the Samaritans to Philip's preaching (8:4–8, 14–17) was a beginning, even though the Samaritans had many beliefs similar to those of the Jews. The conversion of the Ethiopian eunuch was another positive sign of things to come. Now another noteworthy Gentile comes into the picture—a centurion named Cornelius.

The name was a very popular one in ancient Rome. In 82 BC a man named Cornelius Sulla freed ten thousand slaves, and as a token of appreciation they all took the name of their patron. It is quite possible that the Cornelius in this passage was a descendent of one of the freedmen of Cornelius Sulla.

We do know that this Cornelius was a centurion in what was known as the Italian Regiment (10:1). The Roman army was comprised of legions (about six thousand troops) divided into ten regiments. Centurions were responsible for commanding about one hundred soldiers within a regiment.

All biblical references to Roman centurions are positive. Cornelius is described as being a devout and God-fearing person who prayed and gave to people in need (10:2). The phrase *God-fearer* was a technical term that described someone who had essentially converted to Judaism except for one significant step: circumcision. Understandably, many adult men were reluctant to take this final step of conversion to the Jewish faith. But otherwise, it appears Cornelius sought to worship the one true God, accepted the monotheism and ethical standards of the Jews, and attended synagogue services.

As Cornelius was praying at 3:00 p.m., one of the traditional times for Jewish prayer (10:3), an angel came to him in a vision, called him by name, and told him to send people to Joppa and bring back Peter (10:3–6). As a centurion, Cornelius was accustomed to receiving and following orders, so he immediately dispatched two servants and a soldier (10:7–8).

Critical Observation

It is difficult to overstate the significance of what is happening here, as God is beginning to extend the invitation of salvation to the Gentiles. God had a unique purpose in choosing to bless the Jews—they were to be an example and a blessing to all the other families of the earth. Old Testament scriptures had pointed to a day when all nations would be included in the kingdom of God's Messiah. The tragedy was that the Israelites had twisted the doctrine of election into one of favoritism, and they became filled with racial pride and hatred toward others. They came to despise Gentiles to the point of calling them dogs. The traditions they developed over the centuries served to distance them from the Gentiles. Now, by bringing Peter and Cornelius together, God is beginning to unite these two vastly different groups.

10:9–23a

THE VISION OF PETER

As Cornelius's men were making their way to the home of Simon the tanner to find Peter, the apostle was having a divine encounter of his own. At noon on the day after Cornelius had his vision, Peter was on the rooftop, praying while he waited for lunch to be prepared. His hunger played into the vision he received (10:9–10).

He saw a large sheet lowered from heaven that contained all kinds of animals, reptiles, and birds. Many, or perhaps all, were not "clean" as defined in the Law of Moses (and were very specifically prohibited in Leviticus 11), yet a voice called Peter by name and told him to kill and eat (10:13).

Peter's refusal to comply was emphatic (10:14). His hard-line stance was reminiscent of two previous occasions: once when Jesus had tried to tell the apostles of His impending death (Matthew 16:21–22) and again when Jesus tried to wash Peter's feet (John 13:6–8). It seems that Peter was still in the habit of trying to tell the Lord how things should be done in the kingdom. Even after a second and third command, Peter held fast. Then the sheet disappeared back into heaven (10:15–16).

Peter hardly had time to make sense of the vision before Cornelius's messengers arrived and called out for him. Before he could even answer, the Holy Spirit told him to accommodate them because they had been sent by the Spirit. It is interesting to note that the word translated "Do not hesitate" (10:20) can also mean, "Make no distinction." Peter was likely beginning to see the connection between his vision that had challenged the distinction between clean and unclean foods and the timely arrival of Gentile (unclean) visitors. So he went downstairs and introduced himself. The three men explained why they were there, and Peter invited them in as his guests (10:23).

The invitation was certainly a step in the right direction. For one thing, Peter had been waiting for lunch, and probably shared it with his three visitors. In addition, it was too late to begin the thirty-mile trip from Joppa back to Caesarea, so the three men needed overnight accommodations. Most Jews wouldn't consider allowing Gentiles under their roofs, much less overnight. God was beginning to break down some of the divisive barriers.

10:24b–48

GENTILES ARE BAPTIZED INTO THE CHURCH

The next day Cornelius's three messengers led the way back to Caesarea, along with Peter and six believers from Joppa (11:12). The distance took more than a day to travel, so the group arrived four days after Cornelius had his vision (10:30).

Cornelius must have felt strongly that Peter would respond because he had gathered a large group of friends and relatives. As Peter entered, Cornelius met him at the door and fell at his feet in an act of worship. But Peter quickly made him get up, assuring the centurion that they were both equals (10:25–26).

Peter walked right into Cornelius's home (10:27), breaking down old taboos and setting an example both for the Gentiles there and the Jewish believers he had brought with him. By this time it was clear that he had come to understand his vision as a sign that the Gentiles were no longer to be considered unclean (10:28–29).

Cornelius succinctly explained the reason he had sent for Peter, and that he had brought together a group to listen to what God had commanded Peter to say (10:30–33). It is apparent that both Peter and Cornelius were not acting on their own instincts, but following what God had instructed them to do.

Peter began to speak to the crowd about Jesus' life and ministry, His death, and His resurrection. He emphasized the divine plan behind the events that had played out during Jesus' time on earth. Peter could offer not only the facts about Jesus, but also his personal verification as an eyewitness—both before and after Jesus' crucifixion (10:39, 41). And Peter's message provided the totality of the gospel. He concluded with an image of Jesus as the one appointed as God's judge of humanity, yet made it clear that forgiveness and salvation are available for anyone who believes in Him (10:42–43).

Demystifying Acts

In Luke's summary of Peter's sermon (10:34–43) we see the very heart of the gospel message. Theologians call this the *kerygma*, a Greek word that means "preaching" and represents the essential witness and affirmation of the New Testament preachers concerning the gospel of our Lord. The *kerygma* was the core message of the grace of God revealed in Jesus Christ.

Peter was still speaking when the truth of his words was confirmed by the arrival of the Holy Spirit on all who were listening. The Jewish believers were amazed to see Gentiles speaking in tongues and praising God—which demonstrated Peter's wisdom in bringing them to be witnesses (10:44–46).

The next step for those expressing faith in Jesus was baptism. Philip had baptized the Ethiopian eunuch in the solitude of the desert, and the Ethiopian may have been a Jewish proselyte. This would be the first time Gentiles were baptized to be included in the church along with Jewish believers. But apparently there was no objection, because Peter saw to their baptisms right away (10:47–48).

This was a memorable moment in the history of the church. The promise of the prophets centuries before was coming true. God's love, mercy, and grace were reaching everyone—not just the Hebrew nation. But it would take a while for the truth and significance of this event to sink in.

11:1–18

PETER IN JERUSALEM

After staying a few days with Cornelius in Caesarea, Peter went back to Jerusalem. He immediately received criticism from the Jewish believers for visiting and eating with Gentiles (11:2–3). This accusation is somewhat reminiscent of the ones Jesus had regularly received from the religious leaders for eating with tax collectors and sinners.

In explanation, Peter started from the beginning and reviewed his vision, Cornelius's visit from the angel, the coming of the Holy Spirit to the Gentile believers, and the unanimous decision to baptize them (11:4–17). He repeatedly emphasized the work of God and the Holy Spirit as instrumental in bringing about the events.

Peter was persuasive, and his critics relented and praised God (11:18). As hard as it was to understand and acknowledge at the time, God was offering salvation even to the Gentiles. And if God was removing the distinctions between Jews and Gentiles, what right did Peter—or anyone else—have to harbor old prejudices? The dispute was settled, but only temporarily. It would take a long while and many additional debates to work through all the obstacles for allowing Gentiles the same rights and privileges of church membership that the Jews enjoyed.

11:19–30

BARNABAS AND SAUL IN ANTIOCH

At this point Luke goes back to the persecution following the stoning of Stephen and follows a different storyline. He begins by telling about Philip's ministry, Saul's conversion, and Peter's outreach to the Gentiles—all essential to the history of the early church. But meanwhile, noteworthy events were taking place in Antioch of Syria.

Antioch was the third largest city in the Roman world, after Rome and Alexandria. It lay three hundred miles north of Jerusalem, about fifteen miles inland from the Mediterranean Sea. Its population (estimated to be five hundred thousand to eight hundred thousand) contained probably about one hundred thousand Jews along with a number of Gentile proselytes to Judaism. It was also a popular hedonistic destination, accused by the Roman satirist Juvenal of having a corrupting influence on Rome itself.

Yet it was here where some of the victims of the persecution in Jerusalem had settled and had taught the gospel. Many had spoken only to other Jews, but some had reached out to Gentiles as well, and both groups were beginning to see large numbers of people believing (11:21). The presentation of the gospel in the name of Lord Jesus (11:20) rather than Christ is due to the audience. The title "Christ" was equivalent to "Messiah," which would not have had significance to the Gentiles. Many of them, however, would have considered Caesar their "lord," and the teaching of the believers clarified that the title deserved to go only to Jesus.

News of the excitement and growth of the believers in Antioch reached all the way to the church members in Jerusalem. They responded by sending Barnabas to oversee the newly forming church. Here is yet another overwhelmingly positive description of Barnabas (4:36–37; 9:26–27): a good man, full of the Holy Spirit, and full of faith (11:24). As his nickname (Son of Encouragement) warranted, he encouraged the Antioch believers and rejoiced with them.

Tarsus, where Saul was staying (9:30), was about ninety miles away, yet Barnabas went to invite him to Antioch as well. The two were ideal for working among Gentiles, and they spent an entire year with the believers in Antioch (11:26). Tradition indicates that Luke was from Antioch, so it is possible that he was among the new converts who learned of the truth of Jesus from the lips of Barnabas and Saul during this time.

It was in Antioch where believers in Jesus were first called Christians (11:26). The distinction of belonging to Christ's party, or being Christ followers, as the word *Christian* implies, would begin to distinguish the group. Until this point, Christianity had been perceived as an offshoot of Judaism. But now that Gentiles were joining the church, it was clear that was not the case. However, a reference to *Christian* occurs only three times in the New Testament (Acts 11:26; 26:28; 1 Peter 4:16).

The Jews believed the spirit of prophecy had been suspended after the Old Testament writing prophets, and was to be renewed again in the coming messianic age. So early Christians not only acknowledged Jesus as a prophet (3:22; 7:37), but also recognized prophecy as a gift of the Holy Spirit (1 Corinthians 12:28). And prophets operated throughout the early church. The group in this passage (11:26–27) predicted a famine that struck during the reign of Claudius (AD 41–54). Agabus (11:28) would later warn Paul of impending danger (21:10–11).

The genuine faith of the believers in Antioch was evident from their willingness to give to the church in Jerusalem (11:29–30). The Jerusalem church had generously shared its leaders to assist the growth of those in Antioch. Now the Antioch Christians were supporting the Jerusalem church financially.

This is the first biblical mention of the role of "elders" (11:30). The word can mean simply older men, though in this context it seems to refer to church officers. They would be the ones responsible for distributing the gift that had been delivered to them. Jewish synagogues employed elders, and it seems that the position was adopted by the Christian church as well.

Take It Home

Cornelius and Peter were very different people. Yet as they each responded to God's direction, they got together and both learned more about God as a result. Do you know someone who has a very different view of God than you do? If so, do you make the most of opportunities to interact and learn more about his or her opinions of spiritual things? You might not agree with most, if any, of the specifics. But sometimes the very act of discussing matters of faith will be a catalyst for spiritual growth for one, if not both, of you.

ACTS 12:1–24

PETER'S PRISON BREAK

Persecution to Please the Crowds	12:1–3
Peter's Arrest and Prison Escape	12:4–19a
The Death of Herod	12:19b–24

Setting Up the Section

Aside from the death of Stephen and a bit of persecution from Jewish authorities, Luke's history of the early church has been very positive so far in the book of Acts. However, the conclusion of the previous chapter hinted at a famine and some monetary need in Jerusalem (11:27–30). This section continues to report increasing problems for the church—in this case, intensified persecution. And while God continues to provide for some of the believers in miraculous ways, others are beginning to be imprisoned and even killed for their beliefs.

12:1–3

PERSECUTION TO PLEASE THE CROWDS

It is debated whether Luke presents the material in this section thematically or chronologically. King Herod Agrippa I (12:1) was the grandson of Herod the Great and a nephew of the Herod (Antipas) who had killed John the Baptist. He ruled Judea from a headquarters in Jerusalem from AD 41 to 44, the year he died.

The famine mentioned at the end of the previous section (11:27–28) occurred in AD 46. So it is possible that Luke wasn't writing chronologically. Or if Barnabas and Saul were in Jerusalem before the death of Herod *and* during the famine, it would have required two visits—a reasonable possibility for a pair who were on the road so frequently.

Herod had Jewish ties and always tried to sustain a good relationship with those in charge of the Jewish people. As the Jewish believers fell out of favor with the established authorities, Herod found he could impress those in control by mistreating the Christians. He began arresting church members and had James (the brother of John and one of the

Twelve) put to death (12:2). The arrests were due to no other reason than the believers' association with the church. This persecution was fueled by a political motive rather than a religious one.

The Feast of Unleavened Bread (12:3), or Passover, was one of three annual religious festivals that Jewish males were expected to attend, so the population of Jerusalem would swell with those men loyal to their history and traditions. When Herod saw that the death of James pleased the people, he arrested and imprisoned Peter. By now most people knew that Peter was the leading apostle in the church, and that he had been associating with Gentiles. He was the perfect target in Herod's ongoing thirst for popularity.

Critical Observation

Technically, Passover was the meal celebrated to commemorate the exodus of the Israelites from Egypt and God's sparing of the firstborn in all the homes with blood on the doors (Exodus 12). But that specific celebration was followed immediately by the Feast of Unleavened Bread, when all yeast and leavening agents were removed from homes during a week-long celebration. As the two events were commemorated together year after year, they became essentially one in the minds of the people. *Passover* was the popular term for the dual celebrations.

12:4–19a

PETER'S ARREST AND PRISON ESCAPE

This is the third instance Luke records of Peter being imprisoned. The first time he and John only spent a single night in jail; in the second incident he and all the other apostles were miraculously released during the night and were found the next day, preaching in the temple courts (4:3; 5:17–26).

Perhaps Herod had heard of Peter's propensity to escape from prison. The precaution seemed extreme to assign sixteen guards to a single prisoner. But the four squads of four soldiers should have provided ample round-the-clock attention. Peter's likely place of incarceration was the Fortress of Antonia, a Roman stronghold that stood against the north wall of the temple enclosure. A Roman guard usually chained his left hand to a prisoner's right hand, but Peter was chained to guards with *both* hands (12:6).

Herod's plan was to keep Peter in prison until the eight-day celebration of Passover and the Feast of Unleavened Bread was over, and then he would bring him out for a public trial. Since James had recently been killed, it might seem likely that Peter would be concerned for his life. But in spite of the stressful situation, the guards, and the chains, he was sleeping soundly. Peter had a habit of sleeping when he should have been praying (Luke 9:32; 22:45), but in this case Peter's ability to sleep seems to reflect a lack of fear or worry. Perhaps he had confidence in Jesus' previous prediction that he would grow to be an old man (John 21:18). Additionally, we are told that the church was earnestly praying on Peter's behalf (12:5).

What happened next was so unlikely that Peter didn't know if it was actually happening or if he was having another vision (12:9). An angel appeared and a bright light shone in the cell. Still, the angel had to strike Peter to wake him up. Peter did as the angel instructed (12:7–8). The chains fell off his wrists, the various prison doors opened as they came to them, and Peter soon found himself alone and free on the street outside the prison (12:8–10). The reality of the situation suddenly struck him, so he began thinking of a safe place he could go (12:11).

He may have known that other believers were praying for him at the home of Mary, the mother of John Mark (12:12). Peter's inability to get inside at first is comic in its true-to-life appeal (12:13–18). Even though committed church members were earnestly praying for Peter's release, they found it hard to believe when it actually happened. The servant girl was too excited to open the door, and the other believers were too skeptical to go see for themselves. Meanwhile, Peter kept knocking until someone finally let him in.

Demystifying Acts

John Mark was a cousin of Barnabas who would later accompany Paul and Barnabas on their first missionary journey. He and Paul would have a falling out, but it would later be resolved and the two would become close friends. Mark also wrote the Gospel that bears his name. Tradition says he also was Peter's interpreter in Rome and established the church in Alexandria, Egypt.

The assumption that the figure at the door was Peter's angel (12:15) reflects the belief (based partially on Jesus' words in Matthew 18:10) that guardian angels oversee God's people and could take on the appearance of the person being protected. Another explanation is that angel might have been a reference to a human being dispatched by Peter with a message (the same Greek word can mean "angel" or "messenger"). Or a third possibility was that Herod had already killed Peter, and the apostle's spirit had shown itself to the believers.

Since James, the brother of John, had already been killed (12:2), the James referred to in verse 17 was almost certainly the brother of Jesus—a child of Mary and Joseph. James was becoming prominent in the early church in Jerusalem and will appear again later in Acts.

After Peter's previous release from jail, he had been instructed to go to the temple courts and teach. This time, however, the political climate was much different. His life was in danger. Saul had left the area to spend time in Tarsus, and Peter was leaving, too (12:17). We know from later biblical references that, at some point in his life, Peter probably visited Corinth, Rome, and Antioch.

The next morning, Herod discovered Peter was gone. He held the guards responsible, probably assuming the only way Peter could have escaped was through their cooperation with him or through negligence. Either way, their sentence was death (12:18–19).

12:19b–24

THE DEATH OF HEROD

The sudden mention of Herod's decision to leave Jerusalem (12:19) may possibly be attributed to his desire to save face after losing a key prisoner. He decided to visit some of his subjects on the Mediterranean coast who were eager to regain his favor because their food supply depended on him (12:20).

Luke's version of this account is quite concise. The Jewish historian Josephus elaborates considerably more. It seems that Herod stood in the outdoor theater on a festival day, attired in a silver robe that gleamed in the sunshine. The people, eager to flatter him, went so far as to call him a god, and Herod said nothing to correct them. He was then immediately struck with stomach pains and had to be carried out of the theater. According to Josephus, he died five days later.

People have speculated as to the exact diagnosis of the disease that killed Herod, saying it might have been appendicitis that led to peritonitis complicated by roundworms, or possibly a cyst caused by a tapeworm. Luke simply makes it clear that Herod's miserable death was a judgment of God (12:23).

Herod had tried to hinder the growth of the church. Suddenly, he was gone and the Word of God was continually increasing and spreading (12:24). From this point on, it would be spread with more intention.

Take It Home

A logical question that arises from this section is why bad things happen to some people and not others. Why did James die at the hands of King Herod while Peter was freed as the result of an incredible miracle? In this case it seems clear that we must leave such things up to a sovereign God. We certainly can't make a case that Peter was a better person than James, or that James had done anything to warrant death. After all, Peter's time was coming (John 21:18–19). What are some similar questions you tend to struggle with? Do you get frustrated when you can't determine answers, or are you able to leave everything in God's hands and trust that He is in control no matter what happens?

ACTS 12:25–13:52

THE GOSPEL MOVES OUTWARD

The Call of Barnabas and Saul	12:25–13:3
Ministry in Cyprus	13:4–12
Ministry in Pisidian Antioch	13:13–52

Setting Up the Section

Up to this point, any contact between the believers in Jesus and the Gentile community has been quite one-sided. In each case, the contact was clearly God-directed, where Jewish believers were approached by curious Gentiles. But in this section, that will change. The church at Antioch begins to see the opportunity of approaching the Gentiles with the good news of the gospel. So its leaders designate a pair of proven disciples to travel, preach, and build up churches that have begun in various faraway places.

12:25–13:3

THE CALL OF BARNABAS AND SAUL

Barnabas and Saul had spent a year in Antioch (11:26) prior to delivering a financial gift from believers there to the church in Jerusalem (11:30). When they returned to Antioch, they took John Mark with them (12:12). Mark was a cousin of Barnabas (Colossians 4:10).

In this section of Acts, Barnabas seems to be the prominent figure. When he and Saul are mentioned, his name comes first, as it does in the list of prophets and teachers at the Antioch church (13:1). Their names suggest a broad mix of people in the Antioch church: *Simeon* was a Jewish name, and *Niger* suggested a dark-skinned person, possibly from Africa. Niger and Lucius were Roman names, and Manaen's associate (Herod the tetrarch) was Herod Antipas—the man responsible for the beheading of John the Baptist.

It was this group of leaders who discerned God's direction to set aside Barnabas and Saul for a special calling. Apparently little time was wasted. As soon as they finished fasting and praying, they sent them off (13:3).

This commissioning of Barnabas and Saul marks a turning point in Acts. Until now, the church's contact with Gentiles has been almost incidental. When Gentiles got involved in some way, the Jewish believers dealt with it. But here, under the leading of the Holy Spirit, they sent two dedicated church members into predominantly Gentile territory. Barnabas and Saul will still have Jewish audiences as well as Gentile ones, but in most cases from this point forward it will be the Gentiles who are more responsive to their message.

13:4–12

MINISTRY IN CYPRUS

The Holy Spirit led them first to Cyprus, perhaps because Barnabas had ties to the island. Cyprus was a significant location situated on a major shipping route. It was also a province of Rome, and the Senate had assigned a proconsul to govern there. The news about Jesus had already reached Cyprus from people fleeing persecution in Jerusalem, but it had gone out to only the Jewish population there (11:19).

As Barnabas and Saul entered a new community, they would usually go to the synagogue. The people assembled there—both Jews and God-fearing Gentiles—would have a decent knowledge of spiritual truth, which made a good foundation for the presentation of the gospel message. In addition, traveling philosophers or religious figures were frequently invited to speak. The presence of more than one synagogue at Salamis indicates a large Jewish population (13:5).

Paphos (13:6) was the provincial capital on the western coast of the island. It was there where the Roman proconsul, a man named Sergius Paulus, heard about Barnabas and Saul and sent for them.

When the gospel had previously gone out to the Samaritan community, Luke had recorded an unusual confrontation between a local magician and Peter and John (8:9–24). A similar encounter took place in Cyprus. The Roman proconsul had an attendant named Bar-Jesus, who claimed to be a Jewish prophet but was in reality a sorcerer (which is what his nickname, Elymas, meant). When the sorcerer tried to sway the proconsul from the truth of what Barnabas and Saul were teaching, Saul took the lead and passed God's judgment of temporary blindness on the man. It was an appropriate attention-getter for someone who tried to blind others to the truth of God's Word. (Saul knew from experience that temporary blindness could lead to clear spiritual vision [9:1–19].) In addition, the clearly evident power of God convinced Sergius Paulus to believe the truths he was hearing that amazed him so (13:12).

This was another first for Christianity—the presentation of the gospel to someone in authority in Roman aristocracy. The conversion of the proconsul also legitimized a direct ministry to the Gentiles.

Demystifying Acts

It is at this point in Acts that Luke begins to refer to "Saul" as "Paul," and to give him the place of prominence in the group. Both names were probably given to Paul by his parents at birth, a common practice for Jews living among Gentiles. *Paul* (meaning "little") was his Roman name, while Saul was his Jewish name. Paul likely began to use his Roman name when his ministry shifted decisively toward the Gentiles.

13:13–52

MINISTRY IN PISIDIAN ANTIOCH

After spending time in an area familiar to Barnabas, the travelers sailed north to Pamphylia, not far from Cilicia, Paul's home province. At this point John Mark left the other two to return to Jerusalem (13:13). His reason for leaving is not stated. He was young and may have been homesick or fearful of illness or other dangers of travel. Or because of his strong ties to the Jerusalem church, he might not have been completely comfortable with the attention being given to the Gentiles. If so, he would not be the only Jewish believer to express discontent in the weeks and months to come. But whatever the reason for Mark's leaving, it would later cause a rift between Paul and Barnabas (15:36–41).

Pisidian Antioch (13:14) is not to be confused with the Antioch that had sent Paul and Barnabas on this journey, or with another Antioch in nearby Phrygia. The popularity of the name is due to a ruler in 281 BC who had both a father and a son named Antiochus, and founded sixteen cities named in honor of them.

The one hundred-mile journey from the seaport of Perga (13:13) would have taken Paul and Barnabas from sea level to an elevation of 3,600 feet. Bandits roamed the roads, and later Paul would say he was in ill health when he arrived here (Galatians 4:13–14). Yet they went to the local synagogue as usual and were invited to speak (13:15).

What follows is the longest of Paul's sermons (though no doubt in condensed form) to nonbelievers in Acts (13:16–41). The content is very similar to previous messages presented by Peter (2:14–39) and Stephen (7:2–53), providing a broad overview of Israel's history and concluding with the fact that Jesus was the fulfillment of all that had been promised.

Paul's reference to 450 years (13:20) was likely the time span of four hundred years spent by the Israelites in Egypt, forty years spent in the wilderness, and about another decade to conquer and settle in the promised land.

Critical Observation

Paul's clarification that John the Baptist had not been the Messiah (13:24–25) hints of a problem the early church may have faced. Some believe that certain disciples of John the Baptist had moved out of Palestine, teaching that John had been the Messiah. Later passages in Acts (18:24–25; 19:1–7) seem to indicate that some people believed the baptism of John the Baptist was all that was necessary for salvation.

Paul acknowledged the reverence the people held for King David, and said that God had raised up Jesus in much the same way He had raised up David as king (13:33). But in regard to Jesus, Paul also speaks of how God raised Him to emphasize Jesus' victory over death and the grave (13:30, 34, 37).

Paul's closing statements regarding forgiveness, belief, and justification (13:38–39) are explained more fully in his letters to the Romans and the Galatians. His Epistle to the Galatians was written to the people in this area—very likely many who responded to this message in the synagogue. He concluded his sermon with an appropriate quotation from the book of Habakkuk (Habakkuk 1:5; Acts 13:41).

The response to Paul's sermon was quite positive. He and Barnabas were invited to speak again the following week. In the meantime, numerous listeners sought them out to learn more (13:42–43). An enormous crowd turned out to hear them the following Sabbath, which created jealousy among the Jews and caused them to begin badmouthing Paul (13:44–45).

Paul and Barnabas boldly rebuked the Jewish lack of faith and turned their focus primarily to the Gentiles (13:46). The Gentile believers were honored to be included in God's plan, but the Jewish resistance only increased as the jealous ones solicited support from prominent people in the community. As a result, Paul and Barnabas were persecuted and forced to leave the area. They simply shook the dust off their feet and moved on, leaving behind a number of disciples filled with joy and the Holy Spirit (13:52). This event is a key turning point and pattern-setter in Acts. The Jews, for the most part, reject the gospel, so Paul turns to the Gentiles, who will respond positively. This pattern will be repeated again and again until its climax in Acts 28.

Take It Home

Paul and Barnabas (and John Mark, to begin with) were stepping out into new and unfamiliar territory to share their faith with others. Have you ever had a similar experience? If so, which of the three do you best relate to: (1) Paul, who dealt with sickness and opposition to speak boldly to those willing to hear; (2) Barnabas, who seemed quite content to take a secondary position; or (3) John Mark, who retreated to a more familiar setting to continue his ministry?

ACTS 14:1–28

COMPLETION OF THE FIRST MISSIONARY JOURNEY

Ministry in Iconium	14:1–7
Ministry in Lystra	14:8–20
Ministry in Derbe and the Return Home	14:21–28

Setting Up the Section

As Paul and Barnabas take the gospel into areas where it has not been heard, they continue to encounter a wide variety of problems. They have met resistance that will graduate into full-scale violent persecution in places. Yet the message they present and their ability to convey their ideas are so persuasive that the crowds sometimes go overboard in enthusiasm, creating an entirely different kind of problem. In this section, they complete their first journey and return to the church in Antioch.

14:1–7

MINISTRY IN ICONIUM

A noted Roman road (the Via Sebaste) ran from the port city of Ephesus westward to the Euphrates River. At Pisidian Antioch (the most recent stop of Paul and Barnabas) it branched into two roads. One went north through mountainous terrain to the Roman colony of Comana, about 122 miles away, and the other moved southeast across rolling country, past snow-capped mountains, and through the Greek city of Iconium, about eighty miles from Pisidian Antioch, and then ended another twenty-four miles later at the Roman colony of Lystra. So Paul and Barnabas were literally at a fork in the road, and they chose the southeastern route that would take them to people in three very different types of cities in the southern area of the Roman province of Galatia.

Their next stop, Iconium (14:1), sat in a high plateau surrounded by fertile plains and green forests, with mountains to the north and east. As usual, Paul and Barnabas went first to the synagogue and spoke. But the people's reaction was strongly divided. Many people believed and responded—both Jews and Gentiles. But, as in Pisidian Antioch, the Jews who refused to believe caused trouble. This time they tried to influence the Gentiles to join them in resisting Paul and Barnabas.

But God was with His representatives and enabled them to perform great miracles as they stayed in the city and spoke boldly for Him (14:3). They continued to win over many people, but others sided with the Jewish antagonists. When Paul and Barnabas discovered a plot to stone them, they finally moved on, preaching wherever they went (14:5–7).

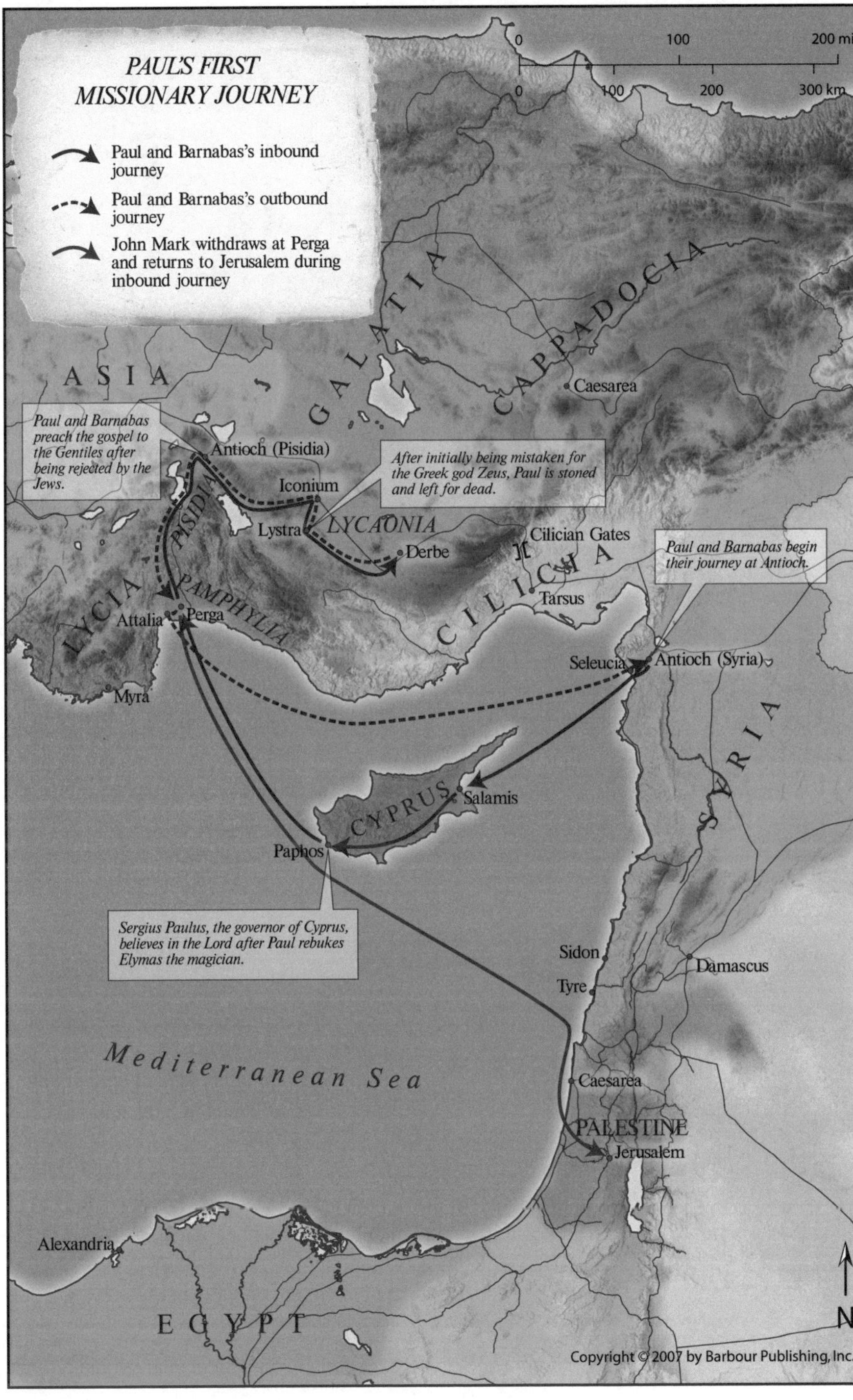
PAUL'S FIRST MISSIONARY JOURNEY
Paul and Barnabas's inbound journey
Paul and Barnabas's outbound journey
John Mark withdraws at Perga and returns to Jerusalem during inbound journey
0 100 200 mi
0 100 200 300 km
ASIA
GALATIA
CAPPADOCIA
Caesarea
Paul and Barnabas preach the gospel to the Gentiles after being rejected by the Jews.
Antioch (Pisidia)
Iconium
After initially being mistaken for the Greek god Zeus, Paul is stoned and left for dead.
PISIDIA
Lystra
LYCAONIA
Derbe
Cilician Gates
CILICIA
Paul and Barnabas begin their journey at Antioch.
LYCIA
PAMPHYLIA
Attalia
Perga
Tarsus
Seleucia
Antioch (Syria)
Myra
SYRIA
Salamis
CYPRUS
Paphos
Sergius Paulus, the governor of Cyprus, believes in the Lord after Paul rebukes Elymas the magician.
Sidon
Damascus
Tyre
Mediterranean Sea
Caesarea
PALESTINE
Jerusalem
Alexandria
EGYPT
N
Copyright © 2007 by Barbour Publishing, Inc.

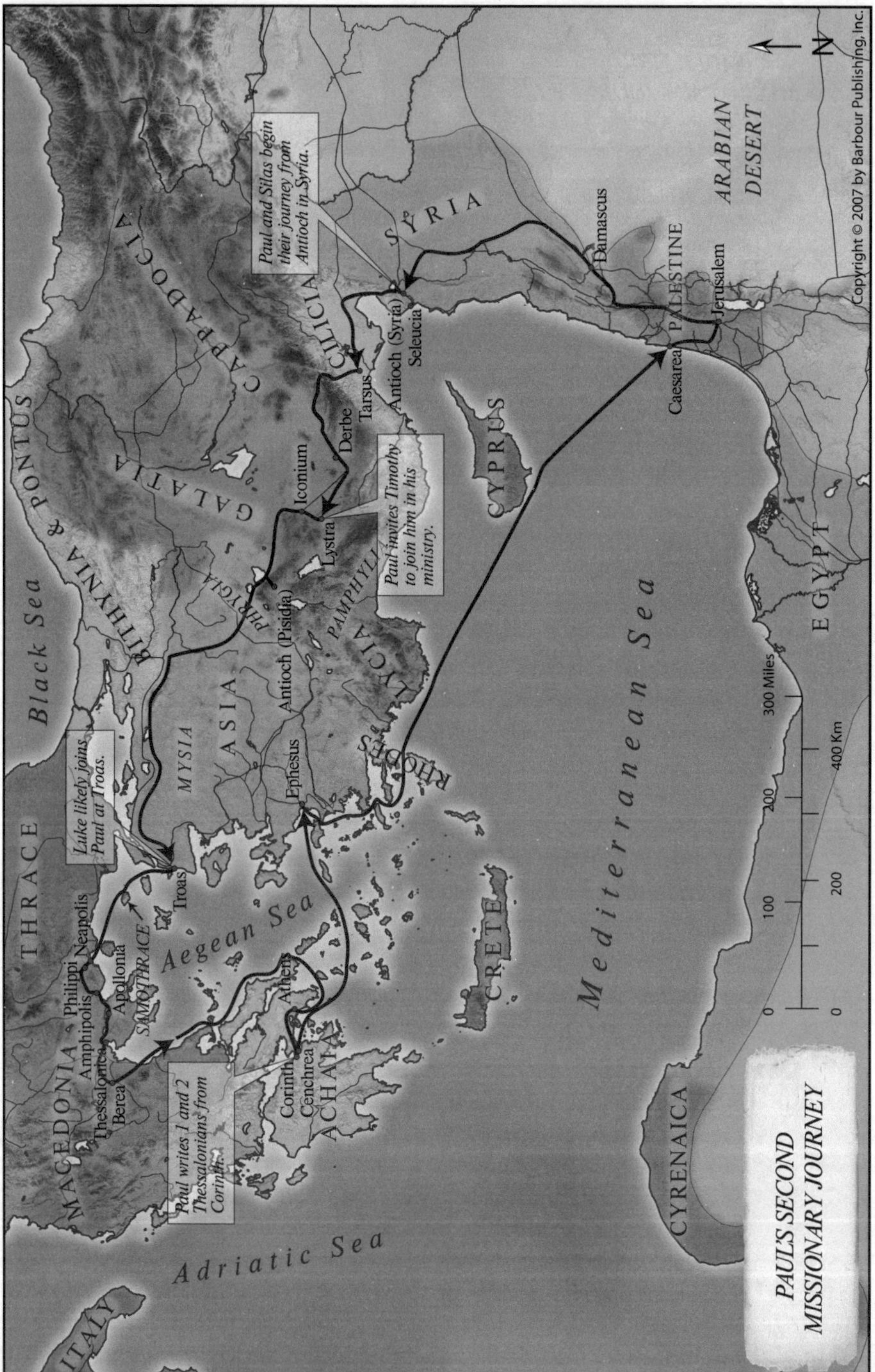
PAUL'S SECOND
MISSIONARY JOURNEY
Paul and Silas begin their journey from Antioch in Syria.
Paul invites Timothy to join him in his ministry.
Luke likely joins Paul at Troas.
Paul writes 1 and 2 Thessalonians from Corinth.
Black Sea
Aegean Sea
Adriatic Sea
Mediterranean Sea
ARABIAN DESERT
MACEDONIA
THRACE
BITHYNIA & PONTUS
GALATIA
CAPPADOCIA
CILICIA
SYRIA
MYSIA
ASIA
PHRYGIA
PAMPHYLIA
LYCIA
ACHAIA
SAMOTHRACE
RHODES
CYPRUS
CRETE
PALESTINE
EGYPT
CYRENAICA
ITALY
Thessalonica
Berea
Amphipolis
Philippi
Apollonia
Neapolis
Troas
Athens
Corinth
Cenchrea
Ephesus
Antioch (Pisidia)
Iconium
Lystra
Derbe
Tarsus
Antioch (Syria)
Seleucia
Caesarea
Jerusalem
Damascus
0
100
200
300 Miles
0
200
400 Km
N
Copyright © 2007 by Barbour Publishing, Inc.

14:8–20

MINISTRY IN LYSTRA

No mention is made of a synagogue in Lystra, which suggests a prominently Gentile population. So Paul preached to a crowd that formed. One among them was a crippled man who had never walked, but Paul saw he had the faith to be healed and commanded him to stand. The man then jumped up and began to walk. This miracle, early in the ministry of Paul, was very similar to one early in the ministry of Peter (3:1–10).

But in this case, without benefit of Old Testament scripture or knowledge of the true God, the people of Lystra believed the Greek gods were walking among them. Hermes (the Roman god Mercury) was supposedly the messenger god, so the people thought Paul must have been the human embodiment of him. They thought Barnabas was Zeus (the Roman Jupiter). They were shouting to one another with excitement, but spoke in a native language that Paul and Barnabas didn't understand. There was a temple to Zeus in Lystra, and only when the priest approached with bulls and wreaths (that would be placed on the sacrificial animals), preparing to offer sacrifices to them, did the two apostles realize what was going on.

Paul and Barnabas did everything in their power to dissuade the people from sacrificing to them. They tore their clothes to indicate extreme grief and distress (14:14). They assured the crowd that they were both just fellow human beings (14:15). They explained that all the good things that occurred were the result of a living God (14:15–17). And still, it was all they could do to calm the people.

Yet the situation quickly went from one extreme to the other. A group of Jews who had opposed Paul in Antioch and Iconium showed up and enlisted support from the people in Lystra. Before long, Paul's stoning that had been planned in Iconium was carried out in Lystra. It was no judicial execution of judgment; it was a lynching. They left Paul for dead. Some people speculate that he did actually die and came back to life, though no evidence exists to prove this theory. But equally miraculous is the fact that he was able to get up and return to the city after such an experience (14:19–20). The next morning Paul and Barnabas left for Derbe, a journey of about sixty miles.

Demystifying Acts

Paul refers to this stoning in 2 Corinthians 11:25 (see 2 Timothy 3:10–11). It may have been the occasion when he was caught up to the third heaven and witnessed amazing things he was not permitted to talk about (2 Corinthians 12:2–6).

14:21–28

MINISTRY IN DERBE AND THE RETURN HOME

Only one verse is devoted to the work of Paul and Barnabas in Derbe (14:21). But after the opposition, persecution, and confusion they had just faced in Iconium and Lystra, it was probably encouraging to preach and see a large number of people become disciples of Jesus.

Paul and Barnabas had gotten within 150 miles or so of Tarsus, Paul's hometown. But he had recently spent time there, so they turned around and retraced their route, strengthening and encouraging the believers as they returned (14:21–26). By this time Paul was speaking from experience when he told them, "that they must enter into the Kingdom of God through many tribulations" (14:22 NLT). It certainly must have taken a great amount of faith and courage to go back through the same cities that had sent hostile delegations to cause them trouble and pain, and surely the believers realized the dedication demonstrated by Paul and Barnabas.

In addition to providing encouragement, Paul and Barnabas addressed the needs of the new churches by appointing elders in each place (14:23). Paul would later declare that elders shouldn't be new converts (1 Timothy 3:6), so he may have chosen believers who had previously served in the Jewish synagogues and would have had a good working knowledge of scripture.

On their arrival back in Antioch (in Syria), they reported to the people who had commissioned them. They had been gone the better part of two years. Their focus was on God's work and how He had opened a door of faith for the Gentiles (14:27–28). Though not stressed at this point, they reported that God's salvation is by faith—not by adapting to Jewish customs or performing any other kind of works. This would soon become a major issue in the church.

Paul and Barnabas stayed a long time in Antioch and were probably glad for the opportunity to rest. Paul wrote his letter to the Galatians from Antioch at about this time.

Take It Home

The behavior of the people in Lystra was extreme, yet somewhat reflective of certain people's opinions in the contemporary church. One moment they had a too-high opinion of Paul and Barnabas as gods; the next they were literally throwing stones at Paul. Have you ever known someone who held a religious figure to an impossibly high standard, only to be immensely let down when the person didn't (couldn't) live up to expectations? What were the circumstances? What was the result? How might the problem have been prevented?

ACTS 15:1–35

THE COUNCIL IN JERUSALEM

The Issue at Hand 15:1–4
Discussing the Issue 15:5–21
Addressing the Issue 15:22–35

Setting Up the Section

Acts 15 begins the second half of the book. It also stands as a pivotal passage in the history of the church. Until this point, the believers in the new church were primarily Jewish, although Gentiles were being converted. But the church had a decision to make. Was it okay to simply express one's belief in Jesus and be included in full fellowship? Or shouldn't Gentiles be expected to adhere to the same high standards as the Jewish believers? Was circumcision and keeping the Law of Moses necessary for salvation? And just as noteworthy as what was decided was how the church leaders arrived at their decision.

15:1–4

THE ISSUE AT HAND

By the time the council in Jerusalem convened, Gentiles had been joining the church for about ten years and were welcomed simply by baptism. The movement began with Cornelius, the God-fearing centurion, and his friends and family whom Peter had baptized in Caesarea (10:44–48). Next came the great number of people in Syrian Antioch who believed when unnamed missionaries began speaking to Greeks (11:20). Barnabas had been sent to confirm the salvation of the Gentiles, and he had recruited Paul to help train the new believers. The church in Antioch had then sent out Paul and Barnabas to travel and preach to people in predominantly Gentile territories, and they returned with news that God had "opened the door of faith to the Gentiles" (14:27).

What had begun as a trickle of Gentile conversions was fast becoming a torrent.

The Jewish believers had little difficulty accepting the Gentiles because many Old Testament passages predicted their inclusion. Yet they were beginning to question exactly how God intended to incorporate the Gentiles into the believing community. It was one thing for the leaders of the Jerusalem church to give their approval to the conversion of Gentiles in general, but could they also approve of conversion without circumcision, faith in Jesus without complete adherence to the Law and traditions, or commitment to the Messiah without inclusion in Judaism?

The first issue that came to the fore was circumcision. The debate began in Antioch, when a group from Judea arrived and started teaching that circumcision was essential for salvation (15:1). This group may have come from the party of the Pharisees (15:5) and might have been the group Paul referred to in Galatians 2:11. Paul and Barnabas, of course, couldn't have disagreed more with their opinion.

It was quickly decided that a delegation including Paul, Barnabas, and a number of others would go from Antioch to Jerusalem to discuss the matter with the apostles and elders. Along the way they spread the word of how Gentiles were becoming believers, and the news made the Jewish believers glad. The apostles and elders in Jerusalem were also glad to see them and to hear of their experiences (15:4).

15:5–21

DISCUSSING THE ISSUE

The Jewish Christians who were Pharisees already had their minds made up. Their representatives insisted that Gentile believers get circumcised and be instructed to obey the Law of Moses (15:5). (The group promoting these teachings would eventually become known as the Judaizers.) Their stance was not surprising. In essentially every encounter the Pharisees had with Jesus, they were holding out for more stringent obedience not only to God's written Word, but also the hundreds of extrabiblical traditions they had developed over the centuries. When Jesus presented a much less legalistic perception of God, they usually were offended and incensed.

Demystifying Acts

The council at Jerusalem had to determine whether Christianity was simply a reform movement within Judaism, or whether Jesus' life, death, and resurrection had initiated a whole new age of salvation. Some of the participants argued that Gentiles must adhere to the same laws and traditions as Judaism in order to find favor with God. But others were beginning to see that the gospel of Jesus was the good news of God's love for the whole world, and that salvation came through faith alone in Jesus Christ and His death on the cross.

The Pharisees' statement evoked a lot of discussion among the church leaders (15:6). In effect, they were suggesting that Moses needed to complete something Jesus had begun, and that the Law should supplement the gospel. But the people who had firsthand experience with the Gentiles knew that was not the case. They each took a turn speaking.

Peter related the story of his encounter with Cornelius and how he had seen that God made no distinction between Jews and Gentiles (15:9). He pointed out that since the grace of God was the source of salvation for the Gentiles, it was also all that was necessary for the Jews as well (15:11). To subject believers to other requirements was tantamount to putting a yoke on them (15:10).

Paul and Barnabas related the signs and wonders they had witnessed God perform among the Gentiles in the various places they had been. The emphasis was not on their efforts, but God's work (15:12).

Last to speak was James, one of the brothers of Jesus who came to faith after the Lord's resurrection. He came to be known as James the Just because of his piety, and was the leader of the "mother church" in Jerusalem. The Jewish roots were still strong in the Jerusalem church, and if anyone was to back the proposal of the Pharisees, it would probably be James. But James referred to the scriptures (Amos 9:11–12) to confirm the experience that the other speakers had described (15:13–18). The inclusion of the Gentiles in the church was not a divine afterthought; the prophets had foretold it. The corresponding evidence between scripture and personal experience was, for James, conclusive.

Critical Observation

During this period of biblical history when miraculous signs and wonders were taking place on a regular basis, God chose to reveal His will to the council in Jerusalem by means of experience, scripture, and reason. The personal experience of Peter, Paul, and Barnabas was a reminder of God's work in history. Then there was an appeal to scripture, God's revealed Word and the only infallible rule in matters of faith in practice. And finally, there was an appeal to reason. In this case there was no prophetic utterance or writing on the wall. The checks and balances of experience, scripture, and reason continue to be the most common way that God reveals His will to His people.

Still, James had a pastor's heart. He knew if Jews and Gentiles were to come together in the church, they would need to be sensitive to one another's feelings. Many Gentile practices were highly offensive to Jewish sensibilities. So James suggested that a letter be written, asking Gentiles to follow a few basic guidelines (15:20)—not because they were "deal breakers" in regard to salvation, but because the elimination of such practices would go a long way in appeasing their Jewish brothers and sisters.

15:22–35

ADDRESSING THE ISSUE

A letter was drafted to go out to Gentile converts. The message was clear and direct, yet tactfully inoffensive (15:23–29). The council members made a number of points. First, they distanced themselves from the Judaizers—the group who had been teaching the necessity of circumcision as a requirement for salvation. Second, they named specifically chosen delegates of the council who would personally verify what was being communicated in writing. Judas and Silas would not only explain the content of the letter, but also minister personally to the Gentile Christians. And third, the council members shared their unanimous decision not to require anything of the Gentile converts other than a few requested cultural abstentions that would have been particularly repulsive to Jewish Christians (15:28–29).

The council could have simply sent out the letter, but it realized the importance of personal contact, and had it hand delivered by personal emissaries. Judging from the names, Judas (Barsabbas) would have been a Hebrew-speaking Jew. Silas (*Sylvanus* in Latin) was Greek-speaking and a Roman citizen (16:36–37). By sending Judas and Silas back to Antioch with Paul and Barnabas, the two would not only verify the decision of the council to the pro-circumcision group (who wouldn't have agreed with it) but would also explain the letter, interpret its meaning, and secure the agreement of the recipients.

Upon the messengers' arrival in Antioch, the believers there gathered to hear the letter read (15:30–31). They were pleased with its positive message. Judas and Silas stayed for a while to strengthen and encourage them, and then returned to Jerusalem. Paul and Barnabas stayed to continue teaching and preaching (15:33–35).

Take It Home

Essentially, the Jewish Christians who were Pharisees were suggesting that faith in Jesus Christ in itself was not enough for salvation. They wanted to add circumcision and obedience to the Mosaic laws. And across the centuries, there have been numerous people who wanted to make the gospel a "Jesus plus" kind of equation. You can be saved if you believe in Jesus. . .plus lead a good life, or give up all your bad habits, or attend church regularly, or give more to the church. And it's not that such additions are necessarily *bad* things, but they aren't requirements for salvation. If you had been at the council of Jerusalem, which of the speakers would you have most related with? Can you see similar issues in the church today, or would you say the contemporary church is relatively free of such influences?

ACTS 15:36–16:40

A SECOND JOURNEY, A DIFFERENT PARTNER

An Irresolvable Dispute	15:36–41
A New Partner, a New Recruit	16:1–5
A New Direction	16:6–15
A Jailer Finds Freedom	16:16–40

Setting Up the Section

Little by little the church has been becoming more accepting of the inclusion of Gentile believers. Paul and Barnabas, still in Antioch where many such converts lived, both had a heart for going out into Gentile territory and spreading the good news about Jesus. So when a disagreement kept them from traveling together, they paired up with other people and doubled their outreach. Paul and his new traveling companion, Silas, prepare to revisit the churches previously ministered to, and they end up widening the scope of their ministry considerably.

15:36–41

AN IRRESOLVABLE DISPUTE

Paul and Barnabas had been a devoted and productive team. After Paul's sudden conversion, it was Barnabas who had first approached him in the Jerusalem church and brought him into fellowship. When Barnabas was sent to observe the church in Antioch and saw it in need of gifted teachers, he went to Tarsus to get Paul to help lead. They had traveled together on a missionary trip that covered roughly seven hundred miles on land and five hundred miles on the sea. So now that the controversy over the matter of circumcision was settled (15:1–35), they discussed taking another trip to return to the communities they had originally visited.

Yet in spite of everything they had been through together, a problem arose, and they were unable to agree on a resolution. For some reason (never stated), John Mark had left them shortly after beginning the first trip. Apparently Barnabas thought that Mark had learned his lesson from his previous failure, and wanted to invite him on this second trip. But Paul felt Mark had deserted them and didn't want him to go. Paul and Barnabas got into such a disagreement that they went their separate ways (15:39).

Luke makes no judgment about who was right or wrong. But the result was a doubling of outreach. Barnabas took Mark (his young cousin) with him and went to Cyprus—an area of familiarity where they would probably face little opposition. Paul paired up with Silas, one of the two representatives of the Jerusalem church who had returned with him to Antioch (15:22). After a short stay, Silas had gone back to Jerusalem. But the fact that he was again in Antioch (15:40) may indicate his interest in the church there. Paul and Silas headed north to Syria and Cilicia, encouraging the churches wherever they went.

Demystifying Acts

Luke records the strong disagreement between Paul and Barnabas, declines to take sides, and then leaves the matter unsettled. But the rest of the story can be determined from other biblical sources. Certainly Paul's opinion was valid: Their ministry was too important to bring along a relative who wasn't committed. But Barnabas, the "Son of Encouragement," knew that people frequently need a second chance. So later we see that Mark had become a valuable asset to Peter (1 Peter 5:13), and many believe that Peter was the source of Mark's Gospel. Mark's ongoing faithfulness even won Paul over eventually (Colossians 4:10; Philemon 24). And in the final days of his life, Paul sent for Mark because he was an attribute to his ministry (2 Timothy 4:11).

16:1–5

A NEW PARTNER, A NEW RECRUIT

Paul and Barnabas had previously sailed to Cyprus, then sailed north, and had approached the cities of Iconium, Lystra, and Derbe from the west. But with Silas, Paul took a land route that took them first through Tarsus, and then into the other cities from the east.

In Lystra was a young believer named Timothy, whose mother was Jewish and father was Gentile (16:1). His mother and grandmother were both exemplary believers (2 Timothy 1:5) who certainly influenced his faith, and it is possible that Timothy had responded to Paul's message on the apostle's previous trip through Lystra. Over a decade later, when Paul wrote to him, people were still considering Timothy too young to be a minister (1 Timothy 4:12), so at this point he must have been quite an outstanding youth. Everyone who knew Timothy spoke highly of him, and Paul invited him along on the journey.

Paul and Silas were delivering news of the decision of the Jerusalem Council—that believing Gentiles didn't need to be circumcised before joining the church (16:4). Yet Paul had Timothy circumcised before taking him along (16:3). We aren't told why Timothy hadn't already been circumcised, yet it was likely in deference to his father's

Gentile culture. But in working with Jewish believers, it would appear callous and even sacrilegious for the son of a Jewish mother to be uncircumcised. So for the good of the ministry, and not as a matter of legalism, Timothy was circumcised. (In a similar circumstance with Titus, a Gentile believer, circumcision itself was the issue. Paul refused to have Titus circumcised [Galatians 2:1–5].) As the trio went from town to town, the churches grew both spiritually and numerically.

16:6–15

A NEW DIRECTION

Paul, Silas, and Timothy soon found themselves in new territory as they set out across Galatia (modern Turkey), headed westward toward the Aegean Sea. They might have turned south, but were told by the Holy Spirit not to enter Asia. When they considered going north through Bithynia, they were also prohibited. So they found themselves in Troas, a seaport on the Aegean Sea (16:8).

Critical Observation

The doctrine of the Trinity has not yet been addressed, but the persons of the Godhead are used interchangeably throughout the book of Acts. For example, in the Ananias and Sapphira story (5:1–11), lying to the Holy Spirit was equated with lying to God (see verses 3, 4, 9). And here we see guidance provided by the Holy Spirit (16:6) as well as the Spirit of Jesus (16:7).

Receiving only negative guidance can be frustrating, yet Paul and his companions were patient and faithful. In Troas Paul was given positive guidance through a vision that made it clear that they should proceed to Macedonia, even farther west (16:9–10). In Troas they also picked up another companion. The writing shifts from third person to first person, indicating that Luke joins the group. Yet he doesn't join the party as a mere observer; he feels called by God to preach the gospel with the others as well (16:10).

From Troas the group sailed to Philippi, a Roman colony in what is now Greece. Luke's description of Philippi (16:12) seems a bit more glowing than that of other places, suggesting that he grew up there and perhaps attended its noted medical school. They stayed a few days in Philippi. There is no mention of a synagogue, so the Jewish community must have been very small. But on the Sabbath, when the group went to find a place to pray, they found a group of women by the river and started a conversation with them.

One of those present was a business woman named Lydia, a seller of purple cloth—something only the wealthy could afford to buy (16:14). She was a Gentile who worshiped God to the extent that she understood Him, but her understanding was greatly increased as Paul spoke and God opened her heart. She was immediately baptized along with her household, which could have included servants and children. And she convinced Paul and his group to stay at her house (16:15), which also indicates that she was a woman of means to have such space available. Lydia is the first known convert on the European continent, and her home may have become the first house church in Philippi.

16:16–40

A JAILER FINDS FREEDOM

Another time in Philippi when Paul and the group were on their way to pray, they passed some men with a slave girl. (Verse 17 is the last use of first person for a while, indicating that Luke stayed in Philippi while the others in the group moved on.) The young girl made a lot of money for her owners by predicting the future through a spirit that possessed her (16:16). It was also not uncommon for opium to be used to promote clairvoyance, so the girl might have been a drug addict. Upon meeting Paul's group, she started following him around day after day, proclaiming who they were and what they were doing (16:17–18). Paul finally had enough and commanded that the spirit leave her.

When it did, her owners were incensed. Rather than being glad that the girl was no longer troubled by the spirit, they only saw that their source of easy income was gone. Instead of admitting it was a money issue, they accused Paul and Silas of promoting Jewish customs that weren't acceptable for Romans (16:20–21). In response, the surrounding crowd joined the attack as Paul and Silas were stripped, beaten, and securely imprisoned (16:23–24).

Peter had been fast asleep in a similar situation (12:6), but in this case Paul and Silas were singing hymns at midnight, which drew the attention of the other prisoners. Then an earthquake shook the foundations of the prison, not harming anyone, but flinging open all the doors and loosening all the chains holding the prisoners (16:25–26).

When the jailer awoke to discover what had happened, he was going to kill himself because he knew the Roman authorities would do as much or worse (16:27). (Herod had previously ordered Peter's guards killed [12:19].) But Paul stopped him with the surprising news that no one had escaped. (The reason for their reluctance to flee is not recorded. Perhaps the prisoners recognized the work of God in connection with the hymns and the miraculous nature of the earthquake.)

The jailer was no longer the authority figure. He fell trembling before Paul and Silas, freed them, and then asked what he needed to do to be saved (16:30). Their succinct answer: Believe in the Lord Jesus (16:31). But they went on to explain the gospel to the jailer and his family, who all believed (16:32–34). After the jailer washed the wounds of Paul and Silas, they baptized the man and his household.

In the morning, word was sent from the city officials to let Paul and Silas go, but they wouldn't leave until the magistrates came themselves to release them (16:37). This was the first they had mentioned that they were both Roman citizens, which alarmed the officials. Roman citizens had rights and should not have been beaten—especially before a trial. But Paul and Silas were probably more concerned about the propriety of the situation. They had just come to Philippi with news of Jesus, and had been treated as common criminals. By demanding an official release, their innocence would be a matter of record.

Their request was accommodated, although the magistrates did ask them to leave the city (16:39). So they made one more stop at Lydia's house to encourage the believers, and then moved on (16:40).

Take It Home

The dispute between Paul and Barnabas (15:36–41) offers an important lesson in conflict management. Too often we may feel that total unity is always the sign of God's presence and blessing. But here, two very faithful, dedicated, and conscientious believers had a difference of opinion. They each did what they felt was right. And in time, they each realized how God had worked through both of them. Can you think of any similar situations in your own life, or in the workings of your church, where a strong disagreement was a potentially damaging problem? What can be done in such circumstances to continue to function as a united body even when not everyone is in total agreement?

ACTS 17:1–34

MOVING THROUGH GREECE

Ministry in Thessalonica	17:1–9
Ministry in Berea	17:10–15
Ministry in Athens	17:16–34

Setting Up the Section

After Paul and Silas paired up to go back to the churches that Paul and Barnabas had previously visited, God's Spirit then directed them to travel through new territory with the good news of Jesus. Along the way they have been joined by Timothy, who is still with them, and Luke, who has remained in Philippi. This leg of the journey will take them south again, through Thessalonica, Berea, and Athens—and they get quite a different reception in each location.

17:1–9

MINISTRY IN THESSALONICA

After being asked to leave Philippi, Paul and Silas moved on and passed through two other prominent cities before deciding to stop in Thessalonica, about one hundred miles away (17:1). The mention of a synagogue in Thessalonica (17:2) may indicate the absence of one in the other towns, explaining why they passed through those locations before stopping. And even though they had just been beaten and imprisoned in Philippi, they didn't alter their usual routine. When they arrived in Thessalonica, they went to the synagogue and spoke to the people assembled there. The response must have been encouraging because they had the opportunity to speak on three consecutive Sabbaths (17:2). And based on other indications (Philippians 4:14–16; 1 Thessalonians 2:8–9), they spent much longer than two or three weeks there.

The appeal of the gospel was widespread. Those responding to Paul's teaching were some of the Jews, a large number of Gentiles, and a considerable number of prominent women in the city (17:4). However, as had been the problem previously, the Jewish leaders grew jealous and took action.

In this instance, they went to the marketplace and incited a mob to go after Paul and Silas. When they couldn't find them at Jason's house where (apparently) they had been staying, they took Jason and some other believers as well. Little is said about Jason, although Paul had a relative of that name (Romans 16:21). Perhaps Jason knew more than he was telling about Paul and Silas but, if so, did not let the crowd know. The mob grabbed Jason and some other believers and charged them with treason before the city officials (17:7). The charge was serious, but apparently the evidence was scant, and Paul and Silas could not be found. So Jason and the others only had to post bond and were released (17:9).

17:10–15

MINISTRY IN BEREA

By nightfall the believers in Thessalonica had reconnected with Paul and Silas and seen them on their way to Berea, about fifty miles southwest of Thessalonica. Berea had a large population, but was of little importance historically or politically.

Yet in a spiritual sense, Berea was one of the more outstanding cities Paul visited. He and Silas went to the Jewish synagogue, as was their custom. But while the Jews of Thessalonica had quickly become jealous and antagonistic, the Jews of Berea were different. They didn't take what Paul was teaching at face value, nor did they hear his new gospel and dismiss it with little thought. Instead, every time Paul said something, they pored over what had been written in their scriptures to see if he was speaking the truth. And as a result, many of the Jews and Gentiles believed—both men and women (17:11–12).

The positive atmosphere was short-lived, however, because the agitators from Thessalonica heard that Paul was in Berea and followed him there to stir up trouble (17:13). Rather than allowing the situation to become a public spectacle as it had previously, some of the believers immediately escorted Paul to Athens—about three hundred miles away, and possibly a sea voyage. Since Paul was apparently the main target of the agitators, Silas and Timothy were able to remain in Berea for a while to help the church get started. They arranged to follow Paul to Athens soon.

17:16–34

MINISTRY IN ATHENS

Alone in Athens, Paul quickly grew dismayed as he saw all the idols. The city was five hundred years past its Golden Age, but remained a center of culture and intellect. Many of the temples and statues that Paul saw are still there today, now admired for their artistic rather than spiritual impact.

With the wide variety of religious beliefs present in Athens, there was a segment of Jewish believers and God-fearing Gentiles, whom Paul addressed in the synagogue. But Athens had another place where people gathered: the marketplace (*agora*). It took Paul little time to meet various philosophers there and discuss their views. When they found his presentation of the gospel hard to grasp, they invited him to speak to the Areopagus, both a location ("hill of Ares") and the name of a court that dealt with matters of morals and the rights and restrictions of people who lectured in public.

This was a prime opportunity for Paul because the Athenians were eager to hear new and different ideas (17:19–21). And Paul found a novel approach to present the gospel. He had seen an altar inscribed with the words To an Unknown God (17:23). This was because they worshiped many gods, and the people were afraid of overlooking one and suffering his wrath. Paul explained that he knew the God they didn't—the God who made the world and everything in it, the Lord of heaven and earth. Paul's God did not live in temples or need anything from humans. He was the Creator who took a personal interest in the lives of those He created (17:24–26).

Demystifying Acts

Epicureans were followers of Epicurus, a Greek philosopher (341–270 BC). He taught that nothing exists but matter and space, so the chief purpose of humankind should be to achieve happiness and pleasure. For a philosopher, that joy was gained through intellectual challenge and growth, but his followers over the years had found pleasure through physical, sensual fulfillment. So what had begun as a philosophy of the highest standards had quickly acquired a bad reputation.

Stoics believed that the true essence of life was the capacity to understand the rational order veiled by natural phenomena. Freedom and joy were the result of detaching from the outer world and mastering one's reactions to his environment. Stoicism didn't allow for sympathy, pardon, or genuine expression of feeling. Famous Stoics included Zeno, Seneca, Cicero, and Marcus Aurelius.

To emphasize his point that God was more personal than all the idols strewn around Athens, Paul quoted Greek literature that his hearers would have been familiar with. Verse 25 had indirectly quoted Epimenides, a poet from Crete who had written, "For in Him we live, and move, and have our being." (Paul quotes him again in Titus 1:12.) Then, in verse 28, Paul quotes a poet from Cilicia (his homeland) named Aratus.

Critical Observation

Even though Paul's listeners were open to new ideas, the Areopagus did not tolerate an anything-goes atmosphere. Socrates had been sentenced to death by poisoning for promoting strange ideas in Athens, so Paul was not entirely free from danger in this setting.

Paul's point was that it is somewhat ironic that humans, as the created offspring of God, try to create gods of stone or precious metal. In fact, the acknowledgement of that fact should lead to repentance (17:29–31). When Paul brought up the topic of resurrection, he started getting resistance from some of his listeners. But he also had the attention of some of the others who wanted to hear more and eventually became believers (17:32–34).

However, no evidence exists that a church was formed in Athens as a result of Paul's visit. Even though a number of people in Athens believed, Paul's later reference to the first converts in this area (1 Corinthians 16:15) was to those in Corinth—his next stop.

Take It Home

Many modern Christians could learn from the first-century Jews of Berea. Rather than take someone's word for something—even someone as trustworthy and insightful as the apostle Paul—they searched the scriptures to verify what he was saying. Do you think most people do the same thing today? Or do they go to church to be told what to believe? To what extent do you tend to verify the "truths" you are taught from the Bible?

ACTS 18:1–22

WRAPPING UP THE SECOND MISSIONARY JOURNEY

Ministry in Corinth	18:1–8
First a Promise, Then a Test	18:9–17
Home Again	18:18–22

Setting Up the Section

Paul and Silas have set out on a second missionary journey, picking up Timothy along the way. But after being pursued from city to city by some troublemakers who would do Paul harm, he had gone ahead of the others into Athens while they stayed a while with the believers in Berea. Paul spoke to a group of philosophers in Athens, but didn't get a particularly enthusiastic reception. So he moves on to the next town: Corinth.

18:1–8

MINISTRY IN CORINTH

Athens is the more familiar city to most modern ears, but in Paul's day Corinth had surpassed it in significance. The Roman military had attacked and destroyed major portions of Corinth in 146 BC, after its citizens had participated in an anti-Roman uprising, and it had remained in ruins for a century. But in 46 BC, Julius Caesar passed through and saw its potential as a Roman colony, so the city was rebuilt. By the time Paul went through, it was probably the wealthiest city in Greece—a major multicultural urban center with a population of 750,000 people.

One thing that made Corinth so popular was its location. The southern portion of Greece would be an island were it not for a narrow five-mile strip that connects the southern portion to the northern part. Sailing around the entire southern part of Greece was hazardous because of heavy winds and rough seas. It had proved more reliable to unload large ships on one side of the isthmus and have porters carry the cargo to the other side. Smaller ships would be dragged fully loaded on wooden rollers across the five-mile stretch. And Corinth lay right in the center of that isthmus, profiting from east and west seafaring traffic, as well as from the travelers going back and forth to the southern section of the peninsula.

In addition to the financial wealth of Corinth, it had a wealth of religious options as well—most of them pagan. A noted temple to Aphrodite, the Greek goddess of love, was there. Prostitution was so rampant in the city that the Greek word meaning "Corinthian girl" came to be a slang term for a promiscuous woman. Corinth was also a center of homosexuality with a temple to Apollo, the epitome of male beauty. Nude statues and friezes in various suggestive poses paid tribute to this god of music, song, and poetry. In addition, the Corinthians could visit temples to Asclepius (the Greek god of healing), Isis (the Egyptian goddess of seafarers), and her Greek counterpart, Poseidon.

There was also a synagogue, so Paul went to it on every Sabbath to reason with the Jews and Gentiles who gathered there (18:4). In the meantime, he had met a couple named Aquila and Priscilla with whom he shared a trade, so he stayed with them. They were in Corinth due to anti-Jewish persecution in Rome (18:2).

Critical Observation

It was a custom in New Testament times to teach every Jewish boy a trade. Jesus had been trained as a carpenter. Paul learned the craft of tent making, which involved working with leather, hair, and wool. It may be that it was Paul's shared trade with Aquila and Priscilla that brought them together at first—not necessarily a shared belief in Jesus (although that would later become evident).

Luke says nothing of Silas and Timothy having met Paul in Athens, as had been their plan (17:15). But apparently they had done so and had been sent out again, because while Paul was in Corinth they were both returning from Macedonia (18:5). It is likely they brought a financial gift from the churches because at that point Paul began a full-time ministry of preaching and teaching, attempting to help the Jewish population see the significance of Jesus.

But it reached a point where Jewish resistance became so strong that Paul gave up on them. Shaking out his clothes (18:6) was akin to shaking the dust off one's feet, as Jesus had previously instructed His disciples to do when they encountered resistance. Their time would be better spent moving on to someone who did want to hear rather than continuing a fruitless debate with someone whose mind was already made up (Luke 9:5; 10:10–11).

Paul didn't have to go far to find new opportunities to speak. Right next door to the synagogue was the home of a believer where he could teach. In addition, the synagogue leader and his entire household became believers, which influenced a number of other Corinthians as well (18:7–8).

18:9–17

FIRST A PROMISE, THEN A TEST

It seems that Paul was facing more opposition than Luke describes here, because the vision he received appears to be in regard to specific threatening circumstances (18:9–10). But its message was consoling in a number of ways: (1) God was with Paul to allow him to keep speaking; (2) no one would attack or harm him in Corinth; and (3) many other believers were in Corinth. So Paul stayed a year and a half. He must have appreciated the opportunity to remain in one place for a while and build relationships rather than move on to another town as quickly as he had been doing. In addition, he might have used Corinth as a base from which he could visit and speak in neighboring districts during that time.

One incident of resistance to Paul while in Corinth is recorded. A group of Jewish people made a cohesive attack to get him in trouble with the Roman authorities. They hauled him into court and accused him of attempting to institute a new and unauthorized religion (18:12–13). Paul was about to defend himself, but didn't even get to speak. Instead, the proconsul, a man named Gallio (who happened to be the brother of the Roman philosopher, Seneca), rebuked the Jewish group and drove them out of court.

Members of the crowd then turned on the leader of the synagogue and began to beat him, which didn't even faze Gallio (18:17). It is unclear whether the attackers were Gentiles who resented the motives and actions of the Jews, or whether the Jews attacked their own synagogue leader because he did a poor job of representing them in court. The synagogue ruler was named Sosthenes, which was also the name of a later associate of Paul (1 Corinthians 1:1). Perhaps the synagogue leader became a convert after this experience.

Although Gallio's ruling essentially allowed Paul to continue his ministry unencumbered, it doesn't seem that Gallio personally became a believer. He later committed suicide.

18:18–22

HOME AGAIN

When Paul finally left Corinth, Priscilla and Aquila went with him (18:18). Priscilla's name is mentioned first, which is not typical and may indicate that she was the more prominent leader or teacher. Before leaving, Paul got a haircut in connection with a vow. The reason and specifics are not recorded.

Demystifying Acts

Occasionally a vow was taken and the person would immediately shave his head in response to an immediate crisis such as a serious illness. More common, however, was the Nazirite vow (Numbers 6:1–21), a temporary time of special devotion to God during which the person would let his hair grow and abstain from certain foods. Perhaps Paul's vow was in connection with his ministry in Corinth, which lasted a year and a half (Acts 18:11). Cutting his hair was the sign that he had concluded his commitment.

Paul stopped briefly in Ephesus, went to the synagogue, and had a good response. The Jewish people there wanted him to stay longer, but he wanted to move on. However, he promised to return if it was God's will (indeed, he would be back soon for a lengthy stay), and he left Aquila and Priscilla there (18:19). Paul appeared to be in a hurry to get back to Jerusalem, perhaps for Passover or some other significant event. The statement that "he went up and greeted the church" (18:22 NASB) suggests it was the church at Jerusalem, which required an ascent in the hills to get there. Then he went down to the church in Antioch (18:22).

And with that, Paul concluded his second missionary journey. Luke devotes little attention to how things were on the home front or how long Paul stayed before starting out again. In fact, the very next verse says that after spending some time in Antioch, Paul set out again on what would become his third missionary trip (18:23).

Take It Home

When you think of initiating conversations about your faith or looking for those who might be interested in the gospel, do you ever consider the people in your workplace? When alone in a strange new city, Paul found a natural bond with fellow tentmakers. Perhaps Aquila and Priscilla were already believers as well, but we don't know for sure. It might have been that the "shop talk" came first and led to more spiritual matters. As you interact with neighbors or coworkers during the next few weeks, keep your eyes and ears open for opportunities to allow the Holy Spirit to work and take your conversations to a more meaningful spiritual level.

ACTS 18:23–19:41

THE THIRD MISSIONARY JOURNEY BEGINS

Introducing Apollos 18:23–28
Clarifying the Truth in Ephesus 19:1–20
Christianity vs. Commerce 19:21–41

Setting Up the Section

Paul has spent a number of years traveling from place to place, preaching the gospel and establishing and building up churches. He made one journey with Barnabas and a second with Silas. In this section he sets out on his third trip, and his emphasis is in Ephesus, a city where he was unable to spend much time previously.

18:23–28

INTRODUCING APOLLOS

Luke's abrupt summary of Paul's second journey (18:18–22) and start of his third one (18:23) seems to be intentional. His focus, therefore, remains on the city of Ephesus. That's where Paul had a positive response from the people at the end of his second trip. That's where he left Aquila and Priscilla while he returned to Jerusalem. That's where he is heading—and will spend almost all of his time—on this third journey. And it's also where we first find Apollos (18:24).

Apollos was a Jewish believer who knew the scriptures very well and had been taught about Jesus. He was a bold speaker in the synagogue, yet he had only experienced the water baptism of John the Baptist to express repentance for sin and evidently didn't yet understand the work or power of the Holy Spirit (18:25–26). So Aquila and Priscilla helped him understand more fully the truths of Christianity. Before long he was eager and ready to move on to Achaia (the territory surrounding Corinth [now southern Greece]) to minister to the believers there. He left with the support and endorsement of the Ephesian church, and was effective there in proving that Jesus is God's Messiah (18:27–28).

19:1–20

CLARIFYING THE TRUTH IN EPHESUS

Not long after Apollos left Ephesus, Paul arrived (19:1). He found other disciples who, like Apollos, had not experienced a full Christian conversion. They were believers, to be sure, but had never even heard of the Holy Spirit (19:1 2). Paul began with what they were familiar with—the baptism of John the Baptist, explaining that John had pointed the way to One coming after him, Jesus. Then Paul baptized them in the name of Jesus. As he did, the Holy Spirit came upon them and they started speaking in tongues and prophesying (19:4–7).

Critical Observation

Ephesus was the capital of Asia Minor in what is modern-day southwest Turkey. It ranked in importance only behind Rome, Athens, and Alexandria. Thanks to a thriving port, it had become the chief link for communications and commerce between Rome and the East. The city contained one of the largest libraries in the ancient world and was a center of learning. But, like Corinth, it was known for pagan worship. Its temple to Diana (Artemis)—about four times the size of the Parthenon in Athens and said by numerous historians to be one of the most beautiful buildings ever built—was one of the seven wonders of the ancient world.

Paul spent three months speaking out in the synagogue, but some of the members stubbornly refused to believe and started publicly disparaging the gospel (19:8–9). So Paul left with those who believed him and moved his ministry to a local lecture hall for the next two years—the longest stay anywhere in his ministry. Word spread about his teachings until everyone in Asia had heard the gospel (19:10).

In addition, the authentic power of God was becoming evident in contrast to other sources of power. Ephesus had developed a reputation for being the magic capital of the world. So God did amazing things through Paul's ministry to validate his teachings. Handkerchiefs and other articles Paul had touched could be carried to sick or possessed people, and they would be healed (19:11–12).

In another graphic example, a group of Jewish exorcists (the seven sons of Sceva) had been going around evoking the name of Jesus to try to cast out evil spirits. Perhaps they wanted to emulate Paul's ability because they used his name as well (19:13), but their efforts backfired when one particular spirit challenged them. The possessed man single-handedly overpowered the whole group and left the exorcists bleeding and naked (19:13–16).

The failure of this group of exorcists was a boost to the church, as the name of Jesus gained more reverence. New believers publicly confessed their previous evil deeds. A group of former sorcery practitioners brought its scrolls and burned them—no small act of contrition considering the combined value added up to fifty thousand silver coins, each one worth about what a laborer would earn for a day's work. So the Word of God spread not only geographically, but grew more influential and respected as well (19:17–20).

19:21–41

CHRISTIANITY VS. COMMERCE

At this point Paul decided (and perhaps felt led) to make his way to Rome (19:21). He would spend a little more time in Ephesus and then take a roundabout route to Jerusalem in order to visit young churches and take up a collection for the believers in Jerusalem who were struggling financially. He sent two associates ahead of him to Macedonia. Erastus was another of Paul's fellow ministers (19:22; 2 Timothy 4:20).

Demystifying Acts

Luke's reporting at this point is focused primarily on Paul, who by this time has a number of assistants in various places. Paul will later mention many of them in his letters, but Luke doesn't acknowledge them all in Acts. For example, Luke mentioned Silas nine times between Acts 15:40 and 18:5, but not at all after that even though Silas remained active in ministry. Paul also had much to say about Titus, but Luke doesn't mention him at all.

Paul was accustomed to facing resistance to his teachings from skeptics and proponents of other beliefs, but in Ephesus he encountered opposition from merchants. Paul's preaching had been so effective that the metalworkers who made idols of the goddess Artemis (Diana) were experiencing a significant decline in income. One of the highlights in the temple of Artemis was an object that was said to have fallen from heaven (19:35). Some believe it may have been a meteorite that resembled a woman with many breasts. (A popular image of Artemis was as a multibreasted fertility goddess.) But fewer and fewer souvenirs were being sold as people believed in Jesus in response to Paul's messages (19:23–26).

So Demetrius, one of the local silversmiths, called a meeting and united his fellow craftsmen. Under the guise of loyalty to Artemis, they soon had incited the entire city. A mob mentality ensued. For two hours, crowds shouted in unison, "Great is Artemis of the Ephesians!" (19:34).

Archaeologists have discovered that the theater in Ephesus seated twenty-five thousand people, so the crowd could have been enormous (19:29). Yet most of the people didn't even know what was going on (19:32). Some were seizing anyone associated with Paul that they could find (19:29). And when someone tried to quiet the people and establish order, they refused to let him talk because he was a Jew (19:34). Many people still didn't differentiate between Judaism and Christianity, but both were detrimental to the sellers of idols.

Evidently Paul was somewhere else in Ephesus. He wanted to go address the crowd, but was restrained by fellow believers who realized the great danger he would be in (19:30). Even the city officials who knew Paul begged him not to appear in front of the crowd (19:31), which shows that Christianity was becoming more of a public influence.

Finally, the city clerk, a position much like a contemporary mayor, subdued the crowd and pointed out that the Christians had done nothing malicious or worthy of mistreatment (19:35–38). He knew Demetrius and the other craftsmen had been behind the pandemonium, and explained how they could legally take appropriate steps to seek the justice they desired (19:38–39). He also warned that Rome could impose penalties or restrictions on the city if its citizens were prone to riot (19:40). And with the situation finally diffused, he sent everyone home.

Paul left the city soon afterward. He would later write of fighting wild beasts at Ephesus (1 Corinthians 15:32). Perhaps this was the incident he had in mind.

Take It Home

Two incidents from this passage make a powerful contrast that is relevant for today's believers. One is the willingness of the former sorcerers, who put their faith in Jesus, to repent and eliminate their occult resources at great personal expense. The other is the attitude of the silversmiths, who resisted the gospel and used a religious guise to attempt to ensure their financial security. Christians can find themselves embroiled in economic dilemmas in a number of ways. Have you (or someone you know) ever had to make a decision to obey God that required a financial sacrifice? (For example, leaving a lucrative job because it required moral sacrifices, refusing to sell or promote certain items that might impair someone's spiritual growth, etc.) What were the results of the decision? How did you (or the person) feel afterward?

ACTS 20:1–38

A FORLORN FAREWELL

Ministry in Macedonia and Greece	20:1–6
An All-Night Sermon. . .and Its Consequences	20:7–12
Good-bye to Ephesus	20:13–38

Setting Up the Section

Paul is on his third missionary journey, and has never spent as much time in one place as he has in Ephesus. But his desire to collect an offering for the church in Jerusalem and start out for Rome has led to his decision to leave. This time his parting is particularly sad because he realized he might never see the Ephesians again. Yet God continues to do great things through Paul's ministry.

20:1–6

MINISTRY IN MACEDONIA AND GREECE

The uproar in verse 1 refers to the riot incited by Demetrius the silversmith and fellow craftsmen because Paul's teachings were causing them to lose money on idol sales (19:23–41). But that's not what prompted Paul's departure; he had already resolved to leave. Timothy and Erastus were already in Macedonia (19:21–22), so Paul set out in that direction.

As should be evident by now, Paul rarely traveled alone. Luke lists several of his companions on this leg of his journey (20:4). They represented the different regions of Macedonia that were taking part in the collection to be delivered to the believers in Jerusalem, who were suffering from a famine in the Middle East. The churches didn't just send money; they sent people to help as well.

In his travels, Paul demonstrated flexibility and sensitivity to the leading of the Holy Spirit. Some scholars believe the three months he spent in Greece (20:3) was winter in

Corinth, and while waiting until ships would sail again, Paul wrote his Epistle to the Romans. Yet at the end of that waiting period, he opted not to sail because he learned of a plot against him. On a ship, it would have been too easy for his enemies to kill him and toss his body overboard, so he decided instead to backtrack through Macedonia. He never resisted suffering when it advanced the promotion of the gospel, but he also used common sense in addition to being sensitive to the leading of God.

In his interaction with the young churches, Paul advocated and demonstrated much encouragement (20:2). They were facing a lot of challenges and obstacles, and Paul could certainly be direct when they got off track. But he also knew the power of encouragement in motivating people to keep going through trying times. The Greek word translated "encouragement" includes aspects of entreaty, exhortation, comfort, and consolation.

At this point in Paul's travels it seems that Luke again joined his group. The story picks up again with a first-person account (20:5–6).

20:7–12

AN ALL-NIGHT SERMON. . .AND ITS CONSEQUENCES

In connection with Paul's seven-day stay in Troas (20:6–7), Luke provides the first clear biblical reference of how Christians met for worship on Sunday rather than Saturday (the Sabbath). The Sunday gatherings were to commemorate Jesus' resurrection that took place on Easter Sunday.

Paul was planning to leave the next day and was spending the evening in fellowship with the other believers. They began by breaking bread (20:7), a reference to a regular celebration of the early church called the *agape* feast ("love feast")—basically a potluck dinner that concluded with the celebration of the Lord's Supper. For some of the poorer members of the church, it may have been the only decent meal they had all week.

Afterward, Paul had much to say, and he was still speaking when midnight arrived. A young man named Eutychus was seated on a high window ledge, perhaps trying to get some fresh air due to the many lamps burning (20:8) and what would almost certainly have been the warmth of a crowded room. As Paul kept talking, Eutychus fell fast asleep, dropped from the third floor, and died when he landed on the ground below. Since Luke was there, the death would have been confirmed.

Paul went to see and threw himself on the body, wrapping his arms around the young man—reminiscent of the Old Testament prophets Elijah (1 Kings 17:21) and Elisha (2 Kings 4:34–35). Just as Peter's faith in the power of God had brought Tabitha back to life (Acts 9:40), Paul's faith restored life to Eutychus.

Paul went back to preaching and continued until dawn. The friends of Eutychus took him home and felt immense comfort (20:11–12).

Critical Observation

The name *Eutychus* means "fortunate." It was a relatively common name among slaves who had been freed, though probably few lived up to the name as well as the young man in this account.

20:13–38

GOOD-BYE TO EPHESUS

Apparently Paul wanted to spend every minute possible in Troas. He sent his companions ahead by ship, knowing that he could take a shortcut across land to catch up with them at Assos. After several days of sailing, they arrived at Miletus. Ephesus was nearby, but Paul had determined not to return there. He had spent almost three years with the Ephesians, and a visit would have taken more time than he had to spend. (He wanted to get to Jerusalem by Pentecost [20:16].) Also, his recent run-in with the guild of silversmiths might have led to legal complications that would have tied him up as well. So rather than going again to Ephesus, he had the elders of the church meet him in Miletus (20:17–18).

At this point comes the only sermon in Acts directed exclusively to Christians (20:18–35). Paul's words to the Ephesian elders are both encouraging and cautionary. Groups of antagonists were out to smear Paul's good name (17:5–9), so he began by defending the sincerity of his motives and reminding them of his personal ministry in Ephesus (20:21). Paul's reference to teaching "from house to house" (20:20) may refer to house churches, many of which probably included one of the elders who had come to see him off.

He continued by sharing his current plans with them (20:22–27). He didn't know for certain what would happen, but he was realistically expecting prison and hardships (20:23). He viewed his ministry the same way a runner sees a race. In spite of any obstacles and difficulties he might face, his goal was to finish the race and complete the task he had been given (20:24).

Paul didn't anticipate ever visiting Ephesus again (20:25), although it seems that he did. (He later refers to events that appear to have taken place after the ones recorded in Acts [Timothy 1:3–4].) So before he left, he wanted to reassure the Ephesian elders of his own innocence and integrity.

Then he challenged them to the same commitment in their own ministries (20:28–31). They were shepherds entrusted by the Holy Spirit with the flock of God. Paul wisely advised the church leaders to watch over themselves as well as their congregations (20:28). After Paul had gone, the flock would come under attack from wolves (20:29)—people who would distort the truth and attempt to lead them astray. Some of the leaders of the early church would indeed fall away from the faith (2 Timothy 4:9–10), so Paul warned them to always be on their guard (20:31).

Finally, Paul reminded the elders of his love, a love borne out in his actions (20:32–35). Both his encouragement and his admonition were rooted in his affection for the Ephesian church. Paul had worked with his hands (20:34) to ensure that the work of God continued.

Demystifying Acts

While speaking to the elders of Ephesus, Paul attributes a quote to Jesus: "It is more blessed to give than to receive" (20:35). It has become a familiar saying and one very closely associated with the Bible. Yet this is the only place it appears. It is found nowhere in the Gospels.

Paul and his traveling companions had to tear themselves away from their Ephesian brothers in order to prepare to sail the next day (21:1). After his farewell speech, Paul prayed for the group, and there wasn't a dry eye among them (20:36–37). Most upsetting was their concern that they might never see Paul again. And as will soon be seen, they had good cause to be concerned.

Take It Home

Try to put yourself in Paul's place by recalling an instance when you had spent a lot of time and devoted a lot of emotional energy to a group of people, and then had to leave for some reason. What kind of farewell did you have? How did people express their emotions prior to your leaving? Have you kept up with them, or did the bonds of friendship diminish after you left?

ACTS 21:1–26

EXPECTING TROUBLE, BUT MOVING AHEAD

Sailing Back to Jerusalem	21:1–9
Advance Warning	21:10–16
Rebutting a Rumor	21:17–26

Setting Up the Section

The majority of the content of Acts 13–20 has been about Paul and his companions' journeys in taking the gospel out of Jerusalem and Antioch into other parts of the world. In this section he heads back toward Jerusalem after his third trip. Although he has faced various hardships throughout his travels, he is warned specifically of trouble ahead if he continues. Yet he is not deterred.

21:1–9

SAILING BACK TO JERUSALEM

Never one to shrink from danger, Paul endured much physical abuse and challenge as he proclaimed the truth of Jesus Christ in numerous new and different places. Yet as he neared the end of his third missionary journey, the signs became more and more ominous.

His clear intent was to first get to Jerusalem, after which he had to go to Rome (19:21). He was aware of repeated warnings from the Holy Spirit that hardships and prison were continual possibilities (20:22–23). He didn't expect to return to the area he had just left (20:25), and his departure left everyone in a state of anxiety and grief (20:36–38). Yet he continued on a direct path to get back to Jerusalem by the day of Pentecost (20:16; 21:1–3).

Demystifying Acts

In addition to Luke's skilled eye as a doctor, he also seems to have had a fondness and appreciation for seafaring. Detailed passages of sea travel have been sprinkled throughout his writing and continue in this passage (note all the references to "we"), and will extend to the very end of Acts.

The stop in Tyre (21:3) put Paul on the mainland, not far from Jerusalem. He found a number of believers there and stayed with them for a few days while the ship unloaded its cargo. And again, the Holy Spirit warned through these believers that he would face trouble in Jerusalem (21:4).

Paul had been through the area of Phoenicia at least once before (15:3), although this is the first mention of his visit to Tyre. Yet after only a week, the church members had a difficult time saying good-bye. A large group of families escorted him out of town and prayed for him before sending him on his way (21:5–6).

The ship's next stop was at Ptolemais, where Paul and his group were able to connect with yet another assembly of believers (21:7). As they got closer to Jerusalem, they were probably finding more and more Christian groups that had sprung up about twenty-five years previously, when persecution in Jerusalem had forced believers out into other communities. But this was only an overnight stop, and they continued the next day to Caesarea.

In Caesarea, Paul and his companions were hosted by a name familiar to some of them: Philip (21:8). Like Stephen, Philip was one of the Seven who had been designated to help the apostles shortly after the coming of the Holy Spirit at Pentecost (6:1–7). Philip had been the first to take the gospel cross-culturally into the region of Samaria (8:5–7, 12). He was the one who had helped the Ethiopian eunuch to understand and believe in Jesus, baptizing him and sending him back to Africa with the truth of the good news (8:26–40). Now, some twenty-five years later, Philip was connected with a group of believers in Caesarea—and not only him, but his four virgin daughters as well, who were all prophetesses (21:9).

21:10–16

ADVANCE WARNING

But it was another prophet who was more prominent during Paul's stay with Philip. A man named Agabus (who has also previously appeared in Acts [11:28]) had come out to meet them. Paul had been warned by other prophets against returning to Jerusalem. Agabus had the same message, but used a more emphatic means of communicating it. His symbolic binding of Paul (21:11), combined with his dire warning, left the group anxious and tearful. But Paul was more upset with their heartbreaking response than with the anticipation of potential trouble in Jerusalem (21:13). One thing that made Paul such a devoted and persistent messenger for God was his willingness not only to suffer, but also to die if it came to that.

One reason for the high emotion was that Jerusalem was their next stop—only about sixty-five miles ahead. But when the group could not persuade Paul to change his plans, it was willing for God's will to be done (21:14). Perhaps Paul was so determined because he was bringing back the money that had been collected from the other churches (that were in primarily Gentile territory). By doing so, he would be emphasizing the unity of the worldwide church, which was very important to him.

Critical Observation

Some people question the leading of the Holy Spirit in this account. On numerous occasions, prophets had warned Paul of impending danger if he went to Jerusalem (21:4, 10–12). Yet Paul was responding to the Spirit in his desire to go (19:21; 20:22–23). Some people believe Paul was so determined to get to Jerusalem that he missed God's will and should have listened to the messengers God put in his path. Others feel the prophets merely confirmed what Paul already knew from the Holy Spirit. Those in the latter group believe the lesson is that just because something appears to be difficult doesn't mean it isn't the will of God.

After a few days in Caesarea (21:10), Paul's group moved on and stayed overnight in the house of a man named Mnason (21:16). He had been a disciple for a long while and was from Cyprus, as was Barnabas. Their next stop would be Jerusalem.

21:17–26

REBUTTING A RUMOR

Paul refers to his delivery of the financial gift from the other churches in various epistles (Romans 15:25–27; 1 Corinthians 16:1–4; 2 Corinthians 8–9). Luke makes no mention of it here, and later acknowledges it only briefly as he records Paul's account of this moment (24:17). Luke's ongoing focus has been on the spread of the gospel and the growth of the church from Jerusalem outward, so his emphasis here is Paul's report to the church in Jerusalem. In addition, the "we" references conclude in verse 18, suggesting that Luke either moved on or changed the tense to emphasize Paul's ministry.

Upon Paul's arrival in Jerusalem, he found much to be the same as when he had last been there. James, the brother of Jesus, was still the leader of the Jerusalem church (15:13; 21:18). Paul's report of the work of God among the Gentiles encouraged them all. The Jerusalem church had good news as well: Thousands of zealous Jewish converts had been added to their number (21:20).

But one major concern had arisen during Paul's absence. Rumors had spread that not only had Paul taken the gospel to the Gentiles, but also that he was telling them to reject Jewish customs and circumcision—which, of course, wasn't true (21:21). There was nothing wrong with such traditions; it was just that they had nothing to do with salvation. Now that Paul was back in town, the church leaders wanted to settle the matter.

An ideal opportunity arose when four men of the church were preparing to conclude a vow they had made to God. Paul had recently done the same thing in Corinth (18:18). (See Acts 18:18–22 inset concerning Nazirite vows.) So the elders recommended that Paul join the four men in their rites of purification. In addition, he would pay for their offerings that were prescribed by Mosaic Law. Each man would bring two lambs, one ram, a grain offering, a drink offering, and a basket of unleavened cakes and wafers (Numbers 6:13–15). After each man's offering was presented to God by the priest, the man would shave his head and his hair would be placed in the fire of the fellowship offering (Numbers 6:16–18).

Paul had no problem accommodating the request, and joined the men in their purification the next day (21:26). The ceremony was one that was entirely voluntary and did nothing to compromise his Christian convictions. Yet his willingness to comply was proof that he wasn't promoting the cessation of Jewish rights and traditions.

In addition, the Jerusalem elders reiterated the previous decision of the council (15:20, 29) that Gentiles hold to certain restrictions: abstaining from food sacrificed to idols, from partaking of blood, from eating the meat of strangled animals, and from sexual immorality (21:25). Both Paul and the other church leaders continued to hold firm to their commitment to salvation by grace, yet allowed both Jews and Gentiles leeway in following their own traditions to promote greater unity in the church.

Take It Home

This passage, perhaps as much as any other so far, has shown Paul's strong determination to continue his ministry for God even in the face of opposition and persecution. (Prophesies of the trouble he would face will be fulfilled in the next section.) Are you inspired by such devotion, or do you tend to disagree with Paul's decision? If you were the one who had been warned by a number of godly people that trouble was in store if you went one direction, would you do it anyway? Or would you choose an alternative course of action? Why?

ACTS 21:27–22:29

TROUBLE IN JERUSALEM (AS PREDICTED)

Same Problem, New City	21:27–32
Paul's Arrest and Defense	21:33–22:21
The Rights of the Accused	22:22–29

Setting Up the Section

In this section, Paul finally arrives in Jerusalem after his third journey. From the moment he planned to come, he was aware that it would be a perilous and threatening trip for him. His first few days were nothing but positive as he shared his exploits with the elders of the church and heard how God had been active in Jerusalem as well. But it didn't take long for trouble to start, and it would be a long while before he would get the matter settled.

21:27–32

SAME PROBLEM, NEW CITY

Shortly after Paul's arrival in Jerusalem, he had been invited to participate in a Jewish purification ceremony to quash some rumors that he was preaching that all Jewish customs should be abandoned (21:21–26). He was glad to do so, and was planning to devote seven days to it (21:27).

But before he could complete the allotted time, he was seen at the temple by a group of Jews from Asia. He was accustomed to being followed from town to town by disgruntled, nonbelieving Jews who simply wanted to create trouble for him and stir up additional opposition to his teaching. Now they had found him in Jerusalem, and they resorted to the same strategy.

They didn't have their facts straight, but it didn't matter. They saw someone they knew from Ephesus, a Gentile man named Trophimus, and accused Paul of taking Gentiles into areas of the temple where only Jews were allowed (21:27–29). Their accusations were entirely unfounded, yet were enough to rile the crowd. They dragged Paul out of the temple, intending to kill him.

21:33–22:21

PAUL'S ARREST AND DEFENSE

The scene was so potentially violent that the Roman commander in charge (a man named Claudius Lysias, according to Acts 23:26) hurried out with sufficient forces to stop those who were beating Paul (21:30–34). He first arrested Paul and placed him in a kind of protective custody, bound with two chains, most likely between two guards (21:33). He then tried to determine from the crowd who Paul was and the nature of his offense, but his efforts were futile due to inconsistent answers and ongoing pandemonium. The mob was still trying to get to Paul, and the soldiers had to actually carry him into the barracks and away from the chanting crowd (21:35–36).

Paul asked the commander for a favor, speaking in Greek, which surprised the Roman leader. Until that moment, the commander thought he might have captured a terrorist—an Egyptian who spoke no Greek—who was on the loose. So Paul's words took Lysias aback (21:37–38).

Critical Observation

In AD 54 an Egyptian man had posed as a prophet and attracted thousands of Jewish followers. He led them to the Mount of Olives, telling them he was about to command the walls of Jerusalem to fall, after which they could storm in and overpower the Romans. But the Romans saw what was happening, confronted the group of rebels, and killed some of them. The Egyptian had escaped, but his supporters were still disgruntled. Lysias may have assumed Paul was that man and the mob was meting out its own justice.

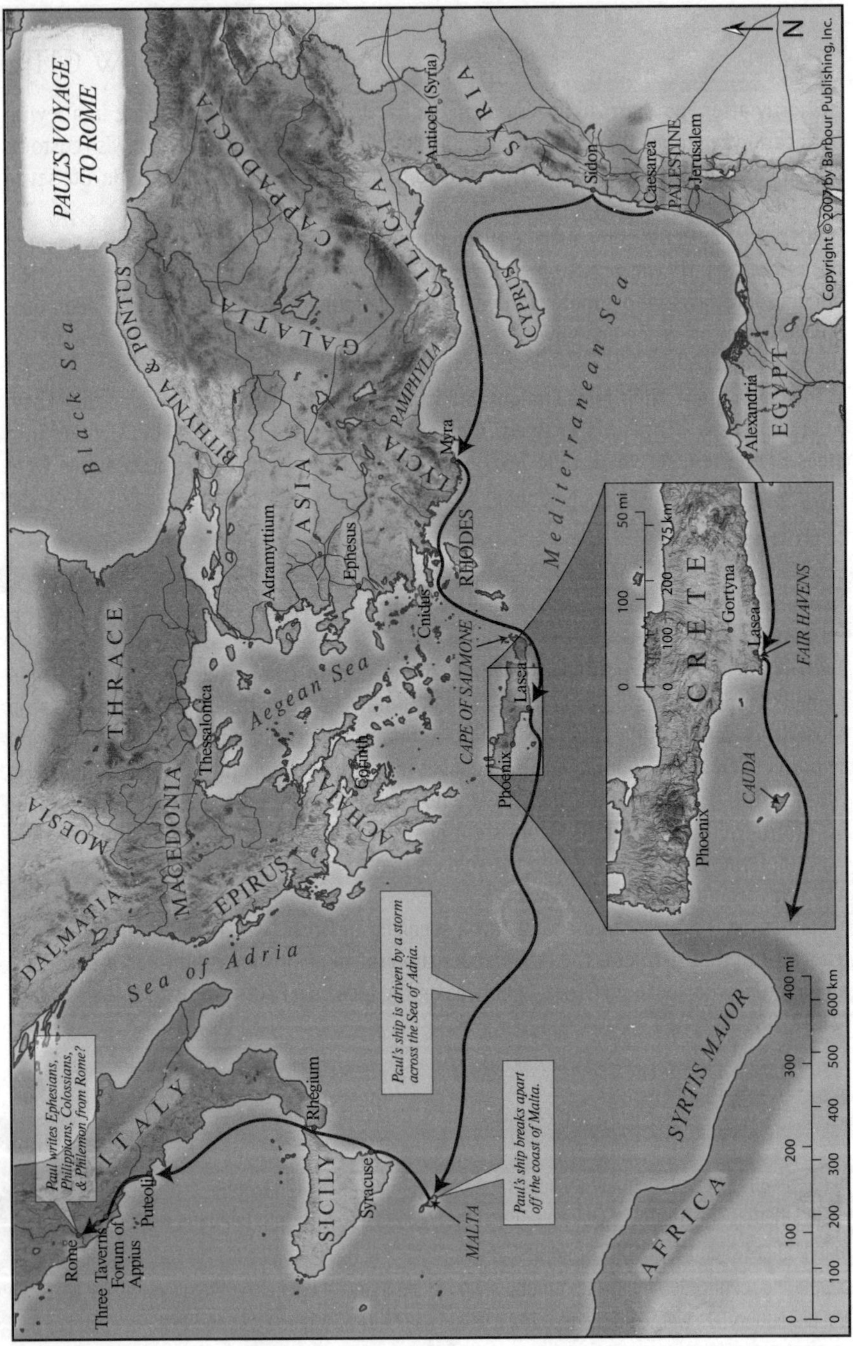

PAUL'S VOYAGE TO ROME
Black Sea
Mediterranean Sea
Aegean Sea
Sea of Adria
MOESIA
THRACE
MACEDONIA
DALMATIA
EPIRUS
ACHAIA
BITHYNIA & PONTUS
GALATIA
CAPPADOCIA
ASIA
LYCIA
PAMPHYLIA
CILICIA
SYRIA
CYPRUS
RHODES
CRETE
CAUDA
FAIR HAVENS
CAPE OF SALMONE
PALESTINE
EGYPT
AFRICA
SYRTIS MAJOR
ITALY
SICILY
MALTA
Rome
Three Taverns
Forum of Appius
Puteoli
Rhegium
Syracuse
Thessalonica
Corinth
Adramyttium
Ephesus
Cnidus
Myra
Antioch (Syria)
Sidon
Caesarea
Jerusalem
Alexandria
Phoenix
Lasea
Gortyna
Paul writes Ephesians, Philippians, Colossians, & Philemon from Rome?
Paul's ship is driven by a storm across the Sea of Adria.
Paul's ship breaks apart off the coast of Malta.
N
0 100 200 300 400 mi
0 100 200 300 400 500 600 km
0 100 50 mi
0 100 200 75 km
Copyright © 2007 by Barbour Publishing, Inc.

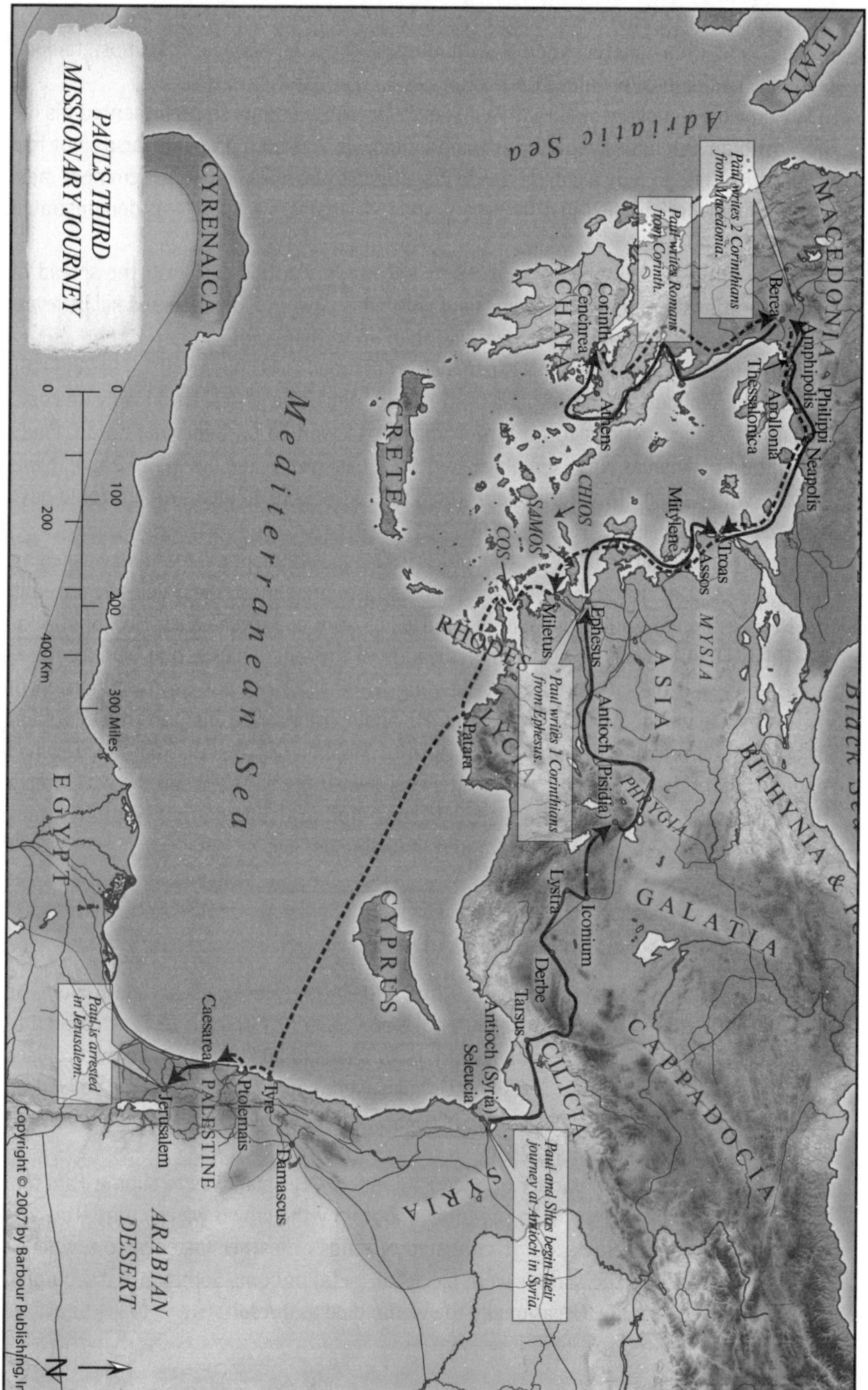
PAUL'S THIRD MISSIONARY JOURNEY
CYRENAICA
Mediterranean Sea
CRETE
ITALY
Adriatic Sea
MACEDONIA
ACHAIA
Corinth
Athens
Paul writes Romans from Corinth.
Paul writes 2 Corinthians from Macedonia.
Berea
Amphipolis
Philippi
Apollonia
Thessalonica
Neapolis
CHIOS
SAMOS
COS
Mitylene
Troas
Assos
MYSIA
ASIA
Ephesus
Miletus
RHODES
LYCIA
Patara
Paul writes 1 Corinthians from Ephesus.
Antioch (Pisidia)
PHRYGIA
GALATIA
Lystra
Iconium
Derbe
Tarsus
CILICIA
CAPPADOCIA
CYPRUS
Antioch (Syria)
Seleucia
Paul and Silas begin their journey at Antioch in Syria.
SYRIA
Damascus
Tyre
Ptolemais
Caesarea
PALESTINE
Jerusalem
Paul is arrested in Jerusalem.
EGYPT
ARABIAN DESERT
0 100 200 300 Miles
0 200 400 Km
N
Copyright © 2007 by Barbour Publishing, Inc.

Still, he granted Paul's request to speak to the crowd. Surprisingly, the crowd got quiet. . .and even quieter when Paul addressed them in Aramaic, the most familiar language of the local people (21:40–22:2).

The crowd's complaint was that Paul wasn't "Jewish" enough, so he presented his life story with an emphasis on his Jewish upbringing. He was born a Jew in Tarsus, but had spent much time in Jerusalem. He had been tutored by Gamaliel, the most eminent rabbi of the time, who had died just five years earlier. (Gamaliel's wisdom was demonstrated in Acts 5:33–40.)

In addition, Paul had been as zealous as anyone in wanting to quash the spread of "the Way" (Christianity). He did everything within his power to imprison and kill believers (22:4–5). The hostile crowd surely was with him up to that point.

Next Paul shared with them his experience on the road to Damascus (9:1–19; 22:6–16). He told them about the bright light from heaven, the voice of Jesus that only he could hear, and the instructions to go into Damascus to wait to be told what to do. Paul's description of Ananias was exemplary: "a devout observer of the law" (22:12 NIV). It was Ananias who had confirmed that Paul would be a witness to all men—which would have included the Gentiles (22:15; see 9:15).

At that point Paul had been baptized. (It wasn't the water baptism that had washed his sins away [22:16], although repentance and baptism are almost always closely linked in the New Testament. Paul had already submitted to Jesus and received the Holy Spirit [9:6, 17–19]; his baptism was an outward verification of the inner change that had occurred.)

So far the hostile crowd was still listening to him (22:22), but the next portion of his testimony would incite it once more. He again emphasized his prior mistreatment of believers, confessing his part in the death of Stephen (22:19–20). Still, the Lord had told him that he would not be accepted by his Jewish peers. As a result, he was sent to the Gentiles (22:21). These instructions had come during a supernatural vision that took place in the very temple Paul was accused of having defiled.

22:22–29

THE RIGHTS OF THE ACCUSED

Paul's explanation was completely truthful and sincere. He wasn't anti-Jerusalem. He had indeed tried to teach in Jerusalem until a contingent of Grecian Jews attempted to kill him, and the other believers had sent him to Tarsus (9:28–30). Yet the crowd refused to listen to his message that Jews and Gentiles were equal and could come to God on identical terms. For those views, the people still wanted him dead and made their wishes known in no uncertain terms (22:22).

Again, the Roman commander ordered Paul indoors. His plan was to submit Paul to a brutal flogging and force him to say more about why the crowd was so irate. This was no small punishment. The scourge consisted of strips of leather fastened to a wooden handle. Embedded in the leather were pieces of metal or bone. Sometimes a scourging crippled a person for life. Occasionally the victim died as a result.

But while the centurion in charge was preparing Paul to be whipped, Paul made a legal appeal (22:25). No one had asked, but Paul was a Roman citizen with rights that were about to be violated. Those rights were well respected by Roman officials, so the centurion went immediately to the commander, who went to Paul for confirmation (22:26–27).

Demystifying Acts

Essentially, Roman citizenship was the right to be treated as equal to the citizens of Rome. Roman citizens were spared humiliating punishments such as crucifixion or scourging, and they had more right to appeal official decisions than did noncitizens. Some people were born into citizenship, as was Paul (22:28). The status of "Roman citizen" could be purchased. Or sometimes a magnanimous emperor would bestow citizenship on individuals, cities, or even an entire province.

Paul affirmed that, yes, he had been born a citizen (22:28). Most likely, his father or some relative farther back had been designated a Roman citizen and had passed the status along to Paul. The Roman commander, on the other hand, had paid a lot of money to acquire citizenship.

The plans to have Paul whipped were immediately canceled. The commander was alarmed because he had almost committed a grievous injustice. He still wanted to find out why Paul had been such a target for the Jews, but now it would be done by means of a trial rather than the use of force.

Take It Home

In this passage we see the importance of being able to tell one's story of spiritual conversion and growth. While it didn't get Paul out of trouble in this case, a hostile crowd settled down to hear what he had to say. In addition, we see that we don't need to know all the answers to difficult theological issues. We simply need to be able to verbalize the things we have seen, heard, and know from personal experience to be true. Sometimes a story of personal experience will be much better received from someone than a sermon or Bible quotation. Personal stories can open doors, preparing a heart for other truths of God. When was the last time you told your story? As you go through the week, look for new opportunities to share with others what God has done for you.

ACTS 22:30–23:35

PAUL'S TRIAL BEGINS

Disorder in the Court 22:30–23:11
The Plot to Murder Paul 23:12–35

Setting Up the Section

After the completion of his third missionary journey, Paul has returned to Jerusalem. He had been participating in a purification ceremony when he was dragged from the temple by an angry group of Jews who thought his work with the Gentiles involved advocating the rejection of all Jewish customs and traditions. The mob tried to kill him, but was stopped by Roman authorities. In this section, the Romans call together the Sanhedrin to help them figure out exactly what is going on.

22:30–23:11

DISORDER IN THE COURT

After planning to flog Paul, the Roman commander, Claudius Lysias, had narrowly avoided trouble when Paul announced that he was a Roman citizen (22:25–29). Paul was spared a scourging, but Lysias still hadn't determined why Paul was the target of such a large and hostile mob. He ordered the Jewish Sanhedrin to assemble and interrogate Paul (22:30).

Many of the members of the Sanhedrin didn't think much better of Paul than those in the angry crowd, including the high priest, Ananias. As soon as Paul had spoken his first sentence, Ananias commanded that he be struck in the mouth (23:2).

Critical Observation

Ananias ruled as high priest from AD 48–59. He was a brutal and scheming man, known for greed and the use of violence. He embezzled money and gave large bribes to the Roman authorities. He was detested by many Jews because he supported Rome. When the war with Rome broke out in AD 66, Ananias's house was burned by Jewish nationalists, and he was forced to take shelter at the palace of Herod the Great in the northern part of Jerusalem. He was eventually found hiding in an aqueduct on the palace grounds and killed.

Ananias was acting in the role of a judge. Paul was quick to point out that *he* was being held to the standards of Jewish law, yet his judge was breaking the law by ordering violence within the court, and his comments included some name calling (23:3). Immediately he was rebuked by those nearby for insulting the high priest (23:4).

Paul quickly explained that he didn't realize that the order had come from the high priest. Some believe Paul had trouble seeing, in which case his poor vision might have prevented him from recognizing Ananias as the high priest. Besides, Paul had been out of Jerusalem for a while and the position of high priest changed quite often. Others feel his reply may have been somewhat sarcastic, and that Paul refused to recognize the authority of anyone who would use the office of high priest to promote unwarranted hostility. But his rapid shift from calling Ananias a "whitewashed wall" (23:3) to his appeal to the group as "brothers" (23:5) suggests sincerity. Whatever his motive, he apologized and submitted to the legal protocol (Exodus 22:28).

Yet Ananias's action must have alerted Paul that he had little chance of receiving a fair trial, so he took the offensive. He knew the Sanhedrin was comprised of a number of Jewish sects, two of the main ones being the Pharisees and the Sadducees. The Pharisees had a high regard for oral tradition; the Sadducees only respected the written law. The Pharisees believed in predestination; the Sadducees believed in free will. The Pharisees believed in the existence of angels and evil spirits; the Sadducees didn't. And the Pharisees believed in the resurrection of the dead, while the Sadducees denied resurrection.

When Paul took a stand for resurrection, he knew he would divide the group. He was right. His statement (23:6) sent the whole council into an uproar. The Pharisees suddenly began taking his side while the Sadducees argued all the more. The conflict intensified to the point where the Roman commander again had to retrieve Paul by force and take him back to the barracks for his own safety (23:10).

After being a target of hostility for two different mobs on two consecutive days, Paul might have felt very disheartened. But the next night he received affirmation from Jesus through a supernatural revelation, encouraging him to keep going. He would indeed be traveling on to Rome, as he had hoped (23:11). Paul didn't see many visions in his ministry, and must have appreciated this unusual blessing that strengthened his weakened spirit.

23:12–35

THE PLOT TO MURDER PAUL

Paul didn't realize it at the time, but he needed some supernatural support. The next morning a group of more than forty Jewish men took an oath not to eat or drink until Paul was dead (23:12–13). This group enlisted the help of the chief priests and elders. The plan was to have Paul summoned back to court. The conspirators would lie in wait, perhaps along some narrow street where Paul could easily be intercepted and killed.

But the right pair of ears happened to overhear the plot. At this point we discover that Paul had a sister and nephew in Jerusalem (23:16), and the young man found out about the ambush planned against Paul. He told Paul, Paul alerted the Roman commander, and Paul's nephew was warned to keep quiet about what he knew.

Demystifying Acts

Luke, who provides so many interesting details in his Gospel and the book of Acts, tells us essentially nothing about Paul's relatives. If he had a sister in Jerusalem, why didn't Paul stay with her? Maybe they weren't believers, yet if not, why take a risk to help Paul? Did they have a connection with the Jewish leadership that allowed them to know so many details of the plot against Paul? And how did a young man gain access to the Roman barracks so easily? We are given the facts but no further explanation.

Remembering that Paul was a Roman citizen, the commander acted immediately. He dispatched two centurions and a detachment of two hundred soldiers, along with seventy horsemen and two hundred spearmen. Even if it encountered the forty assassins, a Roman contingent of 470 soldiers should have had no trouble defeating them. Yet the soldiers weren't looking for a fight. They left at 9:00 p.m., escorting Paul during the night toward Caesarea (a two-day journey) where he would be much safer (23:23).

Paul was being delivered to Antonius Felix, the ruling governor of Judea (23:24). The Roman commander sent a letter to be delivered along with Paul, which would have been expected. Since the message was being sent from one political leader to a superior, Lysias subtly glosses over some of the details of the events he describes. For example, he didn't rescue Paul *because* he was a Roman citizen (23:27). As a matter of fact, he had been preparing to torture Paul during interrogation when he happened to find out about Paul's citizenship (22:23–29).

Still, the letter served to help Paul because Lysias expressed his opinion that Paul was not guilty of any serious crime. There may have been some disagreement about Jewish law, but Paul certainly didn't deserve death or imprisonment (23:29). Lysias also informed Felix that he would be sending Paul's accusers to present their case before him (23:30).

The night travel must have been strenuous for the party escorting Paul. The soldiers traversed thirty-five miles the first night, much of it across difficult terrain—including a long stretch that would have been ideal for an ambush. But after arriving safely in Antipatris, the remaining distance to Caesarea (twenty-seven miles) was far less threatening. So the foot soldiers returned to Jerusalem while the cavalry continued ahead with Paul (23:31–32).

The journey took place without incident. The letter and the prisoner were delivered to Felix, who agreed to hear the case. Paul was held in the palace of Herod until his accusers arrived to prosecute the case (23:35). Unaware of it at the time, this was one of Paul's more pleasant stays. He would be in other prisons in the days to come.

Take It Home

Consider the anger and frustration the Jews felt because they were under Roman control. Yet it becomes more evident in this passage of Acts (and previous ones) that God is actually the One in control. If Paul's Jewish antagonists had had their way, they would have killed him (21:31). But God used a Roman centurion, a Roman commander, 470 Roman soldiers, and a Roman governor to ensure that Paul was spared and would continue to stand for Him. Have you recently felt, like Paul, that people or forces were out to get you? If so, how can the acknowledgement of God's sovereignty help you endure? Is it possible that God might provide for you, using some unexpected people or methods?

ACTS 24:1–27

PAUL'S TRIAL BEFORE FELIX

The Case for the Prosecution 24:1–9
Paul's Rebuttal 24:10–21

Setting Up the Section

In this section, Paul must defend himself before the Roman governor of Judea, Felix. But things could be worse. The Roman commander in Jerusalem has already taken Paul into protective custody to prevent zealous Jewish traditionalists from killing him. And when an elaborate plot was discovered that involved more than forty assassins sworn to murder Paul in Jerusalem, the Romans initiated a change of venue by leaving during the night to escort him to Caesarea. He is being held in the palace of Herod, awaiting his trial.

24:1–9

THE CASE FOR THE PROSECUTION

Felix, the governor, had agreed to oversee Paul's trial, and had sent for Paul's accusers. It was a two-day journey from Caesarea to Jerusalem, so it took five days for the messenger to be dispatched and the group to arrive. In the meantime, Paul was kept under guard.

Felix knew something of Hebrew culture and traditions from his third wife, Drusilla (24:24). She was the daughter of Herod Agrippa I and sister of Agrippa II. Felix had seduced her away from another king, a fact that will later become significant.

When the Jewish entourage arrived, the group included the high priest (Ananias), a number of Jewish elders, and their lawyer (or orator) who was named Tertullus (24:1). They met with Felix and listed their charges against Paul before he was called in.

After Paul was summoned, the trial began. Tertullus opened with what is known as a *captatio benevolentiae*, a flowery and flattering statement meant to capture the goodwill of the judge (24:2–4). He noted Felix's penchant for peace and his reforms, and promised to be brief so as not to weary the busy governor.

Critical Observation

For anyone who heard the description of Antonius Felix as presented by the spokesperson for Paul's opponents, it would seem that he was a wise and beloved leader. That would be far from the truth. Born a Greek subject named Antonius Claudius, he was eventually freed by the emperor Claudius at which time he acquired the name *Felix* ("happy"). He found favor with both Claudius and then Nero, but he was a tyrannical and selfish leader. Far from being a man of peace as portrayed in Acts 24:2, he had squelched several insurrections, using harsh brutality.

As Tertullus turned his attention to the charges against Paul, he was direct and succinct. He alleged that Paul: (1) was a troublemaker who created riots among the Jews throughout the world; (2) was a leader in the Nazarene sect (Christianity); and (3) had intended to desecrate the temple (24:5–6).

Although it may seem that this was a matter for the Jewish courts, each of the charges touched on concerns of the Roman Empire. The Romans demanded order in their territories and would not tolerate anyone going around stirring up riots. They also had a tolerance of Judaism, but now the Jews were trying to distance themselves from the Nazarene sect. It was becoming clear that Christianity was more than just a branch of Judaism, and its leaders might be committing treason against the empire. And even the goings on within the temple needed to be coordinated with the Romans. So far the Jews had been given the right to execute any Gentiles found in the areas where they were not permitted. Yet it was a Roman commander who prevented them from carrying out that sentence on Paul.

Tertullus invited Felix to interrogate Paul himself. And, of course, the Jewish elders who had come with him were backing up everything he said (24:8–9).

24:10–21

PAUL'S REBUTTAL

At this point, Felix motioned for Paul to speak (24:10).

Paul also began with a captatio benevolentiae, but his was considerably more modest and moderate than Tertullus's (24:10). Then he went right to refuting the accusations of the prosecution, one by one.

First, he emphasized that he was not a troublemaker, and that at no time had he attempted to instigate an insurrection. He had gone to Jerusalem as a pilgrim to worship, not as an agitator to cause a riot (24:11–12). He had cut his visits with other churches short in order to be in Jerusalem for the Feast of Pentecost.

Second, Paul stressed the similarities between what his prosecutors believed and what he believed (24:14–16). He pointed out that they worshiped the same God, had the same forefathers, believed in the same scriptures, and maintained the same hope that God would resurrect both the righteous and the wicked. The sect that his opponents accused him of leading was actually a faith quite similar to their own.

Finally, Paul had done nothing that could be construed as defiling the temple (24:17–18). Not only was he not connected to any kind of crowd or disturbance, but he was also ceremonially clean. It wasn't until the Jewish troublemakers from Asia showed up that there was a riot. *They* were the ones who had come into the temple and started the whole melee.

And speaking of those people, if they had a charge against Paul, they should have been present to say so. In lieu of that, the people who *were* there should have cited a specific crime he had committed when he had been standing before the Sanhedrin.

As it came time for Felix to make his ruling, he found himself in a political tight spot. He wanted to curry favor with the Jewish authorities, but he didn't have a legal basis to do so. Lysias, the Roman commander in Jerusalem, had found no fault in Paul. The Jewish

Sanhedrin had been unable to convict him of any crime. And Tertullus had certainly not substantiated his charges.

Yet Felix wasn't yet willing to release Paul, probably because there wasn't anything in it for him (24:26). If Paul had been the average prisoner, he would have offered a bribe and been out in no time. And perhaps Felix had paid special attention to Paul's testimony about delivering gifts and presenting offerings (24:17). But Paul was not about to pay for his own release. So Felix used a stall tactic by saying he would wait to decide until after the arrival of Lysias, the commander in Jerusalem who had written the letter to Felix (24:22). Yet there is no indication that Felix ever sent for Lysias.

In the meantime, however, Felix didn't seem to consider Paul any kind of threat and allowed him a minimum-security environment. Paul was still supervised by a centurion, yet had a degree of freedom and opportunities for friends to visit (24:23).

During Paul's imprisonment, Felix would stop by from time to time. He was still hoping for a bribe (24:26), yet Paul used some of those opportunities to talk about Jesus. Not long after Paul's trial, Felix and his wife, Drusilla, summoned Paul to listen to what he had to say about Jesus. Felix had been governor of Judea for six years and certainly must have been aware of the spread of "the Way" throughout his territory. Paul's words, however, were alarming to Felix who was not known for being either righteous or self-controlled (24:25). He was sitting there beside a woman he had stolen away from another married man, so Felix became afraid as Paul connected such behavior with God's judgment.

Demystifying Acts

Luke doesn't explain the details of the transition between Felix and Festus (24:27). Felix was recalled to Rome after an outbreak of mob violence in Caesarea during which he had allowed Roman troops to kill thousands of Jews and loot the homes of the wealthy. The Jews complained to Rome, and Felix was dismissed from his position as governor. He likely would have been executed had it not been for the influence of his brother, Pallus.

Felix hurriedly dismissed Paul after this first private discussion (24:25). He sent for Paul frequently for subsequent discussions, but kept Paul incarcerated for two years before he was finally forced to step down (24:27). It was the mistreatment of his Jewish subjects that led to his loss of position, and Paul's release would have only created more dissension among them. Festus, who replaced Felix as governor, would prove to be a much better leader.

Take It Home

Paul was probably one of the most knowledgeable, well-trained, and effective speakers of his time. He had spent years by this time telling others—both Jews and Gentiles—about his faith in Jesus and the scriptural evidence that backed his beliefs. And while he inspired many people to believe, there were many others who didn't. Paul spoke to Felix on numerous occasions, and appeared to have his attention and respect. But Felix never acted on what Paul was telling him. How do you feel when you speak out or use your gifts for God, and you don't get the response you hope for? Are you quick to give up? Or, like Paul, do you keep going until you find someone willing to respond?

ACTS 25:1–26:32

A SECOND TRIAL IN CAESAREA

Festus Tries Paul	25:1–12
Festus and Agrippa	25:13–22
Paul and Agrippa	26:1–32

Setting Up the Section

For two years, Paul has been under arrest in Caesarea, the victim of the bureaucracy of the Roman Empire. Charged by a group of Jews in Jerusalem and the target of an assassination plot, he had been brought to Caesarea for trial. The case against him had been weak, yet the governor (Felix) would not pardon him, attempting to endear himself to his Jewish constituents. Felix has just lost his position, leaving his successor, Festus, the problem of what to do with Paul.

25:1–12

FESTUS TRIES PAUL

We know relatively little about Porcius Festus, the successor of Governor Felix in Judea. He lived only two years after his appointment, yet is remembered as being wiser, more reasonable, and more effective than his predecessor.

It didn't take long for Festus to get around to the business of governing. Three days after arriving at his palace, he made the sixty-five-mile, two-day trip to Jerusalem. It was the displeasure of the Jewish people that had led to the dismissal of his predecessor, so Festus showed wisdom in immediately consulting with the Jewish leaders.

At the same time, he was no pushover. The Jews knew they had no real case against Paul, so they begged to have him returned to Jerusalem, secretly planning to kill him along the way (25:3). Festus denied their request, but agreed to a retrial in Caesarea if they still wanted to press charges. They had little choice but to comply.

Festus spent over a week in Jerusalem (25:6), but held Paul's trial as soon as he got back. It was essentially a repeat of the previous prosecution by Tertullus (24:1–9). The Jewish prosecutors made many serious accusations concerning Paul, but couldn't prove any of them. They had accusers, but no witnesses. And all Paul could do was again deny that he had done anything wrong in regard to either Jewish or Roman law (25:8).

As a new governor, Festus didn't want to start his term in office by provoking the Jews if it could be helped. But like Felix, he had no evidence on which to convict Paul (25:9). At this point he did what may seem unusual to a modern court: He consulted the accused. He suggested that Paul might want to return to Jerusalem to be tried. His sensitivity to Paul was likely in recognition of Paul's rights as a Roman citizen.

Festus's attempt to placate the Jews didn't work because Paul knew he would be better off in a Roman civil court than a Jewish religious one. Paul emphatically stated that he would not resist the death penalty if anyone could prove anything against him. But since they couldn't, he would take advantage of his right as a Roman citizen and appeal to a higher court. His next stop would be in Rome before the emperor or his representatives. Even though the current emperor (or Caesar) was Nero, he had not yet developed the reputation of unpredictable leadership and oppression of Christians.

Paul's appeal to Caesar (25:11) must have been a great relief for Festus. Not only would it get Paul out of Festus's jurisdiction in Caesarea, but it also meant he did not have to make a decision that would antagonize the Jews.

25:13–22

FESTUS AND AGRIPPA

Not long afterward, Festus had a visitor: Marcus Julius Agrippa II. He was a descendant of Herod the Great and the person Rome had appointed king over the territory northeast of Judea. Agrippa was accompanied by his sister, Bernice (25:13), who was also his consort. They had tried to squelch rumors of an incestuous relationship by having Bernice marry Polemo II, the king of Cilicia, but she soon returned to Agrippa.

Critical Observation

Herod the Great and his successors are integral antagonists in the New Testament story. The original Herod was the one who had slaughtered the young males of Bethlehem in an attempt to eliminate Jesus as an infant (Matthew 2:16). His son, Herod Antipas, made an impulsive promise at a birthday party that led to his beheading of John the Baptist (Mark 6:17–28) and was the Herod involved with Jesus' trial (Luke 23:8–11). Herod the Great's grandson, Herod Agrippa I, killed James the apostle and had similar plans for Peter (Acts 12:2–4). The Acts 25 passage introduces Agrippa II, son of Herod Agrippa I and the fourth (and final) generation of Herods in scripture. Agrippa II was the last of the family dynasty, and the least odious of the Herods.

The couple was in Caesarea for an extended stay, to welcome Festus to the neighborhood (25:14). They lived in the adjoining province, in Caesarea Philippi. It was protocol for Roman rulers to welcome newcomers and build relationships, and Festus was glad for the interaction with Agrippa. He knew the king was knowledgeable about Jewish culture and customs. Frankly, he didn't understand all that was involved in the Jewish elders' accusations against Paul, and he was glad for the opportunity for a consultation.

It is interesting that Luke provided Festus's outsider perception of everything that had been going on (25:14–21). The governor's account appears honest and straightforward, yet the religious significance had escaped him. He was confused about a dead man named Jesus who Paul claimed was living (25:19), and he had no idea how to respond. Yet his story intrigued Agrippa, who requested the opportunity to hear Paul himself (25:22). Festus agreed to set something up for the next day.

But far from simply having Paul released for a conversation with Agrippa, Festus went out of his way to create an event for his visitors. Everyone of any status in his court and in the city of Caesarea was invited. Agrippa and Bernice entered the room in a formal and courtly manner (25:23). For such an occasion, they would have been wearing their purple robes of royalty and their gold crowns. Festus, too, had a ceremonial uniform, including a scarlet robe. When the officials were all seated, Paul was summoned.

What a contrast he must have made in the great assembly. Paul is thought to have been short and balding. He likely had scars from the beatings and stoning he had already received in his many travels. And he was still wearing the handcuffs by which he would be chained to his guard(s) (26:29).

Festus opened the proceedings by explaining why Paul was being brought before the crowd. It wasn't an official trial, yet he would have to write up the facts of Paul's case to be sent along with him to Rome. Festus was looking for advice from the group—especially Agrippa. Yet Festus also made clear his personal opinion that Paul had done nothing worthy of death—in spite of what Paul's Jewish prosecutors had claimed (25:24–25).

26:1–32

PAUL AND AGRIPPA

Festus yielded the floor to Agrippa, who gave Paul permission to speak. This was a dramatic moment. For four generations, the Herod family had obstructed the work of God through Jesus, John the Baptist, James the apostle, and now Paul. Yet here God's Word is still being boldly proclaimed before the current Herodian leader. This is also the moment when the words of Jesus to His disciples, and later specifically to Paul though Ananias, were first fulfilled about being brought before governors and kings (Matthew 10:18; Acts 9:15).

Paul had been assured, both from Jesus and from Festus (23:11; 25:12) that he would eventually be heard in Rome. Therefore, he had no pressing need to defend himself and could use this opportunity instead to promote the gospel and attempt to sway the opinions of some of the leaders of the Roman Empire.

What follows is the longest of Paul's five defenses that Luke records in Acts. Paul even asked for Agrippa's patience before he began, knowing that he would not be brief (26:3). And just as Paul's defense before Felix had reflected his awareness that there were many Jews in his audience, in this case he tailors his speech for the Gentiles who are listening

Paul's introductory remarks were complimentary, but not flattering (26:2–3). Agrippa was indeed familiar with Jewish customs. Among other things, it was his job to oversee the treasury of the temple and to appoint the high priest. Paul was glad to talk to an authority who knew more about Judaism than Festus, and Festus was glad for Agrippa's help in assessing Paul.

Next Paul spoke of his roots in Judaism (26:4–8). From his childhood he had been devoted to his beliefs, and had eventually become a Pharisee—as dedicated and meticulous as anyone. Yet he felt his faith in Jesus was not in opposition to his Jewish training; rather, Jesus was the fulfillment of what the Jews had been anticipating for centuries (26:6–7). And Jesus' claim to Messiah was based on His resurrection from the dead (26:8). (At this point, Paul expanded his audience, rather than continuing to speak solely to Agrippa.)

Paul followed his exemplary background with a frank confession of his initial fervor to eradicate Christianity before it became a threat to his Jewish upbringing (26:9–11). At the time he didn't believe that Jesus had risen or was the Messiah, and he was near-fanatical in opposing those who did. His reference to casting votes against them (26:10) is usually thought to be a figure of speech rather than literal. It is conceivable that Paul might have been a member of the Sanhedrin at some point, but there is no evidence that he was.

Still, he was as intent as anyone else on targeting those who believed in Jesus, which is what made his conversion story so powerful (26:12–18). This is the third time Luke included the same account (9:1–9; 22:6–11), although in this version he provided a bit of new information. For one thing, Paul mentions that the voice of Jesus he heard was speaking Aramaic (26:14). And in the same verse he cites a Greek proverb about kicking against the goads. Paul included this bit of information while talking to his Gentile audience; it wouldn't have been as meaningful to his fellow Jews. Also significant to his Roman listeners should have been the fact that a voice came from heaven to correct his actions. Additionally, his mission to the Gentiles would include presenting a message of forgiveness of sins and acceptance by God (26:17–18).

Demystifying Acts

A *goad* was a pointed stick used to drive large animals. Whether or not the animals wanted to go in that direction, it did them no good to resist the sharpened goad. "Kicking against the goads" had become a familiar phrase in the Greek world to signify someone who opposed a god or gods. Paul later uses another Greek idiom, "Done in a corner" (26:26).

Everything Paul had said so far was to explain to his high-ranking listeners why he had been arrested. He was simply doing what he had been called to do (26:19–23). It had nothing to do with treason or rebellion. And even though the Jews had seized him and tried to kill him, what he was saying was nothing that hadn't already been prophesied in their scriptures. But thanks to God, he was still alive and able to speak to the assembly.

It was when Paul stressed that Jesus had been the first to rise from the dead for the benefit of both the Jews and Gentiles (26:23) that his discourse was interrupted, beginning a most unorthodox altercation between the bench and the witness stand. First it was Festus who apparently couldn't restrain himself any longer and accused Paul of insanity (26:24). He willingly acknowledged Paul's vast knowledge, but feared Paul's intense study had driven him crazy. Festus's Gentile outlook of life and death allowed no possibility for resurrection.

But Paul calmly denied the accusation of insanity. Rather than taking it personally, he pointed out that everything he was saying was a matter of common knowledge. His assertions were not only true, but also reasonable (26:25). The ministry, death, and resurrection of Jesus had been public and were open to verification. In addition, anyone who believed what the Old Testament prophets had written and compared their prophecies with the historical facts concerning Jesus of Nazareth must acknowledge the truth of Christianity.

Paul knew Agrippa was aware of both Jewish history and the current events concerning Jesus, and asked him directly for his input. Paul's question seems simple enough (26:27). Yet Agrippa was anticipating Paul's follow-up question. If Agrippa admitted to believing in the writings of the prophets, he would surely be asked if he agreed that Jesus had fulfilled those predictions. And he wasn't ready to make such a statement that would lose the support of the majority of the Jews, or let Paul get the better of him in this formal assembly, for that matter.

So Agrippa deflected the attention placed on him with a question of his own (26:28). It is not unreasonable to suppose that his comment was a lighthearted attempt to provide a break in the proceedings. Perhaps Paul's response had a similar tone (26:29). He was clearly serious about his prayers for Agrippa as well as everyone else present and his desire for all of them to be like him. But his final words, "except for these chains," could conceivably have been delivered with a smile.

Whatever the tone of the delivery, Agrippa stood at that point and the assembly was concluded (26:30). Agrippa, Bernice, and Festus hadn't even gotten out of the room before they had agreed that Paul had done nothing for which he should die—or even be imprisoned (26:31). In addition, Agrippa would have released him on the spot if Paul hadn't already made an official appeal to the emperor (26:32).

Agrippa's closing comment confirms the previous results of Paul's trials. Paul had not been found guilty of any crime by the Jewish Sanhedrin (23:9), the Roman commander in Jerusalem (23:29), or two successive Roman governors in Caesarea (24:22–27; 25:25). Now, the king over the territory, a high-ranking Roman authority with long-standing close connections to the Jewish people, could find no fault with Paul. Yet Paul still had another trial to withstand, this one before Caesar himself.

At least Paul would be out of his two-year palace captivity during his transfer to Rome. He had a lengthy voyage ahead of him, and it would not all be smooth sailing.

Take It Home

One significant thing worth noting from this passage is Paul's lack of intimidation. In previous chapters of Acts it has been clear that he has not been intimidated by threats of violence or harm; he has continued in spite of everything that has happened to him. But today's Christians—those in the West, at least—may not relate very well to such physical persecution. Contemporary believers may identify more with this passage where Paul might have been intimidated by status, yet wasn't. He could walk into a room filled with the most important people in his community and his world, share his personal testimony with them, and invite them to consider becoming believers themselves. How would you do in such a setting? Would you be reluctant to be so bold among dignitaries? Or do you think you would respond much like Paul did?

ACTS 27:1–44

PROBLEMS ON THE WAY TO ROME

Sailing West	27:1–12
Into a Hurricane	27:13–26
Shipwrecked, but Ashore	27:27–44

Setting Up the Section

Paul, the prominent figure in the book of Acts, has spent the last two years under guard in Caesarea, waiting for the governor to try him. Felix never got around to it because he was hoping for a bribe. But when Festus, the new governor, arrived, Paul immediately received his trial. Festus didn't fully understand the intricacies of the case and would not make a decision. In response, Paul appealed his case to a higher court—before Caesar himself. If he hadn't done that, he would have been released (26:32). But Paul was eager to go to Rome, and begins his journey in this passage.

27:1–12

SAILING WEST

When Paul first started thinking seriously about going to Rome (19:21), he probably hadn't counted on first spending two years under house arrest and then moving on to Rome as a prisoner. Yet regardless of the conditions, Jesus' promise to him (23:11) was at last being fulfilled.

Luke didn't mention any of Paul's associates who might have come by to see him during his two-year imprisonment, though he had the freedom to receive visitors (24:23). Yet as soon as Paul prepared to sail toward Rome, the book of Acts reverts back to first person (27:1). The last first-person reference was used shortly before Paul's arrest that eventually landed him in Caesarea (21:18), so perhaps Luke had been nearby this whole time.

Little is known about the Imperial Regiment (27:1), as was true about the Italian Regiment mentioned in Acts 10:1. But Julius, the centurion assigned to oversee Paul, would have been responsible for one-sixth of the regiment.

Aristarchus was a believer who had been with Paul both just before his arrest (19:29) and now (27:2), so he, too, may have attended to Paul's needs for the previous two years. He would later be associated with Paul in Rome (Colossians 4:10), so it seems that Paul had friends with him during this long voyage. He was also allowed to get off the ship and visit fellow believers at Sidon, their first stop (27:3). Perhaps Paul's Roman citizenship gave him certain privileges that other prisoners didn't receive.

Prevailing winds in the Mediterranean during fall are usually from the west (27:4), the direction the ship was headed, so sailing was slow. Rather than continuing to follow the coastline, the centurion decided to change ships and attempt to put out to sea. Paul and the other travelers were placed on an Egyptian grain ship (27:6, 38), but their progress wasn't much better. After many days they finally made it to the island of Crete and a harbor called Fair Havens (27:7–8).

Then they had a decision to make. The Day of Atonement was already past (27:9). In AD 59, the year that Paul set out for Rome, the date would have been October 5. The Romans preferred not to sail after mid-September, and any attempts after the first of November were considered suicidal. Everyone agreed that it would be foolish to attempt to make it to Italy. But Fair Havens wasn't a good harbor, and there were no sizable towns around where the crew could pass the winter, so many wanted to sail to Phoenix, a location forty miles farther west.

Paul warned the others that to continue would mean disaster (27:10). But the centurion, who was responsible for the final decision, was swayed by the opinion of the majority, and they moved on.

27:13–26

INTO A HURRICANE

It appeared to be a good decision at first. A gentle wind blew from the south, helping them along. But soon a raging wind came out of the northeast, blowing the ship away from shore (27:14).

Critical Observation

Ancient ships did not have benefit of sextant nor compass, depending instead on astronomical indications and landmarks on shore. In cloudy weather, sailors were at a loss for determining direction (27:20).

A granary ship could be as large as one hundred forty feet long by thirty-six feet wide and thirty-three feet tall, but it wasn't designed for handling storms. The bow and stern were the same width, and it had no rudder, being steered instead by two large paddles coming from each side of the stern. A single mast with a large square sail made it impossible to make progress into the wind, and placed a strain on the ship during high winds.

Fearing that the ship might break apart, the crew took five precautionary measures to save the vessel when they had a few moments of relative calm near the island of Cauda: (1) They managed to haul the lifeboat onto the deck, as it had probably been taking on water (27:16–17); (2) they passed cables transversely beneath the ship and tightened them with winches to hold the ship together like a tied-up package (27:17); (3) they lowered the sea anchor to serve as a brake as they drifted (27:17); (4) they jettisoned much of the cargo to lighten the ship (27:18); and (5) after three days, they tossed out all the ship's nonessential tackle (27:19).

They had no idea where they were, but feared the sandbars of Syrtis (27:17), which were off the coast of northern Africa and had grounded a number of ships. Even after doing everything they knew to do, most had given up any hope of surviving (27:20). There was still food available, yet the sailors weren't eating (27:21).

After many days of enduring the turbulent seas, Paul stood and addressed the others. His opening comment might sound a bit like "I told you so" (27:21), but his intent was likely to convince them of the truth of what he was about to tell them. He explained that an angel had appeared to him, told him not to be afraid, and assured him that God would spare the lives of everyone on board because of Paul (27:23–24). Paul challenged everyone to persevere and have faith that everything would be all right. They would run aground (27:26) and the ship would be destroyed, but all the people would survive (27:22).

27:27–44

SHIPWRECKED, BUT ASHORE

It is no wonder morale was low. Imagine being at sea with 275 other people (27:37) and being tossed by ferocious weather for two entire weeks with no control over where you were going (27:27). It was enough to drive seasoned sailors to despair. And when they realized they were coming upon land (27:27), still with no control, some prayed for daylight while others tried to sneak away in the lifeboat (27:29–30). Paul saw what was going on, alerted the centurion, and the soldiers scuttled the lifeboat.

It wasn't yet dawn, but Paul again tried to lift everyone's spirits. He took some practical steps to prepare them for what was to come. He urged them to eat, he again promised that no one would lose a single hair from his head, and he thanked God publicly (27:34–35). The others were encouraged, ate all they wanted, and then threw all the remaining grain into the sea to again attempt to lighten the boat. They were planning to make it to shore soon, and wanted the ship to sit as high in the water as possible.

By then it was daylight, and they saw a sandy beach on an unidentified stretch of land. Their plan was to run the ship right up onto the shore, but it hit a sandbar they had not seen (27:39–41). As a result, the bow was stuck fast in the sand while the stern was smashed into pieces by the pounding waves.

Demystifying Acts

The stranded ship on the sandbar placed the Roman soldiers in a dilemma. It was an easy swim to shore, and if a prisoner were to escape from their custody the Roman Empire required that the guard be killed. Not wanting to place their own lives in risk, the soldiers were preparing to kill the prisoners (27:42). But by this time, the centurion in charge seemed to trust Paul, and forbade his soldiers from harming anyone.

The centurion instructed those who could swim to make their way to shore first. The others found pieces of the battered ship and used them to float to shore. And just as Paul had promised, everyone arrived safely on the land, which they soon discovered to be the island of Malta.

Take It Home

Just as Jesus had calmed storms and controlled the winds and waves for His disciples on the Sea of Galilee, He saw Paul safely through this threatening sea voyage. We should not fail to notice the angel's promise to Paul: "God has graciously given you the lives of all who sail with you" (27:24 NIV). Paul's situation was probably not a one-time incident when God's protection of His people also spared others around them. Can you recall any instances when nonbelievers might have benefited because of the presence of a righteous person making godly decisions? Can you think of any times when your own decisions have had positive effects on many others?

ACTS 28:1–31

ROME AT LAST

Winter in Malta	28:1–10
From Malta to Rome	28:11–16
Ministry in Rome	28:17–31

Setting Up the Section

Paul's numerous missionary trips had created within him the desire to one day reach Rome and preach there. After a number of legal trials and two years of imprisonment while waiting, he had at last set out on his way—but still as a prisoner. In addition, his ship had encountered a violent storm and wrecked just off the shore of Malta. But he had Jesus' promise that he would arrive in Rome, and in this closing section of Acts he finally gets there.

28:1–10

WINTER IN MALTA

Malta meant "refuge," and lived up to its name for Paul and his fellow shipwreck victims. They found themselves about five hundred miles west of Crete, where they had last put out to sea, and they were only about fifty-eight miles away from the island of Sicily, which was just off the southwest corner of the Italian mainland.

The word for "islanders" (28:2) also means "barbarians," but not in the sense the word is usually used today. In Paul's time it was a term used to indicate anyone who didn't speak Greek. It is evident from Luke's description of the Maltese people that they were far from barbaric.

Indeed, they extended unusual kindness toward the stranded sailors, building a fire on shore to get them warm and dry (28:2). Paul pitched in to help gather wood, and as he was placing it on the fire a poisonous snake amid the brush became startled and struck his arm (28:3). The islanders, who would have known the danger of being bitten by that particular species of serpent, supposed that Paul had been a murderer intended to perish in the sea, yet had somehow escaped (28:4). They watched a long time for the effects of the poison, and when Paul showed no ill effects at all they assumed he must be divine (28:6).

Dike (pronounced Dí-*kay*) was the Greek goddess of justice, frequently portrayed as holding a staff and balance. It was belief in Dike that helped the Maltese natives explain why bad things happened to certain people. Yet their mythology didn't hold true for Paul, and they didn't automatically assume a god (or God) might be protecting Paul. So the only thing that made sense to them was to believe that Paul was a god himself.

Paul continued to mystify the islanders. He and a group (including Luke) were invited to the home of the chief official on Malta. The man's father was in bed with a serious illness. Even in modern times, Malta fever was prevalent in the area, with symptoms lasting an average of four months—and sometimes as long as two or three years. The source was eventually identified as a microorganism in the milk of Maltese goats, and a vaccine was developed. But Paul had no vaccine, and instead laid his hands on the man and prayed for him (28:8). When the official's father was immediately healed, the other sick people on the island flocked to Paul and were also cured (28:9).

Critical Observation

Throughout the book of Acts, Paul displays healing power. Yet in his epistles we discover he had some kind of ailment (a thorn in his flesh [2 Corinthians 12:7–10]) that was never removed. Like Jesus, he used God's power for the benefit of others. But when it came to his own physical problems, he went to God in prayer and submitted to His will.

Paul and the others had to wait out the winter on Malta. But three months later, when they were again ready to sail, the grateful people provided them with all the supplies they needed (28:10).

28:11–16

FROM MALTA TO ROME

Sailing in the Mediterranean would have picked up again around mid-February, which fits the three-month span of time spent on Malta (28:11). Another ship was in a nearby port—probably another grain ship since it, too, was Egyptian. Its figurehead was of Castor and Pollux, sons of Zeus and the twins portrayed in the constellation Gemini. They were thought to protect sailors, and the sighting of Gemini in the night sky was considered a good omen. But the men who had been traveling with Paul knew something of the God who could really protect those at sea.

Arrangements were made, most likely by the centurion, for Paul's group to be transported to Italy on this Alexandrian ship. The first stop was a three-day layover in Syracuse (28:12), a major city on the eastern coast of Sicily. From there they continued north to Rhegium (now Reggio di Calabria), on the "toe" of the Italian mainland, just east of Sicily. A favorable wind the next day carried them 180 miles farther north to Puteoli (now Pozzuoli), a large port protected by the Bay of Naples. A group of believers invited Paul to spend a week with them before going on to Rome, still seventy-five miles away. Evidently, the centurion responsible for Paul had developed enough respect for him to allow him certain privileges rather than moving straight ahead to Rome.

Demystifying Acts

It should be understood that Paul wasn't going to Rome to introduce the gospel, but to deepen the comprehension of the believers there. Puteoli and other communities had a large Jewish population, many of whom had surely traveled to Jerusalem and witnessed the coming of the Holy Spirit years ago. So groups of Christians had already sprung up in various locations (28:14–15). In addition, Paul had written his Epistle to the Romans three years prior to his arrival. So the believers in the area already had a decent understanding of the significance of Jesus' death and resurrection.

After everything Paul had gone through to get to Rome to preach, his entry into Rome is understated (28:14). News of his approach had preceded him. Believers from Rome came flocking to meet him and got as far as the Three Taverns (a way station thirty-three miles outside of Rome) and the Forum of Appius (forty-three miles from Rome). They would have traveled the famed Appian Way, one of the great Roman roads named after Appias Claudius.

The meeting of Paul by the Roman citizens (28:15) is more formal than it may seem. The Greek word used is the same that would apply to an official city delegation going out to greet a general or king. Paul was treated as one of the great heroes of the faith. He was encouraged, not at the attention he received, but at the very sight of believers representing Jesus Christ in the heart of the Roman Empire (28:15). It must have also been encouraging to be granted a large degree of freedom while awaiting his trial in Rome. Although he was always under guard, he was allowed to live by himself (28:16).

28:17–31

MINISTRY IN ROME

One of the first things Paul did during his two-year stay (28:30) was to meet with the Jewish leaders in Rome, perhaps to preempt any problems like those he had faced in other cities. The outspoken segment of Jews who had opposed him in Jerusalem would be likely to arrive after finding out he was in Rome. He quickly summarized what had happened to him and why he had come (28:17–20).

The local Jews said they hadn't heard any bad reports about Paul (28:21). Perhaps they were being tactful because communication between Rome and Jerusalem was usually good, and it had been almost two and a half years since the riot for which he was arrested. (He had been in prison in Caesarea for two years and in transit from Caesarea to Rome for at least three and a half months.) Yet they were curious about Christianity and eager to hear Paul's explanation (28:22).

A meeting was arranged, and a great number of people turned out to hear Paul, who spent the entire day teaching and encouraging them to believe in Jesus. True to the pattern in previous cities, some did believe and others refused to (28:23–24). As those Jews who rejected the gospel were leaving, Paul quoted Isaiah 6:9–10, a prophecy that the Jewish people would close their eyes and ears to (28:26–27). (Jesus had cited the same quotation in reference to His ministry [Mark 4:12].) Paul's last encounter with the Jews thus follows the common pattern throughout Acts. While some responded favorably, most rejected the message, and Paul turned to the Gentiles. They would believe.

It wasn't Luke's intent to write the biography of Paul. Rather, he had recorded the spread of the gospel from Jerusalem to Samaria to the ends of the earth, and from its Jewish roots to the Gentile world (Acts 1:8). As he concludes with the gospel reaching Rome, it may be frustrating that he leaves Paul still under arrest and awaiting trial for two full years. But Luke's central theme comes through loud and clear. Despite his imprisonment, Paul is able to receive visitors and continues to proclaim the kingdom of God "boldly and without hindrance" (28:31). Though Paul is in chains, the gospel cannot be chained and continues to advance despite opposition!

POSTSCRIPT

It was during this two-year period that Paul wrote his Prison Epistles: Philippians, Ephesians, Colossians, and Philemon. Most scholars believe Paul was subsequently exonerated in Rome and released. He took a fourth missionary journey (based on comments in his Epistles) and may even have gone to Spain. But he later found himself in Rome again, this time in a dank prison expecting to die (2 Timothy 2:9; 4:6–8). Tradition says he was beheaded in Rome at the command of Emperor Nero.

Take It Home

Looking back on the ministry of Paul after everything he has been through, his conversion story becomes even more powerful. Luke included it three times in the book of Acts (9:1–19; 22:6–21; 26:12–18). The before-and-after story of Paul is perhaps one of the most dramatic imaginable. Consider your own life before and after becoming a believer. What are some of the biggest differences you have noticed? Do you have a sense of where God may be leading you at this point in your spiritual journey?

ROMANS

INTRODUCTION TO ROMANS

It is easy to forget that the Epistle to the Romans is a letter and not a theological treatise. It is so often used in doctrinal studies and pursuits that we may miss the heartfelt passion that the author, Paul, had for his readers, many of whom he had never met. It isn't the first of Paul's letters chronologically, though it is placed first among his Epistles in the New Testament.

AUTHOR

Paul is the writer of this Epistle. Skeptics have challenged the authenticity of some of Paul's other Epistles, but Romans has never seriously been questioned.

PURPOSE

Paul considered himself an apostle to the Gentiles (11:13), yet he had never been to Rome, the center of the secular Roman Empire. He was planning a visit on his way to Spain (15:23–24, 28), and was writing in anticipation of his arrival. Yet his Epistle is far more than a casual letter. He laid out a fresh and clear explanation of God's plan of salvation for both Jews and Gentiles—one that has continued to inspire and motivate Bible readers for centuries.

OCCASION

Paul was probably writing from Corinth on his third missionary journey, preparing to return to Jerusalem with a financial gift he had collected from the churches in Greece (15:25–29). But he was already making plans for a fourth missionary journey and hoped to include Rome. So while in Corinth (or near there), he wrote his Epistle to inform the church of his plans. As it turned out, he would arrive in Rome as a prisoner (Acts 28:16), but was given a lot of freedom to minister and eventually was released.

THEMES

The themes that permeate the Epistle to the Romans are righteousness from God and justification by faith. Through faith in Jesus Christ, God's righteousness is imparted to human beings. It was how Abraham was justified before God prior to the giving of the Mosaic Law. And it was how Gentiles were able to come to God without being required to be circumcised or observe all the Jewish dietary restrictions and feast days.

HISTORICAL CONTEXT

We know little about the origins of the church in Rome. It is likely that Jewish pilgrims in Jerusalem had become believers on the Day of Pentecost, returned home, and started the church. When Paul finally got to visit (during the early portion of Nero's reign), a group of believers traveled many miles to meet him along the way and escort him back to Rome (Acts 28:14–16).

CONTRIBUTION TO THE BIBLE

The book of Romans has been called the Constitution of the Bible. The privileges and freedoms it describes are good news not only for the Gentiles, who came to God with little knowledge and no traditions, but also for the Jews, who had drifted away from the genuine worship of God and had rejected Jesus. God's love, mercy, and grace are abundant enough for everyone to experience His forgiveness. The realization that people are justified by faith alone has been an eye-opening and life-changing reality for Martin Luther, John Wesley, and other church leaders.

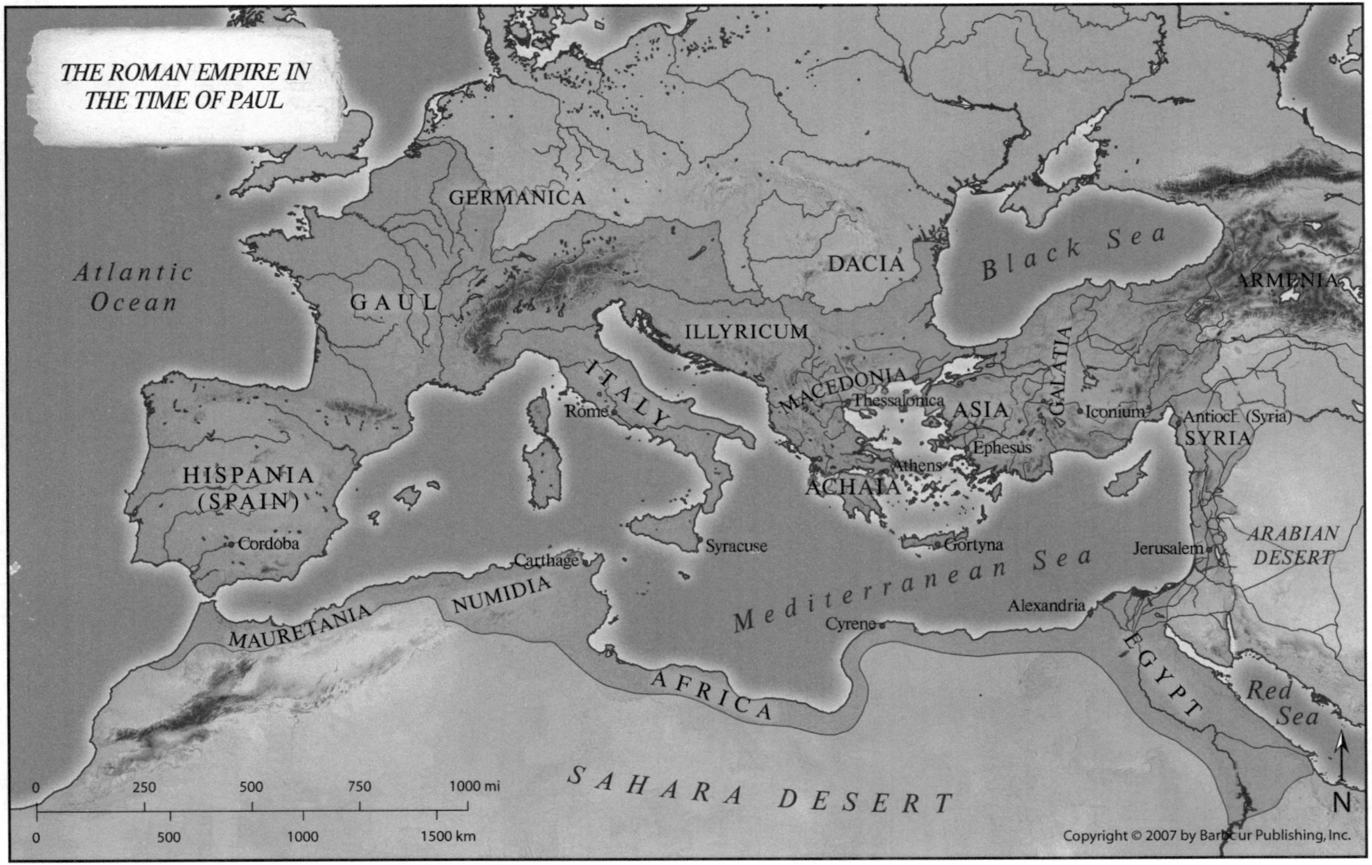
THE ROMAN EMPIRE IN THE TIME OF PAUL
Atlantic Ocean
GERMANICA
GAUL
HISPANIA (SPAIN)
Cordoba
DACIA
Black Sea
ARMENIA
ILLYRICUM
ITALY
Rome
MACEDONIA
Thessalonica
ASIA
GALATIA
Iconium
Antioch (Syria)
SYRIA
Ephesus
Athens
ACHAIA
Syracuse
Gortyna
Jerusalem
ARABIAN DESERT
Carthage
NUMIDIA
MAURETANIA
Mediterranean Sea
Alexandria
Cyrene
AFRICA
EGYPT
Red Sea
SAHARA DESERT
0 250 500 750 1000 mi
0 500 1000 1500 km
N
Copyright © 2007 by Barbour Publishing, Inc.

OUTLINE

ACTING ON WHAT WE BELIEVE	1:1–32
Salutation to the Church in Rome	1:1–7
Paul's Deep Desires	1:8–17
The Wrath of God	1:18–32
GOD HAS NO FAVORITES	2:1–29
Judgment and the Law	2:1–16
Jewish Distinctions	2:17–29
BAD NEWS AND GOOD NEWS	3:1–31
Questions and Answers	3:1–8
The Bad News	3:9–20
The Good News	3:21–26
Justification by Faith Alone	3:27–31
JUSTIFICATION BEFORE THE LAW EXISTED	4:1–25
The Precedent of Faith	4:1–8
The Principle of Faith	4:9–17
The Pattern of Faith	4:18–25
THE FRUITS OF SALVATION	5:1–21
Peace with God	5:1–11
One Trespass, One Act of Righteousness	5:12–21
DEAD TO SIN, ALIVE TO GOD	6:1–23
Choosing to Sin?	6:1–14
The Choice of Masters	6:15–23
THE LINGERING INFLUENCE OF SIN	7:1–25
A Look at the Law	7:1–13
Getting Personal	7:14–25
ASSURANCE AND REASSURANCE	8:1–39
The Spirit of Sonship	8:1–17
Groaning and Waiting	8:18–27
The Inseparable Love of God	8:28–39

SOVEREIGNTY, ELECTION, AND LOVE 9:1–33

Israel's Rejection 9:1–18
God's Sovereignty and People's Choices 9:19–33

EXPLAINING ISRAEL'S REJECTION 10:1–21

Zeal without the Desired Results 10:1–13
Connecting with God 10:14–21

GOOD NEWS FOR ISRAEL 11:1–36

Another Jewish Remnant 11:1–10
The Grafted Gentile "Branches" 11:11–24
The Salvation of Israel 11:25–36

RADICAL TRANSFORMATION 12:1–21

Transformation and Gifts of the Holy Spirit 12:1–8
Love and Other Imperatives 12:9–21

THE BELIEVER'S PLACE IN THE WORLD 13:1–14

The Believer and Governing Authorities 13:1–7
The Debt of Love 13:8–14

WEAK AND STRONG BELIEVERS 14:1–15:13

Dealing with Disputable Matters 14:1–12
Removing Stumbling Blocks 14:13–23
Accepting One Another 15:1–13

PERSONAL COMMENTS 15:14–33

Paul's Ministry to the Gentiles 15:14–22
Paul's Plans 15:23–33

PAUL'S FELLOW MINISTERS 16:1–27

A Series of Greetings 16:1–16
Final Exhortations 16:17–27

ROMANS 1:1–32

ACTING ON WHAT WE BELIEVE

Salutation to the Church in Rome	1:1–7
Paul's Deep Desires	1:8–17
The Wrath of God	1:18–32

Setting Up the Section

Paul wrote his letter to the Romans before ever visiting Rome, yet his heartfelt concern for the believers there is clearly evident throughout this Epistle. After a short salutation and brief personal comments, Paul begins what has become a masterpiece on the topic of righteousness. In this section, he emphasizes the absence of righteousness in humankind, which he will later contrast to the righteousness of God.

1:1–7

SALUTATION TO THE CHURCH IN ROME

Paul consistently begins his letters by identifying himself, as he does in this Epistle (1:1). He had been called by Jesus to be an apostle—someone sent out bearing the authority of another. After Paul's conversion, it didn't take long for him to consider himself a servant (literally, a slave) of Jesus. He had placed himself completely at Jesus' disposal, listening for and responding to his Master's commands. And since it was Jesus who was in control of Paul's life, that's whom he immediately began to write about.

Critical Observation

For the first-century readers to whom Paul was writing, the concept of servanthood was not necessarily drudgery. To be the Lord's servant was an honor. The nation of Israel as a whole was referred to this way (Isaiah 43:10) as was Moses (Joshua 14:7), King David (Psalm 89:3) and the great prophet Elijah (2 Kings 10:10).

The gospel Paul describes had not just appeared; it had been promised long ago in the Old Testament scriptures (1:2). The prophets had foretold the ministry and death of Jesus. Yet many people had missed the significance of His life and death. Among the prophecies was the prediction that the Messiah would not only be the Son of God (1:4), but also a descendant of David (1:3). He was fully human and fully divine, begotten by God, but born of a woman as well. Jesus was not just a great teacher, leader, and healer; He was declared to be the Son of God through the power of His resurrection from the dead (1:4).

In verse 5, Paul mentions two characteristics—grace and apostleship—that he attributes to himself, though he uses the editorial "we." Apostleship is not something available to all believers, but rather a unique calling. What *is* available to all believers is the calling to belong to Christ (1:6). Believers form a family of brothers and sisters who are provided for by a heavenly Father. The call to be saints (1:7) means to be set apart from the secular world. It is something not only desirable, but also achievable for all Christians.

1:8–17

PAUL'S DEEP DESIRES

After Paul's salutation, he first expresses thankfulness for the Christians in Rome (1:8). Paul is grateful that they have already developed a reputation for faithfulness. His reference to all the world means *his* world—the Roman Empire. And although their faith inspires his gratitude, he doesn't thank them, but rather he thanks God. For Paul, thankfulness and prayer are directly connected (1:9–10).

Paul is also praying for the opportunity to visit Rome (1:10). He feels a deep longing to get there (1:11). It is his desire to share his spiritual gifts with the people there, and that he and they will be mutually encouraged as they interact (1:11–12). The ministry of believers to one another is a give-and-take relationship. Paul desires encouragement just as much as the Christians in Rome need to receive it from him. His desire to visit had just been intensified by having had to wait so long (1:13).

Paul follows with three strong personal statements about his desire to preach in Rome. He is obligated, eager, and not ashamed (1:14–17).

Paul isn't ashamed of the gospel because it is the source of both the power of God (1:16) and righteousness from God (1:17). The word he uses for "believing in the gospel" (1:16) means more than simply intellectual assent. It refers to having confidence and placing one's trust in something.

1:18–32

THE WRATH OF GOD

God's wrath is not a popular subject among many people—even believers. Yet just as people are right to become angry in certain circumstances (sexual abuse of children, rape, betrayal of a confidence, widespread slaughter, etc.), so it should make sense that God, too, becomes angry in response to these and other sins. Yet God's wrath is not like human anger, which is frequently petty, controlled by emotion, and given to whims. Rather, God's wrath is always holy and just—a natural expression of His holiness and justice.

Paul lists the reason for God's wrath as the suppression of the truth. God's involvement with humankind should be evident by His creation, if nothing else (1:19-20). While immoral people have a bent toward things that are destructive, those who suppress the truth are perhaps the worst of the bunch. After knowing truth, but resisting it, these individuals grow more comfortable with immorality, or they try to justify or deny their inappropriate actions (as they have since Adam and Eve).

God is the source of truth and righteousness, so all alternatives (foolishness and idols) are shallow substitutes (1:21–23). God's wrath targets the various sins, not the people. Yet when people stubbornly refuse to repent, God will eventually allow their sinful desires to run rampant (1:24–25).

The list Paul provides of sinful desires and shameful lusts (1:26–32) is quite detailed, including homosexuality, envy, murder, deceit, gossip, arrogance, and much more. Such actions are not committed in ignorance, but in willful defiance (1:32).

God's wrath against sin is what allows Him to permit such things to occur. As He lets people go their own way, they see the results of sin all around them. Yet He is still there for all who place their faith in Him.

Paul will have more to say about God's wrath in the next sections, including what can be done to avoid it altogether.

Take It Home

Review Paul's list of sinful actions (1:24–32) and mentally list the ones for which you have been guilty. Be sure to adapt the list to modern times. For example, idolatry may no longer be defined by a statue of Baal in your den, but rather by a big-screen TV during college football season. Would you consider any of the behaviors on Paul's list to be "little" sins? Do you think their inclusion on this list allows you to continue to consider them "little"?

ROMANS 2:1–29

GOD HAS NO FAVORITES

Judgment and the Law 2:1–16
Jewish Distinctions 2:17–29

Setting Up the Section

Paul has just presented a somewhat scathing description of the behavior of humans when they reject God and live according to their sinful desires and natural lusts (1:24–32). It isn't a pretty picture. And neither is his next description of people who feel they have their lives together enough to pass judgment on others. Paul is about to point out that no one—Jew or Gentile—is righteous and law-abiding enough to avoid God's wrath on his or her own merit.

2:1–16

JUDGMENT AND THE LAW

In the previous section, Paul wrote about how people refused to recognize God based primarily on nature and His creation. Here he begins to reflect on how people also reject God by ignoring His special revelation through scripture.

It sounds as if Paul has someone in mind as he begins (2:1). But he had not yet visited Rome to meet the people in the church there. Instead, he uses a literary device (the diatribe style) in which the writer addresses an imaginary pupil or rival and makes his point by making bold statements and asking questions.

Paul's point is that anyone who passes judgment on others is actually condemning himself or herself as well (2:1). It isn't so much the judging itself that is wrong, because believers are instructed to identify and deal with behaviors that are potentially harmful to themselves or others (Matthew 18:15–17; James 5:19–20; etc.). But, like Jesus, Paul warns of the dangers of hypocrisy in evaluations of other people.

Paul may have the Jewish people in mind here because they tended to look down on Gentiles while overlooking their own shortcomings. In any case, the ones passing judgment (2:3) were doing so with stubbornness and an unrepentant heart (2:5). It is far too common to find those who cherish God's kindness, tolerance, and patience for themselves, yet are reluctant to extend it to others (2:3–4).

Even though people tend to be judgmental when they shouldn't be, God is frequently *not* judgmental when He *could* be. His mercy allows people to repent. Then, rather than being self-seeking and pursuing evil, they are able to seek righteousness instead. Rewards are in store for such people, but God's wrath awaits those who continue to reject truth (2:7–10). God will evaluate people's actions—not their religious affiliations or good intentions. He does not show favoritism (2:11–16).

The reference to "apart from the law" (2:12 NIV) refers to Gentiles. They were never given the Law of Moses, so God will not hold them accountable for it. The Jews, however, were given the Law, so God will rightly judge them by those standards. Yet even the Gentiles have been given enough insight into spiritual things that they cannot plead complete ignorance. God's law is inscribed on their hearts and present through the work of their conscience (2:15). Paul will later clarify that the law is not necessary in order for people to be righteous followers of God.

2:17–29

JEWISH DISTINCTIONS

So far, Paul has demonstrated that a person may be moral, yet still lost and in need of salvation. In essence, he has said no one is moral enough to earn salvation. Then he anticipates the next two questions: What about religious people? Won't God accept them?

His answer (2:17–29) addresses the religious pride of the Jewish people of his time. They felt sure God regarded them with special favor because of their national descent from Abraham and because they bore the mark of the Old Testament covenant: circumcision.

Paul introduces a radical thought: Being Jewish is not a matter of race at all but is, instead, a matter of conduct. He begins by citing five positive distinctions that contributed to religious pride.

First, they were proud to be called Jews (2:17). The term was derived from their ancestor, Judah. Not long after the word *Jew* first appeared in the scriptures, it became the national name the Hebrew people were proud to bear.

Second, Paul acknowledges the Jewish reliance on their scriptures (2:17). They possess God's Word, revealed and recorded. God had entrusted to them the oracles of faith.

Third, the Jews had a special relationship with God (2:17). He had made a covenant with them. He had called them to their land, delivered them from bondage in Egypt, and given them the promised land. He called them His own people. They were special to Him.

Fourth, they were strong moralists with a clearly stated set of values (2:18). They distinguished right from wrong and had a high regard for ethics even though they lived amid a culture that encouraged hedonism and self-indulgence.

And fifth, they were very capable of teaching others (2:19–20). Not only did they discern right from wrong, they could share it with others and instruct them in the ways of God.

Critical Observation

At this point in history, the Jews considered (and called) Gentiles "dogs." The Jewish air of spiritual superiority had created a great animosity and antagonism that had resulted in racial conflict. The Jews had been called by God to be a light to the Gentiles, but rather than witnessing God's love, all the Gentiles were seeing was spiritual snobbery, prejudice, and pride.

It might sound as if Paul is endorsing everything the Jewish people were doing. But all these positive traits are listed in "if" clauses. Paul wants to know *if* they had all these positive things going for them, then why aren't their hearts right before God? He boldly exposes the inconsistency between the Jews' personal claims and their actual conduct. His series of questions (2:21–23) leads to the regrettable consequence that, due to preaching what they didn't practice, the Jews were responsible for God's name being blasphemed among the Gentiles (2:24).

Paul also shows that Jewish emphasis on circumcision was misguided. The Jews had an unwarranted confidence in the rite as a sign that they were special to God. Paul points out that the outer sign was supposed to reflect an inner commitment to God. Circumcision meant nothing to those who chose to neglect God's law (2:25–26). In fact, any uncircumcised individual who kept God's Word was preferable to someone who was circumcised but ignored what God had instructed (2:27).

Demystifying Romans

In essence, Paul redefines what it means to be a Jew in Romans 2:28–29—or at the least, he clarifies the original definition. As God had made clear in the Old Testament, when evaluating the worth of a person, He looks at the heart rather than the outward appearance (1 Samuel 16:7). That is still the case (2:29).

Lest it seems Paul has come down too hard on his Jewish peers, he will continue to expand and clarify his thoughts in the following section. There is still much advantage to being Jewish, which he will soon explain.

Take It Home

The first-century Jewish community certainly isn't the only religious group to get its priorities confused. If Paul had been writing to the twenty-first-century church you're familiar with, what do you think he would have said? Do you think today's church lives up to what it proclaims? If so, in what ways? If not, what are the areas you think could be improved?

ROMANS 3:1–31

BAD NEWS AND GOOD NEWS

Questions and Answers	3:1–8
The Bad News	3:9–20
The Good News	3:21–26
Justification by Faith Alone	3:27–31

Setting Up the Section

Paul continues his evaluation of Jewish religious beliefs and points out that God's righteousness cannot be achieved merely through one's commitment to the law and the practice of circumcision. While knowledge of the scriptures and obedience to their teaching is an excellent start, more is necessary. So first, Paul lays out the bad news of the impossibility of achieving righteousness, but he then follows with the good news of God's plan that overcomes that difficulty.

3:1–8

QUESTIONS AND ANSWERS

In light of everything he had been saying in Romans 2, Paul addresses the advantage in being Jewish. Paul himself was a knowledgeable and well-trained Pharisee. And while it isn't his knowledge or Jewish status that lead to salvation (Philippians 3:3–8), he still sees much advantage in his Jewish heritage (3:1–2).

Critical Observation

As Paul lists the advantages of being Jewish, he begins with the word "first" (3:2). But he seemingly gets so caught up in explaining the importance of being entrusted with the words of God that he doesn't get to the rest of his list until much later (9:4–5).

The questions Paul asks and answers have to do with how his teaching supposedly undermined God's covenant with the Jewish people (3:1), nullified God's promises (3:3), and questioned the fairness of God's judgment (3:5). Whether these objections were literal or only anticipated by Paul, he takes them seriously and responds to them. He is saying things that are hard for his Jewish readership to hear, so he is quick to defend the character of God in each case. He affirms that God's covenant has abiding value, God is indeed faithful to His promises, and God is fair in His judgment.

People tend to take a human, rather than a godly, view of spiritual things. So already some were trying to make a case that their sin only caused God to look more glorious and righteous. And if so, then how could God judge them since they were making Him look better (3:5–8)? Paul categorically denies the validity of the argument and moves on, though he will come back to it later (6:1–14).

3:9–20

THE BAD NEWS

Scripture had already spoken on the subject of whether Jews or Gentiles had a better understanding of God's love and righteousness. Paul quotes a series of Old Testament scriptures (mostly from Psalms, with additions from Ecclesiastes and Isaiah) to show the widespread influence of sin. The grim truth is that no one is righteous. No one understands God's love and mercy. No one seeks God (3:10–11).

The rampant, self-seeking effects of sin have victimized both Jew and Gentile. People can observe the law, but it won't make them righteous (3:20). If anything, the law only makes them more aware of their lack of righteousness (3:20). So what are they to do?

3:21–26

THE GOOD NEWS

The hope for people is not in themselves or in the law, but in God. It is impossible to earn righteousness and salvation, yet God will readily provide it. This should have come as no surprise to anyone who knew the teachings of Old Testament scripture (3:21), but it took the life and death of Jesus for people to have the proper insight and understanding.

From God's perspective, there is no difference between Jew and Gentile. Both are sinful. And neither is there a difference in how they restore a proper relationship with God: He justifies them freely, out of grace, because the death of Jesus paid for their sin (3:22–24). People are still unworthy and unable to do anything to contribute to their own justification, so God does it by His grace. They don't deserve it, but He loves them and initiates action.

Demystifying Romans

Justification is a legal term. When God justifies someone, He declares the person to be righteous. He doesn't make the person righteous. Believers will continue to struggle with sin, yet can continue to be assured of God's declaration of righteousness, thanks to the sacrifice of Jesus on their behalf.

The Greek word for "redemption" (3:24) refers to obtaining something by means of purchase. It can refer to payment of a ransom. Jesus' sacrifice (His blood) was the necessary atonement to pay for the sins of humankind—past, present, and future (3:25–26).

The atoning sacrifice (3:25) is also called *propitiation.* The great importance of such a sacrifice is that it appeases God's wrath so that we don't receive the condemnation that we deserve. God doesn't just choose to overlook our sins; they are fully atoned for from this point forward. Additionally, He had left sins unpunished in the past, knowing that justice would be fulfilled when Jesus eventually paid the price for them (3:25–26).

God is just. He doesn't universally negate the consequence of human sin. Yet He also demonstrates great grace and mercy, and justifies those who have faith in Jesus (3:26).

3:27–31

JUSTIFICATION BY FAITH ALONE

After describing and explaining the concept of justification in regard to his theme of righteousness (3:21–26), Paul emphasizes that people are justified only by faith. He summarizes by returning to a question-and-answer format.

Since Paul has clarified that justification has nothing to do with people's works and is instead an act of God based on the sacrificial death of Jesus Christ on the cross, there is no opportunity for boasting. All have sinned (3:23), so anyone who wants forgiveness must have faith in Jesus. Observing the law is a positive action, yet it has nothing to do with justification (3:27).

The one God has but one way for people to come to Him. Jews and Gentiles alike are redeemed by faith. And lest anyone accuse Paul of suggesting that the law was not important or had become outdated, he boldly declares that placing faith in Jesus is exactly how the law is upheld (3:31).

Paul will continue to explain justification by faith by using an example from the law as he continues his argument in the next section.

Take It Home

Notice Paul's emphasis on faith as he presents his argument in this section. Review Romans 3:22–31, and count the number of times he mentions faith. Then read the section once more and let his words sink in. Do you think most believers today agree that faith is really all that is needed to be justified before God? Or do they tend to add other requirements?

ROMANS 4:1–25

JUSTIFICATION BEFORE THE LAW EXISTED

The Precedent of Faith	4:1–8
The Principle of Faith	4:9–17
The Pattern of Faith	4:18–25

Setting Up the Section

Paul has been writing about a most significant topic: the fact that salvation is by faith in Jesus alone, and does not require observance of the Mosaic Law or the sign of circumcision. He realizes many of his Jewish readers will find this hard to accept, so in this section he makes an argument using an example out of the greatest hero of their faith: Abraham.

4:1–8

THE PRECEDENT OF FAITH

Earlier in his letter, Paul demonstrated that righteousness (a right relationship with God) comes only through faith. He said that the Law and the Prophets all bore witness to this fact (3:21). He is writing much like a lawyer trying to make his case. And just as an attorney would want to find witnesses who were credible, respected, well known in the community, and possessing first-hand knowledge of the topic, Paul does the same. He refers his readers back to the story of Abraham.

Critical Observation

The Jewish people had a deep reverence for Abraham. His covenant with God had taken him out of Mesopotamia to the land of Canaan. His faith had resulted in the long-awaited birth of Isaac, who gave birth to Jacob (Israel). From Jacob's twelve sons came the Israelites, so the entire nation of Israel was traced back to Abraham. The Jewish people liked to consider Abraham their father (Luke 3:8). And Jesus used the title "son of Abraham" to indicate someone who was not only a descendant of the patriarch, but who also demonstrated the faith of Abraham (Luke 19:9).

Paul's question (4:1) is intriguing: How, exactly, was Abraham justified by God? The Jews had grown so accustomed to thinking that adherence to the law was the way to God's favor that they could hardly conceive of any other way. But by using Abraham—someone they all had the highest respect for—as an example Paul transports them to a time more than four centuries before God had provided the law. If Abraham could find God's favor without the law, so could other people.

Paul quotes scripture to remind his readers that it was Abraham's faith in God that was credited as righteousness (Genesis 15:6; Romans 4:3, 22). To have something credited means the recipient does nothing to earn what is received—just the opposite of working to get a paycheck (4:4–5).

Paul builds his case further by using a second example from the life and writings of David (Psalm 32:1–2; Romans 4:6–8). Since the Jewish people tended to cite the Law and the Prophets, Paul makes his point with an example from both sections of their scriptures.

4:9–17

THE PRINCIPLE OF FAITH

In addition to their intense emphasis on adherence to the Mosaic Law, the Jewish people were just as insistent about the necessity of circumcision. So again, Paul returns to the story of Abraham. Paul's first-century readers would have been more familiar with the facts of the story (4:9–10) than most modern readers, so he didn't need to spell out for them that God had declared Abraham righteous prior to the birth of Ishmael, at which time he was eighty-six (Genesis 16:16). Yet God did not instruct Abraham to receive the mark of circumcision until just prior to the birth of Isaac, when the patriarch was ninety-nine (Genesis 17:1,11; 21:5). So Abraham's circumcision had no direct connection to his righteousness before God.

There was no problem with circumcision being a sign of Jewishness, and the Jews could continue to honor Abraham as their father (4:12). But circumcision was not proof of a person's righteous standing before God, and Abraham was also to be the father of those who came to God by faith and were not circumcised (4:11).

Paul is not disparaging the Jewish devotion to law; he is simply trying to show how futile it is to attempt to use the law to justify oneself before God. The law could define and point out sin because if the law didn't exist, certain actions would still be wrong but would not be identified as such (4:15). And the law could do nothing to permanently free someone from the penalty of sin (4:14–15).

So Paul affirms that the way to God is entirely through faith that trusts Him and depends on His grace. As with Abraham, God first promises to bless people and then invites them to believe and take Him at His word. He does not say to first obey His law, or to receive a mark on their bodies, and *then* receive His blessing. Therefore, the opportunity for salvation is equally available to Jews and Gentiles (4:16–17).

Demystifying Romans

"The God who gives life to the dead and calls things that are not as though they were" (4:17 NIV) is yet another reference to Abraham. "Giving life to the dead" is an appropriate description of Sarah's pregnancy at age ninety. And God had called Abraham the father of many nations, although it didn't seem for many years that the promise would ever come true.

4:18–25

THE PATTERN OF FAITH

Just because justification is by faith alone does not mean it comes easily. Abraham waited a long twenty-five years between the time of God's initial promise to him and its fulfillment in the birth of Isaac. During that time he was hoping against all hope (4:18). His body was "as good as dead" (4:19 NIV), yet God was at work, and Abraham became the father of the Jews physically and the father of many nations spiritually.

Abraham had faith, to be sure, yet he maintained his faith through trust in God and patience. So it is for all who come to God. After making a statement of faith, it is easy to waver (4:20) when God doesn't respond exactly as we might hope or expect. Ongoing faith is necessary in order to remain convinced that God will do as He has said (4:21).

The pattern remains the same. What was true for Abraham was true for the first-century believers in Rome and is true for believers today. Faith is placed in Jesus, and because of His atoning sacrifice on behalf of humankind, God credits faith as righteousness. Believers stand justified in His sight from that point forward. We may never fully understand it, but it's just that simple.

Take It Home

What Paul teaches in this section will be more meaningful if we have a better understanding of the account of Abraham. Spend time during the next week looking over Abraham's story (Genesis 12–22). What can Abraham's life teach you about being a more faithful believer in God today?

ROMANS 5:1–21

THE FRUITS OF SALVATION

Peace with God 5:1–11
One Trespass, One Act of Righteousness 5:12–21

Setting Up the Section

So far in his letter to the Romans, Paul has been explaining the Christian doctrine of justification by faith. He began by describing our need for salvation (1:18–3:20) and followed with the way of salvation (3:21–4:25). In this section, he begins a lengthy examination of the fruits of salvation—the effect salvation has on believers.

5:1–11

PEACE WITH GOD

Paul has just shown that circumcision and adherence to the Mosaic Law are not necessary for salvation. As he begins to detail a number of benefits resulting from being justified by God, peace is first on his list (5:1)—the awareness that we are no longer God's enemies (5:10) and the confidence that comes from realizing we no longer need to struggle to gain His favor.

It is just as impossible to achieve real and lasting peace for oneself as it is to achieve one's own salvation. With the exception of Jesus, no one was ever good enough to uphold the law perfectly. So rather than working harder and harder to do something that is impossible, people can simply put their faith in God, receive His justification as a gift of grace, and experience peace as a result.

It is also due to Jesus that believers have access to God (5:2). The word *access* refers to ushering someone into the presence of royalty, or a ship sailing into the protection of a safe harbor. Paul is saying that Jesus escorts us into the very presence of God; He brings us safely to our resting place.

Critical Observation

In the tabernacle, and later in the temple, a curtain was hung to prevent anyone from entering the Most Holy Place that held the ark of the covenant, which symbolized the presence of God. Even the high priest could enter only one day each year, on the Day of Atonement (Leviticus 16). But as Jesus died on the cross, the dividing curtain was ripped in two, from top to bottom (Matthew 27:50–51). Thanks to the ultimate sacrifice of His Son, believers would no longer be denied access to God the Father.

Believers have good cause to rejoice. First, they rejoice because they have hope (5:2). The Christian's hope is not blind optimism; it is a joyful and confident expectation of blessing, based on the promises of God.

Suffering can also be seen as a source of rejoicing because of the ultimate outcome. From suffering comes perseverance, out of which grows character, out of which comes hope (5:3–4). The Greek word for "sufferings" means pressures. Note that Paul doesn't say we rejoice *because of* sufferings, but rather rejoice *in* them and *through* them. We don't merely endure the pressures of life with stoic fortitude, but rather learn to rejoice throughout *all* the happenings of life—both pleasant and challenging.

We cannot do this in our own power. The power comes from Jesus, who died for us when we were still powerless (5:6). That fact is the final proof of God's love. A parent might gladly die to save a child, or someone might willingly die on behalf of a friend or loved one. But Jesus died for people when they were sinners and still in a state of hostility toward Him (5:7–8).

One more reason for rejoicing is the fact that we have been reconciled to God (5:11). Jesus' death appeased God's wrath and began to remove the enmity that existed because of the presence of sin. The friendship bonds of former enemies are always stronger than those of merely casual acquaintances.

5:12–21

ONE TRESPASS, ONE ACT OF RIGHTEOUSNESS

Paul then goes back to the very first example of enmity with God: Adam. This is the man he refers to in verse 12. Paul had previously stated that all have sinned and fallen short of God's glory (3:23). Here he goes into more detail as to the occurrence and spread of sin.

Demystifying Romans

Adam was the gateway for sin to enter the world. By eating of the fruit specifically forbidden by God, he faced consequences including exclusion from the paradise of Eden, a sentence of both spiritual and physical death, and a curse on humankind and the earth itself (Genesis 3). From that point forward, death and sin were unavoidable aspects of the human condition.

Adam's actions were representative of all human beings. His defiance of God was the way sin entered the world and death came to all people (5:12). His one trespass led to the condemnation of everyone (5:18). No baby born today has the capacity to live a life of perfect righteousness and obedience.

A common initial response after hearing Paul's explanation about Adam's sin is a cry of unfairness. How can God hold people responsible today for something done centuries ago? But Adam had a position of authority and responsibility, representing many others. Just as a king might declare war and the whole country would feel the effects, Adam's actions affected all of humanity. In addition, most people don't *really* think they could have done any better than Adam. They see their human nature much too clearly and realize their powerlessness to overcome their propensity to sin. Even Paul will later admit his helplessness and inability to avoid sinning (7:15–25).

So the judgment that Adam received for his sin is what each person deserves for his or hers. Yet Adam is only the first of the two men Paul writes about. The second is Jesus Christ (5:15). If people think facing condemnation as a result of Adam's sin is unfair, they must realize that receiving the gift (5:15) that became available to all believers after the death of Jesus is even more undeserved. Yet God reaches out in love to offer His grace and righteousness (5:17).

Adam's one trespass condemned humanity to spiritual and physical death; Jesus' one sacrifice conquered death and the grave, providing eternal life for everyone (5:18). It is important not to take Paul's statement out of context, however. When he says that Jesus' act of righteousness brings life for all (5:18), he is saying that everyone will have the *opportunity* for salvation, not inferring that everyone will be saved. He has already clarified the importance of receiving God's offer of salvation (5:17). Not everyone will choose to do so.

Yet for those who seek restoration, forgiveness, and justification, there is no doubt that they can find it. Paul makes it clear that the weight of our combined sin, as abundant as it is, is no match for God's grace (5:20–21). For a period, sin had reigned and death was the result. But from now on, grace and righteousness reign, providing eternal life.

Take It Home

Paul's words on suffering have considerable significance for many believers today. Have you ever experienced a progression similar to what Paul describes: from suffering. . .to perseverance. . .to character. . .to hope? Can you think of any sufferings you are currently undergoing for which you can rejoice, trusting God to eventually teach you something from them?

ROMANS 6:1–23

DEAD TO SIN, ALIVE TO GOD

Choosing to Sin?	6:1–14
The Choice of Masters	6:15–23

Setting Up the Section

In Romans 5, Paul wrote about the doctrine of original sin and defined the root problem as the sinful human condition that exists within everyone. The reason Jesus died on the cross was to reverse the problem of sin that Adam brought into the world, providing the possibility of new life and a right relationship with God. Now Paul wants to ensure that his readers don't misapply what he has been saying. If the abundance of sin resulted in an even greater abundance of God's grace (5:20), why not try to sin so God can continue to lavish us with His grace?

6:1–14

CHOOSING TO SIN?

After everything he had presented up to this point, Paul asks the question he imagines some of his readers would raise (6:1). And with no hesitation he immediately answers it with an emphatic *no* (6:2). Genuine followers of Jesus Christ cannot continue to live in sin without sensing their own guilt and conviction before God and seeking repentance.

Critical Observation

The belief that God's grace freed Christians to act however they wished, even if that meant ignoring scriptural (and other) laws, was known as *antinomianism* ("against the law"). It was at the other end of the spectrum from legalism.

Three times in Romans 6:1–10, Paul uses the word "know" (6:3, 6, 9) to remind his readers that they have been joined with Christ. He is speaking of baptism, which involves a personal identification with Jesus and signifies inclusion into the covenant community of faith. Baptism also symbolizes death—burial with Christ, followed by resurrection (6:3–4). Believers die to themselves and bury the sinful nature so they can rise and live for Jesus.

If dead to sin, a person can no longer allow it to control his or her life (6:11–12). Yet it requires a conscious decision to act in harmony with, and on the basis of, one's new relationship with Christ. When tempted to revert to an old way of living, a believer must consider that person—and those behaviors—dead. That doesn't mean pretending the old nature has gone away when he knows perfectly well it hasn't. Rather, he must remember that the former identity died with Christ, so he willingly puts an end to its influence on him.

Rather than offering one's body to sin, it should be offered to God (6:13). Grace should rule a believer's life. Instead of giving in to sin and letting it rule, Paul suggests that Christians pursue a positive alternative. The entirety of one's life should be offered to God—limbs, organs, eyes, ears, hands, feet, thoughts, and dreams. It is inconceivable that Christians should go back to their old way of living by willfully persisting in sin and presuming on God's grace.

6:15–23

THE CHOICE OF MASTERS

In verse 15, Paul reaffirms his opening statement (6:1). He says that everyone is a slave to something. While those in the Western world resist the thought of being a slave and prefer the image of rugged individualism, Paul's Roman readers would be well accustomed to slavery as a way of life.

People begin their lives as slaves to sin—whether or not they realize it (6:16). And sin always leads to death (6:16, 23). But because of Jesus, people have another option. They can choose to become slaves to God, where they discover that obedience leads to righteousness. It's giving up one master for another, but the swap makes all the difference in the world (6:17).

Demystifying Romans

From an American viewpoint, the very word *slavery* brings to mind racism, forced subjection, and harsh treatment. When Rome conquered other nations, their prisoners could face similar treatment. But the Romans also had volunteer slavery. For example, people in extreme poverty could offer themselves as slaves to someone in exchange for food and housing. During the first century, the Roman Empire had as many as six million slaves, so Paul's imagery of being enslaved would have been quite clear to his readers. He admitted later, though, that slavery wasn't the perfect analogy to symbolize one's relationship with God (6:19).

Although many people believe the myth, they are not master of their own fate or captain of their own ship. Everyone is a slave to something, whether to sin or to God. Neither option is static. Both are dynamic. But while one is steadily deteriorating into ever-increasing wickedness, the other steadily progresses toward holiness (6:19).

The decision to follow Jesus breaks the bondage of sin and places the person on the path toward righteousness. But that doesn't mean everything will be easy and automatic from that point onward. Slaves—even slaves to righteousness—have to make decisions every day about attitudes, actions, and motivations regarding their service. Believers are no longer slaves to the law, yet their new commitment to righteousness and holiness should inspire them to greater acts of love, mercy, and forgiveness.

One of the best ways to keep a proper mind-set is to look back from time to time and remember the quality of life when sin was still master (6:20–22). Everyone recalls things they aren't proud of, which should inspire greater motivation to pursue obedience and godly living.

This passage concludes with one of the great verses in all the New Testament (6:23). In the Greek language, *wages* referred to a soldier's regular pay, something that was due him, while *gift* was something provided out of kindness and grace. Wages were what a person deserved; a gift was an undeserved prize. For those who allow sin to be master, their wages will be death. But for those who are willing to change masters and become slaves to God, the reward is eternal life.

Take It Home

Even among people who choose to live for God, slavery to sin can continue to be a problem. The church has recognized this in recent years and has provided help for those struggling with addictions such as drugs or alcohol. Other people struggle with smoking, pornography, sexual promiscuity, and other things that continue to interfere with their commitment to righteousness and holiness. Do you struggle with any old problems that you would like to eliminate from your life completely, yet haven't been able to overcome? If so, spend some time this week formulating a plan for how you might become less enslaved to the habit in the weeks to come.

ROMANS 7:1–25

THE LINGERING INFLUENCE OF SIN

A Look at the Law 7:1–13
Getting Personal 7:14–25

Setting Up the Section

In anticipation of a personal visit to Rome, Paul is writing to the Roman believers. He has been outlining the message of the gospel, and has just taught that every person has a master. People are either slaves to sin or slaves to righteousness. In this section, he will continue with that theme as he takes up the subject of God's law and its purpose for the Christian.

7:1–13

A LOOK AT THE LAW

Each of the first thirteen verses of Romans 7 makes a reference to "law," "commandment," or "written code." Paul addresses this question: If a person can't find a right relationship with God by keeping the law and doing all God expects, then what is the place of the Old Testament law in the Christian life?

To answer the question, he uses the metaphor of marriage (7:1–6). According to Jewish law, a woman could not divorce her husband. The only way she would be free to marry another man would be if the first husband died. Otherwise, she would be considered an adulteress.

Paul uses this comparison to symbolize the Christian and the law. A believer "dies" to his or her old ways and is reborn without the same obligation to the law. The new believer is dead to both sin (6:2) *and* the law (7:4), and is united with Christ (7:1–6).

It's not that the law was bad (7:7). Just the opposite. The law was holy (7:12) and spiritual (7:14). While it was impossible to follow the law perfectly and achieve one's own salvation, the law served a positive purpose of exposing and identifying sin (7:7–8).

Demystifying Romans

Beginning in verse 7, and continuing through the rest of Romans 7, Paul changes the tense of his writing. He had been writing primarily in third person, switching occasionally to second person or first-person plural. But for this stretch of writing, he shifts to first-person singular, describing his own personal experience—and exposing his own weaknesses and spiritual struggle.

Paul's use of the phrase, "apart from law" (7:9 NIV), was probably his way of saying, "Before I realized what the law meant." Like the Pharisees who lived unaware of what the law really meant, Paul was "alive" for a while. But after coming to see what the law really said, he was confronted with his sin (7:10–13).

7:14–25

GETTING PERSONAL

The struggle that Paul describes in this section is one that each believer wrestles with as well. The more mature the believer, the more aware of sin he or she becomes. The more progress the person makes toward sanctification, the more he or she will abhor sinfulness and see it for what it is.

What Paul expresses is the inner struggle, the personal civil war that all Christians experience. He is refreshingly honest in this passage as he speaks of his thoughts and feelings.

He admits to feeling unspiritual (7:14). Although a believer no longer has the status of a slave to sin (6:6–7), he or she will continue to struggle with the reality of residual sinful thoughts and behaviors. Paul also admits to being confused (7:15). He can't understand why he does some of the things he does. He does things he doesn't want to do, and doesn't get around to doing the good things he intends to do. Inwardly, God's Word gives him great joy, but when it comes to physically doing the right things, he frequently comes up short (7:15–23).

Critical Observation

Not everyone agrees that Paul is speaking of his own experience in this passage. Some believe Paul is describing a nonbeliever because of some of the terms he uses ("slave" [7:14], "wretched" [7:24], etc.). And they say it's a pretty dismal viewpoint if he is describing a Christian experience. Other people argue that the passage refers to an immature believer who has made a Christian commitment, yet continues to live according to fleshly rather than spiritual desires. Still others believe Paul was writing autobiographically about his own internal struggle to live the Christian life.

The word translated "wretched" could also be interpreted "miserable" or "unhappy" (7:24). There are times when all believers grow weary of their daily struggles and just want to give up. Surely, with all of Paul's exceptional trials, he must have felt the same way at times. Related to this is a sense of hopelessness (7:18, 24). It is one of those sinking feelings where he needs help just to get up and get going again. At times he feels like a prisoner (7:23) in bondage with no escape. Confined. Trapped. Yet at the same time, it is like he is engaged in a battle (7:21–23). Good and evil are battling it out within him, creating an inner conflict.

And finally, Paul confesses to feeling condemned (7:24). He realizes he deserves to have God's judgment of death pronounced on his sins. If he were in a court of law, he would plead guilty to the charges.

What a range of thoughts and feelings, and what an honest expression of emotion. Yet few Christians can say they haven't had similar feelings.

Thankfully, that isn't the end of Paul's story. He concludes the passage with an optimistic message of hope (7:25). Who will rescue him from the dire state in which he finds himself (7:24)? Jesus Christ the Lord.

The key to understanding Paul's complete turnaround is to comprehend the already-and-not-yet nature of the kingdom of God. Jesus inaugurated His kingdom at His first coming, but will not consummate it until His second. Believers who live in between will experience the power of His coming in some measure, but not in full. Therefore, it is possible to be assured of victory in Christ, yet still feel defeated from time to time.

Paul's confident conclusion sets up the magnificent and much-quoted chapter that follows. In Romans 8, Paul's outlook improves considerably.

Take It Home

Everyone goes through periods of spiritual struggle similar to those Paul describes. And the sooner such feelings are admitted and dealt with, the sooner the person is likely to get back on track and move forward again. Do you have someone (or a small group of people) with whom you can be honest when your spiritual life seems derailed for a period of time? Rather than just keep going through the motions as if everything is fine, can you open up with someone the way Paul did in this section? If not, perhaps you might consider finding a trustworthy friend to confide in or forming a small group whose members will be willing to share openly among one another.

ROMANS 8:1–39

ASSURANCE AND REASSURANCE

The Spirit of Sonship	8:1–17
Groaning and Waiting	8:18–27
The Inseparable Love of God	8:28–39

Setting Up the Section

Paul's Epistle to the Romans has been an ongoing defense of justification by faith alone. He has shown that righteousness is the result of one's relationship with God through faith, and not due to adherence to the Mosaic Law, circumcision, or any other external standard. So if believers are not to rely so heavily on such things, what *should* they rely on? Paul's answer in this passage has become one of the most beloved portions of scripture.

8:1–17

THE SPIRIT OF SONSHIP

It may seem that Romans 8 follows naturally after Paul's stark confession of Romans 7:14–25. But the word "therefore" (8:1) actually picks up the thoughts Paul laid out in Romans 3, with chapters 4–7 being somewhat parenthetical. Romans 3:20 described the results of condemnation. Here Paul begins to expound on the results of *no* condemnation.

The Mosaic Law had been powerless to provide a righteous standing before God (8:3). It remains a guide for how believers should live (8:4), yet Paul introduces a new "law"—the law of the Spirit of life (8:2). The Old Testament law could define and prohibit sin, but could never eliminate it. The human nature of the people trying to follow the law could never empower them to live up to its standards (8:3–4).

So Paul begins to contrast the human, sinful nature with that of a person controlled by the Holy Spirit (8:5–17). The difference begins in the person's thoughts and desires. If the sinful nature is in control, the person doesn't want to submit to God—and would be unable to even if the desire was there (8:6–8). But Paul is writing to believers in Rome, so he can assure them that they are under the control of the Holy Spirit. He indicates in this passage that the ministries of Jesus and the Holy Spirit are closely related (8:9–11).

Yet the difference is much more personal than merely determining who is in control. As long as people cling to selfish, natural desires and exclude God, they are unable to experience the relationship that He intends and desires for them. But those who respond to the Spirit of God are led into an intimate relationship—one of Father and child.

Jesus had addressed God as *Abba* ("Father") in His prayers (Mark 14:36). Prior to that, no Jewish person would have addressed God with such a familiar term. Yet here Paul extends the privilege to all believers. The presence of the Holy Spirit is proof that believers are children of God (8:15–16).

Critical Observation

Abba was an Aramaic word for "father." It denoted love and affection, and was the most tender and intimate of the synonyms for father that Paul could have chosen.

"Children" isn't just a title, but a reality. Jesus, as God's Son, is entitled to everything that is the Father's. And as God's *other* children—adopted ones—believers are coheirs with Jesus. They experience similar sufferings, yes, but they also share in the eternal rewards (8:17). This possibility of such a close relationship with God begins to reveal why it's so important not to be misled by legalistic or antinomian doctrines. Paul is advocating the best possible option for followers of God, though he has barely begun.

8:18–27

GROANING AND WAITING

Paul was no stranger to suffering, and in this section he explains some of his reasoning. For one thing, it is a matter of return on investment. The sufferings he experienced would be insignificant in light of the glory that would come later (8:18). In addition, creation itself is suffering. Just as Adam, Eve, and the serpent were recipients of the curse after the fall (Genesis 3:14–19), so was the earth. Rather than remaining the perfect paradise that God intended, creation itself is now in bondage, groaning like a woman in labor to produce fruit and be productive (8:19–22).

Believers groan as well, waiting for the time when God will redeem them fully. God's plan is in action. The agreement has been made. The initial stages have begun of God's adoption of believers and their redemption. Yet the full significance won't be realized until resurrection. So the anticipation and assurance of this reality is the believer's hope in the meantime (8:23–25).

Demystifying Romans

Firstfruits was an offering made when the crops started coming in (Exodus 23:19; Leviticus 23:9–14; Deuteronomy 26:1–11). The first of the produce was offered to God in thanksgiving and anticipation of the rest. The same symbolism is applied to the Holy Spirit in Romans 8:23. The appearance of the Holy Spirit in the life of a believer is representative of everything else God will later bring to fruition.

The presence of the Holy Spirit in the life of the believer is first of all the signs that God has begun His work. In addition, the Spirit acts on behalf of the believer, interceding to bring God and the believer closer together (8:26–27).

8:28–39

THE INSEPARABLE LOVE OF GOD

The world can be an evil place at times, yet God works in all things for good (8:28). This is not to suggest that God creates sin or evil; He works in spite of them. When tragedy befalls a believer, the church should not infer that God was responsible for the pain and confusion. Yet He can see His children through such times and teach them valuable lessons about His love and faithfulness.

The meaning of the word "predestined" (8:29) is debated. (Predestination is also called "election," with an emphasis on being specially selected.) Most agree that God did not create a list of people prior to creation that He had chosen for salvation. Rather, *predestination* means that God has predetermined what He will do for those who call on His name (Ephesians 1:4–6). God's foreknowledge is more than simply knowing ahead of time what will happen. It has an added element of regarding with favor.

Justification (being declared righteous) is a matter of how God sees believers now. Throughout the Christian life, God's people should become progressively more Christlike. Similarly, they are also considered glorified (8:30). Ultimately, that means that their human bodies will be transformed into a state like Jesus' glorious body (Philippians 3:20–21). And even though that hasn't happened yet, the promise stands that it will, so believers are already deemed glorified. Therefore, there is good reason for believers to hold fast to their faith (8:31–39).

God's people will suffer, just as Jesus did. That should come as no surprise. Yet God is with them throughout every painful ordeal. The list of potential threats is so detailed that it encompasses all possibilities—trouble, hardship, persecution, famine, nakedness, danger, sword, angels, demons, present, future, powers, height, depth, and anything in all creation (8:39). God will overcome any problem and prove that His love for His people is too strong to be diminished. And since it is God who has justified, sanctified, and glorified believers, there is really very little for them to ever be worried about.

Take It Home

When was the last time you went through a difficult situation and may have questioned God's love? After reading this passage of Romans, do you think God's love for you was ever in jeopardy? When similar hard times arise in the future, what might you do differently?

ROMANS 9:1–33

SOVEREIGNTY, ELECTION, AND LOVE

Israel's Rejection 9:1–18
God's Sovereignty and People's Choices 9:19–33

Setting Up the Section

Paul has been writing about God's sovereignty over death (Romans 5), over sin (Romans 6–7), and over struggles, persecution, and hardship (Romans 8). In this section, he turns his attention to God's sovereignty in regard to salvation. The Jews had always felt they were God's chosen people. Now that the church was growing into an institution, people were asking how God could be faithful to His promises if the majority of His chosen people—the Jews—were failing to respond to the gospel. Paul answers that question here by using familiar stories to remind them of God's sovereign choices throughout their history.

9:1–18

ISRAEL'S REJECTION

The doctrine of predestination (election) is one that many people avoid, whether consciously or not. But it is closely tied to the doctrine of God's sovereignty. Indeed, believers rejoice in God's sovereignty over sin, struggles, and eventual death. Yet many hesitate to accept His sovereignty in the category of salvation.

Paul begins each of the next three chapters of Romans (9, 10, and 11) with a personal statement that identifies himself with the people of Israel and expresses his profound concern for them. He not only acknowledges their unbelief, but he also agonizes over them with sorrow, anguish, and prayer. In fact, he expresses a willingness to sacrifice his own relationship with Christ if that could somehow bring his peers into the fold instead. But the sentiment was moot; Paul had just completed his emphatic proclamation that *nothing* can separate a believer from the love of God (8:38–39).

Still, how could the people of Israel, with their unique privileges and blessings, reject their own Messiah? If God is sovereign, how could the failure of Israel be explained, and why did it seem that God's promises had come up short?

God was true to His promises. He had never forsaken Israel, and Paul mentions eight specific privileges (9:4–5) the people of Israel had been given:

1) They were the children of God, adopted as His own sons and daughters.
2) They had seen the divine glory of God in the wilderness and had beheld the splendor of His presence.
3) The covenants of God had been given to their ancestors and passed down to them.
4) They prized the Old Testament law as the moral code that outlined what God expected of His people.
5) They had the temple, where they could worship and encounter the presence of God.

6) They had seen God's faithfulness with their patriarchs—Abraham, Isaac, and Jacob.
7) They had provided the human bloodline for Jesus, who was providing salvation for the world.
8) They had been given Christ Himself, whose ministry was first to the Jews and then to the Gentiles (1:16; 2:9–10).

Yet the majority of the Jewish people had forsaken God. Their rejection of Jesus was not due to the failure of God's Word and His promise (9:6). It was not because of the absence of benefits and blessing by God. Rather, it was due to their unbelief.

Paul turns to their history to show how God's sovereignty has been demonstrated throughout the centuries. He points out that Abraham's older child was actually Ishmael, yet God had proclaimed that the promise to Abraham would be fulfilled through Isaac (9:7–9), resulting in more of a spiritual relationship than a physical one. Not long afterward, God had chosen to work through Jacob, the younger twin, rather than Esau. And God's decree came even before the birth of the twins (Genesis 25:23), so His decision wasn't based on anything Esau did wrong or that Jacob did right (9:10–13).

Demystifying Romans

The hate of God (9:13) is not hatred as we define it, and it is not directed toward an individual. What Paul has written about the unconditional love of God still holds true. In essence, the statement "Jacob I loved, but Esau I hated" (9:13 NIV) means that God had chosen (loved) the Israelites and had rejected (hated) the Edomites—the descendants of Esau. In this case, human choice had reinforced God's sovereignty—God first chose Jacob over Esau, but Esau had willingly traded away the rights that came with being the older son (Genesis 25:27–34).

The third example Paul uses from Israel's history is that of Pharaoh. It's a sobering reminder that, without God's mercy, no one can escape the penalty of sin and find new life in God. The hardening of Pharaoh's heart that eventually led to Israel's exodus from Egypt was part of God's sovereign plan (9:17–18).

9:19–33

GOD'S SOVEREIGNTY AND PEOPLE'S CHOICES

Paul anticipates a challenge to what he has been saying. It may seem unfair, if God is sovereign, that He still holds us accountable for our choices. Paul isn't putting down honest questions (9:20), because this is a most difficult topic. Rather, he refers to those who want to quarrel with God. That is not our right, any more than a piece of clay has a right to take issue with the potter (9:21). Paul wants his readers to remember who they are and who God is.

Critical Observation

During Israel's exodus from Egypt (Exodus 7–14), Pharaoh's hardness of heart is referred to fifteen times. In some instances it is said that Pharaoh hardened his heart; in other places we read that God hardened Pharaoh's heart. Was God solely responsible for Pharaoh's refusal to cooperate with Moses (9:18)? Pharaoh had numerous opportunities to respond to God and declined each time. The fault was not with God, but with Pharaoh. Yet God used Pharaoh's stubbornness to bless Israel.

The sovereignty of God in regard to whom He would and would not choose had been prophesied (9:22–29). It had been foretold that God would call those who were not His people (9:25). Even when the nation of Israel rejected Him, He would deliver a remnant who would be saved (9:27). It was only God's mercy that kept Israel from being destroyed as completely as Sodom and Gomorrah (9:29).

The obtaining of salvation by the Jews and Gentiles had been much like the race between the tortoise and the hare. The Jews had zealously pursued a legalistic path to God's favor, yet had never accomplished what they hoped. The Gentiles, on the other hand, hadn't been looking for righteousness at all but had found it through faith in Jesus (9:30–33). The Israelites needed to quit depending on their own efforts and put their faith in God instead.

The Bible teaches two truths about election (predestination): (1) God is sovereign, and (2) people are responsible for their choices. Somehow both teachings are true, and God is certain to reward the believer's struggle to integrate and make sense of them.

Take It Home

How does Paul's outlook on the doctrine of election fit with your own spiritual background? How would you define God's sovereignty for a young child who asked you what it meant?
How would you explain it to a middle school Sunday school class? What questions would you anticipate in response?

ROMANS 10:1–21

EXPLAINING ISRAEL'S REJECTION

Zeal without the Desired Results	10:1–13
Connecting with God	10:14–21

Setting Up the Section

Paul has had much to say about justification by faith so far in Romans. At the end of chapter 9, he had just returned to his running theme of righteousness. As he continues in this passage, he moves from the past to the present and from the aspect of God's sovereignty to individual accountability.

10:1–13

ZEAL WITHOUT THE DESIRED RESULTS

Paul is pained to note how hard many of his fellow Jews are working to be righteous and please God when they don't realize that the only source of righteousness is God. Paul knows personally what it is like to be zealous but misdirected (10:1–2). Their hard work had made them self-righteous, and when presented with the righteousness that is attainable only through Jesus, they are too proud to consider it (10:3–4). Jesus put an end to the law (10:4)—the Messiah to whom all the law and Prophets had pointed. And there were other portions of the law that the Jewish people hadn't understood.

Demystifying Romans

In Romans 10:5–21, Paul makes eleven different direct references to the Hebrew scriptures to support what he is saying. He quotes Leviticus 18:5 (10:5), Deuteronomy 30:12–13 (10:6–7), Deuteronomy 30:14 (10:8), Isaiah 28:16 (10:11), Joel 2:32 (10:13), Isaiah 52:7 (10:15), Isaiah 53:1 (10:16), Psalm 19:4 (10:18), Deuteronomy 32:21 (10:19), Isaiah 65:1 (10:20), and Isaiah 65:2 (10:21).

For example, Moses had taught that justification came by faith, and had emphasized obedience out of love rather than legalistic commitment (Deuteronomy 30:6–10). He had also pointed out the nearness of God's law (Deuteronomy 30:11–14). The people don't have to go out of their way to receive insight from God; He has placed it in their mouths and hearts. Similarly, no one has to complete any grand acts or make a special effort to receive Jesus (the perfect fulfillment of the law). It is foolish pride for people to think that they can do anything to help bring the Messiah down from heaven or to raise Him from the dead. Those actions were completely the work of God (10:6–8).

The Word of God is still essential to their righteousness. However, it is not the written law that will justify them, but the Word that became flesh. And God still desires for that Word to be in their mouths and hearts. Salvation comes through believing in their hearts that God has raised Jesus from the dead and confessing with their mouths that He is Lord (10:9–10).

Paul once again quotes Isaiah 28:16 to show that salvation is by faith (9:33; 10:11). And because this was true, salvation is available to anyone and everyone (Joel 2:32; Romans 10:12–13). Much of the zeal in striving to uphold the law was wasted effort. The Jewish people were complicating something that should have been very simple. They were trying to do something God had already done for them.

10:14–21

CONNECTING WITH GOD

Salvation is a matter of hearing the truth of the gospel and responding, so Paul credits those who were involved with spreading the message. The word for "preach" (10:15) means "to proclaim." Paul isn't referring to the position of church pastor, but to *anyone* who has been sent from God to share the good news. According to the words of Jesus, that would include all believers (Matthew 28:19–20; John 20:21).

Critical Observation

"The feet of those who bring good news" (Isaiah 52:7; Romans 10:15 NIV) was a general reference to the messengers who would come running after a battle or other big event to let the general population know the outcome. More specifically, it had come to refer to the announcement that Israel's exile in Babylon had ended, and the people were returning to Jerusalem. Paul adopted the same saying to apply to those who proclaimed the end of the bondage of sin, thanks to the death and resurrection of Jesus Christ.

The news had gone out through faithful messengers and the truth had been proclaimed. Yet that wasn't enough. The Jewish people needed to respond to what they had heard by calling on Jesus (10:14–15).

But what if Israel hadn't heard the message from God? Paul asks that very question (10:18) and then answers it by quoting from Psalm 19. The psalm describes how God reveals Himself both through what He has created (Psalm 19:1–6) and what He has provided in His written Word (Psalm 19:7–11). The Israelites had heard God's message, but they hadn't responded.

Paul anticipates their next excuse: Maybe they didn't understand what God was trying to tell them. He uses two more Old Testament references to show that the Gentiles (a nation without understanding [Romans 10:19]) had figured it out. The Jews believed themselves to be far superior to the Gentiles, and must have felt a bit insulted at Paul's insinuation.

But neither Paul nor God had given up on the Jewish people, even though they still hadn't responded to the message of the love of God. Paul refers back to the Old Testament one more time to remind his readers of God's ongoing patience (Isaiah 65:2; Romans 10:21). Many of the first-century Jewish people were just as disobedient as their Old Testament counterparts. Yet God perpetually held out His hands to them, ready to receive and embrace them whenever they were willing to respond to what they knew.

Take It Home

Based on Paul's (and Isaiah's) statement in Romans 10:15, do you think your feet would be considered beautiful? Think back to your own spiritual journey and recall the people who contributed to your knowledge of Jesus. Then consider if you are contributing to the spiritual growth of anyone today. If so, reflect on what more you might be able to do for that person. If not, how might you get started in opening up about your own spiritual relationship for the benefit of someone else?

ROMANS 11:1–36

GOOD NEWS FOR ISRAEL

Another Jewish Remnant	11:1–10
The Grafted Gentile "Branches"	11:11–24
The Salvation of Israel	11:25–36

Setting Up the Section

In Paul's ongoing treatise on righteousness and justification by faith alone, he has just finished a rather frank commentary explaining that many of the Jewish people had rejected God and missed the significance of Jesus, the Messiah. Even the Gentiles had better spiritual insight. Now Paul asks a different question: Since the Jews had opted to seek self-righteousness rather than God's justification, had God given up on them?

11:1–10

ANOTHER JEWISH REMNANT

Paul's opening question (11:1) is actually a continuation of the writing style he had been using (10:14, 18, 19). It might appear he was saying that because the Jews had rejected Jesus, God was rejecting the Jews. But that isn't Paul's message at all, as he immediately makes clear.

Paul still identifies strongly with the Jewish people, and his own story is proof that God had not deserted the Jews in favor of the Gentiles (11:1–2). In addition, Paul reminds his readers of the story of Elijah, who had served God during a time when many of the Israelites had turned to idols rather than remaining faithful to the Lord. Even then, God had a remnant of faithful people—seven thousand as a matter of fact (11:2–4; see 1 Kings 19:9–18)!

Paul is equally convinced of another remnant of faithful Jewish believers during his time (the elect [11:7]). The existence of such a remnant is evidence of the grace of God (11:5–6).

Paul again returns to Hebrew scripture to cite examples from Jewish history. Both Moses (Deuteronomy 29:4) and David (Psalm 69:22–23) had written about their people being unable to see what God was doing in their midst. Yet the nation had endured because of a remnant of those faithful to God (11:7–10). The same was true for the first-century Jewish nation.

11:11–24

THE GRAFTED GENTILE "BRANCHES"

Paul goes on to say that the rejection of the Jews was partial, was passing, and had a purpose. A remnant continued to believe, the rejection wouldn't last forever, and some good would actually come from it.

Israel's transgression allowed the gospel to be delivered to the Gentiles. And closely related to that fact, a sense of jealousy developed among the people of Israel (11:11–12). When the Jewish people saw God's acceptance of the Gentiles, many would repent and come to God as well. Indeed, Paul's use of the words "fullness" (11:12 NIV) and "acceptance" (11:15 NIV) indicate a positive future for Israel.

In the meantime, the Gentiles have no right to gloat. Their gospel has Jewish roots and a Jewish Savior. Thanks to God's grace, the Gentiles are grafted into God's olive tree (11:17–18), and they are completely supported by the root.

The Jewish nation should not see the inclusion of the Gentiles as a threat. Just the opposite. If God could make a wild branch become productive, it would be no trouble at all for Him to restore some of the natural branches. All the Jews needed to do was show the same degree of repentance and faith as the Gentiles, and they would quickly be reattached to their source of growth and productivity (11:22–24). Ultimately, the restoration of a Jewish person was an easier process than the call of a Gentile to faith, because the knowledgeable Jew understood the need for forgiveness.

Critical Observation

Note that Paul is careful not to say that one day all unbelieving Jews will be saved and grafted back in. What he says is that the grafting can take place *if* they do not persist in unbelief. The way of salvation is open to both Jews and Gentiles in the death and resurrection of Jesus Christ, but it is up to each individual to choose or reject it.

11:25–36

THE SALVATION OF ISRAEL

Paul is going to shift emphasis in Romans 12, so in wrapping up this section he makes a number of important observations. First, he shows that God's sovereignty is undeniable. Even while Israel was rejecting Him, God was opening the doors of salvation to the Gentiles (11:25). And the long-range results of this would be the salvation of Israel (11:26–27).

Demystifying Romans

What did Paul mean that "all Israel" would be saved (11:26)? Some people believe that all Jews are God's chosen people and will be saved regardless of their response to Jesus, but that opinion disregards the death of Christ and the need for repentance in order to receive salvation. Some interpret the phrase to refer to the "elect," including both Jews and Gentiles, but such an outlook doesn't seem to fit the theme of Paul's writing, which focuses on the rejection of Jesus by the Jews. Another interpretation is that at Jesus' return, a large number of Jewish people will believe and come to faith. The word *all* should not be understood in an absolute sense meaning "without exception," but would rather refer to Israel as a whole.

Second, Paul demonstrates that God's mercy is unfathomable (11:30–32). His love and mercy overflowed to the Gentiles, allowing them access to His kingdom. And He used the inclusion of the Gentiles to get the attention of the Jews. God continues to show His mercy, even after His people reject Him and harden their hearts to His love.

Finally, Paul shows that God's mind is unsearchable (11:33–36). At this point it seems Paul stops preaching and starts worshiping. He notes that people, as finite creatures, are incapable of fully comprehending the infinite God. He had previously spoken of a mystery (11:25), and much of what we believe must simply be taken on faith. Yet that which we cannot grasp with our minds, we can entrust to God with all our hearts.

From this point onward, Paul is going to be less theological and a lot more practical. Now that he has explained how God has declared believers righteous, he is going to provide several ways that such a status should affect their lives.

Take It Home

The doxology that ends this part of Paul's letter is a reminder that when we think about God and His incredible love and mercy, our heartfelt response should be one of praise. Theology and worship should go hand in hand. Worship without sound theology is likely to degenerate into sentimentality or idolatry; theology without worship is dead, dull, and boring. Which aspect is most in need of attention in your own life—your theology or your worship? What can you do this week to bring the two into a better balance?

ROMANS 12:1–21

RADICAL TRANSFORMATION

Transformation and Gifts of the Holy Spirit 12:1-8
Love and Other Imperatives 12:9-21

Setting Up the Section

For eleven chapters in Romans Paul has written at length about the mercy of God. When people were lost in their sin and enemies of God, He opened a way of salvation to them through the gift of His Son. Christ died on the cross, taking their place and paying the penalty for the sins of their lives. It is in light of this awesome mercy of God that Paul now urges his readers to live a life worthy of their calling in Christ Jesus.

12:1–8

TRANSFORMATION AND GIFTS OF THE HOLY SPIRIT

Therefore is usually a significant word in scripture to indicate something important is about to be said. It is particularly true in this case (12:1). Everything Paul has written so far in his Epistle is the basis for what comes next. His focus has been on what God has done for humankind; now he explains what believers can and should do in response.

When Paul refers to believers offering themselves as a worship act, he makes a reference to the Jewish sacrificial system. Part of Jewish worship was the sacrificing of an animal, often on an altar. When believers lay their own wills aside and live their lives for the purpose of pleasing and serving God, they become a living sacrifice. Their lives, lived in dedication to the will of God, become acts of worship (12:2).

What God offers His people is not mere improvement, but radical transformation (12:2). It is not simply an offer to make good people a little better, smoothing out the rough edges of their basically pure hearts. It is rather a matter of transforming sinners into saints, of allowing them to exchange their filthy rags of sin for the royal robes of righteousness in Christ. Holy living involves the body, mind, and spirit.

As believers are transformed and begin to comprehend God's will, they see that God designed the church so its members are interdependent on one another. No one has all the available gifts of the Holy Spirit, so it is incumbent that each person identifies his or her gift(s) to use on behalf of the others in the church. Paul uses the metaphor of a human body to describe how individual parts should work together and operate as a unified whole.

Critical Observation

This passage (12:6–8) is just one of Paul's lists of spiritual gifts. Others are found in 1 Corinthians 12:7–11, 28–31 and Ephesians 4:11–13. The lists vary a bit, suggesting that none is intended to be complete. Paul also uses the analogy of the human body in connection with spiritual gifts in other places (1 Corinthians 12:12–26; Ephesians 4:15–16).

Paul identifies seven of the gifts of the Holy Spirit in this passage. When people think of prophecy (12:6), many immediately think of foretelling the future. While that is one aspect of the gift, a wider sense includes the revelation of the Holy Spirit to a believer, concerning the will of God. For example, when an important decision needs to be made, the gift of prophecy might allow someone to know for certain what God wants His church to do.

The gift of service, or helps (12:7), is the ability to assist and support others inside and outside the family of God in practical ways. The believer with this gift is motivated to faithfully demonstrate Christ's love by meeting practical needs and giving assistance. The Greek word for service (*diakonia*) is the root for our word *deacon*.

Teaching (12:7) is the ability to clearly explain what God has revealed. Many people are willing and even eager to teach, yet it is usually evident which have been given the *gift* of teaching.

Encouragement (12:8) is also a spiritual gift. All believers are commanded to encourage one another (1 Thessalonians 5:11), but certain people stand out. (One example in the early church was Barnabas, whose nickname meant "Son of Encouragement" [Acts 4:36].)

The gift of giving (12:8) is the ability to be sensitive and to provide for the needs of others with great joy and generosity. All believers are encouraged to give consistently to the Lord's work, but the person with the gift of giving has an inner, God-given drive to provide for those with needs.

Leadership (12:8) involves being visionary, goal oriented, and decisive.

Mercy (12:8) is yet another characteristic expected of all believers, yet is endowed to certain people in a special way. It involves the capacity to be compassionate and empathize with others' needs, pains, heartaches, disappointments, and sorrows. Mercy can also include being an agent of healing and restoration.

12:9–21

LOVE AND OTHER IMPERATIVES

In the rest of this section, Paul compresses a number of instructions for practical Christian living. Nowhere else in his writing is a more comprehensive list of concise commands.

The overriding theme is the importance of love, and how genuine love affects the believer's behavior. Love is the foundation for many traits: humility (12:10), a spiritual zeal for service (12:11), patience (12:12), generosity (12:13), and other desired characteristics.

Certainly, the commitment to express love will be met with certain obstacles, among them persecution (12:14), mourning (12:15), and pride (12:16). Paul repeats Jesus' teaching about persecution and nonretaliation (Matthew 5:44; Romans 12:14). It takes a great commitment to love for one to pray for his or her persecutors (12:14, 17).

Paul stresses the importance of being a peacemaker, yet does not insist on peace at any price. Note his two conditions (12:18) that promote peace, though don't guarantee it.

Demystifying Romans

The reference to heaping burning coals on another's head (12:20) gives rise to various interpretations. Some say the phrase refers to an ancient custom. If a fire went out in someone's home, he or she might go to a neighbor to borrow coals, carried in a pan on the head. Transportation was clumsy and might result in some discomfort for the person, yet the coals were proof of another's love. Similarly, receiving good for evil feels so awkward it may have a lasting effect on the recipient. A more common understanding of the phrase, however, interprets the burning coals as symbols of God's judgment. If one's enemy continues to create trouble, and the persecuted only returns good for evil, he or she can be assured that God will mete out appropriate punishment (coals of fire [2 Samuel 22:9; Psalm 11:6; etc.]) in His own time.

One key to maintaining love, peace, and other godly characteristics is to let God deal with injustices. There is no place for personal retaliation (12:19). Otherwise, it is impossible to overcome evil with good (12:21).

Take It Home

Few people today ever fully appreciate just how damaging sin has been in their lives or how costly the price of forgiveness. But the good news of the gospel is that because of the Father's great love for humankind in Jesus Christ, He has made the means of transformation available to every person. To what extent do you think your own transformation has been completed? Which of Paul's instructions (12:9–21) do you find hardest to comply with?

ROMANS 13:1–14

THE BELIEVER'S PLACE IN THE WORLD

The Believer and Governing Authorities 13:1–7
The Debt of Love 13:8–14

Setting Up the Section

Chapter 12 marked a turning point in Romans, where Paul shifted from a theological presentation to a personal appeal for spiritual transformation and love. He listed a number of spiritual gifts and other admirable behaviors for believers to adopt as they related to one another. In this section, he continues with his treatise on practical living and begins to consider relationships with those outside the church.

13:1–7

THE BELIEVER AND GOVERNING AUTHORITIES

Paul's instructions for his readers to submit to the governing authorities (13:1) take on greater significance in light of the fact that there were few Christians in authority at the time. Those in charge were largely unfriendly and even hostile to the church. Yet Paul viewed the governing authorities as not only having been established by God, but also as the servants of God (13:4). The Greek word translated as "servant" can also mean "minister," and is the same word Paul uses to describe the work of a pastor or elder. So Christians are called to submit to their rulers and pray for them, because rebellion against the leaders is considered rebellion against God (13:2).

Demystifying Romans

A number of Old Testament examples demonstrate the power of a godly person working in conjunction with a secular leader. Joseph had worked with the Egyptian Pharaoh to prepare for and survive a terrible famine (Genesis 41). Daniel had found extreme favor with the kings of Babylon even before impressing Darius the Mede by his faith while in the lions' den (Daniel 2–6). And others demonstrated the benefits of submitting to the authorities rather than attempting to undermine them.

Paul also reminds his readers that the purpose of the state is to restrain evil and promote a just social order. Government originated as an ordinance of God. While it cannot redeem the world, it can nevertheless set boundaries for human behavior. The state is not a remedy for sin, but it is a means to restrain sin. So cooperation with the authorities, in cases where no spiritual beliefs are compromised, goes a long way in removing potential problems (13:3–5).

Believers are not to be anarchists or subversives. Rather, they recognize the state as a divine institution with divine authority. Every believer has a civic duty to show respect for elected and appointed officials, knowing that the offices they hold are ordained of God. The respect for the person and office should be demonstrated in tangible ways as well, such as paying taxes (13:6–7).

Critical Observation

While Paul encourages obedience to and prayers for those in civil authority, he is not calling for unequivocal and blind submission to the state. Submission must not require the believer to violate his or her conviction as a Christian or demand a loyalty that is superior to one's allegiance to God. In situations where the state requires something contrary to God's commands, the believer may be called to disobey (Exodus 1:15–21; Daniel 6:6–10; Acts 4:18–20).

The basic principle of scripture is clear: Civil authorities are to be obeyed except for cases where they set themselves in opposition to God's divine law.

13:8–14

THE DEBT OF LOVE

Giving what is due has been a running theme in Paul's letter so far. He has written of the obligation he felt to spread the gospel (1:14–15), the believer's debt to the Holy Spirit to live a holy life (8:12–14), and one's debt to the state to pay taxes (13:6–7). Now he writes that the one outstanding obligation every believer should have is continuing love for one another (13:8). No one ever comes to the point in his or her Christian life where it can be said, "I have loved enough."

Paul ties together love for one another with fulfillment of the law. Some argue that love and law are mutually exclusive—that love has its own moral compass and anything that feels good can't be wrong. But Paul teaches that love cannot operate on its own without an objective moral standard.

For example, a person who truly loves will not commit adultery (13:9), because real love shows respect and restraint. If someone allows physical passion to sweep him or her into an affair, then that person loves too little rather than too much. A person who truly loves will not murder, because love never seeks to destroy. A person who truly loves will never steal, for love inspires giving more than getting.

Why does love sum up all the other commandments (13:9)? Paul says it's because love does not harm its neighbor (13:10). The final five of the Ten Commandments address sins that hurt other people: murder, adultery, stealing, giving false testimony, and coveting (Exodus 20:13–17). The essence of love is to serve one's neighbor and his or her highest good. So the demonstration of love does away with the need to spell out all the individual "You shall nots" of the law. Yet human love is never as complete as it should be, which is why we carry a debt of love at all times.

The importance of love should take on greater meaning in light of the present time (13:11). The Bible divides history into two periods of time—this present age and the age to come. The New Testament writers show that the kingdom of God (the age to come) was inaugurated by Christ at His first coming, but will not be consummated until His second coming. So believers from the first century onward are living between the two comings of Christ.

With each passing day, Jesus' return nears. So as believers anticipate that event when night gives way to day and darkness to light, Paul reminds them to wake up (13:11) and be aware of their behavior (13:12–13). He provides the image of taking off nightclothes and putting on the armor of light, suitable daytime equipment for soldiers of Christ (13:12, 14). As the time grows shorter, the need for love takes on greater urgency.

Take It Home

Sometimes believers are taught to see obedience only as a spiritual discipline, which it is. Yet Paul demonstrates one very practical benefit of obedience: the dispersal of fear. In a practical, civil sense, if people pay their taxes and obey the laws, they have no fear of the authorities (13:3). Likewise, if they submit to God and obey His instructions, they have no fear of being embarrassed when Jesus returns (13:11–14). Can you identify any areas in your own life—civil or spiritual—where increased obedience or submission might result in a lessening of fear?

ROMANS 14:1–15:13

WEAK AND STRONG BELIEVERS

Dealing with Disputable Matters	14:1–12
Removing Stumbling Blocks	14:13–23
Accepting One Another	15:1–13

Setting Up the Section

As Paul continues the practical application section of his letter to the Romans, he deals with conflicts that can arise between people who have different levels of spiritual maturity. What may seem completely appropriate to those in one group can appear wrong (if not outright sinful) to those in another. His exhortation to love one another (13:8) still applies as fellow believers learn to respect one another's opinions.

14:1–12

DEALING WITH DISPUTABLE MATTERS

Scripture is clear as to whether many things are right or wrong. But in this section, Paul addresses those "gray" issues. It's not surprising that these matters were becoming potential problems in the early church. The Jews had a long-established pattern of worship that they naturally planned to continue. The church/worship experience was new to the Gentiles, who had no religious traditions.

Two frequent points of contention were food-related regulations (14:2–3) and the observance of special days (14:5–6). Paul implored his readers not to be so quick to judge one another on these matters. Just because one person found one particular method to be more satisfactory didn't mean that everyone would. Before getting into the specific problems, Paul asked for acceptance of one another and the avoidance of passing judgment (14:1).

Critical Observation

We tend to think that those who follow the most stringent religious disciplines are the most mature. Yet it is interesting to note that the Roman Christians who tended to adhere to the strictest rules and probably felt more superior were those labeled weak by Paul (14:2). Others, generally those who weren't bound to all the Old Testament laws, had experienced the freedom of the gospel to a much greater degree.

No matter the religious practices, a believer had no justification for feeling superior to others. All believers were accountable only to God. Whether or not someone observed all the feasting and fasting days or included meat in a daily diet was inconsequential in terms of his or her salvation and overall relationship with God. After God had accepted someone (14:4), what right did that person have to stand in judgment of a fellow believer?

Believers suffer when they compete with one another. No one is self-sufficient, so all need to acknowledge the right of other believers to worship in a different way. Rather than being critical of one another, people should attend to their own spiritual condition and devote themselves to God (14:6–8).

Paul reminds his readers that there will indeed be a day of judgment (14:10–11). Everyone will stand before God and give an account (14:12). So in the meantime, judgment of one another is a useless exercise.

14:13–23

REMOVING STUMBLING BLOCKS

In addition to judging, another problem between "strong" and "weak" Christians is the exercise of one's religious freedom with a callous disregard for how it might affect others. In the first century, when one group was sensitive to dietary restrictions and whether or not meat had been sacrificed to idols and another group had no concern about such things, sharing a meal together could be awkward.

One might think that the mature believers would be expected to set an example for the others. They were to an extent, but not by blatantly ignoring how their actions would be perceived by less mature members. They weren't to flaunt their spiritual freedom before those who hadn't yet reached that point in their spiritual journeys. Paul explains that the unity of the church is the primary issue; food and other matters are secondary. So even if mature believers (rightly) feel no unease with eating foods others believed were unclean, Paul asks them to forego doing so within group settings. It didn't bother them and it didn't bother God, yet it was a distraction for less mature believers.

Demystifying Romans

The Old Testament prohibition against eating certain foods had been removed by Jesus (Mark 7:14–15) and reinforced to Peter through a vision that symbolized the inclusion of the Gentiles into the early church (Acts 10:9–23). Yet many believers still clung to those teachings, as do certain groups today.

The word translated "stumbling block" (14:13 NIV) is a literal reference to an object in a path over which someone would trip and fall. The more traditional believers were becoming distressed (14:15), finding fellowship with other Christians (and perhaps even with God) to be difficult. What the "strong" believers saw as good was being perceived as evil (14:16). So Paul encourages the more mature in the church to be sensitive to the feelings and beliefs of the others and, out of love, not to practice those things in a mixed group.

Christian freedom is not license. If one's Christian freedoms are impairing the growth of others, it's better to voluntarily do without those things (14:20–21). Paul himself recognized that believers develop at their individual paces, and left it to those who were more mature to not create more difficulty for them. People are not required to reach total agreement in all matters of church function, and should learn to respect one another's differences of opinion (14:22–23).

15:1–13

ACCEPTING ONE ANOTHER

In some of Paul's other writings, he warns against becoming intent on pleasing other people (Galatians 1:10; 1 Thessalonians 2:4; etc.). Those who are too concerned with pleasing others are in danger of falling away from God. That's not what Paul means when he writes of sacrificing one's rights and pleasing his neighbor (15:2). The other instances refer to pleasing people instead of pleasing God. In this case, the desire to find favor with other believers is so that God will be pleased as they continue to grow spiritually.

It is not easy or natural to bear with the failings of the weak (15:1), but it is achievable through knowledge of scripture (15:4), prayer, and praise (15:6). Jesus has already accepted both the stronger and weaker believers, so now they need to learn to accept one another (15:7). He has already set the example to follow, and because of His willingness to set aside His own rights and privileges, He brought salvation not only to the Jews but to the Gentiles as well (15:8–12).

As Paul concludes his writing on the righteousness of God and prepares to make a few closing statements, he prays for joy and peace for all his readers (15:13). Rather than letting their differences of opinion lead to arguments and divisions, they could grow stronger by working through them, with hope and the help of the Holy Spirit.

Take It Home

Deciding where your freedom needs to take a backseat to your responsibility to influence is something that all Christians must navigate in their spiritual journeys. If Paul were writing to the church of the twenty-first century, what issues do you think he would address in regard to mature and immature believers?

ROMANS 15:14–33

PERSONAL COMMENTS

Paul's Ministry to the Gentiles 15:14–22
Paul's Plans 15:23–33

Setting Up the Section

Paul has just finished with the "business" of his letter to the Romans after calling on all the believers to accept one another and not let their differences get in the way of spiritual growth. He has completed his thorough explanation of justification by faith and other doctrinal matters. As he begins to close his letter, he turns his attention to some personal matters, including another affirmation of his genuine concern for the believers in Rome.

15:14–22

PAUL'S MINISTRY TO THE GENTILES

Keep in mind that Paul has not yet set foot in Rome. He knows some of the believers there but has never personally visited. Yet he has just written a very bold letter and wants to ensure it is received well and not misinterpreted. So in this section, he elaborates on the nature of his ministry.

First, he describes his work as a priestly ministry (15:15–16). A priest was responsible for offering the sacrifices of the people, and Paul had been able to offer to God a great number of Gentiles who had converted to Christianity under his ministry. Although the Gentiles were excluded from participating in the temple at Jerusalem and from sharing in the temple sacrifices, they were living sacrifices (12:1).

Paul then speaks of his work as a powerful ministry (15:18–19). Yet he never takes credit for anything that was accomplished. He gives credit to the Holy Spirit and gives glory to Jesus. As Paul had earlier explained, he had chosen to be a servant to Christ (1:1–2; 6:22; 15:17). It is Christ living in Paul whom he credits with the results of his ministry.

Paul also writes that his was a pioneer ministry (15:19–20). Paul had spent ten years in ministry and had gone on three missionary journeys to places where no evangelist had gone before, preaching to people who had never heard the gospel of Jesus. Yet his description is a rather modest summary. His work has prevented him from traveling to Rome, but he is hoping that is about to change.

15:23–33

PAUL'S PLANS

Having clarified his ministry for his readers, Paul outlines his future travel plans. He specifies three destinations: Jerusalem (15:25), Rome (15:24), and Spain (15:24). Assuming he would travel by sea, going to these locations would require a journey of three thousand miles—an ambitious undertaking given the difficulties of first-century transportation.

Paul and others had collected a special offering from a number of Gentile churches in Greece. Before doing anything else, Paul wanted to deliver the gift to the Jewish believers in Jerusalem who were suffering from a severe famine.

Demystifying Romans

Though Paul doesn't say much in his letter to the Romans about the financial gift for the Jerusalem church, he provides a number of details in 2 Corinthians 8–9.

The gift of the Macedonian churches was significant for a number of reasons: It fulfilled the request of the apostles to remember the poor (Galatians 2:10), it demonstrated the solidarity of God's people across various geographic regions and economic levels, and it broke down racial and social barriers. Paul recognized the gift from the Gentile churches to the Jewish believers as a humble, material, and symbolic demonstration of the oneness of the body of Christ.

Paul has wanted to visit Rome for a while (1:15), but has been unable to. Now the time seems right. Paul senses that his missionary service in the eastern Mediterranean area is sufficient. Rome was the center of the empire, and the church there had great opportunities for ministry. Paul wants to visit as well as establish a base of operation prior to going on to Spain. He is also counting on them to help support his ministry as he moves on (15:24).

As far as Paul's hopes to see Spain, we don't know if he ever made it. The entire Iberian Peninsula was under control of Rome and had many flourishing Roman colonies. But if Paul took that trip between his first imprisonment in Rome and the later one that led to his death in AD 64, it isn't on record anywhere.

Critical Observation

Paul was by no means tentative about his traveling. However, his bold statement in 15:29 is not an expression of self-confidence, but rather his faith in Jesus. He knew that when he arrived in Rome both he and the believers there would be blessed.

Paul concludes this section with a heartfelt request for prayer (15:30–33). He had begun his letter with the assurance that he was praying for the believers in Rome (1:8–10), so it is not unusual that he would ask for their support in return. He is quite specific in his prayer requests. He asks for prayers for safety in his travels, for deliverance from his enemies, and above all, for the opportunity to visit with the church in Rome. He does not pray in order to bend God's will to his, but rather to align his plans with God's will.

Paul's request is a reminder that all people need prayer. It is easy to assume that mature spiritual leaders don't really need prayer, encouragement, or affirmation. But the fact that the apostle Paul coveted the prayers of fellow Christians demonstrates the responsibility for believers to pray for all their leaders.

The three concerns of Paul in this section—his apostolic service, his plans for travel, and his need for prayer—all reflect the providence of God in his ministry. As believers are reminded of God's sovereignty, they can take great comfort to realize they are never alone in any of their endeavors.

Take It Home

This personal section at the end of Paul's letter is a good reminder that sometimes we address spiritual matters with a businesslike attitude. Paul had certainly written a deep and insightful letter that dealt with many of the doctrines of the faith. Yet he didn't stop there; he also made it personal. Can you think of ways either you or your church might need to include more of a personal element in your spiritual dealings?

ROMANS 16:1–27

PAUL'S FELLOW MINISTERS

A Series of Greetings	16:1–16
Final Exhortations	16:17–27

Setting Up the Section

As Paul concludes his lengthy letter to the Romans, he personally acknowledges dozens of people who were working for God. It is a personal and intimate conclusion to his Epistle, and was surely an encouragement to those who might have felt unnoticed.

16:1–16

A SERIES OF GREETINGS

When it comes to lists of names in the Bible, whether they comprise tribes, genealogies, the great gallery of faith in Hebrews 11, or other groupings, many people have a natural tendency to skip over them. Yet, in most cases, there are valuable lessons to be discovered by those who slow down and take a look.

In this passage, twenty-six people are mentioned by name, and there are twenty-one titles attached to the various names (sister, servant, helper, etc.). Some names are familiar; many are not. Yet a quick look at the people and Paul's comments may provide some surprising insight.

For one thing, Paul's list reflects the importance of hospitality in the body of Christ. He begins his closing with a personal request that the church in Rome would welcome

Phoebe (16:1–2). Perhaps she was the one entrusted with carrying Paul's letter to the believers in Rome. Paul explains that she had been a big help to him and asks the Roman Christians to do whatever they could to help her.

Hospitality is also evident from the mention of the church in the home of Aquila and Priscilla (16:3–5). Paul had met this couple on his second missionary journey while traveling through Corinth, and had formed a strong bond with this husband-and-wife team (Acts 18:1–3, 18–19). But they were originally from Rome, and had apparently returned home to minister there. They were at the top of Paul's list of greeting.

A second significant point about Paul's list is that it is comprised of people of different rank and race. There are Jews and Gentiles, men and women, slaves and free people. Aristobulus (16:10) was a grandson of Herod the Great and friend of Emperor Claudius. Narcissus (16:11) was a rich and powerful freed slave who served as the secretary to Claudius. Ampliatus, on the other hand (16:8), was one of several common slave names on the list. Rufus (16:13) may have been the son of Simon of Cyrene, the bystander who had been unexpectedly forced into Roman service to carry the cross of Jesus to Calvary (Mark 15:21).

Critical Observation

In the cemetery of Domatilla, one of the oldest Christian catacombs, is a decorated tomb with the single name AMPLIATUS carved in bold and decorative lettering. A Roman male would usually have his three names carved on his tomb, which suggests that Ampliatus was a slave. And if this is the same person mentioned in Romans 16:8, it suggests that this slave held a position of leadership in the church in Rome.

And yet, in spite of the fact that this assortment of people came from different backgrounds, social standings, races, and encounters with Christ, there was great unity within the diversity. Four times in this chapter Paul describes the believers at Rome as being "in Christ." Twice he uses family language of "sister" and "brother." He also refers to "fellow workers" and fellow sufferers, two expressions that strengthen Christian unity.

Paul's list of names also includes the extensive involvement of women. Nine of the named people on the list (one-third) are women. Tryphena and Tryphosa (16:12) may have been twin sisters (based on the similarities in their names). Their names mean "dainty" and "delicate" respectively, yet Paul praises them for working hard for the Lord—a phrase that indicates working to the point of exhaustion. In addition, the list contains the names of Priscilla, Mary, Junia, Persis, Rufus's mother, Julia, and Nereus's sister.

Some people point to other passages of Paul, taken apart from the rest of his writing, and suggest that he taught against women serving in leadership positions in the church. Yet here we see his commendation of Phoebe (16:1), who was most likely a deaconess. (The word for "servant" can also mean "minister.") He referred to Priscilla as a fellow worker. He honors Junia as outstanding among the apostles. He acknowledges the good work of many women in the church and does nothing to criticize their leadership.

Clearly, Paul was not the male chauvinist some have made him out to be. He appreciated the gifts and ministries of women, and he commended them for their service to him and to Christ.

16:17–27

FINAL EXHORTATIONS

Even though this is the longest of Paul's greetings in any of his letters, he still isn't finished with his list of acknowledgments. After greeting many of the individuals who were in Rome, Paul credits a number of people who were with him (16:21–24).

Demystifying Romans

Timothy (16:21) was a young pastor and Paul's protégé, whom Paul mentions frequently in his letters. Jason (16:21) may have been the man who had taken some heat for Paul in Thessalonica (Acts 17:5–9). Sosipater (Romans 16:21) may have been the Sopater who traveled with Paul in Greece (Acts 20:4). Tertius (Romans 16:22) was Paul's secretary who had written the letter to the Romans as Paul dictated. Gaius (16:23) was Paul's host in Corinth; Paul had led him to Christ (1 Corinthians 1:14). The others were evidently believers in Corinth.

Between the list of people Paul greets and the list of Paul's companions, he provides a word of warning. False doctrines were beginning to circulate, promoted by smooth-talking people (16:17–18). Paul challenges his readers to be both wise and innocent (16:19). Naïve people are easily fooled, so wisdom is needed. Yet the more the believers could keep themselves removed from evil things (innocent), the better off they would be.

Paul's doxology (16:25–27) is a final reminder that the mystery of God had been revealed through Jesus Christ. What had been written in the law and proclaimed by the prophets could at last be fully understood. And for that, God was due praise and glory forever.

Take It Home

Paul's lists in this section remind us of how interconnected we are in the body of Christ. Whether it's an appreciation for people we haven't even met or the acknowledgement of those who regularly support and inspire us, it is good to let others know we are thinking about them. Make a list of the people you are thankful for. Then, as soon as you get the opportunity, contact each one to express your gratefulness for his or her influence in your life.

1 CORINTHIANS

INTRODUCTION TO 1 CORINTHIANS

Corinth was a Roman colony and capital of the province of Achaia. Its population probably reached as many as two hundred thousand free citizens, with close to half a million slaves. The city had been in existence since the Bronze Age. It was located in a most strategic position, midway along a five-mile stretch of land between the Saronic Gulf and the Corinthian Gulf. The city would therefore get all the travelers going to the isthmus at the south of Greece, or north to the continent. Additionally, the hazards of sea travel made it advisable for ships to dock, unload, and transfer their cargo to another ship across the isthmus, east to west or vice versa. Small ships would be dragged across the land bridge while still fully loaded.

With all the people and money going through Corinth, it was naturally an influential city. And along with the crowds and wealth came immorality. The city had a reputation for both idolatry and prostitution. The city's less-than- stellar reputation is mentioned in numerous ancient writings. Paul had started a church there during his second missionary journey (Acts 18:1–18). This Epistle to the Corinthian believers alludes to many of the aspects of social life in the city.

AUTHOR

The Epistle of 1 Corinthians both begins and ends with an identification of Paul as the author (1:1; 16:21). The early church was quick to affirm his authorship, and few modern scholars dispute it.

OCCASION AND PURPOSE

During his second missionary journey, Paul remained in Corinth for about eighteen months (about AD 51–52), teaching and establishing the church there. He then returned to his home base at Antioch, and subsequently set off on his third missionary journey. He traveled to Ephesus, the key city in the Roman province of Asia, where he remained for three years, establishing churches there and in the surrounding regions.

While in Ephesus, Paul began to hear of troubles in the young church at Corinth. One of these problems was related to sexual sin, and Paul seems to have written a short letter (now lost) to correct it (5:9). The church was also suffering from division (1:12). In response to the problems in this immature church, Paul wrote this letter, known to us as 1 Corinthians (about AD 55).

Shortly before writing the letter, a delegation from Corinth (Stephanas, Fortunatus, and Achaicus [16:17]) came to Paul with a financial gift from the church. They probably also brought a list of questions from the church, since Paul answers these questions in his letter (7:1). The report of these three men, along with a report from members of the household of a woman named Chloe (1:11), and perhaps a report from his fellow missionary Apollos (1:12; 16:12), prompted Paul to write the letter.

Paul was planning another trip to Corinth. His letter was an attempt to correct some of the problems in the church before he arrived (4:18–21). He also was collecting gifts for the church in Jerusalem because its members were facing tough times, and he wanted the Corinthians to be ready to give (16:1–4).

Paul considered himself the spiritual father of the Corinthian church (4:14–15). It was his love for the believers that motivated him to confront them so directly concerning spiritual and moral issues. Personally, he had experienced weakness, fear, and trembling in his previous association with the church (2:3), but Paul knew it was the power of God that would sustain both him as the messenger and the Corinthian believers as a body.

THEMES

Because of the many ongoing disputes in the church, one of the continuing themes of 1 Corinthians is unity. Paul repeatedly challenges the believers to resolve their conflicts, dissolve their factions, and let God's love rule in the church to bring them together as one body.

Related to unity is the work of the Holy Spirit, especially in regard to spiritual gifts. It is the Holy Spirit who provides the needed wisdom and equips the believers in various ways to minister to one another and the world outside the church.

The sanctification of believers, therefore, is also stressed throughout Paul's letter. Whether supporting their church leaders, addressing sexual sin, foregoing lawsuits against one another, feeling gratitude for their spiritual gifts, or living in anticipation of the resurrection, believers need wisdom from God and the maturity of personal discipline. God has sanctified His people, and in response they are to live accordingly.

CONTRIBUTION TO THE BIBLE

The first letter to the Corinthians is a good example of the importance of integrity within the local church. Much of the focus of scripture is frequently applied to the worldwide church, but here we find a call for each individual body of believers to attend to its own spiritual life and growth.

Paul writes about spiritual gifts in various places, yet his comprehensive explanation in 1 Corinthians 12, using his analogy of the human body, is perhaps his best. The "one body" concept is a universally understood image of the church.

In addition, 1 Corinthians 13 is one of the best-known passages of scripture. Paul's description of love has become a classic piece of literature throughout the centuries since the church at Corinth first read it.

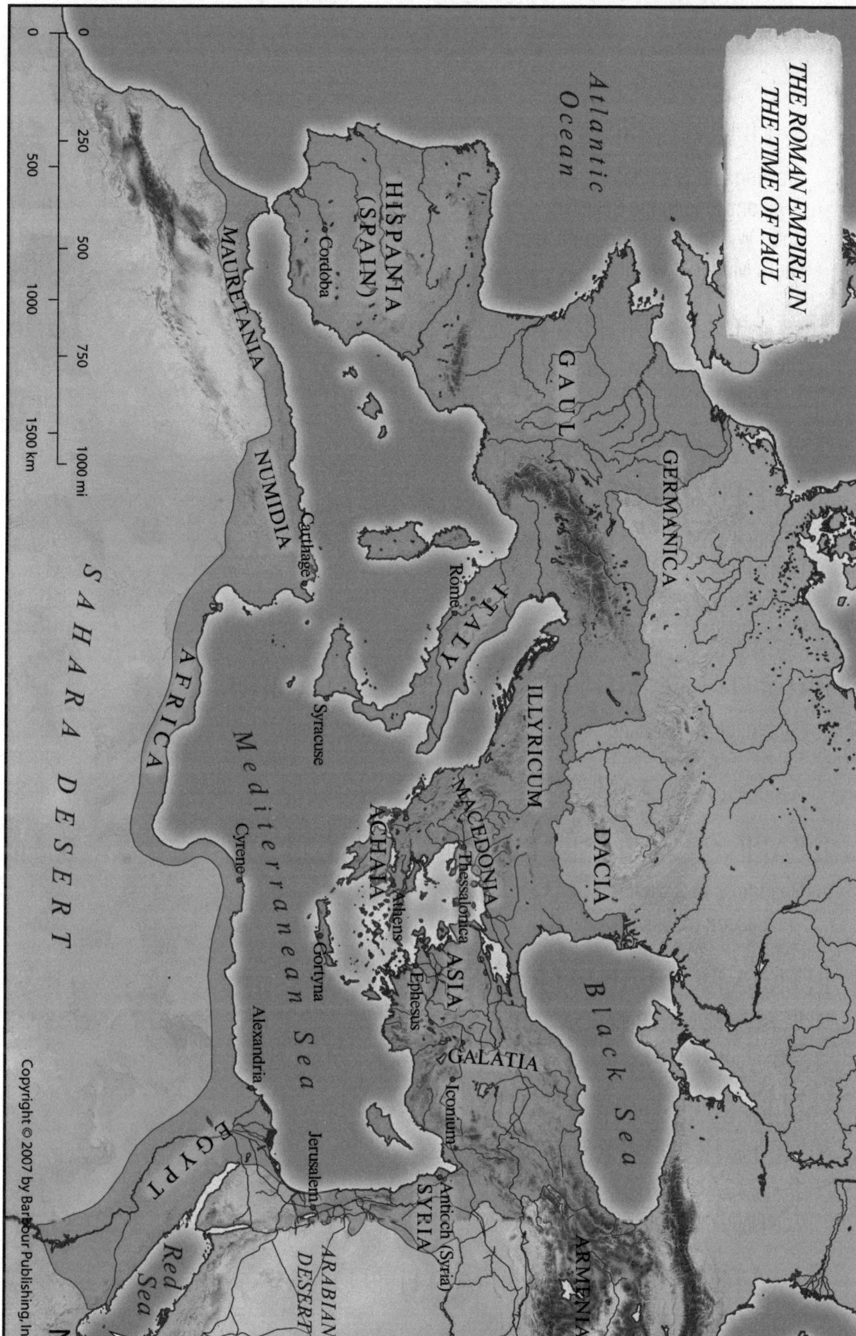
THE ROMAN EMPIRE IN
THE TIME OF PAUL
Atlantic Ocean
HISPANIA (SPAIN)
Cordoba
GAUL
GERMANICA
ITALY
Rome
ILLYRICUM
DACIA
MACEDONIA
Thessalonica
ACHAIA
Athens
ASIA
Ephesus
GALATIA
Iconium
Black Sea
ARMENIA
SYRIA
Antioch (Syria)
Jerusalem
ARABIAN DESERT
Red Sea
EGYPT
Alexandria
Mediterranean Sea
Gortyna
Cyrene
Syracuse
Carthage
AFRICA
NUMIDIA
MAURETANIA
SAHARA DESERT
0 250 500 750 1000 mi
0 500 1000 1500 km
N
Copyright © 2007 by Barbour Publishing, Inc.

OUTLINE

A CHURCH DIVIDED 1:1–2:5

- Greeting and Gratitude 1:1–9
- Divisions among the Believers 1:10–17
- God's Wisdom vs. Human Wisdom 1:18–31
- Paul's Model of Wisdom 2:1–5

THE HOLY SPIRIT'S ROLE IN WISDOM 2:6–16

- The Value of God's Wisdom 2:6–10
- The Illumination of the Holy Spirit 2:11–16

A PLEA FOR COOPERATION RATHER THAN COMPETITION 3:1–23

- Infants in Christ 3:1–4
- God's Field 3:5–9
- God's Temple 3:10–17
- Wise Fools 3:18–23

PROPER REGARD FOR CHURCH LEADERS 4:1–21

- Faithfulness in Serving 4:1–7
- Sacrifice in Serving 4:8–13
- A Model of Service 4:14–21

DEALING WITH SIN IN THE CHURCH 5:1–13

- Unaddressed Sexual Sin 5:1–5
- The Lesson of Leaven 5:6–13

LITIGATION AND LICENTIOUSNESS 6:1–20

- Lawsuits between Believers 6:1–8
- Sexual Impropriety 6:9–20

GUIDELINES FOR MARRIED AND SINGLE BELIEVERS 7:1–40

- The Issue of Marriage 7:1–16
- The Issue of Singleness 7:17–40

QUESTIONS OF CHRISTIAN FREEDOM 8:1–13

- The Problem of Food Sacrificed to Idols 8:1–3
- When to Eat 8:4–6
- When Not to Eat 8:7–13

AN APOSTLE'S RIGHTS 9:1–27

What an Apostle Is Due 9:1–14
What an Apostle Is Willing to Do Without 9:15–27

TEMPTATION AND FREEDOM 10:1–11:1

Lessons from the Past 10:1–13
Lessons from Worship 10:14–22
Specific Guidelines 10:23–11:1

GUIDELINES FOR WORSHIP 11:2–34

Women and Worship 11:2–16
Bad Table Manners at the Lord's Supper 11:17–34

UNDERSTANDING SPIRITUAL GIFTS 12:1–31

An Explanation of the Gifts of the Spirit 12:1–11
Unity and Diversity in the Church 12:12–20
Interdependency in the Church 12:21–31

THE DIFFERENCE LOVE MAKES 13:1–13

The Necessity of Love 13:1–3
The Character of Love 13:4–7
The Permanence of Love 13:8–13

THE PROPER USE OF SPIRITUAL GIFTS 14:1–40

Different Gifts, Different Purposes 14:1–12
Speaking in Tongues Appropriately 14:13–25
Order in the Church 14:26–40

RESURRECTION AND EXPECTATION 15:1–58

A Matter of First Importance 15:1–11
The Power of Resurrection 15:12–34
Perfect, Imperishable Bodies 15:35–58

GIVING AND GREETING 16:1–24

The Gift for Fellow Believers 16:1–4
Some Final Personal Matters 16:5–24

1 CORINTHIANS 1:1–2:5

A CHURCH DIVIDED

Greeting and Gratitude	1:1–9
Divisions among the Believers	1:10–17
God's Wisdom vs. Human Wisdom	1:18–31
Paul's Model of Wisdom	2:1–5

Setting Up the Section

The church at Corinth was undergoing a number of problems. Paul begins by addressing the main source of trouble: division among church members. This issue was evident in a number of specific ways, which Paul will get to in subsequent chapters. But here he deals with the matter from a broader perspective.

1:1–9

GREETING AND GRATITUDE

As was customary for first-century letters, Paul begins by identifying himself and his recipients, and then provides a brief greeting. He refers to his apostleship as well as his calling (1:1), both credentials that attest to his being sent out by God. Later in the letter, he will reveal that his authority is questioned, so from the beginning he makes his intentions clear.

Paul's recipients were Christians in the city of Corinth (1:2). He referred to them as a collective whole, although they may have been members of assorted house churches. Even in the salutation, Paul reminded his readers of their purpose in the Christian life—to be sanctified and holy.

Demystifying 1 Corinthians

Paul adds no details about his companion, Sosthenes (1:1). However, a man by this name appeared in Acts. A synagogue ruler named Crispus had become a believer in response to Paul's preaching (Acts 18:8), and Sosthenes appears to have been his replacement. Perhaps after the unfortunate events described in Acts 18:17, Sosthenes also became a Christian. If Paul's companion isn't this same Sosthenes, we know nothing about him.

The usual Greco-Roman greeting was "rejoice" or "be well" (*chairein*). Paul turned this into a Christian greeting by making it "grace" (*charis*), a Greek word that sounds similar. "Peace" (*shalom* in Hebrew; *eirēnē* in Greek) was the typical Jewish salutation. So Paul combines Greek and Jewish greetings (1:3), and acknowledges their significant theological overtones by citing the origin of grace and peace—the one, true, living God revealed in Jesus Christ.

In his greeting, Paul expresses thankfulness for the believers in Corinth (1:4–6), even though he will soon confront them with a number of problems and shortcomings. Paul trusts God's character and faithfulness to see the Corinthians through their human frailties and flaws (1:7–9).

1:10–17

DIVISIONS AMONG THE BELIEVERS

Before going into detail, Paul appeals to his readers for greater unity (1:10). The Bible urges believers to maintain unity and work toward that goal. The unity of the Spirit can be achieved despite differences and even disagreements.

Yet the Corinthians were divided for various reasons. Foremost among them was the tendency to align themselves with different Christian leaders, as if it were a contest. Paul names four different leaders (1:12), and it's not surprising that they would have appealed to different personalities.

Some believers aligned themselves with Paul. They were probably of Greek ancestry and wanted to be loyal to the one who had founded the church. Others aligned themselves with Apollos. He would have appealed to the intellectuals, because he was well-educated in the city of Alexandria and was known for his oratorical abilities and vast knowledge of the Old Testament (Acts 18:24–28). The third group supported Peter (Cephas), and was probably of Jewish background. Perhaps they were attracted to the forcefulness of Peter's personality or the fact that he had spent three years interacting with Jesus personally. Finally, one group professed devotion only to Christ. While all believers should be aligned with Jesus, perhaps this faction thought they were superior because they acknowledged no human teacher and felt overly spiritual in their walk with the Lord. They were actually using the name of Jesus to separate themselves from others in the church!

Critical Observation

Although the Bible contains 1 Corinthians and 2 Corinthians, apparently these weren't the first two letters Paul had sent to the church in Corinth. He makes references to at least one previous letter he had written (5:9) and one he had already *received* from the church (7:1), yet those correspondences have never been found.

Paul minimizes his own leadership role (1:13–17), and in doing so also downplays the other human leaders of the church. This was to assure his readers that Christ was indeed the leader of the church. Paul was one of the spokespeople, but his preaching was not based on his own wisdom. The power of his message came through the death and resurrection of Jesus.

1:18–31

GOD'S WISDOM VS. HUMAN WISDOM

After contrasting human wisdom with the power of the cross of Christ (1:17), Paul continues the comparison in the next section of his writing. The cross was far from becoming an accepted religious sign. At the time, it was still a horrific symbol of cruelty and death. So for believers to make the cross a major issue seemed foolish to those who didn't understand the necessity and benefits of Jesus' death (1:18–19).

At the time, wisdom was perceived less a matter of genuine intellect and intuition than an ability to articulate a clever-sounding worldview that spoke to the grand themes of life. Two philosophers could expound on their opinions and reach quite different conclusions, yet both be considered wise. God's wisdom had little to do with such showiness. The simple message of the gospel was God's wisdom, yet some people continued to look for wondrous signs and others for bold declarations and hidden truths (1:22–24).

However, there was no comparison. God's "foolishness" is wiser than all of humankind's wisdom (1:25). And God intentionally chooses "foolish" and "weak" things to accomplish His will, which undermines all the arguments of the "wise" and "strong" (1:26–31). As a result, all the credit for a believer's wisdom and strength goes to God rather than oneself.

2:1–5

PAUL'S MODEL OF WISDOM

Paul gives God credit for everything in his ministry. Though well educated and quite knowledgeable about everything he wrote, he refuses to package his message in pretentious speech or high-sounding eloquence. The content of his message is powerful enough without attempting to bolster it in manipulative ways. Paul is able to maintain great humility and vulnerability among those he ministers to (2:2–5). He could have made a dazzling presentation of the gospel, using various secular techniques. But by choosing not to do so, his readers are able to see the supernatural nature of what he is preaching. Paul doesn't want the attention to be on him, but on God (2:4–5).

Take It Home

Paul's emphasis remained on the content of the gospel rather than the presentation of it. Do you think most churches have a similar commitment, or do they try too hard to use human wisdom to attract attention? To what extent do you think it is appropriate for Christian leaders to concern themselves with the presentation of God's Word?

1 CORINTHIANS 2:6–16

THE HOLY SPIRIT'S ROLE IN WISDOM

The Value of God's Wisdom 2:6–10
The Illumination of the Holy Spirit 2:11–16

Setting Up the Section

Paul begins this letter to the Corinthian church by contrasting human wisdom with the wisdom of God. Those who value their own wisdom too highly tend to think that the truth of the gospel is foolishness. Paul continues his clarification in this section, where he explains how the Holy Spirit contributes to a believer's genuine wisdom.

2:6–10

THE VALUE OF GOD'S WISDOM

As Paul continues to differentiate between various definitions of wisdom, he explains that the wisdom of believers is mature, and not at all like what was being presented as wisdom in the secular culture (2:6). The difference is due to the work of the Holy Spirit.

God's wisdom, Paul writes, had been hidden (2:7). But what was once secret has been revealed and is now accessible (2:10). Until the Spirit enlightens someone, however, the person is incapable of realizing the truth about God, Jesus, and the gospel. All the so-called wisdom of the rulers of that time would come to nothing (2:6). Some people think Paul may have been writing of spiritual rulers here rather than (or in addition to) human ones.

Demystifying 1 Corinthians

Paul was not endorsing the new teaching beginning to circulate through the church (later to be labeled Gnosticism) that said the way to God required much deep thought and secret knowledge. Rather, Paul was speaking of a matter of timing. After the coming of the Holy Spirit, access to God's truth required only simple faith rather than intellect or religious zeal.

In Paul's day, the secular culture attempted to approach God through reasoning and argument. The result was a deity created in the people's own image that in no way resembled the real and personal God. In their minds, God was what they called *apatheia*—He had a total inability to feel. They saw God as detached and remote, and the preaching of Christ (with its emphasis on suffering and reconciling the world to Himself through death on a cross) as incomprehensible and foolish.

If the first-century crowds had been able to discern the true wisdom of God, they never would have crucified Jesus (2:8). Indeed, for those who believe, the wisdom of God is profound. But human wisdom alone is not enough. Jesus said He chose His disciples, not the other way around (John 15:16). And the author of Hebrews confirms that Jesus is the author and perfecter of faith (Hebrews 12:2). If people begin to think they are smart enough to comprehend the truths of Christianity on their own, they don't fully understand the ministry of the Holy Spirit in their lives.

2:11–16

THE ILLUMINATION OF THE HOLY SPIRIT

Human observation and careful study can never fully penetrate the deep truths of God. But where human imagination fails, spiritual illumination prevails. Through the power of the Holy Spirit, God reveals the light of the gospel to believers and convicts them of the truths of their faith.

To illustrate his point, Paul asks his readers to consider the human spirit. It is impossible, simply by looking at someone else, to determine that person's deepest thoughts, inner dreams, and strongest desires. But the spirit within the person is aware of such things. Similarly, people had spent centuries trying to understand and relate to God. But it wasn't until the Spirit of God revealed God's truth that people could really comprehend (2:11–12).

Similarly, people without the help of the Spirit can't understand spiritual things (2:14). Those with the Spirit not only are given insight to understand, but also to communicate what they have discerned. Believers learn to translate their spiritual thoughts into spiritual words (2:13). Just as the Holy Spirit provides the enlightenment needed to comprehend the mystery of God's truth, He also enables believers to speak with a type of wisdom far superior to the rhetoric of any orator.

In conclusion, Paul refers to a question from Isaiah: "Who has known the mind of the Lord?" (Isaiah 40:13 NIV). And the answer, from a New Testament perspective, is that with the help of the Holy Spirit, *all believers* can know the mind of Christ. Paul doesn't go into detail here, but his definition of the attitude of Christ (Philippians 2:6–11) is not a bit mystical or mysterious. The mind of Christ is an attitude of humility and sacrifice. And anyone who understands this spiritual truth is accountable only to God—not to those who lack the same spiritual insight (2:15).

Sadly, many in the church at Corinth were still far from understanding the mind of Christ. They had a long way to go in their process of spiritual maturity, as Paul will explain in the next section.

Take It Home

Consider your own opinion about what it means to be "wise." Do you think most people are impressed by a simple demonstration of spiritual maturity and reliance on the truths of God? Or are they looking more for eloquent answers to hard questions? Would you say you tend to display more human wisdom, or do you display godly wisdom that is expressed by spiritual truths (2:13)?

1 CORINTHIANS 3:1–23

A PLEA FOR COOPERATION RATHER THAN COMPETITION

Infants in Christ	3:1–4
God's Field	3:5–9
God's Temple	3:10–17
Wise Fools	3:18–23

Setting Up the Section

In this section, Paul continues his appeal to the Corinthians to quit dividing into factions based on their personal preference of church leadership. As long as jealousy and arguments continued, the church would never unite. And in addition to the church as a whole, Paul speaks to the importance of individual commitment and work for God.

3:1–4

INFANTS IN CHRIST

Paul had just gone into considerable detail (2:6–16) describing the difference between people who attempt to get by with only human wisdom (nonbelievers) and those who have responded to the Holy Spirit and are able to discern the mind of Christ (believers). Here he begins to differentiate between mature and immature believers.

Overall, the church in Corinth was immature. Although the members had been Christians for several years, they were still babes in the faith. They should have possessed a mature hunger for real Christian teaching, but they were still acting immature (3:1–2). They wanted milk (probably a reference to justification and all the other benefits of a Christian relationship), but hadn't moved on to the solid truths of Christianity: choosing righteousness, making sacrifices, submitting to others, and so forth.

Infants can be cute, but not when they are uncompromisingly self-centered, so Paul calls them on their behavior. It must have been particularly disheartening to realize that he was part of the reason the Corinthian believers were jealous and quarreling among one another (3:1–3).

Demystifying 1 Corinthians

Paul considered himself the spiritual father of the Corinthian believers (4:15), and wanted his "children" to mature as they should. Every parent wants to see his or her child grow out of the self-centered stage after a reasonable amount of time.

3:5–9

GOD'S FIELD

To make his point, Paul uses a couple of analogies for the church. The first is that of a field (3:9). Jesus had used the image of a seed and soil as a symbol of the human heart and its response to God's Word (Matthew 13:3–23). Paul makes a similar comparison, but with an application to the entire church instead of a single person. For some of the Corinthian believers to align behind Paul while others supported Apollos—and to argue about which leader was more important—made about as much sense as cheering for one farmer over another in regard to crop growth.

Paul had sown the seed of God's Word in Corinth, and a church had sprung up. Apollos had come along later to "water" the young church. But Paul makes it clear that only God is responsible for any growth (3:6–7). The Corinthians needed to see that Paul and Apollos had played different—but equally important—roles in the ministry of the church. Both would be rewarded by God (3:8), and should be respected by the believers.

3:10–17

GOD'S TEMPLE

Next, Paul uses the illustration of a building to further clarify his point. Jesus is the foundation of anything a believer hopes to construct. Paul had laid that foundation in the sense that he had first preached the gospel in Corinth (3:10–11). And again, Apollos had played a part in the growth by building on the foundation—strengthening the belief of the Corinthian Christians.

But not every builder has the same results. Those who work with valuable materials—the truths of God—would have a lasting ministry. Others who settled for less wouldn't see the same results. The references to wood, hay, and straw probably represent work based on the limited human wisdom Paul described in 1 Corinthians 2. Believers should be capable of better, more productive ministry, yet some settle for less.

Critical Observation

Although God will judge and reward individuals for the work they do (3:12–15), believers are not to operate independently of one another. When Paul wrote, "you yourselves are God's temple" (3:16 NIV), the word *you* was plural. Believers are not individual *temples* of God, but are collectively the *temple* of God.

3:18–23

WISE FOOLS

Up to this point, Paul has been contrasting foolishness and wisdom. He concludes this passage by urging his readers to risk being perceived as "foolish" in order to adopt the true wisdom of God that is found in unity with others in Christ (3:18–20). Christianity is at odds with the worldview of nonbelievers, so believers should not be surprised to find themselves out of step with the secular world as they faithfully follow the Savior.

The Corinthians seemed worried that they might miss out on something if they backed the wrong leader, so they tended to boast about their minister of choice. Paul concludes this section by assuring them that God has provided everything for them (3:21–23)—people, the world, life, death, the present, and the future. Each leader belongs to the entire church. No subgroup can lay claim to a servant of Christ at the exclusion of the other church members. Everything belongs to the church, the church belongs to Christ, and Christ belongs to God. And *that* is something to boast about (1:31)!

Take It Home

Think about your current level of involvement in the church of Christ. Would you say you are contributing to the growth of the church with gold, silver, and costly stones, or with wood, hay, and straw? Do you foresee lasting effects of the work you are doing? (If not, do other people?) What might you do to improve the quality (not the quantity) of your work in the future?

1 CORINTHIANS 4:1–21

PROPER REGARD FOR CHURCH LEADERS

Faithfulness in Serving	4:1–7
Sacrifice in Serving	4:8–13
A Model of Service	4:14–21

Setting Up the Section

In the previous section, Paul had explained to the Corinthian believers some of the wrong ways to respond to their church leaders. He challenged them to quit boasting about human leaders (3:21) and to quit allowing their leadership to create jealousy and quarreling among the church members (3:3–4). In this section, he continues to explain how the church should properly respond to and support its leaders.

4:1–7

FAITHFULNESS IN SERVING

Paul begins his letter to the Corinthians by explaining the wrong way to treat apostles of God. The Corinthians were prone to overly exalt them, and Paul corrects their way of thinking. Next, he brings the discussion full circle and suggests that the Corinthians see their spiritual leaders as servants—servants entrusted with secret things of God (4:1).

Church leaders are stewards. The steward was the highest-ranking servant of a wealthy landowner—the one in charge of the entire estate in his master's absence. The primary responsibility of the steward was faithfulness to his master, so he had to resist kowtowing to the demands of those who served under him.

The church leaders were servants, yet they were servants with authority. It was improper for others to exalt them, yet they were due respect as God's designated stewards. Ultimately, both the leaders and the other church members would have to give an account to the Lord. It meant little to Paul how the Corinthians regarded his ministry, because all that really mattered was God's divine assessment (4:2–5).

Paul further challenges his readers not to impose standards on their leaders that scripture didn't require (4:6). He identifies the Corinthians' problem as one of pride, and then immediately challenges them by asking how they had acquired the things that made them proud (4:7). His point was that they had no right to be proud and boastful, since God had provided them with everything they had.

4:8–13

SACRIFICE IN SERVING

Paul wasn't beyond using a little sarcasm to make his point. He derisively portrays the Corinthian believers as rich and wise kings, filled with strength and receiving honor. In contrast, he describes the apostles as a spectacle, fools, weak, homeless, and scum of the earth. Paul's words are harsh, indeed, yet his illustration isn't far from reality. The Corinthian believers were bickering about minor things while Paul, Apollos, Peter, and other leaders were suffering, going hungry, working hard, and facing persecution.

Demystifying 1 Corinthians

When a Roman general won a great victory, he would parade his triumphant army through the streets of the city, displaying all the spoils of their conquest. Following at the end of the parade was a group of people who had been taken captive. Soon this group would be taken to the arena to fight against wild animals or armed gladiators, where most would die. This is the image Paul uses, describing the proud Corinthians as victorious kings and the church leaders as the doomed prisoners.

4:14–21

A MODEL OF SERVICE

There was an antidote to pride, but it wasn't popular in first-century culture. Paul doesn't use the word *humility* here as he does in other places (Philippians 2:3), but that is his intent. According to Greek philosophy, humility was a trait associated with slaves, a sign of weakness, and not to be associated with men of character. Paul (in imitation of Jesus) had a completely different philosophy that prized humility. It was his humility that allowed him to return cursing with blessing, persecution with tolerance, and slander with kindness (4:12–13).

In fact, Paul pleads with the Corinthians to follow the example he had set in his ministry (4:16). And since Paul couldn't be in Corinth right away, he was sending Timothy to set the same example for them, and to remind them of what Paul believed and practiced (4:17).

Paul isn't afraid to chastise the Corinthian church a bit. Even though there were thousands of people who might weigh in with opinions of how they were doing and what they might need to do, Paul is their spiritual father, in that he had originally gotten the church up and running (4:15).

In the final section of this passage, Paul alerts his readers to a problem that he will revisit later in his letter (9:1–3). When he makes reference to *some* of them (4:18), he is acknowledging his awareness of personal animosity toward him by several in the Corinthian church. This dissentious group had been trying to convince others that Paul was not as sincere or as competent as he purported to be (2 Corinthians 10:10; 11:13). He will deal with them more directly later.

Paul acknowledges that it's easy for the Corinthians to be arrogant when he isn't there to rebut or to defend himself, but he assures them of his intent to visit very soon (4:18–19). If his critics demand a showdown, he will be ready. He hopes it won't come to that, but he will leave it up to them (4:20–21). Do they prefer a whip (a rod wielded by someone in a position of authority)? Or will they rather come to agreement through love with a gentle spirit?

Paul's preference would be the latter. But he isn't afraid to confront the Corinthians on issues he feels are completely out of order, as he will demonstrate in the next section.

Take It Home

When Paul taught others how God intended for them to behave in the world, he was able to urge them to imitate himself (4:16). Can you do the same? Do the people closest to you see the love and humility of Christ evident in your own words and actions? Identify someone you would like to have a stronger influence on, and then consider what you might do to change yourself in order to make a positive impression on that person.

1 CORINTHIANS 5:1–13

DEALING WITH SIN IN THE CHURCH

Unaddressed Sexual Sin 5:1–5
The Lesson of Leaven 5:6–13

Setting Up the Section

To this point, Paul has addressed the problems in the Corinthian church in general terms. But here he gets quite specific. He cites a particular—and particularly offensive—problem, and then provides instructions for how to deal with it. This is the first in a series of specific issues Paul will deal with throughout his letter to the Corinthian believers.

5:1–5

UNADDRESSED SEXUAL SIN

The church frequently came into conflict with the secular culture during the first century. For example, the Greek attitude toward prostitution was rather lax. To most Gentiles, it was a small matter whether someone frequented brothels or participated in an ongoing affair, even if he were married. The Greek word for "sexual immorality" (5:1 NIV), when used by the church, refers to numerous sexual sins they found immoral and inappropriate: fornication, adultery, homosexuality, and more. One of the few specific requests the early church leaders made of Gentile converts was to abstain from sexual immorality (Acts 15:20, 29).

Yet the church in Corinth had reversed the sides of the conflict over sexual propriety. One of its members was living with his father's wife (5:1). Most likely the woman was his step-mother. It is possible that his father had already died and that he and the woman were approximately the same age. But the relationship was still considered incestuous. Pagan society would have looked down on such a bond, and it was prohibited by Roman law. Yet members of the Corinthian church took pride in the tolerance they showed in allowing the relationship (5:2).

The problem in the church went unresolved, largely because the issue of leadership had not been settled. But Paul writes with authority, prescribing specific and immediate action. He doesn't have to be present, he says, because he is acting under the authority of Jesus (5:4).

Paul's concern is not simply for the offending church member. Rather, he views the problem as church-wide. He doesn't address the man, but rather scolds the church as a whole for allowing the problem. And since it hadn't taken action, he dictates what it should do: excommunicate the man for his own good and the good of the church (5:2, 5). It was a severe punishment. Yet Paul later makes a reference to a similar event (2 Corinthians 2:5–11). If he is referring to the same man, it is good news indeed that the man did repent and return to good standing in the church.

Demystifying 1 Corinthians

Paul's instructions to hand the offending church member over to Satan (5:5) can be interpreted in various ways. Most agree that this was primarily a command to expel him from church fellowship into the secular world (the realm of Satan). But the reasons vary. Some believe that by being cut off from worship, the painful isolation would create the strong desire to repent and correct his sinful behavior. Some believe that the expelled man's physical body would suffer as a result of divine chastisement, perhaps even leading to premature death like Ananias and Sapphira (Acts 5:1–11). Some believe the destruction of his sinful nature (or flesh) meant the cessation of his sinful desires. Some propose that the man himself was the sinful nature, and that the spirit of the church would be saved as a result.

5:6–13

THE LESSON OF LEAVEN

Paul had recently warned against judging other people (4:5), but his intent there was in regard to the person's relationship with God. When the issue is obvious immorality in the church, the church leaders have not only the right but also the responsibility to speak up and take appropriate action.

He compares this responsibility to the old Jewish tradition of removing all the yeast from the household during Passover. Just as a tiny amount of yeast in dough has a surprising effect, so does the toleration of just a little sin in the church. It is definitely not something to be proud about! The lingering presence of such "yeast" results in malice and wickedness, while the church without yeast is marked by sincerity and truth (5:6–8).

Critical Observation

The Israelites removed all leaven (yeast) as they prepared the annual Passover dinner. It wasn't enough to put it away; they literally threw it out so it would be far removed from the unleavened bread they were baking (Exodus 12:15; 13:6–7).

In Paul's previous letter (the one that has never been found), he had apparently dealt with a similar problem, but the church members had misinterpreted his instructions. So here, he reiterates his point and makes himself very clear. It is not right to judge those *outside* the church. The church had a ministry to those people. If outsiders choose to ignore the truth of the gospel, then God will be their judge (5:12–13).

Paul's point is to disassociate with immoral people *within* the church (5:11). Perhaps the person is a Christian in name only or a believer who reverted to the ways of his sinful past. Paul prescribes complete removal from such people to the point of not even sharing a meal (5:11). Otherwise, nonbelievers might witness the intimacy between the two and assume that the church approves of such sinful behavior.

Later, Paul will be even more specific concerning the sharing of the meal that was served in connection with the Lord's Supper (10:21; 11:17–34). But first he will return to the topic of sexual immorality as well as lawsuits among believers (chapter 6).

Take It Home

One of the most offensive insults today is to be called judgmental, and few people want that reputation. Conversely, most people like to be considered tolerant of the rights and opinions of others. Yet the refusal to pass judgment in the church at Corinth created a lot of problems both within and outside of the church. Where do you think people should draw the line between tolerance and confrontation? Do you think Christians should be more tolerant or less tolerant of other Christians in comparison to their attitudes toward nonbelievers?

1 CORINTHIANS 6:1–20

LITIGATION AND LICENTIOUSNESS

Lawsuits between Believers	6:1–8
Sexual Impropriety	6:9–20

Setting Up the Section

Paul had begun to respond to specific problems in the Corinthian church he had learned about through correspondence with the believers there. He continues to address their issues in this section, writing about two issues that continue to be problems in many churches today: lawsuits and sexual immorality.

6:1–8

LAWSUITS BETWEEN BELIEVERS

The ancient Greeks loved courtroom drama. In Athens (which was not far from Corinth), the courts of law were a primary source of entertainment. The culture was so litigious that essentially every male citizen was involved with the legal system to some degree, and in the process, tended to cultivate oratorical skill as well. But then, as the citizens became believers and started attending church, they carried their tendencies for lawsuits and rhetoric with them.

Critical Observation

When there was a dispute in ancient Athens, the first attempt to settle the matter was through private arbitration. One arbitrator was chosen by each party, and the two agreed on a third arbitrator to serve as an impartial judge. If that failed to settle the problem, it went to a court known as The Forty. This court referred the matter to public arbitration by Athenian citizens. And if this group couldn't reach agreement, the case went to a jury court that consisted of 201 citizens for small matters and 401 citizens for major issues. Jurors had to be at least thirty years old. Records exist of some cases where the juries numbered in the thousands.

The Jews, on the other hand, had always avoided the public courts. They tended to settle disputes before the leaders of the community or elders in the synagogue. Justice was a matter best left to the spiritual community. So Paul is especially distressed to hear of the Corinthian believers' willingness to allow secular courts to settle their disagreements (6:1–6).

Christians have access to the wisdom of God through the Holy Spirit. They will one day rule with Christ and supposedly be qualified to judge the world (Matthew 19:28) and even angels (Jude 6). Yet the Corinthians couldn't even settle their own minor disputes.

Instead of feeling proud of their legal victories in secular courts, the Corinthian Christians should have been ashamed of extending the problems of the church into the public arena. Paul writes that the result of Christians taking other Christians to court is shame, defeat, and ineffective witness for Christ.

If Christians cannot resolve their disagreements short of secular litigation, there is something fundamentally amiss in the church of Jesus Christ. Even if the Corinthian believers couldn't settle a matter to their satisfaction within the church, for the good of the gospel they should have been willing to be wronged (6:7–8). What offense would be severe enough to sacrifice one's Christian witness to nonbelievers?

Demystifying 1 Corinthians

Paul's instructions in this section apply specifically to Christians involved in lawsuits with other Christians. In such cases, much harm can be done in the resulting misperception of Christian fellowship. But Paul's admonition does not address potential instances of due legal process a Christian might pursue with people outside the church or even with the state. Paul made extensive use of Roman courts and asserted his rights as a Roman citizen. Yet he had the same goal in mind: the spread of the gospel.

6:9–20

SEXUAL IMPROPRIETY

Corinth was a city with a reputation for sexual promiscuity. Prostitution was rampant, much of it connected with the large temple of Aphrodite, the Greek goddess of love. Many of the Corinthian men no doubt visited prostitutes before they became believers, and it appears that some continued to do so even afterwards. (If so, it was no wonder that they had little to say about the man living with his step-mother [5:1–5].)

Paul first lists a number of sexual sins, along with other sins including greed, drunkenness, slandering, and swindling (6:9–11). He acknowledges that numerous believers had once participated in such things, but had since been washed and sanctified. They should have been experiencing the joy and freedom of their salvation rather than desiring to revert to their previous sinful ways.

Paul appears to be responding to specific arguments, suggesting that the Corinthians had given three reasons why they thought they should be included in the anything-goes sexual attitudes of their culture. First was the social argument that everyone else was doing it. They didn't want to be left out of the citywide parties occasionally held at Aphrodite's temple and be considered antisocial. Second was the philosophical argument that sex didn't really matter, because things such as food and sex were physical matters, not spiritual ones (a philosophy known as dualism). The physical body would eventually pass away, leaving only the spirit, so what people did with their bodies was of no lasting concern. And third was a spiritual argument that God's grace was so all-encompassing that the greater a person's sin, the more abundant His grace would be.

Paul counters these arguments one by one and refutes the false thinking of the Corinthians. Everyone else may be doing the wrong things, but believers are not their own. They have been bought with a price and therefore should glorify God with their bodies (6:20). Food may be for the stomach and the stomach for food, but God will destroy them both. The body is not meant for sexual immorality, but for God. And even of all the things that are permissible, not everything is beneficial. Christians should not be mastered by anything (6:12–14).

The Spirit of God dwells in the bodies of believers (6:15–20), so even their physical (bodily) lives should honor God. Clearly, this is not done through sexual promiscuity. And the principle holds true for numerous other behaviors in addition to sex. Freedom in the Christian life is never an excuse to live however one wants. Rather, it is a holy calling to find the power to exhibit self-control in every aspect of life.

Finally, sexual purity is one of God's most precious gifts. Sexual intercourse goes beyond mere biology or physiology and encompasses the totality of one's humanity. So Paul is not being prudish in his instructions. Rather, he is attempting to lift this wonderful gift of God above the cultural standards that tend to debase and demean it.

Many people settle for a cheap imitation of what God intends for sex. In pursuit of selfish gratification, they sacrifice true freedom and miss the ultimate fulfillment of sexual fidelity within the covenant of marriage.

Paul will have much more to say about marriage (as well as singleness) in the next section.

Take It Home

Paul asks the question "Do you not know. . . ?" six times in this section of 1 Corinthians (6:2, 3, 9, 15, 16, 19). In each case, he is chiding the church in Corinth because its members were not following the clear teachings of scripture. They either weren't aware of what its members should do, or were ignoring what they knew. Can you think of anything you are doing that you either suspect or know for sure is not in line with scriptural teaching? What potential harm could come of such behavior?

1 CORINTHIANS 7:1–40

GUIDELINES FOR MARRIED AND SINGLE BELIEVERS

The Issue of Marriage 7:1–16
The Issue of Singleness 7:17–40

Setting Up the Section

Paul had just answered questions concerning sexual behavior. So it was only natural that he would follow by discussing the believers' questions on marriage. He rebuked their improper attitudes, but spent considerably more time prescribing positive behavior.

7:1–16

THE ISSUE OF MARRIAGE

Having just told his readers to flee from sexual sins (6:18), Paul turns to the option of marriage. In previous correspondence, he had received questions about the topic, which isn't surprising because Greek philosophy and cultural values were quite different from the standards God had established for His people.

In fact, the Greek culture distorted scriptural teachings on marriage at both ends of the scale. Those who practiced dualism believed that body and spirit were completely separate entities within a person. In their way of thinking, nothing done to the body had a lasting spiritual effect, so why not engage in hedonism and sexual pleasure-seeking? Another philosophy was asceticism, where the practitioner sought to purify his spirit by depriving his body of any pleasure—sexual or otherwise.

Paul had already addressed the hedonistic group (chapters 5–6), and here he turns his attention to the ascetics. Both extremes were prevalent in the church, so he tries to establish a balance. Rather than attempt to sway everyone to his personal preference of celibacy, or to go the other way and declare the proponents of celibacy to be too legalistic, Paul acknowledges the strengths and weaknesses of both alternatives.

When Paul opens with the statement that it is good for a man not to marry (7:1), he may have been quoting a popular ascetic saying because he follows immediately with the argument *for* marriage. Not only is marriage preferable to rampant immorality, it is a gift from God for some people (7:7). In explaining, Paul's words stood in stark contrast to the highly patriarchal societies of antiquity. When he suggests that neither husband nor wife should deny the other sexual intimacy, this principle of mutual submission is revolutionary. A Christian's body belongs to God (6:19–20), and also to his or her spouse. It is inappropriate to deprive one another of sexual intimacy unless it is a mutually prearranged and temporary agreement to devote themselves to spiritual disciplines (7:2–5).

Critical Observation

One might wonder how Paul knew so much about marriage. He was clearly unmarried at the time of this writing (7:8), although some people speculate he could have had a wife who died young. They base the opinion on the fact that he might have been a member of the Sanhedrin (Acts 26:10), which only accepted married men. Also, he wrote with great understanding and sensitivity for what it meant to be married, suggesting personal experience.

Paul was unmarried and found singleness both satisfying and beneficial in his ministry, yet realized that God had different plans for different people (7:7). Being single and miserable was not a desirable state (7:9).

Yet a commitment to marriage is to be lifelong. God's plan for marriage is for one man and one woman to leave their parents and be joined together in a permanent and exclusive union throughout the course of their earthly lives. Divorce, though allowed by the Mosaic Law in limited circumstances (Matthew 19:8), was never designed nor desired by God.

With the rapid growth of the church, it is not surprising that the question of divorce came up. Paul provides guidelines for when one spouse becomes a believer and the other doesn't. He says if the unbelieving spouse leaves, the believer is no longer bound to the marriage. Yet if the unbeliever is willing to continue in the marriage, the Christian is not to leave his or her spouse. The godly influence of one spouse on the other may result in the other's salvation (7:12–16).

7:17–40

THE ISSUE OF SINGLENESS

Paul provides an underlying principle for marriage and other aspects of life in 1 Corinthians 7:17. Becoming a Christian certainly changes a person's spiritual life and outlook, yet it doesn't mean the person will necessarily change in other ways. Gentiles remain Gentile. Slaves may remain slaves (but are under no obligation to do so if they can obtain their freedom). So happily single people need not rush out looking for a mate, and married believers need not pursue singleness. Instead, everyone should attempt to do whatever God directs (7:17–24).

Demystifying 1 Corinthians

The word translated "virgins" (7:25) allows numerous interpretations. Various opinions of who Paul is addressing include: (1) fathers who were responsible for their unmarried daughters; (2) unmarried couples involved in the ascetic practice of living together before marriage in a purely platonic and spiritual relationship, sharing the same bed but having no physical relations; (3) couples who went through the marriage ceremony but then decided to live as a celibate couple and devote themselves entirely to a spiritual life; and (4) young engaged women who, along with their fiancés, were being pressured by the ascetic group and wondering if they should go through with their weddings as planned.

Paul clearly preferred the single life, yet insists it is not the only option for people to be faithful to God (7:25–28). However, ministry was always foremost on Paul's mind. His reminder that there is little time (7:29) may be a reference to Jesus' return, because Corinth was prosperous at the time, and not yet facing the Christian persecution that would eventually become a problem.

It is logical that a single person is freer to serve God. Marriage is a commitment to another person, and such a commitment requires time and attention or, as Paul wrote, divided interests (7:34). People can serve God, married or single, but God is not honored by the neglect of a spouse.

So while Paul tends to lobby for people remaining single, he still extols the role of marriage (7:36–40). As long as people choose wisely and act appropriately, one choice is as good as the other.

Take It Home

There seemed to be a bias in the early church toward remaining single and serving God more intently rather than getting married. Today the bias might be the other way: Perhaps Christian couples and families are taken more seriously than singles. Have you detected a bias in either direction? Does your church provide equal opportunities for service, whether single or married?

1 CORINTHIANS 8:1–13

QUESTIONS OF CHRISTIAN FREEDOM

The Problem of Food Sacrificed to Idols	8:1–3
When to Eat	8:4–6
When Not to Eat	8:7–13

Setting Up the Section

Paul has been answering questions from a previous letter from Corinth. He has just responded to questions about marriage (7:1) and singleness (7:25). Now he turns to a topic that was a major problem in Corinth, yet not a concern in most modern Western cultures. Still, Paul's approach to the issue provides insight for how to deal with a number of contemporary spiritual problems.

8:1–3

THE PROBLEM OF FOOD SACRIFICED TO IDOLS

Paul had been asked (via mail) to provide some guidelines for how believers should feel about and react to meat that had been sacrificed to idols (8:1). At this time in the city of Corinth, most of the meat available in the community was somehow associated with idol worship. Most of the meat in the marketplace came from sacrificial animals that had been slaughtered at pagan temple ceremonies.

The Corinthian believers no doubt had a number of questions. Did the pagan rituals somehow taint the meat? Could a Christian buy meat that had been sacrificed to an idol? Should a believer eat sacrificed meat if it was served at a friend's home? What about a believer's involvement at various social events, such as weddings and parties, that served the meat and often utilized a temple dining hall for the festivities?

Demystifying 1 Corinthians

For pagan worshipers in Corinth to incur the favor of a god or goddess, an animal would be sacrificed and divided into three portions. One small portion was burned on the altar as an act of worship. The priest received the second portion as payment for his services. The worshiper kept the rest of the meat and could do one of two things with his portion: He could either give a banquet for a number of guests in his home or at the temple, or he could sell the meat in the marketplace.

This issue had become another dividing factor within the church. The members of one group strongly felt that meat sacrificed to idols was indeed tainted and would have nothing to do with it. Nor would they attend any secular social function because they felt they would compromise their witness for Christ and their pursuit of holy living.

Others felt that wherever their food came from, it was ultimately from God. They didn't consider eating meat sacrificed to idols a problem. The conflict between the two groups had become so great that Paul addresses the issue at length, from 1 Corinthians 8–10.

Before he even starts to answer, Paul warns that he isn't attempting to prove one group right and the other wrong (8:2–3). Knowledge without love is prideful. Love is the ultimate goal.

8:4–6

WHEN TO EAT

Paul says that idols have no objective spiritual existence, so essentially the meat had been dedicated to nothing. The one God that Christians serve is the provider of all things (8:4–6). Although other people recognized various gods and goddesses, none of those so-called deities had anything to do with the creation, sustenance, or redemption of the world. Therefore, a Christian was free to eat meat that had been sacrificed to an idol because the idol had no spiritual power or authority.

His comments seem to validate the opinions of the okay-to-eat group. But Paul isn't finished.

8:7–13

WHEN NOT TO EAT

Paul had declared that there was no ontological or theological basis for refusing to eat meat that had been sacrificed to an idol. But the fact remained that some of the Christians in Corinth could not in good conscience eat sacrificed meat in the privacy of their own homes, much less in the pagan temples of the city. Many of them had no doubt been involved with idol worship and ceremonial sacrifices, and wanted nothing to do with that past (8:7). They would have felt compelled to abstain from anything associated with such ceremonies.

Therefore, in consideration of the brothers and sisters in Christ who continued to struggle with the issue, Paul asks other believers to willingly abstain from the practice as well. Even though they had freedom in Christ, the highest calling for the believer is love. And love should constrain them to limit the exercise of their Christian freedom. Concern for one's fellow Christian takes precedence over personal freedom in Christ.

Critical Observation

It is faulty thinking to believe that freedom in Christ entitles a person to do anything he or she wants to. Any fool can do that. True freedom in Christ is having the courage and will to do what *ought* to be done. One of the most important exercises of Christian freedom is willfully abstaining from certain things in order not to cause someone else to stumble in his or her walk with the Lord.

Where does a believer draw the line and set boundaries? Paul indicates that the gray areas of the Christian life will depend on the circumstances and the people affected by one's choices (8:10–12). Personally, Paul is willing to give up eating meat altogether if that's what it takes to bring others closer to Christ (8:13).

It would have required much less thought and care to either create blanket prohibitions of certain practices or to authorize them indiscriminately. But Paul's approach is much truer to reality and to biblical revelation. Christian freedom can certainly be exercised, though believers first need to exercise prayerful thought and godly concern for fellow Christians. They might also seek out wise counsel from other mature believers in order to do God's bidding and bring glory to Him in all areas of their lives.

Take It Home

Eating meat offered to idols isn't much of an issue for most Christians today—at least in the Western world of America and Europe. But what other practices can you think of that tend to create tensions between groups of Christians? How would Paul's advice to the Corinthians apply to such contemporary issues?

1 CORINTHIANS 9:1–27

AN APOSTLE'S RIGHTS

What an Apostle Is Due	9:1–14
What an Apostle Is Willing to Do Without	9:15–27

Setting Up the Section

Paul has just encouraged the Corinthians to willingly forego their Christian rights if by doing so they could prevent more immature believers from stumbling. In this section, Paul gives a personal example of how he had sacrificed his rights for the good of others. By doing so, he also addresses some underlying resentment from a portion of the Corinthian church.

9:1–14

WHAT AN APOSTLE IS DUE

Because of the way chapter divisions have been added to the original scriptures, it appears that Paul is beginning a new thought in 1 Corinthians 9. But chapters 8 through 10 are a continuation of the same theme. Paul had just expressed a willingness to never eat meat again if his choice would keep a weaker believer from stumbling (8:13). As he continues, he will list other things he has given up to minimize problems and dissension in the church.

If anyone was skeptical about Paul's right to be an apostle, it shouldn't have been the Corinthians. Paul's credentials were not only that he had seen the living Jesus on the road to Damascus, but also that he had begun the church in Corinth—sure verification of his calling (9:1–2).

Paul was a proven apostle, and apostles had rights. Although the church should have been supporting him, he never demanded it even though other churches were taking care of the expenses of their leaders—and the leaders' wives as well (9:3–6).

Demystifying 1 Corinthians

In the custom of the time, philosophers and wandering speakers had various means of support. Some charged fees, some enlisted financial backers, some would beg as they went, and others would work. Paul had been taught a trade, as had all educated young Jewish men, and had been willing to work when necessary (Acts 18:1–3). However, the Greek mentality looked down on physical labor, and many Gentiles preferred to leave manual work to their slaves while they pursued art, philosophy, sport, and leisure. This may have been true of some in the Corinthian church.

It was common sense that someone who did so much work should be recompensed in some way. Soldiers were paid for their service to the nation. Gardeners ate the fruit they planted. Shepherds drank their animals' milk. People were sure to feed the oxen that turned the mill wheels (9:7–12). A priest got a share of what was offered at the temple (9:13–14). So how much more should a church take care of its spiritual leader?

Paul's argument is strong that he should be entitled to certain rights and privileges in return for the work and service he is doing for others. Yet he refuses to demand anything because of his high regard for the gospel of Christ (9:12).

9:15–27

WHAT AN APOSTLE IS WILLING TO DO WITHOUT

It might be natural to think that Paul is complaining about what he doesn't have in order to goad his readers into providing him with more support. But that is not his intent. The very point he is trying to make is that the purpose of Christian freedom is to allow believers to choose to do without personal entitlements for the sake of others. It is a matter of love, not privilege.

Paul doesn't require financial support because he is more than satisfied with the reward he has received—the privilege of preaching the gospel without charge (9:18). If he were performing his ministry only because he was getting paid, he wouldn't have found it nearly as fulfilling.

Because of Paul's willingness to minister without remuneration, it not only benefited those he preached to, but also gave him great freedom. He didn't have to justify an expense form or give regular reports to a patron. He used his Christian freedom to live for Christ as fully as possible. When around fellow Jews, he would adhere to all Jewish customs and dietary restrictions, even though he felt no spiritual obligation to do so.

When among Gentiles, he adapted to their less traditional practices and menus. When around immature believers, he would practice no spiritual freedom that might alarm them and cause them to stumble in their progress. In devotion to Jesus, Paul attempted to be "all things to all men" (9:22 NIV).

Critical Observation

The concept of becoming all things to all people in order to win them over to the kingdom of God is frequently misunderstood and misapplied. Paul never neglected or compromised his firm Christian convictions. He wasn't willing to water down his theology in an attempt to appease others. But he was always willing to set aside his Christian freedoms if by doing so he would benefit others.

Many of Paul's readers would have been aware of, if not involved in, the Olympics in Greece, as well as the nearby Isthmian Games that took place every two to three years. So if they missed the point of sacrificing to get ahead on a spiritual level, they would have understood the athletic metaphors (9:24–27). A runner intent on winning would deny himself certain things while in training. Similarly, a boxer would toughen himself up to receive the blows he was sure to receive. But if such efforts resulted in a victory, then the outcome would be worth all the training and sacrifice (9:24–27).

Paul's reference to being disqualified (9:27) is not a suggestion that salvation could be lost. He is emphatic that nothing can separate a believer from the love of God (Romans 8:29–39). But a Christian "runner" who didn't abide by the rules could lose rewards that might be his or hers.

So just as Paul had previously expressed willingness to become a vegetarian in order not to offend a group of weak Christians (8:13), he also proclaims his willingness to set aside other Christian freedoms for the glory of God. He is more than willing to deny himself certain things if the result is the ongoing progress of other believers in their spiritual journeys. He is in the race and striving to win the prize at the end. And he is doing everything in his power to encourage others to do the same.

Take It Home

Paul's willingness to become "all things to all people" (9:22 ESV) allowed him to expand his ministry effectiveness beyond his natural Jewish comfort zone into Gentile territory, and beyond that into the realm of immature believers. He was able to adapt his behaviors without sacrificing his foundational beliefs. Have you had a similar experience where you were able to minister across cultures or across other potential barriers? If so, what were your biggest challenges? What were the results?

1 CORINTHIANS 10:1–11:1

TEMPTATION AND FREEDOM

Lessons from the Past	10:1–13
Lessons from Worship	10:14–22
Specific Guidelines	10:23–11:1

Setting Up the Section

In this section, Paul continues to follow up on the issue of eating food sacrificed to idols. He had previously stated that since idols were nothing of substance, it didn't matter if believers ate meat that had been sacrificed to them (8:4). But he had added warnings to avoid anything that would create spiritual difficulties for immature and growing Christians, and had provided an extensive argument for voluntarily suspending the exercise of Christian freedom for the good of others. As he now continues his train of thought, he warns of the danger of temptation for those who take too much pride in their freedom.

10:1–13

LESSONS FROM THE PAST

Paul had just asked his readers to forego their personal rights in cases where they could promote the gospel and win others to Jesus Christ. In this passage, he continues his argument by including examples from Israel's history.

When believers fail to exercise self-control, they expose themselves to danger. Paul points to several examples as the Israelites wandered in the wilderness of the Exodus. Paul begins by listing four privileges the people of Israel had received that could have led to subsequent blessings, yet didn't (10:1–5): They were guided by God's presence in the form of a cloud (Exodus 13:21–22); they safely escaped the Egyptians by crossing the parted Red Sea (Exodus 14:21–29); they feasted on manna and quail in the desert (Exodus 16); and they were provided with water supernaturally (Exodus 17:1–7).

With God providing such amazing feats for such a crowd of people, one might think the Israelites would have responded with gratitude and praise. But they didn't, and Paul lists four specific ways the people had proved faithless and suffered as a result (10:7–10): They repeatedly complained to Moses and God about their conditions in the desert (Exodus 17:2–3); they committed idolatry by worshiping the golden calf (Exodus 32:1–6); their grumbling turned into rebellion, which resulted in a widespread plague (Numbers 16.41–50); and they engaged in sexual immorality with women of Moab in connection with Baal worship (Numbers 25:1–9).

Paul connects the experience of the Israelites with that of the Corinthian church (10:6, 11). He is illustrating that even those who enjoy the greatest privileges of God are not immune to temptation. The experience of the Israelites should serve as a warning to the Corinthians believers, who were beginning to behave in a similar way. Like the offenses of the Israelites in the wilderness, the pagan temple feasts in Corinth involved idolatry and sexual sin, and tested God's patience.

Demystifying 1 Corinthians

The meaning of testing God (10:9) is to do something wrong to see what He will do in response. Like children who test parents with defiant behavior, believers sometimes flirt with danger or see how far they can go with rebellion before God steps in and does something about it.

It is a mistake to think that the Lord is indifferent or will look the other way when believers do wrong. It is precisely because they are His children that He will be stirred to action. He disciplines those He loves (Hebrews 12:5–6) to guide them back to the path of righteousness.

It is best to heed the mistakes of others to avoid similar failures and consequences (10:11). Everyone faces occasional temptations. No one is exempt. Believers will confront many of the same temptations that others have endured throughout human history, yet they can experience God's faithfulness during such times. Paul assures them that God will not give them more than they can handle, provided they rely on His strength and yield to the power of His indwelling Spirit (10:12–13).

10:14–22

LESSONS FROM WORSHIP

This brief history lesson serves to support what Paul has been saying about eating meat sacrificed to idols. Here he clarifies that while the food itself is morally neutral, the corresponding idolatry is not to be tolerated. To illustrate, Paul uses two more analogies. He begins with the Lord's Supper—something his Gentile readers would be familiar with. The sacrament connected the participant with the risen Lord through the appropriation of the symbols of His broken body and shed blood. And Jewish believers would have understood that after Old Testament sacrifices, those who ate the sacrificial meat in the temple communed with the Lord and appropriated the temporary forgiveness that was associated with those animal sacrifices.

Similarly, pagan sacrifices were not only offered to idols, but part of the meat was given back to the worshiper to hold a feast, with the belief that the god himself would be a guest. So while a believer need not be overly concerned about the meat itself, he or she should not participate in the pagan festivals (10:18–20). The idols may have been only wood and stone, but they had real spiritual forces behind them that believers were to avoid.

So whether Jewish, Christian, or pagan, a meal in connection with a sacrifice was intended to connect the worshiper with the deity. The common loaf of Communion represents a unity in Christ, which necessitates a separation from all false religions. Someone who sits at the table of the Lord in Communion could not then participate in a table that was an instrument of demons and pagan idols (10:21–22).

10:23–11:1

SPECIFIC GUIDELINES

Paul concludes what he had been saying for the past three chapters. The overall rule is that love for others should dictate a believer's choices and behaviors (10:23–24).

Critical Observation

What may be only a matter of dietary choice for a mature believer might be a major spiritual issue for another person. So those who are mature (and supposedly living their lives for God) are asked to sacrifice for the good and salvation of other Christians.

More specifically in the area of meat sacrificed to idols, what a believer did in his or her own home was of no concern. To a Christian, it was just a piece of meat (10:25–26). If believers were invited out to dinner where the meat was served, they could eat it in good conscience (10:27). But if a fellow believer was at the dinner and was troubled by what was served, the more mature believers should refuse to eat, lest he conform and feel that he was sinning.

All areas of life—including eating and drinking—should glorify God (10:31–33). It is easy enough to make an occasional sacrifice that would keep someone else from stumbling. By doing so, who knows when someone might find salvation or spiritual growth as a result?

Take It Home

Many people go through a stage in life where they tend to test God. Did you ever go through such a period? If so, what did you learn from it? Do you think everyone needs to go through the same process, or is it possible to learn from the mistakes of others?

1 CORINTHIANS 11:2–34

GUIDELINES FOR WORSHIP

Women and Worship 11:2–16
Bad Table Manners at the Lord's Supper 11:17–34

Setting Up the Section

After a comprehensive response to the Corinthians' question about eating meat sacrificed to idols (chapters 8–10), Paul moves on to another topic in this section. For the next several chapters he will address various issues of church propriety. In this passage, he addresses gender issues and provides clear instructions for the observance of the Lord's Supper.

11:2–16

WOMEN AND WORSHIP

During Paul's day, it was customary for a woman to wear a veil, similar to a scarf, which covered the head and hung down over her neck. No respectable woman would think of appearing in public without it. Recent immigrations of Arabic people have exposed more Westerners to such dress, and many tend to identify the dress as a religious requirement. However, Paul was writing seven hundred years before Islam came into being. Wearing a veil was widespread among women throughout the ancient Near East as a sign of honor, dignity, security, and respect.

The first-century attitude toward women was that they were inferior and subordinate to men. Jewish women could attend synagogue worship, but they were segregated from the men, in a separate part of the building. Greek women were not allowed to attend school and get an education.

So as women became believers and joined the church, they were viewed with a degree of discrimination and narrow-mindedness. While the question of whether or not a woman should have her head covered or have a particular hairstyle may not seem important to most today, it was a very sensitive matter for the early church. Would the church also impose discrimination and second-class status onto its female members? Would women have all the same rights as men—including dress and hairstyles? Or would some middle ground need to be reached?

Demystifying 1 Corinthians

Bible scholars disagree about the exact problem Paul is addressing. A number of the words in the passage can be translated a variety of ways, and some of the language is metaphorical and symbolic in nature. The apparent meaning of the text has to do with the wearing of a veil, or head covering. Some think Paul is describing the practice of certain women to wear their hair cropped very short in contrast with the custom of the day. Others feel his reference is to women who wore their hair long and flowing in public, which was typical of prostitutes.

Paul first praises the Christians in Corinth for their faithfulness in responding to his teaching about freedom in Christ, but then explains that some of them had carried things too far (11:2). Although God may see males and females as equals and joint heirs of His kingdom, that doesn't mean that all the differences between the sexes have disappeared.

Freedom in Christ is no reason for either gender to abandon appropriate behavior and clothing to send the wrong signals about sexuality. Paul says believers should be careful how they present themselves to a watching world (11:3–6). They should err on the side of modesty.

Among the teachings of Gnosticism, a problematic philosophy that was beginning to influence the first-century churches, was the belief that spiritual purity would transcend one's gender. The Gnostics viewed an androgynous human as a pristine ideal. But Christianity has always recognized that God created men and women as sexual beings with sexual differences. Paul writes that it is unwise to attempt to blur the distinctions. He encourages the Corinthians instead to celebrate the differences between male and female (11:7–10). Modern studies verify specific differences between the genders, physiological and otherwise, so why not find great satisfaction in one's God-created design?

Paul is not, as some accuse him, trying to "put women in their place." Just the opposite. He had already acknowledged the right of women to pray and prophesy in the church (11:5), and he continues by clarifying that men and women cannot operate independently of one another (11:11–12). For a male writing in the first century, Paul's teachings were progressive and radical. He was one of the first advocates for the legitimate role of women in church leadership, but he also wanted to ensure that both women and men were submissive to God and acted appropriately (11:13–16).

11:17–34

BAD TABLE MANNERS AT THE LORD'S SUPPER

Paul usually tries to acknowledge what a church is doing right before correcting its members or challenging them to do better. But when it came to the Corinthians' behavior during celebrations of the Lord's Supper, Paul could find nothing good to say (11:17).

The early church met weekly at a potluck-supper-type meal called the Agape Feast that would culminate with the celebration of Communion. But at Corinth, the wealthy people (who didn't have to work until sunset as did the poorer manual laborers) would go early and eat their fill, leaving little, if anything, for those who needed the food most. Some would drink their fill to the point of drunkenness (11:18–22). The very meal that was supposed to bring people closer to one another and to God had become an embarrassment and yet another source of division within the Corinthian church. And the people's self-centered behavior had not gone unnoticed; God was passing judgment (11:30).

Critical Observation

Since Paul's letter to the Corinthians was written before the Gospels, this passage contains the first recorded words of Jesus. Paul's instructions to the Corinthians about the appropriate procedure for celebrating the Lord's Supper (11:23–26) have become known as the Words of Institution and are used in some form in most Christian churches around the world.

Paul reminds the Corinthians of the proper procedure and purpose of the Lord's Supper (11:23–26). He also instructs the believers to examine themselves before participating (11:28). They should not see the meal without seeing the body and blood of Jesus. And he tells them to consider the others involved (11:27–34).

Jesus died to bring people closer to God. A believer's spiritual rebirth places him or her in the spiritual family of the church with an ongoing calling to be mindful of other believers. And there is no time a Christian should be more aware of this fact than during the solemn reminder of the Lord's Supper.

Take It Home

Paul's instructions for the Corinthians to examine themselves (11:28) apply to the modern church as well. It is easy to get into habits or traditions that require little thought about the things that should be most important in one's life. Think about your own attention to the celebration of the Lord's Supper, and your attitude toward gender differences in the church as well. Can you think of anything you might do to renew your spiritual commitment or heighten your experience in either of these areas?

1 CORINTHIANS 12:1–31

UNDERSTANDING SPIRITUAL GIFTS

An Explanation of the Gifts of the Spirit	12:1–11
Unity and Diversity in the Church	12:12–20
Interdependency in the Church	12:21–31

Setting Up the Section

In this section of Paul's Epistle, he continues to respond to a number of problems that have been creating divisions in the church at Corinth. In the previous section, he addressed some women who were disrupting worship services with the way they prayed and prophesied. He also dealt with the terrible things the Corinthian church members were doing to demean the Lord's Supper. Now he turns his attention to the topic of spiritual gifts—yet another part of church life meant to bring people closer together, but was having the opposite result.

12:1–11

AN EXPLANATION OF THE GIFTS OF THE SPIRIT

Continuing his critique of the worship problems in the Corinthian church, Paul moves on to the practice of spiritual gifts. The Greek word translated "gifts" is *charismata*, the source of our word *charismatic*. The word could also be interpreted as "gifts of grace." Paul says that the church was to be a charismatic, Spirit-gifted community.

Many of the Corinthians had come from pagan backgrounds and had worshiped idols. But the idols were mute, and provided them with no help or direction. The Holy Spirit of God, in contrast, would provide them with knowledge and spiritual substance (12:1–3).

This group of spiritual gifts that Paul lists (12:8–11, 28–30) is not exhaustive. He provides lists in other places as well (Romans 12:6–8; Ephesians 4:11–13).

Critical Observation

Spiritual gifts are not the same as natural abilities. Spiritual gifts are special abilities given by God after a person has become a Christian. The Spirit of God infuses natural skill with a new spiritual dynamic to empower the person to be productive in the work of Christ. As each believer identifies and begins to use his or her spiritual gifts, the church grows stronger.

Scholars have identified ninety-six different New Testament images to describe the church, including the household of God, the people of God, the bride of Christ, and the fellowship of the Holy Spirit. But the symbol that dominates the New Testament is the perception of the church as the body of Christ.

12:12–20

UNITY AND DIVERSITY IN THE CHURCH

Paul emphasizes the importance of unity in the body of Christ. The church, though comprised of many members, is intended to be a single unit (12:12–13), an organic whole regardless of racial or religious backgrounds (Jews or Greeks) or social standing (slave or free).

Unity, however, is not the same as uniformity. Paul is not writing about an institutional unity. Various groups within Christianity, and even within denominations, will have different opinions and emphases that should be respected as long as all agree on the great orthodox spiritual truths that all Christians share.

Then Paul moves on to the obvious fact that there exists diversity in the body of Christ—as there *should* be. Yes, the human body is a single unit, but is comprised of a great many diverse parts. Paul's logic is compelling. No physical body can function as all seeing, all hearing, or all smelling (12:14–20). So why should the church expect to function with a focus on only one spiritual gift?

Still, many believers (whether first century or twenty-first century) tend to separate themselves from others whose gifts appear too different. They understand their own gifts and trust those with similar gifts, which is a natural response. But the work of the Holy Spirit is supernatural. People are not all the same, their gifts will differ according to God's will, and believers should learn to accept one another. They are called to celebrate their diversity within the unity of the church, which provides a place of belonging for a wide range of followers of Jesus Christ.

12:21–31

INTERDEPENDENCY IN THE CHURCH

The various members of the body of Christ are not just to learn to tolerate one another. Like the parts of the human body, there is a principle of mutual interdependence that is critical to proper operation. While some parts of the body function differently from others, there is nevertheless mutuality to common life together. The effectiveness, health, and vitality of the church are dependent on how well its various members function together as a whole (12:21–26).

No individual has the right to say to another, "I don't need you." And whether or not church members realize it, each person is indispensable for collective effectiveness in the world. Indeed, unity and interdependence create a richness and texture for the collective witness of the church.

Demystifying 1 Corinthians

Paul points out a concern that is still a problem for many churches today: The Corinthians' perception of spiritual gifts wasn't accurate. Some of the gifts that *seemed* less important were actually indispensable. Others that appeared quite special were not any more special than the others (12:22–23). Therefore, it is important to trust God in the dispersal of gifts and to put one's gift(s) to use without questioning or comparing.

Not everyone can preach. Not everyone can sing. Not everyone can teach. But everyone is gifted to do *something* (12:29–30). Apparently, the problem in Corinth was a rivalry between spiritual gifts and a jealousy that caused some people to covet the gifts of others. There was no unity, no positive diversity, and certainly no interdependence.

Paul will get to the root of the problem in his next section. But he provides a clue about where he is headed as he concludes this section by telling believers to "eagerly desire the greater gifts" (12:31 NIV).

Take It Home

Rather than focus on your own spiritual gift(s) as you contemplate this section of Paul's writing, think of other believers you know and try to identify *their* gifts. Be sure to differentiate between natural abilities and spiritual gifts. Then, when you get the opportunity, contact those people and thank them for the specific contributions they make to the body of Christ.

1 CORINTHIANS 13:1–13

THE DIFFERENCE LOVE MAKES

The Necessity of Love	13:1–3
The Character of Love	13:4–7
The Permanence of Love	13:8–13

Setting Up the Section

Paul has just finished a rather harsh scolding of the Corinthians—first for their self-centered and unacceptable behavior during the Lord's Supper (11:17–22) and then for the arguments they were having over spiritual gifts (chapter 12). Throughout his Epistle, Paul has tried to emphasize the importance of love in dealing with the various problems of the church. In this passage, he offers a definition of love, and his words have become a cherished portion of scripture as well as a classic piece of literature.

13:1–3

THE NECESSITY OF LOVE

The widespread popularity of 1 Corinthians 13 is understandable, considering the magnificent depiction of love that Paul provides. Yet Paul never intended it to be a stand-alone chapter. In the context of what he had been writing, the importance of love was provided as a solution for the various problems that had been dividing the church. He intended this passage to help the Corinthian believers understand the destructive ways in which they had been using their spiritual gifts, especially in regard to worship. It seems that many people were prideful of their gifts and thought they were better than others because of what God had enabled them to do in the church. Paul counters this notion and points them to a more desirable way (12:31).

The first point Paul makes is that love is absolutely necessary if the church is to function as God intends. People can use their Spirit-given gifts and generate some big actions in the church. They can speak in angelic tongues, understand deep mysteries, give all their possessions to the poor, and sacrifice their very bodies. But actions performed without love don't count for anything (13:1–3).

Love is to be the centerpiece of a Christian's life. Evidently, the Corinthians had been arguing about who was performing the greatest works. Instead, they should have been considering who was showing the greatest love.

13:4–7

THE CHARACTER OF LOVE

The word *love* is tossed around in literature, music, advertising, and visual arts. Surely it was much the same in ancient Corinth, especially with the rampant sexual promiscuity in the culture. Even believers are frequently misled into thinking that love is primarily an emotion—something a person falls into and out of. So Paul provides a description that has nothing to do with hearts and flowers.

True Christian love is not a warm and sentimental feeling. It has little to do with emotion at all. By Paul's definition, it is action in response to the conviction of one's heart and mind. With a series of fifteen succinct descriptive phrases, he explains why this degree of love is necessary for a believer in Jesus Christ (13:4–8). The terms he uses are not romantic sentiments, but rather commitments requiring active choices. This kind of love should be the goal of anyone who desires to live out the majestic and holy calling believers have in Christ.

13:8–13

THE PERMANENCE OF LOVE

Most likely, the arguments about spiritual gifts and divisions in the Corinthian church were centered on those that were most apparent: speaking in tongues, prophecy, healing, and so forth. It would have been quite clear who had those gifts in contrast to the gifts of faith, helping others, administration, etc.

So Paul concludes by clarifying that just because a spiritual gift is clearly from God and being used for the good of the church doesn't mean it is permanent. The time will come when those gifts are no longer needed. Prophecies will cease. Tongues will be stilled. Knowledge will pass away. Only three will always remain: faith, hope, and love. And love is the greatest of the three (13:13).

Many of the gifts of the Spirit are a temporal provision by God in order to equip people for the works of service to which He calls them. Yet those provisions for an imperfect world will one day be rendered unnecessary when the perfection of heaven comes (13:10).

No matter how hard believers try to relate to God, they cannot do so perfectly. Paul compares the process to childhood, when thoughts and reason are far from mature. But one day Christians will leave behind their childish ways and achieve full spiritual maturity.

Paul also compares a believer's image of God to what he or she might see in a mirror of the time. The reflection is helpful, but far from satisfying. It only makes the person wish for a clearer view.

Demystifying 1 Corinthians

The city of Corinth was known for its production of mirrors. But the modern mirror that we are familiar with didn't emerge until the thirteenth century. Mirrors in Corinth were made by polishing bronze until it was completely smooth and reflective. Even so, the bronze mirrors provided an imperfect reflection.

Paul's final promise is that someday believers will see God face-to-face. They will have answers for the things they don't understand. Imperfections will be left behind as they experience God's perfect light.

But in the meantime, they can try to comprehend God's love and apply it to those around them. Now is the time for them to develop faith, hope, and love, because those three gifts will always be around.

Take It Home

Two thousand years after Paul's writing, the church continues to struggle with the human limitations of love. In an attempt to come closer to true self-sacrificial love, review Paul's description in 1 Corinthians 13:4–7. Does that sound like a description of you or anyone you know? If not, identify one specific aspect of love where you could use some improvement. Then focus on that one aspect for a while, asking God for help in becoming a more loving and effective believer.

1 CORINTHIANS 14:1–40

THE PROPER USE OF SPIRITUAL GIFTS

Different Gifts, Different Purposes	14:1–12
Speaking in Tongues Appropriately	14:13–25
Order in the Church	14:26–40

Setting Up the Section

In 1 Corinthians 12, Paul listed a number of spiritual gifts and challenged the believers to use them for the benefit of the church as a whole. He followed in 1 Corinthians 13 with the importance of love in connection with the exercise of gifts. In this section, he returns to a discussion of spiritual gifts and provides some specific guidelines for how they should be properly exercised in a church context.

14:1–12

DIFFERENT GIFTS, DIFFERENT PURPOSES

Paul is about to make some direct and perhaps confrontational comments, so he begins by making himself clear that people should be eager to receive the gifts of the Holy Spirit. And he reiterates what he had just written about the importance of love in connection with spiritual gifts (14:1).

Apparently the believers at Corinth had become enamored with the gift of speaking in tongues. Paul assures them that the gift has its place, yet needs to be used with love and discretion. He contrasts the gift of tongues with the gift of prophecy (14:2–5). The role of the New Testament prophet was to discern God's message to the church through the Holy Spirit. Unlike the modern church, the early believers had no Bibles for reference; even Old Testament scrolls were costly and difficult to secure. So the role of the prophet was very important.

Critical Observation

Believers are divided as to what "tongues" really means. Some believe the gift to the church in Corinth was no different than that to the church in Jerusalem on the Day of Pentecost (Acts 2:1–13): existing languages that could be understood if someone knowledgeable of that language were present. Throughout Corinthians, Paul uses the words *tongues* and *languages* interchangeably. Others believe the tongues in the Corinthian church were divine ecstatic utterances with no earthly equivalent. But either way, Paul's advice was valid. Without an interpreter, the church as a whole benefited little from proclamations that could not be understood.

Although the Corinthians were extolling speaking in tongues, Paul tells them to especially desire the gift of prophecy (14:1). Even though both tongues and prophecy require special revelation from God, there are significant differences. Foremost among them was the fact that everyone in attendance could understand what God was saying through the prophet. But the person speaking in tongues didn't know what he or she was saying, nor did the church. An interpreter was needed, but none was present. The person speaking in tongues would feel edified, but only in a mysterious spiritual way. No one else was benefiting.

Paul provides some practical examples to make his point (14:6–12). First, he asks the Corinthians to suppose he had come to them speaking only in tongues they could not understand. Clearly, they had needed clear knowledge and instruction, as did the newer believers currently in their midst. He uses music as a second example. The cacophony of an orchestra warming up doesn't warrant anyone's attention. But when the notes are arranged to provide a symphony, it means something to the listeners. Third, Paul refers to a military trumpet giving signals to the soldiers. If it is unclear whether the signal is to advance or retreat, how could the army function?

The church needs clear signals. Those with the gift of prophecy, who provide vital information, should not be disparaged. Using the gift of speaking in tongues without having an interpreter is not much different than having a foreign-speaking visitor give the sermon with no translator (14:10–11).

14:13–25

SPEAKING IN TONGUES APPROPRIATELY

Paul never tells the Corinthians *not* to speak in tongues. In fact, he expresses thanks that he had the gift himself (14:18). But he is firm in clarifying the right way to use the gift. He insists that gifts that benefit the church should always be given preference over those that only edify the individual. The people who took undue pride in the gift of tongues thought they were the mature segment of the church, but Paul says they are thinking like children (14:20).

Demystifying 1 Corinthians

In verse 22, Paul comments that tongues are significant for unbelievers. This is in reference to his previous quotation from Isaiah (1 Corinthians 14:21). When God's people stopped believing in Him, they were taken into captivity where they heard strange tongues that symbolized God's rejection. Paul goes on to explain that church attendees who heard people speaking in tongues without explanation would have no idea what was going on (14:23).

People who spoke God's Word in an understandable language would benefit both the believers and unbelievers in the assembly. People would hear and respond, and the church would grow. *That* was the mature outlook.

14:26–40

ORDER IN THE CHURCH

As he starts to conclude this section, Paul writes that all spiritual gifts should be used in an orderly, helpful, productive manner. If speaking in tongues, the public expression should be limited to two or three people, with interpretations for each one. Otherwise, the person(s) should worship silently and privately (14:2–28).

If prophesying, again, the number should be limited to two or three. And the speakers shouldn't compete. They were to take turns so those assembled could hear each one to receive instruction and encouragement. Otherwise, it would appear that believers serve a God of disorder (14:29–33).

Paul's shift to address women at this point (14:34–35) is the cause of much debate, but he doesn't seem to indicate that *all* women should be silent at *all* church functions. He had previously validated their participation in prayer and prophesying (11:5, 13). Most likely his comments were intended to reduce potential confusion in the worship services. It might be that some of the women were asking questions or initiating debates over what was said.

One opinion is that Paul is speaking primarily to women married to believers, asking them to allow their husbands to speak for both of them. Others think he is simply asking the women to keep quiet just as (by limiting the number to three) he was asking some of those who would otherwise speak in tongues or prophesy to keep quiet. His mention of the law (14:34) might have been a reference to Genesis 3:16.

Paul reiterates the right and the privilege of putting all of the gifts of the Spirit into practice (14:39–40)—as long as they are carried out properly. He isn't just expressing his opinion, but using *his* gift to let the Corinthians know how God felt about their worship (14:36–38). And with that, he concludes his writing on spiritual gifts. He had other essential matters to cover before ending his letter.

Take It Home

Do other people do things during worship that make it difficult for you to keep your focus on God? Can you think of anything you do that might inhibit another's worship? How would you feel if those in authority asked you to submit and keep quiet for the good of the church as a whole?

1 CORINTHIANS 15:1–58

RESURRECTION AND EXPECTATION

A Matter of First Importance	15:1–11
The Power of Resurrection	15:12–34
Perfect, Imperishable Bodies	15:35–58

Setting Up the Section

In the previous section, Paul concluded a rather extensive passage examining spiritual gifts and their proper place in worship. He had addressed the Corinthians' past behavior and provided instructions for the current state of the church. In this passage, he turns their attention to the future as he writes of what they can expect at resurrection and beyond.

On the basis of a "dualistic" worldview that viewed the physical world as evil and only the spirit world as good, some of the Corinthian believers were evidently claiming that there would be no resurrection of the body. Paul responds by affirming both the certainty of Christ's bodily resurrection and the centrality of the resurrection for the Christian faith. He also discusses the nature of our glorified bodies.

15:1–11

A MATTER OF FIRST IMPORTANCE

Paul had been dealing with problems and issues that had recently come up in the church at Corinth. So he uses the opportunity to remind the believers of a few things he had already taught them—things that should have been having an effect on their behavior.

He assures them that they had indeed received the gospel (15:1). Salvation is a gift from God. No one ever discovers it on one's own or accomplishes it by clever insight, imaginative thinking, or hard work. In addition, the gospel is the foundation on which they stood. They based the weight of their lives, hopes, and dreams of heaven on what Paul had originally preached to them. By his own estimation, the most important message is that Jesus had died for the sins of humankind, was buried, raised from the dead, and had made numerous undeniable appearances (15:3–8).

Critical Observation

Although the word *gospel* (generally translated as "good news") has come to be closely associated with Christianity, its roots go further back into pagan and Jewish culture. The Romans used the word to mean "joyful tidings." But Paul and other early Christian writers adopted *gospel* to refer to the coming of Christ for the salvation of the world. The "good news" is that Jesus had been resurrected after His death on the cross, providing eternal life for those who believe in Him.

After His resurrection, Jesus had appeared to Peter, the eleven remaining apostles (still referred to as the Twelve), James, a group of more than five hundred, and others. Peter had denied Jesus. James had doubted Him. And Paul was the worst of them all (15:9).

Still, Paul spoke with authority about the effect of the gospel on a person. Although Jesus had already ascended, He showed Himself to Paul on the road to Damascus, and Paul received the grace of God to turn his life completely around and discover his calling (15:9–11). Paul considered himself the least among the apostles, so he could attest to the Corinthians that holding firmly to faith in Christ and His resurrection was their only hope in this life and the life to come.

15:12–34

THE POWER OF RESURRECTION

The debate about whether or not the dead would be resurrected had been going on for a long time. It was a major point of contention between the Pharisees (who said yes) and the Sadducees (who said no). The issue of Jesus' resurrection made the topic that much more relevant (15:12).

Paul says there are only two options: Either Jesus was resurrected, or He wasn't. If Christ had *not* been resurrected, then nobody else would be either. And that would also mean that Christianity was a lie and all preaching was in vain. Sin would still reign. People would have no hope. And to attempt to live a victorious life on earth with no anticipation of eternal life was simply pitiable (15:13–19).

But Paul makes it clear that the other option is the truth. Jesus has indeed been raised from the dead. Adam's sin has separated all humankind from God, but Jesus' sacrifice has redeemed them all and restored an intimate relationship. Jesus has been resurrected, and all believers will follow Him into eternal life after their deaths (15:22–23). The resurrection of Jesus is God's ultimate victory over sin and death (15:24–28).

No one could question Paul's commitment to his belief in Jesus' resurrection. He proved it by facing danger every day (15:31). The beasts he fought in Ephesus (15:32) were probably the people in an angry mob out to find him (Acts 19:28–31). His point is that it would be foolhardy to keep putting his life on the line for a faith that ended at his death. If that were the case, the live-for-today philosophies would make more sense. But the reality of resurrection makes a difference in how believers should live. The Corinthians had no excuse to be indifferent to God (15:32–34).

Demystifying 1 Corinthians

Paul doesn't clarify what he means by his reference to those "baptized for the dead" (15:29), and there have been around two hundred various theories to explain what he was referring to. Just north of Corinth in Eleusis, members of a pagan religion practiced baptism in the sea that was connected with expectations of afterlife bliss. Perhaps Paul was making mention of this mysterious practice. Maybe he meant that the baptism of new believers filled the spots left by the deaths of older believers. Or possibly living believers wanted to be baptized as surrogates for believers who never had the privilege before they died.

15:35–58

PERFECT, IMPERISHABLE BODIES

The attempt to comprehend biblical truths like the resurrection can be overwhelming, and people can begin to pose all sorts of questions (15:35). But just as amazing, Paul points out, is how plants grow from seeds. A shriveled, dead-looking seed can be placed in the ground to produce not the same plant it once was, but the same *kind* of plant with far more fruit than was buried (15:36–38).

In addition, there are all kinds of "bodies"—human, animal, heavenly, etc. The resurrection body will differ from the earthly body in that it will be glorious, imperishable, and spiritual (15:39–44).

Human beings first bear the likeness of Adam in a natural body that eventually returns to the dust of the earth. But after death, believers can look forward to receiving an eternal body with form and structure that bears the likeness of Christ (15:45–49).

Finally, Paul tells his readers why they shouldn't fear death. For believers, it is only a passageway to immortality and eternal life with God. Jesus has removed the sting of sin and the power of death. Victory over death is assured (15:57). Whether dead or alive when Jesus returns, believers' bodies will be changed.

So rather than sit around and speculate about matters that God has already taken care of, Christians should stand firm and get to work (15:58). The assurances of God should not lull them into self-satisfaction, but motivate them to greater love and service.

Take It Home

Today's believers have had two thousand years of history and theology to help them deal with the concept of death and resurrection, and still we have questions. But put yourself in the place of a believer in the first century, when the topic was still very new. What questions would you have had? How would you have felt after hearing Paul's words in this passage?

1 CORINTHIANS 16:1–24

GIVING AND GREETING

The Gift for Fellow Believers 16:1–4
Some Final Personal Matters 16:5–24

Setting Up the Section

Paul is wrapping up his lengthy letter to the Corinthians. Before ending, he has one more matter of business to address, and he wants to convey a number of personal greetings and make a few final requests.

16:1–4

THE GIFT FOR FELLOW BELIEVERS

Before signing off his letter to the Corinthians, Paul wants to answer one final question. Someone had asked about the collection he was taking for the church in Jerusalem. There is no additional information to be found about what he had told the Galatian churches (16:1).

The first day of the week was not yet called the Lord's day, even though Christians had already begun to assemble on that day in memory of the resurrection of Jesus. And it was never called the Sabbath, which was Saturday, the day the Jews met for group worship. Paul tells the Corinthians to regularly bring their financial gifts on the first day of the week. He doesn't want to have to take up a special collection when he gets there; he prefers that the believers make giving to others an ongoing commitment and have their gift ready when he arrives.

Demystifying 1 Corinthians

Tithing is never mentioned in the New Testament. It had been a method of giving prescribed for the Israelites under the Mosaic Law as well as a method of taxation in certain circumstances. Some feel Christians should still tithe because Abraham's tithe to Melchizedek (Genesis 14:18–20) predated the law. Others feel New Testament giving should be less dictated and more heartfelt, based on this passage and 2 Corinthians 8–9.

The church in Jerusalem had been suffering from both persecution and famine. The churches in Greece and Galatia owed their existence to the people God had called out of Jerusalem to go out and minister. So it should have been a natural response for them to help out their sister church financially.

When Paul wrote, he wasn't sure if he would personally take the collection back to Jerusalem (16:4). As it turned out, he did (Acts 21:17; 24:17).

16:5–24

SOME FINAL PERSONAL MATTERS

Paul closes by sharing some of his plans with the Corinthian believers. His phrasing shows that although he was making plans, his ultimate itinerary depended on God. He demonstrates that a believer can use God-given wisdom to keep moving ahead rather than waiting for detailed knowledge of God's will before even getting started.

Paul also acknowledges his fellow ministers, as he usually does in his letters. He is thankful for Timothy (16:10); Apollos (16:12); Stephanas, Fortunatus, and Achaicus (16:15–18); and Aquila and Priscilla (16:19). Divided loyalties between church leaders was one of the problems at Corinth (1:11–12), but Paul always gave credit to *everyone* whom he saw at work for God—whether they were ministering alongside him or elsewhere.

Critical Observation

Although Paul had written a lot of things to correct unwarranted behavior among the Corinthians, he closes with an emphasis on unity and love.

Paul wants to spend a considerable amount of time in Corinth (16:6–7), which is not surprising considering the number and the severity of the issues that demanded his attention. This letter must have been helpful to the Corinthian church, yet its problems would continue. Paul's next Epistle (2 Corinthians) will provide further details of the issues that threatened the unity of the believers in Corinth. Among them would be the resistance to Paul's authority by several of those in the church. Paul will ably defend himself, yet his love and concern for those in Corinth will never waver.

Take It Home

The money Paul was collecting was from primarily Gentile churches to benefit a church with mostly Jewish believers. It was more than a financial gift; it was a symbol of interconnection between two groups who were quite different. Does your church (or your personal) giving ever accomplish a similar goal of reaching out to those beyond your immediate community, based solely on your unity in Jesus?

2 CORINTHIANS

INTRODUCTION TO 2 CORINTHIANS

This epistle from Paul to the Corinthian church is a follow-up letter to 1 Corinthians. The topics he discusses are similar, particularly the concern with the false teachers who continued to plague them. Though Paul addresses both general principles and issues specific to the Corinthian community, there is much here for the church today.

AUTHOR

Paul not only identifies himself as the author of 2 Corinthians (1:1; 10:1) but also provides more autobiographical information than in any of his other letters.

OCCASION

After establishing a church at Corinth (Acts 18:1–11), Paul continued to correspond with the believers there. Some of the correspondence between them has never been discovered (1 Corinthians 5:9; 7:1; 2 Corinthians 2:4; 7:8). In 1 Corinthians, Paul had addressed specific issues that had been raised in previous communications. He firmly advised the church how to handle its problems.

Some time later, while Paul was ministering in Ephesus, he took a trip to Corinth to correct some of the problems that his first letter had not resolved. This was an unsuccessful mission, and Paul was hurt and embarrassed by his reception at Corinth (2:1; 12:14, 21; 13:1–2). In response, he returned to Ephesus and wrote a severe and sorrowful letter (now lost, but referred to in 2:4; 7:8) to the Corinthians, calling them to repent of their disobedience. He sent this letter to Corinth with Titus (7:8–13).

Paul then traveled north from Ephesus to Troas (in modern northwest Turkey), expecting to meet up with Titus and to learn about the response of the Corinthian church. But Titus was not there, so Paul moved on to Macedonia in northern Greece (Acts 20:1; 2 Corinthians 7:5). There he finally met up with Titus who brought the good news that many in the Corinthian church had repented and were greatly appreciative of his ministry. Paul sat down and wrote 2 Corinthians to express his great joy and to encourage the believers further in their faith.

PURPOSE

Although many Corinthian believers had acknowledged and respected the apostolic authority of Paul, there were others who hadn't. A number of self-designated church leaders had appeared in Corinth and set out to undermine Paul. They accused him of being bold in his letters but weak in person. They said that since he didn't charge the Corinthian church for his service to them, his ministry must essentially be worthless. And as they continued attempts to erode Paul's integrity, they began to attract followers from among the Corinthian Christians. Therefore, throughout this Epistle, Paul tends to defend his ministry more than usual. He remains highly supportive and encouraging toward the Corinthian believers, yet targets the troublemakers and rebuts their accusations.

In addition to responding to these criticisms about his apostolic credentials, he needed to ask them to forgive someone who was seeking to restore fellowship with them (2:5–11), and to prompt them to prepare their offering for the church in Jerusalem (chapters 8–9).

THEMES

Paul's appeal to the Corinthians reveals his vulnerability. Even during times of dire distress and deep disappointment, Paul demonstrates the value of trust in "the Father of mercies" and "the God of all comfort" (1:3 NASB).

His writing also reflects ongoing encouragement. Throughout this letter, when Paul had every reason to be offended, he instead focuses on the encouragement and comfort he received not only from God, but from the Corinthians as well.

And as Paul provides a reluctant, but necessary, defense of his ministry, he writes of authenticity. His work for God is based on genuine love for others and commitment to his calling, as contrasted to the self-serving and manipulative tactics of the false apostles in Corinth.

HISTORICAL CONTEXT

Corinth was a much-traveled city and heavily influenced by Greek culture, including its idolatry and sexual promiscuity. Not surprisingly, the church had to deal with members affected by such temptations. Additionally, enough time had passed since the death of Jesus and introduction of the gospel for false teachers to begin to infiltrate the churches. This problem was particularly evident in the Corinthian church.

CONTRIBUTION TO THE BIBLE

Second Corinthians is a valuable book because it reveals not only the trials and tribulations, but also the joy and fulfillment that come from Christian ministry. Paul's directness, his "tough love," his encouragement, and his compassion, had initiated the repentance of many of the believers at Corinth.

In defending his ministry, we see Paul at his most human. In many of his writings, Paul's tremendous zeal and devotion seem almost unreal and unattainable for most people. Yet all believers can identify with the personal sufferings and frustrations Paul expresses in this letter.

Paul's Corinthian Contacts and Correspondence	
First Visit	ca. AD 51; Paul establishes the church; stays 18 months
First Letter	A short letter to respond to immorality in the church (1 Corinthians 5:9)
Second Letter	**1 Corinthians** written from Ephesus: *Dealing with problems and questions in the church*
Second Visit	ca. AD 56–57; Journey from Ephesus; painful visit.
Third Letter	A severe and sorrowful letter (2 Corinthians 2:4; 7:8)
Fourth Letter	**2 Corinthians** written from Macedonia: *Restoration for some; rebuke for others*
Third Visit	ca. AD 57–58; Paul comes and stays 3 months in Corinth; writes **Romans**.

OUTLINE

SETTING THE RECORD STRAIGHT 1:1–2:11

Greetings and Comfort 1:1–11
A Change of Plans 1:12–2:4
Punishment and Forgiveness 2:5–11

PAUL'S CONFIDENCE 2:12–4:18

Sweet Fragrance or Foul Smell? 2:12–17
Proven Competence 3:1–6
Comparing the Covenants 3:7–18
Treasure in a Clay Jar 4:1–12
The Benefit of Suffering 4:13–18

NEW DWELLINGS, NEW CREATIONS, AND NEW ATTITUDES 5:1–7:1

From a Tent to a House 5:1–10
Reconciled to God 5:11–19
Ambassadors for Christ 5:20–6:10
Choosing Sides 6:11–7:1

GRIEVING AND GIVING 7:2–9:15

Godly Sorrow, Godly Joy 7:2–16
Exemplary Giving 8:1–15
A Delegation to Precede Paul 8:16–9:15

MINISTRY: GENUINE AND OTHERWISE 10:1–11:33

Paul's Assessment of His Ministry 10:1–18
Necessary "Foolishness" 11:1–15
Three Comparisons 11:16–33

INEXPRESSIBLE GLORY AND UNAVOIDABLE THORNS 12:1–13:14

Paul's Incredible Vision 12:1–6
Paul's Thorn in the Flesh 12:7–10
Paul's Closing Argument 12:11–13:14

2 CORINTHIANS 1:1–2:11

SETTING THE RECORD STRAIGHT

Greetings and Comfort 1:1–11
A Change of Plans 1:12–2:4
Punishment and Forgiveness 2:5–11

Setting Up the Section

Paul writes this letter with mixed emotions. Although he knows of some problems in the church at Corinth, he also feels a sense of great relief. He had been hoping to receive word from the Corinthians in response to his previous letter (2:4; 7:8), but was unable to locate the messenger, Titus, for a while (2:13). Later, in Macedonia, Titus catches up to Paul and tells him of the Corinthians' repentance and love for Paul (7:5–7). So even though Paul writes of trials and suffering, he does so out of a heart filled with joy.

1:1–11

GREETINGS AND COMFORT

The fact that Paul opens this letter by identifying himself as Christ's apostle by the will of God (1:1) is significant. In later sections he will address the fact that a segment of those in Corinth were challenging his integrity and his call to be an apostle.

Paul may have been away from the Corinthians and uncertain about their response to his previous letter(s), but at least he had Timothy with him (1:1). Timothy was a regular comfort to Paul in his travels. Even though Timothy was quite young when Paul recruited him, Paul considered the young minister a brother.

Paul could experience great comfort because of his understanding of God. All three titles he uses for God (1:3) are not only assurances for Paul, but for all believers as well. Paul will have much to say about suffering in this letter, but he begins with the outcome of his sufferings: comfort. He makes it clear that believers will sometimes share in the sufferings of Jesus, but they will also share in the comfort that only God can provide (1:3–7).

Paul's sufferings are no small matter. He had encountered situations that were literally life-threatening (1:9). As a result, the grace and subsequent comfort of God were very real and dear to him. And because of his personal experience, he could make a very persuasive argument to the Corinthians (1:5–7).

Critical Observation

One example of Paul's sufferings is found in Acts 14:8–20, where Paul is stoned by an angry crowd and left for dead. During the experience, he likely didn't expect God to spare him. He was prepared to face death, which eventually became an ongoing attitude for him (Philippians 1:21–24).

The peril of which Paul refers to (1:10) is unclear. He had previously written of fighting wild beasts in Ephesus (1 Corinthians 15:32), which is usually considered to be a reference to the events of Acts 19:23–41. But nothing had actually happened to Paul during that fracas, so this may be reference to a different experience.

Paul notes that his own weaknesses and limitations only cause God's power to be more apparent (1:10–11). This is a point he will emphasize throughout this letter.

1:12–2:4

A CHANGE OF PLANS

Paul's boasting (1:12–14) had a present dimension; he could declare a clear conscience regarding his conduct among believers and nonbelievers. But it also had a future dimension that looked ahead to the day of the Lord Jesus—the Day of Judgment when Christ would return to establish His kingdom. When that time came, Paul could take pride in his association with the Corinthian church, and the believers could be proud of him. Conversely, Paul's opponents might be proud and boastful now, but would be silenced in the day of the Lord.

Demystifying 2 Corinthians

To *boast* usually has negative connotations, and rightly so. Yet this is the word Paul uses in his defenses throughout 2 Corinthians. Modern readers might not realize, though the first-century believers would have, that Paul had been verbally attacked by a group at Corinth. They wanted to discredit him and had accused him of a number of things. His boasting is simply a statement of his service to Jesus.

Paul never tries to infer that spiritual maturity requires special status or hidden knowledge. His writing style is simple and easy to understand (1:13–14).

While in Ephesus, Paul had made plans to visit Corinth twice, once on the way to Macedonia and once returning from Macedonia (1:15–16). His first visit, however, ended in disaster and disappointment when he was publicly harassed and embarrassed (2:1; 12:14, 21; 13:1–2). False apostles had attacked his authority, and the Corinthian congregation apparently sided with them against Paul. Paul therefore altered his plans and did not visit Corinth a second time, instead returning to Ephesus (2:1). This change of plans only gave his opponents more ammunition. They accused him of waffling on his promises, saying one thing and doing another (1:15–17). Their underlying charge was that since his plans seemed to waver, how could they trust his message?

Paul goes to great lengths to justify his change in plans and to explain that it in no way affected the truth of what he taught (1:15–20). He makes it clear that God's promises are sure. God keeps His word. Likewise, those who serve Him must also keep their word. It would be wrong if Paul had made a foolish promise he had no intention of keeping; but it was quite different to make plans that were subject to the will of God and leading of the Holy Spirit.

Besides, Paul wanted to spare the Corinthians any undue discomfort. His previous visit had been difficult (2:1). Perhaps he felt it was too soon to revisit. It was in this sense that he was sparing them (1:23)—by not wishing to confront them again until he had provided them with enough time to address their problems. Paul seems to realize that being there for someone is not always the best course of action. There are times when love may be better demonstrated by keeping one's distance rather than being present. It is Paul's intent to demonstrate love for the Corinthians rather than cause them further grief (2:4).

So Paul's plans had changed. Yet he was not at all casual in making this choice. Throughout his explanation, he emphasizes God's role in the decision (1:20–23) and what is best for his friends in Corinth (2:1–4). His critics were by no means justified in their accusations.

2:5–11

PUNISHMENT AND FORGIVENESS

Paul refers to a specific individual in this section. Some assume it is the man who was excommunicated for having an improper relationship with his father's wife (1 Corinthians 5:1–5). But it is just as likely that it was someone whom Paul had confronted on his most recent visit to Corinth.

If the latter case is true, it appears that one individual had reacted in an unseemly manner toward Paul. The church members had apparently rushed to Paul's defense to censure the man by excluding him from their fellowship. It also seems that the man had repented, yet the church had not reinstated him (perhaps thinking Paul would want it that way).

But Paul was not one to hold grudges. As long as the church failed to reinstate the offender, the believers would not have unity and would be vulnerable to Satan's attacks. So Paul entreats the Corinthians to forgive and comfort the man, assuring them that his forgiveness would be added to theirs. While Paul had rebuked the previous inaction of the church (1 Corinthians 5:1–5), the Corinthians more recent overzealous attempt to invoke discipline in the church was also a problem.

Paul shows concern for both the individual involved and the church as a whole (2:7–11). Excluding someone from fellowship is a drastic action—necessary at times, but not to become a regular solution for all problems in the church.

Take It Home

It can be a fine line between imposing discipline for the good of an offender and forgiving the offense. As most parents will attest, hasty forgiveness before the offender has repented may not be appreciated or even acknowledged. Where do you tend to draw the line when someone has seriously offended you? What do you think should be the guidelines to apply to a church setting?

2 CORINTHIANS 2:12–4:18

PAUL'S CONFIDENCE

Sweet Fragrance or Foul Smell?	2:12–17
Proven Competence	3:1–6
Comparing the Covenants	3:7–18
Treasure in a Clay Jar	4:1–12
The Benefit of Suffering	4:13–18

Setting Up the Section

Paul here starts to describe what happened when he finally met up with Titus after sending his severe letter to the Corinthians (2:4). He had come to Troas, where he had successful ministry. But he could not find Titus and so was still distraught, wondering how the Corinthians had responded to his stern message (2:12–13). Yet as Paul remembers his anguish, he also recalls the joy he experienced when he finally met up with Titus in Macedonia and learned that the Corinthians had repented. At this thought he breaks into joyful praise to God: "But thanks be to God. . ." (2:14). Paul seems to lose himself in this joy now, launching into an extended discussion of the joys and victory of the Christian ministry (2:14–7:1). He won't resume his discussion of the circumstances of the letter for five more chapters! In chapter 7 he will pick up with, "For when we came into Macedonia, this body of ours had no rest. . ." (7:5 NIV)—exactly where he left off at 2:13! Second Corinthians 2:14–7:1 is therefore an extended parentheses in Paul's letter, a masterful celebration of the trials and joys of the Christian ministry.

2:12–17

SWEET FRAGRANCE OR FOUL SMELL?

In this section and following, Paul addresses two matters of concern for church leaders throughout the centuries. One is a tendency to "burn out" over time due to the continual demands of the position. The other is the temptation to "spice up" the gospel to make it more palatable to a wider cross-section of society.

Even Paul was subject to the pressure of seemingly endless responsibility and accountability. He was always quick to share news of his associates and how much they meant to him. In this case, he had failed to connect with Titus in Troas, which left him without any peace of mind (2:13). Even though he felt that God had opened a door to that city, Paul didn't linger long. Things would be little better for him in Macedonia, although he does catch up with Titus there (7:5–7). And he raises an obvious question: Who is equal to the task he had taken on (2:16)?

Critical Observation

Paul's mention of a triumphal procession (2:14) would have caused his readers to think of Roman generals returning from battle. If victorious, the officer led the way with his armies following, trailed by the people they had defeated and taken captive. Meanwhile, those in the crowd would burn incense. Paul envisioned Christ, having overcome sin and death, leading His followers in a triumphal parade.

The response to the gospel is polarized. For those who believe and respond in faith, the good news is like a sweet aroma. But for the ones who reject the truth that Paul and others proclaim, the message is like the smell of death (2:14–16).

Yet Paul refuses to cater to the whims of his listeners. Unlike others, he didn't minister for the money (2:17). He could therefore speak simply and sincerely.

3:1–6

PROVEN COMPETENCE

In Paul's day, as Christianity was just beginning to spread, it was easy for unscrupulous characters to pose as apostles and proclaim false information, teaching it as truth. So as a safeguard, it was common for a church to vouch for someone traveling to another congregation by means of a letter of recommendation. For example, Paul includes a personal recommendation on behalf of Phoebe within his letter to the Romans (Romans 16:1).

But even as Paul's reputation is being besmirched, he doesn't provide the Corinthian believers with such a letter. Rather, he reminds them that *they* are his "letter" to prove his authority as an apostle. They are the proof that the Spirit of God had worked to authenticate Paul's ministry (3:2–3).

Paul wasn't out to prove himself. Instead, he wanted to prove the adequacy of God. His confidence was not in himself, but in his Lord. Paul's adequacy, therefore, was as a minister (servant) to God. Those who held to the old covenant focused only on the letter of the law. The new covenant initiated by Jesus, however, provides access to the Spirit of God and to life (3:4–6). And it is the Holy Spirit that provides Paul's competence.

3:7–18

COMPARING THE COVENANTS

Paul continues to contrast the old covenant with the new covenant. The old covenant—as spelled out in the Law of Moses—produced condemnation. It set a standard of righteousness that no one could meet (3:6–7). And while the glory of God was occasionally evident under the old covenant, it was a fading glory. Even the glory that lit Moses' face after his time with God did not last. And Paul notes that the old covenant itself was fading away, to be replaced by something much brighter and better (3:11).

The new covenant makes available righteousness and life rather than condemnation and death. The old covenant was like a dim flashlight in a completely dark room—helpful, but only to a certain extent. The surpassing glory of the new covenant is like someone coming in and hitting the switch, flooding the room with light. The old covenant had no glory when contrasted with the new covenant.

Paul uses the veil that Moses had worn over his face (Exodus 34:29–35) to symbolize the spiritual "veil" over the hearts of many of the Jewish people (3:15). In their devotion to the old covenant, they were unable to see the glory that was available to them. The Spirit of God is the One who lifts the veil and enables believers to behold the glory of God in the face of Christ. And it is the hope of glory (3:12) that emboldens believers to proclaim the gospel. With the veil removed, all believers should reflect the glory of the Lord (3:18).

4:1–12

TREASURE IN A CLAY JAR

The power of the Holy Spirit is especially relevant to Paul. He had previously mentioned personal experiences that were impossible to endure (1:8). Yet his reliance on God enabled him not to lose heart or give up in his ministry (4:1). Similarly, the Spirit of God allowed him to continue to proclaim the gospel without distorting it or attempting to deceive his listeners. (Again, Paul had a specific group of people in mind who were guilty of both of those offenses.)

Paul returns to his image of the veiled light of God. His previous application had been made toward the Jewish people (3:14–15). Here he applies the concept to the Gentiles (4:3–4). In all his teachings, he never tries to make himself the object of attention, but faithfully keeps his focus on Jesus Christ as Lord (4:5–6).

Yet the wonder of the gospel is that human believers carry the glory of God within them. Paul describes it as having treasure in jars of clay (4:6–7). The treasure is the glory of God in the person of Jesus Christ. It is quite clear that the glory is God's and not the believer's, although Paul's critics in Corinth were trying to build themselves up with little regard for the truth of the gospel. The image of oneself as a clay pot may not be consoling at first, but when considering the treasure within, it takes on a whole new perspective.

Clay jars are weak, fragile, and subject to being broken. But like the pots used by Gideon's army (Judges 7:15–25), they may be broken for a purpose. If, and when, the jar is broken, the light within shines brightly and does not go unnoticed. Indeed, it may have a powerful effect. Numerous people throughout Christian history have been "broken," only to reveal the great power of the Spirit of God—beginning with the martyrdom of Stephen (Acts 7:54–60) and continuing to the present day.

So the believer is not as fragile as he or she may appear. Paul again writes from personal experience. He knew it was possible to be: (1) hard-pressed without being crushed; (2) perplexed, but not in despair; (3) persecuted, but not abandoned; and (4) struck down, but not destroyed (4:8–9). A believer's afflictions do not result in complete failure or destruction.

People are not made righteous by trying to live for Christ, but by dying to self and to sin so that Christ's life is lived out in them. Paul emphasizes this truth by repeatedly emphasizing death to self in three consecutive sentences (4:10–12). As clay pots, believers must be broken in order for the light of the glory of Christ to shine.

4:13–18

THE BENEFIT OF SUFFERING

In verse 13, Paul references Psalm 116:10. He echoes the psalmist's faith and confidence that he could call on God when in great danger, believing that God would rescue him. Strengthened and encouraged by his faith, he could face and endure persecution, adversity, danger, and even death. In the meantime, he need not be silent about his suffering, for his faith acknowledges the reality of resurrection beyond his suffering and death (4:14).

Demystifying 2 Corinthians

Throughout this passage, Paul uses the first-person plural much of the time (*we, our,* etc.). In some cases, he appears to be speaking of all believers (4:7). In other instances, however, his intent seems more focused on those who are conducting the ministry of an apostle (4:1, 5, etc.).

Paul's suffering was for the benefit of the Corinthians (4:15). As they and others were coming to believe in Christ and being strengthened in the faith, God was receiving praise and thanksgiving.

Paul found comfort in knowing that while his physical body was deteriorating, his inner spirit was being renewed daily. In fact, his body was being destroyed at a more rapid pace than most due to the abuses he received as an apostle determined to spread the gospel. Still, he could endure and remain encouraged as he boldly proclaimed Christ, and he was able to perceive bodily suffering as light and momentary. He could see the unseen glory ahead of him, and encourages his readers to do the same.

Take It Home

Paul's response to the troublesome events of life is quite impressive. His dependence on God is exemplary (4:7–9). If you were asked to comment on the same situations, what would you say? Complete the following statements:

1) When I am hard-pressed by the stresses of life, I. . .

2) When I am perplexed by a spiritual crisis, I feel. . .

3) When I am persecuted by others, I want to. . .

4) When I am struck down after trying my hardest, I feel. . .

2 CORINTHIANS 5:1–7:1

NEW DWELLINGS, NEW CREATIONS, AND NEW ATTITUDES

From a Tent to a House	5:1–10
Reconciled to God	5:11–19
Ambassadors for Christ	5:20–6:10
Choosing Sides	6:11–7:1

Setting Up the Section

Paul is writing to the Corinthians, fully aware that some of them are actively opposing his authority. He is defending himself and his ministry, to some extent, even while addressing his concerns for the genuine believers. In this section, he continues to emphasize the impermanence of human life as he turns his readers' attention to eternal things yet to come.

5:1–10

FROM A TENT TO A HOUSE

Paul had just compared a person's earthly body to a jar of clay (4:7). When the clay pots are shattered by opposition and persecution, the glory of the Lord is made visible to the world. The "shattering" should come as no surprise to believers, since a degree of suffering is typical for all who consider themselves dead to self and alive for Christ.

Here Paul uses the image of a tent to build on what he is saying. The earthly body is temporary and far from perfect. At death, believers leave behind their physical bodies and are provided vastly superior heavenly bodies. The frailty of the human frame is replaced by the permanence of an eternal dwelling place (5:1). It is only natural that people would groan because of their imperfections and the desire for a more perfect body. For now, however, the Holy Spirit is God's pledge to the believer of a future in heaven and a glorious body as well (5:4–5).

Knowing that their earthly bodies are only temporary and that death is only a gateway to something much better, believers have great confidence to live and to proclaim the gospel boldly. If they hasten the day of their deaths by living courageously for Christ, they are only closer to the day they receive their glorious heavenly bodies and go to be with their Lord. They should not fear death (being away from their bodies), but should look upon it as the arrival of what they have long been hoping for (5:6–8).

However, the assurance that they will leave their temporary bodies is no excuse for being careless about the way they live now. The physical body will perish, but the deeds a believer has done in them (whether good or bad) are the basis for future judgment. The resurrection of Jesus should remind people of their own future resurrection, as well as Jesus' promise to return to earth to subdue His enemies. He will then judge everyone according to their deeds, so believers should desire to please God as they live in their earthly bodies (5:9–10).

5:11–19

RECONCILED TO GOD

When faced with the choice of pleasing other people or pleasing God, believers should always choose pleasing God. Some, however, try so hard to win human approval and favor that they corrupt and pervert the truth of the gospel. For such people, the coming Day of Judgment is something to be dreaded.

Knowing that his references to the Day of Judgment would likely evoke fear and dread among those who resisted the truths of God, Paul sought to persuade his readers to turn to Christ and be reconciled to God. The false apostles in Corinth had been telling people what they wanted to hear in order to entice listeners to follow them. Paul, on the other hand, appealed to the conscience of the Corinthians, hoping they would acknowledge his apostleship.

Critical Observation

Paul, as an apostle, was certainly not opposed to attempting to persuade others to put their faith in Jesus. Yet he always did so with a respect for the Lord (5:11). He vocally opposed other methods of persuasion that were unacceptable to God. Salvation was not the result of appealing to fleshly lusts or distorting the truths of the gospel. Paul and his colleagues were fully aware that not only their message, but also their accompanying methods and motives, were evident to God.

If Paul's readers thought he was out of his mind, he wanted them to know it was because he was determined to please God. If they believed him and considered him sane, he let them know it was for their sake that he spoke as he did. Paul and other true apostles were motivated by the love of Christ (5:12–13).

As a result of grace, every Christian has been reconciled to God by identification with Christ in His death, burial, and resurrection. All who are saved have the same general calling (5:14–15). As far as one's standing before God, believers are all the same, in Christ.

Just as believers come to see Jesus through a different lens—as Savior and Lord rather than simply a notable rabbi who had lived and died—so Paul encourages them to see one another differently. According to Paul, believers are new and should be acknowledged as such (5:16–17). Christians dare not view others merely by outward appearances.

Apart from Christ, all people are dead in their sin, enemies of God, and alienated from Him. They do not seek God, but He seeks them through His Son, Jesus Christ. As sinners acknowledge their sin and trust in Jesus for forgiveness and the gift of eternal life, they are reconciled to God. Those who know and trust God are given the privilege and responsibility of proclaiming the gospel, which includes an appeal to others to be reconciled to God through faith in Jesus Christ. In this regard, believers are Christ's ambassadors (5:18–19).

Demystifying 2 Corinthians

In the original language of 2 Corinthians 5:20, the word *ambassador* is used not as a noun, but as a verb. (Believers *ambassador* for Christ.) This responsibility entails: (1) Entreating unbelievers to be reconciled to God (5:20–21); (2) urging believers to properly value the grace of God (6:1–2); and (3) commending oneself as a servant of God without creating stumbling blocks for others (6:3–10).

5:20–6:10

AMBASSADORS FOR CHRIST

Paul describes the importance of ministering to believers as well as unbelievers. Those who are lost need to be reconciled to God and experience the righteous life that He intends for them (5:20–21). In addition, some of those who are already believers need to be reminded of the incomparable gift of grace they have been given.

Paul knew the Corinthian church had been divided into competitive cliques. Some were looking to their leaders or their spiritual gifts as a basis for boasting over others. They needed to experience genuine salvation and then grow up in unity to maturity. Otherwise, they received the gift of God's grace in vain (6:1–2). Because Christ has come, the day of salvation is now.

Paul provides four aspects of the life of an ambassador of Christ (6:3–10). First, he states that true apostles do not create stumbling blocks for others. Note that Paul does not say he avoids offending unbelievers altogether. He knew the truth and power of his message was a problem for many people (1 Corinthians 1:22–23). Yet he is scrupulous to avoid offending anyone unnecessarily or in a way that adversely affects the gospel.

Second, Paul says that ambassadors of Christ suffer for the sake of the gospel. False prophets had minimized sin and its consequences throughout biblical history, as had the false apostles in the church at Corinth. Such people were motivated by greed and self-indulgence, and were quite unwilling to wholeheartedly follow Jesus. But true apostles endure hardships.

Third, Paul writes that ambassadors manifest the character of Christ by the way they suffer. People can suffer for a lot of reasons (1 Peter 4:14–16), but an authentic believer will suffer for the right reason. Throughout their sufferings, ambassadors of Christ are guided by the Word of God, enabled by the power of God, indwelt by the Spirit of God, and characterized by the fruits of godliness (purity, knowledge, patience, kindness, love, etc.). God's authentic apostles manifest Christlikeness in the midst of their adversities.

And fourth, ambassadors of Christ employ godly means and methods. The false apostles in Corinth were religious hucksters who modified the gospel to sell it like a product and satisfy their own desires to feel important. They loved glory and boasted in it. In contrast, authentic apostles know that the crucifixion of Jesus for the salvation of humankind is not a popular message, yet they rely upon the power of the Holy Spirit to convince and convert unbelievers. Ambassadors of Christ do not always seem to succeed or garner the approval of others, yet they are faithful to the God who uses them in their honor and dishonor, for the sake of Christ.

6:11–7:1

CHOOSING SIDES

Throughout both of his letters to the Corinthians, Paul has been hinting at divisions and problems within the body of believers. In this passage, he gets right to the point. The Corinthians had a serious problem regarding their relationships. They had distanced themselves from Paul and other genuine apostles, while at the same time drawing close to those who sounded good but twisted the truth of the gospel. Paul urges those in the church to do as he had done to them: to open their hearts and stop withholding affection (6:11–13).

As Paul continues, his language becomes stronger. His instruction to not be yoked with unbelievers (6:14) is not just a warning, but also an intimation that such an illicit intimacy and partnership with unbelievers already exists. Their association was not just with some misguided church leaders, but with Belial (a term for Satan) and idols. They were much farther from God than they realized (6:15–18).

Christians cannot be yoked together with unbelievers in God's work because of moral incompatibility. Christians are to pursue righteousness; unbelievers are accustomed to lawlessness. Christians have been exposed to the light of God's truth; non-Christians remain in darkness. The distance between the two is so significant that they find no basis for a partnership in spiritual ministry.

The first verse of 2 Corinthians 7 is actually Paul's conclusion to his argument. Paul refers to the Old Testament prophecies as promises because they are yet to be fully realized. They are the basis for his appeal to the Corinthians to put off all defilement—both physical and spiritual. The knowledge that a holy God dwelled in their midst (and would do so even more in His coming kingdom) should have resulted in prompt repentance and pursuit of holiness.

Believers must look to the holy scriptures for guidance so that they can follow the Lord (and His called leaders) in obedience. They are not to avoid association with unbelievers because they are to model Christian living and point others to Christ. Yet Paul's warning is to identify and shun those who claim to be followers of God, but are not. The Holy Spirit works in the lives of believers to provide discernment in such situations.

Take It Home

Religious hucksters wouldn't get by with as much as they do if people weren't so gullible. Even many of today's professing Christians tend to judge leaders on their methods, their personalities, their success rates, or some other trivial standard. Paul has repeatedly attempted to convince the Corinthians not to succumb to such a temptation, but rather to support those who remain faithful and true to God. Can you think of a consistently conscientious and hardworking Christian leader (or lay person) who may not be as flashy or popular as others? If so, try to take some time to call or write that person to offer your appreciation and support.

2 CORINTHIANS 7:2–9:15

GRIEVING AND GIVING

Godly Sorrow, Godly Joy	7:2–16
Exemplary Giving	8:1–15
A Delegation to Precede Paul	8:16–9:15

Setting Up the Section

Earlier in this letter to the Corinthians, Paul had written about the circumstances he was facing (2:12–13). In the midst of that discussion, however, he suddenly launched into an extended discussion of the joys and challenges of Christian ministry (2:14–7:1). In this section he returns to where he left off, writing about his joy at the church's repentance and his reconciliation with them.

7:2–16

GODLY SORROW, GODLY JOY

Paul describes some of the serious problems he faced in Macedonia (7:5), and throughout the letter he describes some significant problems within the Corinthian church. Certain false teachers had managed to gain a following as they proclaimed another gospel and undermined Paul's authority. Some of the Corinthians had even become embarrassed by Paul and his colleagues, and drew back from them.

Yet Paul is surprisingly upbeat in this passage (7:2–4). What enabled him to write with such confidence after so many wrongs had been committed against God and against him?

Paul had just pointed out that he and his colleagues had not closed themselves off to the Corinthians; it was the Corinthians who had withdrawn from the apostles (6:11–13). Yet instead of writing them off and moving to the next ministry opportunity, Paul communicates his desire to restore the relationship he previously had with the Corinthians. It was a state of the heart that needed adjustment. He had already asked them to open their hearts (6:13); here his request is that they make room in their hearts (7:2).

Paul also enumerates evidences of the love the authentic church leaders had for the Corinthians. It would be understandable if the Corinthians had grown suspicious of Paul and others if they knew the apostles had wronged them in some way. But Paul makes it clear that he had not done so. More than that, Paul felt great pride because of his association with the believers in Corinth. Paul could attest to the list of statements he made in 2 Corinthians 7:2–4; the false apostles in Corinth could not.

Paul had crossed over from Troas to Macedonia, looking for his companion Titus and wondering how the Corinthians had responded to his strong letter of rebuke and correction. During this time of great distress (7:5), he finally met up with Titus, who reported that the Corinthians had repented and wanted to be reconciled with Paul. God encouraged Paul not only through the presence of Titus, but especially through the positive report about the Corinthians' repentance. The letter had been hard for Paul to write, knowing that his candor would cause them sorrow. But he had sent it for their own good, so it was with great relief that Paul discovers they had taken his words to heart and repented (7:8–9, 12).

Critical Observation

Paul seems to infer that if he had known about the problems in Corinth and ignored them, he would have actually harmed the people there (7:9). When one believer knows of another who is caught up in some sin, the failure to speak up makes the observer a partner in the other's sin. Writing the letter caused Paul sorrow, but he would have been sorrowful for the Corinthians even if he hadn't written. So by taking the difficult step of writing, he and the Corinthians experienced godly sorrow that led to repentance, restoration, and a renewed bond between them.

Sometimes sorrow is according to the will of God because it produces repentance that leads to salvation and life. Consequently, there are no lasting regrets. In contrast, worldly sorrow leads to death (7:10–12). After denying Jesus, Peter's great sorrow eventually resulted in his repentance and his bold leadership in the early church. Judas, on the other hand, had only regrets and committed suicide.

One other great source of joy for Paul was seeing how excited Titus was after he had delivered Paul's difficult message. Paul had boasted about what kind of believers the Corinthians were. The fact that they responded so well had been a tremendous relief for Titus, and seeing Titus's enthusiasm was pure delight for Paul (7:13–16).

8:1–15

EXEMPLARY GIVING

Paul now turns to the second major reason for writing this letter (chapters 8–9). He is gathering a collection of money for the poor and persecuted believers in Jerusalem, and wants to encourage the Corinthians to give generously. By way of incentive, he points to the generosity of the churches in Macedonia.

Paul's collection was no surprise to the Corinthians. He had told them about it in his previous letter (1 Corinthians 16:1–4). Perhaps the Corinthians had begun to lose heart in the prospect of helping the Jerusalem believers due to the problems in their own church. But since Paul had just heard of their renewed excitement, he broaches the topic again. On his next visit to Corinth, Paul would collect their gift, and he wanted them to be prepared.

The churches in Macedonia (including Philippi, Berea, and Thessalonica) had been models of sacrificial giving. However, the actual amount of their contribution is not mentioned. The size of their donation did not impress Paul as much as the willingness of their giving.

The believers in Macedonia were poor to the point of extreme poverty. In addition, they were facing a severe trial (8:2). Under such circumstances, most would not expect much in terms of a contribution for *others*. Yet, clearly, Paul's expectations were considerably exceeded.

The Macedonians *first* gave themselves to the Lord, and then to the apostles. They realized the great significance of their salvation, and gave back to God what they had. They gave generously, voluntarily, gratefully, and joyfully. They set a high standard for other churches to imitate (8:3–7). The Corinthian church had many strong points (1 Corinthians 1:4–7), and Paul challenges its members to add this level of generosity to the list (2 Corinthians 8:7). Yet he makes it clear that he is not commanding them, but rather encouraging them, to give as proof of their love.

Then Paul provides an even higher standard to strive for: The ultimate example of selfless giving is the Lord Jesus Christ, demonstrated by His atoning work on the cross of Calvary. He was infinitely rich in the presence of His Father, yet gave it all up during His incarnation (Philippians 2:5–8). Because of His sacrificial life and death, He made all who trust in Him exceedingly rich (8:8–9).

Paul was convinced that generous giving was a desirable thing that worked to the donor's advantage. The Corinthians had been the first to begin to give, and if they were not yet ready with their contribution, it was certainly time to finish the matter. The desire to give should continue throughout the process of giving (8:10–12). Paul refuses to use guilt to prompt the Corinthians to give more than they are able, but he doesn't hesitate to urge them to finish what they had started.

Paul concludes his exhortation to give by setting forth two governing principles. The first is the principle of equality (8:13). The secular world is familiar with a structure where the rich get richer and the poor get poorer. But the biblical model is one where political and economic power should be used not to oppress the helpless, but for the good of those who are weak and powerless. Paul never suggests that people give up their rights to own private property or be expected to live on exactly the same standard. But when one believer has more than enough and sees another believer in need, he or she should seek to narrow the disparity rather than widen it.

Paul also promotes the principle of reciprocity (8:14–15). He suggests that although one group of believers may *now* have an abundance and the ability to help another group in need, there may come a day when the tables are turned and they will find themselves in need. Generosity shown toward a brother in need may result in generosity from that same brother at a later time. When people are blessed with prosperity, it is not so they can go overboard in self-indulgence, but rather so they can share with those who have less than they need.

Demystifying 2 Corinthians

In explaining his principle of reciprocity, Paul uses an example from when the Israelites were in the wilderness after leaving the slavery of Egypt (8:15). In an area with essentially no food, God provided for the Israelites by sending manna for them to eat. Each person was allowed a certain allotment per day. Some gathered much. Some gathered little. Yet when the portions were measured, everyone had just the allotted amount (Exodus 16:16–18). Paul seems to believe that those who collected more than enough gave to those who came up short, and he uses the same principle to demonstrate how believers should use their money and possessions.

8:16–9:15

A DELEGATION TO PRECEDE PAUL

Paul had assured the Corinthians that he would soon visit them, but he isn't going right away. He wants to see that they keep their commitment to give not only for the good of others, but for their own reputation and, of course, for the glory of God. So Paul sends this letter to them along with a small group of trusted associates who will help them out. One is Titus, who had recently been to Corinth and has a personal interest in their lives. Although Paul is asking Titus to go, he makes it clear that Titus is eager to make the trip (8:16–17). He will be accompanied by at least two other "brothers" (8:18, 22), who are not named. Some speculate the group might have included Luke, Barnabas, or Apollos. Even though their names aren't provided, these men had outstanding credentials.

Why would Paul send such an esteemed group ahead of him? First, they were to facilitate the financial follow-through Paul had detailed in 2 Corinthians 8 and 9. Their gifts of teaching and exhortation would not only inspire giving, but also help the Corinthians rebut the erroneous teachings they had been hearing from the false apostles. Second, a group (rather than a single person) would ensure the integrity of the financial matters. Paul and his colleagues were scrupulous about money matters. They were consistently trustworthy, but wanted no opportunity for questions to be raised about their integrity.

Just as Paul had told the Corinthians about the selfless giving of the Macedonian churches (8:1–5), he had also told the Macedonians about the commitment the Corinthians had made (9:1–2). So the delegation would help ensure that things were in proper order in case Paul shows up in Corinth later, accompanied by Macedonian believers (9:3–5). Paul wants the Corinthians' gift to be generous and heartfelt, not grudging.

Paul concludes this section of his letter with a number of principles concerning generosity and giving. When dealing with wealth, it is easy to become covetous, and Paul's guidelines serve as reminders of what is really important.

First, he quotes a proverb to teach that the way a person sows is the way he or she reaps (9:6–7). Giving generously is the way to have an abundant return, and the key is an attitude of delight. If people enjoy giving, they do it more frequently and more willingly.

Second, Paul states that when people give generously, God allows them to reap bountifully (9:8–9). When someone shows grace to others by giving, God replenishes the grace so that he or she has more to give.

Paul's third principle is that when people sow generously, they reap more than monetary gain (8:10–14). Cheerful giving transcends financial matters and results in a harvest of righteousness. It is regarded by God as a pleasing spiritual sacrifice. Needy believers may not even know the fellow Christians who give to them, yet they can praise God as the ultimate source.

Finally, Paul suggests that no matter how generous one's giving, it pales when compared with the generosity of God, who gave His only Son (9:15). Even when writing about money, Paul's mind remains on the cross of Christ. The gift of salvation should never cease to produce awe and gratitude, and any degree of generosity believers demonstrate is rooted in the generosity of God.

Take It Home

In this section, Paul has dealt with some difficult matters. He wants believers to do the right thing no matter how hard it might be, whether it involves writing a letter that is certain to create sorrow (7:8–10) or cheerfully giving away one's money (9:6–7). Can you think of something difficult you need to do and have been avoiding. . .perhaps something that can potentially help someone else in the long run, even if it creates hard feelings in the meantime? If so, prayerfully consider if the time is right for you to take action based on Paul's exhortations in this passage.

2 CORINTHIANS 10:1–11:33

MINISTRY: GENUINE AND OTHERWISE

Paul's Assessment of His Ministry	10:1–18
Necessary "Foolishness"	11:1–15
Three Comparisons	11:16–33

Setting Up the Section

So far in this letter, Paul's writing has been authoritative, but rather gentle. After Titus's report from Corinth, Paul must have discovered that he had a lot of support from the believers there. Still, his critics were outspoken, so here he begins to defend himself more emphatically—letting his readers know he feels no shame or regret for his methods or other aspects of ministry.

Critical Observation

Paul's tone changes dramatically in the last four chapters of the letter, causing some scholars to suggest that this section was not an original part of the letter. They claim that perhaps these chapters were originally the severe and sorrowful letter that Paul wrote to the Corinthians earlier (2:4; 7:8), and that later copyists attached it to the end of 2 Corinthians. While possible, this solution is doubtful. It is more likely that Paul's tone changes here because he now turns from addressing the whole church (which has reconciled with him) to those church members who are still opposing him.

10:1–18

PAUL'S ASSESSMENT OF HIS MINISTRY

It seems that every church has its critics, and Corinth was certainly no exception. Paul's letter has hinted at his knowledge of these critics, even as he has tried to encourage and enlighten the majority of believers who would be reading his Epistle.

This passage begins with an accusation that has been leveled against him in his absence: Some said he was only bold and authoritative when writing letters, and would be far less impressive in person (10:1, 10). Paul responds to this charge, yet he was not one to speak impulsively. Rather, his appeal is meek. *Meekness* is a term generally used in regard to those in authority. Meekness involves humility, gentleness, and a confidence that God will defend and vindicate the person so that he or she need not become defensive when challenged or criticized. Both Jesus and Moses were known for their meekness, humility, and gentle demeanor.

In contrast, the false apostles in Corinth sounded authoritative and assertive. They modeled themselves after the world's standards (10:2) and seemed to be somewhat successful. Even today, certain believers seem to respect aggressive leaders more than quiet, humble ones. Although Paul was usually meek, he assures the Corinthians he would be just as bold as necessary when in person. If they took care of their problems in the meantime, however, he wouldn't need to be harsh.

Paul goes on to rebut the use of worldly tactics in the church. The secular world relies on certain things for authority: schooling, status, personal connections, oratorical skill, and so forth. The church, however, uses different "weapons" (10:3–6). The only authoritative source of doctrine is the Word of God, so Paul battles against all arguments and pretensions that oppose God's truth.

In addition to his concern about preserving and promoting the truths of scripture as a basis for doctrine, Paul knew scripture was also the basis for Christian living. The final test of any proposed "truth" is whether or not it results in obeying Christ's commands. Any teaching that turns believers from what is clearly and emphatically taught about God in the Bible is a falsehood. If the Corinthian believers learned to be more diligent and completely obedient, then Paul would be better able to confront the acts of disobedience being committed by the false apostles (10:6).

At this point, Paul begins to get a bit more specific about the accusations that his accusers had leveled at him. They said he referred too frequently to his apostolic authority (10:7–8), yet he did so to assure the Corinthians that his authority came from God and not any other source. His critics could not make the same claim. They also said his letters were just a forceful attempt to cover for his lack of personal charisma (10:9–11). But the false apostles were setting their own standards rather than conforming to biblical ones. They sought to elevate themselves by misrepresenting their own accomplishments and minimizing the value of others. While Paul is honest about his ministry, he is never self-promoting. His attention is always given to building up the church—not his own reputation, image, or power (10:12–16). And any boasting is only to give credit to God (10:17–18).

11:1–15

NECESSARY "FOOLISHNESS"

Paul felt it foolish to spend so much time talking about himself, yet it was the right thing to do in order to answer the accusations of his critics. His concern for the believers in Corinth motivated his actions. Anything that prevented them from being further deceived was well worth any potential discomfort he might feel (11:1–3).

Critical Observation

Paul's language throughout this section is direct, sometimes strong, and definitely personal. He borders on sarcasm and hyperbole. His "foolishness" (11:1) is actually a wise course of action. Those he calls "super-apostles" (11:5) were really false apostles. But the Corinthians were clear about his meaning.

Paul poses himself as the father of the bride, so to speak. The Corinthian believers are the bride, and Paul desires to proudly present them to the groom, Jesus Christ (11:2). Yet his concern for them is not merely parental paranoia. They were facing a very real and immediate danger: Spiritual seduction had historically been a trap for God's people, and Paul didn't want history to repeat itself in Corinth.

The Corinthians had been naively tolerant of the false teachings of the self-proclaimed apostles. Since Paul now had their attention, he quickly set himself apart from those he called "super-apostles" (11:5). Was he inferior to the others, as some had charged? Not at all. The difference was a matter of presentation and style. While the false apostles were proud of their speaking ability, Paul didn't purport to be a trained speaker. What set him apart (and above) the others was the content of his message. God had revealed things to Paul that the others knew nothing about (11:5–6). Evidence of this fact is found throughout his letters as he presents and explains the gospel.

The false apostles had no problem finding people to support them financially, while Paul demanded no payment from the Corinthians. So the ironic charge of the false apostles was that Paul's ministry was worthless. Paul again rebuts their ridiculous charges. If what they said was true, then he was robbing the Macedonian churches because they willingly supported him. Paul knew that by continuing to serve without expecting payment he not only verified that the gift of the gospel is free, but also demonstrated that the so-called apostles in Corinth were operating out of greed and self-interest (11:7–12). The self-centered church leaders were trying to position themselves above Paul, when, in reality, they were nowhere near his level of wisdom, integrity, and devotion.

Paul follows with some of his harshest words for the false apostles. Not only were they deceitful, they were servants of Satan who masqueraded as enlightened leaders (11:13–15).

11:16–33

THREE COMPARISONS

Paul continues to compare himself to the false apostles in Corinth using three different standards. The first was the way they treated people under their authority. In this regard, Paul resorts to sarcasm to explain that he isn't strong enough to exploit or take advantage of others the way the leaders in Corinth were doing (11:16–21). Even though the believers there were willing to put up with such domineering tactics, Paul would not resort to that. If they wanted to shame him for such "weakness," so be it.

The second comparison was the Jewish credentials of the leaders. The others were Hebrews, Israelites, and Abraham's descendants (11:21–22). But Paul was also those things, plus more (Philippians 3:4–6).

The third comparison was the crucial difference: the personal price paid to service others (11:23–33). If Paul didn't quite measure up to his critics (by their standards) on the first point, and was an even match on the second, here he far outperformed them.

Paul's lengthy list of sufferings (11:23–33) is his most detailed. Several of the incidents are mentioned in the account of his missionary travels in Acts or in other places, such as his escape from Damascus in a basket, the stoning, and some of the beatings (Acts 9:23–25; 14:19; 16:22–24). Others we know nothing about. For instance, Acts only tells of one shipwreck of Paul—not three—and it occurred *after* the writing of this letter. So clearly scripture reveals only a small percentage of all Paul experienced at the hands of others.

Demystifying 2 Corinthians

The Mosaic Law prohibited punishment of more than forty lashes (Deuteronomy 25:2–3). It had become Jewish custom to stop at thirty-nine in case of a miscount, so as not to unintentionally break the law (11:24).

As the Corinthian Christians read this list of Paul's sufferings, surely they realized that these were the credentials of a genuine apostle. They were definitely not things the false apostles would have chosen to boast of, even if they had been willing to endure such hardships. Clearly, Paul could have avoided many of these gruesome circumstances if he had backed down when opposed or simply hadn't worked so hard to communicate the gospel to others. Yet he was not only eager to carry the message of Christ's love and forgiveness to as many as possible, he was also willing to suffer along the way.

And still, Paul takes no personal credit. He boasts only in his weakness (11:30), realizing that his ability to endure is through the grace and power of God.

Take It Home

It can be easy to criticize other people before acknowledging the suffering they are going through. Paul's critics in Corinth did so intentionally, but current believers may do so without knowing it. Can you think of some other believer whom others may tend to look down on without giving proper regard to his or her difficult circumstances in life? If so, look for opportunities to prompt the critics to consider the person's situation and respond with more grace and mercy.

2 CORINTHIANS 12:1–13:14

INEXPRESSIBLE GLORY AND UNAVOIDABLE THORNS

Paul's Incredible Vision	12:1–6
Paul's Thorn in the Flesh	12:7–10
Paul's Closing Argument	12:11–13:14

Setting Up the Section

Paul has turned up the heat in his defense against the accusations of his critics, coming on stronger as he boasts in what God has done through him. As he closes the letter, he provides some additional proof of the authenticity of his ministry. He also shares a personal problem, but one that further verifies his role as an apostle.

12:1–6

PAUL'S INCREDIBLE VISION

The fact that Paul says he will "go on" to visions and revelations (12:1) suggests that this is yet another aspect of the bragging of the false apostles in Corinth. It was easy enough for them to *say* that their teachings came from God, which would not only greatly reduce questions and resistance from those who heard them, but also make them appear spiritually superior. However, Paul is about to relate an experience that far outweighs any claims made by the religious phonies, yet he couples it with another story that diminishes his personal glory and shows that he was part of a truly spiritual event.

Demystifying 2 Corinthians

Paul had invoked an oath to testify that he was not lying about what he was saying (11:31). The oath would also apply to his statements about his revelation of the third heaven. As incredible as his story sounded, his oath attested that God knew he was telling the truth.

Although Paul begins to write in third person (12:2–3), he soon makes it clear that he is referring to himself (12:7). He couldn't be sure whether he had undergone a bodily experience as well as a spiritual one, yet he was certain of what had taken place.

He was transported to the third heaven, or paradise (12:2, 4). People referred to the earth's atmosphere as the first heaven, and the stars and realms of outer space as the second heaven. Beyond that was the third heaven, where one would find the presence of God. (Jesus passed through the heavens when returning to God at His ascension [Hebrews 4:14].) Paradise was the place where believers were united with God between death and resurrection (Luke 23:43). While there, Paul heard things that he wasn't even allowed to describe. The experience was surely an encouragement to Paul and a confirmation of his relationship with God.

The false apostles would surely have capitalized on such an experience—both financially and in terms of spiritual status. Yet while Paul relates the event as indisputable evidence that he was a called apostle, he understates it as much as possible. By using third person he doesn't say *I* saw and *I* heard great things. He summarizes all that happened to him in only a few sentences. He remains vague and refuses to provide details that would have drawn people to him as storyteller rather than to the significance of the event itself. He allows fourteen years to pass before he tells anyone what had happened. And when he finally does, he doesn't emphasize the vision, but his own weakness (12:5).

12:7–10

PAUL'S THORN IN THE FLESH

Paul's weakness is evident in what he refers to as a thorn in his flesh (12:7). It was probably some sort of Satan-inspired, God-allowed physical malady. After being privileged to witness heavenly events, even Paul would be tempted to become arrogant, and this impediment was a continual reminder that it was God's grace that kept Paul active—not Paul's own strength or wisdom.

Paul never reveals exactly the problem that he was forced to deal with. It seems likely that it was more than a mere irritation, but rather a nagging, persistent, painful problem that could never quite be put out of mind. It may have been something that affected his appearance, perhaps causing embarrassment. It's also likely that it affected his spirit, attitude, and outlook.

Although Paul willingly endured much suffering, he was no masochist. Just as Jesus had prayed to somehow avoid His agonizing death on the cross (Matthew 26:39), Paul prayed that God would remove his thorn. Three times he pleaded, but was told that Jesus' power was made perfect in his weakness (12:9).

Critical Observation

Some people believe that suffering is a result of God's displeasure toward a person, and that faith is all that is needed to heal one's physical problems. Yet Paul's thorn was not the result of sin in his life or a lack of faith. In his case, Paul suffered from a physically painful ailment of some kind because God had a higher purpose for him.

Rather than removing Paul's thorn, God gave Paul sufficient grace to sustain him throughout his lifelong affliction. Paul's thorn in the flesh was actually an ongoing method by which God's power would be demonstrated. So Paul stopped petitioning God to remove the problem and began to praise God for giving it to him. It was in his human weakness that he learned to find God's strength (12:10).

12:11–13:14

PAUL'S CLOSING ARGUMENT

Like an attorney about to see the jury leave to deliberate, Paul provides his readers a closing argument before ending his letter. He shouldn't have had to defend himself so thoroughly, and he felt foolish for doing so. But his action was necessary because the Corinthians hadn't come to his defense as soon as the "super-apostles" began to criticize him (12:11–13).

Paul reminds the Corinthians yet again that he intends to visit them soon, and assures them that he is not coming with an expectation of personal gain. In fact, he would go out of his way to ensure that neither he nor his associates placed any financial demands on the believers in Corinth (12:14–18).

Paul hopes that his third visit will not create a difficult situation for the Corinthians (12:14). As their spiritual father, he plans to provide for them rather than vice versa. Yet he also suspects he might find a number of problems when he arrives (12:20–21). At this point, Paul reverses his approach to accountability. He had been conscientiously defending his actions to the Corinthians, but now he explains that they would be accountable for *their* actions. Paul had verified that he was indeed an apostle of Jesus Christ, and as such, he sets down truths the Corinthians should accept and live by.

According to the Mosaic Law, any legal accusation had to have more than one witness (Deuteronomy 19:15). Paul was accusing the Corinthians of improper behavior, so it was significant that this would be his third visit, each time with an accompanying witness to what they were doing. He was prepared, if necessary, to be a strict disciplinarian when he arrived (13:1–4).

And although Paul tells the Corinthians to examine themselves in regard to their faith, he doesn't provide a checklist of any kind for them to consider (13:6–9). They were to confirm their relationship with Jesus (13:5) and their commitment to God's truth (13:8). Paul never suggests anything is necessary for one's salvation other than Christ.

Paul's frankness with the Corinthians has a specific purpose: He wants to give them the opportunity to repent and straighten out their spiritual lives before his arrival. If they do, he will have no reason to be harsh with them. If they don't, he will use his God-given authority to discipline them (13:10).

Yet he ends this deeply personal letter with a positive appeal and a reminder of God's grace, love, and fellowship (13:11–14). His final benediction is an assurance of the work of God the Father, God the Son, and God the Holy Spirit.

Take It Home

Do you have any kind of physical problem that might be somewhat comparable to Paul's thorn in the flesh? If so, do you tend to feel a bit resentful because of it, or do you usually tolerate it reasonably well? Can you think of ways to learn to see your human weaknesses as a catalyst for God's grace and strength in your life?

GALATIANS

INTRODUCTION TO GALATIANS

The book of Galatians is a centerpiece of New Testament theology that had a great influence during the Protestant Reformation. (Martin Luther's *Commentary on Galatians* ranks with the most influential books to come out of the Reformation.) Galatians is the only one of Paul's letters addressed to a group of churches rather than a single location. The epistle has been called a spiritual Magna Carta, due to its masterful explanation and defense of justification by faith alone.

AUTHOR

The style of writing and method of thinking is so true to that of Paul that few scholars throughout the centuries have questioned his authorship. The early church held a strong and unwavering belief that Paul was the writer.

PURPOSE

The Epistle to the Galatians was written to emphasize the complete sufficiency of justification by faith alone in one's relationship with God. The Galatian churches (where many new believers were Gentiles) were being strongly influenced to add traditional Jewish beliefs and practices to their newfound faith. While it was quite natural for Jewish believers to continue to worship as they always had in the past, to require the same for Gentiles was, to Paul, tantamount to promoting a different gospel (1:6).

OCCASION

Paul had established a number of churches in Galatia during his missionary travels (1:8, 11; 4:13–14, 19–20; Acts 13–14). When he left, the believers were holding up under suffering (3:4) and doing well (5:7). But not long afterward, Paul had received word that they were being influenced by a group requiring circumcision for salvation, and he was disturbed and dismayed to hear how quickly the Galatians had forsaken his teaching of salvation by faith through grace (1:6–9; Acts 15:1). So Paul wrote this letter to circulate through the churches and call the believers back to the truth of the gospel of Christ.

THEMES

In Galatians, Paul doesn't move from topic to topic as he does in some of his other letters. His focus is on a single theme throughout: Faith in Christ *alone* is all that is necessary for one's justification before God. It had been true for Abraham, and has been God's plan all along. While the law has its purpose, attempting to require *anything* for salvation other than by God's grace through faith in Christ is a serious distortion of the gospel.

HISTORICAL CONTEXT

A centuries-long debate has taken place as to whether Paul was writing to churches in the northern part of the province of Galatia, or to those in the south. The different options allow for different dates for the letter. We know from the book of Acts that Paul took his first missionary journey through southern Galatia, establishing churches in Pisidian Antioch, Iconium, Lystra, and Derbe, before returning to his home base in Antioch, Syria (Acts 13–14). According to the South Galatia theory, Paul wrote his letter to these churches that were established on his first missionary journey. After this journey, Paul attended the Council in Jerusalem (Acts 15:1–35), and then went on a second missionary journey that included the regions of "Phrygia and Galatia" (Acts 16:6). According to the North Galatia theory, on this journey Paul established churches in northern Galatia, and it is to these he is writing his letter. Unfortunately, no specific cities in north Galatia are named in the account in Acts, and no details of events are provided.

A greater number of modern scholars favor the South Galatia option for various reasons: (1) The southern churches are named (Pisidian Antioch, Iconium, Lystra, and Derbe), while the northern are not; (2) Those southern churches were on a route that would have taken Paul through Tarsus, his hometown (Acts 15:41); (3) Paul writes about Barnabas without introducing him (Galatians 2:9, 13), and they had only traveled together on Paul's first journey; and (4) It seems unlikely that the Judaizers would have ignored the more prominent southern cities to go to the north instead.

The various options make it difficult to establish a date for the writing of Galatians. Proponents of the North Galatia theory suggest it was written during Paul's third journey, around AD 53 to 57. And those who hold to the South Galatia theory aren't agreed as to the date of the epistle. If written before the Council of Jerusalem, as some believe, the date could be as early as AD 48–49, making it one of the New Testament's earliest books. Others feel a more accurate date is AD 51 to 53.

CONTRIBUTION TO THE BIBLE

The Epistle to the Galatians should be perceived as each believer's emancipation proclamation. For all the attempts of others to impose a yoke (5:1) of some kind in regard to church practice, Galatians insists that faith is the only instrument needed to free us.

And while spiritually oppressed believers can find great freedom in the teachings of Galatians, it doesn't take much reading between the lines to see that the people attempting to restrict freedom were those who believed themselves to be more mature spiritually. Paul both exposes their error and points out the potential of sin to affect the most devoted believers—even Peter and Barnabas (2:11–13). Galatians reminds us that *no one* should ever presume to be beyond the effects of sin and the danger of losing sight of the wonderful grace of God.

Along these lines, as Paul contrasts the actions of the human, sinful nature with the qualities provided by God, he lists the fruit of the Spirit (5:22–23), and assures his readers that the exercise of such characteristics will never oppose any spiritual law.

OUTLINE

THE THREAT OF A DIFFERENT GOSPEL 1:1–24

No Other Options 1:1–9
The Difference the Truth Makes 1:10–24

THE DIFFICULTY OF LIVING IN FREEDOM 2:1–21

The Truth of the Gospel 2:1–10
An Embarrassing Slip 2:11–14
Justified by Faith in Christ 2:15–21

A CLOSER LOOK AT THE LAW 3:1–25

A New Look at an Old Story 3:1–9
Removing the Curse 3:10–14
The Binding Promise of God 3:15–25

CHILDREN OF GOD 3:26–4:31

Heirs According to the Promise 3:26–4:7
Paul's Personal Plea 4:8–20
Slave vs. Free 4:21–31

TRUE FREEDOM AND SPIRITUAL FRUIT 5:1–26

The Only Thing That Counts 5:1–6
A Choice to Make 5:7–15
In Step with the Holy Spirit 5:16–26

DOING GOOD WITHOUT BECOMING WEARY 6:1–18

Individual and Shared Burdens 6:1–5
Sowing and Reaping 6:6–10
The One Reason to Boast 6:11–18

GALATIANS 1:1–24

THE THREAT OF A DIFFERENT GOSPEL

Setting Up the Section

Paul's epistles have a standard opening that usually include a note of thanksgiving for those reading the letter. However, those complimentary words are absent from his letter to the Galatian churches. The Epistle to the Galatians has a sense of urgency. Paul gets right to the point: His readers are facing serious problems.

1:1–9

NO OTHER OPTIONS

Since Paul will be addressing weighty problems in the church, he begins by identifying himself as an apostle. He would open other letters with a similar reminder that he was one who had been sent (Romans 1:1; 1 Corinthians 1:1; Ephesians 1:1; etc.), but here he places special stress on his authority and the fact that he is speaking for God (1:1).

In other epistles, Paul acknowledges all the people with him, but not here (1:2). Every indication is that there was no time wasted in opening this letter.

Paul's salutation addresses the churches (plural) in Galatia (1:2), while later he refers to the church as singular (1:13). This demonstrates how there is but one church, although it is composed of various bodies of believers. Paul's language also suggests that this epistle was intended to be encyclical—read in one congregation and then passed along to another church in the area. Paul had traveled through southern Galatia during his first missionary journey (Acts 13–14) and again during his second (Acts 16:1–6). If those church members were his intended readers, the letter would have gone to places such as Derbe, Lystra, Iconium, and Pisidian Antioch. Other scholars believe Paul was writing to churches in northern Galatia that were not mentioned in the Acts account or elsewhere.

Twice in his opening Paul notes the connection between—but distinctive identities of—God the Father and Jesus Christ (1:1, 3). In this context, he summarizes the essence of the gospel in a single sentence (1:3–5). It was easy for the early church (as it is for the contemporary church) to begin to place emphasis on things other than the sin of humankind and the need for redemption. Paul makes clear that deliverance from sin is God's doing, not ours, and that He deserves the glory for it.

Paul's opening is something like an overture that contains elements he will return to. And then he goes right to the point of his letter: Certain people within the church were perverting the gospel (1:6–7). The people hadn't been given an option about *which* gospel to believe. Anything that opposed what Paul had taught was not the gospel (1:7). No human credentials were strong enough to discredit the truth of the gospel, and for that matter, no divine credentials either (1:8). Anyone who attempted to teach things contrary to the gospel of Jesus Christ was to be eternally condemned—*anathema*, in Greek. Paul felt so strongly about this offense that he states the curse twice (1:8–9).

Paul is disturbed that the Galatian believers had so soon forsaken their faith (1:6). They had heard Paul preach mere months before. They had seen him perform miracles with their own eyes. They had witnessed the power of the Holy Spirit. How could they have forsaken so much so soon?

Critical Observation

No mention is made of Paul's appeal to the elders of the Galatian churches. Surely elders had been appointed (Acts 14:23), but were likely (by necessity) young believers who may have succumbed to the persuasive but false teachings being introduced. In his later writings, Paul would make it known that no inexperienced Christian should be given the responsibility of church leadership (1 Timothy 3:6–10).

1:10–24

THE DIFFERENCE THE TRUTH MAKES

Paul is writing with the authority of God, by revelation of Jesus Christ, yet he also draws from personal experience. His question in verse 10 suggests that he had been accused of tailoring his message to please his audience. To an extent, the charge was true. He believed in becoming "all things to all people" (1 Corinthians 9:22 ESV). When around Jewish believers, he could join them in their traditional, ceremonial, God-given rites. But he did not attempt to demand such practices of Gentile believers. When traveling with Timothy, a half-Jewish believer who was ministering to the Jews, Paul had him circumcised. But when traveling with Titus, a Gentile believer, he didn't require circumcision. People who lacked Paul's Christian sensibilities might well view his actions as vacillation, moral weakness, or a penchant for playing to the crowd. It has been an age-old tactic to attempt to undermine a message by undermining the messenger.

So Paul goes into further detail about how the gospel had affected his own life. His readers would have equated the meaning of the words *servant* and *slave*, so Paul's reference to being Christ's servant (1:10) was stronger to them than many modern translations suggest. Paul had previously known the slavery of the law (5:1) but had been freed of that yoke. In response, he willingly made himself a slave (servant) to Jesus Christ.

It was no man-made philosophy that turned Paul's life around. Rather, he received the truth of the gospel by direct revelation of Jesus on the road to Damascus, where he was summoned to both salvation and apostleship. It would have been easy enough for him to *say* he had experienced divine revelation (1:12), but the subsequent change in his life was *proof* of what he had experienced.

Paul's critics would have others believe that he was out of step with the genuine apostles because he welcomed Gentile converts into the church without first having them be circumcised. The Council at Jerusalem had sent out letters to Gentile churches about some who went to them without authorization and disturbed them (Acts 15:24), and Paul himself had delivered the letter (Acts 15:25). Yet Paul's critics had the audacity to claim the authority of church leadership and suggest that Paul was among those purporting a false doctrine.

In defense, Paul simply summarizes his life story. He never attempts to hide his sinful past—and especially his zeal as a practicing Jew and early persecutor of the church. In his understanding, the change in his life only magnified the grace of God. However, his comment in Galatians 1:13 suggests that Paul's enemies were telling his story with a different purpose in mind. They hoped to convey that he was still a shady and unreliable character.

Yet Paul's personal history was exactly what made him an expert in the very questions being raised in Galatia. He knew the Jewish mind-set inside and out, as did others. But he also knew the gospel from firsthand experience. As a result, his zeal was redirected. While he had previously gone after the advocates of Christianity, now he used the same passion to promote the truth he had come to know.

Paul's newly discovered Christian truth had come into direct opposition with the traditions of his ancestors (1:14). The beliefs and practices of the rabbinical schools had shaped the Law of Moses into a legalistic system. The problem was not with the law of God, but with the many interpretations that had completely altered its fundamental spirit. Over the centuries the law had become, according to Peter, an unbearable burden (Acts 15:10). In spite of all the zeal and devotion to the law that men like Paul held, it was not a means to salvation. So when Paul discovered the truth of the gospel of Jesus Christ, he wasted no time in responding.

Paul's phrasing in verse 15 is strongly reminiscent of Jeremiah 1:5—another example of God's watchful eye over someone from birth until the time was right for a summons to faith, new life, and new purpose. Paul's original vicious and misdirected hatred of the gospel was no match for God's power and plan. God was pleased to reveal His Son to Paul (1:16), and that's all it took to change Paul's life from that point onward.

Paul's comment about the other apostles in verse 17 may sound a bit arrogant at first, but is not intended to be. He would soon express respect for the other apostles' ministry as equal to his own (2:7–10). Yet since his apostolic calling and commission had been questioned, he made it clear that he did not derive his authority from the other apostles, but from God (1:15–17). It was *not* true, as his critics were seemingly suggesting, that Paul had first been taught by the apostles, but had then broken ranks with them on the issue of circumcision and had begun to follow his own path.

Demystifying Galatians

Paul's mention of going to Arabia (1:17) has generated much speculation. At the time Arabia bordered much of Judea and stretched from an area near Damascus to include most of the Sinai Peninsula. The text does not say that Paul spent three years in Arabia, as some teach. Nor does it say he went there to contemplate his new faith and to meditate for awhile, although that is certainly possible. All we really know for sure is that three years elapsed between Paul's conversion and his first journey as a Christian to Jerusalem, and during that time he made a trip to Arabia.

Paul's return to Jerusalem as a Christian (1:18) is described in Acts 9:26–30. The believers in Jerusalem were understandably suspicious of their former enemy, but Barnabas helped them overcome their fears and introduced Paul to them.

Paul took fifteen days to get to know Peter (1:18). The word translated "get acquainted" can also mean "interviewed," which is almost certainly just as accurate in this context. It is easy to envision Peter providing Paul with firsthand information about Jesus, and to imagine Paul's active mind interrupting, questioning, seeking clarification, and so forth.

Again, Paul makes it absolutely clear that he received no special training from the apostles. He didn't even meet anyone other than Peter and James on his first contact with them (1:18–20).

Cilicia (1:21) was the Asian province where Paul's home city of Tarsus was located. Again, the information he relates to the Galatians agrees with the account of his conversion in Acts 9:1–15. And even with his reputation of terrorizing believers and attempting to prevent the spread of Christianity, the people who first heard him present the gospel were fully convinced of his sincerity and genuine faith (1:23–24). From the beginning, no one had ever questioned his credentials. So the church members in Galatia had no reason to doubt his motives or ministry—especially since they were aware of his additional years of serving faithfully as an apostle and had personally witnessed how much he cared for their church and the others he worked with.

Perhaps more than anyone else in the New Testament, Paul demonstrates what a difference God's revelation of Jesus Christ can make in a person's life. Paul is a consummate example of conversion and repentance from sin, and of what God can do with someone willing to turn from his or her old sinful ways to seek His righteousness.

Take It Home

The Galatian believers' rapid abandonment of their faith in the gospel (1:6) didn't just affect them—it created great disappointment and inner turmoil for Paul, as well as anger toward those who were leading them astray. But at least Paul was willing to confront the Galatians directly and instruct them to ignore the lies they had been hearing. While most people today don't fall away so quickly, it's not unusual for them to lose some of the devotion they had as new believers. Some settle into a pattern of regular growth with normal highs and lows of life, while others seem to continue to drift farther and farther away from the relationship with Jesus that once seemed so vital. Did you undergo any kind of slipping away after your initial commitment to Christianity? How did you work through it? Did you have someone like Paul, who took to heart what you were going through?

GALATIANS 2:1–21

THE DIFFICULTY OF LIVING IN FREEDOM

The Truth of the Gospel 2:1–10
An Embarrassing Slip 2:11–14
Justified by Faith in Christ 2:15–21

Setting Up the Section

Paul has been dealing with a charge by his critics that he is out of step with the Jerusalem apostles as he promotes Gentile freedom without requiring adherence to Jewish ceremonies. Paul's opponents have suggested that his apostleship was derived from those in Jerusalem and should be subordinate to the other apostles, yet his critics accused him of teaching the Gentiles something entirely different. So far Paul has emphatically shown that his gospel and his commission to preach came directly from Jesus, and not from the other apostles.

2:1–10

THE TRUTH OF THE GOSPEL

The book of Acts mentions two different visits that Paul and Barnabas made to Jerusalem (Acts 11:29–30; 15:2). Scholars are divided as to which of the trips is referred to in Galatians 2:1, yet evidence is strong for the earlier visit. It seems likely that if Paul had written Galatians after his second visit, he would have made reference to the Council in Jerusalem that had reached the very conclusion about the Gentiles that he was attempting to defend in this epistle. It would have been the coup de grace against his opponents and would have publicly unmasked them as pretenders who falsely claimed to have the support of the apostles.

Paul had been working in Gentile communities and witnessing God's grace among them. On his trip to Jerusalem, he took an uncircumcised believer named Titus along as an example of his position that Gentiles did not have to be circumcised as a requirement for salvation. The fact that no one in Jerusalem complained of Titus's presence was proof that Paul's position was not out of step with that of the Jerusalem apostles.

Paul always attempted to do things properly. Although he was responding to a revelation he had received, he first met privately with the church leaders to minimize public disagreement and friction that might impede the work he had already accomplished among the Gentiles. It appears from Paul's wording in Galatians 2:4 that the issue of Gentile freedom didn't even come up during this visit to Jerusalem. After all, Peter had had similar encounters with Gentiles that led to their belief in Jesus (Acts 10).

Galatians 2:4–5 seems to be a parenthetical thought. Paul has already dropped some strong hints about his critics and their accusations against him. Here he adds that they had actually infiltrated the church as spies in order to discredit Paul and enslave believers by imposing legalistic restrictions on them. Yet Paul successfully resisted them and continued to hold fast to the truth of the gospel that allowed Christian freedom.

Demystifying Galatians

Although the word isn't used in this epistle, Paul's opponents came to be known as the Judaizers. Most of the early believers in Jesus were Jewish. Some seemed to believe that Christianity should be just a continuation of Judaism with the same adherence to the law and the requirement of circumcision as a sign. The Judaizers had become a vocal group advocating this belief. Paul was never against the law or the practice of circumcision as such, but strongly insisted that such things had nothing to do with one's salvation that was possible only as a result of God's grace through faith (Ephesians 2:8–9).

Paul acknowledges the roles of the Jerusalem apostles (2:6), yet refuses to revere them as some were wont to do. He knew that any wisdom or power that *he* had came from God, and was aware the fact would be true of the other church leaders as well. He realized they all had their callings to attend to. His was among the Gentiles—the uncircumcised. Peter's was among the Jews. Many other apostles were not mentioned, although Thomas, for example, is believed to have gone to India to minister.

The James that Paul refers to (2:9) is not the apostle—he had been put to death by Herod (Acts 12:2). The James of the early church was the brother of Jesus whose faith had led to a leadership role in Jerusalem. Paul would not be swayed by his critics, nor was he unduly impressed by the titles and credentials of the Jerusalem apostles. He had his own sure and certain calling, and his goal was to be faithful to the truth of the gospel (2:5).

2:11–14

AN EMBARRASSING SLIP

The fact that the apostles were human beings with their own frailties and weaknesses became apparent with Paul's next comment (2:11). Paul and Barnabas had been ministering primarily to Gentile believers in Antioch, a prominent city in Syria. Peter had visited and witnessed the unity between Jewish and Gentile believers. Then, later, more people from Jerusalem arrived, claiming to be sent from James. However, several among them were in the militant group who thought circumcision should be required for salvation.

Although previously meals had been shared between Jews and Gentiles, the members of the "circumcision group" segregated themselves. Other Jews soon joined them, followed by Peter, and even Barnabas. It was with clear apostolic authority that Paul corrected these fellow church leaders.

As acting head of the church, Peter should certainly have known better. But Barnabas was a bigger shock. Throughout the book of Acts he appears as an encouraging figure in all circumstances. In addition, he and Paul had been instrumental in founding the Galatian churches. Seeing this entire group distance itself from the Gentile believers must have created both dismay and outrage in Paul.

Paul doesn't attempt to soften the offense of the circumcision group members. He calls it hypocrisy and writes of how Barnabas had been led astray (2:13). He even confronts Peter publicly and challenges his attitudes and actions (2:14). Peter had been living like a Gentile in that he (rightly) didn't feel obliged to follow all the old Jewish ways, including dietary restrictions. Yet suddenly he was positioning himself with the Jews as being somehow superior to the Gentiles.

Some have criticized Paul's public display, suggesting that instead he should have dealt with the matter privately (Matthew 18:15). But later Paul writes that the sin of church elders should be a public matter so that others will witness and take warning (1 Timothy 5:20).

2:15–21

JUSTIFIED BY FAITH IN CHRIST

Paul would soon write that among those who have placed their faith in Christ, there is no distinction between male or female, slave or free, or Jew or Gentile (3:28). At least, God doesn't make such distinctions. Yet the leaders in the early church were forced to deal with the distinctions of these different groups.

Jews by birth (2:15) were those who had grown up with the Mosaic Law, the Old Testament covenants, temple worship, and the promises of God. Some, like Paul, had come to realize that the law was insufficient to accomplish salvation. It had taken Paul a long while to realize that both Moses and Abraham taught justification by faith and not by works. The Jewish people who had not come to that conclusion were still looking for justification by observing the law (2:16)—the equivalent of legalism before they had a word for it.

"Gentile sinners" (2:15 NIV) were those outside the Jewish faith. The term was probably an often-used derogatory phrase among the law-abiding Jews of Paul's day. As an attempt to belittle Him, Jesus had been called a friend of sinners (Matthew 11:19).

It is at this point in his letter where Paul finally gets to the main point. He has let his readers know that the dispute he is addressing concerns the freedom of Gentile Christians from Jewish ceremonial regulations, but not precisely what he understood to be at issue in that dispute.

Here Paul reveals that at issue is how a person is *justified.* It is his first use of the terminology of justification in Galatians. The Judaizers had been teaching that justification was by works—by holding fast to the law, by getting circumcised, and so forth. They would probably have insisted that they believed in justification by faith *and* works, but Paul saw it as just another form of justification by works. It is not correct to say that someone believes in justification by faith if he or she does not mean justification by faith *alone.*

Paul does not deny that good works should be evident in a Christian's life (6:9–10). But nothing—not good works, adherence to the law, circumcision, or anything else—contributes to a person's justification. Anything people attempt to add to justification by God's grace only serves to diminish God's perfect plan of redemption. Therefore, any attempt to require Gentiles to first become Jews in order to become Christians is a denial of the sufficiency of Jesus' atoning work on the cross.

The brevity of Galatians 2:17–18 makes the passage difficult to interpret. Some believe Paul was anticipating the antinomian response to the idea of justification by faith. Antinomianism is at the other end of the scale from legalism. The doctrine perceives that since salvation is indeed by grace through faith, the gospel gives Christians freedom from all other laws and requirements—civil, moral, and even scriptural. Paul refutes this way of thinking in various places, such as Romans 3:31, and it may have been his intent to do so here. Yet if so, his next statement (2:18) makes little sense.

Paul is probably suggesting that if believers forsake all thought of justification by their own works of the law and turn instead to Christ's righteousness, they are likely to be considered sinners by others who have a legalistic mind-set. Although the first-century believers were breaking no biblical mandates, they were going against a lot of Jewish traditions. It might *seem* as if leaders such as Paul were invoking Jesus' name in support of sinful practices, when in actuality they were taking a stand for Christian liberty. So if they decided to rebuild the hindrances they had destroyed (2:18)—as Peter had done by first receiving the Gentiles and then distancing himself from them—*then* they would be perceived as lawbreakers.

Paul is being tactful. Rather than pointing a finger at Peter's discriminatory behavior, he speaks only of himself in making his argument. The Judaizers could charge him with being sinful, but their accusations meant nothing to Paul. However, if he gave in to their pressure, he would indeed have committed a sin against God.

What did Paul mean by saying he had died to the law (2:19)? He isn't suggesting that the law is useless. His defense and admiration of the law is clear in Romans 7:7–13. What Paul means by this is "dying to sin." He had died to the law as a means of justification, of peace with God, and of acceptance by God. He had died to the self-righteousness that had come from knowing the letter of the law and not the Spirit of God. And he had determined to live his life for the Lord, not to fulfill the requirements of the Jewish laws and traditions.

Paul's statement that he had been crucified with Christ (2:20) can be interpreted a couple of different ways. Taken one way, it could mean that believers share in Jesus' crucifixion, death, and resurrection. Just as Jesus underwent suffering and death prior to eternal glory, so shall those who believe in Him.

Yet more likely is the explanation that the old, self-righteous Paul, who based his hope on obedience to the law, had been executed and was dead. It was a new Paul, a new man, who now lived for God. He uses this concept in Romans 6:6, and will come back to this point later in Galatians (5:24; 6:14).

Whatever the particular nuance, Paul's general meaning is clear. Having died with Christ to the law and all thoughts of justification by keeping the law of God, Paul was living according to new realities. No longer driven by self-effort, his purpose and strength now come from a present Christ living in and with him. He had died to the law, so he no longer lived. Yet now Christ lives in him, so in response he lives for God (2:19–20).

Paul makes little distinction between Christ living in him and the Holy Spirit working in him. The Spirit is the Spirit of Christ (Romans 8:9–10). Here Paul assures his readers that Christ lives in him (2:20); later he will say it is the Spirit of God's Son (4:6). Living by faith in Christ is the same as being controlled by the Spirit.

Paul is not promoting some sort of mysticism where two personalities merge—his and Christ's—until Christ takes full control with Paul as merely a vessel. Note all the personal pronouns (*I* and *me*) in verses 19–20. Paul still has his earthly existence. Yet his faith makes possible a real and personal union with Christ, and Christ's presence with him provides power in Paul's life and being.

Critical Observation

Notice that Paul isn't just making a theological argument. It is personal. Paul is responding to the God who lovingly gave His life (2:20). It is one thing to believe that God died for the sins of the world, but when believers comprehend that God died for individuals, allowing for personal relationships with Him, they can experience (as Paul did) a more intense passion and joy in response to their salvation.

Finally, Paul observes that since it required the death of Jesus Christ to purchase his peace with God, then clearly salvation has nothing to do with his own effort or acts of righteousness (2:21). It was the grace—the free gift—of God that achieved his justification. The law had nothing to do with providing righteousness.

Take It Home

This passage has much to consider in regard to personal application. But perhaps one of the weightiest concerns is how even mature church leaders like Peter and Barnabas fell into habits of prejudice and hypocrisy when prompted by a crowd of spiritual-sounding peers (2:11–13). Can you think of a time in your spiritual journey when you were guilty of a similar offense? Is it possible that even now there are times when you aren't as consistent as you need to be?

GALATIANS 3:1–25

A CLOSER LOOK AT THE LAW

A New Look at an Old Story	3:1–9
Removing the Curse	3:10–14
The Binding Promise of God	3:15–25

Setting Up the Section

Paul has been making the case that the gospel of grace and justification by faith alone is, in fact, the true and only gospel. In this section he will begin to demonstrate his point using a biblical, theological argument. As he does, we need to keep in mind that when he makes references to the scriptures, he is referring to what we know as the Old Testament. When he speaks of grace, freedom, and righteousness, he does not present them as new ideas, but as concepts that should have been evident to anyone who was familiar with the law and the prophets.

3:1–9

A NEW LOOK AT AN OLD STORY

The Galatian believers had experienced the freedom of Christ, but were being influenced by the Judaizers to consider a much more legalistic lifestyle. Paul says this was tantamount to being hypnotized (bewitched). After they had personally witnessed what was possible through faith in Christ, it was most unwise of them to consider an alternative. The fact that Jesus died for their sins should completely eliminate any consideration of justification by obedience to the law. Otherwise, they disregarded the weight of His sacrifice on their behalf.

Paul doesn't doubt that their conversion had been genuine, or that they had received the Holy Spirit (3:2). He poses his question, knowing that they would have to answer, "By believing," and in doing so would concede his argument and abandon the Judaizers' viewpoint.

Paul intentionally left no middle ground between justification by faith and justification by works (2:15–16). The inclusion of any works at all as a prerequisite for salvation becomes justification by works. Here Paul provides clearer insight into the Judaizers' error: Whatever they might say about faith and the cross, they really believed that their own effort alone made possible the fulfillment, consummation, and completion of salvation (3:3).

If it were possible to be justified by closely observing the Jewish ceremonies prescribed in the law, believers in Christ would not have suffered the reproach of the Jews. Paul doesn't specify in what ways the Galatians had suffered, yet the message of salvation through Christ's death was offensive to everyone in their culture: The Jews thought it blasphemous and irreverent; the Gentiles thought it ridiculous. If the Galatians were to give up now, their suffering would have been for nothing (3:4). But Paul didn't feel they were beyond help and believed they would come back to the truth.

After all, they had seen God's miracles and received God's Spirit in response to their belief (3:5). It is not likely that the message of the Judaizers had been accompanied by any kind of special signs. The Galatians should have had no trouble detecting which was the authentic gospel.

Critical Observation

Throughout this section it may seem that Paul is taking a strong stand against the law, and indeed he is making a powerful argument against its sufficiency to provide justification before God. But it is in this sense *only* in which law stands in opposition to faith.

At 3:6, Paul begins his biblical argument by quoting from Genesis 15:6. It is very likely that the Judaizers placed much emphasis on Abraham and their relationship to him (as Jewish traditionalists had done in their dealings with Jesus [John 8:33–41]). So Paul reviews the life of Abraham to prove the opposite of what the Judaizers were promoting. He shows that Abraham was an obedient person, on which they all agreed. Abraham believed God, and as a result of his faith was a child of God and was found righteous before God. The crucial difference that Paul wants to convey is that scripture says it was Abraham's *faith* that justified him and produced a life of obedience. It wasn't his obedience that gave him proper standing before God and made him righteous. And in that respect, Abraham stands as the quintessential believer—an example for both Old Testament and New Testament people of God (3:7).

Paul's phrasing in verses 8–9 is remarkable. By saying that scripture foresaw justification by faith and spoke to Abraham, he really means God did it. But what better example is there to demonstrate that the Bible is the Word of God? Paul also says that God announced the gospel to Abraham. Again, something we tend to think of as exclusively a New Testament concept (the gospel) actually predated the giving of the Mosaic Law. Additionally, Paul reminds his readers that all nations were to be blessed through Abraham. Throughout the centuries, the Jewish people had tended to separate themselves from non-Israelites, but it had been God's intention from the beginning to reach out to the Gentiles through them. The writings of the prophets had much to say about God's outreach to the Gentiles—not least among them Jonah's message of repentance to the Ninevites (Jonah 1:1; 3:1–10) and Isaiah's messianic prophecies (Isaiah 2:2–3; 40:5; 42:6; 49:6; etc.).

3:10–14

REMOVING THE CURSE

In Paul's next section he exposes a spiritual dilemma. The law pronounces a curse on those who do not do everything it requires (Deuteronomy 27:26). Yet he implies (with no expectation of disagreement) that no one does everything the law requires. Therefore, everyone is under the curse of the law.

So there are only two options for getting out from under the curse. Paul quotes Leviticus 18:5 for those who promote a works approach to righteousness. If someone argues that it is by obedience to the law and good deeds that God justifies people, then everything depends upon *doing what the law requires.* Obedience must be perfectly consistent with the person committed to keeping every single one of God's laws. Otherwise, the law condemns him as a sinner and lawbreaker; it does not justify him.

But Paul also quotes Habakkuk 2:4, which provides a second option: Those who are righteous live by faith (3:11). Their faith is in Christ, who redeemed them from the curse of the law by personally becoming a curse.

Redemption is one of three great metaphors used in the Bible to describe the work of Jesus as our Savior from sin. One is *propitiation* or atonement, a sacrifice offered for sins that turns away the wrath of God. Christ's death on the cross accomplished this by paying the price of humankind's sin and guilt. The second is *reconciliation*, a bringing together of estranged parties, which Christ achieved by taking away the sin that created separation between humans and God. And *redemption* is buying someone out of bondage by paying a price (ransom). Jesus paid the ultimate price by giving up His life on the cross.

However, the reference to one who is hung on a tree (3:13) originally had nothing to do with crucifixion (Deuteronomy 21:23). Crucifixion was neither an Old Testament nor a Jewish practice. The original reference was to the practice of hanging up, or impaling on a pole, a body *after* execution, with the humiliation of exposure and denial of a proper burial. Yet if the practice of hanging the body of a criminal up *after* death was a shame and curse, how much worse was the experience of being killed on the tree itself and exposed through the entire process of death!

Such was the price of Jesus' redemption of the human race. As a result, all who were under the curse—even Gentiles—can now avoid the just punishment for sin and instead receive peace with God and a righteous status before Him. The Holy Spirit is God's pledge of everlasting life as well as the source of power by which believers can live new lives for God. This justification before God is the "blessing of Abraham" (3:14) that Paul has been describing.

3:15–25

THE BINDING PROMISE OF GOD

Paul next uses an argument based on the nature of covenants (3:15–18). When two people sit down and write out a legal agreement, one of them does not have the right to change the terms of the contract at some future date. Even more binding are the covenants of God. After He made a covenant with Abraham, He wasn't going to renege. And God's promise wasn't just to Abraham, but included his descendants as well (3:16). Abraham's faith had been credited to him as righteousness (3:6), and that arrangement was not going to be annulled or modified—not even by the Law of Moses that came afterward.

The word *seed* (a metaphor for "descendant"), even when in singular form, can refer to a single seed or many seeds (descendants). In one sense, the seed of Abraham includes all believers (3:29). Yet Paul points out that the single most significant seed of Abraham was Jesus Christ (3:16). The promise that God made to Abraham was based, from the beginning, on the work that Christ would do as Redeemer. So from the time of Abraham onward, forgiveness and peace with God were available by faith—faith in what God had promised to do through Christ.

The 430 years (3:17) refers only to the amount of time the Israelites had spent in Egypt (Exodus 12:40–41). From the time of Abraham to Jacob/Joseph would have been about another 215 years. Perhaps Paul chose to use the shorter period of time in order to understate his argument, knowing his critics would realize the covenant with Abraham predated the law by an even longer period of time. Or perhaps Paul considered that God's promise to Abraham applied to all the patriarchs, and dated it from the time Jacob went down to Egypt with his family (Genesis 46). Other places in scripture deal with Abraham, Isaac, and Jacob almost as if they were a single unit.

Then Paul reiterates his point: God had made a promise to Abraham and his descendents. The promise preceded the law by centuries. So when the law was given, it in no way negated or affected the lasting promise of God (3:18).

In addition, Paul connects the law with sin. The law increased transgression (Romans 5:20) in a number of ways: (1) Due to its specific requirements, it produced many more specific violations; (2) Its rules provoked the rebellious spirit within people and produced a more vigorous disobedience (as when a parent tells a child *not* to do something); (3) Like a magnifying glass reveals previously unknown dirt, the law disclosed sin; and (4) It created a far more complete way for people to assert themselves against God by giving sophistication to the perception of works-oriented righteousness.

Demystifying Galatians

What Paul means by the law being put into effect through angels (3:19) is uncertain. There is no explicit Old Testament reference, although Stephen refers to the event as common knowledge (Acts 7:53), as does the author of Hebrews (Hebrews 2:2). We do know that God was accompanied by angels during the giving of the law on Sinai (Deuteronomy 33:2), yet their role in the process is not stated.

The law was also provided by God for the people through a mediator (3:19–20), most likely a reference to Moses. So the promise of God directly to Abraham again takes precedence because the presence of a third party suggests a certain distance.

The fact that the law came later and had a less-direct manner of revelation than God's promise to Abraham was one of Paul's arguments for why it did not supersede or set aside the promise of justification by faith. But Paul then adds that the function of the law was actually to serve the interests of God's promise to bring people to faith in God and in Christ, the Son of God (3:21–25).

Paul again states emphatically that God's law is certainly not in opposition to God's promise. God doesn't contradict Himself. Yet while placing one's faith in God is life-giving, obeying the law is not. (When Paul refers to the law, he almost always means the keeping of the law.) If the law *could* have imparted righteousness, then that method would certainly be preferable to having God's Son die a horrible death (2:21). But God had to step in and do what the law could not do (Romans 8:2–3).

Still, the law has great value. Even though it cannot impart life, it can and does reveal the uselessness of every human effort to save oneself. And it points sinful people to the grace of God and sacrifice of Christ as their only hope of salvation. Being bound by sin (3:22) is the same as being bound by the law (3:23). People are prisoners because the law shows their helplessness to put themselves right with God on account of sin. The law does not allow escape into fancies of justification by good works. No one is good enough.

So in one sense the law is like a prison warden. In another sense, it is like a pedagogue (*paidagogos* in Greek [3:24]). We tend to use *pedagogue* as a fancy word for teacher, but in Paul's day it meant something more specific. A pedagogue was a slave assigned to attend to the family's son from age six or so until puberty. It was the slave's job to provide moral training and protect the child from the evils of the world. Frequently, the discipline imposed could be quite strict. In that sense, the law provides helpful (though sometimes seemingly harsh) direction for a time.

Yet people need not remain under the law's supervision (3:25). Here Paul shifts the emphasis of his theological argument to become more personal. He includes himself among the Galatian believers as he reminds them that the law was provided to lead *us* to Christ (3:24), and that *we* are no longer under the supervision of the law (3:25). While the law is not a good master and is inadequate to provide justification, it is certainly a helpful servant. Thankfully, God provided a much better way for people to attain righteousness. Paul will have more to say about that in his next section.

Take It Home

While Paul frames his argument in theological terms (*the law* vs. *the promise*), contemporary believers may not be so specific. Yet that doesn't mean they are any less susceptible to the problems Paul addresses. When the topic is salvation, any attempt to justify oneself becomes problematic. Until we learn to trust God in faith, we remain slaves to a legalistic system. But God is willing to bestow His grace and freedom whenever we're ready to turn to Him in simple faith. Can you think of anything people do today to attempt to make themselves seem more worthy before God, or even before other church members? Are you possibly guilty of such behavior from time to time? If so, what can you learn from Paul's advice to the Galatian believers?

GALATIANS 3:26–4:31

CHILDREN OF GOD

Heirs According to the Promise 3:26–4:7
Paul's Personal Plea 4:8–20
Slave vs. Free 4:21–31

Setting Up the Section

Up to this point, Paul has been stating that from the beginning, the message of the gospel has been the promise of righteousness before God through faith in Christ (Abraham's "seed"). Justification never had anything to do with good works or obedience to the law. The law, in fact, is a servant of the promise as it exposes people's sin and guilt and points them to the righteousness that God provides as a free gift through faith in Christ.

3:26–4:7

HEIRS ACCORDING TO THE PROMISE

In the previous section, Paul had begun to personalize what he was saying by applying God's justification and freedom both to himself and the Galatian believers (3:23–25). He continues with his personal application here (3:26–29) by using second person (*you*).

The believers in Galatia (primarily Gentiles) were true children of God and true seed of Abraham—not because they observed the requirements of the law that the Judaizers were demanding of them, but rather because they had placed their faith in Christ and had been baptized into His family. The Judaizers believed that Gentiles needed to become Jews before they could become Christians, but the good news of the gospel is that Christ makes *all* who believe children of God. In Christ, Jew and Gentile are already one. Through baptism, all believers are clothed with Christ (3:26–27).

Galatians 3:28 is one of the greatest verses in the Bible on the liberating power of the gospel and its ability to break down walls that formerly divided. Judaism in many ways was a religion of exclusion, where women, Gentiles, and slaves did not have the same rights or access to God as men. The temple in Jerusalem itself was a series of concentric courtyards. Gentiles could not go further than the outer "court of Gentiles," and women could go no further than the next "court of women." Jewish men were allowed the next step in to the "court of Israel," but only priests could enter the temple building itself. Paul's point here is that the gospel breaks down all such boundaries, allowing equal access to God's presence and equal access to salvation for all people, regardless of their race, gender, or social status.

While this verse is a powerful statement of the liberating power of the gospel, its wider significance is debated by Bible scholars. Some see it as affirming the full equality of women and men in terms of church offices, leadership, and family roles. Others claim that this is going beyond what Paul says. Paul is not presuming to say there should be no distinctions between men and women, Jews and Gentiles, or slaves and free people. His topic has been justification, and continues to be, so that should be the context in which this verse is understood. In other words, while there is but one way to find justification before God, this does not eliminate distinct roles for men and women in the church and the home. Those who hold this latter perspective point to other portions of scripture—including Paul's writings—which include instructions directed specifically to males, females, slaves, Jews, etc.

Whichever view is taken on this difficult question, Paul himself would certainly be dismayed if differences of opinion provoked division in the church. After all, Paul's main point here is that we "are all one in Christ Jesus" (3:28).

Critical Observation

A common morning prayer among Jewish men included thanks to God that they had not been born a Gentile, a slave, or a woman. The reason was not necessarily to demean the other groups, but an acknowledgement that those people didn't have all the same rights and privileges available to free Jewish males. Paul's choice of terms in verse 28 was probably intentional to precisely counter the viewpoint of the Judaizers.

Paul's clear statement (3:29) is the very thing the Judaizers would not admit. They were tied to rules and regulations, but Paul continues to logically and meticulously explain why the justification of God is so accessible and rewarding.

Paul refers to the law as both a prison warden (3:23) and a pedagogue to lead people to Christ (3:24). Now he presents it as a guardian who controls an heir until the time of his or her inheritance (4:1–2). Even though God designates believers as heirs, they must wait a while before collecting what He promises. In the meantime, they are still subject to rules and restrictions. The situation may *seem* little different than being a slave (4:1), yet the difference is most significant.

Thanks to Jesus, our period of slavery has ended. When God deemed that the time was right, He sent His Son (4:4). The world had been spiritually ready and in need of a Savior for centuries. But in the first century, it was physically ready as well. The Greek civilization had established a common language across much of the world. The Romans had established peace and built roads. And at a time when the seemingly insignificant Jewish culture intersected with these great empires, Jesus came to earth and the good news of His life, death, and resurrection spread rapidly.

Paul's short and simple description of Jesus (4:4) is surprisingly complete. He was God's Son—preexistent and divine. He was born of a woman—fully human. He was sent—He didn't just happen to arrive; He came to fulfill a mission. And He was born under the law—submissive to the law's demands as He fulfilled the promise of God. It was Jesus' redemption of those under the law that entitled them to full rights as God's children (4:5).

Paul also acknowledges the contribution of the Trinity in the process of salvation (4:5–6). Not only did God send His Son, He also sends the Spirit of His Son. Believers receive not just peace with God—though that alone is a priceless gift—but also become God's sons and daughters. They are actually brought back into a family relationship with God as He originally created people to be. Believers are privileged to address God the Father as *Abba*—an intimate and personal title. In addition, their adoption into God's family bonds them with one another both now (in the church) and eternally, as they discover what it really means to be an heir of God (4:7).

4:8–20

PAUL'S PERSONAL PLEA

In verse 3 Paul mentions "the basic principles of the world" (NIV); here he warns of "those weak and miserable principles" (4:9 NIV). He is referring to the basic principles of unregenerate human life that are at the root of all false religion. Here he refers specifically to the idolatry and paganism from which the Gentile Christians had turned, but the Jewish legalists were just as much in error for attempting to use *their* principles to earn God's righteousness. It was a daring thing for Paul to suggest that first-century Judaism and pagan idolatry were resting on the same foundation! His comments would have infuriated Jews who saw their faith as the complete repudiation of idolatry.

Paul had already made reference to some of the Judaizers' demands of Gentile converts, including circumcision (2:3) and dietary restrictions (2:11–14). Here he adds yet another: observance of the Jewish calendar and celebration of special events (4:10). Again, there was nothing wrong with observing the Sabbath or noting Passovers and years of jubilee. Paul continued to celebrate Jewish events as a Christian. But it was wrong to think that doing so made someone more righteous than another (specifically, a Gentile believer). The Judaizers continued to insist on all the things that tended to separate Jews from Gentiles, and ignored the more important work of God that was attempting to bring them together.

The Galatian Christians had been delivered from the falsehood and futility of legalistic religious ideas and practices. They had experienced the glorious freedom of the knowledge of the living God, of justification by faith in Christ, and of a life founded on love and gratitude. Why would they give all that up to return to the bondage and futility they had escaped? It was almost enough to make Paul give up on *them* (4:11).

As both the prophets and Jesus had done before him, Paul mixes warning (4:8–11) with affectionate appeal (4:12–16). Paul's challenge for the Galatians to become like him (4:12) isn't meant to be boastful. They would have known of Paul's legalistic and anti-Christian background, yet he had experienced the grace of God and had found his purpose and ministry. He had left behind the "credentials" he had once been so proud of, and was now simply living for Christ. Paul wasn't going to hold the Galatians' spiritual reversal personally, yet he was pleading with them to reconsider for their own good.

Demystifying Galatians

Paul occasionally makes reference to personal physical problems in his letters (4:13), yet never specifically identifies his struggle. Some suggest that he may have contracted malaria in the lowlands of Pamphylia, and went to drier, cooler, higher altitudes to recuperate. Others read his comment in 4:15 and believe he must have had a vision problem. Some think he may have suffered from epilepsy. But we aren't likely to ever know for sure.

Paul had problems and trials just as everyone else did, and he greatly appreciated the reception he received in Galatia during an illness (4:13–14). Even though Paul was quite sick, the Galatians had hung on to his words as if he were Jesus Himself. His illness was a trial to them in the sense that they proved they loved the truth so much that they gladly received it from someone they had to physically care for.

Yet it hadn't taken long for them to abandon the joy they initially felt (4:15). Although Paul felt a bit of resistance from them at this point (4:16), a real friend speaks the truth even when it hurts—and especially if that truth is a matter of life and death. The frankness of scripture passages such as this one can be encouraging. Contemporary readers can see that biblical churches were not perfect by any means, even with leaders like Paul, so they should not be surprised when modern churches face similar problems and struggles.

It's easy to label the Judaizers as terrible people, but we need to remember that they were professing Christians. They believed Jesus was the Messiah, that He had risen from the dead, and that it was necessary to have faith in Him. They were also quite evangelistic, and Paul notes their great zeal (4:17). But where they went astray from the gospel was in their insistence to also require obedience to certain ritual requirements and connect that obedience to one's peace and acceptance with God.

The Galatians had been influenced by the zealous efforts of the Judaizers, which dismayed Paul. He challenges them to be just as faithful to the gospel when he is absent from them as when he is present (4:18). Paul's imagery in verse 19 is powerful. He would have at least had the attention of all the mothers in the church by comparing his ministry to childbirth. Giving birth is a joyful experience, because once the trauma is over and the pain has subsided, the parent has a child to be proud of. But in Paul's metaphor, he was being forced to start over and "birth" the same child. It's no wonder he was feeling perplexed (4:20).

However, by expressing his honest feelings (and accusations), Paul is exhorting change. People and groups (such as the Judaizers) often get by with more than they should because nobody says anything in their presence. Paul wrote the truth in a letter that would be read to crowds in the church that would surely have included some of those guilty of exactly the things he describes. Their hypocrisy would become instantly apparent.

4:21–31

SLAVE VS. FREE

After making his personal appeal, Paul returns to a theological argument against the Judaizers' position. The allegory of Hagar and Sarah (4:21–31) continues the line of reasoning he began at Galatians 2:15. It is yet another reference to the founder and hero of their faith, Abraham. The patriarch's first two sons are the focus of Paul's attention. The first was born to Abraham by Hagar, Sarah's maidservant. The second, Isaac, was the product of Abraham and his wife, Sarah. In this culture, the status of the son depended largely on the status of the parents, so Isaac was entitled to far more than Hagar's child, Ishmael.

In addition, there was nothing special about Ishmael's birth. Abraham impregnated Hagar and she delivered the child in the usual way. But Sarah's delivery was much different. She had been barren all her life, yet had God's promise that she would have a child. God waited until she was ninety years old before fulfilling His promise, so Isaac was always special to his parents as a reminder of God's greatness.

Since Paul recalls this story and mentions two covenants (4:24), many believe he is contrasting the covenant God had with Moses and the Israelites with the new covenant that was established through Jesus.

It may well be that Paul is using the term *covenant* with powerful irony, just as he defines the Judaizers' teaching as a different gospel (1:6) when it was no gospel at all. This is another way for Paul to reiterate the point he has been making: There is the way of self-effort and the way of faith in God. Only those who remain faithful and receive the grace of God will experience His powerful and holy love.

Take It Home

Today's Christian community is not so different from the Galatian church. Some people forget the kindness that others have shown them. Some keep going through the motions of worship, but without the joy they previously experienced. Have you witnessed any similar problems of this sort? What do you think Paul would have written to such people if he had been told of their behavior?

GALATIANS 5:1–26

TRUE FREEDOM AND SPIRITUAL FRUIT

The Only Thing That Counts 5:1–6
A Choice to Make 5:7–15
In Step with the Holy Spirit 5:16–26

Setting Up the Section

Paul continues the ongoing argument he has been making to refute the restrictive and destructive philosophies of the Judaizers. He has just made a contrast between slavery and freedom, and now continues with a call to the freedom that only Christ can provide. He will also explain how the Holy Spirit influences the lives of believers in a way that no law can possibly countermand or contradict.

5:1–6

THE ONLY THING THAT COUNTS

It is one thing to acknowledge that freedom is better than slavery, but intellectual assent is not enough. So as Paul concludes his contrast between Sarah and Hagar (or more accurately, Isaac and Ishmael) in 4:21–31, he calls for the Galatians to stand firm in their freedom (5:1). Trying to adhere to the law as a means of righteousness is akin to choosing to wear a yoke of slavery.

Paul was circumcised, and when working among Jewish believers he even had his coworker, Timothy, circumcised (Acts 16:1–3). But in Galatia, where his opponents were insisting that circumcision was a requirement for the salvation of Gentile believers, Paul insists even more strongly that it wasn't. In fact, he says, getting circumcised would be like a personal offense to Jesus (5:2). Adding *any* human requirement to the work of salvation accomplished by Jesus is wrong.

Critical Observation

What Paul seems to suggest in his ongoing response to the beliefs of the Judaizers is that the most troublesome divide in religious thinking may not be between those who call themselves Christians and those who don't. It is likely that an even more egregious division exists between those whose hope of salvation is based on Christ alone and those who think that, in one way or another, salvation is partially based on their own efforts. This latter division is particularly disturbing because it exists largely *within* the church.

Either Christ provides our justification or the law does. There is no middle ground. If it is Christ, it is Christ entirely. If it is the law, it is the law entirely. The latter option would entail performing *all* the demands of the law—not picking and choosing as the Judaizers were doing (3:10; 5:3). They focused on circumcision, diet, and observing special events, yet the law included so much more. Paul becomes emphatic in this section, reverting to first person singular (*I*) to project his personal presence and apostolic authority as much as possible.

Those who don't stand firm in the freedom and grace that Christ provides (5:1) are in danger of falling away from grace (5:4). That doesn't mean God writes off such people, but that they voluntarily give up their freedom by seeking justification by the law—exactly the reason it is such an offense to their Savior (5:4).

The hope Paul writes of (5:5) is not a vague wish, but rather a confident expectation of eternal deliverance based on the presence of the Holy Spirit in believers' lives and His communication of the gospel to their hearts. Christians are already assured of a "not guilty" verdict at Judgment Day, so they can look to the future with eager anticipation rather than fear. In the meantime, issues such as circumcision are irrelevant (5:6). The focus of God's people should remain on faith in Christ, expressed in love. That, writes Paul, is the only thing that counts.

5:7–15

A CHOICE TO MAKE

Why is faith crucial to salvation by grace alone? First, the nature of faith is to look away from itself to another. Only as believers divert attention from themselves to God are they able to maintain a clear focus on His grace. And second, faith is God's gift to those who are being saved (Ephesians 2:8–9), and therefore cannot be regarded as the believer's own contribution to his or her salvation.

Initially, the Galatian believers had understood this. Paul compares their spiritual journey to a race where things were going quite well until someone cut in on the runners and got them off track (5:7). Clearly, the interference was not from God (5:8).

Paul uses the same proverb to awaken the Corinthian church to the problem of tolerating sexual sin in their midst (1 Corinthians 5:6) that he applies here (5:9) to the insidious effect of legalism. If the Galatians allowed works-oriented justification to penetrate their church at all, soon it would crowd out grace altogether.

Paul didn't have many positive things to say about the Galatians in the opening of his letter, and he had recently expressed both fear that he was wasting his time on them (4:11) and perplexity about why they made the decisions they had (4:20). Yet at this point, he is willing to give them the benefit of the doubt that they would do the right thing. The Galatians were making bad decisions when they should have known better, yet Paul realizes they were victims of people who were eloquently promoting untruthful things. It was those people who would be responsible to God (5:10). Paul expects the Galatians to reject the error of the false teaching and return to a genuine, faith-based relationship with God.

Although a *group* of Judaizers had created the trouble in Galatia, Paul uses a singular pronoun in verse 10. Perhaps he was simply alternating between singular and plural (as he had done in 1:7 and 1:9), or maybe he was aware of (or suspected) a specific ringleader and chose not to mention names.

As was stated in connection with 5:2, Paul tolerates (and even endorses) circumcision as a valued Jewish symbol of faithfulness—just not as having anything to do with salvation. Yet his critics could accuse him of inconsistency. They would say either circumcision was right or wrong; Paul couldn't have it both ways.

Yet *they* were trying to have it both ways. If indeed Paul were preaching circumcision as they accused (5:11), then he would have *agreed* with them, so why did they continue to give him a hard time? He would have been their ally, not their enemy. Clearly, that was not the case.

To Paul, the cross of Christ meant everything as the validation of God's great love and the source of grace, mercy, and forgiveness. But to many other people, the very thought was offensive (1 Corinthians 1:23; Galatians 5:11). Anyone who endorsed the validity of circumcision as a way to God negated the importance of the cross—something Paul would *never* do.

Paul is so intent on refuting the Judaizers' views on circumcision that he effectively evokes a curse (imprecation) on them (5:12). In the style of the imprecatory psalms—those where the writers prayed that God would break the teeth of their enemies (Psalm 58:6), dash evil people's babies against the rocks (Psalm 137:8–9), and so forth—Paul wishes castration upon the Judaizers. He isn't specifically asking God to do something bad, yet he wouldn't have minded seeing their misdirected zeal bring harm to themselves rather than the spiritually immature believers in Galatia.

Paul's specific intent is debated. Perhaps he didn't want the Judaizers to reproduce. Maybe it was a spiritual issue, because eunuchs were not allowed to participate in worship (at least, not in the Jewish system [Deuteronomy 23:1]). Or it could be that Paul was adding sarcasm to logic: If a little bit of cutting meant such a big deal to them, then why not be really spiritual and cut a lot? In Paul's extremism, it becomes clear that circumcision truly had very little to do with one's spiritual relationship with God.

In contrast to Paul's feelings toward the Judaizers, he tenderly implores the Galatians to remain free, but not to misuse their freedom (5:13). It would be quite natural for some people, after hearing someone repeatedly emphasize that following the law is not what God expects, to go to the other extreme and ignore all spiritual rules (antinomianism). But Paul immediately clarifies himself and challenges the Galatians to celebrate their freedom by serving and loving one another.

In this context, Paul's reference to "the entire law" (5:14 NIV) means more than just a list of dos and don'ts. Rather, it is the entirety of the spirit, intention, and direction of all the commandments of God. As strongly as Paul had just stressed that the law is *not* the means of justification, it is interesting to note how much he continues to value it as the guideline for how we are to live.

Here, at this late point in Paul's epistle, is the first indication we have that the Galatian church was experiencing divisions and conflicts (5:15). However, the disclosure should come as no surprise. When *any* new teaching is introduced into a group—whether true or false—it is not uncommon for responses to be divided, frequently with controversy, quarreling, and fits of temper. Paul's mental picture of the disharmony in Galatia is quite graphic: wild beasts charging at one another, biting, and hoping to prey on the others (5:15). Paul calls for them to make peace before the damage became irreversible. The choice was theirs, but as he is about to explain, they would have help if they chose wisely.

5:16–26

IN STEP WITH THE HOLY SPIRIT

It would appear to be obvious which of Paul's two options—to either serve one another in love (5:13) or to continue devouring one another (5:15)—is his preference for the believers in Galatia. Yet Paul also knew the frustration of *wanting* to do something one way, but somehow failing to accomplish what he knew was right (Romans 7:14–20). So he reminds his readers of the continual inner struggle between the desires of the sinful nature (the flesh) and those of the Holy Spirit.

As long as believers are still human, they never fully outgrow the lure of the sinful nature to respond to wants, drives, and matters of self. Moral conflict in the Christian life is an ongoing reality. However, the more a believer learns to live by the Spirit, the more his or her self-centered desires are diminished.

Demystifying Galatians

Essentially what Paul means when he writes of living by the Spirit and being led by the Spirit (5:16, 18) is the doctrine of sanctification. When someone becomes a Christian, a process of transformation begins. The Holy Spirit works within to change the heart, which in turn affects behavior. The education, illumination, conviction, and love for God that come with sanctification are ultimately the result of the work of God within believers. Yet people are still responsible for making the right decisions and working out their own salvation (Philippians 2:12–13). So believers won't be able to avoid spiritual conflicts and crises from time to time, but they can always count on the Holy Spirit to help them prevail.

Paul's list of sins (5:19–21) addresses four distinct problem areas. The first three terms refer to sexual immorality, the next two to false gods, the next eight to various sins of personal conflict, and the final two to drunkenness. It also appears that this is not intended to be a complete list, but rather a representation of common problem areas (5:21). This list is quite similar to those Paul provides in other epistles (see 1 Corinthians 5:9–11; 6:9–10; 1 Timothy 1:9–10; and especially 2 Corinthians 12:20–21). The striking similarities have caused Bible scholars to wonder if these lists were circulating among Jewish and Christian ethical teachers, and Paul incorporated them into his letters.

In addition, it is most likely that the sins he lists here would have been specifically targeted to the Galatian Christians. Several of the sins—especially the sexual sin, idolatry, and drunkenness—had become so rampant in the Roman culture that most people tolerated them unless carried to real excess.

Then, in the starkest of contrasts, Paul shifts from the acts of human, sinful nature into a list of the qualities that result as the fruit of the Spirit in a believer's life (5:22–23). Love is first on the list, which makes sense because Paul has already said love is how genuine faith expresses itself (5:6). Some Bible expositors have written that love is actually the only item on the list, with the other named characteristics being how love is expressed in a believer's life. Experience would suggest that where there is true love for God and fellow human beings, joy and peace cannot be far behind.

Unlike the *gifts* of the Holy Spirit that are separate and dispersed among various believers, the *fruit* of the Spirit is found grouped together in a Christian heart and life. Where one is found, the others will likely be found as well.

It seems odd that Paul finds it necessary to add that there is no law against such noteworthy qualities (5:23). Perhaps the best explanation is that Paul's remark is an intentional understatement for rhetorical effect. It forces his readers to think, *Of course these qualities fully meet the demands of the law!* (This is Paul's point in verse 14.)

Note Paul's smooth and natural shift from the Holy Spirit (5:22–23) to Christ (5:24), and then back to the Spirit (5:25). Those who belong to Christ are influenced by the Holy Spirit, and keeping in step with the Holy Spirit helps believers live a more Christlike life.

In another beautiful pairing of God's blessing and personal responsibility, Paul makes it clear that the Holy Spirit directs our course in life, yet believers must also choose to keep in step with the Spirit (5:25).

Finally, this wonderful fruit of the Spirit is available for all believers. Therefore, there is no need (or place) for vanity, jealousy, or competition (5:26). Indeed, such feelings cannot exist in a life filled with love, joy, peace, patience, kindness, goodness, faithfulness, gentleness, and self-control.

Take It Home

It is somewhat sad that Paul felt the need to spell out such a specific list of no-no's for the believers in Galatia (5:19–21). Yet many of those things had become tolerated in Roman society and very possibly were being accepted in the church as well. What, if any, behaviors can you identify in contemporary society that you feel are potential threats to the church? How do you think the church should respond to them?

GALATIANS 6:1–18

DOING GOOD WITHOUT BECOMING WEARY

Individual and Shared Burdens 6:1–5
Sowing and Reaping 6:6–10
The One Reason to Boast 6:11–18

Setting Up the Section

Paul, in a section about the challenges and benefits of Christian freedom, has just made a thought-provoking contrast between the acts of the sinful human nature and the fruit of the Holy Spirit. Clearly, his readers knew the preferable choice, yet Paul was also aware of the power of sin and the grip it could have on people. So as he continues, he provides practical advice for how to deal with existing sin in the church.

6:1–5

INDIVIDUAL AND SHARED BURDENS

Although Paul exhorts the Galatian believers to be led by the Holy Spirit and to refuse to gratify the desires of the sinful nature, he knew that would not always be the case. It is no surprise that Christians will occasionally be caught sinning, even committing habitual sin. So Paul immediately addresses how to handle situations where someone is already beset by sin.

Paul's instructions in verse 1 may not apply to every situation. While all sin is problematic and separates believers from God, there is a difference between more common, tolerable faults (being quick to judge, an unkind word, gossip, tardiness, forgetfulness in some duty, etc.) and sins of far greater consequence to the reputation of Christ and the well-being of others. So Paul isn't encouraging Christians to become nitpickers in regard to the quirks of other believers, but rather to be bold in taking action to help those in serious trouble.

From the beginning, Paul makes a number of assumptions. He readily admits that some members of the congregation are more spiritual than others. At any given time, some will be living by the Holy Spirit while others are out of step. In each person's life, spiritual maturity waxes and wanes. Some people continue to mature throughout their lifetimes, while others may be quite spiritual at some point and then decline (Solomon, for example).

Paul also warns of potential danger to the spiritual, seemingly successful Christian. Believers tend to make assumptions as to who among them is above temptation, yet it is all too common to hear of people who seem to be above reproach being drawn into some sort of sin. Being "spiritual" is an ongoing challenge throughout a person's journey as a Christian. When attempting to help pull someone up from the depths of sin, it is essential for the helper to be careful not to be pulled into the sin as well.

Although Paul prescribes that those who are spiritual help those who fall into a sin, he doesn't provide specifics. He does not say precisely how restoration should take place or what recovery will look like. What works well in one situation might not in another. Those who are "spiritual" should, by definition, remain under the control of the Holy Spirit to know how best to handle each circumstance.

When Paul says to carry one another's burdens (6:2), the word he uses almost certainly means "to bear" or "support." However, the same word is translated one time (Revelation 2:2) as "tolerate" or "put up with." Some people take that to mean that Paul is saying we who are more mature should *bear with* the sins and shortcomings of the weak (similar to what he writes in Romans 15:1). Yet in the context of what he is writing here, surely Paul intends for spiritually mature people to assist (not overlook) weaker, growing believers.

The latter option is certainly what Paul taught by example. After enumerating his personal sufferings in 2 Corinthians 11:23–27, he goes on to describe his additional sympathetic suffering on behalf of the believers he knew in various churches (2 Corinthians 11:28–29). He had his own concerns and responsibilities, to be sure, yet was always aware of and affected by the weaknesses and needs of others.

Paul had previously shown the futility of the law in regard to salvation, yet here acknowledges that it is still the law of Christ (6:2). The Law of Moses had the authority of Christ behind it. Jesus Himself had confirmed that He was the fulfillment of the law (Matthew 5:17). As a result, people should be able to see that the Law of Moses was always intended to be a law of love (5:14).

Unfortunately, spiritual maturity is frequently accompanied by spiritual pride, so Paul warns against arrogance (6:3). He is not suggesting that believers amount to nothing. On various occasions, Paul had found it helpful (if not necessary) to list his own accomplishments and achievements, yet was always quick to give the credit to Christ. God chooses to use people to accomplish great things at times. Yet Paul knew that many other times believers begin to think too highly of themselves when they have no right or reason.

A person's sense of purpose in the Christian life should come solely from his or her relationship to Christ. People who know they are doing what God is calling them to do find great satisfaction regardless of other factors (6:4). It is when they start comparing their own accomplishments and situations to those of others that problems begin to arise. The key to contentment is to respond to one's calling without perceiving the Christian life as a competitive event.

Although Paul had been making a strong argument in favor of justification by faith alone, he still acknowledges the importance of personal responsibility. Not only should each person carry his or her own load (6:5), but believers could take pride in themselves. Indeed, there was a future aspect to what Paul writes here; perhaps he was thinking in terms of believers being judged according to their works. When Judgment Day comes, the evaluation won't be based on how well one person did in comparison to another, but how well each person did in light of God's calling and provision.

Demystifying Galatians

This passage seems to be contradictory. Paul first says to carry each other's burdens (6:2), and then almost immediately says each person should carry his own load (6:5). The similarity is probably intentional, although different words are used. The latter instruction has to do more with one's personal responsibility in life. Believers aren't to coast through their spiritual journeys while others do all the work for them. The former burden has more of an emphasis on morality. So when someone gets mired down in a serious sexual or ethical quagmire, mature fellow believers should be willing to step in and help.

6:6–10

SOWING AND REAPING

Paul was never one to demand payment for his work as a minister. There were times in his travels when he didn't have enough money to support himself, so he went to work in the area in which he had been trained: tent making (Acts 18:1–4). Yet his belief was that churches should take proper financial care of those who were investing their time and spiritual gifts into church leadership (6:6).

Paul was in an ideal position to make such a statement. Because he personally didn't demand financial support from the churches he had founded, he made a good spokesperson on behalf of others in his position. And when churches *did* sacrifice to ensure that Paul could continue his ministry, he always tried to acknowledge their gracious gifts (as in Philippians 4:14–18).

Verses 7–10 may seem out of place after Paul has made such an exhaustive argument defending justification by faith alone. Others of Paul's writings make numerous exhortations to persevere in good works and to expect to give an account for one's actions on Judgment Day, but the message is not expected here at the conclusion of Galatians.

And the full force of Paul's remarks should be noted. He is not making a distinction between people who had professed faith and those who hadn't. Rather, he describes two alternatives: either destruction or eternal life (6:8). And he seems to say that those who persevere in good works get to heaven, while those who fail to persevere get hell instead. In other places he had differentiated between believers and nonbelievers (2 Thessalonians 1:8–10), but here he suggests that the principle of reaping what one has sown applies also within the Christian life and with how Christians will be judged.

Critical Observation

The truths of the Bible are sometimes found at opposite ends of a continuum and juxtaposed, but are not synthesized or harmonized. For example, scripture teaches God's sovereign grace and election (choice) of believers on one hand, and the freedom of human will on the other. We find the assurance of salvation by grace alone contrasted with Judgment Day parables, where Christ's final separation seems to be based on whether or not those involved had done good works (Matthew 25:31–46). There are passages about the reality of the continuing sinfulness of Christians as well as the call for them to be perfect (Matthew 5:48). Such perceived polarities are not really opposites or in conflict with one another, yet they are difficult to harmonize. That is the point. Many spiritual errors develop as a one-sided assertion of "truth" uncorrected by a corresponding truth that would bring balance. So part of spiritual maturity is learning to live with the tensions as we continue to grow in the knowledge of Christ.

The weight of what Paul is saying is intensified based on everything he had written the Galatians to this point about justification by faith alone. Having established that point, clearly he wants his readers to know that love-inspired actions are also important to a believer's life and faith.

And regardless of how Paul's meaning is interpreted, his command is clear: Believers are to commit themselves to good works—especially among one another. A commitment should be made that allows them to continue without giving up (6:9–10).

6:11–18

THE ONE REASON TO BOAST

Paul usually dictated his letters to a scribe rather than write the entire epistle himself. But it was common for him to take over at some point and write a portion of the letter in his own handwriting. Apparently he wanted to personally emphasize this closing section, so he uses large letters (6:11)—either for emphasis, or due to an eye ailment or some other physical problem.

Paul wants to assure the Galatians one more time that he is concerned about their inner, spiritual growth. In contrast, the Judaizers remained focused only on external conformity and their own reputation (6:12–13). They wanted to be accepted by the Jewish community and were unwilling to face the hardships and rejection of those who followed Christ completely. (If the Judaizers could persuade the Gentile converts to be circumcised, those new believers would appear no different than any other Jewish proselytes, and perhaps the Judaizers—who were also Christian converts—would be less likely to be persecuted by the traditional Jews.)

While the Judaizers took great pride in external religious symbolism, Paul's only "boast" was in the reality of Jesus' crucifixion and its results (6:14). Paul once had a list of honors and accomplishments (Philippians 3:4–6). Although religious in nature, they had drawn his heart away from God, so now he considers them crucified. They had lost their charm and allure to Paul, just as he had lost the respect of many who once admired him. For those who rejected Jesus, Paul was an object of either complete disinterest or active contempt.

For Paul to boast in the cross of Jesus was not something many people could understand. We don't find much about crucifixion in classic literature because it was so barbaric and horrific that even the Romans didn't much care to talk about it. As Paul writes elsewhere, it was foolishness to the Gentiles and a stumbling block to the Jews (1 Corinthians 1:23). Yet Paul isn't referring to the actual cross, the literal pieces of wood, but rather to the Savior who was crucified there to bear in our place the punishment of our sins. Nothing else that the world finds important can stand up to the reality and consequence of that event.

No one but God can make someone a new creation, which is really the intent and goal of religious faith. Circumcision in and of itself contributes nothing to one's peace with God. What matters is the supernatural work of grace by which, in Christ, men and women are transformed into new creatures by the Holy Spirit (6:15). Those who are justified by faith in Christ rather than attempting to work toward their own justification—whether Jewish or Gentile—can find God's peace and mercy (6:16).

Although Paul was circumcised, that was not the mark he took pride in. Just as slaves traditionally bore brands or other identifying marks, Paul wore the marks of Jesus—surely a reference to the scars he had received from beatings, stonings, and other such experiences he had endured. Those marks identified who he served and to whom he belonged, so anyone who resisted his message (caused him trouble) was an opponent of Christ Himself (6:17).

And although Paul had shared a message with the Galatians that was probably hard to write and certainly hard to hear, he closes with the final encouraging affirmation that he and they are brothers. He believed they would heed his appeal and remain true to the gospel. And in doing so, they would experience the true grace of Jesus (6:18).

Take It Home

In today's Christian culture, we may do well to consider what Paul meant when he wrote that God cannot be mocked (6:7). There is a tendency to think that we don't always reap what we sow. Many people believe that they will somehow be spared the consequences of their actions. Can you think of examples in your own circle of acquaintances where someone reaped an unwanted result of an action? Such self-deception can frequently be corrected. But what can you learn from such an experience to keep from being deceived about spiritual—and eternal—sowing and reaping?

EPHESIANS

INTRODUCTION TO EPHESIANS

The book of Ephesians is a powerful and uplifting contribution to the canon of scripture. Lacking any specific rebuttals of false doctrines, and addressed primarily to Gentile believers, it has long been beloved by seekers and new believers. Its doctrinal foundation has made it a favorite of Bible scholars as well.

AUTHOR

Paul's authorship was not questioned until the early nineteenth century, at which time certain Bible scholars began to speculate that Ephesians was historically, theologically, and stylistically inconsistent with Paul's other writings. Paul had spent much time in Ephesus (Acts 19:1, 8–10), yet his letter to the Ephesians is impersonal. The discrepancy is easily explained if Paul were addressing a different group of Gentile believers (perhaps newer ones he hadn't yet met), or if he intended the letter to be circulated to different churches. As for theology, Paul never even refers to justification in Ephesians, and his references to reconciliation pertain more to unity between Jews and Gentiles than humankind and God. Yet simply because he emphasizes a different aspect of God's grace in Ephesians is no proof that Paul didn't write the epistle. Any opposition to Paul's authorship is subjective and speculative. Indeed, the logic, the structure of the book, the emphasis on the grace of God, and the full acceptance of Gentile believers are distinct indications that Ephesians was written by the apostle Paul.

PURPOSE

Although some of Paul's epistles address specific problems within a particular church, Ephesians doesn't. Rather, it challenges the reader to set a higher standard for living—the imitation of God (5:1). Paul was writing to a prominently Gentile church, and makes clear that its members have been fully reconciled to God and are entitled to every spiritual blessing that He offers (1:3; 3:16–19).

OCCASION

Paul was a prisoner when he wrote this letter—most likely under house arrest in Rome, awaiting trial before Caesar (Nero). If so, his had been a long, arduous journey, including false arrest in Jerusalem, a series of trials (with ongoing imprisonment) for more than two years, a harrowing shipwreck on the way to Rome, and the current uncertainty of what would happen to him. Yet his letter is filled with enthusiasm, faith, and confidence.

THEMES

A number of topics are repeated with some frequency in this epistle. One is the *Trinity* of God the Father, Jesus Christ the Son, and the Holy Spirit. Where Paul mentions one member of the Trinity, many times he will specify the others as well.

The *mystery* of God is mentioned throughout the letter. Paul explains that, at his writing, it is a revealed mystery—a reference to the gospel of Jesus Christ that can now be understood even though its full meaning had been hidden for centuries.

Ephesians has much to say about the *heavenly realms*, as Paul regularly shifts his readers' attention from their personal, earthly concerns to the spiritual conflict they are involved in.

And Paul's focus remains on the *church*. Although he provides both a theological basis for how to live and practical applications for what to do, his intent is to build up the body of Christ—not a random assortment of spiritually mature Christians.

HISTORICAL CONTEXT

Ephesus was a major city in the Roman Empire. The book of Acts details a number of events that took place there, including passionate opposition to Paul by silversmiths who made their living from the great number of visitors to the temple of Artemis (Acts 19). In spite of the heavy influence of idolatry and sexual promiscuity connected with the temple and the culture, a predominately Gentile church had arisen. Although Paul has nothing bad to say of the church there, John would later report that it had forsaken its first love (Christ) and needed to repent (Revelation 2:1–7).

AUDIENCE

Many scholars believe that Paul did not send this letter exclusively to the church in Ephesus, but that he meant it to be an "encyclical" letter to circulate among various churches. We know from Acts that while ministering in Ephesus, Paul and his disciples started churches throughout the Roman province of Asia (Acts 19:10).

Arguments supporting a circulating letter:

1) Some ancient manuscripts omit the words *at Ephesus* in Ephesians 1:1.
2) There are no personal greetings at the end of the letter. This is particularly surprising since we know from Acts that Paul worked in Ephesus for nearly three years on his third missionary journey (Acts 19).
3) There seems to be no treatment of *specific* church problems. When Paul is writing to an individual church he usually addresses issues and problems specific to that church.
4) Paul writes that he has "heard" of the readers' faith (1:15) and they have "heard" of his ministry (3:2). But Paul knew firsthand of the faith of the Ephesians.
5) In Colossians 4:16, Paul tells the Colossians to read the letter from Laodicea. Some scholars speculate that this is our letter to the Ephesians, and that it is circulating among the churches in Asia Minor.

Together this evidence makes it possible, though not certain, that Paul originally sent this letter to circulate among various churches. Such a possibility does not affect the theological or practical importance of the letter.

CONTRIBUTION TO THE BIBLE

Ephesians in its entirety is a grand epistle of spiritual richness. Yet several of its components have been singled out as favorites of Bible students. One such passage is Ephesians 2:8–9, Paul's clear and concise affirmation of the absolute sufficiency of salvation by grace through faith—and nothing else.

Another favorite selection for memory verses comes at the end of Ephesians 3, where Paul uses physical measurements (wide and long and high and deep) to describe the love of Jesus, and follows that with the assurance that Christ can do immeasurably more than people can ask or imagine.

The submission teachings of Ephesians (5:22–6:9) have generated much discussion throughout the centuries since they were first written. And the closing description of spiritual qualities as the armor of God (6:10–18) is another often-cited section of this epistle.

OUTLINE

THE ALL-SUFFICIENCY OF CHRIST — 1:1–23

- Every Spiritual Blessing — 1:1–14
- A Glorious Inheritance and Incomparable Power — 1:15–23

DEAD IN SIN, ALIVE IN CHRIST — 2:1–22

- Sin and Salvation — 2:1–10
- Brought Near to God — 2:11–22

REVEALED MYSTERY AND GLORIOUS RICHES — 3:1–21

- Mystery and Revelation — 3:1–6
- Confidence before God — 3:7–13
- The Wonder of Salvation — 3:14–21

A GOOD WALK — 4:1–32

- A Call to Unity — 4:1–16
- Putting on the New Self — 4:17–32

LIVING CAREFULLY — 5:1–33

- A Higher Standard of Living — 5:1–7
- Out of the Darkness, Into the Light — 5:8–20
- Husbands and Wives — 5:21–33

STANDING FIRM — 6:1–24

- Parents and Children — 6:1–4
- Masters and Slaves — 6:5–9
- The Armor of God — 6:10–20
- Closing Comments — 6:21–24

EPHESIANS 1:1–23

THE ALL-SUFFICIENCY OF CHRIST

Every Spiritual Blessing 1:1–14
A Glorious Inheritance and Incomparable Power 1:15–23

Setting Up the Section

Paul's letter to the Ephesians has long been considered a masterwork of doctrine and critical thinking. In this epistle, Paul does not address specific problem areas, but directs the thoughts of his readers toward the things God has done for them, and then to what they should do in response. This section will remind believers of many things for which they should be thankful.

1:1–14

EVERY SPIRITUAL BLESSING

Paul begins this epistle, as usual, by identifying himself (1:1). He also uses the title of *apostle*, as he frequently did, as a reminder that he was sent from God. His message is not merely opinion or casual conversation, but carries the authority of the Lord.

As noted in the introduction, several of the oldest manuscripts of Ephesians do not include the mention of Ephesus in the opening of the letter. It is addressed simply to the saints rather than the saints in Ephesus, adding to speculation that this might have been intended as a circular letter. Additionally, Paul does not deal with any specific heresies as he does in other letters, nor does he greet people by name, even though he spent nearly three years in Ephesus (Acts 19:10).

Though *grace* and *peace* (1:2) were traditional greetings, both terms had a personal spiritual significance to Paul and reappear throughout the letter.

At verse 3, Paul begins a sentence that, in the original Greek, doesn't end until verse 14—over two hundred words. One clause builds upon another as Paul loses himself in enthusiasm over what he is writing. As many scholars have noted, this extended paragraph is a doxology. It opens with praise to God the Father, and Paul attempts to keep directing the readers' attention to Him throughout the letter (1:17; 2:18; 3:14; 4:6; 5:20; 6:23).

Ephesians maintains an emphasis upon the person of God the Father and His role in salvation. As Paul opens his letter, he reminds the believers of their rich heritage. He wants them to appreciate what extraordinarily great things had been done for them and given to them, and they had God the Father to thank for it all. He is the source of all good things—peace, joy, hope, love. As believers begin to dwell on what God the Father has done for them, they find inspiration and determination to love Him in return and demonstrate that love through service.

Yet Paul's opening doxology also acknowledges the work of the triune God: the Father, the Son, and the Holy Spirit. Before the creation of the world, before the human race even existed, God was already laying the plan for its salvation from the death and doom humans would bring upon themselves (1:4–8), and that plan would include both Jesus (1:5, 9–10, 12–13) and the Holy Spirit (1:13–14). It is as if the Father, Son, and Holy Spirit met and conferred before the creation of the earth, agreeing on what part each would play in the salvation of the human race. The Father was the planner, choosing those to be saved and determining the way of salvation. The Son was the executor of the Father's plan, bringing it to pass by His incarnation, suffering, death, and resurrection—all on behalf of the ones the Father had given Him. The Spirit would be the communicator of the Father's plan, accomplished by the Son. The Spirit calls the elect to faith in Christ and communicates to their hearts the knowledge of God, of Christ, and of their own salvation.

The salvation of humankind was no afterthought. God knew that human beings would be guilty and inveterate sinners, so He provided a way for sin to be removed, the record cleansed, and perfect righteousness reestablished. Still, that was not all. God loved human beings so much that He chose to include them in His family—not only as servants or friends, but as His sons and daughters (1:4–5). And God is by no means a stingy Father. Believers are lavished with wisdom and understanding. They are made privy to the mystery of His will. While they may not know all the specifics, they can have absolute confidence that all things are proceeding according to God's plan and will ultimately conclude with a universal demonstration of the glory and divine dominion of Jesus Christ (1:7–10).

This passage is rich with theological terms and biblical doctrines: predestination, election, justification, adoption, salvation, sanctification, and more. In addition, the family aspect of God's plan is significant. The connection to Jesus brings all believers together; they are not solo entities. They belong to a family—the church.

The same plan that enables any person's forgiveness and adoption embraces the farthest reaches of the cosmos and everything that happens in it. The salvation of each and every believer is subsumed into God's larger, greater plan for the world and for humankind (1:11–12). The God who planned, accomplished, and applied Christ's salvation to each believer is the same God who now controls the march of history as, day by day and event by event, it makes its inexorable way toward the consummation of all things.

Then, finally, at the conclusion of his long, meandering sentence, Paul relates this mélange of grand, sweeping themes to the daily lives of God's people. The believers in Ephesus were recipients of everything God had promised, and well aware of their inheritance. Yet they could not yet see or experience those things fully. Paul instructs them to wait and look to the future in confident hope (1:13–14). To prevent them from becoming discouraged in the meantime, the Holy Spirit is present among them to assure them that God would someday deliver everything He had promised.

Demystifying Ephesians

The word *redemption* in this instance (1:14) does not mean Christ's payment of His life as a ransom to deliver people from the bondage of sin and guilt (as it usually does in scripture), but rather refers more broadly to the ultimate issue of Christ's redeeming work—the full and absolute deliverance of His people from all the consequences of sin and guilt when He brings them at last to heaven.

In his opening salvo, Paul traces humankind's salvation from its inception in the plan and purpose of God to its ultimate fulfillment in the eternal inheritance of the saints in the world to come. Yet he does not fill in any details. Everything is summarized. Doctrine after doctrine flows among Paul's cascading clauses in this, the longest single sentence in the New Testament. It is God's plan of salvation in a single breath.

Verses 3–14 are a thesis statement—a table of contents for the letter. There is no need to stop and delve into any of these magnificent themes in depth because Paul will come back to them later in the letter. Yet before going any farther, Paul provides a controlling perspective, a theological viewpoint of the sovereignty of God and His grace to sinners. It is this viewpoint that will bring the rest of the letter into clearer focus.

1:15–23

A GLORIOUS INHERITANCE AND INCOMPARABLE POWER

The section that follows (1:15–23) is another long, single sentence. In this case, the passage begins with Paul's thanksgiving for the believers to whom he is writing, his prayer for them (in three parts), and an elaboration of his prayer regarding the power of God.

Paul had spent years in Ephesus (Acts 19:8–10), yet his phrasing (1:15) makes him sound like a stranger. This may be attributed to regular growth in the church, to the point where many new converts would not have known him. Or, as some believe, if Paul intended for this letter to be circulated to numerous congregations, he might have intentionally downplayed personal bonds to address the church as a whole.

Here, as in a number of other places in the New Testament, the point is made that true faith in Christ is evident by showing love for fellow Christians (1:15–16). Paul would soon go on record with his insight into the faith-works debate (2:8–9), but as the Ephesian believers already demonstrated, faith and works *should* go together. Paul wasn't there to see for himself, yet hearing of their actions gave him confidence that they were in fact Christians (1:16).

The report Paul had received about the Ephesian church had inspired thanksgiving, and he responds with prayer on its behalf (1:17–19). When Paul writes of hope (1:18), he isn't referring to a fingers-crossed wish for God to come through. The biblical concept of hope is confident assurance that God will do as He has promised. Christ's work is finished and the Holy Spirit has been given as a deposit and guarantee of a future inheritance (1:14).

Paul desired to see the Ephesian believers grow in the grace and knowledge of the Lord—in wisdom, revelation, and enlightenment (1:17–18). As they grew, they would first see more clearly what God had in store for them. Second, they would learn to appreciate what a wonderful thing it is to be part of the people of God. And third, they would comprehend God's mighty power that assures, secures, and inspires those who realize that it is always available to them and working for them.

The Ephesian believers already possessed the Holy Spirit (1:13), yet Paul writes of a deeper knowledge of Him as well as subsequent wisdom and power available to them. As God's truth more fully captures their hearts, as only the Holy Spirit could make happen, they would live in abounding joy, perpetual thanksgiving, and confident effectiveness.

Critical Observation

It has been written that the mature and holy Christian life has three dimensions: (1) doctrine (the knowledge of the truth about God, man, sin, Christ, the Holy Spirit, salvation, etc.); (2) experience (the life-transforming force of the truth in the heart, producing sorrow for sin, hunger and thirst for righteousness, love for God, joy, and peace); and (3) practice (obedience by keeping the commandments of God and serving Him in the body of Christ). Paul's writings affirm the importance of these spheres of Christian life. Yet while some people tend to minimize the importance of doctrine, that was certainly not Paul's view. Experience and practice are not authentic or effective unless they begin with the knowledge of truth. Awareness of Christian doctrine is imperative.

It should be noted, however, that Paul is not writing about a new or secret knowledge that requires great effort to decode or unveil—a teaching that certain cultic groups would soon promote in the early church. Rather Paul refers only to a deeper awareness of what the Ephesian believers had already been taught. From their introduction to Christianity, they had heard of heaven, the world to come, the grace of God, their inclusion in His household, and His limitless power. These were not brand-new discoveries. Yet as the Ephesians grew in Christian maturity, such truths would become more important to them and begin to burn in their hearts. *That* was the knowledge Paul desired for them.

Believers have access to the same power of God that Jesus had (1:19–23). At one point, Jesus appeared to be at the mercy of Pontius Pilate; now He is King of kings and Lord of lords. Here, Paul hints at spiritual forces of darkness as he writes of authority, power, and dominion. He will later be more specific (3:10; 6:12). Yet whether human or spiritual, current or future, no ruler can ever compare to the power and authority of Jesus Christ.

Paul will also go into more detail about the definition of the church and its relationship to Christ, although his explanation in verses 22–23 is nicely compact. And just as he had done in the previous paragraph, Paul acknowledges each of the three persons of the triune God. Faith in Jesus (1:15) inspires prayer to the Father (1:17) for the sending of the Holy Spirit (1:17). The result of the Spirit's work is that believers are even more certain of the power of God the Father that was demonstrated in raising Jesus from the dead and placing Him over the church (1:19–23).

God has already acted on behalf of believers. It is now important that believers remember that an effective Christian life is built on establishing regular communion with the Father, the Son, and the Holy Spirit.

Take It Home

How often do you take the time to really think about how much God has given you? If indeed He has given His people every spiritual blessing (1:3), how many of those blessings have you thanked Him for lately? Even while offering thanks to God, many people limit their thinking to the more tangible things of life. Paul, however, tends to dwell on truly valuable gifts such as redemption, grace, forgiveness, and the knowledge of spiritual mysteries. It is in recalling the greatness of God's love for us that His Spirit helps us shift from being aware of His work among us to really *knowing* Him.

EPHESIANS 2:1–22

DEAD IN SIN, ALIVE IN CHRIST

Sin and Salvation 2:1–10
Brought Near to God 2:11–22

Setting Up the Section

After a magnificent opening section reminding his readers of the work of God the Father, Jesus Christ, and the Holy Spirit, Paul critiques the believers in Ephesus and explains how they have come to connect with such a holy God. He describes their transformation as a move from death to life, and his intention is to be more literal than symbolic. His words to the first-century Ephesians are just as relevant for the church today.

2:1–10

SIN AND SALVATION

Paul begins this section by reminding the Ephesian Christians of what they once were. Theirs was a church of mostly Gentiles who had placed their faith in Jesus. They had not been raised in godly, believing homes. They could recollect very easily what their lives had been prior to their Christian experience. According to Paul, they had been dead (2:1)—a highly controversial and offensive statement to many who are not believers, but a statement of fact from Paul's perspective.

Many places in scripture portray the absence of faith in Christ as "death." To be dead in a biblical, spiritual sense is not nonexistence, but rather a condition of inner disintegration, of thorough brokenness as a human being. It is an existence devoid of the true purpose, character, and fulfillment of human life created in the image of God. Unbelievers are alive physically, emotionally, and intellectually, yet they are dead.

God had told Adam in the Garden of Eden that if he ate of the fruit of the Tree of the Knowledge of Good and Evil, he would die. After his sin, Adam did not cease to be physically alive, yet he died in a more significant way. From that point forward, the biblical concept of "life" was not understood as simple existence, just as "death" involved more than physical annihilation or destruction.

The reason for the Ephesians' spiritual death, writes Paul, was their trespasses and sins (2:1). Elsewhere Paul makes clear that the wages of sin is death (Romans 6:23). And since all people have sinned (Romans 3:23), they all remain spiritually dead until faith in Christ makes them alive again.

Critical Observation

The understanding of the biblical concepts of life and death, side by side with the more contemporary meanings of the terms, helps us better understand numerous phrases in scripture. For example:

- " 'Let the dead bury their own dead' " (Luke 9:60 NET).
- "It is no longer I who live, but Christ lives in me. So I live in this earthly body by trusting in the Son of God, who loved me and gave himself for me" (Galatians 2:20 NLT).
- "Whoever does not love abides in death" (1 John 3:14 ESV).
- "This lake of fire is the second death" (Revelation 20:14 NLT).

The ruler to whom unbelievers submit so willingly (2:2) is the devil (Satan), whom Paul later identifies more specifically (4:27; 6:11, 16). Paul also will specify the domain of the evil spirits as the heavenly realms (3:10; 6:12), yet here refers to a kingdom of the air (2:2). Perhaps his intent is to emphasize the lower reaches of the devil's influence—and the proximity of evil to the people on earth.

The original sin that permeates human existence is no small problem. It is human nature to sin—to rebel against God rather than trust Him or please Him (2:3). Sin comes from deep within and leaves no part of the person untainted, including his or her desires and thoughts. Sin is not just a matter of misdeed, but also of an unrighteous state of mind, attitudes, and motives. People are born in this sinful condition, and even if they desire to escape are unable to do so in their own power.

But Paul is not out to depress his readers. Quite the opposite. Only by seeing clearly their status of sin, death, and the reality of evil could they truly appreciate the great love, mercy, and grace of God (2:3–5). It was because of sin that the Ephesians had been dead, but then they were made alive because of Christ (2:5). Just as God the Father had raised up Jesus Christ and established His position securely in heaven, so He will for each believer (2:6–7).

Clearly, people can do nothing to deserve this grace of God, which is exactly what makes it grace. Nothing more can be said in explanation of salvation other than God is love and, loving us, He intervened to give us life when we were dead. Such truths of Christianity are not only realistic, but they provide the only truly hopeful teaching to be found.

Salvation is only by God's grace, which Paul emphasizes with repetition (2:5, 8). Some people try to dissect Paul's wording in verse 8 to suggest that while grace is certainly from God, the faith aspect of salvation comes from people. In any reasonable reading of Paul's words, and in any understanding of Paul's teachings, he also takes the origin of faith in Christ out of people's hands and places it within God's graciousness. Believers owe God the entirety of their salvation, both its provision by God and Christ, and its appropriation by the individual.

Paul further emphasizes his point by restating his positive message from the opposite perspective (2:9). Paul's mention of works is to a predominately Gentile group, in which context it would mean simply human effort or human achievement. From beginning to end, salvation is God's doing, which is why boasting is eliminated. No one has any basis for self-congratulations.

Paul has written of predestination and God's sovereignty (1:4–6); here he confirms that God prepared in advance for His workmanship—those He created and who responded in faith to His Son—to do good works. Yet Paul points out that good works are a *result* of salvation, not the *reason* for it (2:10).

2:11–22

BROUGHT NEAR TO GOD

At this point in the letter, Paul confirms that most of his readers are Gentile believers (2:11) as he begins to apply what he has been saying specifically to their experience of salvation. Their situation had been bleak. Not only were they separated from God, they were also excluded from any kind of community of faith (2:12). The Jews at least had their covenant with God and the promise of a Messiah (even though Israel was equally guilty of unbelief).

That's not to say the Gentiles didn't have multitudes of gods. Many Gentiles were intensely religious, and some were proud of their accomplishments and hoped to improve their world. Yet Paul says their gods and all their hopes were false, amounting to nothing. Only in Christ can God and hope be found.

Paul's description of first-century circumstances is not much different from the church of today. The same point he makes about the Gentiles could be made for unbelievers: It could be said that they are separate from Christ because they do not belong to the Christian church. As long as people remain strangers to the covenant of promise (in the Old Testament) or the gospel of Christ (today), they are without God and without hope. Yet recent trends suggest that more and more believers want to allow for people of other faiths to find a way to God that bypasses the sacrifice of Jesus Christ. It's a culturally tolerant view, but a spiritually inaccurate one. Paul would never have agreed.

Now, as then, Jesus is the source of hope for all people. From all appearances, the Gentiles in Ephesus were far away from God, yet they were instantly brought near to Him through the sacrifice of Christ. Jesus came to save the world, not only the Jewish nation (2:13). And again, the proof of God's grace was that the Gentiles had done absolutely nothing to warrant God's love and salvation.

Paul writes about the reconciliation of the Gentiles to God, yet the work of Christ also accomplished reconciliation between the Gentiles and the Jewish nation—the two that Paul refers to in verse 15. This was no small achievement. Hostility between the Jews and Gentiles had been long, deep, and abiding. Fueling the conflict was the exclusiveness of Judaism. Their customs and self-consciousness as a set-apart people led Jews to regard Gentiles as inferior and unclean (spiritually defiled). Not surprisingly, the Gentiles fostered a reciprocal animosity toward the Jews, their religion, and their way of life that seemed so bizarre and offensive. The barrier between the two groups (2:14) is both a metaphoric and literal divider: Gentiles were only allowed into the outermost courts of the temple, and entering the places prohibited to them was punishable by immediate death. (Paul had once been accused of this very offense, attempting to take a Gentile beyond the barrier [Acts 21:27–29].)

If taken out of context, Paul's statement about abolishing the law with its commandments and regulations (2:15–16) can easily be misinterpreted. Some suggest that Paul is saying that Christ did away with the entire law so, therefore, Christians need not obey *any* commandments. The principle of love has made the expectation of obedience obsolete. But clearly, this is an invalid interpretation.

Paul himself is on record saying that upholding the law is part of Christian faith (Romans 3:31). And he is simply reflecting Jesus' teaching: Love for Christ is to be demonstrated by keeping His commandments (John 14:15; 15:10). Later, in this very letter, Paul will quote from the Ten Commandments to make a specific point about keeping the Old Testament law (6:1–3).

So if Paul isn't referring to Jesus' abolishment of the whole law in verses 15–16, what is his meaning? By comparing his statement to the Ephesians with a parallel thought in Colossians 2:13–17, his intent becomes clearer. Christ, by His death on the cross, did away with the *curse* of the law (Galatians 3:13). He did away with the law in the sense that He removed the regulations of Jewish religious life that placed a barrier between Jew and Gentile. (Really, very few laws did so. Most of the separation was due to rabbinical innovations rather than the Law of Moses.) A few of the Mosaic laws needed to be adapted in order to bring the Gentiles into the church without prejudice as members in completely good standing. One example Paul uses in Colossians is the explicit mention of the laws regarding clean and unclean food—laws that Jesus had already revised as He sent disciples out to minister to others (Luke 10:8).

The Old Testament laws regarding clean and unclean food, observance of religious festivals, and certain other rites had a temporary and revelatory purpose. But after Jesus had come to establish a new and better way to approach God, those laws were no longer necessary. It was *those* laws that Jesus abolished, and His purpose was to make peace between the Jews and the Gentiles, forming one united body (2:15–16). So the fruit of the Cross was not only the reconciliation of sinners to a holy God, but also the reconciliation of Jews and Gentiles. Thanks to Jesus' sacrifice, writes Paul, peace is now available to both groups. The same Spirit works through both Jews and Gentiles to provide access to God the Father (2:17–18).

This is not to say that Gentiles received "membership" into Judaism. The unity created by Jesus established oneness among believers that transcended Israel and Judaism. Gentiles are no longer outcasts, but neither are they Jewish proselytes. Rather, they are fellow citizens with the Jews and equal members of God's household (2:19). All believers are part of the same structure, where Jesus is the cornerstone that both supports and unites all the other components. And that structure, or building, as it turns out, is a temple where God resides (2:20–22).

Demystifying Ephesians

The reference to *prophets* as a foundation of this new building (2:20) may evoke images of solitary and eccentric Old Testament figures, but that was not Paul's intent. Most likely he was referring to New Testament prophets who played a vital role in perceiving the will of God in the context of the early church. When apostles and prophets are paired in Ephesians, the apostles are listed first (2:20; 3:5; 4:11). Furthermore, Paul may not have been emphasizing people or their roles, but rather the instructional aspects of both positions. In other words, the foundation of this new temple that unites Jews and Gentiles is the *teaching* of the Word of God by the apostles and prophets.

Once again, Paul brings together the members of the Trinity as he describes this temple of God, where Jesus is the cornerstone and the Holy Spirit dwells among God's people. Believers in Christ—whether Jew or Gentile—have access to God's presence. Yet the biblical image of salvation is lifted up beyond individual redemption and renewal to its corporate dimension. Believers are integrated into the body of Christ, made a living part of something far larger than themselves. No individual Christian can fulfill God's purposes in his or her life without contributing to the life and ministry of that body. People are saved to become part of the church and Christian community—to participate in the life, worship, and ministry of the house of God.

It is helpful to remember that Ephesus was the site of another temple—the renowned temple of Artemis, a stunning marble building that was one of the seven wonders of the ancient world. It would have been natural for Paul's readers to think of this other temple as they considered his words. Artemis resided in her temple in the form of an impressive statue, but God dwells in His in the form of the Holy Spirit who gives comfort and direction to His people. God's temple is less visible and less tangible than the one dedicated to Artemis, but His is just as real and much more lasting. As impressive as the marble structure in Ephesus seems to be, the temple of God that Paul describes to the Ephesians is still standing—stronger than ever.

Take It Home

Do you think Paul's terminology is still applicable to believers and nonbelievers today? For example, would you say the unbelievers you know (or yourself prior to becoming a Christian) are dead (2:1)? What makes you say so? In what ways are unbelievers still foreigners (2:19) to God and His people? In what ways are believers God's workmanship (2:10)?

EPHESIANS 3:1–21

REVEALED MYSTERY AND GLORIOUS RICHES

Mystery and Revelation	3:1–6
Confidence before God	3:7–13
The Wonder of Salvation	3:14–21

Setting Up the Section

Paul has been reminding the predominantly Gentile body of believers in Ephesus of the spiritual blessings that have been provided for them, and he continues to do so in this passage. After just completing a section about how God had brought together Jews and Gentiles, in Christ, into one body, Paul's thoughts seem to turn to the "mystery" of God that had become much clearer in light of the life, death, and resurrection of Jesus.

3:1–6

MYSTERY AND REVELATION

In order to better understand the message of God's grace being communicated to the Gentile believers in Ephesus, it is important to remember who is writing. Paul (Saul of Tarsus) was a former Pharisee and persecutor of the Christian church. Moments before becoming a Christian, Paul couldn't stomach the name of Jesus Christ. He had recently witnessed the stoning of Stephen and was glad to see it happen—the groans and blood coming from that righteous man hadn't affected Paul at all.

Paul would eventually suffer a similar end, but in the meantime he was rejoicing to be counted worthy to suffer for his Lord. He never lost sight of the fact that his dramatic conversion on the Damascus road and subsequent transformation occurred only by the grace of God. He was more amazed than anyone that he had been called to be the missionary of Jesus Christ to the nations. The well-educated and proud Jew who had been conditioned to look down on Gentiles had become their encouraging and devoted servant.

Even as Paul wrote, he was in prison for the sake of the Gentiles (3:1). During his most recent visit to Jerusalem, a group of zealous traditional Jews had accused him of opposing their people, their law, and their temple (Acts 21:28). Paul was also accused of taking a Gentile into the temple beyond the established barriers (previously referred to in connection with 2:14). Paul's message in Jerusalem probably wasn't much different than what he had written the Ephesians so far—that God, in His grace, was bringing together Jews and Gentiles who believed in Him. So the charges against him were false, yet Paul had already been tried before various officials (Acts 21:27–28:31), been threatened with death, spent years imprisoned, undergone a harrowing shipwreck en route to a higher court in Rome, and was currently awaiting trial before Nero. Even so, he didn't consider himself Nero's prisoner, but rather a prisoner of Christ (3:1).

Paul's imprisonment was an honorable one, and proof of his commitment to the Gentiles. So as he writes to the Ephesians, he stops in mid-sentence to remind his readers of his own experience with God's grace (3:1–2).

Paul's use of the word *mystery* has an important distinction from the way the word is used today. To modern ears, a mystery implies something uncertain and vague—a secret only known by very clever people or perhaps a puzzle for which no answer can be found. In New Testament usage, a mystery is still hidden and secret, but only temporarily, and in time is revealed by God so that it can be known and understood. In numerous instances the word *mystery* can almost be a synonym for *revelation*.

Paul uses the word so frequently in this letter that it is not difficult to determine his meaning. He writes of the mystery of God's plan of salvation in its entirety as now revealed in Christ (1:9), the mystery of the gospel (6:19), and here, the mystery of Christ (3:4). In each of these instances, the mystery is clearly the way of salvation for sinners through Jesus Christ. Paul confirms this meaning in Colossians 1:27, where he defines the mystery as "Christ in you, the hope of glory" (NIV). The mystery has become known and is no longer hidden from the world.

Paul frequently emphasizes that he receives his insight into the gospel by direct revelation from Jesus (3:2–5). He is not being boastful, but rather defensive. He knew he had critics who disputed his authority as an apostle. They falsely claimed that he had been taught by the other apostles, yet had strayed from their teaching by opening the gospel to the Gentiles. So Paul inserts regular reminders that he writes and speaks with the authority of Christ.

Although the mystery of Christ had only recently been fully revealed (3:5), God had provided clues for centuries. Long before the ministry of Paul or the incarnation of Christ, the Old Testament prophets had foretold the salvation of God and even the inclusion of the Gentiles in His plan. Paul refers to the gospel in connection with the belief of Moses and Abraham. Yet their understanding could not possibly be as clear and detailed as the comprehension that came *after* Jesus had fulfilled the promise of salvation and unlocked the mystery. Although the ultimate mystery is salvation in Christ, one surprising aspect of the mystery is that salvation would be lavished on the Gentiles as well as the Jews, resulting in a single unified spiritual body (3:6).

3:7–13

CONFIDENCE BEFORE GOD

As soon as Paul really began to comprehend the mystery of God—the gospel—he became its servant (3:7). Like an efficient service person in a restaurant, Paul was pleased to present the gospel to whomever he could. He had received the gift of God's grace and was more than willing to pass it along to others. He knew the message and the power came from God, and it wasn't up to his own strength and capability to spread the word. In fact, he considered himself the very least of all God's people (3:8).

Critical Observation

The Latin word *Paulus*, from which Paul's name is derived, means "little" or "small." Tradition also suggests that Paul was short of stature. Yet Paul had no Napoleonic complex. His ego was also small (3:8). He realized that with God's power he would be plenty big enough to take on any task and endure any trial.

In Paul's case, this was not false modesty. Everyone knew of his pre-conversion reputation. Paul had more than just a message of God's grace; the fact that he was the front person responsible for bringing Gentiles into the church was *proof* of God's grace. Paul, who had once been so protective of the Jewish way of life, was now the primary spokesperson promoting the mystery of God to *everyone* (3:9).

"The unsearchable riches of Christ" (3:8 NIV) refers to God's love, sacrifice for sin, present intercession, promise to come again, and gifts of joy, peace, love, and hope. Even in a Roman prison, Paul is thankful for such riches and confident that they are available to the Ephesian Gentile believers as well.

The church does not exist for itself, but for the glory of God. It serves that purpose by demonstrating the wisdom, grace, goodness, justice, and holiness of God as sinners are transformed by the gospel of Christ and become unified in love. Such a magnificent transformation is bound to be noticed—not only by people who see the changes that the love of Christ can make in a believer's life, but also by rulers and authorities in the heavenly realms (3:10). Paul probably meant that both good and evil beings take notice. We know from 1 Peter 1:12 that holy angels witness matters of human salvation with amazement and wonder. It stands to reason that evil angels see as well, although their response to the progress of the kingdom of God would certainly be different.

Perhaps one of the church's most overlooked privileges is the right to approach God freely and confidently (3:12). For centuries God's people had to offer blood sacrifices and go through priests for access to God. And closeness to God evoked great fear. Modern believers tend to take for granted the perpetual nearness of God they have through prayer and the Holy Spirit. Such access to God greatly diminishes worry and discouragement (3:13). As believers realize that God is working His gracious and perfect purpose out in the world and that all that happens is somehow setting an example for other people and heavenly powers, they can learn to rejoice in their sufferings instead of becoming discouraged by them.

3:14–21

THE WONDER OF SALVATION

In verses 14–19, Paul returns to the prayer he had begun in verse 1. The prayer is similar in content to the one he records in 1:17–19. In between is his description of the wonderful aspects of God and salvation that Paul wanted the Ephesian believers to appreciate more and more. The two prayers serve as bookends for Paul's first section of Ephesians. He asks God to enable those Christians to grow in their understanding of salvation—to deepen their experience of the Father, Son, and Holy Spirit. He wants their transforming experience to be more complete, more powerful, and life transforming.

Paul continues to acknowledge all three persons of the Trinity. He prays to the Father, asking for power from the Holy Spirit and the presence of Christ in the hearts of the Ephesians (3:14–17). Father, Son, and Spirit are intertwined, each relating to the believer in a harmony of grace and love.

Demystifying Ephesians

Paul's reference to heaven and earth (3:15) is sometimes taken to mean both angels and people, with God presiding over both. But a better interpretation may be based on what Paul had just written about Jews and Gentiles forming one body (3:6). More likely, what Paul means is that some of that "family" had already died. So the use of heaven and earth would be his way of referring to the saints above, already in glory, and those still living in the world below.

Paul's mention of glorious riches (3:16) echoes his previous phrase, "the unsearchable riches of Christ" (3:8 NIV). Perhaps there were people in the church then, as now, who would rather have their ministers speak of other, more relevant things: money, marriage, politics, raising children, and so forth. Paul would address those topics, and would do so in helpful and practical ways. Yet he always did so in the context of presenting God's glorious riches.

People can learn to handle money, have a good marriage, raise good kids, etc., and still be dead in sin. So Paul keeps his focus on what Jesus Christ had done on behalf of the Ephesians in providing peace with God, forgiveness of sins, sure hope of everlasting life, and a perfect life after human death. None of those things would ever come from money, marriage, children, politics, or any other source. For Paul, Jesus Himself was the center of everything, the meaning of everything, the way to everything good. (In his Epistle to the Colossians, he makes a classic argument for the supremacy and preeminence of Christ.)

Paul identifies the Holy Spirit as the active agent of the believers' sanctification (3:16). It is His influence within that leads them deeper into godliness. And through the Spirit, Jesus Christ is said to dwell in the hearts of Christians (3:17). Believers need divine insight and power to begin to understand the intensity of God's love—how wide and long and high and deep it is (3:18). Even with God's help, it is a love that cannot be fully understood. Who can really describe what it feels like to be filled with all the fullness of God (3:19)?

Yet Paul also prays that the Ephesian believers would understand (3:18). God empowers believers and helps with their ability to comprehend, but He doesn't download such knowledge into their minds. When it comes to the grasping, comprehending, and proper perception of spiritual truth, scripture teaches that such things are both the gift of God and the responsibility of seekers.

The more believers discover of God, the more they experience His presence, witness His holiness, splendor, love, and grace, and become more holy and loving. Someday they will see Jesus as He really is, face-to-face (1 Corinthians 13:12). Until then, they learn to see more clearly by *trying* to see Him more clearly.

Paul wraps up this first half of his letter with a short doxology (3:20–21). As he reflects on the things he had written about all that God has poured out on His people, Paul could not help but stop and give Him the glory for it. No matter how much believers can comprehend and imagine what God has done for them, He has actually done even more (3:20).

And lest his readers forget, as Paul was finding himself so carried away with all that God had done, he was writing from prison! He demonstrates that the blessings of God and Christ by the Holy Spirit can transcend the troubles of life. Everyone will certainly experience his or her share of trouble, of course, and should feel justified in expressing true feelings that may not sound overtly spiritual. David did. Jesus did. Paul himself was quite open about his "thorn" (2 Corinthians 12:7–10). But even in the midst of their deepest sorrows, believers can realize that their sufferings are minor in comparison to their knowledge of God's glory and the joy and fullness of life that are certain to exist in their future. It is sometimes during their greatest tribulations when Christians actually experience the ecstasy of such knowledge of God.

Paul concludes with the desire that God would receive glory throughout all generations (3:21). That includes modern believers! Today's Christians have access to the same glorious, unsearchable riches that Paul describes to the Ephesians.

Take It Home

It should be impossible to read Paul's prayer (3:14–21) in light of all he had written in Ephesians 3 and come away unaffected. A closer look confirms how right the prayer is and how happy and holy people would be who saw it fulfilled. Spend some time reflecting on what it would be like to be filled with all the fullness of God (3:19) and thinking about all God has done for His people. What can you do so that you will come to an even greater knowledge of the glory of God on a regular basis?

EPHESIANS 4:1–32

A GOOD WALK

A Call to Unity 4:1–16
Putting on the New Self 4:17–32

Setting Up the Section

The first three chapters of Ephesians have been theologically based. In this section, Paul turns from theology to ethics. From this point onward in his letter, Paul will focus on the Christian walk. Now that he has shown what God has done on behalf of believers, he addresses practical ways in which believers should respond.

4:1–16

A CALL TO UNITY

Paul's outline of Ephesians is exactly opposite of what it would be for any other religious philosophy. Most world religions would open with the necessity of being good and doing what God requires, followed by salvation as a result. But as Paul clearly perceived and explained the truth of Christianity, he spent the first half of his letter detailing the salvation of God, the grace that made it possible, and the complete inability of anyone to achieve it on his or her own merit. Only then did he turn to the section on how to live.

Some Bible translations lose the emphasis, but in Greek, Paul opens Ephesians 4 with a strong "therefore." Everything he is about to write from this point forward should be viewed in light of what he had already written. The behavior he will prescribe is based on what God has already done, His great love and power exercised on behalf of humankind, and the sacrifice Jesus made even when people were enemies of God due to their sin.

Verses 1–3 are a single sentence in Greek, so should be considered a single thought. In other words, the qualities of humility, gentleness, patience, and love—as well as efforts to maintain unity with other believers—are all part of the calling believers have received.

The biblical concept of humility, or meekness (4:2), has nothing to do with weakness. As personal experience will attest, it can take great inner strength and the help of God's Spirit to set aside one's rights in favor of a weaker party or the common good. Yet this is the model set by Jesus (2 Corinthians 10:1; Philippians 2:5–8), and one that believers should determine to imitate.

Another significant biblical theme is the connection between personal qualities and ethical choices, as seen in Ephesians 4:2–3. Only someone who is humble will be willing (or able) to lovingly bear with someone else when disagreements arise. Only a gentle and patient person will be successful at preserving the unity of God's people. Secular philosophies suggest that it is possible to maintain spotless public behavior regardless of one's personal character, but the Bible makes clear that right living requires virtue and character. Even godly believers will struggle from time to time, which is why Paul challenges them to make an effort (4:3). Even though the Holy Spirit makes unity possible among people, it requires determination on their part as well.

But Paul is not asking too much of the Ephesians. Unity is God's desire and God's design (4:4–6). Believers *are* one. They are a body, whether they act like it or not. They have the same God, the same experience of salvation, the same future, and the same calling.

Yet at the same time, Christian unity is not a matter of imposing a dreadful sameness upon all believers or reducing individuals to the status of a single cog on a large wheel. When properly understood and experienced, Christianity is anything but monotonous. When individuality and personal initiative are encouraged rather than crushed, the church experiences beautiful harmony, not monotony. Believers receive various gifts apportioned in different ways (4:7–8). As each person applies his or her individual gifts, the resulting variety produces complex and magnificent harmony.

Ephesians 4:8–10 appears to be a parenthetical comment by Paul, yet this short passage has generated countless discussions, debates, and controversies. For one thing, Paul makes a reference to Psalm 68:18, and then appears to misquote it. David's psalm describes the Lord who *received* gifts from men, ascending as a victor loaded with the spoils of his conquests. Paul applies the psalm to Jesus, yet writes that He *gave* gifts to men. His thought seems to be that the Lord distributed those spoils among His people. Paul would have known other biblical passages such as Isaiah 53:12, foretelling that the Messiah would divide His spoils with the strong, and Paul's understanding of the gospel would have allowed him to properly interpret such prophecies.

Paul's mention of the "lower, earthly regions" (4:9 NIV) is another frequently questioned phrase. Some have posited that he is referring to hell (Hades), but that opinion doesn't seem likely. It is probably simply a reference to the earth, intended to emphasize how far away from heaven the Lord Jesus came to fulfill God's plan—Paul's way of acknowledging Jesus' incarnation. Or maybe Paul is noting that Jesus descended into the grave, after which He ascended and bestowed gifts on the church. The common thread among all of the speculations is that Jesus indeed voluntarily lowered Himself for the good of humankind.

And still another debated interpretation: In what way did Jesus' ascension fill up the whole universe (4:10)? Since Paul had been describing the gifts of the risen Savior, maybe his point is that Christ filled the universe with His blessings and His gifts. Then again, he might have been attempting to convey a message similar to that of Philippians 2, about how Jesus came to earth, humbled Himself, and then ascended to receive His reward from God. With every knee bowed to Him and every tongue confessing Him (Philippians 2:10–11), the universe would be filled with His praise.

Paul's statement amounts to saying that the Lord did all that He intended to do in this world. He routed every enemy that enslaved His people. He destroyed every obstacle to their everlasting life and happiness. He completed His work and ascended back to heaven. Now, as head over all things connected with the church, He fills the whole universe with the blessings He brought back with Him as spoils of His holy war.

It is through the grace of this triumphant Christ that each person receives spiritual gifts (4:7), and Paul mentions a few of them. Yet it should be noted that the gifts Paul names (4:11) are those having to do directly with the life of the church as a body. They are the gifts that Christians benefit from when they meet *together*.

Demystifying Ephesians

Paul raises the topic of spiritual gifts here (4:11–13), yet doesn't stop to make much comment or enumerate the various gifts to the extent that he does in other epistles. We can safely presume that his list of gifts in verse 11 is clearly representative—only a sampling. Other lists are found in Romans 12:6–8 and 1 Corinthians 12:7–11, and what Paul says in those passages contributes to the understanding of this brief passage.

These church leadership gifts are essential to the integrity and growth of any body of believers. Some Bible versions translate the responsibility of church leaders as preparing God's people for works of service (4:12). Other versions express the role of church leaders more strongly, as bringing believers to completion for the work of ministry. Although *all* believers receive gifts and have a ministry to perform, everyone is also accountable to those with the leadership gifts. The result should be unity in the faith, deeper knowledge of Christ, and maturity (4:13). Believers will always have something more to strive for, because the ultimate goal is attaining the whole measure of the fullness of Christ.

Paul provides both a positive and negative image of spiritual maturity. Spiritually immature people are like small children who are easily deceived by false teachers and flit back and forth, responding to every new philosophy that comes along (4:14). It doesn't take much to distract them from what they need to be doing and learning.

In contrast, mature believers continue to grow up, becoming more and more like the head of the church, Jesus Christ. Their ongoing commitment is to love one another. They bear with one another in love (4:2). They speak the truth, but do so in love (4:15). And they grow and build up the body of Christ in love as each person does his or her work (4:16). Paul portrays spiritual maturity as a corporate rather than an individualistic vision, as did Jesus when He promised to build His church. In New Testament thinking, believers are almost always addressed in a group (church) rather than as individuals.

4:17–32

PUTTING ON THE NEW SELF

Paul begins this section with another note of transition ("so," "therefore," or some similar translation). This serves as a reminder that he is still building on what he had already written in Ephesians 1–3. He insists on a connection between doctrine and life. What a believer does on any given day should be that person's reflection on who God is, what He has done for the person, and what the person understands His purposes to be. As Paul teaches repeatedly, the Christian life flows out of salvation and forms its character from it at every turn. When people truly begin to comprehend what God has done, they also see more clearly what they must do in response.

One thing Paul insists that the Ephesian Christians do is reject their old way of life, even though many of their peers were still involved in such things (4:17). Paul suggests that the darkness of unbelievers (4:18) is not necessarily due to lack of knowledge about God or inability to understand. Rather, it is a hardness of heart and unwillingness to repent that prevents their salvation, which in turn makes the things of God seem strange and wearisome to them.

The problem with unbelief is that it has lost touch with reality—a fatal flaw. God is in control, and those who acknowledge the fact and respond in faith discover that reality is human existence as created, defined, and judged by the living God. Those who deny God or resist His leading must establish a different reality, one that is not built on truth.

As Paul goes on to describe unbelievers (4:19), he paints their world in very dark colors. No doubt the Ephesians would have lauded the achievements of their civilization in art, building, and government. Thousands of years later, their aqueducts still carry water. Their literature still moves people's hearts and minds. Their buildings remain as inspirations to the world. Yet Paul says nothing at all about those aspects of their lives. When it comes to what is truly important—the moral and spiritual dimension of life as viewed from God's perspective—many would be found wanting and judged accordingly. They weren't even attempting to be disciplined and felt no qualms about indulging in every impure opportunity that came along (4:19). Paul tells the believers in Ephesus to walk away from such people and behavior.

Paul explains that even after placing one's faith in Jesus, a struggle continues between the old self and the new (4:20–24). Although believers die to sin, change their priorities, and begin to live for Jesus, the complete transformation doesn't take place at once. Paul refers to the old self as dead and destroyed (Romans 6:2), because Christ effectively removed people from the sentence of sin and death. Yet the influence of sin continues, and believers must *choose* to ignore the evil desires that remain within them (Romans 6:11–14). Those choices must be made every single day, no matter how long a person lives as a Christian.

To ensure everyone understands what he is saying, Paul gets more specific about exactly what should be discarded as believers begin to live as new creations (4:25–32). First on his list is falsehood. Truth is of utmost importance in Christian doctrine and practice. Lies distort the gospel and poison personal relationships. Yet the deeper such habits have been embedded, the more difficult they are to eradicate.

Quotation marks are around Paul's admonishment against allowing anger to lead to sin (4:26) because he is citing Psalm 4:4. Anger should never be allowed to linger and fester—not even overnight. Paul would soon comment that a believer's struggle is not so much against other people as it is against spiritual forces (6:11–12). Anger, though a common emotion, is one potential avenue to allow spiritual enemies a foothold (4:27).

Critical Observation

The behaviors that Paul extols in this section (4:25–32) are not exclusively Christian concepts. Other philosophies and most civilized societies have promoted truth over falsehood, self-control rather than unleashed anger, and honest work over stealing for a living. Yet Paul places these common, everyday behaviors in the context of a Christian's relationship with God. To him, the difference is more than simple choice, and is instead the result of the old self being replaced by the new self. It is not a matter of simply giving up what is wrong, but also requires replacing the sinful behaviors with godly ones. Paul's ethical teachings are distinctly spiritual, and are based on a genuine experience with the Father, Son, and Holy Spirit.

As believers respond to God's transforming them from old to new, other changes are just matters of common sense. They need to stop stealing and instead work—not just for themselves, but also for the good of others (4:28). They need to start watching their language, realizing that their words can be more harmful than they realize (4:29). And although such instructions make sense, for some people change is much easier said than done.

What many people don't realize is that sin in a believer's life brings grief to the Holy Spirit (Isaiah 30:1; Ephesians 4:30). Not only are Christians wrong to think their sins don't affect others, they are also foolish to suppose that God doesn't notice or doesn't care. The Holy Spirit's very presence in their lives is a sign of their redemption (1:13–14; 4:30). To revert to their old sinful ways is naturally an offense to Him.

Finally, Paul isn't recommending a mild improvement in one's behavior. He says to get rid of *all* bitterness, rage, anger, brawling, slander, and every other form of ill temper (4:31). Those traits should be replaced with ongoing kindness, compassion, and forgiveness (4:32). Thanks to Jesus, God demonstrated such love and grace to humankind. Believers should do no less to one another.

Take It Home

Although everything Paul wrote to the Ephesians applies to believers today, one issue seems particularly relevant—spiritual maturity as a corporate (church) matter rather than an individual one (4:13). Most church members are accustomed to being challenged to become more mature on an individual level, but how does your personal spiritual maturity affect the church as a whole? Can you detect a current influence? If you were to become more spiritually mature, how might the church—either your current body of believers or the worldwide church of Christ—benefit?

EPHESIANS 5:1–33

LIVING CAREFULLY

A Higher Standard of Living	5:1–7
Out of the Darkness, Into the Light	5:8–20
Husbands and Wives	5:21–33

Setting Up the Section

In the previous section, Paul had shifted from a theological perspective of spiritual life to writing about applicable and relevant ways that such a perspective plays out in everyday life. In this section, he continues his instruction concerning daily living, including guidelines for sexual propriety, speech, drinking, and marriage.

5:1–7

A HIGHER STANDARD OF LIVING

In Ephesians 5, Paul continues what he had started in Ephesians 4, as he spells out practical ways to live a more righteous life. He had already said to put on the new self that was created to be like God (4:24). Here he states the same concept in a different way by saying to imitate God (5:1).

Again, he encourages believers to walk appropriately—this time exhorting them to walk in love (5:2). He had made this point in various ways throughout the letter and restates it here: The Christian life is the believer's outworking of God's salvation. There is one acceptable standard of living for God's people; many other standards are not appropriate (5:3).

Paul's intent in verse 3 is most likely that certain things shouldn't even be *mentioned* in Christian company. Rather than being regularly exposed to and beginning to tolerate common sins, Paul recommends that believers keep themselves removed as much as possible, remaining tender and sensitive.

His instructions on speech (5:4) reinforce what he had just written (4:29), because they would have gone against the beliefs of his culture. Paul forbids believers from speech about coarse topics. In contrast, Aristotle considered it a virtue to be skilled at suggestive language and double entendres. So while it is clearly inappropriate to engage in "gutter talk," it is equally wrong to envy the quick-witted, sexually suggestive quips of sophisticates. Neither option is an attempt to imitate God (5:1).

In place of these common sins, Paul says to practice thanksgiving (5:4). By regularly thanking God for what He has provided, people come to see that He is the source of everything good and perfect (James 1:17). Sexual immorality, greed, and rough language direct one's focus away from the goodness and holiness of God; thanksgiving redirects a believer's attention to where it belongs.

Although many sins are common, they are not minor by any means. As Paul continues with his epistle, he connects sinful behavior with idolatry, God's wrath, and future judgment (5:5–7). People don't need wooden or stone images to be idolaters. The biblical definition of idolatry is worship or loyal service to *any* person or thing other than the living God. The human heart—particularly the heart of the old self—is prone to idolatry.

Peer pressure also comes into play in regard to the sins Paul has been describing. He warns of being deceived by the empty words of others (5:6), and of partnering with such people (5:7). Believers are to follow the example of Jesus, who lived and ministered among sinful people. Yet they are also to be ever watchful that they don't fall into the same sin that grips the lives of unbelievers.

5:8–20

OUT OF THE DARKNESS, INTO THE LIGHT

When believers remember the state of their lives before their faith in Jesus, they become less likely to fall back into that sinful lifestyle. Paul challenges his readers to walk as children of light (5:8) and experience the benefits of pleasing God (5:9). Paul doesn't say how to find out what pleases God (5:10), but he suggests that it isn't difficult to discern God's will in such matters. Anyone whose intention is to please the Lord will have no trouble knowing what to do.

Paul had already said to not even speak about the common sins of the world (5:3) and reiterates that thought in verse 12. Yet he also says to expose such sins (5:11). Most likely his meaning is to remain close to the light of God. When believers live as God instructs, their lives reflect His light and reveal fruitless deeds of darkness. The light exposes sin for what it really is (5:13–14).

Paul's citation in verse 14 is probably a portion of an early Christian baptismal hymn. (He will refer specifically to hymns just a bit later [5:19].) If that is the case, it is probably an attempt to remind the Ephesians of the transformation that had taken place in their lives and had been affirmed at their baptisms.

It is far too easy to fall into patterns and habits that don't necessarily lead to sin, yet don't accomplish much either. Paul is attempting to rouse his readers into making something of their lives by capitalizing on every opportunity and making each day count (5:15–16). When he tells the believers to be careful how they walk (live), it is more than a warning to avoid missteps and sin. His command also includes being aware of every potential chance to improve the world around them. The days are evil, he writes (5:16), because sin is prevalent. Believers ought to walk carefully, determine what God's will is (5:17), and do what they can to represent God's kingdom to those around them.

Paul continues with some specific suggestions for how to walk in light. When desiring a consoling influence in one's life, he says, wine is not the answer—at least not to the point of drunkenness (5:18).

Critical Observation

Drunkenness makes people susceptible to numerous subsequent sins by lowering inhibitions. Paul points out that the next step is debauchery—indulgence in sensual lusts (5:18). His point is that if someone is looking for an experience to help him or her rise above the monotony of ordinary life, being filled by God's Holy Spirit is far more effective and beneficial than filling oneself with alcohol.

Spiritual living is exemplified in a number of ways, one of which has always been singing. Church music has long been a source of inspiration. Paul first acknowledges the importance of psalms, hymns, and spiritual songs as edification and encouragement for believers (5:19), but he immediately adds a vertical dimension. Spiritual singing comes from the heart and is ultimately directed to God.

Paul's Trinitarian thinking is again evident in this section of his letter. Believers are to be filled with the Holy Spirit, giving thanks for everything to God the Father, offered in the name of Jesus Christ (5:18–20). Paul again emphasizes thanksgiving as essential to maintaining a proper perspective on spiritual things.

Some people argue that Paul is expecting too much from ordinary people. At this point, it might be wise to consider whether he was really expecting his readers to adhere to the standards he was setting, or whether he was being a bit rhetorical, exaggerating to make a point. No Christian can read what Paul has written here and come away without a measure of disquiet and concern.

The standard Paul sets is for believers to imitate God! Is that not impossible? Yet Paul doesn't stop there—they are to rid themselves of any hint of sexual immorality, all greed, and any degree of coarse speech. He leaves no room for half-measures. And in addition to ridding every shadow of sin from their lives, Christians are not to miss an opportunity to show the love of Christ however possible.

All people come to God from sinful lifestyles. They are weak and continually bombarded by temptations. Is it remotely feasible to expect them to imitate God?

Yet Paul is not suggesting anything Jesus hadn't taught. Christ, too, set the imitation of God as the standard for believers to strive for (Matthew 5:19–20, 48). They realize they have never met that standard and know they will never do so as long as they remain in this world. Nevertheless, the ongoing goal of every follower of Christ is perfection, an ever more complete imitation of God. They will stumble. They will fail at times. Yet they are to grow stronger through their mistakes and keep trying.

Paul himself would not deny the difficulties involved. He was personally determined to press on toward perfection, yet was honest about his own failings (Romans 7:14–25). And in spite of his personal experience, he exhorts the Ephesian believers (and all those since) to imitate God.

5:21–33

HUSBANDS AND WIVES

In this passage Paul discusses how husbands and wives should live in relationship with one another. Not so long ago, the passage was a favorite at weddings. More recently, it has become a battleground of competing interpretations. Some interpreters claim that Paul is affirming God's universal standards for the roles of husbands and wives. Others claim that Paul's commands have a strong cultural element that must be applied differently today—similar to commands related to head coverings (1 Corinthians 11) and foot washing (John 13).

Paul begins by telling believers to submit to one another out of their reverence for Christ (5:21). So is Paul simply recommending mutual submission, as some interpreters have claimed? The context indicates otherwise, as Paul sets out a particular order of submission in relationships: Wives are to submit to their husbands (5:22), children to their parents (6:1), and slaves to their masters (6:5). This clearly goes beyond mutual submission. Furthermore, in other places the concept of submission is used in regard to Jesus' submission to His parents, demons submitting to the power of the disciples, citizens submitting to governing authorities, Christian submission to God, and so forth. Such relationships involve more than mutual submission.

It seems clear, therefore, that Paul is setting out particular role relationships in the Greco-Roman households of first-century Ephesus. The harder question, however, is whether Paul intended these role relationships to be applied to all Christians for all time. This is the point where good Bible scholars and well-meaning Christians differ.

Those who identify themselves as "Egalitarians" claim that Paul is writing to a specific first-century situation where such relationships would have been assumed. Paul wants husbands and wives to respect the orderly institutions of their day in order to be a good witness for Christ. This would also explain why Paul encourages slaves to submit to their masters, instead of calling on masters to free their slaves. Paul placed the proclamation of the gospel first, realizing that major disruptions to the present social order would impede rather than promote the gospel's spread. Social change would occur gradually, as the gospel took hold in people's hearts.

Those who identify themselves as "Complementarians," on the other hand, claim that Paul is here stating God's divinely sanctioned and universal roles for husbands and wives. These roles are complementary rather than identical, with the wife submitting to the husband as the head of the household. Evidence for this view are similar commands throughout the New Testament (Colossians 3:18; Titus 2:5; 1 Peter 3:1) and Paul's linking of male authority to God's order in creation (1 Timothy 2:11–14). Believers certainly have an obligation to love and serve one another (mutual submission), yet that does not nullify the relationships that God has established for the life of humankind and of His church. Paul wants to sanctify and purify both genders in married life. He expects husbands to be distinctly Christian men in their marriages, and he expects wives to be thoroughly Christian women. Whether male or female, the goal in marriage is to be Christlike. The present author believes this interpretation best fits the overall teaching of scripture and represents God's intention for men and women.

It should be noted that as soon as Paul instructs wives to submit to their husbands, he explains what is expected of the husband in the relationship (5:25–30). Husbands are expected to show the same love for their wives that Christ has for the church (5:25). They are to love their wives as their own bodies (5:28, 33). If marriage were merely a matter of hierarchy, no one would want to leave the comfort of his or her own home to become one flesh with a spouse (5:31).

No one can fully comprehend the mysterious metaphor of Christ as a husband and the church as His bride (5:32). Yet we need not have a full understanding to know what Paul means here. Again, Paul sets an immensely high standard for Christians—in this case, Christian husbands—to live up to.

Just as it requires grace when people fall short in their efforts to imitate God, so too is grace necessary in every marriage where two sinful, fallible people attempt to become one flesh. As they attempt to become holy and blameless, without stain or wrinkle (5:27), much love, forgiveness, and grace will be needed.

Paul wants men to accept the authority of headship, but to exert that authority with love and self-sacrifice rather than selfish domination. Similarly, Paul calls for wives to fulfill their femininity willingly, lovingly, and gratefully. Both parties have a special nature to bring into the marriage, which they share with each other in love and humility. There is nothing ordinary about Christian marriage. It is a relationship that human beings can live only by the grace of God. And it is a relationship that they would *want* to live only by His grace.

Take It Home

After reading Paul's challenging words about marriage, it is only natural to examine one's own marriage—or dating relationships. Do Paul's instructions (concerning the wife's submission to her husband) bother you at all? What do you understand them to mean? Even if this is a sensitive subject for you, how do you feel about the rest of what Paul says in this passage on marriage?

EPHESIANS 6:1–24

STANDING FIRM

Parents and Children 6:1–4
Masters and Slaves 6:5–9
The Armor of God 6:10–20
Closing Comments 6:21–24

Setting Up the Section

As Paul concludes this insightful letter, he has some very important things left to say before signing off. Having just addressed the relationship between husbands and wives, he now turns to parents and children, and slaves and masters. Then he will explain how all Christians are engaged in spiritual warfare, and instructs them on what they need to do to stand firm and emerge victoriously.

6:1–4

PARENTS AND CHILDREN

None of Paul's commands in this section would have seemed controversial in his culture. Both Judaism and the Greco-Roman world placed emphasis on the authority of parents (especially fathers) over children, and all would have agreed that it was right for children to obey (6:1).

However, the teachings of scripture stand out by consistently including children in the membership of the church. Jesus had surprised His listeners by saying that the kingdom of heaven belonged to little children (Matthew 19:14). And in this letter, Paul addresses children along with other groups within the church, instructing them of their obligation to serve the Lord by obeying their parents (6:1). Children did not always get as much respect in other segments of society.

Honoring parents (6:2) involves more than mere obedience. It is possible to obey grudgingly, moodily, or only because one has to. Such responses do not honor parents. The one commandment with a promise is the fifth of the Ten Commandments (Exodus 20:12; Deuteronomy 5:16). This is only one of many places in the New Testament where a law is cited from the Old Testament as something believers must obey. Some people promote the idea that the commandments of God have been supplanted by a vague and general law of love. Such an idea never occurred to Paul.

Paul doesn't leave his instructions one-sided. After asking wives to submit to their husbands, he had then clearly instructed husbands how they were to act within the relationship (5:22–33). Similarly, after telling children to obey their parents, he does not leave room for fathers to take license and mistreat their children (6:4).

6:5–9

MASTERS AND SLAVES

In the ancient world, slavery was a way of life. Cruelty on the part of the masters was common enough, yet virtually no one (including the slaves themselves) ever considered abolishing the institution itself. And the lives of many slaves were comparatively good—sometimes better than those of freedmen. Some slaves owned land and even owned other slaves.

Masters who treated their children well tended to also treat slaves with dignity. It was common for masters to grant legal freedom to slaves after a time, although that could involve a lower standard of living for the slave. In fact, some people would even sell themselves into slavery in order to climb the social ladder. In many ways, slavery in the first century was not unlike a boss-employee relationship in the modern world. Some philosophers believe the Western world has only replaced an obsolete form of slavery that was no longer economically viable with a new version. In addition, sin continues to produce slaveries of all kinds, and always will.

Paul follows his pattern of first addressing the group in the subordinate position: wives before husbands, children before parents, and now slaves before masters (6:5). And as there has been much written about the behavior of children outside of the Bible, so also there is plenty of comment about how slaves should conduct themselves. The difference in this case is that Paul addresses the slaves as ethically responsible agents.

Paul makes a strong argument, pointing out that believers all have the same Master to whom they will someday give an account (6:6–8). By faithfully serving their earthly masters, slaves also please their Lord in heaven.

Both slaves and masters are instructed to keep their focus on Jesus. Slaves were not to obey simply because doing so might ingratiate themselves with their masters. And slave owners were not to mistreat their slaves, because in one sense, they were actually fellow servants (6:9). Paul's exhortations are very general; he doesn't provide a long list of dos and don'ts. As in many other places in scripture, it is assumed that if the conscience is awakened and love is ruling in the heart, people will know what to do and how to behave.

Critical Observation

One of the most striking evidences of the difference the gospel made in a culture where slavery was a way of life appears in the catacombs. In a typical ancient Roman cemetery it is very common to find references to the deceased as either a slave or a freedman. But in the Christian tombs there are only names along with an ascription of Christian hope—with no reference as to whether the person was slave or free. In addition, there are numerous cases of slave owners turning to Christianity and, as a result, freeing their slaves. On occasion, thousands of slaves were set free at the same time.

6:10–20

THE ARMOR OF GOD

As Paul approaches his final point (6:10), he turns to a logical question. He has already presented a theological explanation for *why* believers should live for Christ (1–3), as well as *what* they should be doing in various practical ways. Now he turns his attention to *how* they are able to rise above the secular standard of living and devote themselves more fully to God.

He begins by acknowledging adversarial spiritual forces that are under the control of a dark and scheming spiritual leader (6:11–12). Paul has already referred to the devil a couple of times in this epistle (2:2; 4:27), and here he gets more specific.

The existence of evil spirits is taken for granted in much of the world today, and throughout human history people have devised ways to deal with them, mollify them, or defeat them. However, there is a tendency in modern society to dismiss them as superstition and as incompatible with a scientific and sophisticated view of reality. The devil—described by Paul as a very real and dangerous opponent—has become the subject of jokes and cartoons rather than given serious consideration. Even among many evangelical Christians there is a reluctance to express belief in Satan as a personal being. Consequently, the severity of scripture passages such as this one is minimized.

However, the Bible is very clear about the reality of evil spirits, and weaves that teaching into the sum and substance of its doctrine. It was Satan who was instrumental in engineering the fall of humankind into sin and death. It was Satan who did his best to seduce Jesus through various temptations, hoping to hinder or prevent His saving work. It is Satan who, according to Jesus Himself, snatches away the "seed" (the Word of God), attempting to keep people from believing (Matthew 13:19). It is Satan who blinds the eyes of men and women to keep them from seeing clearly the truth of God. As a result, hell was created for the devil and his angels.

If one is to dismiss such biblical teachings about the devil, is it not also necessary to do the same for all teachings about the spiritual realm? If there is no devil, why should we believe there are angels? And if we rule out the devil and angels, why should we think there is a heaven or hell? If we question the teachings of Jesus about Satan, do we also question the other things He taught? And how do we explain the foolishness, empty pride, cruelty, and selfishness of human beings that exceed anything else found in the animal kingdom? Like it or not, what the Bible says about Satan is important to a complete understanding of human and spiritual reality.

As Paul introduces the concept of God's armor (6:11), he is reinforcing what he has already written about putting on the new self (4:24). Whatever people lack that makes them weak, vulnerable, and incomplete, God will supply. They are not strong in themselves, but can become strong with God's power (6:10).

Although Paul describes armor similar to that which a Roman soldier might have worn, his explanation for each piece relates to a spiritual quality. Satan is described as a liar (John 8:44), a lion stalking his prey (1 Peter 5:8), and here as a schemer (6:11). He does not fight fair. A believer's real enemies are not going to easily be dispatched (6:12).

Demystifying Ephesians

It may seem strange that Paul would use the weapons and dress of war to enumerate qualities befitting a Christian—someone called to be a peacemaker. However, it should be noted that Paul was under arrest in Rome when he wrote this letter. He would have been very familiar with the appearance of a Roman legionnaire. It is not unrealistic to think he might have looked up at his own guards as he was writing this passage, noting their uniform piece by piece, and comparing each component to a believer's spiritual armor.

So while Roman soldiers would prepare themselves for battle with a helmet, breastplate, belt, foot guards, shield, and sword, the armor for believers is less tangible. They are to arm themselves with truth, righteousness, readiness, faith, salvation, the Word of God, and prayer. These are metaphors, of course, and there is no need to attempt to make strong and indisputable parallels to a soldier's equipment. Much of Paul's language throughout this section is influenced by Old Testament passages (compare Isaiah 52:7 to Ephesians 6:15).

Taken as a whole, Paul's exhortation to put on the armor of God is intended to convey the fact that all the resources needed by a believer to oppose the devil and his powers have been provided in the gospel of Christ. Putting on the armor means living according to the new life that God has provided in Jesus Christ by the Holy Spirit.

Paul's main thought throughout this section is the importance of standing firm (6:11, 13–14), because the battle will be close and intense at times. For instance, the sword Paul makes reference to in verse 17 is not a large broadsword but rather the short, sharp sword carried by Roman soldiers—their primary offensive weapon for close contact.

As the sword is a weapon, so is prayer. In fact, prayer is given the most prominent place and the most space in Paul's description of a fully armed Christian soldier. The importance of prayer is seen in verse 18, with the repeated emphasis on *all*: *all* petition at *all* times with *all* perseverance for *all* the saints. To pray in the Spirit (6:18) means to pray with the guidance and assistance of the Holy Spirit. While continuing to stand firm, a believer is also to pray and to keep alert.

One possible interpretation of Paul's statement is that prayer is not simply the final piece of a Christian's armor, but also the means by which all the other pieces are made useful. Everything else—truth, righteousness, peace, faith, salvation, etc.—is effective only when employed in a spirit of dependence on God.

The mystery Paul refers to (6:19) means, as before, the gospel itself (1:9; 3:3–4, 9; 5:32). It is something that would not be known unless God had revealed it. Now it is able to be embraced by both Jews and Gentiles alike.

Paul is aware of his own need for prayer (6:19). Writing during his first imprisonment in Rome, he wasn't beyond fear and worry—for others, if not for himself. Yet he was committed to keep going as long as God gave him the words.

The reference to an ambassador bound in chains (6:20) would have been interpreted as an oxymoron. An ambassador was entitled to diplomatic immunity. The arrest of an ambassador would have been a grave insult to the king who had sent him as well as reflect poorly on the leader of the country who had imprisoned him.

6:21–24

CLOSING COMMENTS

Much of Paul's closing (6:21–22) is verbatim to what he writes in his closing statement to the Colossian church (Colossians 4:7–8). The two letters were probably written at about the same time and were possibly both carried by Tychicus to different groups of Christians living in the Roman province of Asia.

Paul had opened his letter with the words *grace* and *peace* (1:2); here he closes with the same sentiment (6:23–24). If this closing sounds a little less personal than some of his other letters, perhaps it is because Paul intended for this one to circulate among several different churches in the same area—to people whom he hadn't even met. Still, his wish for all who read it is an undying love for the Lord Jesus Christ. It is more than a sign-off. Indeed, it would be difficult to think of a more relevant blessing—and challenge—for all who profess faith in God.

Take It Home

What can be done to help you stand firm in your faith? Consider each piece of a believer's armor, and see which, if any, of them could use some reinforcement:

- The belt of truth
- The breastplate of righteousness
- Feet fitted with the readiness that comes from the gospel of peace (6:15 NIV)
- The shield of faith
- The helmet of salvation
- The sword of the Spirit (The Word of God)
- Prayer on all occasions

PHILIPPIANS

INTRODUCTION TO PHILIPPIANS

Paul's letter to the church in Philippi is remembered for its joyful tone of gratitude against the stark background of the fact that Paul was in prison while writing. Paul writes about the peace, joy, and contentment he finds in Christ, no matter what his situation or circumstances.

AUTHOR

According to Philippians 1:1, the apostle Paul is the writer of this letter. The theology and personal comments fit with what we know of Paul from other writings in the New Testament. Early church fathers and historians also affirmed Paul's authorship.

THE ESTABLISHMENT OF THE CHURCH IN PHILIPPI

Philippi was a city in Macedonia (northern Greece), ten miles from the Aegean Sea. The city was named for Philip II of Macedon, father of Alexander the Great. Though a relatively small city, Philippi was a Roman colony, which meant it received special rights and privileges equivalent to those given to the cities of Italy. Many retired Roman military and other colonists from Rome lived there, creating a sense of prestige and civic pride. When Paul says our true "citizenship is in heaven" (3:20 NIV), this meant something in a place where citizenship was of great value.

The story of the founding of the church in Philippi appears in Acts 16. On Paul's second missionary journey he had a vision in Troas, which prompted him to cross the Aegean Sea (Acts 16:8–12). Philippi was the first town in which Paul preached after he crossed the Aegean Sea, making this the birthplace of European Christianity. Paul's normal pattern was to preach first in the Jewish synagogue, but Philippi had few Jewish residents and no synagogue. So Paul began his ministry at a place of prayer beside the river (Acts 16:13). There he met Lydia, a merchant in purple cloth, who became the first convert in the city (together with her household). Lydia subsequently gave Paul and his missionary companions (Silas, Timothy, and Luke) hospitality and a place to stay (16:15). It was also in Philippi that Paul cast out a demon from a fortune-telling slave girl. This provoked the anger of the girl's owners, who were making a tidy profit from her gifts, and they had Paul and Silas arrested, beaten, and imprisoned as troublemakers. That evening an earthquake miraculously opened the prison doors, and Paul led his Philippian jailer to Christ (Acts 16:12–40). In this way, the church at Philippi was founded (about AD 51).

OCCASION

Paul wrote this letter while in prison (1:7, 13, 19). The place of Paul's imprisonment is not clear from the letter, but the ambiguity doesn't affect the interpretation of the book. Some have suggested that this imprisonment was in Caesarea (Acts 23:33; 24:27) or Ephesus (1 Corinthians 4:9–13; 15:32; 2 Corinthians 1:8–10; 4:8–12; 6:4–11), but the evidence points most strongly to Rome. Paul refers to the "praetorian guard" (1:13 NASB)—Caesar's personal guard—and sends greetings from "those of Caesar's household" (4:22 NASB).

Paul was arrested in Jerusalem after completing his third missionary journey (Acts 21–22). He spent two years in a prison in Caesarea before he made his appeal to the emperor and was sent to Rome (Acts 23–28). The year was AD 59 or 60. Most believe that the Philippians heard Paul was in prison in Rome and, wanting more specific information about him and desiring to help, they again raised a large gift and dispatched Epaphroditus to Rome with the money. Because Epaphroditus experienced a substantial delay, Paul had been in Roman prison approximately one year when he arrived. The sacrificial gift touched Paul deeply.

PURPOSE

When Epaphroditus visited Paul, he also brought news of troubles in the Philippian church: The Judaizing threat had appeared (Jewish Christians claiming Gentiles must first become Jews in order to be saved), financial troubles and other problems were creating doubts about the Philippians' newfound faith, and discord had surfaced in the church. Knowing they were in need of help, they asked Paul to send them Timothy, but he could not come immediately. However, Paul sent back with Epaphroditus this letter full of thanksgiving and encouragement, instruction and correction, and doctrine and exhortation.

THEMES

Philippians includes themes such as joy, humility, self-sacrifice, unity, and Christian living. Partnership in the gospel is a theme and nucleus of the letter. This partnership includes the fellowship of the church with the Spirit (2:1), and the fellowship of the believers with Christ's suffering (3:10–11).

OUTLINE

OPENING WORDS 1:1–26

Christian Affections 1:1–11
Motives 1:12–17
O Happy Death! 1:18–26

FAMILY BUSINESS 1:27–2:30

Unity and Faithfulness 1:27–30
Humility 2:1–11
Upright Living 2:12–18
Godly Examples 2:19–30

KNOWING CHRIST 3:1–4:1

Paul's Focus 3:1–11
Always Leaning Forward 3:12–16
Standing Firm 3:17–4:1

BEST AND WORST PRACTICES 4:2–23

Being Like-Minded 4:2–3
Joy and Peace 4:4–7
Keeping the Heart 4:8–9
Credited to Your Account 4:10–23

PHILIPPIANS 1:1–26

OPENING WORDS

Christian Affections 1:1–11

Motives 1:12–17

O Happy Death! 1:18–26

Setting Up the Section

Paul opens his letter to the Philippian church with heartfelt words of gratitude and rich blessings. It is in this section that Paul introduces a main theme of Philippians—partnership in the gospel.

1:1–11

CHRISTIAN AFFECTIONS

While modern letter writers put the addressee first, first-century letters typically listed the sender first and the addressees second, then a greeting. Thus, this letter begins (1:1). Timothy is mentioned because of his connection with the Philippian church and because the believers had asked for Timothy to be sent to them (2:19).

Paul's use of the word *saints* refers to all the Christians in the Philippian community of faith rather than a super-spiritual subset, as the term sometimes implies today. Paul also mentions the church officers here (1:1), a distinction from his other letters. These people were perhaps instrumental in raising the generous offering that was sent to Paul. They will also likely be the ones who ensure that the Philippians follow Paul's instructions in the letter. The fact that this church had these types of leaders, particularly deacons, indicates that it was well established.

Paul replaces the typical greeting with more of a Christian salutation, "Grace and peace" (1:2 NIV). He identifies the source of that grace and peace as God the Father and Jesus Christ. Jesus' life and work remains a recurring theme throughout this letter.

Paul's mention of joy is significant (1:3–4). His was not an easy situation, yet he found joy in the midst of it. Joy is another key theme (1:19, 25–26) in this letter.

In verse 5, Paul acknowledges that the Philippians had participated in his work. They did this by their financial gifts and the resulting emotional support. The good work that God would continue in these believers (1:6) is not another reference to *their own* good work in generous giving, but rather a reference to *God's* salvation and His continued sanctification of His children.

The Philippians had shared God's grace with Paul (1:7) by supporting him as an evangelist and defender of the faith. In both verses 5 and 7, Paul uses a Greek word meaning "to share" or "partner with." Sharing in God's grace means they share a common experience of Christ's love (1:7). Through their experiences they formed an unbreakable bond. His affection for them (1:8) is visible evidence of this bond.

Paul and the Philippians have a mutual admiration. Because Paul loves them as he does, it is easy to pray for blessings on their behalf. The beautiful prayer he prays for them reveals his affection (1:9–11). He wants the best for them.

The day of Christ (1:10) is a reference to the final judgment of Jesus. Paul is praying for their blamelessness in their day-to-day dealings, but also that their lives will be lived blamelessly overall.

1:12–17

MOTIVES

Verse 12 begins the body of the letter. In contemporary terms, Paul is a missionary and the Philippians have supported his work. The next few verses amount to what we know today as the report a missionary sends home to his supporters. The first thing Paul tells his supporters is that their investment is reaping returns and that his imprisonment, which could be seen as an impediment to the spread of the gospel, has actually, in the plan of God, advanced the gospel. Here's how:

- The praetorians, or palace guards, were an elite force serving as the emperor's bodyguards. As Paul met one after another of these soldiers, the knowledge of the gospel began to spread among them. A number of them became Christians, and as a result they began to spread the gospel themselves (1:13–14).
- Being encouraged by Paul's example, Christians in Rome became more daring and fearless in their witness for Christ (1:14). One implication in verse 14 is that evangelism in early Christianity was the work of Christians in general and not left only to the ordained ministry. Much of the evangelism described in the New Testament is the work of apostles and other church officers. But here it seems clear that Paul is talking about Christians in a general sense.

The Christians mentioned in the previous verse include both the rightly motivated and the wrongly motivated (1:15). Paul is willing to say that those who preach Christ out of envy and rivalry are, nevertheless, Christians. He raises no question as to the integrity of the message itself. These people were preaching Christ, but they didn't all have the same opinion about Paul. The genuinely motivated viewed Paul's imprisonment as a consequence of his work. The other group stumbled over it. A real Christian leader, they reasoned, shouldn't be in jail (1:17). Jealous of his prestige, it seems they were trying to outdo him while he was confined. They were taking advantage of an opportunity to preach when Paul could not, perhaps in hopes that in his absence the church would rally around them.

1:18–26

O HAPPY DEATH!

Paul rejoices because the gospel is advancing and for an additional reason—the hope of his own deliverance (1:18–19). When Paul writes about his deliverance, some take him to mean his release from prison (1:19). However, the language he uses is most likely a reference to salvation, and almost certainly his meaning here. In other words, trials and difficulties are part of the means the Lord employs to carry us safely to the end of our pilgrimage. Most scholars believe Paul is quoting from Job 13:16.

Paul will not be put to shame before God (1:20). The eagerness Paul describes here is translated from words that refer to someone straining his or her neck to see what is ahead. (Paul also uses this word in Romans 8:19.) Paul is not worried about God's judgment, nor is he simply celebrating his achievements—he is saying that he has lived the life of a follower of Christ. Having lived such a life, death is the doorway to that happy triumph.

The effectiveness of Paul's work doesn't depend upon whether he lives or dies. In fact, life in this world lived in fellowship with Christ has incomparable advantages, but death has even greater advantages (1:22–25). Paul no longer lives for his own pleasure or makes decisions based on what would be easiest for him. He doesn't expect to go to heaven immediately—his personal preference—but to remain for the sake of the Philippians (and others), who were still in need of his ministry (1:25–26).

Demystifying Philippians

When Paul wrote his letter to the Philippians, he was under arrest in Rome. We know little of the precise details of his imprisonment, but there is reason to believe that by this time Paul was reasonably confident he would eventually be released. In those days, one could never count on a just outcome—Paul had certainly not done anything remotely deserving of Roman punishment, but he was hopeful nonetheless. He would be released and enjoy several more years of ministry before being arrested again and executed in Rome, almost certainly during the reign of the emperor Nero, sometime in the mid-60s, perhaps as early as AD 64.

In the maturity of his Christian life, Paul has come to the place where he actually welcomes death. If he lives he is with Christ, but if he dies he is much more with Christ. For Paul it is proximity to Christ that is the measure of everything.

Paul's welcoming of death may seem strange, but it is not morbid. He is, in fact, happy to spend his life working for the sake of the gospel, and even expects to do so. He is not worried about being exposed to shame in life or death because he is confident that God will approve of him, first because of Christ's perfect righteousness that is his by faith, but also because he has served the Lord faithfully.

PHILIPPIANS 1:27–2:30

FAMILY BUSINESS

Unity and Faithfulness	1:27–30
Humility	2:1–11
Upright Living	2:12–18
Godly Examples	2:19–30

Setting Up the Section

This section marks the beginning of the body of Paul's letter. Greetings and personal information out of the way for now, Paul begins his exhortation about the kind of lifestyle the Philippian Christians are called to live.

1:27–30

UNITY AND FAITHFULNESS

The Philippians needed to be reminded of their calling to live holy lives worthy of the gospel. When Paul writes of their conduct or lifestyle, he uses Greek language from which modern English words such as *politics* are derived. Paul is hearkening to the citizenry of the Philippians. Philippi was a Roman colony, so these people were citizens of Rome, though they didn't live there. Paul is pointing out to them that they are also citizens of the kingdom of heaven. He refers to this citizenship more directly in Philippians 3:20, but the foundation of the theme can also be found here.

The Philippians were facing opposition (1:28). There does not seem to have been a large community of Jews in Philippi—there was no synagogue—so local opposition would likely have come from Gentiles. Here Paul makes a statement mirroring a theme that runs throughout his writings—those who wish to live godly lives will suffer persecution. The Philippians' suffering is proof of their belonging to God and of their being identified with the Lord Jesus (1:29–30).

2:1–11

HUMILITY

Paul's main point of this section is found in the first four verses—a call to holy living.

While Paul asks his readers to make his joy complete, his own joy is not his main concern. His primary concern is the Philippians' unity in love. Rather than rebuke them for disunity, he appeals to the fact that they love him. Their sacrificial actions on his behalf have recently proven the depth and power of that love.

The four brief clauses that complete verse 2 all amount to emphasis on the same thing: spiritual unity. Often in the Bible emphasis is conveyed by repetition, either by repeating the same thing multiple times or emphasizing the point in various ways. Being like-minded does not mean that they should think precisely the same way about everything, but rather that they are one in intentions.

The true obstacle to unity of heart and mind is not based on differences of opinion but is due to selfishness and vanity. Shifting attention away from oneself to others—which, of course, is what Jesus Christ did—is the key to Christian unity (2:4). The fact that Paul has to tell the Philippians this, and later appeal to some members of the church to get along with one another, is proof that Christian unity does not come without effort and attention. Loving unity is as difficult to fulfill as any other part of sanctification.

Verse 5 serves to set up the following verses. When some translations refer to Jesus' mind, it is likely not an actual reference to how or what Jesus thought, but more to His disposition.

The idea in verse 6 is that Jesus, the Son, had in His possession all the attributes and the prerogatives of Almighty God, the Father, but He did not regard His equality with God as something to use to His own advantage.

Critical Observation

Carmen Christi or "Hymn of Christ" is the traditional title for verses 6–11. It has long been thought that these verses were not original to Paul, but are instead the citation of an already existing Christian hymn.

The Greek words translated as Jesus emptying Himself or making Himself nothing (2:7) have led some to believe that Jesus stopped being divine. However, that is not a principle taught elsewhere in the New Testament, and it cannot be the meaning here. Jesus' deity is affirmed both before and after His incarnation—His taking on of human flesh (John 1:1–2, 14, 18). It is Jesus' humility and obedience in the face of His true identity that brings such meaning to His actions (2:7).

The mention of death by crucifixion (2:8) emphasizes the extent of Jesus' sacrifice. Crucifixion was the most degrading and repellent form of execution known to the ancient world.

In verse 9, the focus switches to God's role. Jesus humbled Himself, but God exalted Him. Jesus' teachings include references to this principle—that when we humble ourselves, God will lift us up (Mark 9:35).

Critical Observation

Philippians 2:9–11 describes a universal confession of Jesus' lordship. That does not suggest, however, that each confession is offered willingly. This is more of a statement that Jesus' identity will eventually be acknowledged by all, whether they like it or not.

Paul's mention of every knee bowing to God (2:10) may be a reference to Isaiah 45:23. Paul cites the same text in Romans 14:11, in reference to the Day of Judgment. Both the doomed and the saved will make this confession.

Few passages in the New Testament, apart from the first eighteen verses of the Gospel of John, are as important to the doctrine of the person and work of Jesus Christ as Philippians 2:6–11. It states the following:

1) Jesus existed before there was a baby named Jesus.
2) Jesus is God. The two expressions—"being equal with" and "being in the form of"—mean the same thing.
3) Jesus truly became a human. This is what Christian theology calls the incarnation. As the living God, Jesus did not and could not cease to be God, but He added to Himself true and authentic humanity.

2:12–18

UPRIGHT LIVING

Verses 12–13 are the first part of a subparagraph that extends to verse 18. In typical fashion, Paul follows a general statement of a principle with specific applications of that principle.

The phrase "work out your salvation" (2:12 NIV) is another way of saying "obey." To work out one's salvation is to apply oneself to living in a manner worthy of the gospel of Christ. It is a theme of this whole section. The idea of obedience also connects this statement to the previous verses, which emphasize Christ's obedience, even to the point of death.

Our obedience depends upon God's prior working (2:13). Our work is only made possible by God's grace. This truth reveals the interplay between God's grace and our responsibility. What matters is not that we harmonize the two or that we choose one over the other, but that we believe and live in the reality of both: working to live obedient lives all the while depending upon God's grace in order to be able to do so.

Take It Home

When Paul told his readers to work out their salvation, this was not an encouragement to become a Christian by doing good works. That would be inconsistent with the teachings of the New Testament. But we *are* to work on our own sanctification—the transformation of our lives—and that is a part of salvation in this context. We have been saved, after all, to be conformed to the image of God's Son, and there is work for us to do to that end, even if it is part of that salvation that from beginning to end is the work and the gift of God. This work must be done in and for the community of believers. Unity in love in the body of Christ is always the result of Christians working out their own salvation.

The "awe and reverence" (NET) Paul urges upon us, which is sometimes translated "fear and trembling," is not the same as dread (2:12). It is not insecurity or alarm at the prospect of failure, nor does it require a dark solemnity. You can be in awe of God and be filled with joy at the same time. This awe involves an awareness of your own smallness before the Judge of all the earth. It requires you to accept your proper place as a servant before your God, and then give yourself to obedience with all your heart and mind and strength.

The background of Paul's statement in verses 14–15 is the grumbling of the Israelites in the desert in Exodus 16. In Deuteronomy 32:5, the Israelites in the wilderness are described as a "crooked generation" (NIV). Their grumbling was against God, to be sure, but it was also against their leader—Moses—and against one another. As elsewhere in Paul's letters, Israel is used here as a negative example. This may be due to the fact that as he is writing, the Philippian church is being troubled by Jewish Christians who fail to see that it is not being an Israelite—but faith alone—that makes a person right with God.

How can Christians be described as blameless (2:15) while remaining sinful and still in need of daily confession? Throughout the Bible, terms like *blameless* are applied to people who, while not sinless and perfect, are faithful. A Christian falls short of perfection, to be sure, but he or she is not content with anything but perfect purity and a faultless life.

Verse 15 recollects Jesus' Sermon on the Mount, when Christians are described as the light of the world (Matthew 5:14). Holding out the Word of life is, again, the idea of the ministry of the gospel to others. We are to be light bearers to a dark world. Paul spoke of this earlier in Philippians 1.

Paul refers to being poured out (2:17). In the Jewish sacrificial system, and perhaps the systems of other religions of the day, wine was poured out as a sacrifice on the temple altar, just as the blood of animals were poured out during the animal sacrifices made there. In verses 17–18, Paul uses this reference to the drink offering to convey that even if he should be martyred, he will still rejoice in those he has led to Christ.

2:19–30

GODLY EXAMPLES

At this point Paul returns to his missionary report with information about Timothy (2:19). Timothy was well known to the Philippians since he had been there on Paul's first visit, when the church was founded. Timothy traveled with Paul and was dispatched from time to time to conduct ministry on his own or to encourage a community of believers. Sometimes he was sent to evaluate the circumstances of a particular church when Paul had received a bad report. (The New Testament letters 1 and 2 Timothy are from Paul to this protégé.)

It seems that Paul decides not to send Timothy (2:19, 23) to the Philippians. Still being in prison, Paul probably relied on this close friend and loyal deputy. Apparently, all of Paul's other dependable aides had been dispatched elsewhere (2:21), and he was left with the sort of men he describes in 1:15.

Paul compares Timothy to a son, but that does not mean that Timothy is Paul's biological son. It was common in those days for the relationship between a rabbi and a disciple to be described as that of a father and a son (2:22).

Paul seems to expect a favorable outcome to his legal troubles (2:23–24), but decides it necessary to send Epaphroditus (2:25), who earlier served as the Philippians' emissary to Rome, to inquire after Paul's welfare and to bring him their gift of financial support. Though the journey between Philippi and Rome took roughly forty days, news had reached the Philippians of Epaphroditus's illness (2:26–27). In sending Epaphroditus home, Paul not only ensures the delivery of this letter, but also tends to the natural desire of Epaphroditus to be with his family and friends.

Critical Observation

If Paul thought it better to die than to live—because to die is to depart and be with Christ, as he says in chapter 1—then why is Epaphroditus's healing attributed to God's mercy (2:27)? There are ways in which death is a blessing and ways in which healing is. It was certainly a blessing both to the Philippians and to Paul that Epaphroditus had not died. Though if he had, his death would have been a home-going as much as a departure.

Scholars have wondered why this section concerning Paul's plans for Timothy and Epaphroditus is located here. Shouldn't it have been part of the missionary report in chapter 1? But both Timothy and Epaphroditus serve as examples of the character traits Paul has just been talking about–loving others and putting others first. Timothy and Epaphroditus illustrate the exhortation to love and live in unity that Paul has just completed.

Take It Home

Whether intentional on Paul's part or not, Timothy and Epaphroditus serve as a window on the Christian spirit. Paul appreciates and compliments their highly developed spirit of service and their practical contributions to the work of the gospel and to the lives of other believers. These men were making a difference, and Paul often draws attention to and praises such men. The intention is to make the readers of this letter want to be like these men, to be worthy of praise in the same way Timothy and Epaphroditus were worthy of it.

PHILIPPIANS 3:1–4:1

KNOWING CHRIST

Paul's Focus	3:1–11
Always Leaning Forward	3:12–16
Standing Firm	3:17–4:1

3:1–11

PAUL'S FOCUS

It seems as though Paul is approaching the conclusion of his letter, but one thought leads to another and two more chapters are recorded. In any case, Paul indicates that the Philippians have heard his advice about rejoicing before, but it bears repeating (3:1).

Paul warns the Philippians about dogs. Today, calling someone a dog can be an insult (3:2). But in this first-century context, the term was often used by the Jews to discriminate against the Gentiles. Here, though, Paul twists that usage, referring to the Judaizers who tried to make all new converts live according to Jewish law rather than by simply following in the ways of Christ.

The evil men, or "evil/bad workers" (3:2), Paul refers to is a reference to the Judaizers' emphasis on doing the works of the law. They were demanding circumcision of the new converts to Christianity, thus the reference to mutilation of the body.

Demystifying Philippians

Circumcision was an important Jewish ritual. Other cultures circumcised their baby boys, but the Jewish nation circumcised on the infant's eighth day of life, ritually connecting the physical procedure with the spiritual covenant God made with Abraham. In that covenant, circumcision became a symbol for the connection between God and Abraham's descendants, the Jewish nation (Genesis 17:9–14). Part of Christ's message, and thus Paul's, was that faith is a heart issue. A person can follow religious rituals but not participate in a faith relationship with God (Matthew 23:27–29; Romans 2:29).

Philippians 3:3 sums up much of Paul's teaching that believers in Jesus, whether Jew or Gentile, are the true inheritors of the covenant God made with Abraham and Israel. When one becomes a Christian, he or she does not abandon the God of Israel—on the contrary, Abraham's God becomes one's own. Paul characterizes true Christians this way:

- They worship in the Spirit.
- They glory in Christ as Lord and Savior.
- They reject all confidence in their own achievements to obtain peace with God (3:3).

In contrast, the Judaizers who were troubling the church in Philippi probably expected their Jewish credentials to add authority to their messages. But Paul points out that he has all those credentials and more (3:4). He was born from a pure family line of Israelites, he was a strict Pharisee, and he was zealous for the Jewish and Pharisaic viewpoint to the point of being a persecutor of the church in his earlier days (3:5–6). But Paul came to see that all this religious status and achievement had left him spiritually bankrupt (3:7). His confidence before had been in himself, in his own religious performance. When he encountered Christ it became perfectly obvious that his confidence needed to be in Christ, not in himself.

In fact, Paul counts his previous assets as a religious man not only a loss but rubbish as far as God and salvation are concerned. Rubbish is a polite way of putting it (3:8). Some versions use the term *dung*, which is closer to the mark.

On the positive side, there is much to gain when one gains Christ (3:9). Paul writes that a person gains justification (righteousness before God), sanctification (the transformation of life), and glorification (the resurrection from the dead).

True righteousness can be obtained only by abandoning one's own effort and turning in faith to Jesus (3:9). Because of humanity's sinfulness, true righteousness can only be a gift; it will never be an achievement. One receives not only righteousness by faith in Christ but the transformation of life. He or she becomes more Christlike, not without pain and suffering to be sure, but more and more each day, rejecting sinful desires. There will be suffering, as with Christ, and for the same reason, because it is by this means that life is renewed and God's will is made perfect (3:10).

And finally, in Christ, one obtains eternal life, the perfection of the body and soul at the last day (3:11).

Critical Observation

Clearly, Paul was convinced that people cannot be right with God in themselves—no matter how hard they work at it. Only faith in Jesus brings about that righteousness. This theme runs throughout Paul's other letters as well, which make up a large portion of the New Testament. Therefore, to be righteous in Christ is a central proclamation of the New Testament, the heart of the good news of the gospel.

Paul refers to the "before" and "after" of his life here in Philippians 3. He uses his own personal history to make his theology clear. What happened to him happens to everyone who is saved. His experience is unique for its drama and its aftermath, but as the experience of a sinner saved by grace, Paul is every sinner and every Christian.

3:12–16

ALWAYS LEANING FORWARD

Paul's wish in verse 12 is clear. What he doesn't yet have but what he very much wants is perfection—to be everything he ought to be as a follower of Christ. But Paul is also careful to say that his striving after what he does not yet have is the result of Christ in him (3:13). Once again, Paul's attention is thrown forward to the end, the prize, the culmination of salvation at the resurrection and heaven itself (3:14). And, as with everything else in his Christian life, Paul presses on in Christ Jesus, depending upon Him, confident of God's grace through Him, and seeking to please Him.

The word *mature* (3:15) belongs to the same word group as the word *perfect* in verse 12. Is there a touch of irony in Paul's remark here—a dig at some in the church who seem to think that they are already perfect, which Paul admits he is not?

The second statement in verse 15 can seem confusing, as if Paul is saying that the Philippians are free to disagree with him. But it is possible that the disagreement Paul is referring to is not with himself but with one another in the church. He is returning to the idea of chapter 2 and the importance of practicing unity in love. So Paul would be saying, in effect, "If disagreements continue among you, I trust that God will soon bring unanimity." Whatever views they hold at this particular moment about this or that, the Philippian believers must live in accordance with the truth that they have already received (3:16).

Take It Home

We all have past failures. Whatever they may be, forget what is past—both your failures and your successes—and look to what is ahead. Paul says Jesus lived and died that you might be rich in the Word of God and in prayer, avid in worship, bold and courageous in witness, pure and undefiled in speech and behavior, a lover of God and humanity, and a humble and selfless servant of the kingdom of God. That is why Christ took hold of you, so that you might eventually become like Him in every good and holy way. Every day you are to press on to take hold of all of that! More today than yesterday; more tomorrow than today.

3:17–4:1

STANDING FIRM

It is a common theme in the Bible, and certainly in Paul's letters, that believers should imitate those who live godly lives and to beware of those who do not (3:17–18). Paul wants his readers to be as conscious of their own failings as he is of his, and as dependent upon God's grace to keep going on as he knows he must be.

Paul's readers no doubt knew of whom he was referring when he writes of people whose god was their stomachs (3:19). But it is hard for us to know today precisely whom he means. They certainly seem to be immoral people. They may have been a group of professing Christians who had given to lax morals and had been troubling the Philippian church. They would be enemies of the cross because they imagined that Christ's atonement and forgiveness of sins gave them liberty to live immoral lives. They disgraced the cross before the eyes of the world.

This group would not have been the Judaizers because they were not morally lax, but were the opposite. Still, because the Judaizers are the only enemies specifically referred to in this letter, some commentators suggest that the description of these people in verse 19 could be applied figuratively to the Judaizers: a fleshly mind, a concentration on the accomplishments of this world, and a betrayal of their privileges as the chosen people of God. Their "god" being their stomach could then refer to the Judaizers' claim that one must keep the Jewish dietary laws in order to be saved. The Judaizers were, in Paul's mind, certainly enemies of the cross.

In contrast, Paul makes the connection between the hope of the second coming of Christ and the believer's resurrection with the believer's present godly living (3:20–21). Paul has already spoken of believers going to be with the Lord at death. The emphasis, though, falls primarily and ultimately on the resurrection of the body at the end of history and the consummation of salvation that will occur then.

Take It Home

All of chapter 3, leading up to the warmly personal and encouraging summation in 3:20–4:1, develops the theme of standing firm, both against legalistic doctrine (3:1–16) and immorality (3:17–19). Paul's own testimony of placing his faith in God rather than in his own accomplishments (3:4–14) is an example the Philippians could follow in order to be able to stand firm. It is the same for us today.

PHILIPPIANS 4:2–23

BEST AND WORST PRACTICES

Being Like-Minded	4:2–3
Joy and Peace	4:4–7
Keeping the Heart	4:8–9
Credited to Your Account	4:10–23

Setting Up the Section

The previous section of warning and exhortation ends with verse 1 of chapter 4. What follows is a concluding series of more general exhortations quite typical of Paul's letters. He begins here with somewhat of a rebuke, which is unusually personal for Paul's letters.

4:2–3

BEING LIKE-MINDED

The fact that Paul mentions Euodia and Syntyche by name (4:2) is an indication of how seriously Paul perceives the situation to be in Philippi. The disunity in the church, to which these women obviously were contributing, was a problem that needed to be dealt with directly.

Historically, and still today, there is no denying the influence that women yield in a church. These women had proved their mettle in the work they had done for the cause of the gospel in Philippi. Some have suggested that they were deaconesses, an order of women church workers, that may be referred to in 1 Timothy 3:11 (others think this passage is about wives of deacons). In Romans 16:1, Phoebe is called a "deacon," although this may be a nontechnical use of the term, meaning "servant." We can only guess that these women were deaconesses, since we know very little about this church office and have no more information about them than what Paul mentions here.

It's also unclear as to who Paul is addressing as his "true companion" (NET) in verse 3. He may have been referring to Epaphroditus, mentioned earlier as the one carrying Paul's letter back to Philippi, or to some other prominent leader in the Philippian church. Other scholars have suggested Silas or Luke. Clement of Alexandria, in the second century, even suggested that the reference was to Paul's wife. It is impossible to know for sure.

In any case, Paul does not leave the women to overcome their dispute by themselves. He enlists others in the church to help them. In some respects, he pays a compliment to the Philippian Christians and these two women by addressing the issue so bluntly. It is to the credit of the church that Paul feels free to speak so directly, and it speaks to the maturity of these two women that he is able to address them by name in what is a letter meant to be read to the entire church.

Whatever the issue was with the women, Paul exhorts them to come to an agreement and to become one in their attitude and the direction of their motives, as well as their words and deeds. Paul obviously believes the unity of the church is more important than whatever had separated these women from each other.

Take It Home

Paul's dealings with Euodia and Syntyche remind us to put matters right with anyone with whom we are at odds. In whatever forum you can make it happen, apologize and pledge your love and loyalty. And if you think it is more than you can manage to do, ask someone else to help you. Also, look to Christ for help because it is His will that you be unified among other believers.

4:4–7

JOY AND PEACE

The Philippians were facing both opposition from unbelievers and internal tensions in the congregation. Yet Paul tells them to rejoice (4:4). He has already shown them what it is to have joy. On his first visit to Philippi some years before, he and his associate, Silas, had been arrested, severely beaten, and thrown into prison. And yet they spent their night, bruised and aching, singing hymns to God while the rest of the prisoners listened (Acts 16:25–28).

Given these kinds of situations, Paul is obviously after something more meaningful for Christians than mere happiness with their circumstances. Instead, he writes of true joy, a deep-seated delight in life and in the prospect of the life to come. He writes of joy in the love of God and Christ, in the high purposes for which one may now live his or her life, and in the sense of contentment that comes from the knowledge that we are always in our heavenly Father's all-capable hands—nothing in heaven or on earth can separate us from His love. To have genuine joy, a person must have sources of gladness that are not dependent upon anything in this world of temporary and fleeting things. A human being must be able to look forward and backward without his or her joy being blasted by reality.

Critical Observation

Despite being in prison and facing an uncertain future, Paul writes about his joy and urges the Philippians to rejoice.

- He begins chapter 1 by saying that he prays for the Philippians with joy (1:4).
- In 1:18–19 he rejoices on account of their prayers for him, and he continues his work in hopes of increasing their joy (1:24–25).
- He asks them to make his joy complete (2:2).
- He rejoices with them and urges them to rejoice with him (2:17–18).
- He expects their gladness at seeing Epaphroditus again and urges them to welcome their brother home with joy (2:28–29).
- He urges them to rejoice in the Lord (3:1).
- He describes these believers as his joy and crown (4:1).
- He exhorts them to always rejoice (4:4).

It has often been pointed out that joy is a particular emphasis of the Bible, as it is here. From Psalms to Philippians, joy is a characteristic mark of biblical faith. When Paul tells us to rejoice in the Lord always (4:4), it is a command. Christian joy is an act of obedience. This joy of which Paul speaks is something that should be true of every Christian life.

Paul's next exhortation has to do with gentleness (4:5). This carries with it the ideas of patience and graciousness. Given the fact that the church was facing some opposition, Paul reminds the believers to be gentle-spirited, as Jesus Himself was. In 2 Corinthians 10:1, Paul refers to "the meekness and gentleness of Christ" (NIV), using the same word as here.

Why should Christians be gentle? Because the Lord is near. The word *near* can mean near in terms of either space or time. Either would make sense, and both are reasons for Christians to face the difficulties posed by other people with patience and grace.

There is a proper kind of concern for others. The proof of that is Timothy's concern for the Philippians' welfare (2:20). The same word is used in 4:6 and is often translated "anxious." This anxiety that Paul commands his readers to lay aside (4:6), however, is unreasonable worry—worry that distracts and results from a forgetfulness toward God.

If the Philippian believers heed Paul's exhortations in verses 4–6, God's peace will protect them (4:7). The Greek word translated as "guard" is a military term describing an army surrounding a city. God's peace will fill their hearts as they live their lives thanking Him and looking to Him for their needs.

Critical Observation

Don't be anxious, Paul exhorts in verse 6. Being anxious is the practical opposite of the peace of God. But, of course, in those simple words hangs a great tale. Most people imagine true peace to be the condition of having nothing to worry about. For Paul, true peace is *not* being anxious in the midst of problems, difficulties, sorrows, and disappointments that one must face in life. This peace, God's peace, is a condition that fills a heart in defiance of expectations, no matter the existence of reasonable fears and crushing disappointments.

4:8–9

KEEPING THE HEART

Now Paul turns to the issue of involvement in God's work. When Paul strings terms together as he does here (4:8), the inevitable question is whether each term bears a distinct meaning or whether Paul is adding one to another for effect. There is a fair measure of overlap in meaning between these terms. The difficulty of making precise distinctions is increased by the fact that five of the words in Paul's list are not words he commonly uses, and two of the eight qualities are mentioned only once in the New Testament. It is safe to assume, though, that this list is not definitive but is representative of the kinds of things a believer should focus his or her mind on. The connotation of the verb used to conclude verse 8 (*think*) is that our minds should *continually* be thinking about these kinds of things.

Paul summarizes by saying that his readers are to live according to the teaching they have received from him and the example he has set for them (4:9). Paul is saying that the virtues here are not only to be pondered and reflected on, but practiced, and practiced in the context of the gospel and of faith in Christ.

Take It Home

In verses 7–9, Paul is saying, in different words and more specifically, what the author of the opening chapters of Proverbs said: "Guard your heart with all vigilance, for from it are the sources of life" (Proverbs 4:23 NET).

And Paul is not simply encouraging the act of guarding one's heart; he is instructing us how to do that. We are to devote our hearts—our thinking, especially, as the end of verse 8 makes clear, but our feelings and our will as well—to do what is good and pleasing to God. The result will be that Christ will come down from His high throne and make His presence known within us.

4:10–23

CREDITED TO YOUR ACCOUNT

Though this book is a first-century letter and is prompted by specific circumstances to the situation then prevailing in the Philippian church, this section contains a beautiful account of the Christian faith and the life that is to flow from it—an account that is timeless in its application.

The section opens with Paul's specific thanks for the financial support the Philippians sent his way. Verse 10 refers to Epaphroditus's journey to Rome with the monetary gift for Paul. While Paul's initial statement can sound a little backhanded in the English translation, verses 11–13 clarify that Paul was not sitting and waiting for the Philippians to bail him out of this situation. God remained his hope, yet he was thankful for the help of this community.

Paul teaches that churches should support those who guide them in the faith, but his first-century role in the Christian church was not one that was regularly funded. He had travel and food costs, which sometimes required him to stop and work. He also depended on the hospitality of church members and the gifts he received along the way. While he was probably well-off before his conversion from Pharisee to Christ-follower, he would have understood both ends of the spectrum.

Paul's claim to have found contentment in every situation is testimony to the fact that he well understood that everything, including himself, belonged to God. His was not a contentment that came from self-will or self-discipline. It came from an understanding that Jesus was his strength, no matter the situation (4:12–13).

To make sure that the Philippians understand the measure of his appreciation for their generosity, Paul tells them that he has not forgotten the unique place they have had in his heart from the beginning, some ten years before, when they generously supported his ministry when no one else did (4:14–16). The significance of the mention of Thessalonica is that it is the next major town on the Roman road from Philippi to Athens. So Paul had scarcely left Philippi before their gifts reached him.

Paul's greatest interest is not in what he could receive from the Philippians' generosity but what they will receive from giving (4:17). The term he uses to describe the return on their investment in him can mean the profit gained in business, and here means something like the interest that would accrue on someone's investment account. While the Philippian church was not a wealthy church, the gifts the believers sent Paul were a great blessing to him and fully met his needs. More important, they were pleasing to God (4:18), and they reflected the Philippians' faith in the truth of verse 19, that God would take care of them.

Verse 20 functions as a kind of doxology, and then Paul sends his final greetings. The "brothers" who were there with him probably included Timothy (4:21). Assuming Paul was in Rome, his reference to all the other Christians refers to all the believers there in the Roman Christian church (Romans 16:1–15).

Critical Observation

Paul's mention of Caesar's household reveals a bit of history: The Christian faith had spread even to some who worked for the Roman government (4:22).

Paul gave his life to proclaim the good news of Jesus; he traveled the world with that message. He was Christ's ambassador, preaching to everyone who would listen that God was, in Christ, reconciling the world to Himself. He began this letter with this grace, and he ends with it as well (1:2; 4:23). Only the Bible says that for people to be saved and to rise to eternal life, God has to intervene on their behalf, and in love He did so.

COLOSSIANS

INTRODUCTION TO COLOSSIANS

The New Testament letter to the Colossians presents the person and work of Jesus Christ as the Savior, the Creator, and the Sustainer of the universe and the total solution for humanity's needs, both for time and eternity.

AUTHOR

The author of this letter identifies himself as the apostle Paul (1:1; 4:18). Some modern scholars have questioned this, claiming differences in vocabulary, style, and theology. These differences are minor, however, and are best accounted for by the unique topics covered in the letter. Furthermore, the letter is closely connected to the letter to Philemon, which is widely accepted as authentic, and the two letters were probably sent together (same town, same letter carrier; many of the same companions of Paul are named). No challenges to Paul's authorship were expressed in the early church. We can confidently assert that Paul was the author.

PURPOSE

Paul's purpose in writing Colossians was threefold: (1) to express his personal interest in the Colossians (1:3–4; 2:1–3); (2) to warn them against reverting to their old pagan vices (3:5 and following); and (3) to counteract a particular theological heresy that was being promoted within the church at Colossae (2:4–23). The Colossian heresy wore the mask of Christianity, but it was false.

OCCASION

Several years after the church was established, around AD 61–62, Epaphras traveled to Rome to visit Paul during his first Roman imprisonment. While Epaphras brought some good news regarding the Colossian assembly (1:4, 7–8; 2:5), it appears his primary purpose for visiting was to solicit Paul's help against a certain heresy (or heresies) that was eating its way into the Colossian church.

Paul wrote this letter to counter this false teaching. The epistle was sent to the Colossians by the hand of Tychicus (4:7). In the meantime, Epaphras stayed with Paul, perhaps forced to because of his own imprisonment (4:12; Philemon 23), but surely also for instruction and encouragement from Paul.

THEMES

The main theme of the book of Colossians is the supremacy of Christ and the power of the gospel message. Christ is the object of the Christian's faith because He is God's Son, the Redeemer, the very image of God, the Lord of creation, and the head of the church (1:13–18). It is through Him and because of new life in Him that we are to put away our old manner of life and live according to His grace.

HISTORICAL CONTEXT

Colossae is located about one hundred miles east of Ephesus. At one time the city had been large and populous, but when Paul wrote to the Colossian church, it had become a small town in comparison to its nearest neighbors, Hierapolis and Laodicea (4:13). Though small, Colossae of Paul's day was still a cosmopolitan city with different cultural and religious elements that were mingled together. For the most part, the inhabitants of the area were Gentiles, but there was a considerable quantity of Jews among them.

As far as we know, Paul never visited Colossae, at least not by the time he wrote this epistle (1:4, 9; 2:1). Nevertheless, the community of faith there was a product of his ministry in nearby Ephesus. A young man named Epaphras, who went to Ephesus and evidently heard the gospel from Paul there, is credited with taking the message to Colossae. He was trained and prepared by Paul to go back and plant a church in his hometown (1:7; 4:12).

Though there was a significant Jewish population in the Lycus Valley, the Colossian Epistle suggests that the membership of the church was primarily Gentile. Within the letter to the Colossians, there are not many Old Testament references and almost no reference to the reconciliation of Jews and Gentiles that is found in Ephesians.

OUTLINE

THE PERSON AND WORK OF JESUS 1:1–2:3

Paul's Greeting	1:1–8
Paul's Prayer	1:9–14
The Supremacy of Jesus	1:15–18
The Supremacy of Jesus' Work	1:19–2:3

THE HERESIES 2:4–23

Standing Against False Teachers	2:4–8
The Truth	2:9–15
The Obligations of the Truth	2:16–23

THE WAY TO LIVE LIKE JESUS 3:1–4:1

Think like a Live Person	3:1–4
Live like a Dead Person	3:5–10
The Character of Unity	3:11–17
Modeling Christ	3:18–4:1

IN CONCLUSION 4:2–18

What Message Are You Sending?	4:2–6
What Jesus Are You Worshiping?	4:7–18

COLOSSIANS 1:1–2:3

THE PERSON AND WORK OF JESUS

Paul's Greeting	1:1–8
Paul's Prayer	1:9–14
The Supremacy of Jesus	1:15–18
The Supremacy of Jesus' Work	1:19–2:3

Setting Up the Section

The apostle Paul follows the customary form of greeting for first-century letters. He first identifies himself as the author, with his associate Timothy, and then identifies his recipients, followed by a brief greeting. However, he seasons the greeting with terms that focus on the letter's distinctively Christian character. These first fourteen verses prepare the Colossian readers for the words of warning and the exhortations that will follow. At the same time, these introductory words provide today's readers with insight into the church at Colossae and their growth in Christ.

1:1–8

PAUL'S GREETING

Paul introduces himself as an apostle by God's will. By doing this, he establishes his authority and the Colossians' responsibility to listen. This description further stresses that Paul's position as an apostle is not something he had sought or earned. It was a calling (1:1; see also 1 Corinthians 1:1; Galatians 1:1; 2 Timothy 1:1).

As for his readers, Paul identifies them spiritually in relation to their position in Christ and physically in relation to their geographical location (*at* Colossae)—a reminder of the two spheres in which believers live (1:2).

When Paul speaks of saints (1:2), or "holy" (NIV) brothers, he is not speaking of a special class of Christians who have achieved a certain level of holiness. This is a term used for all believers because of who they are in Christ.

There is an element of prayerful intercession in Paul's greetings. At the same time, he is challenging his readers to a renewed commitment to know, comprehend, and live by the grace of God.

Note that Paul uses possessive pronouns (*our, we* [1:2–3]). This is a reflection of the unity Paul addresses later in this letter.

Critical Observation

As we move into the body of Paul's letter to the Colossians, we get a glimpse of Paul's prayer life. Somewhere in the early portion of almost all of his epistles, Paul begins with either thanksgiving or praise to God. This becomes even more significant when you stop to realize that Paul wrote this letter while under house arrest.

Paul and Timothy had evidently never been to Colossae and did not know the church personally (2:1–2), but verse 4 reveals that they had heard of the faith that existed among the Colossians and of their love for all the saints.

Colossians 1:5 mentions "hope that is stored up" (NIV). Though centered in the person of Christ Himself (1:27), the place of storage is heaven, a place of security and protection where the corruption of this present world cannot touch it.

The term *gospel* (1:5) is the translation of the Greek noun that means "good news," and the Greek verb that means "to bring or announce good news." The reference to the gospel as "the grace of God in truth" (1:6 NET) is naturally aimed at the false teachers who were seeking to add some form of religious works to the gospel. Paul will deal with this in chapter 2.

Verses 6–8 reveal how the Colossians heard the gospel—Epaphras brought the gospel to the city of Colossae. This not only highlights the ministry of Epaphras and puts Paul's approval on his ministry, but also contrasts it against the destructive heresy being taught by the false teachers. What the Colossians had heard and learned from Epaphras was God's truth.

The name *Epaphras* is undoubtedly a shortened form of *Epaphroditus*. His name is mentioned again in 4:12 and in Philemon 23. This Epaphras should not be confused with Epaphroditus, who is mentioned in Philippians 2:25 and 4:18, and was apparently from Macedonia.

Finally, with verse 8, Paul again calls attention to the love of the Colossians linked to the work of the Spirit. This would again highlight the effectiveness of the teaching and ministry of Epaphras, for it was through him that they had learned about the Spirit-led life (Galatians 5:22–23).

1:9–14

PAUL'S PRAYER

In Colossians 1:9–14, Paul moves from thanksgiving to a very specific petition. Paul's prayers are not only brief and explicit, but they are spiritually strategic in nature. To counter the false knowledge of the heretics, Paul prays for a full and more penetrating knowledge of God's will. Two of the terms he uses, *bearing fruit* and *growing*, suggest the figure of a tree to describe God's desire for the church, the body of Christ. It calls to mind the words of Jeremiah 17:8 and Psalm 1:3.

The content and purpose of Paul's prayer is found in his request that God would fill the Colossians. The idea is that they would be filled up and running over.

Paul prays for two things for the Colossians: (1) that his readers would have a full knowledge of God's will (1:9), and (2) that, as a result, they might live in a manner worthy of the Lord (1:10). Both are necessary. Verse 9 without verse 10 is incomplete and falls short of the will of God, but verse 10 without verse 9 is impossible.

In this context, Paul's request focuses on the impact that a proper understanding of the person and work of Jesus should have on one's spiritual walk. In this case, God's will refers to the complete rule of faith and practice.

The ultimate aim of Paul's prayer is to influence the Colossians' conduct day after day. Paul is not saying that one can become worthy of God's love and grace by good works or manner of life. To walk in a manner worthy of the Lord means to walk in a way that is commensurate, fitting, and consistent with who the Lord is and what the Lord has done, is doing, and will do in the future. The implication is that a Christian's life should bring credit to the grace of God in Christ.

In verses 10–12, Paul describes the results of a walk that is pleasing: bearing fruit, growing, being strengthened, and giving thanks to the Father.

The verb translated "bearing fruit" (NIV) is the same verb used in verse 6. Being fruitful in every good work is a call to be balanced and productive. As a result of that productivity, one must never stop growing (1:10). "Being strengthened" (1:11 NIV) carries the idea of strengthening someone who is inherently weak (Ephesians 6:10; 2 Timothy 2:1). More than that, though, the term is in the present tense and points to the constant source that is available to believers through Christ.

Paul also lists giving thanks as a product of a life that is growing by the knowledge of God. Paul does not just tell his readers to be thankful, but points them to four blessings they possess through the work of Jesus. God has:

1) *qualified* us to share in the inheritance of the saints (1:12);
2) *delivered* us from the power of darkness (1:13);
3) *transferred* us to the kingdom (1:13); and
4) given us *redemption*, the forgiveness of sins, through Christ (1:14).

1:15–18

THE SUPREMACY OF JESUS

From his prayerful concern for the Colossians, the apostle moves quickly into the main focus of this letter—the exaltation and preeminence of Jesus in His person and work. Colossians 1:15–18 has been called "The Great Christology," because it sets forth Paul's inspired conviction and understanding of who Jesus Christ is.

- He is the manifestation of God (1:15). To know what God is like, one must look at Jesus (John 1:14–18; 12:45; 14:7–10; Hebrews 1:3).
- He is the firstborn of creation (Colossians 1:15). This is not saying that Jesus was the first to be created by God; "firstborn" refers instead to Jesus' preeminent position over all creation.
- He is the Creator and Sustainer of the universe (1:16). Paul is describing the all-encompassing scope of Christ's authority—thrones, dominions, principalities, and powers—which includes the invisible world of angels and demons. (With the Colossian heresy in mind, Paul stresses the hierarchy of angelic powers.)
- He is before all things (1:17). Note that Paul says Jesus is before all things rather than *was*. This is Paul's way of saying what Jesus said Himself in John 8:58. It also hearkens back to God's claim to Moses to be the "I Am" (Exodus 3:13–14).

In Colossians 1:18, Paul affirms Christ's superiority and supremacy over a new creation, the church. The Colossians must recognize that the Creator of the cosmos is also supreme head of the church as their Savior. He is the source, power, and originating cause of the life of the church.

The statement that Christ was "the first to be raised from death" (CEV), explains why Jesus is the origin and life of the church. The emphasis by context is on Christ's supremacy in time. He is the first one to break the hold of death in a glorified body by virtue of the Resurrection. As such, He is the beginning of a new creation of God.

1:19–2:3

THE SUPREMACY OF JESUS' WORK

In verses 12–14, Paul encourages the Colossians to give thanks for what God has done for them through His beloved Son. Here, he moves from the person of Christ to a powerful declaration of the work of Christ.

God was pleased that His fullness dwelt in Christ (1:19). *Fullness* means "the sum total." *Dwell* means "to reslde, to settle down." Most expositors understand this as a powerful affirmation of Christ's deity (which it is), but the context of this verse is about the work of reconciliation. It might be better to understand *fullness* in reference to *the fullness* of God's plan of reconciliation. Paul is declaring that the fullness of God's saving provision resides totally in the work of Christ through the blood of the cross. Nothing else can be added to the work of the Son.

In verse 20, the phrase "through Him" (NIV) points to Christ as the sole agent of reconciliation. If there is to be reconciliation to God, it must come from God Himself. In this case, reconciliation is not accomplished through the work of both parties, but only one—God reconciles humanity. This verse also makes the point that the cross is a vital and necessary part of reconciliation.

Demystifying Colossians

What does Paul mean when he says all things—heaven and earth—will be reconciled (1:20)? This is not a reference to universal salvation—that all will be saved in the end. This points to the completeness of the plan of God for the whole universe.

Verses 19–20 focus on how the reconciling work of Christ extends to the whole creation. But with the opening words of verse 21, Paul narrows his focus from all of creation to the believers in Colossae. The emphasis is now on God's purpose and plan of sanctification (spiritual growth and transformation). The purpose of God's plan of reconciliation is personal holiness in His people.

Paul's reference to Christ's physical death (1:22) stresses a vital truth of the New Testament–Jesus is the only one perfectly qualified to deal with the problem of sin by dying in our place. He was undiminished deity. This means He gives not just life, but eternal life and God's imputed righteousness. In verse 22, the phrase "holy, without blemish, and blameless" (NET) pertains to this element of sanctification, and the picture of believers being *presented* refers to the final judgment of Christ.

The purpose of God's work of reconciliation in Christ through the cross is holiness. The holy person is one who is set apart to God from the world. The apostle has in mind the growth in holiness that comes through resting in the accomplished work of Christ.

This leads into both a positive affirmation and a negative warning (1:23). The positive element is the fact that the Colossians don't need to *begin* to be established, they only need to *continue* being established. They are already on the right path. The negative warning is the danger of moving away from the truth.

In this context, the word *established* means "to be built a foundation." Christ's person and finished work constitutes the only rock on which one may build his or her life. The idea of being firm in the faith points to the results of being built on such a foundation. In other words, remaining in the faith, the truth of the gospel as Epaphras had presented it to them, is the only way these Colossian believers, or any believer, can become established and steadfast, and thus protected from the shifting sands of the false teachings found in the world.

The hope that is in the gospel is a living hope through Christ's resurrection. The focus on the term *hope* (1:23) includes the confident expectation of spiritual transformation–the result of the indwelling Christ.

Paul's reference to the words the Colossians had heard is to Epaphras, who brought the message to the Colossians as he had received it from Paul. This once more approves the faithful work of Epaphras and becomes a warning against listening to the wrangling of the false teachers.

By mentioning his own service to the gospel, Paul connects with the Colossians.

Epaphras was a servant trained by Paul to carry this message to others, but its path to Epaphras came through the apostolic preaching of Paul, one commissioned directly by the Lord Jesus.

Verses 21–23 stress that the same thing that is true of faith in Christ for salvation is equally true for sanctification—we can't add anything by our own efforts. To add any system of religious works that would somehow serve to justify oneself before God is only to diminish the faith one should have in Jesus.

Paul continues with thoughts on his own suffering. Three things characterize the suffering Paul mentions in verse 24: (1) It was a source of joy; (2) It was for others—for the Colossians and for the sake of the church; and (3) It was related to the sufferings or afflictions of Christ. The false teachers in Colossae may have been claiming that Paul's suffering diminished his ministry, but that was not the case.

Paul claims the preaching of God's message was not an honor and duty that he took upon himself, one that he could either take or leave. Rather, it was an appointment that came directly from God (1:25). The makeup of Paul's message is described as (1) the Word of God, (2) the mystery hidden in the Old Testament but revealed through Jesus, and (3) Christ in the believer, the hope of glory (1:26–27).

What exactly does the apostle mean by "the hope of glory"? It is the confident expectation of the formation of Christ in and through the life of all believers. Glory is the manifestation of the Lord Jesus in us so that we experience Him in attitude, faith, action, and reaction.

How is Christ proclaimed? By instruction and teaching (1:28). Instructing carries with it the idea of warning, counsel, or admonishment. There is a moral appeal for spiritual change, and with teaching there is a doctrinal emphasis. Paul's goal through this instruction and teaching is to present every believer mature in Christ.

The biblical objective of seeing all believers grow and mature in Christ was certainly a captivating force that directed Paul's life, but to accomplish such a goal requires nothing less than God's supernatural power (1:29). "Struggling" (NIV) is a Greek term that means "to engage in an athletic contest." The apostle labored, struggling hard in the task God had given him, but not struggling in his own strength alone.

At the close of chapter 1, Paul declares his struggle to see the Gentiles come to know and grow to maturity in Christ (1:28–29), but as chapter 2 opens, he makes it clear that his message is for everyone (2:1–3). The treasures of wisdom and knowledge are hidden in Christ, but not in the sense that they are concealed. Instead, they are stored up in one place only, and that is in Christ alone.

Take It Home

We can only be truly successful when we learn to live and minister by the unseen presence of the risen Christ and allow Him to work *in*, *through*, and *with* us as the source and power for our ministries. It's often too easy to seek to manipulate, coerce, and force people into spiritual change or Christian service. That may produce some results, but that's not God's method or means. The Lord Jesus, as the unseen power of our lives, works when we relinquish control and draw upon Him through prayer, faith in the truth of Christ, and by means of the control of the Spirit.

COLOSSIANS 2:4–23

THE HERESY

Standing Against False Teachers	2:4–8
The Truth	2:9–15
The Obligations of the Truth	2:16–23

Setting Up the Section

In this passage, Paul addresses the issue of the false teachers among the Colossians. His arguments, however, are never far removed from the doctrinal truth regarding the person and work of Christ. With the exhortation regarding the methods of the false teachers (2:4–5), Paul sets forth the dangers facing the Colossians. With the exhortation to progress in the faith (2:6–7), he sets forth the means of protection: living in Christ. Finally, with the exhortation regarding the philosophy of the false teachers (2:8), his warning focuses on the danger of being tricked by empty philosophy.

2:4–8

STANDING AGAINST FALSE TEACHERS

Why would the Colossian believers listen to the false arguments of these heretical teachers when they knew the One in whom all the treasures of wisdom and knowledge are found (2:3)? Because, as Paul says, the arguments regarding the heresy are false, but they are also persuasive (2:4).

The false teachers employed tricky methods—seemingly reasonable arguments. They were probably promoting *some* of the tenets of biblical Christianity, so their system of knowledge sounded reasonable. Nevertheless, these false teachers were failing to hold fast to Christ as the supreme head from whom the body of Christ draws all her resources (2:18–19).

With verse 5, Paul explains his protectiveness toward the Colossians. He is with these believers in spirit. He rejoices over their "morale" and "firmness" in faith (NET). These terms were sometimes used in military contexts and may here bring out the reality of spiritual warfare. The Greek word translated "morale" (NET) can mean "orderly" (NIV), "disciplined" (TNIV), or even "unbroken ranks" (REB). *Firmness* has the connotation of "steadfastness, solid bulwark, or phalanx." In ancient times, a phalanx consisted of a formation of infantry carrying overlapping shields and long spears. The content of the Colossians' solidarity was their "faith in Christ." Though being attacked by the false teaching, they had not broken ranks to follow the false teaching of the heretics pursuing the church at Colossae.

Verses 6–7 reveal a believer's protection against all false teaching—remaining in Christ. Paul offers four descriptions for remaining in Christ:

1) Being rooted. Through faith, there is an organic union established with Jesus from which comes an ongoing source of life.
2) Being built up. This describes the steady growth of the spiritual structure of the believer's life.
3) Being strengthened. This is a call not to merely hold to faith, but to grow in the knowledge of the faith.
4) Being thankful. Constant, overflowing thankfulness directs one's thoughts to God and what He has done and is doing in and through the Savior.

The idea of being taken captive (2:8) here is to be carried off by an enemy army as booty from a conquest. How is the conquest made? Through empty, deceitful philosophy. This does not imply that Paul is against philosophy as a discipline. His use here of the concept of philosophy is humanity's wisdom versus God's wisdom. In humanity's spiritual blindness, our own powers of reason appear attractive, but lead us away from Christ.

2:9–15

THE TRUTH

The Colossians needed to hear and understand the truth of the gospel because they were being told that there is more to being a Christian than just Jesus Christ. In order to counteract this false philosophy, Paul must tell them exactly who Christ is. Therefore, Paul begins with the character of Christ.

Verse 9 says that the full nature of God dwells within Jesus. This means Jesus is completely full of the divine nature; there is not one aspect of His nature that is lacking any divinity. When Christ came to earth, God came to earth.

As a result of Christ's character, believers now are complete in Him because they become partakers of Him. Salvation is not just a philosophy; it is not just an event. It is the partaking of the very nature of Christ. We do not become God, but His righteousness lives within us. In verse 10, the word for "complete" (NKJV) is the same word for "fullness" (NKJV) found in verse 9. Both carry the idea of lacking in nothing, filled to completion. Believers are given all they need at the point of salvation; there is nothing more that one needs to add.

Paul concludes this thought with a description of the authority of Jesus. In essence, all competing thoughts and all competing philosophy must fall subject to Him. Paul is elevating Christ as above all other competing teachings that the Colossians were being exposed to.

Paul then uses three descriptions of what happened at the Colossians' salvation (2:11–15):

- *Circumcision.* Paul probably uses this description because the Colossians were facing Judaizers, those who taught that one must follow Jewish customs—such as circumcision—to follow Jesus. Paul tells his readers that they have been spiritually circumcised already in Christ, and there is no need to be circumcised physically.
- *Burial.* This is the identification with the death of Christ. Paul uses the word *burial* because it signifies the completion of the death process. The death of Christ is the moment that our punishment was lifted, and sin was dealt a death blow.

Critical Observation

Paul also associates this burial with *baptism*, using the word in its figurative sense, as the identification with that moment of death and rebirth. When Jesus took the penalty for humanity's sin, believers were buried with Him.

- *Resurrection.* The resurrection of Jesus signifies the new life of a believer. Because God raised Jesus from the dead, every believer has been given new life. Salvation is complete. We have been forgiven. As a result, believers now have victory over sin because Christ broke the power over sin and death.

Verse 14 goes on to explain just how that victory happened—the certificate of debt was canceled. Paul uses a common Greek expression for a debt certificate, a legal document declaring that one person owed another a certain sum of money. Paul says God canceled our debt of sin by nailing it to the cross. This means Christ paid the debt that we owed by taking on Himself the penalty for our sins.

Take It Home

In truth, every person has a certificate of debt before God—a list of decrees that need to be paid to Him. But through Jesus' death, God canceled our certificate, taking it out of the way.
We have complete forgiveness in Christ.

Paul concludes this description of salvation by explaining that believers have complete victory over Satan and the stronghold he once had (2:15). In this verse, Paul develops an image that he touched on in verse 8. It is the picture of the victorious soldiers bringing home the captured troops and parading them around to show that the once feared enemy is no longer a threat. The resurrection of Christ is the public display that Satan has no power over death.

2:16–23

THE OBLIGATIONS OF THE TRUTH

In verse 16, Paul declares no one has the right to judge the Colossians based on religious practices because they have been brought into a perfect relationship with God through Jesus Christ.

The false teachers judged the Colossians on the basis of two things: forbidden practices and required rituals. The forbidden practices probably refer to the dietary laws of the Jewish system (2:16), which required abstinence from certain foods and drink (Leviticus 11 and Deuteronomy 14). These false teachers were condemning the Colossians for not following these practices.

The false teachers were also requiring the Colossians to observe the religious celebrations and observances (2:16). *Festival* refers to the yearly religious celebrations. *New moon* refers to the monthly celebrations. The *Sabbath* refers to the weekly Sabbath celebration.

Simply, the Colossians were facing legalism. Believers are not to follow certain rules in order to maintain their faith; they choose their practices and lifestyle *because* of their faith. Therefore, they are able to live out the intent of the law, rather than just the rules of it. This law represents the "shadow of things to come" (2:17 NIV). What is the reality that the law foreshadowed? The reality of Jesus.

Critical Observation

Verse 17 is one of the key verses in this letter. It defines the heart of the issue and a clear resolution to the problem. The law was not intended to save people or to make them holy. The purpose of the law was to point to Christ, who saves and makes us holy.

Paul warns the Colossians not to be disqualified by the false teachers in their midst (2:18). To allow these people to judge them is to lose the prize God had for them—being complete in Christ.

The picture Paul is painting of the heresy is that of a teaching that requires denial of earthly things in order to achieve a spiritual reality. The humility of these teachers is false because it is a denial of the flesh but has no spiritual substance to it. Though it might appear to be a sign of humility to simply deny worldly pleasures, it is no humility at all if it is not based on Christ. To find spirituality by self-will is not the teaching of Jesus.

Verse 18 indicates these false teachers were involved in some type of angel worship. While the actual practice described here has been debated, it is likely that this heresy taught that God was too holy to be worshiped directly, and therefore, a mediator was needed. These teachers may have considered that the angels' role. This is a denial of Jesus' role as that mediator.

Paul also explains that a false teacher bases his teaching on his own subjective reasoning and personal experiences rather than on the Old Testament and Jesus' teachings. Paul declares that anyone who would elevate his visions as more important than the Word of God is arrogant and working out of a fleshly mind, not a mind controlled by God (2:18–19).

Paul gives the root of the false teacher's problem—he denies the Head (2:19), which in this context refers to Jesus (1:18; 2:10). The mystic teacher ignores Jesus and thus takes away His role of being the teacher and sanctifier of the church.

Demystifying Colossians

Observe the way that Paul describes the body of Christ in verse 19. The significance of this is that we are joined together as one body. The reality of this is that what we do individually affects the entire body. If one member of the body buys into false teaching, the entire body will be affected. Paul is telling the Colossians they are all one body, and Christ is the head of that body—they must reject this false teacher together.

Verses 20–23 summarize the warning Paul has just given. In verse 20, Paul says we have died with Christ to the elementary principles of the world. In this context, the world represents the system that is opposed to Christ and His grace. The elementary principles refers to the philosophy already mentioned in verse 8, the system of human logic that says humanity can right itself, by itself, without the work of Jesus.

Not only are believers free from this godless philosophy, but they are also free from the law. The rules Paul refers to do not have any eternal value; they only deal with the here and now. Notice the way Paul explains it—these rules refer to things that will perish (2:22), not the condition of the heart or the state of the soul.

Paul says that these matters seem to appear wise, but they are of no use in the battle against sinful desires (2:23). One can't, in his or her own will, keep from sinning. That is why Jesus came. The discipline of a person has no ability to change the heart; all he or she can do is modify behavior, and even that is not possible without the help of Christ.

COLOSSIANS 3:1–4:1

THE WAY TO LIVE LIKE JESUS

Think like a Live Person	3:1–4
Live like a Dead Person	3:5–10
The Character of Unity	3:11–17
Modeling Christ	3:18–4:1

Setting Up the Section

Paul now shifts gears from the negative to the positive. He tells the Colossians how they are to experience true spirituality in this world. Rather than subjecting themselves to the bondage of the false teachers, they are to understand who they are in Christ, and experience the true freedom that comes from that knowledge.

Instead of thinking that the flesh must be contained by human philosophy, religious legalism, or spiritual mysticism, they are to understand that in Christ, the flesh has been killed on the cross. They must think of themselves as dead to sin and alive to God.

3:1–4

THINK LIKE A LIVE PERSON

Paul begins chapter 3 by explaining that the only logical reality for believers is this: Since they have died to the flesh, the world, and the law, then each must be a new creation. And in all reality they are, because they have been raised with Christ.

Paul is declaring in verse 1, that since his readers are now alive in Christ, they will seek those things that belong to Christ and not the things of the world. That is the reality, as well, for all believers.

The word translated "seek" (NRSV) in 3:1 is a present tense imperative (command) in the Greek, indicating that this is a continual, daily practice of seeking; that is why some translations put the word *keep* in front of the word *seeking* ("keep seeking" NET). It is to be a process that occurs all the time as a manner of life.

What are the things above that believers are to seek (3:1)? They are the spiritual realities that are available through Christ. What does it mean to do this seeking? It is cultivating the desire for spiritual food and God's will, rather than the things of earth.

The heartbeat of this passage is that the Colossians must continually, as a way of life, seek Jesus Christ as the source of all of their spiritual victory. The intentions of their life's passions must be to see Jesus as the source of salvation, sanctification, and their future glorification.

Notice the way Paul describes Christ at the end of verse 1: seated at the right hand of God. This helps us understand Jesus' position of authority and power.

Paul writes that the Colossians should also set their minds on the things above, not on the things of earth (3:2). This means they are to set every aspect of their ability and reason to dwell on their salvation in Christ. Understanding Christ, they will understand who they should be—thus they become transformed.

Notice the contrast between things above and things on the earth in verse 2. This image contrasts the wisdom of humanity with the wisdom of God. Throughout this letter, Paul has been comparing human wisdom with God's wisdom, which produces true righteousness through Christ.

In verses 3 and 4, Paul gives the Colossians the fundamental reason they need to seek Christ with such determination. First, their spiritual lives are hidden in Christ. This means they were crucified and buried with Christ. Next, they will be revealed with Jesus when Christ calls believers home and judges the earth. They will be transformed and stand before God, holy and blameless, robed in the righteousness of Christ.

3:5–10

LIVE LIKE A DEAD PERSON

The Colossians must, as a result of being alive in Christ, be in the daily process of putting sin to death in their own lives. While through the work of Jesus believers stand righteous before God, they are still responsible to grow into that position of righteousness.

First, believers must set their minds on the pursuit of God (3:1–4). Verses 5–11 are the natural result of living in that pursuit.

The difference between what Paul is teaching compared to the false teachers of Colossae is that these believers need to kill the root of the problem of sin through the power of Christ, not merely control the fruit of sin through the power of their will. Some have read this passage to mean that the believer must physically harm himself, or participate in harsh treatment of the body, as mentioned in 2:23. But that is not the case. Paul is telling the Colossians that they must crucify the root of sin through the spiritual process of renewal.

Paul lists two groups of sin that believers are to put to death. The first group can be described as personal sins (3:5):

1) Sexual immorality: any sexual activity outside of marriage
2) Impurity: the contamination of a person's moral character through immoral behavior
3) Passion: uncontrolled lust
4) Evil desire: the scheming side of a person that makes him or her want to plan to participate in sin
5) Greed: This is the intense desire for physical gratification that comes from longing for things in the world. In essence, it is a form of idolatry because it focuses on pleasing self instead of pleasing God.

Paul gives the Colossians two reasons why they should crucify these passions (3:6–7): first, because God is going to pour out His wrath on those sins; second, because it is not who they are anymore. It is a past-tense reality in their lives.

The second group of sins can be described as public sins, or the sins committed against each other (3:8–9). Paul tells the Colossians to put these sins aside much as they would discard an old garment that is not useful anymore:

1) Anger: violent emotional outbursts, temper tantrums, and indignation
2) Wrath: boiling up of the soul that causes one to become enraged

3) Malice: wickedness that causes one to act in an evil way
4) Slander: speaking about someone in a way that destroys his or her character
5) Abusive speech: foul talk used to purposely hurt others

Paul lists these five sins, and then singles out one more—lying (3:9). Lying is purposefully being deceptive to someone, leading him or her away from the truth. Paul lists this sin separately because it includes all of the vices he's already listed. Every sin mentioned involves falsehood in some manner or another. God is a God of truth, not lies, and when believers lie, they act in the exact opposite of the character of God.

The next reality of the Christian life, after taking off the old, is putting on the new. Christianity is not just a putting off of sin, but it is also embracing Jesus. It is the reality of daily becoming a new person.

Verse 10 describes the new person as being renewed. He or she is in a continual process of being transformed from one state of being to another. This process is going on all the time.

This idea of true knowledge (3:10) is the concept of not just mentally knowing God, but experientially knowing God in mind, will, and emotions.

3:11–17

THE CHARACTER OF UNITY

In verse 11, Paul makes a transition from one's union with Christ to union with one another. Race, religion, and class are no longer a barrier to the body; now everyone is one in Christ.

Demystifying Colossians

Here are the distinctions Paul points out:

- **Race:** Greek or Jew. It does not matter if you are a Jew or a Gentile.
- **Religion:** circumcised or uncircumcised. It does not matter if you came to Christ from Judaism or not.
- **Cast:** barbarian or Scythian. A barbarian was a non-Greek speaking tribal person. The Scythians were a Far Eastern Asian people, even more tribal than the barbarians. But even these extreme cultures both lose their stereotypes in Christ.
- **Class:** slave or free. Even considering the social order of the day, the slave and the free are on the same page in Christ.

Paul's next point: Christ is the only source of a believer's salvation. When he says Christ is all and in all (3:11), he probably means that Christ is in all believers. Christians have a new identity in Christ, and are unified by His presence. We are brought into a relationship with Jesus Christ and, through that, a relationship with each other.

The church's unity, Paul points out in verse 12, is not centered around a cause, but rather the eternal work that God has done for the believers. As a result of what God has done for them, the Colossians are chosen (called out by God), holy (set apart), and beloved (before he or she ever asked for it). In light of how God has loved them, Paul tells the Colossians to *put on* the following character traits: compassion, kindness, humility, gentleness, patience, bearing with one another, and forgiving one another. The idea is that they are to wrap themselves around with these essential traits.

Critical Observation

Paul adds to this last point of forgiveness. We are to pattern our grace by the forgiveness we have received from God (3:13)—God forgave us before we could have ever asked for it. He gave grace, not on the basis of our merit or even our request, but on the basis of His love while we were still in rebellion toward Him. Christ is the standard for forgiveness.

Verse 14 serves as Paul's summary: Of all the things the believer is to put on, the governing agent is love. The love that Paul is talking about is God's selfless love that seeks to do the best for people who deserve only death. It is this kind of love that unites the body of Christ.

When Paul refers to the peace of Christ (3:15), he is not talking about an internal feeling of serenity as much as a result of doing the right thing. When humanity rebelled, God sought to make peace by sacrificing His own Son. That same trait must rule within the body of Christ.

Critical Observation

The idea around the word *ruling* is that of an umpire or judge (3:15). An umpire is a person who calls and enforces the rules of a game. When conflict arises, Christ's peace should be the arbitrator.

Paul writes that Christ's Word must take priority among believers in the church (3:16). The word *dwell* used in some translations means to take up residency, to move in and make a home. The Word of Christ is to take up an abundant residence in the hearts of believers. Since the main issue in this letter is the sufficiency of Jesus over all other man-made attempts at righteousness, Paul is declaring that the commands of Jesus should dwell in believers so they have the wisdom to teach (instruct), admonish (warn), and encourage one another.

When Paul lists the types of music in the church in verse 16, he is simply offering a sample, not an exhaustive list. A psalm may be a poem put to music such as David's psalms. A hymn is a song that, in content, specifically praises God. A spiritual song may refer generally to other styles of worship songs.

Paul closes this section of his letter with an exhortation to the Colossians to do everything in the name of Jesus. In this first-century culture, doing something in someone's name meant accomplishing that task as a representative of that person. In verse 17, Paul is telling the Colossians that they are going out as representatives of Jesus, and they are to accomplish every task as if He was doing it Himself (3:17).

At the end of verses 15, 16, and 17 is a command to give thanks. Thankfulness is the sign of a person who is submitted to the Lord Jesus Christ.

3:18–4:1

MODELING CHRIST

In the whole of chapter 3, Paul describes how the Colossians' actions should reflect the new life they have been given in Christ. He now declares that the life of Christ should be modeled in their homes—husbands to wives and fathers to children.

First, the wife is to be subject to her husband (3:18). Some translations declare that wives are to "submit." This word has been the source of much conflict. It means to voluntarily place oneself under someone's authority. It denotes order and authority. It is a voluntary action by the wife, not a forced action by the husband. It is not a position of inferiority, but rather a different role on the same team. The essence of this verse means that a wife finds her identity not apart from her husband, but in conjunction with her husband.

Paul continues his description of the family relationships with two commands to the husbands (3:19)—to love their wives and not be embittered against them. The word *love* here is the self-sacrificing love that causes one to place the needs of others above his or her own. A husband is to give love, and self-sacrificially meet his wife's needs. It is not the role of the husband to dominate his wife and treat her like a slave. He should treat her as more important than himself.

The idea behind the command to not be embittered is that there is no reason to let bitterness boil up to the degree that a husband begins to treat his wife out of that bitterness, rather than the love of Christ. This would refer to a husband who is sharp and rude to his wife.

Take It Home

Implied in Paul's description of the husband and the wife is the concept of teamwork. One of the reasons that God developed marriage was to allow a couple to work together to accomplish that which He has established for them.

A husband's love should serve as a visual representation of God. The common goal is to declare Jesus Christ as redeemer. God has established marriage as a vehicle for this to be accomplished.

Paul continues with instructions for children (3:20). The Greek word translated "obey" combines two very distinct thoughts. It carries the ideas of both *hearing* one's parents and *heeding* their wishes.

The Greek word translated "fathers" (*patters*) in 3:21 could also mean "parents" (Hebrews 11:23), and this may be the meaning here. A different word is used for parents in verse 20, however, so most scholars think Paul here means "fathers" (and most English versions translate it this way). In this case Paul is addressing the one in the family whom God will hold most responsible for what happens in the home.

This instruction is not focusing on the actual duties of raising a child, but rather on the attitude of the parent. The picture painted is that of a father who presumes upon his child's obedience without the appropriate balance between rules and relationship. Paul notes that a father's unappropriate behavior can cause a child to "lose heart" (NASB), or give up.

While still in the arena of relationships, Paul's instruction moves from family relationships to slave and master relationships. This is a relationship of obedience and authority. Typically, this command is linked to employees and employers, but there are other relationships in life that apply. One would be the teacher-student relationship. Another might be the civil law and the citizen. There is a principle in this text that could govern anywhere a person is subject to authority.

In the time of this letter, slavery was a common part of life. A slave was the property of his owner. The master had all the rights, and the slave had none. According to Paul's instruction, even in this situation, the motive of the slave should be wholehearted obedience, the same kind of obedience given to children in verse 20—to listen and to obey.

Paul develops this command by building a contrast between external service and sincerity of heart. The Greek word translated by some as "eyeservice" (NKJV) means to do something only when someone is looking. The Christian slave should work with sincerity of heart. Paul adds another qualifier to the motives of the slaves—fear of the Lord. Every task should be done in light of the reality that God is present (3:22).

Paul then tells the slave how to work—wholeheartedly (3:23). The idea around this word is that all you do derives from the passions of your life, and that everything you have goes into your work.

In a slave-master relationship there are many issues that can get in the way of work. Bitterness, resentment, apathy, lack of respect—all of this can affect the work of the slave. A believing slave must not let those issues get in the way of his service, though. He must understand that obedience is service to God more than service to his master.

Paul continues his thought by explaining to the slave that the true rewards of life come only from God (3:24). The slave, who may never know an earthly family inheritance, is going to get one in heaven—the glories of eternal life. That is why Paul adds that last statement of verse 24—it is God he serves. All of life is to be lived in devotion to Him.

Verse 25 contains the concluding principle for slaves—God will deal without partiality and fairly in the end. Then, whoever does wrong, whether slave or master, they will receive the consequences for that wrong without partiality. This is important to understand in a world that is unfair.

Paul ends this section of instruction with a statement about masters (4:1)—both the master's actions toward the slave and attitude toward God. He is to treat his slave with justice (ethically) and fairness (equality) because that is the way Jesus deals with each of us. Also, the master is not one who holds supreme authority; he, too, is under authority, and must humbly serve his Master, just as the slave has been instructed to do.

COLOSSIANS 4:2–18

IN CONCLUSION

What Message Are You Sending? 4:2–6
What Jesus Are You Worshiping? 4:7–18

Setting Up the section

In this final section of scripture on being raised up in Christ, Paul draws the Colossians' attention outward—to their responsibility to make Christ known, both by praying for those who are actively involved in sharing the gospel and by living out the life of Christ and sharing the gospel in love.

It is not enough to reflect Christ to one another in the church. We are also to take the message of Christ to the world outside of our community of faith. Paul desires to see the Colossians as active participants in the progress of the gospel through responding to the issues and questions of the world.

4:2–6

WHAT MESSAGE ARE YOU SENDING?

The Colossians must understand that they are fully dependent on Christ for everything. This dependence is seen through a life of continual prayer. Paul's instruction is to be devoted to prayer (4:2)—continually faithful, not lacking in endurance. Paul further describes the believer's prayer life as alert. This is a picture of vigilance and undistracted focus.

Gratitude is a part of prayer because of God's gift of mercy and grace. When someone realizes that it is because of God and His great mercy that he or she can even approach God's throne, thanksgiving is a part of that believer's prayer life.

Paul now turns his attention to a specific prayer request. He asks the Colossians to pray that a door of opportunity would open up so that he could share the Word of Christ. Notice that Paul does not pray that his circumstance will change, or that he will be freed from prison so that he can share more. He simply prays for an open door. What Paul desires in this open door is to speak of the mystery of Christ in clarity and boldness. In this context, the mystery of Christ (4:3–4) is a reference to all of redemptive history centered on Jesus.

The Colossians are to pray continually, but also be aware of their behavior and how it comes across to those outside of the faith (4:5–6). This means their lives should reflect the purity and the holiness of God. When Paul states that they be wise (4:5), the idea is that they should be able to apply the truth of God. In making the most of every opportunity there is a sense of aggression in seizing the opportunities that God places in a believer's path. This requires a balance between zeal and tact. How should they accomplish this? By speaking the truth in love, with graciousness (4:6).

Gracious words are words that are meek, compassionate, and reflective of the mercy and compassion of God. Words that are seasoned with salt add to a conversation that will improve or edify the situation. Neither of these descriptions implies diminishing the truth, but rather communicating it with tenderness and mercy.

4:7–18

WHAT JESUS ARE YOU WORSHIPING?

What Colossians offers the child of God is the fundamental understanding of what it means to be a Christian. With this section, Paul's instruction to the Colossians is complete, and now he desires to give the Colossians some closing greetings and remarks. This is not an instructional part of the letter, but it does contain for us some thoughts worth expounding on as we conclude a study of this epistle.

First, Paul desires to keep the lines of communication open. Even though he is in prison and has not personally seen the Colossians, he desires to ensure them that they are a part of his life, and for them to know about the progress of his ministry. Therefore, he is sending two men, Tychicus and Onesimus (4:7–9). Onesimus is the runaway slave that the New Testament book of Philemon is written on behalf of.

Paul not only keeps the lines of communication open between the Colossians and himself, but also between other believers and the Colossians. In verses 10–14, Paul relays the greetings of six fellow laborers.

The first three men are fellow Jews that are, in essence, Paul's ministry team: Aristarchus, Mark, and Justus (Jesus).

The next man who sends his greeting is Epaphras. He is the one God used to begin the church in Colossae. As a result, he carries a deep burden of prayer for these believers. Notice the content of Epaphras's prayer (4:12)—that the church would stand perfect and be assured in God's will.

Within this context, perfection carries the idea of maturity. To be fully assured carries the idea of being fully confident in the understanding of God's will.

Finally, Paul relays the greetings of Luke and Demas (4:14). Luke was a traveling companion of Paul, and that is why he was able to give such detailed accounts of Paul's ministry to Theophilus in the book of Acts. Demas is another traveling companion.

Paul also wants to keep the lines of communication open between himself and the surrounding churches, so he sends his own greeting and provides instruction for distribution of this letter, as well as the one sent to Laodicea (4:15). This request reflects Paul's desire to keep the churches united.

Paul's words to Archippus are an encouragement to faithfully do what he's been called to do without shrinking back (4:17).

Finally, the fact that Paul personally recorded this greeting is a sign of endearment (4:18). It shows that the Colossians are special to him and that he cares deeply for them. This is not just a form letter, but something that is close to his heart.

The essence of his request for the Colossians to remember his imprisonment is a request for continued prayer. Then his final farewell of grace brings the letter full circle, beginning and ending with the grace of God (1:2; 4:18).

Take It Home

There are three basic instructions in this last chapter.

1) Pray continually: Be dependent on God.
2) Live godly lives: Do not add offense to the gospel.
3) Speak the truth in love: Be ready to respond.

Every believer in this world will have an opportunity to respond to a situation with the truth, and there is a way it is to be done—out of a life that is godly and a mouth that is gracious and prepared to share the truth of Christ to this world.

1 THESSALONIANS

INTRODUCTION TO 1 THESSALONIANS

First Thessalonians is a short letter written to a predominantly Gentile church of new converts. It provides all the basic requirements for holy living (a regular "walk" with God), as well as great insight into the importance and specifics of the anticipated return of Jesus. As such, it is a worthwhile study for believers of all ages.

AUTHOR

Early church authorities agree that Paul is the author of this epistle, and little serious opposition has been raised since. With the possible exception of Galatians (for which the date is debated), this is most likely Paul's first letter among those that are included in scripture.

PURPOSE

The church at Thessalonica was facing persecution, yet it was continuing to grow and had developed a dynamic testimony of faith. Paul's letter was an effort to comfort and motivate the believers there with the truth of the Lord's sure return.

OCCASION

Paul had taken the gospel to Thessalonica, but had to leave abruptly when persecution broke out, for the good of other believers in the city (Acts 17:1–10). It would have been natural to wonder if, after his hasty departure, the new Gentile converts would soon drift back to their old ways. Paul had wanted to return on numerous occasions, and had been frustrated when unable to (2:18). So he was overjoyed when Timothy arrived from Thessalonica with a glowing report of their continued faithfulness (3:6–10). This letter was written in response to that report and in anticipation of a personal visit by Paul (3:11).

THEMES

The primary doctrinal issue of 1 Thessalonians is the second coming of Christ. Jesus' return is mentioned at the end of every chapter of this letter, and it is the focus of the end of the epistle.

In addition, Paul's emphasis on holy living is a call to unity, and he uses the term "brothers and sisters" (*adelphoi*) twenty-eight times in 1 and 2 Thessalonians.

HISTORICAL CONTEXT

Originally called Therma, because of many hot springs in the surrounding area, the city of Thessalonica had been renamed in the 300s BC, in honor of the half-sister of Alexander the Great. It was conquered by Rome in 168 BC, and became capital of the province of Macedonia. Today known as Thessaloniki (or Salonica), it is again the capital of Macedonia and one of the few cities from New Testament times that still exists, with a population of three hundred thousand.

The city's strategic location, with access to a major Roman military highway (the Egnatian Way) and a sheltered harbor, attracted many people. As a result, Thessalonica was a wealthy city, though it had also developed a reputation for evil and licentiousness.

CONTRIBUTION TO THE BIBLE

As an early letter of Paul, this epistle shows that even then he was both emotionally vulnerable and theologically strong—a combination that would continue to make him an outstanding writer and church leader. Specifically, the First Epistle to the Thessalonians contains perhaps the clearest picture of the rapture that is connected with Jesus' second coming (4:15–17).

OUTLINE

A FAITH THAT INSPIRES OTHERS 1:1–10

More Than a Standard Greeting 1:1
Good Reasons for Giving Thanks 1:2–10

PAUL'S ASSOCIATION WITH THE THESSALONIANS 2:1–20

Faithful Stewards 2:1–6
Ministering as Loving Parents 2:7–12
Thanksgiving Inspired by Suffering 2:13–20

CONCERN AND ENCOURAGEMENT 3:1–13

The Assistance of Timothy 3:1–8
Paul's Prayer of Thanksgiving 3:9–13

HOLY LIVING 4:1–12

Walking to Please God 4:1–2
Holiness and Sexual Propriety 4:3–8
Brotherly Love and Other Basics 4:9–12

LIVING IN EXPECTATION OF CHRIST'S RETURN 4:13–5:28

The Comfort of Jesus' Coming 4:13–18
The Challenge of Jesus' Coming 5:1–11
Proper Conduct While Awaiting Jesus' Coming 5:12–28

1 THESSALONIANS 1:1–10

A FAITH THAT INSPIRES OTHERS

More Than a Standard Greeting 1:1

Good Reasons for Giving Thanks 1:2–10

Setting Up the Section

Having heard of the persecution and suffering within the church in Thessalonica, Paul wrote to encourage the believers. His opening in this section is filled with genuine praise. Not only were the Thessalonians enduring difficult times, they were also setting an example that other churches were noticing. Theirs was a faith that was helping others grow stronger.

1:1

MORE THAN A STANDARD GREETING

Many Bible readers tend to skip over the personal greetings in the epistles to get to the meat of the letter. The greetings and closings of any letter can be mere formality, but sometimes the words chosen for the salutations and sign-offs reveal love and concern. In addition, much important and practical truth is to be found in the warm greetings of biblical letters.

In this case, the greeting first identifies the writer, Paul (1:1). The great apostle had formerly been known as Saul, but his name shift in the Bible is not explained. There are four main theories about Paul's double name:

1) He had both names from childhood;
2) Perhaps he was short of stature, and Paul ("little") suited him better than Saul ("asked for");
3) He took his second name from Sergius Paulus, an intelligent Roman proconsul whom he had met (Acts 13:4–12); or
4) He chose *Paul* in self-deprecation (1 Corinthians 15:9; Ephesians 3:8).

The first option is most likely. It was common for Jewish males to be given two names at birth. As Paul became the apostle to the Gentiles, he may have simply started using his more Roman-sounding name. Yet we never find the names Saul and Paul used together as is the case in other people, such as Simon Peter.

Paul's greeting also identifies his companions, Silvanus (Silas) and Timothy. *Silas* was probably an Aramaic name, and *Silvanus* a Roman one. He had accompanied Paul on his second missionary journey (Acts 15:40). He was a Jew (Acts 16:20) and a respected church leader (Acts 15:22), who later assisted Peter as well (1 Peter 5:12). Timothy was a younger man, the son of a Jewish Christian mother and a Gentile father (Acts 16:1; 2 Timothy 1:5). Paul may have led Timothy to Christ, and he was a mentor to the younger man (1 Timothy 1:2).

So from Paul's first few words, it becomes evident that he was considerate of others and acknowledged their part in his ministry, that he was a team player, and that he was eager to train and involve others in his work for God.

As for the recipients of his letter, Paul addresses the church (singular) of the Thessalonians (plural). Based on his other letters, we might expect Paul to address "the church at Thessalonica." It appears to be a minor difference, yet his terminology here is a bit more personal and reveals a concern not only for the church, but for each individual of the congregation who was persevering under difficult circumstances.

After acknowledging the *local* sphere of the believers' life—Thessalonica—Paul turns their attention to the *spiritual* sphere of existence. They had an intimate union and spiritual relationship with God the Father and the Lord Jesus Christ (1:1). The linking of both phrases with a single preposition stresses the unity of God the Father and God the Son—Paul's immediate emphasis on the deity of Christ.

Only then does Paul get to his official greeting. *Peace* was the traditional greeting among the Jews, and "grace" (*charis*) sounds like the common Greek greeting *chairein* ("greetings"). Paul not only combines the two, but personalizes them as well. His usage indicates a prayerful concern and desire for his readers to experience what only God can supply. The order is important as well: Without the grace of God, peace is impossible (2 Peter 1:2–4).

1:2–10

GOOD REASONS FOR GIVING THANKS

In essentially all of Paul's letters (Galatians being the exception), he begins by giving thanks for his readers. But the Thessalonian believers received some of his most glowing words. Paul says that he and his associates frequently thought of the godly characteristics of the Thessalonians as they prayed for them (1:2–3). Throughout this chapter, the faithfulness of a struggling church is seen from the perspective of mature and dedicated church leaders.

Demystifying 1 Thessalonians

The Greek sentence structure of verses 2–5 is long and somewhat complicated, but the segment contains three participles that draw attention to how Paul and his associates expressed their gratitude to the Lord: (1) making mention; (2) constantly bearing in mind; and (3) knowing they were chosen by God. Applied to the prayers of Paul and his companions, these phrases include the *means* of giving thanks, the *occasion* for giving thanks, and the *cause* for giving thanks.

The qualities of faith, hope, and love (1:3) are frequently grouped together in the New Testament (most familiarly in 1 Corinthians 13:13) as they are here. They are all Christlike characteristics, as well as fruit of the Holy Spirit. The church can work for God but will be effective only as long as it maintains these godly motives. The church in Ephesus was noted for its hard work and perseverance, yet had lost its first love (Revelation 2:1–7). The church in Thessalonica had no such problem.

The Greek word translated "brothers" (1:4) could also mean "brothers and sisters," and in this context would almost certainly mean "fellow Christians." More than a title, it is an affectionate term used to highlight the Thessalonians' new spiritual relationship as members of the family of God. Paul leaves no doubt by immediately referring to them as beloved by God. They were being persecuted by a hostile world, yet remained under God's fatherly love and care.

Paul knew that the Thessalonian believers were loved and chosen by God—a reference to the doctrine of election. But his was not simply a cognitive awareness. Paul, Silas, and Timothy had first taken the gospel to Thessalonica. It was more than a job to Paul. He hadn't just preached a sermon; his message had been delivered with power, with the Holy Spirit, and with deep conviction (1:5). Paul and his associates realized the way they lived their lives was just as important as what they were saying in their sermons. They didn't depend on looks, personalities, eloquence, oratorical skill, or methodology. Their calling was from God, their strength came from Him, and He was the One they remained accountable to.

Still, their reception in Thessalonica hadn't been entirely positive (Acts 17:1–10). The fact that some of the people there had believed and established a church was proof that they were going against the tide of their community. They had welcomed the message, which would have been Paul's verbal presentation of the gospel since the New Testament was not yet in existence (1:6). And they had imitated Paul and the other teachers not in the sense of mimicking actions, but by seeing their lives as an ideal example to be followed.

Critical Observation

The gospel is spread through actions as well as words. Paul followed the example of Christ (1 Corinthians 11:1). The Thessalonians followed Paul's example (1:6). And as a result, people throughout all of Greece (Macedonia and Achaia) saw the example being set by the Thessalonians (1:7).

Macedonia and Achaia (1:7–8) were Roman provinces that comprised what is now Greece. Because of the faithful witness of the Thessalonians, the gospel was heard through the entire land like the peal of a trumpet. The change in the lives of the Thessalonians was clearly evident. Many had been idolaters and some probably continued to battle the pull of their past. Yet they had welcomed God's message by faith and were putting their trust in Jesus.

The gospel had revealed the foolishness of their faith in empty idols and pointed them to the truth of the living God. The Thessalonians did not put off their old life *in order* to be saved; it was their understanding of and belief in the message of the gospel that led to salvation. Their salvation came only because of their willingness to acknowledge what God had already done for them.

Some might have tried to add Christ to their existing pantheon of idols, which would have been, in essence, to reject Him as the way, the truth, and the life. But the Thessalonians understood Paul's teaching, and as a result turned their backs on idols and became living and ongoing examples of faith for their community and their world. They understood that their Lord was God's Son. He was from heaven. He had been raised from the dead. And He would surely rescue them from God's wrath (1:10).

Such a future perspective helped the Thessalonian believers deal with their present difficulties. They may have been experiencing persecution, but that was nothing in contrast to the coming judgment of God. They were assured that they would be saved from the truly horrible times. Paul would have much more to say about the Second Coming and future events in this letter (and in 2 Thessalonians as well). Paul's original writing isn't divided into chapters and verses, of course, but every chapter in this epistle concludes with a reference to the return of Jesus Christ.

Take It Home

After reading Paul's praise for the Thessalonian believers in this section, it's hard not to ask the question, What would the church look like if everyone imitated *my* faith and behavior? Who have been your models to demonstrate what authentic Christian faith looks like in this world? And whose eyes might be on you, looking for an example of what a follower of Jesus looks like?

1 THESSALONIANS 2:1–20

PAUL'S ASSOCIATION WITH THE THESSALONIANS

Faithful Stewards	2:1–6
Ministering as Loving Parents	2:7–12
Thanksgiving Inspired by Suffering	2:13–20

Setting Up the Section

After a warm and encouraging greeting (1:1), in this section Paul begins to recall his personal experiences in Thessalonica. He has fond memories, and will compare himself to both a loving mother and concerned father. He writes as an evangelist as well as an edifier of believers.

2:1–6

FAITHFUL STEWARDS

A believer's personal life speaks powerfully to the nature of his or her ministry in regard to the motives, methods, and means used to accomplish the work of God. Paul had spent time with the Thessalonians. They knew not only what he said, but also who he was. Consequently, Paul refers to their knowledge of his life numerous times in this short letter (1:5; 2:1–2, 5, 11; 4:2).

What does Paul mean by saying his visit with the Thessalonians had not failed (2:1)?

The original word would have been used to speak of an empty jar. So Paul's meaning is that the Thessalonians had not gone away empty-handed when it came to the things that he had proclaimed: God's truth, essentials of Christian character, sincerity of faith, and so on. The Thessalonians had come away with a deep understanding of the things of God, and their lives had been changed as a result.

Their positive response must have meant a lot to Paul and his traveling companions because he had not been without opposition while trying to spread the gospel. He was still receiving criticism from some who wanted to undermine his credibility because they promoted a more legalistic approach to God. So he takes time to recall his original association with the Thessalonians (2:1–2), and then moves immediately to his current relationship with the church there (2:3–5). Because of the strong opposition they had faced, it had been risky for Paul and his companions to share the gospel with the Thessalonians, but God had provided the courage they needed (2:2).

As an apostle of God (2:6), Paul spoke with authority. Others might have misused the position, yet Paul was always a good steward of the weighty authority he had. He never attempted to wield it to make himself look better, to manipulate his message, or to intimidate his listeners. Some of his critics had used those tactics, but Paul knew *he* hadn't. Even more importantly, the Thessalonians could attest to his conscientious use of authority (2:3).

Traveling speakers generally depended on the gifts of their listeners for their daily needs. Occasionally churches raised collections for Paul, but he never expected or demanded such offerings. In fact, he seemed glad to make the point that he had nothing to gain from his ministry other than seeing the gospel of Christ taken to people who needed to hear it.

Sometimes Paul and his associates would pass through less populated towns in order to establish churches in larger cities, knowing that those churches would then reach out to the smaller towns. Yet they didn't evaluate success in terms of size or numbers. What characterized their ministry and made it fruitful was the authoritative and true revelation of God. Being entrusted with the gospel (2:3–5) was all the motivation and reward that Paul needed. And his ministry was conducted with dignity, simplicity, and vulnerability.

2:7–12

MINISTERING AS LOVING PARENTS

In defending his role as a faithful steward of the gospel, Paul denies several specific accusations (2:5). Then he shifts the emphasis from the negative accusations to his actual feelings toward the Thessalonians.

In this section (2:7–12), Paul compares his ministry to both a loving mother (with an emphasis on gentleness and willingness) and a concerned father (focused on instruction backed up by godly example). The mother he describes is a nursing mother, and the care she shows is the same word used of birds covering their eggs with their feathers. There is not only devotion involved in Paul's meaning, but a loving tenderness as well.

Critical Observation

Various aspects of Paul's ministry are detailed throughout this section:

- Ministry in selflessness (2:5–6)
- Ministry with gentleness (2:6–7)
- Ministry with willingness (2:8)
- Ministry without heaviness (2:9)
- Ministry in holiness (2:10)
- Ministry with admonition (2:11)
- Ministry with God's mission (2:12)
- Ministry centered in Bible exposition (2:1–4, 13)

The word Paul uses for this degree of love and affection (2:8) is very strong and rarely used, though it is found in the parental inscriptions on some ancient graves of small children who had died. Paul was serious about his feelings for the Thessalonians, and those feelings led to his willingness to work hard and share his very life with the recently converted Christians (2:9).

The fatherly aspect of ministry is a bit more diverse. A father certainly shares the mother's desire to love, encourage, and comfort his children (2:11), yet he has primary responsibility for seeing that each child learns to live a worthy life—to find his or her place in the world. Parents want to love and nurture their children, but the long-range goal is to see them grow strong and independent.

The call of God is ongoing—present tense rather than past tense (2:12). Paul wanted his spiritual "children" in Thessalonica to be ready and able to respond to God's calling.

2:13–20

THANKSGIVING INSPIRED BY SUFFERING

Paul is emphatic about something contemporary believers tend to take for granted. He makes it clear that what he had preached to the Thessalonians did not originate with him. He presented it as, and they received it as, the Word of God (2:13). God uses human instruments for transmitting His message, but He is the Author. The Thessalonians had heard a lot of words from Paul's mouth, yet had discerned that the message was indeed God's.

The proof that they had encountered God's truth was evident in their response. They began to receive persecution from their own countrymen, and stood firm rather than backing down (2:14). Just as the believers in Jerusalem had been persecuted by fellow Jews, the Thessalonian believers were persecuted by fellow Gentiles. There was a geographic distinction, but a spiritual commonality in the church of God.

Paul's statement in verses 14–16 can sound like religious bigotry until one remembers that Paul was among the very group he is describing. Though he doesn't go into detail here as he does in other places, his conversion had been so sudden and life-changing that the Christian persecutors he had once been partnered with were the same ones who immediately tried to hinder his newfound zeal for Christ.

Demystifying 1 Thessalonians

It seems that the Thessalonians had opponents from all ranks. Paul had experienced trouble with Jews in the area (Acts 17:5–10), yet he acknowledges that the believers there were suffering at the hands of their own countrymen, who would have been Gentiles (2:14).

The Thessalonians should have been comforted to hear that they were not suffering for any legitimate cause, but only as a result of their faithfulness to God. They were sharing in the suffering of Jesus, of Paul, and of other Christians near and far. Paul projects the future for both groups: The ones who hear the gospel will be saved; the ones who continue to oppose God's message will certainly experience His wrath (2:16).

Paul then shifts from the perspective of what the Thessalonians must have been thinking and feeling to his own thoughts and desires (2:17–20). This section reads as though it is written by a parent to a child, which affirms what Paul has already said (2:7, 11). Physical absence from the Thessalonians had been hard on Paul, and they were continually on his mind (2:17).

Paul attributes to Satan his inability to return. Various Greek words are used to designate Satan, some of which are translated "serpent," "slanderer," or "defamer." The word here is found three dozen times in the New Testament, and each time refers to an adversary or opponent. As the enemy of God, Satan opposes all who belong to Him.

Paul ends this section with a rhetorical question (2:19). He is still using the plural pronoun *our*, showing that he isn't trying to take all the credit for delivering the gospel to the Thessalonians. All those who were with him personally, and who had supported him in prayer, were able to share in the joy of seeing the Thessalonians continue to demonstrate the love and grace of Christ. When Jesus returns, the Thessalonian believers will stand among His faithful followers to receive a reward for all their suffering on His behalf.

And just so there is no doubt as to his meaning, Paul answers his own question (2:20), confirming his appreciation and fondness for the believers in Thessalonica.

Take It Home

Paul was the one in the role of spiritual leadership, yet he was more than open about how much the Thessalonians meant to him. His ministry wasn't just a job. He had established some very real and very strong relationships and wanted to keep them going, even during his absence. Can you think of someone (or some group) that you have had an influence over in the past, yet haven't followed up with in a while? If so, take some time to contact the person(s) to express your feelings.

1 THESSALONIANS 3:1–13

CONCERN AND ENCOURAGEMENT

The Assistance of Timothy 3:1–8
Paul's Prayer of Thanksgiving 3:9–13

Setting Up the Section

Paul spent the previous section answering a number of accusations leveled against him by people who opposed the gospel and his presentation of it. Now that he has set straight the false insinuations of his opponents, he continues to express personal concern for the Thessalonian believers. As their spiritual parent, he wants to see their faith continue to develop. Two key ideas he stresses in this section are spiritual stability and spiritual growth.

3:1–8

THE ASSISTANCE OF TIMOTHY

Paul had a pastoral heart. Not only was he concerned for the evangelism of people in the areas he visited, but he also remained concerned for their ongoing spiritual maturity. Thinking back to his initial encounter with the Thessalonians, he recalls the dilemma he had felt. He and Silas had been the primary targets of persecution (Acts 17:5–10), and felt compelled to leave the city for the good of the believers there. He had repeatedly wanted to return, yet so far had been hindered by Satan (2:18). So in lieu of a personal visit, he did the next best things: He sent a helper to Thessalonica, he prayed earnestly for them, and he sent this letter to encourage, instruct, and warn them.

The helper he sent was Timothy (3:1–3). Paul didn't make decisions impulsively. Rather, he considered all his options and willingly determined what he thought was best (3:1). Timothy's ministry helped put Paul's mind to rest (3:1, 5), and helped provide stability in the persecution-ridden church in Thessalonica (3:2–4).

Still, it was not an easy choice. Timothy was of great value to Paul. The word Paul uses to describe Timothy's leaving (3:1) is the same word someone would use to describe the departure of a loved one who had died. Paul would certainly feel the effects of Timothy's absence, yet his devotion to the Thessalonians was that strong.

Timothy was not only a brother (a fellow believer), but was also Paul's coworker in God's service (3:2). He was active in ministry and a team player. He had been traveling with Paul long enough to know what to do when he arrived in Thessalonica. It would be his job to strengthen and encourage the believers in their faith, even though they had been doing well. The key to spiritual strength and stability is faith, so that was also Timothy's goal (3:2).

Paul mentions his concern for the Thessalonians' faith four times in this section. He wants to ensure that they continue to trust in God's provision and control. Ongoing stability during the ups and downs of life requires faith anchored in the Lord.

Timothy's ministry would be to ensure that the Thessalonians didn't become unsettled (disturbed or shaken) by their trials (3:3). He would remind them that Paul already warned of impending persecution and that such testing of believers is appointed by God (3:3–4). Afflictions are not accidents. Believers are expected to suffer for the sake of Christ when necessary (Philippians 1:29). In addition, sometimes God allows the persecution of His people to demonstrate the evil nature of humankind and the righteousness of His judgment (2:14–16).

Critical Observation

Paul has just written about Satan in his role as an adversary of God's people (2:18). He follows up here by referring to him as "the tempter" (3:5). The title describes Satan's character as well as his strategy. One of the tempter's continual objectives is to negatively affect a believer's faith in the promises and truth of God's Word. He wants believers to doubt God's love. He wants them to depend on works-oriented strategies to handle life rather than placing complete trust in the effective and completed work of Jesus Christ.

When Paul mentions the possibility that his work might be useless (3:5), it is in the sense of being incomplete, or without effect. He knew that work for God is never in vain (1 Corinthians 15:58), but he was also aware of the spiritual opposition believers were up against. Just as Jesus had warned in His parables of Satan's snatching away the Word of God before it could be implanted in someone's heart (Mark 4:14–15), Paul knew his teachings were subject to the influence of the tempter (3:5).

Yet all of the concern and anxiety Paul felt toward the condition of the church in Thessalonica was alleviated by the return of Timothy with an encouraging report (3:6). The word Paul uses here for Timothy's good news is the same that he usually uses in reference to the gospel—this is Paul's only exception. It reflects just what a rejuvenating effect Timothy's report had on Paul.

To hear that the Thessalonians were standing firm was enough to lift Paul's mood even in light of his own personal distress (3:7). It is an example of both Paul's selfless attitude and the kind of influence one person's (or group's) faith can have on someone else.

3:9–13

PAUL'S PRAYER OF THANKSGIVING

Paul had been instrumental in getting the Thessalonian church started, yet he took no credit for it. In fact, he thanked God for the believers' influence on *him*—not the other way around! Paul was a thankful servant, one who always lived with the perspective of God's hand on his life. His heart was filled with gratitude for the work of God in the lives of others.

Paul found words inadequate to express his appreciation for what had happened in the lives of the Thessalonian Christians. His change in mood was dramatic: His concern and distress (3:7) had turned into joy (3:9). This was not superficial euphoria, but heartfelt and sincere joy that could only be experienced in the presence of God.

Praying night and day (3:10) is not a reference to specific times, even though faithful Jews had regular prayer times throughout the day. Nor did Paul mean that he did nothing but pray for days on end. He simply wanted the Thessalonians to know that he prayed for them regularly. His prayer habits illustrate the reality of his faith and his ongoing dependence on God. In addition to consistent prayer, it was prayer in earnest. Paul and his fellow ministers devoted themselves to prayer because they knew God heard and answered.

Paul's prayer for the Thessalonians includes a number of specific desires. First, he wants to see them again, primarily to help them grow and mature in the Lord, completing anything that might still be lacking in their faith (3:10). This is Paul's main objective, and it motivated everything he did. He loved people, yet his driving desire to visit was fueled by his concern for their spiritual growth and stability.

Second, Paul prays that God would remove obstacles that might prevent his return to Thessalonica (3:11). Again, he is referring to the spiritual opposition he had experienced (2:18), so his prayer is for both God the Father and the Lord Jesus to clear the way. There are circumstances where no amount of human desire or effort will accomplish the desired results, and Paul is quick to turn to God's fatherly care to achieve what is best for him.

Third, Paul prays that God will cause the Thessalonian believers to abound in love (3:12). The church was struggling with persecution, and sometimes such circumstances can create a sense of isolation and self-preservation. But if the persecuted believers all unite and continue to place their confidence in God to eventually deliver them, then their love for one another could actually *increase* during those trying times. Knowing what they were going through, Paul's love had increased for them, and he prayed that the same would happen *among* them.

And finally, Paul prays that God would make the Thessalonians strong enough to remain blameless and holy (3:13). He turns their attention from their present sufferings to their future reward.

Demystifying 1 Thessalonians

Believers are declared righteous (holy) at salvation, but this positional sanctification is not what Paul is referring to (3:13). Nor does he mean the perfect condition believers experience after death. Rather, Paul is writing about experiential sanctification, one of the objectives for all spiritually maturing believers. It is an ongoing effort to put on the character of Jesus Christ and become blameless—preparing through faithful service on earth to eventually live in God's perfect eternity.

As believers grow in faith and strengthen their hearts in love, their inner motives and desires improve. They will never be confronted with their sins in heaven because sins are remembered no more (Romans 8:1; Hebrews 10:17), but the quality of their works will be tested (1 Corinthians 3:10–15). The Thessalonians were likely to continue to suffer in the present age, but Paul prays that they would experience only the best that God had to offer in the world to come.

Take It Home

We see from the example of the Thessalonians that an active faith—one lived in the light of the gospel and a personal relationship with God—can inspire loving ministry among others. A stable and growing faith will lead to acts of love. However, it is possible for a person's faith to be real and based on a genuine trust in Christ, yet be temporarily dormant, unfocused, and unfruitful due to failure to continue to grow in the grace and knowledge of Jesus (1 Corinthians 3:3; 2 Peter 1:8–11). How would you evaluate your current level of faith? Are you going strong in spite of all obstacles? Or do you need a bit more clarity and a renewed focus on Jesus?

1 THESSALONIANS 4:1–12

HOLY LIVING

Walking to Please God	4:1–2
Holiness and Sexual Propriety	4:3–8
Brotherly Love and Other Basics	4:9–12

Setting Up the Section

In the previous section, Paul was rejoicing over the arrival of a message from Timothy that affirmed the ongoing faithfulness of the believers in Thessalonica. He had expressed thanksgiving for the church, reviewed his ministry with them, and shown his deep concern for their sufferings. At this point, Paul now begins a series of exhortations regarding appropriate Christian living.

4:1–2

WALKING TO PLEASE GOD

The word translated "finally" (4:1) is a term indicating transition and an alert to the reader that everything to follow is based on what has already been written. Paul had already made it clear that he and the church leaders with him had been earnestly praying for the faith and spiritual growth of the Thessalonians; now he is exhorting them, in keeping with those prayers, to rise to a level of holiness in their daily living. Even though they were doing well, Paul encourages them to improve their consistency even more.

Some people live as if all that is important is salvation and escaping earth to get to heaven. Yet God is deeply concerned with each believer's daily walk—how he or she lives the Christian life. Jesus came not just for the eternal aspect of believers, but also to enable them to live as examples in a dark and sinful world that does not know Him.

Since the church in Thessalonica was predominantly Gentile, Paul's instructions in verses 1-8 are particularly relevant. In contrast to Jewish believers who started their

Christian lives with a good understanding of the law, the Gentiles had come from a culture of gross idolatry that placed little or no restraint on issues of moral character—especially in matters of sex. Slavery had allowed citizens more free time to indulge in decadent living. What Paul is telling the Thessalonians would have been new and groundbreaking information for them.

As he had done in his letter to the Galatians, Paul compares the Christian life to walking. (Some Bible versions translate the word as "living," but "walking" is the more literal translation.)

Critical Observation

Walking is the mode of transportation that moves a person from one sphere to another. It requires taking one step at a time, and while one foot is off the ground with each step, the person is susceptible to being knocked off balance, stumbling, or stepping into trouble.

Walking becomes a visual aid to teach believers how to live. By using the word *walk* (or *live*), Paul puts an emphasis on *actions*, but then he immediately adds that it is to please God (4:1), which demonstrates the importance of *motives*. He first asks for their positive response as a fellow believer, and then urges them, in the name of the Lord Jesus, to respond. He wants their attention, because what he is about to say is very important.

4:3–8

HOLINESS AND SEXUAL PROPRIETY

After a general exhortation (4:1–2), Paul begins to provide specific instructions. He begins with the topic of sexual purity (4:3–8) followed by brotherly love (4:9–10) and orderly living (4:11–12).

By nature, people tend to follow desires that are against the will of God (Ephesians 2:1–3) and can never please Him (Romans 8:8). Paul begins by clarifying that what he is about to say is God's will. The doctrine of sanctification (4:3) has to do with being set apart, consecrated, and dedicated to God. As Paul broaches the topic of sex, he isn't saying it is evil or wrong. Sexual desires are natural and God-given. From the beginning, God created marriage as a sacred union between one man and one woman, and sex is part of that union, serving both as a means of continuing the race and providing pleasure within the marriage. It is only sexual activity outside of God's design that Paul opposes.

Paul's clarifications are very specific: (1) Abstain from immorality (4:3); (2) Learn to control one's body in a holy and honorable way (4:4–5); (3) Don't take advantage of a fellow believer (4:6).

The term translated "sexual immorality" is broad and includes many sexual practices: adultery, premarital and extramarital intercourse, homosexuality, and all other forms of immorality. Many of these would have been practiced openly and even encouraged by many in the Gentile culture. Yet Christians, Paul writes, are to avoid such things.

It isn't just active sexual immorality that is to be avoided, but all passionate lust as well

(4:5). Even then, mere avoidance was not enough. Christians are instructed to maintain control over their bodies in a way that is both holy and honorable. Clearly, one way to avoid sexual impurity is through marriage and a proper understanding of sex as God designed it. Scripture sets marriage apart from the motives, ideas, and values of a world that does not know God.

Paul's reference to one's brother (4:6) is unusual. Essentially every other time he uses the word, he intends it as a synonym for *believer.* In this context, however, he seems to refer to a fellow human being—either male or female. His message is that inappropriate sexual behavior has victims. Adultery on the part of one spouse betrays the other. Premarital sex robs both parties of the gift of virginity at marriage. Prostitution destroys not only lives, but affects entire communities. It may not be as apparent at first, but sexual immorality is just as much a sin as stealing from another person.

And verification of its destructive nature is the fact that God will exact punishment on all such sins (4:6). Sexual promiscuity has its own risks, but even if those involved escape the diseases, broken relationships, and such, they are still accountable to God. Holiness is at the other end of the scale from impurity. God's will for believers is for them to be set apart from the mentality and actions of a secular worldview. Paul never suggests it is easy to leave behind one's involvement in sexual immorality and begin living a holy life for God, but he does promise that believers will have help from the Holy Spirit (4:8).

Demystifying 1 Thessalonians

Greco-Roman ethics were based largely on the principles of self-interest and respect for another's property. The individual was entitled to do what was to his or her advantage (regardless of its effect on others) as long as he or she did not violate another person's property. The people's religion had little, if any, impact on sexual mores. Incest was about the only sexual taboo in their society. So Paul's connection between one's sexual activity and holiness before God was a new concept to many of his readers.

4:9–12

BROTHERLY LOVE AND OTHER BASICS

In contrast to sexual sins, most of which are self-centered and exploitive, Paul directs his readers' attention to brotherly love (4:9–10). Secular society tries to define sexual immorality as "love," but the love that comes from God is genuine and exposes selfish desires for what they are. What Paul calls brotherly love is a deep, affectionate love between friends, which is certainly applicable to marriage partners as well. He doesn't go into detail, because believers who had experienced the love of God and fellowship in the church would already know what he was talking about. This is another instance where the believers already knew what to do, yet Paul exhorts them to do so more (4:10).

Paul's next statements (4:11–12) are a continuation of demonstrating love for one another. He provides some regular, consistent goals: leading a quiet life, minding one's own business, being productive in work, and not being dependent on anyone. The ultimate result would then be the respect of those who aren't believers, and they would be attracted to the kingdom of God.

Paul isn't suggesting Christians should appear boring or disinterested in life. It is quite the opposite. By being quiet Paul means less stressed, not less enthused. Few outsiders would be drawn to an inert and lackluster group promoting joy and abundant life!

A major motivating factor in doing as God instructs is the expectation of Jesus' return. That would be Paul's next topic.

Take It Home

It seems that far too often Christians mostly want to hear *new* truth. Certainly God wants them to continue to grow in the knowledge of His Word, yet sometimes they need motivation to excel more in the truths they *already* know. One goal should be to press on toward a greater and greater appreciation of the truths they are already practicing. Can you think of specific examples in your own life where this goal would be applicable?

1 THESSALONIANS 4:13–5:28

LIVING IN EXPECTATION OF CHRIST'S RETURN

The Comfort of Jesus' Coming	4:13–18
The Challenge of Jesus' Coming	5:1–11
Proper Conduct While Awaiting Jesus' Coming	5:12–28

Setting Up the Section

Paul has already alluded to the return of Jesus several times throughout this letter (1:10; 2:19; 3:13). Here he turns his full attention to what the Thessalonians could expect. They were a church under persecution, and the anticipated return of the One to whom they were being faithful was an ongoing comfort for them. Still, they had a number of questions that Paul answers in this section.

4:13–18

THE COMFORT OF JESUS' COMING

In first-century pagan culture, the Christian concept of resurrection was peculiar and objectionable for many people. Mythology referred to an afterlife, and some Greek philosophers had attempted to teach that pleasant existence would continue after death, but few people in pagan society had real expectation or hope of life after death.

When Paul had first preached about resurrection in Athens, a handful of people had wanted to know more, but many sneered at him (Acts 17:32). It was a goal of the Greeks to shed the body in order to place all one's emphasis on the spirit. They couldn't understand *why* anyone would desire a bodily resurrection, much less *how* resurrection would take place when decomposition and decay was so evident.

The Thessalonian believers had witnessed the lack of hope among their culture, and they had questions. They were expecting the return of Christ at any time, but what about their loved ones who had died since trusting Him? Would their deaths hinder them in any way? Would those who were alive when Jesus returns have an advantage over those who had died?

Paul wants to alleviate the grief of the Thessalonians, but the solution to their grief lay in first removing their ignorance and providing hope (4:13–14). Comfort would follow hope, which would in turn reduce their grief.

Critical Observation

Sleep (4:13) is a common figure of speech for death in scripture, but is applied only to those who are believers because it anticipates an awakening (resurrection). Through faith in Christ, death for the Christian is no longer the threat it was prior to salvation. A sleeper doesn't cease to exist; his or her subconscious is still at work. Similarly, a believer's soul and spirit are active after death until he or she "awakes" to a full bodily resurrection.

Paul diminishes the fear of death by referring to it as sleep, but the reference is only to believers and not to Christ Himself (4:13–14). Jesus had to experience complete separation from God in His atoning work as Savior. Thanks to Him, believers never have to. Because death was very real to Christ, it is no more than sleep to those who have placed their faith in Him.

After assuring the Thessalonians of the reality of resurrection, Paul gives them some further assuring words with which they are supposed to encourage one another (4:18). He says that just as Jesus had died only to rise again and be with God, so would believers. Paul writes that Jesus' return is imminent, and counts himself among those alive and awaiting the moment (4:15).

Paul provides a number of details. Jesus' return won't go unnoticed. It will be accompanied by a shout of command, the voice of an archangel, and the trumpet of God. Those who had died will be resurrected before the believers who are still alive because they are dead in Christ (4:16), just as living believers are in Christ. Though the body is dead, the soul and spirit are still secure in the Lord and kept by the power of God.

As for the believers who are alive, they will be caught up in the air (the word actually means "seized" or "snatched") together with the resurrected dead (4:17). Clouds make an appropriate meeting place for God's people during this event because clouds are frequently associated with the presence and glory of God. Israel was led out of Egypt by a pillar of cloud. Moses received the law in the clouds of Mount Sinai. Jesus ascended into the clouds after His resurrection—and His disciples were told He would return the same way (Acts 1:9–11).

The most promising of Paul's words is that this incredible heavenly gathering will never end. Believers past and present will be with God forever (4:17). This event has come to be known as the rapture.

Demystifying 1 Thessalonians

The word *rapture* is never used in scripture. The term is derived from a Latin word meaning "to catch up." The same word is used by Paul to describe his being caught up into the third heaven (2 Corinthians 12:2–4), and in a (symbolic) reference to Jesus in Revelation 12:5. The mechanics of the transformation of the believers' bodies are never explained, but some kind of change is necessary based on Paul's writings to the Corinthian church (1 Corinthians 15:35–58).

5:1–11

THE CHALLENGE OF JESUS' COMING

The day of the Lord (5:2) is a subject of a great deal of biblical revelation. The phrase is used in the Old Testament about twenty times, along with "the last days" (fourteen times), "in that day" (over one hundred times), Daniel's "seventieth week," and "the time of Jacob's distress." Such references are typically to future things. Paul doesn't expect the topic to be completely new to his readers.

Some of the expectations for the day of the Lord were:

- A time of great judgment and wrath on all the nations and on Israel (Amos 5:18–20; Joel 1:15–2:11)
- The overthrow of God's enemies (Isaiah 2:12–22)
- The purging of the rebels from Israel, resulting in Israel's return to the Lord (Ezekiel 20:33–39)
- After judgment, a time of great blessing as the Lord (Christ) will reign with His people (Zephaniah 3:19–20)

Although much has been written to prepare people for the day of the Lord, it will come suddenly—like a thief in the night or a pregnant woman's labor pains (5:2–3). (According to the pre-tribulation viewpoint of the rapture, all believers would have already met their Savior in the air [4:16–17], so God's sudden and harsh judgment would fall only on those who had purposely rejected Him.)

Throughout this passage, Paul uses analogies of extreme contrast to emphasize the importance of what he is saying: knowledge vs. ignorance (5:1–2), expectancy vs. surprise (5:3), light vs. darkness (5:4–5), sleep vs. alertness (5:6), and soberness vs. drunkenness (5:7–8).

It appears that some of the Thessalonians had heard that Jesus would return soon, and had decided to stop working and just hang around until He took them away with Him. Paul is attempting to motivate them (5:5) to action. They were to remain aware, informed, ready, awake, and sober.

The way Paul phrases his statements in Greek makes a specific point. For example, he isn't stressing "night" as a specific period of time, but rather as a kind of time. In other words, he is referring to the tendency of some people to adapt a nighttime kind of existence, preferring darkness to light. And the spiritual applications then become evident.

Believers should remain spiritually awake. Paul compares essential Christian qualities to a soldier's armor (5:8), as he does in his letters to Rome (Romans 13:12) and Ephesus (Ephesians 6:10–18). The call to sobriety and watchfulness is also part of a soldier's discipline. And in this context, Paul once again groups faith, hope, and love (5:8), as he is prone to do.

In a final dramatic contrast, Paul compares salvation to God's wrath (5:9–11). The fact that God has appointed believers to receive salvation is the basis for there not being a need to fear the day of the Lord and the reason they should live alert and sober. On the day of the Lord, unbelievers will experience the wrath of God as never before, and believers will experience their salvation in a way not yet realized.

There is good reason to believe that Paul's final reference to sleep (5:10) has a different meaning than the sleep of death (4:13). In this different context, he appears to be distinguishing between spiritually mature believers and those who are apathetic or spiritually dull. It explains why he follows with the admonition to encourage and build up one another (5:11). In view of what is certain to happen one day, those who are mature need to reach out to fellow believers who seem to be struggling in their Christian walk.

5:12–28

PROPER CONDUCT WHILE AWAITING JESUS' COMING

As Paul begins to close out his letter, he provides a pithy list of specific guidelines (5:12–22). Church leaders are often admired for the wrong reasons (status, verbal eloquence, physical appearance, etc.), but they *should* be esteemed (loved) because of their work (5:12–13). By showing proper respect, it is easier to learn to live in peace (5:13).

Paul's urging (5:14) is a stronger plea than his previous asking (5:12), as he lists things expected of believers in regard to their dealings with one another (5:14–15). Some of the guidelines seem natural and normal: Help those who are weak, comfort the fainthearted among the congregation, be patient toward everyone.

Following the additional commands, however, can be harder or more uncomfortable. For example, admonishing the undisciplined (5:14) means confronting those who refuse to work. It can be difficult to correct a fellow believer for being too idle, yet such people need admonishment as not only a comment on their conduct, but also as a reminder that such behavior is out of line with the teachings of scripture. It can also be quite difficult not to repay evil for evil (5:15). It is a natural tendency to retaliate for a wrong suffered, no matter what the injury. Believers need reminders that God enables them to exhibit an above-average level of patience—especially with one another.

Next Paul provides a list of instructions for one's personal life (5:16–22). In his first few commands, it's not *what* he says to do that is so challenging, but rather how often he says to do it. He says to be joyful *all the time*. Pray *without ceasing*. In *all* circumstances give thanks. Maintaining a joyful spirit, a prayerful mind, and a thankful attitude are not random goals; they are God's will for believers (5:18). Such things depend on one's focus and faith in God—His person, plan, principles, promises, and purposes set forth in scripture.

So it makes sense that Paul concludes his list with instructions that relate to worship (5:19–22). The Holy Spirit is frequently likened to fire in scripture (Matthew 3:11; Acts 2:3–4; 2 Timothy 1:6). The warning about quenching the fire of the Spirit (5:19) is clearly a prohibition against hindering the work, ministry, and gifts of the Holy Spirit. And Christians should not disparage any authoritative revelation—neither those that were delivered through the gift of prophecy in the first-century church nor those that have been preserved by the Holy Spirit in scripture (5:20).

False prophets were already beginning to infiltrate the churches as Paul wrote this letter, so he warns his readers to examine everything (5:21). Ever since, the church has had to contend with various doctrines that reject or distort the gospel of Christ. Paul's commands are just as important today as they ever were. Believers should test what they hear against the truths of scripture. The teachings that are true and good should be kept and applied. The others should be rejected, as should every other form of evil (5:22).

If Paul's list of guidelines sounds a bit difficult to master, his closing challenge is even more so. He challenges his readers to be completely holy, or as some versions read, sanctified through and through. This holiness would apply to spirit, soul, and body (5:23). Yet Paul doesn't expect believers to simply start living up to such a standard. Rather, he asks them to allow God to make the change. That way, the high standard is not such a struggle because God provides peace (5:23–24).

Paul knew the power of prayer, and he prayed regularly for the churches he had worked among. It is natural that he would ask for prayer in return (5:25). The holy kiss he endorses (5:26) had been a practice in Jewish synagogues, which may have appropriately carried over into the close fellowship of the Christian church.

This is no ordinary letter Paul was writing; it was God's message to the believers in Thessalonica. So Paul strongly charges that it be read to everyone (5:27). And he ends the letter as he started it, with the recognition of God's grace (1:2; 5:28).

Take It Home

Paul has been making references to the return of Jesus throughout his letter, but he dwells more on the topic in this section. Did he provide any information you didn't already know? Do you have any unanswered questions regarding the day of the Lord? Regardless of what you *don't* know, what things *do* you know that can provide encouragement and hope during difficult times, as they did for the believers in the Thessalonian church?

2 THESSALONIANS

INTRODUCTION TO 2 THESSALONIANS

The second letter to the Thessalonian church is a timely follow-up to 1 Thessalonians, and as such, deals with the same concerns for the believers in Thessalonica. (See the introduction to 1 Thessalonians.) Yet some in the church were not responding to the first epistle, so 2 Thessalonians has a more urgent tone.

AUTHOR

Paul's authorship of 2 Thessalonians has not been as widely accepted as that of 1 Thessalonians. The early church never doubted it, but as skeptics arose in the nineteenth century and began to dispute the divine inspiration of the Bible, 2 Thessalonians was one of the books that was challenged based on vocabulary (a few words not otherwise used by Paul) and the writer's approach to future events (warning signs for the day of the Lord and references to the man of lawlessness that weren't found in 1 Thessalonians). Yet most scholars have been convinced that the similarities between the two letters far outweigh the differences, and support the authorship of Paul.

PURPOSE

As persecution in Thessalonica continued to increase, one of Paul's primary purposes in this letter is to offer additional encouragement and comfort. He offers incentive to persevere while also attempting to correct any potential confusion resulting from a forged letter, using his name but twisting his teachings. And while Paul writes, he adds instructions to discipline those who use their spiritual beliefs as an excuse not to work.

OCCASION

Though believed to be written very soon after 1 Thessalonians, the persecution of the Thessalonian church seems to have intensified since the previous letter (1:4–5). So Paul writes this follow-up epistle from Corinth after Silas and Timothy inform him of the recent developments in Thessalonica.

THEMES

The primary intent of 2 Thessalonians is to refute false rumors and clarify the truth about the expected return of Jesus. But in that context, a second emphasis of the letter is the problem of idleness among certain church members.

HISTORICAL CONTEXT

The historical circumstances for 1 and 2 Thessalonians are so similar that most people believe this epistle was written within six months of the first one. (See the introduction to 1 Thessalonians.)

CONTRIBUTION TO THE BIBLE

The Second Letter to the Thessalonians contains scripture's only reference to the "man of lawlessness," at least, by that title (2:3). And the letter's exhortations to avoid idleness provide valuable guidelines for those who continue to anticipate the coming of Christ.

OUTLINE

RESPONDING TO PERSECUTION 1:1–12

A Slightly Different Salutation 1:1–2
Commendation in the Face of Persecution 1:3–4
Comfort and Promise in the Face of Persecution 1:5–10
Worthy of God's Calling 1:11–12

HOLDING TO RELIABLE TEACHINGS 2:1–17

Quashing the Rumors 2:1–5
The Power of God That Restrains Sin 2:6–12
Deliverance for Believers 2:13–17

REMAINING FAITHFUL. . .AND ACTIVE 3:1–18

Confidence in God's Grace 3:1–5
Back to Work 3:6–15
A Personal Farewell 3:16–18

2 THESSALONIANS 1:1–12

RESPONDING TO PERSECUTION

A Slightly Different Salutation	1:1–2
Commendation in the Face of Persecution	1:3–4
Comfort and Promise in the Face of Persecution	1:5–10
Worthy of God's Calling	1:11–12

Setting Up the Section

Paul had written 1 Thessalonians largely to encourage the believers in Thessalonica to remain faithful as they encountered persecution from various sources. But not long after sending the first letter, he heard that the opposition was getting worse, not better. Much of what he says in this opening section is in acknowledgement of what they were facing.

1:1–2

A SLIGHTLY DIFFERENT SALUTATION

Paul's salutation (1:1–2) is essentially the same as the one he uses in 1 Thessalonians, with two small exceptions. First, "God the Father" (1 Thessalonians 1:1) becomes "God our Father" (2 Thessalonians 1:1). And, where he had wished them grace and peace before (1 Thessalonians 1:1), here he adds "from God the Father and the Lord Jesus Christ" (2 Thessalonians 1:2). Both alterations are likely attempts to comfort the persecuted believers by pointing them to the source of all that is worthwhile in their lives.

1:3–4

COMMENDATION IN THE FACE OF PERSECUTION

As is consistent with the grace-oriented thinking of Paul, he begins with an expression of thanks to God for what had miraculously taken place in the hearts and lives of the Thessalonian believers (1:3). Paul and his associates never took for granted the growth and spiritual change in the lives of those they ministered to, nor did they attempt to attribute those things to anything they had done (hard work, methods, plans, etc.). They realized that they were simply instruments of the grace of God, and rejoiced at His work among the various churches.

Paul describes God's work, demonstrated in the love and faith of the Thessalonians, as flourishing (1:3). The word he uses is found only here in the New Testament, and provides an image of the abundant and above-normal output of a fruit-bearing tree. In spite of the increase in persecution the church was experiencing, the believers' love and faith were increasing as well (1:4)—an answer to Paul's previous prayer (1 Thessalonians 3:10, 12).

1:5–10

COMFORT AND PROMISE IN THE FACE OF PERSECUTION

Paul sums up his introduction with two key thoughts (1:5). The first is a statement of fact. He says that the Thessalonians' persecutions and sufferings are clear evidence of righteous judgment that vindicates the work of God in their hearts. Their opponents had rejected the gospel, so the believers' contrasting love and endurance demonstrates their faith in God. Each group would eventually be judged accordingly.

Paul's second comment is a statement of purpose, a call for the believers to endure their sufferings so that they might be considered worthy of sharing in Christ's rule in the kingdom of God. Yes, they are being persecuted, yet their endurance is proof of God's work in their hearts and a guarantee of His promises regarding their future reward in the kingdom. Therefore, they should take comfort.

From there, Paul moves to an explanation of the future righteous judgment of God (1:6–10). Readers of this letter might want to know *why* their suffering and persecutions are evidence of God's future righteous judgment. Because God is absolutely righteous (just), He will do what is right. He will recompense tribulation to those who have persecuted believers (1:6), as well as reward those who remain faithful to Him. He may not take action during a believer's lifetime, but each devoted follower can be assured that God certainly will not ignore or tolerate sin and rebellion. The fact that God will punish the people who troubled the Thessalonians is based on His justice—it is not like human revenge that is based on a sense of indignation or injury.

Critical Observation

Jesus' return is imminent, yet no one knows when it will occur. So in Paul's writing, he sometimes includes himself with the living who will experience transformation rather than death (1 Corinthians 15:51–52; 1 Thessalonians 4:16–17), sometimes with the dead who will experience resurrection (2 Corinthians 4:14), and sometimes in the category of either possibility (2 Corinthians 5:1–8).

In verses 8–10, Paul continues to explain the recompense (judgment) of God, which falls into two categories: affliction and rest. The Greek word used for affliction (1:8–9) suggests a full and complete punishment—a vindication of God. The essence of heaven is being in the presence of God. So although it is difficult for sinful humans to understand, the ultimate punishment is eternal removal from the presence of God (1:9).

It has been noted that 2 Thessalonians 1:9–10 is perhaps Paul's clearest indication of an ongoing eternal punishment for the wicked. The reference to "eternal" *destruction* suggests that Paul does not mean annihilation, but perpetual punishment. Just as believers can look forward to eternal life with God in heaven, those who reject God face an eternal death.

Yet for believers, Paul presents God's judgment as rest (1:7). The word he uses means "a loosening or relaxation" and refers to the kingdom rest that all believers will enjoy after the Lord deals justly with sin and with those who have persecuted His people while ignoring, rejecting, and even mocking His grace and His right to rule.

When will these things take place? On the day the Lord Jesus is revealed from heaven (1:7). The coming of Christ to earth will initiate the recompense, the time of God's "paying back" (1:6)—both for those who afflict others (unbelievers) and the ones afflicted (believers).

Demystifying 2 Thessalonians

Paul's accounts of the return of Jesus differ in his two letters to the Thessalonians. Here Paul portrays a much bolder picture than he had in 1 Thessalonians 4:16–17, with Jesus accompanied by mighty angels and revealed by flaming fire (2 Thessalonians 1:7–8). He provides no timetable because the emphasis should remain on the glory due to Jesus rather than the date. Yet those who hold that 1 Thessalonians 4:16–17 is the rapture of the church believe that Jesus' coming described in 2 Thessalonians 1:6–10 is a separate event, when He will return not only with powerful angels, but with all the saints as well (Revelation 17:14; 19:11–14).

The flaming fire that surrounds Jesus on His return may be a reference to the Shekinah glory of God (Exodus 40:34–38). It may symbolize the judgment of God. Or both may be true.

Another of Paul's comments worth noting is that Jesus will be glorified *in* His people (1:10). That doesn't mean that believers will verbally give Him glory. Rather, Jesus is glorified by their lives and actions rather than mere words.

1:11–12

WORTHY OF GOD'S CALLING

Paul's marvelous description of the return of Christ is intended to provide comfort for the suffering believers in Thessalonica. Yet Paul doesn't want the truth of the Second Coming to only comfort their hearts and minds, but also to impact their hands and feet. Believers are to take hope in the future, yet continue to minister in the here and now. So Paul's prayer (1:11–12) is a call to action.

The Thessalonians would continue to suffer, but they could also continue to live in a manner consistent with their calling. It wasn't too soon for them to begin to glorify Jesus in the way they lived their lives (1:12). And as they glorified Him, He would fulfill the good purposes He had begun in their lives through His grace.

Take It Home

Twice in this section Paul writes about Jesus being glorified in His people (1:10, 12). The first is a reference to the future, but the second is clearly for the church in the present. Think about how believers today tend to glorify Jesus. Do you detect mostly verbal praise, or is Jesus reflected in the entirety of their lives? If an outsider ignored everything you say in church and monitored your behavior during an average week instead, would Jesus be glorified? What might help you glorify Jesus more consistently?

2 THESSALONIANS 2:1–17

HOLDING TO RELIABLE TEACHINGS

Quashing the Rumors	2:1–5
The Power of God That Restrains Sin	2:6–12
Deliverance for Believers	2:13–17

Setting Up the Section

The suffering of the Thessalonian church has been mentioned several times so far in 1 and 2 Thessalonians. We know these believers were facing a lot of persecution from outsiders. But in this section, we discover some false teachings that had begun to circulate regarding the return of Christ, creating even more stress on those who were trying to remain faithful. Paul will set the record straight and then encourage the struggling believers to stand firm.

2:1–5

QUASHING THE RUMORS

Rumors are always problematic, and in church settings especially so. At this point, contemporary readers discover what the Thessalonian believers would have already known: Word was spreading through the congregation that the return of Jesus had already taken place (2:2). Naturally, there was a significant degree of concern and alarm. To make matters worse, the rumor also suggested Paul was the source of the information.

So, as Paul writes about the coming of Jesus and believers being gathered to Him (2:1), he refers (grammatically) to a single event. The coming of the Lord will *include* the gathering of believers to Him. It is Paul's way of immediately pointing out that the sufferings of the Thessalonians (1:4) are not a sign of Jesus' return. Rather, they would know when He arrives because they would instantaneously be gathered to Him. There would be no confusion or overlooked members of the church in a panic.

Paul doesn't want the Thessalonians to be shaken ("unsettled" [2:2 NIV]) in the meantime—his choice of words alludes to a ship that has been torn away from its moorings, out of control amid the strong winds and waves.

He identifies three sources of false reports (2:2). The first is spirits—probably a reference to claims by means of prophetic utterances. Numerous people had the gift of prophecy, but others could easily pronounce a message supposedly from the Spirit of God. The early church leaders had to carefully examine prophetic pronouncements and accept only what was from God.

A second source of false reports is someone's word. Since Paul distinguishes it from prophetic utterances, this source must refer to mere opinion or gossip, perhaps attributed to Paul and his associates.

And the third deceptive source is a letter purporting to be from Paul. Yet the one that had arrived in Thessalonica was in direct contradiction to what Paul had taught them. He reiterates in verse 15 the importance of the Thessalonian believers' remaining aware of what was being taught.

Then Paul clarifies that they should look for two events to take place prior to the day of the Lord: (1) rebellion, and (2) the revealing of the man of lawlessness (2:3).

The current popular view of Paul's first sign is that a *worldwide* rebellion must take place before the day of the Lord begins. In the original Greek, it is not *a* rebellion, but *the* rebellion. A widespread departure from truth and resistance to God will provide the seed for a great system of revolt that will be headed by a man of lawlessness—a reference to the world's last great world dictator, the Antichrist (beast) of Revelation.

Critical Observation

The book of Revelation never uses the term *antichrist*, although this figure has a number of other titles throughout scripture. Here he is called the man of lawlessness (2:3). In other places he is called the little horn (Daniel 7:8), the prince that shall come (Daniel 9:26), the willful king (Daniel 11:36), and the beast out of the sea (Revelation 13:1–10).

Paul describes this figure as a human being, not an angel or "sin personified," as some people teach. He is a man of lawlessness, standing as the epitome of opposition to the laws of God. Yet as soon as Paul introduces this character, he makes clear his destination: destruction. His certain ruin and doom are the result of his religious activity—not only his opposition to God, but his claim to *be* God (2:4). Everything about this future person reeks of Satan, from whom he will get his authority and power (Revelation 13:4).

This shouldn't have been new information to the Thessalonian believers. Paul had taught them these truths in person not too long ago. There is a slight rebuke in his reminder (2:5). The rumors that were spreading should not have shaken the faith of the Christians there.

2:6–12

THE POWER OF GOD THAT RESTRAINS SIN

Paul's first two proofs that the day of the Lord has not yet arrived are the absence of both the widespread rebellion against God and the man of lawlessness. And here he adds an additional proof: the continuing restraining power of God (2:6–7). The reason the man of lawlessness has not yet made his appearance is because God continues to prevent it. The time is not yet right.

It is true that the power of lawlessness is already at work but is being held in check by a restrainer. The first reference to this restraining force (2:6) is a general term, leading readers throughout the centuries to speculate that Paul might be referring to the power of the Roman Empire, the ethical Jewish influence on the culture, or other possibilities. But Paul follows up with a personal reference in his next sentence (2:7). The one who holds back the power of lawlessness must certainly be God Himself.

When God's restraint is withdrawn, the lawless one will soon be revealed (2:8). The temporary nature and sure end of his rule is made clear by two of Paul's statements. The first is, "whom the Lord will destroy by the breath of his mouth" (2:8 NET; see Isaiah 11:4). Whether the phrase "breath of his mouth" is figurative or literal, it highlights the ease with which Jesus will remove the lawless one and his godless system from the earth. He will not cease to exist, but when removed, he will be thrown alive into the lake of fire (Revelation 19:19–20). Paul's second phrase is, "and wipe out by the manifestation of his arrival" (2:8 NET). The very manifestation and splendor of the Savior's presence when He arrives will immediately render the Antichrist impotent and defeated.

However, even though this figure rules for a short time, his activity and actions will be hideous beyond belief. The source behind his coming and influence will be Satan (2:9–10). With the restrainer removed, there is nothing to hinder the work of the devil.

Demystifying 2 Thessalonians

Paul's short summary of the connection between the man of lawlessness (Antichrist) and the source of his power, Satan (2:9–12), is more fully developed by John in Revelation 13:3–8.

The man of lawlessness will be quite convincing in his deceit. He will perform miracles, signs, and wonders—things that usually authenticate divine power, yet are counterfeit in this instance. The tragic irony is that the people so willing to respond to such deceit are those who found no place in their hearts for God's truth (2:10). Even as they respond to the inauthentic signs and wonders, they are perishing—not because they never heard the genuine gospel, but because they rejected it.

Due to humankind's indifference to the truth, God will not only let the people believe a lie, but He will send a deluding influence to promote it (2:11–12). In rejecting God's revelation of Jesus Christ as Savior and Judge, people choose to delight in wickedness.

2:13–17

DELIVERANCE FOR BELIEVERS

Having assured his readers with several convincing reasons why they are not yet in the day of the Lord, Paul returns to the danger they face in failing to hold to what they know to be true. Only by retaining what Paul has taught them will they continue to find comfort and strength in that truth for fruitful living under their stressful circumstances.

Paul was a knowledgeable and well-rounded teacher. He balanced his teaching on prophecy with a focus on practical Christian living. And he had no sooner dealt with the problem of Satan's lies than he returns to a positive emphasis on God's love, thanksgiving, and prayer (2:13–14).

As Paul does in other places, here he shows that salvation is the result of God's sovereignty *and* the belief of the individual (2:13). It cannot be achieved merely on human effort, yet the work of the Holy Spirit requires a response. When unbelievers respond to God's truth, He saves them; when they reject it, they cannot be saved (2:10).

The Thessalonians had begun to waver in their faith, so Paul reminds them to stand firm (2:15). God-breathed teachings had been handed down to His people and incorporated into apostolic traditions. In turn, Paul has handed those teachings on to the Thessalonian believers. They are true and dependable, and a means for standing firm against all forms of false teaching, as well as the various storms of life.

The reason for Paul's prayer at this point (2:16–17) is threefold. First, believing and holding on to the truth should lead to its practice. Second, only God Himself could effectively generate the level of encouragement and stability needed to practice His truth in the midst of a pagan environment. And third, such a wishful prayer is possible only because of what God had done for humankind in the person of His Son, through His grace.

As a result of God's great love, believers receive two wonderful gifts: eternal comfort and good hope. In the midst of the Thessalonians' struggles, these gifts would keep them looking forward to permanent consolation and everything else God has promised His people. They could hardly have asked for anything that would be more appreciated.

Take It Home

Paul isn't afraid to broach the topic of Bible prophecy. As the Thessalonians are suffering, he is able point to the future with significant understanding and clarity. His comprehension of future things led to a much more grounded outlook of the present. How is your own understanding of future things? While some events, dates, and symbols will certainly continue to be mysteries, many other aspects of the future are spelled out clearly in scripture. Do you think a better understanding would have any effect on your day-to-day Christian walk?

2 THESSALONIANS 3:1–18

REMAINING FAITHFUL. . .AND ACTIVE

Confidence in God's Grace	3:1–5
Back to Work	3:6–15
A Personal Farewell	3:16–18

Setting Up the Section

As Paul begins to bring this letter to a close, he emphasizes how his (and his associates') confidence lies not in human plans or promotions, but rather in God Himself. The ultimate success of any ministry depends on the faithfulness of the Lord and His Word, even though He chooses to use frail human instruments to accomplish it.

3:1–5

CONFIDENCE IN GOD'S GRACE

As he had done at the end of his previous letter (1 Thessalonians 5:25), Paul again asks the believers for prayer for himself and his associates (3:1). Paul's team had spread the gospel to Thessalonica and then moved on to carry it to new places. Who better than the Thessalonians, who were currently experiencing the work of God among them, to pray for Paul's ongoing ministry elsewhere? Paul writes with apostolic authority to help the Thessalonians deal with their problems, yet readily confesses his own inadequacy and the need for God's enablement.

Rather than being vague and general, Paul helps the Thessalonians know what to pray for. He has two specific requests. First, he wants God's Word to spread quickly. The word he uses is *run*. With an emphasis on the message rather than the messenger, Paul desires to see the gospel proceed quickly and without hindrance. And connected with this first request is his desire that the message would continue to be glorified—that the gospel, and therefore God Himself, would receive due honor, respect, and praise.

Paul's second specific request is prayer for his deliverance from perverse and evil men (3:2). This request is certainly related to the first, but much more personal. Paul already has God's promise of personal safety in Corinth (Acts 18:9–11), where he was writing this letter, so this request shows he doesn't take such promises lightly or think himself beyond need of the prayers of other believers.

Paul makes a sharp contrast between human lack of faith (3:2) and God's faithfulness (3:3). He assures the Thessalonians that they can count on God for spiritual strength and protection at any time, and he is confident they would continue to faithfully follow the truths they had been taught (3:4). It's more than just a good feeling; it is confidence in God. Paul's confidence is not in the physical stamina of the Thessalonians to endure, but in God's ability to sustain them in growth and obedience.

Biblical references to the heart often mean the entire inner person—mind, emotions, and will. Perhaps that is the case here (3:5), although Paul might have intended it simply as a synonym for the personal pronoun (*your hearts* in place of *you*). Either way, he desires for the Thessalonians to be drawn into a deeper and more inclusive love (like God's) and a more willing and committed endurance (like Christ's).

3:6–15

BACK TO WORK

In his previous letter, Paul had challenged the believers to work conscientiously (1 Thessalonians 4:11–12). It isn't until this point that he really makes clear what the problem is: idleness of some of the church members (2 Thessalonians 3:6). Apparently, a number of believers had heard Jesus was returning and had given up providing for themselves, creating a burden on others in the church. Clearly they weren't quick to correct their actions, because Paul has to address the problem again in this letter, even more strongly.

Critical Observation

The media frequently cover movements of people who think they have figured out the secrets and dates of the end of the world. Some are Christian and others aren't. Some come to tragic ends while others appear somewhat comic. Such groups have formed throughout the centuries since Jesus' *first* coming. The group at the church at Thessalonica is among the first to misinterpret and misapply the teachings of God's Word. Paul's correction is included in scripture as a guideline for others to follow.

Paul has nothing to do with promoting the sit-around-and-wait-for-Jesus philosophy, and he orders his readers to have nothing to do with those who refuse to work and who twist the teaching of scripture (3:6). The word used for Paul's instruction is the same as would be used for a military officer barking out commands. He is quite firm on the topic.

Paul isn't asking the Thessalonians to do anything he doesn't do himself. Even while performing his ministry among them he had provided for himself and had not expected handouts (3:7–8). It's not that he doesn't think he has the right to expect help (1 Corinthians 9:3–4, 6), but it is more important to him to set an example for the believers (3:9). Paul models appropriate Christian behavior for the Thessalonians and challenges them to imitate it (3:7). And it is more than a request; he insists on it as a moral necessity. As for those who are unwilling to work, Paul recommends letting them go hungry (3:10).

Demystifying 2 Thessalonians

Perhaps it was more than simple laziness causing the Thessalonians' reluctance to work for a living. The Jewish people took pride in their work and taught all males a trade. The Greeks, however, considered manual labor to be fit only for slaves. Having come from such a culture, possibly pride was a prominent motive for the nonworking Thessalonians.

The cessation of productive work was already creating problems. With too much time on their hands, some of the believers were becoming busybodies (3:11). So Paul reinforces the importance of their getting back to work and of all the believers to continue doing what is right (3:12–13). If the group of busybodies still refuse to work, Paul instructs the other believers to separate themselves—not to excommunicate and write off the offenders, but to temporarily ostracize them from close fellowship until they saw the error of their ways and repented. The sinning members needed firm correction for their own good, yet they were still brothers, and deserved to be treated with love (3:14–15).

3:16–18

A PERSONAL FAREWELL

The Thessalonians' disputes could be settled by the ultimate peacekeeper (3:16). Yet it requires a real commitment to Christ in order to experience peace at all times and in every way.

Until this point in his letter, Paul has been dictating to a secretary. But as was his custom—as readers discover here—he takes the pen and writes a short section in his own handwriting (3:17–18). And as he had done in 1 Thessalonians, he concludes this epistle as he had begun it—with a prayer of grace for all his readers (1:2; 3:18).

Take It Home

The promised return of Jesus had been misunderstood by some of the Thessalonians, creating a group of inactive busybodies. Do you detect any problems in the modern church based on similar misunderstandings of future events? What do you think is the best way to maintain a balance between joyful anticipation of Christ's return and the necessity of going on with one's daily life and commitments?

1 TIMOTHY

INTRODUCTION TO 1 TIMOTHY

First Timothy is a letter from a faith mentor to one of his dearest disciples. It is a look into the first-century relationships that made up the early church, and the issues with which they grappled.

AUTHOR

The author of this letter introduces himself as the apostle Paul. Of all the letters of Paul, the Pastoral epistles (1 Timothy, 2 Timothy, and Titus) are by far the most disputed in terms of authorship. Differences of language, style, and theology have caused many scholars to doubt that Paul was the original author. Some believe that a disciple of Paul wrote these after his death. Others think he may also have used one of his missionary companions to write out these letters (see Romans 16:22 for an example of this), and this scribe left his own stylistic mark. In any case, the differences are not as great as is sometimes supposed, and there are many features of the letter consistent with Paul's language and style. Evangelical scholars continue to assert that these letters came from the apostle's hand.

OCCASION

Paul wrote this letter from Macedonia sometime after being released from his first Roman imprisonment—around AD 63–64. Paul had left his protégé, Timothy, to minister at the church in Ephesus (1:3). At this particular time, the church was plagued by false teachers and dissension. Paul was going to be delayed in returning to Ephesus to be with Timothy and guide him in person, so he wrote this letter to offer guidance on how to choose and strengthen the leader of the church and train them to preserve godliness and reject false teaching.

PURPOSE AND THEMES

First Timothy is one of the three New Testament books identified as the Pastoral epistles, along with 2 Timothy and Titus. Paul wrote this letter, as he did the other two, to assistants who were leading communities of faith. In the letter, he offers them instructions in their role as shepherds. In the first century, this included standing against heresy and teaching sound doctrine. Understandably then, the themes of 1 Timothy are along those lines—church leadership, sound doctrine, faith in practice, and church order.

Though this letter is addressed to Timothy, there are several indications that the full intention was for the letter to be shared with the congregation and even throughout the region.

OUTLINE

OPENING WORDS	**1:1–20**
Greeting	1:1–2
False Teachers	1:3–11
God's Mercy	1:12–20
THE LIFE OF THE CHURCH	**2:1–15**
Priority on Prayer	2:1–7
Appropriate Worship	2:8–15
CHURCH LEADERS	**3:1–16**
Instructions for Elders	3:1–7
Instructions for Deacons	3:8–13
Instructions for the Congregation	3:14–16
THE LOCAL CHURCH	**4:1–16**
The Problem of Fallen Faith	4:1–5
Timothy, the Teacher	4:6–16
INSTRUCTIONS FOR SPECIFIC GROUPS	**5:1–6:2**
Relationships in the Community	5:1–2
Widows	5:3–16
Elders	5:17–25
Slaves	6:1–2
EXHORTATIONS	**6:3–21**
Heretics	6:3–10
The Faithful	6:11–16
The Rich	6:17–19
In Conclusion	6:20–21

1 TIMOTHY 1:1–20

OPENING WORDS

Greeting	1:1–2
False Teachers	1:3–11
God's Mercy	1:12–20

Setting Up the Section

The opening of Paul's letter to Timothy reveals it to be both personal and official. It also reveals much of Timothy's task in Ephesus—facing teachers of false doctrine.

1:1–2

GREETING

Paul identifies himself by noting the authority with which he writes (1:1). He is an apostle, an envoy, one sent with a specific mission. While all Christians are called to serve God, the first-century use of the term *apostle* referred to a very specific group—those who had accompanied Jesus. While Paul had not been one of the twelve disciples, his conversion experience brought him face-to-face with Jesus (Acts 9:1–9). In Acts 13:2, the Holy Spirit calls Saul and his companion, Barnabas, to the missionary work recorded in the book of Acts. This further legitimizes Paul's claim to be an apostle.

Paul's reference to God as "Savior" is unusual in the New Testament, but occurs repeatedly in the Pastoral epistles (1:1; 2:3; 4:10; Titus 2:10, 13).

Critical Observation

Paul's particular use of the word *Savior* to describe God may have included a specific cultural slant understandable to the readers of his day. At the time, the emperor of Rome was to be not only honored as a leader of state, but worshiped as well. The same term was applied to the emperor. At the time Paul wrote this letter to Timothy, Nero was emperor.

The language that Paul uses to describe the "hope" found in Christ has an element of certainty to it. It communicates a shade of meaning that modern language doesn't always communicate. Rather than hoping something will happen but not being sure it will, the hope Paul refers to is a strong confidence in the source of good things to come.

Paul identifies his recipient as one so dear he is like a son in the faith (1:2). Paul reserves this designation for Timothy and for Titus (Titus 1:4). Timothy had grown up in Lystra, a Galatian city Paul visited on both his first and second missionary journeys. It was on this second journey that Paul requested Timothy to serve with him (Acts 16:1–3). From there they developed the bond that is evident in this letter.

While the greeting is similar to most of Paul's letters, the addition of the word *mercy* is unique to Paul's two letters to Timothy (1:2; 2 Timothy 1:2). Unlike grace and peace, mercy was more of an Old Testament concept referring to God's loving-kindness.

1:3–11

FALSE TEACHERS

Paul had left Timothy in Ephesus to protect the church there from false doctrine (1:3). The very fact that Paul refers to these as false doctrines reveals that at this point in the first century there was a core of Christian doctrine already widely accepted and agreed upon.

Paul's mention of myths and genealogies probably describes two related problems. Both refer to some type of extrabiblical stories that had become accepted as tradition. They provided fodder for debate, but not truth for growing in faith (1:4–5).

The command that Paul refers to in verse 5 is not one specific command, but rather the sum total of the obligations of the Christian walk. The goal of that sum total is love, which comes from three sources:

1) A pure heart. This refers to someone who engages his or her whole self in doing the work to stay spiritually and morally fit.
2) A good conscience. This is the ability to tell right from wrong and to consistently choose right. It is also the absence of unconfessed sin and underhanded motives.
3) A sincere faith. This type of faith calls one to serve not for personal gain, but in obedience to God's will.

The teachers of the law Paul discusses in verses 6–7 may have been Gentiles or Jews. Whichever they were, though, they failed the test of love outlined in the previous verses. What they were teaching was not tightly connected to the scriptures. Their discussions were meaningless (1:6). While they wanted to be seen as authorities, they did not have a handle on the content and meaning of the law (1:7).

This brings Paul to a discussion of the law. Throughout his New Testament writings, Paul maintains the position that the law does not make people right with God or provide forgiveness of sins. The law only served to point out the sin of humanity so that people could realize their need for God, and thus be forgiven and made clean. That is the proper use Paul refers to in verse 8. The list following verse 8, then, makes up those who refuse to see what the law reveals—their need for God's redemption through Jesus (1:9–11).

It has been noted that the first list describes sins against God and the next list describes sins against others, much like the Ten Commandments (Exodus 20:1–17).

Take It Home

Paul's description of the false teachers can be an inspiration to us to remain faithful to the true message of the gospel. In the modern age of the church, it is still just as easy to get involved in controversies or disputes about issues secondary to the message of the gospel. Part of the job of those who lead us is to pull us back on track.

1:12–20

GOD'S MERCY

In verse 12, Paul moves from the sins of others to his own sinful nature, not with self-condemnation but with gratitude that out of his own sinfulness he could have been called to spread the gospel.

Demystifying 1 Timothy

Paul's history as a Pharisee included a vehement opposition to early Christianity. Acts 8:1 paints a picture of Paul approving the stoning of Stephen, the first New Testament Christian martyr. At the time, Paul believed he was ridding the world of false doctrine, but once he came to faith in Jesus, his ideas about what was true and false changed. In writing Timothy, Paul identifies false doctrine as that which stands against the truth of the gospel.

Paul's gratitude focuses on three areas (1:12):

1) God strengthened him. This is not to say that God added to the strength Paul already had, but rather He was the source of Paul's strength.
2) God found him faithful. Paul was not perfect, but because of God's grace He chose to see Paul as faithful.
3) God appointed him for service. It was not just that Paul received the grace of God, he was also a channel of sharing that grace.

In this next section, Paul sets up an interplay between his own sinfulness and God's grace (1:12–16). He claims himself to be the worst of sinners, calling himself a blasphemer, a persecutor, and "a violent man" (NIV). Certainly scripture supports Paul's claims (Acts 8:1–3; 9:1; 22:4; 26:11). But the purpose of Paul's litany of grievances against himself is to illuminate the patience of God in redeeming Paul's life.

Paul's preamble in verse 15—"This saying is trustworthy and deserves full acceptance" (NET)—is a phrase (or a variation of a phrase) he uses only in his Pastoral Letters (1 and 2 Timothy, Titus). It functions much like the Gospel writers, when they quote Jesus as saying, "Verily" (KJV) or "I tell you the truth" (NIV), in that it highlights an important statement. In this case it highlights Jesus' mission to save sinners—Paul claiming himself the worst of them all.

Verse 17 serves as a kind of spontaneous doxology not uncommon in Paul's writing. There is no known external source for this doxology, so it is reasonable that Paul himself wrote it. It highlights God's nature as eternal (no beginning or ending), immortal and invisible (existing as a spirit), and the one true God.

Verses 18–20 close this chapter with a specific instruction for Timothy. Paul's instruction, or charge, has a military connotation, almost like marching orders. It refers to the job Timothy was sent to Ephesus to do—to teach sound doctrine and quiet the false teachers. Within that context, it brings a higher level of seriousness to Timothy's responsibilities in Ephesus.

Paul's mention of prophecies (1:18) may refer to prophecies that Timothy claimed for his own life or things said about Timothy at his ordination (4:14; 2 Timothy 1:6–7).

A second time, then, Paul uses military language, encouraging his spiritual son to fight the good fight. Verse 19 tells how he will do this—with faith and a good conscience.

The two men singled out by Paul—Hymenaeus and Alexander—had evidently been members of the church. Hymenaeus had claimed the resurrection had already taken place (2 Timothy 2:17–18). Alexander was possibly the coppersmith mentioned in 2 Timothy 4:14. When Paul says he handed these men over to Satan, it means they were removed from the church. This practice, while a part of church discipline, was not simply about punishment. The hope was that the men would see their error and return.

Take It Home

Paul's encouragement to Timothy speaks volumes to the church today. Just as faith and a good conscience were Timothy's tools to fight the good fight, so are they ours today. These two—our beliefs and our practices—go hand in hand. They protect us as armor. They provide us the tools with which to fight the enemy.

1 TIMOTHY 2:1–15

THE LIFE OF THE CHURCH

Priority on Prayer	2:1–7
Appropriate Worship	2:8–15

Setting Up the Section

There has been much conversation in the church since Paul wrote the words in this chapter regarding the behavior of the women in the Ephesian community of faith. When applying this teaching universally to the modern church, it's important to keep in mind that Paul was writing for a specific situation—to help Timothy know how to deal with the false teachers assailing the community. It may not be safe to assume that Paul would have given these exact same instructions had Timothy been facing a different situation.

In both chapters 2 and 3, Paul describes the kinds of people who should be leaders in the church. He is not listing the responsibilities of those leaders so much as describing the kind of people they should be.

2:1–7

PRIORITY ON PRAYER

Since Paul does not make more than one point in this section, his "first of all" (2:1) should probably be taken as a statement of priority rather than a structural outline. He is instructing Timothy about prayer.

The different elements of prayer included here are not intended to be a list of all things related to prayer, but a reminder of the scope of prayer—requests, advocacy, thanksgiving. It is noteworthy that Paul includes thanksgiving, as he emphasizes in many of his letters, which is an element of prayer that can be so easily overlooked.

Timothy is urged to pray and give thanks for everyone, but especially for those in authority. Some have noted that those in authority may have included the false teachers Paul was warning Timothy against. These prayers likely involved prayer for the salvation of those in authority (2:3–4). Such an outcome certainly would enable believers to practice godliness without as much fear of persecution.

Both of the descriptions Paul uses—"godliness and dignity" (2:2 NET)—refer to the Christian life lived in community. Godly living is faith in practice. Dignity has to do with the earnestness with which someone walks out his or her spiritual journey. It is these kinds of examples that help others come to the knowledge of the truth—the good news of the gospel (2:4).

When Paul writes that God wants everyone to be saved, he isn't implying that everyone will be, though some have interpreted this passage that way. Taken with the rest of scripture, it is obvious that some reject Christ and face judgment. Nevertheless, God desires that all would come to know Him.

Critical Observation

Paul's encouragement that Timothy pray for his authorities takes on new meaning in light of the fact that Nero was ruling at the time, and persecution of Christians was on the rise. After Nero blamed the Christians for the fire that destroyed much of Rome, the persecution only became more severe. Nevertheless, throughout Paul's teaching, Christians were encouraged to support rather than rail against the government (Romans 13:1–7; 1 Peter 2:13–17).

Verses 5–6 function as a creed or perhaps an early Christian confession. Whether this is an external creed that Paul is quoting or his own creation, it is an affirmation of three important truths:

1) Monotheism—one God to be worshiped by all. While today this concept is familiar and foundational to the three great monotheistic religions (Christianity, Judaism, and Islam), in the first century the worship of many gods (polytheism) was the norm. Only Judaism (and Christianity that arose from it) claimed that there was only one true God.

2) Jesus' unique role as the one mediator between God and humanity. Part of the heresies of the first century involved the role of angels, which some saw as mediators between God and His creation. This is clearly refuted here.

3) Jesus' act of redemption, revealing God's purpose. The price Jesus paid was enough to ransom everyone, if they choose to receive it. This connects with Paul's statement in verse 4, that God wants all people to be saved, thus He did what was necessary at the right time, through the work of Jesus (2:6).

Paul reiterates his appointment as a herald (someone who announces important news), an apostle (one who is commissioned for a specific purpose), and a teacher (2:7). (These three claims are repeated in 2 Timothy 1:11 in the same order). He claims that he was not self-appointed, but that he was commissioned to minister to the Gentiles. Paul's life bore out this calling. He traveled to Gentile lands and spread the gospel to those who did not have the Jewish foundation of Christianity, yet who were equally in need of redemption.

Why would Paul have needed to emphasize the truth of his words as he does in verse 7? Keep in mind that while this letter was written for Timothy, it was intended to be shared among the believers in Ephesus and perhaps even farther. In the face of the false teachers who had undermined Paul's authority and teaching, this emphasis is entirely appropriate.

2:8–15

APPROPRIATE WORSHIP

Paul returns to the notion of prayer that he first introduced at the opening of this chapter. Given Paul's claim of authority in verse 7, these next instructions carry more weight than merely a preference. Paul expects his listeners to act on them.

While contemporary prayer is often accompanied by bowed heads and closed eyes, the first-century posture for Jews and early Christians was often with face and hands looking upward toward heaven. Thus, lifting one's hands in prayer indicated a calling out to God. The fact that the hands were described as holy suggests purity of conduct, which would result in relating to each other without anger or disputes (2:8).

Just as the men receive instructions to pray with holy hands, the women are instructed to adorn themselves with good works rather than elaborate clothing and jewelry (2:9; also see 1 Peter 3:3–5 for similar instructions from the apostle Peter). Neither the wardrobe nor the speech of the women of the Ephesian church was to draw undue attention to themselves (2:9–10). These instructions may have been making reference to the temple prostitutes in Ephesus, but certainly were highlighting the struggle for these women of faith not to blend into the cultural mores that would highlight a woman's body but not her heart and soul. Paul's instructions here are not so much about specific hairstyles or fashion statements, but about the general principle that should guide a believing woman's demeanor and appearance. What is she drawing attention to and for what purpose?

Paul considers the women's faith, evidenced by good works, to be an appropriate adornment. Rather than being attractive through merely outer enhancements, these women of the Ephesian church should be attractive because of how they live and how they portray God's good work in their lives (2:10).

The instruction regarding women being silent in church is likely a specific remedy to the situation Timothy was facing in Ephesus. While it was customary that only men lead prayer in Jewish worship, it is somewhat unusual that Paul specifies only the men to pray. Elsewhere, 1 Corinthians 11:5 for instance, Paul gives guidelines for women both praying and prophesying, so the directive across the board is not for women to always keep silent. In the case of the Corinthians, though, Paul did give specific instructions—the women were to have their heads covered to reflect the authority under which they did their praying and prophesying. It is likely that each of these instructions were geared toward their particular situations rather than laying claim to universal regulations.

Paul is not supporting inequality among men and women, but contending that they have different roles. Both the created order (2:13) and a woman's susceptibility (2:14) suggest that men occupy the role of leadership.

Paul's comments regarding childbearing should be taken within context. While he says that a woman will be saved through childbearing, this doesn't mean that a women's salvation is contingent on bearing children. No other New Testament passages support that. Paul probably had in mind the preservation of a woman's significance when she practices her unique roles—in this case, the role of childbearing.

Some have offered the possibility that the women of this church were being particularly drawn in to the false teaching that was plaguing the whole congregation. While we cannot know this for sure, it does fit well with Paul's comments about the deception of Eve and his protective guidelines for women's participation in leadership roles.

The characteristics to which Paul calls the women of the church—faith, love, holiness, self-control—are no different than the standards he calls all Christians to. These are the distinctives that set these Christian women apart from their cultural counterparts outside of the faith in a way that no amount of alternate dress or hairstyle could.

Take It Home

While Paul's instructions regarding women in the church have given him a discriminatory reputation among some people, it is important to see the reason he is calling for order in the church and what that order is supposed to accomplish. This particular church was facing an attack on its doctrine. It was important for these believers to establish an order for their worship and their communication to preserve the truth and protect themselves from those who didn't speak the truth. If this body of believers allowed themselves to fall into chaos, they would only be prey for any new, louder doctrine that came along. Paul's call for order in the relationships and practices of the body are important to contemporary churches just as they were in the first century.

1 TIMOTHY 3:1–16

CHURCH LEADERS

Instructions for Elders 3:1–7
Instructions for Deacons 3:8–13
Instructions for the Congregation 3:14–16

Setting Up the Section

First Timothy is considered one of the Pastoral epistles (along with 2 Timothy and Titus) because Paul was *pastoring* his protégé in the organization and character of the church and the principles of its leadership. It would make sense then, that Paul would discuss the kind of people that Timothy would choose to lead the church with him. The instructions here are not exhaustive lists, but they offer a glimpse into the kind of mature person that can effectively rise to leadership in the local church.

3:1–7

INSTRUCTIONS FOR ELDERS

Having set some groundwork for conduct in the church, Paul turns to the characteristics of the church's leadership. He refers to another trustworthy saying (1:15; 4:9; 2 Timothy 2:11; Titus 3:8)—aspiring to lead a congregation is noble work (3:1). In this passage, the word translated "aspires" (NET) means to set your heart on something.

The title *elder*, or *overseer*, is a term that applies to anyone who has an oversight function in the church (3:1). Its original use was not specific to the church; the term referred to anyone in a supervisory position. In Paul's letters, the overseer is most often also the teacher.

Paul lists several qualifications for the overseer in verses 2–3:

- Above reproach. This is an opening summary of the character of the overseer. It speaks to a reputation that contains no flaw that could be grounds for accusations.
- Husband of one wife. While some interpret this to mean the overseer must be married, it is more likely that it is a description of his faithfulness to the vows he has made.
- Temperate and self-controlled. He shows good judgment, living a life of balance and moderation.
- Respectable. His behavior should be appropriate to each situation.
- Hospitable. To the first-century Middle Eastern culture, hospitality, even to strangers, was highly valued.
- An able teacher. He should have knowledge of the scriptures and be able to communicate that knowledge.
- Not drunk or violent. There are obvious reasons that an overseer is not to be an immoderate drinker—it would stand in the way of many of the characteristics already listed. But also, this may appear in the list as a reaction to the false teachers that were troubling the church at Ephesus.

- Gentle, not argumentative. He should not easily be threatened or insecure, which often makes someone quick to disagree. He should also be free from harshness.
- Free from the love of money. The overseer mustn't be addicted to wine or money. He must be trustworthy to handle the finances of the church.

The next characteristics Paul lists relate to family life. Again, this is not to say that in order to be a church leader the overseer must have children, but that his management style at home (which will inform his style in the church) should be compassionate, effective leadership (3:4–5). Note that the children of the overseer aren't merely to obey, but are to obey *out of respect*. This distinction reflects on the manner in which the overseer manages his children.

Paul's admonition that the overseer not be a novice Christian is quite understandable (3:6). The word translated "conceited" or "proud" could also mean "deluded," "blinded," or "foolish" (the word originally meant "wrapped in smoke"). Because of the new faith and the quick leadership, a novice Christian may get a distorted view of himself.

The reference to the devil points to the pride that is attributed to Satan's fall. The devil is again mentioned in verse 7, in which Paul recommends that the overseer have a good reputation, even to those outside the community of faith. While we don't have any further information on exactly what Paul means by the devil's trap—whether or not it actually means a trap laid by Satan—we can feel sure that an overseer with a poor reputation in his city or region would be more of a hindrance than a help to the gospel message. That would be the kind of trap the devil would lay.

3:8–13

INSTRUCTIONS FOR DEACONS

Paul now turns to the role of deacons. *Deacon* means "one who serves," and this appears to have been a role associated with day-to-day ministry tasks, rather than leadership or teaching. Though the seven helpers chosen in Acts 6:1–6 to distribute food to poor widows in the Jerusalem church are never explicitly called deacons, they are often viewed as the model for this service ministry in the church.

Critical Observation

Keep in mind that Paul is not setting out to define the leadership roles within the church. He is describing the kinds of service and leadership that are already being provided. He is instructing Timothy to be wise about the kinds of people who are allowed to take on these responsibilities.

Paul lists eight characteristics for deacons, many of which overlap with the list for elders in 1 Timothy 3:2–7:

1) Worthy of respect (3:8). While this is not the same term used for the overseers, it still holds the idea of a person who is serious about what he does, and who carries himself honorably.

2) Not hypocritical (3:8). This is the idea of sincerity, though sometimes it is translated "double-tongued" (NASB) or "two-faced" (NET). It is not simply that their words match their actions, but even more, that their words are the same no matter the audience. They don't say one thing to please one set of ears, then change their story for another audience.
3) Not drinking too much wine (3:8). Sobriety would be necessary for someone of the character and responsibility described by Paul here.
4) Not greedy for money (3:8). It is not that a deacon shouldn't have money, but that he shouldn't be greedy for it, addicted to it, or always anxious for more of it.
5) Holding the mystery of the faith with a clear conscience (3:9). The mystery of the faith is simply the gospel. A deacon should be deeply rooted in the Christian faith and in the lifestyle that best acknowledges and shares that faith. While this should be true of any Christian, it is something that should be proven in the life of someone before they are named a deacon.
6) Blameless (3:10). The kind of testing mentioned here is not an official test that a person must pass to be a deacon. Rather, it is the test of a person who has been observed within the community and seen to model these traits.
7) Husband of one wife (3:12). Just as with the overseers (3:2), this requirement doesn't mean that a deacon *must* be married. Instead, it speaks to his faithful character within his relationships.
8) Managing children and their households competently (3:12). Again, this is not to say that a deacon *must* have children, but that the way he manages his home and his family relationships must be taken into account in determining his ability to lead within the church.

Demystifying 1 Timothy

In the midst of the characteristics for deacons, Paul inserts a short list of four qualities for wives (3:11). Actually the word translated as "wives" could also simply mean "women." Since Paul does not include a list of requirements for elders' wives, this list may have applied to female deacons.

1) **Worthy of respect.** These are serious women. The word Paul uses here is the same that is used for the men.
2) **Not slanderers.** They should not be prone to gossip.
3) **Self-controlled.** These women should be moderate in their lifestyle, just as the overseers should be.
4) **Faithful in everything.** This characteristic is particularly important in a servant role. Dependability in the little things would make all the difference to those whom these women serve.

Though the role of deacon is servant-oriented, Paul makes it clear in verse 13 that God honors the contribution of the deacons.

3:14–16

INSTRUCTIONS FOR THE CONGREGATION

Paul has plans to visit Ephesus in the near future, but gives instructions for the believers' conduct in case his trip is delayed. God's household is the church, though this doesn't refer to a church building but to the Christians who collectively make up the body of Christ. Paul's description of the church as the pillar and support of truth carries the idea of the church as the custodian of God's truth (3:14–15).

Verse 16 contains what is probably a part of an early hymn or confession of the church. Though made up of three couplets, each phrase reveals a part of the mystery of the gospel. This mystery was revealed in Jesus' life, work, and sacrifice:

1) Revealed in a body
2) Justified in the Spirit
3) Seen by angels
4) Preached among the Gentiles
5) Believed on in the world
6) Taken up in glory

While there are differing ideas among commentators as to what each line of the hymn or confession refers to, it is agreed that this first-century writing walks through the life of Christ from His incarnation in Bethlehem to His ascension back into heaven. By including this confession of faith in his letter to Timothy, Paul offers him and his congregation a wonderful tool to moor them to the truth of the gospel in the midst of the false truths they were facing.

1 TIMOTHY 4:1–16

THE LOCAL CHURCH

The Problem of Fallen Faith 4:1–5
Timothy, the Teacher 4:6–16

Setting Up the Section

Chapter 4 picks up right where the last chapter leaves off. Paul takes the logical next step from the responsibility and role of the church to the obstacles that prevent this fellowship from being all that God had called it to be. This section includes both warnings against false teachers and instructions for Timothy in his leadership role.

4:1–5

THE PROBLEM OF FALLEN FAITH

Paul anticipated a future apostasy, a time of people falling away from their faith (4:1; 2 Timothy 3:1). Though he does not list the specific ways the Spirit gave warning of this event, a number of sayings by Jesus and the apostles could be cited (for example Mark 13:22).

The later times Paul makes reference to are the centuries between Christ's resurrection and His eventual return to set up His kingdom (4:1).

Paul clearly attributes this falling away to the work of Satan and his armies, rather than teachers who simply misunderstand the truth. In verse 2, he identifies the teachers as hypocritical liars characterized by a seared conscience. This is the image of a conscience that is deadened to feeling. They no longer sense the spirit or the voice of God.

The false teachers wrongly believed that certain appetites of the body—sexual and even dietary—were evil. Paul counters that God created both appetites to be sated with thanksgiving when they are received prayerfully and practiced biblically (1 Corinthians 10:26; 1 Timothy 4:3–5). The conclusion these troublesome teachers reach—that the physical world is inherently evil, and the more one denies him- or herself, the more spiritual he or she will be—seems to have a semblance of the truth, but is actually a perversion of the reality of the kingdom.

Paul says that nothing God created is to be rejected (4:4). The word translated "rejected" means to be "thrown away," or "regarded as forbidden." Certainly there are some things that should be abstained from, because such things have proved themselves harmful. There is even more of a case for not abusing or overusing God's gifts—being a glutton with food, for instance. These moderations, though, were not the point of the false teachers. Instead, they were calling shameful what God calls good gifts.

Verse 5 declares all these gifts of God to be sanctified by God. Paul's use of the phrase "word of God" is probably a reference to the Creation, when God called all that He created good. If God created the gifts of marriage and food as good things, then our best response is gratitude, not a sanctimonious abstinence that we imagine makes us more spiritual because of our restraint.

4:6–16

TIMOTHY, THE TEACHER

One often thinks of spiritual leaders as those who teach what *not* to do, but here Paul tells Timothy that he should point out the truths of this epistle, and specifically the admonition he has just given (4:1–5)—that God's gifts are good and are to be enjoyed by His children. In doing this, Timothy will nourish himself as well as his congregation on the gospel of Jesus (truths of the faith) and Paul's good teaching.

Paul refers to the false teaching that Timothy must refute as myths and wives' tales (1:4; 4:7). He then gives Timothy the admonition that captures the message of this entire letter: training for godliness. This training is highlighted by a contrast between physical and spiritual training (4:8). Physical training yields temporary benefits, and the spiritual training yields eternal benefits. The function of this word picture is to not only contrast spiritual and physical training, but also the silliness of the false teaching versus the seriousness with which Timothy should take his own spiritual development.

The trustworthy saying in 4:9 (see also 1:15; 3:1; 2 Timothy 2:11; Titus 3:8) may refer back to verse 8, which functions more as a proverb in this context. The contemporary structure of scripture with verse and chapter breaks was not part of Paul's original letter. In this case, he may well have simply reversed the order of his pet phrase for highlighting an important truth.

The hard work described at the opening of verse 10 refers to the daily spiritual exercise required of training in godliness, but notice that the Christian's hope is not in that struggle but in the living God. This is a theme throughout this letter as Paul sets straight the false hope of the teachers who would have the Ephesian Christians believe that they can trust in their own struggle to make themselves holy.

The living God (3:15; 4:10) is worthy of the Christian's hope because He is Savior of all. Salvation is available to everyone because Jesus was a ransom for all (2:6). However, it is obvious that although God is the potential Savior of everyone and desires for everyone to be saved (2:4), only some will exercise the saving faith necessary to experience God as Savior. This is why Paul adds, "especially of those who believe."

Critical Observation

Paul's insistence on salvation being available to all is yet another strike at the false teachers in Ephesus. The spirituality that they proposed had an elitist quality to it, a special knowledge. But Paul reminds Timothy that our hope is in God, who offers His hope to all, not based on rules, but based on the work of Christ.

Verse 11 begins an even more direct instruction from Paul to his protégé. Paul tells Timothy to command, a concept that presupposed authority. This has led many to think that perhaps Timothy was not as outspoken as Paul and needed a reminder that he must take a stand as he leads the Ephesian church into the truths Paul has written.

While Paul does refer to Timothy's youth (4:12), that may communicate a different concept than it would today. Some suppose that Timothy could have been as old as forty when he was leading this congregation. By setting an example in speech, conduct, love, faith, and purity, Timothy will earn any credibility he may lack due to his age. Notice that the first two (speech and conduct) pertain to Timothy's external example, while the last three (love, faith, and purity) have more to do with his internal attitudes that will bear themselves out in his behavior.

From the opening of verse 13, it is obvious that Paul had plans to visit Ephesus and see Timothy's ministry firsthand. Since the scriptures were not reprinted and bound en masse in the first century as they are now, part of Timothy's ministry was the public reading of scripture. Beyond reading the actual text, he also taught doctrine and exhorted his listeners to not only hear and understand what they heard, but act on it as well.

The gift that Timothy received through a prophetic message and the custom of the elders laying their hands on him (1:18; 4:14) probably pertains to his ability, as well as his opportunity, to teach the Word of God.

Timothy was to give attention to, not neglect, this part of his ministry. Paul promises that God will use Timothy's perseverance in sound doctrine to save him, and Timothy's proclamation of that doctrine to save those who hear the message (4:15–16).

1 TIMOTHY 5:1–6:2

INSTRUCTIONS FOR SPECIFIC GROUPS

Relationships in the Community	5:1–2
Widows	5:3–16
Elders	5:17–25
Slaves	6:1–2

Setting Up the Section

The rest of Paul's first letter to Timothy includes very specific instructions for dealing with a variety of groups within the church. Using his gift of exhortation in varying contexts, Timothy was to exhort older men respectfully as fathers, younger men relationally as brothers, older women tenderly as mothers, and younger women with dignity as sisters. The majority of these instructions relate to widows and the church's care for them.

5:1–2

RELATIONSHIPS IN THE COMMUNITY

Verses 1 and 2 serve as a transition between Paul's guidance in the previous chapter regarding Timothy's leadership and the specific instructions that follow regarding widows, elders, and slaves. Since Paul had already framed the church as a household, it makes sense that he would offer guiding principles within the parameters of family relationships.

Critical Observation

The purity that Paul emphasizes in verse 2 involves respect and protectiveness. It is the same quality mentioned in 4:12. There is evidence in Paul's second letter to Timothy that some sexual impropriety may have been taking place in the Ephesian church (2 Timothy 3:6–7). If so, Paul could be offering these guidelines to protect the church and its leaders from these kinds of dangers.

5:3–16

WIDOWS

Considering the historical context of the first century—the low status of women, the importance of the husband in the family inheritance, the obstacles for widows to make money—a widow was often unable to support herself. If a widow had no family to support her, Paul suggests that the church should fill in the gap. On the other hand, if the widow had children or extended family, then the family should carry the primary responsibility. When Paul mentions that a widow's family's caring for her pleases God, he is referring to the fifth of the Ten Commandments (Exodus 20:12; Deuteronomy 5:16), which commands us to honor our father and mother (5:3–4).

To clarify which widows are truly in need of the church's support, Paul offers these parameters—the widow that is left entirely alone, yet continues to live out her faith (5:5). His reference to the widow who seeks pleasure may refer to widows who resort to prostitution to support themselves (5:6).

In the general culture of this day, even outside of the Christian community, there was an acceptance that children were to shoulder the burden of caring for their parents. Paul's exhortation here protects the church community from the shame of being less responsible for its own than the pagan worshipers around them (5:7–8). Those who deny assistance to their aging parents and grandparents are disgraceful not only to their families, but also to their faith.

To prevent women from taking advantage of the church, Paul requires widows to be sixty years old and (formerly) the wife of one husband before including them on the official support list. They should also model good works, including child-rearing, hospitality, servanthood, and benevolence (5:9–10).

The requirement that they have had only one husband does not communicate that it is a shame for a widow to remarry. It may be simply a practical truth that a widow who had only one husband is less likely to have extended family support than a woman who has had two or more marriages (5:9).

The good works mentioned in verse 10 would not only have prepared the widow for service, they would have built her reputation. She is to be known for these good works.

It seems harsh that younger widows should be excluded from ongoing church assistance (5:11), but this refusal on Paul's part isn't based on a lack of mercy. It may be that the vows required of an older widow who is cared for by the church included a vow not to remarry, thus Paul's reference to their first, or former, pledge (5:12). By requiring younger widows to remain in circulation, these guidelines offer them another life with marriage and family.

The "sensual desires" (5:11 NIV), or "passions" (NET), are not necessarily evil, and perhaps could even be defined broadly enough to include the simple desire to have more children. But these passions were potential markers of a woman who was not ready for a life of chastity and celibacy. This woman is still in the process of building her life, thus entertains the possibility of remarriage and not merely serving the church. She may not be as single-minded as her older counterpart.

Paul also points out that assisting these women would allow them too much idle time for unhealthy gossip and socializing (5:13). The word picture he paints is one of destructive behavior both for the women involved and for the community of faith. This is not due to their age or their gender, but to the free time that entices almost anyone to fall into unhealthy behavior patterns. Instead, younger women should fill their lives with children and homes to manage. This will allow them to avoid the excessive idle time that the enemy could leverage (5:14). This seems an obvious reference to Satan, but may also refer to those who would tear down the burgeoning Christian church.

The reference to those who had already turned toward Satan (5:15) may not mean a complete departure from the church so much as someone who had entered into the behaviors that Paul describes in the previous verses: sensual desires, idleness, gossip, and so on.

Critical Observation

There has been some discussion about whether this list that Paul refers to was a kind of order of service that widows joined (5:9). Certainly this would shed some light on the judgment that would fall on a younger woman who backed out of a pledge of service to the church in favor of remarriage (5:11–12). Unfortunately, we don't have enough information to know the details for sure.

In short, the plan Paul presents for the church is that the Christian families take care of any widows in their extended family. Then those widows who have no one will be cared for by the church (5:16). Paul has sometimes been regarded as a person who has a limited view of the roles of women, but in light of this specific situation in Ephesus, he provides a generous amount of information dealing with the care of women in the church.

5:17–25

ELDERS

In contemporary churches, the term *elder* has become specifically defined to certain leadership roles and functions. Keep in mind that at the time Paul wrote to Timothy, these roles were not so fully defined. All of the older men were to be revered. Even more reverence was offered for those who rose in leadership.

When Paul instructs Timothy regarding honor for the elders, this likely means both respect and financial remuneration. In other words, he is to allocate an ample honorarium for those elders who distinguish themselves—particularly in the area of preaching and teaching. The phrase "double honor" (NIV) is not a reference to twice the money, but to the double honor of respect as well as financial compensation (5:17).

To justify such remuneration, Paul quotes two scriptures (5:18). Deuteronomy 25:4 teaches the principle that the laborer should not be denied compensation for his effort. It draws from the illustration of an ox that is harnessed to a large millstone. The animal walks around in a circle accomplishing two things: (1) He is trampling the grain, separating the kernels, and (2) he is turning the mill stone that makes the flour. This animal should be allowed to eat from the grain it is threshing, rather than be muzzled so that it offers work but receives nothing in return. In the same way, those that work in the church should receive payment for their efforts.

The second citation is a direct quote from Jesus' teaching in Luke 10:7 (also Matthew 10:10): "The worker deserves his pay" (NET). The New Testament scriptures as we know them today were still in process when Paul was writing this. Paul may have encountered this teaching of Jesus in written form or oral history still being passed around among Christian communities.

Paul writes that an accusation against an elder is to be verified (5:19). This demand for two to three witnesses reflects the Jewish law. In the Old Testament, two to three witnesses were offered before a person was required to answer a charge (Deuteronomy 17:6; 19:15).

If the accusation stands, then the elder should be rebuked (5:19–20). This rebuke might take place before the whole congregation, but it also could be referred to as a public rebuke even if it took place simply before the other elders. Either way, Paul charges Timothy with the responsibility for taking seriously the doctrine of the church and the leadership of the church.

Demystifying 1 Timothy

It is entirely possible that the false teachers referred to in this letter were elders that fell from the faith. Considering this possibility sheds new light on Paul's words to Timothy regarding elders and regarding the amount of corroboration required to discipline these older men when they faced these kinds of allegations.

Paul's charge in verse 21 is made in the sight of God, Christ Jesus, and the angels. All three included in this short list are attributed with the role of judgment in the Bible (Matthew 25:31–46; 2 Peter 2:4; Revelation 20:1). The "elect angels" probably refers to those angels who did not fall with Satan. The fact that Paul specifically frames his request this way, regarding Timothy not playing favorites, communicates how serious the request was.

Also, Timothy should refrain from appointing leaders hastily. The laying on of the hands (5:22) was often a ritual that went with appointment to office. (Some churches today still include this kind of ritual when they ordain deacons and other church leaders.) Paul had already given some guidelines in choosing leadership in 3:1–13. If Timothy followed these guidelines carefully, these preventive measures could keep him from having to later be forced into a situation where he must avail himself of Paul's advice regarding elders who must be rebuked.

Timothy is also warned about appointing or accommodating sinning leaders. This may relate back to the teaching in 3:6 about not inviting a novice too quickly into leadership. If Timothy allowed someone into leadership who was then revealed to be unfit, then Timothy had a role to play in that person being given authority he was not ready to use righteously.

Paul's words here to Timothy to keep himself pure (5:22) seem to imply that once a leader has been appointed, those who appointed him are partially responsible for how well he carries out the responsibilities of his office. This may or may not have been the intent. Certainly, though, it was essential for Timothy to first keep himself pure so that he could then enable purity in the leadership of his church.

Critical Observation

Paul's concern for Timothy extends to his health, which could be improved with a little wine rather than the water of the day, which could often be contaminated. The fermentation process of wine made it cleaner to drink. While this directive to Timothy does appear abruptly, this kind of parenthetical phrase is often the way of a letter to a dear friend (5:23).

This is not a text that should be misinterpreted as open permission for the use of alcohol, nor does it prohibit its use. Paul has already warned that leaders shouldn't be given to drunkenness (3:3), but in the first century wine was a cultural reality.

While this verse should not be applied as a blanket statement on alcohol use or abuse, it does give us an insight into the everyday concerns of these men, much like our own, and the compassion on Paul's part for Timothy's well-being as a person as well as a spiritual leader.

Verses 24 and 25 pick up where verse 22 leaves off—choosing qualified leaders. The process is difficult, as 5:24–25 reveal, because everyone sins, though some are more conspicuous than others. The judgment Paul refers to can be applied either to the judgment of God or the judgment Timothy and the other church leaders must use when deciding who will serve the church in a leadership position.

Inherent in Paul's words is the idea that what appears on the surface of individuals may not reveal all you need to know in giving them responsibility—that's why it takes time to know people and to know whether they are suited for leadership. The good works of individuals may take time to see, just as their sins may take time to become obvious. This supports the advice Paul has already given Timothy not to choose leaders hastily.

6:1–2

SLAVES

Slaves—noncitizens who served Roman citizens—were common in the Roman Empire of the first century. Slavery in the Roman Empire, though certainly a degrading institution, was very different than slavery in the American South most readers are familiar with. It was not based on race. Many slaves were drawn from the ranks of prisoners of war. Others sold themselves into slavery for financial reasons. Working as a slave in a wealthy household was considered better than living in poverty and destitution. Slaves could achieve very high social status, even serving as managers of large estates. They were often paid and could even purchase their own freedom. Some owned slaves of their own. Imagine the complexity of masters and servants both being a part of the church at Ephesus. While in their households they operated from very different statuses, within the community of faith they were to be considered equal. In fact, a slave could be serving as a leader in a congregation, but his master may join the community as a new convert. In that scenario, the slave might have some leadership over the master, at least as far as the church family is concerned. It is not surprising then, that Paul offers insights regarding these relationships.

Paul often offers biblical counsel for Christian slaves (Ephesians 6:5–8; Colossians 3:22–24; Titus 2:9–10). He instructs these slaves to grant their masters full respect. The same word that is translated "respect" here (6:1) appears as the recognition given to widows (5:3) and the honor that should be given to elders (5:17).

Even if, within the faith community, a slave serves shoulder-to-shoulder with his master, within their working environment it would be the slave's responsibility to grant the respect due and the owner's responsibility to grant the mercy that comes with his position of authority (6:2).

You may notice that in some versions the closing phrase of verse 2 is pulled away from the text. In those versions, this phrase functions more as an introduction to the next section regarding false teachers. Whether it applies to the preceding section or the section to come, it certainly applies to all of Paul's instructions and is one of the themes of Paul's letters to Timothy.

Take It Home

The principles Paul offers to Timothy regarding church leaders are helpful today. It takes time to know the character of the people who serve. Too often we rely on similarities in speech or thought, similar pet peeves, or past experiences. But these characteristics are superficial and can be cultural. We must live and serve with someone for a time to truly understand his or her faith journey.

1 TIMOTHY 6:3–21

EXHORTATIONS

Heretics	6:3–10
The Faithful	6:11–16
The Rich	6:17–19
In Conclusion	6:20–21

Setting Up the Section

This final section of Paul's first letter to Timothy functions much as the closing to many letters. Rather than being a section all on one theme, it is a smattering of information: additional information on false teachers, teachings about wealth, personal notes, and a closing doxology.

6:3–10

HERETICS

The last sentence of verse 2 may pertain more to the following verses than to the specific instructions for slaves offered in verses 1 and 2. Either way, Paul certainly wants Timothy to teach his congregation all the truths included in this letter.

Paul describes the destructiveness of those who do not agree with sound doctrine and godly teaching. The word translated "agree" has the connotation of attachment. It's not that the false teachers simply disagreed with the truth; they were detached from the teachings *about* Jesus, and thus, the teachings of Jesus (6:3).

Regarding the instruction mentioned in verse 3, the word translated "sound" has the idea of health attached to it. The truth or doctrine about Jesus is life-giving truth. It is when that truth is twisted that it becomes destructive. The words "godly teaching" (NIV) refer to the practical instruction and application that is based on the sound doctrine. If the doctrine is in error, then the life lived will be in error.

Paul's description of these false teachers—arrogant, ignorant, craving conflict—paints the picture of someone very unlike what Paul has encouraged Timothy to be as a leader. In the Greek text, these words suggest someone who is almost diseased with his penchant for dispute and dissension (6:4–5).

The reference to material wealth may imply that the teachers charged high fees, or that they simply used ministry to acquire wealth (6:5). We aren't given enough background information here to know the particulars, but we can be sure that this attitude is different from that described by Paul of a godly leader in the church (3:3, 8). The clear word picture that is painted here of those with selfish motives who stir up dissension provides a powerful backdrop for Paul's next teaching on contentment (6:6–8).

In verse 6, instead of a means to financial gain, godliness leads to contentment. Paul uses the same words that he uses in verse 5, but with a twist. Instead of the material wealth on which the false teachers had focused their ministries, godliness brings its own kind of wealth (6:6).

Paul's proverb-like truth in verse 7 is a theme that also appears in Old Testament scriptures such as Job 1:21 and Ecclesiastes 5:15.

Take It Home

In 1 Timothy 6:8, Paul sets the most basic parameters of contentment: the essentials of food and clothing. This speaks to our contemporary cultural bent of wanting more and more and more. Throughout the Bible, this theme is expressed in a variety of ways. God gives us good gifts according to His will. Finding contentment in those gifts is a result of godly understanding.

According to Paul, those who pursue wealth (instead of godliness) will find themselves in a trap that leads to ruin and destruction. It is love of money (6:10), not money itself, that is the root of evil. Lusting after money, that element of greed, is the root. It results in wandering from the faith and in many self-inflicted pains. The idea here is a person impaled on something who continues to force himself against the object, thus increasing his injuries.

It seems apparent that Paul is not talking in theory about people falling away from the faith because of greed. There may have been those in the congregation at Ephesus with whom he or Timothy had firsthand experience (6:9–10).

Paul's warnings about the love of money should not be interpreted as the idea that Christians should disregard financial issues. It is more of a warning against greed than money management. Certainly there are plenty of New Testament scriptures that encourage good money management.

6:11–16

THE FAITHFUL

Typical of Paul's use of contrasts, he instructs Timothy to both flee and to pursue certain things (6:11; 2 Timothy 2:22).

The exhortation to flee probably applies to more than simply the immediately preceding verses on financial greed. It probably refers back to all the issues listed since verse 3 of this chapter.

The list of pursuits is similar to Paul's list of the fruit of the Spirit in his letter to the Galatians (Galatians 5:22–23), and his list of qualifications for church elders earlier in this letter (3:1–3). The list here in 6:11 is not intended to be an exhaustive list, but gives examples:

- Righteousness and godliness. This use of righteousness does not refer to the righteousness that God gives us by faith, but to the righteousness that we offer back through our obedience. Godliness adds to the right actions the right motives, not simply doing the right actions, but desiring to be made like God.
- Faith and love. In Paul's writings, these two can almost stand alone as the prerequisite to all the rest. They involve the ability both to trust someone with your heart and to offer your heart back to him or her.

- Endurance and gentleness. This is the ability to persevere through difficulty and touch with a light hand. From what we know from Paul's letters, Timothy already appears to be somewhat timid. This mention of gentleness may be an affirmation of what Timothy already is.

The word translated "fight" (6:12) has military connotations, but also conveys the image of a contest, perhaps like the Olympics. It carries the idea of an ongoing struggle to win the prize—in this case, eternal life. This third reference to Timothy's good confession may refer to commissioning for ministry, but it also may refer to his baptism in the faith (1:18; 4:14).

Timothy's confession reminds Paul of Jesus' confession before Pontius Pilate. It was before Pilate that Jesus confessed Himself as the Christ (Matthew 27:11). It was before witnesses that Timothy confessed Jesus as the Christ.

Demystifying 1 Timothy

Pontius Pilate was the Roman appointed prefect of Judea (AD 26–36). After examining Jesus both publicly and privately, he reluctantly had Jesus flogged and ultimately crucified. His full name only occurs in the writings of Luke and Paul (Luke 3:1; Acts 4:27; 1 Timothy 6:13).

Paul now cites God and Jesus as the witnesses to his exhortation to Timothy to keep his command. "Command" (6:14 NIV) here is in the singular to include all of Paul's instructions collectively (see also 1 Corinthians 14:37), perhaps including Paul's whole history all the way back to Timothy's commission at his baptism. And Timothy is to keep this command flawlessly until Christ appears, a reference to Jesus' eventual return (6:14). While in some New Testament writings (even Paul's earlier writings) Jesus' return is spoken of in more immediate terms, this particular language is a reference to the distant future. At this writing, Paul is nearing the end of his life and perhaps is acknowledging that he may die before Jesus returns.

Verses 15 and 16 may be part of a first-century Christian hymn or faith confession. It has a Jewish flavor in its style and may be reminiscent of the worship in the Jewish synagogues or local teaching centers. Paul's lofty description of God paints the picture of an authority with whom there is no peer in sight (6:15). He is the immortal, thus eternal. His unapproachable light is His glory through which we cannot see Him, though certainly we can come to know Him. God is not unapproachable—the life and work of Jesus made that point—but God's glory and essence are unapproachable for humanity. He is worthy of honor and the recognition of His power (6:16).

6:17–19

THE RICH

Paul now picks back up on his discussion on wealth from verses 6–10. This is typical for Paul's writing, inserting almost a parenthetical topic in the midst of another. In this case, he inserts an exhortation to Timothy in the midst of an ongoing topic of material goods. This second installment of the discussion on wealth focuses not on those who hope to get wealth (as did 6:3–10), but on those who already have it. Since an underlying theme throughout this letter has been the false teachers, it may be that they were wealthy men and this last word from Paul relates to them.

Those who are rich must fix their hope on God (4:10; 5:5) rather than wealth, which is uncertain. Notice that Paul's words do not make a judgment simply on those who are wealthy. Instead he gives guidelines for rich people to maintain God's perspective on life. They are not to be arrogant because they have wealth, nor are they to depend on their wealth to keep them safe (6:17).

Critical Observation

Paul's statement that God has given all things for us to enjoy is an important one (6:17). Asceticism purported that the more spiritual a person was, the more pleasures of life he or she would abstain from. But with the idea that God gives us all things to enjoy, the spiritual path would also be marked by receiving those gifts and even taking pleasure in them, but within God's will.

Instead the wealthy are to match their amount of wealth with their amount of good deeds. Also, they are to be generous, ready to give at all times. And finally, their attitude must be one of willingness to share what they have (6:18). Each of these things requires a denial of self. It is only natural instinct for a person who has much to protect what he or she has. Yet Paul writes that those who have must maintain their dependence on God and share their resources.

Verse 19 is reminiscent of Jesus' Sermon on the Mount about laying up treasures in heaven rather than merely storing up wealth on earth (Matthew 6:19–21). It is in this way that we live real life. Again, Paul's teaching is reminiscent of Jesus' own words; He came to provide the fullest life to humanity (John 10:10).

6:20–21

IN CONCLUSION

Paul closes both of his letters to Timothy with the similar instructions about guarding his ministry. When Paul writes of what has been entrusted to Timothy's care, the idea is almost like a deposit made into a bank. It is deposited there in order to be kept safe and to sometimes even earn interest. In the same way, Timothy's ministry in Ephesus was given to his care. He is to keep it safe and to allow it to return on the investment.

This idea of avoiding false knowledge and empty chatter is Paul's last blow to the false teachers plaguing the Ephesian congregation (6:20; 2 Timothy 1:14; 2:16). Paul is probably referring to the early Gnostics here. This was an esoteric movement, not full-blown until the second century. They believed themselves to be protectors of secret knowledge. But whether Paul was specifically referring to that particular burgeoning movement or not, these false teachers clearly claimed some sort of special insight that set them apart from the mainstream church. The same is true of cults and false religious movements today.

Paul mentions those who wandered from the faith because of these false teachers (6:21). The word translated "wandered" (NIV) carries the idea of someone who misses the mark. It is not the idea of someone who has left the faith never to return, but rather someone who gets sidetracked and detours, missing the point of the truth.

Paul leaves Timothy with the same closing greeting in both of his letters: "Grace be with you" (6:21; 2 Timothy 4:22). The *you* in this case is plural. Since the expectation was that this letter would be read to the congregation and even shared among congregations, Paul's farewell reflects that reality.

Take It Home

Paul's first-century letter to Timothy about the matters of the community of faith has much to offer us today. Discerning between the truth and the almost-truth is essential to the life of the church. Choosing leaders who have something to offer and can sustain that investment is something we still strive for. Understanding the balance between having good gifts from God to enjoy and using those gifts to invest in His kingdom is a balance we struggle to maintain. May we read Paul's words and all aspire to live the life that is truly life (6:19), being faithful in our doctrine and our behavior. Paul's first letter to Timothy reminds us how to do so.

2 TIMOTHY

INTRODUCTION TO 2 TIMOTHY

AUTHOR

Of all the letters of Paul, the Pastoral Epistles (1 Timothy, 2 Timothy, and Titus) are by far the most disputed in terms of authorship. Differences of language, style, and theology have caused many scholars to doubt that Paul was the original author. Some believe that a disciple of Paul wrote these after his death. Others think he may also have used one of his missionary companions to write out these letters (see Romans 16:22 for an example of this), and this scribe left his own stylistic mark. In any case, the differences are not as great as is sometimes supposed, and there are many features of the letter consistent with Paul's language and style. Evangelical scholars continue to assert that these letters came from the apostle's hand.

PURPOSE

Paul wrote this letter to Timothy, someone who came to faith through Paul's ministry, then worked as a colleague, and finally took on a leadership role at the church in Ephesus. The instructions in this letter serve to give Timothy guidance in leading the church, which included battling with false teachers.

OCCASION

When Paul wrote this letter, he was in prison in Rome and had been deserted by most of his colleagues. He was also aware that his life was reaching its end and may have had some sense of passing the torch of leadership on.

Timothy was in Ephesus, troubled by corrupted doctrine that was affecting his congregation. Paul reached out to Timothy through this letter to offer guidance and to connect and communicate as old friends will do.

THEMES

The themes of 2 Timothy center on the need for boldness in leadership and the need for faithfulness in the Christian walk. Additional themes are instruction in church leadership and how to identify false doctrine and do away with the needless controversy it creates.

CONTRIBUTION TO THE BIBLE

Along with 1 Timothy and Titus, 2 Timothy offers a real-life look at the church, its conflicts, and its leadership in the first century. It offers some key insights regarding scripture itself (3:16–17).

OUTLINE

GREETINGS AND SALUTATIONS	**1:1–18**
The Gospel Is Worthy of Confidence	1:1–7
The Gospel Is Worthy of Proclamation	1:8–12
The Gospel Is Worthy of Protection	1:13–18
PERSEVERANCE	**2:1–26**
The Gospel Is Worthy of Hardships Endured	2:1–13
The Gospel Is Worthy of Faithfulness	2:14–26
THE LAST DAYS	**3:1–17**
The Gospel Is Worthy of Acknowledgement	3:1–9
The Gospel Is Worthy of Standing Against Opposition	3:10–17
IN CONCLUSION	**4:1–22**
The Gospel Is Worthy of Endurance	4:1–8
The Gospel Is Worthy of Participation	4:9–22

2 TIMOTHY 1:1–18

GREETINGS AND SALUTATIONS

The Gospel Is Worthy of Confidence	1:1–7
The Gospel Is Worthy of Proclamation	1:8–12
The Gospel Is Worthy of Protection	1:13–18

Setting Up the Section

Paul opens this letter, as he does many of his other letters, with a salutation and personal greetings. This letter is a peek not only into first-century Christianity, but a personal window into the relationships that made up the church—both those that involved valued solidarity and those that involved obstacles and conflicts.

1:1–7

THE GOSPEL IS WORTHY OF CONFIDENCE

The author identifies himself as the apostle Paul (1:1). *Apostle* means "one who is sent." This is a title of authority. While all Christians are called to serve God, the first-century use of this term referred to a very specific group—those who had accompanied Jesus. While Paul had not been one of the twelve disciples, his conversion experience brought him face-to-face with Jesus (Acts 9:1–9).

The fact that Paul notes he is an apostle *by God's will* means he is responding to a call rather than simply choosing a vocation of his own volition. This reality gives authority to his words and a greater responsibility on the part of his readers to listen and apply his instructions.

The affectionate title, "dearly loved child" (1:2 HCSB), not only conveys Paul's instrumental influence in Timothy's spiritual life but also affords Timothy credibility in the Ephesian church, where he was probably still serving the Lord (1 Timothy 1:3). Certainly it communicates the depth of the relationship between Paul and his protégé.

The threefold greeting of "grace, mercy, and peace" is unique to Paul's two letters to Timothy (1:2). Grace and peace are included in many of Paul's greetings, but here the word *mercy* is added.

In this thanksgiving section of his letter, Paul's mentions his ancestors. This may be in part a foreshadowing of the words he will write in the next few verses about Timothy's family, but it also serves to build a bridge between Paul's past experience in Judaism and his current faith in Jesus (1:3). Paul had certainly served God with as much zeal as a Jewish Pharisee as he did as a Christian missionary. Believing in Jesus did not cause him to reject his religious roots. While his strategy certainly changed with his understanding, it was all connected; he served the same God.

His mention of a clear conscience communicates a sense of no regrets (1:3; Romans 1:9). Someone who didn't understand the grace of God as Paul did could have become mired in the reality that he or she had once vehemently worked against the faith he or she now evangelized. But Paul's clear conscience was that he had served God wholeheartedly at each point in his understanding.

Paul's mention of Timothy's tears (1:4) is probably a reference to the last time they were together—possibly when Paul was taken to prison in Rome. While this may seem an out-of-place reference considering the Western culture in which men are often pressured against expressing strong sentimental emotion, the first-century Judean culture held a different bias.

Paul's longing to see his son in the faith is a portal allowing us to see some of Paul's own loneliness in prison. As he will reveal later in this letter, he has been abandoned by most of his colleagues (1:15; 4:10, 16).

Paul's next words affirm Timothy's faith and the source of his early Christian teaching—his grandmother Lois and mother Eunice (1:5).

Demystifying 2 Timothy

Paul and Barnabas visited Timothy's hometown of Lystra (in Galatia) on their first missionary journey. It is likely where Paul first met Timothy and his family. When Paul visited Lystra again on his second missionary journey, he was so impressed with Timothy's faith that he took him along as a missionary companion. Timothy was one of his closest and most trusted associates from that point onward.

Timothy was the child of a mixed marriage. His mother was Jewish, and his father was a Greek (Acts 16:1). When Paul says that Timothy's faith "first lived in" his grandmother Lois and his mother Eunice (1:5), he may be referring to their Jewish faith, which gave Timothy a solid foundation for receiving the message about Jesus, the Jewish Messiah. Or it may mean that Lois and Eunice first believed Paul's gospel, and then passed that faith on to Timothy. (Acts 16:1 refers to Timothy's mother as "a Jewish woman who was a believer," meaning she was a Jewish Christian.) In either case, Timothy had a solid religious upbringing that centered on God's Word.

Paul calls Timothy's faith sincere; in other words, not hypocritical (1 Timothy 1:5; 2 Timothy 1:5). This kind of sincere faith would have stood in great contrast to those who had not stood by Paul in his most difficult days (1:15; 4:10, 16).

Finally, Paul reminds Timothy of what God has done in his life. The gift of God that Timothy is to keep ablaze is not specified, though it is more than simply his natural gifts and abilities (1 Timothy 4:14; 2 Timothy 1:6). This gift is related to the ministry and calling of the Holy Spirit in Timothy's life.

In encouraging Timothy to *fan the flame*, Paul is not indicating that Timothy had fallen from the faith and needed restoring. Instead, he is affirming something Timothy has already received and is using. It was Timothy's responsibility to be a steward of that gift, to keep it blazing.

Paul's use of the word *spirit* in verse 7 (spirit of timidity. . .spirit of power) probably does not mean the Holy Spirit. Instead, it refers to a gift God's Spirit offers those in whom He dwells. The Holy Spirit inside of Timothy enables Timothy to live with a spirit of power and love and the absence of fear. Taking verses 6 and 7 together, this may be Paul's way of encouraging Timothy to move beyond his own timidity and lead in a bolder fashion.

1:8–12

THE GOSPEL IS WORTHY OF PROCLAMATION

Three times in this chapter Paul warns Timothy against being ashamed—all in the context of suffering or persecution (1:8, 12, 16). These warnings do not mean that Paul felt that Timothy was already ashamed. Instead they are meant to have more of a bolstering effect.

Paul also invites Timothy to join his suffering (1:8; 2:3). In Paul's thinking, when a believer is not ashamed, he proclaims the gospel, resulting in suffering and persecution (3:12). This kind of suffering—that which proceeds from sharing the gospel—is the "holy life" (1:9 NIV) God has called us to live. Paul often reminds his readers that it is the gospel, not good works, that saves the believer. His reference to God's purpose highlights the sovereignty and intentionality of God.

Because of God's grace, which is available in Jesus, Christians anticipate the eternal life that the gospel promises rather than fearing death (1:9). The word translated "appearing" in verse 10 is the noun form of the verb used in 1 Timothy 3:16, which says that Christ "appeared in a body" (NIV). It's also the term Paul uses to refer to the return of Jesus, or His appearing. The gospel of Jesus, in its entirety, brings all these things to light.

Critical Observation

Some translations set 2 Timothy 1:9–10 apart as a poetic chorus, perhaps an early Christian confession. The truths included here fit so well within Paul's text, though, that some have concluded that even if it is a part of hymn text, Paul may have written the hymn or confession himself.

In the face of his own persecution, Paul embraced his role as a spokesperson for the message of grace, the gospel, and he denies being ashamed of it (1 Timothy 2:7; 2 Timothy 1:11–12). The basis of Paul's boldness, however, is not personality or even character—it is God Himself. Paul's relationship with God, in whom he believes, is the key to his ability to stand in the middle of difficult circumstances without being destroyed by them.

Paul's mention of that which he has committed or entrusted to God (1:12) is actually a financial concept, like a deposit at a bank. It paints the picture of someone giving his or her valuables to a friend to hold in safekeeping.

The language at the end of verse 12 has been interpreted in different ways. Either God is able to guard what He has entrusted to Paul (the gospel), or God is able to guard what Paul has entrusted to God. In either case, God is able to do what needs to be done in both the spread of the gospel and in the lives of those who spread it. The day Paul refers to at the end of verse 12 is the second coming of Jesus.

1:13–18

THE GOSPEL IS WORTHY OF PROTECTION

Verse 13 opens with Paul's reference to what Timothy has heard from him. That would encompass all of the teaching shared between this mentor and his protégé, not simply what has been written in this particular letter thus far.

Aware that the threat of persecution may entice fearful Timothy to compromise his message, Paul writes that he should hold on to the "pattern of sound teaching" (NIV). In 1 Timothy 1:16, the same Greek word that is translated "pattern" here, is translated "example." Both concepts work.

The word that is here translated "sound" can also mean "healthy," as in "sound mind," "sound judgment," and "sound investment."

The "deposit" (NIV) that Timothy is charged with protecting in verse 14 is a concept that comes from the same word translated in verse 12 as what has been entrusted to God. In verse 12, though, God is keeping the deposit safe. In verse 14, Timothy is placed in charge of that duty with the help of the Holy Spirit.

As Paul closes out this section of his letter, he galvanizes his warning to Timothy by naming individuals who used to follow Christ but have turned aside along with those in Asia, presumably due to persecution (1:15). We don't have any further information about this incident in Asia or about Phygelus and Hermogenes, but we are safe to assume that Timothy knew the situation. From this text it seems obvious that these men were ringleaders in opposition against Paul.

In contrast to Phygelus and Hermogenes, Onesiphorus is mentioned as a positive example for Timothy. While Onesiphorus is mentioned only here in the Bible, other historical literature refers to him as one of Paul's converts. He was unaffected by any stigma attached to Paul's imprisonment or fear of the consequences that associating with Paul might bring (1:8, 12). He ministered to Paul in Rome and Ephesus (1:17–18). Since only his household is mentioned here and in 4:19, many conclude that Onesiphorus may have already died for his faith.

Demystifying 2 Timothy

If Onesiphorus was already martyred, why did Paul pray for him? This passage is not a proof text for praying for those who are already dead. Paul's reference to "that day" (1:18) is to the final judgment before Christ that everyone—those living and dead—will face. The focus of Paul's statement is on Onesiphorus's behavior while he was living. In light of the way Onesiphorus has lived his life, Paul hopes for mercy to come to his family and mercy to come to him at the final judgment.

In verse 17 Paul refers to Onesiphorus's efforts in searching for him in Rome. The difficult search may have had to do with the lack of support offered by others whom Paul has mentioned. Perhaps they were afraid to offer any information that would associate them with Paul, thus Onesiphorus couldn't get enough information. Or it may have simply been that navigating the Roman penal system was a difficulty (1:17).

Take It Home

Paul and Timothy's journey in faith is one of intertwining relationships and interpersonal investment. Their stories and all the players in them—Lois, Eunice, Phygelus, Hermogenes, Onesiphorus—remind us of the power of community in faith. The support that we offer each other, or fail to offer, has ramifications beyond each individual situation. That's because we are a body—in fact, the body of Christ. How we live and move together sends a message to the world around us.

2 TIMOTHY 2:1–26

PERSEVERANCE

The Gospel Is Worthy of Hardships Endured	2:1–13
The Gospel Is Worthy of Faithfulness	2:14–26

Setting Up the Section

Rather than focus on the doctrines that have been tainted by false teachings, which is a topic that makes up much of the Pastoral Letters, chapter 2 opens with a warm exhortation from Paul to Timothy regarding Christian service.

2:1–13

THE GOSPEL IS WORTHY OF HARDSHIPS ENDURED

At the close of chapter 1, Paul urges Timothy to follow the example of Onesiphorus's faithfulness. The use of "therefore" (NASB), or "so" (NET), suggests that these next thoughts from Paul are a continuation from the previous section (2:1).

Paul's encouragement for Timothy to be strong is not simply an exhortation for Timothy to gather his own self-will and bravado. The fact that Timothy is to be strong in *the grace of Jesus* tempers self-will with the enabling of the indwelling Spirit. Timothy's strength will find its source in grace.

Paul had entrusted the message to Timothy (1:14) and now commands Timothy to entrust it to others who would faithfully protect and proclaim it. The witnesses Paul mentions (2:2) could refer to the elders at Timothy's ordination and baptism (1 Timothy 4:14), but in this case it more likely refers to all those who had heard Paul's teaching along with Timothy. Rather than one specific truth, it encompasses all of the truth that Timothy has been exposed to under Paul's teaching. It is the full scope of that truth that Timothy is now bound to release to listening ears and hearts.

Paul's use of the word *entrust* (2:2) places Timothy in the role of a guardian over this message of the gospel. This is part of Timothy's discipleship under Paul. While some have perceived this particular statement of Paul's to be a kind of apostolic succession (one apostle conferring his special position to someone else), a more likely description is one mentor's encouragement that his disciple go and do something with all he has been taught.

Critical Observation

Paul employs three metaphors for the Christian life (soldier, athlete, and farmer) to help Timothy understand and apply his responsibilities:

- The soldier. Suffering is as common to the Christian as it is to the soldier. In order to please a commanding officer, both the soldier and the Christian will abandon the conveniences of civilian life for the sake of a higher calling. They will endure (2:3–4).
- The athlete. By breaking the rules, a Christian can disqualify himself for effective ministry—thus leaving his contest incomplete—like an athlete can disqualify himself from a race (2:5).
- The farmer. Finally, the hard work of faithfulness to Christ will be rewarded just as the hard work of the farmer is rewarded in the harvest (2:6).

Each of these metaphors is worthy of reflection on its own merit as Paul suggests (2:7), but together they also point to a common truth–the importance of enduring to the end.

In verse 8, Paul defines the gospel by highlighting Jesus' resurrection (He is Lord) and lineage (He is King). These two descriptions also highlight both Jesus' deity (by His resurrection) and His humanity (by His lineage). This may have been an indirect hit from Paul to the false teachers who were troubling Timothy's church. While there is much we do not know about the specific heresies being bandied about, it seems clear that they were based on a misunderstanding of who Jesus was.

The most important message of verses 8 and 9 is not the reference to Paul's imprisonment, but to the fact that God's message cannot be hindered by the schemes or misfortunes of anyone.

Paul clarifies his own role in God's sovereign plan as an instrument to bring the elect to Christ and thus to eternal life (2:10). The "elect" here refers to those who had not yet placed their faith in Jesus.

Paul introduces his next thought with a reference to its trustworthiness (2:11). This kind of setup can also be found in 1 Timothy 1:15; 3:1; 4:9 and Titus 3:8. In some versions of the Bible, the verses that Paul introduces as trustworthy–verses 11–13–are set apart as a poetic chorus, perhaps a hymn of the day of an early Christian confession. It is made up of three couplets: The first contrasts death and life; the second contrasts endurance and rewards; the third highlights total commitment. As a whole, this poem communicates that God will reward both martyrdom and endurance. Although God's faithfulness supersedes our unfaithfulness, He will reject those who reject Him.

2:14–26

THE GOSPEL IS WORTHY OF FAITHFULNESS

Not only is Timothy to remember Paul's teaching (2:8), but he is also to remind others (2:14) of it. Fighting or debating over terminology is useless. The phrase "before God" (NIV) increases the seriousness of the warning.

Second Timothy 2:15 is a key verse. Some scholars have connected Paul's thoughts here to Jesus' parable of the talents (Matthew 25:14–28). The idea of the words *correctly handling*, regarding the word of truth, carries with it the idea of cutting straight. Instead of quarreling over terminology, the Christian should do his or her best to correctly teach God's Word. This carries more than the idea of being studious; here it's the idea of a person who has a great zeal for his or her ethical responsibilities.

The "godless chatter" (2:16 NIV) and the follow-up comparison to gangrene (2:17) is a direct hit on Paul's part against the heresies of the day. In the first century, gangrene was considered fatal, so Paul's use of it here paints an apt description of the spiritual malady of false doctrine (2:17).

Timothy probably knew Hymenaeus and Philetus, whom Paul names as examples of those who "wandered away from the truth" (2:18 NIV). According to 1 Timothy 1:20, Hymenaeus was excommunicated from the church because of his heresy. Knowing this makes the illustration of gangrene even more apropos. Often gangrenous limbs have to be amputated in order for the body to remain healthy.

Demystifying 2 Timothy

The specific nature of the resurrection that these two men misrepresented is unclear, though it was not regarding Jesus' resurrection (2:18). Perhaps they were teaching that the resurrection we are promised in Christ is a spiritual concept rather than an actual event to anticipate. This could have been a by-product of the melding of Christian concepts with the Greek philosophy that all physical things were innately evil. Therefore, a physical resurrection was not to be desired. Whatever the exact nature of their teaching was, it caused many to lose hope.

Paul counters with the notion that God's foundation will stand firm and that "the Lord knows those who are his" (2:19 NIV). The building metaphor seems to be one of Paul's favorites. In this case the foundation refers to the church, which has received God's seal, or mark of ownership. The first inscription that Paul quotes is from Numbers 16:5. Its context for this statement is a rebellion led by a man named Korah. It occurred during the time that the Israelites were on their journey to the promised land (Numbers 16:1–5). The second inscription is not a direct quote from the Old Testament, yet it carries the same theme: that God knows the difference between those who are truly His and those who claim another truth.

In verses 20–21, Paul shifts focus to the proper kind of conduct that flows from the gospel. In his illustration, two categories of objects are described: ordinary wooden and pottery bowls (or utensils), and gold and silver bowls (or utensils). Both of these types of articles would be used in a house, but with different functions. The gold and silver would be used for honorable uses, such as at a banquet table, while the wood and pottery for dishonorable functions, such as carrying garbage. There are two main interpretations. Paul may be referring to the dishonorable actions of the false teachers, which demonstrate their true nature as dishonorable objects. Or he may be calling Christians to purify themselves so that God will use them for greater and more noble tasks (see verse 21). It is possible that both ideas are present.

Next, Paul instructs Timothy to flee from youthful passions, including the desire to win arguments by quarreling (2:22). Since Paul and Timothy knew each other well, Paul could fashion his advice specifically for his young friend. The passions mentioned here are not merely sexual, but include all the extremes of youth. As Paul often does, he contrasts what Timothy should *flee from* with what he should *pursue*: righteousness, faith, love, and peace.

After all of this discussion about controversy and empty debate, Paul closes this section with a final admonition to Timothy against quarreling, in this case a reference to drawn-out verbal bouts. Paul's reference to the Lord's servant points to Timothy, specifically in his role as church leader. Timothy was not to give in to quarrelling. Instead, he was to focus on the truth and the walk that God required of him (2:23–24).

Paul goes on to say that gentleness characterizes the Lord's servant and may lower the defenses of opponents. The tone here is not one of retribution, but of actions committed with the hope of the return of those who have fallen from faith. God alone grants the repentance (Romans 2:4) necessary to escape the devil's trap (2:25–26).

The idea of bringing those fallen back to their senses is that of sobering up after being deluded. The phrase that in English refers to the devil taking these fallen ones captive carries with it the idea of someone taken alive. It is actually the same phrase Jesus used when he told Peter he would catch men instead of fish (Luke 5:10). The difference, of course, is that Jesus intended to make His catches in order to save, and the devil laid his traps in order to destroy. Paul wanted Timothy to be wise in dealing with those caught by both.

Take It Home

Quarreling over words is a topic that comes up several times in Paul's letters to Timothy, and it seems obvious that Paul hopes the believers in Ephesus will not waste their time and energy disagreeing over words and thus be distracted from living the life God has called them to.

In contemporary culture, with denominational differences in doctrine and lifestyle, there are many opportunities to disagree. Paul's words remind us, still, to choose what is important, and to live the life Jesus modeled for us, focusing on the gospel message rather than quarrelling about details.

2 TIMOTHY 3:1–17

THE LAST DAYS

The Gospel Is Worthy of Acknowledgement	3:1–9
The Gospel Is Worthy of Standing Against Opposition	3:10–17

Setting Up the Section

This next section of Paul's letter casts a shadow. There are difficult days ahead, and Paul predicts that the uphill battle against sin will only get steeper over time.

3:1–9

THE GOSPEL IS WORTHY OF ACKNOWLEDGEMENT

Paul opens this section with a call to pay attention—"Mark this" (3:1 NIV). The words "terrible times" (NIV) also mean "hard to bear, dangerous."

The last days referred to in verse 1 specifically represent the time immediately preceding Jesus' return. But in a broader sense, the last days actually encompass the whole era between Jesus' ascension back into heaven until His second coming.

The vice list that follows in verse 2 includes eighteen indictments. Perhaps the first one listed, "lovers of self" (NASB), governs the rest of the list (especially with "boastful," "proud," and "conceited" following 3:2–4). In company with more offensive sins, Paul includes being disobedient to parents (3:2) and slanderous behavior (3:3)—a sober reminder of the wickedness of every sin, even those we may consider less offensive.

There isn't an obvious structure to this list, though a theme could be those who substitute personal pleasure for God (3:4).

Paul sums up the list with a reference to false godliness (3:5). This form of godliness exhibits none of the potential regeneration attributed to faith in Jesus. It was more than faulty or empty religious ritual. It was a turning away from things of the Spirit. Timothy was to turn himself away from people who practice this form of godliness without power.

In verses 6–7, Paul offers more information about the people described in the preceding verses. They would worm their way into positions from which they could deceive susceptible women. The words translated "worm their way" (3:6 NIV) took away any idea that this deception had benign motives. Instead, it was intended to trick and to destroy.

The fate of the women described here is not a statement about females in general, but rather about these specific women who were being easily swayed by false philosophies. They were spiritually immature and ignorant of the truth.

Jannes and Jambres (3:8) are not names you will find in the Old Testament. They were the traditional names given to the Egyptian magicians who contested Moses before Pharaoh (Exodus 7:11, 22) and became symbols of those who oppose the truth. Just as those magicians were exposed in their trickery, those who stand against the truth in Ephesus will be exposed (3:9).

Demystifying 2 Timothy

Exodus 7–9 records Moses' encounter with the Egyptian Pharaoh and his magicians that Paul references in 2 Timothy 3. God had instructed Moses to perform certain miraculous signs to convince Pharaoh that he'd been sent by God. At first, the magicians in Pharaoh's court performed similar signs, but eventually they were unable to accomplish what Moses could accomplish by the power of God's Spirit (Exodus 7–9, specifically, 8:18–19).

3:10–17

THE GOSPEL IS WORTHY OF STANDING AGAINST OPPOSITION

Paul offers Timothy a list of positive traits (3:10) from his own life that contrast with the list of vices in verses 2–5. The fact that Paul practiced the first seven traits in this list—teaching, lifestyle, purpose, faith, patience, love, and endurance—may have invited the persecutions and sufferings that he experienced (3:11). Paul had been persecuted in Antioch, Iconium, and Lystra (Acts 13–14), but this resistance didn't prevent him from returning later to encourage believers in those cities. In fact, it was during his return visit to the city of Lystra that Paul found Timothy (Acts 16:1–3).

Paul follows up these thoughts about his own persecution with verses that paint a picture of a world in which evil people increase, and Christians face persecution (3:12–13). This persecution may or may not come in the physical form, but certainly even Jesus Himself prepared His followers to suffer in His name. The word translated "impostors" can also mean "wizards." This may be a reference back to Jannes and Jambres, the magicians mentioned in verse 8.

With persecution on the rise, Paul instructs Timothy to weather such turbulent times by continuing in what he had believed since childhood, presumably under the influence of his mother and grandmother (1:5; 3:14–15). The mention of the holy scriptures here refers to the Old Testament. While some of the stories of Jesus had been gathered by the time Paul wrote this letter, the New Testament was not yet complete in the form it is today.

Paul provides two indispensable characteristics of scripture:

1) It is inspired by God—God breathed it out.
2) It is profitable to prepare godly people for every good work.

This preparation for every good work happens in four ways: teaching, rebuking, correcting, and training. The first two—teaching and rebuking—are related more to doctrine. The second two—correcting and training—are related more to practice. If all scripture originated with God, who cannot lie (Hebrews 6:18), then it is true.

Critical Observation

Inspiration refers to the supernatural process whereby God influenced people to record scripture. The Christian church reveres the Old and New Testaments (collectively, the Bible) as inspired by God (specifically, through the Holy Spirit) and as authoritative in Christian living. The process of inspiration is further explained in 2 Peter 1:20–21.

2 TIMOTHY 4:1–22

IN CONCLUSION

The Gospel Is Worthy of Endurance 4:1–8
The Gospel Is Worthy of Participation 4:9–22

Setting Up the Section

This final chapter begins with a solemn charge to young Timothy "in the presence of God and of Christ Jesus, who will judge the living and the dead" (4:1 NIV). The opening introduction adds urgency to all that follows. These final words come from a man who has spent time on both sides of Jesus—persecuting Him and proclaiming Him. Writing from prison, Paul shares his mission with Timothy.

4:1–8

THE GOSPEL IS WORTHY OF ENDURANCE

It is likely that Paul wrote to Timothy with the knowledge that he was facing the reality of his imminent death. His reference to Christ's judging the living and the dead is probably a quote from a baptism or confessional creed (4:1).

Paul offers Timothy a charge of five commands (4:2):

1) Preach the Word. There is an underlying urgency to the language of this command, almost in the sense of responding to a crisis.
2) Be prepared. The idea of in and out of season means to be prepared whether you have an obvious opportunity or not; it is to always be ready.
3) Correct. Show the right way life is to be lived.
4) Rebuke. While closely related to correction, the idea of rebuke has a bit more of a confrontational element to it.
5) Encourage. Going a step beyond correction and rebuke, encouraging those in the community adds a positive element of going alongside others as they need it.

Critical Observation

Timothy's five charges should be executed with patience and careful instruction. This speaks to both the manner in which Timothy goes about his ministry—reflecting the patience of God—and the sound doctrine upon which his ministry is to be based. Since doctrinal decay usually precedes moral decay, the rejection of sound doctrine will likely precede the difficult times of immorality Paul warns of in 3:1–5.

"Insatiable curiosity" (4:3 NET) is a phrase that describes those who no longer want the simple truth or sound doctrine (4:3–4). Instead, they want novelty and entertainment. While Paul has already described the false teachers who harassed Timothy's church, here he is turning the tables and highlighting the audience that is attracted to those false teachers. Understanding that audience, though, it makes sense that the teachers who are willing to satisfy that itch for novelty build their popularity by substituting fantastic myths for the truth. The language in verses 3 and 4 is reminiscent of Paul's initial warning to Timothy in 1 Timothy 1:4 about "myths and endless genealogies" (NIV).

In verse 5, Paul takes a right turn and shines the light on Timothy again. He uses these admonitions:

1) Timothy should avoid the kind of nonsense described in verses 3 and 4. Paul's admonition that Timothy *keep his head* means that Timothy should live a sober, morally alert life, staying within legal, moral, and ethical bounds (4:5).
2) Timothy should anticipate and endure hardship, like Paul himself (2:3, 9). In the coming years, Timothy will endure imprisonment as Paul did (Hebrews 13:23).
3) Timothy should do the work of an evangelist—proclaiming the gospel. This is not a formal term or office, as we might describe an evangelist today. Timothy's call as an evangelist is the same call given to all Christians.
4) Timothy should fulfill his ministry, allowing nothing to deter him. This summarizes Paul's final exhortation to Timothy, covering the whole scope of ministry.

Paul then shifts the spotlight from Timothy to himself, describing himself as a *drink offering* (Philippians 2:17; 2 Timothy 4:6). This is language that signifies a sacrifice. Typically a drink offering takes the form of wine being poured out on an altar, a powerful image considering the blood shed by martyrs for their faith.

Paul's death was imminent, thus the mention of his departure (4:6). In this case, though, the word that Paul uses to describe his departure has an almost triumphant quality. Rather than signifying his leaving, it more so signifies the loosening of something that has been bound.

In verse 7, Paul's clear conscience from 2 Timothy 1:3 is evident as he reflects upon the faithful completion of his ministry. There is a sense of finality to the wording, and another example of Paul's use of metaphors. *Fighting the fight* and *finishing the race* are obvious metaphors. But even *keeping the faith* has the connotation of an athlete's promise to keep the rules of the game and a soldier's promise of fidelity to the cause.

In the next verse as well, the *crown of righteousness* is reminiscent of the Olympic wreaths worn by the winners of the contests. Jesus will award the crown on the Day of Judgment, and not just to Paul, but to all believers who persevere. Regarding Jesus' *appearing*, the word that is translated "longed for" in the NIV is a strong verb (the verb form of *agape*) that carries the idea of a deep longing, stronger than mere desire toward something.

4:9–22

THE GOSPEL IS WORTHY OF PARTICIPATION

As Paul draws this letter to a close, he sends greetings and exchanges information on mutual friends. Although Paul twice beckons Timothy to come quickly (4:9, 21), it is not known whether Timothy arrived prior to Paul's execution.

Demas, according to Colossians 4:14, was a close associate of Paul's. The wording here gives the impression that Demas actually deserted Paul on a personal level. Some have supposed he had taken a different, perhaps easier, assignment. Others have supposed he was afraid of suffering Paul's same fate if he associated with him too long. When Paul writes that Demas loved the world, he uses the same verb as in verse 8 (*agapao*)—meaning a deep longing or affection (4:10).

We don't have any further information about Crescens, and with the information given here, we can't be sure whether Crescens and Titus left Paul on good or bad terms. However, it doesn't seem from the text that Paul is associating their leaving with what he has said about Demas. Under whatever conditions they left, only one associate remained—Luke (4:10–11). Since Luke was a physician, he may have remained specifically to care for Paul's physical needs.

Perhaps it was while mentioning those who had left him that Paul was reminded of Mark, who had rejoined Paul's ministry (4:11).

Demystifying 2 Timothy

In verse 11, Paul mentions two Gospel writers with whom he had extensive experience—Luke and Mark. Mark's story is rather touching. Also called John Mark, he had accompanied Paul and Barnabas (Mark's cousin) on their first missionary journey (Acts 12:25). But along the way, Mark left them (Acts 13:13), presumably due to persecution or difficulties, and Paul refused to allow Mark to rejoin them on a subsequent trip (Acts 15:37–39). Paul's disagreement with Barnabas over this decision caused such conflict between them that they parted ways. Understanding this backdrop makes Paul's invitation here, to bring Mark because of his usefulness to Paul's ministry, an indicator that some growth and reconciliation had taken place.

Tychicus, who is mentioned in verse 12, may have hand delivered this letter to Timothy in Ephesus. In fact, it might have been Paul's intention for Tychicus to relieve Timothy so that Timothy could visit him.

Next Paul makes a practical request of Timothy. He requests his cloak and reading—or perhaps writing—materials (4:13). The materials Paul requested may have included parts of the Old Testament or even unfinished drafts of some of his letters.

Take It Home

While we often look to the scriptures for truth and doctrine, it is verses like these that remind us of the human story surrounding the words we read—the real people grappling with life-threatening realities and daily inconveniences. They had friendships that warmed them and hardships that wore them down. Letters like 2 Timothy offer a unique insight into these kinds of everyday realities.

And letters like these allow us to evaluate our own relationships within the body of Christ. Do we stand by our brothers and sisters in their difficulties? Do we shy away when they may need us most? Are we structured as a group in such a way that it allows us to tend to each other's lives as needed? Each friend and colleague that Paul gives Timothy a status on is an example to us—for positive or negative—of how to be the body of Christ.

Paul's comments and warning to Timothy about Alexander the metalworker (4:14–15) may refer to the same person he says was handed over to Satan in 1 Timothy 1:20, but we can't be sure. Paul quotes Psalm 62:12 in saying that God will repay Alexander for standing against him (4:14).

Paul seems to hold Alexander's actions in a different regard than those who merely didn't rise to his support (4:16). Alexander, after all, stood *against* Paul. His was not simply an absence of support. Here, Paul wishes for God's forgiveness of those who deserted him (4:16).

The first defense that Paul mentions is probably the preliminary investigation that would have preceded his formal trial (4:16). His reference to the Gentiles hearing his message (4:17) may simply be a metaphor, since Rome was the center of the Gentile world. In the same way, his rescue from the lion's mouth may also be simply a word picture of escaping great danger (Psalm 22:21; Daniel 6:20) rather than a symbol of Nero or Satan or an allusion to the amphitheatre in which Christians were killed by hungry lions as some have supposed.

Perhaps most important in Paul's description of his first defense is the way the Lord stood at his side, offering strength. This support stands in stark contrast to the lack of support Paul received from his fellow Christians.

In closing, Paul sends his greetings to a few of Timothy's fellow residents in Ephesus—Priscilla, Aquila, and the family of Onesiphorus (4:19).

Demystifying 2 Timothy

Priscilla and Aquila were Paul's friends and ministry colleagues. The couple is always mentioned together in the Bible (Acts 18:2, 18, 26; Romans 16:3–4; 1 Corinthians 16:19; 2 Timothy 4:19), and most often Priscilla's name is mentioned first. Paul first met them in Corinth and stayed with them for a year and a half, learning from their wisdom. They also influenced other first-century church leaders, like Apollos (Acts 18:24–26).

Paul also informs Timothy of the whereabouts of a few more mutual friends, as he has already done in 4:10–12. In this case the news is of Erastus, who is probably the Erastus mentioned in Acts 19:22, and Trophimus, another mutual friend and companion.

Next, Paul sends greetings to Timothy from a few co-laborers in Rome—Eubulus, Pudens, Linus, Claudia, and all the brothers (4:21). Whether or not they were imprisoned with Paul is unclear. The New Testament gives us no other information on them.

Finally, as Paul opens the letter with grace (1:2), so also he closes this letter with the wish that Timothy would be accompanied by the grace of God and His Spirit (4:22).

TITUS

INTRODUCTION TO TITUS

The book of Titus and 1 and 2 Timothy comprise Paul's Pastoral Epistles—not an entirely accurate name for the three letters. Titus and Timothy were not pastors, at least not by the modern definition. Still, both Timothy and Titus were Paul's associates who did a lot of legwork for him, and his letters to them about the expectations of church leaders is a valuable guideline for spiritual leadership.

AUTHOR

Of all the letters of Paul, the Pastoral Epistles are by far the most disputed in terms of authorship. Differences of language, style, and theology have caused many (more liberal) scholars to doubt that Paul was the original author. Some believe that a disciple of Paul wrote these after Paul's death. Yet the differences in style, vocabulary, and theology are not as great as is often supposed, and they can be satisfactorily accounted for by the different themes and by the fact that these letters were written later in Paul's life. Paul may also have used one of his missionary companions to write out these letters (see Romans 16:22 for an example of this), and this scribe left his own stylistic mark. Because of the many Pauline themes and personal touches, evangelical scholars continue to assert that these letters came from the apostle's hand.

PURPOSE

Titus is not mentioned in Acts, as are many of Paul's other associates, but his name appears in various epistles. Paul's ministry had initiated Titus's conversion to Christianity, and the Gentile convert soon had taken on the responsibility of traveling and ministering with Paul, and at other times on his own. This was one of the latter cases, and Paul had left Titus in Crete while the apostle was elsewhere (perhaps Corinth). Paul desired to stay in touch with his protégé and offers him some practical advice for overseeing a church.

OCCASION

Crete is an island in the Mediterranean, about 150 miles long and anywhere from seven to thirty miles wide. In Greek mythology, it is the birthplace of Zeus, and the Cretans claimed that his tomb was on their island as well. The citizens of Crete had a reputation that was less than stellar (1:12).

Titus, a young minister, had been entrusted to oversee the believers there. Paul was writing to both encourage him and give him some practical instructions regarding church leadership (qualifications of elders, basic teachings, dealing with problems, etc.). A proper understanding of the gospel of Christ was especially needed in the hedonistic and idolatrous culture of Crete.

THEMES

Six times in this short letter Paul makes a reference to "good works"—not as a requirement for God's forgiveness and redemption, but in response to God's free gift of salvation. And he regularly connects such proper behavior with sound doctrine.

Paul also directs the reader's attention to "our Savior," a phrase that appears six times in three distinct couplets. Each couplet has a distinct reference to both God and Jesus (1:3–4; 2:10; 3:4, 6).

CONTRIBUTION TO THE BIBLE

Along with 1 Timothy, Titus is a primary source for clearly stated requirements for church overseers (1:5–9). In addition, Paul's concise description of salvation (2:11–14) is a doctrinal delight in its detail as well as its simplicity.

OUTLINE

A CALL FOR AUTHENTIC BELIEFS AND LEADERSHIP	**1:1–16**
Service and Grace	1:1–4
Expectations of Leaders	1:5–16
A CALL FOR AUTHENTIC BEHAVIOR	**2:1–15**
Instructions for Older Believers	2:1–3
Instructions for Younger Believers	2:4–8
Instructions for Slaves	2:9–10
Instructions for Titus	2:11–15
A CALL FOR AUTHENTIC RELATIONSHIPS	**3:1–15**
Proper Respect for All People	3:1–2
The Difference Christ Can Make	3:3–7
People to Avoid	3:8–11
Farewells and Final Arrangements	3:12–15

TITUS 1:1–16

A CALL FOR AUTHENTIC BELIEFS AND LEADERSHIP

Service and Grace 1:1–4
Expectations of Leaders 1:5–16

Setting Up the Section

After Paul had introduced the gospel to such a broad geographic area, it was necessary for him to delegate authority in following up with young and growing churches. To this end, he had placed Titus in Crete—a challenging mission field for anyone. Clearly, the church would need good and strong leadership. So Paul opens his letter to Titus with criteria for church elders and authorizes him to deal with some difficult problems already arising among the believers.

1:1–4

SERVICE AND GRACE

The openings in Paul's letters are all very similar. Paul usually begins by identifying himself as a servant of Christ. But in Titus, he calls himself a servant of God (1:1). This single exception is not too surprising when looking at the writings of Paul as a whole. He frequently gives credit to more than one Person of the Trinity in a single passage, viewing the three as one God at work among humankind. A servant of Christ is certainly a servant of God.

Paul's other self-designation, "an apostle of Jesus Christ" (1:1), is more usual. An apostle is appointed by God to minister. Paul's words to Titus, then, are more than personal opinion. They are from God.

Critical Observation

Paul's elaborate greeting, combined with the description of his apostleship, seems quite formal for a personal letter. This has led some to believe that Paul intended the letter not just for Titus, but for the entire church on the island of Crete where Titus was ministering. If so, then Paul was imparting his authority to Titus.

Paul would soon emphasize the connection between sound doctrine and good behavior in this short letter (1:9; 2:1), and he opens with the importance of not only faith, but also knowledge of God's truth (1:2). His notation that God does not lie (1:2) also presages a later observation that Titus was ministering among people prone to lying (1:12).

Paul refers to Titus as his "true son" (1:4 NIV), as he had done with Timothy (1 Timothy 1:2). It is likely that Paul had been instrumental in the conversion of both individuals to Christianity and felt like a spiritual father to them. It is also likely that Paul had established a teaching relationship and served as a mentor to the younger men who were beginning to hold important spiritual positions.

1:5–16

EXPECTATIONS OF LEADERS

Crete is an island of more than three thousand square miles in the Mediterranean Sea. Paul's ministry there (1:5) is not recorded in Acts. Paul's visit was apparently shorter than he wished, so he left Titus there with significant work to do: answer questions, smooth out problems, appoint elders, and so forth. And along with the assignment, Paul gave Titus the authority to act.

The elders could help with the work that needed to be done—as long as they met certain qualifications. Paul lists over a dozen requirements for the position of elder. (Paul uses the words *elder* and *overseer* [bishop] synonymously. See Titus 1:5, 7). Although not identical to the list he had given Timothy (1 Timothy 3:1–10), Paul's list to Titus (1:6–9) contains many of the same prerequisites for elders (husband of one wife, faithful children, not addicted to wine, not a bully, not greedy, hospitable, sensible, and self-controlled).

Demystifying Titus

Paul's standards for elders are high, but not unreasonable. *Blameless* (1:6–7) doesn't mean sinless, but is more along the lines of being above reproach or accusation for anything. "Having one wife" (1:6) is a frequently debated phrase with three primary interpretations: (1) Paul is prohibiting polygamy; (2) Paul is forbidding divorce; or (3) Paul is addressing the problem of unfaithfulness and promiscuity.

The behavior of an elder is an important aspect of his or her life, including how the person interacts with a spouse, family, fellow church members, and outsiders. Both public and private lives are under constant scrutiny. Yet the expectations don't end there. An elder must also know scripture and hold firmly to its teachings, being able to refute heresy and teach sound doctrine (1:9).

The need for competent and spiritually mature elders was essential because of the threats presented to the believers at Crete. They faced the same problems as other churches, yet those who opposed the truth seemed to be in full force in Crete. There were many who had not only deceived themselves, but were spreading heresy to others (1:10–11).

Their false teachings were only empty words that had no real value. Yet the results were devastating for those who believed the lies instead of God's truth. Many such teachers were only out to make money, yet were devastating entire households in the process.

Paul challenges Titus and the elders to have two voices: one to call God's sheep and another to drive away wolves. They were to silence the false teachers (1:11) by refusing them opportunities to speak in the church—and rebuking them emphatically (1:13). They were also to preempt the false teachers by proclaiming the genuine gospel that *would* have lasting value for their hearers.

A clear indication of some of the false teaching is revealed in Paul's references to the "circumcision group" (1:10 NIV) and Jewish myths (1:14). Other churches had been confronted by groups of vocal Jewish believers requesting (or demanding) that all Christians conform to Jewish laws, customs, and traditions. Especially strong was their insistence that believers be circumcised. But Crete was the wrong place for them to lobby for their beliefs. Titus was an uncircumcised Gentile believer (Galatians 2:1–5) who was ministering with the full endorsement and empowerment of the apostle Paul. He was living proof that an authentic conversion did not require circumcision.

Paul quotes the poet Epimenides (1:12), who had lived in Crete in the sixth century BC. Even though the people of Crete were well aware of their culture's ethical and spiritual shortcomings, Paul knew the power of the Holy Spirit to transform lives. He maintains just as high a spiritual standard in Crete as anywhere else. Yet in order for the believers to persevere and overcome, they had to resist the influence of the false teachers and hold fast to the truth of the gospel.

Paul clarifies that the way to please God is not through strict and restrictive obedience to a set of laws, but rather by experiencing the forgiveness of God and choosing a life of purity as a result. Many of the groups attempting to sway the early church had an ascetic approach to their adherence to the law, thinking God would be satisfied, if not pleased, by their self-imposed miseries. Paul, in contrast, reflects the teachings of Jesus (Matthew 15:10–11, 18–20; Luke 11:39–41).

The mind and conscience work as a filter. If God has cleansed the inner person, then all thoughts and actions are pure. If not, then it is useless to attempt to maintain a "good" life because nothing is pure (1:15).

Paul's mention of those who "claim to know God" (1:16 NIV) may be a reference to nonbelievers, or those who wrongly assumed their good works were sufficient for salvation. Or perhaps Paul had in mind those who had undergone a genuine spiritual conversion but were beginning to respond to the false teachings of the Jewish legalists. By attempting to add any requirement for salvation other than faith in response to the grace of God, a person ceases to know (understand) God.

Paul will stress the importance of doing good works many times in this short letter (1:16; 2:7, 14; 3:1, 8, 14). Yet attempting to require anything for salvation other than what God has already done is, in essence, denying God (1:16). People who do so may act from sincerity, zealous fervor, or other well-intentioned motives, yet their actions are detestable to God. Until the mind and conscience are yielded to God, no amount of effort will compensate.

Take It Home

Review Paul's list of qualifications for church leadership (1:6–9). Which of those standards do you feel is your strong point? Which do you need to work on? You may not be an official church leader, yet any kind of ministry (to children, neighbors, extended family, etc.) would certainly benefit by a more consistent application of these standards.

TITUS 2:1–15

A CALL FOR AUTHENTIC BEHAVIOR

Instructions for Older Believers	2:1–3
Instructions for Younger Believers	2:4–8
Instructions for Slaves	2:9–10
Instructions for Titus	2:11–15

Setting Up the Section

After giving Titus a list of requirements for church leaders (1:6–9), Paul now provides guidelines for different groups within the church. As he does, he also provides some personal encouragement for Titus in the challenging position he held.

2:1–3

INSTRUCTIONS FOR OLDER BELIEVERS

Paul's writings frequently associate biblical truth with appropriate behavior. He has just pointed out that those who don't fully understand the truth about salvation are incapable of producing any pure actions (1:15). Then, as he instructs Titus to teach only sound doctrine (2:1), Paul begins to enumerate how such truth should be reflected in various groups within the church.

He first addresses older men (2:1). Although he doesn't explicitly say so, it is inferred that a positive example set by older men will model genuine faith for younger men, providing the younger men more than mere verbal instructions. (The following instructions for older women to set good examples for younger ones would certainly apply to the other gender as well.)

Being temperate (2:2) has a specific application to the consumption of alcohol, but could also mean to be self-disciplined and reasonable in a broader sense. The other expectations are self-explanatory: worthy of respect, self-controlled, and sound in faith, love, and endurance. Clearly this is not an exhaustive list of dos and don'ts, yet this short list of general commands addresses a wide spectrum of life situations.

Paul's instructions for older women (2:3) are similar. Titus is instructed to leave the teaching of younger women to the older ones (2:4–5)—a much richer investment of idle time than gossip or excessive drinking. Apparently, slander and drunkenness among older women were among the problems that added to Crete's poor reputation (1:12). But those in the church are called to a higher purpose.

Critical Observation

In other places, Paul provides instructions to women concerning church settings (1 Corinthians 14:33–35; 1 Timothy 2). Here, however, he addresses the importance of their role in the home (Titus 2:4–5). The influence of the false teachers in Crete had not just affected the church, but had also ruined entire households (1:11). The need for accurate teaching of scripture and demonstration of godly living was just as great in the home as it was in the church.

2:4–8

INSTRUCTIONS FOR YOUNGER BELIEVERS

Paul's instructions to Titus regarding younger women in the household wasn't surprising for the times and culture. A woman's opportunities were limited during the first century. Yet even within the home, the relationship between doctrine and behavior was important. Paul knew others were watching. The way that young mothers related to husbands and children would influence the way other people perceived the Christian faith. Just as church elders were evaluated based partially on the proper rearing of children (1:6), so, too, were Christian mothers expected to live out their faith at home, where others would detect a difference in their lifestyles and could find no reason to malign the gospel (2:4–5). Then, after their children had grown and moved on to adult lives, the women were called to serve as spiritual mentors to those who were just beginning marriages and families.

Paul's admonition to young men includes only one item (2:6), yet he was not attempting to provide an exhaustive list. This was, after all, a letter to Titus, who would explain and expound on Paul's words as he related them to the believers at Crete. Self-control is certainly an appropriate challenge for most young men, and it encompasses many other positive qualities.

It is at this point that Paul moves from general guidelines for *all* young men to specific ones for Titus, who would have been included in this segment of the church. Titus couldn't just *teach* the gospel; he also had to *model* it (2:7–8). He would certainly face opposition, but he could put his critics to shame by living a spotless life as he ministered to others.

2:9–10

INSTRUCTIONS FOR SLAVES

Paul includes instructions for believing slaves in a number of his writings (Ephesians 6:5–8; Colossians 3:22–24; 1 Timothy 6:1–2). He expected the influence of the gospel to be evident even in the institution of slavery.

Slaves were noncitizens who served Roman citizens, and they were common in the Roman Empire during the first century. (Perhaps as many as half of those in the Roman Empire were slaves.) Many lived as members of the household in which they served.

They were usually paid and occasionally had the opportunity to earn their freedom. Paul tells them to behave in a godly way toward their masters so that the gospel would be attractive (2:9–10).

Demystifying Titus

Many people question why Paul (or scripture in general) seems to condone slavery. But the question itself exposes a misconception. The Bible never endorses slavery, yet since slavery was so widespread in the ancient world, scripture addresses the issue. Slaves were held to certain standards, but so were slave owners. And in most places where the truths of scripture were introduced and implemented, the acceptance of slavery began to decline. Furthermore, the gospel does address the even worse problem of *spiritual* slavery, and how through Christ's sacrificial death all people are able to break the chains of sin and experience freedom and forgiveness. In this regard, there is no distinction between male and female, Jew and Gentile, slave and free person (Galatians 3:28).

2:11–15

INSTRUCTIONS FOR TITUS

At this point, Paul shifts back from outer behavior to "sound doctrine" (2:1). Although the importance of appropriate behavior and good works is emphasized throughout his letter to Titus, Paul makes it clear that God's grace is the foundation for such behavior (2:11).

To make the intangible concept of grace a bit more understandable, Paul defines it as the appearance of Jesus on earth (2:11). Jesus' incarnation was the event that all believers can look back to and see the undeserved gift of God—a Savior who came because He loved them and not because they loved Him. God's only Son was sacrificed on their behalf. Christ's death was the ultimate act of grace, and salvation is by grace alone, through faith (2:14).

As people respond to that act of grace and become believers, their focus turns from past to present. They find the strength to resist the sins and temptations that surround them. On a more positive note, they also choose to live lives that are self-controlled, upright, and godly (2:12). Paul's choice of words reflects a proper relationship with oneself, with others, and with God.

Then Paul moves from a perspective on the present to the future. Believers can choose to go against the moral tide of society not only because of the first appearance of Christ, but also because they eagerly anticipate His second appearance (2:13). Jesus' first coming was a historical reality; His second coming is a blessed hope that should affect all aspects of present-day life.

These doctrinal truths were to be the text of Titus's messages to the people in Crete (2:15). Paul empowered him to encourage and to rebuke as necessary. A young pastor in a culture of self-described liars, evil brutes, and lazy gluttons (1:12) might naturally feel overwhelmed. But Paul reminds his young associate not to be unsettled by his situation. And he will provide more guidelines in his next section.

Take It Home

Choose one of Paul's categories that applies to you—young men, older men, young women, older women, or slaves (substitute "employees" for "slaves" in today's culture). Review Paul's instructions and determine how your behavior compares to the high standards he sets.

TITUS 3:1–15

A CALL FOR AUTHENTIC RELATIONSHIPS

Proper Respect for All People	3:1–2
The Difference Christ Can Make	3:3–7
People to Avoid	3:8–11
Farewells and Final Arrangements	3:12–15

Setting Up the Section

Paul had written this letter to encourage Titus (chapter 1) and provide instructions for various groups within the church (chapter 2). In conclusion, he provides a few more guidelines for the entire church—reminders of how the believers should behave in response to their salvation. Afterward, he signs off as he usually does, with a few personal comments and greetings.

3:1–2

PROPER RESPECT FOR ALL PEOPLE

It has been suggested that the primary teaching job of a pastor is to remind the congregation of what scripture says, not necessarily to impart new information. Believers know what they *should* do, but tend to stray when their minds wander or when their spiritual senses grow dull. So Paul instructs Titus to remind the Christians in Crete how to act.

He lists seven specific qualities expected of Christians: (1) to be subject to rulers and authorities; (2) to be obedient; (3) to be ready to do every good work; (4) to slander no one; (5) to be peaceable; (6) to be gentle; and (7) to show complete courtesy to all people. Paul emphasizes good works three times in this chapter alone (3:1, 8, 14). His feelings about submission to others—even secular authorities—have been expressed in other letters (Romans 13:1–5; 1 Timothy 2:1–2).

3:3–7

THE DIFFERENCE CHRIST CAN MAKE

Paul contrasts the seven Christian qualities with seven characteristics that had been evident prior to the believers' awareness of Jesus: (1) foolishness, (2) disobedience, (3) being deceived by pleasures, (4) enslavement, (5) malice, (6) envy, and (7) both being hated and hating others.

Critical Observation

Paul frequently deals with sin directly and frankly. Yet he doesn't come across as arrogant, legalistic, or condemning. Although his upbringing had been considerably different from most of those who grew up in the hedonistic, secular culture of Crete, he makes no distinction (3:3). He includes himself in those influenced by sin: foolish, disobedient, deceived, enslaved, and so forth.

The juxtaposition of these two lists serves to highlight God's grace in salvation, compelling the reader to respond in grateful obedience. God's kindness, love, and mercy (3:4–5) are all aspects of His grace. Redemption is no small gift of God; it transforms all areas of life. It is not accomplished by works of righteousness (3:5), but rather by the work of the triune God—the Father (3:4), the Spirit (3:5), and the Son (3:6).

Believers are to do good works for others in response to the marvelous and unique good work God has done for them. His act of love took place while people were still disobedient, foolish, and hateful. They were enemies of God, but thanks to Jesus' sacrifice on their behalf, they came to be considered God's friends (Romans 5:10; John 15:13–16).

Salvation is through "the washing of rebirth and renewal" (or "regeneration"), by the Holy Spirit (3:5 NIV). The Spirit is instrumental not only in the conversion experience, but also throughout the transformation from foolish and sinful behavior (3:3) to a life of obedience and godliness (3:1–2). And beyond that, the end result for a believer is eternal life as an heir of God (3:7).

Demystifying Titus

Some people tend to emphasize the importance of water baptism in regard to salvation and use this passage to promote that belief. Yet it is unlikely that Paul is referring to water, much less to baptism, as integral to salvation. He is in the midst of making the point that salvation has nothing to do with human works (3:5). The "washing" here is spiritual. It is the Holy Spirit who is "poured out" on believers (3:6).

The work of the Spirit is not a matter of improving and tweaking the old person until he or she is a child of God. Rather, salvation involves a birth from above, resulting in a new creation (2 Corinthians 5:17). This gift of the Holy Spirit is generous (3:6), and His work is directly connected with the will of God the Father and the authority of Christ (Acts 2:33). Those who place their faith in Christ receive the Spirit. Those who don't do not receive the Spirit.

3:8–11

PEOPLE TO AVOID

Paul isn't just expressing his opinions. He instructs Titus to *stress* these teachings—to insist on them (3:8). They are not only excellent and profitable for anyone who heeds them, they are also trustworthy. Even after salvation, those who want to experience the abundant life that God offers must be careful to devote themselves to doing good. God makes all things possible, but believers must be disciplined and willing.

It is easy to get caught up in various forms of foolishness and nonproductive activity. Paul mentions a few potential problems to Titus. Those in the Greek culture were prone to intellectual debate. While there is nothing wrong with verbal interaction per se, it could become problematic when applied to scripture. It is relatively easy to speculate on theological or philosophical what-ifs while ignoring the clear and straightforward truths of God's revealed Word. Even today, it is easy to *talk about* the contents of the Bible rather than *teach* them.

The Jewish culture could also get off track when it came to teaching scripture. Throughout the centuries, rabbis had added myths and legends to the inspired scriptures, frequently based on the same characters. Genealogies of key figures were sometimes doctored to make Jewish heroes appear more impressive. Other teachers could nitpick for hours about, for example, what was or was not appropriate on the Sabbath.

These were the kinds of things Titus was to insist be avoided. A primary purpose of scripture is to inspire believers to act on what they know to be true. Intellectual pursuits have their place, but they are not to replace loving actions among those in the church as well as toward those outside.

Titus is given a mandate to put an end to such time-wasting controversies and the authority to deal with anyone who would not respond. Those who were being divisive were to receive two clear warnings. If they still did not heed the authority of the church, they were to be cut off from fellowship (3:9–10). There will frequently be those attempting to influence the church who are not of God and are unwilling to receive instruction or correction. Church leaders must be willing to deal with such people directly and quickly. It isn't the leader or the church that condemns the troublemaker; it is the person himself (3:11).

3:12–15

FAREWELLS AND FINAL ARRANGEMENTS

Paul's plans in verse 12 reveal a couple of things. First, he was free to travel, so his writing was taking place prior to his second Roman imprisonment. And second, Nicopolis, a city on the western coast of Greece, wasn't exactly an ideal place to spend the winter. However, it *was* a spot where numerous travelers from various places found themselves forced to stay due to the storm season on the Mediterranean. This fact suggests that Paul intentionally went where groups of people were so he could minister even while traveling was restricted.

Paul had worked with Tychicus (3:12) and spoke highly of him on numerous occasions (Acts 20:4; Ephesians 6:21; Colossians 4:7). Nothing more is said of Artemas in the Bible,

Apparently, Paul was sending one of these men to Crete to minister for a while, allowing Titus to take a break and meet him in Nicopolis.

Before leaving, however, Paul requests Titus's help for Apollos and Zenas, who were traveling through the area. Scripture identifies Apollos (3:13) as a spiritually discerning and devoted church leader (Acts 18:24–28; 1 Corinthians 1:12; 3:5), but this is the Bible's only mention of Zenas. His title of "lawyer" might have meant one of two things: If a Jewish reference, it would mean Zenas was trained in the law and had been a rabbi. If a Gentile reference, it would suggest that he was a person of high standing in Rome who had converted to Christianity.

Although the culture of Crete had a propensity for laziness (1:12), Paul challenges the believers to provide for their daily necessities (3:14). This devotion to doing good could then be spread to people like Apollos and Zenas, who were doing God's work full-time and could benefit from the help of fellow Christians.

In closing, Paul does not identify who is with him, yet he sends everyone's greetings and prays for grace for Titus and all those with him (3:15).

Take It Home

In closing this section, Paul twice names pairs of ministers (3:12–13) where one was a prominent and proven leader and the other a relative unknown. This suggests a mentor-protégé relationship during spiritual training. Have you ever benefited from the wisdom and attention of a spiritual mentor? If so, have you passed along that wisdom to a younger Christian who is seeking maturity? Spend a few minutes identifying people who might help you continue to grow spiritually as well as those who might appreciate your help in their own spiritual journey.

PHILEMON

INTRODUCTION TO PHILEMON

Of the thirteen epistles traditionally attributed to Paul in scripture, his letter to Philemon is the most personal. Most were written to entire churches. The three Pastoral Epistles (1 and 2 Timothy and Titus) were to individuals, but had church-wide applications. Philemon, too, contains public greetings and was intended to be read publicly. Philemon's situation was very specific, yet Paul's advice, as usual, contains wisdom appropriate for all believers.

AUTHOR

Paul identifies himself as the author (verses 1, 9, 19), and there is nothing in the letter theologically or grammatically to suggest otherwise.

PURPOSE

Paul had come upon a runaway slave named Onesimus and had convinced him to return to his owner, Philemon. This letter is Paul's appeal to Philemon to forgive the slave and accept him back into the household.

OCCASION

It appears that Paul was in prison as he wrote (verses 1, 9), which would probably have been during his two-year house arrest in Rome (Acts 28:16, 30). As usual, Paul made the most of his time, ministering through the mail when he couldn't travel in person.

THEMES

The theme of Philemon is forgiveness, not as a great theological concept but as a necessity of an effective Christian life. Whether or not Philemon wanted to forgive the offense of Onesimus as his slave, he was obligated to do so as a Christian brother.

HISTORICAL CONTEXT

Paul's imprisonment and trial (AD 61–63) were during the rule of Nero before he had become such a nemesis to the Christian movement. The letter to Philemon was likely delivered at the same time as the letter to the Colossians (Colossians 4:7–9) and near the time of Ephesians (Ephesians 6:21).

CONTRIBUTION TO THE BIBLE

The short letter to Philemon is important in its view on first-century slavery. Some ask why Paul (or other biblical writers) didn't come right out and condemn the practice. Yet if Philemon heeded Paul's appeal, both slave and master would find themselves equal as servants of Christ. The new relationship would certainly undermine the institution of slavery.

OUTLINE

A SHORT STORY OF FORGIVENESS AND SECOND CHANCES 1–25
A Public Greeting 1–3
Intercession for a Repentant Slave 4–22
Coworkers and Concern 23–25

Setting Up the Section

Paul uses a great deal of tact in this epistle, so the facts of the matter are revealed slowly. But a slave named Onesimus has run away from his master, Philemon, apparently after stealing from him. In God's providence, Onesimus meets Paul, who facilitates his conversion to Christianity and sends him back to Philemon with this letter.

1–3

A PUBLIC GREETING

In most of Paul's salutations he identifies himself as an apostle of Christ. In this instance, however, such an opening would have been too strong. He is asking a favor rather than attempting to impose his position to coerce Philemon's decision, so he identifies himself as "a prisoner of Christ Jesus" (verse 1). He appears to be a prisoner of the Emperor Nero, but he was in chains because of his faithfulness in speaking for Jesus. The fact that Paul adds Timothy to the salutation (even though he writes as an individual throughout most of the letter) also softens the tone of the opening.

Paul will soon be asking a specific favor of a specific person, yet he begins with a greeting that includes the entire church (verses 2–3). The specific appeal is to Philemon, but the importance of forgiveness and acceptance of others is applicable to all believers.

Many people suppose, with good reason, that Apphia is Philemon's wife, and Archippus his son. The fact that Philemon owned at least one slave and had a home large enough to host the church (verse 2), with a guest room to spare (verse 22), indicates that he was probably wealthy.

4–22

INTERCESSION FOR A REPENTANT SLAVE

You in verse 3 (and later in verse 23, as well as *your* in verse 25) is plural. But for the bulk of the letter (verses 4–22), Paul uses the singular pronoun. His appeal is directly to Philemon. As he first shares his feelings, Paul is being tactful, but he isn't being flattering or untruthful. He is truly thankful for Philemon and encouraged by him (verses 4, 7).

Philemon had a track record of encouraging believers. He had refreshed the hearts (verse 7) of many people already; and Paul will soon ask him to refresh *his* heart by granting his request (verse 20).

Critical Observation

There is no evidence of churches as we know them today, where believers leave their homes to gather in a public building, until the third century. Until then, Christians met in homes of devoted believers like Philemon.

Paul chose not to demand the desired response from Philemon, although he felt he had the right to do so (verse 8). He prefers to appeal to Philemon in love. It isn't until this point in the letter (verse 10) that he even mentions Onesimus by name. The slave had apparently become a Christian after conversing with Paul, based on Paul's reference to him as his son (verse 10).

Demystifying Philemon

Paul uses a play on words in verse 11. The name Onesimus means "useful." So Paul is essentially saying, somewhat tongue in cheek, that Philemon's "useful" servant had temporarily become useless, but was now ready to live up to his name.

Paul genuinely liked Onesimus. He would have liked to recruit him as an assistant, much the way he had with Timothy and Titus (verses 12–14). But it was a matter of law, as well as moral obligation, for Paul to return Onesimus to Philemon. Onesimus had already broken faith with Philemon, and possibly had stolen from him as well. Had Paul kept Onesimus rather than sending him back, it would have amounted to yet another theft from Philemon. The slave needed to seek forgiveness from his master and offer restitution.

Yet Paul wanted Philemon to see Onesimus with new eyes. It had been wrong for him to run away, but the experience had led to his conversion, which created an interesting new development. Onesimus had left Colossae as the property of Philemon, but he was returning as a beloved brother (verses 15–16). On a spiritual level, Onesimus and Philemon were now equals. On a human level, they would need to come to an agreement about how they would continue to interact.

Paul did all he could on Onesimus's behalf. He promises to personally pay any unsettled debts to Philemon, and he asks Philemon to receive Onesimus as if he were Paul himself (verses 17–19). The fact that Paul wrote this letter personally (verse 19) would have made his promise legally binding.

It is a bit frustrating to never discover how Philemon responded to Paul's request. Did he punish Onesimus, as was his right to do? Did he take him back as a slave? Did he free him? No one knows. Yet clues abound to suggest that Philemon might have responded as Paul desired.

It would appear that Paul had been instrumental in not only Onesimus's decision to become a Christian, but in Philemon's as well (verse 19). If so, it must have been quite difficult for Philemon to refuse Paul's request. In the first place, the slave and the slave owner had both found salvation in Christ in response to the truth taught by the same preacher. In addition, Paul was offering to do for Onesimus what Jesus had done for them all: pay a debt He didn't owe in order to provide forgiveness and freedom for someone who had done nothing to deserve it.

Paul also expresses confidence that Philemon would grant his request and even go beyond that (verses 20–21). Aside from taking back his fugitive slave, what more could Philemon do other than set him free? And finally, Paul writes that he will soon be making a visit (verse 22). The expectation of soon seeing the apostle in person might have been additional motivation for Philemon to settle the matter. But regardless of Philemon's ultimate decision, Paul's writing in this short letter provides a vastly different view of the worth of a slave than would have been found in the culture of the Roman Empire.

23–25

COWORKERS AND CONCERN

The people with Paul were essentially the same that he mentions at the close of Colossians (Colossians 4:10–14). And his short benediction (Philemon 25) ends this letter, the final of his thirteen letters as arranged in modern Bibles, in very much the same way he concludes all the others—with a prayer for the grace of the Lord Jesus Christ.

Take It Home

It may be difficult for those in the Western world to relate to slavery, yet many people have unresolved relationship issues. Can you think of a rift you have had with someone that could be mended simply by extending your forgiveness? If so, what is preventing you from taking such a step?

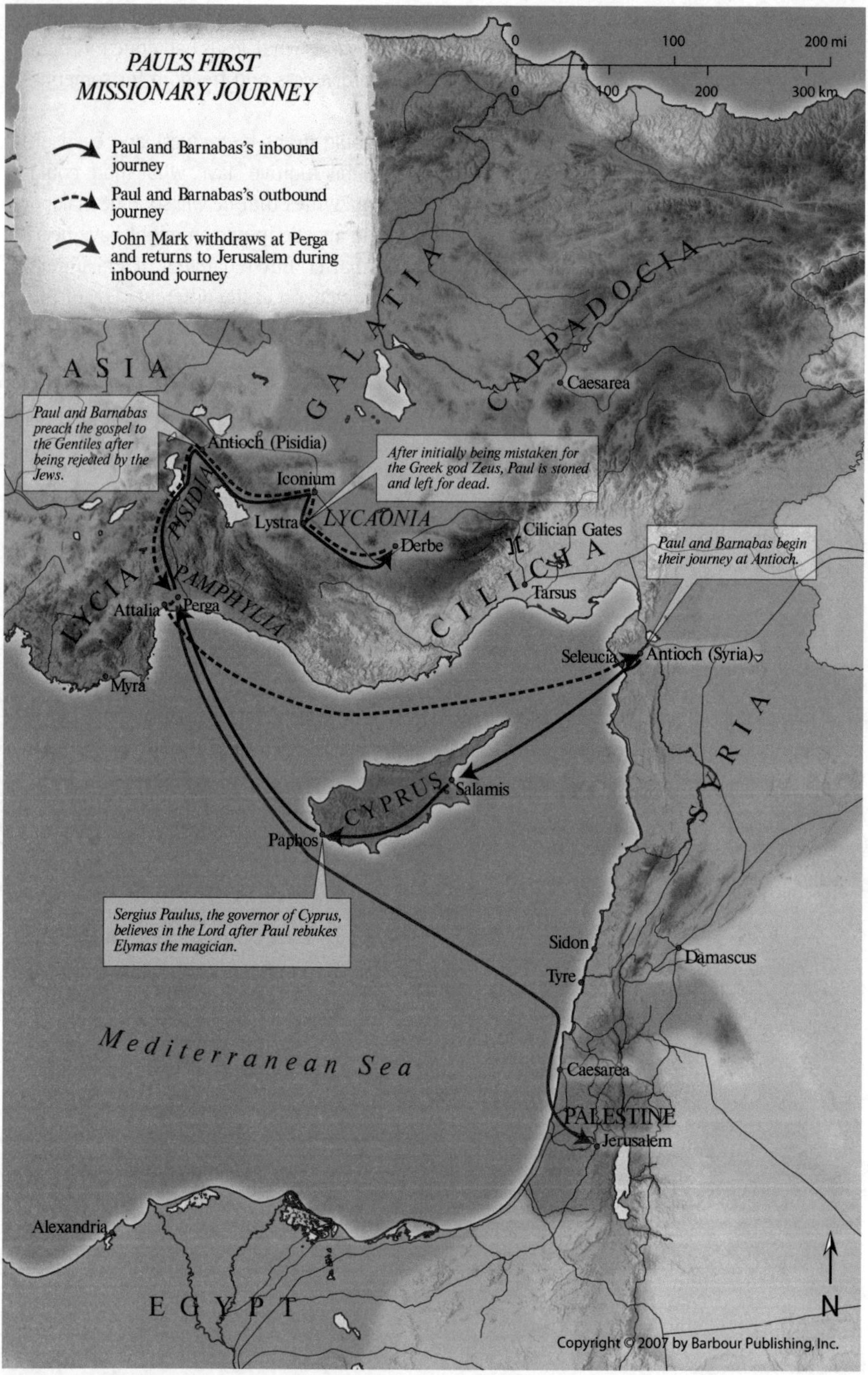
PAUL'S FIRST MISSIONARY JOURNEY
Paul and Barnabas's inbound journey
Paul and Barnabas's outbound journey
John Mark withdraws at Perga and returns to Jerusalem during inbound journey
0 100 200 mi
0 100 200 300 km
ASIA
GALATIA
CAPPADOCIA
Caesarea
Paul and Barnabas preach the gospel to the Gentiles after being rejected by the Jews.
Antioch (Pisidia)
Iconium
After initially being mistaken for the Greek god Zeus, Paul is stoned and left for dead.
PISIDIA
Lystra
LYCAONIA
Derbe
Cilician Gates
Paul and Barnabas begin their journey at Antioch.
LYCIA
PAMPHYLIA
Attalia
Perga
CILICIA
Tarsus
Seleucia
Antioch (Syria)
Myra
SYRIA
CYPRUS
Salamis
Paphos
Sergius Paulus, the governor of Cyprus, believes in the Lord after Paul rebukes Elymas the magician.
Sidon
Damascus
Tyre
Mediterranean Sea
Caesarea
PALESTINE
Jerusalem
Alexandria
EGYPT
N
Copyright © 2007 by Barbour Publishing, Inc.

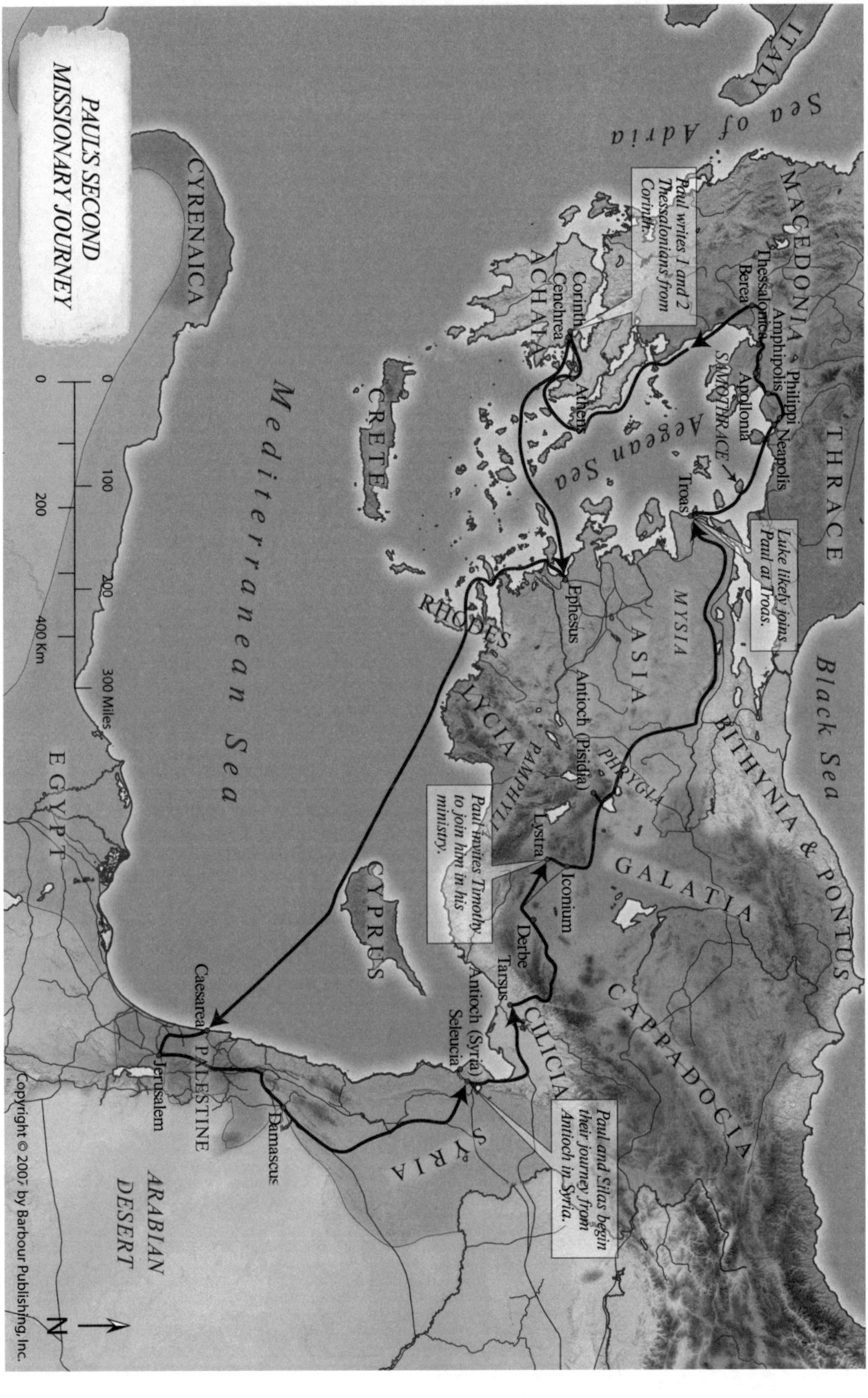
PAUL'S SECOND MISSIONARY JOURNEY
Paul and Silas begin their journey from Antioch in Syria.
Paul invites Timothy to join him in his ministry.
Luke likely joins Paul at Troas.
Paul writes 1 and 2 Thessalonians from Corinth.
ITALY
Sea of Adria
MACEDONIA
THRACE
Philippi
Neapolis
Amphipolis
Apollonia
Thessalonica
Berea
SAMOTHRACE
Troas
Aegean Sea
ACHAIA
Corinth
Cenchrea
Athens
CRETE
RHODES
Ephesus
MYSIA
ASIA
BITHYNIA & PONTUS
Black Sea
PHRYGIA
GALATIA
Antioch (Pisidia)
LYCIA
PAMPHYLIA
Lystra
Iconium
Derbe
Tarsus
CILICIA
CAPPADOCIA
CYPRUS
Antioch (Syria)
Seleucia
SYRIA
Caesarea
PALESTINE
Jerusalem
Damascus
ARABIAN DESERT
CYRENAICA
EGYPT
Mediterranean Sea
0 100 200 300 Miles
0 200 400 Km
N
Copyright © 2007 by Barbour Publishing, Inc.

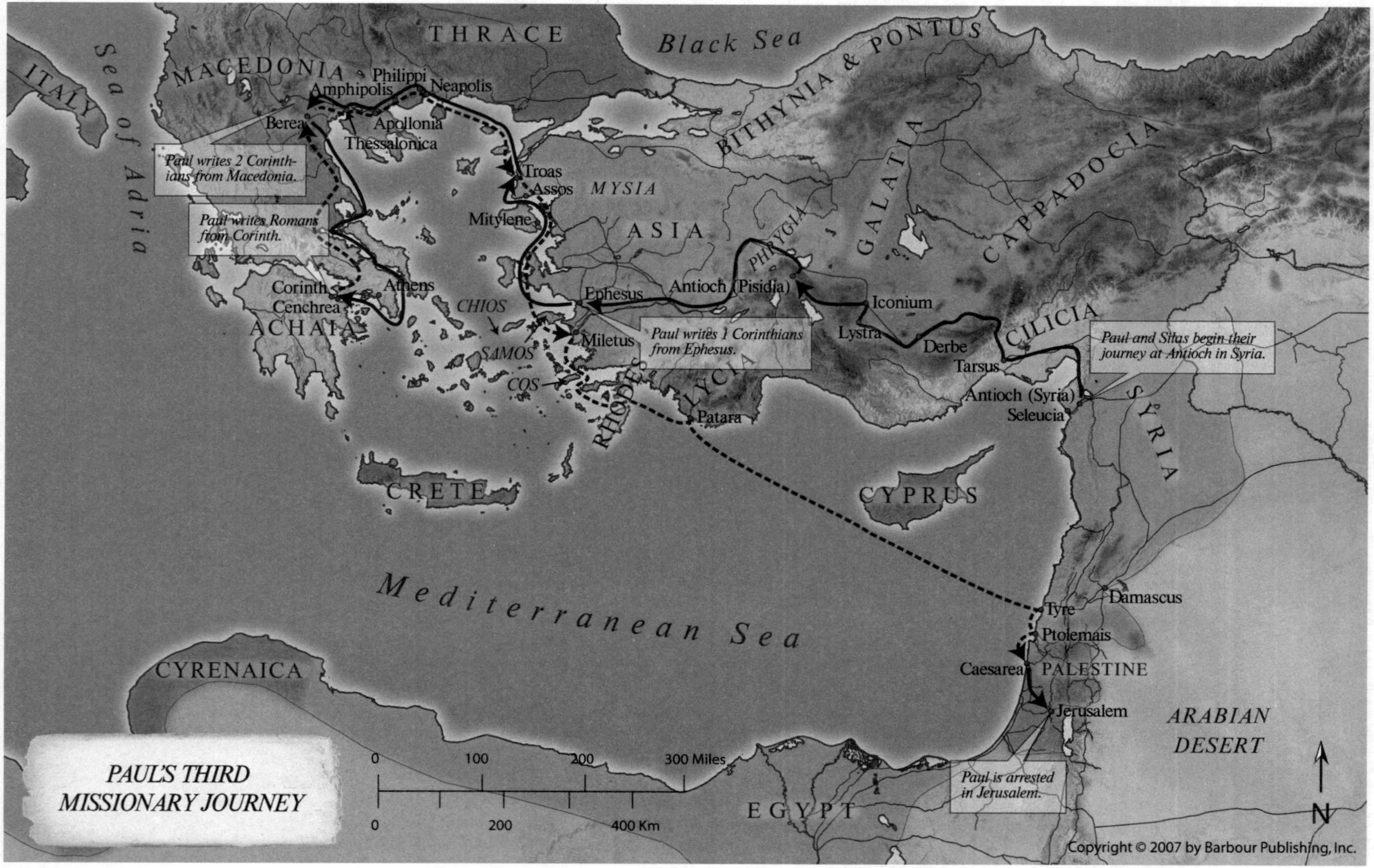
PAUL'S THIRD MISSIONARY JOURNEY
THRACE
Black Sea
BITHYNIA & PONTUS
MACEDONIA
ITALY
Sea of Adria
Philippi
Neapolis
Amphipolis
Berea
Apollonia
Thessalonica
Paul writes 2 Corinthians from Macedonia.
Paul writes Romans from Corinth.
Troas
Assos
MYSIA
Mitylene
ASIA
GALATIA
CAPPADOCIA
PHRYGIA
Corinth
Cenchrea
Athens
ACHAIA
CHIOS
SAMOS
COS
Ephesus
Miletus
Antioch (Pisidia)
Iconium
Lystra
Derbe
Tarsus
CILICIA
Paul writes 1 Corinthians from Ephesus.
Paul and Silas begin their journey at Antioch in Syria.
RHODES
LYCIA
Patara
Antioch (Syria)
Seleucia
SYRIA
CRETE
CYPRUS
Mediterranean Sea
Damascus
Tyre
Ptolemais
Caesarea
PALESTINE
Jerusalem
ARABIAN DESERT
CYRENAICA
EGYPT
Paul is arrested in Jerusalem.
0 100 200 300 Miles
0 200 400 Km
N
Copyright © 2007 by Barbour Publishing, Inc.

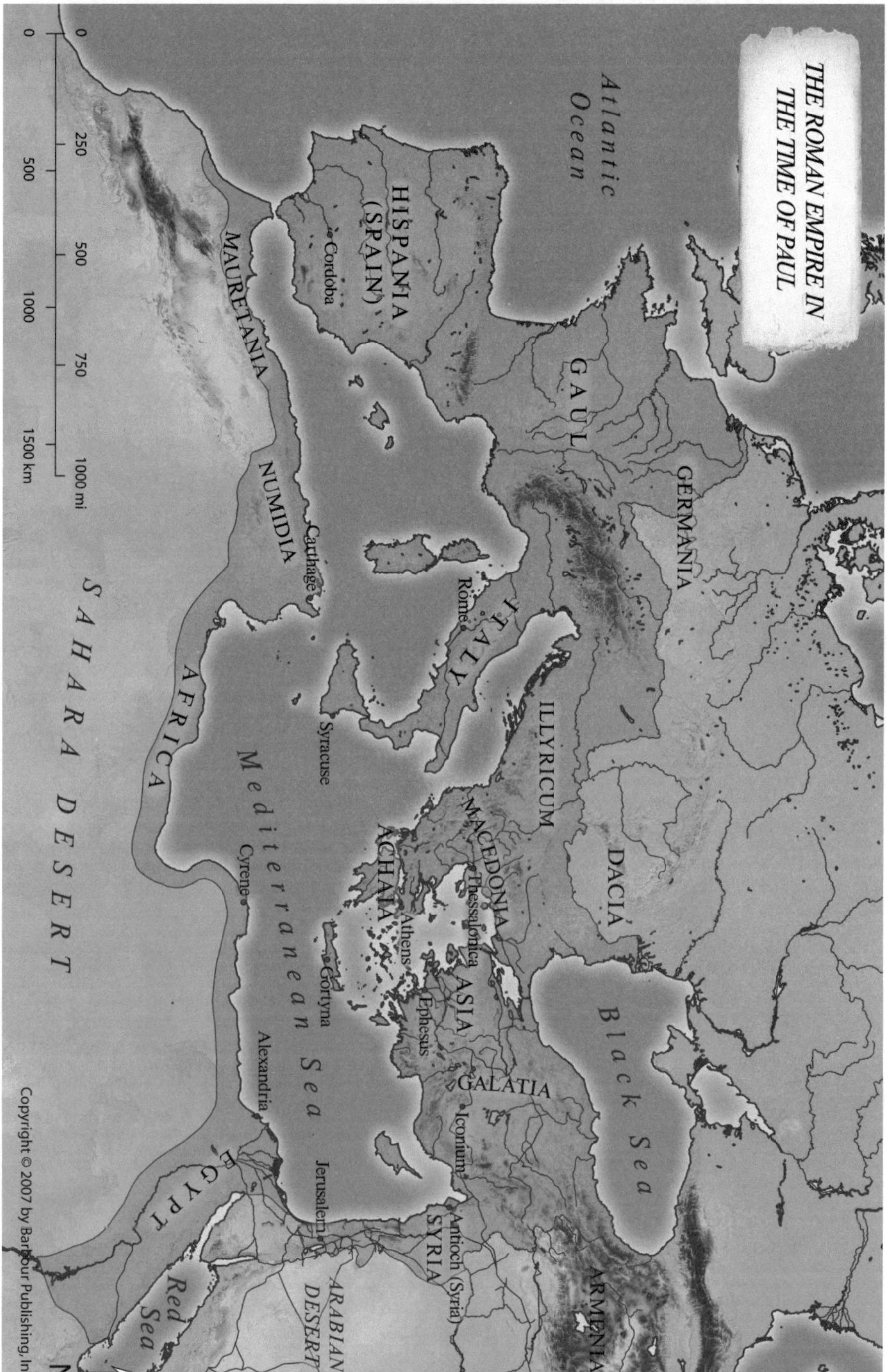
THE ROMAN EMPIRE IN THE TIME OF PAUL
Atlantic Ocean
HISPANIA (SPAIN)
Cordoba
GAUL
GERMANIA
ITALY
Rome
ILLYRICUM
DACIA
MACEDONIA
Thessalonica
ACHAIA
Athens
ASIA
Ephesus
GALATIA
Iconium
Black Sea
ARMENIA
SYRIA
Antioch (Syria)
Jerusalem
ARABIAN DESERT
Red Sea
EGYPT
Alexandria
Mediterranean Sea
Gortyna
Cyrene
Syracuse
Carthage
MAURETANIA
NUMIDIA
AFRICA
SAHARA DESERT
0 250 500 750 1000 mi
0 500 1000 1500 km
N
Copyright © 2007 by Barbour Publishing, Inc.

HEBREWS

INTRODUCTION TO HEBREWS

The book of Hebrews is rightly identified as a letter (or "epistle") because it was written to a specific group of people to address problems and concerns of that community. Like a letter, it contains some personal comments and greetings (13:22–25). But in contrast to most other New Testament letters, Hebrews is fundamentally a sermon—a word of exhortation (13:22). It can be read aloud in less than an hour, and, like most sermons today, is structured around the citation, exposition, and application of scripture. It is not unlike a traditional contemporary sermon.

AUTHOR

No one can say with certainty who wrote Hebrews. Some attribute it to Paul, yet in every other Pauline letter, the apostle opens by identifying himself. In addition, the author's statement about hearing the gospel from others (2:3) does not jibe with Paul's other statements that emphasize his receiving the gospel directly from Christ (Galatians 1:11–12, for example). Furthermore, the language, style, and theological perspective are very different from Paul's elsewhere. Other educated guesses for authorship include Barnabas, Luke, and Apollos. Perhaps the best perspective comes from the insight of the early Christian theologian Origen. Concerning the author of Hebrews, he commented, "God alone knows."

PURPOSE

The original recipients of this letter, as the title indicates, were Jewish Christians. They had suffered persecution for their new faith and had stood firm. . .at first. But as time passed, they had begun to waver and were tempted to return to the comfort of their old, familiar ways. Some had apparently already made the decision to leave the Christian faith and return to Judaism, which placed added pressure on the ones who were still in the church.

OCCASION

No one is certain where the letter was written (perhaps Italy [13:24], although it is equally possible that the *recipients* were in Italy). Still, the occasion of the letter remains clear. The author was well informed about his readers and knew that, while they had once been faithful to Christ and active in the church, some had left to return to the familiarity of Judaism and others were preparing to join them. The writer makes an impassioned plea for them to reconsider, and he lays out a series of strong arguments to verify that Christ is superior to any of their other options. Indeed, Jesus is the *only* option that provides lasting salvation. To reject Him is not only foolish, but spiritually dangerous.

THEMES

Hebrews competes with Galatians for being the most single-minded book in the New Testament. The author makes numerous arguments around a single theme: the absolute necessity of persevering in the Christian faith. Any portion of the letter becomes more pertinent when the reader acknowledges this overriding theme.

HISTORICAL CONTEXT

It appears clear that Hebrews was written prior to the destruction of Jerusalem in AD 70. The author's comment in 2:3 indicates that he is addressing only the second generation of Christians, so a date in the 60s of the first century seems most likely.

CONTRIBUTION TO THE BIBLE

Hebrews presents a masterful explanation of the preeminence of Christ—His superiority to Moses, priests, angels, and everything else. The book also shows not a contrast between the "old" ways of the ancient Israelites with those of the "new" Christian era, but rather the similarity between Old Testament and New Testament believers: Both received the gospel, are saved by grace through faith, look forward to the promised rest of God, and so forth. Hebrews also provides some of the Bible's most direct warnings about the consequences of rejecting Christ and ignoring the work He has completed to provide salvation for humankind.

OUTLINE

THE SUPREMACY OF CHRIST — 1:1–14

The Writer's Thesis — 1:1–4
Jesus Is Superior to the Angels — 1:5–14

SUCH A GREAT SALVATION — 2:1–18

No Better Options — 2:1–4
The World to Come — 2:5–9
Jesus, Humans, and Angels — 2:10–18

JESUS COMPARED TO MOSES — 3:1–19

House Servant vs. Homeowner — 3:1–6
The Consequences of Losing Faith: Then and Now — 3:7–19

REST FOR THE FAITHFUL — 4:1–13

The Same Gospel — 4:1–2
A Sabbath-Rest for God's People — 4:3–13

JESUS COMPARED TO AARON — 4:14–5:10

A Sympathetic High Priest — 4:14–16
The Role of the High Priest — 5:1–10

STEADY GROWTH AND STRONGER HOPE — 5:11–6:20

Time to Grow Up — 5:11–14
A Proper Appreciation for Salvation — 6:1–12
An Example from Abraham — 6:13–20

JESUS COMPARED TO MELCHIZEDEK — 7:1–28

The Story of Melchizedek — 7:1–3
Melchizedek Compared to Levitical Priests — 7:4–10
A Permanent Priesthood — 7:11–28

THE WORK OF A HIGH PRIEST — 8:1–13

Where Christ Serves as Priest — 8:1–6
A New Covenant — 8:7–13

SACRIFICE AND SALVATION 9:1–28

Limitations of the Levitical Priesthood 9:1–15
The Requirement of Blood 9:16–28

THE ONLY MEANINGFUL SACRIFICE 10:1–39

An Annual Reminder of Sin vs. A Clean Slate 10:1–18
Responding to the Priesthood of Christ 10:19–39

NOTEWORTHY FAITH 11:1–40

Faith: Two Definitions and Three Examples 11:1–7
Examples of Faith throughout Israel's History 11:8–40

THE LOVING DISCIPLINE OF GOD 12:1–29

A Positive Appeal: The Benefits of Self-Discipline 12:1–13
A Warning for Those Who Reject Discipline 12:14–29

PRACTICAL APPLICATIONS FOR PERSEVERING FAITH 13:1–25

The Sacrifice of Praise and Good Works 13:1–16
Proper Submission to Authority 13:17–25

HEBREWS 1:1–14

THE SUPREMACY OF CHRIST

The Writer's Thesis 1:1–4

Jesus Is Superior to the Angels 1:5–14

Setting Up the Section

In response to hearing about a number of Jewish Christians beginning to leave the church in order to return to the familiarity of their traditional rites and rituals, the author sends this letter to show them exactly what they are abandoning. In the opening chapters, he describes the superiority of Jesus by making a number of contrasts. In this section he begins by comparing Jesus to angels.

1:1–4

THE WRITER'S THESIS

The first sentence of the Hebrews sermon is an opening salvo. The author immediately begins to set Jesus Christ high above everything and everyone that people might otherwise trust for salvation and security. He does not say, however, that Jesus' message is any different from that of the prophets. The content of the *message* is never contrasted, as will become apparent with a close reading of the letter. But the dignity and authority of Jesus Christ is far greater than any other because He is no less than the Son of God, the heir of all things, and the Creator of heaven and earth (1:2). And the salvation He has accomplished brings to fulfillment all that came before.

The phrase "last days" (1:2) has its background in the Old Testament, referring to the time when God would bring about the restoration of fallen creation. The life, death, and resurrection of Jesus represent the climax of God's plan of salvation, beginning the period of the "last days." At the same time, the writer of Hebrews continues to turn his readers' eyes to the future as he writes about the eventual consummation of their salvation.

The full deity of Jesus Christ is made evident in that He is the Creator of all things, His nature is the same as that of God the Father, and He does what only God can do (1:2–3). After completing His great work of redemption, He is again in heaven at the place of highest honor and authority—God's right hand (alluding to Psalm 110:1–2). The observation that Christ sat down indicates that His work of offering the sacrifice is finished. That point will be reemphasized in 10:12–14, and the reasoning behind this emphasis is that any view of life, any system of salvation, and any approach to God that does not center around Jesus Christ is obviously false and stands self-condemned.

Demystifying Hebrews

"Majesty in heaven" (1:3; 8:1 NIV) is a typical Jewish *periphrasis* for God. In order not to break the third commandment of misusing the name of God, even unintentionally, the Jews began to use other terms to avoid speaking it at all. Some people became almost superstitious about pronouncing God's name.

The comment that Jesus inherited a better name (1:4) does not mean He did not have it by right all along. After all, the writer of Hebrews has just attributed to Christ the creation of the universe, among other things (1:2). But the rewards and inheritance that are due Christ because of His incarnation, death, and resurrection will be shared by those who place their faith in Him.

q 1:5–14

JESUS IS SUPERIOR TO THE ANGELS

The concept of Jesus being better than or superior to other things will be a recurring pattern in Hebrews, occurring in more than a dozen other phrases. The writer begins, however, by citing Jesus' better name and His superiority to the angels.

This would have been a particularly relevant and potentially sensitive subject to many Jewish believers. The Jews held angels in high esteem. Beyond a doubt, angels held important roles as messengers of God. Particularly significant to the Jews was the fact that angels had participated in the giving of the law to Moses on Mount Sinai (Deuteronomy 33:2). So the author uses no fewer than seven citations from Hebrew scripture to make his point.

The first and second citations (Hebrews 1:5), from Psalm 2:7 and 2 Samuel 7:14, respectively, show that Jesus is far more than just another one of God's heavenly messengers. The first quotation is from a psalm that looms large in the New Testament as a prophecy of the incarnation, the ministry, and especially the resurrection of Jesus Christ. The second was originally a covenant promise to David referring to Solomon that was later appropriately applied to Jesus. And by quoting these two passages, the author of Hebrews states boldly that the name of Jesus—the one that is superior to that of the angels—is that of *Son*. Jesus had been God's Son from the beginning, of course. But His incarnation and resurrection were demonstrative examples of that fact. That's why it is said here that Jesus inherited the name (1:4) and that "today" God has become His Father (1:5).

Angels are sometimes referred to as sons of God, just as believers are considered children of God. Yet the singular use of *Son* is a reference applicable to Jesus alone. No angel or person can claim to be *the* Son of God. Angels are only servants of God; Jesus stands high above them as God's Son.

The third Old Testament reference (1:6) is from Deuteronomy 32:43 but is based on the Septuagint—an ancient translation of the Hebrew scriptures into Greek. The Septuagint was translated in the third century before Jesus' birth and would have been the version of scripture familiar to many of the recipients of the letter to the Hebrews. (The text used by those translators had a clause that isn't found in other manuscripts, so the section quoted in Hebrews 1:6 is not found in Deuteronomy 32:43 in most modern Bibles.) The point the writer is making is that the angels, who were exalted by certain people, worshiped Jesus. Christ is not equal to angels; He is their object of worship. This point is made stronger by the writer's reminder that Jesus is the firstborn of God—a title less to do with birth order than to indicate position, authority, and preeminence.

The fourth reference (1:7), from Psalm 104:4, makes a similar point. Not only do angels worship Christ, but they are also His servants—God controls them as He does the winds and the flames. Angels could announce Jesus' birth in Bethlehem and attend to Him in the Garden of Gethsemane, but they couldn't take His place in living and dying for the salvation of humankind.

The fifth reference (1:8–9) is from Psalm 45:6–7, a wedding song for a triumphal king. But since the king is addressed as "O God" and has an eternal throne, the description certainly points to the messianic king. The author of Hebrews shows that Jesus is this king—one of the relatively few texts in the New Testament where Jesus Christ is directly said to be God.

The emphasis is also on this ruler's love of righteousness and hatred of wickedness. Since Christ is being contrasted to angels, it is important to remember that not all angels are good. The focus on righteousness might have been directed to the Jews who still believed that Jesus had been a false prophet who had misled their people.

The next Old Testament reference (1:10–12) is to Psalm 102:25–27. It is a continuation of the previous thought and suggests that while angels are created beings, Jesus is the Creator. To human beings, the life span of a universe appears eternal, but from God's perspective, worlds are created and eventually wear out like a suit of clothes. The reminder that God (Jesus) is eternal and unchanging must have been a welcome consolation to first-century believers during a turbulent time in human history.

Critical Observation

Just as there are numerous denominations and groups that comprise the Christian church today, so were there different sects that professed Judaism in the first century. The Pharisees and Sadducees are mentioned most frequently in scripture, but another group was known as the Essenes. They were nonconformists who tended to isolate themselves in various communities (one being Qumran, the site of the discovery of the Dead Sea Scrolls). Among their nontraditional beliefs were extravagant speculations regarding angels. For example, they believed the archangel Michael would play a decisive role in the coming kingdom. Some Bible scholars think that this section of Hebrews might have been a point-by-point refutation of arguments posed by Jewish Christians who had come out of Essene Judaism and were being tempted to return to it.

The seventh and final reference in this section (Hebrews 1:13) is from Psalm 110:1, and it reiterates the royal status, the divine rule, and the promised inheritance that belong to Jesus Christ. Then, linked with the quote, the author adds his own insight: that angels not only serve God and Christ, but also human beings—those who will inherit salvation (1:14). Some angels minister in the very presence of God, but only Jesus Christ sits at God's right hand.

In addition, here is found the first of many indications in Hebrews that "salvation" is more than the believer's initial commitment. The author will repeatedly speak of salvation as something believers are yet to inherit.

Take It Home

Modern culture has a fascination with angels that may or may not be grounded in biblical fact. From the bumbling Clarence in *It's a Wonderful Life* to the belief by some that we become angels when we die, there are a lot of twisted perspectives. What is your personal belief about angels and their status in comparison to Jesus and to human beings? What questions do you have about angels?

HEBREWS 2:1–18

SUCH A GREAT SALVATION

No Better Options	2:1–4
The World to Come	2:5–9
Jesus, Humans, and Angels	2:10–18

Setting Up the Section

After an emphatic opening showing that Jesus is far superior to any other prophet and even the angels, the author now applies that knowledge to personal faith. Throughout the letter he will repeatedly return to the importance of persevering in the Christian faith.

2:1–4

NO BETTER OPTIONS

In some early translations of scripture, the word used for *drift away* (2:1) was *glide*. Sometimes a departure from faith is not as much a conscious decision as it is a careless sliding past the point where one ought to be (akin to losing a ring from one's finger without noticing). Either way, it is wise to heed the writer's admonition to pay more careful attention.

The author also begins an ongoing argument that the gospel of Christ is not a new teaching. The Jewish readers of this letter were steeped in the ancient scriptures and had no doubts whatsoever about the authority of those writings. They took the Law and Prophets seriously because they believed scripture had been mediated by angels (Acts 7:53; Galatians 3:19), and those who did not submit to it would be subject to severe punishments.

Therefore, after making it clear in Hebrews 1 that Jesus is superior to the angels in numerous ways, the logical question is how the Jewish Christians could ignore what He had taught. If they honored the presence and work of God's angels, how could they possibly overlook or reject the personal appearance and message of God's Son? And if breaking the commands of the old covenant brought severe punishments and discipline, how much greater was the danger of rejecting the much greater revelation given through the Son? In addition to hearing the message itself, the people had witnessed signs, various miracles, and gifts of the Holy Spirit (2:4). So the question begged to be asked: "How will we escape if we neglect so great a salvation?" (2:3 NASB).

What, exactly, should people hope to escape? Although not a popular topic in many churches today, the writer of Hebrews is making a reference to hell and God's judgment of nonbelievers. He will be more specific later (10:26–31).

2:10–18

THE WORLD TO COME

After stating his clear warning, the author returns to the theme he had begun in Hebrews 1: the superiority of Jesus Christ to the angels. He wants his readers to consider the world to come (2:5), and he makes it clear that this is what he has been talking about all along. If indeed the Hebrew believers were being influenced by members of the Essene communities, they would be presented with teachings that included the exaltation of angels in the end times.

The Essenes had not missed the scriptural description of the influence of angels—both good and bad—throughout human history. For example, Michael (the archangel) had come to the aid of Daniel and Israel by opposing other evil angelic beings (Daniel 10:20–21; 12:1). The author of Hebrews does not bother to differentiate good angels from bad, but simply raises the issue and declares that God did *not* appoint the angels to rule in the world to come. Like so much of his argument throughout this sermon, he states the position of the opposition and disproves it biblically without stopping to reconfigure the doctrine from the ground up.

In this case he quotes a portion of Psalm 8 (verses 4–6) to make his point (Hebrews 2:6–8). The psalm can be read as simply a description of how human beings fit into God's creation. Yet the writer perceives the messianic implications of the psalm, acknowledging Jesus as the quintessential human being. Jesus frequently used "Son of man" as a reference to Himself, and in the author's interpretation of the psalm, that title has a double meaning, referring both to human beings generally, and then to Jesus as the fulfillment of humanity's destiny. *All* people have been created a little lower than the angels. Yet this high status is not seen today because of the fallen state of humanity. But through His perfect life, death, resurrection, and ascension, Jesus reversed the results of the fall and achieved this glorified status predicted in the psalm (see Philippians 2:6–11). In Christ the true dignity and destiny of humankind are fulfilled.

Critical Observation

Psalm 8 happens to be a psalm of David, but the author of Hebrews doesn't single him out. A current tendency is to highlight the individuality of biblical authors and analyze their personal outlooks, styles, and theologies. While certain benefits can come from such an approach, the downside is that people begin to look at scripture as just another human book. The Jewish perspective—and the one taken by the author of Hebrews—is to see scripture as God's authoritative Word. If something is included in scripture, it is valid no matter who said it. Throughout the author's writing can be seen his belief that human authorship is a matter of no great importance, but the Word of God certainly is.

The image portrayed by Psalm 8 and Hebrews 2:5–8 is far different from that of some people who see human beings as merely specks in the universe, lost amid the vast cosmos. The psalmist and the writer of Hebrews acknowledge that humans are not only created in the image of God, but are also given authority to oversee creation.

Hebrews 2:9 reprises the author's thought expressed in 1:3–4, which will be a repeated theme throughout this letter. Even though being a little lower than the angels sounds quite impressive to human ears, for Jesus it was a demotion. Yet He had to voluntarily submit to such a status in order to take on human form and sacrifice Himself for all other humans. Because Jesus is now sitting at the right hand of God, believers should acknowledge that setting aside one's own entitlements for the good of others will certainly result in receiving God's reward of glory and honor when it really matters.

2:10–18

JESUS, HUMANS, AND ANGELS

Since the writer of Hebrews is making the point that Jesus is far superior to the angels, he explains why the Son of God had to become a man and suffer and die as a human being. The author is extolling a figure who incurred unprecedented suffering and ignominy in His death. Yet Christ's suffering was the only way God could redeem His people from their sins and deliver them from the wrath to come. Jesus' incarnation was not a pageant or a mere role play. A salvation that would meet the requirement of a just God and atone for the sin of guilty humans required suffering that only a divine-human Savior could endure.

The heavenly Father is referred to here (2:10), as often in the New Testament, simply as God. He is regarded as the source of salvation. The description of Jesus as *author* of salvation (2:10; 12:2) might better be translated as "pioneer" or "trailblazer" (6:20). As the perfect and obedient human being (Psalm 8), Jesus is the "pioneer" of our faith, who brings "many sons and daughters to glory" through His death and resurrection for them (Hebrews 2:10 TNIV).

At first it may appear odd to consider that God *made* Jesus perfect (2:10), since Jesus *was* God. The answer is that Jesus was made perfect or "complete" in His *humanity*. As a human being, He was conceived and born without sin. He lived without sin. And by His obedient suffering, He became the perfect sacrifice for sin and so achieved complete or "perfect" humanity—the position of glory that Adam and Eve failed to achieve because of their rebellion against God. Jesus reversed the results of Adam's fall and became the perfect mediator and High Priest for us. He is now able to save us, as well as to truly sympathize and help us in the midst of trials and temptations.

In Hebrews, sanctification, or being made holy (2:11), does not refer to the moral renewal of a person's life after he or she experiences salvation. Rather, it speaks of the person's reconciliation to God. So here the reader begins to see the great significance of Jesus' incarnation. The Son of God not only forged an identity with very unworthy people, but also was not ashamed to do so. It was an honor beyond anything human beings could ever imagine! And it was something that only Christ could do. No angel was capable of such a feat.

The proclamation of Jesus' solidarity with His people is followed by three citations from Old Testament scripture as proof (2:12–13). The first (2:12) is from Psalm 22:22. The second and third (2:13) are from Isaiah 8:17–18. The Old Testament prophet had expressed faith in the Lord and a willingness to oversee the children of God. Such commitments, when applied to Jesus, were even more powerful. During Jesus' incarnation, He shared the human need to live by faith and put His trust in God the Father.

Jesus was certainly an exemplary human being. Rarely are people both sympathetic and strong. Christ, however, could relate to the limitations of humanity even as He was overcoming the forces that imposed many of those limitations (2:14–15). Had Jesus not accepted the limitations of humanity, He never could have tasted death on behalf of all people (2:9, 14–15). Only Christ was a perfect human being. His humanity allowed Him to die. His perfection made Him an appropriate sacrifice to God. And His willingness to go through with such an awful sacrifice was the only way to break the hold of sin and the devil.

It was Jesus' mission to provide salvation for human beings (Abraham's descendants)—not angels (2:16). Jesus helps in a very real way by seeing His people through whatever they are facing. He relates to human suffering because of His incarnation. He had to take on human form in order to die, and by doing so, He also experienced the emotions, pains, and temptations common to all human beings. His experience perfectly qualifies Him to act as High Priest—an intercessor between sinful humankind and a perfect God (2:17–18). No one can rightly claim that God doesn't understand how he or she feels, because Jesus lived through everything any human being can face—and worse. The writer of Hebrews will have more to say on this topic later in the letter.

Take It Home

Jesus' humanity, and the suffering that went along with it, was what enabled Him to relate more personally and completely to the human experience. Can you think of a similar way in which your own sufferings have, in retrospect, provided you with greater empathy and insight into how someone else was feeling? As a result, have your own sufferings enabled you to be a better minister to someone else who is suffering?

HEBREWS 3:1–19

JESUS COMPARED TO MOSES

House Servant vs. Homeowner 3:1–6
The Consequences of Losing Faith: Then and Now 3:7–19

Setting Up the Section

Knowing of his readers' high regard for angels, the writer of Hebrews has just concluded a section of how Jesus is far superior to the angelic beings. In this section he turns his attention to another hero of the Jewish people—Moses. While his readers had good reason to admire Moses for his faithfulness and great accomplishments, his deeds pale when contrasted to the life of Jesus Christ.

3:1–6

HOUSE SERVANT VS. HOMEOWNER

The writer of Hebrews has just summarized his argument that Jesus Christ is worthier of his readers' praise and admiration than any angel. He continues that thought with the "Therefore" that opens Hebrews 3. The author isn't merely attempting to win a debate; he is attempting to show his Hebrew readers what benefits they could enjoy as a result of Jesus' preeminence. They were not only "brothers" with their Lord and all other believers, but "holy" brothers at that (3:1).

In addition, the writer attempts to clarify the Jews' perception of Jesus. They would have well understood the importance of the role of high priest. The high priest was the figure who stood between the sinful worshiper presenting an offering to God and the holy figure from whom forgiveness was being asked. To have a high priest who had such compassion and empathy and was not ashamed to call them brothers (2:11), was indeed a privilege.

The Jewish Christians were probably less familiar, as are many contemporary Christians, with the concept of Jesus as an apostle (3:1). But the word simply means "one who is sent," and Jesus was certainly sent from God to minister to and save a sinful world. He was God's personal representative and showed humankind in clear and tangible ways what God was like. He demonstrated in no uncertain terms the sometimes overlooked aspects of God's character: love, mercy, grace, forgiveness, and so on.

Since Jesus represents humankind to God as high priest and represents God to people as apostle, He is in a unique position to mediate. This is the great application of the letter of Hebrews. If believers do not stand fast in loyalty to Jesus, what other hope do they have for reconciliation with God?

Critical Observation

It is in this section that many interpretations of Hebrews begin to go seriously astray. Some commentators allege that these verses amount to a contrast between an inferior Mosaic order/administration and the superior administration introduced by Christ and the apostles, resulting in the belief that the Christian era is superior to the Mosaic one. But a close examination of this passage reveals that is *not* what the author is saying.

The author has already briefly contrasted Jesus with the Old Testament prophets (1:1–2) and more explicitly with the angels (1:3–2:18). Here he begins a contrast between Jesus and Moses. The Jews perceived Moses as a great man, great prophet, great leader, and great lawgiver. Yet Jesus fulfilled all those roles as well—to a greater degree than Moses. Both Moses and Jesus were called by God and sent to help His people; both ministered to people who were subject to powerful forces (whether the Egyptian empire or the power of sin) and were being called to freedom; and both brought a message from God to provide clear direction for living in this world while anticipating a better one to come.

But as the writer contrasts Moses with Jesus, his imagery makes his point (3:2–6). Moses was a faithful servant in God's house, but Christ was the builder. Moses was never anything more than a worker in the house over which Jesus ruled as the Son of God. Jesus is clearly superior to Moses.

There is but one house of God and one people of God. Moses himself pointed ahead to the Christ who was to come. Jesus had said that Moses spoke of Him (John 5:45–47), and Paul wrote that Moses' message was the same as his own: salvation through faith in Christ (Romans 9:14–16). So it is a fundamental assumption of the author of Hebrews that God's church has run continually throughout all ages of history. He refers repeatedly to the people of God but never once distinguishes eras or epochs or generations. In all ages, the people of God are those who are saved by persevering faith in Christ.

Demystifying Hebrews

The writer of Hebrews is beginning an argument that will become clearer as he goes on. By the end of the letter, he will state plainly that Jesus Christ is the same yesterday, today, and forever (Hebrews 13:8). Christ Himself was at work in building the church in the ancient epoch. Hebrews 12 clarifies that it was Christ who led the people of God out of Egypt and through the wilderness, who gave the law at Mount Sinai, who talked to Moses in the Tent of Meeting, and whose glory was reflected on the face of Moses. The author is already making that assumption in 3:2–6, although the reader might not yet be aware of such an assumption.

3:7–19

THE CONSEQUENCES OF LOSING FAITH: THEN AND NOW

The writer of Hebrews makes it as clear as possible that any Jewish Christians who were considering abandoning their faith were making a serious mistake. Hebrews 3:7 begins a long hortatory section (where the author makes an urgent appeal by mixing exposition with application) that stretches to 4:13.

He begins by quoting a portion of Psalm 95, which would have accomplished a number of things. First, the passage was a call to worship frequently used in first-century synagogues. More importantly, it recounts the story of the Israelites in the wilderness. By the first century, Moses stood as one of the undisputed heroes of the faith. Yet the psalm is a poignant reminder that the people under Moses' leadership had rebelled. As a result, neither they nor he reached the Promised Land where they were headed. God prevented all the stubborn, complaining people from entering the land, and it was possessed instead by a more faithful generation. In addition, the psalm was more than historic; it was current. The promise and warning for "today" (Hebrews 3:7, 13) are just as relevant in the first and twenty-first centuries as they were in the wilderness.

The story cited by the psalm has obvious parallels to the point being made by the writer of Hebrews. God was trying to elevate His people from one set of circumstances to a much more joyous and rewarding one. Yet as soon as they got started, some of them wanted to turn around and return to their more familiar, though less fulfilling, way of life. The Jewish Christians tempted to return to the stringent adherence to the rites and laws of Judaism could not have missed the writer's point.

The psalm also refers to the ultimate goal of the people as God's rest (3:11). The writer would soon say that the promise of entering God's rest still stands (4:1), so it becomes apparent that the psalmist had something more than the land of Canaan in mind. The rest of God remains, as it has always been, as fellowship with the Lord in heaven.

Here again is the futuristic perspective of Hebrews. Failing to enter God's rest means nothing less than failure to obtain eternal life. Entrance into the Promised Land had been but a symbol of something much greater.

The Jewish Christians receiving this letter would have been more familiar with Psalm 95 than most modern readers. The section quoted by the writer of Hebrews was the latter half of the psalm (verses 7–11). What came before (Psalm 95:1–6) was a rousing call to worship God with joy, thanksgiving, and gratitude. The readers of Hebrews would have known what was expected of them; the writer was simply reminding them.

From the psalm, the writer moves right into a plea for ongoing faithfulness. He never questions the authenticity of their conversions, but addresses them as brothers (3:1, 12) and attempts to reason with them. They had the responsibility for monitoring their own thoughts and beliefs (3:12) as well as regularly (daily) encouraging one another (3:13).

The deceitfulness of sin is an ongoing concern, and believers need to be ever vigilant to prevent becoming apathetic or rebellious toward the things of God. Allowing improper thoughts or attitudes to linger can be disastrous, so the time to act is now (3:15). And again, the author reminds his readers of his main point: Believers need to persevere in their faith so they don't miss out on anything Christ makes available to them (3:14).

It was not enough to know God's plans and purposes. The Israelites who had crossed the Red Sea between walls of water could see beyond a doubt that God was with them. He was ever before them in a pillar of cloud or fire. Yet they had still rebelled against Moses and against God, and were subsequently forbidden from entering the land (3:16–19). The Hebrew Christians also knew God's plans and purposes, but some needed prompting to keep from departing from the truths they knew.

If indeed the recipients of this letter included Jews with an association to the Essenes at Qumran, this historical reference would have been especially pertinent. The Essenes regarded the wilderness generation of Israel as a pattern or paradigm for their lives. But the author of Hebrews is reminding them that the generation that had started out loyal to God had quickly become a tragic example of unfaithfulness and apostasy. Paul makes a similar point in 1 Corinthians 10:1–13.

Throughout Hebrews, the author does not dwell simply on the problem of unbelief, but rather on apostasy—the turning away from the faith by someone who once believed, or at least professed to believe. As indicated in 3:12 and 3:19, there will be an ongoing emphasis on the connections between disobedience and unbelief, and between faith and obedience. What was true for the Israelites in the wilderness remains just as applicable for believers today and in the ages to come.

Take It Home

Can you recall times in your spiritual journey when you went through a period of apathy, disbelief, or rebellion? What was the reason for those feelings? How did your life during those times compare to periods when you felt close to God? What do you think is the best course of action to avoid similar conditions in the future?

HEBREWS 4:1–13

REST FOR THE FAITHFUL

The Same Gospel 4:1–2
A Sabbath-Rest for God's People 4:3–13

Setting Up the Section

The writer of Hebrews began a persuasive argument in 3:7 that continues in this section. He is reminding his hearers of the history of Israel in the wilderness and of the people's failure to enter the rest of God because of their unbelief. He is also warning them that if they turn away from God, they must expect the same consequences. In this section he continues his comparison of the first-century Hebrew Christians to the Israelites of the Exodus.

4:1–2

THE SAME GOSPEL

The author has just noted that the Old Testament Israelites were poised on the brink of entering the *rest* of God. He uses that term (rather than *Promised Land*) because he will bring the same concept into the present and apply it to his readers as well. The Israelites, as well as the first-century Jewish believers who were tempted to abandon the clear teachings of Christianity, were apt to lose much more than a temporary earthly possession. Forsaking their faith could have eternal consequences as well.

Another word the author uses frequently is *promise*, and the first of its fourteen appearances in Hebrews is found in 4:1. He uses the word to encompass the world to come, eternal life, and the final consummation of salvation. This promise was made to God's people in the ancient epoch and is still being made to believers. The author of Hebrews clarifies that the promise will be fulfilled in the next world for those, and only those, who have followed the Lord Jesus with persevering faith all the way to the end of their lives. People in the church whose faith flags and who turn away from following the Lord forfeit that promise.

In another unusual word usage, the writer of Hebrews calls God's message to the Old Testament Israelites the gospel (4:2). That in itself was not unheard of at the time. Paul makes similar statements in his letters (Romans 10:15–16; Galatians 3:8). But the phrasing in Hebrews 4:2 is distinctive. The writer doesn't say that those in the Old Testament had the gospel preached to them, just as those in the first century had heard it. Rather, he says that the New Testament Christians had heard the same gospel as the ancient Israelites. The assumption he makes is that no one would doubt that Israel heard the gospel. Nothing could more profoundly demonstrate his point that the message of salvation in Christ, and the requirement of faith in Christ, has always been the same.

4:3–13

A SABBATH-REST FOR GOD'S PEOPLE

In light of his reasoning, the fact that the Israelites would blatantly ignore God's truth is even more appalling, and that's exactly what the first-century believers were beginning to do. Twice more the author quotes Psalm 95:11 (Hebrews 4:3, 5) as he had in 3:11. He makes it clear that entering God's rest is the issue, and the possibility of failing to enter it is very real.

The fact that the writer uses present tense in verse 3 creates potential problems with interpretation. Some people leap to the assumption that he is saying that the Old Testament saints couldn't enter God's rest because it hadn't yet been made available by Christ's death and resurrection, while believers after Christ can enter God's rest immediately. This view makes no sense, however, in light of the fact that the author had just stated that the promise forfeited by the Israelites was the same promise the current believers must be careful not to abandon. He says the gospel is the same, then and now. And he says, as he will repeat again and again, that the promise (the gospel, salvation, and all things related) ultimately refers to heaven, not just to the partial experience of salvation believers enjoy in this world.

A better interpretation of verse 3 is to read it as a futuristic present tense. For example, Paul and Barnabas had preached, "We must go through many hardships to enter the kingdom of God" (Acts 14:22 NIV). It is clearly a principle that applies to entering the kingdom of God in the future, and the thought remains the same if *rest* is substituted for *kingdom*. That's what the writer of Hebrews intended. It makes little sense to say that New Testament believers have already entered the rest of God when the writer's urgent admonition is that they continue to persevere in faith lest they fail to enter the rest! Hebrews 4:6 and 4:11 both make it clear that the author is looking to the future as he discusses God's rest. Another possibility is that the present tense carries a progressive sense. Believers are entering the rest through the process of salvation but must endure so as to fully enter that rest at the consummation of their salvation. Not to persevere means to fail to enter God's rest (salvation).

The concept of the rest of God was certainly nothing new. From the beginning, God had demonstrated a period of rest at the end of one's work (4:4). After the six days of creation, God rested on the seventh day. So at this point, the rest of God is identified as participation in God's own rest that began immediately after the creation of the world. This is the rest that the Israelites had failed to obtain—not because it wasn't available to them, but because they did not continue to put their faith in God.

Demystifying Hebrews

The writer of Hebrews makes it clear that some people will enter God's rest while others will not, even after hearing the gospel (4:6–7). The difference is a person's *response* to the message. And here he repeats himself about the need to respond while there is still time (3:15; 4:7). God has been making the offer for centuries, in an extended stretch of time called "today" (4:7). This "today" is the whole period of time in which the gospel message of salvation is being offered. It is a limited opportunity. The writer urges his readers to act while there is still time.

The first generation of Israelites missed the opportunity to enter the Promised Land because of their lack of faith. They missed out on God's rest. The author of Hebrews takes this idea of rest and applies it to God's ultimate "Promised Land," what he defines (in various places) as the better country, the enduring city, and the world to come.

The author uses a word that might literally be rendered *Sabbathment* but is usually translated *Sabbath-rest* (4:9). The word is found nowhere else in the Bible and has been detected in no earlier uses than this one. The writer may have invented the word to define what he was talking about. No doubt the term evoked in his mind a connection to the weekly Sabbath. Just as God rested from His work on the seventh day of Creation, so He now invites believers to enter into His rest, signifying both His presence and salvation. Just as the seventh day of Creation represented the completion of God's work and a time of rest, so the Sabbath-rest for believers symbolizes the consummation of their salvation and entrance into God's rest.

Some Christians use this passage to justify doing away with a weekly day of rest for Christians. This, however, is not the author's point (but see Romans 14:5–6; Colossians 2:16–17 for Paul's perspective on the Sabbath). He is simply drawing an analogy between the weekly Sabbath-rest and our salvation. Both involve entering God's rest, which the author uses as a metaphor for the presence of God and the salvation He provides.

Hebrews 4:12 is an often-quoted and frequently memorized verse. As such, it may seem that the writer suddenly shifts topics, from rest to the Word of God. Actually, he is emphasizing a point. He began his discussion of rest at 3:7 by quoting from scripture, attributing not a psalmist, but the Holy Spirit for the text. The psalm is a warning against hardening one's heart and rebelling against God.

So the point he makes in 4:12 is that God's Word is nothing to be taken lightly. It can never be ignored or dismissed with impunity. It is the living voice of God that gets right to the bottom of things. Someone may look fine in the eyes of other people, but God's Word exposes the true condition of the heart, the real character of one's faith, and reveals a genuine spirit.

Critical Observation

The phrase "soul and spirit, joints and marrow" (4:12) is simply a way to refer to the inner life of a human being in all of its aspects. Although some people use this verse as evidence that a person is composed of three parts (spirit, soul, and body), someone else could just as easily cite Mark 12:30 to speculate that people have four parts (heart, soul, mind, and body).

God sees every action. He knows every thought and attitude. No matter how hard people try to hide their sins, the truth will eventually come to light and they will be expected to give an account (4:13). How much better it is to respond to God and await His rest. According to the writer of Hebrews, "today" won't last forever.

Take It Home

The modern church can benefit by a renewed excitement over the celebration of a Sabbath—one day each week set aside for refreshing rest in anticipation of the eternal rest of God that awaits us in the world to come. With a focus on rest and worship, the principle of Sabbath can keep alive one's immediate sense of joy and expectation of even better things to come. Is this typical of your own experience? If not, what needs to change in order for you to make the most of your Sabbath days and preparation for the ultimate rest of God?

HEBREWS 4:14–5:10

JESUS COMPARED TO AARON

A Sympathetic High Priest 4:14–16

The Role of the High Priest 5:1–10

Setting Up the Section

So far in his letter, the author of Hebrews has demonstrated how Christ is superior to the Old Testament prophets, to the angels, and to Moses. In this section he continues his series of contrasts by comparing Jesus to Aaron and other well-respected high priests.

4:14–16

A SYMPATHETIC HIGH PRIEST

Remember that the Jewish Christians who were receiving this letter had been in discussions with certain other Jewish advocates who were pressuring them to return to a more traditional Jewish perspective, which would require that they abandon many of the Christian teachings they had already professed to believe. One topic especially relevant to this dialog was the role of the high priest in regard to a person's salvation. The early Christians were coming to see the traditional rites as only a prefigurement of the final and ultimate provision for salvation made in the life, death, and resurrection of Jesus Christ. But the ongoing Jewish view was that the Levitical priesthood and its ceremonies were still, as had always been the case, God's definitive provision for the salvation of humankind.

The writer of Hebrews has a habit of mentioning a topic early in the letter that he examines later in more detail. He has already presented the image of Jesus in the role of high priest (2:17; 3:1), but in this section he goes into much more depth. He also changes his tone dramatically. After a section with a dire warning of what could happen to those who harden their hearts and give up on their faith, he begins a warm entreaty for them to realize exactly what Jesus had done on their behalf.

The Jews would have been familiar with the procedure of the high priest interceding with God on their behalf. It was a solemn and somber ceremony. One day a year, the high priest—and only the high priest—would enter the Most Holy Place of the temple to sprinkle blood from animal sacrifices on the ark of the covenant (Leviticus 16). The ark was symbolic of the presence of God. Anyone who violated the Most Holy Place or the ark would die (2 Samuel 6:6–7).

But Jesus didn't just step symbolically into God's presence in the temple; He went through the heavens to be literally in the presence of God (Hebrews 4:14). And His qualifications as High Priest were unsurpassed. Not only had He been the spotless, perfect sacrifice whose blood was shed, but He had also shared the human experience with those whom He was defending. He knew exactly the temptations they faced and the weaknesses they felt (4:15). He felt the full force of human difficulties and understands them better than people do, from God's perspective.

Demystifying Hebrews

In order to comprehend the importance of Jesus as High Priest, it is essential to understand the significance of His humanity. Although He displayed great power while on earth, He had to receive power from God as the other human prophets and apostles did. He was a true, authentic person who walked with God. He had the same temptations and troubles as any other person, yet chose to live by faith, trust His heavenly Father, and put on holiness as all believers are called to do. He had a sense of His purpose in life and how His life would end, yet—in His humanity—He was not omniscient or specifically aware of what the next day would bring. He does not make the ideal High Priest because He is God, but rather because He was fully human and lived out His life the way each person must live it.

The writer of Hebrews says that Jesus had been tempted in every way, just as other people are. Obviously that doesn't mean Jesus faced every single possible temptation. He never faced the problems that come with old age, for example. He didn't face the temptations involved in marriage, child rearing, or wealth. Yet the author's point is well taken. Jesus lived a human life that was beset with more stress, trauma, and pain than most people can even conceive. His temptations were many and varied, and He resisted every one of them. People fail to understand the significance of such devotion to God because they so easily give in to temptations. But Jesus never surrendered to temptation. He never sinned, even though His temptations were strong and His pain intense. He endured them all to the bitter end.

Many people memorize Hebrews 4:14–16 as a passage of beautiful sentiment and wonderful hope, which it is. Yet most tend to gloss over the fact that it takes real, sturdy faith to believe that Jesus truly understands how they feel. When life takes a turn for the worse, one of the first things people tend to do is blame God, or at least seek a logical explanation when none exists. It is a great privilege to stand before God with confidence, expecting mercy and grace (4:16).

5:1–10

THE ROLE OF THE HIGH PRIEST

Jewish religious purists might have ruled out Jesus as a likely high priest simply because of the fact that He was from the tribe of Judah, when the priests were required to be descendants of Levi. So in this section, the author takes care to establish that Jesus is in every way fitted to be the believer's great High Priest.

A significant level of maturity was needed in order to be an effective priest. The person needed an awareness of the power of sin and had to be capable of overcoming it in his own life. Yet the role also required a vulnerability borne out of the recognition of his personal weaknesses (5:2). Before priests could offer sacrifices for others, they had to make sacrifices on their own behalf (Leviticus 16:11, 15; Hebrews 5:3).

Additionally, a high priest had to be appointed. He could not take the office on his own (5:1). Originally, God had specified who would serve as high priest. By the first century, however, the role had become entangled with both Jewish and Roman politics and was more of a status symbol than a legitimate spiritual calling. Both Jesus and Paul had encounters with high priests who were lacking in both humanity and spiritual maturity.

With these expectations in mind, the author begins to demonstrate how Jesus met each requirement. Jesus had been called by God, just as Aaron had been. Two prophecies from scripture are quoted as evidence of His divine appointment. The author has already referred once to Psalm 2:7 to show that Jesus is the Son of God (Hebrews 1:5). But not only was He God's Son; He was also designated a priest by God the Father (Psalm 110:4).

In fact, Jesus had quoted from Psalm 110 while asserting His claim to be the Messiah (Matthew 22:41–46). Throughout the Gospels, Jesus makes the point over and over again that He had received His commission from God the Father. Although He willingly offered Himself as a sacrifice, He did not seek the mission for Himself. It was laid upon Him as a charge by God.

The Old Testament verses used by the writer of Hebrews to show how Jesus is a great high priest could be used to prove Christ's kingship as well. The two divinely appointed offices—priest and king—combine in the life and work of Jesus Christ.

Critical Observation

If indeed the letter to the Hebrews was intended to refute some of the teachings of the Essene sect of Judaism, this section would have been particularly appropriate. One of the reasons the Essenes had withdrawn from worship in the Jerusalem temple was their feeling that Israel's current priesthood, under control of the Sadducees, was corrupted beyond repair. In addition, the sect was looking for two messiahs—one to perform in a priestly role and the other as a victorious king. The writer of Hebrews demonstrates that Jesus fulfilled both roles, and was not tainted in any way by corruption.

Jesus had never offered sacrificial animals as the high priests before Him had done. There was no need, because His death would be the only sacrifice ever needed, as the writer of Hebrews will explain later (7:27; 10:10). Instead, Jesus' offerings to God were prayers and petitions, accompanied by loud cries and tears (5:7). The image evokes Jesus' intense prayers in Gethsemane or His cries to the Father from the cross. The tears and cries are reminders that Jesus was never immune to any of the sufferings of life. He succeeded in His life and work, not because He was spared anything other humans must experience, but because He prayed regularly, learned scripture, struggled against enormous temptations, and remained faithful until the very end of His human life.

The writer of Hebrews drops in a couple of references to Melchizedek, the king/priest who had associated with Abraham centuries before (5.6, 10). This is another example of how he tends to briefly introduce a topic before delving into it later. His full discussion about Melchizedek comes in Hebrews 7. At this point, however, where Jesus is being compared to Aaron as a high priest, it should be noted that Melchizedek served as priest long *before* the law was given—before Aaron was even born.

Jesus was God's Son, which held certain entitlements (5:8). Yet He willingly opted to obey through suffering, for the good of humankind. He, more than anyone else, is qualified to rule not only as Lord, but also as High Priest.

In closing this section, the writer of Hebrews connects salvation with *obedience* to God (5:9). It is more usual to associate trust or faith with salvation, but this is not the Bible's sole exception. It is appropriate to use such different terminology because true faith is always expressed through obedience. Not only that, but faith is itself an act of obedience. Everyone who hears the gospel is obliged to believe it as a summons, a command from God. Any response other than belief is a form of disobedience and rebellion. The gospel is more than an invitation to be saved by faith in Christ; it is a command to be obeyed.

Christ rules as king and serves as High Priest. To disobey His truth leaves no other option for salvation. So as the author of Hebrews continues, he will next address the problem of believers who fall away from the faith.

Take It Home

Consider how the knowledge of Jesus serving as your High Priest can help you in practical ways. What situations or emotions are you facing where you would find consolation to realize that Jesus fully understands your feelings? For example, consider the experience of loneliness. It is a crushing burden for many people and a catalyst for the temptation to sin. For many people, the experience has resulted in unbelief, despair, anger, and resentment. Jesus well knew the temptation and sorrow of human loneliness, yet His response was not to succumb to temptation, but rather to get up earlier to spend quality time with His Father (Mark 1:35). How can Jesus' humanity inspire you to overcome or endure a circumstance you are currently facing?

HEBREWS 5:11–6:20

STEADY GROWTH AND STRONGER HOPE

Time to Grow Up	5:11–14
A Proper Appreciation for Salvation	6:1–12
An Example from Abraham	6:13–20

Setting Up the Section

In the author's alternations between exposition and application, this section brings us to another section of application. He is preparing to move on to another segment about the importance of Jesus Christ, but first he pauses to prepare his hearers. His preparation includes a scolding, yet what he has to say is a reminder, in no uncertain terms, of the basic theme of the letter.

5:11–14

TIME TO GROW UP

The author of Hebrews has been developing a deep spiritual thought about Jesus using various scriptures and common knowledge about the work of the high priest. Yet he pauses to concede that his readers might not be ready to hear what he is saying. He compares his teachings to a child's diet (5:13–14). When very young, a baby cannot handle solid food and needs only milk. Soon, however, milk is not enough, and he or she needs to move on to solid food.

The writer was distraught to realize that the Hebrew Christians were still in need of "milk." Yet their situation was not unlike that of many current believers. Their spiritual childishness was a result of their contentment with the status quo. Further progress in their Christian growth and devotion to Christ would only increase the distance between themselves and their Jewish family members, friends, and acquaintances. It was easier not to press the issue.

But as the writer goes on to explain, spiritual stagnation is dangerous. Genuine spiritual growth and vitality requires solid "food." The spiritual and ethical discernment necessary to keep from falling prey to falsehood and the temptations of the world demands a deepening knowledge and the constant exercise of faith. Sitting on the fence between their old Jewish ways and their new Christian commitment wasn't doing any good.

By this time, a number of believers should have been qualified to be teachers. Instead, an outside instructor was still required to teach them elemental truths (5:11–12). Theirs was not an ideal situation.

6:1–12

A PROPER APPRECIATION FOR SALVATION

Although the writer is direct and firm, he does not appear to be angry with his hearers. He is writing out of concern, not merely to criticize. He urges his readers to keep moving forward, beyond the elementary aspects of their faith, into a mature relationship with God.

It wasn't as if they were being asked to forsake everything familiar to them. In fact, the early church had incorporated many of the customs of Judaism into their worship ceremonies. Many of their beliefs were the same as well. The first-century Jewish faith and worldview included repentance from sin, professions of faith, baptism, the laying on of hands (although more in regard to sacrifices and ordination than the bestowal of the Holy Spirit), resurrection, and God's judgment. The Christian church began with Jewish believers who built on what they had already been taught about God.

Yet many of their rites and ceremonies had become hollow traditions. The life, death, and resurrection of Jesus Christ imparted to them the meaning that had been lost. Or more accurately, the awareness of Christ *should* have enlightened their thinking concerning the centuries-old practices they held to. They needed to open their spiritual eyes and begin moving forward into the "meatier" aspects of their faith.

Critical Observation

In this context, the mention of baptisms (6:2) seems to be a clear reference to Old Testament Jewish ceremonial washings rather than the more current application of the word. The author will soon (9:13) make reference to the ritual of the red heifer (Numbers 19) that required bathing and washing one's clothes.

This section is a source of debate among contemporary scholars. Numerous Bible passages affirm that a genuine believer is in no danger of ever losing his or her salvation—and that list includes the final verses of this section (6:16–20). The Hebrew Christians appear to have been genuine believers: They had been enlightened, had reveled in the Word of God, had shared in the Holy Spirit, and more (6:4–5). On the other hand, scripture also points to instances where people seemed to begin the Christian life, sometimes very impressively, yet were later revealed never to have been born again, never to have become genuine followers of Christ (Matthew 7:21–23; 1 John 2:19).

So were the Hebrew Christians true believers or just professing imposters? And if their faith was genuine, was the writer of Hebrews saying they could lose their salvation?

Yet another possibility is that the author is posing a what-if situation. His shift of pronouns (from *we*, *us*, and *you* to *those* and *they* [Hebrews 6:4–6]) might suggest a hypothetical circumstance. Theoretically, if someone were to place faith in Jesus for salvation and then decide to retract that decision, it would clearly be impossible to find any other alternative. Not only would such a change of heart be ineffective, but disgraceful as well—like crucifying Jesus all over again (6:6).

Whatever view the reader takes, the author clearly desires for his hearers to repent, turn back to God, and strive for maturity without further delay. The gift of God is not to be neglected or despised. To do so would be like a soaking rain on dry earth that produces only thorns and thistles, when the same rain should have instead provided nourishment and growth for a life-giving crop (6:7–8). No one would keep investing in worthless land. It is even more tragic when people refuse to produce after experiencing the numerous wonderful gifts of God.

The author's suggested response is practical and doable. Show diligence. Don't be lazy. Imitate those who set good examples (6:11–12). And through it all, remember that God will never be unjust (6:10). God would never condemn anyone unfairly. Therefore, the Hebrew Christians could be confident of improving and expecting good things in their future. The writer again refers to the promise of God that would be experienced only through faith and patience (6:12).

6:13–20

AN EXAMPLE FROM ABRAHAM

The Jews revered Abraham, and the writer has already referred to them as Abraham's descendants (2:16). So after exhorting his readers to incorporate more faith and patience in their lives by imitating those who had previously set good examples (6:12), he follows with a reference to Abraham (6:13). Characteristic of the writer, he drops in a quick example at this point, but later (in chapter 11) he will come back to more fully develop his thoughts about faith and perseverance.

Demystifying Hebrews

It would have been difficult to find a better example than Abraham to demonstrate perseverance in regard to the promise of God. He had left his homeland in Mesopotamia and traveled hundreds of miles to get to Canaan. God had promised that he and Sarah would have a son, yet it was twenty-five years before the promise was ultimately fulfilled—long past the time Sarah could be expected to still bear children. Then, after all that, Abraham was tested to see if he would still be obedient to God when the life of the child was at stake (Genesis 22:1–19). The writer of Hebrews is challenging his hearers to also demonstrate ongoing patience and faith as they await the promise of God.

The specific promise of God to Abraham was that he would have many descendants and become the father of a great nation. Abraham waited, and he eventually received what God had promised. . .to an extent. The birth of Isaac was the event that fulfilled one specific promise (a son), and it made possible the fulfillment of another (that Abraham would be the father of a great nation). So the promise, for Abraham, was not unlike the promise for first-century believers. God was faithfully seeing them through their present trials and challenges, but His ultimate promise was still in their future. Abraham received what was promised (6:15), yet God's promise to Abraham is still being realized.

All believers throughout the centuries have been heirs to God's promise to Abraham (6:17). And they have the same guarantee that the promise will be honored. God cannot lie (6:18), and He has no need to take an oath to ensure His trustworthiness. Yet He did so (Genesis 22:15–18), perhaps as a concession to the human tendency toward disbelief. And since there is nothing greater in the universe, God swore by Himself. There is no stronger assurance available.

The symbol of this assurance is an anchor (Hebrews 6:19)—strong and secure. So when scripture speaks of the hope believers have in God, the concept is a far cry from the fingers-crossed, against-all-odds "hope" of which many people speak. Biblical hope in God refers to the certainty that God's promises will all be fully fulfilled. It is a source of ongoing encouragement (6:18).

The writer will have much more to say about the work of the priests and how Jesus' ministry compares. But at this point he makes one very important observation. He says that Jesus entered the "inner place behind the curtain" in the temple—the Most Holy Place (6:19–20 ESV). The privilege of doing so was given only to the high priest. In Jesus' earthly life, He never went into the Most Holy Place in the temple. So this passage is a clear reminder that the temple in Jerusalem was only a copy—a replica of a greater, heavenly version. Jesus didn't need to sprinkle blood on the ark of the covenant once a year. His sacrifice was offered to God directly, in heaven. It is there where the perfect High Priest still offers intercession for people.

The writer is most assuredly not telling his readers that if they hold fast to Christ they will get something in this world for their pains. Instead, he is saying that if they hold fast to Christ, they will inherit in the world to come. That is why he has already urged them to press on to the end (6:11). He will continue to emphasize this point throughout the letter.

He also makes another reference to Melchizedek (5:10; 6:20), which he will explain in great detail in the following section.

Take It Home

Consider the emphasis in this section about how God honored the promise He made to Abraham. The birth of Isaac occurred as promised yet was against all reason, logic, and expectation. Believers today have the New Testament and teachings of Jesus that reveal a great many more of God's promises. What are some that are most meaningful to you? How might your life change if you believe with greater assurance that God will surely do all He has said He will do?

HEBREWS 7:1–28

JESUS COMPARED TO MELCHIZEDEK

The Story of Melchizedek	7:1–3
Melchizedek Compared to Levitical Priests	7:4–10
A Permanent Priesthood	7:11–28

Setting Up the Section

Continuing his explanation of how Jesus Christ is superior to the Levitical priests in regard to providing salvation, in this section the author focuses on Melchizedek. He has already mentioned the Old Testament character a few times (5:6, 10; 6:20) but will now explain the significance of *when* he appears in scripture and *how* his ministry prefigured that of Jesus.

7:1–3

THE STORY OF MELCHIZEDEK

The writer assumes his readers would know the account of Melchizedek, and most first-century Jews certainly would have. However, the story is foreign to many twenty-first-century believers. The character shows up only briefly in Genesis and is mentioned one other time in Psalms. Yet as the author is about to explain, those brief mentions are more important than they may first appear.

The first mention of Melchizedek is tucked into the story of Abraham. After Abraham and Lot had separated and settled in different places, Lot was among a group of people kidnapped by a coalition of foreign kings (Genesis 14:11–12). When Abraham heard the news, he quickly assembled a rescue party, safely retrieved Lot, and recovered a great many valuables that had been stolen.

Afterward, as Abraham met with the king of Sodom, Melchizedek appeared. He brought a meal and blessed Abraham. In return, Abraham gave him a tenth of all the plunder he had taken from the kings he had defeated (Genesis 14:18–20).

The name *Melchizedek* means "king of righteousness," and he was identified as both king of Salem (the place that would later be called Jerusalem) and priest of God Most High. As the writer of Hebrews points out, the Genesis account says nothing of Melchizedek's lineage, neither his birth and ancestry nor his death and posterity. In this sense, he was without father, mother, genealogy, birth, or death (Hebrews 7:3).

Critical Observation

The brief mention of Melchizedek, the comments that there was no beginning or end to his life (7:3), and the mystery that surrounds him, have led some people to theorize that he was a supernatural figure—perhaps even a preincarnate appearance of Christ to Abraham. One line of thought supposes that the occasional presence of supernatural beings during the early stage of human history spawned the mythology of superhuman figures found in various cultural mythologies. But the fact that the author of Hebrews compares Melchizedek to the Son of God would seem to suggest that they were not the same being.

As strange (and as short) as the description of Melchizedek is, there is still ample information to provide a comparison to Jesus. Melchizedek's home, Salem, was a variation of the word *shalom*, meaning "peace." Both "king of righteousness" and "king of peace" are apt titles for both figures. Melchizedek was both king and priest—exactly the point that the writer of Hebrews had recently made about Jesus (4:14). Some people emphasize that Melchizedek served bread and wine (Genesis 14:18), although the phrase simply refers to a regular meal. And although the New Testament sacraments for the Lord's Supper are meant to be reflective of a normal meal, to say Melchizedek's bread and wine were symbols of Communion stretches the imagery too far.

Clearly, the author is treating Melchizedek as a "type"—an enacted prophecy of the Lord Jesus. The Old Testament is replete with types that served to prepare God's people for the coming of the Messiah. Such types could include people (Moses, David), institutions (the priesthood, royalty, prophecy), events (the Exodus, entry into the Promised Land), or ritual actions (sacrifices, the Passover). These symbolic people and events all embody in a special way the ultimate truths of salvation and the ministry of the Messiah as it would unfold once He appeared in the world. Believers would have found it even more challenging to understand Jesus Christ and His work if they hadn't had all the historical prefigurements.

7:4–10

MELCHIZEDEK COMPARED TO LEVITICAL PRIESTS

The significance of the account of Melchizedek as retold at this point in Hebrews is a matter of historical timing. People were attempting to lure the Jewish Christians back into their traditional rites and ceremonies, including the dependence on their priests for atonement. So the author of Hebrews uses Melchizedek to clarify God's perspective on the importance of priests.

Melchizedek is proof that there were other priests of God besides the Levitical priests (who wouldn't exist for a number of centuries). Those priests would proudly trace their ancestry back to Aaron to justify their authority, yet Melchizedek did not depend on a genealogical right to be a priest. His is the example that foreshadows the ministry of Jesus.

The author then makes an interesting argument. He was writing to people so dependent on the priests to intercede with God on their behalf that many were considering forsaking the gospel and their relationship with Christ to return to that system. So he points out that people acknowledge the authority of their priests by bringing a tithe (7:5). At the same time, they took great pride in being descendants of Abraham. Yet, as the author notes, Abraham offered a tithe to Melchizedek. Symbolically, then, the Levitical priests (through Abraham) deferred to the priesthood of Melchizedek. Jesus was not a high priest in the tradition of Levi/Aaron, but rather in the order of Melchizedek, which was clearly greater.

The fact that no genealogy was provided for Melchizedek, or any record of his birth or death, gave him the perception of ongoing life and ministry. Christ *is* eternal, which is why the comparison to Melchizedek is so appropriate. In contrast, the Levitical priests ministered, died, and were replaced by someone else with the right genetic qualifications (7:8). The priesthood of Melchizedek was exemplary of the priesthood of Jesus that would eventually arrive and never expire.

7:11–28

A PERMANENT PRIESTHOOD

As the author continues his argument, he wants to know, if the Levitical priesthood was intended to be God's definitive, final, sufficient provision for the salvation of His people, then why would scripture so clearly point to someone who would not only be David's lord, but who would also be a priest in the order of Melchizedek (non-Levitical)?

This seemingly simple argument is actually quite masterful. Scripture teaches people to expect one like Jesus and look for a priesthood higher than that of Aaron and the sons of Levi. If Aaron's priesthood alone was enough, then why does scripture prophesy the appearance of a priest in the order of Melchizedek (Psalm 110:4; Hebrews 7:17)?

Demystifying Hebrews

Evidence found at Qumran (one community of the Essenes, who were thought to be influencing the Hebrew Christians) suggests that they believed Melchizedek to be more than human—even angelic. The author of Hebrews seems to be aware of such a train of thought. Even if Melchizedek were an angel—which there is no good reason to assume in the first place—he has shown that Jesus is superior to the angels. And if Melchizedek were a highly regarded human priest, Jesus is of the same order, but a high priest. Either way, the author shows Christ's superior authority.

And as the quote from Psalm 110:4 is introduced, the author reminds his readers that for Christ, the priesthood is forever (7:21). The Law of Moses had made no provision for any such priesthood. This reference by the psalmist is obviously not the Levitical priesthood of the law.

The author is subtly leading up to another very important point. The real issue wasn't just *how* one type of priesthood would replace another; the root of the matter was *why*.

It is here (7:18–19) where the author plainly introduces the great interpretative problem of Hebrews. How could he describe the grand rites and ceremonies of the Mosaic ritual as useless? A reading of Exodus and Deuteronomy would certainly never leave one with that impression.

And this is the crucial point. The author legitimately condemns the old practices because they could not make the worshiper perfect. Their purpose was to point out the sinfulness of human beings and so direct them to God's mercy and grace. Yet the people kept gravitating to a religion based on ritual performance and outward conformity rather than a living faith in God. Numerous Old Testament prophets had attempted to correct such a mentality (Isaiah 1; Jeremiah 7; Amos 5; et al.), but the faulty thinking repeatedly established a foothold in Jewish traditions.

At the time when Hebrews was written, Jewish Christians were still participating (and rightly so) in sacrificial worship in the Jerusalem temple, yet most still had an incorrect or incomplete perception of the significance of such rites. Many Jews of the first century looked at the Mosaic arrangements as a complete way of salvation. They were comfortable with the system, so they felt no need for a redeemer who would die for their sins. Because they perceived their sacrifices as salvation itself, they didn't see that the sacrifices actually symbolized something (or someone) else.

While the author of Hebrews isn't against sacrificial worship, per se, he wants his readers to see the shortsightedness of their hope for peace with God based solely on religious rites and ceremonies. He will build this argument as he continues, but he begins here by showing that scripture clearly reveals another priesthood beyond the Levitical one. And if the Levitical priesthood was all that was necessary, why the need for a future priesthood?

As he identifies Jesus as the king/priest who had come (7:22), his argument begins to make sense. Although from the tribe of Judah rather than Levi, Jesus still qualifies as a priest in the same way Melchizedek did. He is the one who lives forever and continues to intercede before God on behalf of human beings (7:23–25).

In addition, He is superior to the Levitical priests in that He does not need to offer sacrifices on His own behalf (7:26–27). Jesus Christ is a high priest who is holy, blameless, and pure. And He only needed to offer a single sacrifice to God. The sacrifice of Himself was once for all. Its effectiveness covered past, present, and future. The Levitical priesthood was not the last word in salvation; Jesus is.

Take It Home

It may not be easy for today's believers to relate to high priests, sacrificial worship, and unusual figures like Melchizedek. But can you think of any practices in the modern church that might be compared to the offering of sacrifices—something that people tend to cling to, yet in which the genuine meaning may become lost in the ritual?

HEBREWS 8:1–13

THE WORK OF A HIGH PRIEST

Where Christ Serves as Priest 8:1–6

A New Covenant 8:7–13

Setting Up the Section

The author of Hebrews continues his ongoing discussion of comparisons and contrasts between the role of Jesus as High Priest and the priests who came before Him—Aaron and Melchizedek among them. In this section he shifts his perspective a bit, focusing not only on *what* Jesus does in His role of High Priest, but also *where*. And he makes some significant observations pertaining to the new covenant contrasted to the old covenant.

8:1–6

WHERE CHRIST SERVES AS PRIEST

To this point in his current stream of thought, the author of Hebrews has been describing how Jesus compared to previous respected priests in terms of qualification and right to serve. Here he begins an examination of the work itself—yet another indication of the superiority of Jesus.

Remember that the readers were being tempted to believe that the Levitical priesthood was a completely adequate provision for one's salvation. They were missing the point that the Old Testament priesthood was only an instrument of God's grace in Christ—not the means of salvation itself. The tendency of humans to embrace external rites and ceremonies to convey the substance of God's love had been going on for centuries and would continue long after the writing of Hebrews. (The Protestant Reformation was a movement to correct the same fundamental confusion.) So the writer maintains the single theme of his letter—that an ongoing commitment to Jesus Christ, expressed with living faith, is the only way to get to heaven and receive the full promise of God.

The sphere of Jesus' ministry clearly sets Him apart from other priests. The Jewish temple contained no chairs because the work of the priests was ongoing. Yet the author provides an image of Jesus seated (8:1), indicating that His work has been completed. In addition, Christ sits on a throne at the right hand of God the Father. (*The Majesty* was a Jewish term to refer to God without invoking His name, thereby avoiding any unintentional breaking of the commandment to not misuse the name of God.)

Jesus' sacrifice—the offering of Himself to God—was complete (7:27). Yet His service continues (8:2). He didn't die for humankind and then just forget about them; He continues to work on their behalf. And His service is conducted in the very presence of God. It is not limited by time or location, as is the work of earthly priests, but is heavenly and eternal.

Despite all the emphasis many of his readers were placing on the Mosaic laws, the author clearly shows their limited vision (8:3–6). Jesus, he explains, is not just one more in a long line of priests. Jesus, in fact, is the original and true priest. His heavenly priesthood was the blueprint the earthly priests were expected to model. The Levitical system was a copy of the true priesthood; the work of the Old Testament priests was but a shadow of the real thing.

The Jewish people of the first century—especially the nonconformist Essenes—were inclined to regard the life, history, and experience of Israel as a paradigm of their own. They felt a strong association with the wilderness generation under Moses and stressed the Mosaic covenant. And they were inclined to feel that they need not do anything more than duplicate the pattern of life established by their forebears. So the writer of Hebrews begins to address the issue of the covenant.

8:7–13

A NEW COVENANT

Although the first-century Jews felt such an affinity to the Mosaic covenant, they didn't understand the covenant to be the proclamation of the gospel that it was intended to be (4:1–2). The author of Hebrews has already pointed out that the wilderness generation of Israel was not to be emulated (chapters 3–4). After all, that generation perished and failed to obtain God's salvation. They had the rituals the Jews were still so fond of, but they didn't have the faith necessary to finish what they had begun (3:16–19).

He has also shown that the rest, spoken of in regard to the Israelites in the wilderness (Psalm 95:11), was not a reference to the Promised Land. Otherwise, why did God tell the generations of Israelites *after* those in the wilderness that they, too, needed to enter His rest (Hebrews 4:8)?

As the author moves to the topic of the covenant cherished by the first-century Jews, he uses a similar argument. They wanted to believe that the covenant between God and Moses was a lasting one, and they were continuing to try to live according to those rules and regulations. But if that were so, queried the author of Hebrews, why did God later promise a new and better covenant?

Demystifying Hebrews

Just as there was a new and better priesthood than the one established by Aaron, and a new and better rest than that offered by the Promised Land, there would be a new and better covenant than the one established with the unfaithful Israelites in the wilderness. The very fact that scripture promises another covenant to replace the one with the ancestors of the first-century Jews is evidence that the original covenant was inadequate. So clearly it should not be the model people choose to live by. They should have been looking for the new covenant rather than clinging so tightly to the one that had failed.

The crucial point that many of the first-century Jewish community were missing was that the previous covenant failed because God had found fault with the people (8:8). The problem with the Mosaic covenant was not in the covenant itself, but in the unfaithfulness of the people. They did not truly believe God, so they failed to combine the message with true faith (4:2). The same problem was creating problems in the first-century church.

What follows this statement is the longest single quotation of the Old Testament found in the New Testament (8:8–12). The quote from Jeremiah 31:31–34 says specifically that the new covenant would *not* be like the one God had made with Israel in the wilderness. God had been faithful, but Israel had broken their promise. The new covenant would be one where *all* the people would relate to God.

Critical Observation

One reason so many people misunderstand the difference in the old (Mosaic) covenant and the new covenant may be attributed to the adoption in the late second century of the terms *Old Testament* and *New Testament*. It was a way for them to separate scripture that preceded the incarnation of Jesus from that which followed. But in the centuries that followed, believers have instinctively begun to think that there were two theological, spiritual arrangements succeeding one another in time, with the latter significantly superior to the former. Scripture itself does not support such a dichotomy. There was nothing wrong with the old covenant. As the author of Hebrews is attempting to show, concepts such as God's grace, the gospel, and salvation by faith are found in the old covenant as well as the new. As Paul elsewhere points out, the old covenant (the law) was our guardian, or tutor, to lead us to Christ (Galatians 3:24–25). All along it was pointing forward to its fulfillment in Christ.

That the old covenant did not teach a different, inferior means of salvation is evident from various considerations:

1) The author has said it was the gospel that was preached to Israel in the wilderness (4:2). Their failure to obtain the rest of God was not due to any defect in the message, but rather to their failure to believe. They lacked the required faith. The same is true of those under the new covenant.
2) The assumption that modern believers have an easier pathway to God is not supported by Hebrews or anywhere in scripture. Christians have the same responsibility as God's people in the Old Testament. The gospel has been proclaimed, and they are under the obligation to believe it and obey it. The author of Hebrews asks believers in Christ to do what believers had always done to be saved. If they continue in their faith, they will reach God's heavenly country; if not, they could fail to obtain eternal life. Hebrews never contrasts Old Testament believers with New Testament Christians. Rather, it always identifies the spiritual situations of God's people from the beginning of history to its end.

According to the author of Hebrews, the first covenant was the system of ceremonies that included animal sacrifices, the priesthood, and the temple. That first covenant could never truly take away sins (10:4), but was only a shadow (10:1) of good things to come—the salvation available through Jesus Christ, the once-for-all sacrifice for sins.

The first covenant had been broken, and the people had attempted to replace a genuine relationship with God with adherence to a system of rites and ceremonies. The same problem was taking place among the first-century Christians—and continues with certain believers today. The author of Hebrews knew it wasn't enough to be an Israelite, just as it wasn't enough to create a ceremonial practice of Christianity. What is necessary for salvation is a true, living, persevering faith in Christ, the eternal Priest who offers an infinite sacrifice and is able to make perfect those who draw near to God through Him.

Take It Home

The work of a priest is to intercede between a holy God and sinful people. The high priest was the one who entered, to the extent that it was humanly possible, the presence of God. So as you consider that Jesus is a high priest serving in heaven before God Himself, having offered His own life on your behalf, how does that image affect your relationship with God? Does it inspire more confidence? Gratitude? A stronger desire to live a life pleasing to Him?

HEBREWS 9:1–28

SACRIFICE AND SALVATION

Limitations of the Levitical Priesthood	9:1–15
The Requirement of Blood	9:16–28

Setting Up the Section

In the previous section the author had begun a discussion of the superiority of Christ's priestly work to that of the Levitical priests, but had included a brief parenthetical section about the difference between the broken Mosaic covenant and the "better covenant" that had replaced it. In this section he will return to his original thought and describe how the sacrificial blood of Christ would at last provide genuine and lasting cleansing for sin.

9:1–15

LIMITATIONS OF THE LEVITICAL PRIESTHOOD

After portraying an image of Jesus performing as High Priest in a heavenly temple (8:1–6), the author returns to a consideration of the work of an earthly priest. The system of sacrificial worship in the Old Testament was solemn and somber but had limitations. Many of his readers were seriously considering giving up on the freedom offered by Jesus and returning to the Levitical priesthood and its ceremonies. Their mistaken view of what was required for salvation was no small problem.

So the author begins a close-up examination of the earthly priesthood. His readers seemed to associate more closely with the wilderness period of Israel's history, so he chose to describe the tabernacle rather than the temple. The work of the priests was essentially the same. The priesthood of Aaron and his descendants had been established along with the portable tabernacle where the Israelites worshiped as they traveled from Egypt to the Promised Land.

Another reason for referring to the tabernacle was likely the fact that he had already pointed out—those Israelites had heard the gospel presented to them but lacked the faith to believe and apply it. Consequently, they had failed to enter God's rest (4:1–2). If the first-century Jewish Christians didn't renew their faith in Christ, they were in danger of making the same mistake and turning the gospel into a theory of salvation by ritual performance.

The author reviews the basic setup of the tabernacle (9:1–4). The furnishings in the Holy Place and Most Holy Place were described in great detail in Exodus (chapters 35–40). However, most people never got to see those items because only the priests were allowed within those enclosed portions of the tabernacle (and later the temple).

Demystifying Hebrews

The author appears to have made a glaring contradiction with what had been prescribed in the Old Testament. He writes that the Most Holy Place contained the golden altar of incense, when in fact it belonged in the Holy Place (Exodus 30:1–6; Leviticus 16:17–18). However, his intent was most likely to show the inseparable connection between this particular altar with the critical work of the high priest who entered the Most Holy Place only once a year on the Day of Atonement (Hebrews 9:6–10). The close association between the altar of incense and ark of the covenant was no mistake and is identified this way even in the Old Testament (1 Kings 6:22).

It is here (Hebrews 9:4) that we discover the contents of the ark of the covenant. The ark held a gold jar of manna to commemorate the provision of God during the Israelites' wilderness journeys (Exodus 16:33), the stone tablets bearing the Ten Commandments, and Aaron's staff that had budded to verify his authority after being challenged by others (Numbers 17). All were symbols of God's unwavering faithfulness during trying times. And yet the first-century believers were wavering in *their* faithfulness.

The author has hardly begun his review of the tabernacle furnishings when he opts not to go into a lot of detail (Hebrews 9:5). There was little need for him to do so, because his Jewish readers would have been well familiar with the tabernacle and its setup.

Instead, he recalls the events of the Day of Atonement (9:6–8)—the most solemn day of the Hebrew year. The letter to the Hebrews was almost certainly written prior to the destruction of the temple in AD 70, so the observance of the Day of Atonement would still have been an annual ritual. It would have been just as significant for the Jewish Christians as for any Jews—perhaps more so. Just because a Jewish person placed faith in Jesus during this time didn't mean giving up all Jewish practices. We even read of Paul celebrating Jewish rites to show his solidarity with other Christians who continued to observe their traditional Jewish customs (Acts 21:17–26). The problem was not that Jewish Christians continued to participate in their traditional rituals; the problem was with holding to those rites while falling away from their faith in Christ.

The author addresses his readers' faulty perspective as he describes the restricted access to the Most Holy Place and the inability of the sacrifices themselves to bring the worshiper to God (Hebrews 9:8–10). This is not to suggest that believers in the ancient epoch did not have direct access to God or full forgiveness of their sins. Paul makes a strong argument for justification by faith when he shows that Abraham and David received God's forgiveness and drew near to God by virtue of Christ's work—their faith was in anticipation of what Christ would do, while a modern believer can look back and see in retrospect what Christ has done. At this point, however, the author diminishes the importance of the sacrifices' power to take away sin because he is refuting his listeners' viewpoint that those sacrifices, in themselves, could bring the worshiper to God. Without the final and ultimate sacrifice of Christ, those previous sacrifices were worthless.

Translations vary for what the author writes in verse 11. Some Greek manuscripts say Christ came as High Priest of the good things that are already here. Others refer to "the good things that are coming," as the author will say in 10:1. Both affirmations are true from the perspective of the theology of Hebrews, since the salvation Christ has accomplished is both "already" and "not yet." It has arrived through the death and resurrection of Christ but has yet to be completed in the future. A decision on which is the original reading is very difficult. The author's frequent reference to salvation as a future inheritance would favor the second view. But it is also true that a later copyist would have been more likely to change a reference to present salvation into one pointing to the future, rather than vice versa (the "harder reading" is usually the more original one).

The author's next statement, however, is quite clear. Jesus' death was no random tragedy or act of circumstance. It was an intentional and spiritual sacrifice. Although He died on a cross outside the walls of Jerusalem, His sacrifice is represented as having been offered directly to God in heaven (9:11–12). And the author is intentional about acknowledging all three persons of the Triune God in the work of securing the salvation of humankind (9:13–14).

Here again, the term *mediator* is used as a synonym for *guarantor* (9:15), as in 8:6. The author continues to allude to the promised eternal inheritance that no one has yet received, but ongoing faith in Christ ensures believers that they will one day be given everything God has promised.

9:16–28

THE REQUIREMENT OF BLOOD

The Greek word for *covenant* could mean "last will and testament," and the prior reference to "eternal inheritance" (9:15) also brings to mind the concept of a will (9:16–17). A person draws up a will however he or she wishes, and it doesn't take effect until after the death of the person. Similarly, God initiated all the biblical covenants—with Abraham, Moses, David, and the new covenant being described by the writer of Hebrews. People have nothing to offer God, so He is the originator. People *are* expected to respond, however.

The matter of death is also important. In the Levitical system, it was the death of the sacrificial animal—the shedding of blood—that effected God's forgiveness (9:19–22). When the covenant with Moses was confirmed, blood was required to be sprinkled in various places (Exodus 24:1–8).

Critical Observation

Some of the spiritual history referred to in Hebrews is not recorded in the Old Testament (such as the sprinkling of blood on the tabernacle [Hebrews 9:21]). Yet the assumption seems to be that the readers would be familiar with it. It might therefore be assumed that they had other sources of such information that are no longer available.

And ultimately, it was the shed blood of Christ that finalized the new covenant that God established with humankind. It was His death that made possible the inheritance believers had been promised.

This is the contrast the writer has been making all along. Christ's sacrifice was not a copy of the real one, and it was not offered in a temple that was a copy of the real one. Quite the opposite: The earthly priestly system was a copy of the genuine one. Christ's sacrifice was the blood of the perfect, divine substitute, and it was offered in the heavenly sanctuary (9:23–24).

The earthly priests had to enter the tabernacle again and again, year after year, to reenact the ceremony and offer more blood. Not so with Christ. Here again the author uses "once for all" (9:26) to describe Jesus' sacrifice, and he will elaborate more on it in the following section. (This verse is also frequently cited by Protestants to dispute the Roman Catholic claim that in the Mass, Christ continues to be sacrificed again and again.)

Similarly, the following verse (9:27) is among those used to refute the teachings of reincarnation. Hebrews states clearly that people die once and then face judgment.

The statement that Christ's appearance on earth was at the end of time (9:26) suggests that His sacrifice was the pivotal point of human history. Clearly, history wasn't brought to an immediate conclusion, because two thousand years have passed since then. Yet everything needed to bring human history to its fulfillment has now taken place, and only the Lord's return remains.

Notice once again the future-oriented perspective of Hebrews and the definition of salvation as something to be fulfilled at some future point (9:27–28). Salvation as a present possession appears often in the New Testament. Jesus announced the kingdom of God was "at hand" (Mark 1:15) and spoke of salvation as coming "today" to the house of Zacchaeus (Luke 19:9). Paul wrote that with Christ's coming, the culmination of the ages had arrived (1 Corinthians 10:11), and announced that salvation had come to the Gentiles (Romans 11:11). In the Gospel of John, Jesus defines eternal life as knowing God here and now (John 17:3). Many other biblical examples of such usage can be found. But the author of Hebrews places greater emphasis on future salvation—what believers will obtain in the world to come. To him, faith is a matter of persevering and patiently waiting for that time to arrive (9:28).

Take It Home

Because the author of Hebrews places such emphasis on the importance of developing a persevering faith while awaiting the return of Christ, it can be beneficial to examine oneself as to the ability to wait for something. Modern society places great importance on instant gratification of one's desires, immediate access to information, and so forth. Circumstances where waiting is expected grow fewer and fewer. And those that continue (traffic tie-ups, bank lines, and so on) are stereotypical pictures of great frustration. So how do you do when it comes to waiting for something? If you sense a degree of impatience, do you think that such a mentality drifts into your spiritual disciplines as well? (For example, do you ever attempt to hurry God along, urging Him to act sooner?)

HEBREWS 10:1–39

THE ONLY MEANINGFUL SACRIFICE

An Annual Reminder of Sin vs. A Clean Slate 10:1–18
Responding to the Priesthood of Christ 10:19–39

Setting Up the Section

The author has been elaborating on the significance of the person and work of Jesus Christ in the role of High Priest, especially in contrast to the work of the Levitical priests. In this section he continues and concludes that line of thought, reemphasizing some of what he has already said and adding new applications to the information he has been providing.

10:1–18

AN ANNUAL REMINDER OF SIN VS. A CLEAN SLATE

One can be outside on a sunny day, able to see quite clearly while working among the shadows. But when the person steps into direct sunlight, the difference becomes evident. It is this image the author of Hebrews uses to contrast the old covenant with the new one. His reference to the law as a shadow of things to come (10:1) is not his first (8:5). And as he has pointed out previously, the law required that sacrifices be made year after year, again and again.

This time, however, he asks the logical question: If animal sacrifices were sufficient in themselves to remove the sins of the worshiper, why did they need to be continued (10:2)? This is the third of his it-seems-obvious questions. He had already asked why, if perfection could be obtained through the Levitical priesthood, scripture speaks of another priest yet to come (7:11, 17). Shortly later he asks his readers to consider the need for another covenant if there had been nothing wrong or incomplete with the first one (8:7). His question in 10:2 seems just as obvious.

The priests' sacrifices on behalf of the people were not an effective remedy for sin. In fact, the animal offerings were actually annual *reminders* of sin (10:3). The cleansing of the person was only temporary. It wasn't long before sin and guilt again returned to the lives of the worshipers. But those who fully understood the author's reasoning realized that this was not bad news. He isn't saying that the sacrifices were supposed to take away sin but were failing. Rather, what he is making clear is that the sacrifice of animals was never capable of removing sin and was never intended to be a permanent remedy (10:4).

His citation of Psalm 40:6–8 was taken from the Septuagint (10:5–7), and he understood it to be a reference to Jesus. The quotation is especially applicable at this point because it compares the Levitical sacrifices unfavorably with the work of Christ. The Old Testament writings contained numerous revelations that the Levitical rituals served no good purpose apart from the faith and obedience on the parts of the worshipers. The author has made the point before but needs to reiterate it in this context.

Critical Observation

Opinions differ as to whether certain sections of the Psalms should be considered "messianic." A messianic psalm is one that is a prophecy uniquely fulfilled in Christ. Many other psalms are called "royal" psalms. In their original context, these psalms concerned King David or the dynasty of Davidic kings that followed him. They apply to Jesus typologically rather than uniquely; that is, He is the ultimate and final fulfillment of a psalm that originally referred to others. The kingship of Israel, when properly understood and lived out, was symbolic of God's leadership. The king was supposed to be God's appointed person over the nation. David was the greatest model for this, and all the kings that followed him are compared favorably or unfavorably with him. Many psalms, therefore, speak of David's leadership, and these "royal" psalms point forward typologically to God's ideal leader and David's greater son—the Messiah, Jesus Christ. It is not surprising, then, that the early church members were able to see Christ throughout the Psalter.

The author is quite purposeful here (10:8) as he specifies sacrifices, offerings, burnt offerings, and sin offerings rather than grouping all sacrifices together. He indicates the entire sacrificial ritual of the Mosaic Law, aware that his readers were striving to use such methods to deal definitively with their sin before God. He has no quarrel with worshipers who offer sacrifices while acknowledging their trust in the Lord as the true Redeemer. He takes issue, however, with those who hoped that the act of sacrifice would itself cleanse them from guilt.

His perspective reflects God's outlook on sacrifices as well. The heartfelt offering made by a sincere worshiper was like a pleasing aroma that went up to God (Genesis 8:20–21). But when the offerings were made out of obligation or with an attitude of apathy, they produced no sweetness and had no effect (Amos 5:21–22).

The willingness of the first-century Christians to forsake the relationship aspect of their faith in order to practice a ceremonial religion instead was a clear step backward, which was another reason the author recalls Psalm 40:6–8 (Hebrews 10:5–7). It wasn't the animal sacrifice that God desired, but rather an offering of one's heart and faith.

The will of God (10:7, 9–10) that Jesus came into the world to fulfill was, of course, the offering of Himself for sinful humankind. And again, what need would there have been for such a sacrifice if the Levitical sacrifices had been adequate to take away sin and guilt? Christ established a better solution for the sin problem of the world, and in doing so He set aside the prior system (10:9).

As the author begins to wrap up this portion of his argument, he repeats a number of key points in summary. He again uses a favorite phrase to describe Jesus' sacrifice: once for all (10:10). He reminds his readers that the work of the Levitical priests was never really done, yet Jesus completed His work and sat down at the right hand of God the Father (10:11–12). He even repeats his scriptural basis (Jeremiah 31:31–34) to show that his viewpoint is not out of line with God's Word (Hebrews 8:8–12; 10:15–17).

His point is clear: Those who insisted on animal sacrifice as a means of salvation would never find God's favor. But those who place their faith in Jesus will experience the true salvation that God promises and Christ guarantees—a permanent and full forgiveness of sins.

10:19–39

RESPONDING TO THE PRIESTHOOD OF CHRIST

After a lengthy section of exposition, the author turns to another segment of application before moving on to his next thought. The "Therefore" used in verse 19 is a clear indication that he desires his readers to do something about what he has been writing.

No amount of animal sacrifice would ever entitle a worshiper to enter the Most High Place, yet the blood of Jesus was sufficient to allow people to be in God's very presence (10:19–22). It is a renewed and cleansed person who is invited to stand before God. The invitation includes the criteria of sincerity, assurance of faith, and cleansing from a guilty conscience.

Yet once again, it is important not to read this new way (10:20) as contrast between the old way of the Mosaic Law and the new way of Christ and His apostles. It is a common interpretation, but one that violates the author's entire viewpoint. He insists that there had always been but one way, one gospel, and one salvation. The Old Testament saints drew near to God as New Testament Christians did—through faith (11:6).

The old way was not the way of Moses, but the way of death. The new way is the way that produces a new creation, brings a person into a new covenant with God, and provides a new life, heart, and name. The new covenant is not a matter of a better degree of access to God, but of real access, when before there was none. Faithful believers always had access to God, even before the institution of the rituals of the law. In and of themselves, those rites could make no one perfect and bring no one to God.

Demystifying Hebrews

The references to baptism in 10:19–21 (hearts sprinkled and bodies washed) are less about the ceremony of baptism than to what baptism signifies and seals. It is sometimes said that the Israelites were "baptized" as they walked through the Red Sea, although the experience certainly didn't save them or change them in any significant way. Yet the author's statements demonstrate how vividly baptism represented spiritual cleansing to the first generations of Christians in the early church.

And in response to this recent evidence he has presented, the author again presents his persistent theme: the necessity of holding unswervingly to one's faith, ever looking ahead to what has been promised (10:23). He also notes that Christianity was not intended to be a solitary religion; it is a fellowship of saints. Believers are *collectively* looking to the future. As they do, they are to spur one another to deeper love and positive actions (10:24) and to continue to encourage one another and meet together (10:25).

People who call themselves Christians yet show little or no interest in others do not realize what is at stake or how vulnerable they are to fatal errors of thought and life. The author's warning that follows is stark and grim. To choose to continue sinning has terrible results. Committing intentional sins effectively declares oneself an enemy of God (10:27) and tramples underfoot Jesus and everything He has done (10:29). Such people have only the judgment of God to look forward to (10:27), which, without the salvation provided by Jesus, is a dreadful thing (10:31). This warning is stronger than the one previously stated (6:4–8) and will be repeated yet again (12:25–29).

But the author isn't merely trying to scare his readers. He desperately wants to turn them around and prevent them from making a decision that will ultimately harm them. He is aware of the good they have done and reminds them of it (10:32–34). Their hope in everlasting life had motivated them to stand up for the gospel, even when they had to suffer as a result.

Shrinking back from one's faith has always been a problem, as the author points out by quoting from Habakkuk 2:3–4. He takes the liberty of transposing the two lines to place more emphasis on the warning (Hebrews 10:37–38). The quote also reinforces his point that the righteous have always lived by faith—both in the Old Testament system and after the completed work of Christ.

Even though his readers were flirting with spiritual danger, the author is confident that most of them will stand fast. He is being brutally honest with them and very frank about the potential consequences, yet he is convinced that they will continue to believe and be saved (10:39).

Take It Home

What gets more of a response out of you: the motivation of a positive reward, or the threat of the worst that could happen if you fail to act? Why do you think the author uses both positive reinforcement and no-holds-barred warnings of potential consequences?

HEBREWS 11:1–40

NOTEWORTHY FAITH

Faith: Two Definitions and Three Examples 11:1–7

Examples of Faith throughout Israel's History 11:8–40

Setting Up the Section

After a lengthy and somewhat complicated plea for his readers to strengthen their faith and hold out for all the wonderful things God had promised them, the writer now turns to their history as a means of persuasion. He provides example after example of people who demonstrated faith that led to positive results. They were all people who chose to be faithful despite never receiving what they had been promised—something he is asking his readers to do.

11:1–7

FAITH: TWO DEFINITIONS AND THREE EXAMPLES

Hebrews 11 is one of the great chapters of the Bible. The writer has just completed a persuasive, detailed exhortation for his readers to continue their faith in Jesus Christ. Now he turns to a long list of flesh-and-blood examples of those who prevailed after trusting the Lord through thick and thin. He not only tells his readers how to live; he shows them through examples of those who succeeded.

He also provides two definitions for faith. The first is in verse 1: being sure of what we hope for and certain of what we do not see. This definition echoes Paul's observation that hope that is seen is no hope at all (Romans 8:24–25). The "people of old" mentioned in Hebrews 11:2 (NET) are the people who lived prior to the coming of Christ. Some of the examples go back considerably further than others.

The biblical narrative begins with creation, and perhaps the author thought he should start there as well (11:3). It was an event witnessed only by God, and it is a truth that can be known to humans only by divine revelation. Sometimes well-meaning people become so embroiled in debating the science of creation that they fail to emphasize God's involvement in the origins of humankind. According to the writer of Hebrews, that is no small breach of faith.

The author also provides insight into the Cain and Abel story (Genesis 4:1–16). Many people assume that God received Abel's offering because it involved a blood sacrifice and rejected Cain's because it did not. Yet both Hebrews and Genesis suggest that Cain's real sin was tokenism. Abel offered the very best of what he had, while Cain offered only a sampling when he should have given the firstfruits of his crop to God. It was a faulty attitude that led to the rejected offering.

The cryptic comment about Enoch in Genesis 5:24 is better explained here (Hebrews 11:5). Enoch walked with God and was no more because God took him away. The writer of Hebrews verifies that, indeed, Enoch did not face natural death as most everyone else does. (Another exception is Elijah, who isn't mentioned by name in this chapter but is likely one of the people referred to in 11:35 [1 Kings 17:17–24].)

The author's second definition of faith is in Hebrews 11:6: a belief that God exists and rewards those who diligently seek Him. Enoch was spared death because his faith pleased God, and Noah (and family) was spared because he believed God and acted on something he had not yet seen (11:7).

Critical Observation

It is interesting to pause at this point and review the first three examples on the author's list of heroes of the faith. Abel had faith and was murdered. Enoch had faith and did not die. Noah had faith, and everyone died except him. People are instructed to have faith, yet there are no promises or guarantees that they can predict or control the outcome of their lives as a result.

11:8–40

EXAMPLES OF FAITH THROUGHOUT ISRAEL'S HISTORY

Throughout this letter the author has been urging his readers to keep looking ahead to what God has in store for them in the future. And perhaps no one personified such an attitude better than Abraham. His story dominates the section dealing with the patriarchs.

Several examples of Abraham's faith are mentioned. To begin with, he left his homeland solely because God promised to lead him somewhere else. He didn't even know where he was going! But when he arrived, and God promised him the land as an inheritance, he lived there as if it were his even though he never possessed it during his lifetime. (All he actually owned was a small burial plot.) He lived much of his life as a stranger in someone else's country (11:8–10).

A second example is God's promise to provide him with an heir. God waited until Abraham was one hundred years old, and Sarah ninety, to bless them with their son, Isaac, which explains the author's comment that Abraham was too old and as good as dead (11:11–12). By persevering in faith, Abraham saw God act even though it required a miracle for Him to do as He had promised.

A third example involves Abraham's willingness to offer Isaac back to God. There was an element of logic to his faith. After the miraculous birth of his son, Abraham believed that God would certainly honor His promise to provide numerous descendants through Isaac. So when it seemed as if God were going to have Isaac die, the only way the promise could come true would be for God to raise Isaac back to life again. No evidence exists that anyone had ever seen, or even conceived of, a bodily resurrection from the dead. Yet Abraham believed that was exactly what God would do if necessary to be true to His promise (11:17–19).

Tucked away within the stories of Abraham is an important observation that many people seem to miss. The author makes it clear that Abraham was looking for more than a piece of real estate when considering the promise of God. If he just wanted a tangible, physical country, he could have returned to his original homeland. Instead, Abraham was seeking a better, *heavenly* country (11:13–16). He was looking for the very same things that modern believers seek. That's what makes him such a noteworthy model. He never received the complete fulfillment of what he sought during his lifetime, and neither do New Testament believers. Faithful perseverance is just as important for first-century (and twenty-first-century) believers as it was for Abraham.

The examples from the other patriarchs are summed up in just a few sentences (11:20–22), but the readers of Hebrews would have been familiar with all of their stories from Genesis. The main point is that one generation after another died with the certainty that God would fulfill His promise and keep His Word.

Moses is another top figure in Israel's history. And as is the case in numerous instances, the faith of the parents is shown to be influential in the subsequent birth and life of an important spiritual figure (11:23). Of course, Moses didn't get off to such a good start. After being raised by Pharaoh's daughter, his murder of an Egyptian overseer declared his loyalty to the Israelites (Exodus 2:11–15). The short-lived pleasures of the Egyptian court were not to be compared with the eternal inheritance to be enjoyed by those who trust the Lord and do His will.

The author's striking reference to Moses' suffering disgrace for Christ's sake (Hebrews 11:26) is important. Clearly, *Christ* is not identified by name in Exodus, yet the writer of Hebrews informs his readers that it was, in fact, Jesus with whom Moses identified. He had already said that Jesus built the house in which Moses was a servant (3:1–6).

Moses' flight to Midian to escape Pharaoh is portrayed here (11:27), not as an act of desperation, but of discretion. He continued to persevere in his faith during his years in the wilderness. And when called to lead his people, his faith regularly inspired them—as they separated themselves from Pharaoh, as they walked across the dry path through the Red Sea and on to the Promised Land (11:28–29).

Faith was just as important after arriving in the Promised Land as it had been in getting there. Just two examples were provided: the falling of the walls of Jericho and the faith of Rahab, the woman who helped the Israelites and the only survivor (with her family) of the fall of Jericho (11:30–31). The first-century Jewish believers were most likely jolted a bit to be reminded of the faith of a Gentile prostitute—and God's vindication of her—as an example that they would do well to follow.

Even this late in the letter, the author still thinks of himself as speaking rather than writing (11:32). This is no typical New Testament epistle; it is a sermon.

The writer realizes he cannot provide much detail for all the historic examples of faith, and it's interesting to note which people and events he includes in his final summary. What follows (11:32–38) spans the period from the Judges (Gideon, Barak, Samson, Jephthah) to the kings (David) to the heroic resistance of the Maccabees.

Demystifying Hebrews

Some of the author's references to unnamed heroic figures are clear: Shutting the mouths of lions surely refers to the prophet Daniel; quenching the fury of flames points to Shadrach, Meshach, and Abednego; women receiving back their dead seems to indicate both Elijah and Elisha, who each brought a woman's son back to life. Other examples are less clear. For example, scripture says nothing of anyone being sawn in two (11:37), although tradition says that was the way Isaiah died.

The author's inclusion of people like Samson and Jephthah remind believers that living faith can coexist with great character flaws. (Their stories are told in Judges 10:6–16:31.) Faithful people need not be perfect people by any means.

And again, it is noted that faithfulness to God does not always have visible earthly rewards. In the closing verses of this section, the writer speaks of torture, imprisonment, stoning, and poverty. Yet those consequences of life weren't really important in light of the people's remarkable faithful commitment to God.

The final two verses of Hebrews 11 are often misunderstood. The author's clear statement is that the faithful people of Old Testament times did not receive what had been promised to them (11:39). The assumption many people make, then, is that modern believers *have* received it in full.

But the author is not here distinguishing between the situation of believers in the ancient epoch and believers in the new epoch. Rather, he uses the Old Testament heroes as examples because he wants modern believers to identify with their situations. Like those on his list, all believers continue to look to the future for a better country, a better resurrection. One of the last things the author will write is that all believers continue to look for the city that is to come (13:14). All who place their faith in God are to be made perfect *together*—old and new (11:40).

Take It Home

Responding in faith to believe what can't be seen is still essential to the Christian experience. We cannot see into the past to verify God's love for us before we were even born. We cannot see into heaven to ensure it's as good as scripture says. We cannot see the soul. We are still awaiting the return of Christ after two thousand years. None of these things are provable in a laboratory but must be taken on faith. Of all the examples provided in this chapter by the writer of Hebrews, which person(s) most inspire(s) you to continue to persevere in your faith? Why?

HEBREWS 12:1–29

THE LOVING DISCIPLINE OF GOD

A Positive Appeal: The Benefits of Self-Discipline 12:1–13

A Warning for Those Who Reject Discipline 12:14–29

Setting Up the Section

This section of Hebrews continues the author's thought from the previous section. The reason he has just listed so many exemplary people of faith is so his readers would be inspired to imitate them. Here he provides practical insight for what to expect as his listeners begin to recommit themselves to Christ and return to the faith they were being lured away from. He begins with a positive petition but adds a severe warning for anyone who continues to resist God.

12:1–13

A POSITIVE APPEAL: THE BENEFITS OF SELF-DISCIPLINE

After providing such an abundant and commendable group of examples in Hebrews 11, the author tells his audience to imagine being surrounded by those heroes as they lived out their faith in the first-century world (12:1). The historical figures could be perceived as a cheering section that would give the modern believers a home-field advantage of sorts.

Those who are serious about persevering in faith are called to a sometimes-challenging level of self-discipline. The conditions of their spiritual "race" are similar to those of a literal marathon. The first step is to rid oneself of all unnecessary hindrances, and the second is to set a pace that will enable the runner to persevere to the finish line. It is also helpful to remain fixed on Jesus. He has already run the race and knows all about pain, shame, and trials, as well as the joy to be experienced by those who endure (12:2). He is proof that faith will be rewarded.

The first-century believers were starting to give up on their faith with very little effort to persevere. They hadn't come near to suffering to the extent that the faithful people in the past had done—much less to be able to compare to what Jesus had gone through on their behalf (12:3–4). As soon as their faith became a little difficult, they were ready to revert to old familiar ways but would forfeit a genuine relationship with Christ in exchange for mere rites and ceremonies if they did so.

As he was wont to do so frequently throughout his letter, the author pulls out an applicable scriptural passage, this time from Proverbs 3:11–12 (Hebrews 12:5–6). It is a reminder that some of the difficult things in life—godly discipline, rebuke, and even punishment—are in fact necessary and beneficial. Even the correction of God is always carried out in love.

But then, why let it get to the point where God needs to enforce the rules? The author exhorts his readers to take it upon themselves to discipline themselves while enduring hardship (12:7–8). No loving father would stand idly as a child endangered himself or settled for less that what was best for him. First, an involved father would attempt to persuade and encourage the child to excel. If that didn't work, the father would surely impose some means of discipline. And no father is more loving than God, so believers should expect Him to respond if they wander from the security of His will and calling. In fact, discipline is a sign that the person is part of God's family (12:7–9).

No one enjoys being disciplined by an authority figure. When God takes action to get a person's attention, it is not usually pleasant. But neither is it lasting. As soon as the person responds, the disciplinary action is quickly replaced by righteousness and peace (12:10–11).

12:14–29

A WARNING FOR THOSE WHO REJECT DISCIPLINE

The author seems to realize that some people might need a stronger argument, so his encouragement to endure hardship and appreciate discipline turns into a warning for anyone who doesn't take his words to heart.

Peace within the Christian community is not something that occurs automatically or should be taken for granted. Believers are to make every effort to ensure they have a holy lifestyle on an individual basis and a peaceful coexistence with others in the church. Otherwise, people lose sight of God and the things that matter (12:14).

Each Christian must seriously pursue holiness and help other believers do the same. It is important to deal with sin as it arises, or it will quickly become a bitter root that spreads quickly to affect many (12:15).

Sexual immorality is one obvious entry point for sin into the community (12:16). But just as insidious is the attitude of Esau, who personified the Jewish believers beginning to desert the church. Esau had foolishly exchanged his future inheritance for the immediate gratification of his hunger. Similarly, the first-century believers were willing to trade what they had been promised for the readily available pleasures of the world. The writer reminds the church that when Esau realized what he had given up, he tearfully attempted to regain the blessing but was unable to do so (12:17). Esau's tears reflected remorse for the consequences of his actions but not a godly sorrow that leads to true repentance. The first-century believers would do well to consider their attitudes and actions before making a similar mistake.

Demystifying Hebrews

The juxtaposition of denouncing sexual immorality along with the godlessness of Esau may appear awkward. But there was a belief in Jewish tradition that Esau was a sexually immoral person, and the author may have been referring to that line of thought.

The description in verses 18–21 is of the Israelites at Mount Sinai as God gave the law to Moses. The first-century believers were beginning to romanticize life under the old covenant, and this was a reminder of the tremendous fear that had been a part of that system. Those who knew Christ had the benefit of the new covenant with a heavenly perspective rather than an earthly one, and had Jesus as their mediator rather than a human priest (12:22–24). They belonged to the assembly of the firstborn, meaning that they were saints set apart to God and privileged to receive all He offered. They were eligible for the very blessings Esau squandered.

Critical Observation

The same word translated "begged" in verse 19 is translated "refuse" in verse 25. Such an observation suggests that the Old Testament Israelites weren't so much awed by the presence of God as resistant to hearing His Word. Perhaps they didn't make the request (to hear no further Word spoken to them) out of reverence for God, but rather out of the craven fear that comes from unbelief. This view can be supported by their behavior with the golden calf less than a month later. In addition, the quotation by Moses (12:21) was not taken from the Exodus account on Sinai, but from Deuteronomy, where Moses was reflecting on the sin of the people with the golden calf. It seems he was not expressing fear about being in the presence of God, but about what would happen to Israel as a result of their unbelief and disobedience.

Yet those very privileges make the writer's warning even more significant. The notion that God is terrifying and distant in the ancient epoch but is more kind, loving, and accessible to His people after the life of Christ contradicts any number of statements in scripture. With all the additional information about the importance of Christ's sacrifice and ongoing priestly work on behalf of God's people, it is even more egregious now to ignore the Word of God than ever before (12:25–27).

Israel in the days of Moses experienced the grace of God and suffered when they forsook God in disbelief and apostasy—just as was true for believers in the first-century church. God's anger and judgment are still realities, as the author has already reminded his readers in 2:1–4; 6:4–8; 10:26–31, and elsewhere. He is making no attempt to sidestep these serious considerations.

The writer has confidence in the genuineness of the faith of the Jewish believers but is not reluctant to warn them of the dire consequences of apostasy. He never strays far from his focus on the end of time and the salvation that comes in its fullness only when Christ returns. In the context of his current warning, he quotes from Haggai 2:6 to show both the surety and severity of God's power (Hebrews 12:26).

The image of heaven and earth being physically shaken is quickly contrasted with the one thing that is never in danger of being lost or disturbed—the kingdom of God (12:28–29). God is rightly described as a consuming fire (12:29), which is ample cause for those who disdain His work and His Word to fear. But for those who remain reverent and worship Him, the result is thanksgiving and ongoing expectation of all He has promised.

Take It Home

"Fear of the Lord" is a phrase common in the Old Testament and is found in the New Testament as well. It is usually defined more as "respect" than "fright," although people draw the line at different places. How would *you* define a proper fear of the Lord? Do you think most believers today have a proper fear in their spiritual relationships? If not, what do you think ought to be different?

HEBREWS 13:1–25

PRACTICAL APPLICATIONS FOR PERSEVERING FAITH

The Sacrifice of Praise and Good Works	13:1–16
Proper Submission to Authority	13:17–25

Setting Up the Section

This section appears to take an abrupt turn. It seems strange that the writer pauses in the delivery of his long sermon on the absolute necessity of having a persevering faith in Christ to list some specific duties that may not seem to bear directly on what he had previously written. Yet it is characteristic of the Bible to specify particular ways in which a believer should practice and work out the faith to which he or she has been summoned in any given passage. Hebrews is no different in this respect.

13:1–16

THE SACRIFICE OF PRAISE AND GOOD WORKS

There is a sense in which the message of Hebrews—the sermon portion—could be regarded as finished at 12:29. This closing section, then, becomes something of a postscript one might add to a personal letter, but not necessarily an oral sermon.

Much of this section is merely a clarification of the opening statement to persevere in brotherly love (13:1). Most people like to believe they exemplify love for humankind, yet those noble thoughts aren't borne out in everyday actions. It's one thing to "love" a group of unknown or unspecified people; it's quite another to consistently demonstrate love to the specific people one interacts with on a daily basis.

Most likely, the author's comments are in regard to believers, since he begins with the mandate to continue loving one another as brothers. So the strangers that the Hebrew Christians were to entertain (13:2) were probably fellow believers from other places. Whether fellow Christians or not, it is clear that believers should not confine Christian love only to those they know well.

Critical Observation

The author's reference to entertaining angels (13:2) is reminiscent of Abraham and the hospitality he offered three men who turned out to be the Lord and two angels (Genesis 18). Similar hospitality by Samson's parents toward a divine messenger was also rewarded (Judges 13). And there were other instances. The author's point is that hospitality shouldn't be perceived as an obligation or something done in order to receive a return on one's efforts. Rather, hospitality should be offered with the awareness that the host never knows what might be the result. Sometimes he or she will be very surprised.

Similarly, the command to visit prisoners (Hebrews 13:3) might be primarily in regard to believers who had been imprisoned on account of their faith. Underlying all these commands is the golden rule to treat others as one would like to be treated (Matthew 7:12). Brotherly love is more than verbal expressions of regret for others' situations; it requires putting oneself in the situation of another and responding the way one would desire to be treated.

Christian charity in the early church was not always convenient. Believers were bringing others into their homes and going out into their culture to meet others and respond to their needs. Of course, if their faith was beginning to flag (as the author has suggested on numerous occasions), their brotherly love for other Christians might be withering as well, necessitating this closing afterthought.

Certain statements in the New Testament reveal that the early church was troubled by certain ascetic teachers who strongly promoted celibacy—especially among spiritual leaders (1 Timothy 4:3). Other philosophies were much too lax regarding sexual relationships (1 Corinthians 5:1–2). In a single statement (Hebrews 13:4), the author of Hebrews first endorses marriage and then demands that it be given the respect that God intended for such a vital relationship.

He follows with a similar exhortation for a proper attitude toward money, extolling contentment over greed (13:5). God's presence in a believer's life should be the all-important priority that allows a better perspective on life (13:5–6). His readers served a God who would never forsake them and who was always there to help.

The leaders he refers to (13:7) were the first generation of people who had taken the gospel with them as they responded to all that Jesus had taught and had modeled (previously mentioned in 2:3). They had themselves become models of faith and worthy of imitation.

The frequently quoted statement in verse 8 is usually cited to affirm that amid all the uncertainties of this world, the character and promise of Jesus Christ are absolutely unshakable certainties. This is what the first-century believers would have taken it to mean. However, in the context of the New Testament in general, and the other arguments by the writer of Hebrews specifically, the statement is also an important theological confession. Christ is the same *yesterday* as today and forever. It is true that at a particular moment in time, the Son of God appeared as a person in the world to die and rise again, redeeming His people from their sin and guilt. Yet as eternal God, He had been involved with creation, with Abraham, with Moses, and throughout the history of Israel. The blessings and benefits of His redemption have been spread backward as well as forward in time.

Demystifying Hebrews

Any correct understanding of the theology of Hebrews—and scripture as a whole—must acknowledge that Christ did not begin to be His people's savior or object of their faith when He came into the world as the son of Mary. What He accomplished by His incarnation, suffering, obedience, death, and resurrection was the basis for the relationship He had held with His people since the days of Adam and Eve. Otherwise, it could not be said that Christ is the same yesterday, today, and forever (13:8).

As he nears the end of his letter, the writer once more lays out his grand theme (13:9–16). Again he warns his readers of the fatal error of attempting a compromise with Judaism. It wasn't that their rites and ceremonies were worthless (13:9), because numerous church leaders continued to observe them. But in a church that was increasingly Gentile, those old Jewish ways were of no value in providing salvation for anyone. In terms of justification before God, it was dangerous to require *anything* in addition to the work of Jesus Christ.

For believers coming from a Jewish background, the situation in the first-century church must have been quite difficult. They were being asked to downplay the importance of the temple and all its ceremonies. Christians had none of the visible accoutrements that signified a religion to most people of their time–including temples, altars, or priests. Their pagan neighbors thought they were atheists, and their Jewish peers would have scorned their faith without all the outward signs of religious ceremony. So the author of Hebrews reminds his readers that they did indeed have an altar, a priest, and a temple. . .in heaven (13:10–14).

Previously in Israel's history, God had once taken up station outside the camp (Exodus 33:7–11). Similarly, Jesus' sacrifice of Himself outside of Jerusalem rather than in the temple becomes an enacted parable expressing God's judgment on the people's unbelief. The exhortation is clear: It is wrong to continue to attempt to stay connected to the old ways. The time had come to make a clean and permanent break with the way of thinking that considered salvation a matter of the blood of bulls and goats.

Animal sacrifices were no longer necessary. Rather, believers were to offer God a sacrifice of praise (13:15–16)–a confession of His sufficiency and a commitment to do good works. The good deeds have nothing to do with acquiring salvation, but are in response to the forgiveness and righteousness God provides. The language of the Old Testament is brought into the New as yet another proof that the liturgical teaching of the Old Testament is still a valuable model for principles and practices of worship. Offering sacrifices to God is still completely appropriate, but the blood of animals is no longer necessary. Sacrifices of praise connect the worshiper's daily life with his or her worship of God. It is an offering far greater than some cash or a check dropped into the passed plate each Sunday.

13:17–25

PROPER SUBMISSION TO AUTHORITY

In retrospect, seeing how determinedly the author has tried to explain the dangers of reverting to old ways and rejecting Christ, and his persuasive argument to convince his readers to remain true to their faith, it seems safe to assume that the near-schism within the church had already created some tension between those members and the leaders. So the author issues a clear call for obedience to those who were watching over the spiritual integrity of the church (13:17). Their work was demanding enough without a lot of opposition from within.

One result of faithfulness and obedience is a clear conscience (13:18)—something that had become quite rare, and still is. Such a claim is certainly no boast of sinlessness. Rather, a clear conscience is produced by having integrity while establishing one's desires as a Christian and maintaining a fundamental commitment to live in keeping with those desires and high ideals. A clear conscience is achievable only when the believer gratefully receives God's grace and help on a regular basis.

The author has given his audience a lot to think about. His final benediction (13:20–25) is a beautiful summary and reminder that Jesus Christ's shed blood and resurrection are the foundation of God's work in saving people and enabling them to live holy lives. The distinction he makes here is what separates Christianity from all other faiths and philosophies: the conviction that Jesus Christ is *the* way, *the* truth, and *the* life.

Hebrews is one of the longer books of the New Testament, yet the writer considers it a short letter (13:22). He wants his readers to prayerfully consider what he has written, because he plans to follow up his letter with a personal visit (13:19, 23). His brief, final comments confirm the historical nature of the witness of the New Testament with references to real people, times, and places. Yet they do little more than tantalize. The New Testament says nothing else about Timothy's imprisonment (13:23). The author himself remains unknown. And it is impossible to determine whether he is writing *in* Italy, or writing *to* Italy from elsewhere and including the greetings of expatriate Italian believers who were with him (13:24).

Yet the message conveyed in Hebrews comes through clearly, emphatically, and repeatedly: It is essential to keep persevering in faith, looking ahead to the return of Christ, and anticipating the completion of salvation along with the complete rest and promise of God.

Take It Home

The writer of Hebrews was able to declare a clear conscience and a desire to live honorably in every way. Can you say the same thing? If not, what are the areas of life you need to work on? What might you need to confess or address in order to make your conscience entirely clear?

JAMES

INTRODUCTION TO JAMES

AUTHOR

James was the natural son of Joseph and Mary and the younger half brother of Jesus, since they shared a mother but not a father. James is always mentioned first in the lists of Jesus' siblings (Matthew 13:55; Mark 6:3), indicating that he was most likely the eldest of Jesus' half siblings. He is also mentioned in Acts 15:13; 21:18; 1 Corinthians 15:7; Galatians 1:19; 2:9, 12; James; and Jude.

Although he did not believe in Jesus during Jesus' early earthly ministry (John 7:5), after the Resurrection James became the leader of the Jerusalem church from AD 44–62. He presided over the Jerusalem Council (Acts 15), and he was considered by Paul to be a pillar of the church, alongside Peter and John (Galatians 2:9). According to Josephus, a first-century Jewish historian, the Jewish Sanhedrin sentenced James to a martyr's death in AD 62.

PURPOSE

The book of James is one of seven letters in the New Testament called the "general" or "catholic" Epistles (catholic meaning "universal") because it is addressed to a general Christian audience, rather than a specific congregation. Its tone is one of pastoral exhortation. More than fifty of the 108 verses in the letter are imperatives, but James writes his commands in a way that is filled with care and concern for his brothers. Because of its teaching flavor, many scholars consider James more of a sermon in written form than a letter.

OCCASION

James was a Jewish Christian writing to a Jewish Christian audience. The letter is replete with Old Testament teachings and allusions, but it is clear that James wrote from a distinctly Christian perspective and from the experience of one who had spent time with Jesus. The audience was a group of Christians who were experiencing persecution for their faith. James wrote to them to encourage them in the face of trials and to help them know how to stand firm in the faith.

THEMES

James's letter is a pragmatist's dream. He gives his wise instruction in a distinctive rubber-meets-the-road way that only a firsthand witness can. He shows that it is not good enough to have faith without works, but believers must do right acts for the right reasons. James's overall concern is consistency in practicing faith through obedient acts that produce results—truly hearing God equals obeying Him. Submitting to God means living out what one says he or she believes. Loving one's neighbors affects the tongue. Caring for the oppressed is a result of obedience to a just God. James calls for submission to Christ in genuine faith that works.

HISTORICAL CONTEXT

Many scholars date James as early as AD 45–48, which would make it perhaps the earliest New Testament epistle. There are several reasons for this conclusion:

1) The Council of Jerusalem took place about AD 50, yet it is not mentioned in James. In fact, there is no reference to a conflict about requirements for Gentile Christians, the well-known debate of the Council, so it is assumed that James's letter predates it.
2) Church leaders are called by Jewish terms, *teachers* and *elders*, rather than later church terms, *overseers* and *deacons*.
3) The synagogue is mentioned as the meeting place of Christians (2:2).
4) James addresses his letter only to Jewish Christians ("the twelve tribes scattered among the nations" James 1:1 TNIV), which suggests that the mission to the Gentiles had not yet begun. James may well be writing to the Jewish Christians who were dispersed from their homeland during the persecution described in Acts 8.

CONTRIBUTION TO THE BIBLE

James's instructions echo those found in the Old Testament, but they also repeat Jesus' own teachings. James is teaching new believers what it means to live out their faith in Christ as Lord. (The Greek word *pistis*, translated "faith," appears fifteen times in the letter.)

Critical Observation

There are several strong similarities between James's teachings and those of Jesus in His Sermon on the Mount. Besides pointing to the likelihood that James, the half brother of Jesus, is the author of this letter, they show that James's letter works to teach believers a specifically Christian worldview.

James 1:2	Matthew 5:10–12
James 1:4	Matthew 5:48
James 1:5	Matthew 7:7–12
James 1:22	Matthew 7:21–27
James 2:12–13	Matthew 6:14–15
James 3:11–13	Matthew 7:16–20
James 4:11–12	Matthew 7:1–5
James 5:1–3	Matthew 6:19–21
James 5:12	Matthew 5:33–37

OUTLINE

FACING TRIALS AND LIVING OUT FAITH 1:1–27

Greetings 1:1
The Work of Perseverance 1:2–4
Ask and Believe 1:5–8
High and Low Positions 1:9–11
How Temptation Works 1:12–18
Hear and Do 1:19–27

LOVE, FAITH, AND ACTION 2:1–26

No Favoritism 2:1–7
Love Your Neighbor 2:8–13
Dead Faith 2:14–18
The Significance of Faith and Deeds 2:19–26

WISE LIVING 3:1–18

The Tongue's Power 3:1–6
Taming the Tongue 3:7–12
Wisdom vs. Selfishness 3:13–18

PUT IT IN PERSPECTIVE 4:1–17

A Choice to Make 4:1–6
Seeking Submission 4:7–12
If It Is God's Will 4:13–17

WEALTH, WAITING, AND PRAYER 5:1–20

A Warning to the Rich 5:1–6
Patient Waiting 5:7–12
Faithful Prayer 5:13–18
Back from Wandering 5:19–20

JAMES 1:1–27

FACING TRIALS AND LIVING OUT FAITH

Greetings	1:1
The Work of Perseverance	1:2–4
Ask and Believe	1:5–8
High and Low Positions	1:9–11
How Temptation Works	1:12–18
Hear and Do	1:19–27

Setting Up the Section

Early in the church, Christians were gaining their own identity apart from Jews, but this new identity came through much persecution. James urges the believers to persevere in the midst of trials in order to strengthen their faith so they may become righteous in their actions. The call in this chapter is to live with unconditional obedience to God.

1:1

GREETINGS

The writer of the letter simply introduces himself as James. As the most prominent leader in the first-century church in Jerusalem, he would not have needed to explain who he was. Yet instead of clinging to his position, or even to his blood relationship with Jesus, James calls himself a servant. His authority doesn't come through his position as leader or apostle (Galatians 1:19), but as a servant of God and of the Lord Jesus Christ.

The use of the phrase "Lord Jesus Christ" should not be read lightly. James writes to Jewish Christians, and the use of *Lord* indicates deity. Adding *Christ* emphasizes Jesus' role as Messiah.

James addresses the letter to the twelve tribes "dispersed abroad" (NASB) or "scattered among the nations" (NIV). The phrase describes the *diaspora* (scattering), or dispersion of the Jews. While the literal twelve tribes of Israel (the descendants of Jacob's twelve sons) no longer could be traced, references to these tribes had come to represent a regathered Israel. James primarily uses the phrase to represent the Jewish Christians living outside of Palestine, perhaps due to persecution after the stoning of Stephen (Acts 8:1–3).

1:2–4

THE WORK OF PERSEVERANCE

James addresses his "brothers and sisters" (Greek: *adelphoi*) fourteen times in his letter, setting the tone of both pastor and fellow believer. He moves quickly from a joyful greeting to a difficult command—be joyful in the midst of trials (1:2). James's message is clear: Even (or perhaps especially) while suffering, believers should live out their faith. The command echoes Jesus' words in Matthew 5:11–12.

James is writing to people facing trials because of their faith in Jesus. The label "all sorts of" (NET) indicates trials that occur as part of the common human experience, as well as those that come in the form of persecution or difficulties for those who follow Christ.

How can joy and trials coexist? The one experiencing the trial knows that the end result is a stronger character and faith. James says perseverance is developed through trials. God gives believers the ability to endure with patience, and the testing develops perseverance and a stronger faith. It's a lifestyle that leads to a mature and whole spiritual journey. The word *perfect* (1:4 NET) does not mean without fault, but "whole," "complete," or "mature."

1:5–8

ASK AND BELIEVE

Wisdom is a key tool to knowing how to deal with difficult situations. In acknowledging the need for wisdom, James points believers toward God's grace (1:5). God's nature is to give generously and without reservation. His call to live by faith goes out to everyone.

God requires that people ask in faith, believing without doubt. One who doubts is someone with divided loyalties—between depending on self and depending on God. Doubting that God is good and loving makes a person unstable (like being tossed by a wave), which shows up not only in his or her prayers, but also in his or her life.

Demystifying James

Throughout his letter, James uses metaphors to create word pictures for his readers: wind-tossed waves (1:6); withering plants (1:10–11); self-inspection using a mirror (1:23); a dead body (2:26); bridling of a horse (3:3); turning a ship (3:4); forest fire (3:5–6); taming wild beasts (3:7); impossible fountain of fresh and salt water (3:11); impossible vine of grapes and figs (3:12); ephemeral mist (4:14); clothes consumed by moths (5:2); rust behaving like fire (5:3); farmers waiting for rain (5:7); rain watering the earth (5:18).

1:9–11

HIGH AND LOW POSITIONS

James introduces the topic of wealth and materialism, something he expounds on throughout this letter. James is not encouraging poverty and cursing wealth. He is talking about perspective and where believers find their security.

Humble circumstances were a trial many first-century Jewish Christians faced. Many had been forced to leave their homes, losing their property and their source of income. Many possibly also faced self-inflicted poverty when they refused to participate in unethical business dealings. But believers should take pride in their high position because their worth and security are found in Christ.

When singling out the rich (1:10), James references those who abuse wealth and oppress the poor as a means to gain more. (This is something he explores further in chapter 4.) The rich will fade away because money does not bring security. James uses the same wildflower imagery that Jesus uses in Matthew 6:25–34. The rich place their stock in this world, but that beauty will be lost forever. Wealth births the illusion of power, which births the illusion of invincibility, but true security is found in God alone.

1:12–18

HOW TEMPTATION WORKS

Verse 12 serves as a summary statement of ground that James has already covered in chapter 1:

> "Blessed is a man (an echo of Jesus' Beatitudes and reason for joy in 1:2)
> who perseveres (1:3–4)
> under trial (1:2);
> for once he has been approved (stood the test, 1:3),
> he will receive the crown of life which the Lord has promised to those
> who love Him" (NASB).

James's words give believers the courage to face difficult choices and to choose the way of Christ.

James is clear about two things in verses 13–15:

1) Temptation does not come from God. This passage speaks to the holy character of God. God is not tempted by evil, and He is never the source of temptation.
2) Temptation is not sin. Responding inappropriately to temptation is sin, and unconfessed sin brings death. But simply being tempted is a different matter.

James tells his beloved brothers and sisters to stop being deceived (1:16). God is a loving God who wants to help His children, not harm them. God is not the source of temptation, but the source of every good and perfect gift. Not least of these gifts is salvation. God gives new life using the message of truth. This brings believers to a choice: Either sin can be the master (as implied in verses 12–16), or the Creator can be the master (as expected in verses 17–18). God is contrasted with the unstable believer here, because with Him there is no variation or shifting shadow. He is unchangeable, immutable, and unwavering. Believers can rest in knowing His character remains the same, and so His gifts will always be good.

Demystifying James

The Old Testament teaches Jews to bring their "first fruits," or the first and best of their harvests, as an offering to God (Exodus 34:22; Leviticus 23:9–10; Deuteronomy 26:9–11). In verse 18, James calls himself and the believers he writes to "a kind of first fruits among His creatures" (NASB) because they are a new creation, a new people, in Christ.

1:19–27

HEAR AND DO

James condemns dormant, unapplied knowledge. He calls for people to listen to a message of truth and then live a life consistent with that message, and he offers guidelines for what that might look like.

He introduces here the theme of controlling the tongue (he continues to emphasize this theme in chapter 3). The pressure that trials create may make believers quick to react in anger; James says to act differently. Verse 19 is a key verse for the letter because it points to a faith that results in changed behavior.

In verses 21–22, the "message" (NET) refers to Old Testament scripture, but James adds Jesus' teachings to this understanding of the message, which is why it is able to save souls. This is the same meaning James intends when he uses the phrase "perfect law of liberty" (1:25 NET). When James tells readers to hear ("understand," "know," "be aware") this message, he means more than a passive listening; he intends a proactive response on the part of his readers. To hear the Word but not allow it to change one's life is self-deception (see 1:16). If believers listen to the message without allowing the message to grow roots and effect change, they are only fooling themselves. Christians cannot claim new life in Christ while pursuing sin that brings death, and they cannot commit their lives to Christ while continuing selfish living. That is the same as looking in the mirror with no more than a passing glance (1:24–25). James calls for believers to look intently into the perfect law. He is repeating Jesus' teaching in Luke 11:28, which says that those who hear God's Word and obey it are blessed.

Critical Observation

The word translated "peers" in verse 25 (NET) carries the idea of examining something in order to understand it. The word is used of Peter, John, and Mary Magdalene (on three separate instances) looking into Jesus' empty tomb for the first time. In fact, for them, and for us, it involved stooping down to get a closer look. It is with that intensity that we should seek understanding from the scriptures.

James says one's religion is worthless if it is without fruit. As just one example, he says that if faith doesn't change the way a person speaks, then that believer deceives himself (1:26–27). James mentions three areas in which genuine faith will be demonstrated, though it is by no means an exhaustive list: the tongue (1:26), caring for the unfortunate (1:27), and purity (1:27). Pure faith is to care for those who are powerless and defenseless (a theme that is prevalent throughout the Old Testament) and to live in a way that is not influenced by the things of the world.

Take It Home

As believers in Christ, the question isn't *if* we will experience trials and hardship in life, but *when*. So we should prepare as best we can for when the time comes. The Bible is filled with examples of men and women who faced trials and responded in a variety of ways. In order to properly endure and weather hardships, we need to know what we believe—and to live it out. When trials come your way, will you persevere and grow in faith? Or will you resist what God wants to teach you?

JAMES 2:1–26

LOVE, FAITH, AND ACTION

No Favoritism 2:1–7

Love Your Neighbor 2:8–13

Dead Faith 2:14–18

The Significance of Faith and Deeds 2:19–26

Setting Up the Section

In the second chapter of his letter, James again calls for consistency in living out faith. The first half of this chapter deals with consistency in loving others regardless of their socioeconomic status; the second half calls for consistency in one's works and words.

This chapter in James has seemed troublesome to some. At issue is the relationship between faith and works. James agrees that one is saved by faith alone and not by works, but he emphasizes that genuine faith produces fruit. James concludes that workless faith—like faithless works—is unmeritorious before our heavenly Father.

2:1–7

NO FAVORITISM

James introduces a hypothetical situation involving two people who receive two different responses: The one who appears rich receives preferential treatment; the one who appears poor is treated like a lesser-class citizen. James argues that everyone is worthy of preferential treatment, and those who provide it selectively are guilty before God. He concludes this section with a powerful passage that describes one of the clearest—and most difficult—ways to love one's neighbor as oneself: by extending mercy and forgiveness. Thus, James continues his emphasis on living out faith.

James does not have a problem with the rich, though taken out of context it may seem like it. He does, however, have a problem with financial gain that comes through exploitation. He states that the rich who are receiving favoritism are the same people who oppress and dishonor the poor and drag debtors off to jail. What's more, they are also slandering the name of Christ and persecuting Christians. James is not suggesting a *reversal* of discrimination by treating the poor well and the rich poorly; he is teaching a *removal* of discrimination. Preferential treatment has no place among Christians who serve a just God; to be holy as God is holy means treating others as God would treat them—with value and dignity.

James also shows that the fundamental advantage of the poor over the rich is their awareness of their powerlessness. This sentiment echoes James's own words (1:9–10) and echoes Jesus in Matthew 5:3—Blessed are the poor in spirit. Awareness of our own powerlessness is essential before we can trust Christ to do what people are unable to do: save themselves.

Demystifying James

The Jews had started a practice of seating those with privilege or position closer to the front where the Torah and other scripture were kept on scrolls, while other "less important" people were seated in the back. This practice continued in some Christian churches in the first century. Similar preferential treatment takes place in churches still today, but James says it should stop.

2:8–13

LOVE YOUR NEIGHBOR

James writes about the "royal law," the same law he speaks of in 1:25. James refers to the Mosaic Law but adds the definer *royal* to reiterate the significance of the law of Christ, the King—the One who fulfilled the Old Testament law.

To love your neighbor as yourself is an Old Testament command (Leviticus 19:18), and it is an imperative that Jesus gave new meaning to in Matthew 19:19; Mark 12:31; and Luke 10:27. Where the Old Testament law gave instructions on how to treat other Jews, Jesus broadened the meaning of *neighbor* to include even enemies. Jesus' command to love God with all oneself and to love others as oneself is the underpinning of all other commandments. Favoritism, for example, is sin because it isn't in keeping with the law of love. Christians cannot claim to love God and then mistreat the people made in His image.

James argues that showing preferential treatment is no small infraction. He uses adultery and murder as extreme offenses against the royal law to love one's neighbor as oneself (2:11). James explains the law as a unit, so that when someone disobeys one part, he or she has disobeyed the entirety. The Mosaic Law showed the Israelites their need for God and their inability to live holy lives on their own. Jesus, on the other hand, issues a law that brings freedom (2:12). There is freedom from sin's penalty and freedom to serve God by speaking and acting in accordance with Christ's teachings.

James calls for mercy, not judgment (2:13). Mercy and forgiveness are supernatural activities. They are extreme demonstrations of loving our neighbor as ourselves.

2:14–18

DEAD FAITH

The Greek construction of James's rhetorical question at the opening of verse 14 implies a "no" answer. He is not saying that believers are not saved by grace through faith, but he is saying that no one finds salvation through a dead faith. James is clear: Faith must affect every area—and action—in a believer's life. In the same way that Jesus condemned a fruitless fig tree (Matthew 21:18–19), James says that faith without works is dead. *Claiming* to have faith is different from *actually having* faith, because genuine faith is evidenced by actions.

James does not advocate a works-based salvation, though. Workless faith and faithless works are equally dead. James's main concern is consistency of faith, evidenced by its fruit. True faith is active belief and active trust, which result in a changed life. The example in James 2:15–16 shows that action is necessary; otherwise words are empty. What use are words without obedience?

In verse 18, James argues for theological unity: faith *and* works. He essentially says faith without works is impossible. The way people see someone's faith is by how he or she lives it out.

2:19–26

THE SIGNIFICANCE OF FAITH AND DEEDS

James emphasizes the uselessness of faith without its accompanying deeds by saying that even the demons believe in the Triune God—but they do not obey (2:19). He points instead to the example of Abraham, who obeyed out of trust and belief in God. In the beginning of Abraham's narrative, he showed that he trusted God by leaving his home and traveling to an unknown destination (Genesis 12:1–7), and later Abraham showed his faith by preparing to sacrifice Isaac, his son. His faith was made complete (as opposed to a hollow faith) as a result of his obedience. Even the prostitute Rahab acted in obedience that resulted from trust and belief (Joshua 2:4–15; James 2:25). Christians can find narratives throughout the Old Testament of people demonstrating that genuine faith is always accompanied by obedient actions.

Critical Observation

Many scholars find James's theology of justification (2:24–25) problematic because it seems to contradict Paul's theology (Romans 4:1–3). However, understanding that the two apostles use the word *justification* in different ways shows that they are not in conflict. According to James, *justified* means believers are shown to be righteous for having lived a life of faithful obedience.

Paul refers to an initial justification in a moment of gaining righteousness by faith, where James means a final justification, or ultimate declaration of a person's righteousness. It wasn't Abraham's act that made him righteous, but Abraham had an active faith, and that made him accepted by God. Paul sees works as something people do to try to earn salvation, so that faith is an initial saving faith that then leads to obedience; James sees works as a natural outpouring of genuine faith. Paul makes it clear that believers enter the kingdom of God by faith, but James adds that once in the kingdom, obedience is necessary.

JAMES 3:1–18

WISE LIVING

The Tongue's Power	3:1–6
Taming the Tongue	3:7–12
Wisdom vs. Selfishness	3:13–18

Setting Up the Section

This passage includes James's famous teachings on the power of speech. He refers to the combination of thought and speech, and the precariously instantaneous connection between the two by talking about the power of the tongue.

James says the tongue is challenging to tame. It is as unmanageable as a raging fire and as harmful as poison. What's more, it is disproportionately influential: It bears tremendous weight for its relatively small mass. Usually this influence is negative, but when managed properly it can wage a significantly positive force.

3:1–6

THE TONGUE'S POWER

James opens chapter 3 with an instruction that not many should become teachers. His address is to those who seek positions of leadership in the church, likely those who would presume to teach primarily for prestige. His warning is against pride, reminding those who think they should have authority to stay humble.

Critical Observation

There is a parallel of this teaching in Matthew 18:6, when Jesus warns against those who teach others to sin, and in Luke 12:42–48, when He states that much will be expected from those to whom much is given. The truth is not that teachers should be without fault of any kind, but they should be aware of their need to rely on God. James would have recognized the importance of the role of teachers, because Christianity was new. Teachers would be discipling new believers and providing instruction for the fledgling church.

James follows this specific address with general thoughts on living with wisdom and humility. He uses the tongue as an example of being able to control oneself and live wisely. The idea in this passage is that the tongue is seemingly unimpressive, yet it has disproportionate influence on the rest of the body. All are at risk to stumble, but teachers may be at greater risk for judgment because their tongues are their primary means for educating. The ability to control one's words is a mark of maturity for a believer.

To make his point, James uses a series of illustrations, or word pictures, that would have been familiar to his audience. James repeats the imagery of 1:26, suggesting that in the same way a small bit, or bridle, controls a large animal, the tongue can control a person (3:3). In the same way a small rudder directs a large ship at sea, so the tongue can set the course for a person's entire life. And just as a small spark can create a raging fire that would destroy a large forest, the tongue can corrupt the whole person (3:4–6).

Although the illustrations James uses are morally neutral, he is clear that the influence of the tongue is often negative. The image of fire that James uses conveys the potential of an uncontrolled tongue for widespread destruction, perhaps through gossip or slander or boasting. In the same way, the tongue's influence cannot be disconnected from the rest of a person. A person's words reflect his or her heart and character. In its ability to corrupt the whole body, the tongue can easily keep a believer from pure and undefiled religion (1:27).

3:7–12

TAMING THE TONGUE

Verse 7 references the first chapter of Genesis, in which God gave humans the ability to rule over animals. The taming of animals is a common practice, but James shows that humans have trouble controlling their own tongues.

The tongue is restless, meaning it is unstable and its ability to do evil can never be fully restrained (3:8). It is important for believers to be aware of its power in order to avoid careless words. The tongue is also a deadly poison, which is a reference to Psalm 140:3. Words can harm those who speak them, poisoning them through bitterness, and they can harm those they are spoken to or about by wounding like a snake's bite.

By referring to God as "our Lord and Father" (3:9)—a phrase used nowhere else in the New Testament—James reminds his audience of their relationship to God. He also circles back to the topic of consistency by saying believers cannot use their words both to bless and to curse, referencing the creation account by pointing out the problem with believers using words to curse those who are made in the image of God. Because God values all people and has created them in His likeness, believers are to treat other people as though they have value, not use words to assault or destroy. In fact, Jesus said that believers are to bless those who curse them (Luke 6:28).

The tongue reflects what's in a person's heart (Luke 6:45). James uses the inconsistency in both praising and cursing to point to a deeper inconsistency in a person's heart. A pure spring does not produce both freshwater and salt water, and a fig tree does not yield olives (Matthew 7:16; James 3:11–12). In the same way, one who is pure in heart cannot produce words that curse. The idea of cursing is not something to be taken lightly. It is more than using "dirty" language or harsh words to express anger at a person. To curse someone is to proclaim them damned, or cut off eternally from God. To bless God and to curse someone that He made in His image are two actions that cannot go together.

Purity in speech is a natural outpouring of a genuine faith and nonnegotiable for the believer. This is a truth that James undoubtedly would have heard from Jesus when He said that people will have to give an account for every careless word they speak (Matthew 12:36–37).

Demystifying James

While *blessing someone's heart* may be a common colloquialism in some parts of modern culture, the kind of blessing that James wrote of would have had deep meaning to his readers. Blessing would have been part of the daily prayer life of Jews and, thus, Jewish Christians. One of the most common descriptions of God in Jewish literature is "The Holy One, blessed be He," and in the "Eighteen Benedictions," a Jewish liturgy, each ends with a blessing to God.

3:13–18

WISDOM VS. SELFISHNESS

James opens here with a question about wisdom (3:13). He comes back to this subject, tying this passage to the previous section on the tongue, by challenging those who think they are wise to show their wisdom through their actions. True wisdom produces humility, a result of understanding who a person is in relationship to God.

James again highlights the problem of inconsistency in the life of a believer. One who is truly wise cannot harbor bitterness and envy or selfish ambition (3:14). Twice he mentions envy and selfishness, two sides of the same coin. Envy comes when someone selfishly wants what another has, and this leads to strife, a point James makes further in chapter 4.

Wisdom is not something simply to *be*, but rather something to be demonstrated by conduct and actions. However, genuine faith is not something believers can accomplish on their own; wisdom for right living comes from God. And that wisdom from God results in actions that are pure, peaceable, gentle, accommodating, full of mercy, producing good fruit, impartial, and sincere. Worldly wisdom, on the other hand, seeks self-glory and personal gain (3:17–18).

"Wisdom from above"	"Wisdom from below"
Pure	Mixed motives
Peaceable	Ready for a fight
Gentle	Abrasive
Accommodating	Demanding
Full of mercy	Unforgiving
Full of good fruit	Full of bad fruit
Impartial	Prejudiced
Sincere	Manipulative

Take It Home

James is the "show me" book. If you think you are religious, show it by your speech. If you think you have faith, show it by your actions. If you think you have wisdom, show it by your conduct.

What are you showing the people around you? Are you longing for wisdom from above (Proverbs 16:16)? Are you asking the Lord for wisdom from above (James 1:5)? Are you demonstrating the wisdom from above (Colossians 1:9–10)?

JAMES 4:1–17

PUT IT IN PERSPECTIVE

A Choice to Make	4:1–6
Seeking Submission	4:7–12
If It Is God's Will	4:13–17

Setting Up the Section

James is writing to believers who did not always find it easy to get along. There were pockets of disunity, arguments, disagreements, criticisms, and personal attacks taking place among these believers. His words go to the heart of the problem and address what is probably the most basic human sin: pride. He challenges believers to submit to God wholeheartedly.

4:1–6

A CHOICE TO MAKE

Following his comments on wisdom that comes from above (3:15–17), James shows how false wisdom that stems from selfishness leads to fighting. The word translated *conflict* (NET) carries with it a violent image of a battle involving weapons. It's the image of an armed battle, a struggle for control. The word translated "quarrels" indicates an angry dispute without weapons.

Internal battles lead to external battles. The internal battle is a war of evil desires versus a Christian's soul, or the desire to follow selfish nature versus following God's will. The result of choosing these passions or desires (words that come from the same word that can be translated "hedonism") leads to external relational battles that take the form of verbal assaults.

When given over to selfish ambition or pleasures, division and fighting occur. In verse 2, James suggests that people fight because they don't get what they want. Here James also references Jesus' words in Matthew 5:21–22 when he says that the believers murder and envy.

James suggests the problem is a divided loyalty. Without turning to God and to His desires, even believers are left to their own selfish desires. He echoes the necessity for dependence on God by asking Him and trusting Him for needs (James 1:5). He adds that the believers either do not ask, or they ask with selfish motives, pointing again to the necessity for submission to God (4:3).

Take It Home

Can you name five people with whom you genuinely get along? Perhaps you have a great deal in common with them or you've shared many wonderful experiences together. Your friendship runs deep below the surface in these trusted relationships. Now think of five people with whom you do *not* get along (for some, this list is much easier to construct!). Perhaps you've had conflicts with them in the past or personality clashes. Do James's words about the reasons for conflicts lend any understanding to the conflicts that you experience? Do you find yourself engaging in the quarrel, or are you turning your selfish desires over to God?

In 4:4, James exchanges his comforting greeting "my brothers and sisters" (TNIV) with a serious "adulterous people" (NIV). The word he uses would have been understood by his Jewish audience as *adulteresses*, a female form of the verb denoting that they have been unfaithful to their groom, God. By using this powerful word, followed by the imagery of enmity with God and friendship with the world, James is accusing his readers of spiritual unfaithfulness. Echoing Jesus' statement in Matthew 6:24, James makes this strong point: Christians have to make a choice; they cannot love both God and the world's values.

Demystifying James

The concept of God as a groom and the idea of spiritual adultery would have been clear to James's Jewish-Christian audience. The Old Testament is filled with references to the Israelites' covenant with God using marriage images. When God's people turned to other gods, the prophet Jeremiah compared them to an unfaithful wife (Jeremiah 3:20). It is the theme of the entire book of Hosea, in which the prophet's marriage to an unfaithful prostitute mirrors the Israelites' turning away from God. Jesus, too, used this kind of language in calling the Jews who rejected Him an adulterous generation (Matthew 12:39).

James 4:5 opens with a rhetorical question in which James expects a "no" response. The verse is difficult to translate, as it is unclear whether *spirit* should be the subject or the object, and whether the human spirit or God's Spirit is in view. Two possibilities are (1) God, who placed His Spirit in us, is jealous for our loyalty or (2) the spirit that God placed in humans is prone to jealousy. In context with verse 4, it seems likely that verse 5 is a reminder that God is a jealous God (Exodus 20:4–5) and desires the unreserved love of His people.

James 4:6 is a reference to Proverbs 3:34. God gives grace to help believers love Him more when they humbly acknowledge their need for Him. Even if humans are, by nature, sinful and prone to turn from God, His grace is greater.

4:7–12

SEEKING SUBMISSION

In verses 7–10, James presents a series of ten imperatives. He begins by calling believers to submit to God and ends with a repetitive echo to humble oneself before Him, both continued references to Proverbs 3:34.

Between these imperatives come commandments that offer an image of repentance. In each there is an act of will on the part of the believer, combined with an act of God's grace. To give into selfish desires is to yield to the devil. Through Christ there is no need for a human intermediary, so believers can draw near to God. To clean hands and make hearts pure reflects the connection between transforming both hearts and behavior; one without the other is insufficient (Psalm 24:4). James 4:9 is a call to take sin seriously and to seek heartfelt repentance. As God comes near, believers are painfully aware of their shortcomings and the need to depend fully on Him. After repentance, God lifts up believers, something they cannot do on their own.

Humility also leads to the exaltation of others (4:10). Those with a sense of arrogance and self-sufficiency feel worthy to judge. This is a necessary message for James's readers; he has already addressed those who think they are religious but are not, those who think they have faith but do not, and those who think they are wise but are not. Verse 11 continues an emphasis on relationships among believers. James highlights again the importance of controlling the tongue by refusing to harm another's reputation, something that would break a relationship.

God alone is the lawgiver and judge, and at the heart of His law is love (Mark 12:30–31; 4:11–12). James is concerned with condemning speech that divides believers and breaks the law of love. His question, "Who are you to judge?" follows Jesus' words in Matthew 7:1. It's a sharp question that gives believers a proper perspective of who they are in relationship to God.

4:13–17

IF IT IS GOD'S WILL

James offers a powerful warning to those who think they are in control of their lives: Presumptuous living is dishonoring to God. It is not only those who confront God and demand equality with Him who offend Him, but those who often take matters into their own hands.

James's words here are likely addressed to those in business who travel (4:13). Because believers were dispersed, there would likely have been many who had to find a new way to make a living, and traveling to trade was a common first-century practice. The problem James points to is the tendency *not* to include God in the planning. It reinforces the message about submission by pointing to another example of self-sufficiency rather than dependence on God and a desire to do His will. This passage isn't about knowing the Lord's plan and deciding to make other plans; it is about making plans without consulting the Lord at all and taking the future for granted through self-made travel plans and business plans. James calls this arrogant boasting.

Verses 14–16 put believers in the proper place in the divine order, reminding readers that even a "long" life is but a mist. James is not suggesting literally adding the phrase "if it is the Lord's will" at the end of every sentence, but he is giving an imperative to acknowledge that no one should presume even to have the opportunity to travel, conduct business, and pursue success without recognizing that life itself is a gift from God. Self-sufficient boasting is evil because it disregards a need for God.

James ends this chapter with a reminder for believers to live out what they believe—to do the good they know to do (4:17).

Take It Home

"My life is my own." Few Christians would have the audacity to say those words, but most of us live as though we believe them. We often plan our days, our weeks, our months, and our years with a great deal of presumption. We sense that we are in control of our time and activities. In a results-oriented culture, we have convinced ourselves that the secret to success (in our education, career, family, future, and more) rests in the right formula. James reminds us that we are not in control of our lives. How seldom we acknowledge that our every breath is an unearned gift from God. Time is not our own, business is not our own, and the results of our efforts are not our own. In fact, our very lives are not our own (1 Corinthians 6:19–20). Let us live every day with that on our minds and make every plan contingent on, "If the Lord is willing."

JAMES 5:1–20

WEALTH, WAITING, AND PRAYER

A Warning to the Rich 5:1–6
Patient Waiting 5:7–12
Faithful Prayer 5:13–18
Back from Wandering 5:19–20

Setting Up the Section

In the final chapter of his letter, James continues his focus on having an eternal perspective. He begins with a focus on material wealth and a warning to the rich who find their security in the here and now. Then he encourages believers to endure in the present by focusing on Christ. Finally, he points readers to trusting in God by praying earnestly.

5:1–6

A WARNING TO THE RICH

In warning rich people, James is most likely addressing wealthy nonbelievers, possibly the oppressive landowners he references in 2:6. The misery that is coming is the future suffering on the Day of Judgment. It is important to note, though, that James does not single out everyone with wealth, but only the *unrighteous* rich.

Demystifying James

James's words to the rich reflect God's heart for the poor. His Jewish audience would have been familiar with the many passages in the Old Testament that direct God's people to care for the poor. They would also have been aware that those laws were often ignored. Old Testament prophets such as Amos and Isaiah spoke out against mistreating and ignoring the poor. James's use of the words *weep* and *wail* echoes the language of those prophets (5:1).

In verses 2–3, James highlights the impermanence of this world and all it has to offer and emphasizes the foolishness of placing security in earthly possessions. The word *riches* indicates more than just money and points to the many things that it can buy: clothing, gold and silver, treasures, indulgence in luxury, and crops and livestock.

Verse 2 echoes Jesus' words in Matthew 6:19–26. The warning is against hoarding wealth while others have need. Crops and hoarded food are rotting while others face hunger; excess clothing (a first-century luxury) is eaten by moths while the poor go without; and precious metals tarnish in storage instead of going to help others.

In addition to hoarding, James speaks out against people who acquire their possessions by unjust means. Workers lived day to day, so withholding pay might mean a laborer could not feed his family, possibly leading to eventual starvation (the murder referenced in 5:6).

The rich also often used the legal system to gain wealth and condemn the poor. God hears the cries of workers because He hates injustice and values human life.

James's words of warning in verse 5 again emphasize an eternal perspective. He condemns self-indulgence in the present, reminding the rich that their luxury comes at a greater price than they are willing to realize.

Take It Home

The Bible has a lot to say about money. We are encouraged to be financially responsible and have financial plans (Proverbs 21:20; 24:3–4; 27:23–27), but we are also encouraged to be generous givers (Proverbs 11:24–25; 21:13; 28:27; Luke 12:33–34). Jesus said, "What do you benefit if you gain the whole world but lose your own soul?" (Matthew 16:26 NLT). Are you hoarding, or are you saving wisely and giving to others in need? Do you allow others to use what you have? Are you aware of the needs of others within your community? Do you have an eternal perspective on wealth? Do you trust God for your future, or do you trust money for your future?

5:7–12

PATIENT WAITING

James focuses again on his Christian "brothers and sisters" who are facing poverty and political oppression, exhorting them to be patient and strong in the midst of hardships. To suffering saints, James calmly whispers, "Wait."

This message continues to point to an eternal perspective. James uses the farmer as an example. The early, or spring, rains occur soon after a crop is planted; the late, or autumn, rains occur just before harvesting. It is not the rains that the farmer waits for, though, but the crop itself. He has planted, labored, and invested a great deal, and then he waits. Just as the farmer waits patiently for the fruit of his labor, so must Christians wait patiently for the return of the Lord.

It would be easy to grumble against or turn against other believers during difficult times, but James urges his brothers not to do this (5:9). James reminds believers that the Lord's coming is near. He is the judge standing right at the door, and He is coming to vindicate the righteous and to hold the unrighteous accountable.

The word translated here as "patience" occurs four times (5:7, 8, 10) in this letter. James uses the prophets as an example of exhibiting patience while suffering as a result of following God's will.

In verse 11, James returns to the notion of perseverance. Job's endurance is the same word used in 1:3–4, a strong perseverance in the face of trials.

Critical Observation

Job complained, but he remained faithful to his God. In the end he was blessed. James does not promise material blessings, but he does point to the promise of God's mercy and compassion. The word for "mercy" in 5:11 is only used elsewhere in Luke 6:36: "Be merciful, just as your Father is merciful" (NIV).

In verse 12, James warns briefly against oaths, echoing Jesus' words in Matthew 5:33–37. Oaths were commonly forfeited by legal loopholes, but Christians should be consistent in their honesty, avoiding even half-truths. Again, James emphasizes the weight of words and consistency. The oaths, in this context, were more than words. They were promises, often promises made before God within a worship setting.

5:13–18

FAITHFUL PRAYER

In closing, James circles back to his opening call for prayer. He points to praying in all circumstances: whether facing trouble or in happy times (5:13). He also directs those who are sick to call church leaders to pray. Notice that it is not the faith of the sick person that James mentions, but the faith of those who pray. Presumably, the sick person exercises faith by calling the elders.

Demystifying James

Interpretations of 5:14–15 vary. One view that has strong support is the notion that the oil referenced (5:14) had medicinal properties in New Testament times, such that even Luke, a doctor, records its application in the parable of the Good Samaritan (Luke 10:30–37). The same Greek word for *oil* is used in Luke 10:34 and James 5:14. Another view is that the oil could have had a symbolic purpose of anointing, or setting someone apart, for God's care. Either way, the main focus is still prayer, emphasizing that it is God who does the healing.

James also dispels a widespread belief that illness is caused by a person's sin. He writes "if," indicating that sin could be a factor contributing to one's sickness, but it is not necessarily the cause (5:15). He also gives the opportunity to confess sins to one another, reminding believers of their call to bear one another's burdens (Galatians 6:2; James 5:16).

James calls the prayer of a righteous person effective and uses Elijah as his example (5:17). In 1 Kings 17:1, the prophet Elijah spoke with Ahab, the wicked king of Israel. As a sign of God against Ahab's wickedness, Elijah prophesied that there would be no rain for three years. Three years later, in 1 Kings 18:1, God sent him back to Ahab promising rain again. Elijah was not supernatural; he was human. What set him apart is that he prayed earnestly.

5:19–20

BACK FROM WANDERING

James 5:19 describes someone who wanders from the truth. This is the same word Jesus uses in Matthew 18:12, in reference to the one sheep who wanders away from the ninety-nine. The idea is more than just an unintentional straying from the path, but a complete departure from faith in Christ.

James does not want Christians to misunderstand prayer and think that the purpose is primarily for themselves. Instead, he emphasizes focusing on others' relationships with God in prayer. He offers a picture of Christian community in which members are accountable to one another. James's letter closes with a continued concern for living out a faith that works and also with concern for the welfare of others.

1 PETER

INTRODUCTION TO 1 PETER

First Peter is a great book to shatter any false expectations about who God is and what it means to serve God. It gives us realistic expectations about what this world has to offer and what perspective can help us through the tough times.

AUTHOR

This letter was written by Peter, one of Jesus' twelve disciples, who became a leader of the first-century Christian church. Because of the high quality of the Greek language used in this letter, some have doubted that Peter, the common fisherman, could have been the author. This argument is not strong, however. Greek was widely spoken in Galilee, and so Peter may well have been fluent in the language. Peter also notes at the end of the letter that he wrote "with the help of Silvanus" (or, Silas; 5:12). Like other New Testament writers (see Romans 16:22; Galatians 6:11), Peter may have dictated the letter to Silas, who improved the style and quality of the Greek.

OCCASION AND PURPOSE

Peter writes to believers living in Asia Minor to encourage them to faithfully endure persecution in light of the glorious salvation Christ has accomplished for them, and to see their suffering as a normal part of their service to God.

Peter addresses this letter to "God's elect, strangers in the world, scattered throughout Pontus, Galatia, Cappadocia, Asia, and Bithynia" (1:1)—the provinces of Asia Minor (present-day Turkey). The churches in this region were made up of both Jewish and Gentile Christians, though they were primarily Gentile. Several of Peter's statements suggest his audience is mostly Gentile (1:14; 2:10; 4:3–4)

Peter's purpose is stated in 1 Peter 5:12, where he tells the believers to stand firm in the true grace of God. The believers were experiencing a great deal of opposition and persecution because of their faith (1:6; 3:13–17; 4:12–19). Peter addresses them as "strangers" (NIV) or "exiles" (TNIV), living in a world that was growing increasingly hostile to Christians. By standing firm in the grace of God, they would be able to endure their "fiery ordeal" (4:12), knowing that there was a divine purpose behind their suffering and pain.

The letter was probably written in the early to mid AD 60s, shortly before or during the severe persecutions instigated by the Roman emperor Nero. Some have said that the context of the letter is the later empire-wide persecutions of Domitian (AD 81–96) or Trajan (AD 98–117). But in Peter, the persecutions seem to be local trials and hatred, not official state-sanctioned persecution. In later persecution, sacrifices to the emperors were a key issue. This does not appear to be the case in this letter. While Christianity had not yet been banned officially, there was a growing hatred for Christians, especially because (1) they lived differently, (2) they refused to worship pagan gods, and (3) they boldly preached the gospel. Peter says, "Do not be surprised" at such persecution, because you are resident aliens in this world (2 Corinthians 5:20; Philippians 3:20; 1 Peter 4:12).

Peter claims to be writing from "Babylon" (5:13), which is probably a cryptic reference to Rome. The reasons for this are as follows:

1) Literal Babylon on the Euphrates was almost deserted by New Testament times.
2) "Babylon" appears to be used as a symbolic title for Rome in Revelation 17:3–6, 9, 18, and in other literature.
3) Church tradition says nothing about Peter's travels to Babylon but tells us he went to Rome and was martyred there.
4) John Mark is with Peter when he writes this letter (5:13). Mark is mentioned with Paul during his first imprisonment in Rome (Colossians 4:10) and probably came to him there during his second imprisonment (2 Timothy 4:11).

THEMES

Major themes in 1 Peter include submission to authority, suffering because of faith in Christ, and shepherding the flock of believers. In these themes we are given the proper expectations that we are to have when we consider what it means to be a Christian.

OUTLINE

GOD'S PLAN FOR HUMANITY 1:1–2:3

Our Encouragement 1:1–12
Our Battle 1:13–21
The First Action of Faith—Love 1:22–2:3

GOD'S PLAN FOR THE CHURCH 2:4–25

Unified for a Reason 2:4–10
Integrity that Leads to Praise 2:11–17
Submission and Sacrifice 2:18–25

GOD'S PLAN FOR THE CHRISTIAN 3:1–22

The Heart of Submission 3:1–7
Grace in a Graceless Age 3:8–12
Suffering Properly 3:13–22

GOD'S PLAN FOR SUFFERING 4:1–19

God Uses Suffering in Holiness 4:1–6
God Uses Suffering in Relationships 4:7–11
God Uses Suffering in Endurance 4:12–19

LIVING SOBERLY 5:1–14

Elders Living Soberly in an Intoxicated World 5:1–4
The Flock Living Soberly in an Intoxicated World 5:5–14

1 PETER 1:1–2:3

GOD'S PLAN FOR HUMANITY

Our Encouragement	1:1–12
Our Battle	1:13–21
The First Action of Faith—Love	1:22–2:3

Setting Up the Section

This letter begins with the traditional greeting, identifying Peter as an apostle of Jesus and stating to whom he is writing. The author is the same Peter who was called by Jesus to be an apostle and the same Peter who struggled with learning how to follow God by faith and not in the power of his own emotional zeal.

1:1–12

OUR ENCOURAGEMENT

Verses 1–2 function as an introduction to a core foundation truth: God has called every believer to be conformed to the image of Jesus. As that is happening, the person being transformed will be different and, at times, persecuted.

Peter wrote to churches made up of both Jewish and Gentile Christians, who reside as "aliens" throughout the region of Asia Minor. All of the provinces mentioned in this verse are located in modern-day Turkey (1:1).

Critical Observation

Some say that this letter was written primarily to Jewish Christians, because Peter uses the word *scattered* or *dispersed* to describe the readers. This word often refers to the scattering of the Jews from their homeland to all parts of the Mediterranean region. Yet while Peter draws on this and many other terms that are elsewhere applied to Israel, here he uses them with reference to the church made up of both Jews and Gentiles—the new people of God in the present age. Statements in the letter concerning the believers' past life suggest that the majority of them were Gentiles (1:14; 2:10; 4:3–4).

The most important thing in this introduction is not the list of provinces, but the description of the people:

- Alien—someone living temporarily in a land that is not his or her home.
- Scattered—the people of the church who are dispersed throughout many regions.
- Chosen—selected with a purpose in mind.

Notice that the calling Peter refers to in verse 1 was a result of the foreknowledge of God, by the sanctifying work of the Spirit (1:2). The word *foreknowledge* does not mean that God knows the future as much as He actually *makes* the future.

The calling of God was accomplished by the sanctifying work of the Spirit. The word *sanctifying* denotes an ongoing process. The Spirit of God is constantly working in the lives of believers, conforming them to the image of Jesus.

There is a final part of this process. This calling and sanctifying are done so that people might obey Jesus and be cleansed by His blood. In this world we take our marching orders from Jesus Christ.

Demystifying 1 Peter

After Moses first read the Law of God, the Israelites affirmed that they wanted to obey. Moses sprinkled some blood onto them (Exodus 24:3–8). The picture here in 1 Peter 1:1–2 is that these Old Testament Jews had the blood of the covenant applied to them, and so they became children of the covenant.

Verses 3–12 reveal the future, present, and past encouragement of God's salvation. Verse 3 begins with praise. The word that is translated "praise," or "blessed," is the same word from which we get the word *eulogy*. It means to tell how great someone is.

Critical Observation

The fact that Peter refers to God as Jesus' Father is significant (1:3). A first-century Jew would have said that Abraham was his father. This meant that he shared in the blessed nature of Abraham. In saying God was Jesus' Father, Peter's wording stresses the fact that Jesus shared in God's nature.

Mercy is the part of God's nature that causes Him to look with compassion upon the most vile of sinners (1:3). As His great act of mercy, God caused us to be born again into a living hope.

In verse 4, Peter highlights the point of inheritance. The believer's hope is not simply in going to heaven, but in the inheritance awaiting there. It is imperishable; it cannot be destroyed. It is also undefiled, or sin-free. It is unimpaired by time and will not lose its value. Finally, it is unconditionally reserved—guarded. The point of a reservation is that it's guaranteed.

Believers not only have a protected inheritance, they are also a protected people (1:5). If God is going to protect their inheritance in heaven, then He is going to protect them on earth as well.

The salvation that will be revealed in the last time is the final part of salvation (1:5). In this case, the term *salvation* is referring not to the moment of salvation, but to the final salvation, when believers go to live with God forever. Until that day comes, believers are protected by God.

Peter's point is that in this world there will be trials, but these trials are momentary in the grand view of eternity (1:6). The faith displayed during trials will be the faith that will one day deliver us from this world.

Peter states that his readers greatly rejoice (1:6). These believers really did believe that waiting for them was the eternal inheritance that is far beyond any possession on earth. Whenever we think of this inheritance, our hearts can shout for joy, because what we have in heaven has been given to us out of the great love and mercy of God.

Verse 7 is a continuation of the truth of verse 6. Suffering is a tool in the hands of God to bring about revelation and glory. Jesus is our example. Through Him, God revealed His character and put His glory on display.

The overall point in verses 8–9 is that believers love Christ and believe in Christ even though they have never seen Him. As a result, they will gain the salvation from the world that they are living in.

Take It Home

Peter describes trials as lasting a little while (1:6). This is a perspective check. When you are in a trial, it seems as if that is all there is. Yet, compared to heaven, any trial is only momentary. What do you do while you are suffering? Keep your eyes on the person and work of Christ. Believe in what He has done for you and trust in the provision that He has given you that will be revealed in the last days.

To show the great value of the understanding that we have because of Christ, Peter makes four points of comparison between the prophets and his readers.

1) The prophets longed to know what we know (1:10).
2) The message of the prophets was consistent with the New Testament message: grace as well as judgment.
3) Not only did the prophets talk of God's grace, but the Spirit of Christ was within them (see 2 Peter 1:21).
4) The words of the prophets serve us more than them (1 Peter 1:12). When you read their message in light of the Cross, then you can see the fullness of what is written without the hindrances that the prophets had when they wrote it.

At the end of verse 12, we read that this gospel that has been preached to us is a message that the angels longed to look into. The word *long* means to crave. It is the idea of looking at something with deep desire.

1:13–21

OUR BATTLE

In verse 13, Peter uses the metaphor of someone "girding his loins" to illustrate working in the field or preparing for battle. In the first century, if a man wanted to work in the field, he would gather up his robe and pull it between his legs, then tie it around his waist. This would get the excess cloth out of the way so he could work. Similarly, a warrior would gather up his clothes and tuck them into his waist to fight more effectively.

In comparison, our minds are filled with excess thoughts about the cares of the world. The thoughts of our minds must be disciplined so that the focus is on the things of heaven.

Next, Peter tells his readers to keep sober. This is the idea of self-control, not having a mind or a heart that is inebriated with the love of this world.

As part of being obedient children, Peter tells his readers not to be conformed to their former desires. Now they need a different way of living—holiness (1:14–15). As believers, they are to reflect the very character of God in everything they do.

Critical Observation

Peter does not mean that your holiness will be equal to the perfect holiness of God. Instead, the holiness of God is now to be the pattern for how you are to react and respond to the world. Instead of justifying sinful responses to the world, we now place the holiness of God as the standard for our responses.

In verse 16, Peter quotes Leviticus 11:44, a verse from the passage outlining the dietary laws that set the Jews apart from the cultures around them. Today, we are not bound by these laws. Instead, we are bound by our commitment to imitate the character of Jesus.

In the context of verse 17, the word *judge* holds more the meaning of evaluation than condemnation. Peter is saying you cannot fool God; He knows how you are living. Since that is true, live reverently.

Critical Observation

One of the themes throughout Peter's letter is the idea that Christians are citizens of heaven, not earth. Verse 17 supports that theme by referring to Christians as strangers, or exiles, here on earth.

Verses 17 and 18 work together. In 17 we are told that God sees us for who we really are, and in verse 18 we are told that after seeing us exactly as we are, He redeems us, or purchases us out of slavery. Rather than mere human effort, redemption came in the form of Jesus' blood. In verse 19, Peter draws on the image of the Old Testament sacrificial system, offering animal sacrifices to maintain peace with God. The animals offered were to be without any blemish (Leviticus 3:1)—in His perfection, Jesus fit the bill.

Because of that redemption, we have faith and hope in God (1 Peter 1:20–21). We can partake of this faith and hope because of the resurrection of Jesus. The Resurrection was the sign that God was satisfied and redemption was complete.

1:22–2:3

THE FIRST ACTION OF FAITH—LOVE

In verses 13–21, Peter gives us the theological application—to keep our minds fixed on our inheritance, our behavior centered on being set apart from the world, and our hearts focused on who God really is and what He has done for us.

Critical Observation

Verse 22 serves as a transition to how our salvation should change our response to others. Peter makes a connection for us between obedience to the truth and the purification of our souls. This purification doesn't mean we no longer sin, but God cleans up our souls and makes us responsive to Himself.

How does this purification occur? We obey the truth. The word *obey* carries the idea of listening to something and then responding to it. Peter is saying that since we believed the message of the gospel and confessed that Jesus is who He said He is, that belief caused our souls to be purified. And the result? Love for one another.

The love mentioned here is unhypocritical love, a genuine, self-sacrificing affection that comes from the care and love that we have received from God. Our purification is not just about what we do and do not do; it is about why we do and do not do those things.

Verse 23 is a point that Peter has made already in this letter (1:4, 7, 18)—our salvation finds its source in the eternal Word of God. To illustrate his point, Peter quotes from Isaiah 40:6–8 (1 Peter 1:24–25). Just before this quote appears in Isaiah, God had declared judgment on Israel for rejecting Him, but in chapter 40, His message of salvation emerges.

The first few verses of chapter 2 are a continuation of the close of chapter 1. Peter says we must put aside our natural responses to the world around us. The sins listed here are the enemies of love. When we see what God has done for us, it should humble us and cause us to reach out to others with the same love. We should crave this new way of life.

Understand in verse 3 the importance of us tasting the kindness of the Lord. If one has not been touched by the grace of God, then he or she has not experienced the love Peter is saying we should offer to others.

1 PETER 2:4–25

GOD'S PLAN FOR THE CHURCH

Unified for a Reason	2:4–10
Integrity that Leads to Praise	2:11–17
Submission and Sacrifice	2:18–25

Setting Up the Section

How do we live out this purification of our souls? How do we identify ourselves to the world around us? How do we relate to the governmental structure of our cultures? These are the kinds of questions Peter addresses in this passage.

2:4–10

UNIFIED FOR A REASON

When we come to Christ, we come to Him not just as our Savior but as our living stone (2:4). This image of the cornerstone carries the idea of Jesus being the centerpiece of our lives. According to Peter, the world has rejected Jesus in this role.

Peter calls Jesus a *living* stone, just as he wrote about a *living* hope in 1:3 and the *living* Word in 1:23. Why? Because the cornerstone aspect of Christ's ministry was set in place by His resurrection. Since we get our lives from Him, we have identities that come from this relationship (2:5)—we, too, are living stones, pieces of a building that God is making. This speaks to our corporate identity.

We are called to be a spiritual house for a holy priesthood. A major role of the priest in the Old Testament was to offer sacrifices on behalf of the people. Our role is to offer spiritual sacrifices (2:5). Within the context of the church, when we love each other, care for each other, and sacrifice for each other, we are offering up to God the sacrifice and praise that He finds acceptable.

The truth that Peter has just proclaimed about Christ is not new. Both Isaiah 28:16 and Psalm 118:22 teach that there will be those who reject this stone and those who accept this stone (2:6–7). Rejection can lead to injury. To stumble means to get hurt (2:8).

Some have interpreted Peter's words at the end of verse 8 about destiny to mean that those who don't believe have been doomed to that fate. That is not necessarily so. It could just as easily mean that their rejection has been predicted by God because God said that there would be those who disobey. Their doom is simply the consequences of their choices.

Unlike those set apart for doom, the believer is different. The terms Peter mentions in verse 9 are terms that were used to describe the Jews in the Old Testament. Peter uses them to describe all Christian believers, even Gentiles.

We have an identity, mission, useful purpose, and a new lifestyle because of Christ. We are to tell the world about how God transitioned us from death to life and that this transition is a transition of love, mercy, kindness, and compassion. This is what we are to proclaim to the world.

2:11–17

INTEGRITY THAT LEADS TO PRAISE

Notice how Peter describes the believers: aliens and strangers (2:11 NIV). The word *alien* means a person who is not a part of the life of society in which they are presently living. In a spiritual sense, this is true of Christians.

The term *stranger* carries the idea of temporarily dwelling in a land with no intention of putting down roots. Certainly, this is how Christians look at their sojourn on earth.

The way Christians should be distinct is through their lifestyles—distancing themselves from sinful desires as an ongoing part of their spiritual walk. It is the role of the believer to maintain excellent behavior so that any false accusations of wrongdoing would ring completely untrue (2:12). While Christians may often be attacked because of their faith, their own behavior should not provide any fuel for the attack. We are not commanded to be free of accusation, but free of being guilty of accusations.

God wants our good deeds to be revealed so that our lives point the way to Jesus. The day Jesus appears is the Day of Judgment. On that day, the character of Jesus Christ will be the standard that will judge the world (2:12).

In this life, the attitude and action of the believer is to submit to human authorities. Our distinctness from our culture does not mean we are above the structure of the world. The government is sent by God to punish evil and praise good behavior, to keep lawlessness from ruling (2:14).

Critical Observation

Keep in mind which government Peter called these people to submit to—a government that did not respect Christianity, that supported practices that were offensive to God, and in months and years to come would begin a persecution of the church that would last for hundreds of years. Nevertheless, Peter wants them to see God's design for government and to submit for the Lord's sake. Of course there is a line in the sand—if the authority calls us to disobey God then we must reject their rule. But, short of that circumstance, we are not above the day-to-day ruling of the law.

Our response to government is designed not only to serve God but also to silence those who accuse us of wrongdoing (2:15). The *ignorance* mentioned includes the false understanding of Christianity spread among outsiders. The submission of the believers to government was meant to prove these foolish people wrong.

In verse 16, Peter tells the believers that they are free to be God's slaves rather than slaves of sin—they are free to uphold the laws of the state as God's servants. Peter wants his readers to see themselves as free from sin, free from having to please men, and free from the bondage of their own lusts *so that* they can be free to serve God and do what He says.

It is dangerous to see Christian freedom as a means to serve yourself. Your freedom in Christ is not a cover for evil. Freedom is the opportunity to be set free from the bondage of serving self in order to love and serve others (2:17).

Verse 17 is a summary statement of the preceding passage (1:17–2:16). When we use our freedom in this manner, God receives the praise and the world sees the power of the gospel at work on earth.

2:18–25

SUBMISSION AND SACRIFICE

According to most historians, almost half the population in the Roman Empire was some type of slave or servant. This was a key to the economic stability of the Roman Empire.

The slaves mentioned in verse 18 were not the slaves in the field but, instead, the domestic helpers. This is why many preachers apply this passage to employees.

If a servant became a Christian and began to put his or her priority on heavenly things, he or she could be tempted to take the job lightly or to judge an unbelieving master rather than submitting to him. Peter's point is that salvation in Christ is not an excuse to ignore the order and structure of the world. Peter is telling his readers to show respect and honor to their masters because the masters have authority—whether the master uses that authority well or not (2:19–20).

Why would we want to serve well in difficult situations? Because God is pleased when we obey Him, no matter the circumstances (2:19). This truth offers comfort to the servants who have to live in horrible conditions. They are in the favor of God as they suffer.

Peter clarifies the kind of suffering he is referring to by asking, "If you receive punishment for your own wrongdoing, is that suffering?" (2:20). Suffering because you were a bad servant does not offer the hope of God's blessing. Yet God rewards those who persevere through difficult times, revealing Jesus' attitude.

The first thing that we have to see is the relationship between suffering and Christianity. Verse 21 is a statement that the believers have been called for the purpose of suffering. God designed our salvation to include a life of serving others in this world. We do this by following Jesus' example.

In verse 22, Peter offers a snapshot of the service of Jesus in the face of suffering by quoting Isaiah 53:9, part of the description of the suffering Messiah. Jesus never sinned, yet He was accused and punished severely. In the midst of that, Jesus did not respond in kind (1 Peter 2:23). He was verbally and physically abused, yet He did not threaten abuse in return.

Jesus did this by continuing (not once, but over and over again) to *entrust* Himself into God's care. This *entrusting* is like walking onto an airplane and entrusting your well-being to the pilots and mechanics who manage the plane.

Jesus believed in and trusted in the fact that God would make all things right in the end. He was content to let the Father take care of the situation. In the meantime, Jesus continued to serve those who sought to kill Him—He prayed for their forgiveness and died to preserve their souls (2:24). He is the perfect example of someone who trusted God enough to continue to serve no matter the circumstances.

We were a straying people who wandered away from God (2:25). Jesus suffered for us so that we might be able to be pulled toward God and live for Him and live out His sacrificial love for this world.

Take It Home

God calls us to serve people and to love them, finding our place in the structure of the world. We do this because it pleases God, not because people deserve it. When we serve, we do so knowing that even though there might be injustice now, perfect justice will come one day in the future. It is not our job to dispense justice right now.

How can we better entrust our well-being into the hands of God when we face injustice?

1 PETER 3:1–22

GOD'S PLAN FOR THE CHRISTIAN

The Heart of Submission	3:1–7
Grace in a Graceless Age	3:8–12
Suffering Properly	3:13–22

Setting Up the Section

What do the roles of husbands and wives reveal to the world about God? Peter reminds his readers not just of the acts of submission, but of the heart of submission—to God first, then within our relationships.

3:1–7

THE HEART OF SUBMISSION

Peter begins this section by connecting these thoughts about marriage to the overall thought that he introduced in 2:11–12: Christians should live in every area so that they are showing the world the character of Jesus. He uses the phrase "In the same way. . ." (3:1).

Demystifying 1 Peter

There have been some who have tried to say that Peter uses the word likewise to draw a connection between verse 1 of chapter 3 with the last few verses of chapter 2. They teach that Peter's point is that just as Jesus suffered in life, so the wife must also be ready to suffer in marriage. But this is not Peter's point. His "likewise" is not referring to Christ's suffering (2:21–25), but to the life of reverence to God and submission to one another (introduced in 2:18) that Christians are intended to live.

Notice that the wives are to submit to their *own* husbands (3:1). Verse 1 is not a description of how all women are to relate to all men; thus you must read the remainder of this section within that context.

Submit means to honor the position of another. Its opposite would be to resist. Just as chapter 2 reveals how a Christian should act so that others will be affected, so here Peter reveals that as a woman functions within her marriage in this way, others will be influenced by her example.

Submission is an attitude that leads to an action; this is why Peter describes the attitude rather than the action of submission. In verse 2, Peter identifies the marks of a submissive life: a sincere and pure heart along with reverent behavior.

Just as the servants of chapter 2 were to honor their authorities out of obedience to God, here the wife is to honor her husband's position out of love for God. When the wife shows kindness and devotion to her husband, she is showing the world the kindness that God has shown her.

In the first century, often the women were the first to hear the gospel message, because the men were busy working. Yet, in that culture it was the custom for the women to adopt the faith of their husbands. Peter says in verses 1–2 that the evangelism of a woman's husband doesn't take place by her convincing her husband, but by her showing her husband the love and service of Christ.

In verses 3–4, Peter is not condemning a woman for dressing nicely, but he makes the point that women should not make their looks the sum total of their worth. He contrasts those who focus on external beauty with those who focus on the inner attitude. This part of the woman's life must be adorned with a gentle and quiet spirit.

In verse 4, Peter is describing a woman who doesn't have the need to push her beliefs on someone else. A quiet spirit is one that does not need to dominate a room.

Peter's idea here is not a new thought. Ancient women were known by this behavior (3:5–6). Sarah honored Abraham by referring to him respectfully according to the customs of the age in which she lived (see Genesis 18:12). Women today are the spiritual descendants of Sarah when they follow her example, unafraid of the vulnerability it might cost them to put someone else before themselves.

Next, Peter addresses husbands. They are to live with their wives in an understanding manner (3:7). The phrase translated "considerate" (NIV) or "in an understanding way" (NASB), can also be translated "according to knowledge." The husband is to be a student of his wife so that he can care for her and love her according to who she is specifically.

Peter's mention of the wife as the "weaker" partner is not an insult toward women or a statement of the moral or spiritual superiority of men (as some throughout church history have claimed). "Weaker" refers instead to the fact that women are generally physically weaker than men, and so a husband's role is to ensure that his wife is protected, cared for, and treated with dignity and honor. Another possibility, however, is that "weaker" means "less-empowered" and refers to the low social status of women in the first century. In this case, Paul would be saying that husbands should show honor and respect for their wives in contrast to a society that often demeans and abuses women.

The husband is to treat his wife with honor so that all will see that he values her, respects her as a precious gift from God. This honoring is not based on merit, but on the fact that she is a fellow heir of the grace of God.

The way that a man treats his wife has a direct effect upon his spiritual life. Love and respect your wife, Peter says, so that "nothing will hinder your prayers." We cannot have a harmonious relationship with God unless we are reconciled to others.

3:8–12

GRACE IN A GRACELESS AGE

Verse 8 opens with "Finally," and this signifies that Peter is coming to a logical conclusion. Thus far Peter has communicated in several different ways that the way we live in this world communicates the gospel—or not. In verse 8, he reviews the attitudes and the actions that must govern our relationships within the body of Jesus Christ.

All of these terms in verses 8–9 are products of grace. The assumption of this passage is that we are all in relationships with people who do not deserve kindness, yet God tells us to be kind and to treat people with compassion. When we do, we are giving them grace.

Humility is the only trait listed here that deals with self. It enables all the rest of the traits. It is impossible to show any of the above-mentioned qualities if one is not humble in the way that one lives.

Peter continues his conclusion with a "not" rather than a "do"—do not return evil for evil (3:9). Revenge is forbidden, but Peter goes further—we are called to give a blessing instead. A blessing is a gift that is meant to be an encouragement or investment into others; it's something that will benefit them.

Why offer blessing instead of revenge? Because God wants us to demonstrate the same grace we have received to the world around us. In verse 10, Peter illustrates this point by quoting Psalm 34:12–16, a psalm in which David realizes he does not need to retaliate against his enemies. The point of this psalm is to tell the believers that they must understand their responsibility in being committed to showing the world love rather than evil.

Demystifying 1 Peter

David wrote Psalm 34 when he ran for his life from King Saul and tried to find refuge in the city of Gath. There He escaped detection by pretending to be out of his mind.

In the midst of all this, David realized that those who understood how to live in this world are the ones who understand that peace and holiness are the keys to living.

3:13–22

SUFFERING PROPERLY

This passage picks up again Peter's central theme of enduring suffering for the cause of Christ.

Peter's first point is that we have been given protection from God. The heart of his question in verse 13 is a redefinition of being hurt. Yes, someone can harm us physically, but our souls are protected. Even if there is an earthly cost to serving and suffering, the cost cannot take away our salvation.

Peter's second point is that we are to remember God's promise (2:14). In the midst of suffering for doing what is right, we can think that God is hurting us because things are going badly. The point is that we have the very promise of God that He will see us through the suffering and repair us from any damage we might endure to bring us to the promise of heaven.

Verse 15 should be seen in connection with verse 14. The focus of our emotional and mental energy should not be fear or intimidation, but instead ensuring that Jesus has the center place in our lives. When we do this, our lives will stand out. It would be difficult to live for God in this manner and not have people ask why we are not afraid and why we keep serving those who hate us. We need to be ready to give an account of the hope that is in us. Then we will have the opportunity to share our hope in a spirit of gentleness and reverence. Our attitude must reflect the heart of the message that we are sharing.

Finally, we must have a conscience that is pure (3:16). To maintain that clear conscience, we must live with integrity in this world so any accusations against us won't stick.

Verse 17 reminds us that suffering that occurs as a result of seeking to serve Christ and love others is a tool in the hand of God. With this in mind, Peter points us to the suffering of Jesus as an example of the way God uses suffering (3:18). The first product of Jesus' suffering is redemption. The second is deliverance.

In verses 18–20, Peter explains that through His suffering, Jesus preached to spirits in prison who were disobedient during the days of Noah.

Some believe that these verses refer to the fact that Jesus went to Hades when He died and preached the gospel. Others believe the spirits in prison are the fallen angels (see also 2 Peter 2:4–10; Jude 6), and that Jesus' preaching was not to announce redemption, but to assert that all angels, authorities, and powers are in submission to Him and nothing can stop the deliverance that He provides. A third view is that Christ preached long ago to the people of Noah's day (either through Noah or in a preincarnate state), and that these people ("spirits") are now in Hades.

Whatever the case, Jesus' suffering brought about salvation. Just as Noah's family passed through the water and were delivered, when we pass through the waters of baptism and all that they symbolize, we are delivered (3:21). Peter rids his readers of any magical ideas about baptism by making it plain that the efficacy of baptism does not lie in the outward symbolism but in the inner response of faith toward God.

Jesus' suffering brought about redemption, deliverance, and salvation to a new life and a glory that is to be revealed. Suffering is a powerful tool in the hands of a mighty God.

Take It Home

First Peter 3:17 reminds us that if suffering comes, God has allowed it to come, but it is better to be in the will of God and to suffer than to be out of the will of God. We must stay the course and not use suffering as a signal to disengage from doing what is right. If you are in a situation where doing what is right will cause you to suffer, stay the course, because your suffering is not in vain. It is not a waste in your life; it is actually a part of God's will.

1 PETER 4:1–19

GOD'S PLAN FOR SUFFERING

God Uses Suffering in Holiness 4:1–6

God Uses Suffering in Relationships 4:7–11

God Uses Suffering in Endurance 4:12–19

Setting Up the Section

Peter's goal in both of his letters is to prepare the church to endure suffering. He does this by showing the reader the intrinsic value of suffering. When we suffer in this world, God uses it to mold us into the image of Christ. The reality of being molded into the image of Christ is a very important part of our formation. In this section, Peter wants us to see how suffering is used to achieve this goal.

4:1–6

GOD USES SUFFERING IN HOLINESS

When verse 1 says a person is "done with sin" (NIV), this does not mean that person has become perfect. Peter is saying that the moment we share in God's understanding of suffering and we step up and begin to suffer for what is right, we are no longer pursuing the flesh but instead are living for the will of God.

The point that Peter is making in verses 1–2 is that suffering is the road or the path that God uses to deal with our sin. For this reason, suffering is not a liability in our lives; it is actually an asset.

There are two reasons we should embrace suffering:

1) The time is over for us to live for the lusts of the flesh. Every sin mentioned in verse 3 is a sin of personal pleasure. When people seek to live for righteousness in this world, they stop living simply for their own pleasure. They live, instead, aware that they will give an account to Jesus for their lives (4:2–5).
2) There is a reward that will follow—eternal life. Redemption cannot be stopped even if the world treats us like the scum of the earth (4:6).

Critical Observation

The term *Gentile* (NASB) is used in verse 3 to refer to not simply a non-Jew, but to a person who lives a godless life. That is why some translations simply say non-Christian (NET). In the Old Testament, the nations that surrounded Israel lived lives filled with pagan practices. These pagan practices could be summarized in the term *Gentile.* When Peter uses this term, he is saying that when people live solely for their own passions and flesh, they are not living as God's people.

4:7–11

GOD USES SUFFERING IN RELATIONSHIPS

With verse 7, Peter takes a turn in his teaching about suffering to show us how this news of judgment and mercy is meant to make us purposeful in our relationship with God. The first phrase—"the culmination of all things is near" (NET)—sets the stage for verses 7–11.

The word *end* denotes specifically the end of a plan—in this case, the plan of redemption. In light of all that will happen at the end of that plan, Peter mentions four priorities that should be a part of the Christian's life:

1) Prayer (4:7). Since God is bringing the world to His end, we must not stop communing with God. *Sound judgment* was a word used to describe people who were able to process the world through the eyes of God. The *sobriety* Peter writes of means to be vigilant and alert—the opposite of drunk.
2) Love (4:8). Notice the way verse 8 begins: "Above all." Love is the paramount quality that must shine in the life of the Christian, because it is at the core of the nature of God. We are to love deeply, with increasing energy. The language here is a picture of stretching forward with intense energy and effort—this is how God has loved us. This love that covers sins is not permissiveness toward sin, but more of a *dealing with* sin.
3) Hospitality (4:9). Hospitality means to show love to strangers—a high value in Ancient Near Eastern society (as it is today in the Middle East). In Peter's day there were many traveling preachers who moved from town to town and may have arrived unannounced at a believer's home. Since many Christians were very poor, having another mouth to feed would have been an enormous personal sacrifice. Hospitality is not just an act; it is a selfless act.
4) God's glory (4:10–11). We are to use the gifts that God has given us in the power of God so that God will receive the glory. Every believer has been given a special gift to use to serve others (4:10). Verse 11 places the gifts into two major categories: speakers and servants.

If we live according to these priorities, we can serve others, even in difficulty, because we believe that God is moving the world to His end and we can live for His glory rather than protecting our own glory.

4:12–19

GOD USES SUFFERING IN ENDURANCE

The remainder of chapter 4 focuses on persevering through suffering.

The reality is that suffering is intrinsic to living for Jesus (4:12). With this in mind, Peter tells us not to be surprised at the trials that come. We have to expect to have people resist us when we seek to do what the scriptures declare.

His description of trials is sometimes translated "fiery ordeals," which means "the burning experiences." The image is an ongoing trial that causes deep grief and heartache. Keep in mind, though, that fire not only burns, but it also purifies.

Some versions of the Bible use the word *testing* rather than *suffering* in verse 12. When a trial comes and a person has to endure it and keep his or her eyes on Jesus, that trial becomes a test for that person's own faith (see 1:6–7).

The result of our trials is revealed in 4:13. We all will suffer in many different degrees, and as we do, we must rejoice, because we are suffering more and more like Jesus. Since we know that Jesus is coming back and that His righteousness will rule, we can rejoice that we are in the effort with Him.

In verses 14–16, we find a message of hope—suffering in this world is not a sign of sin but a sign of blessing. The insults Peter mentions in verse 14 refer to being insulted for the name of Christ. The blessing has at its root the idea of being refreshed.

The idea behind God and the Spirit of glory resting on you is that God is applying His glory to your life so that when you suffer, His glory is being seen. In other words, your suffering is a usable moment in the hands of God, for God is allowing His glory to rest upon you. We can be agents of God's glory—in other words, the expression of His character and nature.

Verse 15 serves as criteria for the kind of suffering that blessing accompanies. Some suffering is a result of people doing evil, and as a result they suffer the consequences. Yet, if one suffers for the sake of Christ, then they must be encouraged.

The term *Christian*, which Peter uses in verse 16, was coined in the first century to refer to those who desired to follow Jesus. Verses 17 and 18 seem complex, but they make a simple point—if the trials the church is undergoing are severe, how much more severe will be the judgment awaiting the wicked. The word *judgment* used with reference to the church means the ongoing process of dealing with sin rather than the final pronouncement of judgment.

To make this point even clearer, Peter includes a loose quote from Proverbs 11:31 (1 Peter 4:18). In this proverb, the author states that the road to eternal life is not an easy road. If our life is hard as God's children, picture what life will be like for those without that life-giving relationship.

As we suffer, we must consciously place our souls into the hands of a faithful Creator (4:19). Peter uses the term *Creator* to remind us that we are going to get a new life in the next world, and that life is far better than the best that this world can offer.

Take It Home

To apply this passage, keep the following points in mind:

1) Seek to understand how God uses suffering.
2) Within the depths of your heart, believe that God truly is going to use your suffering.
3) Daily submit your mind, will, and emotions into the hands of God, trusting in the protection that He offers.
4) Press on standing for Christ no matter the resistance you face.

If you keep these four things in mind, you will endure the trials that come.

1 PETER 5:1–14

LIVING SOBERLY

Elders Living Soberly in an Intoxicated World 5:1–4

The Flock Living Soberly in an Intoxicated World 5:5–14

Setting Up the Section

Peter begins this final section of his letter talking about the role of the elders within the church. He also offers believers some final instructions concerning living in this world. By reminding the elders of their importance, mission, and future, Peter reveals the proper environment necessary for the flock to live soberly in a world that is drunk on its own pleasure and self-deception.

5:1–4

ELDERS LIVING SOBERLY IN AN INTOXICATED WORLD

Prior to this passage, Peter said judgment is coming first to the household of God (4:19). In light of this, Peter presents the role of the elders within the context of the trials the flock will face.

Peter appeals first as a fellow elder (5:1). Peter is not only a fellow elder, but he is also a witness of the sufferings of Christ. This may mean that Peter literally saw Jesus suffer or that Peter has experienced the kind of suffering that is associated with serving Jesus. Both are true, and both give Peter credibility.

Peter also claims himself a partaker of the glory that is to be revealed. Just as we have to face the fact of our suffering, we also have the guarantee of the day of our vindication, the day that our reward is made ours, and the day that we inherit the kingdom of God fully.

The command to the elders is simple—shepherd God's flock. It is key to understand that God owns the sheep. This means that the elders are to care for the congregation in the manner the owner wants them to be cared for—the elders are overseers, not owners. God describes the elders this way:

- Willing (5:2). This is the idea of a mule that is being dragged by its owner. A proper elder does not have to be dragged into his work.
- Not greedy, but eager (5:2). The work is not merely a means to creating a certain lifestyle.
- Humble (5:3). To lord yourself over someone means that you will exact control or dominate that person.

Critical Observation

The position of a shepherd in the first century was not a position of honor. The fact that Peter uses this term to describe leaders brings an automatic idea of humility and service.

Rather than using the position to *tell* people what to do, the elder should *show* them an example of what to do (5:3). They must show the flock how they are to live. When Jesus comes, there will be a reward for all those who served the way Peter has described in verses 2–3. This reward is an unfading crown of glory; their work will not go unrecognized by God (5:4).

Peter identifies Jesus as the Chief Shepherd (5:4), a reminder that the elders are not the leaders of the church, but the stewards of it. When the Chief Shepherd appears, which refers to the second coming of Jesus, for all eternity the true elders of the church will have honor in heaven.

5:5–14

THE FLOCK LIVING SOBERLY IN AN INTOXICATED WORLD

Beginning in verse 5, Peter switches gears from the leadership of the elders to the response of the flock. The church needs to respond properly to the leadership of the church, each other, and ultimately to God.

First, the younger men. Verse 5 says "likewise" or "in the same way." Peter has given instructions to the elders as to how they should operate in the midst of suffering; in the same way, the young men are going to get their instruction.

The word often translated "young men" could be used to mean younger men, young men, or young women—someone who is younger than someone else. Therefore, even though many translations put the word *men* in the text, the clearest rendering is a young person.

The point is that the younger must submit to the older. In order for the elders to do their job, those who are under their care must receive and accept their shepherding. Peter offers his reasoning for this humility by loosely quoting Proverbs 3:34. God puts His hand out to the one who shows no humility and holds him back. In other words, God puts obstructions in the path of proud men so that they will have conflict until they humble themselves.

As Peter makes his case that humility is needed toward leaders and each other, then it stands to reason that we must be humble in our relationship with God (1 Peter 5:6–7). The mighty hand of God is an image that is used frequently in the Bible. Here it refers to what Peter stated in 4:17—namely, that God is at work in the lives of His children, using the trials of the world to deal with their sin. To humble yourself under the mighty hand of God is to acknowledge the trial that you are in and to surrender to the process rather than running away. We are to be ready to have God give us the honor in His time rather than fighting for it in our own schedule.

We humble ourselves under God's hand by casting all our anxiety upon Him (5:7). The anxiety that Peter is talking about is the feeling of pain, worry, and pressure that we feel when we are surrounded by people who cause us to suffer for our faith. If we cast our anxieties upon God, we are looking to God to provide the strength and hope that is necessary to do what is right in the midst of a trial.

In verses 8–9, Peter addresses evil. Even though God uses the evil in our lives, we must be careful as to how we are going to endure this evil—do we become anxious, or entrust ourselves to God? First, we need a sober spirit—characterized by self-control. Without that, we overreact and become derailed by suffering. We are also to be on the alert—to be ready for trials, to even anticipate them.

It is Satan who is seeking to overwhelm us when we live for God. Observe the way that the devil is described in verse 8.

1) The Adversary. An opponent who is out to get you, particularly in a legal scenario. This is someone who wants to take something away from you.
2) The Devil. This name means "slanderer." The devil is one who seeks to slander, lie, and deceive people.
3) A Lion. Consider a roaring lion. When a lion roars, it does so in order to dominate. A lion runs after a herd of animals to cause the animals to run until the weak and feeble fall behind. Satan does the same with the church.

In verse 9, Peter says to resist Satan. This is a picture of an army holding its ground so that the enemy cannot take possession of that land. We must stand firm in the same manner—but our faith is the valuable real estate we are protecting. Part of our power to resist is the knowledge that we are not alone in our suffering.

In verses 10–11, Peter offers one more piece of helpful advice—look to the future. This suffering is for a short time compared to eternity. This is such great news that Peter ends in words of praise (5:11).

Peter concludes this letter by saying that he sent this letter through Silvanus, a formal name for Silas who traveled with Paul (see Acts 15:35–41). Silas was faithful, which means that he, too, endured the trials of following Jesus.

While Babylon was a historic place in the history of Israel (see 2 Kings 24:8–17), Peter's reference to *Babylon* here in verse 13 was probably a reference to Rome. Some have suggested it may have been an attempt on Peter's part to conceal his own location. Others simply see it as an apt parallel given the antagonistic role of Rome at the time.

Mark, also mentioned in verse 13, was probably John Mark, a leader in the first century church who traveled with Paul and Barnabas (Acts 13:5, 13; 15:37–39; Colossians 4:10; 2 Timothy 4:11).

The kiss described in verse 14 was a typical greeting among Christians of this day.

Peter's final wish for peace would have echoed the hopes of all those who faced persecution. His teachings in this letter, if followed, provide a path to finding that peace in the midst of the turmoil of life.

Take It Home

Peter and Silas testified that this letter represents the true grace of God. In other words, this is the truth, so hold on to it.

1) We have been saved by God.
2) An inheritance is waiting for us.
3) In this world we will face trials for following Jesus.
4) In the midst of these trials, love the brethren.
5) In the midst of the trials, serve your enemies.
6) God uses the trials to work out our sin.
7) Walk humbly with God and people.
8) Walk soberly in this world prepared for suffering.
9) Remember that God will restore you before you go to heaven.

Let us remember these words so that we can walk faithfully with Christ.

2 PETER

INTRODUCTION TO 2 PETER

Late in the first century, the church was in an increasingly vulnerable position. In addition to the continuing threat of persecution, false teachers began to arise and distort the true message. At the same time, the apostles, who had established the church and provided its early leadership, were beginning to die off or suffer martyrdom. This letter deals with the problems that come when false teachers sneak into the Christian fold with the goal of turning people away from the message of Christ and enticing them with their own false message grounded in worldly wisdom and human achievement.

AUTHOR

The writer of this book identifies himself as Peter, one of Jesus' twelve disciples. Many have questioned Peter's authorship because of language differences with 1 Peter, among other things. However, conservative scholars still agree that while acknowledging the difficulties of the letter's authorship, Peter is a viable option.

PURPOSE

Peter's goal in writing is to fortify the church against false teaching. He wants to give the standard of truth to the church so that once he and the rest of the apostles are gone, the church will be able to stand strong against heresy. In order for the standard of truth to be established, Peter must show the true knowledge of God, the nature of the false teachers, and how to stand firm in the midst of both.

OCCASION

Peter is near the end of his life. This letter was probably written from Rome, about three years after Peter's first letter, around AD 67.

THEMES

Themes in 2 Peter include false teachers (2:1–22; 3:3–5) and Jesus' return (3:3–14).

HISTORICAL CONTEXT

False teachers had sought to overrun the church and destroy the foundation of the doctrine under which the church was established. Peter writes about the importance of the gospel so that the church would be strengthened and secure in the midst of false teaching. The letter has many words, phrases, and themes in common with the letter of Jude, and scholars debate which was written first and which author borrowed from the other.

CONTRIBUTION TO THE BIBLE

The trials that Peter deals with in his first letter focus on conflict against the church coming from the outside in the form of persecution. Second Peter is different in that it deals with the conflict and the trials that arise *within* the church because of false teaching.

OUTLINE

THE TRUE KNOWLEDGE OF GOD EXPLAINED 1:1–21

The Divine Power—The Knowledge of God Given 1:1–4
The Divine Life—The Knowledge of God Gained 1:5–11
The Divine Message—The Knowledge of God Affirmed 1:12–21

THE TRUE KNOWLEDGE OF GOD ATTACKED 2:1–22

The Mission of the False Teachers 2:1–3
The Rescue of the Godly 2:4–9
The Destruction of the False Teachers 2:10–22

THE TRUE KNOWLEDGE OF GOD PROTECTED 3:1–18

The First Reminder—Judgment Is Coming 3:1–7
The Second Reminder—Mercy Is Here for a Time 3:8–10
The Third Reminder—Live Godly, Wait Patiently 3:11–18

2 PETER 1:1–21

THE TRUE KNOWLEDGE OF GOD EXPLAINED

The Divine Power—The Knowledge of God Given	1:1–4
The Divine Life—The Knowledge of God Gained	1:5–11
The Divine Message—The Knowledge of God Affirmed	1:12–21

Setting Up the Section

In the first four verses, Peter declares that he is the true apostle, states the authentic message that is to be believed, and reveals what the authentic Christian life really is. He does this so the readers will not succumb to the perversion of the gospel that was being preached in their midst. The truths outlined in these verses, as well as in all of chapter 1, represent the core doctrines that were being twisted by false teachers.

1:1–4

THE DIVINE POWER—
THE KNOWLEDGE OF GOD GIVEN

The writer identifies himself in three ways (1:1):

1) Simon Peter
2) A bond-servant (NASB), or slave, in absolute submission to his master
3) An apostle, called by Jesus as one of the original twelve disciples

Next, Peter clarifies that he is writing to all believers rather than one specific church. He states that the faith the church has received is the same faith the apostles received. Not only is it the same faith, but also the same source of faith—the righteousness of Jesus Christ.

Peter wishes grace and peace for his readers. *Grace* is the unearned gift and favor of God (1:2). *Peace* is a term that means more than the absence of conflict; it means a right relationship with God. The fact that Peter wants grace and peace to be multiplied (growing exponentially) means he wants the believers to know the unending experience of God's blessing and peace.

The knowledge Peter refers to is an intimate and experiential knowledge of God (1:2). It is best illustrated in the kind of familiarity that comes through a marriage relationship. The more people know and experience God, the more they experience His grace and peace.

The divine power of Jesus is the power that dwells in God alone (1:3). When Peter refers to life in this text, he is referring to new life found in Christ alone.

Critical Observation

Believers have everything they need for godliness. The life God calls His followers to live comes through the divine power of Jesus. Again, keep in mind the context of this letter; false teachers were extolling a system of works that leads to godlessness. Peter wants the readers to find their godliness in the power of Christ alone—not through human effort.

This life and godliness are given by the divine power of Jesus and come through true knowledge of Him. The idea in verse 3 is very simple–the new life and the godliness that believers need to please God come through a relationship with the One who calls them.

This divine power leads to a divine promise (1:4). One does not have to become holy to gain God's favor; He calls us when we are unholy so that we will become holy by partaking of the divine nature of Jesus. As a result, salvation leads to holiness, rather than the other way around. Believers should be growing in their reflection of the divine nature of Jesus Christ.

1:5–11

THE DIVINE LIFE—THE KNOWLEDGE OF GOD GAINED

The point of 2 Peter 1:1–11 is to define for the readers the nature of true salvation. Peter's goal seems to be that his readers pursue what they have been given in Christ and, in light of their salvation, stand strong in the face of false teaching.

Critical Observation

Notice that verse 5 is based on verses 3 and 4, which are not commands but rather a description of what God has done for us. Verse 5 states that one should apply all diligence—to pursue that which has already been given in Christ.

Peter mentions seven things believers are to add to their faith: excellence, knowledge, self-control, perseverance, godliness, brotherly affection, and unselfish love (1:5–7 NET). He does not offer these qualities as a checklist for holiness; instead, it is a grouping of character traits that believers now have the ability to live out because of the righteousness they have been given in Christ.

The word translated *add* in verse 5 originally meant to pay the expenses of a chorus in staging a play but came to mean providing support or aid of any kind (generally rich or lavish support provided at one's own expense). In the context of verse 5, it carries with it the idea of cooperating with God as He produces these important qualities in His children.

Peter says, in essence, if you are not pursuing these things and if they are not being fleshed out in your life, then your profession of faith is not valid (1:8). On the other hand, if you pursue them and are growing in them, then your profession is good. This is not a requirement for perfection, but a constant movement in the right direction. The Christian life is to produce a changed life so the whole world can see the character of God forming in a believer.

In verse 8, Peter refers to a believer's knowledge of Jesus. This is a knowledge that is forged in a relationship, not a simple acknowledgement or familiarity with a set of information.

In verse 9, Peter describes the fallout of someone who does not pursue the traits described in verses 5–7. That person is blind, shortsighted, and suffers from amnesia. He or she cannot see the reality of the present world, the inheritance that waits, or what Jesus has done for him or her in the past.

Verses 10 and 11 make it crystal clear what is at stake in such blindness and powerlessness and fruitlessness—the confirmation of one's calling into faith. The danger described in verses 8 and 9 is not the danger of slipping into the kingdom with no rewards. It is the danger of not being a citizen of the kingdom at all. The calling of God is a calling to transformation. Peter is saying that if one does not love and desire transformation, then he or she should question the calling.

1:12–21

THE DIVINE MESSAGE— THE KNOWLEDGE OF GOD AFFIRMED

In the first eleven verses of chapter 1, Peter lists the proper pursuits of the Christian life. Beginning in verse 12, he explains this focus.

Verses 12–15 are about remembering one's call and source of righteousness. The Christian life is the pursuit of the righteousness that one has been given in Jesus. As sin surfaces, God wants believers to remember that they have been given the righteousness of Jesus. Therefore, they can pursue a change of mind, will, and emotions through the Word of God, prayer, and their faith community.

The tenets of Christianity are not based upon people gathering to create a new religion. Instead, the tenets of Christianity are based upon what the apostles saw and heard—the majesty of Jesus Christ. They saw Jesus, touched Jesus, lived with Jesus, and saw the very glory of God shine forth from Him (1:16).

In verses 16–18, Peter refers to the event that is often called the Transfiguration (Mark 9:2–8). Jesus brought Peter, James, and John to a mountain, and He physically changed before them, revealing His glory. Elijah and Moses—both key figures in the storyline of the Bible—appeared with Jesus. This was a defining moment for the apostles.

Demystifying 2 Peter

Notice that in reference to the Transfiguration in Matthew, Mark, and 2 Peter, there is a difference in the wording of the voice from heaven. In Mark 9:7, God says to listen to Jesus. In 2 Peter 1:17, He declares He is well-pleased with Jesus. Matthew 17:5 records both statements. There is no contradiction here, since each writer selects what is important from his own perspective concerning the event.

After making the claim that what they received was from God, Peter draws the readers' attention to the prophecies of the Old Testament. His experience on the mountain with Jesus only verifies what was recorded by the writers of the Old Testament (2 Peter 1:19). Therefore, Peter calls the Christians to pay attention to the scriptures.

In verse 19, the dawn and the Morning Star refer to the time when Jesus comes back to establish His kingdom and to give people new bodies that can never sin. In Revelation 22:16, Jesus calls Himself the Morning Star. The picture here is that until the time believers enter into eternity, scripture is the source of direction for life.

The prophets did not come up with their teaching through their own wisdom (2 Peter 1:20–21). The prophets did not offer their own interpretation of God or what it means to be a child of God. The prophets were moved by God through the hand of the Spirit. In other words, the God who defined Jesus for the apostles is the same God who moved the writers of the scriptures, and therefore there is complete continuity in the message.

2 PETER 2:1–22

THE TRUE KNOWLEDGE OF GOD ATTACKED

The Mission of the False Teachers	2:1–3
The Rescue of the Godly	2:4–9
The Destruction of the False Teachers	2:10–22

Setting Up the Section

This section continues where chapter 1 leaves off, comparing the Old Testament prophets to the false teachers who had invaded the lives of Peter's readers.

2:1–3

THE MISSION OF THE FALSE TEACHERS

False prophets had risen in Israel, just as they were appearing in the first-century church (Deuteronomy 13:1–3; Isaiah 28:7; Jeremiah 23:14; Ezekiel 13:1–7; 2 Peter 2:1). Note, though, that Peter switches quickly from the term false *prophets* to false *teachers*. These teachers were not prophets revealing God's truth.

Most certainly they will face judgment before God, since they have denied the One who bought them. They have refused the redemption offered them and influenced others to do the same (2 Peter 2:1–2). Peter's use of "the way of truth" may be an allusion to Psalm 119:30.

The opening verses of this second chapter offer six descriptions of these teachers and their motives (2 Peter 2:1–3). They are deceptive, Christ-denying, destroyed, sensual, slandering, and self-indulgent people who seek to care for themselves over God and the people of God.

2:4–9

THE RESCUE OF THE GODLY

In verse 3, Peter announces sure destruction on these false teachers. He pulls from three examples in the Old Testament to make his point (2:4–6). He starts from Genesis 6 and then moves to Genesis 19 to call the people back to the scriptures.

His first example is from Genesis 6—fallen angels God judged for rebellion and immorality (Genesis 6:1–5; Jude 6). The fate described here is a reference to a place reserved for the most wicked to be held until they can be judged.

As a result of the angels' sin and all that humanity became in that era, God flooded the earth to wipe out the rebellious race—Peter's second example of God's judgment (Genesis 6–7; 2 Peter 2:5). God's protection of Noah and the survival of only a few faithful make this illustration particularly relevant to Peter's readers. Noah is described here as a preacher, contrasting him with the false teachers in this situation.

The final picture of God's judgment is Sodom and Gomorrah, cities renowned for their affluence and immorality (Genesis 19; 2 Peter 2:6). God's judgment took the form of fire from heaven, burning the cities to the ground.

Demystifying 2 Peter

Lot was Abraham's nephew and an inhabitant of Sodom and Gomorrah. He and his family were given warning to escape before fire destroyed the cities (2:7–8). Lot's story is told in Genesis 18–19, including the unfortunate fate of his wife. The Genesis account does not present Lot as an upright man as Peter seems to here. It may be that Peter's words here describe someone whose righteousness was affected by the wickedness around him rather than someone who was grieved by it.

Through these examples, Peter is demonstrating that while false teachers experience limited success, no one will have to endure them forever. God will judge the false teachers, and He will deliver the righteous (2:9).

2:10–22

THE DESTRUCTION OF THE FALSE TEACHERS

Peter has now moved from the past to the present.

Verse 10 reveals the two main problems with the false teachers. First, they engage in overt immorality. And, second, they despise authority. Peter describes them as daring and self-willed (2:10). The idea around the word *daring* is that of recklessness. It carries the idea of a person who is so arrogant and so bold that he or she will do whatever he or she wants, no matter the cost.

Demystifying 2 Peter

To make his point, Peter describes one of the despicable acts of these teachers—insulting the "glorious ones" (2:10 NET; Jude 8–10). This is a puzzling statement. Who are the glorious ones? Some interpret this to mean church leadership. Others, and possibly the majority, interpret this as a reference to the fallen angels mentioned in 2:4. In both interpretations, the statement is made as an example of the brazen nature of these false teachers.

Verse 11 compares the insolence described in verse 10 with the actions and attitudes of heavenly angels. While they are agents of God and of heaven, and more powerful than the glorious ones, they are presented here as unwilling to cast judgment—a responsibility that belongs to God alone. The false teachers reveal their arrogance by taking liberties that even angels wouldn't take.

In verses 12–13, Peter compares these teachers to unreasoning animals. Rather than living by the Spirit, they simply follow their own fallen instincts–and, like wild animals, they are caught and destroyed. The fact that they are carousing in broad daylight would have been an offense not only to the Christian community, but to the first-century Roman culture at large.

The feast mentioned in verse 13 is regarded by many to refer to the love feast celebrated by the church. In this case, the immorality of these teachers was practiced in full view even at gatherings of the community of faith.

In a religious sense, a stain or blemish carries the idea of something that is not acceptable to God. Keep in mind that in Leviticus 21:21, God declared that no animal could be sacrificed to Him that had any spot or blemish.

Peter describes the nature of the false teachers as constantly immoral (2 Peter 2:14). When Peter says that these teachers have eyes full of adultery, he doesn't mean they are looking to commit adultery as much as the fact that all they can see is adultery. They believe that everything in the world belongs to them, and they want to have it all.

Worse still, they prey upon the spiritually weak so they can seduce them into their sensual lifestyle. The word translated "entice" (2:14 NET) implies something caught with bait. It is an intentional fishing expedition. This intentionality is also captured in the next idea that they have schooled themselves in immorality. They have become experts in sin.

What these false teachers offer is immorality in the name of God, thus replacing the righteousness of Jesus Christ with sin. Because their hearts are greedy, they pursue money, power, and pleasure and then peddle this to others as gifts from God.

To sum up this point, Peter writes two words to describe the false teachers: "cursed children" (2:14 NET). They live under God's curse. To make his point even clearer, Peter associates them with the Old Testament prophet, Balaam, well-known for his desire to turn a profit based on his religious standing. In the same way, these false teachers have a gift for teaching, but they are not using that gift for the glory of God. Instead, they are using it to glorify themselves.

Demystifying 2 Peter

The account of Balaam is recorded in Numbers 22. Balaam was a prophet who was willing to take money in order to entice God to curse the Israelites. Balak, the king of Moab, at the request of the Midianites, tried to use Balaam's prophetic gift to curse the Israelites. At first Balaam tried to comply, but God would not let him. In the process of stopping Balaam, God used a talking donkey to confront him.

Peter uses more word pictures to sum up the character of these men—springs without water, mists driven by a storm that pass over a place but never drop any rain (2:17). Since many of the readers of this letter lived in desert climates, these pictures were vivid. Peter is showing the people that false teachers might appear to be helpful, but in the end they do not bring people to the water of life.

Verse 18 describes the true method of the false teachers and the content of their teaching. Their words are empty, sometimes translated "vain," or "vanity." They have no value. These teachers have nothing beneficial to say, yet they say it with great pride and arrogance.

Notice that they entice by immorality. They pull people in to desire money, possessions, and power, and tell them that this is God's desire for them. The objects of their teaching are not all Christians, but also those who "have barely escaped from a lifestyle of deception" (2:18 NLT). These people are just coming out of an immoral lifestyle, and they are being enticed by teaching that allows them to have a moral version of their same perversion.

Critical Observation

False teachers promise freedom, but the truth is that they are slaves to their own immorality (2:19). Peter explains that a person is a slave to that which he or she surrenders. These false teachers present themselves as those who have chosen liberty in Christ over the old Jewish law. But the truth is that their liberty has become a license to sin. That is not what freedom in Jesus is about. There are certainly ethical restrictions on the behavior of those who seek to live like Jesus, even if those restrictions are ultimately guided by love. It is within those restrictions that followers of Jesus find freedom from the sins that ruled their behavior in their old lives. Because the false teachers are in bondage to sin, their promises of freedom are empty.

Peter's words in verses 20–21 have prompted much debate. How could it be better for someone never to have known the way of righteousness? The answer is that knowledge creates responsibility (see James 3:1, where teachers are said to receive a stricter judgment). Those who have heard and understood the message, yet willfully reject it, will be judged more harshly than those who have never heard or understood. The false teachers had heard the gospel, knew the gospel, and could even speak the gospel message, yet they never obeyed it.

Verse 22, which is a quote from Proverbs 26:11, points to the fact that since the false teachers have not been truly converted, they will return to their way of unrighteousness. False teachers will return to the sin that they claim they have left because they do not order their hearts by the Word of God.

2 PETER 3:1–18

THE TRUE KNOWLEDGE OF GOD PROTECTED

The First Reminder—Judgment Is Coming	3:1–7
The Second Reminder—Mercy Is Here for a Time	3:8–10
The Third Reminder—Live Godly, Wait Patiently	3:11–18

Setting Up the Section

Chapter 3 transitions from a description of the false teachers to encouragement for the readers. It is a chapter of reminders meant to help the church understand who God is, how to stay true to His message, and how to live in a world with false teaching.

3:1–7

THE FIRST REMINDER—JUDGMENT IS COMING

In verse 1, Peter mentions that this is the second letter he has written to these same readers. While we could assume this refers to 1 Peter, the description here doesn't seem to fit. First Peter isn't a letter of reminder in the same way this letter is. Therefore, this may be a reference to a letter that no longer exists.

Peter also says he wants to stir his readers' minds—to make them think. He describes them as sincere, or pure. This means that Peter seeks to strengthen the sincere minds that they already possess. How does Peter make sure their minds stay in the truth? By making sure that they remember the scriptures—the prophets and the teachings of Jesus as recorded by the apostles (3:2). Given that this letter addresses specifically those who deny Jesus' return, the commandment mentioned here is probably that which calls Christians to live their lives *according* to the reality of Jesus' return.

Critical Observation

False teachers will inevitably question the words of both the apostles and the prophets, and for this reason Peter knows that the saints must stay true to what the prophets wrote and the apostles spoke. The believers do not need more revelation; they need to order their lives by the existing revelation that they have been given.

"In the last days" is a common phrase in the New Testament, referring to the time marked at the beginning of Jesus' time on earth and continuing until His return (3:3).

In verse 3, Peter refers to the false teachers as "mockers" (NASB) because they deride, or attack, God's truth—starting with the return of Jesus. They ask in doubt, "Where is Jesus? I thought He said He would return" (3:4). Their implication is that God has not had an active part in the history of the world. Things have continued to simply go their way, and He has not kept His promise.

First, Peter offers an argument based on Creation, referring to the first chapter of Genesis. God spoke the world into being (3:5). He formed it out of water, but He also used water as a means of judgment. Next, he points to the flood, another example that things have not always gone on without any intervention from God, as the false teachers imply (3:6). The world is not on an unlimited fixed course but instead is being run by the sovereign hand of God.

Peter's final point is that God will intervene by judgment on the ungodly (3:7). Just as God has intervened in the past, so He can, and will, in the future. He spoke the world into existence, judged it according to humanity's actions, and certainly has the power and authority to do so again.

3:8–10

THE SECOND REMINDER—MERCY IS HERE FOR A TIME

Verse 8 is a reference to Psalm 90:4. This psalm was written by Moses and was a foundational psalm in early Christian teaching. Within Peter's context, it emphasizes the fact that God is not bound by time. The false teachers are incorrect in their assumption that because Jesus has not yet returned, He isn't going to at all.

According to verse 9, the patience of God shouldn't be interpreted as a lack of involvement, but instead as the ultimate involvement, because God is using this time to draw humanity to Himself. When Peter says that God doesn't want anyone to perish, it does not imply that all will enter the kingdom of heaven—verse 7 reveals God's judgment. But Peter is saying that the Lord is patient toward those who are not mockers and not opposed to the will of God—as he has described the false teachers.

Demystifying 2 Peter

In the Old Testament, the Day of the Lord was the future time when God would vindicate His holy name, bring judgment on those who refuse to believe, and gather His people into a new kingdom of righteousness and peace (Zephaniah 1:14–18; Malachi 4:1–3).

In the New Testament, beginning with Jesus, the day took on the connotation of Jesus' final return and judgment (Matthew 24:42–44; Acts 2:20; 1 Thessalonians 5:2–4).

In 2 Peter 3:10, Peter makes the point that there will be an end to the time of mercy—the Day of Judgment. Peter's comment that this day will come like a thief refers back to Jesus' own description of the unexpected timing of God's judgment in Matthew 24:42–44.

No one knows when this day will come, though Peter reveals some events that will take place:

1) The heavens will pass away—the sky, sun, moon, and stars.
2) The elements will be destroyed—at the time of Peter's writing, these elements would be understood as earth, air, fire, and water.
3) The earth and its works will be burned—humanity and all it has built up to sustain itself as a civilization. This may be a reference to Malachi 4:1, which speaks of a day that will burn like an oven.

3:11–18

THE THIRD REMINDER—LIVE GODLY, WAIT PATIENTLY

If God's judgment is to come as described in the preceding verses, then how should Peter's readers live in light of that reality? In the final verses of this letter, Peter reminds them how they are to live their lives in light of who God is.

The words *holy* and *godly*, in verse 11 (NIV), are in the plural. Peter is not giving the people a checklist for their lives, but is instead saying that they must pursue holiness and godliness in a variety of ways.

The word *hastening* in verse 12 (NASB) means, just as it does today, to speed something up. Within this context, speeding up is not a reference to the amount of time in which we wait for Jesus' return, but rather *how* we live as we are waiting. We must be a part of what God is doing on the earth. Waiting for that day is not a lack of activity, but it is active waiting as believers participate in God's kingdom.

Peter again describes the judgment of God in terms of fire—an all-consuming and powerful blaze (3:10, 12). This is not something that should strike fear in his readers' hearts, though, because the destruction is meant for the ungodly.

In verse 13, Peter reveals two things: There is a new world coming, and righteousness will be a part of it. This "new heavens and new earth" is a phrase from the prophecy of Isaiah (Isaiah 65:17; 66:22). The faithful will not simply escape this world; they will live where righteousness lives.

It follows then, if God is preparing a new world in which righteousness is the controlling factor, those who want to live in that new world will desire righteousness in their current lives. Peter wants his readers to focus on the peace that comes from walking in full harmony with God. He also says to be diligent, spotless, and blameless (3:14). This is an image from the Old Testament. The Passover lamb could not have any spot or blemish. In regard to his readers, Peter is saying that when Jesus returns, He must find believers living pure lives on earth.

Demystifying 2 Peter

In verses 15–16, Peter refers to Paul's writings, saying he and Paul are preaching the same message. At the end of verse 16, Peter places Paul's writings in the same category as all of the scriptures—which in this case refers to the Old Testament.

We can't be sure which of Paul's letters Peter's readers would have seen. At this time, Paul's letters were not gathered into one body of work as they are organized in the New Testament today. We also can't be sure which specific passage, if any, Peter is referring to. But certainly throughout Paul's writing, he encourages believers to live holy lives in light of God's commands and Jesus' return, just as Peter is doing here.

Notice that Peter admits Paul's letters can be difficult to understand, and misinterpretations can lead to destruction, which is true of all scripture (3:16). The false teachers take the difficult concepts and twist them to their own use.

Peter's final words are of warning and direction: It is the responsibility of the believer to be on guard (3:17). This means a believer must be personally vigilant over his or her own spiritual life.

In closing, Peter turns his attention to the spiritual growth of his readers–in the grace and knowledge of Jesus. Verse 18 is the application point of Peter's second letter. He opens the letter praying that grace and peace will be multiplied to his readers (1:2). At the closing, then, he comes full circle, instructing them to continue to grow in grace and also in knowledge. His inclusion of knowledge here is a reminder that dealing with false teaching requires tending to one's own knowledge of the truth.

Peter closes this letter with a benediction. Because Jesus is Lord and Savior, He is the One who deserves all the honor. Peter's mention of "that eternal day" (3:18 NET) refers to the final Day of Judgment, the coming of Jesus.

Take It Home

To grow in grace means to grow in gratitude and expression of all that you have received from God. Not only must we grow in grace, but we must also "grow in the grace and knowledge of our Lord and Savior Jesus Christ" (3:18 NIV, NET). This is imperative.

This world gives only temporary happiness, but the world to come will give eternal joy. We must live for that day, pursuing peace and purity, joining in God's kingdom. We must continue to pursue our understanding of the gift of grace and the One who gives it. This is the only way we can avoid being led astray by a twisted gospel message.

1 JOHN

INTRODUCTION TO 1 JOHN

The New Testament book we refer to as 1 John is a letter to a community of faith. Much of this letter is written to combat heresy regarding the identity of Jesus. The conflict over this heresy caused part of the congregation to split from the rest. John writes to ground the community in a true picture of not only Jesus' identity, but the identity of the children of God in light of who Jesus is.

AUTHOR

Determining the author of 1 John is somewhat different from determining the author of 2 and 3 John. In the case of 1 John, no author is identified in the work itself. However, the author does identify himself as an eyewitness of Jesus' ministry. He also speaks with an apostolic kind of authority and writes in a similar style to the Gospel of John. There is good evidence, both historical and internal, that supports the traditional view of John the apostle as author.

PURPOSE

The purpose statement for 1 John can be found in 5:13. We can deduce from this verse that the author is writing to believers and that his purpose is to assure them that they do indeed possess eternal life. Although this letter is written in response to a specific situation (the false teachers who had withdrawn from fellowship), it has a relevant message for the church at large.

OCCASION

John appears to be writing to a community to which he is well-known (and to which he may belong). Because this Christian community has undergone a serious split, and a substantial part of the community has withdrawn from fellowship over doctrinal issues, John writes to reassure them of their faith.

The group that has split off is continuing to propagate its own beliefs, seeking to persuade more community members to join them. John writes to warn members of the community to resist the proselytizing efforts of these false teachers by bolstering their understanding of the truth.

THEMES

While this letter is written to combat theological opponents, the themes of walking in light and confessing Jesus as Christ are repeated throughout all of it.

In John's attempts to assure the believers of their eternal life (5:13), he also repeatedly emphasizes two basic components of that assurance: obedience to God and the love of fellow Christians.

OUTLINE

GOD IS LIGHT 1:1–10

The Prologue 1:1–4
Walking in the Light 1:5–10

OBEYING THE LIGHT 2:1–29

Darkness and Light 2:1–11
Reassurance 2:12–17
False Teachers 2:18–29

GOD IS LOVE 3:1–24

Love vs. Sin 3:1–10
Loving One Another 3:11–24

UNDERSTANDING GOD'S LOVE 4:1–21

The Test of Love 4:1–6
The Anatomy of Love 4:7–21

GOD IS LIFE 5:1–21

The Life of Jesus 5:1–12
Eternal Life 5:13–21

1 JOHN 1:1–2:2

GOD IS LIGHT

The Prologue 1:1–4
Walking in the Light 1:5–10

Setting Up the Section

The use of a prologue to begin a work is characteristic of both the Gospel of John and 1 John. This section of John's first letter lays the foundation for the rest.

1:1–4

THE PROLOGUE

The prologue of 1 John opens with a reference to "that which was from the beginning." While there is agreement that this is a reference to Jesus, some see this as a reference to His eternality, while others view it as a reference to the beginning of His earthly ministry.

It has been suggested that John's use of *we* in the opening verse is simply a style preference rather than an actual reference to a group. However, since that preference doesn't continue throughout the letter, it is more likely that the *we* references in the opening of the prologue refer to a group of people, including all eyewitnesses of Jesus' earthly life and ministry. The group probably includes John and the other apostles.

Some question whether the use of *word* in the prologue is a reference back to the famous prologue in the opening of John's Gospel, in which John refers to Jesus as *the Word* (John 1:1–14; 1 John 1:1). Here, though, the verses that follow expound on the idea of *life* rather than *word*. So in this case, *word* probably refers to the message of Jesus rather than Jesus Himself.

Verses 2–3 clarify that it is the eyewitness testimony about the earthly career of Jesus that is being announced in this letter. Why? So that the readers might have fellowship with John and the other apostolic eyewitnesses. People who are in fellowship share some reality in common—in this case, the commonality is the life of Jesus. This commonality would have brought comfort to those who had just experienced a sharp doctrinal disagreement in their fellowship.

Demystifying 1 John

To those who are watching closely, much of John's wording is a jab at the false teachers (not referred to directly until 2:18–19), who not only split from the community of faith, but are still trying to convince members of the community to join them. This gives added significance to John's point in verse 3. The reason for proclaiming the truth about Jesus from eyewitnesses is for the sake of fellowship.

While this word (*fellowship*) will not be repeated throughout the letter, it does provide a kind of foundation. The fellowship John describes here among the community members is based on their own fellowship, not only with God the Father, but also with the Son, Jesus. This connection is made over and over again in a variety of ways—as we have been loved by the Father and Son, so must we love each other.

In verse 4, John states his purpose for writing: that the joy of all these witnesses might be complete. This joy will come from continuing fellowship with one another and with the Father and the Son, as opposed to breaking that fellowship by siding with the false teachers.

1:5–10

WALKING IN THE LIGHT

The summary statement for the next section is the message defined in verse 5: "God is Light, and in Him there is no darkness at all" (NASB). This is a description of one of God's qualities–completely sinless. It is also the introduction of the imagery of light and darkness–important images in John's theology.

Verse 6 begins a series of six "if" clauses, which end in 2:1. These divide into three pairs, each pair consisting of a hypothetical "If we say. . ." statement that has a negative connotation and probably represents the ideas of the false teachers (1:6, 8, 10), and then a "But if. . ." statement with a positive connotation that probably represents the counterclaim of John (1:7, 9; 2:1).

John's problem with the false teachers is their contradictory behavior: They continue walking in darkness, yet at the same time, they are making the claim to have fellowship with God (1:6).

If we say. . .	But if. . .
we have fellowship with God, yet walk in darkness, we lie (1:6).	we walk in the light, we have fellowship with each other and are cleansed by Jesus' blood (1:7).
we have no sin, we deceive ourselves (1:8).	we confess our sins, we are forgiven (1:9).
we have not sinned, we call God a liar (1:10).	we sin, Jesus is our advocate (2:1).

In contrast to verse 6, verse 7 introduces the counterclaim–if we actually do walk in the truth, we will be assured of fellowship with God. In this context, fellowship is something shared between believers as a result of a righteous lifestyle.

Verse 8 bounces back to the claim of being without sin. This is the situation of the false teachers. They are deceiving themselves. The attempt of the false teachers to deceive others (2:26) begins with their self-deceit about being guiltless of sins at all.

In verse 9, the confession John writes about is an ongoing lifestyle of confession, not just a one-time confession at conversion (as this verse is often applied). John's readers have already experienced conversion.

Verse 10 contains the last of the three pairs of "if" statements. It is almost a repetition of the claim in verse 8 but is stated a little differently. The false teachers had apparently developed a version of perfectionism by which they were able to deny that, after professing to be Christians, they could be convicted of sin. John counters this by pointing out that the one who claims this makes God a liar.

1 JOHN 2:1–29

OBEYING THE LIGHT

Darkness and Light	2:1–11
Reassurance	2:12–17
False Teachers	2:18–29

Setting Up the Section

This section contains three claims to intimate knowledge of God (2:4, 6, 9). As with the three "if we say" clauses in chapter 1 (1:6, 8, 10), these claims indirectly reflect the claims of the false teachers. The focus of the subject matter shifts from awareness and acknowledgment of sin to obedience of God's commandments. The concept of fellowship, introduced in the prologue (1:4), is replaced by an emphasis on knowing and loving God along with one's fellow believers.

2:1–11

DARKNESS AND LIGHT

The seriousness of the claim of no sin in the last verses of chapter 1 causes John to break the pattern of "if" statements with a parenthetical note at the beginning of 2:1. This note makes it clear that John is not simply implying that occasional acts of sin are acceptable; the purpose here is that the readers not sin at all.

The latter part of verse 1 includes the final counterclaim to the "if" statements beginning in 1:6. In this case, the counterclaim is that if one sins, Jesus speaks in his or her defense. This is the picture of someone coming alongside to represent us, like a mediator.

The word John uses to describe the work of Jesus—translated "atoning sacrifice"—involves the idea of a sacrifice for sins that turns away the divine wrath (2:2). Jesus does not turn away God's wrath by ignoring one's sin, but by offering His own punishment in one's stead—His life.

Keep the situation in mind: A group has left the fellowship because of a doctrinal disagreement, and they continue to attempt to convince others in the fellowship to join them. There would certainly be those in the community who wondered if the group that left was right in their opinion. John is writing to bolster those remaining, not only in their doctrine, but in their practice. His point in verse 3 answers the question, "How do we know that we know God?" John's answer is that obedience to God's commands gives the assurance that one has come to know God.

In the first of three claims, John alludes to the false teachers by describing the one who says he knows God but isn't following His commandments (2:4). According to John, this person's claim to know God is false; it's those who obey God's Word who truly know Him (2:5). In this case, God's Word is a reference not only to the facts of the scriptures, but to God's ethical demands. It is these demands a believer will attempt to obey (but presumably the false teachers would not be concerned about obeying).

The second of the three claims appears in verse 6: The person who claims to reside in God should live like Jesus. This is the first occurrence of this concept of residing, but it appears often throughout the rest of the letter. The implication in John's claim here is that the false teachers do not walk as Jesus walked, so how can they claim to reside in Him?

The commandment John speaks of in verse 7 refers to the teaching specified as the "new commandment" of John 13:34–35 (that believers should love one another).

Demystifying 1 John

John describes what he is writing as *not* a new commandment in 2:7, then as a new commandment in verse 8. Most likely, John means that this commandment does not originate with him. Yet it still can be called a new commandment, since that is the way Jesus Himself described it (John 13:34; 1 John 2:8).

The light/darkness contrast in verse 8 is a little broader than in John's Gospel, where he writes that the "light shines in the darkness, but the darkness has not understood it" (John 1:5 NIV). In the Gospel, the light refers to Jesus Himself. In this context, though, the obedience of John's readers is a part of the light that is shining.

The false teachers claim to be in the light. But if someone hates his fellow Christian, as far as John is concerned, this person—regardless of his or her claim to the contrary—still lives in darkness (1 John 2:9). The opposite of hating one's fellow believer is, of course, the fulfillment of the new commandment—to love one another. This is an important theme in this letter (John 13:34; 1 John 2:10).

Critical Observation

The idea of making someone stumble (2:10) has been cited by some as a reference to the "stumbling block" in Leviticus 19:14. The idea of the stumbling block is used figuratively in the New Testament to refer to something that is a temptation to sin or an enticement to false belief (Romans 9:33; 1 Peter 2:8; Revelation 2:14), which fits the context here.

The use of the verb *hate* in verses 9 and 11 may seem strong, but for John the failure to show love for others in the Christian community to which one belongs is a very serious matter. Such a person may be described as spiritually blind (John 9:39–41). Some see the description in 1 John 2:11 as a reference to Proverbs 4:19, with its description of the wicked who stumble in the darkness.

Critical Observation

In the New Testament, blindness is frequently a spiritual condition associated with deliberate disbelief. Particularly applicable to verses 9–11 is John 12:39–40, where deliberate refusal to believe, in spite of the miracles Jesus had performed, led to an inability to believe. Just as those who refuse to come to the light are left in darkness, so those who refuse to love fellow members of the Christian community are said to be in darkness.

2:12–17

REASSURANCE

In verse 12, John addresses his readers directly as little children. He writes to assure them that their sins have been forgiven. This is a reference to the whole group (little children) followed by two subgroups (fathers and young people [2:13]). Whether these two subgroups are distinguished by age or spiritual maturity is not clear, but John's words are applicable to all.

John first addresses the fathers. The expression "him who is from the beginning" (2:13 NIV) could refer either to God or to Jesus. Since God the Father is clearly referred to in the next verse, a reference to Jesus is more likely. Those who are addressed as fathers have remained faithful to the apostolic testimony about who Jesus is. When John turns to those he addresses as young people, the emphasis is on their victory over the evil one (Satan).

Critical Observation

This is the first time we encounter "the evil one" in this letter (2:13). Here, as with the four remaining occurrences in 1 John, it is a reference to Satan (2:14; 3:12; 5:18, 19).

In verse 14, John repeats himself, probably for the sake of emphasis. There is a new thought introduced here, though: The Word of God resides in these believers.

John presents only two alternatives in verse 15: A person either loves the world or loves the Father. In this case, the *world* does not refer merely to creation or to the world's population for whom Christ died (John 3:16). Instead, this use of *the world* represents those who stand against John and the teachings of Christ.

In 1 John 2:16, John defines everything the world has to offer:

1) The desires of the flesh. This probably does not refer simply to sensual desires (lustfulness or promiscuity). It refers to everything that is the desire of human beings—all that meets their wants and needs.
2) The desire of the eyes. This is more than merely human desires; this is related to what we want for ourselves. We see it, and we want to have it.
3) The pride of life (NASB) has to do with our possessions and accomplishments, those things we brag about, even if in our minds.

Verse 17 makes it clear that all these things are transitory. While it is true that the world and worldly desires will pass away in the future, for John they have already begun to disappear in the present. The person who does the will of God is the believer (in contrast to the false teachers). It is in doing God's will (obedience) that the believer demonstrates to himself and to those around him that he is a believer. This amounts, for John, to one means of assurance.

2:18–29

FALSE TEACHERS

Critical Observation

Many interpreters see a new section or perhaps a new major part of the letter starting with verse 18. If so, the theme verse would be the opening phrase: "Children, it is the last hour. . ." (NET).

The arrival of the last hour (a period of time rather than a moment in time) is signaled by the appearance of the false teachers, described as antichrists (2:18). To understand John's use of the term *antichrist*, note that it is more than just someone who opposes Christ, but one who is hostile and seeks to replace Christ. This reveals how John sees the false teachers with their innovative but false view of Jesus.

Demystifying 1 John

The Letters of John contain the only New Testament uses of the term *antichrist*. Although the word itself is unique to 1 and 2 John, the concept behind it and the figure to which it refers are not. Paul describes this individual, in 2 Thessalonians 2:3, as "the man of lawlessness" and "the son of destruction" (NASB). Jesus Himself refers to "the abomination of desolation" in Mark 13:14 (see also Matthew 24:15). This individual is also referred to as "the beast" in Revelation 13:1.

John describes the departure of the false teachers from the community (1 John 2:19). John's point here is that the withdrawal of the false teachers reveals that they never genuinely belonged. He implies that their departure is part of God's sovereign purpose, perhaps intending this as reassurance to his readers in the face of the turmoil that may have followed.

The anointing in verse 20 refers to the Holy Spirit who indwells believers, rather than a ceremonial one-time anointing.

Verse 21 contains more reassurance for John's readers. Because of the false teaching, some may have come to doubt that they really know the truth concerning Jesus. John writes to reassure them that they do know the truth.

Critical Observation

The phrase "no lie comes from the truth" (2:21 NIV) refers to the teaching of the false teachers. The contrast between truth and falsehood is introduced in 1 John 1:6, where the person who claims fellowship with God yet walks in darkness is characterized as a liar. But here the line is drawn much more distinctively. The picture that is painted of a false teacher is not simply one who is ignorant, but one who is hostile toward the truth as it is taught by John.

The false teachers have already been identified as antichrists (2:18). They are now identified as liars (2:22). This is the first time in the letter that John explicitly states the position of the false teachers—they deny Jesus is the Messiah. Most often this is understood to mean that these teachers reject the orthodox interpretation of the Incarnation: that Jesus' divine and human natures were fully united. What logically follows for John, then, is that if the false teachers deny that Jesus is the Messiah, then they have no relationship with the Father (2:23).

Verses 24–26 include a wordplay in the Greek manuscript. The Greek word translated *remain* can also be translated *reside*. One is to stay somewhere, and the other is to take up residence. The teaching of the apostles must remain (reside) in the readers in order for the readers to remain (reside) in the Son and in the Father. If that happens, then they will have eternal life (2:25). Verses 27–28 continue the *remain/reside* wordplay. John reminds his readers that the Holy Spirit resides in them. The "anointing" they have received is the indwelling presence of the Holy Spirit. This provides assurance that they do also indeed reside in Him—Jesus.

Verse 26 focuses again on John's primary reason for writing: to protect his faithful followers from the false view of Christ espoused by these departed teachers.

Critical Observation

At the end of verse 27 is a statement that can be taken as a declaration of fact or as a command: "you reside in him" (NET). In this chapter it transitions between a section of encouragement and a section of exhortation. While the phrase is true with either interpretation, it most likely ends the encouragement and so should be read that way, as an assurance to the readers that they do reside in Jesus.

Verse 28 references Jesus' second coming. At this point, John switches from reassurance to exhortation. He wants his readers to remain in the truth so that they don't have to shrink away from Jesus in shame when He appears. Anyone who does not remain demonstrates that whatever profession he has made is false, and he is not a true believer.

The "If" that opens verse 29 is not to cast doubt on whether Jesus is righteous, but instead whether the readers of the letter have realized this fact. The expectation reflected here is that all those who are truly God's children will practice righteousness. For John, conduct is the clue to authenticity of this relationship.

Take It Home

John stresses ethical behavior as important for the Christian, in contrast to the teaching of the false teachers, who argue that a Christian's moral or ethical behavior is unimportant. This serves to remind the church that actions have always, and still do, speak much louder than words. Speaking for Christ is important. Living for Him is essential.

1 JOHN 3:1–24

GOD IS LOVE

Love vs. Sin 3:1–10
Loving One Another 3:11–24

Setting Up the Section

Within this section, the first 3 verses are a parenthesis in which John reflects on what it means to be fathered by God, a subject he has already mentioned at the end of 2:29. The flow of the argument against the false teachers is then resumed by verse 4.

3:1–10

LOVE VS. SIN

Verse 1 begins a parenthetical comment that extends through the end of verse 3. John refers to believers as God's children. The last part of the verse asserts that the world's treatment of believers is a reflection and outgrowth of its treatment of Jesus Himself.

The concept that John uses here to describe God's relationship to believers, as a father to children, points on the one hand to God's personal, relational, and loving nature. On the other hand, it defines the status of Christians: They are members of God's household.

What believers will be is to be revealed at some later point (3:2). In light of the reference to Jesus' second coming in 2:28, this is probably what John refers to in verse 2, when believers see Him "as He is" (NASB).

Because of this hope, believers are expected to purify themselves; that is, to separate themselves from sin and live with moral purity just as Jesus did (3:3). The assurance of the previous verse, that believers will see Him just as He is, has moral and ethical behavioral implications for their lives in the present. This serves to further rebut the false teachers' claims that what the Christian does in the present life is of no consequence. With this verse ends the parenthetical section that opens chapter 3.

Verse 4 opens with a statement on lawlessness, which carries the idea of opposition or rebellion. Keep in mind that the "law" for John is the law of love, as given by Jesus in the new commandment of John 13:34–35. This is the command to love one's brother, a major theme of 1 John.

Critical Observation

Those who sin (3:4) are sharply contrasted with those who reside in Christ (3:6), which is typical of John's writing style. John is referring to the false teachers in verse 4. The only specific sin in all of 1 John that John charges the false teachers with is failure to show love for fellow believers (3:17).

In verse 5, John reminds the readers of the basics they all know: that Jesus came to take away sins. He also affirms Jesus' sinlessness. This, in turn, leads into the issue of sin for those who reside in Jesus.

Verse 6, along with verse 9, can seem to mean that genuine Christians do not sin. Obviously, this is not the case, as John points out in 2:1. More likely, John is saying that genuine Christians do not continue to sin with no remorse.

Throughout this letter, the ones attempting to deceive John's readers, as mentioned in verse 7, are clearly the false teachers. The deception that John is guarding them from is a misunderstanding of this: The practice of righteousness is the evidence that a person is a member of God's family.

The strong contrasts that have characterized this section come to a head in verses 8 and 10. He who is sinful refers to the false teachers. They claim to be in relationship with God, yet they refuse to live righteously as Jesus did. Such people do not belong to God but to the devil.

Jesus, however, came to destroy the devil's works. This is not a figurative statement. Here, the verb *destroy* means to "bring to an end, abolish, or do away with."

As already stated in 2:29, in a spiritual sense, one's paternity (whether one is a child of God or a child of the devil) is revealed by whether one practices righteousness.

3:11–24

LOVING ONE ANOTHER

The message described in verse 11—loving one another—is a restatement of Jesus' command to the disciples in John 15:12, which is itself a restatement of the new commandment of John 13:34.

In 1 John 3:12, Cain serves as the example of what not to do—instead of loving his brother, he took his brother's life. Here John illustrates the stark contrast between righteous and evil actions, just as he contrasted darkness and light in John 3:19–21.

Critical Observation

The mention of Cain and his brother, with its allusion to Genesis 4:1–16, is the only direct reference to the Old Testament in 1 John.

Since the way Cain treated Abel is the way unbelievers generally treat believers, John tells his readers not to be surprised when the world mistreats them (1 John 3:13). In contrast to the hostility they may experienced in the world, however, followers of Jesus also have assurance that they have crossed from death to life. This assurance comes from the love of fellow believers (3:14). As in 2:3 and 2:5, obedience to the new commandment to love one another becomes the basis for this assurance. Love for fellow believers is in fact a form of God's love for us, because as far as John is concerned, all love comes from God (4:7–11).

But the person who refuses to love fellow believers remains in a state of spiritual death (3:14). Such a person is surely an unbeliever, as verse 14 makes clear. Ultimately, these verses will apply to the false teachers (3:17), and the fact that they remain in a state of spiritual death demonstrates (again, as in 2:19) John's belief that they were never genuine believers to begin with.

In verse 15, John writes that the person who hates a fellow believer is as guilty as if he or she had murdered him. This is strong language, but failure to show love to fellow believers is a serious matter to John. Failure to show love for fellow believers is an indication that eternal life is not present within the individual. Once again, one's behavior is a measure of one's spiritual status.

In contrast to the hatred shown by the false teachers for fellow believers, and the hatred of Cain for his brother, verse 16 states the standard of love is established by Jesus Himself—He laid down His life. Jesus' sacrifice on behalf of believers forms a strong motivation for them to lay down their lives for fellow believers. For John, this act of selfless sacrifice on Jesus' part becomes the very standard by which love is measured.

Critical Observation

References to Jesus "laying down His life" are unique to the Gospel of John (John 10:11; 15:13) and 1 John (3:16). From John's perspective, Jesus' sacrifice was a voluntary one; He was always completely in control of the situation surrounding His arrest, trials, and crucifixion (John 10:18).

John next describes the opposite of sacrificial love. The individual who has ample material possessions and yet fails to show compassion for a fellow Christian in need demonstrates that he or she does not have God's love residing within. John's point is made by asking a rhetorical question: How can the love of God reside in this kind of person? The question assumes the answer: The love of God cannot reside in a person who doesn't show God's love.

Verse 18 describes love in two pairs of words. In each pair, the first word is produced by the second: Words are produced by the tongue, and actions (deeds) that show a believer's love for another are produced by the truth. John exhorts his readers to love one another not merely with words, but with real actions that spring from their relationship to the truth.

The prepositional phrase that opens verse 19 ("by this" NET) refers to the previous verse: By expressing love for one another, Christians assure themselves that they belong to the truth, because the outward action reflects the inward reality of one's relationship with God.

Verse 20 describes believers condemning themselves because of a guilty conscience concerning sin (3:20). In this case, their actions in showing love for fellow believers will assure them that God will accept and forgive them even if their own consciences are guilty.

On the other hand, if a person's conscience does not condemn him or her, then that person can have confidence in prayer (3:21). This is not to say that an obedient lifestyle on the part of the believer merits or guarantees answered prayer. It simply means that, insofar as believers' consciences make no accusation against them, and they are living in obedience to God's commandments, their will and God's will coincide, and they can reasonably expect to receive answers to their requests. This combination of confidence and answered prayer appears also in 5:14–15.

This same word, *confidence*, also occurs in connection to Christ's second coming (2:28; 4:17). So this may also be a reference to the Christian's assurance of a positive outcome at the judgment when Jesus returns.

John closes the chapter specifying God's commandment to believe in Jesus and love one another. The person who does these things, the genuine believer, is in a mutual and reciprocal relationship with God. The assurance of this mutual relationship between God and the believer is God's Spirit. The believer's assurance in 1 John is based on three things:

1) Believing in Jesus (3:23)
2) Loving one another (3:23)
3) The gift of God's indwelling Spirit (3:24)

1 JOHN 4:1–21

UNDERSTANDING GOD'S LOVE

The Test of Love 4:1–6
The Anatomy of Love 4:7–21

Setting Up the Section

Since the book of 1 John has a rather free structure, many interpreters divide it in a multitude of ways, breaking sections in a variety of places. With almost no exception, though, the opening six verses of chapter 4 are kept together as a section standing on its own. It opens this chapter, which focuses on understanding God's love.

4:1–6

THE TEST OF LOVE

Since having the Spirit of God is a ground of assurance for the believer (2:27; 3:24), it is important to know how to test the spirits. Every spirit is not from God (4:1).

The false prophets mentioned in verse 1 is a reference to the false teachers and their false understanding of Jesus. These teachers claim to be inspired by the Spirit of God, yet John takes strong exception to their teaching. In light of all this, John proposes the test described in verse 2: Does the Spirit confess Jesus as having come from God? Note that this test is both confessional (concerning what a person believes) and Christological (concerning what a person believes about Jesus). Presumably, the false teachers would not be able to make this confession, since this is designed to test their truth.

Demystifying 1 John

While verse 2 describes how to recognize the Spirit that does come from God, verse 3 describes the other side of the coin. A spirit that does not come from God does not acknowledge Jesus' identity. This is where the false teachers probably had their problems. By the time John was writing this letter, many heresies and sects had begun to distort Jesus' identity. For example, some could confess the Messiah would come in the flesh but could not connect this with Jesus. John identifies this kind of spirit with the Antichrist. Earlier John had called the false teachers antichrists (2:18). Now he says the false spirit behind them is the spirit of the Antichrist.

While in verse 1 John addresses his readers as friends, in verse 4 he addresses them as children. He offers them the assurance of victory over the false teachers because of the power of the Holy Spirit.

He makes a slight change to his language in verse 5. Whereas in verse 1 he asserts that the false teachers had gone into the world, in verse 5 he claims that they are *from* the world. This determines their perspective and also ensures that the world pays attention to them. (Compare this with John 15:19.)

In verse 6, John introduces another way to test the spirits. Those who are of God include all the faithful Christians who have held on to the orthodox testimony about who Jesus is. Those not from God is a reference to the false teachers, who refuse to listen to this testimony about Jesus. John makes this statement, not as a lone man demanding ultimate authority, but as one of the apostles whose message is connected with all those who witnessed Jesus' life (1:1–2).

4:7–21

THE ANATOMY OF LOVE

In verse 7, John addresses his readers again as friends. He also returns to the theme of loving one another, the major theme of the second half of the letter. By "everyone who loves," John means those who love fellow believers sacrificially, as Jesus loves us (3:16). He again connects one's behavior toward fellow believers to an indication of whether that person has come to know God. Since God is love, those who truly know Him will reflect that love toward fellow members of the Christian community. According to verse 8, the reverse is also true.

In verse 9, God's love is revealed in believers through the giving of His Son (compare John 3:16). While all Christians are children of God, Jesus is God's Son in a unique, one-of-a-kind sense.

Critical Observation

John uses the term *world* in a variety of ways, depending on the context. In formulas like the one in verse 9, which echoes John 3:16 and speaks of God sending His Son to be the Savior of the world, the term is used in a neutral sense. In other places, like 1 John 2:15, John uses the same term to refer to the opposition of the world. In this case, it holds a negative connotation and has in mind that part of the population that stands against John's teaching.

John reminds his readers in verse 10 that real love comes from God, and no one can love God without Him loving us first, providing His Son to sacrifice for us. The initiative lies with God.

For the sixth and last time in this letter, John addresses his readers as friends in verse 11. God's example of self-giving, sacrificial love—the giving of His own Son—serves as the model for believers to follow in loving one another.

Since no one has seen God at any time, how is it possible for believers to know that God resides in them? Verses 12–16 offer three grounds of assurance for the believer:

1) The indwelling Holy Spirit. This indwelling of the Spirit (4:13) leads a person to testify to what God the Father has done through His Son, who was sent to be the Savior of the world (4:14). This expression recalls the testimony of the Samaritan woman at the well in John 4, which led to the same confession about Jesus by the Samaritans (John 4:42).

2) The confession that Jesus is God's Son (1 John 3:23; 4:15). This confession insures both God's residence within the believer and vice versa.
3) Love shown to fellow believers (4:16). When a believer shows love toward another believer, this provides assurance to the first believer that he or she resides in God, and likewise, that God resides in him or her.

In verse 17, John switches topics to Christian growth or sanctification, the outgrowth of loving each other. As believers love one another, their love is perfected, and that in turn allows them to have confidence when Jesus returns. They will not fear punishment, but they will be like Him.

Fear and mature love are mutually exclusive (4:18). A Christian who fears God's punishment (on the Day of Judgment, mentioned in verse 17) needs to grow in his or her understanding of love.

Critical Observation

The phrase, "fear has to do with punishment" (4:18) could be understood several ways. In the immediate context of the Day of Judgment (4:17), it seems virtually certain that eternal punishment (or fear of it) is what is meant.

Although verse 19 appears to be a declarative statement, it contains an implicit exhortation: Because God first loved believers, believers *ought* to love Him and others in return.

In verse 20, John reverts to hypothetical statements like those in 1:6 and 2:4. Like the former statements, this one almost certainly has the false teachers in view: They claim to love God but fail to love fellow Christians. This leads John to conclude that such a person is a liar. Why? Because the person who does not love his fellow Christian, whom he has seen, cannot love God, whom he has not seen. Once more, in closing the chapter, John stresses the connection between loving God and loving one's fellow Christian (4:21). The two go hand in hand.

1 JOHN 5:1–21

GOD IS LIFE

The Life of Jesus 5:1–12
Eternal Life 5:13–21

Setting Up the Section

In this section, John will explain that the means by which believers conquer the world (including, of course, the false teachers, who are now part of the world according to 1 John 4:5) is their faith: faith in what Jesus has done during His earthly life and ministry, including His sacrificial death on the cross. For John, this is a faith the false teachers do not possess.

5:1–12

THE LIFE OF JESUS

Once again (echoing 4:2–3) John stresses that confession of Jesus as the Christ is the standard that determines whether or not one is fathered by God. The second part of verse 1 reads like a proverb: If one loves the parent, one will love the child. While this is likely a general statement applying to any parent, in the present context it has application to loving God and loving God's children.

At face value, verse 2 says just the opposite of 4:20. In chapter 4, John states we can know we love God when we love our fellow Christians. Here John seems to be saying we can know that we love fellow Christians by loving God. It appears the debate is really over two things at once: whether or not we really love God (addressed by 4:20 and aimed at the false teachers) and how we can know that we really love God's children (addressed here and aimed at the readers). These two verses are like looking at the same coin from two different sides. They both work together.

A believer's love for God is expressed by his or her obedience (5:3). The description that God's commands are not weighty or burdensome may be a reference to the words of Jesus in Matthew 11:30 (which are a reiteration of Deuteronomy 30:11). John can describe God's commandments as not being weighty, because the commandment is to love one another, and God Himself is the endless source of this love. It is the love of God living inside Christians that makes the commandments unburdensome.

In the first part of verse 4, John uses the word *overcome*. He has already used this same word to describe victory over Satan in 2:13–14 and over the false teachers (described as false prophets) in 4:4. Here, John most likely has in mind victory over the false teachers.

In the latter part of verse 4, John also refers to a past conquering. Although some interpreters connect this with the past victory achieved over the false teachers, it may refer to Jesus Himself, who has already overcome the world by His victory over death. Thus, when John says faith has conquered the world, he is speaking of believers' faith in Jesus, who overcame the world by His sacrificial death on the cross, resurrection, and return to the Father.

Although verse 5 is phrased as a rhetorical question, the answer is clear. John now affirms that it is the person who believes that Jesus is the Son of God who has conquered the world.

In verse 6, John says Jesus came by water and blood. A common interpretation sees the water as a reference to Jesus' baptism, while the blood is a reference to Jesus' death on the cross. Others see it as a reference to the outpouring of blood and water that came forth from Jesus' side after He died on the cross (John 19:34). While this phrase is a bit puzzling to contemporary readers, the terminology was probably familiar to John's original audience. His contention that Jesus came not by "water only" would be a strike at the false teachers. It may be that they affirmed Jesus' baptism but not His death and resurrection.

In 1 John 5:7–8, John calls on three witnesses to support his claims about Jesus: the Spirit, the blood, and the water. In the previous verses, the Spirit was listed separate from the water and the blood, but here they stand together.

The mention that the three witnesses are in agreement (5:8) means that they work together to achieve the same result—to establish the truth that Jesus is Christ (Messiah) and Son of God. Many see in the number of the witnesses (three) the Old Testament requirement that evidence had to be confirmed by two or three witnesses (Deuteronomy 19:15; John 8:17–18).

The testimony attributed to humanity (1 John 5:9) likely refers to the testimony of John the Baptist at the baptism of Jesus (John 1:32; 3:31–33; 5:36), which the false teachers were quoting to support their claim that Jesus "came by water" at His baptism (1 John 5:6). In this case, John mentions a fourth witness in addition to the three mentioned in verse 8: God Himself. John is saying that the false teachers, in their appeal to the human testimony of John the Baptist, are wrong because God's testimony surpasses human testimony.

Critical Observation

Verse 10 is a parenthesis in John's argument, which is then resumed in verse 11. John, in this context, is not distinguishing between the person who has made a personal commitment to Jesus and the person who has failed to do so, but between the person who has made a true confession of Jesus as the Christ, the Messiah, and the person who has made a false one, referring to the false teachers.

In verse 11, God's testimony (mentioned in verse 9) is revealed. The testimony is the eternal life that John and his readers possess, while the false teachers do not. It is important to remember that in John's debate with the false teachers, the controversy is not over the *reality* of eternal life (whether it exists at all), but over which side in the debate *possesses* it. John began with a testimony that the eternal life had been revealed (1:2), and it is consummated here with the acknowledgment of that eternal life as the final testimony in his case against the false teachers.

Possession of eternal life is connected to one's relationship to God's Son (5:12). The contrast between the readers of the letter, who are being reassured that they do indeed possess eternal life, and the false teachers, who in the opinion of John do not, is once again portrayed in stark terms. Someone either has the Son—He is present in the person's life—and thus has eternal life, or does not have the Son, in which case he or she does not have eternal life.

5:13–21

ETERNAL LIFE

John begins his conclusion by telling his readers why he has written the letter (5:13). The expression *these things* refers to what has preceded. Once again John writes to reassure his readers that they possess eternal life.

In verses 14–15, John asserts the confidence that believers can have regarding prayer. Asking according to God's will brings assurance that God hears believers when they pray, and this gives assurance that they will receive answers to their requests.

In verse 16, John asks his readers to pray for the fellow believer who commits a sin, described here as a sin that doesn't result in death. While John's readers were expected to be familiar with this description of sin (resulting in death or not resulting in death), there has been some question since the original writing about what this sin is exactly. Theories include:

1) This is a specific sin. If so, we can't know from the information here what it is.
2) The sin is falling away from the faith, rejecting God after having once believed.
3) The sin is the refusal to believe in Jesus as God's Son.

Since in most of this letter John's negative aspersions have shed light on the position of the false teachers, it seems that the sin resulting in death is the sin of the false teachers whom John has consistently regarded as unbelievers (2:19; 3:14–15, 17). Refusal to believe in Jesus as the Christ, the Son of God, is the one sin that cannot be forgiven, because it denies the only means of forgiveness.

In verse 17, John does not leave the impression that any sin is insignificant. He reminds his readers that all unrighteousness is sin. Without the atoning work of Jesus, all sin leads to death.

Demystifying 1 John

John's claim that anyone fathered by God does not continue in sin (5:18) is essentially the same claim he makes in 3:9. In the immediate context in chapter 3, John is contrasting the children of God and the children of the devil. Here John writes that Jesus, who is born of God, keeps His children safe from the evil one.

If someone continues in the practice of sinning, in John's way of thinking it calls into question that person's salvation. It is God's life within the Christian that enables obedience.

In verse 19, John affirms that the whole world is still under the controlling influence of the evil one. However, believers do not belong to the world any longer. They belong to God and His Son.

John's closing can seem rather abrupt. It is possible that he is offering a general warning against idolatry in verse 21. However, John has spent virtually the whole letter discussing, in one form or another, the false teachers who are continuing to trouble the community. It is likely that this is a reference to the false image of Jesus that these teachers are putting forth.

Take It Home

John's letter is a continual effort to call this group of Christians back to an accurate view of Jesus, and thus an accurate view of the life they are to live as believers. The evil one is still at work today. It remains necessary for God's children to take account of the life within them, and the manner in which they practice the faith they are called to.

2 JOHN

INTRODUCTION TO 2 JOHN

Second John is a personal letter written to warn a sister congregation some distance away. In its original Greek manuscript, it is shorter than any other New Testament book, except 3 John (with 219 words). The length of both 2 and 3 John is governed by the size of a single sheet of papyrus, which would have measured about 25 by 20 centimeters.

AUTHOR

As with the Gospel of John, the author does not explicitly identify himself as the apostle John. Instead, he uses the designation *the elder.* He obviously assumes the readers know him. However, the style of writing is unmistakably similar to that of 1 John. Also, as early as the second century, Christian historians and theologians recognized the author as the apostle John, one of the original twelve disciples.

PURPOSE

The purpose of this letter is to warn its readers of the missionary efforts of false teachers and the dangers of welcoming them whenever they should arrive.

OCCASION

Both 1 and 2 John are written in response to the same kinds of false teachers. This letter offers specific instructions about how to deal with the traveling preachers who were being sent out to local congregations. There is no conclusive evidence for the actual date, but this book was probably written around the same time as 1 John (around AD 90), while John was in Ephesus.

THEMES

Second John has the same themes that can be found in other writings by John: how to know the truth, how to live a life of love within that truth, and how to identify false teaching regarding the Christian faith.

OUTLINE

THE GREETING	1–4
THE MESSAGE	5–12
FAREWELL	13

2 JOHN 1–4

Setting Up the Section

This Second Letter of John is written in a format characteristic of first-century letters. It begins with an introduction (verses 1–3), which mentions the sender and the addressee, and includes a greeting. Many letters of this period follow the greeting with an expression of thanksgiving or a wish for the health of the addressee. Although no explicit expression of thanksgiving is found in 2 John, John's expression of joy in verse 4 may be roughly equivalent.

1–4

THE GREETING

In verse 1, John identifies himself as the elder. He identifies his original addressee as "an elect lady and her children" (NET), which refers to a particular local church at some distance from the community where John is living at the time.

He also refers more specifically to all who know the truth. This focuses on those members of the community who have held fast to a correct view of Jesus in the face of opposition by the false teachers described in 1 John (1 John 2:3, 13; 4:16).

In one sense, the truth mentioned here suggests a primarily doctrinal focus—a point of belief about Jesus. In verse 2, however, the connection of truth with the expression "lives in us" (NIV) suggests that, for John, the truth is personalized and is a manifestation of the Spirit who resides permanently with believers.

John's greeting, while it fits the standard format of a first-century letter, also contains a significant amount of reassurance for the readers. Rather than wishing or praying for his readers to have grace, mercy, and peace with them (for instance, "may grace be with you"), verse 3 is more of a promise that these three important elements of faith, specifically from the Father and the Son, will certainly be with his readers.

The fact that John acknowledges that *some* of the members of the church are living according to God's truth does not necessarily mean that he is leaving out those *not* walking in the truth. It simply means that he does not have personal knowledge of all the members of the church to which he is writing (verse 4).

The use of the verb *walk* in verse 4 refers to conduct, behavior, or lifestyle. It is common in the New Testament (1 John 1:6; 3 John 3–4). In the context of this opening to John's letter, it refers to the resulting conduct of an individual who has truth residing within.

5–12

THE MESSAGE

Verse 5 is an echo of 1 John 2:7. Both verses refer to a commandment that the readers have had from the beginning. The new commandment (John 13:34) is that believers love one another.

In verse 6, John explains what the love of God consists of: obedience to God's commandments. (This coordinates with 1 John 5:3.) Believers express their love for God by obeying His commandments and especially by loving one another.

The deceivers (verse 7) refer to the false teachers described at length in 1 John (2:18–19; 4:1). These false teachers are compared to the ultimate deceiver (Satan) and the Antichrist. This is not to mean they are identified as Satan or the Antichrist described in Revelation, but they are like these individuals in that they accomplish Satan's work and prepare the way for the Antichrist. They "do not acknowledge Jesus Christ as coming in the flesh" (NASB).

In verse 8, John urges his readers not to lose what they have worked for, which refers to their pastoral and missionary efforts in their community and surrounding communities. If the false teachers are unopposed and allowed to recruit in the community to which John is writing, all the effective work accomplished up to this point by the recipients of the letter would be in danger of being lost. Thus, there would be no basis left on which to be rewarded.

Critical Observation

The *reward* that John wants the readers to receive is a term for a workman's wage—the payment he is due in exchange for his labor. The idea of rewards for Christians who serve faithfully occurs in a number of places in the New Testament (Matthew 5:12; Mark 9:41; Luke 19:11–27; 1 Corinthians 3:8).

In verse 9, the false teachers are described as those who have gone beyond the apostolic eyewitness testimony about Jesus. Such a person does not have God, as opposed to the individual who remains in the apostolic teaching about Jesus. To *have* in this sense means to be indwelt by the Holy Spirit, who is in a dynamic relationship with both the Father and the Son at all times. John does not regard this to be true of the false teachers.

The warning not to welcome those without the teaching of Christ (verse 10) could simply be a prohibition against showing hospitality to the traveling representatives of the false teachers. It is possible, though, that the house refers to a church. If that is so, then this is an instruction to prohibit the false teachers to speak to the house church and spread their false teaching.

John's command not to welcome, or greet, these individuals is not intended to represent an insult. In this context, to greet someone means to greet him or her as a fellow Christian, and this is impossible, because as far as John is concerned, the false teachers are not genuine believers. Therefore, they should not be publicly greeted as such. Giving one of the false teachers' representatives a greeting in public could be construed as giving endorsement to that person's views about Jesus. This would be, in effect, to share in his evil deeds (verse 11).

In verse 12, John indicates he has much more to say but prefers to do so in person. This is a quick letter sent in light of the urgency he feels about the danger of these false teachers.

13

FAREWELL

In verse 13, John sends final greetings. It is significant that it is the *children* of the elect sister, and not the sister herself, who send the greetings here. This probably refers to members of a sister church to which 2 John is written. Evidently, John is staying in that community while writing this letter.

Take It Home

John's letter reminds us of the importance of knowing what we believe, not for the sake of winning an argument, but for the sake of walking with God in truth.

3 JOHN

INTRODUCTION TO 3 JOHN

Third John, like 2 John, is written in the standard correspondence format for the first century. It is slightly shorter than 2 John and is the shortest book of the New Testament. It is the only one of the three New Testament letters to be addressed to a named individual.

AUTHOR

As with the Gospel of John, the author does not explicitly identify himself as the apostle John, but instead uses the designation *the elder*. As early as the second century, though, Christian historians and theologians recognized the author as the apostle John, one of the original twelve disciples.

PURPOSE

John wrote this letter to commend two church leaders, Gaius and Demetrius, and to send a warning about Diotrephes, a man who opposed John's leadership.

OCCASION

The problem with Diotrephes was not a problem with heresy (as in 1 and 2 John) as much as authority. He was evidently trying to diminish John's authority as well as censure those sent by John. It was this behavior that prompted John to write to Gaius.

THEMES

John's third, short letter deals with the themes of hospitality toward the traveling teachers who spread the gospel in the first century. It also speaks to pride and its affect on leadership within a community.

OUTLINE

THE GREETING	1–2
THE MESSAGE	3–12
FAREWELL	13–15

3 JOHN 1–2

Setting Up the Section

Third John begins with an introductory formula (verses 1–2), that mentions the sender and the addressee. The greeting, a standard part of the introduction, is omitted, but unlike 2 John, the letter includes a health wish (verse 3).

1–2

THE GREETING

As in 2 John, John refers to himself as the elder (verse 1). The addressee's name, *Gaius*, was common in the Roman Empire, and it is unlikely that the person addressed here is the same as one of those with that name associated with Paul (Acts 19:29; 20:4; Romans 16:23; 1 Corinthians 1:14). This individual is well-known to John, but it is not certain whether they had met in person, since the report of Gaius's conduct toward the brothers is heard secondhand by John. Nor is it certain whether Gaius belonged to the same local church as Diotrephes (3 John 9) or was himself the leader of another local congregation. It is clear, however, that John regards Gaius as a valuable ally in the controversy with the false teachers and their false view of Jesus (verse 3).

John affirms in verse 2 that Gaius is well-off spiritually. He prays that Gaius's physical health would match his spiritual health. Notice, it is the spiritual health that is to be the standard by which one's physical health is measured, not the other way around.

3–12

THE MESSAGE

In verse 3, the word *truth* may refer to either doctrine or behavior. Certainly John makes no effort to correct Gaius's doctrine. But according to verse 5, it is Gaius's faithful work on behalf of the brothers—the traveling missionaries who need support—that is commended by John. Therefore, in this context, the emphasis is on Gaius's behavior rather than on his doctrine.

In verse 4, John may be referring to Gaius as one of his own converts (like Paul refers to his spiritual children in 1 Corinthians 4:14–15), but more likely John simply regards those under his spiritual authority as his children.

Addressing Gaius as a dear friend in verse 5, John commends him for his faithful service to the traveling missionaries (the brothers), even though he did not know them personally. The missionaries have returned and informed John of Gaius's support (verse 6). It seems likely that the church mentioned here is also John's church, where he is currently located.

John writes that the missionaries have gone out on behalf of the name of God (verse 7). They have been sent out to combat the false teachers and have accepted nothing from non-Christians, or pagans. Their mission is not evangelization but concerns an in-house debate over Jesus' identity as the Son of God.

Critical Observation

The word translated *pagan* here occurs only four times in the New Testament (the other three are in Matthew 5:47; 6:7; and 18:17). It refers to Gentiles. Since the issue here is support for the traveling missionaries and there is no indication that John would want to forbid receiving support from Gentile converts to Christianity, the word must refer to Gentile unbelievers. The traveling missionaries sent out to combat false teaching have been accepting nothing by way of support from non-Christians. Why support from non-Christians should be refused is not entirely clear, although a number of interpreters see the possibility of confusion with missionaries representing pagan deities.

The first person plural in verse 8 includes John himself, Gaius, and all genuine Christians, who should all support the traveling missionaries in their efforts to resist and counteract the teaching of the false teachers.

In verse 9, Diotrephes appears to be an influential person (perhaps the leader) in a local church known to Gaius, but to which Gaius himself does not belong. John's description of Diotrephes suggests an arrogant person who has refused to acknowledge John's prior written communication. This communication probably concerns the traveling missionaries mentioned in the next verse, and Diotrephes has refused to acknowledge John's authority to intervene in the matter. (For Diotrephes this may have been an issue of John's authority and local jurisdiction over such things.)

The church mentioned here, which John says he may visit (verse 10), is not the same as the one mentioned in verse 6, to which John apparently belongs (or of which he is in charge). It seems probable that Gaius belongs to (or is in charge of) one local church while Diotrephes is in another.

Concerning Diotrephes, John gives a warning in verse 10. Because Diotrephes does not recognize John's authority, if John visits he will expose Diotrephes' behavior. Since Diotrephes made unjustified charges against John, John will bring charges of his own against Diotrephes.

John's instruction not to imitate what is bad is clearly a reference to Diotrephes' behavior (verse 11). By implication, John calls into question the genuineness of Diotrephes' faith. In John's terminology, it is clear that the phrase "has not seen God" is equivalent to "is not a genuine Christian."

Demetrius, mentioned in verse 12, is apparently someone Gaius has not met. He has a good reputation, and it is possible he is the leader of the traveling missionaries. John commends Demetrius to Gaius.

Demystifying 3 John

Demetrius may well have been the leader of a delegation of traveling missionaries and may even have been the bearer of this letter to Gaius. The writing of letters of introduction to be carried along by representatives or missionaries in New Testament times is also attested in Paul's writings (1 Corinthians 16:3).

13–15

FAREWELL

As in the closing of 2 John, John says that he has many things to write to Gaius but prefers to speak in person. It appears that John anticipates a personal visit in the near future. This may be the same visit mentioned in connection with Diotrephes in verse 10. Gaius's church and Diotrephes' church may have been in the same city or in neighboring towns, so that John anticipates visiting both on the same journey.

John closes with greetings similar to 2 John 13. *Friends* is an alternative to *brothers* as an early Christian designation, especially within John's community. It may have come about from Jesus' teaching in John 15:13–15, "You are my friends if you do what I command."

JUDE

INTRODUCTION TO JUDE

AUTHOR

The author of this letter is Jude, the brother of James. Most likely these brothers are the same brothers listed in Matthew 13:55 and Mark 6:3 as Jesus' half brothers (born to Joseph and Mary after Jesus' birth). It was common in the history of the church to shorten the name of Judas to Jude, in the interest of changing one's name from that of the great betrayer, Judas Iscariot. While these two brothers did not have faith in Jesus as Lord during His lifetime (John 7:5), they became leaders in the first-century Christian church, and each wrote a New Testament letter.

PURPOSE

This epistle is a passionate plea for the readers to contend for their faith. In light of a growing heresy in the church that understood grace as a license for immorality, Jude wrote to an unidentified group of Christ-followers to call them back to faith.

OCCASION

We don't know exactly when Jude was written, but many estimate around AD 65. The content of Jude and 2 Peter are closely related, and this has prompted discussion about which came first and which provided reference for the other.

While it had been Jude's intent to write to this particular group of believers on the topic of salvation (verse 3), what prompted this letter was news of false teaching.

THEMES

Truth and discernment are two key themes of this book. A believer's security in God's love opens and closes the letter, but the meat of the content pertains to the false teachers in the midst and the need for believers to stand firm in the truth.

OUTLINE

CONTENDING FOR THE FAITH	1–4
THE DESCRIPTION OF FALSE TEACHERS	5–16
THE DEFENSE AGAINST FALSE TEACHERS	17–23
THE DOXOLOGY	24–25

JUDE 1–4

Setting Up the Section

In this section, Jude gives his reasons for writing and a strongly worded identification of the enemies of the faith.

1–4

CONTENDING FOR THE FAITH

Jude describes himself as a bond servant (or, slave; Greek: *doulos*) of Jesus Christ (verse 1). A bond servant is a lifelong loyal servant of his master. He also identifies himself as the brother of James. In this case, James is the half brother of Jesus. This kind of introduction is an act of humility on Jude's part, not touting his familial connection with Jesus, but rather his faith in Jesus.

Jude's identification of his readers (verse 1), while it does not specifically identify the people or the community, paints a beautiful picture of those who follow Jesus: chosen, loved by God, and kept by Jesus.

In verse 2, Jude writes an encouraging prayer request that his readers would receive their full capacity of three things:

- *Mercy.* The mercy of God displayed upon His children when He comes to judge the world.
- *Peace.* Supernatural contentment no matter the circumstances one faces.
- *Love.* The love of God manifested to us so that we will one day stand in His presence.

Jude's original purpose for writing had changed (verse 3). Rather than being a relaxed letter to friends, this letter deals with a problem the introduction of false doctrine into the community.

Jude sounds like a general giving a passionate speech to motivate his troops or a coach to motivate his players. He encourages his readers to *contend* for their faith, to passionately struggle, to protect it from destruction. This is not a onetime event, but an ongoing effort. He describes this faith as something that has been once for all delivered to the saints. The idea behind the phrase "once for all" is the concept of finality. Jesus was the complete fulfillment of the truth, and there is no more to add to it.

In verse 4, Jude tells his readers that the enemy has infiltrated the camp. The idea is that these men have subtly slithered in, escaping notice. These men came in under the guise of Christianity but distorted the message.

Jude's description of these teachers is written in strong language. It is possible, because of the deceitful tactics of the teachers, that he is denouncing men who have become respected, perhaps even leaders. Yet, Jude states, they are without God.

JUDE 5–16

Setting Up the Section

Jude wants his readers to see the true nature of false teachers so that they will not try to please them or keep them close. False teachers are not people to be reasoned with; they are a danger to the congregation and, as Jude will point out, need be avoided.

5–16

THE DESCRIPTION OF FALSE TEACHERS

In verses 5–7, Jude offers three examples of God's judgment on those who failed in contending for their faith. In doing so, he sheds light on the nature of the false teachers.

First, in verse 5, Jude refers to the redemption of the Israelites from Egypt. God delivered His children from Egypt, but after that deliverance, the people failed to believe that God would give them the land that He promised. Thus they died without entering the land (Numbers 32:10–13).

Next, in verse 6, Jude points out God's judgment on the angels. This is not a description of Satan's fall, but more likely a description of the angels in Genesis 6:1–4 who interacted with humanity and took women for wives.

Sodom and Gomorrah are Jude's third example. They committed the same sin as the angels—immorality (verse 7). The words translated *sexual immorality* here describe extreme, unbridled sexual sin.

If Jude is using these examples to describe the false teachers, then we can assume that these men were once orthodox in their faith but had fallen away from that faith and into immoral living. He assigns the fall of these men to their dreaming (verse 8). This may refer to their claims to have had visions that distort God's commands as given in scripture and thus claiming license to live immorally.

Jude tells us that the angel Michael (verse 9) did not even speak in his own authority to the devil. This is a reference to a story not included in scripture, but that was probably well-known to Jude and his readers. The story centered on who had jurisdiction over Moses' body after he died, the angel Michael or the devil. The point Jude is likely making here is that Michael did not act on his own authority even against the devil, but rather left that task to God Himself. (The words attributed to Michael here may have been drawn from Zechariah 3:2.) If Michael was this careful in how he spoke and acted, how much more so should mortal men watch their words in light of God's power? Yet these false teachers were cavalier in their attitudes, theologies, and philosophies (verse 10).

Demystifying Jude

Jude lists three more examples from the Old Testament that shed light on these false teachers (verse 11):

1) Like Cain, who offered up his sacrifice to the Lord on his own strength without faith, the false teachers try to please God on their terms and seek to do their work in the flesh (Genesis 4:1–16).
2) Like Balaam, the prophet who led the people of God astray for money, the false teachers follow their passion for wealth at the expense of the people (Numbers 22:1–34).
3) Like Korah's followers, who rebelled against Moses and were swallowed up in the earth, these teachers will be judged (Numbers 16:1–35).

In verses 12–13, Jude describes these troublesome teachers as sunken reefs (concealed danger), self-focused feasters, waterless clouds (empty promises), fruitless trees (twice dead because they came to faith, then fell away), waves carrying impurities to the beach (see Isaiah 57:20), and shooting stars that fall into the darkness.

Demystifying Jude

Verses 14–15 announce judgment by quoting 1 Enoch, a Jewish book written between the Old and New Testaments and not included in the Christian Bible. The man Enoch, however, is mentioned in Genesis 5 as the descendant of Adam through Seth, Adam's son born after Cain and Abel. One of Enoch's claims to fame is as the father of Methuselah. The other is that rather than record his death, the scriptures say that he walked with God and God simply took him from the earth (Genesis 5:18–24).

While it may seem strange to hear a New Testament writer quote from a book not included in the scriptures, it is important to remember that this book was valued by both Jude and his readers, and that the New Testament canon had not been formalized when Jude was writing this letter. Jude does not claim that it is scripture, but simply describes a scene recorded in it.

Finally, in verse 16, Jude gives a further, colorful description of the false teachers, painting them as negative, selfish men out for their own profit. Rather than men guided by the truth, they are represented more as disgruntled scam artists.

JUDE 17–23

Setting Up the Section

Up to this point Jude has been making his case against the false teachers, but here he focuses on his main point. Discernment and mercy are requirements for this community—discernment so one does not get carried away by false teaching and mercy to reach out to those who have been influenced by heresy.

17–23

THE DEFENSE AGAINST FALSE TEACHERS

In verses 17–19, Jude warns the community of danger by quoting the apostles. We can't know which of the apostles' writings Jude's readers were aware of, but we can certainly see from the New Testament scriptures available to us that the apostles often warned of false teachers (see Acts 20:29; 2 Corinthians 11:3; Colossians 2:4; 1 Timothy 4:1–3; 1 John 2:18–19).

Jude next offers five ways to stay faithful (Jude 20–22). These are not onetime events, but ongoing requirements:

1) Build yourself up in faith.
2) Pray in the Holy Spirit.
3) Stay within the love of God.
4) Wait eagerly for the return of Christ.
5) Show mercy to those unstable in their faith.

In verses 22–23, Jude addresses three different kinds of people who need to be reached: those who doubt because of false teaching, those who have gone past doubt and committed themselves to a false system, and those who are completely contaminated by heresy. All need to be reached but require different tactics.

Jude tells us to hate the garment that has been polluted by the flesh (verse 23). The garment spoken of here is the undergarment, which is closest to the body. The image of garments, both blemished and clean, appears throughout the scriptures. In the Old Testament, the law required the literal garments of a defiled person to be burned, and perhaps Jude's comment is an allusion to that custom. In both the New and Old Testaments, though, garments often were used to talk about the lifestyle of a person, laying aside the old garments in exchange for the new.

JUDE 24–25

Setting Up the Section

As Jude brings his Epistle to a close, he focuses on the sustaining power of God.

24–25

THE DOXOLOGY

God's children will survive the false teachers they face because of the person in whom they place their faith. Jesus is able to keep us from falling and help us to stand clean in His presence (verse 24). The idea behind the word *able* is the concept of power, which is the focus of these verses. God is powerful enough to protect His children's souls from the threatening sin that is in the world.

Not only will God's strength allow us to survive, but we will stand spotless before Him. Jude is describing the great work of redemption.

In his final words of praise, Jude describes God as worthy of all honor for eternity past and future (verse 25). Yet, in His completeness, He saves us, protects us, and uses us to reach out to others and share the lifesaving news of the gospel.

Take It Home

If we are going to be contenders for the faith and guard the gospel that we have been entrusted with, we must apply the survival skills that Jude offers. Are you doing what it takes to stay in the sphere of God's love? What is your attitude toward those who might be trapped in a false belief system? Will you reach out to them with mercy?

REVELATION

INTRODUCTION TO REVELATION

The word *revelation* means "unveiling," or "disclosure." This is a book that reveals how the person, righteousness, and judgment of Jesus are going to be revealed in all of the fullness and power of God.

Understanding a symbolic book like this requires putting together whole sections rather than reading select verses in isolation. The meaning of Revelation comes from unfolding the entire book chapter by chapter. The message is God's sovereignty over all.

AUTHOR

As with most New Testament books, through the centuries there has been discussion as to the author of this letter. While the writer identifies himself as John (1:1), some have wondered if it is safe to assume that this means the apostle John. Many of the arguments on this topic center around the language differences from the other New Testament books attributed to the apostle (the Gospel of John and 1 John). There has been no irrefutable evidence, though, to sway conservative scholars from accepting John's authorship.

PURPOSE

The church in the first century was suffering. Many of the original apostles had been martyred for the faith, and John had been arrested and placed in exile on the island of Patmos. The fires of persecution were burning, and the immediate future seemed to hold only increasing difficulty. The first-century Christians needed spiritual, mental, emotional, and physical stability to stand firm in their trials.

The overall purpose of this letter is to encourage those Christians. They needed to know that the kingdom of God would overcome the kingdoms of the world, and that all those who oppose God and oppress God's children would be brought to justice.

OCCASION

Since so many of the images in Revelation are often interpreted in relation to governments and political leaders, discussions about when the book was written focus on which emperor was ruling at the time. Many suggest that Nero must have been ruling, but most suggest that John wrote during the time of Domitian, which would have placed the writing of this vision letter around AD 90–95. One of the biggest supports for this date is the fact that emperor worship—which is repeatedly alluded to in John's visions—was a much greater issue during Domitian's rule than during Nero's.

THEMES

First, John's book reveals significant aspects of the character and future work of Jesus Christ, the Lamb of God.

Also, the eternality and sovereignty of God is a major theme. The idea that God is outside of time and sovereign over human history is encouraging, because we can know that He is above the things in the earth that drive us down. God is holding all things together, and therefore, no matter how much it looks like evil is winning, that is not the reality.

CONTRIBUTION TO THE BIBLE

Revelation is the only book of prophecy in the New Testament and the only book that focuses so heavily on the end times. It offers us a symbolic, but rich, vision of the end of the age that is mentioned in places in the other New Testament writings.

OUTLINE

ETERNAL HOPE 1:1–20

Greeting and Introduction 1:1–8
The Revelation of Power 1:9–20

LETTERS TO THE CHURCHES 2:1–3:22

Ephesus—Passion for Christ 2:1–7
Smyrna—Dependence upon Christ 2:8–11
Pergamum—Perseverance in the Truth 2:12–17
Thyatira—Purity of Leadership 2:18–29
Sardis—Faith That Leads to Life 3:1–6
Philadelphia—Deliverance through Trials 3:7–13
Laodicea—Dangers of a Lukewarm Faith 3:14–22

OH WORSHIP THE KING 4:1–11

The Door of Revelation 4:1
The God of Revelation 4:2–3
The Revelation of Worship 4:4–11

THE LION AND THE LAMB 5:1–14

The Scroll and the Lion 5:1–5
The Lamb and the Salvation 5:6–7
The Worship and the Praise 5:8–14

THE FOUR HORSEMEN OF THE APOCALYPSE 6:1–17

The White Horse 6:1–2
The Red Horse 6:3–4
The Black Horse 6:5–6
The Pale Horse 6:7–8
Prayer in Persecution 6:9–11
The Cosmic Disturbance 6:12–17

THE DRAMATIC PAUSE 7:1–17

The Angels and Servants 7:1–8
The Believers Are Rescued 7:9–17

THE WRATH OF GOD 8:1–13

Preparation for Justice 8:1–5
The First Four Trumpets 8:6–13

THE DAY OF THE LORD 9:1–21
More Trumpets and the First Woe 9:1–11
The Last Trumpet and the Second Woe 9:12–21

THE MESSENGER, THE MESSAGE, AND A MEAL 10:1–11
The Messenger 10:1–3
The Message 10:4–7
The Meal 10:8–11

TWO WITNESSES AND ONE LAST TRUMPET 11:1–19
The Measuring 11:1–2
The Messengers 11:3–14
The Seventh Trumpet 11:15–19

THE SEVEN SIGNS 12:1–17
The Woman and the Dragon 12:1–6
A Battle with the Enemy 12:7–17

THE ANTICHRIST AND THE FALSE PROPHET 13:1–18
The Beast's Ancestry, Authority, and Adoration 13:1–4
The Beast's Arrogance 13:5–6
The Beast's Activities and Admirers 13:7–10
The False Prophet's Presence and Purpose 13:11–14
The False Prophet's Plan 13:15–18

THE PROTECTION AND POWER OF GOD 14:1–20
The Protection 14:1–5
The Proclamations 14:6–13
The Harvest 14:14–20

PRELUDE TO DESTRUCTION 15:1–8
The Agents of Wrath 15:1–4
The Attire of Wrath 15:5–6
The Attitude of Wrath 15:7–8

THE SIX BOWLS 16:1–21
The First Six Bowls 16:1–12
Preparations for War 16:13–16
The Seventh Bowl 16:17–21

THE DESTRUCTION OF BABYLON 17:1–18

The Vision of the Prostitute 17:1–6
The Angel's Explanation 17:7–14
The Relationship between the Beast and the Prostitute 17:15–18

THE FUNERAL OF HUMANITY 18:1–24

The Warning 18:1–8
The Weeping 18:9–19
The Wrath 18:20–24

WORSHIP AND WRATH 19:1–21

Praise for the Judgment of Babylon 19:1–6
The Wedding Celebration 19:7–10
The Return of the Messiah 19:11–16
The Reign of the Messiah 19:17–21

THE COMPLETION OF THE PROMISES OF GOD 20:1–15

Satan Bound 20:1–3
Saints Ruling 20:4–6
The Completion of the Promise to the Serpent 20:7–10
The Completion of the Promise to Humanity 20:11–15

ALL THINGS BRIGHT AND BEAUTIFUL 21:1–27

The New Heaven and Earth 21:1–8
The City of God 21:9–21
The Temple, Sun, and Moon 21:22–27

EDEN RESTORED 22:1–21

The Tree of Life 22:1–5
Epilogue 22:6–21

REVELATION 1:1–20

ETERNAL HOPE

Greeting and Introduction 1:1–8
The Revelation of Power 1:9–20

Setting Up the Section

The book of Revelation, while a type of literature known as "apocalyptic" (a Greek word meaning "revelation"), is written in the form of a letter. It opens with a greeting typical for a New Testament Epistle.

John opens his letter with the truth of God's power and eternal nature. This would have been an encouragement to his readers who were facing increasing persecution for their faith. The first-century Christians needed spiritual, mental, emotional, and physical stability to stand firm in their trials. They would have been strengthened by the knowledge that God has a plan, and no matter how much it looks like evil is winning, that is not the reality.

1:1–8

GREETING AND INTRODUCTION

The first two verses of Revelation reveal three things:

1) The book is a revelation of Jesus Christ and His sovereign control of the universe.
2) John is the one who received this revelation.
3) The letter is an eyewitness account.

Verse 3 is a beatitude. In it John claims this book as a prophecy to be heard and obeyed. The word *prophecy* here does not mean a prediction of the future, though much of Revelation has to do with future events. Instead, it is prophecy in the sense that it is God's truth communicated to humankind.

Demystifying Revelation

Verse 4 begins a section of letters to seven churches in Asia. These seven churches are all located in the western part of what we know today as Turkey. They all face differing circumstances and struggle with a variety of issues. Though these letters address the specific situations of each church, all together they offer a wealth of application for the church at large today.

Letters in the first century typically had a greeting that identified the sender and the addressees. The greeting in Revelation is what theologians call a Trinitarian greeting. It starts with a description of the Father, the supreme sovereign Lord of the entire world, past, present, and future (1:4). The seven Spirits before His throne represent the Holy Spirit (1:4). And at the first part of verse 5, we have a threefold description of Jesus:

1) *The faithful witness.* Jesus was faithful in the past to carry out God's plan of redemption, and He will be faithful in the future by bringing about the plan of God for the consummation of the ages.
2) *The firstborn of the dead.* Because Jesus was faithful to the plan of God, God raised Jesus from the dead. This is the ultimate in hope for the believer, because all those who place their faith in Jesus can be assured of rising from the dead as well.
3) *The ruler of the kings of the earth.* Even though John's readers were dealing with cruel rulers, and it would seem as if these rulers were in ultimate control, Jesus has supreme control and the earth is under His rule.

At the end of verse 5 and the beginning of verse 6, John states two things about Jesus: First, He loves us and releases us from our sins by His blood. Next, He allows each true believer to be a part of the kingdom of God, and thus to be a priest to God the Father. Because of Jesus, there is no longer need for any other human mediators to connect us to God. Therefore, all believers are the object of Jesus' love, released from sin, a part of the kingdom of God, and able to pursue God directly through Jesus Christ. That is why John offers praise in the form of a doxology at the end of verse 6.

As a conclusion to the work of Jesus, John finally states that this same Jesus who loves us, releases us, includes us in the kingdom, and makes us able to serve God will also come again (1:7). Notice that at the return of Jesus the people will mourn (an allusion to Zechariah 12:10). They will be mourning the judgment that is coming as a result of their sin.

There are several titles given to God the Father in verse 8, and each conveys the depth and the strength of God:

1) *Alpha and Omega*: This statement refers to the eternal and unchanging nature of God. *Alpha* is the first letter of the Greek alphabet, and *omega* is the last. This means that God lives in an eternal state.
2) *Who is, who was, and who is to come*: God, although living outside of time, still dwells in time and therefore simultaneously interacts with those living in the present, those in the past, and those in the future.
3) *The Almighty*: This refers to the fact that God has His hand on everything and, therefore, is able to completely rule the world.

John's readers can take hope in these truths—God is the One who secures us in time and space because He is eternally secure in heaven.

1:9–20

THE REVELATION OF POWER

In verse 9, John reveals that he is writing from the island of Patmos, a place to which criminals were banished. John's crime was proclaiming the Word of God. He writes that every believer partakes of the following:

1) *Tribulation*—the trials that come when a person seeks to follow God.
2) *Kingdom*—the spiritual world that one experiences in part on earth and then experiences fully upon death.
3) *Perseverance*—the ability to persevere in the trials that come along with following Jesus.

There are some that say that the Lord's Day (1:9) is a figurative statement referring to the final judgment day (1:10). More likely it is simply the first reference to Sunday, the new day of worship (as opposed to Saturday, the Jewish Sabbath) based on Jesus' resurrection. So here, John is caught up in the spiritual world on the day commemorating Jesus' resurrection.

Demystifying Revelation

It is important to interpret John's letter of Revelation as apocalyptic literature, a type of Jewish literature that often used symbolic images to describe spiritual as well as historical realities. This vision of John is not necessarily meant to be a literal description of people and events (the Antichrist, for example, will not literally look like a "beast"), but instead it is meant to be a figurative description that bares light on the character of Jesus and the nature of the salvation He is providing. This metaphorical language happens in other passages of scripture as well, such as when Jesus calls Himself bread or a gate (see John 6:35; 10:7). We are not supposed to think that Jesus actually looked like a piece of bread, but are instead supposed to understand aspects of His character and mission from the illustration. So it is with Revelation.

In verse 10, John says he was "in the Spirit." This may imply a kind of trance, but it certainly describes a state of mind in which John was open to the Spirit's leading through visions. In this open and spiritual state of mind, John hears a voice that sounds like a trumpet. This voice instructs him to write down his vision and send it to the seven churches listed in verse 11.

Verses 12–13 introduce a new image—seven golden candlesticks, or lampstands, which represent the churches John will address. And in the midst of those candlesticks is the Son of Man.

In John's vision, Jesus' description and even position are telling. The fact that He was standing in the middle of the churches signifies that the churches belong to Him (1:13). The term *Son of Man* (Daniel 7:13–14; Revelation 1:13), when used about the Messiah, refers to the fact that Jesus not only had a divine nature but a physical body as well. John is saying that he saw a man, but not just any man—He is a God-man. Jesus' full-length robe with a golden sash was the apparel of a priest. His white hair signifies both age and wisdom. In fact, it is the same type of description used of the Ancient of Days, a reference to God Himself in Daniel 7:9. This paints the picture of someone who has the wisdom of the world because He has existed forever (Revelation 1:14).

The fire images introduced in verse 14 and continuing into verse 15 are pictures of judgment. In this vision, Jesus is looking at the world with the eyes of judgment. The feet of Christ represent the reality that Jesus can judge the earth and will execute that judgment personally. His feet are glowing with the power of justice and righteousness.

The fact that His voice sounded like roaring waters implies that Jesus spoke with authority and power (1:15; see Ezekiel 43:2). The seven stars in Jesus' hand refer to the Spirit of God at work in each of the churches, and the sword from His mouth is a symbol of God's Word with the continuing connotation of judgment (Revelation 1:16). Jesus' shining face implies His glory (1:16).

John's response to this vision is not simply a reverent bow, but rather a complete collapse caused by the overwhelming glory he has experienced. Jesus tells him not to be afraid but to remember that He is eternal ("First and Last," mirroring verse 8), resurrected, and in control (1:17–18). These are three key truths that John can cling to so that he does not need to fear for his life in the presence of Jesus.

The use of *Hades* here refers to the realm of death, which Jesus triumphs over. This is a different meaning than hell, the place of punishment.

John's role, as described in verse 19, is to describe this vision, reveal the state of the churches, and communicate the later description of the future to come.

The angels (1:20) of the churches may simply refer to the spirits of those churches as opposed to an actual type of guardian angel. It is important to note that the churches are described as lampstands—not the light itself, but that which reveals the light.

Take It Home

While Revelation is apocalyptic in nature, it is important to remember that, like any New Testament book, it serves to reveal Jesus to us. We make the most of studying this book when we stop trying to figure out the "when" of Jesus' return (which we have already been told is impossible; see Mark 13:32–36) and instead focus on who Jesus is and who we are to be in light of that revelation.

REVELATION 2:1–3:22

LETTERS TO THE CHURCHES

Ephesus—Passion for Christ	2:1–7
Smyrna—Dependence upon Christ	2:8–11
Pergamum—Perseverance in the Truth	2:12–17
Thyatira—Purity of Leadership	2:18–29
Sardis—Faith That Leads to Life	3:1–6
Philadelphia—Deliverance through Trials	3:7–13
Laodicea—Dangers of a Lukewarm Faith	3:14–22

Setting Up the Section

While some see these churches as only symbolic, it is more likely these were messages to specific congregations. What we do know about the cities addressed here meshes with the specific messages John writes. The situations of these churches vary, and thus John addresses many issues that churches face still today.

These letters do not represent a collection of letters that were once circulated separately, but were from the beginning part of the book of Revelation. The whole book was meant to circulate among the seven churches.

2:1–7

EPHESUS—PASSION FOR CHRIST

The church at Ephesus is committed to doctrinal purity; the believers have persisted as disciples of Jesus (2:1–3). Yet their love for doctrine and truth is stronger than their passion for the person of Jesus (2:4). The concept of not staying true to their first love may include not only their love for Jesus, but also their love for each other, which is to mirror their love for Jesus.

Demystifying Revelation

The Ephesus of John's day was the most important city in the Roman province of Asia, located in what is today western Turkey. It was home to 250,000–500,000 people. Because it stood at the crossroad of many trade routes, it was an eclectic city with many religions present.

The apostle Paul spent more than two years in Ephesus establishing this church. The New Testament book of Ephesians is his letter to the congregation. According to tradition, Ephesus is where John spent his later years.

The Ephesian church receives two commands (2:5):

1) They must consider how far they have fallen.
2) They must repent.

If they don't comply, Jesus will pronounce judgment, and their effectiveness as a church of God will be lost (2:5).

The Ephesian church is credited for standing against the Nicolaitans. All that is known of this group is found here. While it is clear from this passage that the Nicolaitans represent a heresy, we have only speculations as to the origin and specifics. Some have argued that this was a heresy spawned from Nicolas, one of the seven servants chosen to serve the widows in the Jerusalem church (Acts 6), who later fell into heresy and used his position to lead many astray. Others think that this group is not associated with Nicolas and just used his name to gain credibility.

This letter to Ephesus ends with "The one who has an ear. . ." (Revelation 2:7 NET), a statement used throughout these letters to the churches. It means that if anyone understands the real meaning of what he or she hears, then he or she must respond.

While the close of verse 7 refers back to the tree of life from the Garden of Eden (Genesis 3:24), God's paradise refers to the future when God restores heaven and earth from the fall of humanity.

2:8–11

SMYRNA—DEPENDENCE UPON CHRIST

Jesus addresses this church from His role as the resurrected One. He identifies them by the distresses they have experienced—suffering, poverty, and slander. Christianity was outlawed at the time John was writing and was particularly held in contempt in a place known for its loyalty and worship of the emperor.

Demystifying Revelation

Smyrna was a beautiful city with much trade based on a well-protected harbor. It had been destroyed and rebuilt before 200 BC. After that, it was rebuilt according to a plan, much as a planned community today. Most likely, the church in Smyrna was a product of Paul's Ephesian ministry (Acts 19:10) and was founded by the apostle himself or one of his converts. At the end of the first century, life was difficult and dangerous for Christians in Smyrna. As a loyal Roman ally, the city was a key center for emperor worship, so any other religious loyalties could easily be perceived as political threats.

In Revelation 2:9, John makes reference to those who call themselves Jews but are not. What he means is that, in light of the revelation of Jesus, being a Jew has more to do with how a person lives than with his heritage or bloodline. This is key to one's interpretation of John's writing in Revelation. One who understands John's use of the Jewish nation to mean the new nation of faith—the church—will interpret passages relating to the Jews as symbolically to be about the church as a whole. How one chooses to interpret this affects many portions of this book.

In light of the persecution of the day, the reference to prison in verse 10 may infer more than simple containment. It may be a reference to a type of holding cell where a detainee awaits execution (2:10). The mention of ten days would have been understood by John's original readers as an allusion to Daniel's request to be tested for ten days in order to see that God's commands regarding food would make him and his cohorts stronger than the rest of the men taken to Babylon (Daniel 1:12–15). This was a test that proved God faithful, as would the test of the Smyrnaeans.

Jesus wants this congregation to be faithful until death so that they may receive the crown of life. The word translated *crown* here is not a king's crown, but the winning wreath given to the winner of a game. In the case of the Smyrnaeans, if they persevere in the midst of their difficulties, they will not be hurt by the second death—in other words, they will be the ultimate victors over hell (the second death [Revelation 2:10–11]).

2:12–17

PERGAMUM—PERSEVERANCE IN THE TRUTH

In the letter to the church at Pergamum, Jesus is described as the One with a sword in His mouth, an image that symbolizes the Word of God. This symbol may have had multiple meanings to John's original readers in that the sword also served as a symbol of Rome. In light of that fact, this image could serve as a reminder that Jesus' authority exceeds any earthly power (2:12).

Demystifying Revelation

Pergamum was about a hundred miles north of Ephesus, with Smyrna located about halfway in between. As Asia's ancient capital, it was considered Asia's greatest city, not because of its position on trade routes but because of its governmental standing. It was a city with many pagan practices, renowned for its altar to the god Zeus as well as multiple temples to the emperor.

The people in this church remained true to Christ in the face of great temptation. The believers did not give in to the emperor worship that was rampant, but instead they remained true even in the face of martyrdom. No additional information is given about Antipas's identity, but it's obvious from verse 13 that he was faithful even in death.

The reference to Satan is a reminder that their persecution is a product of spiritual warfare rather than simple governmental persecution (2:13).

The accusation against this church is that they allowed false teachers to exist in their presence (2:14). The references to Balaam and Balak are from an Old Testament account in which a king named Balak tried to hire a prophet named Balaam to curse the Israelites. When Balaam's attempt failed (Numbers 22–24), he instructed Balak to tempt the Israelites to forsake their religious commitments so the ensuing consequences would have the same effect as a curse (Numbers 31:15–16). Both behaviors listed here in Revelation 2:14—food sacrificed to idols and sexual immorality—were related to idol worship.

The reference to the Nicolaitans offers no more explanatory information than in the previous letter to the church at Ephesus (2:6). In this case, though, there seems to be a possible connection to the idol worship mentioned in connection with Balaam (2:14–15).

Jesus calls the church to repent, at the risk of war if they don't, thus the apt vision with the sword—an image of God's Word, but also a military weapon (2:16). On the other hand, if this church prevails against their sin, they will have hidden manna (2:17). This refers to the manna that was hidden in the ark of the covenant by Moses, one of the most precious relics of the ancient Jews.

Demystifying Revelation

The white stone in verse 17 may refer to an invitation. In the Roman culture, a white stone was given to the winner of a competition. The stone had the winner's name inscribed on it, and it was used to get the winner into the awards banquet. The party that these believers are going to will be "by invitation only," and they will receive this stone as the invitation. On it will be a new name that no one knows.

In the Greek culture there was a thought that the gods all had secret names in which their powers were kept. Jesus may be using that imagery to illustrate that they will have a name that has power to it, and this name is hidden from the world. It is a name that has to be revealed. This name is given to the people as their new name because they are given a new life in Jesus Christ.

2:18–29

THYATIRA—PURITY OF LEADERSHIP

Opening the letter to the church at Thyatira is a vision of Jesus similar to the description given in chapter 1 of Revelation. This vision of Jesus' eyes and feet highlights His all-knowing nature and His commitment to hunt down and conquer evil (1:14–15; 2:18).

While this church's good works are acknowledged, the church is also accused of tolerating Jezebel (2:19–20). This is probably an alias John uses for this troublesome woman, relating her to the wicked queen of the Old Testament by the same name

(1 Kings 16:30–31). This woman's teaching pulls people away from the Word of God to immorality and idolatry. On one hand, this church has people who are serving God in a strong fashion. On the other hand, they have allowed a false teacher in their midst to lead them astray (Revelation 2:20).

Demystifying Revelation

Many speculate that the church at Thyatira was founded somehow through Paul's ministry in Ephesus. At the time of the writing of Revelation, the city of Thyatira was entering its greatest season of prosperity. As a Roman outpost city, it served a purpose of protecting the Roman Empire from invading forces from the north. The various businesses were divided into guilds that all had their own gods. In order to do business in the city, a person had to go through a guild. Thus, before business was conducted, one would have to perform the worship customs of the god of the guild.

Verses 21–23 reveal how God deals with evil. Those who follow this woman will join her in illness and suffering as an added prompt toward their repentance.

There are those in Thyatira who have not succumbed to Jezebel's false teaching, and they are commended (2:24–25). The additional burden that will not be added to them probably refers to anything further than the service they have already been called to as disciples of Jesus (2:24). The reward for their perseverance, though, will be authority in Jesus' name (2:26).

The iron rod probably refers to a shepherd's implement with a metal tip (2:27). While a shepherd is a gentle leader, he maintains ultimate control over his flock. This image coupled with the image of the clay jars broken to pieces implies judgment. This may mean that the authority given to the faithful will be participation in Jesus' final judgment.

The morning star, also a reward given to the faithful by Jesus, refers to the power of a new life, the resurrected life that Christ had shown when He rose from the dead (2:28).

3:1–6

SARDIS—FAITH THAT LEADS TO LIFE

Unlike the preceding churches, the judgment against the church at Sardis appears in the first verse of the address. It is a church that thinks it is alive, but in all reality it is dead (3:1). Sardis, the city, had twice been overtaken by enemies because of its failure to remain on watch. So it seems apt that the command offered to the Christian church in that city is to wake up (3:2).

The church of Sardis has a noticeable difference from the other churches addressed so far. All of the other churches have some corrupt people but others who are faithful. In this case, the faithful are in the minority (3:3–5).

Demystifying Revelation

Sardis was a wealthy city full of gold taken from the nearby Pactolus River. The city was located on a high hill at the intersection of five roads. Like the other cities addressed in Revelation 2–3, the church of Sardis was probably founded through Paul's ministry in Ephesus.

Through the years there have been a variety of meanings suggested for the white clothing mentioned in verse 4. Most likely, the white clothes represent justification through faith in Jesus. These few faithful individuals mentioned here have done nothing to forfeit that justification, thus staining their clothes (3:4). Also, they will be confessed before the Father, which means they will be acknowledged as belonging to Jesus and thus allowed to enter into heaven (3:5).

Finally, they will not have their name erased. Some people think that this is a reference to them not losing their salvation, but that is not the case. In some ancient cities, everyone had their name in a book, and when they died their name was crossed out or erased from the book. Jesus is saying that those who overcome will not have their names erased, because they will never die. Eternal life is their destiny.

3:7–13

PHILADELPHIA—DELIVERANCE THROUGH TRIALS

The descriptions in verse 7 apply to Jesus. He is described as the One who has the key of David, meaning He has all authority. Though Jesus' reference to an open door can be interpreted in a variety of ways, the fact that no one can shut the door is an obvious reference to the fact that no one can undo what He decrees (3:7–8).

The Jews will bow before the believers in this city as a testimony to the reality that Jesus is the Messiah (3:9). The implication is that with the life and death of Jesus, the definition of God's chosen people has changed. No longer is it simply a matter of family heritage, but of faith in Jesus.

Demystifying Revelation

Little is known about the church of Philadelphia apart from this passage. Like most of the other churches, it was probably founded through Paul's ministry to Ephesus. One interesting note is that this church lasted for centuries. The people stood firm in the face of major persecution.

The church at Philadelphia will be protected from the testing that will come. This may mean they will escape trials, but it can also mean that Jesus will see them through the trials they face. They will have protection from all of the evil that will come to the earth (3:10).

The crown mentioned in verse 11 is not a crown of royalty, but a crown of victory, much like the garlands or wreaths worn by the winners of an Olympic competition.

The comparison of one who conquers to a pillar in verse 12 is a reference to strength. Earthquakes were common in this region. Typically, the pillar of a building was all that remained after a quake. Because of this, a pillar is an excellent image for something that will remain secure no matter what happens around it.

Critical Observation

While later in Revelation John writes that there will be no temple in heaven, in verse 12 he refers to the temple. This is a reminder that John is recording a series of symbolic visions. Each image stands alone, supporting a specific point of truth. To find apparent inconsistencies between those visions is only to recognize that they, indeed, are separate.

The believers described in Philadelphia, those who will be kept through testing, will have three names written on them: the name of God, New Jerusalem, and Jesus. This means they will be claimed by these three things. In their earthly lives they may have been insignificant, but in heaven they will be members of the New Jerusalem.

3:14–22

LAODICEA—DANGERS OF A LUKEWARM FAITH

In the opening of the letter to the church at Laodicea, several names are used for Jesus that have not been used yet in Revelation. All three stress His authority.

The judgment against this church is that they are lukewarm (Revelation 3:15). The water supply to Laodicea came from a hot spring, so the water in the city was indeed lukewarm. In this case, of course, it is the spiritual condition of the church that is being described. Rather than denying Christ, they made an empty profession. According to verse 16, this is nauseating to God.

Demystifying Revelation

Laodicea was an economic banking center for Asia. Due to its location, it became a major financial site for the Roman Empire. The city was famous for the soft black wool it produced. Laodicea was also known as an important center of ancient medicine. The nearby temple of the Phrygian god Men Karou had an important medical school associated with it. That school was most famous for developing an eye salve, which was exported all over the Greco-Roman world. All three of these industries (clothing, banking, and eye medicine) are used in Jesus' condemnation.

Verse 17 further carries the charge against this church, declaring that these people claimed to need nothing, yet they were poor, blind, and naked. These three assertions were direct hits at the industry of the Laodiceans: banking, medicine, and clothing. Banks cannot remove the bankruptcy of the soul. Wool cannot cover the nakedness of sin. Eye salve cannot remove the blindness toward the gospel. Thus, to trust in the things of the world is foolish. According to verse 18, only Christ can actually take care of spiritual poverty, blindness, and nakedness.

Verse 19 echoes a truth found elsewhere in the New Testament—God disciplines those He loves. The repentance referred to here is not an ongoing daily repentance, but a once-for-all, turning-from-your-old-ways kind of change.

Verse 20 is a well-known verse, including a word picture of Jesus asking to be let in. The words translated "share a meal" (NET) do not refer to a meal shared with a stranger, but with a meal shared among friends who know each other well.

The reward offered in verse 21 is unlike the wreaths or crowns already mentioned that are given to winners of a competition. Instead, this is the offer to rule with Jesus.

REVELATION 4:1–11

OH WORSHIP THE KING

The Door of Revelation	4:1
The God of Revelation	4:2–3
The Revelation of Worship	4:4–11

Setting Up the Section

From this point on, John's writing transitions from the letters to the church to the vision of heaven. He begins with a vision of God Himself.

4:1

THE DOOR OF REVELATION

Verse 1 opens with an introductory phrase that John often uses in Revelation to begin a new vision—"After this I looked. . ." (NIV).

The door of verse 1 is the third door mentioned in Revelation. The first is the door of opportunity in Philadelphia. The second is the door of fellowship in Laodicea. This door is one of revelation. John is going to pass through a door that will allow him to see the God of the universe and all of the glory that controls the world.

The voice that sounded like a trumpet is the voice of Jesus calling John into the vision. Notice that the revelation Jesus is about to reveal is of things that *must* happen. They are certain.

4:2–3

THE GOD OF REVELATION

John saw the throne of the Almighty (4:2). His description of the throne is not meant to be literal. The images are used to describe the meaning of the throne. This symbolic language describes the universe from a heavenly point of view.

John describes God by using the names of jewels. Different versions of the Bible translate these names differently (jasper, carnelian, diamonds, rubies, etc.). Also, we can't be sure if the ancients used the same names for precious and semiprecious stones that we use today. Nevertheless, the importance of John's description is in the images of beauty and value that are attributed to God. John gives no literal, physical description of God, because God cannot be described. Instead, the character and nature of God are described, because that is what anyone could ever see of God (4:3).

There was a rainbow, or a halo, around the throne. This is reminiscent of the rainbow that signified the eternal covenant that God made with Noah (Genesis 9:12–13; Revelation 4:3).

4:4–11

THE REVELATION OF WORSHIP

In verses 4 and 5, John paints a picture of worship. The first picture is twenty-four elders sitting on thrones around God. There are many interpretations of this picture, ranging from the elders as a special class of angels to the elders as the church before God.

For those who make a case that these elders represent the church, John's description, then, is of the redeemed—they have white robes (19:8), they are wearing crowns (James 1:12), and they reign with God (2 Timothy 2:12). Why are there twenty-four? Some say there were twenty-four priests that represented the entire nation of Israel. And some have said that the elders represent the twelve tribes plus the twelve apostles. Each interpretation includes its own difficulties. However the specifics are interpreted, this vision reveals the majesty of worship.

Critical Observation

The key to understanding the picture painted of the throne of God in Revelation 4:5 is the account of the Jews at Mount Sinai in Exodus 19. When God descended upon the mountain, it shook with thunder and lightning. All of this was a picture of the holiness of God. John is telling us in this passage that God is holy and His holiness reigns in heaven.

John also sees seven lamps of fire. Unlike the lampstands mentioned in Revelation 1:12–13, these are outdoor torches. John identifies these torches as the seven Spirits of God, a phrase that denotes the Holy Spirit (see Zechariah 4:1–10).

Since there is no sea in heaven (Revelation 21:1), the body of water mentioned in verse 6 is not a literal sea. Instead, it is a descriptive term showcasing the brilliance of heaven. Today a clear glass or a large mirror is easy to come by. In John's day, though, a large glass as clear as crystal was an extravagance beyond imagination. This points to the immense glory and power of the One who sits on the throne.

There are also living creatures centered around the throne (4:6). Their positions suggest both their closeness to God and the fact that they attend to Him. One general description that covers all of the creatures is that they are full of eyes both front and behind. Eyes are used for seeing, and thus these angels are aware of what is all around them. Some have suggested that the creatures are cherubim, but this is not known for certain.

According to verse 7, each of these creatures has a different face: lion, calf, man, and eagle. Each symbol shows that all of creation is represented before the throne, and thus all of creation is worshiping God. Creation's purpose is to bring glory to God.

These creatures, representative of the creation of God, call out God's holiness. They repeat the word *holy* three times, emphasizing that God is holy. They also acknowledge that God is almighty and eternal; He began all things, and He will bring all things to a conclusion.

Verses 9–11 offer a picture of worship. The angels give glory, honor, and thanks to the One who sits on the throne. To give someone glory is to put that person on display. To honor is to praise someone for what he or she has done. To give thanks is more than simply recognizing an attribute of someone, but to go one step further and be grateful for who that person is or what he or she has done. The heart of the worship is centered on displaying God, acknowledging His attributes, and thanking Him for what He has done.

In addition to the angels, the elders also worship. They fall before God in reverence and lay their crowns before Him. All of their actions—throwing themselves down, offering crowns—communicate God's greatness. They are placing themselves below Him. This indicates that they do not look at God as a peer; instead, they see themselves as His servants. When they fall before God, they offer up words of praise.

Take It Home

The elders' song of worship gives words to their actions and acknowledges God as the source of all creation. There is no way to understand the judgment of God without understanding that God is the center of the universe. Everything bows to Him, putting Him in the position of granting His approval to all He has created. Giving that approval, or not, is the act of judgment.

REVELATION 5:1–14

THE LION AND THE LAMB

The Scroll and the Lion	5:1–5
The Lamb and the Salvation	5:6–7
The Worship and the Praise	5:8–14

Setting Up the Section

In chapter 5, John's visions transition from God the Creator to Jesus the Redeemer. Here the nature of Jesus will come into view when we see the final judgment of the world taking place. Jesus will be the Judge; thus He is called the Lion. Yet Jesus is also the Savior of the world; thus He is called the Lamb. As the Lamb, He took the sin of humanity so that they might stand redeemed before God.

5:1–5

THE SCROLL AND THE LION

The scroll John describes has seven seals. Sealing a scroll was not an unusual practice. Some scrolls may have had seven seals on the outside that had to be broken in order to unroll the parchment. In this case, though, it seems the seals open each section of the scroll. The angel is looking for someone worthy to open the scroll, read it, and carry out the plan of God (5:1–2).

When no one could be found to break the seals, John weeps (5:4). The kind of weeping described here is a loud, wailing grief.

While John reveals in verse 1 that the scroll is in the hand of the person sitting on the throne, it seems that he doesn't fully see that person until verse 6. John has seen a vision of Jesus but not the revelation of Jesus that the elder is referring to. This elder begins to explain to John that Jesus is the One who is worthy to open the scroll.

The phrase "Lion of the tribe of Judah" is found only here in the Bible. In Genesis 49:9, Jacob speaks a prophecy over each of his sons. When he speaks of Judah, he refers to him as a lion cub. Jesus, of course, finds His ancestry in the tribe of Judah.

The "root of David" means that Jesus was born into the family line of David. Both Matthew and Luke give genealogies of Jesus, tracing Him through David's bloodline (Matthew 1; Luke 3).

5:6–7

THE LAMB AND THE SALVATION

The lamb that appears to have been killed symbolizes Jesus' crucifixion (5:6). The fact that the lamb has seven horns and eyes suggests completeness. The number seven often carries that connotation in the Bible.

Horns are often a symbol of power; most powerful animals have horns. In this image, then, Jesus is represented as the One who possesses complete power.

In the same way, the seven eyes represent complete vision. According to the text here, these eyes are the seven Spirits of God. While this may be a reference to the Holy Spirit, it is more likely this all-seeing attribute is credited to Jesus.

Critical Observation

The lamb is the meekest of animals, the least fierce, and evokes the least amount of fear. Yet, it was through becoming a Lamb that Jesus conquered. Jesus proved His strength by being meek. The triumph of God does not come through power, but rather through love and meekness.

The end of verse 7 is the high point of John's vision—the Son of God takes the scroll from the hand of God. This means that the plan of God is ready to be carried out, and the person of Jesus Christ is the One who will implement the plan.

5:8–14

THE WORSHIP AND THE PRAISE

The elders and the creatures fall down in worship of Jesus. The only appropriate response to this moment is praise. In this case, the instruments and implements they use are harps and bowls of incense (5:8).

Harps, possibly small lyres, are often associated with worship in Revelation. The bowls with incense symbolize the prayers of the saints who have been under the persecution of evil in the world and as a result of the persecution have been killed (6:10).

As with so many new things in Revelation, the elders and creatures are singing a new song (5:9). In this case, new is not a chronological designation but more so the quality of the song. This song is meant for this particular situation, not simply reused from another. The song celebrates the fact that Jesus is worthy to take the scroll. He is the One to accomplish the plan of God—dying for people from every nation in the world. Not only did Jesus die to bring humanity to God, but He also enabled believers to stand before God holy and just.

In both verses 9 and 10, the song acknowledges that the redeemed belong to God. In verse 10, they are appointed as a kingdom and as priests. This is similar to John's greeting in Revelation 1:6.

In verse 11, John's vision widens so that he sees and hears innumerable voices as one voice singing. His numbers are not meant to be equations of a specific number, but are instead a description of the vastness of those in the vision. The song itself claims Jesus' worthiness, as does the song in verses 9–10. The first four descriptive words are qualities of Jesus: power, wealth, wisdom, and might. The last three describe the response to Jesus: honor, glory, and praise (5:12).

Then, added to the innumerable amount of worshipers, every creature joins in the singing (5:13). The final "Amen" is added by the elders who began the song in verse 9. There is no distinction drawn in their worship between the One sitting on the throne (God) and the Lamb (Jesus). They worship them as one.

REVELATION 6:1–17

THE FOUR HORSEMEN OF THE APOCALYPSE

The White Horse	6:1–2
The Red Horse	6:3–4
The Black Horse	6:5–6
The Pale Horse	6:7–8
Prayer in Persecution	6:9–11
The Cosmic Disturbance	6:12–17

Setting Up the Section

Beginning in chapter 6, and continuing into chapters 7 and 8, the scroll is unrolled and its seals are broken. Rather than reading the scroll, John experiences it in visions.

The unrolling of the scroll marks the judgment of God upon the earth—justice brought to the world. The first four seals on the scroll reveal the sin of humanity unleashed on the earth.

6:1–2

THE WHITE HORSE

Jesus, the Lamb, breaks the first seal on the scroll, at which point one of the four creatures shouts an invitation to come (6:1). This invitation is not directed to John, but to the white horse and the first horseman. This horseman holds a bow and is given a crown. As in Revelation 2:10, this is a crown of victory rather than royalty. The implication, of course, is that this horseman will find victory in his efforts.

This horse and rider serve the purpose of conquering. The idea here is simple: The first judgment that must come to humanity before the final consummation of the ages is that of military conquering. There are three popular views as to who will conquer or be conquered:

1) This horse represents Christ and the gospel in the world.
2) This horse represents the Antichrist.
3) This horse represents the spirit of conquest, or military figures.

We cannot know for certain, but we can note that the bow seems a significant part of the vision, and that a bow is not a typical Roman weapon. So this vision has implications beyond a political statement regarding the Roman Empire. This is a vision of a conqueror and destruction.

Critical Observation

Some associate this first vision with one group of warriors in John's day who were known for using bows—the Parthians. They were a feared group of warriors who tormented much of the East and Middle East for hundreds of years. The Parthians were noted for two things: their horsemanship and their skilled archery. They would ride into a city, shoot their arrows with deadly accuracy, and then ride out so fast they could not be killed. They rode white horses that they trained to jump and maneuver in incredible ways.

While John's vision is probably not intended to be this specific (one army or one country), the Parthians may have been the closest comparable image for John's original readers.

6:3–4

THE RED HORSE

As with the first seal, the Lamb opens the second seal, and the second creature offers the same invitation to the next horseman to come (6:3).

The power to remove the peace that is on the earth is granted to this horseman on a red horse. Since God is sovereign over all things, it is He who grants the permission. The imagery here is not that this horseman does the butchering, but that he removes peace, and without that peace, humans butcher one another. The great sword is the image of the machines of war being unleashed on the earth, acted out by people left to their own devices without any divine intervention.

6:5–6

THE BLACK HORSE

With the next seal broken by the Lamb and the next invitation from the third creature, a horseman rides in on a black horse with a scale in his hand. Since verse 6 reveals the exorbitant prices of wheat and barley, this horseman symbolizes famine. The scale is for measuring out food.

The announcement in verse 6 is not ascribed to any one of the four creatures. In fact, the announcement itself is only said to have been like a voice from among the creatures.

A quart of wheat was what one person needed in a day. According to the prices called out in verse 6, a person would work all day to simply get the grain that he or she needed. If there was one income for a family, the problem was obvious. In addition, barley was used by the poor to mix with their wheat to make it go further. According to the information given in verse 6, the market prices were well beyond what anyone could afford.

The oil and the wine were protected. These are basic ingredients for cooking and for purification. We see that they have been left out of the judgment, but no reason is offered for this. Because the olive trees and grape vines are still producing, this famine will affect the poor, but some will survive.

6:7–8

THE PALE HORSE

The fourth horse and rider, also summoned by the Lamb breaking the seal and the voice of a creature, is described as pale, or ashen. This signifies a pale green color, the color of a corpse.

This horseman is not holding a weapon of any kind, but his name is Death, and he is followed by Hades, the place of departed spirits. As with the third horseman, permission is given for the destruction to take place involving 25 percent of the earth. This destruction will come by a variety of means.

6:9–11

PRAYER IN PERSECUTION

The next seal marks a change. The first four reflect the coming of a particular kind of destruction. The fifth involves the prayers of a particular group of people—the persecuted (6:9).

The first evidence of the difference between this seal and the four preceding is that no one summoned the vision. In the first four seals, one of the living creatures called "Come," and the horsemen came. For the fifth seal, John simply notices the souls who have been violently killed for their faith.

These souls are under an altar—they are already dead. They have been persecuted to death. John gives two reasons why these souls have been killed: (1) because of the Word of God and (2) because of the testimony they had been given by Jesus.

The Word of God refers to the message of the scriptures (6:9). The central message is the redemptive work of Jesus Christ. The testimony that these souls maintained refers to the active and verbal faith that they lived out in the world. These people were distinctively Christian, and they were killed because of it. The lives of these people became offerings of worship; thus they are under the altar.

While their persecution is a reality, the focus is on their prayers for justice (6:10). Sin is running rampant, and many people are being killed for their faith in Jesus Christ. Those who have been killed want justice. In light of the teachings throughout the scriptures about vengeance and its place in God's hands (not humanity's), it would be a mistake to understand the prayers of these souls as merely a cry for revenge. It is, rather, a cry for God to rule. This is a prayer that longs to see the power in the hands of the One who rightfully controls the universe. The souls even address God as *sovereign*, a term often used for the master of slaves. They recognize His power and authority.

The answer to their prayers comes in two parts. The first part is in God rewarding them for their sacrifices. Their reward is rest. Once dead they are allowed to enjoy the peace of heaven. The other part of their reward includes a long white robe, which probably represents victory as it does in the vision of the white horse of the first seal (6:1–2).

They are told to rest until the "full number" (NET) of martyrs was reached. This does not imply that God has a certain quota of martyrs that have to die before He will enact His justice, but it does reveal the reality that more people will be sacrificing their lives for Him (6:11).

6:12–17

THE COSMIC DISTURBANCE

There are two parts to the disturbance of the sixth seal: first, the cosmic light show and, second, the response of the people.

The reason the sun and moon are both a part of this vision is that God is going to move at the same time all over the world; in some places it will be night and in other places it will be day. Notice the sun will be black as sackcloth. This is a reference to the black sackcloth worn by mourners. The garments were made out of the hair of black goats, so they were naturally very dark. If the sun ever became that dark, there would be no light. Without light, the entire world will be disoriented.

Critical Observation

Keep in mind that John's visions are not the first his readers have heard of the apocalypse. Jesus Himself spoke of terrible events at the end of the world (Matthew 24; Mark 13; Luke 12). The Old Testament prophets offered their own apocalyptic visions as well (Joel 2:11, 31; Zephaniah 1:14, 18; 2:2). It is quite likely that John's readers made a connection between his visions recorded here and the teachings of Jesus and the prophets. Rather than new and disturbing images, John is likely describing a confirmation of God's sovereignty from the ancient days to the ultimate future.

If the sun goes away, the natural fallout will be that the light given from the moon will also cease to exist, since it merely reflects the sun's light. John records that the moon looks like blood (6:12). The idea is that there is a covering of the moon to such a degree that it will give no light. Instead, there will be darkness and the moon will look as if it has been covered in blood. Remember that blood is maroon in color when in large quantities, so this describes a darkening of the moon more than a reddening of it.

The two images of sackcloth and blood are meant to convey the destruction that is coming. Blood symbolizes death, and sackcloth represents the mourning that comes along with it.

There are two ways in which the word *stars* can be translated in verse 13. It could mean the actual stars in the sky falling, but it more likely refers to meteors falling from the sky to the earth. While some have interpreted the result of the falling stars as a violent effect, like an earthquake, the illustration John actually gives is of ripe figs that easily fall when the wind shakes their limbs.

Verse 14 paints the picture of the sky opening up so that the atmosphere, the blue canopy that is over the earth, will split open and form a hole. Then verse 15 indicates that these events will affect everyone on earth and cause widespread panic. Verse 16 reveals the hopelessness of the situation. It is clear that no person has control of his or her own fate. Each is at the mercy of the powerful sovereignty of heaven and earth (6:17).

REVELATION 7:1–17

THE DRAMATIC PAUSE

The Angels and Servants 7:1–8
The Believers Are Rescued 7:9–17

Setting Up the Section

Chapter 7 describes a pause between the sixth and seventh seal. This pause sets up the events just prior to the wrath of God being poured out on the earth. It is a moment God stops the clock to provide divine protection.

7:1–8

THE ANGELS AND SERVANTS

John describes four angels holding back the wind (7:1). The fact that they are standing at the four corners of the earth implies that they cover the whole earth.

To this point, John has not described any winds that need to be held back, so these angels may be holding back all that was released in the first four seals. At the least, they are stopping the natural order of the world. The sun is not shining, the stars are not shining, meteors are falling to the earth, and now the wind has stopped blowing.

In verse 2, another angel ascends and carries the seal of God's ownership. This angel instructs the four angels holding the wind to hold back their damage until the servants (slaves) of God are identified by a seal on their foreheads (7:3). This seal will mark them so that they will not be hurt during the judgment of God.

Critical Observation

According to Revelation 14:1–5, the servants marked with a seal are those who have kept themselves pure, followed the Lamb, been purchased by God, and been offered as firstfruits.

Many interpreters of Revelation hold that the 144,000 people represent Israel. Keep in mind, though, that John is sending this letter to dispersed Christians, not all of whom are Jewish. Also, keep in mind that John has made statements elsewhere that can be interpreted to mean that God's chosen people are no longer determined by heritage or ancestry, but by faith (2:9; 3:9). In light of this, others interpret this 144,000 as the faithful of the Christian church.

Verses 5–8 provide a list of the tribes of Israel. These lists are based on the sons of Jacob (whose name was later changed to Israel). While the tribes are usually listed in order of the age of the sons, in this case Judah is listed first, though Judah was not the oldest son. This is significant in that Jesus is from the tribe of Judah. This may have been intentional on John's part, though it is difficult to find an intentional meaning in the order of the rest of the list.

A tribe is missing from this list—Dan. Some say this is because of the idolatry engaged in by that tribe.

7:9–17

THE BELIEVERS ARE RESCUED

What follows is John's vision of an amazing and diverse crowd in the serenity of heaven. Many think this refers to the Rapture, when God removes His church from the world. Others believe it refers to those who have been killed during the unleashing of evil. Regardless, these are people who have come from the world and are now rescued from their misery and are in the presence of the Lord (7:9).

These people are worshiping the Lamb. Their long white robes are more akin to glorious celebration than everyday clothing. The palm branches they wave are typical symbols of triumph (7:9). They are worshiping the Lord because of the salvation He has given (7:10). All the angels worship as well, proclaiming their own doxology to God (7:11–12).

In verses 13–14, an elder both asks and answers the question of the identity of this throng in white robes. His answer includes the now familiar phrase "great tribulation." This could mean simply the ongoing tribulation that these people have faced on earth, as opposed to the specific period now referred to as "the Tribulation." Undoubtedly these are the redeemed, because their robes have been washed clean in Jesus' blood.

The elder's description continues in verses 15–17 with the fate that awaits these worshipers. They will be provided for, and even shepherded, by the Lamb. Reminiscent of Psalm 23, Jesus will provide for them, and the sorrows and difficulties of this life will be left behind.

Take It Home

We can be encouraged by this vision in two ways. It signifies the following:

1) Believers will not face the wrath of God.

2) Enduring trials for our faith here in this life will not be forgotten in eternity.

For John's original readers facing persecution, this would have been a precious thought. For contemporary readers, it offers an eternal perspective in the midst of the suffering we face.

REVELATION 8:1–13

THE WRATH OF GOD

Preparation for Justice 8:1–5
The First Four Trumpets 8:6–13

Setting Up the Section

What we have here is the beginning of the wrath of God. The judgment of Jesus is going to be carried out. This is the great moment of justice that suffering believers have been praying for.

8:1–5

PREPARATION FOR JUSTICE

In John's vision, God is about to deal with the sin that is in the world. At the opening of the seventh seal, the response is silence (8:1). And a new vision begins.

The seven angels in verse 2 are specific angels. They are those who stand before God. And in this case, they are the ones with the responsibility of carrying out justice on the earth. The trumpets symbolize the instruments of that judgment (8:2).

Critical Observation

The difference between the seventh seal and the former seals is who is implementing the punishment. During chapters 6 and 7, humankind and nature are having their way. During this vision of the trumpets, it is the angels who have been given the role of executing the judgment of God on earth.

Verse 3 is a dramatic image of the prayers of the saints ascending into heaven. In 5:8 the incense embodies the prayers of the saints, but that is not case here in chapter 8. In chapter 5, prayers for justice are given to God from the martyred saints. The idea here is that all of the prayers for justice are given to God so that God can answer them all. He is going to begin the process of retribution for the persecution of the church.

In verse 4, the prayers ascend from the angel's hand. Heaven and earth are united in this request. And in verse 5, fire from the altar is added and the prayers are empowered. This can be seen as a picture of the power of God added to the prayers.

8:6–13

THE FIRST FOUR TRUMPETS

As with the seals, the first four trumpets are distinguished from the last three. In this case, the first four are concerned with natural events and the last three with people. The trumpets are distinguished from the seals in that the trumpets are God's intervention rather than the world's actions upon itself. These trumpets do not describe the final judgment. In each case, only part of the world is affected. To John's original readers, though, they are reminders that God will indeed deal with sin.

- THE FIRST TRUMPET (8:6–7): The angels prepare to blow the trumpets, but only the first trumpet is sounded, followed by hail and fire mixed with blood. One-third of the earth is burned. In this case, *one-third* may not mean an exact amount, but instead may be a way of saying that a portion of the earth was affected, but not the majority.

Critical Observation

Each of John's visions stands somewhat on its own. An example is the first trumpet (8:7), in which one-third of the grass and trees are destroyed. Then in the account of the fifth trumpet, God commands that the grass not be destroyed (9:4). Revelation is best understood when it is read as a series of apocalyptic visions each standing on its own. While similar elements may appear in the visions, they are not meant to be treated as scientific facts that should be paralleled and measured. This is a vision, much akin to a dream—truth told in images for a first-century audience. These visions communicate over and over, in a variety of ways, that God will deal with sin in the end.

- **The Second Trumpet** (8:8–9): At the blowing of the second trumpet, something like a mountain of fire is thrown into the sea. We are not told exactly who did the throwing. This time a third of the sea becomes blood and a third of the creatures and ships are destroyed. This event is more than just pollution of the water, since ships are destroyed and sea life dies.
- **The Third Trumpet** (8:10–11): At the blowing of the third trumpet, a star falls from the sky and lands on a third of the rivers and springs, making a third of the water toxic. The plant with the same name as the star, *Wormwood*, is a bitter plant often used as a metaphor for something bitter to the taste, though it is not usually considered a poison.
- **The Fourth Trumpet** (8:12): The fourth angel's trumpet sound struck a third of the sun, moon, and stars. This affects the structure of the universe. Everything from the remaining plant life and even the tides in the oceans would be changed. Certainly, as described, the natural amount of daylight would be altered.

Thus far, the attacks have dealt only with the earth and have only indirectly affected human population. With each phenomenon, God is removing hiding places and protection in nature.

After the first four trumpets and judgments, a flying eagle proclaims three woes, perhaps in light of the three trumpets yet to blow (8:13). This is a curse and a proclamation of things to come. The appearance of the eagle (which may mean one of several kinds of birds of prey, as the term was used in the first century) provides an interlude in the trumpets.

REVELATION 9:1–21

THE DAY OF THE LORD

More Trumpets and the First Woe 9:1–11
The Last Trumpet and the Second Woe 9:12–21

Setting Up the Section

Just as the last three seals pertain to things of heaven rather than earth, the last three trumpets deal with the realm of the supernatural—in this case, though, it's the demonic rather than angelic realm.

9:1–11

MORE TRUMPETS AND THE FIRST WOE

The Fifth Trumpet and the First Woe (9:1): It was common for people or angels to be referred to as stars in Jewish imagery (Isaiah 14:12). Therefore, John is likely employing a common image for his day of an angel of some kind. The angel descends to the earth and receives a key to the opening of the abyss, which evidently has a narrow opening that then widens beyond the entrance (Revelation 9:2).

Demystifying Revelation

The pit, or abyss, is a place that is referenced nine times in the scriptures, seven of which are in the book of Revelation. The pit seems to be a place where God holds all of those who have died without faith. The glories of heaven are not fully open, and neither are the tortures of hell. The abyss is a place where people exist until the final judgment.

The smoke from the abyss is enough to block out the remaining light of the sun (8:12; 9:2). In addition, locusts poured from it. The locusts here represent the judgment of God just as they did in the plagues in Egypt and in the prophecy of Joel (Joel 2:25). In this case, though, the locusts are prohibited from plant life, which is their typical food source. These locusts were given power, presumably by God, to sting like scorpions. They could go after, but not kill, people without God's seal (Revelation 9:5). The effects would be torturous to the point that those affected would wish to die.

The five-month period of torment may correspond to the typical life span of the locust, or it may simply be a way to communicate that the torment would last a few months. This is the way the number five is used elsewhere in scripture (Acts 20:6; 24:1; Revelation 9:5).

Verses 7–11 describe the locusts. The description combines human and animal features, and reveals the locusts to be more akin to demons than insects. The importance of the comparison to horses is not that the demons looked like horses, but that they were prepared for battle like horses. This is to say that they were determined to accomplish the task.

In the same way, John's mention of crowns is not to say that the beings wear crowns, but that they resemble something wearing crowns. The crowns here may symbolize the authority to act and to get things done. The teeth like lion's teeth reveal more about the fierceness of the creatures than their physical description. And the breastplates reveal how well-protected the beings are. The loud noise made by their wings reveals their great number (9:7–9).

Critical Observation

Verse 11 is a difficult verse to understand because it is the only reference to this king—called the angel of the abyss. This is either referring to the fact that there is one who will control these creatures and they will be carrying out a mission on earth, or it is a cultural issue emerging that is contemporary to John's day.

At the time John was writing this letter, the emperor of Rome liked to think of himself as a reincarnated form of the god Apollo. Interestingly, Apollo was known as the god over the locusts. The locusts in this verse are from the underworld, and thus they are the power of evil being used by God, a message that would be relevant to John's readers. Both names listed in verse 11, *Abaddon* and *Apollyon*, can be translated as "destruction."

9:12–21

THE LAST TRUMPET AND THE SECOND WOE

Since the appearance of the eagle announcing the three woes in 8:13, the trumpets have been identified as woes (9:12). What is identified as the second woe here is also the sixth trumpet.

The voice that follows the sixth trumpet comes from the horns on the golden altar before God (9:13). This is probably the same altar mentioned in 8:3, the place where the prayers of the saints have registered with God.

The four angels who are bound at the Euphrates River are the angels that God has set aside to pour out His wrath on the earth. They have not been able to perform their designed purpose until this moment in time (9:14–15).

Demystifying Revelation

The river Euphrates was the easternmost border of the Roman Empire. The army that occupied this part of the empire was the Parthian army, which was ready to attack at any moment. This army was feared by the people, and this description would have evoked fear in the minds of John's readers.

These angels are going to release an army on the earth to destroy a third of the population—millions of people.

When John claims there are two hundred million soldiers on horseback, this is probably an actual number (9:16). John is not estimating—he had been told the number.

John describes his vision in verses 17–19. It is not certain whether he is describing three different colors of breastplates or breastplates that are each three colors. However, the description of the horses—heads like lions, tails like snakes—expresses the ferocity and danger of this army. These are warriors bent on total destruction.

According to verses 18–19, it seems the riders do not play any active part in the destruction of the people; it is the horses who breathe the fire, smoke, and sulfur on the people. The fire, smoke, and sulfur represent three different, yet destructive, plagues.

Verse 20 transitions from the plight of the cavalry to a description of those who survived the plagues. Notice that John's description of the idols underscores the appalling reality that even in light of the destruction around them at the hand of God, these people failed to repent. His list of their sins in verse 21 doesn't seem to be in a specific order, and they don't correlate with another specific list in the scriptures—murders, magic, sexual immorality, and theft.

REVELATION 10:1–11

THE MESSENGER, THE MESSAGE, AND A MEAL

The Messenger 10:1–3
The Message 10:4–7
The Meal 10:8–11

Setting Up the Section

Just as there was a pause between the sixth and the seventh seal, there is now a pause between the sixth and seventh trumpet. This pause is composed of two main sections: First an angel and a little book, then two witnesses come to declare the glory and wrath of God.

The section provides a specific warning. God has judged people in general. Now He will judge the leaders of the world system that sets its agenda against God.

10:1–3

THE MESSENGER

Verse 1 describes an angel descending from heaven (10:1). Clouds, like those he is dressed or wrapped in, sometimes symbolize those coming back to earth from heaven to carry out a task for God.

The rainbow appearing above his head signifies that he is going to bring judgment and salvation. In the Old Testament, the rainbow is a sign that God would never again flood the earth (Genesis 9:12–16). Yet this sign is meant to remind people of how God saved and judged people at the same moment.

The face of this angel is like the sun, which means that he is a source of power, and his legs are like pillars of fire, which means he has the power of judgment within him.

The angel holds a little scroll (10:2). This scroll is open, which means that what is on the scroll is about to be read and executed. The fact that the angel places one foot on the sea and the other foot on the land shows that he has authority over the entire earth. What he is about to announce is meant for everyone in the world.

The imagery of thunder speaking is also used in Psalm 29:3 to describe the voice of God. Many believe that the thunder in this passage is the Lord speaking, and He repeats Himself seven times, though that information is not given definitively in verse 3.

10:4–7

THE MESSAGE

John understood the words spoken by the seven peals of thunder and intended to write them down, but he is instructed not to do so (10:4). While some seals used thus far in Revelation that functioned to claim someone, in verse 4, to *seal* means to hide what has been said.

Take It Home

One of the gifts of this passage is the realization that God has not given us all the information. There is always the temptation to take the information in Revelation and decide how God will act and when certain events will occur. But we are not given all that knowledge or understanding. God keeps mysteries for Himself, and He will reveal them in His own time.

The angel in verse 5 is identified as the same angel as in verse 2, who has authority over the land and the sea. He swears an oath by raising his right hand, a gesture common in both ancient and contemporary days. His oath is that when the seventh trumpet is blown—when all is done that needs to be done—there will be no delay before the fulfillment of the mystery of God (10:6).

The seventh trumpet mentioned in verse 7 is not actually blown until 11:15. What begins here is not a description of the chronological events in between the sixth and seventh trumpets, but is instead more like parenthetical information. John is not in control of his vision. Instead, he writes it down as he experiences it.

The "mystery of God" (10:7) is usually understood to refer to the gospel message, though it could have an even broader meaning than that. The prophets referenced here are not necessarily confined to the Old Testament prophets, but to those who have spoken God's truth, including the gospel message.

Critical Observation

While John eating the scroll is an unusual request by contemporary standards, it is not without precedent in the scriptures. In the book of Ezekiel, the prophet himself is asked to eat a scroll (Ezekiel 2:8–3:3). The idea is that eating the scroll is devouring the truth, or taking the words to heart.

10:8–11

THE MEAL

When John is instructed to eat the scroll (10:9), he does as he is asked, and it changes him. The scroll tastes sweet but is bitter in his stomach. This is an apt image of God's commandments in the lives of His children. The picture here is that the commands of God are always good, and they are always something that the child of God can rejoice in. But at the same time, these words are powerful, and they will be difficult to grapple with because they tell of the wrath of God. This is the twofold nature of God's words.

This is the first time in these visions that John is a participant in the experience in heaven rather than simply an observer. As a participant, John has the opportunity to experience fully how God is going to work on and in this earth. Verse 11 explains why John has been asked to participate—he is to prophesy.

Also, up until this point, the judgment of God has not been directed toward anyone in particular, just humanity in general. Now God is using John to announce that specific judgments are on their way. The Word of God is to be in John's heart so that he can carry out the job God has called him to do.

REVELATION 11:1–19

TWO WITNESSES AND ONE LAST TRUMPET

The Measuring	11:1–2
The Messengers	11:3–14
The Seventh Trumpet	11:15–19

Setting Up the Section

In this chapter we will see a measuring of the temple and two witnesses emerging to give testimony. As with much of Revelation, these events can be interpreted either literally or symbolically. If taken symbolically, many interpret the measuring of the temple to reflect a description of the emerging Christian church based on the familiar temple of Jerusalem. By the same token, a symbolic interpretation often sees the two witnesses as a reflection of the martyrs of the church who give testimony with their lives, rather than two specific men. Whichever interpretive path, this section continues the theme of God's judgment as He begins to hold the world outside of the church accountable.

11:1–2

THE MEASURING

In the first century, as often today, a building was measured any time it was changing hands. It was a means of guaranteeing a fair exchange. In this vision, John is given some type of measuring stick and is asked to measure the temple as a sign that God will take the temple back (11:1). If this were a literal temple, it would most likely refer to the temple at Jerusalem. It can also be interpreted as a reference to the church, God's redeemed, but the language is written in terms of the temple.

John is instructed not to measure the court of the Gentiles (11:2). This refers to the outer area of the Jewish temple, a courtyard in which non-Jews were allowed. If John's image is meant as a picture of the church, then it may be that he is speaking of Christians to be the chosen nation. There would still be an outer court for those outside of the faith, which in this case would include all nonbelievers.

Regardless of the literal or symbolic path of interpretation, John delineates a forty-two-month period of time (three and one-half years) in which those outside of the Christian faith would trample God's city. A connection can be drawn to other scriptures in which a time period of forty-two months is delineated (Daniel 7:25, "time, times and a half a time" equals a year, two years, and one-half a year). This time frame comes into play in several places in Revelation as well. For John's readers, a time frame in itself is significant. It speaks to the fact that their suffering will not go on indefinitely. There will be an end to the persecution of God's people.

11:3–14

THE MESSENGERS

While the identities are not revealed, God will send two witnesses in the midst of the persecution. In verse 3, the time period is defined in terms of days but is the same amount of time as the forty-two months mentioned in verse 2.

The attitude of the witnesses is reflected in the clothes that they will wear—sackcloth, the clothes of mourning. This symbolizes the sorrow and grief that are about to come to the earth.

Some believe the witnesses are simply symbols that represent believers. Others believe that these two are Moses and Elijah. Still others think the witnesses are apostles, martyrs, or other prophets. The significance of the number of witnesses may relate the Old Testament command that two witnesses must confirm a story in order for it to be considered credible. The fact that there are two witnesses here reflects the fact that whoever these witnesses are, their testimony is enough to prove God's truth credible.

Verse 4 offers a description taken from Zechariah 4:3, 11–14. While there is only one lampstand in the Zechariah passage and two in John's description, the point remains that the lampstands are connected directly to olive trees. This means there will be an endless supply of oil and the lamps will never burn out. This could mean that the two witnesses bear testimony to an endless supply of life. While their identity is not known, it is evident they are special people who have been prophesied in the Old Testament as the ones to bring life to a dead Israel.

Because it is God's will that these men preach the Word of God, they will have the ability to protect themselves from any attack (Revelation 11:5–6). They can prevent rain and perform miracles if necessary, like turning water to blood and causing plagues. These references bring to mind Moses and Elijah who exhibited these types of miracles (Exodus 7:19–20; 1 Kings 17:1).

For the two witnesses, this ability to protect themselves is temporary. When their job is done, they are killed by what is referred to as "the beast" from the abyss (11:7–8). The beast is a figure that is prominent in the last half of Revelation. It is empowered by Satan and filled with evil.

For those who interpret Revelation in a more literal sense, the killing of the prophets will happen in Jerusalem, where the Lord was crucified. Jerusalem is also referred to as Sodom and Egypt, one a city famous for immorality and the other a country known for holding God's people in bondage. So those who interpret Revelation figuratively see this city as representative of the world's cities in general.

The fact that the corpses lay for three and a half days without being buried is an act of shame and triumph by those who were glad of their deaths (11:9). Due to the customs of the day, John's original readers would have felt the pain of this disgrace of no proper burial.

The general population rejoices that these two witnesses are dead (11:10). Because of the message they had and the power that was at their disposal, the forty-two months that they were on the earth were horrible for the unrepentant. Therefore, to those unrepentant, their deaths are almost like a holiday—people exchange gifts and celebrate. But this only happens for three and a half days.

Then the witnesses come back to life. First, God breathes life into them; then He calls them to heaven (11:11–12). All those watching are seized by fear. In a sense, this is a review of the gospel—new life and the conquering of death. While we can't be sure if everyone in the crowd watching hears God call out, or if just the two witnesses hear His voice, it is obvious to everyone that those who were dead have found new life.

Verses 13–14 draw this woe to an end. Those who had celebrated the death of the two witnesses have now experienced an earthquake that collapses part of the city and kills seven thousand. The unrepentant now honor God's power and authority. The third woe associated with the seventh and final trumpet is on the way.

11:15–19

THE SEVENTH TRUMPET

The seventh trumpet is not just one short event; it actually comprises the rest of the judgment of God and then the final end of the age with the new heaven and the new earth. It also serves as a prompt for the next series of visions recorded by John.

The seventh angel blows the seventh trumpet, and instead of immediate destruction, there is loud praise from voices in heaven (11:15). The reference to loud voices implies a group, but we are not told the specific identity of the group. Perhaps it is everyone who is in heaven. The focus of this praise is this: The kingdom of this world has become Jesus' kingdom.

The twenty-four elders, not mentioned since the last of the seals (7:11), worship God and give thanks because:

1) He has begun to reign on earth.
2) His wrath has punished the rebellious nations. All of the kings that try to rule the world challenge God, and therefore God defends His honor by judging the nations.
3) He has judged the living and the dead. God gives each person the reward he or she deserves (11:17–18).

The people in heaven are seeing God bring about the final day of reckoning. For this they worship the Lord.

Verse 19 contains meaningful Old Testament Jewish imagery. The temple of heaven opens up and the ark of the covenant appears. In the Old Testament, the ark was the symbol of God's presence and God's covenant with humankind. In the Old Testament tabernacle, the temple of that day, the ark resided in the innermost chamber, the Holy of Holies, sealed off from everyone except the high priest. Here God is allowing people into the real Holy of Holies and is, in essence, saying that His covenant is complete.

The thunder, lightning, and hail are reminiscent of the power of God that was present the first time He revealed His covenant with the children of Israel, unveiling the Ten Commandments on Mount Sinai (Exodus 19–20).

Take It Home

When the trumpet blows, the people praise God because they know that He is now bringing all things to their appointed end and the kingdom of heaven to its appointed beginning. This is great news and worth praising God over. At this point there is a shift in John's visions from heaven to the kingdom of the earth and the fate of Satan.

For John's original readers, the idea of God establishing a place where He alone rules and justice is complete is a reason to hope. It is the same for contemporary culture. Amid the imagery and symbolism of Revelation is the message that God is moving toward a specific end and that His children are cared for within that plan, even though temporary suffering is a reality.

REVELATION 12:1–17

THE SEVEN SIGNS

The Woman and the Dragon 12:1–6
A Battle with the Enemy 12:7–17

Setting Up the Section

Chapter 12 begins a series of seven visions that will extend into chapter 14. These visions do not have a repeating symbol, like the seven seals or seven trumpets. But they are similar in that they flesh out the conflict between God and His church and the forces of evil that would seek to destroy both.

12:1–6

THE WOMAN AND THE DRAGON

In the first of the seven signs, a woman is described as a picture of Israel (12:1–2). She has been called by God and is clothed with the sun, which means she is reflecting the power of God. The moon is under her feet, which indicates that she is the nation God has marked as special, and she has twelve crowns that correspond to the twelve tribes of Israel. She is with child, which is the picture of the Messiah. Her labor pains represent the struggles that were a part of the life of Israel.

Demystifying Revelation

For John there is always a connection between Old Testament Israel and the New Testament church. In his theology, the church has become God's chosen nation. Here in chapter 12, the image of the woman represents Israel, but later in Revelation a woman will represent the church. Understanding John's visions requires that his readers stay sensitive to the fact that images can sometimes maintain their meanings between visions, but at other times the same image can carry a different message.

The next sign John sees is that of a dragon, not an uncommon concept in ancient literature (12:3). This dragon is red, the symbol of blood. This fits the image of Satan—he is a murderer. He seeks to kill and devour.

The dragon has seven heads. *Seven* is a number that symbolizes perfection or completion. This many heads may imply that the evil one is all over the world. In other words, his evil is everywhere. On each head are seven diadems, or crowns. These crowns are not merely the wreaths worn by the victor of a contest; they are the crowns of royalty and symbolize the dragon's ability to rule. Whatever authority the dragon has, though, is limited and delegated. God has allowed it.

In addition to the seven heads, there are also ten horns, which in the most basic sense imply great strength. Some interpreters understand the ten horns to represent the ten nations that will rule under the Antichrist during the final days. Others believe the ten horns represent the leaders or rulers that have been a tool of Satan to attempt to oppose the Messiah.

The dragon's tail sweeps away one-third of the stars (12:4). Some see this as a reference to Satan taking one-third of the angels with him when he fell from heaven. Others simply think it represents a show of power by the dragon. He has only one goal in mind in this particular vision, and that is to destroy the child, an image of the Messiah.

In verse 5, the Messiah arrives on the earth in order to rule with an iron rod. This is not a picture of a tyrannical rule as much as it is a firm hand in the power of a king. The child is immediately caught up into heaven, or He ascends into heaven. This ascension means that the Son is waiting for the day when He will rule.

Critical Observation

Some question the fact that John's vision includes this obvious reference to Jesus' birth, cutting directly to the ascension without any reference to His ministry or death and resurrection. But there is no explanation given here. It is important to remember, though, that the purpose of this section is to give hope to the church by highlighting God's power over Satan rather than to give a review of Jesus' life.

In verse 6, the 1,260 days, or three and one half years, show up again (11:1–3). In this case, the woman, a picture of Israel, hides for three and a half years. She hides in a place that has been prepared by God in order for her to be cared for. Satan has power, but he cannot oppose the plan of God.

Take It Home

What do we see in this text? We see that God is finally going to bring an end to the delegated and defeated power of Satan on this earth.

What do we learn from this? We learn that Satan has some limited power, and we must be careful dealing with him. Also we see that his goal is to attack Jesus, but he cannot win, because God still has control over him.

12:7–17

A BATTLE WITH THE ENEMY

Verses 7–8 describe the battle between Satan, the dragon, and Michael. Michael is the angel who was given to Israel to protect her as a nation and as a people (Daniel 12:1). Thus, this battle can be understood as a direct attack by Satan on Israel.

Both Michael's and the dragon's armies are referred to as angels, a designation that simply means "messenger" (Revelation 12:7).

The reality is that Satan is not strong enough to overtake Michael. The original readers of this letter would find great hope in this description. Without this kind of encouragement, their suffering could push them into thinking that Satan was finally going to do away with not only Israel, but all of the people of God.

According to verse 9, at the end of the war Satan is thrown out along with all of his army. The idea here is that God stops Satan from ever attacking again. In verse 9, John uses several of Satan's designated names:

- *Serpent*—the first term used to describe Satan (Genesis 3:1)
- *Satan*—accuser, adversary (Job 1:6)
- *Devil*—deceiver, slanderer (Matthew 4:1)

After this final expulsion from heaven, there is an announcement: Salvation—the power and the kingdom of God, as well as the authority of Jesus Christ—has come. Satan is finally prevented from ever entering heaven for the purpose of interrupting the plan of God. This final expulsion provides a great outburst of praise in heaven (12:10–12).

Notice that this announcement is spoken in first person plural—the accuser of *our* brothers and sisters. It is probably proclaimed by a group of angels, but any of the heavenly members in the vision could be the source.

According to verse 11, the people's power to overcome Satan is found in three things:

1) *The blood of Jesus.* It was the death of Jesus that took the power of death away from all those who place their faith in Jesus alone.
2) *The word of their testimony.* The people continued to proclaim Jesus no matter the consequences. The proclamation of the gospel is the power that will see Satan defeated.
3) *Not loving this life over the next.* Satan uses death as a means to intimidate people into denying Jesus. Nevertheless, the saints who deal with the complete onslaught of Satan realize that their only hope is to proclaim Christ, no matter the cost.

Verse 12 contains a woe to the people of earth, warning them that Satan is now truly a being with nothing to lose. He knows his final defeat is simply a matter of time (12:12). The heavens are rejoicing because Satan is cast out forever, and the believers know how to handle him. The rest of the world, however, will have to endure his wrath for a short while. This will be a bad time on earth. But these days will not go unpunished.

As the vision continues in verse 13, when Satan realizes that he can't reach the child, he goes after the woman. In other words, Satan sets out to persecute Israel. He surely knows that he will not defeat her, but he can inflict pain and suffering.

In verse 14 God provides divine protection for Israel. The protection is found in the symbolic picture of an eagle. The eagle has large wings and is strong enough to carry the people of God. This image is reminiscent of Exodus 19:4, a description of Israel's deliverance from Egypt.

So not all of Israel is destroyed. Some are protected for the three and one-half years ("time, times and half a time"). This would be the second part of the three and a half years when Satan is allowed to unleash his fury.

At the end of verse 14, Satan is referred to as the serpent rather than the dragon. He has been referred to as the serpent in verse 9, so there is little doubt that the serpent and the dragon are one and the same.

Two more attempts are made by Satan, the dragon. First, he spits floodwaters to sweep the woman away from her wilderness safe house, but the earth swallows the floodwaters (12:15–16). Then, when he is unable to attack, he goes after her children. In other words, he turns on the church (12:17).

REVELATION 13:1–18

THE ANTICHRIST AND THE FALSE PROPHET

The Beast's Ancestry, Authority, and Adoration	13:1–4
The Beast's Arrogance	13:5–6
The Beast's Activities and Admirers	13:7–10
The False Prophet's Presence and Purpose	13:11–14
The False Prophet's Plan	13:15–18

Setting Up the Section

At this point in Revelation, we have seen the judgment of God on the earth in a general sense. This judgment has been carried out toward the earth and the people of the earth.

In chapter 10, God begins to deal directly with Satan and all those who have intentionally and directly supported his efforts to oppose Jesus. This final judgment on Satan is the reason worship breaks out at the end of chapter 11.

Chapter 12 describes the plight of Israel (the woman), Jesus (the child of the woman), Satan (the dragon), and the church (the other offspring of the woman). Satan, as revealed in this chapter, has one goal—to destroy the Messiah. Because he cannot destroy the Messiah, he seeks to do away with Israel. Because he cannot do away with Israel, he goes after the church.

In chapter 13, the story line continues with a final move of Satan in trying to oppose the Messiah through a false messiah—otherwise referred to by the contemporary church as the Antichrist. (Chapter 14 will show that this attempt will not be successful.) Also in chapter 13, we will see the description of the man whom the Antichrist will possess, referred to as the false prophet.

13:1–4

THE BEAST'S ANCESTRY, AUTHORITY, AND ADORATION

It is already established that the dragon is Satan, and he has in mind to do away with the Messiah. If he can't accomplish that, then he will do away with Israel and the church. The way in which Satan will try to do away with all three of these is found here in Revelation 13.

At the end of chapter 12, Satan is standing on the sand of the seashore. This represents Satan standing at the edge of the abyss.

In essence, he is summoning the beast, the one who has been called the Antichrist. This is the offense that will cause Satan, and all who directly follow him, to be judged in a direct and painful way by God. The offense of Satan is that he offers a false messiah to the world in order to deceive and destroy.

The beast is described in verse 1 as having ten horns and seven heads (as does Satan, the dragon, in 12:3), with crowns on its horns. Typically, the horns on an animal represent the strength of that animal to attack and defend. There are also diadems or ruling crowns, but they are on the horns of the beast rather than the heads. Some believe each of these crowns represents nations or kingdoms that will make up his ruling empire.

On each of the beast's multiple heads is written a blasphemous name. This may mean seven different names or the same name on each head. This beast is a culmination of all that is evil in this world.

In verse 2, we find a description of the power and authority that is given to the beast. He is described in terms of a leopard, a bear, and a lion. Each of these animals was used by governments to describe their power. The leopard describes swiftness in battle, the bear is the strength and stability that comes with enough power, and the lion describes the fighting power of a nation.

Critical Observation

While the beast is described as having seven heads, he has only one mouth ("like that of a lion," NIV). This is a reminder that John is describing a vision. His interest is not in making all the visual pieces fit, but rather in describing them and allowing them to flesh out the truth.

Some interpret the beast in John's writing to represent the Roman leadership in the first century. They would see the multiple heads as the Roman emperors, citing the myth that Nero was too evil to die and would therefore be resurrected. They connect this myth with the wounded head described in verse 3.

This beast will have a consuming power that could be used to overrun the world—and all the power is given to him by Satan. The territory Satan has been allowed (the earth) will be given to the beast so he will be able to rule the entire world without much restraint. The wickedness that is on the earth will rule all at once.

The man the beast represents—often referred to as the Antichrist—will have absolute authority over the entire world. It is delegated authority in the sense that God could stop it at any point, but nevertheless, it is a moment in time when evil will rule. God is centralizing all of the wickedness into one place to deal with it completely.

According to verse 3, one of the beast's heads has been fatally wounded, then healed, or brought back to life. This adds to his popularity. He is seen as supernatural, and this causes people to be deceived into following him. In the remainder of John's description of the beast, this head that has been restored becomes his calling card.

The people will begin to ascribe to him and to Satan the worship due to God. This is the ultimate in blasphemy. The question, "Who is like the beast?" may be a satiric reference to Psalm 35:10, "Who is like you, O LORD?" (NIV), highlighting this blasphemous worship.

13:5–6

THE BEAST'S ARROGANCE

The beast has been given everything he has. In other words, he is still bound to the ultimate sovereign control of God. There is nothing in this man that God has not allowed and that God cannot take away.

He is allowed to rule for forty-two months, the now familiar amount of time for several significant events in Revelation—three and one-half years (11:2; 13:5).

The pride of this man goes beyond the pride that most powerful leaders struggle with from time to time. This man considers himself to be God (13:5). He believes he possesses all the authority of God, and he acts on that belief by blaspheming God and all who dwell in heaven with Him (13:6).

Critical Observation

Keep in mind that one of the struggles for John's readers in their political climate was the pressure to worship the emperor as deity. This emperor worship was seen as blasphemy. This passage would likely have touched on that hot-button issue in their minds.

13:7–10

THE BEAST'S ACTIVITIES AND ADMIRERS

This man, depicted by the image of the beast, is more than talk; he also acts in a deadly and powerful manner. At the focus of his attack are believers in the one true God. All of the saints present on earth will be in his radar, and if he finds them, he will kill them. The situation John describes in verse 7 is such that, if it continues, there will be no believers left on the earth.

According to verse 8, this beast rules the world. The beast is the fulfillment of evil, the ultimate fulfillment of every evil power that has existed. The focus in verse 8 is that those who are not believers will worship the beast. Those who are true believers will not, for they will see that he is not the Messiah. The beast is the ultimate moment of separation; he will be the dividing rod of humanity. The true believers will not submit, and the world will.

Verse 9 contains a common New Testament warning: "He who has an ear, let him hear." It is used fifteen times in the New Testament. It means that if anyone understands the real meaning, he or she must respond. Some will read this and not get the message. Others will understand the message, and it will change them.

Verse 10 contains instructions. In essence, if you are marked out to be arrested, then go. Do not resist. If you are to be killed, do not fight back. Submit to what happens. There is a day of reckoning coming, and you are to wait for that day. The idea is to leave the fighting to God. By trusting in the faithfulness of God to bring about retribution, you will persevere.

13:11–14

THE FALSE PROPHET'S PRESENCE AND PURPOSE

At the time the beast comes to power, another beast will rise to power with him. He will be called his prophet. This prophet's purpose is to make sure that everyone worships the beast and to ensure that all humans are sealed with the mark of the beast. This prophet is a critical part of the attack of Satan.

Some believe that this second beast will be a nation or a government. But that theory is difficult to accept because the Greek says *another* beast (13:11). The way it is constructed denotes another of the same kind. Therefore, the most natural way to read this is that another man is on the scene performing critical works.

The first beast came out of the sea, which denotes the abyss or the mysterious place of Satan. This second beast comes out of the earth, which denotes he is satanic in his power (13:11). To the first-century readers, the earth was a little less foreboding than the sea. It was a picture of an evil place but not the place of hell. This would suggest that this will be an evil man but not as evil as the first.

The second beast has two horns (13:11). Horns symbolize power and sometimes nations. Interpreted the latter way, this man will have the authority of two nations under him. It also may simply parallel the two witnesses who were killed and then resurrected (chapter 11). The horns on this man are the horns of a lamb, which may be a parallel of Jesus, the Lamb. This suggests that he appears gentle and meek, but that appearance is deceptive. The reason for the guise is that his role is to get people to worship the beast, and he therefore has to be a salesman. He must make all of the evil of the beast look good to humanity. Even though he will have two horns like a lamb, he will speak like a dragon—he will speak the words of Satan. He will appear harmless, but in reality his words will be deadly.

This second beast exercises the delegated authority of the first (13:12). In application, the second beast is indwelt with the same evil power as the first, and therefore he will be given some of the responsibilities to carry out the first beast's will on the earth. All of this power is centered on one goal—to get every living being to worship the Antichrist rather than Jesus Christ.

Verse 13 offers their strategy for accomplishing this. The second beast, the false prophet, will perform miracles. These miracles will draw attention to the first beast, and particularly to the fact that the beast was wounded yet survived. In this way, the healing of the one damaged head becomes a point of tribute and worship. The main tactic is this: The prophet gets everyone's attention with his own powers, and when he has their attention, he speaks as front man. The spin of his message? The fact that the first beast was restored to life shows his ultimate power in the world, and therefore everyone should worship him. Note that both verse 12 and verse 14 identify the first beast as having a fatal wound that was healed.

The second beast, the false prophet, will also be able to mimic the prophets of the past by calling down fire from heaven (13:13). Because of these powers, he will be able to convince people that he preaches the truth, and everyone who is not a true believer will be fooled (11:14). He will encourage people to make an image of the beast so that all can worship him in their homes. In this way, he will have the entire world consumed with the first beast, the one with the restored head, the Antichrist. He will be a household word, even a way of life.

13:15–18

THE FALSE PROPHET'S PLAN

The prophet's plan for carrying out these tasks has two parts. The first part is supernatural, and the second part is economic.

According to verse 14, the prophet instructs people to make an image of the first beast and to put it in their homes. Then, according to verse 15, the prophet gives the image, or idol, the power to speak. The word *speak* is often translated "spirit." This seems to mean that not only can the image speak, but it has a spirit within it that will be watching everyone in his or her home. If anyone strays from total allegiance, that person will somehow be killed, apparently by the idol itself.

The second part of the plan—the economic part—is found in verses 16–17. The prophet will control access to the food supply of the world so that all people, no matter who they are, will look to him to gain access to food. The way to participate in the global economy will be through taking his mark. This mark is a mimic of the mark given to protect the 144,000 in Revelation 14:1. This mark will be placed on the right hand or forehead and will allow people to participate in the global economy. Without it there can be no participation, and people will starve to death.

The mark is either a name or a number. Verse 18, which reveals the number 666, opens with a call for wisdom. Wisdom is the application of the knowledge of God into real life. If Christians are wise, they are living for God and should be discerning as to who the beast really is. They must not be fooled into thinking that this is Christ reigning or that it is the advent of the kingdom of God. Instead, they must see that all of this is merely the power of a person. That is why the mark given to the people does not reflect the glory of God but instead the glory of humanity.

For centuries, people have searched for the meaning behind the numbers 666. Since numerical values were often applied to letters in the ancient world, many have looked for a name that, when converted to numbers, would equal 666. No solutions to that equation have been widely accepted. And in truth, this number may represent some symbolism that has thus far not been taken into account.

REVELATION 14:1–20

THE PROTECTION AND POWER OF GOD

The Protection 14:1–5
The Proclamations 14:6–13
The Harvest 14:14–20

Setting Up the Section

In chapter 14, we see God's response to the attack of the two beasts described in chapter 13. The beast's goal has been to stop the Messiah, destroy the Jews, and persecute the church. Here God claims His own and begins the final harvest.

14:1–5

THE PROTECTION

God prevents the plan of the beast from coming to completion by sealing 144,000 people to keep them from being killed by the beast. He will seal them with a sign on their foreheads (14:1).

Demystifying Revelation

The idea around the sign on the forehead is that God is marking these individuals as being His and His alone. The marking of the forehead is an Eastern practice, both in the first century and today. A person places the mark of the god he or she serves on his or her forehead. When God marks His name on these people, He is declaring them His exclusive property.

In verses 2–3, John hears the singing of a song that resembles rushing waters, thunder, and harps. The song is powerful and beautiful. It is sung before the throne of God, and the only people able to sing it are the 144,000 whom God purchased from the earth (7:4–8).

There are two notable things in this passage. The first is that this song is exclusive to this particular group of people. The second is that these people have been purchased from the earth—God has redeemed them.

Critical Observation

Many believe the 144,000 represent a remnant of Jews brought to faith to represent the restoration of Israel. Others see this number as a symbol of completion. They see the 144,000 as a representation of all the redeemed who are now the spiritual children of Abraham—in other words, the church.

Verses 4 and 5 offer five characteristics of these worshipers:

- **Sexually Pure.** The first description is that these individuals are not married and have not allowed themselves to indulge in immoral relationships.

Critical Observation

The New Testament does not represent sex within marriage as anything sinful, though certain vows included abstaining from sex. This description of sexual purity raises some questions about how to interpret John's comments. For those who interpret this passage symbolically, this description simply implies that this group has been spiritually faithful to God—spiritual virgins. For those who interpret it as a literal group of 144,000 Jews, this description implies that the group is all male and that they have never married.

- **Devoted to Jesus.** These individuals not only believe that Jesus is the Messiah, but they are also completely devoted to obeying Him and doing His will.
- **Purchased as Firstfruits.** Firstfruits were the first of the harvest offered to God as an act of worship. Offering the firstfruits indicates that the worshiper understands that all things belong first to God. Here, these people were the firstfruits offered to God and to the Lamb, Jesus.
- **Righteous.** When the text states that no lie is found in their mouths (14:5), it means that because their hearts are righteous, their words and actions are righteous as well. To say a person speaks no lie is to say that his or her heart is governed by truth.
- **Blameless.** The final characteristic is that these Jews are blameless. This means that people live lives that are beyond reproach. To be righteous is to have a heart that is pure before God, and to be blameless means that your life is pure before the world.

14:6–13

THE PROCLAMATIONS

In verses 6–12, John witnesses three angels each making a proclamation.

First proclamation: The Gospel (14:6–7). John sees an angel that appears in mid-air, or midheaven. This is the place in the sky where the sun is at high noon, the highest point in the sky. The image is that this angel will be in the center point of the sky preaching the gospel to the whole world. There are three parts to the angel's message:

1) Fear God. The fear of the Lord means to treat the Lord with awe and reverence. The call is to acknowledge God's control and power over the earth. At this time, the beast is ruling and the world is giving its respect and reverence to him. Yet the angel has stated that fear must be given to God and not to the beast.
2) Give God glory. To give glory to God is to announce the marvelous wonders that He has done. The glory of God is the manifestation of His attributes. To give God glory is to announce His attributes to the world.
3) Worship God. The beast may be manipulating the earth, but God is the *maker* of

the earth. To worship God is to acknowledge who He is. In this case, He is to be acknowledged as the maker of the universe.

At this point there is another announcement; this one about the destruction that is to come.

Second Proclamation: The Destruction (14:8). This proclamation states that Babylon has fallen. The angel is letting everyone know that God is going to do away with the beast's empire. It will fall. Notice the terminology: This nation makes people drink the wine of her immorality. Every thought and every desire of this nation is so wicked and evil that its heart is bent on destroying God.

Demystifying Revelation

This is the first of several times in Revelation that Babylon is mentioned (16:19; 17:5; 18:1–24). The actual city of Babylon began after the flood with the story of the tower of Babel (Genesis 10:10; 11:9). Throughout the history of the Bible, Babylon represented pride, power, and wickedness. Some say that John was using Babylon here to represent Rome. Certainly his original readers would have seen Rome as the oppressive power they were experiencing. But there is a much broader interpretation as well. Babylon can represent the pride and wickedness of humanity that opposes God.

Third Proclamation: The Punishment (14:9–12). Punishment is awaiting those who take the mark of the beast and worship him. Keep in mind that the mark of the beast represents humanity. It is not just a number—it is a religion and a life philosophy. Those who receive the mark of the beast will experience the following punishments:

1) Drink of the wine of God's wrath. This refers to both His power to punish and the totality of all of His anger.
2) Be eternally tormented with fire and brimstone. This refers to the burning of hell. This hell is a place the angels and Jesus will be able to view.
3. Be tormented continually. Their lives will be tormented, both day and night, without rest.

The ones who keep their eyes on the way of God and the work of Jesus will avoid this torment. Those who want to stay true to the Lord during this time risk almost certain death, and for that reason John is told that those who die for the Lord are blessed.

Take It Home

Verse 13 serves as a reminder (and encouragement) to John's readers that while they may face trials even to the point of death, what they have done with their lives will continue on beyond the grave. This theme is woven throughout Revelation and serves to remind all readers of this letter that God's economy exists outside of this life. That which we do for Him is not destroyed or discredited even if it is rejected by the surrounding culture.

14:14–20

THE HARVEST

Some interpret John's vision in verse 14 to be a picture of Jesus bringing judgment to the earth. Others view it as an angel using his sickle to do God's bidding by bringing in a harvest.

The first interpretation is based on the use of the name *Son of Man,* which often describes Jesus in the Gospels. The second interpretation focuses on the fact that this being is described as *like* a son of man (meaning like a human being), which is more similar to the description of an angel. Then verse 15 begins by referring to another angel, as if an angel had just been mentioned.

In the vision, someone like a son of man sits on a white cloud (Daniel 7:13–14; Revelation 14:14). He is wearing a crown and holding a sickle. Another angel then appears to announce that it is the right time for the harvest. For John's original readers, this idea of it being the right time would have been meaningful. Since they are facing persecution, they would surely be eager to know when God is going to intervene on their behalf.

In verse 16, the one who is sitting on a cloud swings his sickle over the earth and reaps a harvest in one swing. Because there is no mention of wrath, those who interpret the person on the cloud as Jesus hold that this reaping is the time when the followers of God are being brought to heaven. For those who hold that the one doing the reaping is an angel, this harvest is undefined.

Verses 17–20 describe a grape harvest. Another angel appears with a sickle, this one coming out of the temple. Then another angel, this one from the altar, joins him and offers the instruction to gather the grapes because they are ripe. When the angel gathers the grapes, he tosses them into God's winepress. This is most likely a picture of judgment, since it is a winepress of wrath. We aren't told who presses the grapes, but the huge amount of blood that pours from the winepress reveals a devastating judgment.

John describes the amount of blood as deep enough to reach the height of horses' bridles stretching for nearly two hundred miles. The Greek reads 1,600 *stadia* (see NIV). A stade was about 607 feet, so the distance was about 180 miles. The greatest concern here is not the exact distance; it is the immeasurable extent of God's judgment falling on those who refuse to believe.

REVELATION 15:1–8

PRELUDE TO DESTRUCTION

The Agents of Wrath 15:1–4

The Attire of Wrath 15:5–6

The Attitude of Wrath 15:7–8

Setting Up the Section

Chapters 15–16 include another sevenfold image. In this instance, the image is of seven angels pouring out the contents of bowls. The contents contain God's wrath—His final judgment.

15:1–4

THE AGENTS OF WRATH

This is the third time in Revelation that John introduces a sign. The first was the image of a woman that represented Israel (12:1). The second immediately followed: Satan in the form of a red dragon (12:3). This third sign is the angels of destruction with seven final plagues (15:1). These angels hold the wrath of God, which will be used to destroy Satan—it will settle the issue of sin once and for all. After this, the judgment of God will be complete.

An area that resembles a sea of glass appears in Revelation 4:6 and now here in 15:2. This time, though, it is mixed with fire. Some have speculated that this "sea" represents the evil in the world, with those who have overcome that evil standing beside it. Others have supposed that this "sea" is the same one mentioned in Revelation 4:6—a glasslike platform that surrounds the throne of God offering an image of His purity—with the added feature here of God's anger (fire).

The victorious ones described in verse 2 had endured three things:

1) The beast—the evil of the man himself
2) The beast's image—the power of the image that would draw attention to the beast
3) The number of his name—the identification with his teaching and worldview

In John's vision, these conquerors are standing before the throne of God holding harps. They are prepared to worship God. The song that they sing is referred to as the song of Moses and the song of the Lamb (15:3–4). While the words to this song are not the same as the song attributed to Moses in Exodus 15, it is a similar theme—deliverance and justice. Through their song, those who have avoided the wrath of God are worshiping Him because He will make Himself known in the world. The next section in this prelude to final destruction is the description of the angels who will do the destroying.

15:5–6

THE ATTIRE OF WRATH

In verse 5, John includes what is actually an Old Testament reference to the presence of God. The tabernacle was the portable temple the Israelites used for their worship as they were traveling. The innermost part of the tabernacle, a shrine to the one true God, was the place where His Spirit resided. This innermost chamber was called the Holy of Holies, and it was a room off-limits to everyone but the high priest, and he could enter only once a year on the Day of Atonement. Understanding this reveals the significance of the fact that this room was now opened.

Critical Observation

In Exodus 38:21, this inner room is referred to as the "tabernacle [tent] of the Testimony" because it held within it the ark of the covenant, which contained the Ten Commandants. When this room is opened, as described here, it not only reveals God's presence but also His moral code. It is out of this moral code that people will be judged—it won't be an irrational or emotional moment, but a moment based on basic moral standards.

The seven angels with the seven plagues enter the main stage (15:6). Everything about the description of this scene implies that these angels and these plagues are sanctioned by God Himself. The angels are dressed in clean linen cloths that reflect purity. (The cleanliness of linen often refers to the holiness of the person.) The golden sashes allude to the sashes worn either by priests or warriors. Both would have meaning within this context of exercising God's judgment.

15:7–8

THE ATTITUDE OF WRATH

In verse 7, the four living creatures that exist close to the throne of God give the seven angels bowls filled with judgment. The word translated *bowls* is the same word used for the bowl that contained the prayers of the saints in Revelation 5:8.

Demystifying Revelation

Understanding the temple is a key to understanding many of the terms John uses to describe his visions in Revelation. For instance, there were bowls in the temple that served a significant role in worship. In the sin offering (Leviticus 4), blood was put in a bowl and then sprinkled and poured out during the ceremony. The bowls are used similarly here in the vision of the seven angels with seven plagues. In this case, the angels do not receive bowls with blood; instead, they receive bowls with anger and judgment. The eternal God who cannot be in the presence of sin will fill these bowls with His wrath, and they will be poured out on the earth.

Verse 8 describes the temple as filled with smoke. In the scriptures, smoke has often accompanied majesty and power. It was one of the signs of the presence of God (Exodus 40:34–35) and one of the signs of the awesome wrath of God. In this closing verse of chapter 15, God's glory, all the attributes of His character, and His power fill the temple, and there is no room for anything else until the plagues are poured out by the angels. All must stop and watch the mighty power of God on display.

REVELATION 16:1–21

THE SIX BOWLS

The First Six Bowls	16:1–12
Preparations for War	16:13–16
The Seventh Bowl	16:17–21

Setting Up the Section

In the judgments up to this point, there has been partial destruction. A portion of the stars, a portion of the earth, or a portion of the sea was destroyed, but not the whole of anything. In this case, total destruction will begin. All of the people who worship the beast are affected, all of nature is affected, and the end is destruction.

Seven bowls of judgment are described in the upcoming chapters, and they symbolize the final events of God's punishment of those who reject Him.

16:1–12

THE FIRST SIX BOWLS

In verse 1, John describes a loud voice from the temple. This means that the actions that are about to take place are being driven and controlled by God directly. In the same way, the judgments that are about to fall are falling upon those who have directly scorned God. For these people, following the beast is a conscious attack against God.

Critical Observation

Isaiah 66:1–6 has a warning for Israel. The warning is to any of the Jews who refuse to accept the message of the Lord and instead serve the sin of the world. That message is simply that the Lord will call out from heaven and kill the rebels. Isaiah 66:6 describes the sound of the Lord destroying people.

This points out that God the Father is the One who will avenge His honor and name. Thus, in the following verses in Revelation, we see Him shouting from heaven about the coming wrath. God made a promise that He would destroy the dragon/serpent and its power over the earth in Genesis 3:14–15. At the cross, the power of sin had been broken in the lives of those who call out to God by faith. But still, God plans on removing the power of evil from the earth altogether.

The First Bowl (16:2): The first bowl is a physical attack against all of the people who worship the beast. This wrath is not just anger; it is actual punishment in the form of pain—ugly and painful sores. This attack will render those who worship the beast useless. Then, once those who are opposed to God are out of commission and the beast is unable to help them, they are available to watch the judgment of God fall upon the earth.

The Second Bowl (16:3). Not only do the people get sores, but the water is turned to blood, much as it had been in the famous plagues of Egypt (Exodus 7:17–21). Earlier in Revelation, during the second trumpet (8:8–9) the water was turned to blood, but this is a little different. In this case, *all* of the water of the world is turned to blood, which means that life can no longer be sustained. Also, this is the blood of a dead man, meaning the blood has already coagulated. It is thick and stale and useless. As a result, all of the creatures of the sea die. Not only has the water supply ended, but also a major source of food.

God has rendered the people useless and in agonizing pain. Now the water supply is corrupted and so, too, all of the life that depended upon it. Any hope of survival is diminishing.

The Third Bowl (16:4–7). When the third bowl is poured out by the angel, the rest of the water supply is affected—the rivers and the streams. There is nothing to drink. When this happens, an angel offers up a word of praise, but it is praise for the retribution. As this angel expresses it, God's retribution has been justly poured out on those who shed the blood of God's followers and even opposed God Himself.

The "angel of the waters" (NET) mentioned in verse 5, the one who spoke the praise, is not mentioned anywhere else in the Bible. We can't know details of his identity other than this designation.

Notice in verse 7 that it is the altar that speaks. Earlier in Revelation, a voice came from the horns of the altar (9:13), but in this case, it's the actual altar offering praise.

Critical Observation

The third trumpet also dealt with the water supply (8:10–11), but in that case, only a part of the water became toxic. In this case, all the waters were ruined.

The Fourth Bowl (16:8–9). In some of the past judgments described in Revelation, the sun has been diminished (6:12; 8:12; 9:2). But in this judgment, the intensity of the sun increases so much that it is scorching people.

Unfortunately, rather than crying out to God, the hearts of the people are unchangeable. They blaspheme the name of God. This means they degrade His character and call Him evil.

While the first four plagues poured out by angels affected the natural world, the next plague is more political in nature.

The Fifth Bowl (16:10–11). The fifth angel turns his attention upon the beast. In fact, he pours his bowl on the beast's throne and darkness takes control. John doesn't give a specific explanation for what caused the people's pain. Their sores are still present according to verse 11. Also, there could be many who were burned from the scorching sun but were not killed by it. While all the details are not known, it is obvious that people are miserable, in pain. Yet they curse God rather than acknowledge Him as the One who could ease their suffering and the One who has the power to control the plagues.

The Sixth Bowl (16:12). The sixth plague removes the water from the Euphrates. This might not seem like such a bad thing given the fact that the river is filled with blood. But it is important because the next judgment is the great war of Armageddon that will destroy the armies of the beast once and for all. Drying up the riverbed removes an important obstacle for attacking armies.

John mentions that the kings from the East are the threat that will come across the dry riverbed left behind in the path of the Euphrates, but this is the only time these kings are mentioned. The Euphrates River did serve as the boundary of the Roman Empire, so in the minds of John's readers, assaulting enemies could easily lay beyond the river. And without the river to block them, the empire was much more open to attack. Still, as for these kings from the East, no more explanation is given than is mentioned in verse 12.

16:13–16

PREPARATIONS FOR WAR

As with the previous sets of seven events in Revelation, there is a pause between the sixth bowl and the seventh bowl. (There is a pause between the sixth and seventh seals and the sixth and seventh trumpets as well.) In this case, the pause allows the armies of the world to gather in one place.

Out of the mouths of the dragon, beast, and second beast, come demons that go to all of the kings of the world (16:13–14). These demons are spirits that perform remarkable miracles to entice the enemies of God to gather. Why would these armies need to be enticed to wage war against God? Because they are infested with sores, their water supply has dried up, and the sun is scorching people to death. The only way these people are going to move is by some form of deception. The deception is that the beast is stronger than the One doing this to them, and if they unite they will be victorious.

Critical Observation

The fact that the three demons are compared to frogs (16:13) is an interesting element in Revelation. Some have supposed that this is actually a form of mockery aimed toward Satan and his armies.

Before the seventh seal and the seventh trumpet an announcement is made. The series of bowl visions contain the same kind of element. In the case of the seals and trumpets, an announcement of salvation was made to the world. In this case, an announcement is made that the coming of the Day of the Lord is like a thief in the night (16:15). The reality is that no one will know the day when the fury will strike. Therefore, those who are ready and know that this day will come are the ones who walk through life prepared. Those who do not account for this day are the ones who walk around the world vulnerable and naked—which means that at the very least they will be ashamed when they are caught unprepared. This announcement is the final act of judgment upon these people.

The froglike spirits are successful, according to verse 16, and the armies of the beast gather in one place—Armageddon. The name probably stands for Har Mageddon, which means "the mountain of Megiddo." There is no known mountain with this name, so some have considered it to be merely an element of John's vision—a symbol of God's judgment. Others, however, identify it as the plain that lies beside the ancient city of Meggido.

Demystifying Revelation

Megiddo was a much desired spot because it was a junction for roads running north and south as well as east and west—with control of these trade routes the location was a boon to merchants of all kinds. Because it was such an advantageous location, many battles were fought in the vicinity.

16:17–21

THE SEVENTH BOWL

When the seventh angel pours his bowl of wrath upon the earth, a loud voice comes from the throne in the temple shouting, "It is done" (16:17). While the speaker is not identified, it is likely that it is God, even if simply based on the fact that the voice came from the throne. This is similar to the announcement of Jesus at His death—"It is finished" (John 19:30). When Jesus uttered those words, He was saying the payment for sin was paid in full. When God expresses these words, He is saying there will be no more judgment—the serpent and all evil are being punished on the earth.

God uses two things to destroy the earth. The first is a severe earthquake (16:18). Notice the precision with which John describes just how severe this earthquake is. There has never been an earthquake like it. The earthquake does several things: It kills people and rearranges the landscape of the earth, islands disappear, and mountains fall into the opening where the ground split into three parts (6:19–20).

The great city that the earthquake destroys may refer to humanity in general. The fact that it breaks in three parts (as opposed to simply dividing into two parts) implies complete destruction. The whole picture here, including the second reference John makes to Babylon (which serves as an excellent picture of human arrogance, see Genesis 10:10; 11:9), builds a picture of more than specific cities, but of the destruction of the part of civilization that demands to remain godless (Revelation 16:19).

Next come hailstones that weigh up to one hundred pounds according to some translations. They fall from the sky, crushing the people beneath. And while these people are receiving their judgment, they are cursing God (16:21).

Take It Home

Two things about this passage are important to understand. First is the destruction of sin. Sin is rebellion that disconnects us from our Creator.

The second is how quickly and simply God can destroy those who follow after sin. He requires no nuclear holocaust, no human-made weapons. The Creator of the universe can use His creation to destroy those who have rejected Him. He has the power to rearrange the earth, which reveals His true sovereignty.

We fear or worry about many things in life—things that can't hurt us. When we truly acknowledge God's power, it should give us pause. We should respect the power that could crush us yet offers us the opportunity over and over again to change our ways and be treated as beloved children.

REVELATION 17:1–18

THE DESTRUCTION OF BABYLON

The Vision of the Prostitute	17:1–6
The Angel's Explanation	17:7–14
The Relationship between the Beast and the Prostitute	17:15–18

Setting Up the Section

Thus far in Revelation, John's message has carried the theme of God's sovereignty. No matter what powers *seem* to exist, God is the One with the ultimate power and with the choice to decide when to display that power.

With chapter 17, the theme of the remainder of the book becomes the final judgment of God. He has chosen to display His power against evil, and the final throw-down is in sight.

Chapter 17 is built upon the vision of a woman, a prostitute, who seems to symbolize the same thing that Babylon symbolizes in 16:19—civilization convinced it doesn't need God.

17:1–7

THE VISION OF THE PROSTITUTE

This prostitute, revealed to John in verses 1–2, is the leader of the immorality of the world. She leads the kings to commit acts of immorality and causes the people of the world to be led astray. The description "sits on many waters" is the same used by the prophet Jeremiah for the Old Testament city of Babylon (Jeremiah 51:13). As Revelation 17 and 18 play out, the image of this woman is identified with Babylon in many ways.

Critical Observation

The fact that the woman in Revelation 17 is referred to as a prostitute rather than an adulteress is telling. Throughout the Old Testament, when the nation of God strays into sin, it is often described as an adulteress. This, of course, is because these people were considered God's bride.

But here the people who are living outside of God's law are simply referred to as a prostitute. They were never in a relationship with God, so they were not forsaking that relationship.

In verse 3, after having the prostitute described to him, John sees her for himself. After being carried away, he sees the woman on a scarlet beast. This is presumably the same beast described in 13:1, with seven heads, ten horns, and labeled with blasphemous names.

The woman is dressed in purple and scarlet, the colors of royalty (17:4). She is glittering with her accessories of gold, pearls, and precious stones. Many interpret this description, particularly the royal colors, to mean that the prostitute symbolizes a kingdom. She holds a golden cup, but inside the cup are immoral, disgusting things.

There is a title written on her forehead (17:5). This is one of several times in Revelation that people are identified by their mark, or seal, on their foreheads (7:3; 9:4; 14:1). Rather than understanding her name as being *Mystery*, her name *was* a mystery. More explanation is given later in this chapter, when an angel explains some of the symbolism to John (17:15–18).

The next thing written on her forehead is *Babylon*, a city that has already been mentioned several times in Revelation. In this case, the name Babylon is not used to identify a place but more to identify a godless culture.

It is clear, though, that not only is this woman (or whom she represents) evil herself, but she births evil. Identified as the mother of all prostitutes, she represents the source of all of the immorality in the world. In addition, she is the source of all of the evil that seeks to desecrate God. And as verse 6 states, she clearly opposes the children of God as well.

Verse 6 draws an even more vivid description. The woman is drunk with the blood of the saints, which implies she is responsible for their deaths. The language here is not that of something done long ago, but rather something that is still continuing. She enjoys the destruction of that which she has partaken. And John is amazed at what he sees.

17:7–14

THE ANGEL'S EXPLANATION

The angel offers some explanation of the scene that has astonished John (17:7). While John has described the woman prominently in the vision, the angel reveals that it is the beast—identified by his heads and horns—that seems more prominent.

Several times in the angel's explanation, the beast is described, with some variations, as the one who "was, now is not, and will come" (17:8). This is a way of saying that he has been resurrected, but it is a false resurrection. It is probably meant to stand in contrast to the description of Jesus in Revelation 1:4, "Grace and peace to you from him who is, and who was, and who is to come" (NIV). This beast lived, died, and is going to come back to life—a sign of false divinity. But in the end, this coming back serves the purpose of his final destruction.

Demystifying Revelation

Much of John's visions in Revelation would have had political implications in the ears of his original readers. There was a myth that the evil Nero would be resurrected. Many saw this resurrection coming true in the cruel rein of Emperor Domitian. It was probably during this reign that John was writing.

Just as in 13:18, when the number for the beast is cited, the angel states that the mind that grasps the explanation of this vision requires wisdom (13:18; 17:9). Lest we think these should be simple concepts, they are not. They are truths that require a lot of understanding.

According to the angel, the seven heads on the beast are seven mountains on which the woman sits—as well as seven kings (17:9–10). For some contemporary interpreters, this means that the heads on the beast represent seven nations or emperors that this woman controls. To others, this is an obvious reference to Rome, which was often described as a city of seven hills. Certainly, in the days of John, Rome would have fit much of the description of Babylon given in this book.

Verse 10 mentions the seven kings, five of which have fallen. Those who see the heads of the beast as nations interpret this verse as a reference to five kingdoms who have stood against Israel but are no longer in control. For those who see the heads of the beast as rulers, this verse references emperors or perhaps empires. Others offer the option that the number 7 may, as it has before, represent completion. Rather than a specific nation, ruler, or kingdom, it could denote all that has stood against God.

In verse 11, we read that there will actually be one more to rule. Whether interpreted as a ruler, a nation, or a symbol of evil, this eighth king refers to the beast himself. Somehow, he belongs to the seven yet rules again. The angel's interest in this explanation, though, doesn't seem to be identifying the beast in a definite way or explaining the symbolism without question. The focus seems to be that this beast is on his way to destruction at the hand of God.

Next, the angel begins to explain the horns (17:12–14). The ten horns represent ten kingdoms as a confederacy that will rule with the beast for a definite time—a quite short period of time. They will be completely united with the beast in opposition to the Lamb, but they will be defeated.

Jesus is described as Lord of lords and King of kings, a name similar to that which describes God in Deuteronomy 10:17. He will be accompanied by His chosen and faithful followers. This is not to be understood as His army; the Lamb needs no army to defeat evil. Rather, it is the family of those He has redeemed.

17:15–18

THE RELATIONSHIP BETWEEN THE BEAST AND THE PROSTITUTE

In the explanation, the angel reveals that the waters on which the prostitute sits represent the influence she has over the entire world. Many believe this is a description of a world religion. For the first time, the entire world will share a common belief system. Others see it as a description of an immeasurably large empire (17:15).

In either interpretation, the main players turn on each other. The beast, with his army, first shames the prostitute, then destroys her (17:16). This is a picture of the nature of evil and of the sovereignty of God. Evil's nature is to turn even on its own. God's sovereignty is such that His will is done even by those who defy Him. God uses the hatred of the beast to do away with the spirit of evil that rules the world.

In verse 18, the angel who is making this explanation offers John some clues to the identity of the prostitute. The angel says that she is a great city who rules over the kings on the earth. In John's culture, this certainly would have been taken as a reference to Rome. In regard to the end times, it can be seen as an organized, but false, world religion or simply as a reference to organized humanity, yet outside of the law of God.

REVELATION 18:1–24

THE FUNERAL OF HUMANITY

The Warning	18:1–8
The Weeping	18:9–19
The Wrath	18:20–24

Setting Up the Section

Chapter 18 records the destruction of Babylon. There are similarities here with the Old Testament accounts of the destruction of Tyre (Ezekiel 26–28) and with the destruction of the actual city of Babylon (Jeremiah 50–51).

When Babylon is destroyed, the entire infrastructure of humanity will be destroyed. This will create an undoing of the world that will leave humans hopeless. For John's original readers, this prophecy would have held some significance regarding the Roman Empire, but it is also the picture of all human civilizations that focus on earthly accomplishments rather than the power of the Creator.

18:1–8

THE WARNING

Chapter 18 opens with an angel coming from heaven with authority, splendor, and an announcement that Babylon has been destroyed (18:1–2). This opening part of the announcement is in the past tense, as if the event is completed. The angel describes Babylon four ways:

1) It is the home for demons and unclean birds. The unclean birds were probably scavenger birds, like buzzards, that preyed on dead things. This was despicable to the Jews. It was also an apt image of a deserted place (18:2).
2) It is a source for all of the evil in the world. This is pictured by the nations drinking the wine of Babylon's immorality (18:3).
3) It is a source for all of the wicked leadership in the world, thus the image of the kings committing adultery with her (18:3).
4) It is a source for all of the ill-gotten gain in the world. This can be seen by the mention of the merchants making their profits from Babylon's lavish wickedness (18:3).

At verse 4, there is a shift in the tense of the passage. Chapter 18 opens with the proclamation of Babylon's destruction as a completed event. With verse 4, the voice from heaven sends out an address while Babylon is still in the process of being destroyed. The warning is to stay away from the city because it is already condemned.

While verses 4–5 are addressed to the people of God, verses 6–8 seem to be addressing those who can inflict justice. They are a request for punishment, not simply according to the amount that Babylon has inflicted pain, but double that. In fact, the punishment this voice is calling for is not according to Babylon's cruelties, but according to her demand for luxury. As extravagantly as she has lived, so let her punishment be (18:7).

Critical Observation

Babylon's claim not to be a widow and not to have to mourn may reflect the nation's arrogance and demand for profitable times (18:7). She seems to believe that no power can take away the extravagance with which she lives. Babylon is a diva of a nation, looking down on all others.

According to verse 8, her due punishment will come all at one time through four plagues: death, mourning, famine, and fire.

18:9–19

THE WEEPING

While no one runs to Babylon's rescue, according to verses 9–11, there are some who mourn her passing—those who profited from her trade. The kings who traded with her stand at a distance and verbalize their lament over her quick (one hour) demise (18:10).

In verse 11, the merchants join the lamentation for the simple reason that Babylon is not there to buy their cargoes any longer. Verses 12–13 list the kinds of merchandise that made up that cargo. Most are easily recognizable still today. The precious stones could denote stones such as granite, as well as what we consider precious stones today. The colors of the cloth—scarlet and purple—are both colors the scriptures associate with splendor, even royalty, and also with sin. Citron wood is a hardwood well-known for its deep grain. The mention of bodies denotes slaves and what we would refer to today as human trafficking.

Verse 14 caps off this list of cargo with a parenthetical announcement addressing the destroyed city directly and adding a general description of the splendor lost.

The section closes with more mourning of the merchants but includes more specifically the sea merchants who lost their overseas business (18:15–19). Their lament echoes the previous laments in the description of the city as lavish and in their sorrow for the loss of profits. The economic foundation of their existence has been destroyed.

18:20–24

THE WRATH

Verse 20 is another parenthetical address, in this case perhaps by John himself (see also verse 14). This statement addresses the saints, apostles, and prophets attributing this great act of judgment to God. It is a call to rejoice.

John's vision in verse 21 involves an angel who picks up a millstone and throws it into the sea. This image is reminiscent of the Old Testament prophet Jeremiah's actions in Jeremiah 51:63, which are also a picture of the destruction of Babylon.

Demystifying Revelation

The typical millstone in that day was four to five feet in diameter and a couple of feet in thickness. It would have been quite heavy and would have sunk instantly when thrown into the water. In other words, it would seem to disappear. That is an apt description of the sudden destruction of Babylon. The entire system of the world will be done away with in an instant.

When the millstone is thrown down, it is done with violence. The judgment comes in an intense and destructive moment that changes the foundation of life forever (18:21). Verses 22–23 list the things that will never happen again in light of Babylon's destruction: Musicians won't play, craftsmen won't practice, and everyday life—like grinding grain into flour, marrying, and even lamps lighting homes—will cease.

While the previous verses were addressing Babylon, verse 24 is a statement *about* Babylon (much like verse 20). The deaths of prophets and saints and all those killed on earth have been attributed to her. In light of such a broad scope of destruction being credited to Babylon, many believe that the destruction represents not just the destruction of one city or power, but a representation of all the world's cities that have chosen to operate outside of God's laws.

REVELATION 19:1–21

WORSHIP AND WRATH

Praise for the Judgment of Babylon	19:1–6
The Wedding Celebration	19:7–10
The Return of the Messiah	19:11–16
The Reign of the Messiah	19:17–21

Setting Up the Section

Chapter 19 includes the great marriage ceremony of the Lamb and the return of Jesus. It is a chapter of both worship and victory, including the final destruction of the beast and his prophet.

19:1–6

PRAISE FOR THE JUDGMENT OF BABYLON

Chapter 19 opens with a great multitude singing God's praise. These are probably angels, but John doesn't specify. In this song, God is worshiped for His twofold work of judgment and of salvation:

1) Salvation and glory and power belong to God.
2) God's judgments are true and righteous.
3) He has judged the great prostitute who corrupted the earth with her immorality.
4) He has avenged the blood of His servants on her, blood that was on the great prostitute's hands (19:1–2).

Critical Observation

The song opens with the word *Hallelujah*, such a familiar word of praise in contemporary culture, yet this is the first time it is used in the New Testament. It does appear in the Psalms, and in that case is often related to the destruction of the wicked and the salvation of the children of God.

When the multitude sings out a second time, a picture of smoke rising from the battle is a sign of the permanence of the destruction (19:3). Then, for the final time in Revelation, the twenty-four elders and four living creatures, those who have been described as the ones closest to God's throne, take part in the worship. They offer their agreement. *Amen* means "so let it be." It is a statement of finality. And they offer their own praise (4:10; 19:4).

Take It Home

Yet another unidentified voice calls out in verse 5 for all God's servants to praise Him. The attitude of the worshipers indicates that they fear the Lord. Their praise is simple—the acknowledgment of the reign of God. Today we can still answer this call to worship, acknowledging God's present and evolving reign as His established kingdom (19:6). When we worship as the servants of God, we join this multitude.

19:7–10

THE WEDDING CELEBRATION

Throughout the scriptures, the picture of a bride has often represented God's faithful people. In the Old Testament, the prophet Isaiah spoke of Israel as God's bride (Isaiah 54:6). Here, in Revelation 19:7, the bride is a picture of the church, and the Lamb is a picture of Jesus. Redeemed believers are welcomed into heaven, and they have the privilege of having union with Christ forever.

The bride of the Lamb is dressed in clean, fine linen, which represents the good works of the faithful. This kind of imagery is common for those who are spiritually clean (Zechariah 3; Revelation 19:8).

In verse 9, the angel instructs John to write. Several times John is instructed to create a written record of what is happening, and only once is he forbidden from doing so (10:4).

Critical Observation

Those who are invited to take part in the great wedding banquet are called *blessed.* This would have had particular meaning to John's original readers. Facing persecution and even death, they had to wonder if blessings would indeed be theirs. The words of the angels, attributed to God, would have been a good reminder to these believers (and to believers through the ages) that in His kingdom there is a different timetable and a different measure of blessing not determined by the particular circumstances of the moment.

The angel also tells John that these are the words of God, and this declaration prompts John to worship the angel himself (19:10). The angel's response makes several things clear:

1) Angels are not to be worshiped.
2) Angels are fellow servants with Christians, all bearing witness to Jesus.
3) The testimony about Jesus is the spirit of prophecy.

The entire prophetic message of God from the beginning of the world has pointed to Jesus. He is central to everything for this life and the next.

19:11–16

THE RETURN OF THE MESSIAH

The portrayal of Christ's coming takes the form of a series of symbolic pictures that highlight aspects of an event too great to comprehend in advance. When heaven is opened, the first thing John sees is a white horse, with Faithful and True riding it (19:11). This is a representation of Jesus, the almighty Conqueror, the Word of God (John 1:1–3), coming to subdue the rebellious of earth, which are led by the powers of hell.

His blazing eyes relate to judgment (Revelation 19:12); His many crowns to His position as King of kings and Lord of lords (19:12, 16). He has a name that only He knows, yet His names are given in verses 11, 13, and 16.

His blood-dipped robe is that attributed to God by the Old Testament prophet Isaiah (Isaiah 63:1–6; Revelation 19:13). First-century rabbis claimed God would wear this kind of robe on the day of His vengeance on Rome.

Verse 14 mentions the armies that follow Jesus, also on white horses. These armies are the angels that surround Him. While the description of their white clothes does resemble the description of the redeemed in verse 8, the church is just described as the bride (19:14). For them to appear as an army here would be too quick of a switch.

Verse 15 employs several descriptions that have already appeared in John's visions. The sword extending from Jesus' mouth is His true weapon, rather than His armies (1:16). The iron rod of His rule depicts His absolute authority (12:5). Finally, the winepress of God's wrath is an image of judgment also used in chapter 14 (14:19–20).

Some translations are unclear as to whether Jesus' name appears both on His thigh and on His clothing (19:16). The name probably does appear twice, but there is some question as to how it appears on His thigh. There is no question, though, that He is coming to earth to enforce the reign of the Word of God.

19:17–21

THE REIGN OF THE MESSIAH

Verses 17–21 paint a picture of final disaster. An angel appears midair and calls to the birds to come and feast on the flesh of everyone—from those in highest power to the slaves who serve (19:18). This represents everyone who took the mark of the beast, including the beast himself and his false prophet (described in chapter 13 as a secondary beast).

This is a judgment scene that exhibits the power of the Word of God. The picture holds one dominant reality: Christ's victory over those who oppose Him is total. The Antichrist and the false prophet are thrown into the fiery lake of burning sulfur—this is complete destruction.

Demystifying Revelation

This fiery lake is a picture of hell, which in the New Testament is commonly called *Gehenna* (Matthew 5:22; 29, 30; 10:28; et al.). The Greek word is a transliteration of a Hebrew phrase meaning "the valley of Hinnom," a valley on the south side of Jerusalem where the Jews of Jeremiah's time offered human sacrifices by fire (Jeremiah 7:31). This was an appalling act that brought God's judgment upon them. The valley later came to be used as the city's garbage heap, where fires burned constantly. Such a place of constant stench and burning became an appropriate symbol for the place of eternal judgment.

REVELATION 20:1–15

THE COMPLETION OF THE PROMISES OF GOD

Satan Bound 20:1–3
Saints Ruling 20:4–6
The Completion of the Promise to the Serpent 20:7–10
The Completion of the Promise to Humanity 20:11–15

Setting Up the Section

To this point in Revelation, we have seen all those who stood on the side of the beast destroyed, except one. That is Satan himself. In this section, Satan receives his judgment.

There are many interpretations of the events John describes here, as well as a variety of timetables proposed for those events. The underlying truth remains, though, that John's visions reinforce God's ability and decision to deal with sin once and for all.

20:1–3

SATAN BOUND

Chapter 20 opens with an unnamed angel descending from heaven holding a key and a chain. The obvious picture here is that the angel has authority over the abyss. It is interesting to note that, while we might expect John's vision to include the most famous of angels to deal with Satan himself, in this case it is simply an unnamed angel who is given the task.

The abyss mentioned here is a kind of spiritual holding cell. It is not the final place of judgment.

In verse 2, Satan is identified by several terms that have already been used in Revelation—*dragon*, *serpent*, *devil*, and *Satan*. He is thrown into the abyss for one thousand years (20:3).

Critical Observation

As with much of Revelation, this passage has been interpreted in many ways, much depending on whether the details are viewed symbolically or literally. Some see the binding as a future event that will take place literally after the return of Christ to earth. Others see it as a symbolic binding that occurred at Christ's death and resurrection when he achieved victory over Satan. The length of time is also debated. Many believe the thousand years denotes the actual number of years that Satan will be bound. For others, it is simply a good round number, one that communicates that God will bind Satan's power and influence for the right amount of time that He will determine.

20:4–6

SAINTS RULING

The next part of John's vision includes those who have been martyred for their faith. The typical form of execution in first-century Rome was a beheading with an ax or sword, as the wording in verse 4 mentions. In this case, though, the language probably implies more generally those who were martyred for their faith, whatever the method.

John further describes the restraint of these sufferers: They had not worshiped the beast nor received his mark. Because of this, they were mistreated by the authorities of their world and thus will be given authority by God. They are resurrected to rule with Jesus.

John calls this the first resurrection. He mentions that the rest of the dead will come to life after the thousand years is complete, but he does not refer to that as the second resurrection. Instead, he only speaks of a second death, from which these martyrs are saved (20:5–6).

20:7–10

THE COMPLETION OF THE PROMISE TO THE SERPENT

At the end of the one thousand years, Satan is released from the abyss and begins to gather his army. Gog and Magog are hostile leaders included in a prophecy of the Old Testament prophet Ezekiel (Ezekiel 38–39). Their names are used here to represent the world's evil. The picture in verse 7 is that of an innumerable army gathered from all over the earth (Revelation 20:7–8).

The fact that this kind of army can be gathered seems to imply that even though Jesus has ruled the earth for a thousand years, not everyone has followed wholeheartedly.

According to verse 9, the armies of Satan are able to gather in an advantageous position. They encircle the saints and the "beloved city" (20:9 NET). This beloved city stands in stark contrast to the description of wicked Babylon as the "great city" (17:18; 18:10). Many interpret this beloved city to be Jerusalem. Others interpret it to represent the actual body of believers who now embody God's presence as the temple once did.

Notice the understated description of the victory in verse 9. It is no problem for

God to defeat Satan when the time is right to do so—fire comes down and the army is destroyed.

Consequently, the devil is thrown into the lake of fire and sulfur to accompany the beast and false prophet who are already there. Their torment will be continuous. God had promised Eve that the serpent would be dealt with eventually, and that promise is fulfilled here (Genesis 3:15; Revelation 20:10).

20:11–15

THE COMPLETION OF THE PROMISE TO HUMANITY

The throne in verse 11 is distinguished from the other thrones mentioned in Revelation in that it is large and white. It is such a powerful place of righteousness that nothing will be able to stand before it. While John does not identify who sits on the throne, most likely it is God the Father.

Demystifying Revelation

Some have noted that things seem out of order in these verses. Verse 11 has heaven and earth fleeing, yet in verse 13 the sea gives up its dead. There have been several solutions offered for this perceived problem. The mention of heaven and earth fleeing could be simply a metaphor explaining the power of the One who sits on the throne. Others suggest that these events could be happening simultaneously. A final solution is to recognize that John is not arguing for a strict chronology but is writing for emphasis. This is a vision meant to enlighten, not a history lesson with a strict timeline. Verse 11 provides a picture of the power of God's presence, while verse 13 gives the picture that none of those who have died will be overlooked in this resurrection to judgment. Even those lost or buried at sea will be held accountable.

Verse 12 states that this judgment is going to be for everyone who ever lived. John declares that he saw the dead, the great and the small, standing before the throne.

The books mentioned here are apparently records of all the deeds by which these lives will be judged. The book of life, separate from the other books, represents the names of those who have been redeemed and will find their home in heaven.

Verse 13 reinforces the idea that no one will be overlooked in this judgment. All those who have died, no matter their fate, will be called up.

The power that held physical bodies in bondage (death) and the place where all the wicked went until the Day of Judgment (Hades) will both be destroyed in the lake of fire (20:14). There is no reason for these two things to exist, because sin is finally being removed from the earth.

Verse 15 paints the picture of two distinct fates. The book of life is the determining factor.

REVELATION 21:1–27

ALL THINGS BRIGHT AND BEAUTIFUL

The New Heaven and Earth	21:1–8
The City of God	21:9–21
The Temple, Sun, and Moon	21:22–27

Setting Up the Section

Having described the fate of evil in the previous chapters, the remaining two chapters of Revelation describe visions of a new world established and ruled by God. This is the fate of the faithful, a spiritual destiny described here in earthly terms.

21:1–8

THE NEW HEAVEN AND EARTH

John's vision opens with not only a new earth, but a new heaven. He is describing a whole new existence in the presence of God. The fact that the sea no longer exists is a mysterious image. It may relate to the fact that the dragon came from the sea (21:1). The sea was also viewed by ancient peoples as a place of danger and death, where evil spiritual forces lived. In the new heaven and earth there will be no danger or death.

The New Jerusalem is described as a bride coming down from heaven (21:2). The bride is completely prepared, at her best for her husband.

The great pronouncement in verse 3 is that God is now living among His people. Any separation is gone. Heaven and earth have joined together to make one place; there will be no more pain, sin, tears, or death. All of the misery that the children of God had to endure on their way to heaven will be wiped away. God will restore every believer (21:3–4).

In verse 5, God speaks directly, one of the few times in Revelation. John has to be reminded to write down the proclamation that God is making all things new. Then God continues with a confirmation that what needed to be accomplished is complete. He also identifies Himself as the One with the authority to make this claim—the Alpha and Omega. *Alpha* is the first letter of the Greek alphabet, and *omega* is the last letter. This imagery shows God's nature to be eternal.

Finally, this eternal God says He will forever be a source for the water of life—free of charge (21:6). His eternal nature provides people with the new life necessary for participating in this new world.

According to verses 7–8, those who do not succumb to evil and remain true to God are the ones who will engage in this complete relationship with God. There are those who will not, however, and their fate is the second death in the lake of fire as described in the previous chapter. The list given in verse 8 opens with cowards, the opposite of those who persevered and conquered.

21:9–21

THE CITY OF GOD

In verse 9, there is a reference not only to the bride of the Lamb, but to the *wife* of the Lamb. This parallels the idea of God's work being complete. The wedding has taken place, and the relationship is solidified.

Jerusalem is called the bride because the children of God are now all one, and all in the city are married to God. In the past, it was called the bride because of its splendor; now it is called the bride because the redeemed inhabit it.

John again sees Jerusalem descending from heaven (21:10). The city is described as a clear jewel. The stone that is now known as jasper is not transparent, so the name *jasper* may have been applied to a different stone in John's day (21:11). Nevertheless, the description here of the city of God is that of a beautiful, costly jewel.

A more physical description of the city is given in verses 12–14. The walls, though unnecessary in a world without enemies and natural disasters, still denote a protected and safe place.

The twelve gates, guarded by angels and labeled with the twelve tribes of Israel, can easily be seen as a fulfillment of God's promises to His chosen people throughout history (21:13). The gates are positioned to reflect the way the twelve tribes encamped around the tabernacle in Numbers 2.

The inclusion of the names of the twelve apostles is an inclusion of the Christian church, the redeemed of God (Revelation 21:14).

The angel measures the city, and while it is described as square, it is actually an even cube, given that the height is also the same as the length and width—about fourteen hundred miles each (21:15–16).

Critical Observation

The next number given is related to the wall of the city. Verse 17 describes it as 144 cubits, or about 200 feet. The angel doesn't state whether the measurement is of the height or the depth of the wall, but either of these is difficult to reconcile with the measurements given of the city in verses 15–16. This is a good reminder that John's visions point to the underlying truth rather than the specific details.

New Jerusalem's walls are made of jasper (21:18). In Revelation 4:3, God is described as jasper, so there may be an allusion here to God as the city's protector.

Demystifying Revelation

It's puzzling, by contemporary standards, that the city is described as pure gold yet transparent (21:18). Gold, as we know it, is opaque. This may be more of a reference to something very shiny and completely pure. Glass was not crystal clear in the first century, and mirrors were dark and inconsistent in comparison with their modern counterparts. This description may reflect John's attempt to describe something so fine that it would have been unimaginable to his own cultural background.

The stones described in verses 19–20 seem to correlate with the stones in the Jewish high priest's breastplate as described in Exodus 28:17–20. It would be difficult to define each of the stones since not only has the study of stones become much more specific through the centuries, but even in the first century, stones were identified differently in the Hebrew language than in the Greek. It is certain, though, that these stones are of great value, which is the reason they are used as the foundation of the city. The New Jerusalem is not a place built on simple brick, but even the foundation is made of precious jewels.

The gates into the city are not only made of pearl, but each is one giant pearl. And again, as in verse 18, the main street is pure gold, clear and perfect (21:21).

Take It Home

John's vision of the world God creates for His people is one of perfection from the bottom to the top. To the original readers of this letter, this would have spoken to a hope that the imperfect and even cruel world that they endured was not a reflection of God's vision for them, nor the only thing they had to look forward to.

For modern believers, also, this perfect city reminds us to keep looking up to God's standards for life. We cannot imagine the way God actually intended our world to be, but we can participate in that kingdom with our obedience and with our eager anticipation of God's ultimate justice and reign.

21:22–27

THE TEMPLE, SUN, AND MOON

Verses 22–27 reveal three things missing from the New Jerusalem: the temple, the sun and moon, and the presence of sin.

There is no temple because the Lord dwells in this place (21:22). God is the temple. There is no sun or moon because God's glory and the light of the Lamb provide all the light needed. There is no night or any need for locked gates for protection (21:23–26).

Verse 24 reveals the wide breadth of redemption. The nations of the earth and the kings of the earth add grandeur to this place, but because of redemption, they bring none of their sin.

Finally, there is no sin (21:27). The description of sin here may apply specifically to idolatry. Also, there is no untruth. The expectation is that those who are included in the Lamb's book of life bring no sin to this place.

REVELATION 22:1–21

EDEN RESTORED

The Tree of Life 22:1–5

Epilogue 22:6–21

Setting Up the Section

Chapter 22 continues John's vision of the new heaven and earth begun in chapter 21. Then the chapter closes with an epilogue of observations about the collection of visions that make up the book of Revelation and the promise that Jesus is coming again.

22:1–5

THE TREE OF LIFE

In verses 1–2, an angel shows John a vision of a river made up of the water of life. The water sparkles brilliantly, is clear as crystal. It originates with God's throne and flows down the center of the main street (22:1–2). The scriptures offer allusions to the water of life in other places. The Old Testament prophecies of Ezekiel and Zechariah include mention of such (Ezekiel 47; Zechariah 14:8), as well as Jesus' teaching in the Gospels (John 4:7–14; 7:37–38).

The tree that is on this river is the tree of life. The Genesis creation account includes the description of two trees—the tree of the knowledge of good and evil and the tree of life. Many see this tree John describes by the river as the latter tree from the Garden of Eden. Somehow, in John's vision, this tree grows on both sides of the river (22:2). Also, it produces a different fruit each month (rather than twelve different fruits all year long).

The leaves of this tree are described as bringing healing to the nations. After the description in chapter 21 of the idyllic surroundings with no tears, sickness, or sin, one can wonder what these leaves will actually heal. Neither John nor the angel answers this question, so we can only appreciate the fact that these leaves are health-giving in some way.

Verse 3 says there will be no more curse, which some see as a fulfillment of Zechariah's prophecy in Zechariah 14:11. God and the Lamb are there with their people who both offer worship and bear God's name on their foreheads (Revelation 14:1; 22:4).

Critical Observation

The Old Testament prophet Ezekiel described the name of the eternal city of God as, "The Lord is there." Certainly John's vision in chapter 22 bears out that name.

Because God will be the center of this city, there will never be any darkness. No lamps are necessary; no sun is needed to light the way. God is the light for this eternal place. The idea that the inhabitants will reign with God is not to indicate that there will be multitudes to reign over, for everyone there will be a child of God. But it is an indication that everyone there will be considered royalty, children of the King (22:5).

22:6–21

EPILOGUE

In verse 6, the angel confirms the credibility of what has been revealed to John. While his claim that the words are reliable and trustworthy could simply apply to the immediately preceding verses, it is likely that they can be understood as a claim for this whole book of visions. This prophecy is of God.

The quote in verse 7 can be attributed to Jesus. The word *soon* is used here as in the verse above. In this case, *soon* means not so much that these events will happen sooner rather than later, but that they are the next event on God's schedule.

With verse 8, it is clear that John is speaking rather than the angel, offering his own testimony to the credibility of this prophecy. Then he again shows reverence to the angel, who reminds him that only God should be worshiped (19:10; 22:9).

John is told not to seal up the words of this book (22:10). They are to be shared and understood. Keeping a book unsealed means the words will be proclaimed, and God will give understanding to the people who hear it. According to the angel, though, some who hear the words of this book will continue on in their sin (22:11). In essence, the angel says, let each person respond as he or she will respond, for God will be the One who will judge people by their deeds.

Verses 12–13, just like verse 7, are the words of Jesus. He repeats His promise to come soon and to reward each person according to the life he or she has lived. He also states the same claim that was attributed to God in Revelation 1:8. In this case, Jesus adds two additional descriptive phrases, but all three mean the same thing—He is the beginning and the end.

Verses 14–15 are probably spoken by John, but this is not completely clear. These two verses first claim blessings on the ones who keep their clothes clean—keep their lives righteous—and thus have access to the tree of life and city in which it dwells. Then verse 15 draws a comparison with those who choose to live outside of the city, which in this case implies they are living outside of God's laws. The sins listed here have appeared elsewhere in the descriptions of those who followed the beast (9:21; 21:8).

Demystifying Revelation

It seems odd that there would be talk of all this sinfulness, when just verses ago John includes such a beautiful description of the new heaven and earth after sin is removed. The information in this closing section, though, is outside of the vision. It is a movement back toward the reality faced by John's readers who are attempting to live according to the kingdom of God in a world that resembles this description of those outside the new city gates.

Verses 16–17 again offer an invitation to come to Jesus and drink of the water of life. Jesus describes Himself as both the root of David (that from which David's bloodline sprang) and a descendant of David (that which sprang from David's bloodline). He is the One who came before David and before the great political empire of Israel. He is also the One who is the human descendant of David. He is the center of everything.

Jesus' claim to be the bright morning star may be a reference to Numbers 24:17, a prophecy stated by a prophet Balaam, who claimed a star would come out of the family of Jacob, father of the twelve tribes of Israel.

The warning in Revelation 22:18–19 covers both those who would add to John's prophecy and those who would diminish it. Neither will be tolerated.

John closes this prophecy with both a promise from Jesus that He is coming and a prayer from John that Jesus will come (22:20–21). Notice that in verse 20 Jesus is described as the One who testifies to these prophecies and confirms His intent to return. This must have resonated greatly with those first-century Christians enduring persecution, wondering about God's timetable, praying that their good deeds would not be forgotten by God, even if they were disdained by their own culture and government.

Take It Home

Verse 21 is a typical close to a letter of this era but an unusual close to such a dramatic writing. These closing words are a good reminder to all that no matter the situation—whether facing persecution or any of the situations described in the churches at the beginning of Revelation—we all are in need of the grace of the Lord Jesus.

The point of this book is not to show us who the beast is, but to show us how Jesus is going to overcome the beast. It is not to offer us a mysterious timetable over which we can quarrel, but to unite us in our eager anticipation of God's kingdom. It is not an apocalypse meant to scare us into obedience, but a promise of God's character no matter what the circumstances of the moment might present to the contrary.

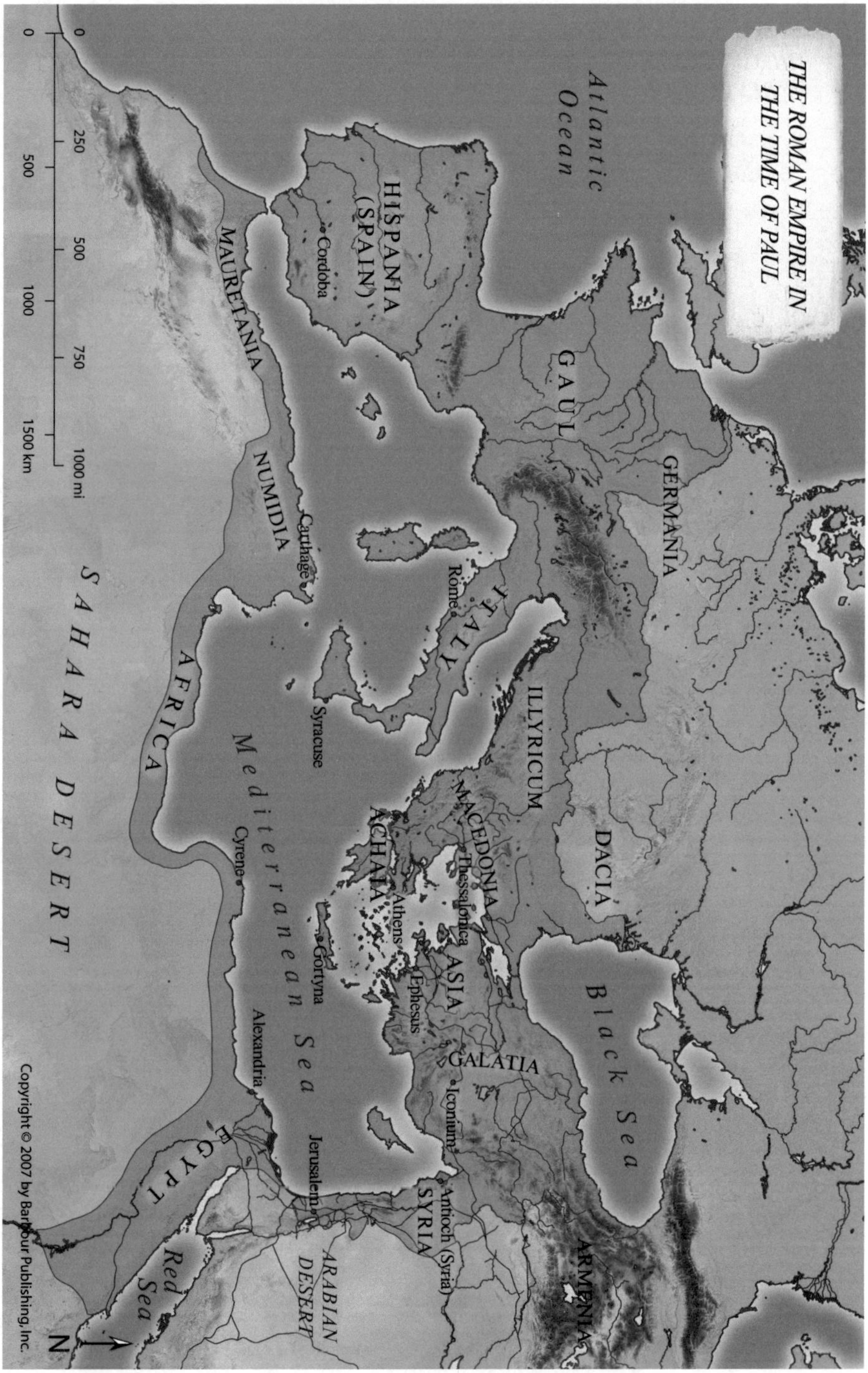
THE ROMAN EMPIRE IN THE TIME OF PAUL
Atlantic Ocean
HISPANIA (SPAIN)
Cordoba
GAUL
GERMANIA
MAURETANIA
NUMIDIA
Carthage
ITALY
Rome
Syracuse
ILLYRICUM
DACIA
MACEDONIA
Thessalonica
ACHAIA
Athens
ASIA
Ephesus
Gortyna
GALATIA
Iconium
Black Sea
Mediterranean Sea
Cyrene
Alexandria
AFRICA
SAHARA DESERT
EGYPT
Red Sea
Jerusalem
SYRIA
Antioch (Syria)
ARABIAN DESERT
ARMENIA
N
0 250 500 750 1000 mi
0 500 1000 1500 km
Copyright © 2007 by Barbour Publishing, Inc.

THE CHURCHES OF REVELATION
one of the seven churches addressed in Revelation
0
50 mi
0
50 km
THRACE
Byzantium
Chalcedon
Nicomedia
Sea of Marmara
Sangarius River
Nicea
Cyzicus
BITHYNIA
Abydos
Ilium (Troy)
Troas
MYSIA
Assos
Adramyttium
Tembrius River
LESBOS
Mytilene
Pergamum
Selinus River
Thyatira
ASIA
Hermus River
CHIOS
Sardis
Philadelphia
Smyrna
LYDIA
Apamea
Cayster River
Hierapolis
Ephesus
Tralles
Meander River
Laodicea
Magnesia
Colosse
Lycus River
SAMOS
Priene
IKARIA
Miletus
CARIA
PATMOS
Halicarnassus
Indus River
LYCIA
RHODES
COS
Cnidus
John is exiled to the island of Patmos, where he writes the book of Revelation.
Xanthus River
Rhodes
Xanthus
Myra
Patara
N
Copyright © 2007 by Barbour Publishing, Inc.

CONTRIBUTING EDITORS

Dr. Peter Barnes is the pastor of Westlake Hills Presbyterian Church in Austin, Texas. He has a Master of Divinity degree from Gordon-Conwell Theological Seminary, and a Doctor of Ministry from Fuller Theological Seminary. He is author of *The Missional Church: Restoring a Vision for the Mission of God through the Local Church in the 21st Century*. Peter and his wife, Lorie, have three adult sons.

Robert L. Deffinbaugh, Th.M., graduated from Dallas Theological Seminary with his Th.M. in 1971. Bob served for over 35 years as a teaching elder at Community Bible Chapel in Richardson, Texas. Since his retirement from full-time preaching, Bob continues serving as an elder and works for Bible.org as a ministry facilitator. Many of Bob's sermons are posted on Bible.org. He also serves on the staff of Biblicaleldership.com.

Dr. Ian Fair was a missionary in South Africa for 14 years, has preached for 39 years, taught Bible classes for 39 years, and has served as an elder and deacon. Recently retired from Abilene Christian University, Dr. Fair continues to teach as an adjunct professor.

Dr. Hall Harris W. III is professor of New Testament Studies at Dallas Theological Seminary and is also the project director and general editor for the NET Bible (New English Translation). For over twenty-five years, Hall has taught courses in intermediate level Greek grammar and syntax, exegetical method, and various courses in the Gospel and Epistles of John. He received a Th.M. from Dallas Seminary and a Ph.D. from the University of Sheffield, England.

The late **J. Hampton Keathley III, Th.M.** was a 1966 graduate of Dallas Theological Seminary and a former pastor of 28 years. Hampton wrote many articles and on occasion taught New Testament Greek at Moody Bible Institute, Northwest Extension for External Studies in Spokane, Washington. In August 2002 he succumbed to lung cancer and went home to be with the Lord.

Dr. Stephen Leston is pastor of Kishwaukee Bible Church in DeKalb, Illinois. He is passionate about training people for ministry and has served as a pastor at Grace Church of DuPage (Warrenville, Illinois) and Petersburg Bible Church (Petersburg, Alaska).

Jeff Miller holds a Th.M. degree from Dallas Theological Seminary and is completing his doctorate at Duke University Divinity School. Jeff is coauthor of the *Zondervan Dictionary of Bible and Theology Words* and *A New Reader's Lexicon of the Greek New Testament* (Kregel Publications). He has also written nearly fifty articles. He is best known for his ministry to men, along with his book *Hazards of Being a Man* (Baker Books). Jeff is Senior Pastor of Trinity Bible Church in Richardson, Texas where he lives with his wife, Jenny, and two daughters. Visit Jeff at www.jeffreyemiller.com.

Dr. Robert Rayburn holds a Master of Divinity degree from Covenant Theological Seminary and a doctorate in New Testament from the University of Aberdeen, Scotland. His commentary on Hebrews was published in the *Evangelical Commentary of the Bible.* He is pastor of Faith Presbyterian Church (PCA) in Tacoma, WA.

CONSULTING EDITOR

Dr. Mark Strauss is professor of New Testament at Bethel Seminary San Diego. He is the author of various books and articles, including *How to Read the Bible in Changing Times; Four Portraits, One Jesus; The Gospel of Mark* in the *Zondervan Exegetical Commentary* series, *The Gospel of Luke* in the *Zondervan Illustrated Bible Background Commentary,* and *The Essential Bible Companion.* He also serves as Vice Chair of the Committee for Bible Translation for the *New International Version* and as an associate editor for the *NIV Study Bible.* He lives in San Diego with his wonderful wife, Roxanne, a marriage and family therapist, and three delightful children, two in college, one in high school.

WITH SPECIAL THANKS TO BIBLE.ORG

Bible.org is a nonprofit 501(c)(3) Christian ministry headquartered in Dallas, Texas. In the last decade, Bible.org has grown to serve millions of individuals around the world and provides thousands of trustworthy resources for Bible study including the new NET BIBLE® translation.

Bible.org offers thousands of free resources for:

- Spiritual formation and discipleship
- Men's ministry
- Women's ministry
- Pastoral helps
- Small group curriculum and much more...

Bible.org can be accessed through www.bible.org.

NOTES

NOTES

NOTES

NOTES

NOTES

NOTES

NOTES

NOTES

NOTES

NOTES

NOTES

NOTES

Also Available

Bible commentaries are often daunting—but they don't have to be. *The Layman's Bible Commentary—Old Testament* addresses key passages with thousands of notes covering the Pentateuch through the Minor Prophets. This single-volume commentary is concise and easy to understand—it's perfect for Bible students who aren't Bible scholars.

Paperback / ISBN 979-8-89151-264-0